Neotropical Birds

Neotropical Birds

Ecology and Conservation

Douglas F. Stotz

John W. Fitzpatrick

Theodore A. Parker III

Debra K. Moskovits

WITH ECOLOGICAL AND DISTRIBUTIONAL DATABASES BY

Theodore A. Parker III

Douglas F. Stotz

John W. Fitzpatrick

A Project of
Conservation International and
the Field Museum of Natural History

The University of Chicago Press
Chicago and London

DOUGLAS F. STOTZ is conservation ecologist for the Field Museum of Natural History. JOHN W. FITZPATRICK is Louis Agassiz Fuertes Director of the Cornell Laboratory of Ornithology. The late THEODORE A. PARKER III established and directed the Rapid Assessment Programs (RAP) for Conservation International and was a research associate of the Museum of Zoology at Louisiana State University. DEBRA K. MOSKOVITS is director of environmental conservation programs, Field Museum of Natural History.

The University of Chicago Press, Chicago 60637
The University of Chicago Press, Ltd., London

Printed in the United States of America
05 04 03 02 01 00 99 98 97 96   1 2 3 4 5
ISBN: 0-226-77629-8 (cloth)
0-226-77630-1 (paper)

Library of Congress Cataloging-in-Publication Data

Neotropical birds : ecology and conservation / Douglas F. Stotz . . . [et al.] ; with ecology and distributional databases by Theodore A. Parker III, Douglas F. Stotz, and John W. Fitzpatrick.
p. cm.
"A project of Conservation International and the Field Museum of Natural History."
1. Birds—Latin America. 2. Birds—Habitat—Latin America. 3. Birds—Ecology—Latin America. 4. Birds, Protection of—Latin America. 5. Birds—Ecology—Latin America—Databases. 6. Birds—Latin America—Geographical distribution—Databases. I. Stotz, Douglas F. (Douglas Forrester), 1956– . II. Conservation International. III. Field Museum of Natural History.
QL685.7.N46 1996
598.298—dc20   95-31571
CIP

This book is printed on acid-free paper.

Dedicated to the memory of

THEODORE A. PARKER III *and* ALWYN H. GENTRY

cherished friends and ardent explorers who

opened our eyes, changed our lives, and inspired a

generation of conservation biologists

Contents

Illustrations

MAPS (*following index*)

PLATES *(following page 12)*

COLOR PLATES

BLACK-AND-WHITE PLATES

FIGURES

Preface

We undertook this project with two goals. First, we hoped to compile an enormous volume of new, largely unpublished information on the ecology of Neotropical birds. Much of the data now available on these four thousand bird species could not reach the literature through typical channels of technical publishing, so a synoptic reference tool seemed the right approach. Second, we had each spent much of our adult life witnessing firsthand the disappearance of some of the greatest living treasures on earth. While all four of us shared an interest in tropical birds, we found in one another an even more abiding common interest in the natural communities that support them. It seemed to us that bird communities provided a remarkably accurate barometer of habitat conditions. We saw both the need and the opportunity to organize knowledge about Neotropical avian ecology into a conservation framework.

The tragic death of Ted Parker in 1993, while surveying hill forests of western Ecuador, occurred only shortly before these databases and text were sent out for review. Nothing we could write or say adequately expresses our sorrow and grief at the passing of this exceptional person, friend, and coauthor. He enriched each of our lives, along with those of a whole generation of birders and conservationists on two continents. Even at his most exasperating moments, Ted always was engaging and inspiring. He was a gifted individual whose vast knowledge about Neotropical birds was surpassed only by his insatiable appetite for more information and his impatience at the slow pace and political quagmires of conservation.

Ted was widely respected not only for his boundless enthusiasm and remarkable ears and eyes, but also for his unmatched field experience throughout the habitats of Central and South America. The knowledge he gained on his own complemented close personal associations he formed with other field ornithologists from throughout the world. And Ted had the uncanny capacity to absorb untold volumes of detail while unraveling the patterns within them. This combination of unique attributes allowed him to synthesize an unparalleled body of comparative information about tropical birds and their habits. Only a little of this synthesis had been published when he died. It is little consolation that his death occurred after the databases and much of the manuscript for this book had been completed and proofread.

Ted Parker's knowledge formed the core of the ecological database, although the origins of the database lie in a project begun by the Nature Conservancy in the mid-1980s. From 1988 to 1991, through initiatives of Conservation International and coaxing from Moskovits, Ted poured considerable energy into a greatly expanded version of the original data file. In amending, modifying, and proofing Parker's original draft of the ecological table, Stotz drew from his own extensive experience in the Neotropics, plus the published and unpublished work of many additional colleagues. Stotz, Parker, Fitzpatrick, and Moskovits reviewed countless drafts of the database thereafter.

Stotz compiled the geographical table using published and unpublished sources, including Parker's experiences and notes. We are extremely grateful to many colleagues and museums for access to their specimens and field records for this table.

As the databases took shape, preliminary comparisons of endemism, habitat specialization, and conservation status among different regions and habitats became possible. We carried out most analyses on personal computers using Paradox 4.0 (Borland International 1992a), Paradox for Windows (Borland International 1992b), or SAS (1985a, 1985b, 1985c). First drafts of the text began through extensive discussions among all four authors, with considerable input from Brent Bailey of Conservation International. Draft chapters were composed by Stotz (chapters 4, 5, 6, 7, 8), Fitzpatrick (chapters 1, 3, 9, 10), and Parker (chapter 2). Moskovits assembled the authors and ensured the completion of the databases and text. Moskovits, Fitzpatrick, and Stotz rewrote and edited each chapter.

All text benefited especially from critical comments by Jennifer Shopland, Louise Emmons, Brent Bailey, Thomas Schulenberg, Scott Robinson, Robert Ridgely, and David Willard. Robin Foster and the late Alwyn Gentry (who died in the same plane crash as Parker) provided invaluable discussions, revisions, specific botanical information, and firsthand experience for the habitat descriptions in chapter 2.

Part 4—the databases—begins with a text chapter providing historical overview and context for the project. The Guide to the Databases offers brief descriptions of the habitat categories, zoogeographic regions and other variables used throughout the tables and in the analyses discussed in the text. The habitats and regions form the most important units used in our analyses for comparing ecological assemblages.

Parts 1 through 3 discuss some of the ecological patterns that can be drawn from the databases of part 4. We emphasize patterns that have important implications for conservation, especially regarding endemism and habitat specialization in different areas. Chapter 1 emphasizes the importance of communities, as opposed to species, as units of conservation, and discusses birds as biological indicators. Part 1 then examines ecological patterns and conservation issues from the perspective of the major vegetation types in the Neotropics. First, in chapter 2, we present our classification and descriptions of Neotropical vegetation types. We then present our ecological analyses by major vegetation categories: humid forests (chapter 3), dry forests (chapter 4), grasslands (chapter 5), and aquatic habitats (chapter 6). Conservation status of a special class of birds—the long-distance migrants—is explored in part 2. Chapter 7 examines Nearctic migrants, and chapter 8 considers their mirror image in the Southern Hemisphere, austral migrants.

In part 3 we summarize our conclusions and views on establishing conservation priorities from these biological data. Chapter 9 suggests a set of general criteria for establishing both local and global priorities, and chapter 10 uses these criteria to compare explicitly different regions and vegetation types within the Neotropics. We introduce the concept of "cornerstone habitats" and identify which regions and communities of the Neotropics demand most immediate conservation attention.

In attempting to tackle such a large subject, projects like this one are hampered by the scale itself. Double-checking the accuracy of data tables with over four thousand species and dozens of fields presents mechanical as well as scientific challenges. Errors of omission and commission no doubt still exist. The deliberate pace at which this project progressed, however, allowed us to ferret out many of the mistakes. The ecological and distributional databases continued to be modified even as analyses and writing proceeded. Specific numbers changed in most analyses with each generation of the ecological database. We tried to ensure that all text tables and analyses are drawn from the final version of the data tables, but we openly acknowledge that some corrections may have escaped our attention. Such errors in detail would not affect any overall conclusions.

Although we accept complete responsibility for our mistakes, this book could not have come about without the generous input of an enormous number of colleagues and friends. We are sincerely grateful to every one. We cannot possibly name all who provided encouragement, advice, hours of discussion, and logistical support or shared with us some of their personal observations. Among the many who contributed to the final product are Brent Bailey, Rob Bierregaard, Hélio Camargo, José Maria Cardoso da Silva, John Carr, Barry Chernoff, Terry Chesser, Mario Cohn-Haft, Silvia Correa, Victor Emanuel, Louise Emmons, Davis Finch, Adrian Forsyth, Robin Foster, Al Gentry, Luis Gonzaga, Gary Graves, Mort Isler, Phyllis Isler, Neils Krabbe, Scott Lanyon, Fred Lohrer, Gitogo Maina, Russ Mittermeier, Silvio Olivieri, Ken Parkes, Bruce Patterson, Carsten Rahbek, Van Remsen, Mark Robbins, Scott Robinson, Ken Rosenberg, Tom Schulenberg, Peter Seligman, Jennifer Shopland, Wesley Silva, Mel

Traylor, Paulo Vanzolini, Jacques Vielliard, Bret Whitney, Dave Willard, Ed Willis, Glen Woolfenden, the library staff at the Museu de Zoologia da Universidade de São Paulo, and the staff in the Department of Photography at the Field Museum of Natural History. For help with entering records into the computer databases, and for creating the map figures, we thank Conservation International's staff, especially Alberto Lora, Chris Rodstrom, and John Lovell. Many institutions supported us through the six years this work was in progress, including Conservation International, the Field Museum of Natural History (Ellen Thorne Smith Fund), Archbold Biological Station, the Museu de Zoologia da Universidade de São Paulo, Fundação Amparo à Pesquisas do Estado de São Paulo (FAPESP), and Louisiana State University Museum of Natural Science. Archbold Biological Station provided the refuge for our weeklong get-togethers between 1989 and 1992 to write, talk, compare notes, trade drafts, and rewrite. Finally, we sincerely thank Susan Abrams for never doubting that this book would someday get done, Joe Alderfer for his graphics advice and support, Alice Bennett for editing and improving the text and especially for her sharp eyes and heroic efforts in clarifying our text tables and making our abbreviations more consistent, and Larry McQueen for the painting on the cover.

Perhaps the most frustrating feature of a project of this scale is that it permits us to address conservation priorities only at the regional level. Governments and conservation agencies must work at local levels when inventorying sites, comparing alternative tracts for protection, and ultimately designing and implementing preserves. We remain acutely aware of this shortcoming. We urge users of the data tables to devise their own analyses, tailoring them to local needs and local comparisons. The information that went into these tables was garnered from experience at the local level throughout the Neotropics. Although we could not analyze and write about many specific local communities, we feel that the real measure of this project's success will be its usefulness in zeroing in on the remaining best places around the Neotropics—places where Ted Parker might have stood listening to the birds around him and thinking, "This place *has* to be preserved."

Note to Readers

We wrote this book with the interests of a wide audience in mind—from conservationists and politicians to tropical ecologists, ornithologists, and birders. The geographic area we cover spans the Neotropical realm, from the West Indies and the United States border with Mexico to Tierra del Fuego at the southern tip of South America.

We believe that bird communities can effectively inform priority allocation and site selection for conservation. In these pages we highlight conservation implications of many aspects of Neotropical bird communities and present basic ecological information on Neotropical birds.

We begin the text chapters (parts 1 through 3) with a brief summary of the key results and conservation issues discussed. We base all analyses of the bird communities and their conservation implications on the databases presented in part 4. To understand the terminology and criteria used throughout the text, and the categorization of the data, we refer readers to the Guide to the Databases in part 4, where they will find definitions for the zoogeographic regions and subregions, conservation priorities, and other ecological and distributional variables we use throughout the book. We describe the avian habitats and microhabitats in chapter 2.

The largest single source of information for the databases was the personal, unpublished information of the late Theodore A. Parker III. We strongly encourage authors referring to any material contained in part 4, especially information on the ecology or distribution of specific birds, to cite that section separately, as T. A. Parker III, D. F. Stotz, and J. W. Fitzpatrick, "Ecological and Distributional Databases," in *Neotropical Birds: Ecology and Conservation,* by D. F. Stotz, J. W. Fitzpatrick, T. A. Parker III, and D. K. Moskovits. We thank our readers for their consideration.

The databases presented in part 4—the essence of this book—are also available on diskettes to enable readers to engage in their own analysis, perform their own sorts, and print out custom lists. The "intro.use" file on diskette explains how the databases are set up and how they differ from the printed versions in part 4 of this book. The file also provides hints on how to use the tables and on ways of analyzing the data.

The diskette containing the databases presented in part 4 of this book may be purchased separately from the University of Chicago Press. For price and ordering information, please call 1/800/621-2736 during regular business hours. The bibliographical information for the diskette is as follows: T. A. Parker III, D. F. Stotz, and J. W. Fitzpatrick, "Ecological and Distributional Databases for Neotropical Birds," in *Neotropical Birds: Ecology and Conservation*, by D. F. Stotz, T. A. Parker III, J. W. Fitzpatrick, and D. K. Moskovits (Chicago: University of Chicago Press, 1996). ISBN 0-226-64676-9

Neotropical Birds

1 Introduction: Neotropical Bird Communities and Conservation

Paradise

Of all the realms on earth that could be called paradise, perhaps the Neotropics most deserve the title. Explorers and scientists have marveled for centuries at the bewildering diversity of life forms found together within tropical biomes of the New World. The Neotropics encompass earth's most extensive humid forest, largest river system, greatest wetland, longest mountain chain, driest desert, and richest ocean current.

South America has the highest absolute number of living species among the seven continents, by a substantial margin. Spectacular as they are, however, species counts alone do not convey the importance of the Neotropics as a cradle of diversity. Ancient Gondwanan origins, plus ample geographic opportunity for relicism and radiation, helped build and maintain enormous numbers of higher taxa in both plants and animals. Among birds, for example, 90 of the world's approximately 150 families occur in the Neotropics, and 28 of these families are endemic to the realm. No other region of the planet comes close in diversity or endemism.

Paradise Lost

Even in the late twentieth century, places still exist in the Neotropics that recall romantic images of paradise as lovely as any painted on canvas or described in myth. Today, however, one must go to remote corners of the realm to find them. During our own lifetimes we have watched the earth's last great wilderness systems become the dominion of modern humans and their technology, where missionaries, loggers, miners, settlers, road builders, and city planners now rule.

Some of the original great forests, such as those of eastern Brazil, are functionally gone. Even the vast Amazon, while still mostly forested, has been crisscrossed with highways. Steadily the cleared margins of these roads swell to meet one another, isolating a growing number of forest fragments between them. Even more devastating has been the conversion of a remarkable complex of open-country habitats in central South America into planted pines, soybeans, and sugarcane, interspersed with citrus groves, overgrazed pasture, and other crops.

The loss of paradise in the Neotropics is well chronicled. Popular press and countless television documentaries flood the public with stories about the richness of the tropics and their accelerating destruction. "Endangered species" and "tropical deforestation" are buzzwords of the late twentieth century.

Conservation Priorities

Few would dispute the global importance of trying to save some pieces of native wilderness in the Neotropics, and considerable effort already is under way. Most important throughout the process is the need to follow clear priorities that guide and focus conservation research and action. In this book we concentrate on one particular aspect of conservation—site selection for protected reserves in the Neotropics. Our primary goal is to devise an expedient means for identifying the Neotropical areas of highest priority for protection, based on their biological value.

Conservation priorities are most meaningful when placed in a geographically relevant context—goals appropriate for Brazil, for example, are different from those for Mexico, or for international organizations based in the United States or Europe. When a geographic region is deemed important, different sites potentially available for protection have to be assessed. Which site best represents the biological region being protected? On a local scale, how do we compare candidate sites effectively when limited resources and dwindling time demand triage?

The world cannot afford to spend a long time studying these difficult questions. We need fast routes to locating the most important, most sensitive, or most endangered areas. After working in virtually all the terrestrial habitats of the Neotropics, we became convinced that birds provide important clues to help establish conservation priorities in selecting sites for conservation. Birds can help us differentiate biological communities and evaluate the condition of an area. Intact communities are now the exception and someday may not even be recognized without a reference guide to what they once looked like. Moreover, some locally endemic communities are so sensitive to human disturbance that they are almost gone today. Birds can help identify these sensitive communities while there is still time to save them.

Deriving Conservation Priorities from Biological Data

A considerable body of literature now exists on the use of biological data for establishing conservation priorities and for locating the most important natural areas to be protected (for examples, see Eisenberg 1980; Gilbert 1980; Terborgh and Winter 1980, 1983; A. W. Diamond 1985; J. M. Diamond 1985a; Stiles 1985a; Gentry 1986a; Hubbell and Foster 1986; Soulé and Kohm 1989; Fjeldså 1991). We emphasize a community approach to conservation. Specifically, we suggest using concentrations of species that share some level of rarity or risk to locate candidate areas for protection. This approach differs from focusing on centers of high biotic diversity, which often attract the attention of media and conservationists. Protecting centers of high diversity can provide the illusion of enormous "bang for the buck": large numbers of species protected per conservation dollar. However, many of these species are widespread and in little need of protection. Additionally, many centers of absolute diversity are under less immediate threat than are other equally distinctive ecological assemblages that have a lower number of species. In the Neotropics, the Amazon basin presents a good example of such a situation, a high-diversity region with little immediate threat and a relatively low level of endemism (see chapter 3).

We arrived at our approach to conservation priorities by witnessing, between 1970 and 1990, the accelerating destruction of such habitats as the Brazilian cerrado, the mid-montane forests of the Andes and the Caribbean, and the dry forests of western South America. Small in area, sometimes low in species diversity, such regions are enriched with species that occur nowhere else in the world. Some of these individual slices of evolutionary history are about to be lost forever.

We emphasize in this book that the first major waves of extinctions in the Neotropics are not occurring in centers of diversity such as the Amazon. Rather, extinctions are occurring within centers of local endemism, especially among species that have evolved ecological specializations that limit their ability to adapt to human modifications of their habitats. The most vivid examples are on the islands, such as Guadalupe Island and the Greater and Lesser Antilles. Extinction already has removed whole trophic levels from these communities (e.g., Steadman, Pregill, and Olson 1984).

Larger extinction waves are approaching. Like their predecessors, they will occur on islands, but these will be mainland "islands," pockets of local endemism and habitat specialization within continental Middle and South America. The most pressing conservation goal today is to reduce these new extinction waves to a minimum. To do so, we need to locate where they are most likely to occur and avoid allowing the few individual species that already have reached the brink of extinction to distract us from the larger crisis.

Biological Communities and Flagship Species

Communities, not individual species, are the proper cornerstones of natural resource conservation. Individual species cannot be protected effectively outside the biological context afforded by the community they occupy. Similarly, biological communities exist in the matrix of other communities that constitute an ecosystem. Communities will be substantially degraded if not maintained within the context of their encompassing ecosystems. Interchange among communities greatly enriches those communities, in terms of both species diversity and the biological interactions that drive the systems. Although this concept has become a modus operandi in conservation biology, the ecosystem approach to conservation is still persistently ignored by government agencies, many private conservation organizations, and much of the popular press.

In the United States, for example, expensive conservation efforts still focus on rescuing the California Condor (*Gyps californicus*) and Whooping Crane (*Grus americanus*). Yet only meager attention and minimal dollars have been directed toward restoring the Mojave Desert wilderness or the northern Great Plains, the ecosystems where these two spectacular species once flourished. We pour money into rescuing the Hawaiian Crow (*Corvus hawaiiensis*) but spend almost nothing at the state or federal level on restoring and protecting the great koa forests where this species and countless others hang in the balance.

Compared with the temperate zone, elevated species diversity and pronounced local endemism characterize most tropical ecosystems. This makes it imperative that conservation in the Neotropics be approached from a community viewpoint rather than a focus on individual species. Except in a few cases (mostly involving game hunting or the pet trade), noteworthy threatened and endangered species in the tropics exist amid assemblages of less visible but also imperiled forms.

Even some endangered game species, hunted nearly to extinction, represent the high-profile end of entire endangered communities. In the western Andes, for example, the critically endangered White-winged Guan (*Penelope albipennis*) will never flourish in the wild without the localized, semideciduous forest habitat it depends on. This habitat is disappearing along with the guan (see chapter 4); or more appropriately, the guan is disappearing along with its habitat. The habitat, not the guan, represents the "unit" in need of protection. The entire list of bird species endemic to these forests of northwestern Peru and adjacent Ecuador, not just the guan, identifies the habitat tracts of semideciduous forest most worthy of protection. The White-winged Guan is only the tip of the mast—it is the whole ship that is sinking.

Most conservationists embrace the idea of individual "flagship species" as an important public relations device. Where a flashy species is available, it provides a way of communicating to a wide audience the plight of a local ecosystem. Outstanding examples do exist of the use of this technique to accomplish ecosystem conservation (e.g., the accomplishments of the RARE Center for Tropical Conservation in raising public awareness and saving forest habitats in the West Indies). We applaud single-species flag-waving for fund-raising and consciousness-raising. However, we do not consider single-species rescue missions to be an effective conservation strategy. Using the single-species strategy in the Neotropics is dangerous for at least three reasons:

1. Almost all genuinely endangered Neotropical species are threatened with extinction because of critical loss or degradation of their habitat. Focusing on researching, rehabilitating, and propagating a single species deflects attention and resources away from the myriad *other species* also threatened within the same habitat. Except in the most extreme cases, conservation strategies should be designed to protect threatened and endangered species by rescuing and protecting their biological context, not solely their reproductive potential.

Captive breeding without concerted habitat protection is only one notable case in point. The single-species fallacy can be pursued even in the absence of captive breeding. Again, a good example is under way in the United States: the endangered Red-cockaded Woodpecker (*Picoides borealis*) was native to a mature, fire-adapted pine ecosystem now almost gone from the southeastern United States. Conservationists and foresters are attempting to foster the woodpecker's survival in young pine stands by removing competitors from the roosting and nesting cavities, and by drilling roost cavities within previously unused and otherwise unsuitable habitat. Meanwhile, the destruction of suitable native pineland continues, and the species is declining everywhere within its range (James 1991). Has anything biologically meaningful been accomplished by maintaining an ecological specialist in an artificial habitat while its original ecosystem is eliminated?

2. Some of the most threatened New World ecosystems lack charismatic flagships and could go unprotected because of single-species conservation priorities. For example, the virgin campo grasslands of the Brazilian plateau contain a host of ecologically specialized endemic plants and animals. The continued existence of these species hinges on preserving portions of the richly diverse, but rapidly vanishing, South American prairies (see chapter 5). What are the avian flagships of the campo? A tiny, straw-colored flycatcher (*Culicivora caudacuta*), a reddish brown terrestrial ovenbird (*Geobates poecilopterus*), and several other nondescript birds, all of which could fit together inside a breadbox. Viewed as a community, this assemblage of drab creatures is among the most distinctive and threatened in the Neotropics. Starring as central figures on a television nature broadcast, however, they would cast individual shadows too small to capture attention.

3. Single-species conservation efforts invariably focus on the few species and habitat tracts that are most critically endangered. These preservation measures often amount to salvage operations. The danger in valiantly rescuing critically endangered species, regardless of cost, is that we are forced to overlook the species and ecosystems that are only slightly less rare. Concentrating efforts on critically endangered species, and not attending to the second and third priority communities in advance, will serve to *increase*, rather than decrease, the total number of species threatened with global extinction. Instead, we should focus on anticipating which communities are about to become endangered and do whatever is necessary to keep viable natural communities from becoming rare.

For example, the upper tropical forests along the base of the eastern Andes do not contain even one endangered bird species. However, this razor-thin life zone is being decimated at unprecedented rates. Furthermore, these spectacular forests contain literally hundreds of ecologically specialized, locally endemic birds that are extremely sensitive to habitat loss (see chapter 3), and a huge number of species may soon be threatened. This life zone ranks as one of our highest conservation priorities, despite lacking any endangered birds today (see chapter 9).

Birds as Ecological Indicators

Certain organisms can play a key role in helping to identify integral biological communities in need of protection. Such *indicator* species share at least one of the following biological features: endemism, habitat specialization, and rarity or sensitivity to habitat disturbance. Having one or more of these characteristics typically places an organism at higher risk of extinction. Areas with many such species contain vulnerable biological communities and should figure prominently in a list of priority sites for protection.

But how can we locate such areas across the entire

Neotropics? Bewildering assortments of life forms occupy even some of the most depauperate Neotropical communities. Our level of knowledge about distribution and abundance, and even species identities, is still rudimentary for all but a few groups of animals and plants. How could we accomplish the research necessary to identify the areas most immediately threatened and most biologically important?

Our operating hypothesis is that ornithological surveys provide a means of assessing, quickly and accurately, the ecological characteristics and conservation status of most terrestrial communities. Many characteristics of birds make them ideal biological indicators, as discussed below.

Conspicuous behavior. Most birds are diurnal and behaviorally active, so they can be inventoried relatively easily. Open-country species (e.g., finches, flycatchers, some furnariids, raptors) are easily observed. Forest inhabitants (e.g., trogons, puffbirds, jacamars, woodpeckers, antbirds) tend to be highly vocal. Many forest species (e.g., antbirds, furnariids, tanagers) join in noisy mixed-species flocks, which are easily located and censused. Even many solitary, secretive, or nocturnal species tend to have distinctive songs or calls that carry great distances.

Rapid and reliable identification. Nonspecialists require only a moderate amount of training and practice to identify most birds. Technical knowledge and specimen preparation are required only rarely, and dissection is not necessary for species-level identification. Most birds can be recognized by color pattern alone, whereas essentially all other groups of living organisms require considerable technical training, detailed dissection, microscopic examination, or availability of ephemeral characters (e.g., flowering or fruiting parts of plants).

Ease of sampling. Representative species lists of birds can be obtained for most habitats in just a few days of study. Birds also are active throughout the year. Although some seasonal movements occur (see part 2), birds do not present the severe seasonal sampling problems inherent in surveys of plants, insects, reptiles, or amphibians. Tools needed to carry out adequate surveys (binoculars, tape recorders, mist nets, and field guides) are readily accessible.

Bird communities in forest and scrub habitats are especially amenable to quantitative sampling with mist nets (black nylon mesh nets, usually 6 m or 12 m long and 2 m high, strung between poles to capture birds unharmed as they fly through the understory). Mist nets provide an excellent means of obtaining nearly complete species lists for understory communities. With standardized methods, mist nets become a scientific tool (albeit with weaknesses; see Remsen and Parker 1983) for comparing bird composition and relative abundances at different sites and in different habitats (e.g., Karr 1976, 1979; Terborgh and Weske 1975; Lovejoy et al. 1986).

Perhaps most important from a conservation standpoint, mist nets provide a reliable means for documenting the presence of many rare and difficult-to-detect species. Rare species are often ecological specialists and therefore represent an important group of indicator taxa within the community. Mist nets enhance the ability of even inexperienced field-workers to document the presence of rare species at any season. Birds in the hand can be identified readily, photographed, and released unharmed. Those that present special problems can be collected and prepared as voucher specimens for preservation and study in museums.

Many ornithologists now have considerable experience with the vocalizations, behavior, and habitat preferences of Neotropical birds. These biologists can survey tropical bird communities in a fraction of the time needed for equivalent inventories of any other animal or plant group.

Wealth of knowledge. Species-level taxonomy is far better known for birds than for any other animal or plant group. Scientists describe valid new species from the Neotropics at the rate of only about two per year (Vuilleumier and Mayr 1987; Vuilleumier, LeCroy, and Mayr 1992), and even this low rate is declining. For most purposes we have completed the job of finding and naming species, which is not true for any other group.

Considerable knowledge about identification, geographic distribution, ecology, and behavioral characteristics of Neotropical birds now appears in field guide format. The entire West Indies, all eight countries in Middle America, and half of the thirteen South American countries now have good to excellent illustrated field guides to their birds. Except for a few endemics from Peru southward and in southeastern Brazil, the vast majority of the 4,037 Neotropical bird taxa treated in this book (see part 4, database B) are illustrated in color in commonly available literature. By comparison, Emmons's (1990) excellent field guide is the only good one available for Neotropical mammals, and it treats the two dominant groups (bats and rodents) only to generic level. For other groups of widespread and diverse organisms (e.g., butterflies, reptiles, flowering plants), the level and availability of taxonomic knowledge are far below those for birds.

Diversity and ecological specialization. The numbers, distributions, and degree of specialization among birds make them excellent biological indicators. Virtually every major Neotropical habitat contains a distinctive bird community, and endemics and specialists are numerous. Of the 3,751 breeding species treated in this book, 1,600 (42.7%) are endemic to one of the twenty-two zoogeographic regions, 1,070 (28.5%) are endemic to a single subregion, and 1,267 (33.8%)

are restricted to one habitat. Most important for their use as indicators, 717 of these species (19.2%) are restricted to both one habitat *and* one zoogeographic region (see chapter 9).

A common misconception about birds is that the ability to fly results in broad dispersal across habitats. Indeed, besides penguins, only nine Neotropical species are truly flightless (three grebes, three ducks, two rheas, and a cormorant), and 690 species (17%) engage in seasonal long-distance migrations from one region or habitat to another each year (chapters 7 and 8). The rest are mostly sedentary and habitat specific. In fact, most non-migratory tropical birds probably are physically incapable of long-distance or sustained flight. Resident species in forest and brush have relatively short, rounded wings compared with those of migrants (Saville 1957; Fitzpatrick 1985) and may even have reduced pectoral muscles (Hartman 1961).

Data on banded birds from many studies in Central and South American forests show that passerines, woodpeckers, jacamars, puffbirds, and tinamous occupy small home ranges throughout the year (e.g., Munn and Terborgh 1979; Powell 1979; Greenberg and Gradwohl 1985; Munn 1985; Bierregaard, unpubl.; Terborgh and Fitzpatrick, unpubl.). Results of numerous censuses, mist-netting projects, and ad lib observations around the tropics further reveal that most nonmigratory species are extraordinarily faithful to small subsets of the available habitats and elevations. Two brief examples illustrate the habitat-specific and sedentary nature of tropical forest birds:

1. The warbler genus *Basileuterus* contains twenty-one species, ranging from Mexico to southeastern Brazil. In central Peru, five species are distributed up the forested eastern Andean slopes in series, elevationally replacing one another with little overlap (Terborgh 1971). No *Basileuterus* occurs below 600 m elevation, even where the tropical forest meets the montane forest along a continuous gradient. Although these birds can fly perfectly well, *Basileuterus* populations are now isolated from one another by any valley that dips below about 600 m in elevation. The importance of faithful restriction to certain elevational zones in many Andean birds is well documented in a landmark trio of papers (Terborgh 1971, 1977; Terborgh and Weske 1975). We explore the conservation implications of elevational segregation in chapter 3.

2. Recently A. Capparella (1988, unpubl.) documented the remarkable degree to which bird populations of the forest understory are genetically isolated from conspecifics across Amazonian rivers just a few kilometers wide. He showed that in some species populations on opposite banks of a river, which cannot be distinguished morphologically from one another, differ genetically to the same degree as do many species of North American warblers in the genus *Dendroica*. Gene flow is absent across these narrow water gaps today and apparently has been reduced for an extremely long time.

The remarkably sedentary nature of most tropical birds has important implications for design and placement of preserves (chapter 9). Since most Neotropical bird species do not stray from fixed and relatively narrow sets of ecological and geographic limits, the commonly recognized tropical communities usually contain at least a handful of characteristic "indicator species" (see below).

High sensitivity to disturbance. Responses of birds to habitat disturbance or fragmentation vary considerably among species (e.g., Robbins et al. 1989). If habitat degradation has begun (e.g., fragmentation, selective logging, proliferation of openings or edges, or structural changes to the understory), highly sensitive species will be missing. Others may appear specifically because of the habitat alterations (see "trash species" in chapter 3). Therefore a comparison of "observed" versus "expected" species at a given habitat tract provides a test of its condition.

Indicator Species Lists

Indicator species are those that, taken as a group, exclusively define a specific ecological and geographic province. Lists of indicator species (see database I) provide a standard for assessing the type and condition of the biological community being studied.

Good indicators for identifying appropriate sites for the conservation of a habitat share four characteristics: (1) they typically occur in only one or a very few habitats; (2) they are relatively common; (3) they can be detected easily; and (4) they show high sensitivity to habitat disturbance (i.e., they become rare, or disappear, in habitats that are altered, overhunted, or fragmented).

Not all habitat-restricted species make good ecological indicators. Some can be so rare or difficult to observe that even the most competent observers may fail to detect their presence. For example, spotting a Harpy Eagle (*Harpia harpyja*) while surveying a forest locality—besides being an exhilarating experience—suggests that a large area of pristine forest with abundant arboreal mammals exists in the region. However, *not* encountering a Harpy would not indicate the inverse, because these large raptors naturally occur in low density and are difficult to detect in the dense forest canopy.

For this book we generated lists of indicator species occupying many of the important habitats and regions (see part 4, database I). We produced these lists from database A using computer searches of the complete table, choosing entries with a specified combination of ecological traits and geographic provinces.

What do these lists convey? Separately, the presence of any one indicator species at a given site says little.

Many forest species use openings or secondary habitats temporarily during the day, or during certain seasons, despite being strictly dependent on primary forest over the long term. Toucans, many hummingbirds, cotingas, tanagers, and other canopy species occasionally use secondary forest, often to visit flowering or fruiting trees. Nevertheless, some of these species are good indicators because they are common, are easily observed, and correlate with the presence of pristine habitat in the region. Therefore it is important to think of a list of indicators as a *complete ecological assemblage*. These taxa identify a tract of habitat as pristine only when virtually all of them are present.

Although birds are only a small part of any natural community, their numbers and composition reflect traits of the habitat that clearly affect other species as well. A central assumption of this book is that diversity, zones of endemism, and ecological specialization among bird communities correlate broadly with those of most other terrestrial organisms in the Neotropics (discussed in chapter 3). However, bird communities can be measured with only a fraction of the time and effort required for other groups. This suggests that birds can be used as a principal indicator group for assessing the type and quality of any terrestrial Neotropical habitat for designation as a protected site.

Deriving Communities and Their Properties from the Databases

Our major data table (database A, "Zoogeographic and Ecological Attributes of Bird Species Breeding in the Neotropics") encodes ecological and geographic attributes of each Neotropical bird species, allowing computer-aided searches and sorts for species with shared properties. When sorted according to zoogeographic province, groups of bird species with similar habitat and microhabitat descriptors form genuine ecological assemblages. Together with features such as elevational limits, foraging stratum, and relative abundance, database A can be used to define profiles of every important bird assemblage within the Neotropics.

Degree of habitat specialization of a given species can be inferred by the number of habitats (up to seven) recorded. The habitat specialists ($N = 1{,}267$) have only a single habitat listed, while the few real generalists ($N = 10$) have all seven "habitat fields" filled. This feature allows us to compare proportions of habitat specialists among various ecological assemblages. We emphasize this comparative approach throughout the text, because assemblages that are rich in habitat specialists are likely to be most vulnerable to habitat loss or alteration.

Vulnerability of an avian assemblage to human activity also can be derived from the "conservation status" and "notes" of its respective species in database A. As shown in our treatments of the major habitat types (chapters 3 to 6) and conservation priorities (chapters 9 and 10), database A can be used to pinpoint the regions and habitats that contain the most threatened ecological communities.

Database B ("Distribution of Neotropical Bird Species by Country") was prepared as an aid to individual planners within the political units in the Neotropics. It fulfills two main goals. First, cross-referencing databases A and B allows within-country users to analyze only the subset of bird species or communities that occurs within their country. From the perspective of natural resource planning, this reduces the number of species to manageable and locally meaningful levels. Second, listing the countries where each species is found permits users in every country to gain a broader perspective on their avifauna. Most important, planners in each country can identify the species that are uniquely "theirs." Endemics restricted to a single country represent the unique prizes that are paramount in setting in-country priorities for conservation (see chapter 9). Assemblages of such species may point to globally significant, cornerstone habitats within the country (chapter 10). To be maintained, these cornerstones will require international recognition and support, as well as great attention from within the country.

PART

1

Birds and Vegetation: Distribution and Threats

2 Neotropical Vegetation Types as Avian Habitats

Synopsis

We distinguish forty-one principal habitats in the Neotropics, a classification based on the birds' discrimination of different vegetation types. We believe our categories can be used as a base for describing the habitats of other terrestrial taxa as well. Finer-grained distinctions in vegetation communities may be derived from database A, by searching for a given habitat type (e.g., lowland evergreen forest) within a specific zoogeographic region or subregion (e.g., the very wet Chocó Lowlands in Colombia).

In this chapter we briefly describe the general characteristics of each of the twenty-nine terrestrial vegetation types—fifteen forest, fourteen nonforest—and twelve aquatic habitats we recognize. With help from two tropical botanists, Robin Foster and the late Alwyn Gentry, we have attempted to highlight typical botanical features for each habitat. Our goal is to make each category recognizable by, and useful to, tropical biologists, whatever their taxonomic specialties.

The birds' use of the different habitats is summarized in table 2.1. The codes presented in table 2.1 and below correspond to the codes used in part 4, database A. The total number of species using each type is listed, along with the number of species that use the given habitat as their primary or sole habitat.

Neotropical Avian Habitats

Forest Habitats

Tropical Lowland Evergreen Forests (F1)

Lowland evergreen forests (see plate 1) occur up to 900 m in the Neotropics, wherever rainfall is abundant (more than 2,000 mm per year near the equator) and soils are suitable (for example, sufficiently deep or well drained; Gentry 1988a). These forests at present range from southern Veracruz, Mexico, south through Middle America to coastal Ecuador, northern Venezuela, the Orinoco and Amazon basins, the Atlantic coast of Brazil, and northern Argentina (Jujuy, Misiones). Remnants also persist on some larger Caribbean islands (Prance 1989).

Throughout much of the Neotropics, these forests reach 25–40 m in height, with emergents of 50–60 m (Breedlove 1973; Terborgh 1983; Gentry 1990a). They are typically rich in buttressed trees, canopy and undergrowth palms, woody vines, and vascular epiphytes including aroids, bromeliads, ferns, and orchids (Schimper 1903; Emmons and Gentry 1983; Gentry and Dodson 1987). Richards (1952) described a multilayered character of such forests, typically consisting of three tree strata besides one or two layers of shrubs and herbs. Just as often there is no clear layering, however, especially when the forest is dynamic, with a high rate of tree turnover.

Climate and soil affect the structure and composition of the forests. Several types can be distinguished based on seasonality and quantity of soil moisture, including the pluvial, wet, and moist forests distinguished by Gentry (1978). For the purposes of this book, we combine all these lowland forest variants into one broad category (F1), encompassing humid forests of the Central American lowlands, the Amazonian floodplain and upland *terra firme* forests, and the humid forests along the Atlantic coast of Brazil and the Paraná/Paraguay river drainages. Also included are a variety of forest types in Amazonia sometimes recognized as distinct from the typical upland forests, such as liana forests (those with an unusual abundance of woody vines) and bamboo forests, which are characterized by extensive understory thickets of the tall, spiny bamboo *Guadua angustifolia* (see Prance 1989). White sand forests are considered separately (see F12).

Lowland evergreen forests are renowned for their extraordinary diversity of plant species. As many as 265 species of trees and lianas greater than 2.5 cm dbh

Table 2.1 Use of Neotropical Habitats by Birds

Habitat	Habitat Code	Number of Bird Species: Total Users	Primary Habitat	Habitat Restricted
Forests				
Tropical lowland evergreen	F1	1,410	1,012	408
Flooded tropical evergreen	F2	166	76	22
River-edge/river island	F3	193	80	14
Montane evergreen	F4	1,162	840	357
Elfin	F5	166	61	27
Polylepis woodland	F6	55	18	6
Tropical deciduous	F7	635	300	64
Gallery	F8	474	99	12
Southern temperate	F9	57	31	12
Pine	F10	119	60	18
Pine-oak	F11	179	75	8
White sand	F12	60	16	6
Palm	F13	10	4	2
Mangrove	F14	87	15	4
Second-growth habitats	F15	920	54	2
Scrubs/grasslands				
Arid lowland	N1	342	167	41
Arid montane	N2	265	114	40
Semihumid/humid montane	N3	107	31	7
Cerrado	N4	46	18	3
Campo grasslands	N5	68	23	9
Low, seasonally wet	N6	103	58	1
Southern temperate	N7	68	36	8
Northern temperate	N8	35	24	3
Puna	N9	69	41	18
Paramo	N10	53	35	12
Riparian thickets	N11	118	35	1
River island scrub	N12	29	11	6
Pastures/agricultural lands	N13	132	22	0
Second-growth habitats	N14	324	69	1
Aquatic				
Freshwater marshes	A1	187	124	55
Saltwater/brackish marshes	A2	39	8	2
Coastal sand beaches/mudflats	A3	28	5	2
Coastal rocky beaches	A4	20	6	5
Riverine sand beaches	A5	7	5	2
Freshwater lakes and ponds	A6	91	35	15
Alkaline lakes	A7	14	5	2
Rivers	A8	43	13	2
Streams	A9	29	8	0
Bogs	A10	15	3	1
Coastal waters	A11	71	59	21
Pelagic waters	A12	69	50	47

have been found in 0.1 ha of lowland forest in Pacific Colombia (Gentry 1986b). Upper Amazonian forests, although they grow on poorer soils, may be richer still (Foster 1990; Gentry 1990b). Floodplain and *terra firme* forests in upper Amazonia are floristically distinct, though the transition between them can at times be gradual. Young floodplain forests are inundated at near-yearly intervals for short periods (Terborgh 1983; Foster, Arce B., and Wachter 1986). Often conspicuous in these forests are trees of *Ficus insipida, F. maxima,* and *Clarisia biflora* (Moraceae; family names and taxonomic treatment follow Gentry 1993a), *Cedrela odorata* and *Guarea guidonia* (Meliaceae), *Terminalia oblonga* (Combretaceae), and *Gallesia integrifolia* (Phytolacceae). Various species of *Heliconia* (Musaceae) often dominate the understory. Older floodplain forests, inundated rarely or at intervals of many years, include such prominent trees as *Ceiba pentandra* (Bombacaceae), *Brosimum alicastrum* (Moraceae), *Dipteryx micrantha* and *Apuleia leiocarpa* (Leguminosae), *Luehea cymulosa* (Tiliaceae), *Hura crepitans* (Euphorbiaceae), and *Sloanea fendleri* (Elaeocarpaceae). The higher, poorer soils of the *terra firme* forest usually represent uplifted, older, eroded floodplain terraces. Characteristic trees include numerous representatives of Sapotaceae, Lecythidaceae, Burseraceae, Caryocaraceae, Vochysiaceae, Annonaceae, and Chrysobalanaceae (Prance 1990). The very young successional forests along the riverbanks are considered separately (F3), as are the season-long or permanently inundated forests (F2), discussed below.

Little remains of the lowland tropical evergreen and semideciduous forests of coastal Brazil, which once occupied about 1 million km^2 and stretched along Brazil's entire eastern coast. By the 1970s, estimates of habitat destruction along different parts of the coast ranged from 65% to 93% of the original forest (Mori, Boom, and Prance 1981). Although we lump this habitat into F1, endemism in the coastal region is high: 53.5% of a sample of forest tree species were unique to the region (Mori, Boom, and Prance 1981). Many of the primary tree families in these coastal forests are the same as in the *terra firme* forests of Amazonia; for example, Sapotaceae, Chyrsobalanaceae, Lecythidaceae, Caesalpinaceae, and Lauraceae. However, the predominance of Myrtaceae in the Atlantic forests distinguishes them from other lowland humid forests (Mori et al. 1983).

Evergreen forests of the Paraná and Paraguay river basins are floristically less diverse than those of coastal Brazil and Amazonia. Cabrera (1971) describes the flora of a Paraná forest site near Iguazú, Argentina, consisting of more than a hundred tree species averaging 20–30 m in height. Among the most common trees are *Balfourodendron riedelianum* (Rutaceae), *Nectandra saligna* and *Ocotea pulchella* (Lauraceae), *Chrysophyllum gonocarpum* (Sapotaceae), *Cabralea oblongifolia* (Meliaceae), and *Lonchocarpus leucanthus* and *Holocalyx balansae* (Leguminosae). Bamboos are abundant (and important to a variety of bird species), including *Guadua trinii, Merostachys claussenii,* and several species of *Chusquea.*

Color plate 1. Montane evergreen forest (F4). Cuzco, Peru (photo, J. W. Fitzpatrick).

Color plate 2. Montane evergreen forest (F4). Cuzco, Peru (photo, J. W. Fitzpatrick).

Color plate 3. Elfin forest (F5), interior. Cajamarca, Peru (photo, J. W. Fitzpatrick).

Color plate 4. Elfin forest (F5), edge with puna (N10); note bog (A10) in foreground. San Martín, Peru (photo, Susan A. Lohr).

Color plate 5. *Polylepis* forest (F6). Lima, Peru (photo, D. E. Willard).

Color plate 6. Tropical deciduous forest (F7), dry season. Aragua, Venezuela (photo, J. W. Fitzpatrick).

Color plate 7. Tropical deciduous forest (F7), rainy season (note tree in right foreground, which is the same tree as in color plate 6). Aragua, Venezuela (photo, J. W. Fitzpatrick).

Color plate 8. Southern temperate forest (F9), *Nothofagus* forest. Magellanes, Chile (photo, B. D. Patterson).

Color plate 9. White sand forest (F12), campina. Amazonas, Brazil (photo, R. B. Foster).

Color plate 10. Mangrove forest (F14). Florida, United States (photo, R. Bowman).

Color plate 11. Mangrove forest (F14), stilt roots of *Rhizophora mangle*. Puntarenas, Costa Rica (photo, R. B. Foster).

Color plate 12. Arid lowland scrub (N1). Aragua, Venezuela (photo, J. W. Fitzpatrick).

Color plate 13. Campo grassland (N4). Brasília, Brazil (photo, J. W. Fitzpatrick).

Color plate 14. Puna (N9) with vicuñas. Ayacucho, Peru (photo, Susan A. Lohr).

Color plate 15. Paramo (N10). Carchi, Ecuador (photo, R. B. Foster).

Color plate 16. Riparian thickets (N11). Madre de Dios, Peru (photo, J. W. Fitzpatrick).

Plate 1. Tropical lowland evergreen forest (F1). Pando, Bolivia (photo, T. A. Parker III).

Plate 2. Flooded tropical evergreen forest (F2). Amazonas, Colombia (photo, J. W. Fitzpatrick).

Plate 3. River island forest (F3). Loreto, Peru (photo, T. A. Parker III).

Plate 4. Montane evergreen forest (F4). Cuzco, Peru (photo, J. W. Fitzpatrick). See also color plates 1 and 2.

Plate 5. *Polylepis* woodland (F6). Cuzco, Peru (photo, T. A. Parker III). See also color plate 5.

Plate 6. Tropical deciduous forest (F7). El Oro, Ecuador (photo, T. A. Parker III). See also color plates 6 and 7.

Plate 7. Gallery forest (F8). Brasília, Brazil (photo, J. W. Fitzpatrick).

Plate 8. Southern temperate forest (F9), Araucaria forest. Rio Grande do Sul, Brazil (photo, T. A. Parker III). See also color plate 8.

Plate 9. Pine forest (F10). Jalisco, Mexico (photo, J. W. Fitzpatrick).

Plate 10. Pine-oak forest (F11). Western Mexico (photo, T. A. Parker III).

Plate 11. Oak forest (F11). Jalisco, Mexico (photo, J. W. Fitzpatrick).

Plate 12. White sand forest (F12), restinga. São Paulo, Brazil (photo, T. A. Parker III). See also color plate 9.

Plate 13. Palm forest (F13). Pando, Bolivia (photo, T. A. Parker III).

Plate 14. Mangrove forest (F14), mangrove knees (*Avicenna* sp.). Bahia, Brazil (photo, D. F. Stotz). See also color plates 10 and 11.

Plate 15. Second-growth forest (F15). Madre de Dios, Peru (photo, J. W. Fitzpatrick).

Plate 16. Arid lowland scrub (N1). Lambayeque, Peru (photo, T. A. Parker III). See also color plate 12.

Plate 17. Arid montane scrub (N2). Cuzco, Peru (photo, T. A. Parker III).

Plate 18. Arid montane scrub (N2). Cuzco, Peru (photo, T. A. Parker III).

Plate 19. Humid montane scrub (N3). Cajamarca, Peru (photo, J. W. Fitzpatrick).

Plate 20. Cerrado (N4). Santa Cruz, Bolivia (photo, T. A. Parker III).

Plate 21. Campo grassland (N5). Brasília, Brazil (photo, J. W. Fitzpatrick). See also color plate 13.

Plate 22. Low, seasonally wet grassland (N6). Roraima, Brazil (photo, D. F. Stotz).

Plate 23. Southern temperate grassland (N7). Magellanes, Chile (photo, B. D. Patterson).

Plate 24. Northern temperate grassland (N8). Arizona, United States (photo, D. F. Stotz).

Plate 25. Puna (N9). Arequipa, Peru (photo, T. A. Parker III). See also color plate 15.

Plate 26. Paramo (N10). Merida, Venezuela (photo, D. E. Willard). See also color plate 14.

Plate 27. Riparian thickets (N11). Loreto, Peru (photo, T. A. Parker III). See also color plate 16.

Plate 28. River island scrub (N12). Loreto, Peru (photo, T. A. Parker III).

Plate 29. Agricultural land (N13). Santa Cruz, Bolivia (photo, T. A. Parker III).

Plate 30. Agricultural land (N13). Cuzco, Peru (photo, J. W. Fitzpatrick).

Plate 31. Second growth-scrub (N14). Amazonas, Brazil (photo, J. W. Fitzpatrick).

Plate 32. (*above left*) Freshwater marsh (A1). Madre de Dios, Peru (photo, T. A. Parker III).

Plate 33. (*above*) Freshwater marsh (A1). Loreto, Peru (photo, T. A. Parker III).

Plate 34. Saltwater marsh (A2). Georgia, United States (photo, R. Bowman).

Plate 35. Coastal mudflats (A3). Falcón, Venezuela (photo, J. W. Fitzpatrick).

Plate 36. Coastal rocky beach (A4). St. Lucia (photo, T. A. Parker III

Plate 37. Riverine sand beach (A5). Madre de Dios, Peru (photo, J. W. Fitzpatrick).

Plate 38. Freshwater lake (A6). Cuzco, Peru (photo, T. A. Parker III).

Plate 39. Alkaline lake (A7). Arequipa, Peru (photo, T. A. Parker III).

Plate 40. River (A8). Rio Mamoré, Bolivia (photo, T. A. Parker III).

Plate 41. Stream (A9). Cuzco, Peru (photo, D. E. Willard).

Plate 42. Coastal waters (A11). Ica, Peru (photo, T. A. Parker III).

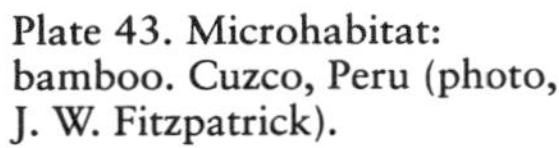

Plate 43. Microhabitat: bamboo. Cuzco, Peru (photo, J. W. Fitzpatrick).

Plate 44. Microhabitat: terrestrial bromeliads. São Paulo, Brazil (photo, T. A. Parker III).

Plate 45. Microhabitat: cliffs. Rio Grande do Sul, Brazil (photo, T. A. Parker III).

Plate 46. Microhabitat: streamside. Amazonas, Venezuela (photo, D. E. Willard).

Flooded Tropical Evergreen Forests (F2)

A variety of Neotropical forests are flooded permanently or annually. Most of these forests are structurally and floristically similar to the upland forests (F1) but differ in supporting flood-tolerant trees and undergrowth plants. This category includes both *várzea* forests (see plate 2), along Amazonian whitewater rivers, and *igapó* forests, primarily on sandy soils bordering blackwater and clearwater rivers of Amazonia.

Prance (1989) distinguishes four types of *várzea* forests. These are less diverse than the upland forests but equally tall, with numerous heavily buttressed trees and abundant arboreal epiphytes (huge aroids, bromeliads, and ferns). The rich undergrowth includes a variety of broad-leaved Cyclanthaceae, Marantaceae, and Zingiberaceae, and characteristic trees include *Pseudobombax munguba* (Bombaceae), *Calycophyllum spruceanum* (Rubiaceae), *Cecropia paraensis* and various species of *Ficus* (Moraceae), *Carapa guianensis* and *Trichilia singularis* (Meliaceae), *Cassia grandis, Albizia niopoides,* and *Pithecellobium multiflorum* (Leguminosae), *Crataeva tapia* (Capparidaceae), *Cordia tetrandra* (Boraginaceae), and *Piranhea trifoliata* (Euphorbiaceae) (Prance 1979, 1989; Adis 1984).

Igapó forests typically are inundated for periods of five to six months or longer. They vary greatly in height; the tallest have canopies averaging nearly 35 m. The undergrowth is open, with few herbs and shrubs, and arboreal epiphytes are uncommon. Up to forty-eight species of trees were recorded on 1 ha sites in Amazonian Brazil (Adis 1981). Typical *igapó* tree species include *Aldina latifolia, Parkia pectinata, Swartzia polyphylla, Macrolobium acaciaefolium,* and *Copaifera martii* (Leguminosae), *Allantoma lineata* and *Eschweilera pachysepala* (Lecythidaceae), *Caraipa grandiflora* (Guttiferae), *Couepia paraensis* and *Licania apetala* (Chrysobalanaceae), *Eugenia inundata* (Myrtaceae), *Piranhea trifolia* (Euphorbiaceae), *Ruprechtia tenuiflora* and *Triplaris surinamensis* (Polygonaceae), *Tabebuia barbata* (Bignoniaceae), and *Virola elongata* (Myristicaceae) (Adis 1984; R. B. Foster, pers. comm.; Prance 1979, 1989).

Also included under the F2 habitat category are filled-in floodplain lakes (swamp forests) such as upper Amazonian *Ficus trigona* swamps (Terborgh 1983) and *Erythrina fusca* swamps, or various swamp forests associated with slow-moving rivers in Middle America (Breedlove 1973; Hartshorn 1988). Palm swamps (F13) and mangroves (F14) are considered separately.

River-Edge (and River Island) Forests (F3)

These early successional forests (see plate 3) border rivers throughout the lowland tropics and into mountain river valleys. They replace riparian shrubby thickets of *Tessaria* (Compositae), *Salix* (Salicaceae), and *Gynerium* (Gramineae) (see N11) on recently formed islands and riverbanks. Species of *Cecropia* (Moraceae) dominate these forests (usually in even-aged stands 10–25 m tall) or are mixed with *Ochroma pyramidale* (Bombacaceae), *Guazuma crinita* (Sterculiaceae), *Sapium* spp. (Euphorbiaceae), *Erythrina* spp., and mimosoid trees or shrubs such as *Acacia, Albizia, Senna,* and *Mimosa* (Leguminosae). Dense thickets of giant herbs such as *Heliconia* (Musaceae), *Calathea* (Marantaceae), *Renealmia,* and *Costus* spp. (Zingiberaceae) or species of *Piper* (Piperaceae) cover the ground beneath. River-edge forests form a narrow zone (rarely more than 100 m wide) between the riverbank and more diverse forests on higher ground (see F1). In upper Amazonia, floods regularly inundate this habitat, but runoff is rapid and vegetation rarely is submerged for more than a few days or weeks. In the mountains, inundation from flash floods more often lasts hours than days.

Montane Evergreen Forests (F4)

The exact elevation at which the transition from lowland to montane forests occurs varies from region to region and sometimes from ridge to ridge. The transition probably has less to do with actual elevation than with the elevations at which clouds most frequently touch the mountains, so that the probability of drought stress is greatly reduced. These elevations differ significantly between a small peak sticking out of the lowlands of central Panama and one along the eastern slopes of the Andes. Some mountains, such as the western Andes in Ecuador, seem to have two different elevations where the clouds usually hit, resulting in a complex gradient of forests (R. B. Foster, pers. comm.).

In this varying transition zone, mostly between about 600–700 and 1,200–1,500 m throughout the humid highlands of Middle and South America, many montane plant species and some genera replace lowland plant species and genera (Gentry 1988a; Prance 1989). On higher mountains or ranges, the main replacement of lowland plant genera with montane genera occurs mostly between 1,500 and 2,000 m. At any elevation, the most obvious feature of montane forests is the profusion of mosses and other epiphytes (including bromeliads, ferns, and orchids) that cover the exposed branches and trunks of most trees. The transition from lowland to highland flora and fauna is often abrupt. As one hikes from foothill forests of Amazonia into Andean forests at 900–1,200 m, the sudden appearance of moss-covered trees, as well as tree ferns and montane bamboos, is striking.

Hartshorn (1983) characterizes montane evergreen forests (see plate 4) as low to intermediate in height, with two tree strata. In forests above 1,500 m, canopy trees are 25–30 m tall, having short, stout, unbuttressed trunks with rough bark. Their crowns are relatively small, compact and rounded, with many thick, short, twisting branches. The understory is open, with trees 5–15 m tall, often having crooked trunks. Grubb (1974) distinguishes between lower montane forests (700–1,800 m), where trees with mesophyll leaf types and herbaceous vascular epiphytes are dominant (see color plates 1 and 2), and upper montane forests (1,800–3,400 m), where microphyllous trees and bryophytic epiphytes and lichens are more numerous.

Conspicuous tree and shrub genera of montane forests in the Andes, especially above 1,500 m, include *Alzatea* (Alzateaceae), *Brunellia* (Brunelliaceae), *Clethra* (Clethraceae), *Clusia* (Guttiferae), *Cinchona* (Rubiaceae), *Drimys* (Winteraceae), *Hyeronima* (Euphorbiaceae), *Ilex* (Aquifoliaceae), *Myrsine* (Myrsinaceae), *Nectandra* and *Ocotea* (Lauraceae), *Oreopanax* and *Schefflera* (Araliaceae), *Podocarpus* (especially *montanus* and *oleifolius*) (Podocarpaceae), *Prunus* (Rosaceae), *Rhamnus* (Rhamnaceae), *Solanum* (Solanaceae), *Symplocos* (Symplocaceae), and *Weinmannia* (Cunoniaceae). Tree ferns (especially *Cyathea*) often are conspicuous, and highland palms, especially *Ceroxylon* and *Dictyocaryum,* occur locally. Natural landslides and other edges are invaded by *Chusquea* bamboos, alders (*Alnus acuminata*) or *Croton* spp. (Euphorbiaceae), and also vines, shrubs, and small trees of the following genera: *Baccharis* (Compositae), *Bocconia* (Papaveraceae), *Centropogon* (Capparidaceae), *Fuchsia* (Onagraceae), *Oreopanax* (Araliaceae), *Embothrium* and *Roupala* (Proteaceae), *Rubus* (Rubiaceae), *Solanum* (Solanaceae), various melastomes (esp. *Tibouchina* and *Miconia*), and bushes of *Weinmannia* (Cunoniaceae) and *Viburnum* (Caprifoliaceae) (Weberbauer 1911; Tosi 1960; also see Cuatrecasas 1957, 1958; Diels 1937; Troll 1959).

Highland forests in Middle America contain many of the same genera. However, oaks (*Quercus acatanagensis, Q. corrugata, Q. costaricensis,* and *Q. seemannii*), sweet gum (*Liquidambar* spp.), and other Laurasian elements often are numerous, and conifers such as *Abies guatemalensis* and *Pinus ayacahuite* (Pinaceae) often are locally dominant (Breedlove 1973; Hartshorn 1983; Rzedowski 1978).

Montane forests in southeastern Brazil appear very similar in structure to those in the Andes. Arboreal epiphytic growth in the form of large bromeliads and mosses is conspicuous above 1,000 m, and bamboos are unusually abundant (and important to birds), especially tall stands of *Merostachys* spp. and extensive thickets of *Chusquea* spp. (esp. *C. pinifolia*). Segadas-Viana (1968) describes the vegetation of the Itatiaia range and lists the dominant trees in forest above 1,500 m as *Cabralea canjerana* (Meliaceae), *Drimys winteri* (Winteraceae), *Myrsine gardneriana* (Myrsinaceae), *Roupala lucens* (Proteaceae), and *Weinmannia discolor* (Cunoniaceae).

Elfin Forests (F5)

Elfin forests (see color plates 3 and 4) occur locally on humid, windswept ridges in Middle America, from as low as 500 m on Cerro Jefe, Panama (Lewis 1971), to above 3,200 m on the upper slopes of volcanoes from Chiapas, Mexico, south to Chiriquí, Panama. In the humid Andes, stunted forests form an almost continuous band (from ca. 3,200–3,800 m) below the paramos, from Venezuela to central Bolivia. They also occur as low as 900 m on exposed Andean ridge crests, especially those of outlying ridges; on the rain-drenched mountaintops of many Caribbean islands; and on the higher tepuis in southern Venezuela and adjacent portions of Guyana and Brazil.

Beard (1955) defined elfin forest or woodland as a single-storied, impenetrable tangle of trees and shrubs 1–10 m tall. Hartshorn (1983) described it as a "short, gnarled, sodden forest where the canopy appears sculptured and streamlined by the relentless wind." Prance (1989) emphasized the microphyllous or nanophyllous character of this stunted forest, where bryophytic epiphytes and lichens cover the branches of trees and shrubs and carpet the ground. Vascular epiphytes are not as numerous or conspicuous as in taller montane forests at lower elevations.

At the highest elevations, elfin forests may be stunted from the diebacks caused by occasional drought stress or fire, besides the wind pruning. At all elevations there is a tendency for the harder quartzites, sandstones, and granites to end up as the tops of ridges and mountains because they are most resistant to erosion. Even at low elevations, the acid soils over these rocks often lead to vegetation stunting and downward migration of the slow-growing, upper montane plant genera.

Characteristic elfin forest tree and shrub genera include *Befaria* (Ericaceae), *Brunellia* (Brunelliaceae), *Clusia* (Clusiaceae), *Gynoxys* (Compositae), *Ilex* (Aquifoliaceae), *Miconia* (Melastomataceae), *Rhamnus* (Rhamnaceae), *Escallonia* (Escalloniaceae), and *Weinmannia* (Cunoniaceae) (Prance 1989; R. B. Foster, pers. comm.). Hartshorn (1983) mentions *Clusia alata* (Clusiaceae) and various Araliaceae (*Didymopanax pittieri, Oreopanax nubigeneum,* and *O. sanderianus*) as common trees in a Costa Rican elfin forest. Bamboos (*Chusquea* spp.) and tree ferns (*Cyathea* spp.) are often conspicuous floristic elements in Andean treeline forests. Floristically, it usually is a stunted version of the upper montane forest, with the same genera being represented by different species.

Polylepis *Woodlands (F6)*

This distinctive, high-elevation forest type (see plate 5 and color plate 5) occurs above cloud level (ca. 3,500–4,500 m) in the Andes, from western Venezuela south to northern Argentina and Chile (Simpson 1979). *Polylepis* woodlands often occur as islands of woody vegetation surrounded by paramo or puna grass and shrub communities; they are usually restricted to steep, rocky slopes in sheltered valleys but also occur locally on exposed, windswept plains of the Andean altiplano. These *Polylepis* spp. (Rosaceae) are highly drought tolerant and probably fire resistant. They also are represented in some upper montane forests, but monospecific stands normally occur in isolated patches well above treeline. The most extensive tracts of this threatened ecosystem survive in the Cordillera Blanca and in adjacent mountains of west-central Peru, where large stands of *P. incana, P. racemosa,* and *P. weberbaueri* grow on steep slopes in association with lesser numbers of other trees, especially *Buddleja incana* (Loganiaceae) and *Escallonia hyprophila* (Escalloniaceae), and a variety of shrubs, including species of *Baccharis, Barnadesia.* and *Gynoxys* (Compositae), *Berberis* (Berberidaceae), *Brachyotum* (Melastomataceae), *Hesperomeles* (Rosaceae), *Hypericum* (Guttiferae), *Lupinus* (Leguminosae), and *Ribes* (Saxifragaceae) (Fjeldså 1987; Cerrate 1979). The largest *Polylepis* trees in these forests are 18 m tall, with trunks 90 cm across (Fjeldså 1987). Mosses and lichens grow on the branches and trunks of *Polylepis* in humid areas, particularly on the eastern slopes of the Cordillera Blanca and above the upper montane forests of southeastern Peru. Epiphytic mistletoes (e.g., *Tristerix chodatianus* and *T. longebracteatus*) are conspicuous in the *Polylepis* trees. In drier areas of southern Peru and Bolivia, *Polylepis besseri, P. tomentella,* and *P. tarapacana* grow in scattered patches of open woodland surrounded by puna vegetation, or as scrub on arid, shrub-covered slopes (Fjeldså 1987; Pearson and Ralph 1978; Cabrera 1976). Vuilleumier and Ewert (1978) describe woodlands of *Polylepis sericea* that occur on rocky slopes within the paramos of Venezuela.

Tropical Deciduous Forests (F7)

Deciduous forests (see plate 6 and color plates 6 and 7) occur widely in dry to arid regions of the Neotropics. They dominate landscapes along the Pacific slope of Middle America from southern Sonora south to northwest Costa Rica and are also well developed along the Pacific coast in southwest Ecuador and northwest Peru, as well as across Caribbean Colombia and Venezuela. In addition, extensive deciduous forests cover the interior of central South America south of Amazonia, particularly within the caatinga of north-central Brazil and the chaco of southern Bolivia, Paraguay, and northern Argentina. Smaller pockets of this forest type occur in several Andean valleys in Peru, and intermittently south to the eastern slopes of the Andes in southeastern Bolivia and northern Argentina.

These forests contain a diverse association of deciduous and semideciduous trees; the canopy varies from 10 to 25 m in height, although trees as tall as 50 m occur in riparian areas (Hartshorn 1983). Secondary forest in this habitat is usually completely deciduous, whereas mature forest has more evergreen species. Rainfall does not exceed 2,000 mm and is usually much lower. During the long dry season of four to seven months, most trees and understory plants lose their leaves (see color plate 6), unless their roots reach the water table. Many species flower conspicuously then, attracting numerous avian and insect nectarivores. Spiny Mimosoideae and Caesalpinoideae legume trees dominate the canopy in many areas; Bignoniaceae are the dominant lianas; and Rubiaceae may be prominent in the understory, particularly in taller, denser forests (Gentry 1993b; Hartshorn 1983). Arboreal epiphytes are sometimes conspicuous, mostly *Tillandsia* spp. (Bromeliaceae), but are not as common or diverse as in humid forests.

Typical trees in tall, deciduous forests in Chiapas, Mexico, and Guanacaste, Costa Rica, include *Pochota quinata* and *Pseudobombax ellipticum* (Bombaceae), *Casearia arquata* (Flacourtiaceae), *Bursera excelsa* and *B. simaruba* (Burseraceae), *Calycophyllum candidissimum* (Rubiaceae), *Cedrela oaxacensis* (Meliaceae), *Cochlospermum vitifolium* (Cochlospermaceae), *Cordia alliodora* (Boraginaceae), *Enterolobium cyclocarpum, Gliricidia sepium, Lysiloma aurita,* and *Pithecellobium saman* (Leguminosae), *Guazuma tomentosa* (Sterculiaceae), *Hura polyandrum* (Euphorbiaceae), *Luehea candida* (Tiliaceae), *Spondias mombin* (Annonaceae), *Tabebuia chrysantha* and *T. rosea* (Bignoniaceae), and *Triplaris melanodendron* (Polygonaceae) (Breedlove 1973; Hartshorn 1983). Tall forests of this kind in northwestern Peru and southwestern Ecuador often are dominated (at least visually) by Bombacaceae (*Ceiba trichistandra, Cavanillesia platanifolia, Eriotheca ruiziana*), *Erythrina* spp. (Leguminosae), and *Tabebuia chrysantha* (Bignoniaceae); *Capparis* (Capparidaceae) is unusually diverse and conspicuous (Gentry 1986b, 1993b; Tosi 1960).

Shelford (1963) distinguished "short-tree" and "tall-tree" deciduous forests. Thorn forests in western Mexico and the caatinga of north-central Brazil, for example, are shorter (often ca. 10 m tall) and floristically less diverse than those described above but contain species of many of the same tree genera (Gentry 1982a, 1993b; Andrade-Lima 1957, 1964, 1981). In both regions, spiny trees and columnar cacti are common; terrestrial bromeliads are especially prominent in caatinga forests (Parker, pers. obs.).

Several types of deciduous forests characterize the chaco. Mesquites (*Prosopis alba* and *P. nigra*), *Geoffroea decorticans* and *Pithecellobium scalare* (Leguminosae), *Celtis* spp. (Ulmaceae), *Schinus* spp. (Annonaceae), *Sideroxylon obtusifolia* (Sapotaceae), and *Zizyphus mistol* (Rhamnaceae) dominate spiny forests 12–15 m tall on somewhat salty soil. Columnar cacti (*Cereus coryne* and *C. validus*) often are conspicuous, as are terrestrial bromeliads (*Bromelia serra, Dyckia ferox*). Characteristic trees in taller forests (to 25 m) on richer soils of the chaco include *Aspidosperma quebracho-blanco* (Apocynaceae) and *Schinopsis balanse* (Anacardiaceae), as well as *Bulnesia sarmientoi* (Zygophyllaceae), *Caesalpinia paraguaruensis, Gleditsia amorphoides,* and *Enterolobium contortisiliquum* (Leguminosae), *Calycophyllum multiflorum* (Rubiaceae), *Celtis pubescens* (Ulmaceae), *Chorisia insignis* (Bombacaceae), *Pisonia zapallo* (Nyctaginaceae), *Ruprechtia laxiflora* (Polygonaceae), and *Tabebuia impetiginosa* (Bignoniaceae) (Cabrera 1976; Short 1975). Many of these species occur in dry forests in the Andean foothills of southern Bolivia and northern Argentina. For a discussion of the chaco plant communities and the chaco avifauna see Short (1975).

Gallery Forests (F8)

Gallery (or riparian) forests (see plate 7) occur along watercourses throughout the drier regions (annual rainfall less than 1,600–2,000 mm) of the Neotropics, or where other conditions (e.g., fire) inhibit the growth of woody vegetation away from the river. These levee or swampy floodplain forests are rarely more than 100 m wide and typically reflect the vegetation of the nearest floodplain or bottomland forest (R. B. Foster, pers. comm.). Eiten (1972) and Prance (1989) describe gallery forests in central Brazil and list the following characteristic tree species: *Cariniana estrellensis* (Lecythidaceae), *Maclura tinctoria* (Myicaceae), *Hirtella martiana* and *Licania gardneri* (Chrysobalanaceae), *Ilex paraguariensis* (Aquifoliaceae), *Dulacia singularis* (Olacaceae), *Qualea ingens* (Vochysiaceae), *Ternstroemia candolleana* (Theaceae), and *Xylosma venosum* (Flacourtiaceae). Palms often are a conspicuous element in gallery forests. When they grow in pure, extensive stands, however (e.g., *Mauritia flexuosa*), they are treated separately as palm forests (see F13 below).

Also included in this habitat are riparian woodlands that occur as islands in grassland away from watercourses, or in dry regions from northern Mexico to central Argentina, or that border streams and rivers in dry to arid regions of Middle America. Below 1,200 m in northwestern Mexico, these woodlands often contain willows (Salix spp., esp. *S. goodingii*), cottonwoods (*Populus* spp., including *P. fremontii* and *P. dimorpha*), hackberries (*Celtis reticulata*), and mesquites (*Prosopis velutina*); the introduced *Tamarix chinensis* (Tamaricaceae) is widespread and common. Sycamores (*Platanus* spp.) become numerous at higher elevations, especially within the oak zone. Farther south, more tropical elements appear, including Montezuma cypress (*Taxodium mucronotum*), figs (*Ficus* spp.), and palms (e.g., *Sabal ureseana, Erythea aculeata*) (Minckley and Brown 1982).

Southern Temperate Forests (F9)

Forests of *Araucaria angustifolia* (Araucariaceae) (see plate 8) once covered large areas of eastern Paraná, Rio Grande do Sul, and Santa Catarina, Brazil, above 900 m. Now this forest survives mostly as isolated islands of trees amid grassland and farmland; few large areas of *Araucaria* are protected (e.g., Parque Nacional Aparados da Serra). Relict patches of *Araucaria angustifolia* occur at high elevations, usually above 1,500 m in the mountains of Rio de Janeiro and São Paulo, and at about 1,000 m within evergreen forests in western Paraná and adjacent Misiones, Argentina.

Besides *Araucaria,* other canopy trees of this forest include *Podocarpus lambertii* (Podocarpaceae) and various broad-leafed species, such as *Campomanesia xanthocarpa* and *Eugenia pyriformis* (Myrtaceae), *Sebastiana klotzchiana* (Euphorbiaceae), *Ocotea pulchella* (Lauraceae), and *Matayba eleagoides* (Sapindaceae) (Belton 1984; Waechter, Cestaro, and Miotto 1984). The understory is usually dense, with tree ferns (e.g., *Dicksonia sellowiana* and *Cyathea* spp.) and dwarf bamboos (*Chusquea* spp.) conspicuous in humid areas. Common trees in an *Araucaria angustifolia* forest in Misiones included *Balfourodendron riedelianum* (Rutaceae), *Ilex paraguariensis* (Aquifoliaceae), and *Nectandra raligna* (Lauraceae) (Cabrera 1971).

Impressive forests of southern beeches (*Nothofagus* spp., Fagaceae), *Araucaria araucana,* and a variety of other large trees occur on Andean slopes (600–2,000 m) south of 30° S, and in the lowlands of southern Argentina and Chile (see color plate 8). North of 37° S, stands of huge, evergreen *Araucaria araucana,* 45 m tall, with trunks 2 m in diameter, grow on Andean slopes above 1,000 m. Mixed with the *Araucaria* are *Nothofagus antarctica, N. dombeyi,* or *N. pumilo* (Fagaceae), and *Austrocedrus chilensis* (Cupressaceae), and a variety of smaller trees and shrubs including *Berberis buxifolia* (Berberidaceae), *Pernettya mucronota* (Ericaceae), *Maytenus distichia* (Celastraceae), *Ribes magellanica* (Saxifragaceae), and *Escallonia virgata* (Es-calloniaceae). Bamboos, especially *Chusquea culeou,* form dense thickets in the understory. In central Chile, forests often are dominated by *Nothofagus obliqua* and *N. glauca.* Farther south, tall forests of *Nothofagus* (depending on the site, *N. dombeyi, N. obliqua, N. pu-milio, N. antarctica,* or *N. betuloides*) and conifers, *Fitzroya cupressoides* and *Pilgerodendron uviferum* (Cupressaceae), *Podocarpus nubigena* and *Saxegothea conspicua* (Podocarpaceae), occur with *Eucryphia cordifolia* (Eucryphiaceae), *Laurelia* spp. (Monimiaceae), *Aextoxican punctatum* (Aextocicaceae), and *Drimys winteri* (Winteraceae). The smaller trees and shrubs in these forests include *Berberis* spp. (Berberidaceae), *Ribes magellanica* (Saxifragaceae), *Viola buchtienii* (Violaceae), and bamboos, *Chusquea* spp. (Cabrera 1976; Veblen, Schiegel, and Oltremari 1983; Vuilleumier 1985; Schmaltz 1991).

Pine Forests (F10)

These uniform forests contain one to several species of pines (*Pinus*) or firs (*Abies*), or both, and occur primarily above 2,000 m in the mountains of Mexico and Guatemala (see plate 9). In Nicaragua, local patches occur as low as 500 m. Pines also dominate some islands in the Bahamas, locally in the lowlands and highlands of Cuba, and above 1,500 m in the mountains of Hispaniola.

Extensive stands of *Pinus ponderosa* (var. *arizonica*) occur at high elevations in the Sierra Madre Occidental, Mexico. These conifers often form nearly pure stands but occur locally with other pines—*Pinus ayacahuite, P. engelmannii, P. leiophylla* (var. *chihuahuana*), and *P. durangensis,* junipers (*Juniperus deppeana*), occasional oaks (*Quercus* spp.), and other small trees: for example, *Ceanothus huichagorare* (Rhamnaceae), *Arctostaphylos pungens,* and *Arbutus arizonica* (Ericaceae) (Marshall 1957; Pase and Brown 1982b). Pockets of fir (*Pseudotsuga menziesii, Abies religiosa, A. hickeli, A. guatemalensis,* and *A. oaxacana*) and spruce (*Picea chihuahuana*) cover the cooler canyons and north-facing slopes at uppermost elevations (Pase and Brown 1982b; Binford 1989).

In Oaxaca, nearly pure forests of *Pinus hartwegii* occur locally at elevations above 3,200 m (Binford 1989). In the mountains of northern Baja California, forests of *Pinus jeffreyi* replace pine-oak communities above 2,800 m; other conifers at higher elevations in Baja include *Pinus monophylla* and *Juniperus occidentalis*.

Few (if any) virgin forests of pine remain anywhere in the Neotropics.

Pine-Oak Forests (F11)

Mixed forests or open woodlands of pines and evergreen oaks (see plate 10) form well-defined communities in mountainous areas from northern Mexico south to Nicaragua, mainly from 900 to 2,800 m. Marshall (1957) lists eight species of evergreen oaks characteristic of drier pine-oak woodlands in the northern Sierra Madre Occidental of Mexico, including *Quercus arizonica, Q. grisea,* and *Q. viminia,* which grow in association with several species of pines (*Pinus engelmannii, P. durangensis,* and *P. leiophylla*), other conifers (*Cupressus arizonica* and *Juniperus deppeana*), and a variety of scrubby trees and shrubs (*Arctostaphylos pungens* and *Arbutus xalapensis* (Ericaceae), *Ceanothus huichagorare* (Rhamnaceae), *Cercocarpus breviflorus* (Rosaceae), and *Quercus toumeyi* (Fagaceae). Pase and Brown (1982b) offer additional botanical information on this "Madrean evergreen woodland."

Humid pine-oak forests in Oaxaca are dominated by *Quercus rugosa, Q. laurina* (Fagaceae), *Pinus termifolia, P. chiapensis, P. pseudostrobus,* and *Abies hickeli* (Pinaceae), *Arbutus xalapensis* (Ericaceae), *Litsea glaucescens* (Lauraceae), *Buddleia cordata* (Loganiaceae), and *Montanoa arborescens* (Compositae) (Binford 1989; Breedlove 1973). Such forests are often tall (to 35 m) and epiphyte laden. Sweet gums *(Liquidambar styraciflua)* are locally numerous in this habitat in eastern Oaxaca, Chiapas, and farther south to northern Nicaragua (Breedlove 1973).

Also included in this category are evergreen oak woodlands (*encinales*) devoid of pines (see plate 11) that occur from sea level to over 1,500 m in Baja California and at low elevations (900 to 1,500+ m) elsewhere in Mexico. Most of their representative tree species grade into and mix with pines at higher elevations.

White Sand Forests (F12)

Included here are the forests and scrubs on white sand in Amazonia (campina) (see color plate 9), and the structurally similar restinga of coastal eastern Brazil (see plate 12). The white sand habitats of Amazonia are very patchily distributed, covering about 60,000 km^2 in Brazil (Pires 1974) and an equivalent area outside Brazil. The major center of campina lies in the upper Rio Negro region, but it occurs locally throughout Amazonia. Typically the soil contains virtually no clay; nutrient levels are extremely low, even when compared with the low-nutrient, lateritic soils that dominate Amazonia (Anderson 1981), and water retention is poor.

The appearance of white sand forests varies tremendously from site to site: some are open scrubs, with only small shrubs among bare patches of sand; others form a closed canopy, with trees 20–30 m in height. Floristically, white sand forests are very distinct from those in *terra firme* (F1). Endemism is high, even among different forest patches, but plant diversity is low. Among woody plants, the dominant families include Leguminosae, Euphorbiaceae, Sapotaceae, Guttiferae, Rubiaceae, and Myristicaceae. Some families that are important in other Amazonian lowland forests, such as Moraceae, Palmae, and Lecythidaceae, are represented poorly here (Anderson 1981).

The restinga of eastern Brazil once stretched along much of the coast, from Maranhão south to Santa Catarina. Patches of similar vegetation also occurred as far north as the mouth of the Amazon. The habitat now is becoming rapidly endangered, as much of it is transformed into residential development, especially around Rio de Janeiro and São Paulo.

In its broadest sense, restinga refers to the vegetation

covering deposits of white sand behind the dunes along the coast; it ranges in width from a few hundred to several thousand meters. The forests on these sands are sclerophyllic and short (usually under 5 m in height), with many terrestrial bromeliads. Although structurally similar to the vegetation in Amazonian white sand forests, the restinga is floristically unrelated (Pires 1974), with relationships mainly to the rainforests of eastern Brazil (Lacerda, de Araújo, and Maciel 1993). Important genera of trees and shrubs include *Eugenia, Gomidesia, Myrcia,* and *Psidium* (Myrtaceae), *Miconia* (Melastomataceae), *Piptadenia* (Leguminosae), *Nectandra* and *Ocotea* (Lauraceae), *Myrica* (Myricaceae), *Humiria* (Humiriaceae), *Anacardium* (Anacardiaceae), and *Clusia* (Clusiaceae) (Alfonso 1977; Lacerda, de Araújo, and Maciel 1993).

Palm Forests (F13)

Small to extensive stands of *Mauritia flexuosa* cover old Amazonian lakebeds or poorly drained areas in savannas to the north and south (plate 13). In drier areas, watercourses are often lined by nearly pure stands of *Mauritia.* Other palms that grow in large, monospecific stands include *Euterpe* (in western Ecuador), *Maximiliana, Copernicia, Dictyocaryum, Orbignya,* and *Raphia* (Myers 1990).

Mangrove Forests (F14)

Dense, low forests of one to several species of mangroves (see plate 14 and color plate 10) border coastal lagoons, estuaries, and rivers along the Pacific coast from Sonora, Mexico, south to Tumbes, Peru, and on the Atlantic coast from Florida, the West Indies, and Tamaulipas, Mexico, south to southeastern Brazil at 29° S (West 1977). These forests are permanently or occasionally flooded by brackish waters. The most widespread and common species are red mangroves (*Rhizophora mangle, R. racemosa,* and *R. harrisonii,* Rhizophoraceae), which typically colonize standing water nearest the sea; black mangroves (*Avicennia germinans, A. nitida,* and *A. tomentosa,* Verbenaceae), which grow in periodically flooded areas; white mangrove (*Languncularia racemosa,* Combretaceae); and *Pelliciera rhizophorae* (Theaceae), on the Pacific coast. Many mangrove forests are 4–9 m tall, but in some areas they have closed canopies at 20–25 m. Stilt roots and branches of red mangroves form impenetrable tangles (see color plate 11), which serve as cover and nesting sites for a variety of waterbirds.

Second-Growth Forests and Woodlands (F15)

Here we include most forms of second growth consisting primarily of trees. These habitats are usually human created (see plate 15). However, naturally "disturbed" habitats, such as early successional forests on landslides, or forested areas damaged by hurricanes, also are included. Natural disturbances make up a very small portion of the total area of "second-growth forests." Successional forests along rivers are treated separately (F3).

The tropical bird literature is filled with habitat references such as open woodlands, orchards, coffee plantations, parks, and trees around houses. We were conservative in assigning species to such "habitats"; most true forest species visit second-growth areas only occasionally, and we doubt they could survive in them permanently. Some frugivores and nectarivores may use briefly abundant food supplies but then return to primary forest or forest edge to breed. We believe it is misleading to assign F15 to species such as the Brazilian Ruby (*Clytolaema rubricauda*), clearly a forest species, although it may become seasonally abundant in *Eucalyptus* (Myrtaceae) when that is in bloom. Examples include many species of hummingbirds and other nectarivorous species attracted (seasonally) to flowering coffee or the trees that shade it (e.g., *Erythrina* spp., Leguminosae).

Nonforest Habitats

Arid Lowland Scrubs (N1)

Arid lowland scrubs include a variety of plant communities dominated by shrubs, scattered small trees, cacti, and (locally) terrestrial bromeliads forming a nearly continuous cover of low vegetation (see plate 16 and color plate 12). Extensive areas of scrub occur in the deserts of northern Mexico, northern Colombia and Venezuela, western Peru and Chile, the caatinga of northeastern Brazil, the chaco of Paraguay and northern Argentina, the monte of western Argentina, and in Patagonia. In most of these regions, scrub grades into some form of deciduous forest or grassland. *Lowland scrub* communities, usually containing many widespread tropical plant genera, are often replaced by *montane scrub* above 1,000 m.

The Sonoran Desert of northwestern Mexico encompasses one of the largest areas of desert scrub in the Neotropics. Although plant geographers recognize at least six subdivisions of this desert (Turner and Brown 1982), many plant taxa are widespread. Characteristic shrubs and trees include creosote bush (*Larrea tridentata,* Zygophyllaceae), saltbush (*Atriplex* spp., Chenopodiaceae), paloverde (*Cercidium microphyllum, C. praecox,* and *C. floridum*), ironwood (*Olneya tesota*), mesquite (*Prosopis glandulosa* and *P. velutina*), and catclaw acacia (*Acacia greggii,* Leguminosae), bursage (*Ambrosia dumosa*) and brittlebush (*Encelia farinosa,* Compositae), and *Lycium* spp. (Solanaceae). Cacti are usually common and conspicuous, especially tall, columnar forms such as the saguaro (*Carnegiea gi-*

gantea), cardon (*Pachycereus pringlei*), and organ pipe (*Stenocereus thurberi*), as well as a great variety of smaller forms such as cholla and prickly pear (*Opuntia* spp.). In west-central Baja California, the Vizcaino region is characterized by peculiar forms such as boojum tree (*Fouquieria* [*Idria*] *columnaris,* Fouquieriaceae) and a thick-stemmed tree, the copalquin (*Pachycormus discolor,* Anacardiaceae) (MacMahon and Wagner 1985).

Another important area of lowland desert scrub extends from southwestern Ecuador south to Ancash, Peru. The rich flora includes a mixture of shrubs and small trees, among them *Capparis angulata, C. cordata,* and *C. ovalifolia* (Capparidaceae), *Cercidium praecox, Parkinsonia aculeata,* and *Prosopis julifora* (Leguminosae), *Froelichia interrupta* (Anacardiaceae), *Cryptocarpus pyriformis* (Nyctaginaceae), *Galvezia limensis* (Scrophulariaceae), *Grabowskia boerhavifolia* (Solanaceae), and *Monnina pterocarpa* (Polygonaceae). Columnar cacti, including *Armatocereus* spp., *Monvillea* spp., and *Neoraimondea gigantea* (Rauh 1985), are conspicuous. Farther south, in the coastal deserts of Peru and Chile, "fog loma" vegetation in the form of winter-green annuals and bulbous perennials, sometimes also including terrestrial bromeliads (*Tillandsia* spp.) or cacti (species of *Haageocereus, Islaya,* or *Copiapoa*), grows on desert sand and rock where winter fog is heaviest. Isolated patches of trees (esp. *Acacia macracantha* and *Caesalpinia tinctoria,* Leguminosae) and shrubs (e.g., *Carica candidus* [Caricaceae], and *Tournefortia undulata* [Boraginaceae]) covered with mosses and lichens also occur locally (Ferreyra 1977; Rauh 1985).

A semiarid climate, with rainfall ranging from 300 to 800 mm, characterizes the caatinga of northeastern Brazil. Its vegetation is short—generally under 7 m in height—and is completely deciduous in the dry season (Andrade-Lima 1981). Many of the shrubs are armed with spines. Cacti (Cactaceae) abound, especially *Cereus jamacaru* (a columnar species), *Pilosocereus gounellei,* and various species of *Melocactus* and *Opuntia.* Terrestrial bromeliads (*Bromelia laciniosa* and *Neoglaziovia variegata*) are a prominent feature of the caatinga (Andrade-Lima 1960, 1981). The dominant shrubs or small trees include *Croton sonderianus, Cnidoscolus phyllacanthus,* and *C. bahiae* (Euphorbiaceae), *Spondias tuberosa (*Annonaceae), *Aspidosperma pyricollum* (Apocynaceae), and a variety of leguminous species, among them *Caesalpinia pyramidalis, Mimosa* spp., and *Cassia excelsa* (Egler 1951; Andrade-Lima 1981).

The monte desert of west-central Argentina, and drier parts of the adjacent chaco to the north, supports desert scrub communities similar to those of northern Mexico. Creosote bushes (*Larrea cuneifolia* and *L. divaricata,* Zygophyllaceae) is the dominant vegetation over wide areas; other characteristic shrubs include *Atriplex* spp. (Chenopodiaceae), *Bougainvillea spinosa* (Nyctaginaceae), *Bulnesia retama* and *Plectrocarpa tetracantha* (Zygophyllaceae), *Cassia aphylla, Cercidium praecox, Prosopis alpataco,* and *P. torquata* (Leguminosae), *Chuquiraga erinacea, Flourensia tutuosa,* and *Grindelia* spp. (Compositae), *Lycium* spp. (Solanaceae), and *Monttea aphylla* (Portulacaceae) (Cabrera 1976; Mares, Morello, and Goldstein 1985). As in other desert scrub areas, cacti are often conspicuous, especially the columnar *Trichocereus terscheckii* and species of *Cleistocactus* and *Opuntia*; terrestrial bromeliads (*Bromelia, Dyckia, Tillandsia*) also may be common.

To the south, Patagonian scrub, interspersed with areas dominated by grassland, covers vast areas. Cabrera (1976) describes a variety of shrub/grass communities, including those with an almost continuous cover of such shrub species as *Chuquiraga rostulata* and *Senecio covasii* (Compositae), *Ephedra ochreata* (Ephedraceae), *Mulinum spinosum* (Umbelliferae), and others with a mixture of *Acaena* spp. (Rosaceae) and *Adesmia* spp. (Leguminosae) shrubs with a rich variety of grasses. Other common shrubs include *Berberis grevilleana* (Berberidaceae), *Fabiana patagonica* and *Lycium chilense* (Solanaceae), *Grindelia chiloensis* (Compositae), *Junellia scriphioides* (Verbenaceae), and *Larrea nitida* (Zygophyllaceae).

Arid Montane Scrubs (N2)

The arid and semiarid highlands of Middle and South America support a diverse assemblage of plant communities structurally similar to those of the lowland habitats described above. Shrubby vegetation, often mixed with cacti, terrestrial bromeliads, and grasses, typifies dry mountainous regions at elevations of 1,000–4,000 m, from northern Mexico to the southern Andes of Argentina and Chile (see plates 17 and 18). Many characteristic plant genera are also represented in lowland scrub communities, especially those shared by the high Andes and Patagonia.

The highland plains, basins, and mountain slopes of north-central Mexico at 1,000–2,000 m support an endemic flora of more than a thousand plant species (Brown 1982a), many of which characterize the Chihuahuan Desert. Although creosote bush (*Larrea tridentata,* Zygophyllaceae) forms vast, uniform stands on level or gently rolling terrain, other shrubs, such as *Flourensia cernua* (Compositae) and *Acacia neovernicosa* and *Prosopis glandulosa* (Leguminosae), are equally widespread. Rocky slopes above the plains support a richer assemblage of plants, including a variety of such distinctive floristic elements as ocotillo (*Fouquieria splendens*) and many species of leaf succulents including *Agave* (Amaryllidaceae), *Hechtia* (Bromeliaceae), and *Dasylirion* and *Yucca* (Liliaceae) (Brown 1982a; MacMahon and Wagner 1985). Common woody shrubs include *Acacia greggii* (Leguminosae), *Coldenia greggii* (Boraginaceae), *Condalia* spp. and *Zizyphus obtusifolia* (Rhamnaceae), and *Leucophyllum minus* (Scrophulariaceae) (Brown 1982a). Chihuahuan desert scrub grades into juniper or oak woodland at higher elevations and has invaded large areas once covered with pristine grasslands.

In the drier mountains of Mexico, above about 1,700 m, desert scrub is replaced by a shrubby form of vegetation called "interior chaparral" by Pase and Brown (1982a). The dominant vegetation consists of a variety of shrubby oaks (*Quercus* spp.), madrone (*Arbutus* spp.), and manzanita (*Arctostaphylos pungens*) (Ericaceae), *Ceanothus greggii* (Rhamnaceae), mountain-mahogany (*Cercocarpus breviflorus,* Rosaceae), silk-tassels (*Garrya* spp., Cornaceae), and sages (*Salvia* spp., Labiatae).

Along the coast, from northern California to northwestern Baja California, a structurally similar but floristically different chaparral covers the mountains and lowlands. Many shrubs are of the same genera as plants of the interior chapparal, but the species are different. Dominant plants include *Adenostoma fascicultum* and *A. sparsifolium,* mountain-mahogany (*Cercocarpus betuloides* and *C. ledifolius*) and chaparral holly (*Heteromeles arbutifolia*) (Rosaceae) (Keeley and Keeley 1988).

Binford (1989) describes montane scrub communities in the highlands of Oaxaca, southern Mexico, including extensive thickets of *Acacia bilimecki, A. farnesiana,* and *Prosopis chilensis* (Leguminosae), interspersed among bushes and cacti (esp. *Lemaireocereus* spp.), and a scrub juniper/oak association of *Juniperus flaccida* and *Quercus* spp.

The dry parts of the Andes, particularly south of Ecuador, support a great variety of scrub habitats. Various cacti, terrestrial bromeliads, and scattered shrubs form the dominant vegetation in the arid western Andes of Peru and northern Chile, from 700 to 3,000 m (Rauh 1985). More arid lower slopes support a sparse cover of cacti such as *Armatocereus procerus, Haageocereus aureispinum,* and *Neoraimondia roseiflora,* whereas a richer mixture of cacti (*Espostoa melanostele*), bromeliads (*Puya* spp.), and shrubs (*Carica candicans* [Caricaceae] and *Jatropha macracantha* [Euphobiaceae]) occurs above 1,500 m.

In southern Bolivia and northwestern Argentina, the arid upper Andean slopes support similar communities of shrubs, bromeliads, and cacti (e.g. *Trichocereus pasacana, T. terscheckii*), cacti being especially abundant in many areas. Dominant shrubs include *Adesmia inflexa, Caesalpinia trichocarpa, Cassia crassiramea, Cercidium andicola,* and *Krameria iluca* (Leguminosae), *Baccharis boliviensis, Gochnatia glutinosa, Proustia cuneifolia,* and *Chuquiraga erinacea* (Compositae), *Bougainvillea spinosa* (Nyctaginaceae), *Bulnesia* spp. (Zygophyllaceae), *Justicia pauciflora* (Acanthaceae), *Junellia juniperina* (Verbenaceae), and *Lycium venturii* (Solanaceae) (Cabrera 1976).

Distinctive plant communities also occur locally in rocky places on the plateaus and low mountains of the Brazilian shield, from about 750 to 2,000 m. Collectively know as *campo rupestre,* this habitat supports many endemic plant species with small ranges, including a variety of Velloziaceae and Eriocaulaceae (Giulietti and Pirani 1988).

Semihumid/Humid Montane Scrubs (N3)

A fairly dense shrub zone forms at elevations above 2,500 m (see plate 19), especially in moist intermontane valleys, and extends up to puna grasslands at about 4,000 m. Some of these are degraded semihumid forests (R. B. Foster, pers. comm.). The shrub assemblage at a representative site in central Peru included *Ambrosia arborescens, Baccharis odorata, Barnadesia dombeyana, Eupatorium sternbergiarium, Flourensia macrophylla, Mutisia acuminata,* and *Senecio elatus* (Compositae), *Berberis flexuosa* (Berberidaceae), *Cassia tomentosa, Dalea* spp. and *Lupinus* spp. (Leguminosae), *Carica candicans* (Caricaceae), *Dodonaea viscosa* (Sapindaceae), *Ephedra* spp. (Ephedraceae), *Euphorbia* spp. (Euphorbiaceae), *Hesperomeles cuneata* and *Kageneckia lanceolata* (Rosaceae), *Monnina* spp. (Polygonaceae), and *Ribes peruviana* (Saxifragaceae). Small trees, such as *Schinus molle* (Annonaceae) and *Caesalpinia spinosa (Leguminosae),* cacti (esp. *Trichocereus peruvianus*), maguey (*Furcraea andina,* Amaryllidaceae), and terrestrial bromeliads (*Puya* spp.) are also characteristic (Cerrate 1979).

Cerrado (N4)

This biogeographic domain encompasses nearly 2 million km^2 in central Brazil, adjacent eastern Bolivia, and northeastern Paraguay (Cavalcanti 1988; Eiten 1972, 1978; Sarmiento 1983; Killeen, Louman, and Grimwood 1990). The name has been used widely for the nonforest vegetation that covers much of the Brazilian shield, ranging from open grasslands (*campo sujo*) to dense woodlands (*cerradão*). The latter occur alongside semideciduous tropical forests at the southern periphery of Amazonian Brazil. In our list of habitats we separate open campo grasslands with a sparse cover of shrubs and trees (N5) from denser cerrado vegetation "of woody plants too dense to permit a jeep to be driven through" (see plate 20) (Eiten 1972). Trees and shrubs with thick, fire-resistant bark, twisted trunks and limbs, and large, thick leaves dominate this open woodland, which has a nearly continuous ground cover of grasses, sedges, and forbs. Floristic elements of deciduous forests and lowland scrub (e.g., caatinga) such as terrestrial bromeliads, cacti, and other spiny plants are scarce or absent (Eiten 1972). The cerrado supports an extremely rich diversity of vascular plants; a single hectare may contain 250 to 350 species (Heringer 1971; Eiten 1984; Silberbauer-Gottsberger and Gottsberger 1984). Eiten's (1972) list of characteristic cerrado plants includes 62 genera of trees, 78 genera of shrubs, and more than 90 genera of forbs. Widespread trees include *Andira humilis, Bowdichia virgiloides* (Leguminosae), *Davilla elliptica* (Dilleniaceae), *Magonia pubescens* (Sapotaceae), *Zeyheria montana* (Bignoniaceae), and *Qualea grandiflora, Q. parviflora,* and *Q. multiflora* (Vochysiaceae). Some common and widespread cerrado species, among them *Curatella americana* (Dilleniaceae), *Byrsonima crassifolia* (Malpighiaceae), and *Palicourea rigida* (Rubiaceae), are also typical of grasslands within Amazonia and across northern South America (Eiten 1972).

Campo Grasslands (N5)

Upland grasslands with little or no woody vegetation occur locally on the Brazilian and Guianan shields (see plate 21 and color plate 13). Eiten (1972) considered *campo limpo*—essentially pure grassland—and *campo sujo*—with scattered trees and shrubs—to be floristically part of the cerrado vegetation described above. Goldsmith (1974) described eight types of campo communities found in northeastern Mato Grosso, Brazil, including dry grassland on sandstone hills and lateritic outcrops and (periodically) moist grassland on gentle slopes bordering gallery forests. The latter, known as "valley side campo" (Goldsmith 1974; Eiten 1975, 1978), supports a rich variety of herbaceous vegetation of more than 200 species in 50 families (Goldsmith 1974). Goldsmith (1974) recorded 29 species of grasses in 14 genera at sixty campo sites in Mato Grosso, including the genera *Abolbodo, Andropogon, Axonopus, Mesosetum, Paspalum, Panicum, Digitaria, Leptocoryphium, Loudetia, Olyra, Schiza, Thasyra, Tristachya,* and *Trachypogon.* He also found 9 genera of Cyperaceae, as well as representatives from the Xyridaceae, Eriocaulaceae, Commelinaceae, Rapataceae, Iridaceae, Musaceae, and Zingiberaceae.

A complex of grasslands and savannas covers northern Venezuela and northeastern Colombia (llanos), southeastern Venezuela (Gran Sabana), the northern part of Roraima, Brazil, and parts of the Guianas. Many of these grasslands are seasonally flooded, especially in the llanos, and they are described below (see N6). But there are also extensive areas of dry campos throughout the region. In much of the area, scattered *Curatella americana* are the only trees. As the tree cover becomes denser, other species become more common (Sarmiento 1983). Dominant grasses in these dry campos include *Trachypogon vestitus, Axonopus pupusii,* and *Paspalum pectinatum* (Coupland 1992). *Andropogon* spp., *Bulbostylis* spp., *Trachypogon* spp., *Leptocoryphium lanatum,* and *Panicum olyroides* may be common (Sarmiento 1983). In Brazil and the Guianas, the grasslands are dominated by various species of *Trachypogon* (Sarmiento 1983).

Low, Seasonally Wet Grasslands (N6)

Low-lying grasslands cover vast areas of northeastern Colombia, Venezuela north of the Río Orinoco, northern and southeastern Bolivia, and adjacent Brazil, most of which are seasonally flooded and periodically burned (see plate 22). This ecosystem encompasses more than 100,000 km^2 in Bolivia alone, where over 600 species of vascular plants (including 81 grasses and 55 sedges) have been found in one locality (Beck 1984; Haase and Beck 1989). These authors, along with Beard (1953), describe a variety of grassland types in northern Bolivia and Venezuela. In both regions "bunchgrass savannas" occur on well-drained, slightly higher ground that becomes dry and hard during the dry season; characteristic grasses in this habitat in Bolivia include *Paspalum ionanthum, Leptocoryphium lanatum, Thrasya petrosa,* and *Trachypogon plumosus.* Scattered, fire-resistant trees, such as *Curatella americana* (Dilleniaceae), and clumps of *Miconia* (Melostomataceae) bushes dot the landscape. In wetter areas, *Trachypogon* species are mixed with a variety of other grasses (e.g., *Aristida torta, Saciolepis myuros, Sorghastrum stipoides*) and sedges (e.g., species of *Bulbostylis, Rhynchospora,* and *Kyllinga*). Many genera in the South American grasslands do not reach Central America, where the wooded grasslands are less diverse (R. B. Foster, pers. comm.).

Southern Temperate Grasslands (N7)

Grasslands (see plate 23) covered much of extreme southeastern Brazil in southern Rio Grande do Sul, Uruguay, and northern Argentina, extending locally south to Tierra del Fuego. Conversion of the pampas to pastureland was nearly complete by the early 1800s. Much has since become cropland, especially devoted to raising wheat.

Cabrera (1976) and Soriano et al. (1992) described several types of grassland found in northeastern Argentina. The northern prairies of Santa Fé, Entre Rios, and northern Buenos Aires typically consisted of *Stipa neesiana, S. tenuissima, Poa lanigera, Eragrostis ciliensis, Aristida murina, Briza subaristata, Melica brasiliana, Piptochaetium montevidense,* and various species of *Paspalum.* Other well-represented grass genera included *Axonopus, Bothriochloa, Digitaria,* and *Schizachyrium.* Scattered shrubs, especially species of *Baccharis* and *Eupatorium* (Compositae), *Heimia* (Lythraceae), and *Margyricarpus* (Rosaceae), were common. Farther west and south, *Poa ligularis* (up to 1 m high) occurred widely with species of *Stipa* (incl. *filiculmis, tenuissima,* and *trichotoma*) and *Panicum urvilleanum,* as well as several of the grasses and bushes mentioned above.

The grasslands of northern Patagonia (Neuquen–northeastern Santa Cruz) contain a variety of *Festuca, Poa,* and *Stipa* species mixed with shrubs in the genera *Adesmia* (Leguminosae), *Mulinum* (Umbelliferae), and *Senecio* (Compositae). *Festuca pallescens,* 20–60 cm tall, covers extensive areas, constituting up to 90% of the vegetation (Cabrera 1976; Soriano 1983); *Agrostis* spp., *Bromus* spp., *Poa lanigera,* and *Stipa speciosa* are also common in this habitat. Farther south, *Festuca gracillima* (to 70 cm tall) is equally dominant and widespread.

Common Patagonian grassland shrubs include *Chuquiraga rostulata, Grindelia chiloensis,* and *Senecio covasii* (Compositae), *Ephedra ochreata* (Ephedraceae), *Junellia scriphioides* (Verbenaceae), *Larrea nitida* (Zygophyllaceae), *Lycium chilense* (Solanaceae), and *Mulinum spinosus* (Umbelliferae) (Cabrera 1976).

Northern Temperate Grasslands (N8)

Extensive grasslands occupy large areas of northern and central Mexico at elevations of about 1,100 to 2,300 m. Overgrazing has seriously degraded most of the once widespread Mexican grasslands, allowing the subsequent invasion of desert shrubs and small trees. Brown (1982b) recognized four types of subtropical grassland in Mexico: "semidesert grassland" (or *pastizales;* see Flores Mata et al. 1971); "plains grassland" (see plate 24); "subalpine grassland"; "montane meadow grassland"; and a tropical "Sonoran savanna grassland."

Semidesert grasslands once covered large areas on the Mexican plateau. They consisted primarily of perennial bunchgrasses, including various species of *Bouteloua* (esp. *B. eriopoda*), *Hilaria mutica,* and *Sporobolus wrightii* (in poorly drained areas), as well as *Muhlenbergia porteri, Aristida* spp., and *Trichachne* spp. Other important plants include *Nolina, Dasylirion,* and *Yucca* (esp. *Y. elata,* Liliaceae), *Agave* (Amaryllidaceae), *Opuntia* (Cactaceae), and ocotillo (*Fouquieria splendens,* Fouqueriaceae). Bushes and small trees have become increasingly common in overgrazed areas, especially mesquites (*Prosopis glandulosa* and *P. juliflora*) and *Acacia greggii* (Leguminosae), *Berberis trifoliata* (Berberidaceae), *Celtis pallida* (Ulmaceae), *Condalia ericoides* and *Zizyphus obtusifolia* (Rhamnaceae), *Ephedra* spp. (Ephedraceae), and *Juniperus monosperma* (Cupressaceae) (Brown 1982b).

"Plains grasslands" occur above 1,200 m in extreme northern Mexico and range up to 2,300 m where they meet oak woodland, pinyon-juniper woodland, or montane conifer forest. Overgrazing and too frequent burning have drastically altered this once extensive ecosystem. Shortgrass prairies of various *Bouteloua* species, and *Buchloe dactyloides, Eragrostis intermedia, Hilaria jamesii, Koelaria cristata,* and *Panicum obtusum,* now usually are mixed with cacti and shrubs such as *Atriplex canescens* (Chenopodiaceae), *Yucca glauca* (Liliaceae), and *Artemesia* spp. and *Gutierrezia* spp. (Compositae).

Smaller grassy patches occur on the high volcanoes of central and southern Mexico and at upper elevations in the Sierra Madre Oriental. These "subalpine grasslands" or *zacatonales* are composed primarily of bunchgrasses in the genera *Calamagrostis, Festuca, Muhlenbergia,* and *Stipa* (Flores Mata et al. 1971; Brown 1982b). "Montane meadow grasslands" occur within conifer forests of the Sierra Madre Occidental (Brown 1982b).

Large areas of tropical grassland that once covered level plains along the rivers and streams of Sonora below 1,000 m were essentially destroyed by 1940 (Tomlinson 1972; Brown 1982b). Now these areas are best considered lowland desert scrub.

Puna Grasslands (N9)

Semiarid grasslands, pure or mixed with scattered bushes (and locally small trees) (see plate 25 and color plate 14), cover the upper mountain slopes and high plains of the Andes above 4,000 m, from northern Peru south to northern Argentina and Chile. The dominant vegetation over vast areas consists of coarse grasses, especially bunchgrasses of the genera *Festuca* and *Calamagrostis* in Peru and Bolivia (Weberbauer 1936), or *Festuca orthophylla, F. chrysophylla,* and *Poa gymnantha* in northern Argentina (Cabrera 1976). Other genera of grasses represented by numerous species in the puna include *Agrostis, Bromus, Calamagrostis, Dissanthelium,* and *Muhlenbergia.* Composites are also well represented in most puna sites (Weberbauer 1945). Common shrubs include *Chuquiraga rotundifolia, Parastrephia lepidophylla, Baccharis tricuneata B. incarum, Senecio graveolens,* and *S. spinosus* (Compositae), *Lupinus microphyllum* (Leguminosae), and *Margyricarpus strictus* (Rosaceae). Cabrera (1976) listed the following additional taxa: *Adesmia* spp. (Leguminosae), *Berberis empetrifolia* (Berberidaceae), *Chuquiraga oppositifolia* (Compositae), *Ephedra andina* (Ephedraceae), and *Junellia* spp. (Verbenaceae).

Also characteristic of the puna are the frost-resistant cushion plants *Azorella* (Umbelliferae), *Distichia, Pycnophyllum* (Caryophyllaceae), and *Oxychloe* (Juncaceae), which form dense mats on the ground or on rocks (Weberbauer 1936). Cacti (e.g., *Tephrocactus* spp.) usually are present but inconspicuous. Terrestrial bomeliads occur locally, including relict stands of the largest bromeliad in the world, *Puya raimondii,* whose

12 m flower stalks produce up to 20,000 flowers; this species provides food and cover for a variety of Andean birds. *Polylepis* woodlands also occur within the puna zone, but we treat them as a separate habitat (see F6).

Paramo Grasslands (N10)

These humid grasslands mixed with shrubby vegetation (see plate 26 and color plate 15) occur above montane and elfin forests along the highest mountains of Costa Rica and Panama and from Venezuela south to Ecuador, then patchily south to northern Bolivia. Although many paramo plant genera are also found in drier parts of the Andes (and even Patagonia), numerous endemic species are restricted to the much wetter paramos along the upper limit of humid forest. The genus *Espeletia* (Compositae) is perhaps the most distinctive and visible floristic element of paramos from Venezuela to northern Ecuador, but nearly all other typical paramo plant genera range south into Bolivia or farther. Grasses include many species of *Agrostis, Calamagrostis, Festuca,* and *Stipa*. Shrubby members of the Compositae (*Espeletia, Gynoxys, Senecio*) and Ericaceae (*Pernettia*) are especially well represented; also conspicuous are species of *Astragalus* and *Lupinus* (Leguminosae), *Berberis* (Berberidaceae), *Brachyotum* (Melastomataceae), *Hesperomeles* (Rosaceae), *Hypericum* (Guttiferae), *Loricaria* and *Werneria* (Compositae), *Rubus* (Rubiaceae), and *Valeriana* (Valerianaceae). Ferns (*Blechnum* spp.) and terrestrial bromeliads (*Puya* spp.) characterize the uppermost vegetation of many paramos (Sturm and Rangel Ch. 1985).

Riparian Thickets (N11)

Shrubby thickets of bushes and small trees line the banks of streams and rivers throughout the Neotropics (see plate 27) and are especially important to birds in drier regions. In desert areas of northern Mexico, dense stands of the introduced *Tamarix chinensis* (Tamaricaceae) mix with tall bushes and small trees, including *Baccharis glutinosa* (Compositae), and shrubby forms of *Prosopis pubescens* (Leguminosae), *Salix goodingii,* and *Populus fremontii* (Salicaceae). When these thickets exceed 2–3 m in height and trees rather than bushes dominate, we consider them gallery forests (see F8). In South America, *Tessaria integrifolia* and *Baccharis* spp. (Compositae), *Salix humboldtiana* (Salicaceae), and *Gynerium sagittatum* (Gramineae) form dense cover along watercourses, extending from the lowlands to sometimes over 3,000 m in the Andes. Thickets of *Gynerium* and *Tessaria* also occur locally in other regions.

River Island Scrub (N12)

Newly formed islands in the larger rivers of Amazonia are quickly colonized by grasses (*Paspalum* spp.), bushes, and small trees. Large thickets of shrubby *Tessaria integrifolia* (Compositae) appear within a few months of the formation of a new island. These may gradually be replaced by stands of the giant cane *Gynerium sagittatum* (Gramineae), the longer-lived and taller willows (*Salix humboldtiana,* Salicaceae), and other small trees, especially *Cecropia membranaceae* (Moraceae) and several other species, such as *Ochroma* (Bombacaceae), and *Acacia* (Leguminosae) (see plate 28 and color plate 16). This vegetation averages 3–6 m in height. Vines (e.g., *Ipomoea* spp., Convolvulaceae) usually cover the trees. In large braided rivers these islands usually have short life spans. The shifting course of the river washes them away while forming new ones.

Pastures and Agricultural Lands (N13)

Extensive areas in southeastern Brazil and northern Argentina are covered by pasturelands, which are presumably degraded native grasslands. In some cases nonnative grasses now dominate the habitat, but some grassland bird species readily adapt to them. Intensively grazed areas in northern Mexico and in the high Andes have been similarly altered by humans. Lesser numbers of bird species breed in agricultural lands (see plates 29 and 30) such as fields of hay, wheat, and dry rice, but such "habitats" may be very important to a variety of migratory and wintering (Austral and Nearctic) species.

Second-Growth Scrub (N14)

The category of second-growth scrub (see plate 31) encompasses the full range of low vegetation types dominated by bushes, scattered small trees, grasses, or large herbs. As with second-growth woodlands or forests (see F15), most second-growth scrub results from human activities. It includes the vegetation growing along road edges, in areas recently cleared of forest, and generally in areas where the original plant cover has been removed. Included are hedgerows, overgrown agricultural fields and pastures, vacant lots in populated areas, and the like. The vegetation of natural landslides in mountainous, humid regions we classify as "semihumid/humid montane scrub," but many birds in this habitat also colonize second-growth scrub.

Aquatic Habitats

Freshwater Marshes (A1)

Emergent aquatic vegetation often covers extensive areas bordering lakes, ponds, slow-moving rivers, and streams (see plate 32). Composition varies from pure stands of cattails (esp. *Typha domingensis,* Typhaceae), grasses (e.g., *Paspalum* spp.), or sedges and bullrushes (*Scirpus* spp., Cyperaceae) to a mixture of smaller species forming floating mats, such as pondweeds (*Potamogeton,* Potamogetonaceae), duckweeds (*Lemna,* Lemnaceae), and milfoils (*Myriophyllum,* Haloragaceae). Seasonally flooded areas support a variety of shorter marsh plants, including species of *Juncus* (Juncaceae), *Eleocharis* (Cyperaceae), and *Distichlis* (Gramineae) (Minckley and Brown 1982). Most of the stillwater vegetation above occurs widely in the Neotropics, some species ranging from northern Mexico to Tierra del Fuego. For example, *totorales* or reedbeds of *Typha domingensis* (Typhaceae), and *juncales* of *Scirpus californicus* (Cyperaceae) occur throughout most of the Neotropics, from sea level to above 4,000 m in the Andes.

Extensive grassy marshes form along the shores of river channels throughout much of Amazonia, wherever slower currents allow. These consist primarily of the aquatic marsh grasses *Echinochloa polystachya, Paspalum repens,* and *P. fasciculatum* or, where currents are even slower, of *Eichhornia* species (Pontederiaceae). Richer communities of these and other aquatic or semiaquatic grasses, sedges, and other plants form in areas where water fluctuations are more pronounced; typical plants include the grasses *Echinochloa polystachya, Hymenachne amplexicaulis, Leersia hexandra, Luziola spruceana,* and *Oryza* spp., the sedge *Scirpus cubensis,* and floating mats of *Azolla filiculoides* and *Salvinia* spp. (Salviniaceae), *Ceratopteris pteridoides* (Parkeriaceae), *Ceratophyllum demersum* (Ceratophyllaceae), *Eichhornia crassipes* (Pontederiaceae), *Pistia stratiotes* (Araceae), and *Utricularia foliosa* (Lentibulariaceae) (Junk 1970; Junk and Howard-William 1984).

Marshes composed of many of the plants above also form, and persist for many years, around the edges of floodplain and oxbow lakes (Junk 1970; Junk and Howard-William 1984). They consist especially of grasses, such as *Paspalum repens, Leersia hexandra,* and *Panicum grandis*; sedges, such as *Scleria microcarpa, Scirpus cubensis,* and *Cyperus giganteus.* Other plants including *Heliconia marginata* (Musaceae), *Calathea lutea,* and *Thalia geniculata* (Maranthaceae) and floating plants such as *Victoria amazonica* and *Nymphaea* spp. (Nymphaeaceae) also may be locally common (see plate 33). In later successional stages these marshes are gradually replaced with bushes and small trees.

Apparently some marsh-dwelling birds strongly prefer marshes with certain types of aquatic vegetation (e.g., reedbeds vs. sedges or grasses). We point out some of these preferences in the notes section of database A.

Saltwater and Brackish Marshes (A2)

Many aquatic plant genera listed above, and some of the same species, form extensive coastal and estuarine (tidal) marshes (see plate 34), especially various *Scirpus* species (Cyperaceae) and widespread forms such as *Salicornia* spp. (Chenopodiaceae), *Distichlis* spp., and *Phragmites australis* and *Spartina* spp. (Gramineae) (Cabrera 1976; West 1977; Minckley and Brown 1982).

Coastal Sand Beaches and Mudflats (A3)

Coastal beaches and mudflats (see plate 35), especially those of estuaries, are important habitats for a variety of waders and shorebirds, especially Nearctic migrants. A variety of aquatic birds forage on mudflats but require the nearby cover of mangroves or some type of marsh vegetation; most of these species are listed under those habitats. A few landbirds use the "strand" vegetation that forms on upper beaches above the tideline.

Coastal Rocky Beaches (A4)

Rocky beaches (see plate 36) are typical of long stretches of the Pacific coast of western South America, south of central Peru. They also are found along the west coast of Baja California, Mexico, and locally to the south. Most bird species that prefer rocks regularly washed by seawater also use jetties in areas otherwise lacking such habitat.

Riverine Sand Beaches (A5)

Seasonally, river levels along many lowland tropical rivers drop several meters and expose broad expanses of sand or mud (see plate 37) for up to several months at a time as small islands or beaches. Although these are mostly devoid of vegetation, some stands of herbaceous growth generally develop during the months of exposure. A 100 m by 20 m strip of riverine sandy beach in southeastern Peru had nearly a hundred species of plants, dominated by Gramineae and Compositae (Foster, Arce B., and Wachter 1986). A few Neotropical shorebirds and landbirds forage and nest exclusively on these sandy beaches bordering rivers and large streams, particularly in Amazonia. Many Nearctic shorebirds also forage on riverine beaches and mudflats, particularly across Amazonia during their southward migration.

Freshwater Lakes and Ponds (A6)

This category encompasses a variety of lake types, including the large oxbows of Amazonia, high-altitude freshwater lakes of the Andes (see plate 38), and human-made bodies of water scattered throughout the Neotropics, especially in dry regions. Bird species confined to the broad fringe of marsh vegetation that often borders such lakes are listed under "freshwater marshes" (A1).

Alkaline Lakes (A7)

Large, generally shallow alkaline lakes (see plate 39) occur at high elevations in the central and southern Andes, and also in Patagonia. A few also are found on the Mexican plateau and in the West Indies. In most regions such lakes are ephemeral, containing water for only a few months (or years) following periods of good rainfall. A few bird species are confined entirely to the saline waters of this habitat. We also include here several Neotropical shorebirds that are essentially restricted to the mudflats bordering these lakes.

Rivers (A8)

We define rivers as bodies of running water wider than 10 m. They include whitewater and blackwater rivers of Amazonia, most of which are relatively broad, deep, and slow moving (see plate 40), and also the rapid clearwater rivers of the Andes, Patagonia, and higher parts of Middle America. The open water and submerged vegetation and rocks of Neotropical rivers are used by some aquatic bird species, most of which also are found on lakes, ponds, and even coastal waters. Many riverine bird species require the cover of vegetation overhanging riverbanks but nonetheless feed exclusively on aquatic organisms and are therefore included here.

Streams (A9)

We define streams as bodies of running water less than 10 m wide (see plate 41). They support a variety of birds that forage for aquatic organisms from the ground, rocks, or perches in adjacent vegetation. Most bird species listed here occur along streams in a variety of forest and nonforest habitats (e.g., kingfishers). Those strongly associated with only one or a few forest or nonforest habitats (e.g., Sharp-tailed Streamcreeper, *Lochmias nematura,* in montane forest) are listed under those habitats but are assigned "streamside" (vegetation or other foraging substrates) as a microhabitat.

Bogs (A10)

Bogs occur in the high Andean elevations (see color plate 4), on poorly drained soils that are constantly supplied with water. Bogs remain perennially damp or wet, even during the prolonged droughts that are frequent in drier regions. Soils are usually gravelly or sandy with a deep layer of organic material (peat). In the Andes, Juncaceae, Cyperaceae, and mosses of the subclass Bryidae dominate the bogs; tuft-forming grasses and herbs are less abundant elements (Weberbauer 1945).

Coastal Waters (A11)

Coastal waters include bays, estuaries, and other areas that overlie the continental shelves (see plate 42). In some cases coastal waters extend far out to sea, especially at the mouths of major rivers, but coastal bird species only rarely occur beyond 20 km from shore. Along the coast these birds feed on submerged aquatic vegetation in shallow water, or on fish or invertebrates that typically occur close to shore. Most seabirds are found in waters within a few kilometers of the coast, or else they are highly pelagic.

Pelagic Waters (A12)

Pelagic waters are offshore areas past the edge of the continental shelves. These deep oceanic waters provide habitat for seabirds that can survive far from land for long periods. Pelagic birds often concentrate along the edges of continental shelves, where the upwelling of nutrients results in large concentrations of fish and crustaceans. Although most true seabirds are rarely seen from land, many species can occur close to shore where currents bring nutrient-rich waters to the surface; for example, along the coasts of Peru and Chile. However, pelagic birds differ from coastal species by being able to find scarce and widely dispersed food resources over vast areas of relatively "dead" ocean as well.

Microhabitats

Distinctive features of habitats that are critical to certain bird species are designated as microhabitats. Bamboo thickets, for example, are a patchily distributed vegetation element in humid tropical forests throughout the world; many Neotropical bird species are entirely dependent on them for food and cover. Similarly, Oilbirds (*Steatornis caripensis*) and cocks-of-the-rock (*Rupicola* spp.) require caves or crevices in rocky outcrops (for nesting) in or near forests, and a variety of species rarely are found far from terrestrial bromeliads in dry forests. Our list of microhabitats is brief; we hope their inclusion stimulates other workers to increase our general knowledge of these and other microhabitat associations.

Bamboo. Dense thickets of various large, woody species of bamboo (Gramineae) (see plate 43) occur locally within evergreen forests throughout the Neotropics; they are most common and conspicuous in upper montane forests in the Andes and Middle America, where *Chusquea* spp. often cover large areas along natural and human-made edges. Tall (to 20 m) thickets of spiny *Guadua angustifolia* and other species grow patchily within forests around the periphery of Amazonia, especially in southeastern Peru and southwestern Brazil. Montane forests in southeastern Brazil, and lower forests in adjacent parts of Argentina and Paraguay, often are dominated by extensive stands of *Guadua, Merostachys,* and *Chusquea* species, and the bamboo bird community in these regions is accordingly large. Many species of large bamboos produce seeds at regular but long intervals of several years to twenty years or more (Janzen 1976); most bamboo seed specialists are therefore nomadic (see chapter 8). The dense foliage and tangled branches in bamboo thickets provide numerous foraging substrates for insectivorous birds, some of which specialize in searching dead leaves and other debris trapped while falling from the forest canopy. Cavities in bamboo stalks serve as refuges for a variety of avian prey items (Pierpont and Fitzpatrick 1983).

Treefalls. Small forest openings formed by fallen trees are quickly overgrown by low vegetation that provides habitat for a variety of organisms (Schemske and Brokaw 1981). Bushes and small trees grow up among the decaying trunks and branches, often forming impenetrable thickets one to several meters high. Sunlit gaps are rapidly colonized by fast-growing trees, many of which (e.g., various species of Melastomataceae) produce large quantities of edible fruit and sustain large insect populations. Although many avian gap specialists are insectivores that forage low in dense vegetation, most depend on the undergrowth of surrounding forest as well. Increased sunlight in forest openings also results in the proliferation of canopy and midstory vines.

Vine tangles. Woody vines make an important contribution to the high floristic diversity of Neotropical forests (Emmons and Gentry 1983). Pires and Prance (1985) recognize unusually vine-rich forests in Amazonia and coastal Brazil as a distinct vegetation type, but we prefer to treat vines as a microhabitat that varies greatly in abundance from forest to forest throughout the Neotropics. Lowland forests with pronounced dry seasons support greater diversity and larger numbers of vines than occur in wetter regions; vines rapidly become less conspicuous with increasing elevation in the humid mountains. Canopy and midstory vine tangles serve as cover and foraging substrates for several species of bird, many of which search for prey hiding in curled dead leaves and other debris trapped among the dense branches (Gradwohl and Greenberg 1982, 1984; Remsen and Parker 1984).

Ground bromeliads. An unusually dense ground cover of bromeliads (Bromeliaceae) (see plate 44) characterizes many dry forests and scrub habitats. Nearly impenetrable thickets of spiny bromeliads in the genera *Bromelia* and *Dyckia* occur in dry forests of the Brazilian caatinga and in the chaco of Paraguay and northern Argentina. Terrestrial bromeliads, especially species of *Puya* and *Tillandsia,* are also important floristic elements in arid, mountainous regions, where they often form the dominant vegetation on steep slopes or cliffs. A variety of insectivorous birds spend much of their time foraging among the closely spaced leaves of these plants.

Rocky outcrops and caves. Cliffs (see plate 45) and caves occur locally throughout mountainous and hilly regions of the Neotropics. Many bird species strongly associated with one habitat (e.g., Andean Cock-of-the-Rock, *Rupicola peruviana,* in montane forest) require cliff faces for nest sites. The granite domes of Pantepui provide the only breeding sites for several cliff-nesting species in the region.

Streamside. Birds restricted to the streams in only one or a few forest or nonforest habitats are assigned to the specific habitat(s), with "streamside" as a microhabitat (see plate 46). In contrast, we designate streams (A9) as the habitat for species that forage along or in streams in a wide variety of forest or nonforest settings.

Army ants. Although not a microhabitat, we list army ants here because they are a distinctive feature across several habitats and are critical to certain bird species. Army ants serve as "beaters" for a variety of Neotropical birds, some of which spend all or most of their lives following columns of ants, primarily *Eciton burchellii* and *Labidus praedator,* as they swarm across the forest floor, killing almost every small animal that fails to escape. Obligate ant-following birds capture invertebrates and small vertebrates as they flee the oncoming ants. The occurrence of these birds depends on the existence of the appropriate species of army ants in a forest (Harper 1988; Bierregaard and Lovejoy 1989). This specialized foraging behavior has been studied in great detail by Willis (e.g., 1967, 1969, 1973, 1979a; Willis and Oniki 1978). The movements of the ants are unpredictable but are related to rainfall and breeding cycles.

3 Neotropical Humid Forests

Synopsis

Neotropical humid forests are famous for their species richness. Total avian diversity in twenty-one of the twenty-two zoogeographic regions is directly proportional to the diversity of of their humid forest birds. The single exception is Central South America, with its large radiation of birds in open habitats.

Geographic and climatic barriers divide Neotropical humid forests into discrete units, each with a distinct avifauna. Elevation has an even greater impact on species composition: bird species overlap is greater between the forests of southern Brazil and Central America than between the two endpoints along an elevational transect in forested Andean slopes. Few bird species occur in both humid forest and nonforest habitats. Levels of endemism are roughly equal in humid forest and open habitats; however, forest bird species are much more likely to be habitat restricted (i.e., to occur in only one of the forty-one possible habitat types) than are nonforest species.

Lowland humid forests in the Neotropics have the highest single-site bird species diversity in the world. Most species are associated with *terra firme* forest, but other forest habitats can contribute substantially to local species richness.

The principal threats to lowland forests and their birds involve clearing for agricultural development and, locally, logging for timber. Among lowland forests, the greatest immediate threat is faced by the lowlands in the Atlantic Forests of eastern Brazil and those in the West Indies. The Amazon basin and the Tepuis are the least threatened humid forest regions in the Neotropics.

Montane forests, as a whole, are just as rich in bird species as are the lowland forests, even though single-site species diversity declines with elevation. Montane forests have more endemic species than do the lowlands, with two to four times the number of endemics as in the geographically associated lowlands. In the Andes and in the Madrean Highlands, bird species composition changes approximately 10%–15% with each 100 m gain in elevation. In the smaller, more isolated mountain ranges of eastern Brazil, southern Central America, and the Tepuis, montane bird species have broader elevational ranges.

"Upper tropical" forested slopes, between 500 and 1,500 m elevation, support both the highest overall species diversity and the largest proportion of species with narrow elevational distributions. Throughout the Neotropics, this is also the zone undergoing most rapid and thorough clear-cutting for conversion to agriculture. In the Chiriquí-Darién and Atlantic Forest regions, conservation efforts must focus on these threatened lower slopes, where the forest endemics are concentrated. In the Central and Northern Andes, and in the Madrean Highlands, forest endemics are distributed evenly up the entire slope. In these regions, conservation efforts must preserve entire elevational transects.

From northeastern Mexico to Bolivia and southeastern Brazil grow some of the most luxuriant rainforests in the world. Tropical moist forests cover about 5 million km^2 in the Neotropics (Myers 1980 and sources therein) and harbor the realm's most species-rich bird communities. Over 90% of the bird species in terrestrial habitats in the Neotropics occur in humid forests, and more than 80% rely on these forests as their primary habitat.

Where the forested Andes meet the Amazon basin, single-site diversity of birds is higher than anywhere else on the planet (Haffer 1990). Many other major groups of Neotropical organisms—for example, canopy trees (Gentry 1982b, 1988b), butterflies (Lamas 1985), reptiles (Dixon 1979), frogs (Duellman 1988), bats (Koopman 1981, 1982), and other mammals (Emmons 1984)—also reach peak diversity in these western Amazonian forests.

Bird communities in humid forests include some of the most localized and ecologically specialized species known. Specialized species also tend to be vulnerable species (as we show in chapter 9), and steady elimination of humid forests from Mexico to Brazil has caused numerous bird species to decline precipitously in recent years. Many forest specialists are now widely regarded as threatened or endangered (e.g., Diamond and Lovejoy 1985; Collar et al. 1992).

The overwhelming importance of humid forests to tropical diversity makes it difficult to assign relative conservation priorities to regions. Tropical rainforests *everywhere* are receiving increased publicity, so it is especially important to distinguish communities that are threatened with immediate losses from those that are in less urgent predicaments. Indeed, forest regions across the Neotropics differ dramatically in their proportions of threatened or vulnerable bird species. Therefore birds can provide an index by which to compare forest regions according to need for emergency conservation action. Some tropical forests receiving widespread publicity, such as the Amazon basin, are actually not immediately threatened (chapter 10; see also Mares 1992).

Table 3.1 Ratios of Forest to Nonforest Bird Species in the Twenty-two Zoogeographic Regions in the Neotropics

Region	Region Code	Total Species	Forest Species	Non-forest Species	Ratio
Southern Amazonia	AMS	892	753	159	4.7
Northern Amazonia	AMN	896	747	166	4.5
Northern Andes	NAN	772	680	158	4.3
Central Andes	CAN	804	594	270	2.2
Gulf-Caribbean Slope	GCS	689	545	166	3.3
Atlantic Forest	ATL	682	524	154	3.4
Northern South America	NSA	652	485	179	2.7
Central South America	CSA	645	349	285	1.2
Chocó Lowlands	CHO	401	341	58	5.9
Madrean Highlands	MAH	379	311	135	2.3
Chiriquí-Darién Highlands	CDH	279	255	49	5.2
Pacific Arid Slope	PAS	358	234	124	1.9
Greater Antilles	GAN	250	167	72	2.3
Equatorial Pacific	EPC	289	157	115	1.4
Tepuis	TEP	142	131	37	3.5
Baja-Sonora	BSR	239	115	119	1.0
Pampas	PAM	249	77	136	0.6
Lesser Antilles	LAN	110	65	26	2.5
Southern Andes	SAN	198	60	137	0.4
Mexican Plateau	MPL	122	54	92	0.6
Subtropical Pacific	STP	206	43	110	0.4
Patagonia	PAT	181	25	104	0.2

Note: Regions are ordered by their diversity of forest birds.

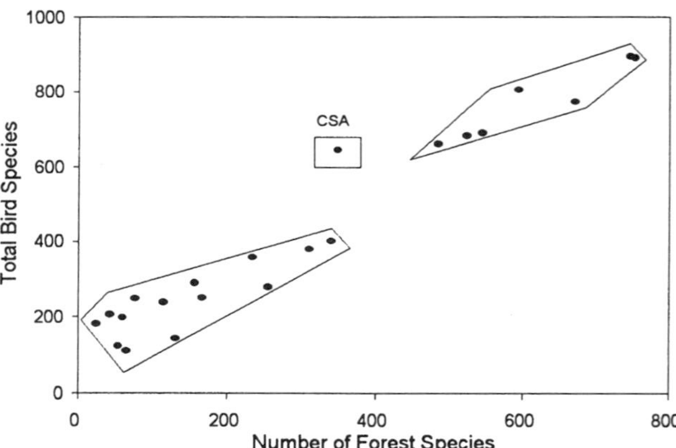

Figure 3.1 Relationship of forest to total species richness in birds, by Neotropical zoogeographic region. Note that Central South America has a higher number of species than expected based on its diversity of forest birds.

Forest versus Nonforest Habitats

For purposes of this chapter, we include under "humid forest" all forest habitats (F1 through F15—includes secondary forests) except the dry, tropical deciduous forests (F7). The dry forest avifauna is mainly a mixture of species from adjacent humid forests and scrubs and shows diversity patterns quite different from those in humid forests. We exclude dry forests from the analyses in this chapter and discuss them separately (chapter 4).

Species richness. Humid forests have two to three times more species of birds than nonforest habitats. Among nonaquatic Neotropical birds, 2,820 species use some form of humid forest, while only 1,017 use nonforest habitats. The ratio of species using humid forest versus nonforest habitats varies geographically (table 3.1). These ratios serve as good indicators of the proportion of each region originally occupied by humid forest, and in sixteen of the twenty-two regions humid forest species outnumber nonforest species. Regions with extensive humid forests contain two to six times more forest birds than nonforest birds, while regions of open country are dominated by nonforest species (table 3.1). Where humid forest is scattered amid more extensive nonforest habitats (e.g., Equatorial Pacific Coast and Central South America) roughly equal numbers of forest and nonforest species occur.

With one very interesting exception, the number of forest-inhabiting species within Neotropical regions is the main determinant of the region's absolute diversity (fig. 3.1). The exception is Central South America (CSA), where species diversity is comparable to that of the seven principal forest regions but an unusually large proportion of species occur in nonforest habitats. Central South America is the only high-diversity

Table 3.2 Number of Bird Species Occurring in Humid Forests in the Neotropics

Habitat	Habitat Code	Total Users[a]	Primary Habitat	Habitat Restricted	Habitat-Restricted Endemics
Montane forests					
Montane evergreen	F4	1,162	841	357	220
Elfin	F5	166	61	27	25
Polylepis	F6	55	18	6	4
Southern temperate	F9	57	31	12	10
Pine	F10	119	60	18	7
Pine-oak	F11	179	75	8	4
Subtotal		1,441	1,086	428	270
Lowland forests					
Tropical lowland evergreen	F1	1,410	1,012	408	198
Flooded tropical	F2	166	76	22	8
River-edge	F3	193	80	14	6
Gallery	F8	474	99	12	10
White sand	F12	60	16	6	5
Palm	F13	10	4	2	0
Mangrove	F14	87	15	4	3
Second-growth habitats	F15	920	54	2	2
Subtotal		2,070	1,356	470	232
Total		2,820	2,442	898	502

[a] Total species using each forest type are not additive, since many species use more than one habitat and therefore appear more than once in this column.

region with an avifauna that is not overwhelmingly dominated by humid forest species. Diversity and conservation in this remarkable region are discussed in many places in this book (especially chapters 4, 9, and 10).

Habitat restriction. Remarkably few bird species use both humid forests and other habitats. Birds tend to specialize, and this specialization is most pronounced in humid forest communities. Of the 2,820 bird species in Neotropical humid forests, 70% occur only in humid forests, and 32% are habitat restricted (occur in only one type of humid forest throughout their range; table 3.2). Comparable proportions for nonforest birds are 42% exclusively in nonforest habitats, and only 15% habitat restricted (table 3.3). This tendency to specialize makes forest species especially vulnerable to habitat loss. As a general rule, forest communities are both more diverse and more vulnerable than nonforest communities.

Endemism. Although humid forest birds are much more prone to habitat specialization, they are only slightly more prone to endemism than are nonforest birds. The mean number of zoogeographic regions occupied by forest species is 2.38, compared with 2.81 regions for nonforest species (fig. 3.2). Of the 2,442 species that use humid forests as their primary habitat, 1,093 (45%) are endemic to a single zoogeographic region, compared with 258 endemics among the 684 nonforest species (38%).

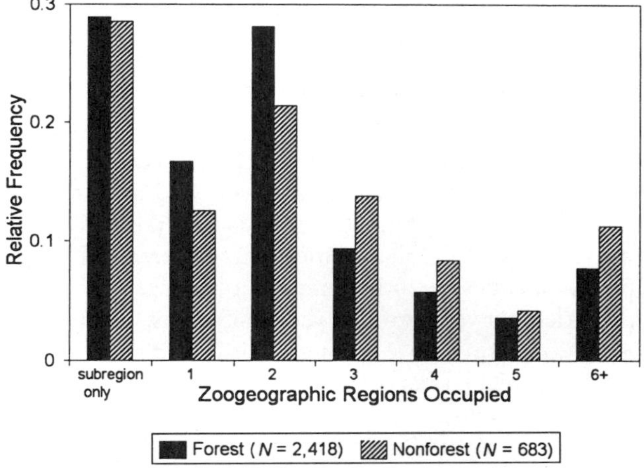

Figure 3.2 Geographic range of birds in forests and open habitats in the Neotropics.

That both forest and nonforest species are prone to endemism in the Neotropics is of utmost importance in establishing conservation strategies using the community approach (chapter 9). Independent assemblages of birds exist throughout the Neotropics, in open country as well as forests. Each endemic assemblage represents a separate, locally evolved ecosystem. Each one requires special, local attention for its preservation (for excellent examples and discussions about such local assemblages, see papers by A. W. Diamond, Delgado, Scott and Brooke, and Stiles in Diamond and Lovejoy 1985).

Table 3.3 Number of Bird Species Occurring in Nonforest Habitats in the Neotropics

Habitat	Habitat Code	Total Users[a]	Primary Habitat	Habitat Restricted	Habitat-Restricted Endemics
Montane nonforest					
Arid montane scrub	N2	265	114	40	31
Humid montane scrub	N3	107	31	7	6
Puna	N9	53	35	12	11
Paramo	N10	69	41	18	14
Riparian thickets	N11[b]	32	7	0	0
Subtotal		408	228	77	62
Lowland nonforest					
Arid lowland scrub	N1	342	167	41	29
Cerrado	N4	46	18	3	3
Campo grassland	N5	68	23	9	7
Low, seasonally wet grassland	N6	103	58	1	0
Southern temperate grassland	N7	68	36	8	6
Northern temperate grassland	N8	36	24	3	2
Riparian thickets	N11[b]	87	28	1	1
River island scrub	N12	29	11	6	1
Pastures	N13	132	22	0	0
Second-growth habitats	N14	324	69	1	0
Subtotal		776	456	73	49
Total		1,017	684	150	111

[a] Total species using each habitat type are not additive, since many species use more than one type and therefore appear more than once in this column.

[b] Species using riparian thickets are split into montane and lowlands, with species having center of abundance at or above the Upper Tropical Zone considered montane.

Generalists and Edge Species: the "Trash" Avifauna

Only 436 species, or 12% of the Neotropical avifauna, regularly occur both in humid forest and in nonforest habitats. These habitat generalists probably lived in forest edges, floodplains, moist scrub, tree-fall openings, landslides, or other natural openings within the presettlement vegetation of the Neotropics. Today most of these generalists are among the 1,209 species (32.3% of Neotropical taxa) that occur in severely human-altered habitats: secondary forest (F15, $N = 920$), pastures and cultivated land (N13, $N = 132$), and brushy second growth (N14, $N = 324$).

Birds of secondary habitats have proliferated around human-caused disturbances ever since people began altering the landscape. Certainly the future of these species is secure as habitat alteration accelerates across the Neotropics. Many appear in our lists of indicator species for degraded habitats (see part 4, database I). In most other respects, although they include some of the most common and conspicuous bird species of the American tropics, these edge and generalist species do not figure prominently in this book.

Humid Forests: Geography, Inundation, and Elevation

Humid forests occur in a multitude of discrete regions and vegetation formations throughout the Neotropics. As habitat for different bird communities, the most important distinctions among Neotropical humid forests originate with geographic isolation, plus differences in rainfall, soil moisture, soil type, and elevation (through its effects on temperature and light availability; Grubb 1977). Many of the different forest types are easily distinguished by geography and their characteristic plants alone (chapter 2).

Geography. The principal humid forests in Central and South America are separated from one another by geographic or habitat barriers, including ocean, mountains, major rivers, and expanses of nonforest habitat. These barriers inhibit faunal mixing, and they have played a substantial role in elevating the overall diversity across the forests of the Neotropics.

Among mainland forests, both distance and habitat boundaries contribute almost equally to the separation of faunas. Out of a total pool of 1,410 species that use lowland humid forests, only 71 (5%) occur in all six of the lowland forest regions of the Neotropical mainland. Among adjacent zoogeographic regions, only the two regions of the Amazon basin (Southern Amazonia, AMS, and Northern Amazonia, AMN)—which are separated by the Amazon River alone—share as many as 85% of their species. The remaining humid forest regions in the lowlands share no more than 60% of their species, the number of species in common being inversely related to the distance separating the regions (table 3.4).

Table 3.4 Tropical Lowland Evergreen Forest (F1) Bird Species Shared among the Seven Principal Humid Forest Regions of the Neotropics ($N = 1,410$)

Region	Region Code	Number of Forest Species	GCS	CHO	NSA	AMN	AMS	ATL
Greater Antilles	GAN	111	11	5	13	8	8	5
Gulf-Caribbean Slope	GCS	428		253	245	185	177	110
Chocó Lowlands	CHO	307			191	155	149	91
Northern South America	NSA	370				240	221	147
Northern Amazonia	AMN	583					493	193
Southern Amazonia	AMS	586						209
Atlantic Forest	ATL	435						

Note: Four species occur in all seven regions; 71 species occur in six regions, excluding the Greater Antilles.

Isolation by ocean is the most important contributor to the formation of separate forest avifaunas. Long isolation of the Caribbean islands, plus an available dispersal route northward from South America through the Lesser Antilles, produced a noteworthy endemic avifauna in the Greater Antilles (GAN). Nearly two-thirds of the Greater Antillean humid forest birds (111 species), are endemic to those islands. These birds include numerous endemic genera and two endemic families (Todidae and Dulidae). The Lesser Antilles (LAN) have a smaller forest avifauna, with only 22 forest endemics. A significant part of the endemic avifauna in the Caribbean became extinct after human arrival on the islands (Steadman, Pregill, and Olson 1984), and many more species now balance on the verge of extinction (see below).

In South America, topographically and geographically distinct temperate forests also harbor specialized bird communities that are distinct from those of adjacent subtropical humid forests. We grouped these peculiar humid forests into two types: the *Polylepis* woodlands of the high central Andes (F6) and the *Nothofagus, Podocarpus,* and *Araucaria* forests of subtropical and south temperate South America (F9).

Moisture. Much of the variation in humid forests across the Neotropics arises from differences in rainfall, soil, and drainage (Walter 1971; Grubb 1977; Gentry 1982b). Elfin (F5) and upper montane (F4) forests may receive as little as 1,000 mm annual rainfall but often are cloaked for days on end in dense, windblown fog. These misty forests support luxuriant epiphytic plant communities, plus a host of specialized bird species that have become dependent on epiphytes. Montane forests at lower elevations receive up to 6,000 mm average annual rainfall. Where such wet conditions coincide with nutrient-rich soil, some of the most productive plant associations are found (e.g., Janzen 1973a, 1973b). As discussed below, huge assemblages of birds specialize on this transitional zone, occupying a narrow and highly threatened ecological zone along the bases of Neotropical mountains. These specialists join a diverse contingent of tropical lowland species, so that the highest overall species diversity occurs in the montane foothills.

In contrast, certain tropical forests of the Amazon basin that grow on nutrient-poor white sand soils (F12), drained by blackwater rivers, support relatively depauperate ecological communities with only a few avian specialists. *Terra firme* forests (F1) occur on widespread, relatively well drained, nutrient-poor soils (e.g., oxisols) between major rivers or valleys. Bird communities of these forests are extremely diverse, but many of the species are widespread. Swamp forest and *várzea* (F2), river-edge forest (F3), and gallery forest (F8) all differ in their relationships to permanent or seasonal inundation. Each forest type has a handful of unique bird specialists, together with much larger numbers of widespread species. *Mauritia* palms (F13) and mangroves (F14) support specialized forest communities in freshwater swamps and tidal flats, respectively.

Elevation. Spectacular ecological transitions occur between treeline and tropical elevations in the wet mountains of Middle and South America. Many of these can be traversed in only a few hair-raising kilometers of highway. In southern Mexico and Middle America, for example, habitats grade from spruce-fir and pine forests at the top, through broadleaf evergreen forests, then through a lower pine-oak zone, and finally to tropical evergreen or deciduous forests. In this region, only three of the ninety-nine bird species of the coniferous mountaintops also occur in the lowland forests (Swallow-tailed Kite, *Elanoides forficatus,* Singing Quail, *Dactylortyx thoracicus,* and Stygian Owl, *Asio stygius*). In the eastern Andes a similar transect runs from mossy, elfin forests at treeline through drenched cloud forests and the upper tropical forests to the humid lowland forests of the Amazon basin. The two extremes of this extraordinarily diverse eastern Andean transect do not have a single bird species in common.

The avifaunas of the humid lowland tropics and those of the forested mountains differ markedly in their evolutionary history as well as in their patterns of endemism, distribution, and habitat use. These differences have important implications for conservation priorities in lowland versus montane communities.

Lowland Humid Forests

Lowland forests of South America are famous for their enormous single-site species diversity, which is the highest in the world. Thorough inventories at single sites in the central Amazon basin reveal nearly four hundred bird species (e.g., Moskovits, Fitzpatrick, and Willard 1985; Stotz and Bierregaard 1989), and the numbers climb to five hundred or more in western Amazonia (e.g., Terborgh, Fitzpatrick, and Emmons 1984; Parker, Donahue, and Schulenberg 1994; recent summary by Haffer 1990). These fantastic numbers often lead scientists and conservationists to single out lowland tropical forests as the regions most likely to suffer mass extinctions because of deforestation (e.g., Myers 1986; Pimm 1986).

The reasoning behind a disproportionate concern for lowland forests is clear. With more species than montane forests or nonforest sites, lowland forests have the greatest total number of species potentially affected by habitat loss. With more complex food webs, lowland forests might be more easily destabilized than less diverse habitats after the loss of a few species. With few exceptions, however, forested habitats of the humid Neotropical lowlands are not as immediately threatened as are those of the Neotropical mountains.

Types of Lowland Forests

Several distinct forest types cloak the humid lowlands of the Neotropics (chapter 2). *Terra firme* forests (F1) are by far the dominant type, both in land area covered and in number of bird species they contain. Other lowland forests occur as strands along rivers (F2, F3, F8) or as patches within a matrix of *terra firme* (F12, F13) and have few specialists associated with them (table 3.2). The avifauna of a typical *várzea* site (F2) in Amazonia, for example, has just a handful of specialists and only about half the total number of species found in adjacent *terra firme* forest.

Despite having relatively few habitat specialists, river-edge forests contribute significantly to the overall species richness at individual lowland sites in Amazonia (Remsen and Parker 1983; Terborgh, Fitzpatrick, and Emmons 1984). As many as one-quarter of the total bird species in sites that encompass both riverine and *terra firme* habitats may depend on the river-edge habitats. Interestingly, habitat specialization by birds along rivers is restricted almost exclusively to Amazonia. Very few species are specifically associated with riverine forests in the lowlands of Central America or in eastern Brazil (table 3.5). Even in other major forested river systems, such as the Mississippi basin of North America or the Congo basin of Africa, few bird species depend on the riverine forests (Remsen and Parker 1983). The reason for this specialization in Amazonia is not clear, but increased habitat specialization throughout the Amazonian avifauna may be a response to the high overall diversity in the region, as suggested on theoretical grounds by Rosenzweig (1992). The greater importance of riverine habitats in the Amazon may also result from their huge area compared with the relatively small, discontinuous river systems that drain eastern Brazil and Central America (Remsen and Parker 1983). Lack of severe seasonal fluctuations in water levels in both the Mississippi and Congo drainages, which results in the small areal extent of these riverine habitats, may have prevented the evolution of a significant riverine habitat avifauna in these regions (Remsen and Parker 1983).

Gallery forests (F8) also are depauperate in habitat-restricted birds. Fewer than 3% of the species that use gallery forest are restricted to it (table 3.2). A gallery forest avifauna consists of a mixture of edge-inhabiting generalists, species from nearby continuously forested areas, and species from adjacent open habitats. As a result, the gallery forest avifauna is diverse but low in endemism and habitat specialization.

Because gallery forests tend to be swampy or seasonally flooded, they often survive intact long after the surrounding landscape has been transformed into agricultural fields or plantations. Even when the forests are greatly damaged—by selective logging, burning, or lowering of water tables—threats to this unspecialized forest avifauna generally remain low. The biggest exception is in Central South America (CSA), where twenty-two endemic bird species use gallery forests as their primary habitat and eight are restricted to it. These forests are being degraded rapidly along with the open country habitats around them, as discussed in chapter 4.

Distinctive scrubs and scrubby forests (F12) grow on nutrient-poor white sands of the Amazon basin and coastal Brazil (chapter 2). In Amazonia these patchy "campina" habitats still fare well. Low soil nutrients make these areas unsuitable for agriculture, and most of the campinas lie in the still remote basin of the upper Rio Negro. The fifteen species whose primary habitat is campina vegetation are not currently at risk, although the patchy nature of the habitat renders these bird communities quickly vulnerable were agriculture to develop.

In contrast, the white sand forests (restinga) in eastern Brazil are already at risk. Three bird species use restinga as a primary habitat, and all are endemic to this region. Second homes for affluent urbanites, who are attracted to the famous beaches of coastal Brazil, are rapidly replacing this rare habitat (Willis and Oniki 1992).

Palm forests (F13) occur as isolated, sometimes extensive patches in wet areas throughout the humid low-

Table 3.5 Habitat Restriction and Endemism in Humid Lowland Forest Habitats in Neotropical Zoogeographic Regions

Region	Region Code	Primary Habitat	Habitat Restricted	Habitat-Restricted Endemics	Primary-Habitat Endemic
Tropical lowland evergreen forest (F1)					
Greater Antilles	GAN	58	1	1	45
Gulf-Caribbean Slope	GCS	325	80	15	43
Chocó Lowlands	CHO	247	72	13	22
Northern South America	NSA	262	51	4	8
Northern Amazonia	AMN	465	217	45	57
Southern Amazonia	AMS	466	216	48	56
Atlantic Forest	ATL	313	88	57	124
Flooded tropical evergreen forest (F2)					
Greater Antilles	GAN	0	0	0	0
Gulf-Caribbean Slope	GCS	9	0	0	0
Chocó Lowlands	CHO	7	0	0	0
Northern South America	NSA	21	2	0	0
Northern Amazonia	AMN	69	18	4	6
Southern Amazonia	AMS	70	18	4	6
Atlantic Forest	ATL	10	0	0	0
River-edge forest (F3)					
Greater Antilles	GAN	0	0	0	0
Gulf-Caribbean Slope	GCS	11	0	0	0
Chocó Lowlands	CHO	8	0	0	0
Northern South America	NSA	26	0	0	0
Northern Amazonia	AMN	65	8	1	2
Southern Amazonia	AMS	77	13	6	14
Atlantic Forest	ATL	14	0	0	0
Gallery forest (F8)					
Greater Antilles	GAN	3	0	0	0
Gulf-Caribbean Slope	GCS	19	0	0	3
Chocó Lowlands	CHO	5	0	0	0
Northern South America	NSA	21	0	0	3
Northern Amazonia	AMN	29	1	1	2
Southern Amazonia	AMS	23	0	0	0
Atlantic Forest	ATL	13	0	0	0
Central South America	CSA	51	8	8	22
Pacific Arid Slope	PAS	14	0	0	1
Baja-Sonora	BSR	20	2	1	6

lands of South America. *Mauritia* palms form single-species stands in swamps and old lake beds within the continuous rainforest of the Amazon basin, and also in the open country of Central South America and the Guianan Shield. Five bird species use these palm stands as their primary habitat.

Mangrove forests (F14) constitute an essentially aquatic habitat. As with other aquatic habitats (see chapter 6), birds that use mangroves tend to be habitat generalists that range over wide geographic areas. Only eight bird species that use mangroves are endemic, and only four are restricted to mangroves. Therefore, even though many waterbirds nest in mangroves, birds overall are poor indicators of the condition of mangrove habitats (see also chapter 6).

Conservation of Lowland Forests

Lowland humid forests occur in three broad zones in the Neotropics: (1) the trans-Andean forests of Central America (zoogeographic region GCS, Gulf-Caribbean Slope) and the Chocó Lowlands region of western Colombia and northwestern Ecuador (CHO); (2) the cis-Andean Amazon and southern Orinoco basins (AMN and AMS); and (3) the Atlantic Forest (ATL) of eastern Brazil, eastern Paraguay, and northeastern Argentina. Small areas of humid lowland forest occur on various islands of the Greater Antilles (GAN) and Lesser Antilles (LAN) and in scattered patches within the open habitats of Northern South America (NSA) east of the Andes.

Agricultural development and, locally, logging for commercial timber threaten lowland forests throughout the Neotropics. The extent and immediacy of the threat to forest habitats, however, vary greatly among the different zones. Extensive clearing threatens entire ecosystems in the Atlantic Forest and Lesser Antilles and may reach those levels soon in the Gulf-Caribbean Slope of Central America and the Chocó Lowlands.

Clearings for roads, towns, and agriculture are still local in the Amazon basin (AMS and AMN). This vast region remains largely forested, even in areas suffering extensive development pressures (e.g., Rondônia, Brazil).

The conservation status of the endemic avifaunas highlights the differences in the present-day condition of lowland forest regions (table 3.6). The two Amazonian regions (AMN, AMS) and the Central American Gulf-Caribbean Slope have received the most publicity in connection with tropical deforestation and threats to biodiversity. Yet these regions are among those showing the lowest percentage of avifauna at risk (CP status 1, 2, or 3; see part 4, Guide to the Databases). Below we focus on each zone separately, to examine conditions responsible for the broad patterns of threat and to pinpoint issues of local concern.

Amazonia. Several features set the Amazonian lowlands apart from the other lowland forest regions. Overall diversity is extremely high in Amazonia and is lowest among the mainland forest regions in the nearby Atlantic Forest region (table 3.7). Only about 10% of lowland forest species (146) occur in all three of the major areas of lowland forest—the Amazon basin (AMN and AMS), the trans-Andean forests of Central America (GCS) and the Chocó Lowlands, and the Atlantic Forest. An additional 219 bird species are shared between Amazonia and one of the other two forest zones (only two species, Tropical Parula, *Parula pitiayumi*, and Golden-crowned Warbler, *Basileuturus culicivorus*, occur in the Atlantic Forest and trans-Andean forests but not in Amazonia).

Two bird families (Psophiidae, Opisthocomidae) are completely restricted to the Amazonian lowlands. A number of other families, especially suboscine passerines, are represented by disproportionately high numbers in the Amazonian forests. Mixed-species flocks of birds in the Amazon are larger and much more highly structured than anywhere else in the Neotropics (Munn and Terborgh 1979; Munn 1985; Powell 1985). Army ants (*Eciton burchelli* and *Labidus praedator*) attract far more "professional" swarm followers in the Amazon than elsewhere (Willis and Oniki 1978). As mentioned above, flooded forests contain habitat specialists in the Amazon, but nowhere else.

Yet despite their overwhelming biological diversity, most areas of the Amazonian lowlands do not warrant the most urgent conservation efforts. Vast tracts of Amazonia, especially in the diverse, upland *terra firme* forests (F1), remain intact. Except in one area, the Amazonian forest avifauna will persist relatively unthreatened for some time still.

The one exception is southeastern Amazonia, south of the Amazon River and east of the Rio Madeira. Extensive deforestation has driven a high percentage of the endemics in the Pará and Madeira-Tapajós sub-

Table 3.6 Conservation Status of Humid Lowland Forest Endemics by Region

Region	Region Code	Lowland Forest Endemics	Conservation Priority			
			CP-1	CP-2	CP-3	CP-4
Greater Antilles	GAN	88	4	12	16	56
Lesser Antilles	LAN	21	4	6	3	8
Gulf-Caribbean Slope	GCS	54	0	4	22	28
Chocó Lowlands	CHO	23	0	6	12	5
Northern Amazonia	AMN	74	0	1	18	55
Southern Amazonia	AMS	79	0	4	31	44
Atlantic Forest	ATL	169	19	42	58	50

Note: Humid lowland forest includes F1, F2, F3, F8, F12, F13, F14, and their edges.

Table 3.7 Numbers of Bird Species Occuring in Humid Lowland Forests in Neotropical Zoogeographic Regions

Region	Region Code	Total Users	Primary Habitat	Habitat Restricted	Habitat-Restricted Endemics
Greater Antilles	GAN	136	65	1	1
Gulf-Caribbean Slope	GCS	515	371	82	16
Chocó Lowlands	CHO	340	272	73	13
Northern South America	NSA	477	341	55	5
Northern Amazonia	AMN	743	644	250	54
Southern Amazonia	AMS	745	649	251	59
Atlantic Forest	ATL	490	358	89	58

Note: Humid lowland forest includes F1, F2, F3, F8, F12, F13, F14, and their edges.

regions into threatened status (see table 3.8). Immediate conservation efforts in Amazonia should focus on protecting the remaining large forested patches in this southeastern section. Amazonia does, however, still offer the chance to save huge, viable portions of an extremely rich and virtually undamaged ecosystem. This rare opportunity, especially in western Amazonia, where human population pressure is still low, cannot be squandered.

Central America. Although deforestation has advanced more in Central America than in Amazonia, the level of threat to Central America's endemic humid lowland avifauna is not much greater than in corresponding bird communities in Amazonia (table 3.6). Two factors probably explain this anomaly. (1) In Central America, lowland forest endemics tend to be more tolerant of second growth than are endemics in the other four mainland regions (table 3.9). This difference is particularly striking between the Gulf-Caribbean Slope and the two Amazonian regions: well over half (65%) of the forest endemics in the Gulf-Caribbean Slope use secondary forest, but only 11% of the endemics in Amazonia do so. Birds that use secondary habitats are, of course, less vulnerable to extinction than are birds restricted to primary habitats (table 3.9). (2) Birds in Central American lowland forests appear to have smaller territories, hence higher population densities, than do birds in Amazonia (Terborgh et al. 1990). Higher native densities may allow Central American forest birds to survive in relatively smaller fragments of forest than in the Amazon, where many species quickly disappear from small fragments (Bierregaard and Lovejoy 1989). How far these differences between Central American and Amazonian forests can be generalized to other taxa remains unknown.

Table 3.8 Conservation Status of Forest Birds Endemic to Amazonian Subregions

Subregion	Subregion Code	Conservation Priority CP-1	CP-2	CP-3	CP-4
Northern Amazonia					
Throughout region	o	0	0	1	15
Guianan	GUI	0	0	6	27
Rio Negro West	RNW	0	1	11	13
Southern Amazonia					
Throughout region	o	0	0	10	24
Pará	PAR	0	3	6	0
Madeira-Tapajós	MID	0	1	6	3
Rio Madeira West	RMW	0	0	9	17

Table 3.9 Second-Growth Use and Level of Risk in Lowland Forest Birds of Three Major Lowland Forest Zones of the Neotropics

	Amazonia (AMN, AMS)	Atlantic Forest (ATL)	Trans-Andean (GCS, CHO)
Second-growth users	274 (32%)[a]	206 (42%)	299 (51%)
At risk	7	32	26
Primary forest only	595	290	292
At risk	89	117	83
Total lowland forest users	869	496	591
At risk	96	149	109

[a] Percentage of lowland forest bird species in region that use second growth.

Deforestation of Central American humid lowlands also has been implicated in the population decreases in some species of Nearctic migrant birds (e.g., Terborgh 1980; Rappole et al. 1983; Hall 1984; Morton 1992). We discuss Nearctic migrants and their conservation issues in chapter 7.

Atlantic Forest. The Atlantic Forest region has been largely deforested. At least 80% of the forest present when Europeans arrived in the 1500s had been destroyed by the late 1970s (Mori, Boom, and Prance 1981), and destruction continues. Rio de Janeiro, the bustling metropolis of coastal Brazil, lies at the heart of what was once a vast forest that covered more than one million km^2. Today one can travel hundreds of miles up the coast from Rio toward Bahia without seeing a single significant patch of native lowland forest. Occasional hilltops with second growth are all that remain of this once magnificent forest.

South of Rio de Janeiro some forest patches still stand, mostly protected by the steep slopes of the Serra do Mar and, until recently, lack of access to the coastal strip. Yet even in the state of São Paulo, where the largest tracts of intact forest in eastern Brazil survive, some 85% of the original forest has been leveled. This history of rampant devastation has left the Atlantic Forest region (ATL) by far the most endangered zoogeographic region in the Neotropics. The 32 bird species endemic to the Rio de Janeiro (RDJ) or Northern (NOR) subregion of the Atlantic Forest region are *all* considered at risk. Of these, 26 (81%) are considered threatened or endangered (CP-1 or CP-2; see Guide to the Databases in part 4 for definitions of CP rankings).

With 199 endemic bird species overall, the Atlantic Forest region is the third largest concentration of endemic birds in the Neotropics. Almost all of the endemics are forest species, and over one-third are restricted to one forest type: 57 endemics are restricted to lowland forests and 13 to montane forests, with an additional 48 species restricted to a combination of the two. In contrast to the sharp break between lowland and highland avifaunas in the Andes (see below), the mountains in eastern Brazil show little species turnover along the slopes, and few birds are restricted to the mountaintops. The highest concentrations of species diversity and of endemics in the Atlantic Forest lie in the tropical and lower montane forests.

Despite the tremendous importance of lowland and lower montane forests to biodiversity in this region, most of the existing parks in the Atlantic Forest (especially eastern Brazil) protect *high* elevation forests. Of the 67 Atlantic Forest endemic birds classified as CP-1 or CP-2, 59 (88%) use lowland humid forests and 41 (61%) are restricted to these lowland forests. Even today, deforestation of the lower elevations continues unabated.

Many forest birds that are widespread in the Neotropics are represented in the coastal humid lowlands of the Atlantic Forest by disjunct populations. Most of these are well-differentiated subspecies, genetically isolated and distinct from the Amazon forest populations. Therefore species-level tallies actually underestimate the importance of the coastal lowland forests of Brazil to Neotropical biodiversity.

It is critical that local and international conservation priorities devote immediate, substantial efforts to protecting what remains of the lowland forests of the Atlantic Forest. Deforestation threatens the entire, very distinctive forest communities of eastern and southeastern Brazil. The most endangered avian assemblages are endemic species restricted to lowland forest remnants from Espírito Santo northward. In these patches lives the most imminently endangered avifauna in the Neotropics (see also chapters 9 and 10).

West Indies. The West Indies also need urgent conservation action (chapter 10). Relentless habitat destruction on virtually every island has seriously endangered the endemic avifauna. In the Greater Antilles, 43% of the endemic forest avifauna is at risk, and 22% is threatened or endangered. The risk is roughly evenly divided among the Greater Antillean islands, and even endemics that occur on more than one island show equivalent levels of risk (table 3.10). In the Lesser Antilles, 67% of the endemics are at risk, and over half (13 of 24) are threatened or endangered. Here species that are restricted to a single island are much more likely to be at risk (11 of 12 are CP-1, CP-2, or CP-3) than are those that occur on more than one island (5 of 12 are CP-1, CP-2, or CP-3).

Table 3.10 Conservation Status of Birds Endemic to the Greater Antilles, by Subregion

Subregion	Subregion Code	Conservation Priority			
		CP-1	CP-2	CP-3	CP-4
Throughout region	o	1	4	7	20
Bahamas	BAH	0	1	0	2
Cuba	CUB	4	5	3	13
Puerto Rico	PUE	1	2	2	9
Hispaniola	HIS	2	6	6	10
Jamaica	JAM	1	3	8	15

Montane Humid Forests

Evergreen broadleaf forests dominate the mountains from northern Mexico south to Tierra del Fuego. These montane forests, contiguous with lowland forests in many areas, extend to treeline at about 3,500 m elevation. Humid montane forests are most extensive on the Atlantic or east-facing slopes through most of the Neotropics. Like the Pacific lowlands, Pacific and west-facing mountain slopes in the Neotropics generally receive less rainfall because of cool ocean currents or rain shadow effects, or both. Important exceptions are the very wet, forested slopes from southern Costa Rica to northern Ecuador and the temperate forests of southern Chile.

The largest continuous expanse of montane forest lies along the Andes from Colombia and Venezuela south to Bolivia. Other important areas are in Central America, the tepuis, the Atlantic coast of Brazil, and on many islands of the West Indies.

In the following sections we examine patterns of diversity, endemism, and habitat specialization in the montane forest avifauna from two perspectives. First, we compare montane forests with their adjacent lowlands to illustrate an underappreciated fact: montane forests are equally diverse and contain *more* endemics and specialists than do the better-publicized tropical lowland forests. Second, we examine diversity and endemism at different elevations up the mountain slope to identify which, if any, elevations should take priority as the most important reservoirs of vulnerable species.

Bird Diversity in Montane versus Lowland Forests

Species richness. At tropical latitudes, the most diverse humid montane forests occur in five major regions: the Madrean Highlands (MAH), the Chiriquí-Darién Highlands of Costa Rica and Panama (CDH), the Northern and Central Andes (NAN, CAN), and the mountains of the Atlantic Forest (ATL). Montane forests of the Tepuis region (TEP) are isolated and depauperate (e.g., Mayr and Phelps 1967; Willard et al. 1991), and those of the West Indies (GAN, LAN) are even more so (table 3.11). The temperate forests of the Southern Andes (SAN) also are depauperate compared with forests of the tropical Andes.

Despite differences in scale, the pattern of decline in species diversity with elevation is remarkably similar among all five major montane regions (fig. 3.3). Different absolute numbers of species in these five regions correlate with differences in overall land area represented: the northern and central Andes are extensive mountain regions, with numerous separate massifs, while forested regions of Middle America, Chiriquí-Darién, and southeastern Brazil contain smaller and more isolated mountains.

Table 3.11 Diversity and Endemism in the Principal Neotropical Montane Forests

Region	Region Code	Montane Forest Species	Endemics	Percentage Endemic
Northern Andes	NAN	640	200	31
Central Andes	CAN	546	138	25
Madrean Highlands	MAH	257	90	35
Chiriquí-Darién Highlands	CDH	224	66	29
Atlantic Forest	ATL	211	104	49
Tepuis	TEP	111	35	32
Greater Antilles	GAN	85	68	80
Lesser Antilles	LAN	15	4	27

Note: Montane forest includes F4, F5, F6, F9, F10, F11 and their edges.

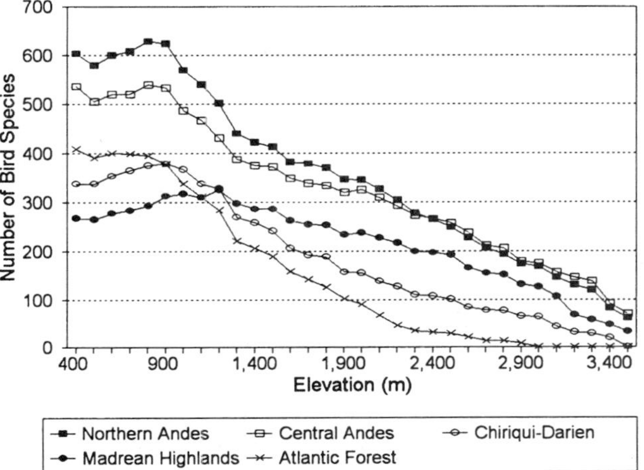

Figure 3.3 Elevational diversity gradients of forest bird species in five Neotropical montane regions. Although absolute values differ, all regions show the same basic pattern, with a plateau or slight increase up to about 1,000 m, followed by a gradual, nearly constant rate of decline to treeline.

Bird diversity is highest in the Northern Andes (NAN; table 3.11), where decline in species richness upslope averages approximately 5% with every 100 m gain in elevation between 1,000 and 3,000 m (fig. 3.3). A plateau in species numbers between 500 and 1,000 m represents the appearance of lower montane species as they overlap the uppermost recorded elevations of those lowland species that extend somewhat upslope. This overlap of lowland and montane species is illustrated for the Central Andes in figure 3.4.

Terborgh (1971) maintained that species numbers decline steadily with elevation in the Central Andes, but our own recent work in southeastern Peru suggests a different pattern (Fitzpatrick, Willard, and Stotz, unpubl.). If we restrict the analysis to birds of *terra firme* forest (F1 and F4), a peak in species diversity occurs at the foothills, between 500 and 1,000 m (fig. 3.5). Higher overall diversity at the lowest elevations in Amazonia, below 500 m, results primarily from increased habitat diversity. Although *terra firme* forest is effectively the only natural habitat on the forested Andean slopes, various additional types of forest and scrub thrive along the river and lake edges (e.g., F2, F3, N11, N12) on the flatter lowlands.

Habitat specialization. Montane forests contain proportionally more habitat specialists than do lowland forests (table 3.2). Across the Neotropics, montane forests provide habitat for a total of 1,441 bird species, of which 428 (30%) are restricted to a single habitat. Lowland forests are used by many more total species (2,070), but only 23% (470) occur in only one habitat type.

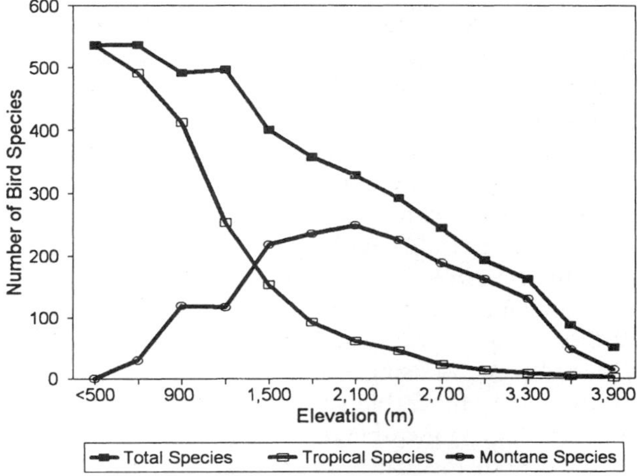

Figure 3.4 Elevational diversity gradients of montane and tropical forest bird species in the Central Andes region. Overall and tropical species richness declines monotonically, but montane species reach a peak around 2,000 m.

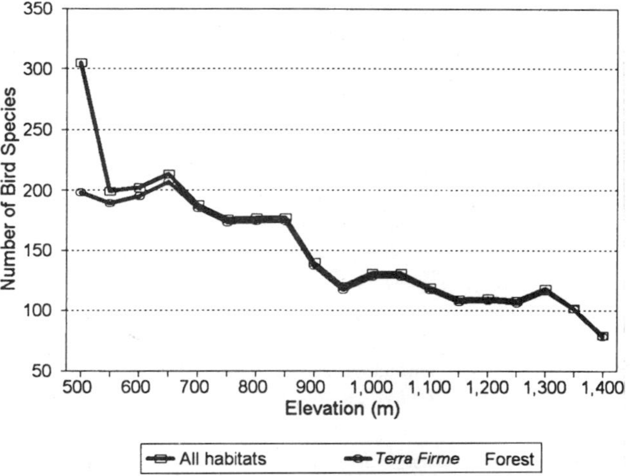

Figure 3.5 Elevational diversity gradients of bird species in all habitats and in *terra firme* forest only, on the Cerro de Pantiacolla, Madre de Dios, Peru.

Montane endemism. Throughout the forested Neotropics, endemism is especially pronounced in the mountains. Table 3.12 compares bird diversity and endemism in mountains versus lowlands for the three major continental forest areas. The tropical Andes (NAN and CAN) and the Amazon basin (AMN and AMS) have nearly identical numbers of forest bird species (791 vs. 788) and similar numbers of habitat-restricted forest birds (313 vs. 311). However, the Andes have more than twice as many *endemic* forest birds as the Amazon (318 vs. 152, or 40% vs. 19% endemism).

Montane endemism is even more pronounced in Middle America (table 3.12). In the Madrean and Chiriquí-Darién Highlands, 38% of the forest birds are endemic, compared with only 11% in the Caribbean lowlands, even though the two regions have almost identical forest bird diversities.

In the Atlantic Forest region the pattern is somewhat different. The proportion of endemics is higher in the mountains than in the lowlands (55% vs. 34%), as it is in the other montane areas. However, montane habitats in eastern Brazil are so depauperate (only 222 forest species) that the total number of endemic birds in the montane forests of the Atlantic Forest is well below that in the lowlands (table 3.12).

Habitat-restricted endemics in humid forest. Across the Neotropics as a whole, 717 bird species (about 19% of the total avifauna) are restricted to one habitat type *and* occur in a single zoogeographic region. These are the most vulnerable species: 40% of endangered, threatened, or vulnerable (CP-1, CP-2, and CP-3) species belong to this category. The general relationship between endemism, habitat restriction, and conservation status in the Neotropics is explored later (chapter 9).

Of the 717 habitat-restricted endemics, 502 (70%) are restricted to some type of humid forest (table 3.2). The importance of montane forests is again evident: over half of the forest-restricted endemics live in the mountains (270, or 54%), despite the much smaller land area at the higher elevations. Table 3.13 identifies the eleven zoogeographic regions that contain at least 10 of these local specialists.

The Northern Andes has the highest number of habitat-restricted forest endemics (98), followed by the Central Andes and the Atlantic Forest (74 and 73). These three regions also contain the only endemic communities restricted to the humid elfin forests at treeline. In Middle America, the Chiriquí-Darién Highlands is the region with the highest concentrations of forest-restricted endemics. Also noteworthy are 20 montane forest endemics in the Tepuis region and the assemblages of pine and pine-oak forest birds in the Greater Antilles and the Madrean Highlands.

Although number and proportion of forest-restricted endemics are highest in the mountains, some lowland forest regions also have significant assemblages. In particular, the lowlands of the Atlantic Forest region has 57 forest-restricted endemics, the northern and southern regions of Amazonia have 45 and 48, respectively, the Gulf-Caribbean Slope has 15, and the Chocó Lowlands region has 10.

Andean versus Amazonian endemism. Species turnover across the Marañón-Amazon River barriers differs strikingly between the Andes and the Amazon basin (table 3.14), even though the two sides of the river contain equivalent numbers of bird species. The Northern and Central Andes have similar diversity (772 and 804 species) and similar numbers of forest-inhabiting species (681 and 610). The Northern and Southern Amazon also have nearly identical overall diversity (896 and 892, respectively) and number of forest species (751

Table 3.12 Avian Diversity, Habitat Restriction, and Endemism in Montane versus Lowland Forests within Three Main Geographic Areas of the Neotropics

	Montane Forests		Lowland Forests	
	N	Prop.	*N*	Prop.
	Northern and Central Andes		Amazon Basin	
Total forest species	791		788	
Habitat restricted in forest	313	0.396	311	0.395
Endemics	318	0.402	152	0.193
	Middle American Highlands		Caribbean Lowlands	
Total forest species	397		436	
Habitat restricted in forest	85	0.214	82	0.188
Endemics	151	0.380	48	0.110
	Atlantic Forest Mountains		Atlantic Forest Lowlands	
Total forest species	222		409	
Habitat restricted in forest	34	0.153	83	0.203
Endemics[a]	121	0.545	141	0.345

Note: Data include only those species whose primary habitat is humid forest.

[a] Seventy-seven species endemic to the Atlantic Forest occur in both montane and lowland forest.

Table 3.13 Principal Concentrations of Habitat-Restricted Endemics in Neotropical Humid Forests

			Humid Forests						
Region	Region Code	Total	Montane Evergreen (F4)	Tropical Lowland Evergreen (F1)	Elfin (F5)	Pine (F10, F11)	Flooded Tropical Evergreen (F2)	River-Edge (F3)	Other
Northern Andes	NAN	98	85	3	10				
Central Andes	CAN	74	53	3	14				4
Atlantic Forest	ATL	73	13	57	1				2
Southern Amazonia	AMS	60		48			4	6	2
Northern Amazonia	AMN	54		44			4	1	5
Chiriquí-Darién Highlands	CDH	36	35	1					
Tepuis	TEP	20	20						
Gulf-Caribbean Slope	GCS	16		15					1
Chocó Lowlands	CHO	13		13					
Greater Antilles	GAN	12	6	1		5			
Madrean Highlands	MAH	10	6			4			

Note: Listed are the eleven zoogeographic regions containing ten or more endemic birds that are restricted to humid forest, and any habitat containing at least five such restricted species.

and 759). Similarity between these northern and southern avifaunas across the Marañón-Amazon Rivers reflects the equivalent sizes, ecological histories, physiographic and habitat structures, and resource bases of these adjacent biomes.

North-south *turnover* highlights the importance of endemism in the mountains. Fewer than 10% of the species occupying either region of the lowland Amazon are endemic to their region. In the mountains, however, more than a quarter of the species in the Northern or Central Andes are endemic to their region (222, or 28%, and 216, or 27%). The same percentages hold when these comparisons involve forest species only (table 3.14).

Almost half the Central Andean species do not occur north of the Marañón gap (349, or 44%), and a similar proportion of Northern Andean birds are not found south of the Marañón (316, or 41%). In contrast, only

Table 3.14 Endemism and North-South Regional Turnover in the Amazon Basin versus the Andes

	Northern Amazon	Southern Amazon	Northern Andes	Central Andes
Total species	896	892	772	804
Species in one region, not in the other	136	132	316	349
Species endemic to the region	76	79	222	216
Species endemic to one subregion	62	48	145	174
Forest species	751	759	681	610
Forest species in one region, not in the other	116	124	289	218
Forest species endemic to the region	75	79	206	151
Forest species endemic to one subregion	60	45	130	122

about 15% of the Amazon basin species occur on only one side of the Amazon River. Again, these strikingly different rates of species turnover characterize the forest-restricted species as well.

Patterns of north-south turnover illustrate a central point of this chapter. Tropical mountains contain large numbers of forest species occupying small geographic ranges. Habitat loss in the mountains threatens a much greater proportion of the community than does a similar loss of habitat in the lowlands.

Montane Avifaunas and Elevation

Elevational distributions. One reason for the abundance of local endemics in the mountains is that few species range from the luxuriant forests of the valley bottoms all the way up to the mossy, stunted forests of the ridgetops. Limits to elevational distributions on tropical mountain slopes often are extraordinarily abrupt, even in continuous montane forest (Terborgh 1971). Figure 3.6 illustrates these sharp elevational limits among four species of forest-inhabiting manakins (Pipridae), based on mist-net capture data (Fitzpatrick, Willard, and Stotz, unpubl.) along an elevational transect in southeastern Peru.

Elevational distributions of many forest birds are extremely narrow, especially in the eastern Andes. For example, the median width of elevational distributions in the Central and Northern Andes is 1,300 m (fig. 3.7), and fully one-quarter of the species have elevational ranges narrower than 900 m of vertical elevation (e.g., Green Manakin, *Chloropipo holochlora*, in fig. 3.6).

Restriction of so many forest specialists to narrow elevational zones along the mountain slope has extremely important conservation consequences. Even though a number of Andean species have geographic ranges that span 3,000 km and five countries (Bolivia, Peru, Ecuador, Colombia, and Venezuela), many of

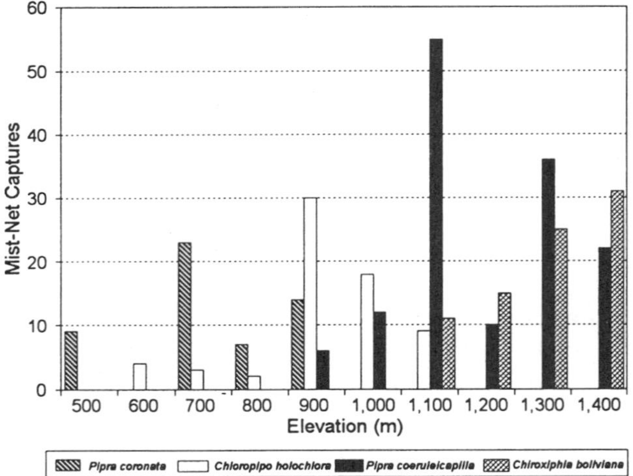

Figure 3.6 Elevational distributions of four species of manakins (Pipridae) on the Cerro de Pantiacolla, Madre de Dios, Peru.

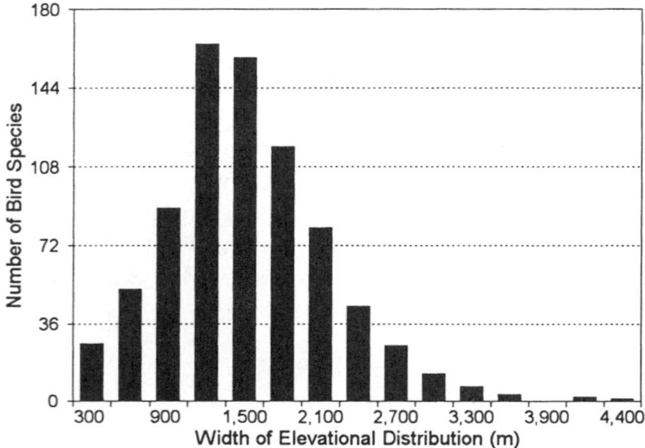

Figure 3.7 Elevational distribution widths of montane forest birds in the Central and Northern Andes.

these species actually are extinction-prone specialists. Because they are squeezed into narrow elevational ranges, accurately plotted distributions of these species would appear as hair-thin lines on a map of South America (Graves 1988).

Fragmentation of these narrow ranges occurs today with the clearing of only a few hundred meters of forest. Huge gaps now exist in the distributions of most such species along the length of the Andes. Their distributions have become "dashes and dots" rather than continuous ribbons.

Elevational cohorts. We can characterize avian diversity along elevational gradients by dividing an entire slope's avifauna into "elevational cohorts." This depiction of montane forest communities tracks separate cohorts of species up the slope. The species are grouped according to their minimum elevational limits. An elevational cohort consists of species whose minimum elevation falls within a particular 500 m interval. For example, the 750 m cohort (cross-hatched in fig. 3.8) includes all species with a minimum elevation from 500 m to (but not including) 1,000 m. With these elevational cohorts, it is possible to track groups of birds along an elevational gradient and see how species are added to and lost from the community as elevation changes.

For all Neotropical mountain ranges, the dominance of lowland forest species at the lowest elevations and their lingering numbers well up the mountain slope significantly affect the overall shape of the diversity curve (e.g., fig. 3.8). Removing tropical species from the samples allows us to see better the relative sizes and persistence of montane forest species cohorts along the elevational gradient (fig. 3.9).

The striking elevational diversity of the forested Andean slopes stands out clearly. Species replacements occur steadily all the way up the slope, from tropical elevations to treeline. These results make a persuasive case for parks that protect the entire elevational transect. No single elevation contains the majority of species, and no cohort retains much of its diversity across more than about 1,000 m.

Elevational cohorts reveal both similarities and profound differences in the way montane forest bird communities are assembled along the different mountain slopes in the Neotropics (fig. 3.9). Lower montane cohorts contain more species, but they attenuate rapidly up the slope. As discussed below, this attenuation underscores the need to incorporate foothill forests into the design of montane forest preserves.

Forested slopes of the huge mountain massifs in the Central and Northern Andes are sectioned into numerous elevational cohorts, several of them quite diverse. Cohort size drops off gradually but steadily with elevation. In contrast, the small and isolated mountains of the Chiriquí-Darién Highlands and, especially, the At-

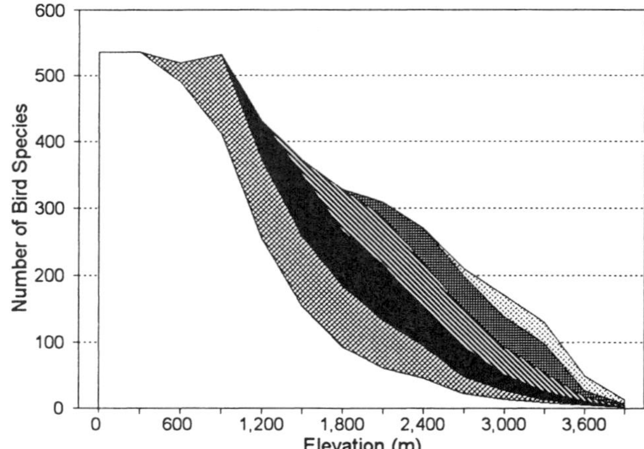

Figure 3.8 Elevational distributions of forest birds by elevational cohort in the Central Andes, including tropical species. See text for definition of elevational cohorts.

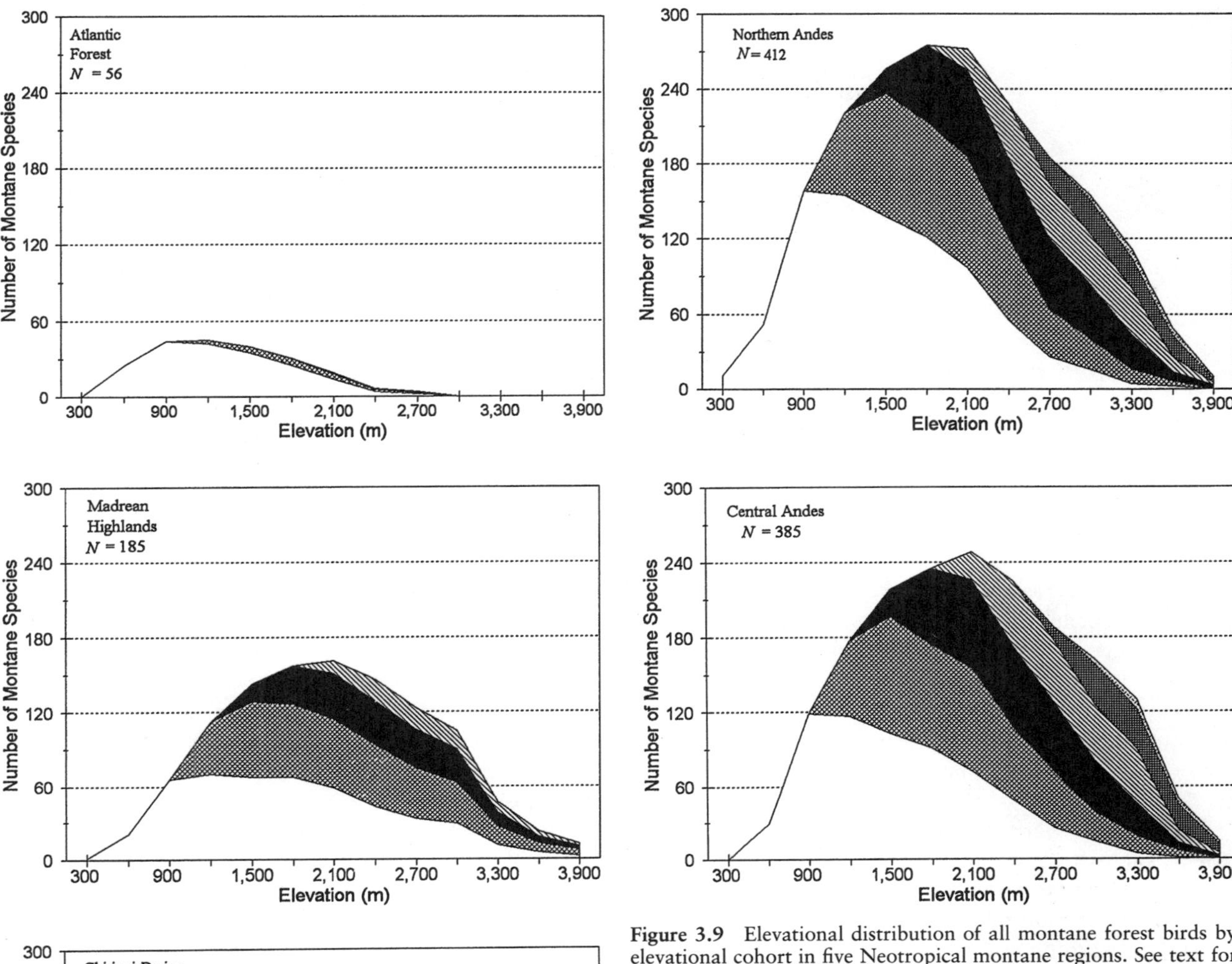

Figure 3.9 Elevational distribution of all montane forest birds by elevational cohort in five Neotropical montane regions. See text for definition of elevational cohorts.

lantic Forest slopes have only a few major cohorts. The largest cohort is the lowest one (500–1,000 m), and attenuation of all cohorts is abrupt at about 2,000 m.

In its elevational patterns, the montane forest avifauna of the Madrean Highlands more closely resembles the Andes than the nearby Chiriquí-Darién slopes. Like the Andes, these Middle American mountains have substantial diversity divided among multiple cohorts (fig. 3.9). Unlike the Andes, however, here the lowest-elevation cohorts retain much of their diversity well up the slope, rather than attenuating sharply. For example the 750 and 1,250 m cohorts have largely disappeared at 3,000 m in the Andean regions but make up about half of that elevation's diversity in the Madrean Highlands. This difference reflects the broader elevational distributions on the lower montane slopes of the Madrean Highlands (fig. 3.10), presumably a result of the reduced overall diversity in Middle America compared with the Andes.

With the broader elevational limits in the Madrean Highlands, a greater proportion of the total forest diversity in Middle America is encompassed by preserves that cover only a portion of the mountain slopes. To maximize the number of species protected, such preserves should be placed in the middle and lower elevations of the mountains.

Endemism and elevation. Montane forests are rich in local endemics—locally distributed species that are extremely vulnerable to extinction. The continued survival of such species, especially in Colombia, now depends on the persistence of just a few preserved habitat

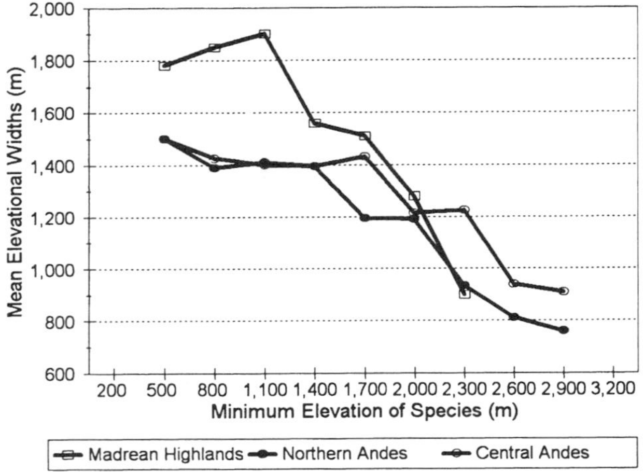

Figure 3.10 Elevational distribution widths of forest birds by minimum elevation in three Neotropical montane regions.

patches. For this reason regional conservation priorities must focus special attention on the zones of endemism along mountain slopes (see also chapter 9). But where are these zones? Do diversity patterns among endemic species mirror those of the entire montane forest community? Here again, differences exist among the five major Neotropical montane regions (fig. 3.11; cf. fig. 3.9).

In both the Madrean Highlands and the Northern Andes, the distribution of endemic cohorts closely resembles that of the total montane forest avifauna. Peak diversity of all montane birds and of montane endemics (i.e., excluding lowland species) occurs at about 2,000 m. This mid-montane fauna is dominated by a few large cohorts of lower montane endemics that enter below 2,000 m. In the Northern Andes, the forests along the west slope of the Western Andes and the deep inter-Andean valleys contribute a significant portion of the endemics to this diversity.

In the Central Andes the pattern is different. Here forest endemics occur all the way up the slope of the highest mountains to the uppermost elfin forests (F5) and *Polylepis* woodlands (F6). In this complex region, almost equal-sized cohorts of endemics enter the montane avifauna from 500 m to above 3,000 m. Peak diversity overall occurs at about 2,000 m, as in the previous regions, but peak diversity of endemics is at 3,000 m. Even at 3,300 m, diversity of endemics has declined only 10% from its peak (fig. 3.11). In the Central Andes, therefore, preservation of endemic diversity requires equal attention to *all* forested elevations.

In the smaller mountain ranges of Chiriquí-Darién, and especially in the Atlantic Forest, relatively little land area exists at the uppermost forested elevations. Probably because of species-area effects, total species richness declines upslope much more steeply than on the larger massifs (fig. 3.3). Correspondingly, the number of endemics reaches a peak at lower elevations than in the Andes or farther north in the Madrean Highlands (fig. 3.11). Endemics peak at 900 m in the Atlantic Forest. Given its very small total area, the Chiriquí-Darién region is remarkable in supporting a high diversity of endemics over a considerable span (1,200 to 3,000 m).

Conservation Status and the Montane Foothills

The huge assemblages of forest specialists throughout the mountains of the Neotropics occupy only a tiny fraction of the total land area covered by the lowland forest fauna. Montane habitat zones are naturally fragmented and narrow, often perched like shoestrings along the middle or upper elevations of long mountain ranges. Endemism and restriction to narrow life zones render the montane avifauna in most regions much more vulnerable to extirpation than the avifauna in the adjacent lowlands. Rapid turnover of species and communities upslope requires that preserves be wide enough to incorporate, and effectively buffer, several elevational zones. In addition, the abundance of local endemics in montane forests emphasizes the importance of protecting numerous, separate habitat patches (Terborgh and Winter 1982; Orejuela 1985). At best, many montane species will be protected in only one or a few preserves.

Differences in the profiles of bird communities up the slopes of tropical mountains (figs. 3.9, 3.11, 3.12) suggest that optimal design and placement of preserves differ from region to region. To maximize the number of species and assemblages protected, preserves in the Andes must incorporate the entire elevational gradient. No single elevational "slice" contains more than about half of the species endemic in either the Northern or the Central Andes. The same pattern holds in the mountains of Costa Rica and Panama (fig. 3.11). In the Central Andes the upper elevation forests demand special attention as centers of endemism and specialization. In contrast, forest birds in the Madrean Highlands and the Atlantic Forest have wide elevational distributions, and diversity attenuates sharply in the upper third of the elevational gradient.

Given the varying patterns of distribution in the different montane regions, what are the elevations in most urgent need of protection? The answer is clearly the lower elevations, from 500 to 1,000 m. Concentrations of species with high conservation priority (CP-1, CP-2, or CP-3) are unmistakably skewed toward these lower elevations in *all* montane regions (fig. 3.12; cf. figs. 3.9 and 3.11). The skew toward the lower slopes is especially striking in the Central Andes. Although diversity and endemism are highest between 2,000 and 3,000 m, threatened and vulnerable species are concentrated between 1,000 and 2,000 m, with two huge cohorts

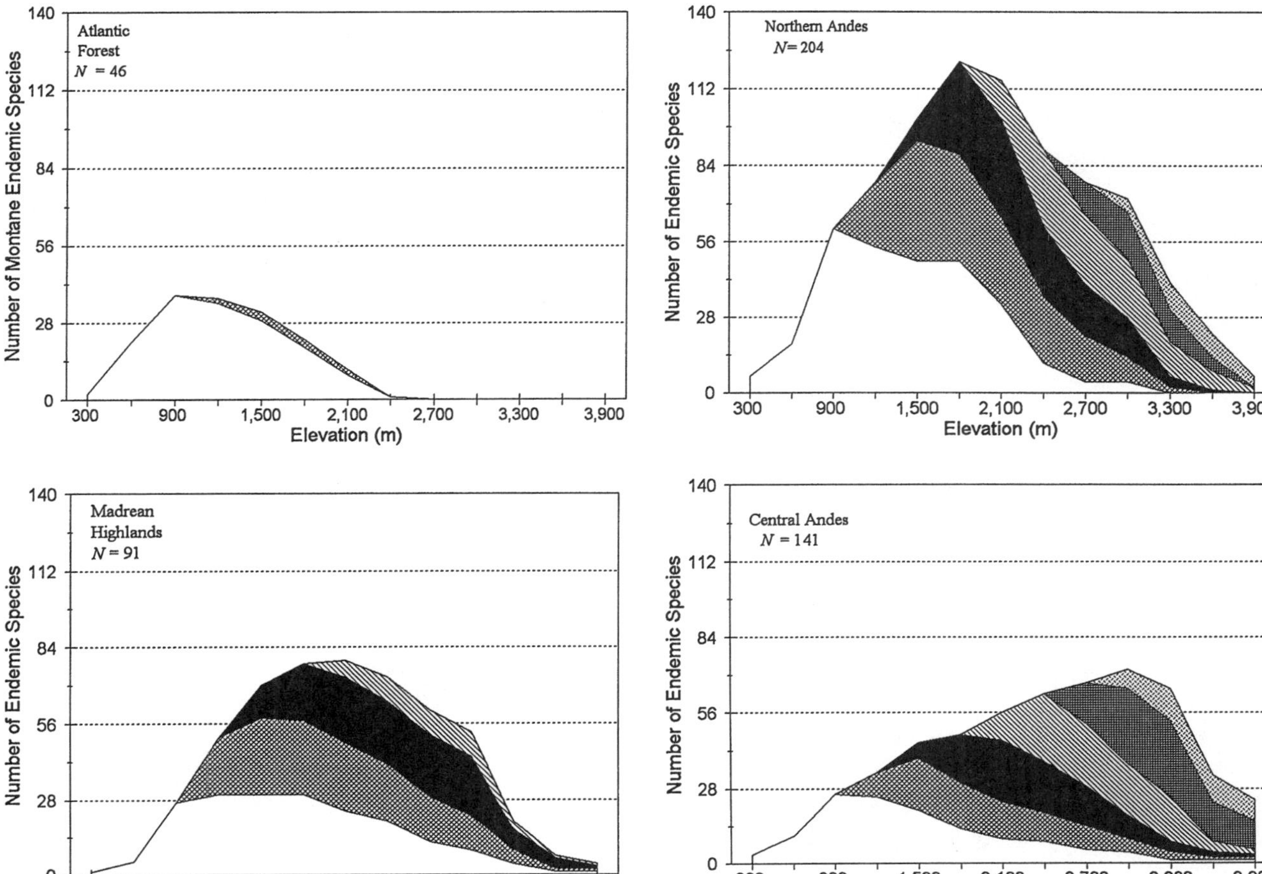

Figure 3.11 Elevational distribution of montane forest birds by elevational cohort in five Neotropical montane regions; endemic species only. See text for definition of elevational cohorts.

dominating (fig. 3.12). The same pattern holds throughout the Neotropics: *all five major montane regions contain conspicuous assemblages of threatened and vulnerable species in the lower-elevation forests on their slopes*. Why?

Not surprisingly, montane species with the narrowest elevational ranges are among the most vulnerable forest species in the Neotropics (table 3.15). Such species are especially at risk when their elevational zones coincide with forests, soils, or climates of high commercial and agricultural value, as in the montane foothills. Continuing loss of habitat exposes these narrowly distributed species to fragmentation, leading to local and regional extirpation because of island effects and degradation of habitat along the edges of forest patches.

Partly because of their high overall diversity (fig. 3.3), the foothills and lower slopes of both Central and South America include an especially large number of forest birds with narrow elevational ranges (fig. 3.13a). On these lower montane slopes also grow some of the richest, most beautiful forests in the world. A large number of the bird species that use these forests from 800 to 1,700 m are habitat-restricted specialists (fig. 3.13b). The combination of habitat restriction and narrow elevational ranges among lower montane species enriches this fauna with species vulnerable to habitat loss. Severe human exploitation of timber and soils at these elevations caused the "expression" of this vul-

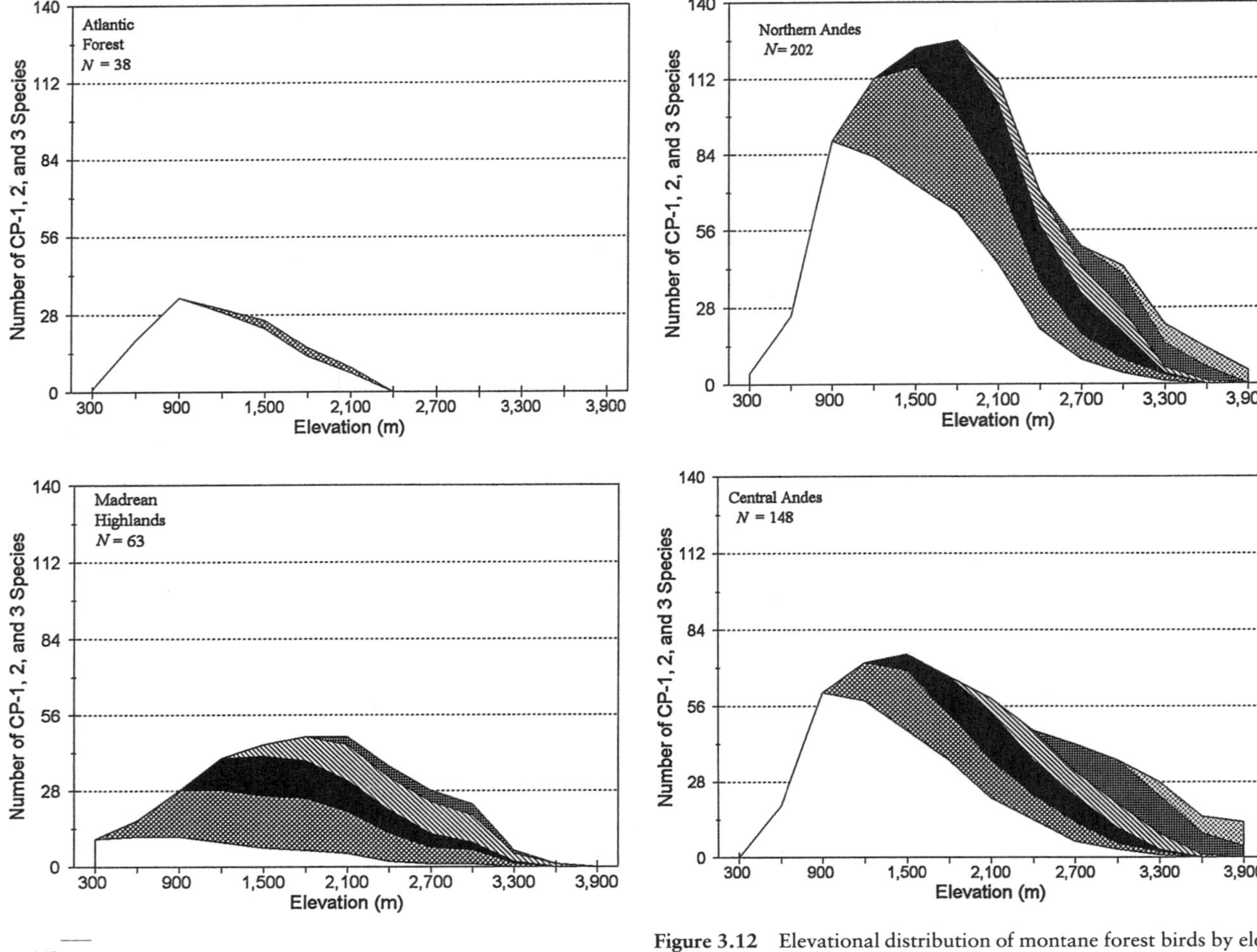

Figure 3.12 Elevational distribution of montane forest birds by elevational cohort in five Neotropical montane regions; species of conservation concern (CP-1, CP-2, and CP-3) only. See text for definition of elevational cohorts.

nerability, explaining the disproportionate threat to lower montane birds.

Pristine forest tracts spanning elevations between 500 and 1,700 m have become extremely rare. Except in a very few already established parks in Middle America and the Andes, essentially no virgin stands of foothill forest remain within easy access of human commercial exploitation. This humid and very productive life zone, narrow to begin with, might today be the fastest-disappearing forest type in the Neotropics (Hartshorn 1992).

The situation is further complicated along the foothills of the Andes, where ecological specialization of yet another sort occurs. Here certain bird species occur in narrow zones at lower montane elevations (500 to 1,500 m) only on isolated mountain ridges, and not on the main Andean slopes (e.g., Southern Helmeted Curassow, *Crax unicornis,* Gray-tailed Piha, *Lipaugus subalaris,* Koepcke's Hermit, *Phaethornis koepckeae,* and Rufous-webbed Brilliant, *Heliodoxa branickii*). These species are especially vulnerable: their distributions are not only elevationally narrow, but also naturally fragmented because the foothill ridges tend to be small and isolated. Species restricted to these outlying ridges are very prone to local extirpation as their limited forest habitat is cleared.

Many outlying mountain ridges probably possess unique assemblages of these specialized species (see

Table 3.15 Conservation Status and Width of Elevational Distributions in Forest Birds of the Central and Northern Andes

Elevational Width (m)	Conservation Priority CP-1	CP-2	CP-3	CP-4	N	Mean CP Status
≤500	3	18	25	10	56	2.75
550–1,000	4	26	71	77	178	3.24
1,050–1,500	1	22	82	208	313	3.59
1,550–2,000	1	4	39	154	198	3.75
2,050–2,500		3	9	83	95	3.84
2,550–3,000			3	34	37	3.92
>3,000			2	20	22	3.91

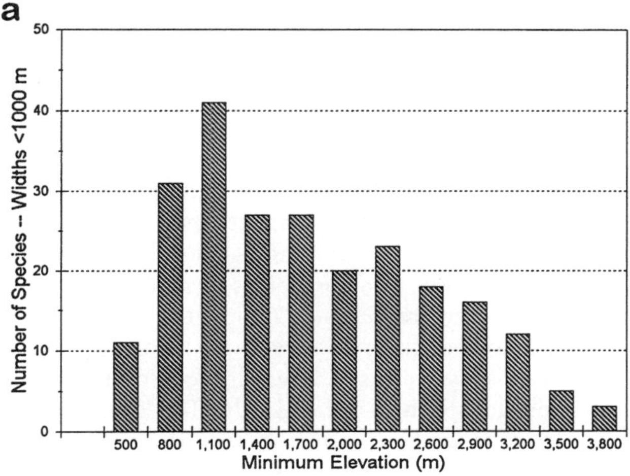

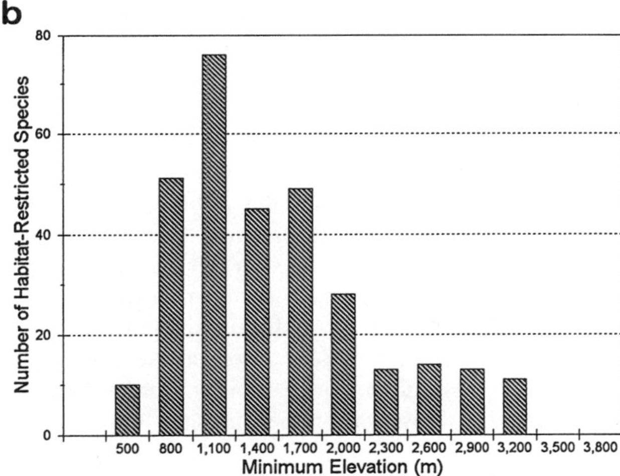

Figure 3.13 Frequency distribution of minimum elevations of montane forest birds in the Central and Northern Andes: (a) species with elevational distributions narrower than 1,000 m; (b) habitat-restricted species.

J. M. Diamond 1985b for examples in New Guinea). The larger ridges even harbor their own endemic taxa (e.g., Cerros del Sira, Dept. Huanuco, Peru; Weske and Terborgh 1971; Graves and Weske 1987). Fortunately, many isolated ridges are in remote locations, still inaccessible to large-scale commercial logging. Such protection is temporary, however. Conservation of the unique assemblages of ridgetop isolates depends on concerted efforts to inventory these ridges from Colombia to Bolivia and ensure that they are incorporated into protected preserves. They might otherwise be overlooked as too small to matter.

4 Neotropical Dry Forests and Arid Scrubs

Synopsis

Dry, deciduous forests and natural arid scrubs are distributed across the Neotropics in six main areas, separated by expanses of humid forest, mountains, or grassland. Avian species richness in these dry forests and scrubs is much lower than in the humid forests, and birds that occur in the dry formations are less likely to be restricted to a single habitat type. However, levels of endemism in both deciduous forest and scrub equal or surpass those in humid forests. Among habitat-restricted species, endemism is consistently higher in dry habitats than in humid forests. Fully 90% of the species restricted to deciduous forests are local endemics.

Conservation measures should focus on core areas within the main dry forest regions. Although arid scrub species and the unspecialized portion of the dry forest avifauna are relatively safe, 80% of the habitat-restricted species are at risk. The two regions with the largest concentrations of dry forest specialists (Equatorial Pacific Coast and Central South America) are undergoing dramatic transformations into agricultural landscapes.

Accelerating destruction of native habitats in the "cerrado" region of central Brazil merits special discussion. This complex of habitats—deciduous forest, grassland, cerrado woodland, and gallery forest—is being obliterated by the rapid advance of mechanized, large-scale agriculture. Although many endemics in the cerrado region are not habitat specialists, over three-quarters are at risk, and 40% are threatened or endangered. Publicity abounds over the plight of the Amazon rainforest, while right next door—in the cerrado—one of the greatest ecological catastrophes in Latin America proceeds unnoticed.

Although dominated by humid forests, the Neotropics also contain large expanses of deciduous forest, lowland and highland desert scrubs, and a variety of transition habitats between these arid or semiarid formations. At first glance the birds that inhabit these dry areas seem to form an unspecialized assortment of species, frequently occurring in adjacent habitats. On the contrary, however, arid zone birds form a unique set of assemblages that represent a major, though little emphasized, conservation priority in the Neotropics.

As we discuss in this chapter, dry forest birds are remarkably localized geographically. The small assemblages that depend on dry forests are almost all endemic to a single zoogeographic zone. Although species diversity in these drier habitats does not approach that of humid forests (chapter 3), proportional endemism among species restricted to deciduous forests or arid scrubs is substantially higher than in the humid lowland forests.

Many of the arid zone environments are disappearing as fast as, or faster than, the humid forests that surround them. Because tropical dry habitats are less species rich, however, their destruction does not receive much publicity. The arid zones in the Neotropics, and their signature bird species and communities, are quietly disappearing. Below, we discuss the patterns of diversity, endemism, and threat among these arid assemblages and highlight priority habitats and regions in urgent need of conservation measures.

Main Areas of Arid Formations

Dry forests and natural scrubs are distributed in six main areas of the Neotropics (fig. 4.1): (1) lowlands and slopes of the Greater Antilles; (2) Pacific Arid Slope of Central America (PAS), from southwestern United States to northwestern Costa Rica; (3) northern Yucatán peninsula (YUC subregion in GCS); (4) Caribbean lowlands of Colombia and Venezuela (ARC subregion in NSA); (5) Pacific Coast of South America (EPC and portions of CAN and STP), from central Ecuador to central Chile, including interior valleys in the Central

Figure 4.1 Neotropical arid regions with dry forest and desert scrubs.

Andes, the western Andean slopes of Peru, and the Galápagos Islands; and (6) lowlands and low plateaus of central and southern South America (CSA, PAT, portions of PAM), from northeastern Brazil to Tierra del Fuego, excluding the humid Atlantic Forest region.

In addition, smaller, isolated arid formations occur in Central and South America, along the rain shadows of high mountains. These dry intermontane valleys or lowlands are scattered locally throughout the cordilleras of the Andes, Central America, and numerous small islands of the West Indies.

Each of the main Neotropical arid regions contains at least a few endemic birds, many of which are limited to distinctive and equally endemic vegetation complexes. Few bird species are shared among the different dry forest regions (only three species occur in all six continental lowland regions of deciduous forest).

The Precipitation Gradient

Precipitation plays a key role determining the basic structure of forest and scrub habitats. Gradients in precipitation are reflected in the dramatic changes in vegetation from humid evergreen forest, to dry deciduous forests, to several types of scrub or desert formations. The most striking such gradient occurs along the Pacific coast of South America. Average annual rainfall can surpass 10,000 mm in the superhumid forests of the Chocó region of Colombia but declines progressively southward. Vegetation turns from lush rainforests to deciduous forests in southwestern Ecuador and northwestern Peru, then to desert scrub in northern Peru. Finally, rainfall is almost nonexistent in the desolate Atacama desert of southern Peru and northern Chile. Precipitation increases again southward, through the savannas of central Chile to the wet *Nothofagus* forests of southern Chile.

Another spectacular rainfall gradient occurs in extreme northern South America, in the vicinity of Lake Maracaibo. Northward from the base of the Santa Marta Mountains to the Guajira peninsula, and from the Venezuelan Andes to the Paraguaná peninsula, vegetation changes steadily from humid forest through dry forest and spiny shrublands to parched coastal deserts.

On a smaller scale, similar gradients are associated with elevation along the Pacific coast of Central America. Cool ocean currents keep the lower elevations dry, especially in winter; the vegetation is mostly arid scrub along the base of the Sierra Madre Occidental. As elevation increases, mountains wring out the moisture trapped in air masses coming off the ocean. Arid scrubs give way to deciduous woodland or pine-oak forests at the cooler, more humid intermediate elevations, and the vegetation then turns to humid montane forests at the higher elevations.

Diversity Patterns in Dry Forest

Bird diversity generally correlates with habitat complexity, and therefore also with precipitation. The total number of species using all Neotropical dry forests combined (635 species) barely exceeds the number found at single sites in lowland humid forest of southeastern Peru (for example, Explorers' Inn; Parker, Donahue, and Schulenberg 1994). However, Janzen (1988) has suggested that tropical dry forests may contain a set of biotic activities, life histories, and interactions even more diverse than that in humid forests despite the lower species diversity.

Besides the lower overall diversity in dry forests, arid and humid habitats also differ in their regional diversity. Unlike the relatively uniform humid, lowland forest regions, arid regions differ greatly from one another in species composition. No single arid formation contains even a third of the total dry forest species pool (table 4.1). More striking, no two of the principal dry forest regions share more than half of their species (most pairs share fewer than 10%; table 4.2). In contrast, adjacent humid forest regions can share as many as 85% of their species (percentages ranging upward from 20% for the mainland regions; table 3.4). This pattern illustrates the distinctiveness of the dry forest

Table 4.1 Principal Regional Concentrations of Birds Using Dry Forest and Arid Scrub

Region	Region Code	Total Users[a]	Primary Habitat	Habitat Restricted	Habitat-Restricted Endemics
Dry forest					
Greater Antilles	GAN	81	30	5	5
Pacific Arid Slope	PAS	170	71	7	7
Gulf-Caribbean Slope	GCS	197	73	5	5
Equatorial Pacific Coast	EPC	129	58	11	11
Northern South America	NSA	174	64	5	3
Central South America	CSA	202	85	27	23
Total		635	300	64	58
Arid scrub (N1 or N2)					
Greater Antilles	GAN	46	15	2	2
Baja-Sonora	BSR	93	52	9	2
Mexican Plateau	MPL	72	36	1	0
Gulf-Caribbean Slope	GCS	72	25	2	2
Pacific Arid Slope	PAS	79	30	5	2
Madrean Highlands	MAH	93	45	7	5
Equatorial Pacific Coast	EPC	78	42	8	6
Subtropical Pacific	STP	74	39	5	0
Central Andes	CAN	151	93	26	18
Southern Andes	SAN	90	53	8	3
Northern South America	NSA	63	22	1	1
Central South America	CSA	106	55	17	14
Patagonia	PAT	55	26	5	3
Total		484	281	81	61

[a] Totals of columns, other than for habitat-restricted endemics, are not additive, since many species occur in more than one zoogeographic region and therefore appear more than once in these columns.

Table 4.2 Dry Forest Bird Species Shared among the Six Principal Regions of Lowland Arid Habitats in the Neotropics ($N = 298$)

Region	Region Code	*N*	PAS	GCS	NSA	EPC	CSA
Greater Antilles	GAN	30	4	6	5	2	1
Pacific Arid Slope	PAS	71		32	12	5	5
Gulf-Caribbean Slope	GCS	73			27	10	9
Northern South America	NSA	64				10	14
Equatorial Pacific Coast	EPC	58					8
Central South America	CSA	85					

Note: Includes all species whose primary habitat is dry forest (F7).

regions: each has a unique fauna, and each needs a locally tailored conservation strategy for the dry forest fauna as a whole to be preserved.

Regional distinctiveness of the major dry forest areas is not accompanied by increased habitat restriction among the component species. In fact, the percentage of dry forest species that use dry forest as their primary habitat is much lower than the corresponding percentage of humid lowland (F1) and montane (F4) forest species (47% vs. 86%). The extent of habitat restriction within the dry forest avifauna is even more limited. Birds of humid forests are nearly four times as likely as their dry forest counterparts to be restricted (fig. 4.2).

Reduced habitat specialization among dry forest birds probably reflects the intermediate position of this habitat along the precipitation and vegetation gradients within which it occurs. Dry forests represent a mix of faunal elements drawn from both arid and humid habitats. Indeed, most good examples of dry forests are in habitat mosaics. These include evergreen gallery forests (F8), which provide an especially diverse pool of species, as well as more arid habitats, which add species that can use dry forests even during periods of seasonal leaf loss.

Diversity Patterns in Arid Scrubs

Because of their overall similarity, we combine lowland (N1) and montane scrub (N2) in analyzing the patterns of diversity, endemism, and threat in scrub regions. In general, scrubs show patterns similar to those of the dry forests. In arid scrub habitats, overall bird diversity is extremely low: a total of only 484 species use Neotropi-

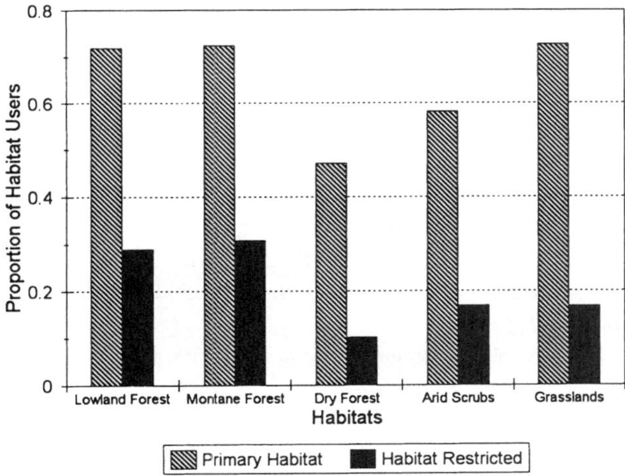

Figure 4.2 Habitat specialization of birds in five Neotropical vegetation types, showing proportion of species that use the vegetation type as their primary habitat and that are restricted to that habitat.

cal scrub habitats (table 4.1), including 342 in lowland scrub (N1) and 265 in montane scrub (N2). Regional scrub diversity is also low. Even the richest arid region (Central Andes, CAN) has only 31% of the total arid scrub fauna (table 4.1).

Levels of habitat fidelity by species using arid scrubs are slightly higher than that of dry forest birds but still low compared with that of humid forest birds (fig. 4.2). Of the 484 species that use arid scrubs, 281 (58%) use them as primary habitats, and only 81 (17%) are restricted to them. The notable lack of specialization among scrub avifaunas in every Neotropical region helps place them among the least threatened of all tropical bird communities.

A few differences between scrub and dry forest diversity patterns are worth noting. In contrast to the remarkably similar numbers of species among dry forest regions, scrub regions vary widely in total bird diversity, levels of endemism, and number of primary habitat users (table 4.1). Levels of endemism in scrubs generally resemble those of humid forest habitats (fig. 4.3). In two of the regions—Subtropical Pacific (STP) and Southern Andes (SAN)—less than 10% of the avifauna is endemic, while in two other regions—Greater Antilles (GAN) and Equatorial Pacific Coast (EPC)—endemics make up nearly half (40% to 47%) of the scrub avifauna.

Levels of threat also differ substantially between dry forests and arid scrubs (table 4.3, fig. 4.4). Central South America and Equatorial Pacific Coast, the two regions with the most threatened dry forest avifauna (table 4.4), show little threat to their scrub communities (table 4.5). Only in the Central Andes, where much of the scrub has been degraded or converted to subsistence plots of corn and potatoes, is the scrub avifauna significantly threatened. Local or patchy distribution of some species, along with the long-standing existence of a large human population in the altiplano, contribute to this elevated level of risk to the Central Andean scrubs.

Conservation Threats to Arid Habitats

In both dry forests and arid scrubs, although habitat fidelity is low (see above), endemism is high—comparable to or higher than that of humid forests. Furthermore, endemism increases with the level of dependence on the habitat, especially among dry forest birds (fig. 4.3). Of the 300 species that use dry forest as their primary habitat, 173 (58%) are endemics. Fully 90% (58 of 64) of the species restricted to dry forests are endemics (table 4.1).

Elsewhere (chapters 3, 9) we point out that exceptionally high levels of endemism and specialization in montane forests place those communities at greater risk than the more widespread lowland forests. For the avifaunas of dry forests and arid scrubs, however, al-

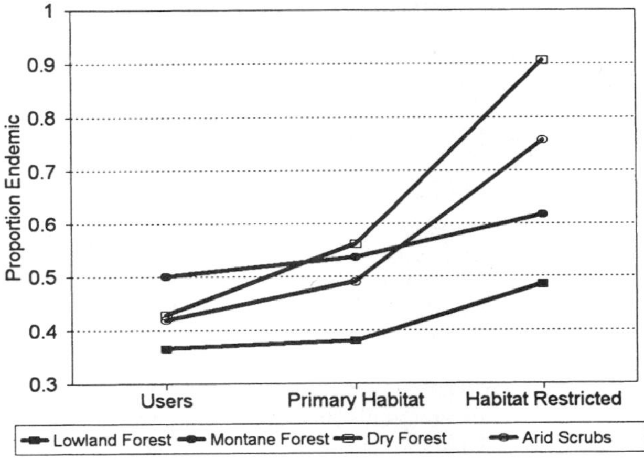

Figure 4.3 Relation between endemism and habitat specialization in four Neotropical vegetation types.

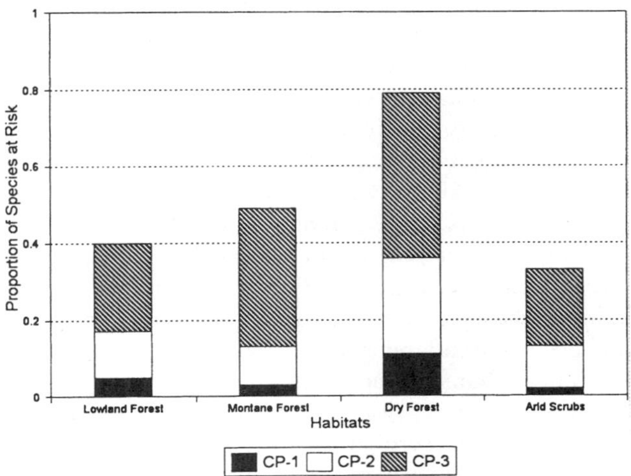

Figure 4.4 Proportion of habitat-restricted bird species considered at risk in four Neotropical vegetation types.

Table 4.3 Conservation Status and Habitat Specialization in the Avifauna of Four Major Neotropical Habitats

Conservation Priority	Humid Lowland Forests (F1)				Humid Montane Forests (F4)				Dry Forests (F7)				Arid Scrubs (N1, N2)			
	U[a] (1,410)	P (1,011)	R (407)	RE (197)	U (1,162)	P (840)	R (357)	RE (220)	U (635)	P (300)	R (64)	RE (58)	U (484)	P (281)	R (81)	RE (61)
CP-1[b]	2	3	5	10	1	2	3	5	2	3	11	12	1	1	2	3
CP-2	7	8	12	22	7	8	10	14	8	10	25	25	3	5	11	15
CP-3	19	19	23	35	26	28	36	40	15	22	43	42	11	11	20	23
CP-4	72	70	60	34	65	62	51	40	75	65	22	20	85	84	67	59

Note: Entries represent percentage of total species in that habitat specialization category. The total number of species is in parentheses.

[a]U = user; P = primary habitat; R = habitat restricted; RE = habitat-restricted endemic.

[b]Conservation priorities: 1 = urgent, endangered; 2 = high, threatened; 3 = medium, vulnerable; 4 = low, not at risk (see Guide to the Databases for details).

Table 4.4 Conservation Status of Dry Forest Birds, Including Endemics, in the Main Arid Regions of the Neotropics

Region	Region Code	CP-1	CP-2	CP-3	CP-4	Total	Percentage CP-1–3
All primary users							
Greater Antilles	GAN	1	1	6	22	30	27
Pacific Arid Slope	PAS	1	5	8	57	71	20
Gulf-Caribbean Slope	GCS	0	2	8	63	73	14
Equatorial Pacific Coast	EPC	1	10	13	34	58	41
EPC, excl. Galápagos	EPC-GAL	1	10	12	30	53	43
Northern South America	NSA	1	1	5	57	64	11
Central South America	CSA	5	7	20	53	85	38
CSA, excl. cerrado	CSA-CER	3	6	17	53	79	33
Endemics							
Greater Antilles	GAN	1	1	5	11	18	40
Pacific Arid Slope	PAS	1	4	7	12	24	50
Gulf-Caribbean Slope	GCS	0	1	7	11	19	42
Equatorial Pacific Coast	EPC	1	9	9	17	36	53
EPC, excl. Galápagos	EPC-GAL	1	9	8	13	31	58
Northern South America	NSA	1	0	4	14	19	26
Central South America	CSA	5	7	17	13	40	72
CSA, excl. cerrado	CSA-CER	3	6	14	13	36	64

(CP-1 through CP-4 are grouped under the heading "Conservation Priority".)

Note: Includes all species using dry forest (F7) as their primary habitat.

though endemism is high, diversity and habitat fidelity are much lower than in humid forests. The conservation status of drier habitats therefore cannot be inferred from the diversity patterns alone. To clarify the conservation issues for dry forests and arid scrubs, we compare the degrees of threat, specialization, and endemism in these drier habitats with those in humid lowland and montane forests (table 4.3, fig. 4.4).

Arid scrub avifauna. For the arid scrub avifauna, threat of extinction is low (tables 4.3, 4.5). Even among habitat-restricted endemics, fewer than one-quarter of the species are endangered or threatened (CP-1 or CP-2), and only a handful more are vulnerable (CP-3). This low level of current risk reflects, in part, the unsuitability of most arid scrublands for agriculture and most other human land uses other than grazing livestock. Except in irrigated areas near major river valleys, water scarcity and poor soil fertility have kept arid scrubs relatively intact across the Neotropics. Even endemic birds have declined little.

Scrub species are further protected by their tolerance for alternative habitats: only 81 of the 484 arid scrub users (17%) are habitat restricted (table 4.1). Indeed, most of the arid scrub avifauna is relatively tolerant of habitat disturbance (only a few of the species are rated "highly sensitive" in database A). Therefore most scrub species persist well even in the face of moderate agricultural development.

The regions with highest bird diversity coincide for arid scrub and dry forest, but areas of greatest relative threat do not (cf. tables 4.4 and 4.5). This lack of concordance probably results from the generally lower levels of threat in the scrub communities (17% to 27% CP-1 to CP-3 among the major centers of diver-

Table 4.5 Conservation Status of Arid Scrub Birds, Including Endemics, in the Main Arid Regions of the Neotropics

		Conservation Priority					
Region	Region Code	CP-1	CP-2	CP-3	CP-4	Total	Percentage CP-1–3
All primary users							
Greater Antilles	GAN	0	1	2	12	15	20
Baja-Sonora	BSR	0	0	0	52	52	0
Madrean Highlands	MAH	0	2	3	40	45	11
Equatorial Pacific Coast	EPC	0	1	5	36	42	14
Central Andes	CAN	1	2	12	78	93	16
Northern South America	NSA	1	0	2	19	22	14
Central South America	CSA	0	2	4	48	55	11
Gulf-Caribbean Slope	GCS	0	0	2	23	25	8
Pacific Arid Slope	PAS	1	1	0	28	30	7
Mexican Plateau	MPL	0	0	0	36	36	0
Subtropical Pacific	STP	0	1	3	35	39	10
Southern Andes	SAN	0	0	1	52	53	2
Patagonia	PAT	0	0	1	25	26	4
Endemics							
Greater Antilles	GAN	0	1	2	5	8	38
Baja-Sonora	BSR	0	0	0	3	3	0
Madrean Highlands	MAH	0	1	3	6	10	40
Equatorial Pacific Coast	EPC	0	1	3	19	23	17
Central Andes	CAN	1	2	8	29	40	27
Northern South America	NSA	0	0	2	3	5	40
Central South America	CSA	0	1	3	17	21	19
Gulf-Caribbean Slope	GCS	0	0	2	3	5	40
Pacific Arid Slope	PAS	1	1	0	2	4	50
Mexican Plateau	MPL	0	0	0	0	0	0
Subtropical Pacific	STP	0	1	0	1	2	50
Southern Andes	SAN	0	0	1	3	4	25
Patagonia	PAT	0	0	0	4	4	0

Note: Includes all species using arid scrubs (N1 or N2) as their primary habitat.

sity), along with the occurrence of a few moderately threatened species in the depauperate arid scrub communities, which raises their apparent level of threat (table 4.5).

Dry forest avifauna. Among the unspecialized dry forest birds, proportions of species "at risk" (CP-1, CP-2, CP-3) are similar to or lower than the proportions in humid lowland and montane forests (table 4.3). However, the specialist component of the dry forest avifauna shows an exceptionally high level of threat. Among habitat-restricted species, including the restricted endemics, *levels of threat are higher in dry forest than in any other Neotropical habitat.* Nearly 80% of this specialist avifauna is considered at risk, versus 49% in montane and 40% in lowland forests (fig. 4.4).

It is dangerous to be a deciduous forest specialist in the Neotropics. Two factors greatly contribute to this predicament: the relatively small geographical extent of the dry forest regions within the Neotropics, and severe habitat disturbance by humans in most of the dry forest zones.

Even before the spread of human development, post-Pleistocene climate conditions had reduced most deciduous forests to small patches, isolated from one another by large expanses of humid habitat (for example, see Pregill and Olson 1981). The exception is in Central South America, the "arid diagonal" (Vanzolini 1974) that extends from northeastern Brazil southwestward to the chaco (fig. 4.1), where significant dry forest formations of several kinds support the largest radiation of open country birds in the Neotropics (see fig. 3.1). Natural areas in this region especially are being rapidly decimated. The moderate rainfall and relatively fertile soils characteristic of deciduous forest regions have encouraged the rapid conversion of this habitat into agriculture throughout the Neotropics. Dense human settlements that accompany rural agriculture add to the pressure on the habitat, including the use of dry forest trees for firewood.

Assessing the Most Important Dry Forests

Bird species diversity is comparable among the five mainland regions of dry forests, with about 60 to 80 species using these forests as their primary habitat in each region (table 4.1). However, two regions—Equatorial Pacific Coast (EPC) and Central South America

(CSA)—emerge as having substantial cohorts of species restricted to dry forests. Almost all of these habitat-restricted species are also endemic (34 of 38, or 89.5%; table 4.1). Unfortunately, these are the two regions undergoing the most extensive habitat devastation.

Central South America. In Central South America, two-thirds of the endemic species whose primary habitat is dry forest are classified "at risk" (CP-1, CP-2, or CP-3), and over one-quarter (12 of 42) are seriously threatened or endangered (table 4.4). This proportion is equally high both within and outside the important cerrado subregion (see below), where large-scale, mechanized agriculture dominates the landscape. Decades of increasing pressure from expanding human populations, especially in northeastern Brazil, have destroyed nearly all forests in the area. Grazing by goats and cattle and harvesting of firewood have dramatically altered the structure and composition of dry forests throughout Central South America.

Equatorial Pacific Coast. The coastal mainland of Ecuador and adjacent Peru contains one of the most diverse and localized concentrations of dry forest endemics in the Neotropics. Even widespread species that occur in this region have very distinctive endemic subspecies, indicating that the area has been a focal center of diversity and evolution in dry forest birds for a long time. Today the avifauna of this Equatorial Pacific Coast is under severe threat from deforestation and development. Even including the well-protected Galápagos Islands, 53% of the primarily dry forest users are at risk (table 4.4). When endemics from the Galápagos are excluded from the pool, the proportion of endemics at risk rises to 58%, nearly as high as in Central South America.

Transitional avifauna. Each of the major arid regions has an assemblage of species that is restricted neither to dry forest nor to arid scrub but to a combination of the two. These 45 species occupy transitional, tall scrubs in addition to the two discrete ends of the arid vegetation gradient. Although they are somewhat more generalized than the 64 dry forest specialists and 101 arid scrub specialists, these birds show a very high level of endemism (44 of the 55, or 89%), and their principal areas of endemism coincide with those of the specialists: 18 in Equatorial Pacific, 9 in Central South America, and 6 in Northern South America. Because these species use a broader array of habitats, they are less vulnerable than are the habitat-restricted assemblages. Only 13 of the 55 species (24%) are ranked as CP-1, CP-2, or CP-3. These species add numbers to the list of birds dependent on the major arid habitat formations of the Neotropics, but they do not change the patterns we have discussed.

Assessing quality and condition of dry forests. Dry forest habitats are seriously degraded throughout the Neotropics; it is important to develop a tool for assessing quality and condition of the remaining patches of dry forest. As we have shown here, many of the bird species frequently found in dry forests also use other habitats and so present a poor measure of habitat quality. Of the bird species that are restricted to dry forests, however, almost all are both endemic and at risk. Therefore we suggest using these habitat specialists, rather than a larger list of "typical" species, in making critical appraisals of different patches of dry forest for conservation. A second important indicator assemblage should be the transitional endemics described above; these also tend to be endemic and at least partially dependent on the dry forest ecosystem. Finally, the additional presence of relatively widespread taxa that use dry forests as primary habitat may help identify the richest local areas. Total number of species should not take precedence, though, over the presence of specialists and endemics.

Our "indicator species list" for dry forests (part 4, database I) reflects this peculiar aspect of inventorying dry forests. It contains mostly endemic taxa for which dry forests are the primary habitat, and it also notes the habitat-restricted species. For evaluation of the diversity of different patches, we list certain widespread species that use dry forest as their primary habitat.

Cerrado: The Unheralded Crisis

We categorize cerrado habitat as distinct from dry forest or scrub, and we excluded cerrado in the preceding analyses. Botanical and structural differences set this peculiar savanna-woodland habitat apart from typical deciduous forests of the Neotropics (Eiten 1972). The term "cerrado" refers both to a habitat type (see chapter 2), and to a region of eastern Brazil that extends from Maranhão south to the pantanal of Mato Grosso. This region of upland cerrado separates the Amazonian and Atlantic forests.

In our definition of the cerrado habitat, we include only formations within central Brazil, with extensions into northeastern Paraguay and eastern Bolivia. Elements of the cerrado flora (see Ferri 1971) and avifauna (Haffer 1974), however, extend north into the savannas of northern South America and south into the chaco.

As a geographic region, the cerrado is a diverse mosaic of habitats, including gallery forest, open grasslands, deciduous forest, and even patches of humid, *terra firme* forest (at least formerly), all within a matrix of true cerrado woodland. At both the Amazonian and the Atlantic borders, the cerrado habitat grades into forest through a distinctive taller woodland known as *cerradão.*

Most generalizations about the dry forest avifauna discussed above hold for the cerrado habitat. Overall diversity is low, and habitat specialization is extremely

Table 4.6 Habitat Use and Specialization by Bird Species Endemic to the Cerrado Subregion (CER; N = 41) and Their Conservation Status

Habitat	Habitat Code	Users	Primary Habitat	Habitat Restricted	At Risk (CP-1–3)[a]
Gallery forests	F8	13	10	6	6
Campo grasslands	N5	14	10	6	10
Tropical deciduous forests	F7	9	6	6	6
Cerrado	N4	7	5	3	4
Arid montane scrubs	N2	5	5	5	3
Low, seasonally wet grasslands	N6	5	3	0	2
Other		4	2	0	1
Total		41	41	26	32

[a] At-risk species assigned to primary habitat.

low. Only 46 species regularly use cerrado, and only 3 species are restricted to this peculiar habitat.

Despite the limited specialization on cerrado as a *habitat,* 41 species of birds are endemic to the cerrado region. Of these, 26 (63%) are restricted to a single habitat (table 4.6), but the primary habitats of these endemics include all the major components of the habitat mosaic. Gallery forest and grasslands have most species (14 and 13, respectively; table 4.6). This pattern substantiates the idea that the "cerrado" avifauna constitutes a regional assemblage rather than a specific habitat assemblage. Such a treatment is consistent with the concept of the cerrado region as a single "morphoclimatic domain" (Ab'Saber 1967; Vanzolini 1972).

Although endemism in the region is high, low habitat specificity among the total cerrado fauna might lead us to expect a low level of risk among cerrado birds. Unfortunately, the reverse is true: over 75% of the endemic cerrado avifauna is considered at risk (32 of 41 species; table 4.6), and over 45% of the species are considered threatened (CP-2, N = 17) or endangered (CP-1, N = 2). In fact, the cerrado is one of the most threatened biotic regions in the Neotropics (see chapter 10).

The basis for this threat lies mainly in landscape-scale mechanized agriculture, which has hit the cerrado region to an extent unprecedented in the Neotropics. Since the 1960s, enormous areas of central Brazil have been converted from native habitats (especially campo and cerrado) into croplands.

We find it noteworthy and ironic that so much attention in the 1980s and 1990s has been focused on the destruction of Amazonian rainforest, where the immediate threat to local biodiversity is among the lowest in the Neotropics (chapter 10). In the immediately adjacent cerrado region, the largest and most diverse expanse of open country biota in the Neotropics is being devastated. This unique flora and fauna are at risk of disappearing altogether, essentially without public notice.

5 Neotropical Grasslands

Synopsis

We recognize six types of grasslands across the Neotropics. Centuries of agricultural use have degraded them all, no doubt resulting in significant changes to their original avifaunas. The avifauna of tropical grasslands as a whole is the least diverse among the Neotropical terrestrial habitats, with a total of 298 species, or barely 8% of the total.

Two regions supporting the greatest diversity of grassland birds are Central South America, with its campo and seasonally flooded grasslands, and the Central Andes, containing the high-elevation puna grasslands. About 25% of the birds occurring in grasslands are restricted to grasslands as a whole, and nearly 75% have some type of grassland as their primary habitat. Very few bird species are restricted to a single grassland type, yet few grassland species in the tropics also tolerate the widespread human-created grasslands, namely agricultural pastures.

Endemism is extremely high (80%) among grassland-restricted birds. In regions where native grasslands have suffered extensive conversion to agricultural fields, these endemics are at serious risk. The Northern Andean paramos, and especially the extraordinary—but vanishing—campo grasslands of Central South America, are in urgent need of conservation action. Few grassland birds of the Andean puna zone or the northern and southern temperate grasslands are currently at risk, indicating that these habitats are much more secure.

Few truly pristine grasslands remain anywhere in the New World tropics, and all are threatened to some degree. The great grasslands of Mexico, Venezuela, Brazil, Argentina, and the Andean countries have been used for agriculture for centuries. In Brazil and extreme northeastern Bolivia, large areas of upland campos—open grasslands similar to the dry prairies in the midwestern United States—have been lost (along with the cerrado) to large-scale mechanized agriculture (Cavalcanti 1988). Total destruction of the campo habitat is imminent outside a few small areas already protected. The short-grass prairies of northern Mexico and southern Argentina have been degraded over a much longer period, with large areas replaced by scrubby vegetation. Humans have altered even the most remote Andean paramos and punas, primarily through overgrazing and burning.

No baseline data exist with which to measure the long-term impact of human land use on Neotropical grassland birds. Settlement and agriculture of Neotropical grasslands probably have led to sharp declines in many bird populations. The more specialized grassland birds avoid other habitats, especially human-modified ones.

Diversity and Specialization in Grassland Avifaunas

We divide Neotropical grasslands into six types: two tropical, two temperate, and two high elevation (table 5.1; see descriptions in chapter 2). Several of these grassland types correspond to geographic regions. The major exception is seasonally wet grassland, which dominates the llanos of Northern South America and occurs widely south of the Amazon, in Central South America.

Only 297 bird species use these habitats, making the grassland avifauna the least diverse of the avifaunas in the terrestrial ecosystems in the Neotropics. With one glaring exception, diversity is roughly equal among the different grassland types across the Neotropics (table 5.1). The northern temperate grasslands in northern Mexico are the exception, with fewer species than the others and only two endemic specialists—Masked Bobwhite, *Colinus virginianus ridgwayi*, and Worthen's Sparrow, *Spizella wortheni*. Interestingly, these Mexican grasslands do harbor large numbers of wintering migrant birds during the northern winter (see chapter 7).

Central South America (CSA), with its formerly extensive campo and seasonally flooded grasslands, and the Central Andes (CAN), with a vast, puna-covered altiplano, are the two main geographic centers of diversity for grassland birds (fig. 5.1). It is noteworthy that although Northern South America (NSA) and Northern Amazonia (AMN) have fairly large grassland avifaunas, they have no endemic species. This reflects the predominance of seasonally flooded grasslands in these two regions, a habitat with few endemics and no habitat-restricted endemics (see below). Northern Amazonia also contains isolated patches of campo grassland, but these lack most of the campo specialists found in central Brazil (the species that do occur in these grasslands have differentiated little if at all, suggesting a recent connection among the Amazonian and Central South American campos [Haffer 1974]).

Habitat specialization is about as rare in grassland birds as in birds of other arid habitats, but with one important difference. Of the total sample of grassland users, 17% (51 of 298) are restricted to a single grassland type (table 5.1). This compares with 17% habitat restriction in arid scrubs, and only 10% in dry forests (table 4.1). However, about 25% of grassland users are restricted to grasslands as a whole (i.e., occur only in one or more of the six grassland types), and roughly three-quarters of grassland users rely on some form of grassland as their primary habitat (table 5.1). No doubt this feature of the avifauna reflects the structural similarities of the native grasslands. Birds can use the same general foraging or nesting behavior in several grassland types. Taken together, grasslands support an avifauna as specialized as that of humid lowland forest (see fig. 4.1; cf. tables 5.1, 3.3), and much more specialized than that of dry forest or arid scrub.

Most of the 81 species that use grasslands, but not as a primary habitat, are species of arid scrubs (N1, N2; $N = 23$), secondary habitats (N13, N14; $N = 20$), or forest edges ($N = 5$). Scrub habitats still are under minimal threat (chapter 4), and secondary and edge habitats increase rapidly across the Neotropics as the original habitats are altered. Most of the present Neotropical grassland avifaunas, therefore, include a little-threatened group of widespread habitat generalists. However, this grassland avifauna component should not be confused with the highly threatened set of endemic grassland species discussed below.

Human-modified grasslands. The specialized habitat requirements of most grassland birds are illustrated by their intolerance of agricultural fields and pastures (N13), despite the outward structural similarity of some croplands and improved pastures to native prairies. Of the 217 bird species that use grasslands as a primary habitat, only 51 (24%) are also found in grazed pastures. Among all grassland users, the fraction is equivalent (74 out of 298, or 24.8%; table 5.2).

Birds that rely on secondary habitats ($N = 40$) and arid scrubs ($N = 15$) as their primary habitat dominate agricultural lands. The largest contingent of grassland species that do use pastures is found among the birds of temperate zone grasslands (N7, N8): 26 of the 60 species (or 43%) also occur in pastures. In contrast, avifaunas of lowland and montane grasslands of lower latitudes avoid pastures for the most part. Only 13 of the 99 bird species that use puna, paramo, or campo as their primary habitat also occur in pastures and farmlands.

Where soils of original campo or puna are tilled, or where native grasses and forbs are replaced by exotic crops and forage, the diversity of grassland birds plummets. Native bird species require native grasslands for survival.

Endemism and Conservation Status of Grassland Avifaunas

The threat to the avifauna in grasslands, based on our conservation priority rankings, is similar to the threat in forested habitats and much higher than that in arid scrubs. Of the 217 species using grasslands as their primary habitat, 74 (34%) have high conservation priorities (CP-1 to CP-3; table 5.3). This compares with 30%, 38%, 35%, and 17% for equivalent samples in humid lowland and montane forests, dry forest, and arid scrubs, respectively (table 4.3).

Of the bird species restricted to a single grassland habitat, 80% (41 of 51) are endemic to one zoogeographic region. This degree of endemism is surpassed only by the exceptional endemism among dry forest specialists (see fig. 4.2). As a group, these restricted grassland endemics show levels of threat somewhat lower than those in forest, but still higher than in arid scrub (34 of 77 grassland restricted endemics, or 44%, are CP-1, CP-2, or CP-3; table 5.3; cf. table 4.3).

Puna and paramo. From a conservation perspective, an important feature of grassland avifaunas is that the level of threat differs widely among regions. Despite several thousand years of intensive human occupation of the Andean puna, grassland birds in the region are still at low risk (fig. 5.2). That few species of birds are endangered in puna grasslands probably results from generally low human population densities in the high Andes, combined with the persistence of traditional agricultural practices over much of the region. In the puna, birds nest and forage in the uncultivated margins and mountaintops between farms. Moreover, these species have been able to adjust to the effects of human population slowly, over many centuries, rather than

Table 5.1 Avian Diversity and Habitat Specialization in the Neotropical Grasslands

Habitat	Habitat Code	Users[a]	Primary Habitat	Grassland Restricted[b]	Habitat Restricted	Habitat-Restricted Endemics
Campo	N5	68	23	15	9	7
Low, seasonally wet	N6	103	58	12	1	0
Southern temperate	N7	68	36	10	8	6
Northern temperate	N8	36	24	3	3	2
Puna	N9	69	41	22	18	14
Paramo	N10	53	35	15	12	11
Total		298	217	77	51	40

[a] Species that use more than one habitat appear more than once in this column, so column is not additive.

[b] Grassland-restricted species may occur in more than one grassland habitat; they are listed in their primary habitat only.

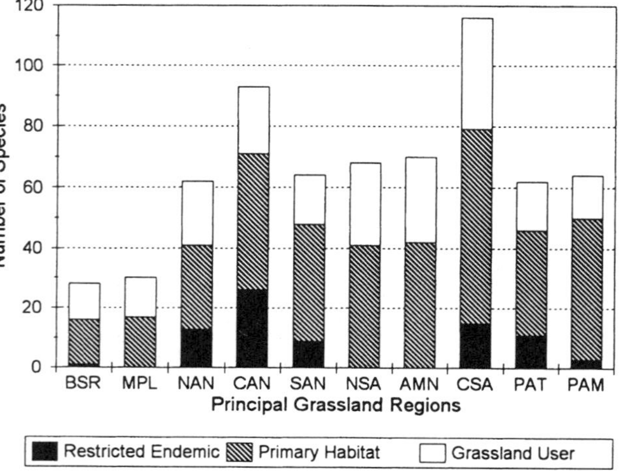

Figure 5.1 Diversity and habitat specialization of grassland avifaunas in Neotropical zoogeographic regions that have significant natural grasslands.

Table 5.2 Primary Habitats of Birds That Use Pastures and Agricultural Land in the Neotropics

Habitat	Habitat Code	All Users[a]	Grassland Species[b]
Gallery forests	F8	5	1
Arid lowland scrub	N1	9	2
Arid montane scrub	N2	6	1
Cerrado	N4	3	1
Campo grasslands	N5	4	4
Low, seasonally wet grasslands	N6	16	16
Southern temperate grasslands	N7	15	15
Northern temperate grasslands	N8	11	11
Puna grasslands	N9	4	4
Paramo grasslands	N10	5	5
Pastures	N13	22	11
Second-growth habitats	N14	18	3
Freshwater marshes	A1	7	0
Others		7	1
Total		132	74

[a] Species are listed only once in each column, under their primary habitat.

[b] Grassland species are any species that use grasslands.

having to face immediate, radical alteration of the habitat. The puna avifauna, even its specialists, represents the least threatened grassland community in the tropics.

Although the paramos of the northern Andes have significantly fewer bird species than does the central Andean puna (fig. 5.1), the number of threatened species is equivalent in the two regions (fig. 5.2 and 5.3). The higher proportion of the paramo avifauna at risk mirrors the greater threat facing this unique ecosystem. Humid alpine vegetation in the paramo is more diverse, structurally and botanically, than is the drier vegetation of the puna, and it has suffered greater alteration from its native condition (especially through cattle grazing and range burning). In the high Andes of Colombia and Ecuador, intense habitat exploitation has modified the environment much more than in the arid altiplanos of Peru and Bolivia. Conservation action must focus in the paramos before the region can be salvaged only through habitat restoration.

Campo. In the lowland grasslands of South America, 80% of the endemic birds are at risk. Campo grasslands once existed as large "islands" within the more extensive open woodlands (cerrado) and forests on the Brazilian plateau (see chapter 4). Today they are the most threatened grasslands. *All* endemic campo bird species are at risk; nearly 90% are threatened (CP-2). Although several types of campos exist, they all attract cattle ranchers or farmers. Most of the campos that survive outside the few existing parks and biological reserves have been degraded. Some campo grasslands still survive in the Amazon basin, but most campo bird specialists are confined to central Brazil.

Native grassland communities at risk. Major problems face grassland birds today. Besides being strongly dependent on a restricted set of native habitats, which are disappearing almost everywhere, grassland birds are saddled with the now-familiar fact that most habitat specialists are endemics. As grassland regions become major centers of agricultural development, these

Table 5.3 Relation between Habitat Specialization, Endemism, and Conservation Priority in Neotropical Grasslands

Conservation Priority	Number of Species %					
	All Users	Not Primary Habitat	Primary Habitat	Grassland[a] Restricted	Habitat Restricted	Habitat-Restricted Endemics
CP-1	2 (0)	0 (0)	2 (1)	2 (3)	2 (4)	2 (5)
CP-2	28 (9)	2 (2)	26 (12)	16 (21)	10 (20)	9 (22)
CP-3	55 (18)	9 (11)	46 (21)	16 (21)	11 (22)	8 (20)
CP-4	213 (71)	70 (86)	143 (66)	43 (56)	28 (55)	21 (52)
Total	298	81	217	77	51	40

[a] Grassland-restricted species may use any number of grassland habitats but use no nongrassland habitat.

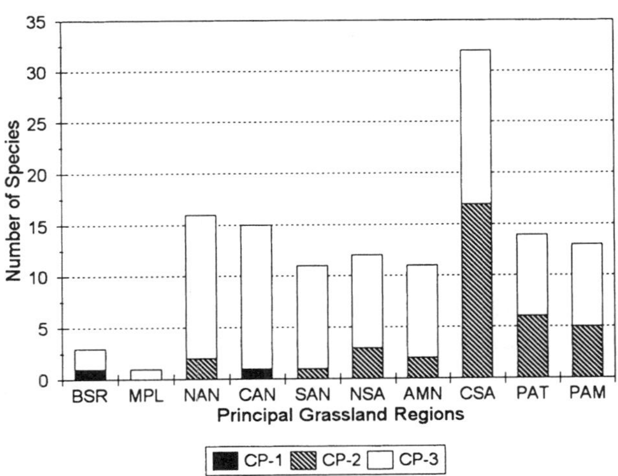

Figure 5.2 Grassland bird species of conservation concern in Neotropical zoogeographic regions that have significant natural grasslands. Only species that use a grassland type as their primary habitat are included.

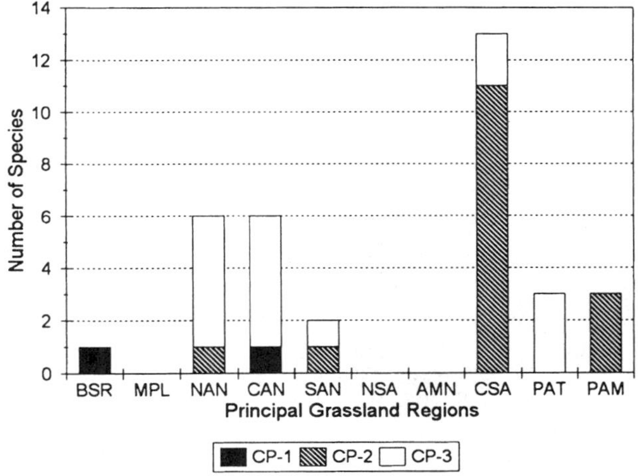

Figure 5.3 Endemic grassland bird species of conservation concern in Neotropical zoogeographic regions with significant natural grasslands. Only species that use a grassland type as their primary habitat and are endemic to a single zoogeographic region are included.

specialist bird species fail to adapt, and entire, distinctive native grassland communities are threatened as a result.

Nowhere is this process more advanced than in the cerrado region of central Brazil, center of the major avian radiation of open country specialists in the Neotropics. Intense agricultural development in this region places its grassland birds at alarmingly high risk (see chapter 4).

In most other grassland regions, the avifaunas—especially the endemics—are at least moderately threatened (see Bucher and Nores 1988; Fjeldså 1988). Only in the Central Andes do major, intact assemblages of grassland species persist. Even here, however, continued efforts to set aside native puna and paramo are necessary before these montane grasslands go the way of the Brazilian campo or the North American prairie.

6 Neotropical Aquatic Communities

Synopsis

Birds are poor indicators for type and condition of aquatic ecosystems. Unlike freshwater fishes, for example, birds do not show specific affinities for distinct river drainages, and they often occupy multiple habitats. Total species richness of birds in aquatic habitats is low compared with that in terrestrial habitats, and endemism and habitat specificity are extremely low. Diversity of aquatic birds is influenced more by the nature and condition of habitats surrounding the water than by the quality of the water itself.

Birds do point to a few areas as important centers for conservation attention, however. Neotropical waterbird diversity is highest in Central South America, where large marsh ecosystems serve as major breeding sites for resident species. Certain areas in both Central and Northern South America support huge aggregations of migrant waterbirds during their nonbreeding seasons. Migration is prominent among aquatic birds: 35% of the species that breed in Neotropical freshwaters show latitudinal migration, and 40% of the North American migrants to the Neotropics use aquatic habitats.

With broad habitat tolerance and widespread distributions, most freshwater birds continue to fare well in the Neotropics. Environmental toxins are known to affect breeding success, however, and many aquatic birds are uppermost in their food chains. Present-day tolerance of poor water quality could lead to longer-term declines in waterbird populations. Furthermore, agricultural practices include drainage of shallow wetlands in the llanos of Northern South America and the Pantanal region of Central South America. The most important conservation need at present may be long-term monitoring of waterbird populations.

Among waterbirds, only seabirds show high risk of extinction as a group. Conservation concerns for seabirds include pollution (especially from oil spills), overexploitation of fish resources, and introduction of predators to breeding islands. These habitats and concerns are mentioned only briefly in this book.

We have argued that birds are ideal indicators of habitat type and condition in terrestrial environments. In aquatic environments this does not hold true. Waterbirds are poor predictors of general diversity and endemism in aquatic systems, and they tolerate considerable habitat degradation. Nonetheless, they are useful indicators of the health of certain types of aquatic environments, especially freshwater marshes.

We review conservation of seabirds only briefly here. They face a separate set of problems, very different from those of freshwater or terrestrial avifaunas. For a discussion of their conservation, we recommend *The Status and Conservation of the World's Seabirds* (Croxall, Evans, and Schreiber 1984).

Aquatic Birds as Poor Indicators

Some groups of freshwater fish show distinct patterns of endemism along single river drainages (Weitzman and Weitzman 1982; Vari 1988). Birds do not. Even the two primarily piscivorous bird families, the herons (Ardeidae) and the kingfishers (Alcedinidae), show no species restriction to major river systems: neither family has a single species restricted even to one zoogeographic region. Of the 56 bird species that depend on open freshwater (lakes, streams, or rivers), only 9 (16%) are restricted to one zoogeographic region. Of these, only one—Rufous-throated Dipper (*Cinclus schulzi*), an insectivorous species from Andean southern Bolivia and northern Argentina—uses primarily rivers or streams. The other 8 species (which include 5 grebes, Podicipedidae) live in high-elevation or south temperate lakes.

Bird diversity is relatively low in aquatic habitats: 394 species overall, with only 292 in freshwater habitats (including marshes). Regional variation in diversity is slight compared with most terrestrial habitats. Central South America, with its expansive marshes, has the highest diversity of species that use, or are restricted to, freshwater habitats (table 6.1).

Waterbirds show low sensitivity to some of the worst degradations of aquatic environments. Anyone who has bird-watched around sewage treatment plants realizes that aquatic birds can tolerate highly polluted water. Near the city of São Paulo, the Rio Tietê is among the most polluted in the Neotropics; yet where surrounding habitat remains intact, so does the avifauna. Just east of the city, egrets and cormorants fish in the murky black waters, while yellowlegs and other shorebirds feed nervously on the polluted shore. Whistling-Ducks and White-cheeked Pintails float in quiet backwaters with their broods. In the marsh vegetation fringing the river, the nests of Yellow-throated Spinetails are a common sight, and rails and gallinules call amid the reeds. In fact, all the expected herons and ducks, and most of the expected marsh birds, remain common close to São Paulo, along heavily polluted stretches of the Rio Tietê. A few kilometers farther west, though, the river is restricted to a concrete channel, and all the habitat is gone, along with all the waterbirds. Only a few Black Vultures remain to enjoy the odor of a dead river.

For the most part, aquatic birds reflect the quality of the vegetation that surrounds the water rather than the quality of the water itself. As a result, birds act as indicators *only* for these riparian habitats. Over the long term, birds may respond to water quality because they are susceptible to waterborne toxins, especially heavy metals and pesticides that are concentrated as they move up the food chain. These generally affect breeding success, killing the next generation rather than the adult birds. With long-lived aquatic birds like herons and ducks at the top of food chains, the deadly effects of water pollution may be slow to appear.

Endemism and Habitat Specificity among Aquatic Birds

Fewer aquatic birds are habitat specific, and more are geographically widespread, than are Neotropical birds generally (fig. 6.1). To examine patterns in more detail, we consider each aquatic habitat individually (table 6.2; we have lumped several related habitats). Even in freshwater marshes—which have the greatest diversity, habitat specificity, and levels of endemism—only 18 (15%) of the 121 species that use marshes as their primary habitat are endemic to a single region. With such limited endemism, it is nearly impossible to specify unique species assemblages that define geographic communities.

Migrant Birds in Aquatic Habitats

Many waterbirds migrate: of the 273 species of birds that use freshwater habitats and breed in the Neotropics, 101 (35%) undergo true latitudinal migration. In addition, of the 186 species of migrants that breed entirely outside the Neotropics (part 4, database C; also chapter 7), 74 (40%) use aquatic habitats. Even among the resident aquatic birds, numerous species move regularly in response to changes in the aquatic habitats, such as fluctuations in water level or resource abundance, and the presence of open, unfrozen water. For example, many waterbirds of the Amazon basin move widely in the basin in response to the seasonal changes in water levels.

The most important aquatic habitats among both migrants and residents are freshwater marshes and lakes. Coastal mudflats are very important to migrating shorebirds but are relatively unimportant to resident species. When the northern migrants are present, favorable stretches might have twenty species of shorebirds foraging throughout the intertidal zone and a half dozen species of gulls and terns loafing onshore In late May, June, and July these same mudflats may have nothing more than a few Collared Plovers scurrying about, and perhaps a Snowy Egret fishing in the shallows.

The movement patterns of some aquatic migrants are well known, especially those of ducks (Anatidae) and shorebirds (Charadriidae and Scolopacidae). Wintering and migrating populations of some of these species concentrate in specific small areas (Myers 1983; Myers et al. 1987). Besides being critical to the survival of migrant birds, these sites often teem with resident aquatic birds. For example, in southern Brazil, Uruguay, and northern Argentina, wetlands in the pampas are key wintering grounds for both Nearctic shorebirds and austral migrant waterbirds, especially ducks. They are also the year-round residence for a large variety of aquatic species.

Conservation of Aquatic Birds

Despite their low habitat specificity, low endemism, and relatively high tolerance for water pollution, both endemic and nonendemic aquatic species are at slightly greater risk than Neotropical birds as a whole. Of the 306 species that use aquatic habitats (excluding oceanic waters), 92 (30%) are at risk, threatened, or endangered. This unexpectedly high degree of risk reflects the extreme pressure that encroaching towns and agriculture exert on aquatic habitats.

Aquatic habitats do not show concentrations of threatened species that are restricted by geography or habitat. The largest such concentration is of only four species, in the marshes of central Mexico (where an-

Table 6.1 Number of Bird Species Using and Restricted to Aquatic Habitats by Region

		All Aquatic Habitats					Freshwater Habitats				
Region	Region Code	Users	Primary Habitat	Habitat Restricted	Endemic	Habitat-Restricted Endemics	Users	Primary Habitat	Habitat Restricted	Endemic	Habitat-Restricted Endemics
Baja-Sonora	BSR	75	56	28	10	6	41	25	9	1	0
Greater Antilles	GAN	66	52	26	4	3	39	28	12	3	2
Pacific Arid Slope	PAS	78	54	28	2	1	52	30	12	0	0
Gulf-Caribbean Slope	GCS	98	60	29	2	1	75	40	17	2	1
Chocó Lowlands	CHO	57	33	16	0	0	48	25	11	0	0
Equatorial Pacific	EPC	75	52	23	7	2	45	26	6	2	0
Subtropical Pacific	STP	105	83	33	13	8	66	48	10	0	0
Central Andes	CAN	60	39	13	15	5	58	39	13	15	5
Southern Andes	SAN	52	35	7	1	0	49	35	7	1	0
Northern South America	NSA	122	72	35	3	2	98	51	22	2	2
Northern Amazonia	AMN	105	56	27	0	0	99	52	25	0	0
Southern Amazonia	AMS	99	52	25	1	1	95	50	24	1	1
Central South America	CSA	124	74	32	1	1	123	74	32	1	1
Atlantic Forest	ATL	116	70	35	5	0	99	55	26	5	0
Pampas	PAM	110	73	27	6	1	105	68	25	5	1
Patagonia	PAT	95	78	34	10	5	56	43	9	2	1

Note: Regions are listed from north to south.

Table 6.2 Diversity, Habitat Specificity, and Endemism of Aquatic Birds by Habitat Type

Aquatic Habitat	Users	Primary Habitat	Habitat Restricted	Habitat-Restricted Endemics
Oceanic waters	118	109	89	27
Saltwater marshes	39	8	2	2
Freshwater marshes	187	124	55	14
Lakes	93	40	22	12
Streams and rivers	56	21	9	1
Bogs	16	3	1	0

other species, Slender-billed Grackle, *Quiscalis palustris,* recently has become extinct). To detect important aquatic centers of diversity and endemism in aquatic environments, it will be necessary to focus on a group of truly aquatic organisms—such as freshwater fish—that are much more sensitive than birds to local conditions. Some fish families may be sufficiently well known (e.g., the Curimatidae; Vari 1988) to act as indicators of type and condition of aquatic habitats.

Seabirds

Seabirds face three main threats: pollution; overexploitation of resources, especially overfishing; and most important, introduction of mammals to isolated breeding islands. For the 109 seabirds breeding in the Neotropics, pollution has played a relatively minor role. Thus far the region has not been devastated by oil disasters of the dimensions of some in North America or Europe. The potential for such oil spills exists, however, and seabirds are especially vulnerable because of their highly clumped breeding distributions.

Overfishing also has had a relatively minor impact on Neotropical seabirds. An exception is the regular overexploitation of the Peruvian anchovy, the dominant fish along the Humboldt Current off the coast of Peru. Combined with the extreme natural fluctuations in resource availability brought by El Niño years, the overfishing has caused sharp declines of several seabirds over the past few decades, including Red-legged Cormorants (*Phalacrocorax gaimardi*), Peruvian Diving-Petrel (*Pelecanoides garnotii*), and Humboldt Penguin (*Spheniscus humboldtii*) (Tovar 1983, 1985; Duffy, Hays, and Plenge 1984; Hughes 1985; Hays 1987).

By far the most serious threat to seabirds worldwide is the introduction of mammals onto islands with breeding colonies. Most devastating are the predators—cats, rats, mongooses, pigs—that destroy the nests, eggs, and young of ground-nesting seabirds. In some other instances, feral herbivores like goats and

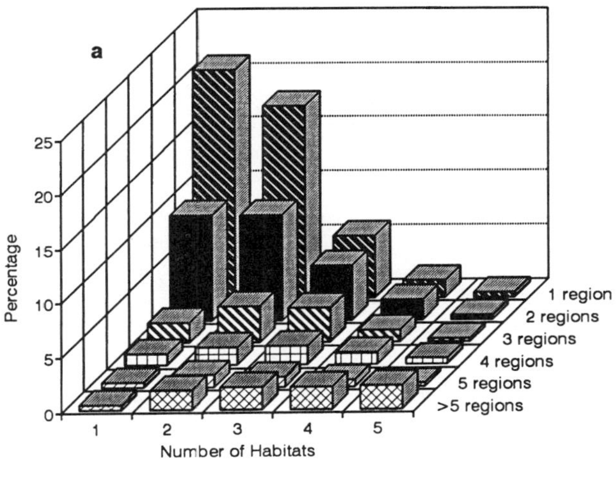

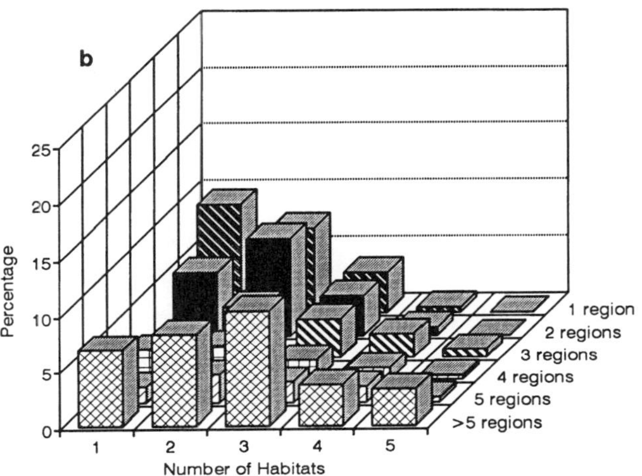

Figure 6.1 Number of zoogeographic regions and habitats occupied by Neotropical birds: (a) all breeding species; (b) birds in freshwater habitats.

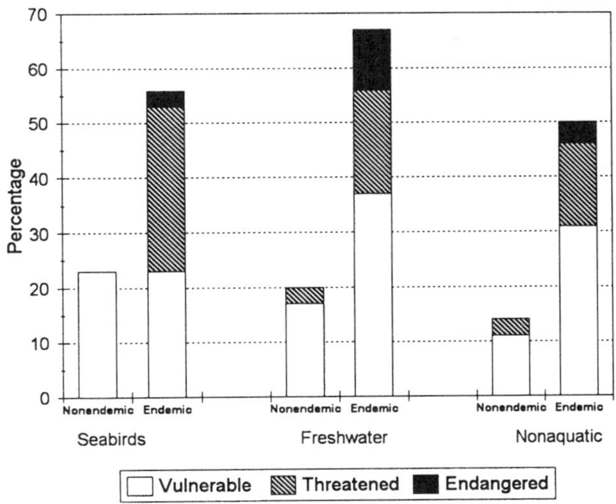

Figure 6.2 Conservation priority status of seabirds, other aquatic birds, and nonaquatic birds of the Neotropics; proportion in each CP category.

rabbits so damage the habitat that seabirds cannot breed successfully.

Such disturbance is especially dangerous to seabirds with small breeding ranges: the introduction of predators to just one island can lead to the extinction of some species. The extinct Guadalupe Storm-Petrel, *Oceanodroma macrodactylus*, once restricted to Isla Guadalupe in Mexico, apparently was eliminated by cats. More than a third of the seabirds endemic to a single region are threatened (fig. 6.2). Introduced mammals pose the main threat to 10 (59%) of these species.

PART

2

Bird Migration and Conservation in the Neotropics

7 Nearctic Migrants in the Neotropics: How Big Is the Threat?

Synopsis

Over 420 species of Nearctic birds migrate to wintering grounds in the Neotropics. Diversity of migrants is highest in northern Central America and declines southward. Even at their peak of diversity in the Central American lowlands, Nearctic migrants make up less than one-quarter of the total avifauna. Migrant passerines are disproportionately concentrated in Central America and the West Indies; nonpasserines are more evenly distributed, with 16 species reaching Patagonia. Compared with resident birds in the Neotropics, wintering Nearctic migrants have wider geographic distributions and broader habitat tolerances; they use secondary habitats more frequently and primary forests less frequently; and they generally rely less on montane forest habitats than on lowland forests (except for the montane pine forests in Mexico).

Pine and pine-oak forests are the most common primary habitats of wintering Nearctic migrants in the Neotropics. Lowland evergreen forest, secondary forest, and coastal habitats come next in importance. In addition to these five, seven other habitats are each used as primary habitat by more than 10 migrant species.

Recent concern that declines among many North American birds stem primarily from habitat loss on Neotropical wintering grounds is poorly substantiated, and this is unlikely for most species. Only a small group of Nearctic migrants may be threatened primarily by conditions on their Neotropical wintering grounds. The most likely candidates are migrants restricted to the lowland forests of Central America or the Greater Antilles, or to the pampas grasslands of southern South America.

We advocate determining conservation priorities in the Neotropics based on the needs of resident species and communities, *not* on the needs of migratory birds. Migrants constitute a tiny portion of the Neotropical avifauna, they concentrate in only a few habitats and regions, and throughout their wintering grounds they face considerably less risk than do the resident avifaunas.

Most birds in northern temperate zones migrate, and more than a quarter of the species that breed within the United States winter entirely south of the country. Until recently the migrants wintering in the Neotropics were little studied in winter. The first organized attention to Nearctic migrants on their Neotropical wintering grounds was a symposium at Front Royal, Virginia, in 1977 (Keast and Morton 1980). Several subsequent symposia and a plethora of papers (e.g., papers in Ouellet 1988; Hagan and Johnston 1992) reflect recognition that migrants represent an important, if mobile, element in tropical avian communities, and that conditions on their wintering grounds could play an important role in the population dynamics of these species.

Beginning in the early 1970s, various studies have suggested severe declines in the populations of many birds that breed in eastern North America but winter in the Neotropics (e.g., Aldrich and Robbins 1970; Whitcomb, Whitcomb, and Bystrak 1977; Robbins 1979; Ambuel and Temple 1982; Hall 1984; Robbins et al. 1989; Robbins, Sauer, and Peterjohn 1993). Island effects resulting from forest fragmentation (Whitcomb, Whitcomb, and Bystrak 1977; Whitcomb 1977; Robbins 1979; Lynch and Whigham 1984; Askins, Philbrick, and Sugeno 1987; Porneluzi et al. 1993), nest predation (Andrén et al. 1985; Wilcove 1985; Holmes and Sherry 1992; Robinson 1992; Böhning-Gaese, Taper, and Brown 1993), cowbird parasitism (Brittingham and Temple 1983; Robinson et al. 1993), and other threats within the breeding range have received much attention as possible causes for these population declines. Over the past two decades, destruction of tropical forests has been cited increasingly as a primary factor in these declines (e.g., Terborgh 1980; Lovejoy 1983; Rappole et al. 1983; Hall 1984; Askins, Lynch, and Greenberg 1990; Morton 1992). Some remain skeptical, however, unconvinced that tropical deforestation is primarily responsible (Hutto 1988; Kaufman 1990; Böhning-Gaese, Taper, and Brown 1993) or even that the reported declines are real (Hutto 1988; Hagan et al. 1992; Hussell, Mather, and Sinclair 1992). We include ourselves among the skeptics, as detailed below.

For a fine discussion of many issues involved in the apparent population declines of Nearctic migrants wintering in the Neotropics, we recommend John Terborgh's *Where Have All the Birds Gone?* (Terborgh 1989). Terborgh reviews the various demographic and environmental problems faced by migratory species and speculates on many probable causes. He also suggests solutions to some of these problems. We call special attention to his emphasis on the effects of habitat alteration and fragmentation in the United States.

In this chapter we examine patterns of habitat use and geographic range of Nearctic migrants on their Neotropical wintering grounds in order to evaluate potential threats from habitat loss. We also examine whether threats to the migrants currently at risk occur primarily on the breeding or wintering grounds. Our goal is to place potential problems confronting different kinds of wintering northern migrants within their appropriate contexts and scale. How do the needs of migrants compare with the needs of resident birds? How representative are migrant birds as indicators for the need to conserve Neotropical communities as a whole, or even in any one geographic region? How important a role should the concern over migratory birds play in developing conservation strategies for the Neotropics?

Migrant Databases

Information analyzed in this chapter is provided in four migrant databases (see part 4). These databases include all the species of Nearctic migrants that regularly winter in the Neotropics. Database C contains Nearctic migrants that do not breed anywhere in the Neotropical region as we define it. Database D contains the northern migrants that have breeding populations in the Neotropical region and use additional zoogeographic regions or habitats in the winter. Database G lists Nearctic migrants with breeding populations in the Neotropical region but that do not use additional zoogeographic regions or habitats in winter. Finally, Database F provides a list of pelagic species that are without breeding populations in the Neotropics and that winter strictly at sea. Databases E and H, which contain austral migrants, are discussed in chapter 8.

Databases C and D provide data on the distribution, elevational range, and ecology of the Nearctic migrants during their winter residence. Two other databases consist of simple species lists; in one case (database G), the data are unchanged between breeding and winter seasons, and in the other (database F) the species are outside the scope of this book. For more details on the structure, variables, and uses of these databases, see the Guide to the Databases (part 4).

Geographic Distribution

We treat 422 nonpelagic species as northern migrants in the Neotropics. Of these, 174 species winter completely or almost completely in the Neotropics; 136 others have a substantial portion, and 97 only a trivial fraction, of their temperate North American breeding population wintering south of the United States. Another 15 species with no breeding populations in the United States or Canada migrate partially or completely from their breeding ranges in the West Indies or Central America to wintering ranges farther south.

We concentrate on Nearctic migrants not breeding in the Neotropics (database C) for most analyses, but we also mention a few unique patterns involving those that do breed in the Neotropics. By focusing on species with no breeding populations in the Neotropics, we avoid confusion between overwintering and resident populations. In some cases resident populations have misled researchers regarding the main wintering range of a northern, migratory species. For example, Terborgh (1989) treats southern South America as the main wintering range of Cinnamon Teal (*Anas cyanoptera*). In fact, the breeding populations of Cinnamon Teal from the western United States and Canada winter almost entirely in Mexico (Bellrose 1976; see also Phillips 1975); birds in southern South America breed there and actually are austral migrants (chapter 8) that undertake a limited northward migration in the austral winter.

The number of species of wintering Nearctic migrants increases northward within the Neotropics (fig. 7.1). This overall pattern is a composite of several sets of migrants. A major set consists of species that also winter widely in temperate North America. These, of course, are most numerous in adjacent Mexico and the West Indies. If we eliminate these northerly winterers and focus on those that winter entirely within the Neotropics, different patterns emerge. Figures 7.2 and 7.3 show numbers of passerines and nonpasserines, respectively, that winter entirely within the twenty-two Neotropical regions. Migrant passerines (mainly warblers, flycatchers, and vireos associated with forest or scrub habitats) concentrate in the lowlands of Central America and the West Indies (fig. 7.2). Few of these winter south of Venezuela, where montane forests become more important for migrants than lowland habitats (Hayes et al. 1990; Stotz et al. 1992; Robinson, Fitzpatrick, and Terborgh 1995). Nonpasserines (e.g., hawks, ducks, shorebirds) are more evenly distributed throughout the regions (fig. 7.3). This distribution re-

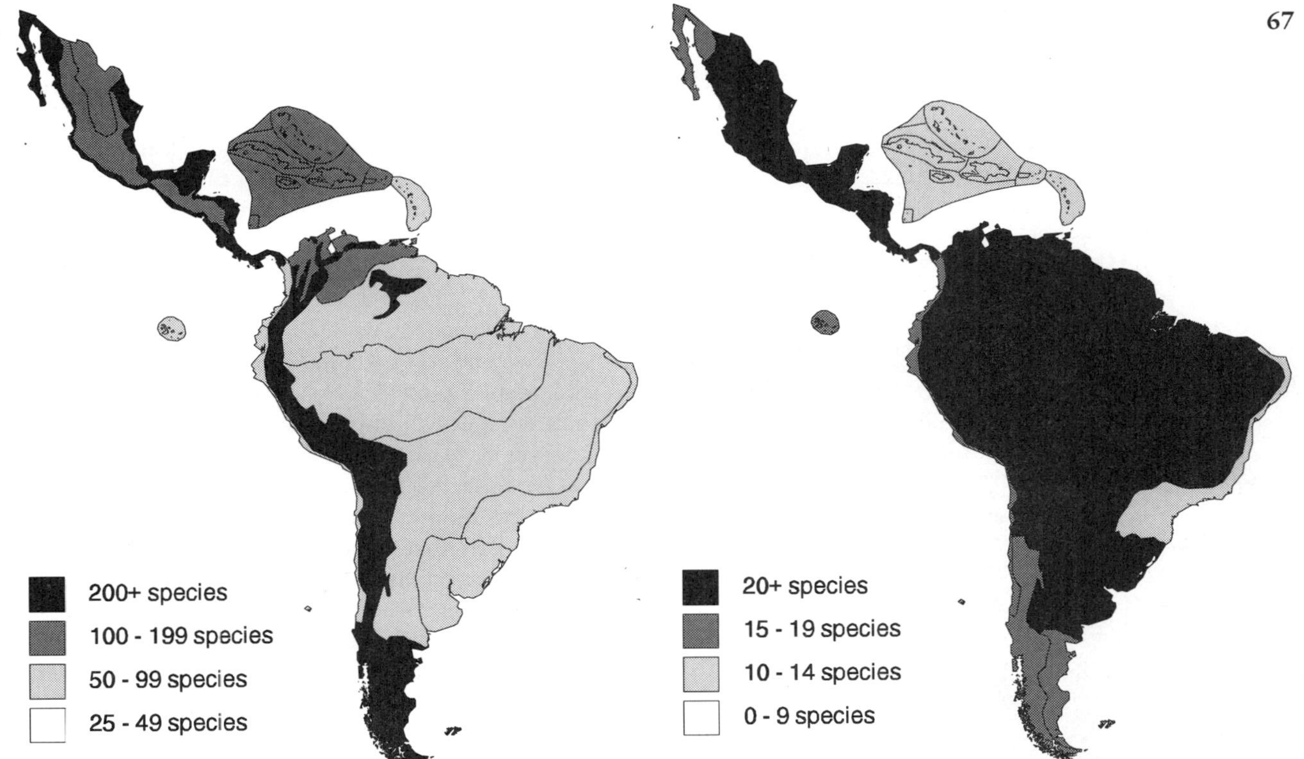

Figure 7.1 Regional diversity of wintering Nearctic migrants in the Neotropics.

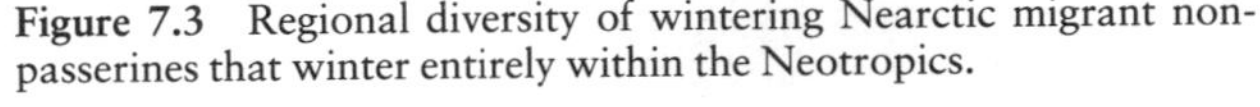

Figure 7.3 Regional diversity of wintering Nearctic migrant non-passerines that winter entirely within the Neotropics.

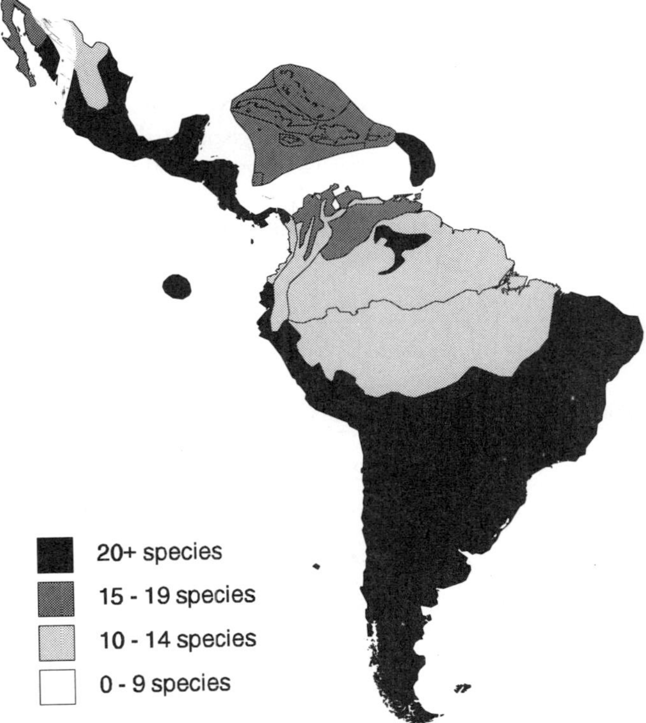

Figure 7.2 Regional diversity of wintering Nearctic migrant passerines that winter entirely within the Neotropics.

flects the numerical dominance of sandpipers (Scolopacidae) within the migrant nonpasserine sample. Most sandpipers are widespread in coastal regions, and many winter all the way south to Tierra del Fuego. Sandpipers that have more limited geographic distributions in winter are restricted mainly to the grasslands and marshes of southern South America.

In chapters 3 and 9 we demonstrate a close relationship between the conservation status and the geographic range of a species. Most threatened or endangered species are restricted in range, and few widespread species are seriously threatened. In this respect northern migrants fare quite well as a group. Some researchers have pointed out that many migrant species are forced into small areas during the winter (e.g., Askins, Lynch, and Greenberg 1990). In fact, by tropical standards northern migrants are geographically widespread (fig. 7.4a). Fewer than 20% of northern migrants are restricted to a single zoogeographic region, and over 35% winter in more than four regions. In contrast, over 44% of resident bird species in the Neotropics are restricted to one zoogeographic region, while fewer than 14% span more than four (fig. 7.4b).

To test whether the pattern above results from the inclusion of widespread northerly species not entirely tropical during the winter, we ran the same analysis considering only the species that winter almost entirely within the Neotropics (i.e., those with status A; see the Guide to the Databases in part 4). These purely tropical winterers are even more widespread than are migrants as a whole (fig. 7.5). Only 21 species (12%) of Nearctic migrants that winter exclusively in the Neotropics are restricted to a single zoogeographic region. More than three times as many resident bird species are endemic to the Gulf-Caribbean Slope (GCS) alone. Among resi-

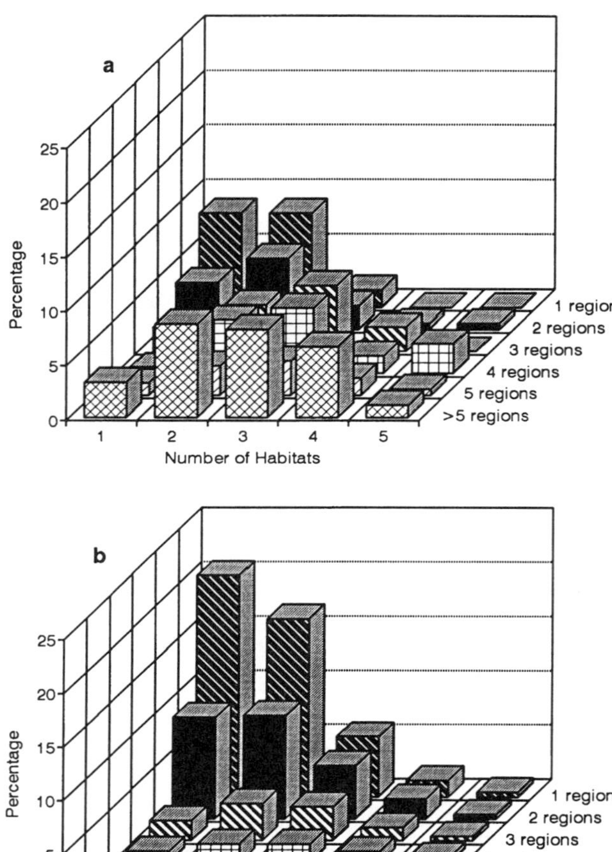

Figure 7.4 Number of zoogeographic regions and habitats occupied by Neotropical birds: (a) Nearctic migrants (winter distribution); (b) all breeding species.

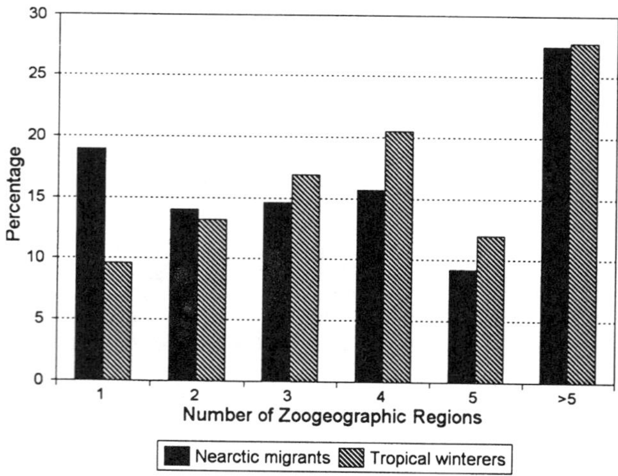

Figure 7.5 Number of zoogeographic regions occupied in winter by Nearctic migrants and by Nearctic migrants that winter entirely within the Neotropics.

dent birds, only species endemic to a single zoogeographic region show an elevated tendency to be at risk of extinction (chapter 9). Therefore the threat to Nearctic migrants from habitat alteration cannot be general because most of them occur in two or more zoogeographic regions in winter.

Habitat Use

Besides occupying smaller geographic ranges, threatened species tend to be habitat specialists. On average, species classified as CP-1, CP-2, or CP-3 use fewer habitats than do species not currently considered to be at risk (chapter 9). Again in this respect, migrants appear to be safer than residents. Figure 7.4 shows that migrants are less habitat restricted than are resident species, and species that winter entirely within the Neotropics are even less habitat specific than are migrants as a whole. About 34% of the resident avifauna is restricted to a single habitat, but only 13% of northern migrants and 9% of northern migrants wintering entirely in the Neotropics are equally habitat restricted in winter. With wide geographic ranges and generalized habitat use, wintering migrants show an ecological profile that would *not* place them under immediate threat from habitat alteration on their wintering grounds.

Although the potential effect of tropical deforestation on populations of "Neotropical migrants" has received considerable attention (e.g., Hall 1984; Powell and Rappole 1986; Morton 1992), Nearctic migrants in the Neotropics are less strongly associated with forest than are the resident birds. Most migrants do not occur in forest habitats (table 7.1): of the 407 northern migrants that breed in the United States or Canada,

Table 7.1 Use of Habitats by Nearctic Migrants in the Neotropics

Habitat	Habitat Code	Users N (%)	Primary Habitat N (%)
Unknown	?		1 (0)
Mangroves	F14	15 (4)	2 (0)
Salt marshes	A2	45 (11)	7 (2)
Marine waters, coastal beaches	A3–4, A11–12	87 (21)	57 (14)
Freshwater marshes	A1	74 (18)	44 (11)
Lakes and streams	A6–9	65 (16)	28 (7)
Lowland scrub	N1	56 (14)	23 (6)
Montane scrub	N2, N3	48 (12)	11 (3)
Grasslands	N5–10	46 (11)	31 (8)
Gallery forests, riparian thickets	F8, N11	99 (24)	30 (7)
Deciduous forests	F7	73 (18)	17 (4)
Lowland evergreen forests	F1–3	85 (21)	47 (12)
Montane forests	F4, F5	40 (10)	14 (3)
Pine or pine-oak forests	F10, F11	86 (21)	58 (14)
Second-growth habitats	F15, N13–14	187 (46)	38 (9)

Table 7.2 Use of Habitat Classes by Migrant and Resident Birds in the Neotropics

Habitat	Habitat Code	Northern Migrants (Percentage Using as Primary Habitat)	Residents (Percentage Using as Primary Habitat)
Humid forests	F1–6, F9–14	29	61
Other forests	F7, F8	12	11
Grasslands	N5–10	8	6
Scrubs	N1–4, N11–12	8	10
Marine habitats	A2–4, A11–12	16	3
Freshwater habitats	A1, A5–10	18	5
Second-growth habitats	F15, N13–14	9	4

only 194 winter in or at the edges of primary forest habitats. Of these, only 56 are restricted to primary forests. Among northern migrants as a whole, aquatic and forest habitats are approximately equal in importance, and grasslands and scrubs are used by many species. Nearly half of the migrants use disturbed habitats; 38 species (8%) use them as their primary habitat.

Migrants' lack of reliance on forest contrasts sharply with the pattern shown by the resident birds of the Neotropics, which predominantly use humid forest habitats (chapter 3; table 7.2). Nearly two-thirds of the residents use some type of humid forest as their primary habitat; for migrants this figure is barely one-third (table 7.2). A much higher proportion of the migrants use aquatic habitats, while terrestrial nonforest habitats are slightly more important to migrants than to residents.

Of the primary native habitats, gallery forests are used by the largest number of migrant species (88), but only a few use this as their primary habitat. Pine and pine-oak forests are the primary habitat for the largest number of species (table 7.1). Along with gallery and pine and pine-oak forests, coastal habitats and lowland evergreen forests are each used by more than 20% of the migrants.

When we restrict the analysis to migrants wintering almost entirely within the Neotropics (status A), the importance of aquatic habitats declines and that of forest habitats increases (table 7.3). About 60% of purely tropical winterers prefer some type of primary forest. Lowland evergreen forest, especially in Central America, is most important, followed by pine and pine-oak forests.

Pine and pine-oak forests are the primary habitats for over half the migrant species restricted to undisturbed forests (table 7.4). The great importance of pine and pine-oak forests as a wintering habitat for northern-breeding birds has gone almost unnoticed, or at least unheralded, in the literature (however, see Hutto 1992). We suspect that two factors contribute to this oversight. First, 62 of the 86 northern migrants that use pine or pine-oak forests (table 7.1) also have resident populations in the Neotropics, obscuring the winter range of migratory populations. Instead, attention tends to focus on species that occupy wholly different ranges during winter. Second, only two species in eastern North America, Yellow-throated Warbler (*Dendroica dominica*) and Pine Warbler (*Dendroica pinus*), winter primarily in pine and pine-oak forests, and only the former winters predominantly in the Neotropics (in Caribbean pine forests). Scientists and authors from research centers in eastern North America, who dominate

Table 7.3 Primary Habitat of Nearctic Migrants Wintering Entirely within the Neotropics

Habitat	Habitat Code	Species Using as Primary Habitat *N* (%)
Unknown	?	1 (1)
Salt marshes	A2	1 (1)
Marine waters, coastal beaches	A3–4, A11–12	11 (6)
Freshwater marshes	A1	5 (3)
Lakes and streams	A6–9	3 (2)
Lowland scrub	N1	11 (6)
Montane scrub	N2, N3	6 (3)
Grasslands	N5–10	9 (5)
Gallery forests, riparian thickets	F8, N11	14 (8)
Deciduous forests	F7	13 (7)
Lowland evergreen forests	F1–3	41 (23)
Montane forests	F4, F5	13 (7)
Pine or pine-oak forests	F10, F11	29 (16)
Second-growth habitats	F15, N13–14	18 (10)

Table 7.4 Primary Habitat of Forest-Restricted Nearctic Migrants

Habitat	Habitat Code	Species Using as Primary Habitat *N* (%)
Mangroves	F14	1 (2)
Gallery forests	F8	7 (12)
Deciduous forests	F7	5 (9)
Lowland evergreen forests	F1–3	8 (14)
Montane forests	F4, F5	5 (9)
Pine forests	F10	18 (32)
Pine-oak forests	F11	12 (21)

the field, find most of "their" familiar bird species on wintering grounds outside pine and pine-oak habitats. From the standpoint of migrants alone, pine and pine-oak habitats of Mexico and Middle America warrant more attention than any other type of forest (table 7.4).

As noted by Terborgh (1989), few migrants winter in cloud forest, and almost none winter in elfin forest. Diversity of forest-dwelling migrants declines monotonically with increasing elevation and drops off rapidly above 1,500 m (fig. 7.6). The decline in wintering migrants with increasing elevation is even more pronounced among the nonbreeding northern migrants: only 7 of these species winter at elevations above 3,000 m (fig. 7.6). The species with breeding populations in the Neotropics have a very different pattern of diversity with elevation; because of the preponderance of montane pine and pine-oak species in this subset of migrants, their diversity reaches its peak at about 2,000 m and falls off much more gradually upslope (fig. 7.6).

Although numerically more important in Central America, wintering migrants occur across all the major tropical habitats in South America as well. They mainly inhabit edges and ephemeral habitats in South America, but a number of migrant species set up territories and join mixed-species flocks in the heart of primary forests in Central America. Northern migrants seem to play a minor role in the organization of avian communities in South America, yet they may play a crucial role in the communities of Central America. Keast (1980) and Fitzpatrick (1980) suggest that the high diversity of migrants in Central America may be partly responsible for the relatively depauperate resident avifauna there, through competition between migrant and resident species.

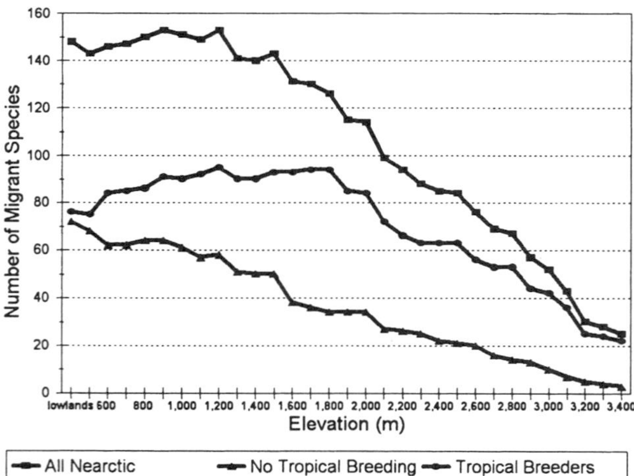

Figure 7.6 Elevational diversity gradient of wintering forest-dwelling Nearctic migrants in the Neotropics. The "All Nearctic" line includes all the forest-dwelling species. This is decomposed into two additional lines: Nearctic migrants without breeding populations in the Neotropics, "No Tropical Breeding" and Nearctic migrants with breeding populations in the Neotropics, "Tropical Breeders."

Perhaps the most important conclusion regarding the habitats of Nearctic migrants in the tropics is that no single type dominates. A total of twelve major habitats, including scrub, grassland, various aquatic habitats, and several types of forest, are preferred by at least 15 species of northern migrants. Ten of these habitats are the principal home to 10 or more migrant species that winter exclusively within the Neotropics. It is clear, then, that although lowland forests are important for some migrants, they do not warrant the disproportionate attention they have received as the winter home of northern migrants. By placing overwhelming stress on lowland forests to the exclusion of other habitats, conservationists ignore the fact that a large proportion of both resident and migrant bird species depend on nonforest habitats. Undue concentration of conservation efforts on lowland forests could result in a major *loss* in diversity among both migrants and residents as the other habitats quietly disappear.

Migrants versus Residents: Specific Comparisons

As a group, northern migrants are less tied to single habitats or regions than are resident species across the Neotropics. But migrants and residents also differ markedly in distribution: northern migrants are overwhelmingly more diverse in the northern Neotropics, while resident birds reach peak diversities near the equator. Few migrants inhabit montane forests, where resident birds not only abound but reach peak levels of endemism.

The Gulf-Caribbean Slope (GCS) of Central America stands out as the region with greatest winter concentration and species richness of migrant passerines in the Neotropics. Rapid destruction and fragmentation of the forests in this region (Myers 1980; Sader and Joyce 1988) has drawn much attention to the plight of migrants there. A comparison of range and habitat use by the migrant and resident avifaunas could help guide conservation efforts in this vulnerable area.

Before launching into this analysis, however, we stress a point often overlooked in discussions about Nearctic migrants. These species constitute only a small portion of the overall avian diversity of the Neotropics (about 10%). Even in the Gulf-Caribbean Slope region, where Nearctic migrants have their highest number of species (219), the 691 species of residents dwarf the diversity of migrants.

Differences in geographic range and habitat specificity between resident and migrant passerines are less marked in the Gulf-Caribbean region than across the Neotropics as a whole, but the same trends exist (fig. 7.7). Migrants wintering in this region are more widespread than are residents. Among species that occur in primary forests (fig. 7.8), the proportion restricted to these habitats is much lower among migrants

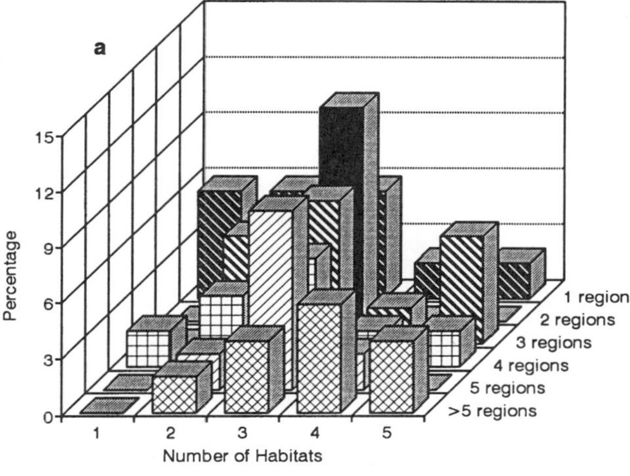

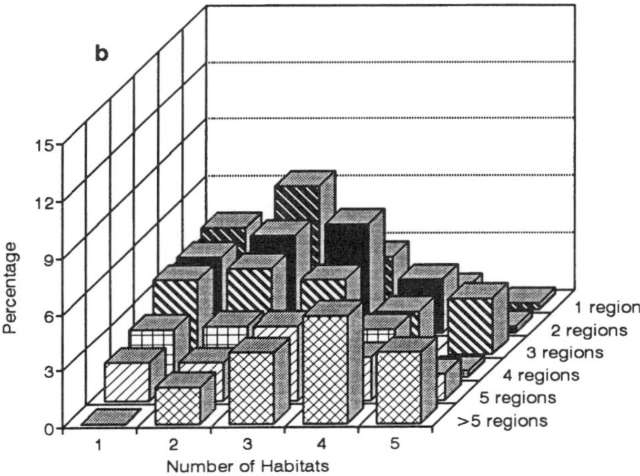

Figure 7.7 Number of zoogeographic regions and habitats occupied by birds of the Gulf-Caribbean Slope region: (a) Nearctic migrants (winter distribution); (b) all breeding species.

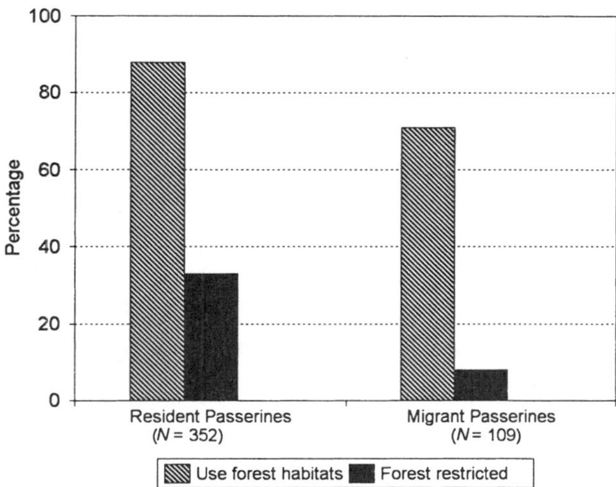

Figure 7.8 Proportion of resident and migrant passerines in the Gulf-Caribbean Slope region that use, or are restricted to, primary forests.

(12 of 112, or 11%) than among residents (117 of 352, or 33%).

Because the fates of warblers (Parulinae) on their wintering grounds is the focus of especially great concern (Hall 1984; Powell and Rappole 1986; Reed 1992), we compare geographic and ecological distributions of migrant and resident warblers. Again, the same patterns observed in other comparisons emerge. In both respects, migrant warblers (fig. 7.9a) are substantially more widespread than are resident warblers (fig. 7.9b). Indeed, resident Neotropical warblers show pronounced endemism, with 50 of 82 species (61%) occurring in only one zoogeographic region (fig. 7.9b). Furthermore, although migrant warblers are largely forest dependent (81% use humid forests as their primary habitat), they are much *less* restricted to primary forests than are resident warblers: only 26% of migrant warblers are confined to primary forests versus 56% of the residents.

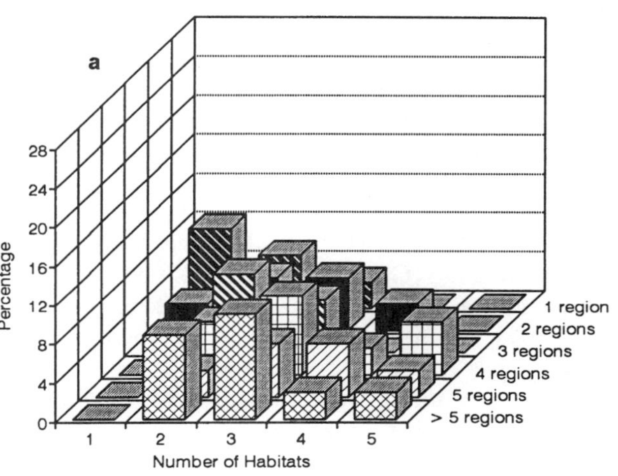

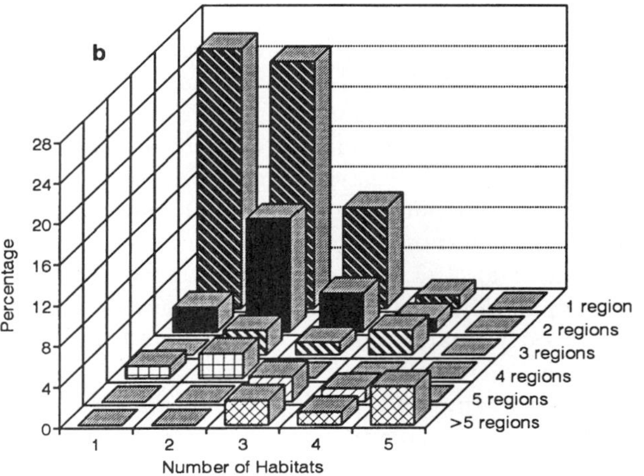

Figure 7.9 Number of zoogeographic regions and habitats occupied by Neotropical warblers (Parulinae): (a) Nearctic migrants (winter distribution); (b) all breeding species.

Which Nearctic Migrants Are Threatened?

As a group, migrants are more widespread, less habitat specific, and therefore less sensitive to habitat disturbance than are the much more diverse resident birds of the Neotropics. We cannot escape the general conclusion that, compared with resident tropical species, northern migrants are in substantially less danger of becoming extinct because of habitat loss, especially deforestation, in the tropics. This said, however, we do recognize that habitat destruction affects northern migrants unevenly. Just as with residents, the migrant species hardest hit by habitat loss are those with narrowly restricted geographic and ecological ranges, especially where these ranges coincide with the most aggressive conversion of tropical habitats. Vulnerable northern migrants fall into two classes: passerines that winter in Middle American forests, and shorebirds that migrate to the Argentine pampas.

Of the 422 Nearctic migrant bird species, only 50 are considered at risk (table 7.5). We exclude from further analyses the endangered Whooping Crane (*Grus americana*), today only casual in the Neotropics. We also exclude an additional 17 species whose breeding populations in the Neotropics are at risk, but whose migrant populations are not (table 7.5). Of the remaining 32 migrant species, most (24) are considered only vulnerable (i.e., ranked as CP-3 in database A or C) rather than endangered (CP-1) or threatened (CP-2). Surprisingly, only 10 of the 32 migrants at risk use forest as their primary habitat, and only 4 require lowland tropical forest (table 7.6).

For each of the 32 species at risk, we qualitatively assessed the relative threat posed by conditions on its wintering and breeding grounds (table 7.5). Only 7 species are threatened primarily on their wintering grounds (fig. 7.10). Two additional species seem affected equally on wintering and breeding grounds. Even these 9 candidates—4 warblers, 3 shorebirds, and 2 thrushes—have important caveats that render our assessment of tropical effects uncertain. Bachman's Warbler (*Vermivora bachmani*; probably extinct) must have suffered from extensive habitat destruction in Cuba, its only known wintering site (Terborgh 1989; Rappole et al. 1983). However, Remsen (1986) provides a plausible explanation for the demise of this species based primarily on loss of extensive canebrakes in North America. Worm-eating Warbler (*Helmitheros vermivorus*) and Swainson's Warbler (*Limnothlypis swainsonii*) are uncommon and declining. Both species winter exclusively in lowland forests where habitat destruction has been extensive—Worm-eating winters primarily in Central America and Swainson's in the Greater Antilles. However, both warblers have also lost extensive habitat in North America. Finally, as pointed out by Robbins, Fitzpatrick, and Hamel (1992), the ecologically specialized and rapidly declining Cerulean Warbler (*Dendroica cerulea*) may be affected equally by the destruction of forests on the Andean foothills and by the fragmentation of habitat on its breeding grounds.

Table 7.5 Nearctic Migrants at Risk, and the Primary Threats to Their Survival

Species	Conservation Priority	Threats[a]
Botaurus lentiginosus	3	+
Hydranassa rufescens	3	+
Aix sponsa	3	+
Anas fulvigula	3	+
Anas strepera	3	A, C
Aythya valisneria	3	A, C
Pandion haliaetus	3	D
Haliaeetus leucocephalus	3	D
Aquila chrysaetos	3	C, D
Falco peregrinus	3	D
Grus americana	1	A, B
Grus canadensis	3	+
Rallus limicola	3	+
Laterallus jamaicensis	2	+
Charadrius melodus	2	A
Charadrius montanus	3	A, B
Limosa fedoa	3	A
Limosa haemastica	3	B
Numenius americanus	3	A
Numenius borealis	1	C, B
Bartramia longicauda	3	A, B
Catoptrophorus semipalmatus	3	+
Tryngites subruficollis	3	B
Sterna antillarum	3	A
Sterna dougalli	3	D
Columba leucocephala	3	A
Asio flammeus	3	+
Nephoecetes niger	3	+
Anthus spragueii	3	A, B
Catharus bicknelli	3	B
Hylocichla mustelina	3	E, B
Sitta canadensis	3	+
Cistothorus (platensis) stellaris	3	+
Regulus calendula	3	+
Calcarius mccownii	3	A, B
Ammodramus bairdii	3	A, B
Ammodramus savannarum	3	+
Spiza americana	3	E, B
Vermivora bachmani	1	B, A
Vermivora chrysoptera	3	F, A
Vermivora crissalis	2	A
Dendroica cerulea	3	B, A
Dendroica chrysoptera	2	A
Dendroica kirtlandii	1	A
Limnothlypis swainsoni	3	B, A
Helmitheros vermivorus	3	B, A
Vireo atricapillus	2	E
Vireo bellii	3	E
Icterus (galbula) abeillei	3	+
Icterus (spurius) fuertesi	3	+

[a] A = breeding habitat loss or restriction; B = wintering habitat loss or restriction; C = hunting or shooting; D = environmental toxins; E = cowbird parasitism; F = competitive interactions; + = threats to Neotropical breeding populations.

Table 7.6 Primary Winter Habitat of Threatened or Vulnerable (CP-1, 2, or 3) Nearctic Migrants

Habitat	Habitat Code	Primary Habitat
Mangroves	F14	1
Salt marshes	A2	3
Marine waters, coastal beaches	A3–4, A11–12	8
Freshwater marshes	A1	
Lakes and streams	A6–9	3
Lowland scrub	N1	2
Montane scrub	N2	1
Grasslands	N5–10	11
Deciduous forests	F7	1
Lowland evergreen forests	F1	5
Montane forests	F4	2
Pine or pine-oak forests	F10, F11	4
Second-growth habitats	F15, N13–14	3

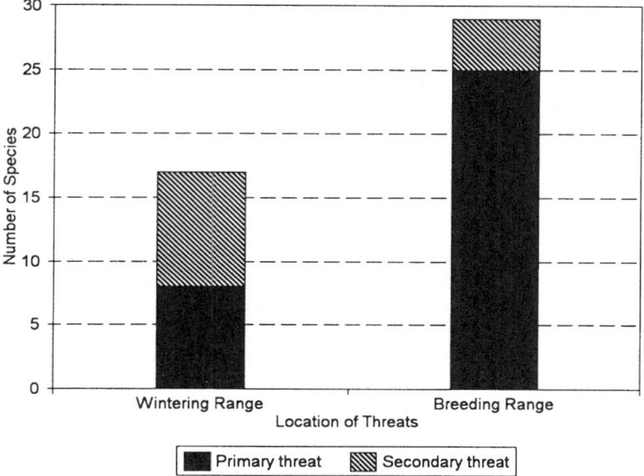

Figure 7.10 Location of threats to northern migrants of conservation concern.

Bicknell's Thrush (*Catharus bicknelli*), only recently recognized as a distinct species (Ouellet 1993), is at risk because of its small wintering range. The bird is known only from the island of Hispaniola, and its status in winter is virtually unknown. Continued deforestation in Hispaniola places the species at risk. Meanwhile the Wood Thrush (*Hylocichla mustelina*), although still common, is apparently declining (Robbins et al. 1989). It faces serious threats on both its wintering and its breeding grounds. It winters in lowland forests—almost exclusively the interior of primary forests—of Central America, where habitat loss is severe. In the breeding grounds, it is greatly affected by forest fragmentation, which has resulted in high rates of predation and nest parasitism (Robinson 1992).

Three shorebirds, rare or uncommon today, breed in the Arctic and winter primarily in the grasslands of southern South America. Eskimo Curlew (*Numenius borealis*) was driven to the brink of extinction primarily by market hunting in North America at the end of the previous century and has not recovered. Hudsonian Godwit (*Limosa haemastica*) and Buff-breasted Sandpiper (*Tryngites subruficollis*) also were once much more abundant and have failed to recover since the ban on shorebird hunting in North America. Wintering shorebirds, including these three species, abound in the Argentine pampas (Myers 1980), but the native habitats on these wintering grounds are disappearing. We speculate that conversion of both wet grasslands and upland pampas into rice and grain fields could be limiting these three species during winter. We stress, however, that little attention has been paid to this possibility, especially compared with the presumed plight of forest-inhabiting migrants farther north. The role of habitat loss and resource limitation among the shorebirds in the pampas is an ecological and conservation question badly in need of study.

Two recent assessments of relative vulnerability among Nearctic migrants that winter in the Neotropics deserve mention here. Reed (1992) examined the susceptibility of 57 species of warblers and vireos to extinction on both wintering and breeding grounds, based on a classification scheme for rarity (Rabinowitz 1981; Rabinowitz, Cairns, and Dillon 1986) using range size, habitat specificity, and population size. Reed concluded that few migrant species were highly susceptible on their wintering grounds and that when vulnerability differed between breeding grounds and wintering grounds, it was more often higher on the breeding grounds. Our classifications of the same species (table 7.5) support Reed's conclusion that problems in the wintering habitat are rarely as serious as problems in the north.

Morton (1992) estimated the vulnerability of 37 forest-dwelling migrants scattered across nine families based on four features of their winter ecology and distribution: winter range size, winter territoriality or mixed flock attendance, foraging specialization, and tendency to use secondary habitats. He scored each factor on a scale from 0 to 5, and any bird with a score of 12 or more (of a possible 20) Morton judged "highly vulnerable to continued tropical deforestation." Of the 37 migrants analyzed, 20 species scored 12 or higher.

Morton's implication that over half of all forest-dwelling migrants are imminently threatened by tropical deforestation is extremely misleading. The most obvious flaw in his analysis is that he weighted all the factors equally. Range size and tolerance of secondary habitats are much more important in determining vulnerability than are the two behavioral variables. Moreover, unlike Reed (1992), Morton incorporated no factor reflecting population density or rarity, which clearly plays a role as habitat area is lost. Most important, in a similar analysis applied to tropical *residents*, most score as high as or higher than the migrants. Not a single Nearctic migrant has a score of 20 on Morton's scale, but hundreds of tropical resident species do. For example, Checker-throated Antwren (*Myrmotherula fulviventris*), a dead-leaf specialist that lives in undergrowth of humid lowland forest of southern Central America and the Chocó, scores 20 on Morton's scale. However, we consider this species of low conservation priority (CP-4), the ICBP *Red Data Book* (Collar et al. 1992) does not treat it as even "near-threatened," and Hilty (1985) does not place it on his list of Colombian birds that have undergone serious population declines. This and countless similar examples convince us that Morton's scale provides no meaningful or objective measure of vulnerability among migrants. Rather, we contend that both ecological and geographic characteristics of migrants make them much less vulnerable than residents to tropical habitat alteration.

We remain convinced that the main threats to northern migrants occur on their breeding ranges. Habitat destruction on the wintering grounds certainly affects certain species, but only a handful of these are currently threatened. Furthermore, most migrants that are currently at risk winter not in Neotropical forests, but in grasslands and aquatic habitats—especially freshwater lakes and marshes. Sadly, these habitats receive far less attention than do forests, even from conservation groups expressing concern over North American migrants on their wintering grounds.

Should the Needs of Migratory Birds Set Overall Conservation Priorities?

Although no consensus exists on this point, evidence from breeding bird censuses suggests that populations of Nearctic migrants do appear to be declining somewhat more than those of resident North American species (e.g., Robbins et al. 1989; but see conflicting data in Hussell, Mather, and Sinclair 1992). Interestingly, Hagan et al. (1992) found the most significant declines among migrants that winter in southeastern North America, not the Neotropics. It is true that migrants face a harsh journey twice a year, encounter habitat alteration and destruction at both ends of the trip, and face the problem of recolonizing each end of their "global home range" each year. However, any conclusion that tropical habitat conversion is causing widespread declines among North American birds is premature at best.

Specifically, the recent focus on tropical lowland deforestation as a cause of population declines among North American migrants is overemphasized. Migrant birds are more widespread than Neotropical residents, more tolerant of secondary habitats, and less restricted to primary forests. Because Nearctic migrants do not breed in the Neotropics, their resource demands in wintering habitats are lower than those of the local resident avifauna, many of which have their primary nesting periods while the winterers are present.

A focus on tropical deforestation as a principal threat to migrants has led the public, and even some scientists, to ignore (1) the enormously destructive effects of habitat alteration and fragmentation in the North American breeding ranges of many of these species (Terborgh 1989); (2) the importance of nonforest habitats for migrants in their wintering grounds (table 7.3); and (3) the importance of pine and pine-oak habitats, as opposed to lowland evergreen forests, for the majority of migrants restricted to primary forests in their wintering grounds (table 7.4).

Nonforest habitats, including grasslands and marshes, are vital to many species of migrants. Native grasslands are among the Western Hemisphere's most threatened habitats, both in the Neotropics (chapter 5) and in North America. Their suitability for grazing and growing cereal crops has led to their overwhelming exploitation for agriculture. Aquatic habitats face additional threats from pollution and drainage.

We support the idea that Nearctic migrants in the tropics provide a publicity "hook." The plight of migrants has resulted in a call to arms among the North American public, who now contribute substantial energy and money to the effort to maintain tropical habitats. Without perceiving any effects on their own backyard birds, many North Americans might view tropical habitat destruction as an irrelevant problem. We further acknowledge the important observation that some species of Nearctic migrants, even if not already declining, may begin to decline in the future because of tropical habitat alteration going on today (Terborgh 1989).

This said, we advocate viewing Nearctic migrants primarily as participating elements of native *tropical* communities, not as a separate group of besieged birds. Concern for northern migrants should not drive tropical conservation efforts. This concern would make us focus on the wrong habitats, and even on some of the right habitats for the wrong reasons. If habitat destruction continues unabated in the Neotropics, entire biological communities will have been destroyed. With the loss of these communities, uncountable losses of Neotropical biodiversity will ensue, potentially including the loss of hundreds of species of resident tropical birds. When these first extinction waves arrive, they are unlikely to include *any* North American migrant birds. Besides forming only a small portion of these tropical communities, migrants winter disproportionately in only a few parts of the Neotropics and are buffered by their broad habitat tolerance. Conservation efforts in the tropics must resist the temptation to follow the migratory pathways of birds, and instead focus on the entire range of biological communities.

8 Austral and Intratropical Bird Migration in the Neotropics

Synopsis

In southern South America, austral migrants seasonally move northward in what mirrors the more familiar southward migration of North American species. The number of these austral migrants is about half that of North American migrants. Austral migrants differ from their northern counterparts in several ways: they migrate over shorter distances (fewer than 15% reach Amazonia); they are dominated by different taxonomic groups (mainly flycatchers, ducks, and emberizine finches); and proportionately fewer migrants are from higher latitudes.

Austral migrants share the same features that place northern migrants at relatively low risk: wide geographic range in winter, broad habitat tolerance, and frequent use of disturbed habitats. The single exception is an assemblage of austral migrants that winters in the native grasslands of Central South America. Rapid disappearance of these grasslands (chapter 5) threatens migrants and residents alike.

Smaller-scale regional movements of birds are common in some areas and among some groups in the Neotropics. In Middle America and southeastern Brazil, seasonal elevational movements of many frugivores and nectarivores are a prominent feature in montane bird communities. These species are at increased risk because deforestation has been much more severe in the lowlands than in the mountains. Other regional movements exist, but most are poorly documented. A suite of birds that respond to erratic and rare bamboo flowering is at risk as forest destruction and fragmentation make such flowering less common and less predictable.

About 237 species of nonpelagic birds (databases E and H in part 4) are known to move northward during the austral winter. This number will likely increase to over 250 species as our knowledge improves. Some important studies presenting relevant data include Humphrey et al. (1970), Willis (1979b, 1988), Sick (1985), Fjeldså and Krabbe (1990), Davis (1993), and Hayes, Scharf, and Ridgely (1994). A recent overview of the timing, extent, and geography of austral migration is Chesser (1994).

Following the same format we used for Nearctic migrants in the Neotropics (chapter 7), here we analyze patterns of geographic range and habitat use by austral migrants and evaluate the threats they face. We also compare patterns of austral and northern migrants and explore some potential conservation problems tied to seasonal migration. These analyses are based on two migrant databases in part 4. Database E lists austral migrants that occupy new zoogeographic regions, habitats, or elevational ranges in winter. Database H lists austral migrants that do not use new regions or habitats but leave portions of their breeding range to winter within the remainder. Additional details on these databases are found in the Guide to the Databases in part 4.

Geographic Distribution and Habitat Use

Of the 237 austral migrants (excluding seabirds that winter in pelagic waters), 114 (48%) reach their southern breeding limit in Patagonia or the southern Andes and another 105 (44%) breed only as far south as the chaco or pampas of northern Argentina, while 13 (5%) reach only as far south as the Atlantic forests of southern Brazil, northeastern Argentina, and eastern Paraguay. Of the 5 remaining species, 4—Slaty Elaenia (*Elaenia strepera*), Subtropical Doradito (*Pseudocolopteryx acutipennis*), Western Slaty Thrush (*Turdus nigriceps*), and Dusky-capped Flycatcher (*Myiarchus tuberculifer*)—withdraw northward from the humid Andean forests of northern Argentina, and one, Gray Gull (*Larus modestus*), moves north along the Pacific coast from northern Chile to Peru and Ecuador. Most species leave their southern breeding grounds in February or March and return in September or October.

In sharp contrast to the many Nearctic birds that

leave temperate regions for tropical wintering areas, most austral migrants do not winter at tropical latitudes. Instead they winter in temperate South America. Few austral migrants embark on long northward movements: only 32 migrate as far north as Amazonia, no more than 14 migrate north of the Amazon basin, and no species regularly winters north of Costa Rica or the southern Lesser Antilles. The full extent of migratory movements from southern South America is difficult to document, however, because more than two-thirds of the species of austral migrants (159 species) move into areas already occupied by resident populations of conspecifics (database H).

Like Nearctic migrants, austral migrants show a pattern of wide distribution and limited habitat specificity on their wintering grounds (fig. 8.1; compare fig. 7.4). As discussed earlier, this pattern generally renders species less susceptible to the effects of habitat degradation. On their wintering grounds, austral migrants are roughly evenly split among forest, aquatic, and open habitats (table 8.1).

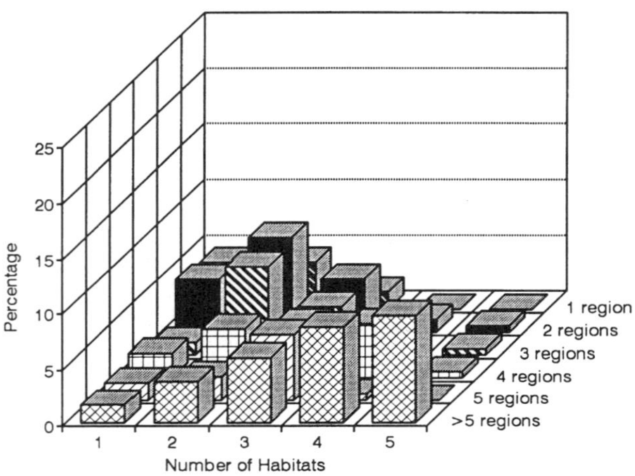

Figure 8.1 Number of zoogeographic regions and habitats occupied by austral migrants (winter distribution).

Table 8.1 Primary Winter Habitat of Austral Migrants

Habitat	Habitat Code	Primary Habitat
Marine waters, coastal beaches	A3–4, A11–12	15
Freshwater marshes	A1	32
Lakes and streams	A6–9	14
Lowland scrub	N1	20
Montane scrub	N2	14
Grasslands	N5–10	40
Gallery forests, riparian thickets	F8, N11	6
Deciduous forests	F7	11
Lowland evergreen forests	F1–3	39
Montane forests	F4, F5	14
Temperate forests	F9	6
Second-growth habitats	F15, N13–14	26

Austral Migrants: Comparisons with Neotropical Residents and Nearctic Migrants

Some patterns displayed by austral migrants differ from those of Nearctic migrants. Three of the most striking differences are distance traveled between breeding grounds and wintering grounds, taxonomic makeup of the migrants, and proportion of the avifauna that is migratory along the latitudinal gradient.

Nearly all of the 32 species of austral migrants that winter as far north as the Amazon River breed no farther south than northern Argentina. By contrast, 18 species of northern migrants winter primarily in southern South America, and nearly one-quarter of all northern migrants regularly winter south of Amazonia. Most of these extremely long-distance migrants are shorebirds. The 10,000 kilometer migration of such birds as Hudsonian Godwit (*Limosa haemostica*) and Buff-breasted Sandpiper (*Tryngites subruficollis*) finds no parallel among the austral migrants. Among northern migrants, over half winter in ranges entirely disjunct from their breeding ranges. Among austral migrants, only 14 species (7%) have completely disjunct summer and winter ranges.

The family composition of Nearctic versus austral migrants differs substantially (fig. 8.2). Almost one-third of austral migrants belong to a single avian family, the Tyrannidae (New World flycatchers). Only two other families or subfamilies, the Anatidae (ducks and geese) and Emberizinae (sparrows and finches), include many austral migrants. In contrast, the Nearctic migrant contingent includes several families or subfamilies with many migrants, such as Parulinae (wood-warblers), Scolopacidae (sandpipers), and Laridae (gulls and terns), along with the same three families that dominate the austral migrants. The largest group of

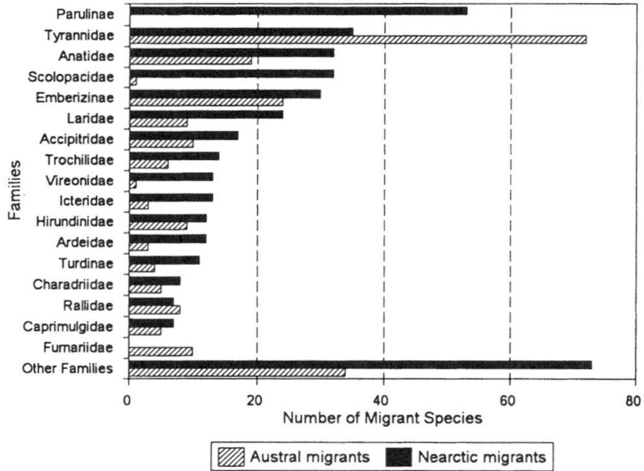

Figure 8.2 Number of migrant species by family in Nearctic and austral migrants.

northern migrants (Parulinae, wood-warblers) is completely unrepresented among austral migrants.

Taxonomic differences between Nearctic and austral migrants primarily reflect differences in the avifaunas of northern North America versus southern South America. We detect no tendency for members of a particular family to be migratory in one hemisphere and not in the other. Birds that depend on open water (e.g., ducks and shorebirds) or on active insects (e.g., flycatchers and vireos) are almost all migratory in both north and south temperate regions. These ecological groups form the bulk of all migrants.

Within northern temperate regions, the proportion of breeding species that migrate shows a strong latitudinal gradient, dropping from about 70% near the Arctic Circle to virtually zero at the Tropic of Cancer (Tramer 1974; Slud 1976). A similar but considerably less dramatic gradient occurs in the southern temperate regions of South America. The percentage of migrants drops from 50% in Tierra del Fuego (Humphrey et al. 1970) to about 10% at the Tropic of Capricorn in São Paulo (Willis 1988; Stotz, pers. obs.).

Conservation Status of Austral Migrants

As with Nearctic migrants, the combination of extensive wintering ranges and low habitat specificity among austral migrants means that, as a group, these birds are not particularly threatened by changes on their wintering grounds. Only 25% of austral migrants use humid forests during winter, and most species are tolerant of secondary habitats, even on their breeding grounds. For example, in remnant forest patches in São Paulo, Willis (1979b) found that migrant bird species were more likely to persist in the face of forest fragmentation than were resident members of the same ecological guild.

Despite the positive outlook for austral migrants as a whole, for a few the outlook is grim. At particular risk is the assemblage of species that rely on grassland habitats. South American native grasslands are seriously threatened everywhere (see chapter 5). Intense habitat destruction menaces several bird species (e.g., *Sporophila* spp.) at both ends of their migration. These species mostly breed in the marshes and grasslands of northern Argentina and winter in the grasslands of central Brazil. In both regions, extensive conversion of marshes and native grasslands into agricultural land threaten to obliterate these species.

Research is urgently needed on the winter distributions and habitat use of austral migrants, many of which are very poorly known. For example, Black-bellied Seedeater (*Sporophila melanogaster*) is a fairly common breeding species in marshes in the southern Brazilian highlands, where its breeding habitat seems secure, but its wintering range and habitat remain uncertain. Recent evidence (Ridgely and Tudor 1989; Parker, pers. obs.) suggests that this species winters in the disappearing campo grasslands of central Brazil. If true, *S. melanogaster* instantly becomes a species of immediate concern rather than one that is relatively safe. Many other examples exist and together define an important priority for ornithological fieldwork throughout South America.

Regional Movements

Besides conspicuous, continental-scale migrations, there are many smaller-scale, seasonal movements of populations within the Neotropics. In general these movements are poorly documented and not yet understood. Evidence for local migrations consists mainly of reports that particular species are seasonally absent from a region or site. In the notes to database A (part 4), we point out species that seem to undergo these movements and describe their movements to the extent they are known.

Best documented are seasonal movements up and down elevational gradients. Stiles (1988) has found downslope movements in the nonbreeding season for more than 20% of the montane avifauna in Costa Rica. These elevational migrants are primarily frugivores or nectarivores. Presumably they are responding to predictable seasonal changes in resource availability. Moving out of severely cold and dry mountains, they spend the winter in the warmer, lower elevations where food may be more abundant.

Stiles suggests that elevational movements on a similar scale may exist in the Andes but have gone unnoticed because most fieldwork there coincides with the North American summer. We disagree. Beginning in the mid-1960s, considerable Andean fieldwork, with extensive bird collections, has spanned all months of the year. We doubt that forest birds of the tropical Andes could undergo the extensive elevational movements Stiles noted in Costa Rica without being detected. A few Andean species do make prominent seasonal elevational movements (e.g., the hummingbird Mountain Velvetbreast, *Lafresnaya lafresnaya*). However, our own observations at many elevations and seasons in eastern Peru convince us that such movements are the exception. Probably the rarity of elevational movements in the tropical Andes reflects smaller seasonal variation in climatic conditions closer to the equator.

Preliminary data from the mountains of São Paulo (Stotz, unpubl.) suggest a pattern of elevational movements remarkably like that Stiles found in Costa Rica. About 20% of the avifauna seems to make elevational movements. Frugivorous and nectarivorous species predominate among these elevational migrants.

As Stiles notes, movement up- and downslope may render some species more susceptible to population declines resulting from deforestation, because habitat loss at either end of the elevational gradient would hurt the population. Although latitudinal migrants generally have wide distributions and low habitat specificity, elevational migrants in both Costa Rica and southeastern Brazil include a disproportionate number of restricted-range and forest-dependent species. Species with these attributes almost certainly are at greater risk than others, even without elevational movements. Those that migrate elevationally may be the most threatened of the montane-breeding species, since in both Costa Rica and Brazil lowland forests have undergone much more rapid and thorough destruction than have montane forests.

A small but distinctive set of Neotropical birds depends on bamboo seeds. These specialists apparently travel great distances between stands of flowering or seeding bamboo. The characteristic irregularity with which certain bamboo species produce seeds (Janzen 1976) means that even in their pristine condition Neotropical forests presented a patchy resource for these bird species. Deforestation has greatly exacerbated this pattern and threatens to eliminate certain species because it dramatically increases the distance between resource patches. Among the species most at risk are certain parrots (e.g., Lined Parakeet, *Bolborhynchus lineola*), doves (e.g., Maroon-breasted Ground-Dove, *Claravis mondetoura*, and Purple-winged Ground-Dove, *C. godefrida*), and various emberizine finches, including Slate-colored Seedeater (*Sporophila schistacea*), Buffy-fronted Seedeater (*S. frontalis*), Temminck's Seedeater (*S. falcirostris*), and both species of *Amaurospiza* and *Haplospiza*. Other than *Sporophila schistacea*, these birds do not appear to tolerate deforested habitats. In eastern Brazil, *Claravis godefrida* is already endangered, and *Sporophila frontalis* and *S. falcirostris* apparently have declined, presumably because of forest destruction and fragmentation.

Some lowland species make seasonal (or irregular) movements that are not part of a general latitudinal migration (i.e., neither "northern" nor "austral") and not connected with elevational shifts. Azure Gallinule (*Porphyrula flavirostris*) provides a remarkable, well-documented example (Remsen and Parker 1990). This species apparently breeds in marshes along the Amazon and in the Guianas roughly from May to July. It then leaves, at least from the Guianas and the eastern part of Amazonia, moving southward to spend the austral summer as a nonbreeder in the marshes of southwestern Amazonia and the pantanal region of Brazil and Paraguay. Other examples include species such as Greater Ani (*Crotophaga major*) and Swallow-Tanager (*Tersina viridis*), which are absent from much of Amazonia during the local dry season. Where these populations go, and why, remains unknown.

Few species known to make local or regional movements in South America currently are at risk, other than those tied to bamboo flowering. However, any species with low tolerance of habitat disruption is likely to be more susceptible to forest fragmentation if it also undergoes seasonal movements. This susceptibility underscores the importance of improving our knowledge of movement patterns of birds throughout the tropics. Frugivorous and nectarivorous species appear to be among the most mobile of tropical birds. Seasonal movements of these birds presumably influence community composition and ecosystem function through their roles as pollinators and seed dispersers. The loss of these mobile, ecologically important birds could have far-reaching effects on the structure and diversity of the plant communities throughout the Neotropics.

PART

3

Priorities for Protection

9 Guiding Principles for Conservation in the Neotropics

Synopsis

Goals of biological conservation should be to protect natural communities, preserving as closely as possible their natural distributions and maintaining the biological, ecological, and evolutionary processes within them. Using bird communities, we develop a set of criteria to establish site-selection priorities for conservation on both global and in-country scales. Principal attention should be devoted to the most vulnerable communities, so that they may be saved before they become irreversibly degraded.

We recommend the following strategies for setting global priorities: (1) Focus on assemblages of endemics and habitat specialists. Bird species with limited geographical and ecological distributions face greater risks than do more widespread species. Centers of endemism for birds tend to correspond with endemism in other taxa. (2) Focus on distinct communities rather than on sheer number of species. Too much attention devoted to areas with the highest species richness (tropical humid forests) narrows the scope of conservation to a small subset of biological communities. This would leave some much more imperiled biological communities with little or no protection. (3) Preserve ecotones, tension zones, and gradients. Such areas protect two or more distinct ecosystems, contain species that specialize on transition zones, and supply the needs of many species that move between different habitats seasonally. (4) Preserve genetic and geographic diversity. Geographic variability of species is an important feature of biological diversity. Maintaining a full range of attributes across the species' ranges helps preserve natural processes within and among populations.

Within-country conservation priorities must be relevant to the specific political unit, but they also should reflect the overriding importance of global considerations. We recommend the following: (1) Protect in-country areas of endemism. Suites of endemics that are nearly or completely restricted to a particular country depend solely on that country for their survival. They can be protected nowhere else. These endemic communities should be viewed as national treasures of uppermost priority among the country's biological resources. (2) Protect threatened and vulnerable communities. Most ecosystems range over more than a single country, but any globally threatened community should represent a high conservation priority in the country where it occurs. (3) Protect suites of habitat-restricted species. These species generally run the highest risk of becoming rare or being extirpated. (4) Preserve ecotones, gradients, and zoogeographic transitions, as explained above. (5) Protect peripheral isolates if they represent truly discrete, geographically isolated populations. Such isolates contribute to the genetic diversity of a species. In contrast, widespread species whose distribution barely overlaps the border of a country do not warrant special conservation attention.

Biological diversity consists of both individual units (species) and the processes and interactions that interweave them. These processes evolved and persist in the form of functioning ecological communities. Only these communities can provide all the resources necessary to support individual species. When the processes and interactions disintegrate, no amount of human intervention can protect certain species from decline and disappearance. It follows that communities, rather than individual species, should be the focus of conservation action. *The goals of biological conservation are to protect natural communities, preserve as closely as possible their native distributions, and maintain the natural processes that brought them about.*

Conservation involves more than preventing endangered species from becoming extinct. Of equal importance is preventing common species from becoming uncommon. The politics and economics of conservation often focus too narrowly, concentrating on exceedingly rare or rapidly declining species. As discussed earlier (chapter 1), the long-term fallacy of this narrow focus is that it diverts attention and resources toward a tiny fraction of the native biota. Almost always, a larger but lower-profile list of gradually declining species is ignored.

At present, remarkably few bird species in the Neotropics are on the brink of extinction. Most of these endangered species have declined because of habitat destruction (table 9.1). With steady loss of habitat in the late twentieth century, many species and communities in the New World tropics are *becoming* rare and fragmented. The goals of this book, and of our conservation philosophy in general, are to identify the species and communities most likely to become endangered and funnel efforts into preventing that from happening.

Table 9.1 Critically Endangered Birds of the Neotropics, and Primary Reasons for Their Decline

Species	Main Threats
Pterocnemia (pennata) tarapacensis	HD[a]
Crypturellus (erythropus) saltuarius	HD
Nothoprocta kalinowskii	HD (small range)
Podilymbus gigas	Hybridization
Podiceps (nigricollis) andinus	HD (small range)
Podiceps taczanowskii	Pollution, drainage
Oceanodroma macrodactyla	Introduced mammals
Mergus octosetaceus	HD
Leptodon forbesi	HD
Chondrohierax (uncinatus) wilsonii	??
Harpyhaliaetus coronatus	??
Buteo ridgwayi	HD
Penelope albipennis	HD, hunting
Penelope perspicax	HD
Aburria jacutinga	HD
Oreophasis derbianus	HD
Crax alberti	HD
Crax blumenbachii	HD, hunting
Crax (mitu) mitu	HD
Colinus (virginianus) ridgwayi	HD
Odontophorus strophium	HD
Rallus antarcticus	HD
Cyanolimnas cerverai	HD
Columba inornata	HD, hunting
Zenaida graysoni	Introduced mammals
Claravis godefrida	HD (bamboo)
Anodorhynchus glaucus	HD
Anodorhynchus hyacinthinus	Pet trade, HD
Anodorhynchus leari	HD, pet trade
Cyanopsitta spixii	Pet trade
Ognorhynchus icterotis	HD
Touit melanonota	HD, poorly known
Hapalopsittaca (amazonina) fuertesi	HD
Amazona brasiliensis	HD
Amazona guildingii	HD, pet trade
Amazona imperialis	HD, pet trade, hunting
Amazona pretrei	HD
Amazona versicolor	HD, hunting
Amazona vittata	HD, introduced birds
Siphonorhis americanus	Introduced mammals
Glaucis dohrnii	HD
Phaethornis (superciliosus)margareittae	HD
Heliangelus zusi	HD (small range)?
Dryocopus galeatus	HD
Campephilus imperialis	HD
Campephilus principalis	HD
Xiphocolaptes franciscanus	HD
Philydor novaesi	HD
Myrmotherula erythronotos	HD?
Terenura sicki	HD
Pyriglena atra	HD
Rhopornis ardesiaca	HD
Grallaria alleni	HD
Grallaria milleri	HD
Merulaxis stresemanni	HD
Phylloscartes ceciliae	HD
Phylloscartes lanyoni	HD
Phylloscartes roquettei	HD
Hemitriccus furcatus	HD (bamboo)
Calyptura cristata	HD
Cotinga maculata	HD
Ferminia cerverai	HD
Mimodes graysoni	Introduced mammals
Ramphocinclus brachyurus	HD
Atlapetes pallidiceps	HD
Nemosia rourei	HD?
Buthraupis aureocincta	HD?
Leucopeza semperi	HD?, introduced mammals?
Carduelis cucullata	Pet trade, HD?
Corvus leucognaphalus	HD?

[a] HD = habitat destruction.

Threatened communities should dictate conservation priorities. This means that conservationists and lawmakers must focus on the biological communities most vulnerable to destruction. In the Neotropics, such communities can be identified by the status of their birds. In the context of database A, we define vulnerable communities as those containing the largest numbers or proportions of bird species classified as conservation priority 1 ("endangered"), 2 ("threatened"), or 3 ("vulnerable"). These vulnerable assemblages—not the individual species—are the flags that mark habitats and regions around the New World tropics in need of immediate conservation action.

Global versus In-Country Priorities

Conservation priorities depend in part on setting a proper geographic scope. Priorities may differ depending on whether the agency, private or governmental, acts for an international effort with global concerns or for an individual political unit such as a state or country.

The priorities we spell out below under "Global Priorities" focus on conservation needs across the Neotropics as a whole. We recognize, however, that each country's conservation priorities and actions must be tailored to that country's own biological communities and to the specific realities and threats facing those communities within the country. In the second section, "In-Country Priorities," we suggest how an individual country may generate its unique set of conservation priorities. We also indicate how these would differ from global ones.

Our global and local recommendations are drawn directly from data in databases A and B (part 4). As we stated in chapter 1 and expand briefly below, we assume that diversity, ecological specialization, and endemism in bird communities overlap broadly with those in most other terrestrial organisms. Therefore, although we base our recommendations on birds—which are comparatively easy to observe and identify—the regions we specify should provide effective protection to the diversity of plants and other animals as well.

Global Priorities

To minimize the loss of biological diversity and ecological processes globally, without reference to political boundaries, several guiding principles emerge from our study of avian distributions in the Neotropics.

1. Focus on Endemics and Habitat Specialists

We agree with the many authors who advocate using concentrations of both endemic species and habitat specialists as flags for protected areas (e.g., J. M. Diamond 1985a; Gentry 1986a; Terborgh and Winter 1983). For purposes of this book, we define *endemic species* as those found in only one of the twenty-two zoogeographic regions of the Neotropics. Many endemics are categorized further as *locally endemic*, because they are confined to a single "subregion" (see Guide to the Databases) within the larger zoogeographic region.

Besides their great intrinsic interest as evolutionary units with peculiar characteristics (Kruckeberg and Rabinowitz 1985), endemic species are of special importance in conservation for at least five strategic reasons. We list these here with reference to birds, then discuss them briefly:

- endemic species constitute a significant portion of the avifauna—saving endemics means saving many species;
- endemics tend to be habitat restricted—they are less capable of surviving environmental alteration than are widespread species;
- small geographic ranges and a tendency toward specialization result in a more rapid proportional decline in endemics than in widespread species as habitat is lost—endemics are overrepresented in lists of vulnerable and threatened species;
- many zones of endemism contain elevated species richness—judiciously located preserves, with suitable habitat to protect endemic species, will preserve most widespread species as well;
- endemic birds mark the locations of unique biotic communities—assemblages of endemic birds correlate with endemics of most other groups of organisms.

Numbers of endemics. Endemic species represent a significant component of the Neotropical avifauna. Of the 3,751 bird species that breed in the Neotropics, 1,600 (42.7%) occur in only one zoogeographic region (table 9.2). Because the twenty-two zoogeographic regions were defined in part around zones with unique fauna (see Guide to the Databases), none of them lack endemics: numbers range from 2 endemic breeding species in the Mexican Plateau up to 222 in the Northern Andes. Proportions of endemics making up the regional avifaunas range from 1.6% (2 endemics out of 122 species) in the Mexican Plateau to exactly 50% (125 out of 250) in the Greater Antilles (table 9.2). More than two-thirds of the bird species that are restricted to one zoogeographic region actually are confined to much smaller subregions (1,070 out of 1,600 endemics). Preserving the full diversity of birds (and thus habitats) in the Neotropics requires attention to every major geographic region within the realm.

Habitat restriction among endemics. Endemic bird species are significantly more likely to be habitat restricted than are widespread species (table 9.3; fig. 9.1). The mean number of habitats used by endemics is 1.9 (1.7 for subregion endemics), compared with 3.2 for widespread species (table 9.3).

The frequent association between narrow geographic range and ecological restriction or specialization has attracted attention from population biologists and biogeographers for decades (reviews by Kruckeberg and Rabinowitz 1985; Rabinowitz, Cairns, and Dillon 1986). This important pattern exists for a combination of reasons, some of which can be teased out by more detailed examination of database A. Full discussion of the topic is beyond our present scope, but it is important to note that the relationship holds in every habitat, forest or nonforest (table 9.4): *Throughout the Neotropics, concentrations of endemics contain a preponderance of ecologically restricted species.* These specialists make up the assemblages most likely to falter as habitats are altered and destroyed. Indeed, as shown below, some of these communities already have started to falter.

Vulnerability of endemics. Endemism, habitat specificity, and conservation status are tightly linked (fig. 9.1). Vulnerability of endemics to habitat loss offers a compelling reason for using them to guide conservation priorities. Of the 70 endangered species (CP-1) in the Neotropics, 59 (84.3%) are subregion endemics and 52 (74.3%) are restricted to a single habitat. Of 1,122

Table 9.2 Number of Bird Species, Endemics, Habitat-Restricted Endemics, and Vulnerable Species by Zoogeograpic Region

Region	Region Code	Total Species	Endemics	Habitat-Restricted Endemics	Endemics "at Risk" (CP-1, CP-2, CP-3)
Atlantic Forest	ATL	682	199 (0.29)[a]	76 (0.11)	141 (0.21)
Northern Andes	NAN	772	222 (0.29)	111 (0.15)	133 (0.17)
Central Andes	CAN	804	216 (0.27)	115 (0.14)	108 (0.13)
Central South America	CSA	645	112 (0.17)	56 (0.09)	67 (0.10)
Greater Antilles	GAN	250	125 (0.50)	22 (0.09)	56 (0.22)
Madrean Highlands	MAH	379	101 (0.27)	20 (0.05)	42 (0.11)
Gulf-Caribbean Slope	GCS	689	74 (0.11)	24 (0.03)	36 (0.05)
Southern Amazonia	AMS	892	79 (0.09)	60 (0.07)	34 (0.04)
Equatorial Pacific	EPC	289	73 (0.25)	20 (0.07)	33 (0.11)
Chiriquí-Darién Highlands	CDH	279	69 (0.25)	36 (0.13)	26 (0.09)
Northern Amazonia	AMN	896	76 (0.08)	56 (0.06)	21 (0.02)
Northern South America	NSA	652	41 (0.06)	11 (0.02)	19 (0.03)
Chocô Lowlands	CHO	401	24 (0.06)	14 (0.03)	19 (0.05)
Pacific Arid Slope	PAS	358	36 (0.10)	13 (0.04)	18 (0.05)
Lesser Antilles	LAN	110	24 (0.22)	7 (0.07)	16 (0.15)
Subtropical Pacific	STP	206	19 (0.10)	11 (0.06)	12 (0.06)
Baja-Sonora	BSR	239	18 (0.08)	10 (0.04)	8 (0.03)
Pampas	PAM	249	8 (0.03)	2 (0.01)	5 (0.02)
Southern Andes	SAN	197	23 (0.11)	16 (0.08)	5 (0.03)
Patagonia	PAT	182	22 (0.13)	13 (0.07)	4 (0.02)
Tepuis	TEP	142	36 (0.25)	21 (0.15)	2 (0.01)
Mexican Plateau	MPL	122	2 (0.02)	2 (0.02)	2 (0.02)
Total		3,751	1,599 (0.427)	716 (0.192)	807 (0.215)

Note: Regions are listed in decreasing order by number of endemics at risk.
Figures for endemics exclude *Popelairia letitiae,* known from two males from "Bolivia," which could be endemic to either the Central Andes (CAN) or Southern Amazonia (AMS).

[a]Number in parentheses gives proportion of total regional avifauna in class.

Table 9.3 Number of Habitats Occupied in Relation to Zoogeographic Range

Number of Zoogeographic Regions Occupied	Number of Species	Number of Habitats Occupied: 1	2	3	4	5	6	7	Mean Number of Habitats
1, subregion only	1,070	509	382	133	34	11	1	0	1.74
1, >1 subregion	530	208	216	78	26	1	1	0	1.87
2	936	337	338	176	67	16	2	0	2.03
3	380	63	129	125	50	13	0	0	2.53
4	223	39	68	56	40	16	4	0	2.72
5+	508	57	126	130	106	62	17	10	3.16
Mean number of regions		1.75	2.22	3.04	3.95	6.00	6.96	12.30	
Total	3,647	1,213	1,259	698	323	119	25	10	

Note: We excluded 104 species because, although they breed in the Neotropics, they also occur extralimitally as breeders (mostly in North America or on oceanic islands).

species ranked endangered, threatened, or vulnerable (CP-1, CP-2, or CP-3; table 9.5), 808 (72%) are endemic to a single zoogeographic region or subregion and 445 (39.7%) are both endemic *and* restricted to a single habitat. Subregion endemics are especially vulnerable: of the 1,070 endemics restricted to one subregion, 630 (58.8%) are endangered, threatened, or vulnerable (table 9.5).

In contrast to the preponderance of endemics among the threatened species, only 792 (31.2%) of the 2,540 species *not* considered at risk (table 9.5) are endemics, and only 272 (10.7%) are habitat-restricted endemics. Among the entire pool of 1,600 endemic species across the Neotropics, half (50.5%, N = 808) are ranked endangered, threatened, or vulnerable. In contrast, only 15.3% (N = 314) of the 2,047 species distributed in two or more zoogeographic regions are similarly ranked (table 9.5).

Ecological communities rich in local endemics have the lowest resilience to habitat loss. As habitats become fragmented or degraded, communities of limited geographic extent are bound to be the first to lose species. Endemic species have "nowhere else to turn." Because endemics have small ranges, the available habitat can

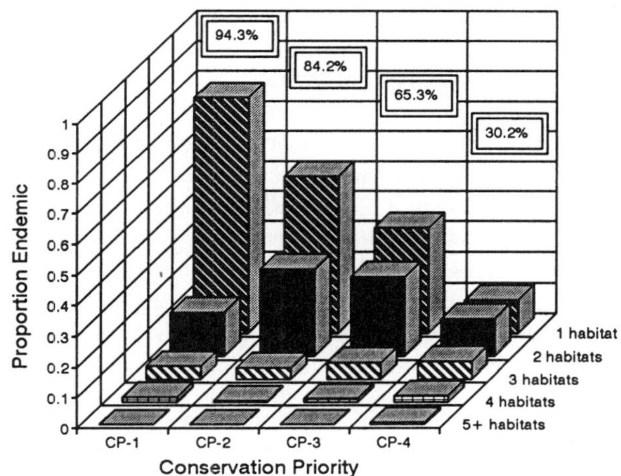

Figure 9.1 Relation of endemism and habitat specificity to ranking in conservation priority. Rear grid shows the percentage of birds in the respective conservation priority class that are endemic to a single zoogeographic region.

be completely devastated more easily and rapidly than for species of more continental scale. The Atlantic Forests of Brazil present a case in point: this distinctive area of endemism contains a higher number and proportion of endangered species than any other in the Neotropics. Habitat fragmentation increases the risk of local extirpations for any species. For those with small ranges, local extirpations can annihilate a large proportion of the total population.

Centers of endemism and diversity. Endemics are the most vulnerable taxa in a region, but they coexist with many species that are more widespread or generalized. Properly designed habitat preserves that offer protection to endemics and specialists will automatically include a large and representative section of the total local diversity. Many of the centers of endemism across the Neotropics coincide with centers of elevated overall diversity (e.g., Cracraft 1985; Haffer 1974, 1990).

Endemic centers define the zoogeographic regions and subregions. For each center, it is important to protect large tracts of representative habitats, replete with the common as well as the rare species. Such reserves then will function as source pools for future communities, just as present-day communities have been shaped by history, chance, and the available species pools (Hubbell and Foster 1985). Focusing on suites of endemic species and ensuring their survival protects the less threatened species as well, and therefore the entire community (Wright and Hubbell 1983). The reverse, however, is not true.

Table 9.4 Endemism and Habitat Restriction among the Birds of the Principal Habitat Types of the Neotropics

Habitat	Habitat Code	Total Users	Endemics *N*	Endemics Habitat Restricted	Endemics Proportion Habitat Restricted	Nonendemics *N*	Nonendemics Habitat Restricted	Nonendemics Proportion Habitat Restricted
Forest								
Tropical lowland evergreen	F1	1,410	523	197	0.377	887	209	0.235
Montane evergreen	F4	1,162	585	220	0.376	577	137	0.237
Elfin	F5	164	100	25	0.250	64	2	0.031
Tropical deciduous	F7	635	275	58	0.211	360	6	0.017
Gallery	F8	473	114	10	0.088	359	2	0.006
Tropical flooded evergreen	F2	166	17	8	0.471	149	14	0.094
Nonforest								
Arid montane scrub	N2	265	77	31	0.403	188	9	0.048
Arid lowland scrub	N1	342	121	29	0.240	221	12	0.054
Campo grassland	N5	68	17	7	0.412	51	2	0.039
Freshwater marsh	A1	187	29	12	0.414	158	43	0.272

Table 9.5 Conservation Priority in Relation to Zoogeographic Range

Number of Zoogeographic Regions Occupied	Number of Species	Conservation Priority 1	2	3	4	Mean CP
1, subregion only	1,070	59	199	372	440	3.11
1, >1 subregion	530	7	47	124	352	3.55
2	936	4	32	140	760	3.77
3	380	0	5	45	330	3.86
4	223	0	4	23	196	3.86
5+	508	0	3	43	452	3.82
Mean number of regions		1.06	1.24	1.70	3.01	
Total	3,647	70	290	747	2,540	

Note: We excluded 104 species because, although they breed in the Neotropics, they also occur extralimitally as breeders (mostly in North America or on oceanic islands).

Zones of overall biotic endemism. Although definitive data and comparative studies remain woefully meager, zones of endemism for birds appear to coincide with those for other organisms across the Neotropics. The reality and cause of some of these coincident patterns are still debated (e.g., within the Amazon basin: Connor 1988; Endler 1982; Gentry 1986a; Haffer 1974, 1985, 1990; Prance 1982). However, it is clear that the twenty-two different zoogeographic regions and fifty subregions we recognize have had separate evolutionary histories. Speciation patterns reflect these separate histories in all organisms, not just birds. In this respect, birds are coarse-grain indicators of centers of endemism compared with certain plant families (Gentry 1986a), and birds are far less prone to endemism than are many groups of insects. Yet because no group of animals or plants is as thoroughly sampled as birds, none can serve as so reliable a beacon for unique centers of diversity across the Neotropics as a whole.

2. Preserve Communities over Species Numbers

In general, ensuring permanent protection for the maximum number of discrete communities also will protect the maximum number of species. However, trade-offs exist between protecting communities and protecting species numbers. As limited resources for conservation must be distributed among ever-growing arrays of threatened regions and habitats, local governments and international agencies might be forced to choose between suffering the loss of species or the loss of unique communities.

We strongly believe that protecting distinct biotic communities should rank above protecting the highest possible "species count." Examples from a global perspective might involve choosing between investing conservation dollars in small, highly endemic, and badly damaged ecosystems such as the Greater Antilles or the Brazilian cerrado and making an equivalent investment in the Amazon forest. The smaller, distinctive communities lack the enormous species diversity of higher-profile regions: small parks that could preserve outstanding examples of cloud forests on Hispaniola, or cerrado communities in central Brazil, or dry forests of western Ecuador would preserve species pools only a fraction as large as parks of equal size or cost in the Amazon (table 9.2). However, regions like the mountaintops of Hispaniola or the cerrados of Brazil soon will cease to exist as functional ecosystems unless emergency protection is initiated. These entire evolutionary complexes are in immediate peril.

3. Preserve Ecotones, Tension Zones, and Gradients

Ecosystems rarely consist of completely self-contained units. Instead, they interdigitate across ecotones, gradients, or mosaics, all reflecting underlying environmental transition. Such transition areas provide exceptional opportunities for conservation: single preserves can provide havens for exceptionally high diversity, by encompassing elements of two ecosystems along with their interactions.

Some species favor the edge or mosaic conditions that characterize these transition areas. Preserving environmental gradients such as watersheds, mountain slopes, and habitat mosaics at the junction of two or more major vegetation formations is a major global priority. Because such preservation is most easily done within single countries, we discuss the issue below in more detail as an important priority for country planners.

4. Preserve Genetic and Geographic Diversity

The extremely sedentary life history of many tropical birds, especially in the forest understory, makes them prone to local adaptation and differentiation (Wright 1943, 1978). In many widespread Amazonian species, for example, substantial differentiation occurs across large areas of seemingly continuous forest (Haffer and Fitzpatrick 1985). Even more remarkable is the recent discovery of species-level genetic differentiation among Amazonian populations, including some that had been considered to belong to the same subspecies (Cappella 1988 and unpubl.).

Many widespread species in the Neotropics occur in multiple, widely disjunct populations (e.g., Sharpbill, *Oxyruncus cristatus*, fig. 9.2; see also Chapman 1939),

Figure 9.2 Disjunct distribution of *Oxyruncus cristatus*.

which can even dwell in vastly different habitats or elevations. Some of these populations exhibit obvious morphological differences; others show subtle visible differences or none at all. It is now clear from an abundance of modern biochemical studies that whatever historical factors brought them about, today these separate populations are genetically isolated from one another. Regardless of our concept of "species," for the many hundreds of avian taxa that break up into thousands of disjunct populations, each population is currently on a distinct evolutionary track (McKitrick and Zink 1988).

Biological diversity consists of myriad separate evolutionary tracks and geographic variants. Even when conservation efforts focus on individual species rather than communities, a species is not "saved" when it exists in good numbers in only one place. To protect the full array of life, and to ensure continuing capacity for each population and species to change, representative populations must be protected throughout the species' entire range.

Most species share certain aspects of their ecological history with other species in their community. Therefore the process of seeking out and protecting isolated populations is not as onerous as it might seem. In the Neotropics, disjunct populations of numerous polytypic birds are distributed among many of the same areas that hold high numbers of endemic species. Haffer (1974) even used this observation to argue that Amazonian centers of endemism reflect ancestral regions where forest contraction produced refuges, amplifying the differentiation of taxa. Regardless of their origin (see Capparella 1988; Connor 1988; Endler 1982; and Gentry 1986a for alternative hypotheses), the distributions of locally endemic populations, subspecies, species and even genera coincide remarkably across the Neotropics. This overlap in endemism across taxa has allowed us (and many others before us) to divide the realm meaningfully into twenty-two regions and fifty subregions. The overlap also reinforces the importance of endemics as markers for centers of biological diversity.

In-Country Priorities

For land-use planners, government officials, and conservationists primarily interested in a single state or country, we suggest a series of procedures for using databases A and B to identify communities that most warrant attention within that country. These recommendations are amplifications of the global priorities above. Effectively, conservation within a particular country should reflect the overriding importance of global conservation priorities. However, in-country programs can be tailored to the needs and realities of the country.

Our most general recommendation to individual countries, and to smaller political units within them, is that in-country conservation priorities *emphasize genuinely threatened biological communities most characteristic of the ecosystems in the country*. This is not as obvious a recommendation as it might seem at first. Throughout the world (and especially in the United States) conservation efforts within individual political units often emphasize species that are rare or localized within that unit but common or widespread outside the political boundaries.

As discussed above, isolated populations of widespread species may be extremely important in preserving genetic diversity, especially where widely disjunct, independent entities are involved. However, these genuinely isolated, distinct populations (e.g., the birds of the isolated grasslands of southern Suriname) must be distinguished from the "political accidents" where the continuous range of a species barely enters the area of a country (e.g., the southern Venezuela Tepuis birds, which barely spill into Brazil). The common "political accidents" should be recognized as such and assigned low priority where conservation funds are limiting.

1. Protect In-Country Areas of Endemism

We believe that the most important conservation priorities within a single country are areas with globally unique endemics: species or communities found nowhere else in the world. These represent the country's special national heritage, sources of both national pride and national responsibility. With or without flashy species to advertise them, in-country centers of endemism provide the most significant flagships for conservation action and education. Table 9.6 lists the principal Neotropical centers of endemism (see also fig. 9.3) and the countries responsible for them. From the perspective of birds, at least, the areas listed in table 9.6 are the most important within-country regions for unique biological diversity.

A good example to explore is Costa Rica. This small country encompasses a variety of habitats and an extremely large list of bird species (853 species, database B). In part because the country is relatively small, many of its habitats occur in limited areas within the country. Most of these habitats are widespread elsewhere in the Neotropics. Yet Costa Rica harbors an essentially endemic life zone: the humid montane forests of middle and upper elevations in the central massifs (cordilleras Tilarán, Central, and Talamanca). Habitat gradients on these spectacular mountain slopes hold a large number of endemic species restricted to narrow habitat zones. These genuinely threatened species depend on Costa Rica for their continued existence (table 9.6).

Humid montane forests constitute a uniquely high conservation priority *in Costa Rica* because of its importance globally. In contrast, the tropical dry forests of northwestern Costa Rica, along with the humid for-

Table 9.6 Principal Areas of Endemism among Neotropical Birds

Endemic Region or Subregion	Region or Subregion Code	Number of Endemics	Countries Responsible
Southern Atlantic Forest	SOU	101	Brazil, Argentina, Paraguay
Andean Altiplano	AWA	70	Peru, Bolivia, Argentina, Chile
Chiriquí Highlands	CHR	51	Costa Rica, Panama
Humid eastern slope, northern Andes	EAS	50	Colombia, Ecuador, Peru
Equatorial Pacific (mainland)	MAN	45	Ecuador, Peru
Humid western slope, northern Andes	WES	43	Colombia, Ecuador
Cerrado	CER	41	Brazil, Bolivia, Paraguay
Humid eastern slope, Peruvian Andes	MTC	36	Peru
Tepuis	TEP	36	Venezuela, Guyana, Brazil
Guianan lowland forest	GUI	34	Guyana, Suriname, French Guiana, Brazil, Venezuela
Humid eastern slope, Andes of southern Peru and northern Bolivia	COC	31	Peru, Bolivia
Galápagos Islands	GAL	28	Ecuador
Arid Caribbean coast	ARC	27	Venezuela, Colombia
Jamaica	JAM	27	Jamaica
Chaco	CHA	27	Paraguay, Bolivia, Brazil, Argentina
Humid lowlands west of Rio Madeira	RMW	26	Brazil, Peru, Bolivia
Humid lowlands west of Rio Negro	RNW	26	Brazil, Ecuador, Colombia, Peru
Central American highlands	CAH	26	Mexico, Guatemala, Honduras, Nicaragua, Belize, El Salvador
Cuba	CUB	25	Cuba
Hispaniola	HIS	24	Dominican Republic, Haiti
Chocó Lowlands	CHO	24	Colombia, Ecuador
Patagonia	PAT	23	Argentina, Chile
Southern Andes	SAN	22	Chile, Argentina
Central Atlantic forest, south of Rio São Francisco	RDJ	22	Brazil
Caatinga	CAA	20	Brazil
Northern Mexican mountains	NMM	20	Mexico
Coastal mountains of Venezuela	VNZ	19	Venezuela
Yucatán Peninsula	YUC	17	Mexico, Belize, Guatemala
Santa Marta Mountains	SMT	16	Colombia
Marañón Valley	MAR	15	Peru
Arid slopes from Sinaloa to Oaxaca, Mexico	SIN	15	Mexico
Southern Mexican highlands	SMH	15	Mexico
Humid slopes of Andes of Bolivia and northern Argentina	SCT	14	Bolivia, Argentina
Puerto Rico	PUE	14	United States
Humid Pacific coast of southern Central America	HPC	13	Costa Rica, Panama
Venezuelan Andes	VAN	13	Venezuela
Baja California	BAJ	12	Mexico
Humid lowlands between Rios Madeira and Tapajós	MID	10	Brazil, Bolivia
Panamanian mountains (Tacarcuna, Pirre)	TAC	10	Panama, Colombia
Northern Atlantic forest, north of Rio São Francisco	NOR	10	Brazil
Humid lowlands of Pará, Brazil	PAR	9	Brazil
Pampas	PAM	8	Argentina, Uruguay, Brazil
Cauca, Magdalena, Sinu, and Nechi valleys	CMV	8	Colombia
Humid lowlands of southern Central America	SCA	7	Guatemala, Honduras, Nicaragua, Costa Rica, Panama
Humid lowlands of Mexican Gulf coast	GCM	7	Mexico
Pacific lowlands, Chiapas, Mexico to Guanacaste, Costa Rica	CHG	7	Mexico, Guatemala, El Salvador, Honduras, Nicaragua, Costa Rica
Socorro Island group	SOC	6	Mexico
Juan Fernández Islands	JFI	6	Chile

Note: Listed are all subregions having five or more endemic birds, plus all regions having five or more endemics and not broken into subregions.

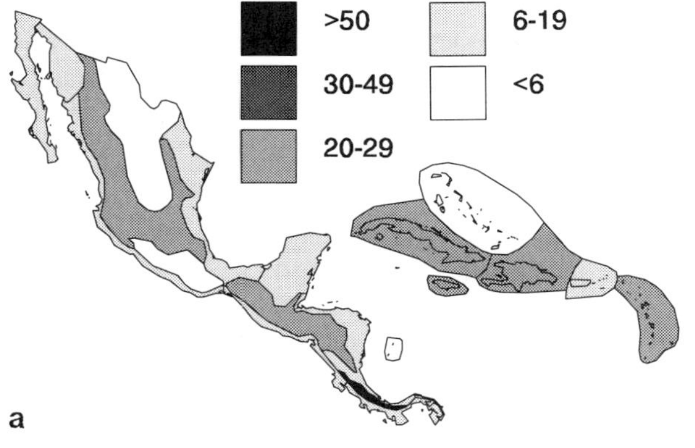

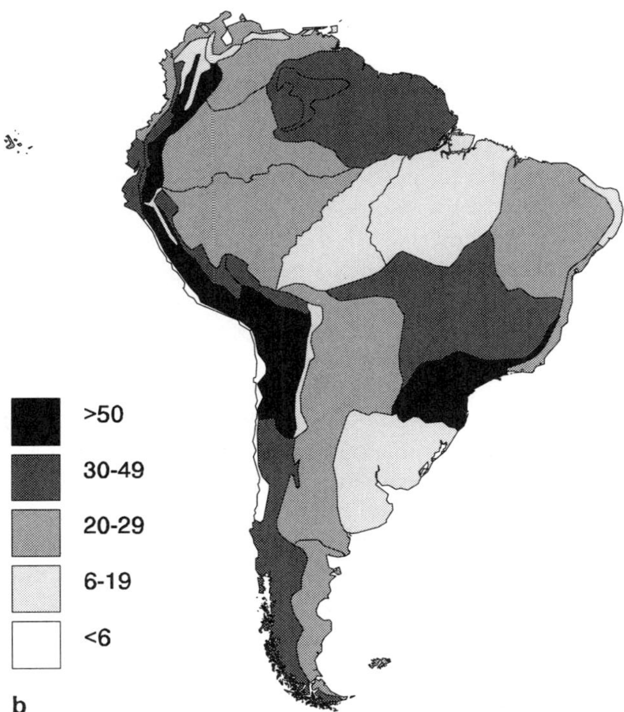

Figure 9.3 Number of locally endemic bird species in the subregions of: (a) Middle America and the West Indies; (b) South America.

ests that cover most of the country's lowlands, have relatively few endemic species. These habitats extend widely through Middle America. Conservation efforts in Costa Rica should therefore focus on protecting the country's unique, globally threatened montane forests.

However, we cannot overlook the remarkable efforts under way in Costa Rica to protect and restore tropical dry forests. Initiated by Dan Janzen, these efforts have introduced the concept of large-scale habitat restoration to the international conservation community, with tremendous success. This Costa Rican deciduous forest project is a critical experiment and demonstration of habitat restoration as a fundamental approach to tropical conservation. The importance of Janzen's work lies much more in its ramifications for future habitat restoration than in returning to its natural state an area of deciduous forest in Costa Rica. The forests in question are relatively widespread, have few local endemics, and are not as dependent on Costa Rica as are the biologically rich, humid montane forests of southern Central America.

In contrast to those in Costa Rica, deciduous forests in the arid Equatorial Pacific lowlands of Ecuador (EPC) are an important in-country area of endemism. The region is home to numerous scrub and dry forest species endemic to a tiny portion of the Ecuadorian coast. Except for a minuscule extension of this habitat into northwestern Peru, the entire existence of this unique dry forest community depends on protection provided by the Ecuadorian people and government.

Seven countries contain five or more of these important subregions of endemism (table 9.7). Two of the countries—Brazil and Mexico—contain four or more of these regions entirely within their political boundaries (fig. 9.4; tables 9.6, 9.7). *From a global perspective, the top few countries in table 9.7 represent the most important political units for conservation action in the Neotropics.* From an in-country perspective, these ta-

Table 9.7 Distinct Areas of Local Endemism in the Neotropics, by Country

Country	Zones of Local Endemism	Uniquely Owned	Shared with One Other Country	Locally Endemic Species in Country[a]
Brazil	13	4	0	316
Mexico	9	6	0	122
Colombia	8	2	3	177
Peru	8	2	2	237
Argentina	8	0	3	165
Bolivia	7	0	2	137
Ecuador	6	0	3	159
Venezuela	5	2	1	125
Panama	4	1	2	74
Chile	4	1	2	68
Costa Rica	4	0	2	75
Guatemala	4	0	0	37
Paraguay	3	0	0	80
Honduras	3	0	0	28
Nicaragua	3	0	0	18
Guyana	2	0	0	43
El Salvador	2	0	0	6
Suriname	1	0	0	29
French Guiana	1	0	0	27
Jamaica	1	0	0	26
Cuba	1	1	0	25
Hispaniola	1	1	0	24
U.S.A. (Puerto Rico)	1	1	0	16
Belize	1	0	0	24
Uruguay	1	0	0	16

Note: Includes all areas containing five or more local endemics;
[a]Number of species restricted to single zoogeographic subregion that regularly breed in country.

Figure 9.4 Number of zoogeographic subregions restricted to each country.

bles identify focal areas for conservation action in each country. This mode of analysis, combined with emphasis on habitat specialists, provides a priority-ranking system based on globally significant habitat centers (chapter 10).

2. Protect Threatened and Vulnerable Communities

Most Latin American countries do not rank near the top in tables 9.6 or 9.7, because they do not encompass entire areas of endemism. For these countries, and for small political units within countries, we recommend that highest conservation priority be placed on habitats containing assemblages of threatened or vulnerable species. Most important are assemblages limited to a single zoogeographic region, many of which straddle political boundaries and therefore do not appear as in-country areas of endemism (conservation priority 1, above).

The major habitats and assemblages of endangered, threatened, and vulnerable species throughout the Neotropics are discussed specifically in chapter 10.

3. Protect Habitat-Restricted Species

Most vegetation formations within a country or other political unit contain species restricted to that single habitat. Assemblages of habitat specialists are vulnerable: their continued existence in the country depends on the persistence of key preserves specifically targeting the habitat. These assemblages are threatened further by the tendency of their ranges to become fragmented. We recommend two methods for determining relative priority of different habitats for conservation action within a country:

1. Identify the country's concentrations of specialists: This concentration is obtained by using both database A and database B to tally, for each habitat, the total number of habitat-restricted species within the country. Preserving habitat tracts containing these assemblages would address the most diverse communities of specialists.
2. Identify the unique role individual countries can play as protectors of continentwide biodiversity at the community level.

Species numbers alone favor forested habitats—forests contain larger absolute numbers of species and therefore are bound to have more specialists. With this method, we emphasize the country's global opportunity for protecting specific habitats: For each habitat type in the Neotropics, databases A and B can be used to calculate the *proportion* of the habitat's bird specialists that occur within each country.

For example, the campo grasslands of the Neotropics contain nine bird species that occur in no other habitat. For these specialists, Brazil is the only country in which all nine species occur. Brazil is therefore uniquely important as a global protector of the campo grassland community. Campo emerges as a top habitat priority for the country, despite the limited diversity of campo species. Additional examples where habitat specialists are proportionally well represented within a country, although not unique to it, are tropical forests and coastal mangroves in Suriname, pine savannas in Nicaragua, coastal chaparral in Mexico, pampas grasslands in Uruguay, and *Nothofagus* forests in Chile. Identification of globally significant, "cornerstone" habitats is discussed in chapter 10.

4. Preserve Ecotones, Gradients, and Zoogeographic Transitions

In defining conservation site-selection priorities within a country, strict adherence to individual habitat classifications could result in overlooking areas that are exceptionally important because of their high "between-habitat" diversity. Because most transition areas are small and local, they usually are limited to single countries or even smaller political units. Therefore they warrant high conservation priority at the in-country level. We call special attention to three kinds of transitional areas, each of which can be of special significance even without compelling conservation priorities within their individual habitats.

Ecotones. We cannot overstate the importance of

preserving habitats in areas where two or more naturally occur side by side. One obvious benefit is that multiple habitats might be preserved within one reserve. More important, though, is that some species actually use habitat boundaries as their principal habitat. In the humid eastern Andes, for example, a recognizable assemblage of species is restricted to the wet transition zone at treeline (e.g., *Schizoeaca* thistletails, *Asthenes* canasteros, and several *Ochthoeca* chat-tyrants). Many predators (and even their prey) use dense vegetation along ecotonal boundaries for daytime roosts and hunt in the open at night.

In the lowlands, habitats on either side of the gallery forest/campo grassland ecotone contain species that live primarily at the edge rather than deep inside either of the well-defined habitats. Therefore areas in Brazil, Venezuela, and Colombia that contain mosaics of open grassland and gallery forest need to be preserved with each habitat *and the transitions* intact. This specific ecotone is especially important: agricultural cultivation of such open habitats usually extends directly up to the gallery forest border, destroying the natural function of the forest edge as a unique resource for a transition fauna.

Gradients. The most spectacular transition zones in the New World tropics occur along environmental gradients, areas where species turnover occurs almost continuously across broad expanses of habitat. The best examples are on mountain slopes, where gradients in temperature, rainfall, humidity, soil, and seasonality sometimes combine to produce biotic communities that change along their entire transect. Other environmental gradients producing continuous changes in faunal and floral character are found in rain shadows (e.g., arid northwestern Venezuela), fog belts (e.g., arid and semiarid western Peru), and regions of shifting soil type (e.g., the Bolivian chaco).

For birds, perhaps the most persuasive reason to preserve elevational gradients lies in their daily and seasonal movements and in their role as pollinators and dispersers of many forest plants. Patches of a single habitat type, excised and isolated from contiguous habitat elsewhere on a montane gradient, are not sufficient for many species of fruit-eating and nectar-feeding birds that move seasonally (Stiles 1985a, 1985b, 1988; see also chapter 8). Even mixed-species flocks that move up and down mountain slopes in a single day undoubtedly play an important role in expanding local diversity of tree species beyond what it would be were only a single elevational slice available.

In preserving fully representative habitat gradients, *processes*, as well as species elements, are recognized as important components of biodiversity. Gradients present ecological tension and interchange. It is at these species boundaries that competitive interspecific interactions are most intense and environmental constraints and natural selection act most precipitously. By harboring genetic variety, habitat gradients preserve opportunity for continued evolutionary modification at the local level.

Other roles place habitat gradients among the most important natural areas to save in the Neotropics. Perhaps the best examples are gradients along mountain slopes and valleys, many of which encompass entire watersheds, from mountaintop to valley bottom. Protection of the natural vegetation along these gradients reduces the rate at which rainwater runs off. Besides preserving species, such protected natural areas reduce erosion, ensure a safe and consistent water supply, and provide inexpensive and reliable flood protection for communities downstream.

Zoogeographic transitions. Where major zoogeographic zones come into contact, species of plants and animals that are otherwise broadly allopatric often occur side by side, resulting in uniquely diverse ecological communities (e.g., at Tambopata Reserve in southeastern Peru, where the approximately 573 bird species constitute the world's largest single-site list; Parker, Donahue, and Schulenberg 1994). Zoogeographic transitions commonly bring closely related species pairs together across ecological tension zones such as elevational gradients, river barriers, or even seemingly homogeneous habitat. Hybridization among related forms that are approaching species-level separation often occurs along these zoogeographic boundaries (e.g., reviews in Haffer 1974, 1985; Short 1975). Interactions among species at zoogeographic tension zones remain poorly studied but represent some of the most dynamic community processes in the Neotropics at the evolutionary level. This alone argues for their protection.

5. Protect Peripheral Isolates

Of lowest priority compared with the preceding are local, peripheral populations of species that are common outside the country. As with previous examples, the first step is a search for assemblages of these isolated populations.

For example, the wet grasslands of extreme southeastern Peru along the Río Heath contain many open country species that are common and more widespread on the campos of Bolivia and Brazil but in Peru occur *only* along that river. These species represent a distinct ecological assemblage in the context of Peru's avifauna and define an area worth protecting. However, no species or subspecies are endemic to this zone, and the total number of grassland specialists found in it is not a large proportion of the total list of grassland specialists in South America. The Río Heath grassland, then, warrants protection, first to preserve Peru's in-country biodiversity, and second as an isolated, environmentally distinctive corner of a much larger system (tropical grasslands) now endangered over its entire extent.

However, the many assemblages of true endemics and habitat specialists found elsewhere in Peru, but in no other country, should be assigned higher conservation priority than the Río Heath grasslands. Similar examples of country-specific, local isolates of widespread communities are the spiny deserts of southern Brazil, the campo grasslands of Suriname, and the humid lowland forest of Veracruz, Mexico.

We emphasize that isolated, peripheral populations do merit some attention and protection. Many peripheral populations may have been isolated for evolutionarily long periods. Almost always such populations are along range boundaries and geographic limits to the distributions of species and their habitat. These isolates have a high likelihood of being genetically distinct and may play potentially important roles as "founder populations." Protection of peripheral isolates contributes to the maintenance of overall natural genetic diversity. For example, Garrido (1992) discusses isolated populations of widespread Caribbean species on small cays off Cuba. Many have undergone habitat shifts and are threatened today, not just by direct habitat destruction, but also by the invasion of other forms of the same species more tolerant of human disturbance.

10 Centers of Diversity at Risk: Translating Principles into Action

Synopsis

Here we compare regions and ecosystems in an effort to determine which ones need most urgent conservation action. To begin, we rank all twenty-two zoogeographic regions in the Neotropics, using a series of eleven criteria grouped into three general categories: overall avian *diversity*; *uniqueness* (endemism) of the avifauna; and level of *threat* to the area's biota. Diversity alone, without regard to endemism or threat, is a poor guide because some of the high-diversity regions are still relatively secure, and the high diversity is based primarily on wide-ranging species. We advocate that conservation attention be guided principally by comparative levels of threat, especially to locally endemic biota. Birds are excellent indicators of these criteria.

Four regions consistently rank near the top regardless of the criterion used. These are Atlantic Forest, Central South America, Northern Andes, and Central Andes. All four are rich in endemic species as well as ecological diversity and have undergone severe habitat alteration that continues unabated today.

To identify more precisely which ecological communities should command immediate attention, we develop the concept of *globally significant cornerstone habitats*. These are regional habitats containing large proportions of the endemics that are restricted to that vegetation type. Of the four hundred regional habitats occupied by birds across the Neotropics, thirty-nine contain over 80% of all habitat-restricted endemics. These thirty-nine regional habitats are major reservoirs of Neotropical biodiversity and need protection to the fullest extent still possible. Five regions combine to contain over half of these key biological communities: Central South America, Central Andes, Northern Andes, Greater Antilles, and Madrean Highlands.

Present-day threat to biological diversity is a critical factor for determining conservation priorities. Using birds as a measure of this criterion, the twenty-two zoogeographic regions fall into five groups. Two regions stand out as the most seriously threatened: Atlantic Forest and Northern Andes, both of which have suffered severe habitat loss and degradation in all their ecological communities. Extinctions hover around these two regions. In the second group are three regions—Greater Antilles, Central South America, and Central Andes—in which some communities face serious and immediate threats and nearly all are at risk. The third group—Lesser Antilles, Chocó Lowlands, Equatorial Pacific, Gulf-Caribbean Slope, and Madrean Highlands—consists of regions with only a few vegetation types, but with a large proportion of species at moderate risk. In the fourth group—Chiriquí-Darién Highlands, Southern Amazonia, Northern South America, Northern Amazonia and Pacific Arid Slope—a few ecological communities are at risk but most remain secure. In the seven remaining zoogeographic regions, ecosystems currently face only limited threat.

It is time now for us to translate the many comparisons and principles from preceding chapters into specific conservation priorities for the Neotropics. Which communities and geographic regions are the most endangered, in most urgent need of additional action and protection? Which regions or ecosystems exhibit patterns of habitat modification that suggest they are next in line for endangered status? Faced with a variety of equally valid but very different criteria, is it possible to rank conservation needs in different Neotropical regions on a single, absolute scale?

We believe that species richness by itself is not a sufficient criterion for conservation priority (chapter 9). Ranked by diversity alone, the forested regions, especially Amazonia, obviously dominate. To emphasize this point we were tempted not to provide anywhere in this book a ranking of regions by their sheer numbers

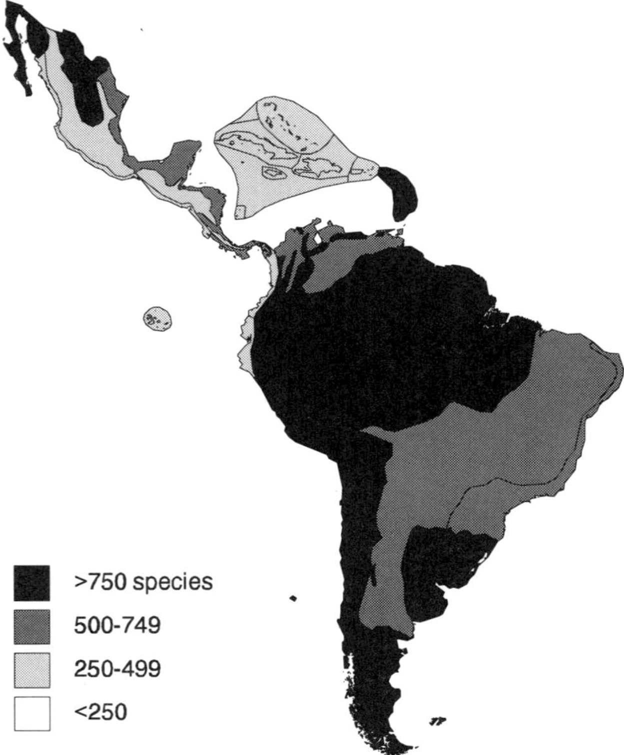

Figure 10.1 Number of bird species in each zoogeographic region.

of species. We do so here (table 10.1; fig. 10.1) in part to emphasize how different this ranking looks from those derived by the other criteria we have discussed.

This chapter begins with a series of comparisons, ranking the twenty-two geographic regions by the most important conservation criteria discussed in chapter 9. These criteria emphasize numbers and proportions of species that either are already "at risk"—endangered (CP-1), threatened (CP-2), or vulnerable (CP-3)—or are potentially vulnerable because of endemism or habitat restriction. We conclude with general comparisons that summarize individual rankings into three overall criteria: diversity, uniqueness, and threat.

Remarkably, certain Neotropical regions consistently emerge near the top in conservation priority by virtually any criterion. Real danger zones exist among regions that are high in both diversity and endemism. The Atlantic Forest, Central South America, the Northern Andes, and the Central Andes all contain extremely diverse ecological communities, filled with threatened or vulnerable species facing significant threats today.

Numbers of Species at Risk

The easiest way to identify the most important centers of diversity at risk is to compare regions and regional habitats by their absolute numbers of species classified "at risk." Table 10.1 lists these totals for each of the twenty-two regions.

Four regions—all in South America—have exceptionally high numbers of species at risk. Six other regions constitute a second tier (see table 10.2).

The Andes from Peru northward and the Atlantic forests of Brazil tower over all other Neotropical regions in their total number of species that are under immediate threat. Despite having fewer total species, Central South America also joins this top roster of regions whose diversity is under the most serious threat. These four regions alone account for over half (645, or 57%) of the 1,122 total Neotropical bird species we consider at risk. At a global scale, these are the hot spots of threatened avian diversity.

The six regions in group 2 add 299 species at risk. In all, ten of the twenty-two Neotropical regions account for 944 (84%) of all the bird species at risk.

Even when we focus only on endangered and threatened species (CP-1 and CP-2), the same group of four highest-priority regions emerges. Thirteen regions have 10 or more species under immediate threat (table 10.3).

The Atlantic Forest accounts for 22 of the 70 endangered species (31%) and 57 of the 292 threatened species (20%) in the Neotropics (table 10.1). These statistics are especially striking because total species richness in the Atlantic Forest ranks only sixth, behind all the other forest regions of the Neotropical realm (table 10.1).

The Northern Andes is another region of extremely high conservation priority. This region contains almost as many critically endangered species as the Atlantic Forest and has more vulnerable species (CP-3) than any other Neotropical region.

Somewhat surprisingly, given their prominence in the popular press, the Northern Amazon and Southern Amazon regions rank below most other forested areas in absolute numbers of endangered, threatened, or vulnerable species. This low ranking exists even though these regions have by far the highest total number of species. Compared with other areas around the Neotropics, conservation threats are not yet high in the Amazon.

Ecological Assemblages at Risk

For endangered, threatened, and vulnerable species, respectively, tables 10.4, 10.5, and 10.6 break the regional numbers down by vegetation type. In many respects, taken together these three tables represent the most important conclusions of our book. These tables identify the ecological assemblages that contain the highest numbers of species at risk across the Neotropics.

Specific comments and comparisons about many of these threatened ecological assemblages appear in preceding chapters (chapters 2–9) and will not be repeated here.

Table 10.1 Diversity, Endemism, Habitat Restriction, and Conservation Status of Birds in the Twenty-two Zoogeographic Regions

Region	Region Code	Total Species[a]	Endemics	CP-1[a]	CP-2[a]	CP-3[a]	Total at Risk (CP-1–3)[a]	Habitat-Restricted Species[a]	Habitat-Restricted Endemics	Habitat-Restricted Endemics at Risk (CP-1–3)
Northern Amazonia	AMN	896	76	0	7	69	76	286	56	20
Southern Amazonia	AMS	892	79	1	11	82	94	286	60	31
Central Andes	CAN	804	216	3	39	166	208	270	115	63
Northern Andes	NAN	772	222	11	57	179	247	263	111	84
Gulf-Caribbean Slope	GCS	689	74	0	12	93	105	119	24	15
Atlantic Forest	ATL	682	199	22	57	109	188	147	76	70
Northern South America	NSA	652	41	4	11	69	84	97	11	10
Central South America	CSA	645	112	9	41	82	132	100	56	41
Chocó Lowlands	CHO	401	24	0	12	52	64	90	14	14
Madrean Highlands	MAH	379	101	3	19	53	75	41	20	13
Pacific Arid Slope	PAS	358	36	2	10	29	41	47	13	10
Equatorial Pacific	EPC	289	73	1	19	38	58	46	20	14
Chiriquí-Darién Highlands	CDH	279	69	0	4	63	67	70	36	16
Greater Antilles	GAN	250	125	9	22	44	75	48	22	17
Pampas	PAM	249	8	0	9	25	34	34	2	1
Baja-Sonora	BSR	239	18	2	2	19	23	52	10	4
Subtropical Pacific	STP	206	19	1	10	32	43	43	11	8
Southern Andes	SAN	197	23	0	3	21	24	34	16	3
Patagonia	PAT	182	22	1	6	17	24	45	13	1
Tepuis	TEP	142	36	0	1	19	20	31	21	1
Mexican Plateau	MPL	122	2	0	1	6	7	14	2	2
Lesser Antilles	LAN	110	24	5	8	13	26	21	7	7
Total		3,751	1,599	70	292	760	1,122	1,267	716	445

Note: See table 9.2 for additional statistics on all twenty-two zoogeographic regions; regions are listed in order by total number of species.
[a] Species that occur in more than one zoogeographic region are listed more than once, so entries do not sum to totals.

Table 10.2 Total Number of Species at Risk

Region	CP-1, CP-2, or CP-3 Species
Group 1	
Northern Andes	247
Central Andes	208
Atlantic Forest	189
Central South America	132
Group 2	
Gulf-Caribbean Slope	105
Southern Amazonia	94
Northern South America	84
Northern Amazonia	76
Madrean Highlands	75
Greater Antilles	75

Table 10.3 Number of Species Threatened or Endangered

Region	CP-1 or CP-2 Species
Group 1	
Atlantic Forest	79
Northern Andes	68
Central South America	50
Central Andes	42
Group 2	
Greater Antilles	31
Madrean Highlands	22
Equatorial Pacific	20
Northern South America	15
Lesser Antilles	13
Pacific Arid Slope	12
Chocó Lowlands	12
Southern Amazonia	12
Subtropical Pacific	11

Relative Threat

Overall species richness should not determine conservation priority. Nevertheless, species richness obviously plays a major role in determining the absolute number of endangered, threatened, or vulnerable species occurring in a region. Also needed is a measure of *relative* or proportional threat, so that communities may be compared along a scale that is independent of their overall diversity. The simplest such measure is to compare regions by the proportion of their avifauna ranked as endangered, threatened, or vulnerable (fig. 10.2).

Three regions rank especially high in relative threat, each with over 12% of its avifauna classified as either endangered (CP-1) or threatened (CP-2). Five additional regions have more than 5% of their avifauna in these two high-risk categories (table 10.7).

Proportional to their total numbers of species, the Greater and Lesser Antilles join the Atlantic Forest as the most immediately threatened major ecosystems in the Neotropics (fig. 10.3a).

The Northern Andes, Central Andes, and Central

Table 10.4 Principal Assemblages of Critically Endangered (CP-1) Bird Species in the Neotropics

Region	Region Code	Tropical Lowland Evergreen Forest (F1)	Evergreen Montane Forest (F4)	Tropical Deciduous Forest (F7)	Arid Scrubs (N1, N2)	Gallery Forest (F8)	Pine or Pine-Oak Forest (F10, F11)	Fresh-water Marshes (A1)	Fresh-water Lakes (A6)	Other	Regional Total
Atlantic Forest	ATL	18	1							3	22
Northern Andes	NAN		8		2				1		11
Greater Antilles	GAN	2	2	1			2	2			9
Central South America	CSA			5		3				1	9
Lesser Antilles	LAN	2	2	1							5
Northern South America	NSA	2		1	1						4
Madrean Highlands	MAH		1				1		1		3
Central Andes	CAN				1				1	1	3
Pacific Arid Slope	PAS			1	1						2
Baja-Sonora	BSR									2	2
Equatorial Pacific	EPC			1							1
Southern Amazonia	AMS					1					1
Subtropical Pacific	STP							1			1
Patagonia	PAT							1			1
Total CP-1 species		24	14	10	4	3	3	3	3	6	70

Note: Four species occur in more than one region, so row totals do not sum to 70.

Table 10.5 Principal Assemblages of Threatened (CP-2) Bird Species in the Neotropics

Region	Region Code	Tropical Lowland Evergreen Forest (F1)	Evergreen Montane Forest (F4)	Tropical Deciduous Forest (F7)	Grasslands (N5–N10)	Montane Scrubs (N2, N3)	Freshwater Aquatic (A...)	Pine or Pine-Oak Forest (F10, F11)	Elfin Forest (F5)
Atlantic Forest	ATL	38	7	2	4		1		1
Northern Andes	NAN	5	41		2	2	1		5
Central South America	CSA	4		7	17	1	3		
Central Andes	CAN	2	15	2		6	2		4
Greater Antilles	GAN	3	7	1	1		2	5	1
Madrean Highlands	MAH		6	1		2	3	7	
Equatorial Pacific	EPC	2	3	10			1		
Gulf-Caribbean Slope	GCS	8		2			1		
Chocó Lowlands	CHO	11							
Northern South America	NSA	5		1	3		2		
Southern Amazonia	AMS	6	1		1		2		
Pacific Arid Slope	PAS	3		5					
Pampas	PAM				6				
Lesser Antilles	LAN	6		2					
Patagonia	PAT				5		1		
Total CP-2 species[a]		80	68	31	26	13	13	12	8

Note: Includes all regions containing assemblages of five or more CP-2 species sharing a habitat. Species are assigned to primary habitat in all zoogeographic regions they occupy.

[a] Regional and CP-2 species totals are not sums of table entries because some species occur in more than one region, and small assemblages and some regions have not been included in the table.

South America remain near the top. These three areas, along with the Atlantic Forest, are of extreme conservation priority on both absolute and relative scales.

The Equatorial Pacific and the Madrean Highlands emerge as high-priority areas when ranked by relative threat. These regions are less speciose than many others in the Neotropics, but they are important centers of endemism (see below).

Thus far in this section we have considered only the proportion of the avifauna already in serious trouble (CP-1 or CP-2). However, today's vulnerable species (CP-3) are tomorrow's threatened or endangered ones. What do we learn by ranking the regions according to their proportions of vulnerable species alone? Thirteen of the twenty-two regions have more than 10% of their avifauna classified as vulnerable (table 10.8).

The highest-priority regions are now becoming familiar. Northern Andes, Central Andes, Greater Antilles, Atlantic Forest, and Central South America are the most threatened areas in the Neotropics, regardless of how we rank them.

It is revealing that the Chiriquí-Darién Highlands region ranks among the three highest regions in proportion of vulnerable species, despite having no endangered (CP-1) and only four threatened (CP-2) bird species. Costa Rica and adjacent Panama provide an excellent example of a region that needs focused conservation attention even without species that are currently on the brink of extinction. Only Costa Rica's outstanding national park system protects this unique montane community from outright obliteration (Stiles 1985a). The rate of deforestation outside these parks continues to be extremely high. The enormous diversity of vulnerable species in the forests of Costa Rica and western Panama will soon be limited to fragmentary ranges subject to independent fluctuations, natural catastrophes, and local extinctions. Other regions that deserve more attention than their endangered and threatened avifauna might suggest are the Subtropical Pacific, the Gulf-Caribbean Slope, and the Southern Andes.

As expected, proportional degree of threat to a region does not correlate with total species richness (fig. 10.3a). For example, Northern Amazonia and Southern Amazonia, with the highest number of species, are proportionately the least threatened of any community in the Neotropics. Several less diverse regions, such as the Greater Antilles, Lesser Antilles, and Chiriquí-Darién Highlands, are either threatened or endangered at the community level (fig. 10.3).

ENDEMISM

Global uniqueness of biological communities within a region should be a major factor dictating the relative conservation priority of that region. As discussed in chapter 9, centers of endemism at the species level in birds correlate with endemism at the subspecies and population levels, and also with endemism in other groups of organisms. All other criteria being equal, a region with a large number or high proportion of endemics demands special attention: these are communities that cannot be saved anywhere else (fig. 10.4).

Fourteen of the twenty-two zoogeographic regions have more than 10% of their total avifauna endemic (table 10.9).

Even by this ranking, in which conservation threats are not factored in, the same regions already mentioned appear near the top. The Greater Antilles towers over the others as the Neotropical region with the highest degree of endemism. Atlantic Forest, Northern Andes, and Central Andes are other threatened regions that are also high in endemism.

The Tepuis region—with high endemism but still largely intact—illustrates that an important refinement is needed beyond the straight ranking of regions by endemism. Sometimes endemic species are common or occupy habitats that do not place them at risk. In the Tepuis especially, most endemics remain largely "out of reach" to humans. In ranking conservation priorities, the number of endemic species is not as important as their *status*.

ENDEMISM AT RISK

Neotropical zoogeographic regions differ markedly from one another both in the number (fig. 10.5) and in the proportion (fig. 10.6, table 10.10) of endemics classified "at risk." Table 10.10 ranks the eighteen regions with more than 20 endemic species (see also table 9.2) by the percentage of endemics at risk. Although this

Gallery Forest (F8)	*Polylepis* Forest (F6)	Arid Lowland Scrub (N1)	Cerrado (N4)	Other	Regional Total[a]
				4	57
				1	57
5		1	3		41
	6			2	39
		1		1	22
					19
		1		2	19
1					12
		1			12
					11
				1	11
		1		1	10
		1		2	9
					8
					6
6	6	6	3	20	292

Table 10.6 Principal Assemblages of Vulnerable (CP-3) Bird Species in the Neotropics

Region	Region Code	Evergreen Montane Forest (F4)	Tropical Lowland Evergreen Forest (F1)	Tropical Deciduous Forest (F7)	Fresh-water Marshes (A1)	Montane Scrubs (N2, N3)	Elfin Forest (F5)	Gallery Forest (F8)	Arid Lowland Scrub (N1)
Northern Andes	NAN	124	20				9		
Central Andes	CAN	87	11	7		14	7		
Atlantic Forest	ATL	31	53		8				
Gulf-Caribbean Slope	GCS	7	53	8					
Southern Amazonia	AMS		44						
Central South America	CSA		11	20	6			7	
Northern Amazonia	AMN		34					5	
Northern South America	NSA	6	26	5					
Chiriquí-Darién Highlands	CDH	44	14						
Madrean Highlands	MAH	30	5						
Chocó Lowlands	CHO	8	42						
Greater Antilles	GAN	8	11	6					
Equatorial Pacific	EPC			13					5
Subtropical Pacific	STP								
Pacific Arid Slope	PAS		11	8					
Pampas	PAM				7				
Southern Andes	SAN								
Tepuis	TEP	8							
Total CP-3 species[a]		240	196	66	23	22	15	15	15

Note: Entries indicate all assemblages of five or more CP-3 species sharing a habitat within a region, excluding coastal habitats; assemblies smaller than five are not listed to highlight the larger clusters. Species are listed under primary habitat in all zoogeographic regions in which they occur.

[a]Regional and CP-3 species totals are not sums of table entries because some species occur in more than one region, and small assemblages and some regions have not been included in the table.

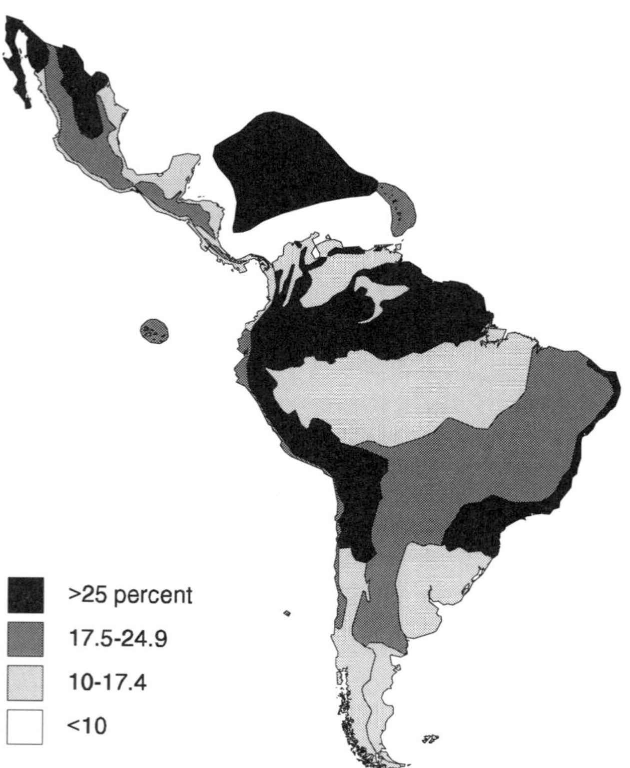

Figure 10.2 Percentage of avifauna at risk in each zoogeographic region.

Table 10.7 Percentage of Avifauna Endangered or Threatened

Region	CP-1 or CP-2 Species (*N*)	Total Species (*N*)	Percentage of Total
Group 1			
Greater Antilles	31	250	12
Atlantic Forest	79	682	12
Lesser Antilles	13	110	12
Group 2			
Northern Andes	68	772	9
Central South America	50	645	8
Equatorial Pacific	20	289	7
Madrean Highlands	22	379	6
Central Andes	42	804	5

ranking provides a slightly different group at the top, the basic pattern is little changed from previous rankings. The Atlantic Forest, Northern Andes, and Central South America still rank extremely high. Both regions of the Amazon fall near the bottom, because much of the forest remains intact and the sheer size of the Amazon basin means that even many endemics have wide ranges.

Immediate and Long-Term Threat: Stages of Endangerment

Conservation priorities should be established as a way of anticipating endangerment and preventing it (chapter 1). We compare the proportions of endemics that are

Pine or Pine-Oak Forest (F10, F11)	Paramo (N10)	Low, Seasonally Wet Grasslands (N6)	River-Edge Forest (F3)	*Polylepis* Forest (F6)	Southern Temperate Grass-lands (N7)	Fresh-water Lakes (A6)	Flooded Tropical Evergreen Forest (F2)	Campo Grass-lands (N5)	Regional Total[a]
	8								179
	8			10					166
									105
									93
		5	9						83
		5						6	81
							6		69
									69
									67
10									53
									52
									44
									38
						5			32
									29
									25
					5				21
									19
14	13	11	11	10	8	8	7	7	760

on the verge of being rare (vulnerable species, CP-3) with those already at immediate risk (CP-1 or CP-2). A close correlation would indicate that future threats to a regional avifauna (indicated by number of CP-3 species) can be predicted by the degree to which its present avifauna is endangered.

The correlation is not perfect (fig. 10.7), but it is suggestive. Vulnerability and endangerment are especially strongly related among those regions dominated by tropical evergreen forest.

The pronounced level of threat now evident among bird communities in the Lesser Antilles reveals a pattern that we suggest may be general among ecosystems worldwide. A trajectory of endangerment appears to exist among the regions of endemism within the Neotropics (fig. 10.7):

Stage 1 threat: the ancestral condition. In a few regions the endemic fauna is not yet threatened. These regions represent the "ancestral" condition for all Neotropical communities. The Tepuis region is a perfect example; it is still an essentially virgin community. Northern Amazonia also remains in an early stage of change and threat.

Stage 2 threat: vulnerable communities. The next level of threat is represented by regions with a few endangered endemics (very low proportions of CP-1 and CP-2) but significantly elevated proportions of vulnerable endemics (CP-3). Regions in this category are the Chiriquí-Darién Highlands, Gulf-Caribbean Slope, Southern Amazonia, and Central Andes.

Stage 3 threat: endangered communities. Several Neotropical regions have reached an extremely threatened condition. More than 20% of their endemic birds are endangered or threatened, and half to two-thirds of the remainder are vulnerable, that is, are becoming rare. The forested regions in this category are Northern Andes, Chocó Lowlands, and Atlantic Forest. Among open-country regions, Central South America clearly is the most endangered.

Stage 4 threat: severely endangered communities. The Lesser Antilles have the most endangered endemic fauna in the Neotropics, with nearly 60% of the endemic birds already threatened or endangered. Why is the proportion of the remaining endemics that are vulnerable (CP-3) not as high as those regions in stage 3 (fig. 10.7)? We think this reflects an important general feature of avian communities: not all species are sensitive to habitat disturbance and therefore prone to become threatened. In the Lesser Antilles, our data suggest that essentially all bird species sensitive to human impact already have become rare. Although some still are only vulnerable, most already are threatened or endangered. The Atlantic Forest region may be approaching this level of threat today.

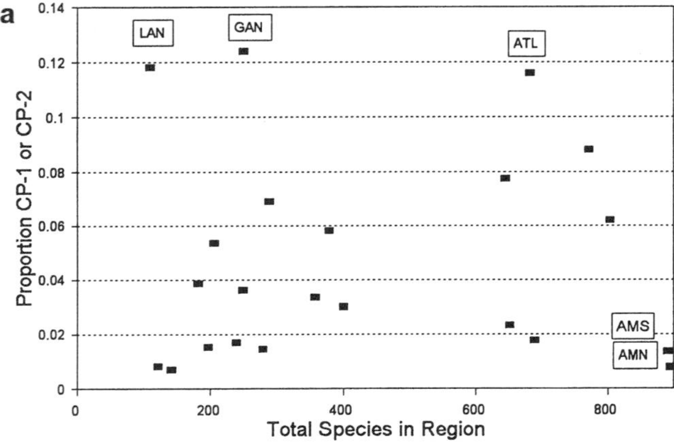

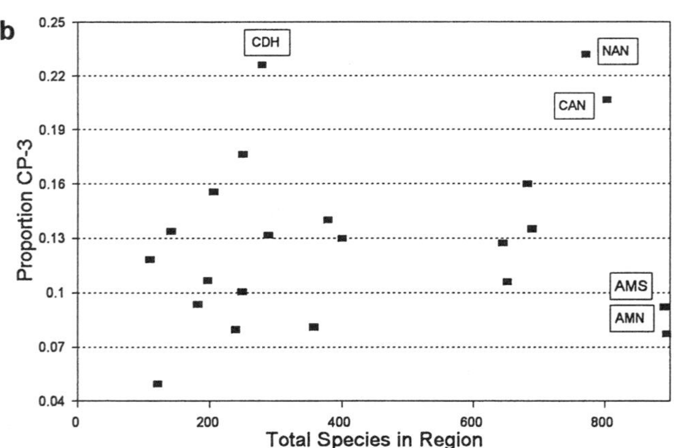

Figure 10.3 Relation between the proportion of avifauna threatened and species richness in birds, by tropical zoogeographic region: (a) proportion of bird species endangered (CP-1) or threatened (CP-2) vs. regional bird diversity; (b) proportion of bird species vulnerable (CP-3) vs. regional bird diversity.

Table 10.8 Percentage of Avifauna Vulnerable

Region	CP-3 Species (%)
Group 1	
Northern Andes	23
Chiriquí-Daríen Highlands	23
Central Andes	21
Greater Antilles	18
Subtropical Pacific	16
Atlantic Forest	16
Madrean Highlands	14
Group 2	
Equatorial Pacific	13
Central South America	13
Gulf-Caribbean Slope	13
Chocó	13
Tepuis	13
Southern Andes	11

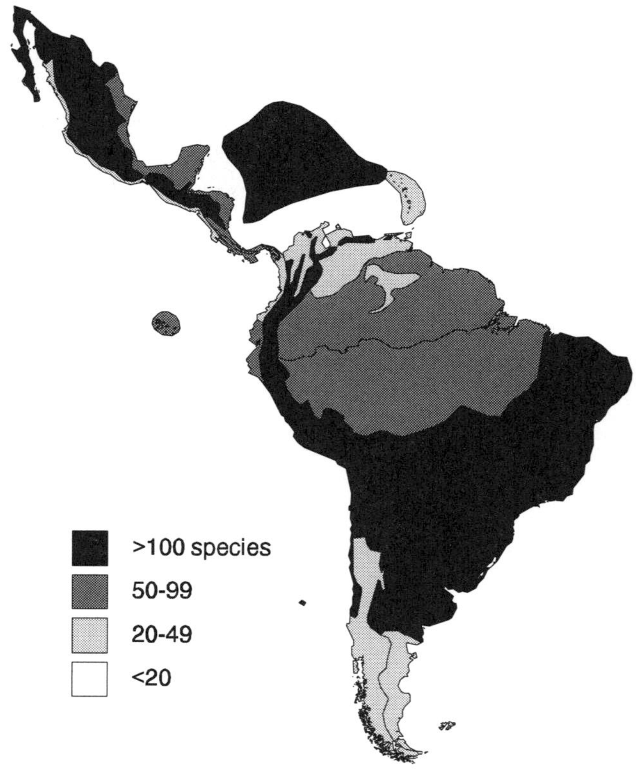

Figure 10.4 Number of endemic bird species in each zoogeographic region.

Table 10.9 Endemic Species

Region	Number of Endemics	Percentage of Total Avifauna
Group 1		
Greater Antilles	125	50
Atlantic Forest	199	29
Northern Andes	222	29
Central Andes	216	27
Madrean Highlands	101	27
Equatorial Pacific	73	25
Tepuis	36	25
Chiriquí-Darién Highlands	69	24
Lesser Antilles	24	22
Central South America	112	17
Group 2		
Patagonia	22	12
Southern Andes	23	12
Gulf-Caribbean Slope	74	11
Pacific Arid Slope	36	11

Stage 5 threat: ecological collapse. To take a non-Neotropical example, the Hawaiian Islands have reached a fifth stage on this trajectory to functional collapse (Ralph and van Riper 1985; Scott et al. 1986). As human influences continue to destroy major areas of native habitat in the archipelago and alter the character of the remaining tracts, significant portions of the endemic species have become extinct (Olson and James

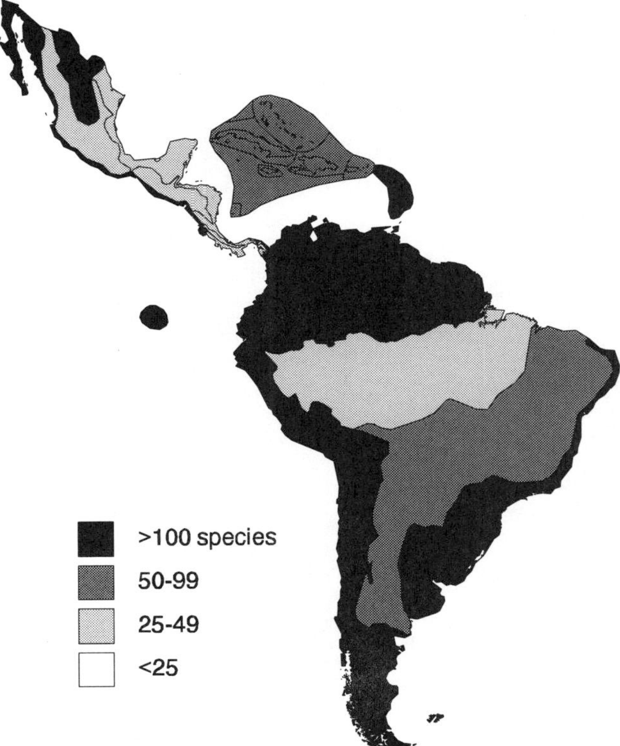

Figure 10.5 Number of endemic bird species at risk.

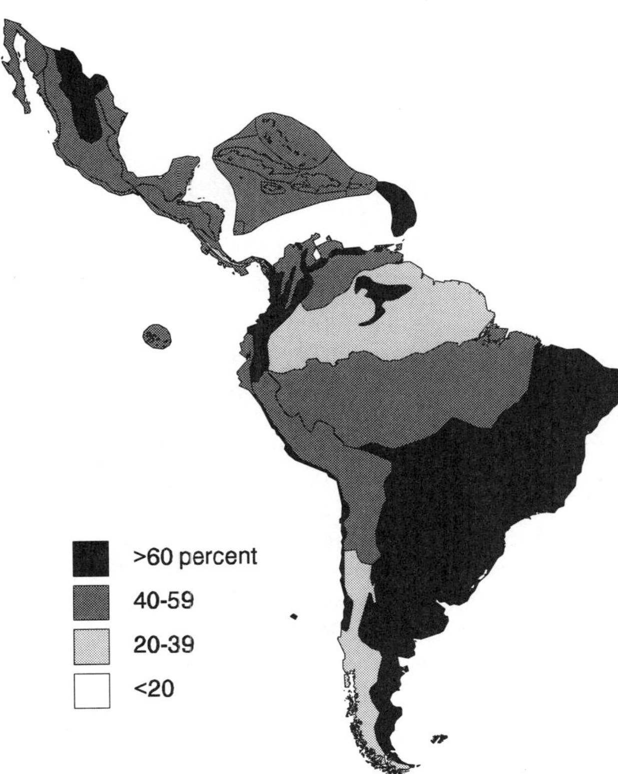

Figure 10.6 Percentage of endemic bird species at risk.

Table 10.10 Percentage of Endemic Species at Risk

Region	Percentage CP-1 or CP-2	Percentage CP-3	Percentage at Risk
Group 1			
Chocó Lowlands	29	50	79
Atlantic Forest	34	37	71
Lesser Antilles	54	13	67
Northern Andes	23	37	60
Central South America	29	30	60
Group 2			
Central Andes	13	37	50
Pacific Arid Slope	25	25	50
Gulf-Caribbean Slope	7	42	49
Northern South America	15	32	46
Greater Antilles	24	21	45
Equatorial Pacific	21	25	45
Southern Amazonia	5	38	43
Madrean Highlands	20	22	42
Group 3			
Chiriquí-Darién Highlands	3	35	38
Northern Amazonia	1	26	28
Southern Andes	13	9	22
Patagonia	18	0	18
Tepuis	0	6	6

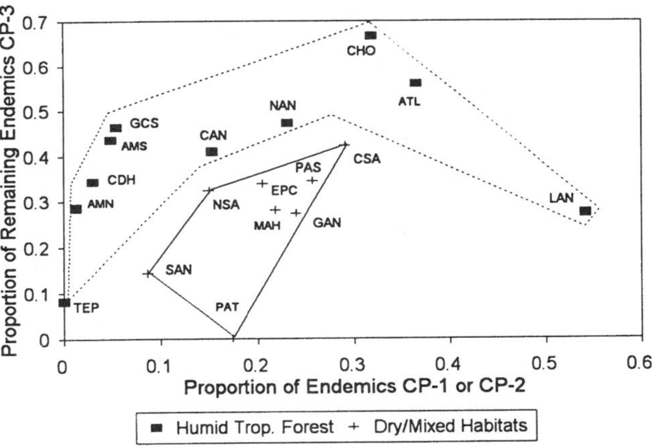

Figure 10.7 Relation between vulnerability and endangerment in the Neotropics. Proportion of endemic birds that are endangered (CP-1) or threatened (CP-2) vs. vulnerable (CP-3), by Neotropical zoogeographic region.

1982, 1991; James and Olson 1991). Virtually all the rest are threatened or endangered. Although no Neotropical region has reached this stage, many islands in the Caribbean seem to be close, especially if we include the macrofauna that is known to have been driven extinct after early human colonizations (Steadman, Pregill, and Olson 1984).

Habitat-Restricted Endemics

Habitat-restricted endemics are probably the most vulnerable of all species when native vegetation is lost or degraded. As discussed in chapter 9, these species are both local and inflexible. Ecological specialists generally make up 30% to 60% of the endemic fauna within the twenty-two Neotropical regions. The eighteen regions listed below have more than 20 endemic bird species. In ten of these regions (groups 1 and 2 below), at least 50% of the endemics are habitat restricted (table 10.11).

Some regions with a high proportion of habitat-restricted endemics are still in relatively good condition; their endemic avifaunas are not under serious threat. More informative for establishing conservation priorities is a ranking by the level of threat to habitat-restricted endemics. This highlights the degree to which the species known to be most extinction prone (habitat-restricted endemics) actually are threatened by today's habitat loss or overharvesting. Because many regions have only a few habitat-restricted endemics, the proportion at risk can be extremely high (100% in three cases). To help eliminate this artifact, we divide the twenty-two regions into two categories, based on the total numbers of habitat-restricted endemics (table 10.12).

Among the higher-diversity areas, the Atlantic Forest ranks highest in degree of threat to its endemic specialists, and the Equatorial Pacific joins an otherwise familiar set of high-priority regions. Among lower-diversity areas, the Lesser Antilles and Chocó Lowlands show the most dire threats among their small communities of habitat-restricted endemics.

Table 10.11 Prevalence of Habitat-Restricted Endemics

Region	Number of Habitat-Restricted Endemics	Percentage of All Endemics That Are Habitat Restricted
Group 1		
Southern Amazonia	60	76
Northern Amazonia	56	74
Southern Andes	16	70
Group 2		
Patagonia	13	59
Tepuis	21	58
Chocó	14	58
Central Andes	115	53
Chiriquí-Darién Highlands	36	52
Northern Andes	111	50
Central South America	56	50
Group 3		
Atlantic Forest	76	38
Arid Pacific Slope	13	36
Gulf-Caribbean Slope	24	32
Lesser Antilles	7	29
Equatorial Pacific	20	27
Northern South America	11	27
Madrean Highlands	20	20
Greater Antilles	22	18

Table 10.12 Percentage of Habitat-Restricted Endemics at Risk

Region	Percentage CP-1 or CP-2	Percentage CP-3	Total Percentage at Risk
More Than Fifteen Habitat-Restricted Endemics			
Group 1			
Atlantic Forest	62	30	92
Greater Antilles	55	23	77
Northern Andes	33	42	76
Central South America	36	38	73
Equatorial Pacific	40	30	70
Group 2			
Madrean Highlands	45	20	65
Gulf-Caribbean Slope	4	58	62
Central Andes	17	37	55
Southern Amazonia	7	43	50
Chiriquí-Darién Highlands	3	42	44
Northern Amazonia	2	34	36
Group 3			
Southern Andes	6	13	19
Tepuis	0	5	5
Fourteen or Fewer Habitat-Restricted Endemics			
Group 1			
Lesser Antilles	86	14	100
Chocó Lowlands	46	54	100
Mexican Plateau	50	50	100
Northern South America	50	30	80
Pacific Arid Slope	50	29	79
Subtropical Pacific	56	11	67
Group 2			
Pampas	50	0	50
Baja-Sonora	22	22	44
Patagonia	8	0	8

Cornerstone Habitats and Global Significance

In preceding sections we ranked whole zoogeographic regions according to features of their total bird communities, pooling all the habitats. Each region, however, encompasses several vegetation types. To establish where to direct conservation action first, it is essential to identify specific vegetation types and communities under most serious threat. Within Central South America, for example, how threatened are the grassland communities compared with the forest ones? Where should attention be directed to preserve most effectively the dry forest ecosystems of the Neotropics? Which regions are of highest priority for preserving elfin forest, or gallery forest, or arid lowland scrub?

To address whole communities, we focus again on habitat-restricted species. Geographic concentrations of specialists provide the clearest indication of important centers of diversity for any given vegetation type. If an assemblage of habitat specialists is present in a "regional habitat," then even larger numbers of less specialized users of the habitat are likely to be present in the same area.

One approach is to compare the number of specialists in a given regional habitat with the total number of specialists using that vegetation type across the Neotropics. Regional habitats that contain a high proportion of the specialists in that vegetation type obviously belong at the top of any priority ranking. Such regional habitats usually represent the core examples of each Neotropical community: they are the principal cradles of diversity.

Although it is important to preserve representative tracts of any vegetation type within each zoogeographic region, the global significance of each region's various habitats will vary. Certain vegetation types may be represented only peripherally in one region (e.g., campo grasslands in northern Amazonia) but reach a true center of diversity in the middle of another (e.g., campo grassland in Central South America). Furthermore, some vegetation types (e.g., *Nothofagus* forest) occur in only one region or a few regions, whereas others (e.g., lowland forest) are spread widely through many regions. Finally, certain vegetation types (e.g., montane forest) are rich in endemic species whereas others, even in the same region, may show little endemism.

We suggest that proportional representation of habitat specialists provides one of the best indexes to the global importance of a region. We introduce here the concept of *cornerstone habitats* to indicate regional habitats that possess significant conservation value as measured by their local and global role in harboring unique centers of diversity:

Cornerstone habitat—A regional habitat containing a high proportion of all species restricted to that vegetation type.

Globally significant cornerstone habitat—A regional habitat containing a high proportion of all *endemic species* restricted to that vegetation type.

Risk index for cornerstone habitat—Within a cornerstone habitat, the percentage of its habitat-restricted endemics listed as vulnerable (CP-3), threatened (CP-2), or endangered (CP-1).

Example: arid lowland scrub. The concept of "cornerstone habitat" can be made clear through an example. Conservation planners interested in arid lowland scrub ought to ask: Where should investment be placed to preserve the most important examples of arid lowland scrub in the Neotropics? This question is not trivial; lowland scrub covers significant portions of sixteen of the twenty-two zoogeographic regions.

Database A (part 4) indicates that arid lowland scrub (N1) is the primary habitat for 167 bird species, of which 41 are restricted to this habitat. Of these restricted species, 32 are endemic to a single region. Analysis of these 32 species points to seven regions that serve as "cornerstones" to the survival of the arid scrub communities in the Neotropics (table 10.13). Three of these are "globally significant cornerstone habitats" because they contain large assemblages of endemics that specialize in arid lowland scrub. Central South America, Equatorial Pacific, and Baja-Sonora harbor 20 of the 32 habitat-restricted endemics in the arid scrub (60%), while no other region contains more than 3. Adding Patagonia, Pacific Arid Slope, Gulf-Caribbean Slope, and Greater Antilles totals another 9 endemics, for a combined total of 29 (91%) of the restricted endemics.

A feature of this analysis bears emphasis, because it illustrates both the flexibility and limitations of using database A to search for important communities. We know that a distinctive assemblage of dry country

Table 10.13 Avifauna of Cornerstone Lowland Scrub Habitats, Compared with Those of Other Lowland Scrub Regions in the Neotropics

Region	Number (Proportion) of Arid Scrub Species		
	Primary Habitat (N = 167)	Habitat Restricted (N = 41)	Habitat-Restricted Endemics (N = 32)
Globally significant cornerstone scrub habitats			
Central South America	48 (0.29)	12 (0.28)	9 (0.26)
Equatorial Pacific	40 (0.24)	8 (0.19)	6 (0.17)
Baja-Sonora[a]	42 (0.25)	7 (0.16)	5 (0.14)
Cornerstone scrub habitats			
Pacific Arid Slope	27 (0.16)	4 (0.09)	2 (0.06)
Patagonia	18 (0.11)	5 (0.12)	3 (0.09)
Gulf-Caribbean Slope	23 (0.14)	2 (0.05)	2 (0.06)
Greater Antilles	15 (0.09)	2 (0.05)	2 (0.06)
Total (proportion) arid lowland scrub species in cornerstone habitats	149 (0.89)	37 (0.90)	29 (0.91)
Other zoogeographic regions containing arid lowland scrub			
Central Andes	19	2	1
Northern South America	22	1	1
Chocó Lowlands	4	1	1
Subtropical Pacific	25	2	0
Mexican Plateau	27	0	0
Madrean Highlands	23	0	0
Southern Andes	12	0	0
Atlantic Forest	12	0	0
Northern Amazonia	12	0	0
Southern Amazonia	11	0	0
Northern Andes	8	0	0
Lesser Antilles	4	0	0
Chiriquí-Darién Highlands	3	0	0

[a]Includes three endemics that also occur in Sonoran desert region of the southwestern United States.

birds occupies desert scrub and xeric woodlands of extreme northwestern Venezuela and adjacent Colombia. Yet this endemic community does not emerge as a cornerstone habitat when analyzed in the manner just presented. Northern South America has only one habitat-restricted species in the arid scrub (Vermilion Cardinal, *Cardinalis phoeniceus*; table 10.13). This community does not emerge as a reservoir of endemics because nearly all the scrub endemics there also are found in the adjacent arid woodlands and mangrove edges and therefore are coded as occurring in two or three habitats (mostly dry forest, F7).

Database A and most of our examples are conservative. Only the most narrowly restricted species are coded as occupying only one habitat. We conducted an analysis similar to that in table 10.13, but using a characteristic *combination* of dry country habitats (N1 and/or F7). In this way we broadened the ecological community examined. Searching across these two arid habitats increased the number of "habitat-limited" endemics overall, because they could be limited to either habitat alone *or* to the combination.

This new analysis does point to the Northern South American scrubland community as a reservoir of endemics. However, results of this broader search change our conclusions about cornerstone scrub habitats only slightly (table 10.13): Equatorial Pacific and Central South America remain as the two "globally significant cornerstones" (with 41 and 40 dry country endemics, respectively); the Pacific Arid Slope (13 endemics) and Greater Antilles (9 endemics) remain as "cornerstones," now joined by Northern South America (8) and the Gulf-Caribbean Slope (9). The Baja-Sonora (5) and Patagonia (3) regions drop out of the cornerstone list.

Ranking regions by cornerstone habitats. For each of the major habitats in the Neotropics, we provide a list of the zoogeographic regions that qualify as cornerstone habitats (tables 10.14, 10.15, 10.16). The number of cornerstone habitats in a region (fig. 10.8) reflects both its level of ecological variability and its global role as a reservoir of diversity. Across the Neotropics, the two most diverse regions in habitat types are the Central Andes and Central South America. The former has dry inter-Andean valleys, several habitats above treeline, and a mix of humid forest habitats. The latter has campo grasslands, cerrado, dry forest, and scrubs intermingled with gallery forests. Not surprisingly, given these ecological variations, these two regions lead in cornerstone habitats with eight and seven, respectively (table 10.17).

Northern Amazonia has five cornerstone habitats (although two are distinctive forest types of limited geographical extent associated with large rivers). Six regions have four cornerstones, two have three, and four have two. Finally, five regions have one cornerstone habitat each. These regions are dominated geographically by the single habitat for which they represent a cornerstone.

Regions lacking cornerstones. Of the twenty-two zoogeographic regions, only the Mexican Plateau and the Lesser Antilles lack cornerstone habitats. Both are regions of exceptionally low diversity (122 and 107 bird species, respectively, the lowest in the Neotropics). A composite avifauna occupies the Mexican Plateau, with elements from North America, Baja-Sonora, and the Pacific Arid Slope. On the Lesser Antilles, the 24 endemics are ecologically generalized (only 7 are habitat restricted). This is a pattern typical of isolated island faunas (MacArthur 1972), although still incompletely understood. The remaining avifauna of the Lesser Antilles is composed of widespread Caribbean species and seabirds.

Table 10.14 Cornerstone Forest Habitats of the Neotropics

			Habitat-Restricted Endemics			
Habitat	Primary Habitat	Habitat Restricted	*N*	Prop.	CP1–3	Risk Index
Tropical lowland evergreen forests (F1) (1,012 primary users; 408 habitat restricted; 198 restricted endemics)						
Atlantic Forest	313	88	57	0.29	54	0.95
Southern Amazonia	466	216	48	0.24	23	0.48
Northern Amazonia	465	217	45	0.23	12	0.27
Gulf-Caribbean Slope	325	80	15	0.08	10	0.67
Chocó Lowlands	247	72	13	0.07	13	1.00
Total restricted endemics			178	0.90	112	
Montane evergreen forests (F4) (840 primary users; 357 habitat restricted; 222 restricted endemics)						
Northern Andes	499	217	85	0.38	64	0.75
Central Andes	385	180	54	0.24	31	0.57

Table 10.14 (*continued*)

Habitat	Primary Habitat	Habitat Restricted	Habitat-Restricted Endemics *N*	Prop.	CP1–3	Risk Index
Chiriquí-Darién Highlands	168	61	35	0.16	15	0.43
Tepuis	78	27	20	0.09	0	0.00
Atlantic Forest	90	14	13	0.06	10	0.77
Total restricted endemics			207	0.93	120	
Tropical deciduous forests (F7) (300 primary users; 64 habitat restricted; 59 restricted endemics)						
Central South America	85	27	23	0.39	20	0.87
Equatorial Pacific	58	11	11	0.19	9	0.82
Pacific Arid Slope	71	7	7	0.12	5	0.71
Gulf Caribbean Slope	73	5	5	0.08	2	0.40
Greater Antilles	30	5	5	0.08	3	0.60
Total restricted endemics			51	0.86	39	
Elfin forests (F5) (61 primary users; 26 habitat restricted; 25 restricted endemics)						
Central Andes	34	15	14	0.54	6	0.43
Northern Andes	39	12	11	0.42	5	0.45
Total restricted endemics			25	0.96	11	
Flooded tropical forests (F2) (76 primary users; 22 habitat restricted; 8 restricted endemics)						
Northern Amazonia	69	18	4	0.50	3	0.75
Southern Amazonia	70	18	4	0.50	1	0.25
Total restricted endemics			8	1.00	4	
Pine forests (F10) (60 primary users; 18 habitat restricted; 7 restricted endemics)						
Greater Antilles	13	8	5	0.71	4	0.80
Madrean Highlands	36	3	2	0.29	1	0.50
Total restricted endemics			7	1.00	5	
River-edge forests (F3) (80 primary users; 14 habitat restricted; 7 restricted endemics)						
Southern Amazonia	77	13	6	0.86	5	0.83
Gallery forests (F8) (99 primary users; 12 habitat restricted; 9 restricted endemics)						
Central South America	49	8	8	0.89	7	0.88
Southern temperate forests (F9) (31 primary users; 12 habitat restricted; 9 restricted endemics)						
Southern Andes	23	12	8	0.89	1	0.13
Pine-oak forests (F11) (75 primary users; 8 habitat restricted; 4 restricted endemics)						
Madrean Highlands	71	7	4	1.00	0	0.00
Polylepis woodlands (F6) (18 primary users; 6 habitat restricted; 4 restricted endemics)						
Central Andes	18	6	4	1.00	4	1.00
White sand forests (F12) (16 primary users; 6 habitat restricted; 5 restricted endemics)						
Northern Amazonia	12	4	3	0.60	1	0.33

Note: Cornerstone habitats are defined here as regional habitats containing at least two habitat-restricted endemics and at least 5% of the habitat-restricted endemics using that habitat.

Table 10.15 Cornerstone Nonforest Habitats of the Neotropics

			Habitat-Restricted Endemics			
Habitat	Primary Habitat	Habitat Restricted	*N*	Prop.	CP1–3	Risk Index
Arid lowland scrub (N1) (167 primary users; 41 habitat restricted; 32 restricted endemics)						
Central South America	48	12	9	0.28	1	0.11
Equatorial Pacific	40	8	6	0.19	2	0.33
Baja-Sonora	42	7	5	0.16	0	0.00
Pacific Arid Slope	27	4	2	0.06	2	1.00
Patagonia	18	5	3	0.09	0	0.00
Gulf-Caribbean Slope	23	2	2	0.06	2	1.00
Greater Antilles	16	2	2	0.06	2	1.00
Total restricted endemics			29	0.91	9	
Arid montane scrub (N2) (114 primary users; 40 habitat restricted; 31 restricted endemics)						
Central Andes	73	23	17	0.55	8	0.47
Madrean Highlands	22	7	5	0.16	2	0.40
Southern Andes	41	8	3	0.10	1	0.33
Central South America	7	5	5	0.16	3	0.60
Total restricted endemics			30	0.97	14	
Puna grasslands (N9) (41 primary users; 18 habitat restricted; 14 restricted endemics)						
Central Andes	38	15	11	0.79	1	0.09
Southern Andes	18	6	3	0.21	0	0.00
Total restricted endemics			14	1.00	1	
Paramo grasslands (N10) (35 primary users; 12 habitat restricted; 11 restricted endemics)						
Northern Andes	26	10	9	0.82	6	0.67
Central Andes	21	3	2	0.18	1	0.50
Total restricted endemics			11	1.00	7	
Campo grasslands (N5) (23 primary users; 9 habitat restricted; 7 restricted endemics)						
Central South America	21	7	6	0.86	6	1.00
Southern temperate grasslands (N7) (36 primary users; 8 habitat restricted; 6 restricted endemics)						
Patagonia	28	6	4	0.67	0	0.00
River-island scrub (N12) (11 primary users; 6 habitat restricted; 1 restricted endemic)						
Northern Amazonia	11	6	1	1.00	1	1.00
Humid montane scrub (N3) (31 primary users; 7 habitat restricted; 7 restricted endemics)						
Central Andes	22	3	3	0.43	2	0.67
Subtropical Pacific	5	2	2	0.29	2	1.00
Total restricted endemics			5	0.71	4	
Cerrado (N4) (18 primary users; 3 habitat restricted; 3 restricted endemics)						
Central South America	18	3	3	1.00	2	0.67

Note: Cornerstone nonforest habitats are defined here as regional habitats containing at least two habitat-restricted endemics (except river-island scrub, N12), with these making up at least 5% of all restricted endemics occupying that habitat across the Neotropics.

Table 10.16 Cornerstone Freshwater Aquatic Habitats of the Neotropics

Habitat	Primary Habitat	Habitat Restricted	Habitat-Restricted Endemics *N*	Prop.	CP1–3	Risk Index
Freshwater marshes (A1) (124 primary users; 55 habitat restricted; 12 restricted endemics)						
Central South America	63	28	1	0.08	1	1.00
Greater Antilles	29	11	3	0.25	3	1.00
Northern South America	46	21	2	0.17	1	0.50
Pampas	60	23	1	0.08	0	0.00
Atlantic Forest	51	24	0	0.00	0	0.00
Madrean Highlands	14	7	2	0.17	2	1.00
Gulf-Caribbean Slope	41	17	1	0.08	1	0.00
Northern Amazonia	45	21	0	0.00	0	0.00
Southern Amazonia	42	21	1	0.08	0	0.00
Total habitat-restricted endemics			11	0.92	8	
Freshwater lakes (A6) (35 primary users; 15 habitat restricted; 6 restricted endemics)						
Central Andes	12	7	3	0.50	3	1.00
Patagonia	13	5	1	0.17	1	1.00
Northern Andes	6	4	1	0.17	1	1.00
Southern Andes	13	4	0	0.00	0	0.00
Subtropical Pacific	13	4	0	0.00	0	0.00
Total habitat-restricted endemics			5	0.83	5	

Note: Table includes all regions with at least two habitat-restricted endemics or with significant numbers of habitat-restricted species; note that aquatic habitats contain few restricted endemics.

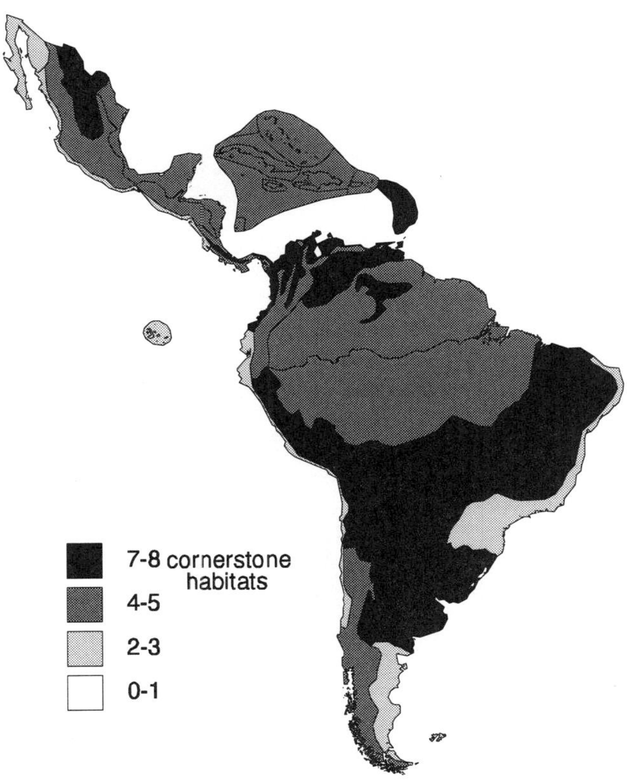

Figure 10.8 Number of cornerstone habitats in each zoogeographic region.

Cornerstone Habitats as Conservation Indicators

In this book we have divided the Neotropics into twenty-two zoogeographic regions and forty-one habitats, yielding a theoretical maximum of 902 regional habitats. Occupancy by at least a few bird species indicates that about 400 of these regional habitats actually exist in the real world (e.g., no elfin forests exist in Northern Amazonia, etc.). Of the 400 regional habitats, 134 contain one or more bird species restricted to both the region and the habitat; that is, 134 regional habitats contain all 727 habitat-restricted endemic birds in the Neotropics (table 10.1).

Only 39 regional habitats, or fewer than 10% of the total, contain 84% of all habitat-restricted endemic birds in the entire Neotropical realm (table 10.18; fig. 10.9). Among birds, at least, these regional habitats are the most important centers of specialization and endemism in the New World tropics. Preserving significant tracts within each of these regional habitats will produce the largest payoffs for preservation of Neotropical terrestrial biodiversity.

At the local level, the concept of cornerstone habitats as conservation flagships can help focus conservation efforts on globally significant vegetation formations within regions. In-country agencies or conservation organizations should be encouraged to emphasize preser-

Table 10.17 Ranking of Zoogeographic Regions by Number of Cornerstone Habitats

Region	Region Code	Number of Cornerstone Habitats	Cornerstone Habitat Codes
Central Andes	CAN	8	F4, F5, F6, N2, N3, N9, N10, A6
Central South America	CSA	7	F7, F8, N1, N2, N4, N5, A1
Northern Amazonia	AMN	5	F1, F2, F12, N12, A1
Greater Antilles	GAN	4	F7, F10, N1, A1
Northern Andes	NAN	4	F4, F5, N10, A6
Southern Andes	SAN	4	F9, N2, N9, A6
Southern Amazonia	AMS	4	F1, F2, F3, A1
Madrean Highlands	MAH	4	F10, F11, N2, A1
Gulf-Caribbean Slope	GCS	4	F1, F7, N1, A1
Atlantic Forest	ATL	3	F1, F4, A1
Patagonia	PAT	3	N1, N7, A6
Equatorial Pacific	EPC	2	F7, N1
Baja-Sonora	BSR	2	F10, N1
Pacific Arid Slope	PAS	2	F7, N1
Subtropical Pacific	STP	2	N3, A6
Chocó Lowlands	CHO	1	F1
Chiriquí-Darién Highlands	CDH	1	F4
Tepuis	TEP	1	F4
Pampas	PAM	1	A1
Northern South America	NSA	1	A1

Note: The Lesser Antilles and Mexican Plateau lack cornerstone habitats; see text. The following habitats support too few habitat-restricted species to merit identification of cornerstone habitats: mangroves (F14), palm forests (F13), northern temperate grassland (N8), low, seasonally wet grassland (N6), riparian thickets (N11), agricultural land and pastures (N13), and all aquatic habitats except freshwater marshes and lakes.

Table 10.18 Thirty-nine Important Regional Habitats of the Neotropics and Their Numbers of Habitat-Restricted Endemic Bird Species

Region (*N*)	Region Code	F4	F1	F7	N2	F5	N1	N9	N10
Central Andes (5)	CAN	54			17	14		11	
Central South America (5)	CSA			23	5		9		
Northern Andes (3)	NAN	85				10			9
Southern Amazonia (3)	AMS		48						
Greater Antilles (3)	GAN	6		5					
Madrean Highlands (3)	MAH	6			5				
Atlantic Forest (2)	ATL	13	57						
Northern Amazonia (2)	AMN		45						
Gulf-Caribbean Slope (2)	GCS		15	5					
Equatorial Pacific (2)	EPC			11			6		
Chiriquí-Darién Highlands (1)	CDH	35							
Tepuis (1)	TEP	20							
Chocó Lowlands (1)	CHO		13						
Southern Andes (1)	SAN								
Pacific Arid Slope (1)	PAS			7					
Baja-Sonora (1)	BSR						5		
Lesser Antilles (1)	LAN		4						
Northern South America (1)	NSA		4						
Patagonia (1)	PAT								
Total		219	186	51	27	24	20	11	9
Proportion of all restricted endemics using habitat		0.99	0.94	0.86	0.84	0.96	0.69	0.79	0.82
CP-1, 2, or 3 habitat-restricted endemics represented		130	120	39	13	11	3	1	6
Total CP-1, 2, or 3 restricted endemics, all regions		132	131	47	16	12	9	1	7
Proportion		0.98	0.92	0.83	0.81	0.92	0.33	1.00	0.86

Note: All regional habitats containing four or more habitat-restricted endemics are indicated; number of endangered (CP-1), threatened (CP-2), and vulnerable (CP-3) habitat-restricted endemics contained within these thirty-nine habitats, and the proportions of the Neotropical totals for these categories, are shown in the lower portion of the table.

vation of important tracts representing these cornerstone habitats in their area. In many regions such a focus will result in broader emphasis on some habitats (especially nonforest ones) that may not be in the mainstream of conservation attention but should be.

For example, in the Central Andes, a large habitat preserve placed along the forested eastern slopes will protect only two of the seven cornerstone habitats in the region (montane and elfin forests). Of course these are diverse and important habitats, very worthy of protection. However, five other globally significant cornerstone habitats also require concerted attention within the Central Andes. Conservation efforts in this area need to include key examples of isolated *Polylepis* woodlands, freshwater lakes, puna grasslands, and the two kinds of arid scrub. Although these habitats contain endemic assemblages uniquely characteristic of the Central Andes, they receive much less attention than do the more spectacular humid montane forests of the eastern slopes.

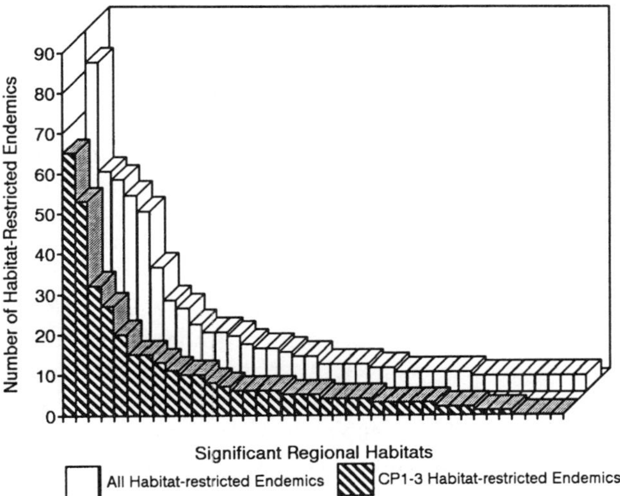

Figure 10.9 Distribution of habitat-restricted endemics and habitat-restricted endemics at risk across regional habitats.

Overall Priority Rankings: Diversity, Uniqueness, and Threat

We can now derive a summary ranking of conservation priorities among the twenty-two zoogeographic areas discussed in this book (tables 10.19 and 10.20). Conserving biological diversity requires attention to communities and processes, with three parallel missions: protect centers of high absolute *diversity*, protect centers of ecological *uniqueness*, and protect, with greatest haste, those communities that are under the most immediate *threat*. These themes suggest a three-

F2	F8	F9	N5	F3	F10	F6	F11	N7	Totals
						4			100
	8		6						51
									104
4				6					58
					5				16
							4		15
									70
4									49
									20
									17
									35
									20
									13
		8							8
									7
									5
									4
									4
								4	4
8	8	8	6	6	5	4	4	4	600
1.00	0.89	0.89	0.86	0.86	0.71	1.00	1.00	0.67	0.84
4	7	1	6	5	4	4	2	0	356
4	9	2	7	6	5	4	2	2	396
1.00	0.78	0.50	0.86	0.83	0.80	1.00	1.00	0.00	0.90

part clustering to the ranking criteria presented in preceding sections.

Table 10.19 summarizes each of ten rankings into first-priority (group 1) and second-priority (group 2) groups, organized under the three headings of diversity, uniqueness, and threat. To gather these rankings into an overall evaluation of conservation priority among regions, we scored the clusters from table 10.19 as follows: each region received two points for every group 1 ranking and one point for every group 2 ranking (table 10.20).

Diversity

Absolute diversity. Forested habitats dominate this list, with the Amazonian and Andean regions ranked highest. Clearly, preservation of forested regions will affect by far the largest number of species. Many of these species are widespread and not under immediate threat.

Cornerstone habitats. The Central Andes and Central South America rank highest in number of major vegetation types and centers of endemism. Other mosaic regions also rank high, including the Amazon basin.

Uniqueness

Percentage of endemics. The Greater Antilles, the Atlantic Forest, the forested Andean regions, and the arid Equatorial Pacific lead this group. These are regions of small geographic area, characterized by the insularity of their habitats. The two Amazonian regions rank very low in proportional endemism.

Percentage of endemics habitat restricted. Habitat specialization among endemics is highest in the two Amazon regions, where most endemics are forest or river-edge specialists. Many of the other high-ranking regions (e.g., Southern Andes, Baja-Sonora, Patagonia, Subtropical Pacific) contain unique concentrations of nonforest specialists.

Threat

Total endangered and threatened species (CP-1, CP-2). The Atlantic Forest and Northern Andes stand out in absolute number of species that are nearing extinction, followed by Central South America and the Central Andes. A large middle group includes both forest and nonforest regions. The Amazon regions do not appear at all.

Table 10.19 Summary Rankings for Determining Conservation Priorities among Twenty-two Regions in the Neotropics, Based on Features of Their Avifauna

Diversity		Uniqueness		Threat					
Total Species	Cornerstone Habitats	Percentage of Avifauna Endemic	Percentage of Endemics Habitat Restricted	Total CP-1 or CP-2	Total CP-3	Percentage of Avifauna CP-1 or CP-2	Percentage of Avifauna CP-3	Percentage of Endemics CP-1–3	Habitat-Restricted Endemics CP-1–3
Group 1									
AMN	CAN	GAN	SAN	ATL	NAN	GAN	NAN	CHO	ATL
AMS	CSA	ATL	AMS	NAN	CAN	ATL	CDH	ATL	GAN
CAN	AMN	NAN	AMN	CSA	ATL	LAN	CAN	LAN	EPC
NAN	GAN	CAN		CAN	GCS		GAN	NAN	NAN
GCS	NAN	EPC			AMS		STP	CSA	CSA
ATL	AMS	TEP			CSA		ATL		LAN[a]
NSA	SAN	MAH							CHO[a]
CSA	MAH	CDH							MPL[a]
		LAN							NSA[a]
		CSA							PAS[a]
									STP[a]
Group 2									
CHO	ATL	PAT	TEP	GAN	AMN	NAN	EPC	CAN	MAH
MAH	PAT	SAN	PAT	MAH	NSA	CSA	CSA	PAS	GCS
PAS	GCS	GCS	BSR	EPC	CDH	EPC	GCS	GCS	CAN
	EPC	PAS	STP	NSA	CHO	MAH	CHO	GAN	AMS
	BSR		CAN	GCS	MAH	CAN	MAH	EPC	CDH
	PAS		CDH	PAS	GAN		SAN	NSA	AMN
	STP		NAN	LAN	EPC		TEP	AMS	PAM[a]
			CSA	CHO				MAH	BSR[a]
			CHO	AMS					
				STP					

Note: See tables 9.2, 10.1–10.3, and 10.7–10.12 for raw data, rankings, and spelled-out regional names. Regions are listed in decreasing rank, and divided into group 1, group 2, or unranked based on discontinuities in the ranked values.

[a] These eight regions show high proportions of habitat-restricted endemics that are CP-1–3, owing in part to their low overall diversity.

Table 10.20 Scores for Overall Conservation Priority among Twenty-two Neotropical Regions, Based on Elements of Avifaunal Diversity, Avifaunal Uniqueness, and Existing Threat

Region	Region Code	Diversity (max = 4)	Uniqueness (max = 4)	Threat (max = 12)	Total Score
Northern Andes	NAN	4	3	11	18
Atlantic Forest	ATL	3	2	12	17
Central South America	CSA	4	3	10	17
Central Andes	CAN	4	3	9	16
Greater Antilles	GAN	2	2	9	13
Equatorial Pacific	EPC	1	3	7	11
Madrean Highlands	MAH	3	2	6	11
Southern Amazonia	AMS	4	2	5	11
Gulf-Caribbean Slope	GCS	3	1	6	10
Chocó Lowlands	CHO	1	1	7	9
Lesser Antilles	LAN	0	2	7	9
Northern Amazonia	AMN	4	2	2	8
Subtropical Pacific	STP	1	1	5	7
Northern South America	NSA	2	0	5	7
Chiriquí-Darién Highlands	CDH	0	3	4	7
Pacific Arid Slope	PAS	2	1	4	7
Southern Andes	SAN	2	3	1	6
Tepuis	TEP	0	3	1	4
Baja-Sonora	BSR	1	1	1	3
Patagonia	PAT	1	2	0	3
Mexican Plateau	MPL	0	0	2	2
Pampas	PAM	0	0	1	1

Note: Scores are based on groupings summarized in table 10.19. Each region received two points for each group 1 ranking and one point for each group 2 ranking.

Total vulnerable species (CP-3). Attention to this category anticipates rarity and is fundamental to a wise conservation strategy. The Northern and Central Andes and the Atlantic Forest contain by far the most diverse communities considered "the next to go."

Percentage of avifauna endangered or threatened (CP-1, CP-2). The Greater Antilles, Atlantic Forest, and Lesser Antilles—three isolated and highly endangered communities—tower above the others in the proportion of their total avifauna already nearing extinction.

Percentage of avifauna vulnerable (CP-3). In this measure of advancing conservation threat, the Chiriquí-Darién Highlands fall just below the highly endangered Northern Andes. The Subtropical Pacific reaches group 1 ranking here.

Percentage of endemics at risk (CP-1, CP-2, CP-3). If any single criterion represents a "flagship ranking" for conservation purposes, this may be it. The Greater Antilles, Chocó Lowlands, Atlantic Forest, and Lesser Antilles have the highest proportion of their endemic birds at some level of risk.

Percentage of habitat-restricted endemics at risk (CP-1, CP-2, CP-3). Group 1 includes both high-diversity and low-diversity regions (see above). Among the high-diversity regions of endemic specialists, the Equatorial Pacific joins the familiar list of highly endangered areas.

Conservation Priorities in the Neotropics

We believe that conservation priority should ultimately be determined by degree of present-day threat. By this view, conservationists should ignore measures of species richness or uniqueness in determining priorities for action.

Our measures of threat divide the twenty-two Neotropical regions into five groups. Two regions—Atlantic Forest and Northern Andes—stand out as the most threatened ecosystems in the Neotropics (table 10.20, "Threat" column). Three additional regions—Central South America, Greater Antilles, and Central Andes—also rank high in virtually every criterion we can devise to measure present-day threat. We define the five levels of threat to zoogeographic regions in the Neotropics as follows (see fig. 10.10):

Group 1: *All ecosystems critically threatened; many catastrophic declines occurring, some extinctions probable and imminent; immediate action including protection of specific key areas essential for continued existence of systems and assemblages.*
- Atlantic Forest
- Northern Andes

Group 2: *Most ecosystems seriously threatened, some critically so; some catastrophic declines occurring, a*

Figure 10.10 Regional levels of threat to ecosystems in the Neotropics.

few extinctions imminent; immediate action needed in all ecosystems to stem widespread declines.
Greater Antilles
Central South America
Central Andes

Group 3: Most ecosystems threatened and declining; catastrophic declines limited to specific taxa most sensitive to human impact; immediate and long-term action needed in all ecosystems to prevent further declines.
Lesser Antilles
Chocó Lowlands
Equatorial Pacific
Gulf-Caribbean Slope
Madrean Highlands

Group 4: Certain ecosystems threatened or vulnerable, but few catastrophic declines apparent; targeted protection needed to prevent further declines.
Chiriquí-Darién Highlands
Southern Amazonia
Northern South America
Northern Amazonia
Pacific Arid Slope

Group 5: Most ecosystems still functionally intact, few immediate threats; long-term protection recommended.
Baja-Sonora
Mexican Plateau
Subtropical Pacific
Southern Andes
Tepuis
Pampas
Patagonia

Some conservationists believe that overall conservation priorities should be driven at least in part by measures of species richness and uniqueness (endemism). These measures are incorporated into our final summary ranking, presented in the last column of table 10.20.

We close by emphasizing that the five zoogeographic regions ranking highest by threat alone also rank among those that are most diverse and most distinctive in the Neotropics. To accomplish the maximum long-term good, conservation action in the Neotropics should be directed preferentially and immediately to the *Northern Andes, Central South America,* the *Atlantic Forest,* the *Central Andes,* and the *Greater Antilles.* Ecosystems warranting special attention within these regions are specifically identified in table 10.18 and in our discussions of individual habitats within preceding chapters.

PART

4

Ecological and Distributional Databases

Theodore A. Parker III
Douglas F. Stotz
John W. Fitzpatrick

11 The Development of Ornithology for Conservation in the Neotropics

All of us were childhood birders in the 1960s and students in the 1970s. We first learned about Neotropical birds through resources available to our generation: excellent historical collections, a century and a half of primary regional literature, the great taxonomic compendiums of Ridgway, Cory and Hellmayr, and Peters, and a few key reference guides.

Our early musings about Neotropical ornithology were shaped by the writings of Hudson, Chapman, Wetmore, Carriker, Zimmer, Gyldenstolpe, Phelps and Phelps, Meyer de Schauensee, Blake, Olrog, Snow, Haffer, Skutch, and a few others. Many of these authors combined some personal experience with tropical avifaunas with more extensive study of taxonomy and distribution done in some of the great natural history museums of the Western world. We had the privilege of using these great collections ourselves. We pay special homage to the insightful observations of Chapman (1917, 1929) and Wetmore (1926, 1972); the critical taxonomic base provided by Hellmayr in his multivolume *Catalogue of the Birds of the Americas;* the first great Neotropical field guide, by Blake (1953); the enormously important reference volumes on South American birds by Meyer de Schauensee (1966, 1970); and the lifetime of dedicated exploration in South America by M. A. Carriker Jr.

As our own experiences in the Neotropics accumulated, we recognized major shortcomings in the historical collections and literature, especially when interpreted in a modern ecological context. Perhaps most important was a lack of firsthand experience by most authors over broad areas of Central and South America, a shortcoming imposed until just a few years ago by limitations in road and air travel. These limitations prevented even the best ornithologists of earlier eras from making their own comparisons among bird communities across the tropics. These scientists could not write about the range of ecological requirements of individual bird species or differentiate among subtle habitat gradients except by inference from museum specimens and locality data. Until just a few years ago little quantitative information existed on relative abundances, community compositions, species assemblages, habitat preferences, or behavior of Neotropical birds.

Unfortunately, field data traditionally recorded on avian specimen tags before the 1960s were woefully meager at best, and downright incorrect in some important cases. Precise data on geographic locality, elevation, habitat, fat and gonadal conditions, stomach contents, and cranial pneumatization rarely were recorded. Because of the small amount and uncertain reliability of ecologically important information, most of the historical literature and specimens are of limited use today in quantifying avian communities in the Neotropics. Their importance remains, of course, as permanent vouchers of bird communities, many of which were in habitats long since put asunder by humans.

Neotropical Ornithology, 1960–90

An explosion of exploratory research in Neotropical ornithology has continued unabated since about 1960, spearheaded most prominently by several generations of professors and students at Louisiana State University. Biologists from North America, Latin America, and Europe have carried out extensive regional surveys, taxonomic revisions, ecological analyses, behavioral studies, and conservation assessments in virtually every country of Central and South America. A review of this thirty-year episode of discovery is outside our present scope, but a taste of its fruits is available in the volume *Neotropical Ornithology,* commemorating the life and contributions of the late Eugene Eisenmann (Buckley et al. 1985).

Two important results of this recent period bear on our own project. First, extensive new information became available on geographical and ecological distributions of birds, at once revealing and eclipsing the flaws in the historical data on Neotropical birds. Second, this blizzard of new information on where to find tropical birds coincided with vigorous growth in birding by amateurs worldwide. An entire industry was spawned, with companies specializing in taking birders through some of the most exotic and remote corners of the Neotropics.

The growth of birding in the Neotropics began a positive feedback loop that continues to this day. A handful of skilled, professional bird-tour leaders rapidly accumulated new information on avian ecology, adding knowledge to the technical literature while enhancing their own ability to show tropical birds to tourists. A number of these tour leaders had graduate training in ecology and evolution, which helped ensure reliable observations and note taking. Some began using sound recording equipment, making it easier to lure secretive birds into view and producing valuable new information on the vocalizations of previously little known species. Many of these recordings are deposited in the Library of Natural Sounds at the Cornell Laboratory of Ornithology, where anyone can obtain access to them. All this new information, together with increasing numbers of skilled observers, has made it possible to inventory the avifauna at a given tropical locality with unprecedented thoroughness and speed.

Open exchange of information now occurs among a large circle of colleagues familiar with different geographic areas in the Neotropics. The burst of information about birds in these areas has led to the production of exhaustive illustrated guides covering several important areas of the Neotropics (most notably those of Hilty and Brown 1986; Ridgely and Gwynne 1989; Stiles and Skutch 1989; Fjeldså and Krabbe 1990; and Howell and Webb 1995). The databases in this volume represent an effort to synthesize this new information, along with much unpublished information of our colleagues' as well as our own, into a rapidly accessible and analyzable format.

The Conservation Era: ICBP's *Red Data Book*

Accompanying the new explosion of information on Neotropical birds in the 1970s and 1980s was the realization that many species were rapidly declining and that a few had become exceedingly rare. Indeed, a small handful of Neotropical species had reached, or passed, the brink of extinction. These were first cataloged by Vincent (1966–71) in the first edition of the *Red Data Book,* produced by the International Council for Bird Preservation (ICBP, now BirdLife International). A second, expanded edition of the *Red Data Book* (King 1981) listed a total of 114 Neotropical species and subspecies as endangered (41), vulnerable (20), rare (24), or indeterminate (29). Collar and Andrew (1988) provided brief paragraphs on 350 Neotropical species considered at risk or potentially so. That summary was a precursor to the publication of a greatly expanded third edition of the *Red Data Book* (Collar et al. 1992).

Although the two works serve different purposes, obvious similarities in timing and coverage between the project of Collar et al. (1992) and our own make it enlightening to compare the two. The *Red Data Book* (RDB) is an extremely important, elegantly written, scholarly encyclopedia covering 327 species that its authors consider the most seriously threatened in the Americas. Separate chapters on each species thoroughly document known distribution, ecology, recent population trends, and conservation measures under way. Our databases, which cover all Neotropical taxa, summarize key elements of these same data in tabular format so that patterns of cooccurrence and shared attributes may be sought. Our text (parts 1–3) explores some of these patterns, with an eye toward establishing regional and local conservation priorities. Readers interested in up-to-date information on the ecology and status of specific threatened species can glean a general picture from our databases but should consult the RDB (1992) for details. Our text refers little to individual species; we emphasize communities.

Although Parker was a coauthor of the RDB, time constraints prevented his being consulted for that volume's assessment of conservation priorities. Therefore the two works supply essentially independent assessments of conservation status for the 314 species treated in common, plus 316 additional taxa classified as "near threatened" by Collar et al. (1992, appendix D). General agreement between these assessments is clear from table 11.1.

The *Red Data Book* and this work differ most in classifying levels of threat below "endangered." Discrepancies at this level are to be expected, because these assessments represent efforts to see into the future. In the absence of hard data, attempts to classify levels of threat can only be educated guesses about future declines and extinction probabilities. Our concern over the early stages of threat reflects our objective of pinpointing regional habitats that are especially vulnerable. This led us to assign conservation priorities 2 and 3 to far more species than the comparable levels in the RDB (292 vs. 228, and 760 vs. 327, respectively). Some 526 species are considered at risk in our analysis but are not mentioned anywhere in the RDB. Most of these species exhibit combinations of small geographic range, habitat specialization, accelerating habitat destruction, and extreme sensitivity to human disturbance that convince us they are well on the way to becoming endangered.

The biggest discrepancies between rankings of specific species are explained by taxonomy. All nine taxa considered endangered by one set of authors and not listed at risk by the other reflect different taxonomic treatments: we do not split the endangered Jamaica Petrel (*Pterodroma caribbaea*) from the Black-capped Petrel (*P. hasitata*), Trinidad Piping Guan (*Aburria pi-*

Table 11.1 Conservation Priority Ratings in the Third Edition of the *Red Data Book* and in This Volume

CP Status in This Volume (*N*)	Category of Threat in the *Red Data Book*				
	Endangered	Indeterminate	Vulnerable/ Rare	Near-Threatened	Not Treated
CP-1 (70)	38	5	19	1	7
CP-2 (292)	41	27	107	84	33
CP-3 (760)	6	18	48	170	526
CP-4 (2,626)	0	2	3	64	2,557
Total	85	52	177	316	3,118

Note: Includes 314 of the 327 species covered in the *Red Data Book* (Collar et al. 1992); the remainder are North American (Nearctic) breeders or not recognized as distinct taxa in this volume.

pile) from continental taxa, or Alagoas Antwren (*Myrmotherula snowi*) from Unicolored Antwren (*M. unicolor*); and we treat the endangered Puna Rhea (*Pterocnemia tarapacensis*), Cuban Hook-billed Kite (*Chondrohierax wilsonii*), Masked Bobwhite (*Colinus ridgwayi*), White-collared Kite (*Leptodon forbesi*), Margaretta's Hermit (*Phaethornis margarettae*), and Snethlage's Woodcreeper (*Xiphocolaptes franiscanus*) as species, but Collar et al. (1992) do not. Of the 33 species we consider seriously threatened (CP-2) that are not listed in the RDB, two-thirds also reflect differences in taxonomy.

Seven taxa considered endangered by one system are judged to be only at the lowest level of risk (CP-3, "near threatened") by the other: we treat White-necked Crow (*Corvus leucognaphalus*) as endangered; and Collar et al. (1992) treat Dark-rumped Petrel (*Pterodroma phaeopygia*), Plain-flanked Rail (*Rallus wetmorei*), Little Woodstar (*Acestrura bombus*), Floreana Mockingbird (*Nesomimus trifasciatus*), Slaty Becard (*Pachyramphus spodiurus*), and Blackish-headed Spinetail (*Synallaxis tithys*) as endangered.

Collar et al. (1992) list 3 species as rare or vulnerable and an additional 64 as "near threatened" that we consider to be safe (CP-4). Some of these species (e.g., Venezuelan Bristle-Tyrant, *Phylloscartes venezuelanus*) occupy very small ranges, but our experience indicates that their habitats are secure. Others are widespread but rarely encountered (e.g., Agami Heron, *Agamia agami,* and Buff-fronted Owl, *Aegolius harrisii*), and we judge their long-term prospects to be good.

Minor variances in judgment as to rarity and threat should not mask the overall agreement between these two classification schemes. We embrace the sage words of Nigel Collar in his introduction (p. 14): "The plain fact of inclusion in this book is more significant for a species than the category it occupies." Any species suspected to be at risk by an assembly of experienced observers deserves attention.

For our purposes, the relative ranking of any one species is less important than are patterns of concordance among the assemblages of species. Whether one chooses to use the rankings in this book or those of Collar et al. (1992) for individual species, it is clear that the same patterns of regional threat will emerge (e.g., Bibby et al. 1992). These are the areas in the Neotropics that desperately need conservation action, now.

12 A Guide to the Databases

Two extensive data tables form the base for the analyses, discussions, and recommendations in parts 1 through 3. One (database A) presents key aspects of the ecology of Neotropical birds, from the zoogeographic regions and foraging strata for each bird to its research and conservation priorities. The other (database B) lists the status of each bird within the political units of the Neotropics. In addition, a series of smaller databases (databases C though H) provide data on wintering ecology and distribution of austral and northern migrants in the Neotropical region. A final database (database I) lists indicator species by region and habitat (see chapter 1).

In the preface we presented a brief history of the compiling of the databases. Here we concentrate on the sources beyond our personal experience that we relied on to amass the information, the taxonomic decisions we made during the process, and the variables and codes we used in each database. To manipulate the databases and analyze our results, we used a variety of programs for personal computers, especially SAS (1985a, 1985b, 1985c), Paradox 4.0 (Borland 1992a), Paradox for Windows (Borland 1992b), and Quattro Pro 4.0 (Borland 1992c).

Compiling of the Databases

Primary published sources included all the major reference works on Neotropical birds (see Database Sources). Important for Andean and Amazonian species were many unpublished expedition reports (written for the government agencies that issued research permits) and unpublished locality lists, primarily from Brazil, Bolivia, and Peru. Additional data on elevational distribution were gleaned from specimens housed in the Field Museum of Natural History (Chicago) and the Louisiana State University Museum of Natural Science (Baton Rouge). We also relied heavily on unpublished field notes at present stored in the LSUMNS (Parker) and the FMNH (Stotz). Compiling the data in database A was made easier by discussions with numerous colleagues, especially J. V. Remsen Jr. and J. P. O'Neill (LSUMNS); T. S. Schulenberg, D. E. Willard, and S. M. Lanyon (FMNH); M. B. Robbins and R. S. Ridgely (Academy of Natural Sciences, Philadelphia); and J. Fjeldså and N. Krabbe (Zoological Museum, University of Copenhagen). Schulenberg contributed most of the systematic and ecological information on the genus *Scytalopus*.

Together the authors have more than fifty years of experience in fieldwork and research on Neotropical birds: Parker 1972–93, Stotz 1978–94, Fitzpatrick 1974–86, and Moskovits 1975–82. At least one of us has visited each country in the Neotropics (including all the larger islands in the West Indies) except French Guiana, and we have extensive experience in Peru, Mexico, Bolivia, Brazil, Ecuador, and Venezuela.

Data on habitat, microhabitat, elevational distribution, center of abundance, and relative abundance were drawn from the relatively few published sources that we consider accurate and reliable. Unpublished references and personal field experience by Parker and Stotz constitute the basis for the bulk of the entries.

Taxonomic Decisions

We use the biological species (Mayr 1963) as the basic taxonomic unit in our analyses, despite recent suggestions for alternatives (e.g., Cracraft 1983; Donoghue 1985; McKitrick and Zink 1988). Treating geographically isolated populations as separate species—except in instances when these distinct populations represent special conservation concerns, as described below—would have deflected attention from the conservation issues we wish to emphasize. We can more effectively discern patterns useful in guiding conservation action by focusing on biological species.

Although we agreed to follow the biological species concept, we remained divided over many individual questions of higher-order taxonomy. Taxonomy in birds is currently in flux, with exciting discoveries being made with new biochemical techniques, morphological studies, and methods of analysis. Therefore, for the sake of consistency and simplicity we chose to follow standard taxonomic treatments at the higher levels. Although none of us are entirely pleased with the results, we believe that presenting the birds in a familiar, accessible format, consistent with most standard treatments of Neotropical birds, most closely conforms to our goals. We intend this book not as a taxonomic treatment of the Neotropical avifauna, but as an attempt to use birds in specifying ecological assemblages in the Neotropics in need of conservation action.

For the most part we follow the sequence and taxonomy of Morony, Bock, and Farrand (1975) for the level of genus, family, and order, keeping departures from this standard reference to a minimum. Some changes were necessary, however: (1) Opisthocomidae is treated as a member of the Cuculiformes and follows the Cuculidae as suggested by Sibley and Ahlquist (1990); (2) Furnariidae follow the classification of Peters (1951) rather than the radical departure based on Vaurie (1971a) used by Morony, Bock, and Farrand (1975) (see review of Vaurie 1980 by Fitzpatrick 1982, who discusses the taxonomy of Vaurie); (3) the family Conopophagidae is eliminated—the gnateaters, *Conopophaga,* are placed at the end of Formicariidae, and the antpipits, *Corythopis,* are included in Tyrannidae, following *Pseudotriccus* (Traylor 1979, based on work of Ames, Heimerdinger, and Warter 1968); (4) Tyrannoidea (Tyrannidae, Pipridae, Cotingidade, Oxyruncidae, and Phytotomidae) follows Traylor (1979); and (5) Black-capped Mockingthrush, *Donacobius,* is moved from Mimidae to the start of Troglodytidae (AOU 1983).

Our taxonomic approach results in the retention of some genera that recently are not treated as distinct, such as *Aerornis* and *Nephoecetes* among the Apodidae, and *Ochetorhynchus* in the Furnariidae. We also retain the possibly erroneous placement of some species. The Blue Finch, *Passerina caerulescens,* for example, probably does not belong in the genus *Passerina* (Parker, pers. obs.). As we stated above, however, these taxonomic questions are outside the realm of this book. Justifying individual taxonomic decisions would have diverted attention from the main conservation issues we want to stress.

To simplify access to information on particular species, we sequence species alphabetically within each genus. Although unusual among ornithologists, this convention is common for other vertebrate groups, where both genera within families and species within genera are alphabetized.

The databases include taxa listed as valid species by the sixth edition of the AOU checklist (AOU 1983) and subsequent supplements (AOU 1985, 1987, 1989, 1991, 1993), and with the few exceptions listed in table 12.1, species considered valid by Meyer de Schauensee (1970). We also include species that have been newly described or split from other taxa since the publication of these two basic taxonomic references. Species whose taxonomic status is considered doubtful by these two references (appendix A in Meyer de Schauensee 1970 and appendix C in AOU 1983) were not addressed unless recent work suggested the taxa are valid.

We also include in the databases taxa not considered separate species in most of the recent treatments. These taxa are listed by trinomials. In the text, and on the computer disks enclosed, we put the name of the species in which these taxa are customarily placed (or would be placed were they to be lumped) in parentheses.

In databases A–E, these taxa are indented below the binomial with which they are associated. For example, *Crypturellus (erythropis) columbianus* is shown as:

Crypturellus erythopis
  columbianus

These additional taxa fall into three groups:

1. Taxa recently treated as distinct species or newly described taxa, for which the evidence of specific status appears equivocal; for example, *Phaethornis (superciliaris) margarettae.*
2. Taxa that appear to be separate species based on vocalization differences, close approach of populations without hybridization, or other evidence, but for which detailed analyses and taxonomic conclusions remain unpublished; for example, the genus *Scytalopus,* for which we use a modification of the treatment of Fjeldså and Krabbe (1990) suggested by T. S. Schulenberg (pers. comm.).
3. Geographically isolated, morphologically distinctive populations that show differences in conservation status or ecology worthy of note by conservationists. For example, the two widespread forms of *Onychorhynchus,* Amazonian Royal Flycatcher (*O. coronatus*) and Northern Royal Flycatcher (*O. mexicanus*), were once considered separate species; today they usually are treated as conspecific (*O. coronatus*), and we do not dispute this view. However, two additional forms of *Onychorhynchus* with distinct plumage—the Pacific Royal Flycatcher, O. *(coronatus) occidentalis,* in the threatened dry forests of western Ecuador and Peru, and Atlantic Royal Flycatcher, O. *(coronatus) swainsoni,* in the disappearing Atlantic Forest of eastern Brazil—are of conservation interest. We believe they should be treated separately, and we therefore include all four *Onychorhynchus* as distinct forms.

Undoubtedly, as new genetic and behavioral data are obtained in the near future many forms within currently polytypic species will be recognized as distinct. We have indicated some examples in the notes in database A, to suggest possible areas of taxonomic re-

Table 12.1 Species Considered Valid by Meyer de Schauensee (1970) Not Included in Databases A and B

Species	Our Treatment		References
Falco kreyenbergi	Morph	*F. peregrinus*	Ellis and Garat 1983
Sterna eurygnatha	Subspecies	*S. sandvicensis*	AOU 1983
Pyrrhura hypoxantha	Aberrant	*P. molinae*	Forshaw 1973
Pyrrhura berlepschi	Subspecies	*P. melanura*	Ridgely and Robbins 1988
Glaucidium nanum	Morph	*G. brasilianum*	Marín A., Kiff, and Peña 1989
Phaethornis maranhaoensis	Male	*P. nattereri*	Hinklemann 1988
Coeligena orina	Juvenile	*C. bonapartei*	Bleiwiess 1988
Pteroglossus sanguineus	Subspecies	*P. torquatus*	Haffer 1974
Pteroglossus erythropygus	Subspecies	*P. torquatus*	Haffer 1974
Pteroglossus mariae	Subspecies	*P. flavirostris*	Haffer 1974
Ramphastos citreolaemus	Subspecies	*R. vitellinus*	Haffer 1974
Ramphastos culminatus	Subspecies	*R. vitellinus*	Haffer 1974
Ramphastos aurantiirostris	Subspecies	*R. tucanus*	Haffer 1974
Ramphastos cuvieri	Subspecies	*R. tucanus*	Haffer 1974
Picumnus borbae	Subspecies	*P. aurifrons*	Short 1982
Colaptes campestroides	Subspecies	*C. campestris*	Short 1982
Colaptes melanolaimus	Subspecies	*C. melanochloros*	Short 1982
Melanerpes rubrifrons	Morph	*M. cruentatus*	Short 1982
Synallaxis poliophrys	Aberrant	*S. frontalis*	Vaurie 1971b
Philydor hylobius	Juvenile	*Automolus roraimae*	Dickerman et al. 1986
Myrmeciza stictothorax	Aberrant	*M. atrothorax*	Schulenberg and Stotz 1990
Percnostola macrolopha	Female	*P. lophotes*	Parker 1982; Terborgh, Fitzpatrick, and Emmons 1984
Phlegopsis barringeri	Hybrid	*P. nigromaculata/erythroptera*	Graves 1992
Pipra obscura	Female	*P. vilasboasi*	Snow 1979
Serpophaga araguayae	Male	*Myiopagis caniceps*	Silva 1989
Serpophaga griseiceps	—	*S. munda*	Traylor 1979
Tyranniscus australis	—	*Phyllomyias sclateri*	Traylor 1979
Tachyphonus nattereri	Subspecies	*T. cristatus*	Zimmer 1945
Ramphocelus icteronotus	Subspecies	*R. flammigerus*	Isler and Isler 1987
Psarocolius yuracares	Subspecies	*P. bifasciatus*	Haffer 1974
Spinus santacrucis	Subspecies	*Carduelis magellanicus*	Howell, Paynter, and Rand 1968

search. However, we treat separately only the taxa that present special conservation concerns.

In a few special cases, we also use trinomials for taxa treated as valid species by AOU (1983) or Meyer de Schauensee (1970). These include:

1. Forms traditionally treated as conspecific in most recent references, such as Peters's *Check-list of Birds of the World,* but recognized as distinct species by AOU (1983) with no clear evidence or discussion regarding the species status; for example, the Blue-hooded Euphonia (*Euphonia musica*) complex.
2. Taxa treated as distinct species by our basic references and other literature, which we suspect to be conspecific based on plumage and behavior but for which there are no definitive taxonomic studies to confirm our suspicion; for example, Concolor Woodcreeper, *Dendrocolaptes (certhia) concolor.*

Database Descriptions and Definitions of Variables

Database A: Zoogeographic and Ecological Attributes of Bird Species Breeding in the Neotropics

Presented here are the 3,751 taxa of birds that breed in the Neotropical realm, that is, from northern Mexico to the southern tip of Argentina, including the West Indies. Information recorded in this database pertains to the distribution and ecology on breeding grounds only. Nonbreeding habits of migrants are listed separately, in the migrant databases (see below). Thirteen types of variables are listed for each bird.

Taxonomic Variables (Order, Family, Genus, Species)

Self-explanatory. Our taxonomic decisions are described in the section above; on a few occasions, we use trinomials.

Sensitivity to Disturbance (Snst)

Some bird species are considerably more vulnerable to human disturbance than others. We assign the qualitative variables listed below based on our observations and unpublished field notes. Species highly vulnerable to human disturbance are good indicators of the health of the environment.

H	High	L	Low
M	Medium	?	Unknown

Foraging Strata (Strat)

The level at which the bird forages within its habitat is specified, from terrestrial to aerial. When birds use more than one stratum, the range is shown (e.g., understory to canopy = U/C). Foraging strata may have specific implications for conservation when the forest is logged or cattle are allowed to roam through (essentially destroying the understory layer).

T	Terrestrial	C	Canopy
U	Understory (undergrowth)	A	Aerial
M	Midstory	W	Water

Center of Abundance (CntAb)

Center of abundance is the heart of the species' elevational distribution; it is the elevational zone in which the bird species is most common. This is especially informative for montane species that may range over several thousand meters up and down a slope but are most concentrated in a particular portion of their elevational range.

Most species in montane regions probably reach their population peak close to the mean elevational distribution (i.e., [min + max]/2). However, some species, especially those of the lower slopes of the mountains, or of treeline zones, have their population centers considerably offset from their mean elevations.

The elevation zones we use are:

LT	Lower Tropical Lowlands, lower than 500 m; tropics.
LS	Lower Subtropical Lowlands, lower than 500 m; subtropics.
HT	Hill Tropical Hills and lower slopes, 500–900 m; tropics.
UT	Upper Tropical Higher slopes, 900–1,600 m; tropics.
US	Upper Subtropical Higher slopes, 500–1,600 m; subtropics.
MM	Middle Montane Mountains, middle range, 1,600–2,600 m.
UM	Upper Montane Mountains, upper range, above 2,600 m.

Relative Abundance (Rel)

Relative abundances are based primarily on subjective impressions that stem from our collective field experience. Some have been confirmed by quantitative census work. "Common" species occur throughout their ranges in moderate to large numbers and are found easily during brief periods of fieldwork. These species occur in large numbers within small areas of preferred habitat, with densities of fifteen or more individuals per km^2 typical in lowland forest (Terborgh et al. 1990). "Uncommon" species are less numerous but are found readily in the proper habitat. Most uncommon species at a lowland evergreen forest site in southeastern Peru were represented by one to four pairs per km^2 (Terborgh, Fitzpatrick, and Emmons 1984; Munn 1985; Terborgh et al. 1990). "Rare" species are genuinely scarce and seldom encountered, even during prolonged stays in the field. Many have very large territories, some are nomadic, most are patchily distributed, and nearly all occur in small numbers throughout their ranges. Rare resident species usually are represented by fewer than one individual per km^2.

Variables used are:

C	Common	R	Rare
F	Fairly common	P	Patchily distributed
U	Uncommon		

We use a question mark to qualify uncertain status or indicate unknown abundance and a slash to indicate intermediate categories (e.g., common to fairly common) and to qualify abundance (e.g., common but patchily distributed).

Elevation (Min and Max)

We list the minimum and maximum elevational distribution for each species, with qualifiers (+, ?) when needed. In contrast to many authors, we exclude elevational records far outside the normal limits for the species. Instead, we indicate these records and geographic variation in the notes section of the database tables.

In both elevational fields we use *L* to denote species reaching either their minimum or their maximum elevation in relatively low-relief lowland areas. In lowland Amazonia, elevation ranges from sea level at the edge of the Atlantic Ocean to about 500 m along the base of the Andes. However, the distribution of birds in the lowlands does not reflect elevation per se. Instead, local topography, particularly as it affects the distribution of habitats, plays a much bigger role. So we do not attempt to distinguish among elevational distributions of birds in the lowlands.

Determining elevational distributions was particularly difficult. For montane species of the tropical Andes, Parker first referred to published and unpublished accounts of recent (1965–93) intensive inventories along elevational gradients in Ecuador, Peru, and Bolivia. Usually, lower and upper limits for Andean forest species were fairly uniform (within 50–100 m) from southeastern Colombia to northern Bolivia.

Elevational distributions were more difficult to pinpoint for some Middle American birds and for birds of montane southeastern Brazil. In these areas we relied on the very few publications with usable data, data from museum specimens, and our own field notes. Other problematic regions were the Caribbean, Tepuis, and southern Andes.

Microhabitats (Micro)

A bird's affinity for a specific feature of a habitat type is defined under microhabitats. For most birds we do not list a microhabitat. Seven types of microhabitats are considered and are described briefly in chapter 2.

These are:

A Army ant swarms
B Bamboo
G Ground bromeliads
R Rocky outcrops and caves
S Streamside
T Treefalls
V Vine tangles
B/V Bamboo/vine tangles

Habitats

We have distinguished forty-one habitat categories in the Neotropics, based on how birds appear to distinguish the vegetation types. These habitats (see chapter 2) consist of twenty-nine vegetation types—fifteen forest (F1–F15; includes human-disturbed or second-growth forests) and fourteen nonforest (N1–N14; scrubs and savannas, including pastures and disturbed, second-growth scrubs),plus twelve aquatic habitats (A1–A12; marshes, rivers, lakes, oceanic waters).

Up to seven habitats are recorded for each bird species. We list habitats in decreasing order of importance for a species. The first habitat is treated in the text analyses as the primary habitat of the species; this is the habitat the species uses most commonly over most of its range. This habitat preference tends to be sharp, but some species may use two or more habitats equally, in which case the order is somewhat arbitrary. We do not provide an exhaustive habitat list: we include only habitats the species uses or breeds in regularly within a significant portion of its range. For example, we list secondary forest only for birds that regularly breed in the habitat or that regularly use it without adjacent undisturbed forest. The habitat is not listed for species that merely visit second-growth forest, or that use it only when it is adjacent to undisturbed forest.

Habitat gradients, enclaves, and contact zones present problems. Because birds are assigned a habitat only if they occur in the habitat proper, transitional habitats in the field can share species that do not share a habitat in the database. Although this conflict is locally misleading, on a larger scale the species in transitional habitats are characteristic of different habitat types.

Four habitats always occur as enclaves within a matrix of *terra firme* (F1) forest. These are: *várzea* (F2), river-edge (F3), white sand (F12), and palm (F13) forests (see chapter 2). In eastern Brazil, palm forests (F13) are surrounded by dry forest (F7) instead. We have therefore approached the assignment of these four habitats differently from that of the others, assigning them only if the species shows a predilection for the specific forest type. For example, in southern São Paulo, White-bearded Manakin, *Manacus manacus*, and Swallow-tailed Manakin, *Chiroxiphia caudata,* are common in the taller restinga (F12). However, we assign this habitat only to *M. manacus*. This species occurs in restinga throughout eastern Brazil and is present in both tall and short restinga; it also occurs in the Amazonian white sand formations (Oren 1981); and it is rare in, or absent from, undisturbed humid forest in eastern Brazil. In contrast, *Chiroxiphia caudata* does not occur in restinga north of Rio de Janeiro; it disappears from the shorter, more open restinga and is far more common in the surrounding humid forest than in the restinga. As a result, we treat *C. caudata* as a humid forest bird that "spills over" into restinga only because of the proximity of the two habitats, and we do not assign it to restinga in the database.

Although some bird species occur mainly at the edges of undisturbed forest, they could not survive away from pristine habitat. To differentiate such primary forest-edge birds from ones that clearly have adapted to secondary forests, we add an E to the end of the habitat code (e.g., F1E for *terra firme* forest edge). A question mark follows habitat codes when the presence of the bird in that habitat is suspected but not confirmed.

For migrant bird species, we list only breeding habitats in database A. We cover their wintering ecology separately in the migrant databases.

Zoogeographic Regions and Subregions (Sub)

We divided the Neotropical realm into twenty-two regions (map 1, following index) that reflect areas of endemism in birds and probably in other taxa as well. Usually we relied on major vegetation structure and physiographic features to define the regional boundaries. For example, the zoogeographic region we term Amazonia North (AMN) is delineated by the Amazon River, the topographic and vegetation shift from the Amazonian lowlands to the Andean foothills, and the vegetation shift from the tropical rainforests of Amazonia to the open habitats of the llanos, at the Orinoco River.

We divided lowland and montane regions at elevations where extensive relief disappears, that is, where the foothills level out into relatively flat terrain. This elevation varies throughout Latin America. Along the west coast of South America and in eastern Brazil, the break comes at about 100–200 m. Along the base of the Andes and the Tepuis, the break is near 500 m, except in Patagonia and in the southern part of the Chaco, where broad, flat plateaus occur above 1,000 m. In Central America, the lowland versus montane definition is complex and varies substantially within the region.

Within regions, the locations of natural geographical subsets of avian endemism are defined as subregions (maps 2 and 3, following index). Many of our subregions coincide with the centers of distribution identified by Haffer (1974) and generally correspond to the areas of endemism defined by Cracraft (1985). Like Cracraft, we use a restricted definition of endemism, and we identified areas with overlapping distributions of these endemics. Not all regions have subregions, and no region has more than five subregions.

Species endemic to one region but occurring in more than one subregion are designated subregion "o". No subregion designation is given to species that occur in only one Neotropical region but are not endemic to that region because they also breed in an area not covered by this book (mostly North America north of Mexico, or oceanic islands outside the Neotropics). The subregion category therefore identifies all true Neotropical endemics. Only endemic species have entries in the subregion field.

For each Neotropical bird, we record all regions in which the species is known to breed, or in which breeding is inferred based on the bird's presence in appropriate habitats or seasons. When the breeding status or occurrence of a bird in a given region is highly questionable, the regional code is followed by a question mark. The regions are listed roughly from north to south, in the order presented below.

The twenty-two regions, and corresponding subregions (maps 1–3, following index), are described below. Total numbers of bird species vary from 896 in Amazonia North, to 110 in the Lesser Antilles. Along with each region's short description, we provide the total number of species breeding in, and endemic to, the region (see also chapter 9).

1. Greater Antilles (GAN) (250 species, 125 endemic)

The four main islands of the Greater Antilles (Cuba, Hispaniola, Jamaica, and Puerto Rico), along with smaller island groups (Bahamas, Cayman Islands, and Virgin Islands). We recognize the following subregions:

CUB Cuba
Cuba and its satellite islands.

HIS Hispaniola
Hispaniola with satellite islands.

JAM Jamaica
Jamaica with satellite islands, including Cayman Islands.

PUE Puerto Rico
Puerto Rico with satellite islands, and Virgin Islands.

BAH Bahamas
All islands and cays of the Bahamas, and the Turks and Caicos Islands.

ISA Isla Providencia and Isla San Andrés
Islands about 200 km east of the coast of Nicaragua (which are politically part of Colombia). These are included because a handful of GAN birds live on the islands.

2. Lesser Antilles (LAN) (110 species, 24 endemic)

The island chain stretching from Anguilla to Grenada and Barbados. We do not recognize subregions as such, but we identify single islands to which birds are endemic in the subregion field.

Single Islands

DOM	Dominica	MON	Montserrat
GRE	Grenada	STL	St. Lucia
GUA	Guadeloupe	STV	St. Vincent
MRT	Martinique		

3. Baja-Sonora (BSR) (239 species, 18 endemic)

All of Baja California, along with the coastal plain and arid foothills of Sonora, south to the Río Yaqui valley and east to the lower limit of pine-oak woodland. We recognize two subregions:

BAJ Baja California
The states of Baja California Norte and Baja California Sur.

SON Sonoran Desert
The part of Sonora mentioned above.

4. Mexican Plateau (MPL) (122 species, 2 endemic)

The open arid formations and riparian areas of north-central Mexico, from the United States border south to the states of Aguascalientes, Guanajuato, and San Luis Potosí, bordered on the east by the Sierra Madre Oriental and on the west by the Sierra Madre Occidental. We recognize no subregions.

5. Pacific Arid Slope (PAS) (358 species, 36 endemic)

The dry lowland regions of the Pacific slope, from southern Sonora south to Guanacaste, Costa Rica. We recognize four subregions:

SIN Sinaloa-Oaxaca
Southern Sonora south to the Isthmus of Tehuantepec.

CHG Chiapas-Guanacaste
Isthmus of Tehuantepec south to Guanacaste Province, Costa Rica.

SOC Islas Revillagigedo (Socorro island group)
The Revillagigedo island group off the Pacific coast of Mexico.

CIS Cocos Island
Cocos Island, off the Pacific coast of Costa Rica.

6. Madrean Highlands (MAH) (379 species, 107 endemic)

The mountains of northern Middle America, from the Sierra Madre Occidental and Oriental, in Mexico, south to Nicaragua. Also includes the complex basin and range system in central Mexico. We recognize three subregions:

NMM Northern Mexican Mountains
Mountains of northern Mexico from northern Sonora and Chihuahua south to the volcanoes of Colima in the west, and from Coahuila to San Luis Potosí in the east. Includes the intervening highlands and volcanoes from Guanajuato south to the Balsas depression.

SMH Southern Mexican Highlands
Mountains and intervening high elevation basins, from and including the Balsas depression, southern Puebla, and central Veracruz, south to the Isthmus of Tehuantepec. Includes the isolated western ranges of the Sierra Madre del Sur.

CAH Central American Highlands
Mountains of central Middle America, from the Isthmus of Tehuantepec southeast through the montane regions of Guatemala, Belize, and Honduras, to the southern border of Nicaragua.

7. Gulf-Caribbean Slope (GCS) (689 species, 74 endemic)

The eastern slope lowlands of Middle America, from the United States border of Mexico south to the Colombian border of Panama. Includes the humid lowland regions of the Pacific slope of Panama and Costa Rica, south of Guanacaste. We recognize four subregions:

GCM Gulf Coast–Mexico
The Gulf lowlands of eastern Mexico, from the United States border south to Veracruz and northern Chiapas.

YUC Yucatán Peninsula
The Yucatán peninsula, including the Mexican states of Yucatán, Campeche, and Quintana Roo; northern Belize; and the Petén region of Guatemala.

SCA Southern Central America
The Caribbean lowlands, from Guatemala south to the border of Panama and Colombia.

HPC Humid Pacific Coast
The Pacific lowlands of Costa Rica and Panama, from the Gulf of Nicoya south to the Colombian border.

8. Chiriquí-Darién Highlands (CDH) (279 species, 69 endemic)

The mountains and high basins of Costa Rica and Panama. We recognize two subregions:

CHR Chiriquí
The montane areas of Costa Rica and south to the Chiriquí region of western Panama.

TAC Tacarcuna
The montane regions of Panama, south of the Chiriquí. Includes a variety of small peaks and ridges through much of Panama, as well as Cerro Tacarcuna and Cerro Pirre in eastern Darién.

9. Chocó Lowlands (CHO) (401 species, 24 endemic)

The wet lowland forests of Colombia and Ecuador, west of the Andes, from the Gulf of Urabá near the border with Panama, south to Esmeraldas and Pichincha in Ecuador. We recognize no subregions.

Note: The western slopes of the Andes often are included in the Chocó region (e.g., Cracraft 1985). However, the avifauna on the slopes, including most of the endemics, is primarily of montane origin. We therefore consider the western slope of the Andes as a subregion (WES) of the Northern Andes (see NAN) and restrict Chocó to the lowlands.

10. Equatorial Pacific (EPC) (289 species, 73 endemic)

The arid and semiarid lowlands of western Ecuador and Peru, and the Galápagos Islands. We recognize two subregions:

MAN Manabí-Tumbes
The Pacific lowlands, from Manabí, Ecuador, south to Lambayeque, Peru.

GAL Galápagos
The Galápagos Islands, off the coast of Ecuador.

11. Subtropical Pacific (STP) (206 species, 19 endemic)

The desert regions of Peru and Chile, and the Juan Fernández Islands. We recognize three subregions:

PER Peruvian Desert
The lowlands of Peru, from Lambayeque south to the border with Chile.

CHL Chilean Desert
The lowlands of Chile, from the border with Peru south to Maule.

JFI Juan Fernández Islands
The Juan Fernández island group, off the coast of Chile.

12. Northern Andes (NAN) (772 species, 222 endemic)

All the montane regions, from the coastal cordilleras of Venezuela, south to Porculla Pass and the Río Marañón, in Peru. We recognize five subregions:

VNZ Venezuelan Coastal Mountains
Various montane ridges in northern Venezuela, north of the Río Orinoco, extending from Falcón to the Paria peninsula in Sucre.

VAN Venezuelan Andes
The Andes of Venezuela, including the Merida Andes and the Sierra de Perija.

SMT Santa Marta
The Sierra Nevada de Santa Marta, northeastern Colombia.

EAS Eastern Slope Andes
The Eastern and Central Andes of Colombia, and the eastern slope and central valleys of Ecuador and northern Peru, south to the lower limit of humid forest above the Río Marañón. The continental divide separates EAS from WES (below) south of the Magdalena valley.

WES Western Andes
The Western Andes of Colombia and the Pacific slope of the Andes, from Nariño, southern Colombia, south to Porculla Pass, Peru.

13. Central Andes (CAN) (804 species, 216 endemic)

The montane regions and associated valleys from Porculla Pass and the Marañón Valley, Peru, south to Tucumán and Catamarca, Argentina, and northern Atacama, Chile. We define the following subregions:

MAR Marañón Valley
The arid portion of the valleys of the Río Marañón and its tributaries, from Amazonas south to Huanuco.

MTC Marañón-Cuzco
The humid forest region from the southeast side of the Río Marañón, beginning near Bagua, northwestern Peru, south to and including the Río Urubamba and its tributaries in Cuzco.

COC Cuzco-Cochabamba
The humid forest region from the upper reaches of the Madre de Dios drainage, southeastern Peru, south and east to the Cochabamba border with Santa Cruz and Chuquisaca, Bolivia.

SCT Santa Cruz–Tucumán
The humid forest region from Santa Cruz and Chuquisaca, Bolivia, south to the southern extent of humid forest in Tucumán and Catamarca, Argentina.

AWA Altiplano and Western Andes
The altiplano, the Pacific slope of the Andes, and the associated arid interior valleys, from Porculla Pass and the Río Marañón, Peru, south to Salta and Antofagasta. The upper edge of the humid forest, which averages about 3,500 m elevation, separates AWA from the eastern side of the Andes.

14. Southern Andes (SAN) (197 species, 23 endemic)

The Andes, from Atacama (Chile) and La Rioja (Argentina) south. Also includes the isolated ranges in Córdoba and San Luís, Argentina; the lowland temperate forest and lake region in Chile, south of Maule; and Tierra del Fuego. We recognize no subregions.

15. Northern South America (NSA) (652 species, 41 endemic)

The lowland areas north of the Ríos Orinoco and Meta west to the Gulf of Urabá (Colombia), and east to include the Orinoco delta. Also includes the near offshore islands in the southern Caribbean: Netherlands Antilles, Trinidad, Tobago, and various small islands belonging to Venezuela. We recognize two subregions:

ARC Arid Caribbean Coast
Arid coastal region, stretching from Atlantico, Colombia, to Monagas, Venezuela, south to the Río Orinoco.

CMV Cauca-Magdalena Valley
The mainly semiarid, low-lying portion of the Cauca, Magdalena, Sinú, and Nechi valleys, in Colombia.

16. Tepuis (TEP) (142 species, 36 endemic)

The montane and Gran Sabana regions of southern Venezuela, and associated highlands near the borders of northeastern Brazil and Guyana, south and east to the Acary Mountains of Guyana. We recognize no subregions.

17. Amazonia North (AMN) (896 species, 76 endemic)

The area from the Ríos Orinoco and Meta in Venezuela (except the montane areas included in the Tepuis) south to the Rios Amazonas and Solimões in Brazil, and the Río Marañón in Peru, west to the base of the Andes, and east to the Atlantic Ocean. We recognize two subregions:

GUI Guianan
Lowlands north of the Rio Amazonas, from the Rio Negro and Rio Branco east to the Atlantic Ocean.

RNW Río Negro West
Lowlands north of the Rio Solimões and Río Marañón, from the Rio Negro and Rio Branco west to the base of the Andes.

18. Amazonia South (AMS) (892 species, 79 endemic)

The area south of the Río Marañón, Rio Solimões, and Rio Amazonas, west to the base of the Andes and south and east to the edge of Amazonian forest in Santa Cruz, Bolivia, and Mato Grosso, Goiás, and Maranhão, Brazil. We recognize the following subregions:

PAR Pará
Amazonian forest region south of the Rio Amazonas and east of the Rios Tapajós and Teles Pires, east to Maranhão and Goiás.

MID Madeira-Tapajós
Region south of the Rio Amazonas, between the Rio Madeira and Río Beni (Brazil and Bolivia), and the Rio Tapajós (Brazil), south to the edge of Amazonian forest in Beni and Santa Cruz, Bolivia.

RMW Rio Madeira West
Lowland region west of the Rio Madeira and Río Beni, south and west to the base of the Andes.

19. Central South America (CSA) (645 species, 112 endemic)

The lowland, open habitats stretching from Maranhão east to Rio Grande do Norte, and south through interior eastern Brazil, eastern Bolivia, and Paraguay to Río Negro in central Argentina. This region separates the humid Amazonian forests from the humid forests of coastal eastern Brazil. We recognize three subregions:

CAA Caatinga
The arid and semiarid region of northeastern Brazil, from the Atlantic coast on the north to southern Bahia on the south.

CER Cerrado
A complex of semiarid habitats, occurring from Goiás and Minas Gerais south and west to northeastern Santa Cruz in Bolivia, northeastern Paraguay, and Mato Grosso do Sul (excluding the pantanal) and western São Paulo in Brazil.

CHA Chaco
A complex of three main vegetative formations: pantanal, chaco, and monte. It ranges from eastern Bolivia (Santa Cruz and southern Beni) and western Brazil (the pantanal of Mato Grosso and Mato Grosso do Sul), west to the base of the Andes, and south to Río Negro in Argentina.

20. Atlantic Forest (ATL) (682 species, 199 endemic)

The humid coastal forest region of eastern Brazil, from Ceará south to the escarpment of central Rio Grande do Sul. Also includes the humid forests of the middle Río Paraná drainage of eastern Paraguay, extreme northeastern Argentina in Misiones, and interior southern Brazil from Goiás and Minas Gerais to Rio Grande do Sul. We recognize four subregions:

FDN Fernando de Noronha
Fernando de Noronha island, off the coast of northeastern Brazil.

NOR Northern Coastal Brazil
The humid forest region of northeastern Brazil, from Ceará south to the Rio São Francisco. Throughout much of this region, humid forests form a mosaic with the arid formations of the caatinga region, which are included in Central South America.

RDJ Rio de Janeiro–Bahia Lowlands
The lowland forest region from the Rio São Francisco on the north, south along the coastal plain to the lowlands around the city of Rio de Janeiro.

SOU Southern Atlantic Coast
Forested region from Rio de Janeiro south to Rio Grande do Sul, including the forests of the Paraná drainage. Also includes the montane forests in Espírito Santo, southern Goiás, and eastern Minas Gerais, and the patches of humid forest on the planaltos of Minas Gerais and southern Goiás.

21. Pampas (PAM) (249 species, 8 endemic)

The region from the base of the escarpment in Rio Grande do Sul (Brazil), south through Uruguay to the Río Colorado in southern Buenos Aires (Argentina), west to La Pampa (Argentina), and northeast through Santa Fé to Corrientes (Argentina). We recognize no subregions.

22. Patagonia (PAT) (182 species, 22 endemic)

The lowland, open region from Río Negro, Argentina, south to Tierra del Fuego and west to the base of the Andes as well as the Islas Malvinas (Falkland Islands). We recognize no subregions.

For zoogeographic regions not delimited by some geographic barrier such as a river or deep valley, transition zones between regions can create definition problems. When the zoogeographic region is associated with a vegetation type, regions were assigned to birds based on the species' characteristic habitat type (see also Habitats, above). Similarly, in transition zones between montane and lowland zoogeographic regions, assignments were based on a species' use of specifically montane habitats (e.g., humid montane forest) or its occurrence up to high elevations (above 2,000 m). This problem is especially evident in Central America, where much of the lowland avifauna climbs into the foothills.

Coastal and oceanic waters are assigned to the adjacent zoogeographic region except in three cases:

1. The coastal and oceanic waters of Costa Rica and Panama, south of the Gulf of Nicoya, are assigned to the Pacific Arid Slope (PAS) rather than to the Gulf-Caribbean Slope (GCS). This assignment avoids placing species restricted to Pacific waters in a region with Gulf and Caribbean species.
2. The waters off the entire coast of eastern Brazil are assigned to the Atlantic Forest (ATL) region; no coastal habitat of northeastern Brazil is placed in Central South America (CSA). This avoids splitting a natural group of birds into two poorly defined units.
3. The coastal and oceanic waters off southern Chile are assigned to Patagonia (PAT) rather than to the Southern Andes (SAN). As above, this assignment avoids dividing a natural group of birds.

Conservation Priority (CP)

We determined conservation priorities subjectively for most species. Where possible, this variable reflects published data on a particular species' population status (population size and trends) and on its vulnerability to various threats. Most of the data available came from unpublished notes from colleagues and from our own fieldwork. For the many species for which population data were not available, we estimated the conservation priority based on status of the species' habitat (e.g., destruction rates, amount of unaltered habitat still remaining, and level of protection to these remaining patches in each species' range); the species' range size, elevational distribution, relative abundance, habitat tolerance, and sensitivity to disturbance; and any pressures on the species imposed by hunting or the pet trade.

We use four qualitative measures of conservation priority:

1 Urgent: species already is *endangered;* in need of conservation action to survive.
2 High: species is *threatened,* usually because of range and/or habitat restriction; already showing signs of serious population decline.
3 Medium: species is not in short-term danger but is *vulnerable* if present trends in habitat destruction continue.
4 Low: species is of widespread distribution, is a habitat generalist, and/or uses nonthreatened habitats; not at risk.

Research Priority (RP)

Research priorities are based on the knowledge of the life history, distribution, and taxonomy of a species. Only a few Neotropical species have been studied in detail (mostly in Costa Rica). Poorly known and seemingly rare species with small geographic ranges were given high research priority, as were some fairly common species that occur patchily within large ranges. Most species with high research priority have some ecological peculiarity that might be important for conservation. Species with low research priority are either well-known or nonthreatened species of widespread distribution.

1 High
2 Medium
3 Low

Notes (Notes)

Special notes on taxonomy, distribution (range and elevation), or conservation concerns are included when necessary.

Database B: Distribution of Neotropical Bird Species by Country

Included here are the 4,037 taxa of birds that breed, migrate through, or visit the Neotropics. For each of the twenty-nine Latin American political units that we consider independently, we indicate whether the species is vagrant, migrant, resident, or endemic to the area.

This database provides instant access to lists of locally endemic species whose protection depends exclusively on the actions of a single political unit. It also presents a quick synopsis of the species' distribution. Four types of variables are recorded for each bird.

Taxonomic Variables (Order, Family, Genus, Species)

The order, family, genus, and species are indicated, based on taxonomic decisions described above. In a few cases we use trinomials.

Political Units

We consider a total of twenty-nine political units in the Neotropics separately. Oceanic islands claimed or administered by mainland Latin American countries are included under those countries except for Easter Island (Chile) and various subantarctic islands claimed by Chile or Argentina. Clipperton Island off the Pacific coast of Mexico, administered by France, also is excluded despite its inclusion in a recent guide to Mexican birds (Howell and Webb 1995). The avifauna of the Islas Malvinas (Falkland Islands) is treated under Argentina. The islands not treated here have seabirds that occur nowhere else in the Neotropics, have no land birds, and therefore do not show faunal affinities with the Neotropics. In alphabetical order, the units are:

Argn	Argentina
Baha	Bahamas
Beli	Belize
Boli	Bolivia
Braz	Brazil
Chil	Chile
Colo	Colombia
Cost	Costa Rica
Cuba	Cuba
Ecua	Ecuador
Elsa	El Salvador
Fren	French Guiana
Guat	Guatemala
Guya	Guyana
Hisp	Hispaniola (includes Haiti and the Dominican Republic)
Hond	Honduras
Jama	Jamaica
Lant	Lesser Antilles (includes all the islands in the Lesser Antilles)
Mexi	Mexico
Nant	Netherlands Antilles
Nica	Nicaragua
Pana	Panama
Parg	Paraguay
Peru	Peru
Puer	Puerto Rico
Suri	Suriname

Trin Trinidad
Urug Uruguay
Vene Venezuela

Occurrence Status

Within each political unit, the status of the bird is given:

- X Breeding species. Also included are species for which actual breeding evidence is lacking, but for which breeding seems likely based on the species' status as resident or summer resident.
- XN Nonbreeding species that occur regularly.
- XR Endemic breeding species. These species do not breed elsewhere, although they may occur as vagrants or even as regular nonbreeders in other countries.
- X? Species that occur regularly, but with uncertain breeding status.
- XI Introduced species.
- XD Dubious species; of doubtful taxonomic validity.
- XF Formerly a breeding species in the area.
- V Vagrants: generally fewer than five records for the country.
- S Sight records only. In this database, species whose occurrence in a country is supported by recognizable photographs or sound recordings are classified with those supported by specimen records as documented and are not listed as sight records. The "sight record only" categories are equivalent to those above, differing only in the weaker documentation of the species' occurrence.
- SX Breeding species (known by sight records only).
- SN Nonbreeding species that occur regularly (sight records only).
- S? Uncertain breeding status (sight records only).
- SI Introduced (sight records only).
- SV Vagrant (sight records only).
- ? Occurrence uncertain. Specimen exists or existed, but the country of origin or identification is uncertain. Also includes records from major, reliable references (e.g., AOU checklist, Meyer de Schauensee, Peters, some country-specific references) that we were unable to trace or confirm.
- + Recently extinct (since 1920).

Migrant Databases

The ecological information on migrant birds in the Neotropics is divided among six databases. The first three—databases C, D, and E—include all migrants except seabirds, whose wintering ranges differ substantially from the breeding ranges. We provide data on distribution, elevational range, and habitat use during the period of winter residence. We exclude information on transitory periods because most birds, except shorebirds, occur over a wide range of habitats during migration. From a conservation viewpoint, effects of habitat alteration tend to be of less concern along the migration route than they are on the wintering grounds (but see Myers 1983; Myers et al. 1987; and chapter 6). The distribution by country for all Neotropical migrant birds is included in database B.

The information listed for migrants in databases C, D, and E is equivalent to that provided for breeders in database A (with some variables omitted to limit redundancy, as noted under the description of each database). A new variable—status (Stat)—is given for Nearctic migrants (databases C, D, and G). The four status categories reflect the extent to which a species' wintering range occurs within the Neotropics:

- F (Fraction) Wintering range almost completely outside the Neotropical region, with a very small fraction (less than 5%) of the North American breeding population wintering in the Neotropics.
- S (Some) Wintering range substantially Neotropical, but with significant wintering populations remaining in the United States or Canada. This includes species with the bulk of their wintering populations in the Neotropics (e.g., Lesser Yellowlegs, *Tringa flavipes*; Vermilion Flycatcher, *Pyrocephalus rubinus*), as well as species wintering primarily in the United States and Canada (e.g., Eastern Phoebe, *Sayornis phoebe*; Lark Bunting, *Calamospiza melanocorys*).
- A (All) Wintering range entirely or almost entirely encompassed within the Neotropical region. This includes species with few individuals wintering in the southernmost United States (e.g., Hammond's Flycatcher, *Empidonax hammondii*; Cape May Warbler, *Dendroica tigrina*; and Common Tern, *Sterna hirundo*).
- T (Total) Wintering and breeding ranges entirely within the Neotropical region; no breeding populations in the United States or Canada.

Species in categories A and T may become endangered or even extinct because of excessive mortality in the Neotropical wintering area. Similarly, high mortality in the tropics might cause species in category S to show serious population declines. Population levels of species in category F are unlikely to be affected by events within their small wintering populations in the tropics.

Databases F, G, and H consist of species lists only. Nonbreeding seabirds that winter exclusively in pelagic waters are listed in database F, and birds that migrate but do not occupy different ecological or distributional areas in winter appear in databases G (Nearctic partial migrants) and H (austral partial migrants). A description of the six migrant databases follows:

Database C: Nearctic migrants (no breeding in the tropics). Included are 187 species that occur regularly in the Neotropical region, but only as nonbreeders. Birds that winter exclusively in pelagic waters are listed elsewhere (database F). The variables Strat, CntAb, Rel, Micro, and Sub are omitted from this database.

Database D: Nearctic migrants (some breeding in the tropics). Included are 138 species that breed partly or fully within the Neotropical region and extend their distribution southward in the winter into zoogeographic regions, habitats, or elevational ranges not occupied by breeding populations. Status categories indicate the extent to which breeding populations in the United States and Canada move to the Neotropics in winter. For example, a species with extensive Neotropical resident populations, such as the Short-eared Owl, *Asio flammeus,* is assigned category F because only a small portion of the breeding population of the United States and Canada reaches the Neotropics. The variables Strat, CntAb, Rel, Micro, Sub, CP, and RP are omitted from this database. This information is in the main ecology database (database A).

Database E: Austral migrants. Included here are 78 species that breed in the Neotropical region but extend their distribution northward in winter into zoogeographic regions, habitats, or elevational ranges not occupied by breeding populations. The variables Strat, CntAb, Rel, Micro, Sub, CP, and RP, are omitted from this database. This information is available in the main ecology table (database A).

Database F: Nonbreeding seabirds. Included here are 49 species that occur regularly within the Neotropical region only in pelagic waters and that do not breed within the region. Database B provides details on the distribution of these species within the Neotropics. As noted earlier (chapter 6), important conservation issues for seabirds are, as a whole, significantly different from those for terrestrial and freshwater birds and are not discussed in this book. We include this list for completeness.

Database G: Nearctic partial migrants. Included here are 97 species with northern populations that are partially or entirely migratory but winter entirely within the breeding distribution of the species as a whole. For example, populations of Rose-throated Becard, *Pachyramphus aglaiae,* breeding in southern Arizona, southern Texas, and northern Sonora withdraw southward in the winter, disappearing into the range of resident populations farther south. Individuals of certain species in this database may winter in local areas not occupied by breeding populations; however, wintering individuals do not regularly occupy different zoogeographic regions, habitats, or elevational ranges than in the breeding season. For example, House Wrens, *Troglodytes (aedon) aedon,* regularly winter in the lowlands of northern Mexico and Sonora, two regions that lack breeding populations of this species. However, House Wrens breed in southern Mexico, which is treated here as part of the same zoogeographic region as northeastern Mexico (Gulf-Caribbean Slope), and they breed in northern Baja California, treated as part of the same zoogeographic region as the lowlands of Sonora. Species in this database also are assigned a status category.

Database H: Austral partial migrants. In this mirror image of database G are included 159 species with southern populations that are partially or completely migratory but winter entirely within the breeding distribution of the species as a whole. For example, Tropical Kingbird, *Tyrannus melancholicus,* is migratory over a wide area in southern Brazil, Argentina, and Paraguay. These populations apparently winter in Amazonia, where they cooccur with a substantial resident population of the same species. As in database G, individuals of some species included in this database winter in local areas from which they are absent as breeders. However, these species do not extend into new zoogeographic regions, habitats, or elevational ranges.

Database I: Indicator species. Presented here are seventy-eight lists of indicator species, grouped by zoogeographic region and arranged by habitat within each region. Lists that are not specific to a single zoogeographic region—deciduous forests, mangrove forests, and second growth—are placed at the end. Lists for indicator species of bamboo—a microhabitat—are also provided within the context of the particular zoogeographic region.

We chose as indicator species those birds whose presence at a site indicates that the site is a high-quality example of the particular habitat type (see discussion in chapter 1). The ideal list of indicator species would be composed of several species that are restricted to the habitat in question, are highly sensitive to disturbance, and are easily sampled. The lists for the various humid forest habitats approach such an ideal. For most other habitats, however, limited levels of habitat specialization and of sensitivity to human disturbance required us to relax our standards. Nonetheless, for all primary habitats, species included on the indicator species list are ones most strongly associated with the habitat and most susceptible to disturbance, while also common enough to serve as good indicators.

Lists are presented at the regional level, not the local

level. We also include species that occur in only part of the region, but that serve as good indicators for that portion. This means that some species may not occur at a particular site within the region, and appropriate field guides must be used to confirm the geographic distribution of the species. For example, the antwrens *Myrmotherula haematonota* and *M. gutturalis* are part of the Northern Amazonia Tropical Lowland Evergreen Forest indicator species list. *Myrmotherula haematonota* is restricted to forests west of the Rio Negro/Rio Branco. East of these rivers it is replaced by *M. gutturalis*. Obviously, not finding *M. haematonota* outside its range—at a forest site in Amapá, eastern Brazil, for example—has no ecological significance. However, the absence of *M. gutturalis* would indicate that a significant portion of this habitat's typical avifauna could be missing at the site. Absence of a number of other indicator species would confirm that the site is of poor quality.

Use of indicator species lists is complicated by the different forms of human disturbance. Some of the species on the lists may be quite susceptible to hunting (e.g., cracids, tinamous) and may be absent from a site that contains an otherwise relatively intact avifauna. Evaluation of the condition of a habitat patch using indicator species should be couched within regional comparisons. How does a particular site compare with other patches in the same region? Heavily hunted species may be largely or completely extirpated from certain regions and would be poor indicators of the condition of a habitat within those regions. In less disturbed areas, however, these same species could be the first alert for signs of serious disturbance.

Mangrove forests and second-growth habitats are not separated into regional lists because these communities vary little geographically. As with the other indicator species lists, users must consult appropriate field guides for the particular area of interest. Tropical deciduous forests also are not separated geographically. Because of the nature of these forests, habitat-restricted endemics are used as the indicator species for this habitat, as discussed in chapter 4.

Database A

Zoogeographic and Ecological Attributes of Bird Species Breeding in the Neotropics

	Snst	Strat	Cntab	Rel	Min	Max	Micro	Habitats	Sub	Zoogeographic Regions
RHEIFORMES										
Rheidae										
Rhea americana	L	T	LT	U/F	L	1200		N5, N6, N4, N7		CSA, PAM, PAT
Pterocnemia pennata										
pennata	M	T	LS	U	L	2000		N7, N1		SAN, PAT
tarapacensis	M	T	UM	R	4000	4500		N9	AWA	CAN
TINAMIFORMES										
Tinamidae										
Tinamus guttatus	H	T	LT	F	L	850		F1		AMN, AMS
Tinamus major	M	T	LT	F	L	1000		F1, F2, F15?		GCS, CHO, NSA, AMN, AMS
Tinamus osgoodi	H	T	UT	R	900	2100		F4		NAN, CAN
Tinamus solitarius	M	T	LT	U	L	1200		F1	o	ATL
Tinamus tao	H	T	LT	U	L	1900		F1, F4		NAN, CAN, NSA, AMN, AMS
Nothocercus bonapartei	H	T	MM	F	1300	2500		F4		CDH, NAN
Nothocercus julius	H	T	UM	U	1700	3350		F5, F4		NAN, CAN
Nothocercus nigrocapillus	H	T	MM	U	1550	3000		F4	o	CAN
Crypturellus atrocapillus	L	T	LT	F/P	L	900		F1E, F15	RMW	AMS
Crypturellus bartletti	H	T	LT	F	L	500		F2, F1		AMN, AMS
Crypturellus berlepschi	M	T	LT	F	L	500		F1E, F15	o	CHO
Crypturellus boucardi	M	T	LT	F	L	800+		F1, F15		PAS, GCS
Crypturellus brevirostris	H	T	LT	F	L	500		F2, F1		AMN, AMS
Crypturellus casiquiare	H	T	LT	?	L	L		F1?	RNW	AMN
Crypturellus cinereus	L	T	LT	F	L	700		F2, F3, F15		AMN, AMS
Crypturellus cinnamomeus	L	T	LT	C	L	1850		F8, F7, F15		PAS, GCS
Crypturellus duidae	M	T	LT	?	L	500		F12, F1?	RNW	AMN
Crypturellus erythropus										
columbianus	?	T	LT	?	L	600?		F1?	CMV	NSA
erythropus	L	T	LT	F	L	1300		F7, F8, F1E, F15, F12		NSA, AMN
idoneus	M	T	LT	?	L	1300		F7	ARC	NSA
saltuarius	?	T	LT?	R?	L	L?		F7?	CMV	NSA
Crypturellus kerriae	H	T	HT	U	300	800		F1	o	CHO
Crypturellus noctivagus	M	T	LT	F	L	700+		F1, F15	o	ATL
Crypturellus obsoletus	L	T	UT	F	L	2600		F4, F1		NAN, CAN, AMS, ATL
Crypturellus parvirostris	L	T	LT	C	L	1200		N4, N1, N14		AMS, CSA, ATL
Crypturellus ptaritepui	H	T	UT	?	1350	1800		F4	o	TEP
Crypturellus soui	L	T	LT	C	L	1500		F1E, F15, F3		GCS, CHO, NSA, AMN, AMS, CSA, ATL
Crypturellus strigulosus	H	T	LT	F	L	L	T?	F1	o	AMS
Crypturellus tataupa	L	T	LT	F	L	1400		F7, F1E, F15		AMS, CSA, ATL
Crypturellus transfasciatus	M	T	LT	F	L	1500		F7	MAN	EPC
Crypturellus undulatus	L	T	LT	C	L	900		F3, F8, F7, F15		AMN, AMS, CSA
Crypturellus variegatus	H	T	LT	F	L	900		F1		AMN, AMS, ATL
Rhynchotus rufescens	L	T	LT	C	L	2500		N5, N6, N7, N13, N2		CAN, AMS, CSA, ATL, PAM
Nothoprocta cinerascens	L	T	LT	F	L	L		N1	CHA	CSA
Nothoprocta curvirostris	L	T	UM	F	2800	3700		N10, N9, N2, N13		NAN, CAN
Nothoprocta kalinowskii	H?	T	UM	R	3000	4600?		N2	AWA	CAN
Nothoprocta ornata	M	T	UM	F	3450	4700		N9		CAN, SAN
Nothoprocta pentlandii	L	T	UM	F	800	4100		N2, N13		NAN, CAN, SAN
Nothoprocta perdicaria	M	T	UT?	F	400	2000+		N2		STP, SAN
Nothoprocta taczanowskii	M	T	UM	U	3000	4300+		N2	AWA	CAN
Nothura boraquira	M	T	LT	F/C	L	500+		N1	o	CSA
Nothura chacoensis	M	T	LT	?	L	L		N1	CHA	CSA
Nothura darwinii	M	T	LS	F	L	4300		N7, N9		CAN, SAN, CSA, PAT
Nothura maculosa	L	T	LT	C	L	1200		N5, N7, N13		CSA, PAM, PAT

CP	RP	Notes
2	2	Probably declining in many areas.
3	2	Declining locally; monitor.
1	1	Declining; survey.
4	3	Occasionally to 1,100 m.
4	3	Occasionally to 1,500 m (Colombia); in low-lying forest in Amazonia.
2	1	Poorly known; may contain two species.
3	2	Scarce and declining outside reserves.
4	3	Patchy in lowlands.
4	3	Occasionally to 700 m.
4	3	Mainly above 2,500 m.
4	3	
4	3	
4	3	
4	3	Possibly regular to 900 m.
3	2	Locally to 1,500 m; deforestation.
4	3	Probably a morph of *bartletti*.
4	2	Associated with forest on white sand?
4	3	
4	3	
4	2	Poorly known; habitat not threatened.
2	1	Deforestation.
4	2	
3	2	Deforestation.
1	1	Known only from single specimen; taxonomy uncertain;deforestation.
2	2	Habitat destruction.
2	2	Declining outside reserves; deforestation.
4	3	Patchy in lowlands.
4	3	
4	3	
4	3	Patchy in *terra firme* forest? occasionally to 2,000 m.
4	3	Patchy in W Amazonia, but extensive range.
4	2	Status of isolated populations in Peru uncertain.
2	2	Rapid deforestation.
4	3	
4	3	Occasionally to 1,300 m (Venezuela).
4	3	
4	3	
4	3	
1	1	Poorly known; may be subspecies of *ornata*.
4	3	
4	3	
4	3	
2	2	Habitat degradation.
4	3	
4	3	Possibly conspecific with *maculosa* (see Short 1975).
4	3	
4	3	

Abbreviations Used

Snst - Sensitivity:
L - Low; **M** - Medium; **H** - High.

Strat - Foraging Strata:
T - Terrestrial; **U** - Understory; **M** - Midstory; **C** - Canopy; **A** - Aerial; **W** - Water.

Cntab - Center of Abundance:
LT - Lower tropical; **LS** - Lower subtropical; **HT** - Hill tropical; **UT** - Upper tropical; **US** - Upper subtropical; **MM** - Middle montane; **UM** - Upper montane.

Rel - Relative Abundance:
R - Rare; **U** - Uncommon; **F** - Fairly common; **C** - Common; **P** - Patchily distributed.

Min - Minimum Elevation:
L - Lowlands; **?** - Uncertain value; numeric values in meters.

Max - Maximum Elevation:
L - Lowlands; **?** - Uncertain value; **+** - species occurs at least to given elevation but likely occurs higher; numeric values in meters.

Micro - Microhabitats:
A - Army ants; **B** - Bamboo; **T** - Treefalls; **G** - Ground bromeliads; **C** - Rocky outcrops and caves; **S** - Streamside; **V** - Vine tangles; **B/V** -Bamboo/vine tangles.

Habitats:
F1 - Tropical lowland evergreen forest; **F2** - Flooded tropical evergreen forest; **F3** - River-edge forest; **F4** - Montane evergreen forest; **F5** - Elfin forest; **F6** - *Polylepis* woodland; **F7** - Tropical deciduous forest; **F8** - Gallery forest; **F9** - Southern temperate forest; **F10** - Pine forest; **F11** - Pine-oak forest; **F12** - White sand forest; **F13** - Palm forest; **F14** - Mangrove forest; **F15** - Secondary forest; **N1** - Arid lowland scrub; **N2** - Arid montane scrub; **N3** - Semihumid/humid montane scrub; **N4** - Cerrado; **N5** - Campo grasslands; **N6** - Low, seasonally wet grassland; **N7** - Southern temperate grassland; **N8** - Northern temperate grassland; **N9** - Puna grassland; **N10** - Paramo grassland; **N11** - Riparian thickets; **N12** - River island scrub; **N13** - Pastures/agricultural lands; **N14** - Second-growth scrub; **A1** - Freshwater marshes; **A2** - Saltwater/brackish marshes; **A3** - Coastal sand beaches/mudflats; **A4** - Coastal rocky beaches; **A5** - Riverine sand beaches; **A6** - Freshwater lakes and ponds; **A7** - Alkaline lakes; **A8** - Rivers; **A9** - Streams; **A10** - Bogs; **A11** - Coastal waters; **A12** - Pelagic waters.
E - Edge (used as a modifer to particular habitats).

Sub - Subregions:
ARC - Arid Caribbean Coast; **AWA** - Altiplano and Western Andes; **BAH** - Bahamas; **BAJ** - Baja California; **CAA** - Caatinga; **CAH** - Central American Highlands; **CER** - Cerrado; **CHA** - Chaco; **CHG** - Chiapas-Guanacaste; **CHL** - Chilean Desert; **CHR** - Chiriquí; **CIS** - Cocos Island; **CMV** - Cauca-Magdalena Valley; **COC** - Cuzco-Cochabamba; **CUB** - Cuba; **DOM** - Dominica; **EAS** - Eastern Slope Andes; **FDN** - Fernando de Noronha; **GAL** - Galápagos; **GCM** - Gulf Coast-Mexico; **GRE** - Grenada; **GUA** - Guadeloupe; **GUI** - Guianan; **HIS** - Hispaniola; **HPC** - Humid Pacific Coast; **ISA** - Isla Providencia and Isla San Andrés; **JAM** - Jamaica; **JFI** - Juan Fernández Islands; **MAN** - Manabí-Tumbes; **MAR** - Marañón Valley; **MID** - Madeira-Tapajós; **MON** - Montserrat; **MRT** - Martinique; **MTC** - Marañón-Cuzco; **NMM** - Northern Mexican Mountains; **NOR** - Northern Coastal Brazil; **PAR** - Pará; **PER** - Peruvian Desert; **PUE** - Puerto Rico; **RDJ** - Rio de Janeiro-Bahia Lowlands; **RMW** - Rio Madeira West; **RNW** - Rio Negro West; **SCA** - Southern Central America; **SCT** - Santa Cruz-Tucumán; **SIN** - Sinaloa-Oaxaca; **SMH** - Southern Mexican Highlands; **SMT** - Santa Marta; **SOC** - Islas Revillagigedo (Socorro Island group); **SON** - Sonoran Desert; **SOU** - Southern Atlantic Coast; **STL** - St. Lucia; **STV** - St. Vincent; **TAC** - Tacarcuna; **VAN** - Venezuelan Andes; **VNZ** - Venezuelan Coastal Mountains; **WES** - Western Andes; **YUC** - Yucatán Peninsula.
o - Endemic to region, but not restricted to a single subregion.

Zoogeographic Regions:
AMN - Northern Amazonia; **AMS** - Southern Amazonia; **ATL** - Atlantic Forest; **BSR** - Baja-Sonora; **CAN** - Central Andes; **CDH** - Chiriquí-Darién Highlands; **CHO** - Chocó Lowlands; **CSA** - Central South America; **EPC** - Equatorial Pacific Coast; **GAN** - Greater Antilles; **GCS** - Gulf-Caribbean Slope; **LAN** - Lesser Antilles; **MAH** - Madrean Highlands; **MPL** - Mexican Plateau; **NAN** - Northern Andes; **NSA** - Northern South America; **PAM** - Pampas; **PAS** - Pacific Arid Slope; **PAT** - Patagonia; **SAN** - Southern Andes; **STP** - Subtropical Pacific; **TEP** - Tepuis.

CP -Conservation Priority:
1 - Urgent; **2** - High; **3** - Medium; **4** - Low.

RP - Research Priority:
1 - High; **2** - Medium; **3** - Low.

	Snst	Strat	Cntab	Rel	Min	Max	Micro	Habitats	Sub	Zoogeographic Regions
Nothura minor	H	T	HT	R	700	1000		N5	CER	CSA
Taoniscus nanus	H?	T	HT	R/U	700	1000		N5, N4	CER	CSA
Eudromia elegans	M	T	LT	F	L	3000		N1, N2		SAN, CSA, PAT
Eudromia formosa	M	T	LT	F	L	L		F7?	CHA	CSA
Tinamotis ingoufi	M	T	LT	U?	L	800		N7	o	PAT
Tinamotis pentlandii	M	T	UM	U	4000	4700		N9	AWA	CAN
SPHENISCIFORMES										
Spheniscidae										
Aptenodytes patagonicus	H	W	LS	R	L	L		A12		PAT
Pygoscelis papua	H	W	LS	R	L	L		A12		PAT
Eudyptes chrysocome	H	W	LS	U	L	L		A12		PAT
Eudyptes chrysolophus	H	W	LS	U	L	L		A12		PAT
Spheniscus humboldti	H	W	LT	R	L	L		A11, A12	o	STP
Spheniscus magellanicus	H	W	LS	F	L	L		A11, A12		STP, PAT
Spheniscus mendiculus	H	W	LT	F	L	L		A11, A12	GAL	EPC
PODICIPEDIFORMES										
Podicipedidae										
Tachybaptus dominicus	M	W	LT	C	L	2600		A1, A6		GAN, LAN, BSR, PAS, MAH, GCS, CHO, EPC, NAN, NSA, AMN, AMS, CSA, ATL, PAM, PAT
Podilymbus gigas	H	W	UT	R	1500	1500		A6	CAH	MAH
Podilymbus podiceps	M	W	LS	C	L	3100		A6, A1		GAN, LAN, BSR, MPL, PAS, MAH, GCS, CDH, CHO, EPC, STP, NAN, CAN, SAN, NSA, CSA, ATL, PAM, PAT
Rollandia micropterum	H	W	UM	U	3800	4300		A6	AWA	CAN
Rollandia rolland	M	W	UM	C	L	4500		A6		STP, CAN, SAN, PAM, PAT
Podiceps gallardoi	H	W	LS	U/P	500	1200		A6	o	PAT
Podiceps major	M	W	LS	F	L	1200		A6, A11		STP, SAN, PAM, PAT
Podiceps nigricollis										
andinus	M	W	UM	R	2500	3100		A6	EAS	NAN
nigricollis	M	W	MM	C	L	2500+		A6		BSR, MPL
Podiceps occipitalis	M	W	LS	C	L	5000		A6		NAN, CAN, SAN, CSA, PAT
Podiceps taczanowskii	H	W	UM	R	4080	4080		A6	AWA	CAN
Aechmophorus clarkii	M	W	MM	C/P	750	2500		A6		MPL
Aechmophorus occidentalis	M	W	MM	C/P	750	2500+		A6		MPL
PROCELLARIIFORMES										
Diomedeidae										
Diomedea chrysostoma	H	W	LS	F	L	L		A12		PAT
Diomedea immutabilis	H	W	LT	R	L	L		A12		BSR
Diomedea irrorata	H	W	LT	F	L	L		A12	GAL	EPC
Diomedea melanophris	H	W	LS	C	L	L		A12, A11		PAT
Procellariidae										
Macronectes giganteus	L?	W	LS	C	L	L		A12, A11		PAT
Pterodroma arminjoniana	H	W	LT	U	L	L		A12		ATL
Pterodroma cooki										
defilippiana	H	W	LS	F	L	L		A12	JFI	STP
Pterodroma externa	H	W	LS	C	L	L		A12	JFI	STP
Pterodroma hasitata	H	W	LT	R	L	L		A12	o	GAN
Pterodroma longirostris										
longirostris	H	W	LS	U	L	L		A12	JFI	STP
Pterodroma neglecta	H	W	LS	U	L	L		A12		STP
Pterodroma phaeopygia	H	W	LT	U	L	L		A12		EPC

CP	RP	Notes
2	1	Declining; habitat destruction; survey.
2	1	Habitat destruction; survey.
4	3	
4	3	
4	2	
4	2	Study needed of distribution and behavior.
4	3	
4	3	
4	3	Formerly *E. crestatus.*
4	3	
2	1	Population declining; monitor.
3	2	Monitor.
3	2	Monitor.
4	3	Mainly below 900 m.
1	1	Restricted to single lake; apparently extinct.
4	3	
3	2	Habitat degradation.
4	3	
2	2	Winter range unknown, probably coastal; monitor.
4	3	
1	1	Probably extinct.
4	3	
4	3	
1	1	Restricted to a single lake; pollution and drainage.
4	2	Status of breeding population uncertain.
4	2	Status of breeding population uncertain.
4	2	Status of breeding population uncertain.
3	3	Small population on Guadalupe Island vulnerable (see Dunlap 1988).
3	2	Relatively small population; monitor.
4	3	
4	3	
4	3	Breeds on IlhaTrinidade and Martin Vaz Rocks.
2	2	Small population; monitor.
3	2	Excludes *P. cervicalis* (Imber 1985); introduced predators?
2	2	Formerly widespread as breeder, now only Hispaniola; monitor.
3	2	Threatened by introduced predators?
3	2	Poorly known; breeds in Juan Fernández Islands.
3	2	Declining; introduced predators; monitor in the Galápagos.

Abbreviations Used

Snst - Sensitivity:
L - Low; **M** - Medium; **H** - High.

Strat - Foraging Strata:
T - Terrestrial; **U** - Understory; **M** - Midstory; **C** - Canopy; **A** - Aerial; **W** - Water.

Cntab - Center of Abundance:
LT - Lower tropical; **LS** - Lower subtropical; **HT** - Hill tropical; **UT** - Upper tropical; **US** - Upper subtropical; **MM** - Middle montane; **UM** - Upper montane.

Rel - Relative Abundance:
R - Rare; **U** - Uncommon; **F** - Fairly common; **C** - Common; **P** - Patchily distributed.

Min - Minimum Elevation:
L - Lowlands; **?** - Uncertain value; numeric values in meters.

Max - Maximum Elevation:
L - Lowlands; **?** - Uncertain value; **+** - species occurs at least to given elevation but likely occurs higher; numeric values in meters.

Micro - Microhabitats:
A - Army ants; **B** - Bamboo; **T** - Treefalls; **G** - Ground bromeliads; **C** - Rocky outcrops and caves; **S** - Streamside; **V** - Vine tangles; **B/V** -Bamboo/vine tangles.

Habitats:
F1 - Tropical lowland evergreen forest; **F2** - Flooded tropical evergreen forest; **F3** - River-edge forest; **F4** - Montane evergreen forest; **F5** - Elfin forest; **F6** - *Polylepis* woodland; **F7** - Tropical deciduous forest; **F8** - Gallery forest; **F9** - Southern temperate forest; **F10** - Pine forest; **F11** - Pine-oak forest; **F12** - White sand forest; **F13** - Palm forest; **F14** - Mangrove forest; **F15** - Secondary forest; **N1** - Arid lowland scrub; **N2** - Arid montane scrub; **N3** - Semihumid/humid montane scrub; **N4** - Cerrado; **N5** - Campo grasslands; **N6** - Low, seasonally wet grassland; **N7** - Southern temperate grassland; **N8** - Northern temperate grassland; **N9** - Puna grassland; **N10** - Paramo grassland; **N11** - Riparian thickets; **N12** - River island scrub; **N13** - Pastures/agricultural lands; **N14** - Second-growth scrub; **A1** - Freshwater marshes; **A2** - Saltwater/brackish marshes; **A3** - Coastal sand beaches/mudflats; **A4** - Coastal rocky beaches; **A5** - Riverine sand beaches; **A6** - Freshwater lakes and ponds; **A7** - Alkaline lakes; **A8** - Rivers; **A9** - Streams; **A10** - Bogs; **A11** - Coastal waters; **A12** - Pelagic waters.
E - Edge (used as a modifer to particular habitats).

Sub - Subregions:
ARC - Arid Caribbean Coast; **AWA** - Altiplano and Western Andes; **BAH** - Bahamas; **BAJ** - Baja California; **CAA** - Caatinga; **CAH** - Central American Highlands; **CER** - Cerrado; **CHA** - Chaco; **CHG** - Chiapas-Guanacaste; **CHL** - Chilean Desert; **CHR** - Chiriquí; **CIS** - Cocos Island; **CMV** - Cauca-Magdalena Valley; **COC** - Cuzco-Cochabamba; **CUB** - Cuba; **DOM** - Dominica; **EAS** - Eastern Slope Andes; **FDN** - Fernando de Noronha; **GAL** - Galápagos; **GCM** - Gulf Coast-Mexico; **GRE** - Grenada; **GUA** - Guadeloupe; **GUI** - Guianan; **HIS** - Hispaniola; **HPC** - Humid Pacific Coast; **ISA** - Isla Providencia and Isla San Andrés; **JAM** - Jamaica; **JFI** - Juan Fernández Islands; **MAN** - Manabí-Tumbes; **MAR** - Marañón Valley; **MID** - Madeira-Tapajós; **MON** - Montserrat; **MRT** - Martinique; **MTC** - Marañón-Cuzco; **NMM** - Northern Mexican Mountains; **NOR** - Northern Coastal Brazil; **PAR** - Pará; **PER** - Peruvian Desert; **PUE** - Puerto Rico; **RDJ** - Rio de Janeiro-Bahia Lowlands; **RMW** - Rio Madeira West; **RNW** - Rio Negro West; **SCA** - Southern Central America; **SCT** - Santa Cruz-Tucumán; **SIN** - Sinaloa-Oaxaca; **SMH** - Southern Mexican Highlands; **SMT** - Santa Marta; **SOC** - Islas Revillagigedo (Socorro Island group); **SON** - Sonoran Desert; **SOU** - Southern Atlantic Coast; **STL** - St. Lucia; **STV** - St. Vincent; **TAC** - Tacarcuna; **VAN** - Venezuelan Andes; **VNZ** - Venezuelan Coastal Mountains; **WES** - Western Andes; **YUC** - Yucatán Peninsula.
o - Endemic to region, but not restricted to a single subregion.

Zoogeographic Regions:
AMN - Northern Amazonia; **AMS** - Southern Amazonia; **ATL** - Atlantic Forest; **BSR** - Baja-Sonora; **CAN** - Central Andes; **CDH** - Chiriquí-Darién Highlands; **CHO** - Chocó Lowlands; **CSA** - Central South America; **EPC** - Equatorial Pacific Coast; **GAN** - Greater Antilles; **GCS** - Gulf-Caribbean Slope; **LAN** - Lesser Antilles; **MAH** - Madrean Highlands; **MPL** - Mexican Plateau; **NAN** - Northern Andes; **NSA** - Northern South America; **PAM** - Pampas; **PAS** - Pacific Arid Slope; **PAT** - Patagonia; **SAN** - Southern Andes; **STP** - Subtropical Pacific; **TEP** - Tepuis.

CP -Conservation Priority:
1 - Urgent; **2** - High; **3** - Medium; **4** - Low.

RP - Research Priority:
1 - High; **2** - Medium; **3** - Low.

	Snst	Strat	Cntab	Rel	Min	Max	Micro	Habitats	Sub	Zoogeographic Regions
Halobaena caerulea	H	W	LS	F	L	L		A12		PAT
Pachyptila belcheri	H	W	LS	F	L	L		A12		PAT
Pachyptila turtur	H	W	LS	U	L	L		A12		PAT
Procellaria aequinoctialis	H	W	LS	F	L	L		A12		PAT
Puffinus auricularis	H	W	LT	F	L	L		A12	SOC	PAS
Puffinus creatopus	H	W	LS	C	L	L		A12		STP, PAT
Puffinus gravis	H	W	LS	U	L	L		A12		PAT
Puffinus griseus	H	W	LS	C	L	L		A12		PAT
Puffinus lherminieri	H	W	LT	C	L	L		A12		GAN, LAN, GCS, EPC, NSA
Puffinus opisthomelas	H	W	LT	F	L	L		A12	BAJ	BSR
Puffinus pacificus	H	W	LT	F	L	L		A12		PAS
Hydrobatidae										
Oceanites gracilis	H	W	LT	F	L	L		A12		EPC, STP
Oceanites oceanicus	H	W	LS	C	L	L		A12		PAT
Garrodia nereis	H	W	LS	R	L	L		A12		PAT
Fregetta grallaria	H	W	LS	U	L	L		A12		STP
Halocyptena microsoma	H	W	LT	F	L	L		A12	BAJ	BSR
Oceanodroma castro	H	W	LT	F	L	L		A12		EPC
Oceanodroma homochroa	H	W	LT	U	L	L		A12		BSR
Oceanodroma hornbyi	H	W	LS	U	L	L		A12	o	STP
Oceanodroma leucorhoa	H	W	LT	U	L	L		A12		BSR
Oceanodroma macrodactyla	H	W	LT	R	L	L		A12	BAJ	BSR
Oceanodroma markhami	H	W	LS	U	L	L		A12	o	STP
Oceanodroma melania	H	W	LT	F	L	L		A12	BAJ	BSR
Oceanodroma tethys	H	W	LT	F	L	L		A12		EPC, STP
Pelecanoididae										
Pelecanoides garnotii	H	W	LS	U	L	L		A11, A12	o	STP
Pelecanoides magellani	H	W	LS	C	L	L		A11, A12	o	PAT
Pelecanoides urinatrix	H	W	LS	U	L	L		A11, A12		PAT
PELECANIFORMES										
Phaethontidae										
Phaethon aethereus	H	W	LT	U	L	L		A11, A12		GAN, LAN, BSR, PAS, GCS, CHO, EPC, STP, NSA, ATL
Phaethon lepturus	H	W	LT	R	L	L		A11, A12		GAN, LAN, ATL
Pelecanidae										
Pelecanus erythrorhynchos	H	W	LT	C\P	L	L		A6, A1, A11		MPL?, GCS
Pelecanus occidentalis	H	W	LT	F	L	L		A11		GAN, LAN, BSR, PAS, GCS, CHO, EPC, NSA
Pelecanus thagus	H	W	LT	C	L	L		A11, A12	o	STP
Sulidae										
Sula dactylatra	H	W	LT	F	L	L		A12		GAN, LAN, BSR, PAS, GCS, CHO, EPC, STP, NSA, ATL
Sula leucogaster	H	W	LT	C	L	L		A11, A12		GAN, LAN, BSR, PAS, GCS, CHO, NSA, AMN, AMS, ATL
Sula nebouxii	H	W	LT	C	L	L		A11		BSR, PAS, CHO, EPC
Sula sula	H	W	LT	F	L	L		A12		GAN, LAN, PAS, GCS, EPC, NSA, ATL
Sula variegata	H	W	LT	F	L	L		A11, A12	o	STP
Phalacrocoracidae										
Phalacrocorax albiventer	H	W	LS	F	L	1000		A11, A6		PAT
Phalacrocorax atriceps	H	W	LS	F	L	L		A11		PAT
Phalacrocorax auritus	M	W	LT	F	L	L		A11, A6		GAN, BSR, MPL, GCS
Phalacrocorax bougainvillii	H	W	LS	C	L	L		A11		STP, PAT

CP	RP	Notes
4	3	
4	3	
4	3	
4	3	
2	2	Poorly known; monitor; introduced predators?
4	3	
4	3	Small breeding population in Islas Malvinas.
4	3	
4	3	
3	2	Monitor.
4	3	
4	2	Breeding grounds barely known.
4	3	
4	3	
4	2	Breeding population in Juan Fernandez Islands poorly known.
4	2	Restricted breeding range; monitor.
4	3	
3	2	Monitor.
2	2	Breeding grounds unknown; monitor.
4	2	May contain multiple species; monitor breeding population off Mexico.
1	1	Extinct? survey Guadalupe Island (see Jehl and Everett 1985).
2	2	Breeding grounds barely known; monitor.
4	3	
3	2	Race *kelsalli* scarce; survey.
2	1	Apparently declining; survey.
4	3	
4	3	
4	3	
4	3	
4	2	Irregular as breeder.
4	3	
4	3	
4	2	Monitor breeding colonies.
4	2	
4	3	
4	2	Monitor breeding colonies.
4	2	Monitor breeding colonies.
4	2	
4	2	Relationship to *P. albiventer* uncertain.
4	2	Locally to 2,000 m (Mexico).
3	2	Monitor population fluctuations.

Abbreviations Used

Snst - Sensitivity:
L - Low; **M** - Medium; **H** - High.

Strat - Foraging Strata:
T - Terrestrial; **U** - Understory; **M** - Midstory; **C** - Canopy; **A** - Aerial; **W** - Water.

Cntab - Center of Abundance:
LT - Lower tropical; **LS** - Lower subtropical; **HT** - Hill tropical; **UT** - Upper tropical; **US** - Upper subtropical; **MM** - Middle montane; **UM** - Upper montane.

Rel - Relative Abundance:
R - Rare; **U** - Uncommon; **F** - Fairly common; **C** - Common; **P** - Patchily distributed.

Min - Minimum Elevation:
L - Lowlands; **?** - Uncertain value; numeric values in meters.

Max - Maximum Elevation:
L - Lowlands; **?** - Uncertain value; **+** - species occurs at least to given elevation but likely occurs higher; numeric values in meters.

Micro - Microhabitats:
A - Army ants; **B** - Bamboo; **T** - Treefalls; **G** - Ground bromeliads; **C** - Rocky outcrops and caves; **S** - Streamside; **V** - Vine tangles; **B/V** -Bamboo/vine tangles.

Habitats:
F1 - Tropical lowland evergreen forest; **F2** - Flooded tropical evergreen forest; **F3** - River-edge forest; **F4** - Montane evergreen forest; **F5** - Elfin forest; **F6** - *Polylepis* woodland; **F7** - Tropical deciduous forest; **F8** - Gallery forest; **F9** - Southern temperate forest; **F10** - Pine forest; **F11** - Pine-oak forest; **F12** - White sand forest; **F13** - Palm forest; **F14** - Mangrove forest; **F15** - Secondary forest; **N1** - Arid lowland scrub; **N2** - Arid montane scrub; **N3** - Semihumid/humid montane scrub; **N4** - Cerrado; **N5** - Campo grasslands; **N6** - Low, seasonally wet grassland; **N7** - Southern temperate grassland; **N8** - Northern temperate grassland; **N9** - Puna grassland; **N10** - Paramo grassland; **N11** - Riparian thickets; **N12** - River island scrub; **N13** - Pastures/agricultural lands; **N14** - Second-growth scrub; **A1** - Freshwater marshes; **A2** - Saltwater/brackish marshes; **A3** - Coastal sand beaches/mudflats; **A4** - Coastal rocky beaches; **A5** - Riverine sand beaches; **A6** - Freshwater lakes and ponds; **A7** - Alkaline lakes; **A8** - Rivers; **A9** - Streams; **A10** - Bogs; **A11** - Coastal waters; **A12** - Pelagic waters.
E - Edge (used as a modifer to particular habitats).

Sub - Subregions:
ARC - Arid Caribbean Coast; **AWA** - Altiplano and Western Andes; **BAH** - Bahamas; **BAJ** - Baja California; **CAA** - Caatinga; **CAH** - Central American Highlands; **CER** - Cerrado; **CHA** - Chaco; **CHG** - Chiapas-Guanacaste; **CHL** - Chilean Desert; **CHR** - Chiriquí; **CIS** - Cocos Island; **CMV** - Cauca-Magdalena Valley; **COC** - Cuzco-Cochabamba; **CUB** - Cuba; **DOM** - Dominica; **EAS** - Eastern Slope Andes; **FDN** - Fernando de Noronha; **GAL** - Galápagos; **GCM** - Gulf Coast-Mexico; **GRE** - Grenada; **GUA** - Guadeloupe; **GUI** - Guianan; **HIS** - Hispaniola; **HPC** - Humid Pacific Coast; **ISA** - Isla Providencia and Isla San Andrés; **JAM** - Jamaica; **JFI** - Juan Fernández Islands; **MAN** - Manabí-Tumbes; **MAR** - Marañón Valley; **MID** - Madeira-Tapajós; **MON** - Montserrat; **MRT** - Martinique; **MTC** - Marañón-Cuzco; **NMM** - Northern Mexican Mountains; **NOR** - Northern Coastal Brazil; **PAR** - Pará; **PER** - Peruvian Desert; **PUE** - Puerto Rico; **RDJ** - Rio de Janeiro-Bahia Lowlands; **RMW** - Rio Madeira West; **RNW** - Rio Negro West; **SCA** - Southern Central America; **SCT** - Santa Cruz-Tucumán; **SIN** - Sinaloa-Oaxaca; **SMH** - Southern Mexican Highlands; **SMT** - Santa Marta; **SOC** - Islas Revillagigedo (Socorro Island group); **SON** - Sonoran Desert; **SOU** - Southern Atlantic Coast; **STL** - St. Lucia; **STV** - St. Vincent; **TAC** - Tacarcuna; **VAN** - Venezuelan Andes; **VNZ** - Venezuelan Coastal Mountains; **WES** - Western Andes; **YUC** - Yucatán Peninsula.
o - Endemic to region, but not restricted to a single subregion.

Zoogeographic Regions:
AMN - Northern Amazonia; **AMS** - Southern Amazonia; **ATL** - Atlantic Forest; **BSR** - Baja-Sonora; **CAN** - Central Andes; **CDH** - Chiriquí-Darién Highlands; **CHO** - Chocó Lowlands; **CSA** - Central South America; **EPC** - Equatorial Pacific Coast; **GAN** - Greater Antilles; **GCS** - Gulf-Caribbean Slope; **LAN** - Lesser Antilles; **MAH** - Madrean Highlands; **MPL** - Mexican Plateau; **NAN** - Northern Andes; **NSA** - Northern South America; **PAM** - Pampas; **PAS** - Pacific Arid Slope; **PAT** - Patagonia; **SAN** - Southern Andes; **STP** - Subtropical Pacific; **TEP** - Tepuis.

CP -Conservation Priority:
1 - Urgent; **2** - High; **3** - Medium; **4** - Low.

RP - Research Priority:
1 - High; **2** - Medium; **3** - Low.

	Snst	Strat	Cntab	Rel	Min	Max	Micro	Habitats	Sub	Zoogeographic Regions
Phalacrocorax brasilianus	L	W	LT	C	L	3500		A11, A6, A8		GAN, LAN, BSR, MPL, PAS, GCS, CHO, EPC, STP, CAN, SAN, NSA, AMN, AMS, CSA, ATL, PAM, PAT
Phalacrocorax gaimardi	H	W	LS	U	L	L		A11		STP, PAT
Phalacrocorax magellanicus	H	W	LS	F	L	L		A11		STP, PAT
Phalacrocorax pelagicus	H	W	LS	R	L	L		A11		BSR
Phalacrocorax penicillatus	H	W	LS	F	L	L		A11		BSR
Nannopterum harrisi	H	W	LT	R	L	L		A11	GAL	EPC
Anhingidae										
Anhinga anhinga	M	W	LT	F	L	900		A6, A8		GAN, PAS, GCS, CHO, EPC, NSA, AMN, AMS, CSA, ATL, PAM
Fregatidae										
Fregata ariel	H	W/A	LT	?	L	L		A12		ATL
Fregata magnificens	H	W/A	LT	C	L	L		A11, A12, F14		GAN, LAN, BSR, PAS, GCS, CHO, EPC, NSA, AMN, AMS, ATL
Fregata minor	H	W/A	LT	C	L	L		A12		PAS, EPC
CICONIIFORMES										
Ardeidae										
Botaurus lentiginosus	M	T	LS	U	1500	2700		A1		MPL, MAH
Botaurus pinnatus	M	T	LT	U/P	L	1100		A1		PAS, GCS, CHO, NAN, NSA, AMN, CSA, ATL, PAM
Ixobrychus exilis	M	U	LT	U/P	L	3100		A1, A2, F14		GAN, BSR, PAS, MAH, GCS, EPC, STP, NAN, NSA, AMN, AMS, CSA, ATL
Ixobrychus involucris	M	U	LT	U/P	L	L		A1, A1		STP, NSA, AMN, CSA, ATL, PAM, PAT
Tigrisoma fasciatum	M	T/W	HT	U/P	L	2400		A8, A9		GCS, CDH, CHO, NAN, CAN, NSA, AMN, CSA, ATL
Tigrisoma lineatum	M	T/W	LT	F	L	1000		A1		GCS, CHO, NSA, AMN, AMS, CSA, ATL
Tigrisoma mexicanum	M	T/W	LT	U	L	800		A1, A8, A9		PAS, GCS
Zebrilus undulatus	H	T	LT	R/P	L	L		F2		NSA, AMN, AMS
Nycticorax nycticorax	L	T/W	LT	F	L	4400		A1, A2, A6, A8, A9		GAN, BSR, MPL, PAS, MAH, GCS, CDH, CHO, EPC, STP, NAN, CAN, SAN, NSA, AMN, AMS, CSA, ATL, PAM, PAT
Nycticorax pileatus	M	T/W	LT	F	L	900		A1, A6, A8		GCS, NSA, AMN, AMS, CSA, ATL
Nycticorax violaceus	M	T/W	LT	F	L	L		F14, A2, A1, A6		GAN, LAN, BSR, PAS, GCS, CHO, EPC, NSA, AMN, AMS, ATL
Cochlearius cochlearius	H	W	LT	F/P	L	800		A6, A8, F14		PAS, GCS, CHO, NSA, AMN, AMS, CSA, ATL
Ardeola ibis	L	T	LT	C	L	2200		N13, N6		GAN, LAN, BSR, MPL, PAS, MAH, GCS, CDH, CHO, EPC, STP, NAN, CAN, NSA, AMN, AMS, CSA, ATL, PAM, PAT
Syrigma sibilatrix	M	T	LT	F	L	1200		N6, N5, N7, N13, A1		NSA, CSA, ATL, PAM
Butorides striatus										
striatus	L	T/W	LT	C	L	1900		A1, A2, F14, A8, A9		LAN, GCS, CDH, CHO, EPC, STP, NAN, CAN, NSA, AMN, AMS, CSA, ATL, PAM
sundevalli	L	T/W	LT	F	L	L		A1, A2, F14	GAL	EPC
virescens	L	T/W	LT	C	L	1850		A6, A1, A8, A9, F14		GAN, LAN, BSR, MPL, PAS, MAH, GCS
Hydranassa caerulea	M	T/W	LT	F	L	1500		A1, A2, F14		GAN, LAN, BSR, PAS, GCS, CHO, EPC, STP, NSA, AMN, AMS, CSA, ATL
Hydranassa rufescens	H	T/W	LT	U/P	L	L		A3, F14		GAN, BSR, PAS, GCS
Hydranassa tricolor	M	T/W	LT	F	L	700		A2, A1, A3, F14		GAN, LAN, BSR, PAS, GCS, CHO, EPC, STP, NSA, AMN, AMS
Egretta alba	L	T/W	LT	C	L	1500		A1, A2, A3, A4, A6		GAN, BSR, PAS, GCS, CHO, EPC, STP, CAN?, SAN, NSA, AMN, AMS, CSA, ATL, PAM, PAT

CP	RP	Notes
4	3	Usually called *P. olivaceus*, see Browning (1989b); occasionally to 4,000 m.
3	2	Monitor populations; recent rapid decline.
4	3	
4	2	Monitor.
4	2	Monitor.
2	1	Monitor.
4	3	Wanders to 3,700 m.
4	2	Monitor.
4	3	
4	3	
3	2	Breeding populations apparently declining in Mexico.
4	2	Locally to 2,600 m (Colombia); distribution poorly known.
4	2	Distribution poorly known.
4	2	Distribution poorly known.
3	1	Mainly montane; endangered in southeastern Brazil; survey.
4	3	Occasionally to 1,600 m (Colombia); usually near forest.
4	2	Monitor; usually associated with woodland or gallery forest.
4	2	Poorly known, but widespread and frequently overlooked.
4	3	
4	3	Usually near woodland or forest.
4	3	
4	3	Occasionally to 2,600 m (Colombia); usually near forest.
4	3	Occasionally to 4,500 m; rapidly expanding range.
4	3	
4	3	
3	2	May be melanistic morph of *B. striatus*.
4	3	
4	3	Very local in interior of Mexico.
3	2	Monitor.
4	3	Occasionally to 2,600 m.
4	3	Occasionally to 4,100 m.

Abbreviations Used

Snst - Sensitivity:
L - Low; **M** - Medium; **H** - High.

Strat - Foraging Strata:
T - Terrestrial; **U** - Understory; **M** - Midstory; **C** - Canopy; **A** - Aerial; **W** - Water.

Cntab - Center of Abundance:
LT - Lower tropical; **LS** - Lower subtropical; **HT** - Hill tropical; **UT** - Upper tropical; **US** - Upper subtropical; **MM** - Middle montane; **UM** - Upper montane.

Rel - Relative Abundance:
R - Rare; **U** - Uncommon; **F** - Fairly common; **C** - Common; **P** - Patchily distributed.

Min - Minimum Elevation:
L - Lowlands; **?** - Uncertain value; numeric values in meters.

Max - Maximum Elevation:
L - Lowlands; **?** - Uncertain value; **+** - species occurs at least to given elevation but likely occurs higher; numeric values in meters.

Micro - Microhabitats:
A - Army ants; **B** - Bamboo; **T** - Treefalls; **G** - Ground bromeliads; **C** - Rocky outcrops and caves; **S** - Streamside; **V** - Vine tangles; **B/V** -Bamboo/vine tangles.

Habitats:
F1 - Tropical lowland evergreen forest; **F2** - Flooded tropical evergreen forest; **F3** - River-edge forest; **F4** - Montane evergreen forest; **F5** - Elfin forest; **F6** - *Polylepis* woodland; **F7** - Tropical deciduous forest; **F8** - Gallery forest; **F9** - Southern temperate forest; **F10** - Pine forest; **F11** - Pine-oak forest; **F12** - White sand forest; **F13** - Palm forest; **F14** - Mangrove forest; **F15** - Secondary forest; **N1** - Arid lowland scrub; **N2** - Arid montane scrub; **N3** - Semihumid/humid montane scrub; **N4** - Cerrado; **N5** - Campo grasslands; **N6** - Low, seasonally wet grassland; **N7** - Southern temperate grassland; **N8** - Northern temperate grassland; **N9** - Puna grassland; **N10** - Paramo grassland; **N11** - Riparian thickets; **N12** - River island scrub; **N13** - Pastures/agricultural lands; **N14** - Second-growth scrub; **A1** - Freshwater marshes; **A2** - Saltwater/brackish marshes; **A3** - Coastal sand beaches/mudflats; **A4** - Coastal rocky beaches; **A5** - Riverine sand beaches; **A6** - Freshwater lakes and ponds; **A7** - Alkaline lakes; **A8** - Rivers; **A9** - Streams; **A10** - Bogs; **A11** - Coastal waters; **A12** - Pelagic waters.
E - Edge (used as a modifer to particular habitats).

Sub - Subregions:
ARC - Arid Caribbean Coast; **AWA** - Altiplano and Western Andes; **BAH** - Bahamas; **BAJ** - Baja California; **CAA** - Caatinga; **CAH** - Central American Highlands; **CER** - Cerrado; **CHA** - Chaco; **CHG** - Chiapas-Guanacaste; **CHL** - Chilean Desert; **CHR** - Chiriquí; **CIS** - Cocos Island; **CMV** - Cauca-Magdalena Valley; **COC** - Cuzco-Cochabamba; **CUB** - Cuba; **DOM** - Dominica; **EAS** - Eastern Slope Andes; **FDN** - Fernando de Noronha; **GAL** - Galápagos; **GCM** - Gulf Coast-Mexico; **GRE** - Grenada; **GUA** - Guadeloupe; **GUI** - Guianan; **HIS** - Hispaniola; **HPC** - Humid Pacific Coast; **ISA** - Isla Providencia and Isla San Andrés; **JAM** - Jamaica; **JFI** - Juan Fernández Islands; **MAN** - Manabí-Tumbes; **MAR** - Marañón Valley; **MID** - Madeira-Tapajós; **MON** - Montserrat; **MRT** - Martinique; **MTC** - Marañón-Cuzco; **NMM** - Northern Mexican Mountains; **NOR** - Northern Coastal Brazil; **PAR** - Pará; **PER** - Peruvian Desert; **PUE** - Puerto Rico; **RDJ** - Rio de Janeiro-Bahia Lowlands; **RMW** - Rio Madeira West; **RNW** - Rio Negro West; **SCA** - Southern Central America; **SCT** - Santa Cruz-Tucumán; **SIN** - Sinaloa-Oaxaca; **SMH** - Southern Mexican Highlands; **SMT** - Santa Marta; **SOC** - Islas Revillagigedo (Socorro Island group); **SON** - Sonoran Desert; **SOU** - Southern Atlantic Coast; **STL** - St. Lucia; **STV** - St. Vincent; **TAC** - Tacarcuna; **VAN** - Venezuelan Andes; **VNZ** - Venezuelan Coastal Mountains; **WES** - Western Andes; **YUC** - Yucatán Peninsula.
o - Endemic to region, but not restricted to a single subregion.

Zoogeographic Regions:
AMN - Northern Amazonia; **AMS** - Southern Amazonia; **ATL** - Atlantic Forest; **BSR** - Baja-Sonora; **CAN** - Central Andes; **CDH** - Chiriquí-Darién Highlands; **CHO** - Chocó Lowlands; **CSA** - Central South America; **EPC** - Equatorial Pacific Coast; **GAN** - Greater Antilles; **GCS** - Gulf-Caribbean Slope; **LAN** - Lesser Antilles; **MAH** - Madrean Highlands; **MPL** - Mexican Plateau; **NAN** - Northern Andes; **NSA** - Northern South America; **PAM** - Pampas; **PAS** - Pacific Arid Slope; **PAT** - Patagonia; **SAN** - Southern Andes; **STP** - Subtropical Pacific; **TEP** - Tepuis.

CP -Conservation Priority:
1 - Urgent; **2** - High; **3** - Medium; **4** - Low.

RP - Research Priority:
1 - High; **2** - Medium; **3** - Low.

	Snst	Strat	Cntab	Rel	Min	Max	Micro	Habitats	Sub	Zoogeographic Regions
Egretta thula	L	T/W	LT	C	L	1500		A1, A2, A3, A4, A6		GAN, LAN, BSR, PAS, GCS, CHO, EPC, STP, NSA, AMN, AMS, CSA, ATL, PAM
Ardea cocoi	L	T/W	LT	F	L	900		A1, A6, A8		GCS, CHO, STP, NSA, AMN, AMS, CSA, ATL, PAM, PAT
Ardea herodias	L	T/W	LS	F	L	2000		A1, A2, A3, A6, A8, F14		GAN, BSR, PAS, GCS, EPC, NSA
Agamia agami	M	T	LT	U/P	L	600		F2, F8, A6, A9		GCS, CHO, NSA, AMN, AMS, CSA
Ciconiidae										
Mycteria americana	L	T/W	LT	F	L	800		A1, A2, A6		GAN, BSR?, PAS, GCS, EPC, NSA, AMN, AMS, CSA, ATL, PAM
Ciconia maguari	L	T	LT	U	L	900		N7, N6, N13, A1		STP, NSA, AMN, AMS, CSA, PAM
Jabiru mycteria	M	T/W	LT	F	L	700		N6, A1, A6		PAS, GCS, NSA, AMN, AMS, CSA, PAM
Threskiornithidae										
Harpiprion caerulescens	M	T	LT	F	L	600		N6, N13		CSA, PAM
Theristicus caudatus										
branickii	L	T	UM	U/P	3700	5000		N9		NAN, CAN
caudatus	L	T	LT	F	L	1200		N6, N13		NSA, AMN, AMS, CSA, PAM
melanopis	L	T	LS	U/P	L	3000		N13, N7		STP, SAN, PAT
Cercibis oxycerca	M	T	LT	U	L	L		N6		NSA, AMN, AMS
Mesembrinibis cayennensis	M	T	LT	F/C	L	1200		F2, F8, A1, A6, A8		GCS, NSA, AMN, AMS, CSA, ATL
Phimosus infuscatus	M	T	LT	C	L	800		A1		NSA, AMN, AMS?, CSA, ATL, PAM
Eudocimus albus	M	T/W	LT	F/C	L	L		A1, A6, F14		GAN, BSR, PAS, GCS, CHO, EPC, NSA
Eudocimus ruber	M	T/W	LT	F	L	L		A1, A6, F14		NSA, AMN, AMS, ATL?
Plegadis chihi	L	T/W	LT	F	L	2500		A1		MPL, MAH, GCS, STP, NSA, CSA, ATL, PAM, PAT
Plegadis falcinellus	L	T/W	LT	U	L	L		A1		GAN, PAS
Plegadis ridgwayi	M	T/W	UM	F	3100	4800		A1, A10	AWA	CAN
Ajaia ajaja	M	W	LT	F	L	800		A1, A6		GAN, PAS, GCS, CHO, EPC, NSA, AMN, AMS, CSA, ATL, PAM
PHOENICOPTERIFORMES										
Phoenicopteridae										
Phoenicopterus chilensis	M	W	LS	F	L	4400+		A11, A7, A6		EPC, STP, CAN, SAN, PAM, PAT
Phoenicopterus ruber	M	W	LT	U/P	L	L		A11		GAN, GCS, EPC, NSA, AMN
Phoenicoparrus andinus	H	W	UM	U?	3750	4700		A7	AWA	CAN
Phoenicoparrus jamesi	H	W	UM	U	4000	4700		A7	AWA	CAN
ANSERIFORMES										
Anhimidae										
Anhima cornuta	M	T	LT	F	L	800		A1		NSA, AMN, AMS, CSA
Chauna chavaria	M	T	LT	U/F	L	1200		A1	ARC	NSA
Chauna torquata	L	T	LT	C	L	L		A1		CSA, PAM
Anatidae										
Dendrocygna arborea	M	T/W	LT	R	L	L		A1, F14, A6, A2	o	GAN
Dendrocygna autumnalis	L	T/W	LT	C	L	1500+		A1		BSR, PAS, GCS, CHO, EPC, NSA, AMN, AMS, CSA
Dendrocygna bicolor	L	T/W	LT	F/C	L	1000		A1, A6		BSR, PAS, GCS, EPC, STP?, NSA, AMN, AMS, CSA, PAM
Dendrocygna viduata	L	T/W	LT	C	L	1000		A1, A6, A9		PAS, NSA, AMN, AMS, CSA, ATL, PAM
Cygnus melanocoryphus	L	W	LS	F	L	1200		A6, A1, A11		STP, SAN, CSA, PAM, PAT
Coscoroba coscoroba	L	W	LS	F	L	L		A6, A1		STP, SAN, CSA, PAM, PAT
Chloephaga hybrida	M	T/W	LS	U/F	L	L		A11	o	PAT
Chloephaga melanoptera	M	T/W	UM	F	3100	4700		A10, A6, A7		CAN, SAN
Chloephaga picta	L	T	LS	F	L	1500	S	N7, N13		SAN, PAT
Chloephaga poliocephala	L	T/W	LS	F	L	1500?	S	N7, N13		SAN, PAT

CP	RP	Notes
4	3	Occasionally to 4,100 m.
4	3	Occasionally to 3,000 m (Colombia).
4	3	Very local in interior of Mexico.
4	2	Occasionally to 2,600 m (Colombia); associated with forest.
4	2	Occasionally to 3,700 m; monitor; some populations declining.
3	2	Monitor.
4	2	Declining in parts of range.
4	3	
3	2	Apparently declining in some areas.
4	3	
3	2	Probably declining; Peruvian population threatened--survey.
3	2	Monitor.
4	3	Associated with forest.
4	3	Wanders to 2,600 m.
4	2	Monitor.
3	2	Monitor; mainly coastal.
4	3	
4	3	
4	3	Regularly wanders to Pacific coast.
4	2	Monitor.
4	2	Monitor.
3	2	Declining locally.
2	1	Survey.
2	1	Survey.
4	3	Locally sensitive to persecution.
3	1	Survey.
4	3	
2	1	Declining; associated with forest?
4	3	
4	3	Formerly to 2,600 m (Colombia).
4	3	
3	2	Monitor.
3	2	Seasonally to 1,000 m; monitor.
4	3	
3	2	Monitor; occurs lower in south seasonally.
4	3	Monitor hunting.
4	3	

Abbreviations Used

Snst - Sensitivity:
L - Low; **M** - Medium; **H** - High.

Strat - Foraging Strata:
T - Terrestrial; **U** - Understory; **M** - Midstory; **C** - Canopy; **A** - Aerial; **W** - Water.

Cntab - Center of Abundance:
LT - Lower tropical; **LS** - Lower subtropical; **HT** - Hill tropical; **UT** - Upper tropical; **US** - Upper subtropical; **MM** - Middle montane; **UM** - Upper montane.

Rel - Relative Abundance:
R - Rare; **U** - Uncommon; **F** - Fairly common; **C** - Common; **P** - Patchily distributed.

Min - Minimum Elevation:
L - Lowlands; **?** - Uncertain value; numeric values in meters.

Max - Maximum Elevation:
L - Lowlands; **?** - Uncertain value; **+** - species occurs at least to given elevation but likely occurs higher; numeric values in meters.

Micro - Microhabitats:
A - Army ants; **B** - Bamboo; **T** - Treefalls; **G** - Ground bromeliads; **C** - Rocky outcrops and caves; **S** - Streamside; **V** - Vine tangles; **B/V** -Bamboo/vine tangles.

Habitats:
F1 - Tropical lowland evergreen forest; **F2** - Flooded tropical evergreen forest; **F3** - River-edge forest; **F4** - Montane evergreen forest; **F5** - Elfin forest; **F6** - *Polylepis* woodland; **F7** - Tropical deciduous forest; **F8** - Gallery forest; **F9** - Southern temperate forest; **F10** - Pine forest; **F11** - Pine-oak forest; **F12** - White sand forest; **F13** - Palm forest; **F14** - Mangrove forest; **F15** - Secondary forest; **N1** - Arid lowland scrub; **N2** - Arid montane scrub; **N3** - Semihumid/humid montane scrub; **N4** - Cerrado; **N5** - Campo grasslands; **N6** - Low, seasonally wet grassland; **N7** - Southern temperate grassland; **N8** - Northern temperate grassland; **N9** - Puna grassland; **N10** - Paramo grassland; **N11** - Riparian thickets; **N12** - River island scrub; **N13** - Pastures/agricultural lands; **N14** - Second-growth scrub; **A1** - Freshwater marshes; **A2** - Saltwater/brackish marshes; **A3** - Coastal sand beaches/mudflats; **A4** - Coastal rocky beaches; **A5** - Riverine sand beaches; **A6** - Freshwater lakes and ponds; **A7** - Alkaline lakes; **A8** - Rivers; **A9** - Streams; **A10** - Bogs; **A11** - Coastal waters; **A12** - Pelagic waters.
E - Edge (used as a modifer to particular habitats).

Sub - Subregions:
ARC - Arid Caribbean Coast; **AWA** - Altiplano and Western Andes; **BAH** - Bahamas; **BAJ** - Baja California; **CAA** - Caatinga; **CAH** - Central American Highlands; **CER** - Cerrado; **CHA** - Chaco; **CHG** - Chiapas-Guanacaste; **CHL** - Chilean Desert; **CHR** - Chiriquí; **CIS** - Cocos Island; **CMV** - Cauca-Magdalena Valley; **COC** - Cuzco-Cochabamba; **CUB** - Cuba; **DOM** - Dominica; **EAS** - Eastern Slope Andes; **FDN** - Fernando de Noronha; **GAL** - Galápagos; **GCM** - Gulf Coast-Mexico; **GRE** - Grenada; **GUA** - Guadeloupe; **GUI** - Guianan; **HIS** - Hispaniola; **HPC** - Humid Pacific Coast; **ISA** - Isla Providencia and Isla San Andrés; **JAM** - Jamaica; **JFI** - Juan Fernández Islands; **MAN** - Manabí-Tumbes; **MAR** - Marañón Valley; **MID** - Madeira-Tapajós; **MON** - Montserrat; **MRT** - Martinique; **MTC** - Marañón-Cuzco; **NMM** - Northern Mexican Mountains; **NOR** - Northern Coastal Brazil; **PAR** - Pará; **PER** - Peruvian Desert; **PUE** - Puerto Rico; **RDJ** - Rio de Janeiro-Bahia Lowlands; **RMW** - Rio Madeira West; **RNW** - Rio Negro West; **SCA** - Southern Central America; **SCT** - Santa Cruz-Tucumán; **SIN** - Sinaloa-Oaxaca; **SMH** - Southern Mexican Highlands; **SMT** - Santa Marta; **SOC** - Islas Revillagigedo (Socorro Island group); **SON** - Sonoran Desert; **SOU** - Southern Atlantic Coast; **STL** - St. Lucia; **STV** - St. Vincent; **TAC** - Tacarcuna; **VAN** - Venezuelan Andes; **VNZ** - Venezuelan Coastal Mountains; **WES** - Western Andes; **YUC** - Yucatán Peninsula.
o - Endemic to region, but not restricted to a single subregion.

Zoogeographic Regions:
AMN - Northern Amazonia; **AMS** - Southern Amazonia; **ATL** - Atlantic Forest; **BSR** - Baja-Sonora; **CAN** - Central Andes; **CDH** - Chiriquí-Darién Highlands; **CHO** - Chocó Lowlands; **CSA** - Central South America; **EPC** - Equatorial Pacific Coast; **GAN** - Greater Antilles; **GCS** - Gulf-Caribbean Slope; **LAN** - Lesser Antilles; **MAH** - Madrean Highlands; **MPL** - Mexican Plateau; **NAN** - Northern Andes; **NSA** - Northern South America; **PAM** - Pampas; **PAS** - Pacific Arid Slope; **PAT** - Patagonia; **SAN** - Southern Andes; **STP** - Subtropical Pacific; **TEP** - Tepuis.

CP -Conservation Priority:
1 - Urgent; **2** - High; **3** - Medium; **4** - Low.

RP - Research Priority:
1 - High; **2** - Medium; **3** - Low.

	Snst	Strat	Cntab	Rel	Min	Max	Micro	Habitats	Sub	Zoogeographic Regions
Chloephaga rubidiceps	L	T/W	LS	R	L	L		N7, N13	o	PAT
Neochen jubata	M	T	LT	R	L	L		A5, A1		NSA, AMN, AMS, CSA
Tachyeres brachypterus	L	W	LS	F	L	L		A11	o	PAT
Tachyeres leucocephala	M	W	LS	F	L	L		A11	o	PAT
Tachyeres patachonicus	M	W	LS	C	L	1200		A11, A6, A8		SAN, PAT
Tachyeres pteneres	M	W	LS	C	L	L		A11	o	PAT
Cairina moschata	M	W	LT	F	L	1000		A6, A8, A1, F14		PAS, GCS, CHO, EPC, NSA, AMN, AMS, CSA, ATL
Sarkidiornis melanotos	M	W	LT	R/P	L	1200		A6, A1		EPC, STP, NSA, AMN, AMS, CSA, ATL
Callonetta leucophrys	M	W	LT	U	L	700		A1, A6		CSA, PAM
Aix sponsa	M	W	LT	U	L	900+		A6, A9		GAN
Amazonetta brasiliensis	L	W	LT	C	L	1200		A1, A6		NSA, AMN, AMS, CSA, PAM
Merganetta armata	M	W	UM	F	1500	4300		A8, A9		NAN, CAN, SAN
Anas bahamensis	L	W	LT	F	L	L		A1, A2, A6, A7, A11		GAN, LAN, EPC, STP, NSA, AMN, AMS, CSA, ATL, PAM
Anas cyanoptera	L	W	UM	C	L	4600		A1, A6		BSR, MPL, STP, NAN, CAN, SAN, NSA, CSA, PAM, PAT
Anas flavirostris	M	W	LS	F	L	4400		A1, A6, A8		NAN, CAN, SAN, PAM, PAT
Anas fulvigula	L	W	LS	U	L	L		A1, A2		GCS
Anas georgica	L	W	LS	F	L	4600		A1, A6		STP, NAN, CAN, SAN, CSA, PAM, PAT
Anas platalea	M	W	LS	F	L	3500		A1, A6		STP, SAN, PAM, PAT
Anas platyrhynchos										
diazi	M	W	US	F	800	2500		A1	o	MPL
platyrhynchos	L	W	LS	U/P	L	1000		A6, A1		BSR
Anas puna	M	W	UM	F	3100	4600		A1, A6	AWA	CAN
Anas sibilatrix	M	W	LS	F	L	1200		A6, A8		STP, SAN, PAM, PAT
Anas specularioides	M	W	LS	U	L	4700		A6, A7, A11		CAN, SAN, PAT
Anas specularis	M	W	LS	U	L	1800		A8, A6	o	SAN
Anas versicolor	L	W	LS	F	L	1000		A1, A6		STP, SAN, CSA, PAM, PAT
Netta erythrophthalma	L	W	LT	R/P	L	3700		A6		STP, NAN, CAN, NSA, CSA, ATL
Netta peposaca	L	W	LS	F	L	1200		A6, A1		STP, SAN, CSA, PAM
Aythya americana	M	W	MM	U/P	1000	2300		A6, A1		MPL, MAH
Mergus merganser	M	W	US	R/P	1900?	1900?		A8		MAH
Mergus octosetaceus	M	W	LT	R	L	1100		A9, A8		CSA, ATL
Heteronetta atricapilla	M	W	LS	U	L	L?		A1, A6		STP, CSA, PAM
Oxyura dominica	M	W	LT	U/P	L	800		A1		GAN, LAN, PAS, GCS, CHO, EPC, NSA, AMN, AMS, CSA, ATL, PAM
Oxyura jamaicensis										
ferruginea	M	W	UM	F	2000	4400		A6		STP, NAN, CAN, SAN, PAT
jamaicensis	M	W	LT	F	L	2200+		A6		GAN, LAN, BSR, MPL
Oxyura vittata	M	W	LS	F	L	800		A6		STP, SAN, PAM, PAT
Falconiformes										
Cathartidae										
Cathartes aura	L	T/A	LT	C	L	2500		N13, F7, F8, F15, F10, N1, N6		GAN, BSR, MPL, PAS, MAH, GCS, CDH, CHO, EPC, STP, NAN, CAN, SAN, NSA, TEP, AMN, AMS, CSA, ATL, PAM, PAT
Cathartes burrovianus	M	T/A	LT	F/P	L	1000		N6, N14, A1		PAS, GCS, NSA, AMN, AMS, CSA, ATL, PAM
Cathartes melambrotus	M	T/A	LT	C	L	900		F1		AMN, AMS
Coragyps atratus	L	T/A	LT	C	L	2800		N14, N6, N1, N13, F3E		BSR, MPL, PAS, MAH, GCS, CDH, CHO, EPC, STP, NAN, CAN, NSA, TEP, AMN, AMS, CSA, ATL, PAM
Sarcoramphus papa	M	T/A	LT	F	L	1500		F1, F7, F8, N6		PAS, GCS, CHO, EPC, NSA, AMN, AMS, CSA, ATL

CP	RP	Notes
2	1	Rare on mainland; declining; introduced predators.
2	1	Declining throughout; survey.
4	3	
4	3	
4	3	
4	3	
4	3	Usually associated with forest.
2	1	Declining; survey.
3	2	Poorly known (including elevation); monitor.
3	2	Usually in wooded areas; monitor Cuban population.
4	3	
3	2	Regularly to lowlands in south; declining locally; monitor.
3	2	Monitor; declining in some areas.
4	3	Monitor, especially North American migrants.
4	2	May contain two species.
3	2	Monitor; status of Mexican population uncertain.
4	3	In Andes, only above 3,200 m; monitor.
4	3	
3	2	
4	3	
4	3	Monitor.
3	2	Monitor; probably declining.
4	2	In Andes, only above 4,000 m; monitor.
2	1	Declining? survey.
4	3	Monitor.
3	2	Andean population small and declining.
3	2	Monitor.
4	2	
4	2	Bred once in Chihuahua (Van Rossem 1929).
1	1	Deforestation, dams; survey.
4	2	Western range poorly known.
4	3	Locally to 2,600 m (Colombia).
4	2	Locally to lowlands in south.
4	2	Monitor breeding populations in Greater Antilles.
4	3	
4	3	Wanders to 3,200 m+.
4	2	Distribution poorly known.
4	3	
4	3	Occasionally to 3,500 m, but mainly below 900 m.
4	2	Monitor.

Abbreviations Used

Snst - Sensitivity:
L - Low; **M** - Medium; **H** - High.

Strat - Foraging Strata:
T - Terrestrial; **U** - Understory; **M** - Midstory; **C** - Canopy; **A** - Aerial; **W** - Water.

Cntab - Center of Abundance:
LT - Lower tropical; **LS** - Lower subtropical; **HT** - Hill tropical; **UT** - Upper tropical; **US** - Upper subtropical; **MM** - Middle montane; **UM** - Upper montane.

Rel - Relative Abundance:
R - Rare; **U** - Uncommon; **F** - Fairly common; **C** - Common; **P** - Patchily distributed.

Min - Minimum Elevation:
L - Lowlands; **?** - Uncertain value; numeric values in meters.

Max - Maximum Elevation:
L - Lowlands; **?** - Uncertain value; **+** - species occurs at least to given elevation but likely occurs higher; numeric values in meters.

Micro - Microhabitats:
A - Army ants; **B** - Bamboo; **T** - Treefalls; **G** - Ground bromeliads; **C** - Rocky outcrops and caves; **S** - Streamside; **V** - Vine tangles; **B/V** -Bamboo/vine tangles.

Habitats:
F1 - Tropical lowland evergreen forest; **F2** - Flooded tropical evergreen forest; **F3** - River-edge forest; **F4** - Montane evergreen forest; **F5** - Elfin forest; **F6** - *Polylepis* woodland; **F7** - Tropical deciduous forest; **F8** - Gallery forest; **F9** - Southern temperate forest; **F10** - Pine forest; **F11** - Pine-oak forest; **F12** - White sand forest; **F13** - Palm forest; **F14** - Mangrove forest; **F15** - Secondary forest; **N1** - Arid lowland scrub; **N2** - Arid montane scrub; **N3** - Semihumid/humid montane scrub; **N4** - Cerrado; **N5** - Campo grasslands; **N6** - Low, seasonally wet grassland; **N7** - Southern temperate grassland; **N8** - Northern temperate grassland; **N9** - Puna grassland; **N10** - Paramo grassland; **N11** - Riparian thickets; **N12** - River island scrub; **N13** - Pastures/agricultural lands; **N14** - Second-growth scrub; **A1** - Freshwater marshes; **A2** - Saltwater/brackish marshes; **A3** - Coastal sand beaches/mudflats; **A4** - Coastal rocky beaches; **A5** - Riverine sand beaches; **A6** - Freshwater lakes and ponds; **A7** - Alkaline lakes; **A8** - Rivers; **A9** - Streams; **A10** - Bogs; **A11** - Coastal waters; **A12** - Pelagic waters.
E - Edge (used as a modifer to particular habitats).

Sub - Subregions:
ARC - Arid Caribbean Coast; **AWA** - Altiplano and Western Andes; **BAH** - Bahamas; **BAJ** - Baja California; **CAA** - Caatinga; **CAH** - Central American Highlands; **CER** - Cerrado; **CHA** - Chaco; **CHG** - Chiapas-Guanacaste; **CHL** - Chilean Desert; **CHR** - Chiriquí; **CIS** - Cocos Island; **CMV** - Cauca-Magdalena Valley; **COC** - Cuzco-Cochabamba; **CUB** - Cuba; **DOM** - Dominica; **EAS** - Eastern Slope Andes; **FDN** - Fernando de Noronha; **GAL** - Galápagos; **GCM** - Gulf Coast-Mexico; **GRE** - Grenada; **GUA** - Guadeloupe; **GUI** - Guianan; **HIS** - Hispaniola; **HPC** - Humid Pacific Coast; **ISA** - Isla Providencia and Isla San Andrés; **JAM** - Jamaica; **JFI** - Juan Fernández Islands; **MAN** - Manabí-Tumbes; **MAR** - Marañón Valley; **MID** - Madeira-Tapajós; **MON** - Montserrat; **MRT** - Martinique; **MTC** - Marañón-Cuzco; **NMM** - Northern Mexican Mountains; **NOR** - Northern Coastal Brazil; **PAR** - Pará; **PER** - Peruvian Desert; **PUE** - Puerto Rico; **RDJ** - Rio de Janeiro-Bahia Lowlands; **RMW** - Rio Madeira West; **RNW** - Rio Negro West; **SCA** - Southern Central America; **SCT** - Santa Cruz-Tucumán; **SIN** - Sinaloa-Oaxaca; **SMH** - Southern Mexican Highlands; **SMT** - Santa Marta; **SOC** - Islas Revillagigedo (Socorro Island group); **SON** - Sonoran Desert; **SOU** - Southern Atlantic Coast; **STL** - St. Lucia; **STV** - St. Vincent; **TAC** - Tacarcuna; **VAN** - Venezuelan Andes; **VNZ** - Venezuelan Coastal Mountains; **WES** - Western Andes; **YUC** - Yucatán Peninsula.
o - Endemic to region, but not restricted to a single subregion.

Zoogeographic Regions:
AMN - Northern Amazonia; **AMS** - Southern Amazonia; **ATL** - Atlantic Forest; **BSR** - Baja-Sonora; **CAN** - Central Andes; **CDH** - Chiriquí-Darién Highlands; **CHO** - Chocó Lowlands; **CSA** - Central South America; **EPC** - Equatorial Pacific Coast; **GAN** - Greater Antilles; **GCS** - Gulf-Caribbean Slope; **LAN** - Lesser Antilles; **MAH** - Madrean Highlands; **MPL** - Mexican Plateau; **NAN** - Northern Andes; **NSA** - Northern South America; **PAM** - Pampas; **PAS** - Pacific Arid Slope; **PAT** - Patagonia; **SAN** - Southern Andes; **STP** - Subtropical Pacific; **TEP** - Tepuis.

CP -Conservation Priority:
1 - Urgent; **2** - High; **3** - Medium; **4** - Low.

RP - Research Priority:
1 - High; **2** - Medium; **3** - Low.

	Snst	Strat	Cntab	Rel	Min	Max	Micro	Habitats	Sub	Zoogeographic Regions
Vultur gryphus	M	T/A	UM	U	L	5000+	R	N9, N2, N1, N7, A4		STP, NAN, CAN, SAN, PAT
Accipitridae										
Pandion haliaetus	M	W	LT	U	L	L		A11, A6, A8		GAN, BSR, PAS, GCS
Leptodon cayanensis	M	C	LT	U	L	1000		F1, F2, F7		PAS, GCS, CHO, NSA, AMN, AMS, CSA, ATL
Leptodon forbesi	M?	C	LT	R?	L	600		F1	NOR	ATL
Chondrohierax uncinatus										
uncinatus	L	C	LT	U/P	L	2800		F1, F7, F8, F4		LAN, PAS, MAH, GCS, NAN, CAN, NSA, AMN, AMS, CSA, ATL
wilsonii	M	C	LT	R	L	500+		F1	CUB	GAN
Elanoides forficatus	M	C/A	LT	U	L	1800		F1, F7, F10		MAH, GCS, CDH, CHO, NAN, CAN, NSA, AMS, CSA, ATL
Gampsonyx swainsonii	L	C	LT	U/P	L	1200		F1E, F7E, F15, N6, N1		PAS, CHO, EPC, NSA, AMN, AMS, CSA
Elanus leucurus	L	C/A	LT	U/P	L	2600		N13, N14, N6, N1, N2		BSR, MPL, PAS, GCS, NSA, AMN, CSA, ATL
Rostrhamus hamatus	M	W/A	LT	F/P	L	800		F3, F8, A1, F2		CHO, NSA, AMN, AMS
Rostrhamus sociabilis	L	W/A	LT	C	L	1000		A1		PAS, GCS, CHO, NSA, AMN, AMS, CSA, ATL, PAM
Harpagus bidentatus	M	C	LT	F	L	1500		F1, F4		GCS, CHO, NSA, AMN, AMS, ATL
Harpagus diodon	M	C	LT	F	L	1400		F1, F7, F4		AMS?, CSA, ATL
Ictinia plumbea	M	C/A	LT	C	L	1700		F1, F7, F8		PAS, GCS, CHO, NSA, AMN, AMS, CSA, ATL
Haliaeetus leucocephalus	M	T/W	LS	R	L	800		A11, A8		BSR
Geranospiza caerulescens	M	M/C	LT	U	L	800		F7, F8, F2, F14		PAS, GCS, CHO, EPC, NSA, AMN, AMS, CSA, ATL
Circus buffoni	M	T/A	LT	U/P	L	900		N6, N5, N14, A1		STP, NSA, AMS, CSA, PAT
Circus cinereus	L	T/A	LS	F	L	4400		N7, N9, N14, N2, A1		STP, NAN, CAN, SAN, CSA, PAM, PAT
Circus cyaneus	L	T/A	LS	F	L	L?		N8, A1		BSR
Accipiter bicolor	M	C	LT	U	L	2000		F7, F8, F1		GCS, CHO, EPC, SAN, NSA, AMN, AMS, CSA, ATL
Accipiter collaris	H	C	UT	R	600	1800		F4		NAN, CAN
Accipiter cooperii	M	C	US	F	600	3000+		F7, F8, F11		BSR, MPL, MAH
Accipiter gentilis	H	C	UM	R	2100	3400		F10, F11		MAH
Accipiter gundlachi	M	C	LT	R	L	900+		F1, F7, F10	CUB	GAN
Accipiter poliogaster	H	C	LT	R	L	L		F1		NSA, AMN, AMS, CSA, ATL
Accipiter superciliosus	H	C	LT	U	L	1200		F1, F4		GCS, CHO, NSA, AMN, AMS, ATL
Accipiter striatus										
chionogaster	M	C	MM	F	500	3000		F10, F11, F4, F7	CAH	MAH
erythronemius	M	C	MM	F	L	3500		F4, F1, F9, F15		NAN, CAN, CSA, ATL
striatus	L	C	US	F	1000	3100		F11, F8		GAN, MPL, MAH
Leucopternis albicollis	H	C	LT	F	L	1500		F1, F4, F7		PAS, MAH, GCS, CDH, CHO, NAN, CAN, NSA, AMN, AMS, CSA
Leucopternis kuhli	H	M/C	LT	R	L	600		F1	o	AMS
Leucopternis lacernulata	H	M/C	LT	U	L	900		F1	o	ATL
Leucopternis melanops	H	M/C	LT	U	L	1000		F1		AMN, AMS
Leucopternis occidentalis	M	C	LT	U	L	1500		F1, F7		CHO, EPC
Leucopternis plumbea	H	U/M	HT	U	L	800		F1		GCS, CHO, EPC
Leucopternis polionota	H	C	HT	U	L	1500		F1	o	ATL
Leucopternis princeps	H	C	UT	U	300	2500		F4, F1		CDH, CHO, NAN
Leucopternis schistacea	H	U/M	LT	F	L	L		F2		AMN, AMS
Leucopternis semiplumbea	H	M/C	LT	U	L	1000		F1		GCS, CHO
Buteogallus aequinoctialis	M	T/C	LT	U	L	L		F14, F1		NSA, AMN, AMS, ATL
Buteogallus anthracinus	M	C	LT	F	L	1800		F7, F8, F1		GAN, LAN, BSR, PAS, MAH, GCS, NSA
Buteogallus subtilis	M	T/C	LT	F	L	L		F14		PAS, GCS, CHO, EPC

CP	RP	Notes
3	1	Probably declining; monitor.
3	2	Monitor.
4	3	Occasionally to 2,000 m? (Venezuela)
1	1	Deforestation; relationship to *L. cayanensis* uncertain.
4	3	
1	1	Declining; survey.
4	2	Occasionally to 3,300 m (during migration?); monitor.
4	3	
4	2	Spreading with deforestation; sometimes considered race of *E. caeruleus*.
4	2	Seasonal movements poorly known.
4	3	
4	3	Occasionally to 1,800 m (Venezuela).
4	2	Seasonal movements poorly known.
4	3	Occasionally to 2,600 m (Colombia).
3	2	Status of breeding population poorly known.
4	3	Occasionally to 1,500 m.
4	2	Locally to 2,000 m; monitor.
4	3	
4	2	Monitor,especially breeding population in Mexico.
4	2	Locally to 2,700 m; may contain multiple species.
3	2	Poorly known.
4	3	
4	2	To lowlands rarely in winter; monitor.
2	1	Survey.
3	1	Poorly known; seasonal movements?
4	3	Occasionally to 1,800 m (Venezuela), but mainly below 900 m.
4	3	
4	2	Seasonal movements of southern populations unknown.
4	3	
4	3	
4	2	Distribution poorly known.
2	1	Deforestation; survey.
4	2	Relationship to *L. kuhli* needs study.
2	1	Locally to 2,100 m; monitor; deforestation.
4	2	
3	1	Mainly montane; monitor; deforestation.
4	2	Occasionally to lowlands; monitor.
4	3	
4	2	
4	2	
4	2	
4	2	

Abbreviations Used

Snst - Sensitivity:
L - Low; **M** - Medium; **H** - High.

Strat - Foraging Strata:
T - Terrestrial; **U** - Understory; **M** - Midstory; **C** - Canopy; **A** - Aerial; **W** - Water.

Cntab - Center of Abundance:
LT - Lower tropical; **LS** - Lower subtropical; **HT** - Hill tropical; **UT** - Upper tropical; **US** - Upper subtropical; **MM** - Middle montane; **UM** - Upper montane.

Rel - Relative Abundance:
R - Rare; **U** - Uncommon; **F** - Fairly common; **C** - Common; **P** - Patchily distributed.

Min - Minimum Elevation:
L - Lowlands; **?** - Uncertain value; numeric values in meters.

Max - Maximum Elevation:
L - Lowlands; **?** - Uncertain value; **+** - species occurs at least to given elevation but likely occurs higher; numeric values in meters.

Micro - Microhabitats:
A - Army ants; **B** - Bamboo; **T** - Treefalls; **G** - Ground bromeliads; **C** - Rocky outcrops and caves; **S** - Streamside; **V** - Vine tangles; **B/V** -Bamboo/vine tangles.

Habitats:
F1 - Tropical lowland evergreen forest; **F2** - Flooded tropical evergreen forest; **F3** - River-edge forest; **F4** - Montane evergreen forest; **F5** - Elfin forest; **F6** - *Polylepis* woodland; **F7** - Tropical deciduous forest; **F8** - Gallery forest; **F9** - Southern temperate forest; **F10** - Pine forest; **F11** - Pine-oak forest; **F12** - White sand forest; **F13** - Palm forest; **F14** - Mangrove forest; **F15** - Secondary forest; **N1** - Arid lowland scrub; **N2** - Arid montane scrub; **N3** - Semihumid/humid montane scrub; **N4** - Cerrado; **N5** - Campo grasslands; **N6** - Low, seasonally wet grassland; **N7** - Southern temperate grassland; **N8** - Northern temperate grassland; **N9** - Puna grassland; **N10** - Paramo grassland; **N11** - Riparian thickets; **N12** - River island scrub; **N13** - Pastures/agricultural lands; **N14** - Second-growth scrub; **A1** - Freshwater marshes; **A2** - Saltwater/brackish marshes; **A3** - Coastal sand beaches/mudflats; **A4** - Coastal rocky beaches; **A5** - Riverine sand beaches; **A6** - Freshwater lakes and ponds; **A7** - Alkaline lakes; **A8** - Rivers; **A9** - Streams; **A10** - Bogs; **A11** - Coastal waters; **A12** - Pelagic waters.
E - Edge (used as a modifer to particular habitats).

Sub - Subregions:
ARC - Arid Caribbean Coast; **AWA** - Altiplano and Western Andes; **BAH** - Bahamas; **BAJ** - Baja California; **CAA** - Caatinga; **CAH** - Central American Highlands; **CER** - Cerrado; **CHA** - Chaco; **CHG** - Chiapas-Guanacaste; **CHL** - Chilean Desert; **CHR** - Chiriquí; **CIS** - Cocos Island; **CMV** - Cauca-Magdalena Valley; **COC** - Cuzco-Cochabamba; **CUB** - Cuba; **DOM** - Dominica; **EAS** - Eastern Slope Andes; **FDN** - Fernando de Noronha; **GAL** - Galápagos; **GCM** - Gulf Coast-Mexico; **GRE** - Grenada; **GUA** - Guadeloupe; **GUI** - Guianan; **HIS** - Hispaniola; **HPC** - Humid Pacific Coast; **ISA** - Isla Providencia and Isla San Andrés; **JAM** - Jamaica; **JFI** - Juan Fernández Islands; **MAN** - Manabí-Tumbes; **MAR** - Marañón Valley; **MID** - Madeira-Tapajós; **MON** - Montserrat; **MRT** - Martinique; **MTC** - Marañón-Cuzco; **NMM** - Northern Mexican Mountains; **NOR** - Northern Coastal Brazil; **PAR** - Pará; **PER** - Peruvian Desert; **PUE** - Puerto Rico; **RDJ** - Rio de Janeiro-Bahia Lowlands; **RMW** - Rio Madeira West; **RNW** - Rio Negro West; **SCA** - Southern Central America; **SCT** - Santa Cruz-Tucumán; **SIN** - Sinaloa-Oaxaca; **SMH** - Southern Mexican Highlands; **SMT** - Santa Marta; **SOC** - Islas Revillagigedo (Socorro Island group); **SON** - Sonoran Desert; **SOU** - Southern Atlantic Coast; **STL** - St. Lucia; **STV** - St. Vincent; **TAC** - Tacarcuna; **VAN** - Venezuelan Andes; **VNZ** - Venezuelan Coastal Mountains; **WES** - Western Andes; **YUC** - Yucatán Peninsula.
o - Endemic to region, but not restricted to a single subregion.

Zoogeographic Regions:
AMN - Northern Amazonia; **AMS** - Southern Amazonia; **ATL** - Atlantic Forest; **BSR** - Baja-Sonora; **CAN** - Central Andes; **CDH** - Chiriquí-Darién Highlands; **CHO** - Chocó Lowlands; **CSA** - Central South America; **EPC** - Equatorial Pacific Coast; **GAN** - Greater Antilles; **GCS** - Gulf-Caribbean Slope; **LAN** - Lesser Antilles; **MAH** - Madrean Highlands; **MPL** - Mexican Plateau; **NAN** - Northern Andes; **NSA** - Northern South America; **PAM** - Pampas; **PAS** - Pacific Arid Slope; **PAT** - Patagonia; **SAN** - Southern Andes; **STP** - Subtropical Pacific; **TEP** - Tepuis.

CP -Conservation Priority:
1 - Urgent; **2** - High; **3** - Medium; **4** - Low.

RP - Research Priority:
1 - High; **2** - Medium; **3** - Low.

	Snst	Strat	Cntab	Rel	Min	Max	Micro	Habitats	Sub	Zoogeographic Regions
Buteogallus urubitinga	M	T/C	LT	F	L	1600		F7, F1, F8, F3		PAS, MAH, GCS, CHO, EPC, NSA, AMN, AMS, CSA, ATL
Harpyhaliaetus coronatus	M	?	HT	R	L	1200+		F7, N4	o	CSA
Harpyhaliaetus solitarius	H	C	UT	R	600	2200		F4		MAH, CDH, NAN, CAN, TEP
Heterospizias meridionalis	L	T/C	LT	F	L	1200		N6, N5, N14		GCS, EPC, NSA, CSA, ATL, PAM
Busarellus nigricollis	L	T/C	LT	F	L	800		F2, F8, A1		PAS, GCS, CHO, NSA, AMN, AMS, CSA
Geranoaetus melanoleucus	M	T	UM	U	L	4400		N1, N2, N5, N7		STP, NAN, CAN, SAN, TEP, CSA, PAM, PAT
Parabuteo unicinctus	L	C	LT	U	L	1900		N1, N2, F7, N6		BSR, MPL, PAS, MAH, GCS, EPC, STP, NSA, CSA
Buteo albicaudatus	L	T	LT	F	L	2200		N6, N5, N8, N1, N2, N14		BSR, PAS, MAH, GCS, NSA, AMN, AMS, CSA, ATL, PAM
Buteo albigula	M	C	UM	U	1700	3400		F4, N2, N1		NAN, CAN, SAN
Buteo albonotatus	M	C	LT	U/P	L	2800		F8, F7, F11, F3, F1E		BSR, MPL, PAS, MAH, GCS, EPC, NSA, AMN, AMS, CSA
Buteo brachyurus	M	C/A	LT	F	L	1200		F1, F7, F8, F11		PAS, GCS, CHO, EPC, NSA, AMN, AMS, CSA, ATL
Buteo galapagoensis	M	C	LT	U	L	L?		F7, N1	GAL	EPC
Buteo jamaicensis	L	T/C	LS	C	L	3500+		F7E, F10, F11, F4E, N1, N2, F15		GAN, LAN, BSR, MPL, PAS, MAH, CDH
Buteo leucorrhous	M	C	MM	U/P	1400	3300		F4		NAN, CAN, CSA, ATL
Buteo lineatus	L	C	LS	F	L	1100		F8, F15, F11		BSR, GCS
Buteo magnirostris	L	C	LT	C	L	2500		F1E, F7, F8, F3, F12, F15, N14		PAS, GCS, CHO, EPC, NSA, AMN, AMS, CSA, ATL, PAM
Buteo nitidus	M	C	LT	F	L	1300		F8, F7, F1E, F3		BSR, PAS, GCS, NSA, AMN, AMS, CSA, ATL
Buteo platypterus	M	C	LT	F	L	1500		F1, F4, F7		GAN, LAN
Buteo poecilochrous	M	T	UM	F	2000	4700+		N2, N9		NAN, CAN
Buteo polyosoma	L	T/C	LS	F	L	3400		N1, N2, N3, F7E, F9E		EPC, STP, NAN, CAN, SAN, CSA, PAT
Buteo ridgwayi	M	C	LT	R	L	2000+		F4, F1, F7, F10	HIS	GAN
Buteo swainsoni	M	T	US	F/P	500	1600		N8, N1		BSR, MPL
Buteo ventralis	M	?	LS	?	L	1200		F9E, N2, N1	o	SAN
Morphnus guianensis	H	C	LT	R	L	1200		F1		GCS, CHO, NSA, AMN, AMS, ATL
Harpia harpyja	H	C	LT	R	L	900		F1		GCS, CHO, NSA, AMN, AMS, CSA, ATL
Aquila chrysaetos	M	T	US	R	L	2700+		N8, N2, N1		BSR, MPL, MAH
Spizastur melanoleucus	H	C	LT	U/P	L	1200		F1, F3, F4		MAH, GCS, CHO, NSA, AMN, AMS, CSA, ATL
Spizaetus ornatus	M	C	LT	U	L	1200		F1, F4		PAS, GCS, CHO, EPC, NSA, AMN, AMS, CSA, ATL
Spizaetus tyrannus	M	C	LT	U	L	2000		F1, F7, F4		PAS?, GCS, CHO, EPC, NSA, AMN, AMS, CSA, ATL
Oroaetus isidori	H	C	MM	U	1700	2800		F4		NAN, CAN
Falconidae										
Daptrius americanus	H	C	LT	F/P	L	1400		F1, F4		PAS, GCS, CHO, NSA, AMN, AMS, CSA
Daptrius ater	L	T/C	LT	C	L	800		F3, F15, F1E		AMN, AMS
Phalcoboenus albogularis	M	T	US?	U?	L	1500		N7, N1, N2		SAN, PAT
Phalcoboenus australis	M	T	LS	R	L	L		N7, A4	o	PAT
Phalcoboenus carunculatus	M	T	UM	F	3000	4000+		N10, N14	o	NAN
Phalcoboenus megalopterus	M	T	UM	F	2900	4600+		N9, N10, N14		CAN, SAN
Caracara plancus	L	T	LT	C	L	2600		N1, N2, N6, N7, N14, N13		GAN, BSR, MPL, PAS, MAH, GCS, CDH, CHO, EPC, STP, NAN, CAN, SAN, NSA, AMN, AMS, CSA, ATL, PAM, PAT, PAT
Milvago chimachima	L	T/C	LT	C	L	1800		N6, N12, N14, N13		GCS, CHO, NSA, AMN, AMS, CSA, ATL, PAM
Milvago chimango	L	T/C	LS	C	L	1000+		N7, N14, N1, N2		STP, CSA, PAM, PAT
Herpetotheres cachinnans	L	C	LT	F	L	1500		F1E, F8, F3, F2, F7		PAS, GCS, CHO, EPC, NSA, AMN, AMS, CSA, ATL
Micrastur buckleyi	H	?	LT	R?	L	700		F1		AMN, AMS

CP	RP	Notes
4	3	
1	1	Declining; reason for decline uncertain; survey.
3	2	Locally to 2,800 m, occasionally to lowlands; monitor.
4	3	Occasionally to 1,800 m (Colombia).
4	3	Occasionally to 1,350 m (Guatemala).
4	2	Non-Andean populations probably declining.
4	2	Monitor.
4	3	
4	3	To lowlands in south; southern populations migratory?
4	2	Breeding distribution poorly known.
4	3	Occasionally to 2,500 m.
3	2	Monitor.
4	3	
4	2	Locally to lowlands? distribution poorly known.
4	3	
4	3	
4	3	Occasionally to 2,300 m (Central America).
4	2	Status of breeding populations unknown.
4	3	Occasionally to 900 m?
4	3	Occasionally to 4,000 m+.
1	1	Declining; deforestation.
4	2	
4	3	
3	2	Monitor; declining in much of range.
3	1	Locally to 2,000 m+; extinct in parts of range; survey.
3	1	Probably declining; monitor in Mexico.
4	2	Locally to 2,000 m, occasionally to 3,000 m.
4	3	Occasionally to 2,500 m+.
4	3	
3	2	Occasionally to 800 m and 3,500 m; monitor.
3	2	Declining in parts of range; causes unknown.
4	3	Occasionally to 1,500 m (Peru).
4	2	Occasionally to 3,000 m; poorly known.
2	1	Monitor.
4	3	Occasionally lower elevations.
4	3	Occasionally lower elevations.
4	3	See Banks and Dove (1992) for use of *Caracara* for genus; locally to 3,000 m (Colombia).
4	3	Occasionally to 2,600 m (Colombia).
4	3	
4	3	Occasionally to 2,400 m (Colombia).
3	1	Locally (?) to 1,800 m; poorly known.

Abbreviations Used

Snst - Sensitivity:
L - Low; **M** - Medium; **H** - High.

Strat - Foraging Strata:
T - Terrestrial; **U** - Understory; **M** - Midstory; **C** - Canopy; **A** - Aerial; **W** - Water.

Cntab - Center of Abundance:
LT - Lower tropical; **LS** - Lower subtropical; **HT** - Hill tropical; **UT** - Upper tropical; **US** - Upper subtropical; **MM** - Middle montane; **UM** - Upper montane.

Rel - Relative Abundance:
R - Rare; **U** - Uncommon; **F** - Fairly common; **C** - Common; **P** - Patchily distributed.

Min - Minimum Elevation:
L - Lowlands; **?** - Uncertain value; numeric values in meters.

Max - Maximum Elevation:
L - Lowlands; **?** - Uncertain value; **+** - species occurs at least to given elevation but likely occurs higher; numeric values in meters.

Micro - Microhabitats:
A - Army ants; **B** - Bamboo; **T** - Treefalls; **G** - Ground bromeliads; **C** - Rocky outcrops and caves; **S** - Streamside; **V** - Vine tangles; **B/V** -Bamboo/vine tangles.

Habitats:
F1 - Tropical lowland evergreen forest; **F2** - Flooded tropical evergreen forest; **F3** - River-edge forest; **F4** - Montane evergreen forest; **F5** - Elfin forest; **F6** - *Polylepis* woodland; **F7** - Tropical deciduous forest; **F8** - Gallery forest; **F9** - Southern temperate forest; **F10** - Pine forest; **F11** - Pine-oak forest; **F12** - White sand forest; **F13** - Palm forest; **F14** - Mangrove forest; **F15** - Secondary forest; **N1** - Arid lowland scrub; **N2** - Arid montane scrub; **N3** - Semihumid/humid montane scrub; **N4** - Cerrado; **N5** - Campo grasslands; **N6** - Low, seasonally wet grassland; **N7** - Southern temperate grassland; **N8** - Northern temperate grassland; **N9** - Puna grassland; **N10** - Paramo grassland; **N11** - Riparian thickets; **N12** - River island scrub; **N13** - Pastures/agricultural lands; **N14** - Second-growth scrub; **A1** - Freshwater marshes; **A2** - Saltwater/brackish marshes; **A3** - Coastal sand beaches/mudflats; **A4** - Coastal rocky beaches; **A5** - Riverine sand beaches; **A6** - Freshwater lakes and ponds; **A7** - Alkaline lakes; **A8** - Rivers; **A9** - Streams; **A10** - Bogs; **A11** - Coastal waters; **A12** - Pelagic waters.
E - Edge (used as a modifer to particular habitats).

Sub - Subregions:
ARC - Arid Caribbean Coast; **AWA** - Altiplano and Western Andes; **BAH** - Bahamas; **BAJ** - Baja California; **CAA** - Caatinga; **CAH** - Central American Highlands; **CER** - Cerrado; **CHA** - Chaco; **CHG** - Chiapas-Guanacaste; **CHL** - Chilean Desert; **CHR** - Chiriquí; **CIS** - Cocos Island; **CMV** - Cauca-Magdalena Valley; **COC** - Cuzco-Cochabamba; **CUB** - Cuba; **DOM** - Dominica; **EAS** - Eastern Slope Andes; **FDN** - Fernando de Noronha; **GAL** - Galápagos; **GCM** - Gulf Coast-Mexico; **GRE** - Grenada; **GUA** - Guadeloupe; **GUI** - Guianan; **HIS** - Hispaniola; **HPC** - Humid Pacific Coast; **ISA** - Isla Providencia and Isla San Andrés; **JAM** - Jamaica; **JFI** - Juan Fernández Islands; **MAN** - Manabí-Tumbes; **MAR** - Marañón Valley; **MID** - Madeira-Tapajós; **MON** - Montserrat; **MRT** - Martinique; **MTC** - Marañón-Cuzco; **NMM** - Northern Mexican Mountains; **NOR** - Northern Coastal Brazil; **PAR** - Pará; **PER** - Peruvian Desert; **PUE** - Puerto Rico; **RDJ** - Rio de Janeiro-Bahia Lowlands; **RMW** - Rio Madeira West; **RNW** - Rio Negro West; **SCA** - Southern Central America; **SCT** - Santa Cruz-Tucumán; **SIN** - Sinaloa-Oaxaca; **SMH** - Southern Mexican Highlands; **SMT** - Santa Marta; **SOC** - Islas Revillagigedo (Socorro Island group); **SON** - Sonoran Desert; **SOU** - Southern Atlantic Coast; **STL** - St. Lucia; **STV** - St. Vincent; **TAC** - Tacarcuna; **VAN** - Venezuelan Andes; **VNZ** - Venezuelan Coastal Mountains; **WES** - Western Andes; **YUC** - Yucatán Peninsula.
o - Endemic to region, but not restricted to a single subregion.

Zoogeographic Regions:
AMN - Northern Amazonia; **AMS** - Southern Amazonia; **ATL** - Atlantic Forest; **BSR** - Baja-Sonora; **CAN** - Central Andes; **CDH** - Chiriquí-Darién Highlands; **CHO** - Chocó Lowlands; **CSA** - Central South America; **EPC** - Equatorial Pacific Coast; **GAN** - Greater Antilles; **GCS** - Gulf-Caribbean Slope; **LAN** - Lesser Antilles; **MAH** - Madrean Highlands; **MPL** - Mexican Plateau; **NAN** - Northern Andes; **NSA** - Northern South America; **PAM** - Pampas; **PAS** - Pacific Arid Slope; **PAT** - Patagonia; **SAN** - Southern Andes; **STP** - Subtropical Pacific; **TEP** - Tepuis.

CP -Conservation Priority:
1 - Urgent; **2** - High; **3** - Medium; **4** - Low.

RP - Research Priority:
1 - High; **2** - Medium; **3** - Low.

	Snst	Strat	Cntab	Rel	Min	Max	Micro	Habitats	Sub	Zoogeographic Regions
Micrastur gilvicollis	H	U/M	LT	F	L	900		F1		AMN, AMS, ATL?
Micrastur mirandollei	M	M/C	LT	U/P	L	800		F1		GCS, CHO, AMN, AMS, ATL?
Micrastur plumbeus	H	?	HT?	?	L	900		F1	o	CHO
Micrastur ruficollis	M	U/M	LT	F	L	2600		F1, F4		PAS, MAH, GCS, CDH, CHO, EPC, NAN, CAN, NSA, AMN, AMS, CSA, ATL
Micrastur semitorquatus	M	M/C	LT	F/P	L	1500		F1, F7, F8		PAS, GCS, CHO, EPC, NSA, AMN, AMS, CSA, ATL
Spiziapteryx circumcinctus	M	C	LT	U	L	1000+		N1, F7	CHA	CSA
Falco deiroleucus	M	T/A	HT	R/P	L	2000	R	F1		GCS, CHO, NSA, AMN, AMS, CSA
Falco femoralis	L	T/C	LT	U	L	4400+		N6, N9, N5, N7, N8, N14		MPL, PAS, GCS, STP, NAN, CAN, SAN, NSA, AMN, AMS, CSA, PAM, PAT
Falco mexicanus	M	T/A	US	U	L	2300	R	N8, N2		BSR, MPL, MAH
Falco peregrinus	M	T/A	LS	R	L	2600	R	A11, N2, F7E, F9E		BSR, MPL, MAH, EPC, STP, CAN, SAN, CSA, PAT
Falco rufigularis	L	C/A	LT	F	L	900		F1E, F7E, F8E, F15		PAS, GCS, CHO, EPC, NSA, AMN, AMS, CSA, ATL
Falco sparverius	L	T/C	LS	F	L	4400		N8, N1, N7, F7, F8, N13, N9		GAN, LAN, BSR, MPL, PAS, MAH, GCS, CHO, EPC, STP, NAN, CAN, SAN, NSA, TEP, AMN, AMS, CSA, ATL, PAM, PAT

Galliformes

Cracidae

	Snst	Strat	Cntab	Rel	Min	Max	Micro	Habitats	Sub	Zoogeographic Regions
Ortalis canicollis	L	U/C	LT	C	L	1200+		F7, F8	CHA	CSA
Ortalis cinereiceps	L	T/C	LT	F	L	1100		F1E, F8, F15		PAS, GCS, CHO
Ortalis erythroptera	M	T/C	LT	U	L	750+		F7, F8?	MAN	EPC
Ortalis garrula	L	T/C	LT	C	L	800		F7, F8, F1E, F15	CMV	NSA
Ortalis leucogastra	L	T/C	LT	F	L	1050		F7, F15, F8	CHG	PAS
Ortalis motmot										
araucuan	M	U/C	LT	U	L	700		F1E, F7, F8	o	ATL
colombiana	M	U/C	UT	R	L	2500		F1E, F7		NAN, NSA
guttata	L	U/C	LT	C	L	1800		F1E, F3, F8, F15		AMN, AMS
motmot	L	U/C	LT	C	L	2000		F1E, F3, F8, F15, F4E		NAN, AMN, AMS
superciliaris	M	U/C	LT	U?	L	1000?		F7, F1E		AMS, CSA
Ortalis poliocephala										
poliocephala	L	T/C	LT	F	L	1800		F7, F1E	SIN	PAS
wagleri	M	T/C	LT	F	L	2000		F7, F8	SIN	PAS
Ortalis ruficauda	L	T/C	LT	C	L	1600		F7, F8, F1E, F15	ARC	NSA
Ortalis vetula	L	T/C	LT	C	L	1850		F1E, F8, F15	o	GCS
Penelope albipennis	H	C	HT	R	L	900		F7	MAN	EPC
Penelope argyrotis	M	M/C	UT	F	900	2400		F4, F15?	o	NAN
Penelope barbata	M	M/C	MM	F	1550	3000+		F4		NAN, CAN
Penelope dabbenei	M	C	MM	?	1800	2500		F4	SCT	CAN
Penelope jacquacu	H	T/C	LT	F	L	1400		F1		AMN, AMS
Penelope jacucaca	H	?	LT	?	L	L		F7, F8	CAA	CSA
Penelope marail	M	C	LT	F	L	700+		F1	GUI	AMN
Penelope montagnii	M	M/C	UM	F	1800	3450		F4, F15?		NAN, CAN
Penelope obscura	M	T/C	UT	F	L	2100		F4, F1		CAN, CSA, ATL
Penelope ochrogaster	H	C	LT	U	L	L		F8	CER	CSA
Penelope ortoni	M	C	HT	?	200	1500		F4, F1	WES	NAN
Penelope perspicax	H	?	MM	R	1300	2100		F4	WES	NAN
Penelope pileata	H	C	LT	F	L	L		F1	o	AMS
Penelope purpurascens	M	U/C	LT?	F	L	2000		F1, F7, F8, F4, F11		PAS, MAH, GCS, CDH, NAN, NSA
Penelope superciliaris	M	T	LT	F	L	1100		F1, F12		AMS, CSA, ATL
Aburria aburri	H	C	UT	U	700	2100		F4, F1		NAN, CAN

CP	RP	Notes
4	3	Locally to 1,500 m (Colombia).
4	2	Population status in eastern Brazil?
2	1	Deforestation; survey.
4	3	Most common below 1,600 m.
4	3	
4	2	Poorly known.
3	1	Poorly known.
4	2	Mainly above 2,000 m in Andes; some populations declining.
4	2	Monitor.
3	2	Breeding distribution poorly known; includes *F. kreyenborgi* (pale color morph).
4	3	Locally to 1,600 m; occasionally to 2,000 m.
4	3	
4	3	
4	3	
2	1	Deforestation; survey.
4	3	
4	2	Relationship to *O. vetula* and *O. poliocephala* uncertain.
3	2	Local; deforestation.
2	1	Deforestation.
4	3	
4	3	Occasionally to 2,500 m, mainly below 900 m.
3	2	Deforestation.
3	2	Monitor.
3	2	Monitor; deforestation.
4	3	
4	3	
1	1	Deforestation, hunting.
4	2	Occasionally to 300 m; declining in many areas; monitor.
2	1	Deforestation.
2	1	Occasionally to 850 m; declining; deforestation; survey.
4	2	Occasionally to 1,600 m; declining locally; monitor.
2	1	Deforestation; survey.
4	3	
4	3	Occasionally to 1,350 m.
3	2	Monitor, especially in Atlantic Forest.
2	1	Deforestation.
2	2	Declining with deforestation.
1	1	Possibly extinct; survey.
3	2	Survey.
3	2	Declining, especially outside reserves; monitor.
4	3	
2	2	Occasional to 600 and 2,500 m; declining; deforestation.

Abbreviations Used

Snst - Sensitivity:
L - Low; **M** - Medium; **H** - High.

Strat - Foraging Strata:
T - Terrestrial; **U** - Understory; **M** - Midstory; **C** - Canopy; **A** - Aerial; **W** - Water.

Cntab - Center of Abundance:
LT - Lower tropical; **LS** - Lower subtropical; **HT** - Hill tropical; **UT** - Upper tropical; **US** - Upper subtropical; **MM** - Middle montane; **UM** - Upper montane.

Rel - Relative Abundance:
R - Rare; **U** - Uncommon; **F** - Fairly common; **C** - Common; **P** - Patchily distributed.

Min - Minimum Elevation:
L - Lowlands; **?** - Uncertain value; numeric values in meters.

Max - Maximum Elevation:
L - Lowlands; **?** - Uncertain value; **+** - species occurs at least to given elevation but likely occurs higher; numeric values in meters.

Micro - Microhabitats:
A - Army ants; **B** - Bamboo; **T** - Treefalls; **G** - Ground bromeliads; **C** - Rocky outcrops and caves; **S** - Streamside; **V** - Vine tangles; **B/V** -Bamboo/vine tangles.

Habitats:
F1 - Tropical lowland evergreen forest; **F2** - Flooded tropical evergreen forest; **F3** - River-edge forest; **F4** - Montane evergreen forest; **F5** - Elfin forest; **F6** - *Polylepis* woodland; **F7** - Tropical deciduous forest; **F8** - Gallery forest; **F9** - Southern temperate forest; **F10** - Pine forest; **F11** - Pine-oak forest; **F12** - White sand forest; **F13** - Palm forest; **F14** - Mangrove forest; **F15** - Secondary forest; **N1** - Arid lowland scrub; **N2** - Arid montane scrub; **N3** - Semihumid/humid montane scrub; **N4** - Cerrado; **N5** - Campo grasslands; **N6** - Low, seasonally wet grassland; **N7** - Southern temperate grassland; **N8** - Northern temperate grassland; **N9** - Puna grassland; **N10** - Paramo grassland; **N11** - Riparian thickets; **N12** - River island scrub; **N13** - Pastures/agricultural lands; **N14** - Second-growth scrub; **A1** - Freshwater marshes; **A2** - Saltwater/brackish marshes; **A3** - Coastal sand beaches/mudflats; **A4** - Coastal rocky beaches; **A5** - Riverine sand beaches; **A6** - Freshwater lakes and ponds; **A7** - Alkaline lakes; **A8** - Rivers; **A9** - Streams; **A10** - Bogs; **A11** - Coastal waters; **A12** - Pelagic waters.
E - Edge (used as a modifer to particular habitats).

Sub - Subregions:
ARC - Arid Caribbean Coast; **AWA** - Altiplano and Western Andes; **BAH** - Bahamas; **BAJ** - Baja California; **CAA** - Caatinga; **CAH** - Central American Highlands; **CER** - Cerrado; **CHA** - Chaco; **CHG** - Chiapas-Guanacaste; **CHL** - Chilean Desert; **CHR** - Chiriquí; **CIS** - Cocos Island; **CMV** - Cauca-Magdalena Valley; **COC** - Cuzco-Cochabamba; **CUB** - Cuba; **DOM** - Dominica; **EAS** - Eastern Slope Andes; **FDN** - Fernando de Noronha; **GAL** - Galápagos; **GCM** - Gulf Coast-Mexico; **GRE** - Grenada; **GUA** - Guadeloupe; **GUI** - Guianan; **HIS** - Hispaniola; **HPC** - Humid Pacific Coast; **ISA** - Isla Providencia and Isla San Andrés; **JAM** - Jamaica; **JFI** - Juan Fernández Islands; **MAN** - Manabí-Tumbes; **MAR** - Marañón Valley; **MID** - Madeira-Tapajós; **MON** - Montserrat; **MRT** - Martinique; **MTC** - Marañón-Cuzco; **NMM** - Northern Mexican Mountains; **NOR** - Northern Coastal Brazil; **PAR** - Pará; **PER** - Peruvian Desert; **PUE** - Puerto Rico; **RDJ** - Rio de Janeiro-Bahia Lowlands; **RMW** - Rio Madeira West; **RNW** - Rio Negro West; **SCA** - Southern Central America; **SCT** - Santa Cruz-Tucumán; **SIN** - Sinaloa-Oaxaca; **SMH** - Southern Mexican Highlands; **SMT** - Santa Marta; **SOC** - Islas Revillagigedo (Socorro Island group); **SON** - Sonoran Desert; **SOU** - Southern Atlantic Coast; **STL** - St. Lucia; **STV** - St. Vincent; **TAC** - Tacarcuna; **VAN** - Venezuelan Andes; **VNZ** - Venezuelan Coastal Mountains; **WES** - Western Andes; **YUC** - Yucatán Peninsula.
o - Endemic to region, but not restricted to a single subregion.

Zoogeographic Regions:
AMN - Northern Amazonia; **AMS** - Southern Amazonia; **ATL** - Atlantic Forest; **BSR** - Baja-Sonora; **CAN** - Central Andes; **CDH** - Chiriquí-Darién Highlands; **CHO** - Chocó Lowlands; **CSA** - Central South America; **EPC** - Equatorial Pacific Coast; **GAN** - Greater Antilles; **GCS** - Gulf-Caribbean Slope; **LAN** - Lesser Antilles; **MAH** - Madrean Highlands; **MPL** - Mexican Plateau; **NAN** - Northern Andes; **NSA** - Northern South America; **PAM** - Pampas; **PAS** - Pacific Arid Slope; **PAT** - Patagonia; **SAN** - Southern Andes; **STP** - Subtropical Pacific; **TEP** - Tepuis.

CP -Conservation Priority:
1 - Urgent; **2** - High; **3** - Medium; **4** - Low.

RP - Research Priority:
1 - High; **2** - Medium; **3** - Low.

	Snst	Strat	Cntab	Rel	Min	Max	Micro	Habitats	Sub	Zoogeographic Regions
Aburria cujubi	H	C	LT	F	L	L		F3, F1	o	AMS
Aburria jacutinga	H	C	LT	R	L	900		F1, F3	o	ATL
Aburria pipile	H	C	LT	F	L	900		F3, F1, F8		NSA, AMN, AMS, CSA
Chamaepetes goudotii	M	C	UT	U/P	900	3300		F4		NAN, CAN
Chamaepetes unicolor	H	C	UT	F	1000	3000		F4	CHR	CDH
Penelopina nigra	H	C	UT	F	900	3150		F4, F11	CAH	MAH
Oreophasis derbianus	H	U/C	MM	R	1800	3100		F4	CAH	MAH
Nothocrax urumutum	H	T	LT	F	L	800		F1, F2		AMN, AMS
Crax alberti	H	T	LT	R	L	1200		F1, F4?	CMV	NSA
Crax alector	M	T	LT	F	L	1400		F1, F4	o	AMN
Crax blumenbachii	M	T	LT	R	L	L		F1	RDJ	ATL
Crax daubentoni	M	T	LT	F	L	1500		F8, F7	ARC	NSA
Crax fasciolata	M	T	LT	F	L	900+		F1, F8, F7		AMS, CSA
Crax globulosa	M	T	LT	R	L	L		F2, F3		AMN, AMS
Crax mitu										
mitu	H	T	LT	R	L	L		F1	NOR	ATL
tuberosa	H	T	LT	U	L	900		F1		AMN, AMS
Crax pauxi	H	T	UT	R?	900	2200		F4	o	NAN
Crax rubra	M	T	LT	U	L	800		F1, F7		PAS, GCS, CHO
Crax salvini	H	T	LT	U	L	800		F1	RNW	AMN
Crax tomentosa	H	T	LT	U	L	600		F1, F8	o	AMN
Crax unicornis	H	T	UT	R	450	1200+		F4	COC	CAN
Phasianidae										
Meleagris gallopavo	M	T	MM	R?	1200?	2500+		F11, F10		MAH
Agriocharis ocellata	M	T	LT	R	L	L		F1E, F7	YUC	GCS
Dendrortyx barbatus	H	T	UT	R	950	2150		F4, F11	NMM	MAH
Dendrortyx leucophrys	M	T	MM	U	1000	2900		F4, F11		MAH, CDH
Dendrortyx macroura	M	T	UM	U	1800	3700+		F4, F11	o	MAH
Oreortyx pictus	M	T	MM	F	1250	2800		N2, F11		BSR
Callipepla squamata	L	T	LT	C	800	2100+		N2, N8, N14		BSR, MPL
Lophortyx californica	L	T	LT	C	L	2800		N1, N2, N14, F10		BSR
Lophortyx douglasii	M	T	LT	F	L	1550+		N1, F7		BSR, PAS
Lophortyx gambelii	L	T	LT	C	L	1600		N1, N14		BSR, MPL
Philortyx fasciatus	L	T	LT	F	L	1800		N1, N2, F7, N14		PAS, MAH
Colinus cristatus	L	T	LT	C	L	1500		N1, N6, N14		PAS, GCS, NSA, AMN
Colinus nigrogularis	L	T	LT	C	L	L		N1, N6, N14	o	GCS
Colinus virginianus										
ridgwayi	M	T	LS	R	L	L		N8	SON	BSR
virginianus	L	T	LT	F	L	2500		N14, N1, N8		MPL, MAH, GCS
Odontophorus atrifrons	H	T	MM	F?	1200	2800		F4	o	NAN
Odontophorus balliviani	H	T	MM	U	1000	3050		F4	COC	CAN
Odontophorus capueira	H	T	HT	F	L	1600		F4, F1	o	ATL
Odontophorus columbianus	H	T	MM	F	1300	2400		F4	VNZ	NAN
Odontophorus dialeucos	H	T	UT	U?	1050	1450		F4	TAC	CDH
Odontophorus erythrops	H	T	LT	F	L	1600		F1, F4		GCS, CDH, CHO, NAN
Odontophorus gujanensis	H	T	LT	F	L	900		F1		GCS, CHO, NSA, AMN, AMS
Odontophorus guttatus	H	T	UT	F	L	2200		F4, F1		MAH, GCS, CDH
Odontophorus hyperthyrus	H	T	MM	U	1600	2700		F4	o	NAN
Odontophorus leucolaemus	H	T	UT	U	700	1850		F4	CHR	CDH
Odontophorus melanonotus	H	T	UT	?	1200	1500		F4	WES	NAN
Odontophorus speciosus	H	T	MM	F	1050	2650		F4		NAN, CAN
Odontophorus stellatus	H	T	LT	F	L	1050		F1		AMN, AMS

CP	RP	Notes
3	2	Survey.
1	1	Extirpated from much of range; elevational migrant; deforestation; survey.
4	2	Declining locally; may contain multiple species.
4	3	Occasionally at 500 m (Chocó).
3	2	Occasionally to 500 m; monitor; declining outside reserves.
3	2	Occasionally to 250 m; declining locally; survey.
1	1	Occasionally to 1,550 and 3,350 m; survey.
4	3	
1	1	Declining; deforestation; survey.
4	3	
1	1	Known mainly from reserves; survey.
3	3	
3	3	Monitor.
2	1	Declining; survey.
1	1	Isolated forest patches in northeastern Brazil, possibly extinct.
4	3	Occasionally to 1,350 m.
2	1	Occasionally to 500 m; survey.
2	2	Locally to 1,500 m; declining outside reserves; monitor.
3	2	Probably declining locally.
4	2	Monitor.
2	1	Elevational range poorly known; survey.
3	1	Survey northern Mexico populations.
2	1	Declining outside reserves; survey.
2	1	Deforestation; survey.
3	3	Occasionally to 300 m; survey.
3	2	Locally to 1,300 m; habitat degradation; monitor.
4	2	Monitor Baja population.
4	3	
4	3	Introduced into Chile.
4	3	
4	3	
4	3	Occasionally to 2,500 m.
4	3	Locally to 3,100 m (Colombia); may contain two species.
4	3	
1	1	Grassland habitat nearly destroyed; remnant habitat degraded.
4	2	Mexican populations small, local, and poorly known.
3	2	Declining with deforestation.
4	3	
3	2	Declining outside reserves.
3	2	
2	2	Survey.
3	2	Declining with deforestation; may contain two species.
4	3	Locally to 1,800 m.
4	2	Only above 1,000 m from Costa Rica south; monitor.
3	2	Monitor.
3	2	
2	1	Declining with deforestation.
4	3	
4	3	

Abbreviations Used

Snst - Sensitivity:
L - Low; **M** - Medium; **H** - High.

Strat - Foraging Strata:
T - Terrestrial; **U** - Understory; **M** - Midstory; **C** - Canopy; **A** - Aerial; **W** - Water.

Cntab - Center of Abundance:
LT - Lower tropical; **LS** - Lower subtropical; **HT** - Hill tropical; **UT** - Upper tropical; **US** - Upper subtropical; **MM** - Middle montane; **UM** - Upper montane.

Rel - Relative Abundance:
R - Rare; **U** - Uncommon; **F** - Fairly common; **C** - Common; **P** - Patchily distributed.

Min - Minimum Elevation:
L - Lowlands; **?** - Uncertain value; numeric values in meters.

Max - Maximum Elevation:
L - Lowlands; **?** - Uncertain value; **+** - species occurs at least to given elevation but likely occurs higher; numeric values in meters.

Micro - Microhabitats:
A - Army ants; **B** - Bamboo; **T** - Treefalls; **G** - Ground bromeliads; **C** - Rocky outcrops and caves; **S** - Streamside; **V** - Vine tangles; **B/V** -Bamboo/vine tangles.

Habitats:
F1 - Tropical lowland evergreen forest; **F2** - Flooded tropical evergreen forest; **F3** - River-edge forest; **F4** - Montane evergreen forest; **F5** - Elfin forest; **F6** - *Polylepis* woodland; **F7** - Tropical deciduous forest; **F8** - Gallery forest; **F9** - Southern temperate forest; **F10** - Pine forest; **F11** - Pine-oak forest; **F12** - White sand forest; **F13** - Palm forest; **F14** - Mangrove forest; **F15** - Secondary forest; **N1** - Arid lowland scrub; **N2** - Arid montane scrub; **N3** - Semihumid/humid montane scrub; **N4** - Cerrado; **N5** - Campo grasslands; **N6** - Low, seasonally wet grassland; **N7** - Southern temperate grassland; **N8** - Northern temperate grassland; **N9** - Puna grassland; **N10** - Paramo grassland; **N11** - Riparian thickets; **N12** - River island scrub; **N13** - Pastures/agricultural lands; **N14** - Second-growth scrub; **A1** - Freshwater marshes; **A2** - Saltwater/brackish marshes; **A3** - Coastal sand beaches/mudflats; **A4** - Coastal rocky beaches; **A5** - Riverine sand beaches; **A6** - Freshwater lakes and ponds; **A7** - Alkaline lakes; **A8** - Rivers; **A9** - Streams; **A10** - Bogs; **A11** - Coastal waters; **A12** - Pelagic waters.
E - Edge (used as a modifer to particular habitats).

Sub - Subregions:
ARC - Arid Caribbean Coast; **AWA** - Altiplano and Western Andes; **BAH** - Bahamas; **BAJ** - Baja California; **CAA** - Caatinga; **CAH** - Central American Highlands; **CER** - Cerrado; **CHA** - Chaco; **CHG** - Chiapas-Guanacaste; **CHL** - Chilean Desert; **CHR** - Chiriquí; **CIS** - Cocos Island; **CMV** - Cauca-Magdalena Valley; **COC** - Cuzco-Cochabamba; **CUB** - Cuba; **DOM** - Dominica; **EAS** - Eastern Slope Andes; **FDN** - Fernando de Noronha; **GAL** - Galápagos; **GCM** - Gulf Coast-Mexico; **GRE** - Grenada; **GUA** - Guadeloupe; **GUI** - Guianan; **HIS** - Hispaniola; **HPC** - Humid Pacific Coast; **ISA** - Isla Providencia and Isla San Andrés; **JAM** - Jamaica; **JFI** - Juan Fernández Islands; **MAN** - Manabí-Tumbes; **MAR** - Marañón Valley; **MID** - Madeira-Tapajós; **MON** - Montserrat; **MRT** - Martinique; **MTC** - Marañón-Cuzco; **NMM** - Northern Mexican Mountains; **NOR** - Northern Coastal Brazil; **PAR** - Pará; **PER** - Peruvian Desert; **PUE** - Puerto Rico; **RDJ** - Rio de Janeiro-Bahia Lowlands; **RMW** - Rio Madeira West; **RNW** - Rio Negro West; **SCA** - Southern Central America; **SCT** - Santa Cruz-Tucumán; **SIN** - Sinaloa-Oaxaca; **SMH** - Southern Mexican Highlands; **SMT** - Santa Marta; **SOC** - Islas Revillagigedo (Socorro Island group); **SON** - Sonoran Desert; **SOU** - Southern Atlantic Coast; **STL** - St. Lucia; **STV** - St. Vincent; **TAC** - Tacarcuna; **VAN** - Venezuelan Andes; **VNZ** - Venezuelan Coastal Mountains; **WES** - Western Andes; **YUC** - Yucatán Peninsula.
o - Endemic to region, but not restricted to a single subregion.

Zoogeographic Regions:
AMN - Northern Amazonia; **AMS** - Southern Amazonia; **ATL** - Atlantic Forest; **BSR** - Baja-Sonora; **CAN** - Central Andes; **CDH** - Chiriquí-Darién Highlands; **CHO** - Chocó Lowlands; **CSA** - Central South America; **EPC** - Equatorial Pacific Coast; **GAN** - Greater Antilles; **GCS** - Gulf-Caribbean Slope; **LAN** - Lesser Antilles; **MAH** - Madrean Highlands; **MPL** - Mexican Plateau; **NAN** - Northern Andes; **NSA** - Northern South America; **PAM** - Pampas; **PAS** - Pacific Arid Slope; **PAT** - Patagonia; **SAN** - Southern Andes; **STP** - Subtropical Pacific; **TEP** - Tepuis.

CP -Conservation Priority:
1 - Urgent; **2** - High; **3** - Medium; **4** - Low.

RP - Research Priority:
1 - High; **2** - Medium; **3** - Low.

	Snst	Strat	Cntab	Rel	Min	Max	Micro	Habitats	Sub	Zoogeographic Regions
Odontophorus strophium	H	T	MM	R	1500	2050		F4	EAS	NAN
Dactylortyx thoracicus	H	T	UT	U	L	3100		F4, F1, F11, F7		MAH, GCS
Cyrtonyx montezumae	M	T	US	U	1100	3100		F11, N2, N8		MPL, MAH
Cyrtonyx ocellatus	M	T	MM	U	750	3050		F11, N2, F10	CAH	MAH
Rhynchortyx cinctus	H	T	HT	U	L	1400		F1, F4		PAS, GCS, CDH, CHO, NSA
GRUIFORMES										
Gruidae										
Grus canadensis	L	T	LS	R	L	L?		A1, N8		GAN
Aramidae										
Aramus guarauna	M	T	LT	C	L	L		A1		GAN, PAS, GCS, CHO, NSA, AMN, AMS, CSA, ATL, PAM
Psophiidae										
Psophia crepitans	H	T	LT	U	L	700		F1		NSA, AMN
Psophia leucoptera	H	T	LT	U	L	1050		F1	RMW	AMS
Psophia viridis	H	T	LT	U	L	L		F1	o	AMS
Rallidae										
Rallus antarcticus	M	T	LS	R	L	L		A1, A3		STP, PAT
Rallus elegans										
elegans	M	T	LT	U	L	L		A1		GAN, GCS
tenuirostris	M	T	MM	F	1550	2800		A1	SMH	MAH
Rallus limicola	M	T	MM	U	L	2800		A1		BSR, MPL, MAH, NAN
Rallus longirostris										
longirostris	H	T	LT	F	L	L		A2, F14		GAN, LAN, GCS, EPC, NSA, AMN, AMS, ATL
obsoletus	H	T	LT	F	L	L		A2, F14, A1		BSR, PAS
Rallus semiplumbeus	M	T	UM	U	2500	3400		A1	EAS	NAN
Rallus wetmorei	M	T	LT	?	L	L		A2, F14	ARC	NSA
Ortygonax nigricans	M	T	LT	U/P	L	2200		A1		CHO, NAN, AMN, AMS, CSA, ATL
Ortygonax sanguinolentus	M	T	LS	C	L	4200		A1		EPC, STP, CAN, SAN, CSA, ATL, PAM, PAT
Pardirallus maculatus	M	T	LT	U/P	L	800		A1		GAN, PAS, GCS, EPC, NSA, AMN, AMS, CSA, ATL, PAM
Amaurolimnas concolor	M	T	LT	R/P	L	1000		F8, F15, F2		GCS, CHO, AMN, AMS, CSA, ATL
Cyanolimnas cerverai	H	T	LT	R	L	L		A1	CUB	GAN
Aramides axillaris	H	T	LT	U	L	1200		F14, F1?, F7		PAS, GCS, CHO, EPC, NSA, AMN
Aramides cajanea	H	T	LT	F	L	1200		F2, F8, A1, F14		PAS, GCS, CHO, NSA, AMN, AMS, CSA, ATL
Aramides calopterus	H	T	LT	R	L	800		F1, A9		AMN, AMS
Aramides mangle	H	T	LT	U	L	900?		F14, F15?		CSA, ATL
Aramides saracura	M	T	LT	U	L	1600		F1, F4, A9, F9	o	ATL
Aramides wolfi	H	T	LT	?	L	900		F14, F8		CHO, EPC
Aramides ypecaha	M	T	LT	F	L	L?		F8, A1		CSA, PAM
Anurolimnas castaneiceps	L	T	LT	U/P	L	900		F15, F1E		AMN, AMS
Porzana albicollis	M	T	LT	F	L	1550		N6, A1		NSA, AMN, AMS, CSA, ATL, PAM
Porzana carolina	L	T	LS	U	L	L		A1		BSR
Porzana flaviventer	M	T	LT	U/P	L	600		A1		GAN, PAS, GCS, NSA, AMN, AMS, CSA, ATL, PAM
Porzana spiloptera	L	T	LT	U?	L	L		A1		CSA, PAM
Laterallus albigularis	L	T	LT	F	L	1600		A1		GCS, CHO
Laterallus exilis	L	T	LT	C	L	1200		A1, N13		GCS, CHO, NSA, AMN, AMS, CSA, ATL
Laterallus fasciatus	M	T	LT	F	L	L		F3, N11, N14		AMN, AMS
Laterallus jamaicensis	M	T	LT	R/P	L	4100		A1, A2		GAN, BSR, GCS, STP, CAN, CSA
Laterallus leucopyrrhus	M	T	LT	U	L	900		A1		ATL, PAM
Laterallus levraudi	M	T	LT	?	L	600		A1	ARC	NSA
Laterallus melanophaius	L	T	LT	F	L	1100		A1		NSA, AMN, AMS, CSA, ATL, PAM

CP	RP	Notes
1	1	Extensive deforestation in range; survey.
4	2	Monitor.
4	2	Monitor; overgrazing and burning.
4	2	Occasionally to 400 m; monitor; overgrazing and burning.
3	2	Poorly known; monitor; deforestation.
3	2	Status of breeding population unknown.
4	3	
3	3	Hunting; deforestation.
3	3	Hunting; deforestation.
3	2	Hunting; deforestation.
1	2	Poorly known; apparently declining; survey.
3	2	Poorly known in Neotropics.
2	2	Habitat degradation,drainage; survey.
3	2	Local in lowlands; breeding populations vulnerable.
4	3	
3	2	Habitat degradation; status of Colorado River population in Mexico?
2	2	Occasionally to 2,100 and 4,000 m; habitat degradation.
3	3	
4	3	Mainly below 800 m.
4	3	
4	3	Occasionally to 2,000 m; very local.
4	2	Range poorly known; local.
1	1	Habitat threatened by fires; survey.
4	3	Occasionally to 1,800 m (Venezuela).
4	3	Occasionally to 2,300 m (Colombia).
4	2	Poorly known.
3	2	Status inland in northeastern Brazil uncertain.
4	3	
4	2	Monitor.
4	3	
4	3	Occasionally to 1,500 m (Colombia).
4	3	
4	3	
4	2	Occasionally to 2,500 m; distribution poorly known.
4	2	Poorly known; status unknown.
4	3	
4	3	Occasionally to 1,700 m (Venezuela)?
4	3	
2	1	Neotropical populations poorly known; very local; may contain two species.
4	2	Poorly known.
3	2	Poorly known.
4	3	

Abbreviations Used

Snst - Sensitivity:
L - Low; **M** - Medium; **H** - High.

Strat - Foraging Strata:
T - Terrestrial; **U** - Understory; **M** - Midstory; **C** - Canopy; **A** - Aerial; **W** - Water.

Cntab - Center of Abundance:
LT - Lower tropical; **LS** - Lower subtropical; **HT** - Hill tropical; **UT** - Upper tropical; **US** - Upper subtropical; **MM** - Middle montane; **UM** - Upper montane.

Rel - Relative Abundance:
R - Rare; **U** - Uncommon; **F** - Fairly common; **C** - Common; **P** - Patchily distributed.

Min - Minimum Elevation:
L - Lowlands; **?** - Uncertain value; numeric values in meters.

Max - Maximum Elevation:
L - Lowlands; **?** - Uncertain value; **+** - species occurs at least to given elevation but likely occurs higher; numeric values in meters.

Micro - Microhabitats:
A - Army ants; **B** - Bamboo; **T** - Treefalls; **G** - Ground bromeliads; **C** - Rocky outcrops and caves; **S** - Streamside; **V** - Vine tangles; **B/V** -Bamboo/vine tangles.

Habitats:
F1 - Tropical lowland evergreen forest; **F2** - Flooded tropical evergreen forest; **F3** - River-edge forest; **F4** - Montane evergreen forest; **F5** - Elfin forest; **F6** - *Polylepis* woodland; **F7** - Tropical deciduous forest; **F8** - Gallery forest; **F9** - Southern temperate forest; **F10** - Pine forest; **F11** - Pine-oak forest; **F12** - White sand forest; **F13** - Palm forest; **F14** - Mangrove forest; **F15** - Secondary forest; **N1** - Arid lowland scrub; **N2** - Arid montane scrub; **N3** - Semihumid/humid montane scrub; **N4** - Cerrado; **N5** - Campo grasslands; **N6** - Low, seasonally wet grassland; **N7** - Southern temperate grassland; **N8** - Northern temperate grassland; **N9** - Puna grassland; **N10** - Paramo grassland; **N11** - Riparian thickets; **N12** - River island scrub; **N13** - Pastures/agricultural lands; **N14** - Second-growth scrub; **A1** - Freshwater marshes; **A2** - Saltwater/brackish marshes; **A3** - Coastal sand beaches/mudflats; **A4** - Coastal rocky beaches; **A5** - Riverine sand beaches; **A6** - Freshwater lakes and ponds; **A7** - Alkaline lakes; **A8** - Rivers; **A9** - Streams; **A10** - Bogs; **A11** - Coastal waters; **A12** - Pelagic waters.
E - Edge (used as a modifer to particular habitats).

Sub - Subregions:
ARC - Arid Caribbean Coast; **AWA** - Altiplano and Western Andes; **BAH** - Bahamas; **BAJ** - Baja California; **CAA** - Caatinga; **CAH** - Central American Highlands; **CER** - Cerrado; **CHA** - Chaco; **CHG** - Chiapas-Guanacaste; **CHL** - Chilean Desert; **CHR** - Chiriquí; **CIS** - Cocos Island; **CMV** - Cauca-Magdalena Valley; **COC** - Cuzco-Cochabamba; **CUB** - Cuba; **DOM** - Dominica; **EAS** - Eastern Slope Andes; **FDN** - Fernando de Noronha; **GAL** - Galápagos; **GCM** - Gulf Coast-Mexico; **GRE** - Grenada; **GUA** - Guadeloupe; **GUI** - Guianan; **HIS** - Hispaniola; **HPC** - Humid Pacific Coast; **ISA** - Isla Providencia and Isla San Andrés; **JAM** - Jamaica; **JFI** - Juan Fernández Islands; **MAN** - Manabí-Tumbes; **MAR** - Marañón Valley; **MID** - Madeira-Tapajós; **MON** - Montserrat; **MRT** - Martinique; **MTC** - Marañón-Cuzco; **NMM** - Northern Mexican Mountains; **NOR** - Northern Coastal Brazil; **PAR** - Pará; **PER** - Peruvian Desert; **PUE** - Puerto Rico; **RDJ** - Rio de Janeiro-Bahia Lowlands; **RMW** - Rio Madeira West; **RNW** - Rio Negro West; **SCA** - Southern Central America; **SCT** - Santa Cruz-Tucumán; **SIN** - Sinaloa-Oaxaca; **SMH** - Southern Mexican Highlands; **SMT** - Santa Marta; **SOC** - Islas Revillagigedo (Socorro Island group); **SON** - Sonoran Desert; **SOU** - Southern Atlantic Coast; **STL** - St. Lucia; **STV** - St. Vincent; **TAC** - Tacarcuna; **VAN** - Venezuelan Andes; **VNZ** - Venezuelan Coastal Mountains; **WES** - Western Andes; **YUC** - Yucatán Peninsula.
o - Endemic to region, but not restricted to a single subregion.

Zoogeographic Regions:
AMN - Northern Amazonia; **AMS** - Southern Amazonia; **ATL** - Atlantic Forest; **BSR** - Baja-Sonora; **CAN** - Central Andes; **CDH** - Chiriquí-Darién Highlands; **CHO** - Chocó Lowlands; **CSA** - Central South America; **EPC** - Equatorial Pacific Coast; **GAN** - Greater Antilles; **GCS** - Gulf-Caribbean Slope; **LAN** - Lesser Antilles; **MAH** - Madrean Highlands; **MPL** - Mexican Plateau; **NAN** - Northern Andes; **NSA** - Northern South America; **PAM** - Pampas; **PAS** - Pacific Arid Slope; **PAT** - Patagonia; **SAN** - Southern Andes; **STP** - Subtropical Pacific; **TEP** - Tepuis.

CP -Conservation Priority:
1 - Urgent; **2** - High; **3** - Medium; **4** - Low.

RP - Research Priority:
1 - High; **2** - Medium; **3** - Low.

	Snst	Strat	Cntab	Rel	Min	Max	Micro	Habitats	Sub	Zoogeographic Regions
Laterallus ruber	L	T	LT	F	L	1500		A1		PAS, GCS
Laterallus spilonotus	M	T	HT	C	600	1500		F4, A1?	GAL	EPC
Laterallus viridis	L	T	LT	F	L	1300		N6, N5, N13		NSA, TEP, AMN, AMS, CSA, ATL
Laterallus xenopterus	M	T	LT	U	L	1000		A1	o	CSA
Micropygia schomburgkii	H	T	LT	U/P	L	1250+		N5, N6		GCS, NSA, TEP, AMN, AMS, CSA
Coturnicops notatus	L	T	LS	R	L	1500		N6, A1, N13, N7?		NSA, AMN, CSA, ATL, PAM, PAT?
Coturnicops noveboracensis	L	T	MM	U	2300	2800		A1		MAH
Neocrex columbianus	M	T	LT	U/P	L	2100		N6, A1		GCS, CHO, NSA
Neocrex erythrops	M	T	LT	U/P	L	2600		N6, N13, A1		GCS, CHO, EPC, STP, NSA, AMN, AMS, CSA
Porphyriops melanops	M	W	LS	F	L	3100		A1, A6		STP, NAN, SAN, CSA, ATL, PAM, PAT
Gallinula chloropus	L	T/W	LS	C	L	4000		A1		GAN, LAN, BSR, MPL, PAS, MAH, GCS, CDH, CHO, EPC, STP, NAN, CAN, NSA, AMN, AMS, CSA, ATL, PAM
Porphyrula flavirostris	M	T	LT	U/P	L	500+		A1		NSA, AMN, AMS, CSA, ATL
Porphyrula martinica	L	T	LT	F	L	1200		A1		GAN, LAN, PAS, MAH, GCS, CHO, EPC, STP, NSA, AMN, AMS, CSA, ATL, PAM
Fulica americana	L	T/W	LS	C	L	3400		A1, A2, A6		GAN, BSR, MPL, PAS, MAH, GCS
Fulica ardesiaca	L	T/W	UM	C	2000	4500		A1, A6		EPC, STP, NAN, CAN
Fulica armillata	M	W	LS	C	L	1000		A1, A6		STP, SAN, CSA, PAM, PAT
Fulica caribaea	L	W	LT	C	L	L		A6, A1, A2		GAN, LAN, NSA
Fulica cornuta	H	W	UM	U	3100	5000		A6, A7	AWA	CAN
Fulica gigantea	H	W	UM	U	3500	5000		A6	AWA	CAN
Fulica leucoptera	M	W	LS	F	L	4500		A1, A6		STP, SAN, CSA, PAM, PAT
Fulica rufifrons	M	W	LS	U	L	L		A1		STP, CSA?, PAM, PAT
Heliornithidae										
Heliornis fulica	M	W	LT	U	L	L		A6, A9		PAS, GCS, CHO, NSA, AMN, AMS, CSA, ATL
Eurypygidae										
Eurypyga helias	M	T	LT	U	L	1200		F2, A9		GCS, NSA, AMN, AMS, CSA
Cariamidae										
Cariama cristata	M	T	LT	F	L	2100		N4, N5, F7		CSA, ATL
Chunga burmeisteri	M	T	LT	F	L	800+		F7, N1	CHA	CSA
CHARADRIIFORMES										
Jacanidae										
Jacana jacana	L	T	LT	C	L	900		A1		GCS, CHO, NSA, AMN, AMS, CSA, ATL, PAM
Jacana spinosa	L	T	LT	C	L	1500		A1		GAN, PAS, GCS
Rostratulidae										
Nycticryphes semicollaris	L	T	LT	R	L	L?		A1, N13		STP, CSA, PAM
Haematopodidae										
Haematopus ater	M	T	LS	F	L	L		A4		EPC, STP, PAT
Haematopus bachmani	M	T	LS	U	L	L		A4		BSR
Haematopus leucopodus	L	T	LS	C	L	1000		A3, A6		STP, SAN, PAT
Haematopus palliatus	M	T	LT	F	L	L		A3, A4		GAN, LAN, BSR, PAS, GCS, CHO, EPC, STP, NSA, AMN, ATL, PAM, PAT
Recurvirostridae										
Himantopus mexicanus	M	T	LT	F	L	1600		A1, A2, A3		GAN, LAN, BSR, MPL, PAS, MAH, GCS, CHO, EPC, STP, CAN, NSA, AMN, AMS, CSA, ATL, PAM, PAT
Recurvirostra americana	M	W	LS	C	L	2500		A1, A2		BSR, MPL
Recurvirostra andina	H	W	UM	U	3600	4600		A7, A6, A1	AWA	CAN
Burhinidae										
Burhinus bistriatus	L	T	LT	F	L	900		N6, N1, N5, N13		PAS, GCS, NSA, AMN
Burhinus superciliaris	L	T	LT	U	L	L		N6, N1, N13		EPC, STP

CP	RP	Notes
4	3	
3	2	Habitat destruction; monitor.
4	3	
3	2	Poorly known; habitat destruction.
3	1	Habitat destruction.
2	1	Almost unknown; survey; migratory?
2	1	Status of Mexico breeding population unknown; survey.
3	2	Poorly known.
3	2	Poorly known.
4	3	2,500-3,100 m in Colombia.
4	3	
4	2	Migratory behavior and range poorly known.
4	3	Wanders to 3,500 m.
4	3	
4	2	Locally to lowlands; taxonomy follows Fjeldså (1982).
4	3	
4	2	Status uncertain; relationship to *F. americana* uncertain.
2	1	Monitor; habitat destruction.
3	2	Monitor.
4	3	
4	3	
4	2	Monitor.
4	3	Occasionally to 1,800 m (Venezuela).
4	3	
4	3	
4	3	Occasionally to 3,000 m.
4	3	
3	2	Distribution and seasonal movements poorly known.
4	3	
4	2	
4	3	Local inland (Patagonia).
4	2	Monitor.
4	2	Locally to 4,100 m; restricted to coastal regions in Amazonia.
4	3	
3	2	Occasionally lower; monitor.
4	3	
3	2	Monitor.

Abbreviations Used

Snst - Sensitivity:
L - Low; **M** - Medium; **H** - High.

Strat - Foraging Strata:
T - Terrestrial; **U** - Understory; **M** - Midstory; **C** - Canopy; **A** - Aerial; **W** - Water.

Cntab - Center of Abundance:
LT - Lower tropical; **LS** - Lower subtropical; **HT** - Hill tropical; **UT** - Upper tropical; **US** - Upper subtropical; **MM** - Middle montane; **UM** - Upper montane.

Rel - Relative Abundance:
R - Rare; **U** - Uncommon; **F** - Fairly common; **C** - Common; **P** - Patchily distributed.

Min - Minimum Elevation:
L - Lowlands; **?** - Uncertain value; numeric values in meters.

Max - Maximum Elevation:
L - Lowlands; **?** - Uncertain value; **+** - species occurs at least to given elevation but likely occurs higher; numeric values in meters.

Micro - Microhabitats:
A - Army ants; **B** - Bamboo; **T** - Treefalls; **G** - Ground bromeliads; **C** - Rocky outcrops and caves; **S** - Streamside; **V** - Vine tangles; **B/V** -Bamboo/vine tangles.

Habitats:
F1 - Tropical lowland evergreen forest; **F2** - Flooded tropical evergreen forest; **F3** - River-edge forest; **F4** - Montane evergreen forest; **F5** - Elfin forest; **F6** - *Polylepis* woodland; **F7** - Tropical deciduous forest; **F8** - Gallery forest; **F9** - Southern temperate forest; **F10** - Pine forest; **F11** - Pine-oak forest; **F12** - White sand forest; **F13** - Palm forest; **F14** - Mangrove forest; **F15** - Secondary forest; **N1** - Arid lowland scrub; **N2** - Arid montane scrub; **N3** - Semihumid/humid montane scrub; **N4** - Cerrado; **N5** - Campo grasslands; **N6** - Low, seasonally wet grassland; **N7** - Southern temperate grassland; **N8** - Northern temperate grassland; **N9** - Puna grassland; **N10** - Paramo grassland; **N11** - Riparian thickets; **N12** - River island scrub; **N13** - Pastures/agricultural lands; **N14** - Second-growth scrub; **A1** - Freshwater marshes; **A2** - Saltwater/brackish marshes; **A3** - Coastal sand beaches/mudflats; **A4** - Coastal rocky beaches; **A5** - Riverine sand beaches; **A6** - Freshwater lakes and ponds; **A7** - Alkaline lakes; **A8** - Rivers; **A9** - Streams; **A10** - Bogs; **A11** - Coastal waters; **A12** - Pelagic waters.
E - Edge (used as a modifer to particular habitats).

Sub - Subregions:
ARC - Arid Caribbean Coast; **AWA** - Altiplano and Western Andes; **BAH** - Bahamas; **BAJ** - Baja California; **CAA** - Caatinga; **CAH** - Central American Highlands; **CER** - Cerrado; **CHA** - Chaco; **CHG** - Chiapas-Guanacaste; **CHL** - Chilean Desert; **CHR** - Chiriquí; **CIS** - Cocos Island; **CMV** - Cauca-Magdalena Valley; **COC** - Cuzco-Cochabamba; **CUB** - Cuba; **DOM** - Dominica; **EAS** - Eastern Slope Andes; **FDN** - Fernando de Noronha; **GAL** - Galápagos; **GCM** - Gulf Coast-Mexico; **GRE** - Grenada; **GUA** - Guadeloupe; **GUI** - Guianan; **HIS** - Hispaniola; **HPC** - Humid Pacific Coast; **ISA** - Isla Providencia and Isla San Andrés; **JAM** - Jamaica; **JFI** - Juan Fernández Islands; **MAN** - Manabí-Tumbes; **MAR** - Marañón Valley; **MID** - Madeira-Tapajós; **MON** - Montserrat; **MRT** - Martinique; **MTC** - Marañón-Cuzco; **NMM** - Northern Mexican Mountains; **NOR** - Northern Coastal Brazil; **PAR** - Pará; **PER** - Peruvian Desert; **PUE** - Puerto Rico; **RDJ** - Rio de Janeiro-Bahia Lowlands; **RMW** - Rio Madeira West; **RNW** - Rio Negro West; **SCA** - Southern Central America; **SCT** - Santa Cruz-Tucumán; **SIN** - Sinaloa-Oaxaca; **SMH** - Southern Mexican Highlands; **SMT** - Santa Marta; **SOC** - Islas Revillagigedo (Socorro Island group); **SON** - Sonoran Desert; **SOU** - Southern Atlantic Coast; **STL** - St. Lucia; **STV** - St. Vincent; **TAC** - Tacarcuna; **VAN** - Venezuelan Andes; **VNZ** - Venezuelan Coastal Mountains; **WES** - Western Andes; **YUC** - Yucatán Peninsula.
o - Endemic to region, but not restricted to a single subregion.

Zoogeographic Regions:
AMN - Northern Amazonia; **AMS** - Southern Amazonia; **ATL** - Atlantic Forest; **BSR** - Baja-Sonora; **CAN** - Central Andes; **CDH** - Chiriquí-Darién Highlands; **CHO** - Chocó Lowlands; **CSA** - Central South America; **EPC** - Equatorial Pacific Coast; **GAN** - Greater Antilles; **GCS** - Gulf-Caribbean Slope; **LAN** - Lesser Antilles; **MAH** - Madrean Highlands; **MPL** - Mexican Plateau; **NAN** - Northern Andes; **NSA** - Northern South America; **PAM** - Pampas; **PAS** - Pacific Arid Slope; **PAT** - Patagonia; **SAN** - Southern Andes; **STP** - Subtropical Pacific; **TEP** - Tepuis.

CP -Conservation Priority:
1 - Urgent; **2** - High; **3** - Medium; **4** - Low.

RP - Research Priority:
1 - High; **2** - Medium; **3** - Low.

	Snst	Strat	Cntab	Rel	Min	Max	Micro	Habitats	Sub	Zoogeographic Regions
Charadriidae										
Vanellus cayanus	M	T	LT	F	L	800		A5		NSA, AMN, AMS, CSA
Vanellus chilensis	L	T	LT	C	L	2600		N6, N13, A1		CHO, STP, SAN, NSA, AMN, AMS, CSA, ATL, PAM, PAT
Vanellus resplendens	M	T	UM	C	3100	4600		N9, N13, A1, A9, A10		NAN, CAN
Charadrius alexandrinus	H	T	LT	F	L	L		A3, A6, A7		GAN, BSR, MPL, PAS, GCS, STP, NSA
Charadrius alticola	H	T	UM	U	3700	4700		A7, A6	AWA	CAN
Charadrius collaris	H	T	LT	F	L	800		A5, A3		LAN, PAS, GCS, CHO, EPC, STP, NSA, AMN, AMS, CSA, ATL, PAM
Charadrius falklandicus	M	T	LS	F	L	1200		A6, A7, A3, A4		STP, PAT
Charadrius modestus	M	T	LS	F	L	2000		N7, A3		STP, SAN, PAT
Charadrius vociferus	L	T	LT	C	L	2400		A1, N13, A3, A5		GAN, BSR, MPL, PAS, GCS, EPC, STP
Charadrius wilsonia	M	T	LT	U	L	L		A3		GAN, LAN, BSR, PAS, GCS, CHO, EPC, STP, NSA, AMN, AMS, ATL
Phegornis mitchellii	H	T	UM	R	3500	5000		A10		CAN, SAN
Eudromias ruficollis	L	T	LS	F	L	4500		N7, N1, N9, N13		EPC, STP, CAN, SAN, CSA, PAT
Pluvianellus socialis	H	T	LS	U	L	1200		A7, A6	o	PAT
Scolopacidae										
Catoptrophorus semipalmatus	M	T	LT	U	L	L		A2, A3, A4		GAN, LAN, GCS, NSA
Gallinago andina	M	T	UM	F	3100	4400		A1, A10		NAN, CAN
Gallinago imperialis	H	T	UM	R	2800	3600		F5, A10		NAN, CAN
Gallinago nobilis	M	T	UM	U	2700	4200		N10, A10	o	NAN
Gallinago paraguaiae	L	T	LS	C	L	1500		A1, N13		STP, SAN, NSA, AMN, AMS, CSA, ATL, PAM, PAT
Gallinago stricklandii	M	T	UM	U	L	4200		N10, N7, A10		NAN, CAN, SAN, PAT
Gallinago undulata	H	T	LT	U/P	L	1600		N6, N5, A10		NSA, AMN, CSA, ATL
Thinocoridae										
Attagis gayi	H	T	UM	U/P	4000	5500		N9, A10		CAN, SAN
Attagis malouinus	H	T	US	U	L	2000		N7, A10		SAN, PAT
Thinocorus orbignyianus	M	T	UM	F	1000	4700		N9, A10, N7		CAN, SAN, PAT
Thinocorus rumicivorus	M	T	LS	C	L	3700		N7, N9, N13		EPC, STP, CAN, SAN, PAT
Chionididae										
Chionis alba	H	T	LS	F	L	L		A4, A3		PAT
Laridae										
Catharacta chilensis	H	W	LS	F	L	L		A11, A12		STP, PAT
Catharacta skua										
antarctica	H	W	LS	F	L	L		A11, A12		PAT
Gabianus scoresbii	M	T/W	LS	U	L	L		A11, A3, A4	o	PAT
Larus atricilla	M	T/W	LS	C	L	L		A11, A3, A4		GAN, LAN, BSR, PAS, GCS, NSA
Larus belcheri										
atlanticus	H	T/W	LS	U	L	L		A11, A3	o	PAM
belcheri	H	T/W	LS	F	L	L		A11, A4, A3		EPC, STP
Larus cirrocephalus	M	T/W	LS	U/P	L	1000		A1, A2, A3		EPC, STP, CSA, ATL, PAM
Larus dominicanus	M	T/W	LS	C	L	L		A11, A3, A4, A6		EPC, STP, SAN, ATL, PAM, PAT
Larus fuliginosus	H	T/W	LT	U	L	L		A11, A4	GAL	EPC
Larus heermanni	H	T/W	LS	C	L	L		A11, A3		BSR, PAS
Larus livens	M	T/W	LS	F	L	L		A11, A3	o	BSR
Larus maculipennis	L	T/W	LS	C	L	1200+		A1, A2, A6, N13		STP, SAN, ATL, PAM, PAT
Larus modestus	H	T/W	LS	C	L	L		A11, A3	CHL	STP
Larus occidentalis	M	T/W	LS	C	L	L		A11, A3, A4		BSR
Larus serranus	M	T/W	UM	C	2800	4700		A6, A7, A8, N13		NAN, CAN, SAN
Creagrus furcatus	H	W	LT	U	L	L		A11, A12	GAL	EPC
Phaetusa simplex	H	W	LT	F	L	L		A8, A6		NSA, AMN, AMS, CSA, ATL, PAM

CP	RP	Notes
4	3	
4	3	
4	3	Locally to 2,000 m in south; wanders seasonally to sea level.
4	3	Locally 2,000-2,500 m (Mexico); monitor populations.
4	3	Wanders to Pacific coast.
4	3	
4	3	
4	3	
4	3	
4	3	
4	2	Seasonally to 2,000 m in south; survey.
3	2	Monitor; declining in some areas?
4	2	Survey.
3	2	Local as breeder; possibly declining; monitor.
4	3	Locally to lowlands in winter.
3	2	Range poorly known; inaccessible habitat.
4	2	Monitor.
4	3	
3	2	May contain two species; southern populations vulnerable.
2	2	Habitat degradation.
3	2	To 2,000 m in southern Andes; monitor.
3	2	Seasonal in lowlands? monitor.
4	3	In south, regularly to lowlands in winter.
4	3	
4	3	Breeding status uncertain.
4	3	
4	3	
4	3	
4	3	
2	1	Status uncertain; survey.
4	3	
3	2	Occasionally on Andean lakes; distribution poorly known.
4	3	Locally to 1,000 m (Patagonia).
3	2	Small population; monitor.
4	3	
4	2	Monitor.
4	3	
4	2	Breeds inland in desert to 2,000 m; forages along coast.
4	3	
4	3	Occasionally along Pacific coast.
3	2	Relatively small populations; monitor.
4	3	Occasionally wanders to 3,500 m.

Abbreviations Used

Snst - Sensitivity:
L - Low; **M** - Medium; **H** - High.

Strat - Foraging Strata:
T - Terrestrial; **U** - Understory; **M** - Midstory; **C** - Canopy; **A** - Aerial; **W** - Water.

Cntab - Center of Abundance:
LT - Lower tropical; **LS** - Lower subtropical; **HT** - Hill tropical; **UT** - Upper tropical; **US** - Upper subtropical; **MM** - Middle montane; **UM** - Upper montane.

Rel - Relative Abundance:
R - Rare; **U** - Uncommon; **F** - Fairly common; **C** - Common; **P** - Patchily distributed.

Min - Minimum Elevation:
L - Lowlands; **?** - Uncertain value; numeric values in meters.

Max - Maximum Elevation:
L - Lowlands; **?** - Uncertain value; **+** - species occurs at least to given elevation but likely occurs higher; numeric values in meters.

Micro - Microhabitats:
A - Army ants; **B** - Bamboo; **T** - Treefalls; **G** - Ground bromeliads; **C** - Rocky outcrops and caves; **S** - Streamside; **V** - Vine tangles; **B/V** -Bamboo/vine tangles.

Habitats:
F1 - Tropical lowland evergreen forest; **F2** - Flooded tropical evergreen forest; **F3** - River-edge forest; **F4** - Montane evergreen forest; **F5** - Elfin forest; **F6** - *Polylepis* woodland; **F7** - Tropical deciduous forest; **F8** - Gallery forest; **F9** - Southern temperate forest; **F10** - Pine forest; **F11** - Pine-oak forest; **F12** - White sand forest; **F13** - Palm forest; **F14** - Mangrove forest; **F15** - Secondary forest; **N1** - Arid lowland scrub; **N2** - Arid montane scrub; **N3** - Semihumid/humid montane scrub; **N4** - Cerrado; **N5** - Campo grasslands; **N6** - Low, seasonally wet grassland; **N7** - Southern temperate grassland; **N8** - Northern temperate grassland; **N9** - Puna grassland; **N10** - Paramo grassland; **N11** - Riparian thickets; **N12** - River island scrub; **N13** - Pastures/agricultural lands; **N14** - Second-growth scrub; **A1** - Freshwater marshes; **A2** - Saltwater/brackish marshes; **A3** - Coastal sand beaches/mudflats; **A4** - Coastal rocky beaches; **A5** - Riverine sand beaches; **A6** - Freshwater lakes and ponds; **A7** - Alkaline lakes; **A8** - Rivers; **A9** - Streams; **A10** - Bogs; **A11** - Coastal waters; **A12** - Pelagic waters.
E - Edge (used as a modifer to particular habitats).

Sub - Subregions:
ARC - Arid Caribbean Coast; **AWA** - Altiplano and Western Andes; **BAH** - Bahamas; **BAJ** - Baja California; **CAA** - Caatinga; **CAH** - Central American Highlands; **CER** - Cerrado; **CHA** - Chaco; **CHG** - Chiapas-Guanacaste; **CHL** - Chilean Desert; **CHR** - Chiriquí; **CIS** - Cocos Island; **CMV** - Cauca-Magdalena Valley; **COC** - Cuzco-Cochabamba; **CUB** - Cuba; **DOM** - Dominica; **EAS** - Eastern Slope Andes; **FDN** - Fernando de Noronha; **GAL** - Galápagos; **GCM** - Gulf Coast-Mexico; **GRE** - Grenada; **GUA** - Guadeloupe; **GUI** - Guianan; **HIS** - Hispaniola; **HPC** - Humid Pacific Coast; **ISA** - Isla Providencia and Isla San Andrés; **JAM** - Jamaica; **JFI** - Juan Fernández Islands; **MAN** - Manabí-Tumbes; **MAR** - Marañón Valley; **MID** - Madeira-Tapajós; **MON** - Montserrat; **MRT** - Martinique; **MTC** - Marañón-Cuzco; **NMM** - Northern Mexican Mountains; **NOR** - Northern Coastal Brazil; **PAR** - Pará; **PER** - Peruvian Desert; **PUE** - Puerto Rico; **RDJ** - Rio de Janeiro-Bahia Lowlands; **RMW** - Rio Madeira West; **RNW** - Rio Negro West; **SCA** - Southern Central America; **SCT** - Santa Cruz-Tucumán; **SIN** - Sinaloa-Oaxaca; **SMH** - Southern Mexican Highlands; **SMT** - Santa Marta; **SOC** - Islas Revillagigedo (Socorro Island group); **SON** - Sonoran Desert; **SOU** - Southern Atlantic Coast; **STL** - St. Lucia; **STV** - St. Vincent; **TAC** - Tacarcuna; **VAN** - Venezuelan Andes; **VNZ** - Venezuelan Coastal Mountains; **WES** - Western Andes; **YUC** - Yucatán Peninsula.
o - Endemic to region, but not restricted to a single subregion.

Zoogeographic Regions:
AMN - Northern Amazonia; **AMS** - Southern Amazonia; **ATL** - Atlantic Forest; **BSR** - Baja-Sonora; **CAN** - Central Andes; **CDH** - Chiriquí-Darién Highlands; **CHO** - Chocó Lowlands; **CSA** - Central South America; **EPC** - Equatorial Pacific Coast; **GAN** - Greater Antilles; **GCS** - Gulf-Caribbean Slope; **LAN** - Lesser Antilles; **MAH** - Madrean Highlands; **MPL** - Mexican Plateau; **NAN** - Northern Andes; **NSA** - Northern South America; **PAM** - Pampas; **PAS** - Pacific Arid Slope; **PAT** - Patagonia; **SAN** - Southern Andes; **STP** - Subtropical Pacific; **TEP** - Tepuis.

CP -Conservation Priority:
1 - Urgent; **2** - High; **3** - Medium; **4** - Low.

RP - Research Priority:
1 - High; **2** - Medium; **3** - Low.

	Snst	Strat	Cntab	Rel	Min	Max	Micro	Habitats	Sub	Zoogeographic Regions
Gelochelidon nilotica	H	W	LT	U	L	L		A2, A11		GAN, BSR, PAS, GCS, EPC, ATL?, PAM
Hydroprogne caspia	H	W	LT	F	L	L		A1, A2, A11		BSR, PAS
Sterna anaethetus	H	W	LT	U	L	L		A12		GAN, LAN, PAS, GCS, NSA
Sterna antillarum	M	W	LT	F	L	L		A11, A2		GAN, LAN, BSR, PAS, GCS, NSA
Sterna dougallii	H	W	LT	U	L	L		A11, A12		GAN, LAN, GCS, NSA
Sterna forsteri	H	W	LS	F	L	L		A11, A6?		BSR, GCS
Sterna fuscata	H	W	LT	F	L	L		A12		GAN, LAN, BSR, PAS, GCS, EPC, STP, NSA, ATL
Sterna hirundinacea	H	W	LS	F	L	L		A11		STP, PAT
Sterna hirundo	M	W	LT	C	L	L		A11		GAN, NSA
Sterna lorata	H	W	LT	U	L	L		A11, A2		EPC, STP
Sterna superciliaris	H	W	LT	F	L	800		A8, A6, A1		NSA, AMN, AMS, CSA, ATL, PAM
Sterna trudeaui	M	W	LS	F	L	L		A1, A2, A11		STP, PAM, PAT?
Thalasseus elegans	H	W	LT	C	L	L		A11		BSR, PAS
Thalasseus maximus	H	W	LT	C	L	L		A11		GAN, LAN, BSR, PAS, GCS, NSA, PAM
Thalasseus sandvicensis	H	W	LT	F	L	L		A11		GAN, LAN, GCS, NSA, ATL, PAM
Procelsterna cerulea	H	W	LS	R	L	L		A12		STP
Larosterna inca	H	W	LS	F	L	L		A11	o	STP
Anous minutus	H	W	LT	U	L	L		A12		PAS, NSA, ATL
Anous stolidus	H	W	LT	F	L	L		A12		GAN, LAN, PAS, GCS, CHO, EPC, STP?, NSA, ATL
Gygis alba	H	W	LT	F	L	L		A12		PAS, EPC, ATL
Rhynchopidae										
Rhynchops niger	H	W	LT	F	L	600		A8, A11		BSR, PAS, GCS, EPC, NSA, AMN, AMS, CSA, ATL, PAM
Alcidae										
Brachyramphus craveri	H	W	LS	U	L	L		A12	BAJ	BSR
Brachyramphus hypoleucus	H	W	LS	U	L	L		A12	BAJ	BSR
Ptychoramphus aleuticus	H	W	LS	U	L	L		A11, A12		BSR
COLUMBIFORMES										
Columbidae										
Columba araucana	M	C	US	U	L	1500		F9	o	SAN
Columba caribaea	M	C	US	U	300	1500+		F4, F1	JAM	GAN
Columba cayennensis	M	C	LT	C	L	800		F8, F3, F12, F1E, F15		GCS, CHO, EPC, NSA, AMN, AMS, CSA, ATL, PAM
Columba corensis	M	C	LT	F	L	L		F7, N1	ARC	NSA
Columba fasciata	M	C	UM	F	900	3600		F4, F11, F15		BSR, MAH, CDH, NAN, CAN, TEP
Columba flavirostris	M	C	LT	F	L	1800		F7, F8		PAS, GCS, CDH
Columba goodsoni	H	C	LT	U	L	1000		F1, F4	o	CHO
Columba inornata	M	C	UT?	R	L	2000		F1, F4, F7, F14	o	GAN
Columba leucocephala	M	C	LT	F	L	2000+		F14, F7, F1		GAN, LAN, GCS
Columba livia	L	T/C	LT	C	L	4500		N14, F15, N13		GAN, LAN, BSR, MPL, PAS, MAH, GCS, CDH, CHO, EPC, STP, NAN, CAN, SAN, NSA, AMN, AMS, CSA, ATL, PAM, PAT
Columba maculosa	M	C	LS	C	L	3800		F7, F15, F4E, N6, N1, N3		CAN, SAN, CSA, PAM, PAT
Columba nigrirostris	M	C	LT	F	L	1500		F1, F4		GCS, CHO
Columba oenops	M	C	UT	U	900	2300		F7, F8	MAR	CAN
Columba picazuro	M	C	LT	C	L	1100		F8, N6, N13		CSA, ATL, PAM
Columba plumbea	H	C	LT	F	L	2100		F1, F4		CHO, NAN, CAN, NSA, AMN, AMS, CSA, ATL
Columba speciosa	M	C	LT	F	L	1400		F1, F4, F8		GCS, CHO, NAN, CAN, NSA, AMN, AMS, CSA, ATL
Columba squamosa	M	C	UT	U	L	2500+		F4, F1		GAN, LAN, NSA
Columba subvinacea	H	C	LT	F	L	1800		F1, F2, F4		CDH, CHO, EPC, NAN, NSA, AMN, AMS

CP	RP	Notes
4	3	
4	3	
3	2	
3	2	Declining; monitor breeding populations.
3	2	Declining; survey West Indies breeding populations.
4	3	Local.
4	3	
4	2	Monitor; locally inland in Patagonia, breeds?
4	2	
3	2	Survey.
4	3	
4	2	Monitor.
4	2	Monitor breeding colonies.
4	2	Monitor breeding colonies.
4	2	Monitor breeding colonies.
4	2	Monitor breeding colonies.
4	2	Monitor breeding colonies.
4	2	Monitor breeding colonies.
4	3	
4	3	
4	2	
3	2	Monitor breeding colonies.
3	2	Monitor breeding colonies; may contain two species.
4	2	Local as breeder.
2	1	Monitor.
2	1	To lowlands in winter; monitor; hunting pressure.
4	3	Occasionally to 2,100 m (Colombia).
4	2	Monitor.
4	2	Locally to lowlands; monitor; hunting pressure in many areas.
3	2	Locally to 2,100 m; declining in most of range; monitor.
3	2	Monitor; deforestation.
1	1	Declining in most of range; conservation measures.
3	2	
4	3	
4	3	
4	3	
2	1	Monitor.
4	3	Spreading with deforestation.
4	3	Occasionally to 2,550 m (Bolivia).
4	3	
3	2	Monitor; declining on many islands because of hunting.
4	2	Locally to 3,300 m.

Abbreviations Used

Snst - Sensitivity:
L - Low; **M** - Medium; **H** - High.

Strat - Foraging Strata:
T - Terrestrial; **U** - Understory; **M** - Midstory; **C** - Canopy; **A** - Aerial; **W** - Water.

Cntab - Center of Abundance:
LT - Lower tropical; **LS** - Lower subtropical; **HT** - Hill tropical; **UT** - Upper tropical; **US** - Upper subtropical; **MM** - Middle montane; **UM** - Upper montane.

Rel - Relative Abundance:
R - Rare; **U** - Uncommon; **F** - Fairly common; **C** - Common; **P** - Patchily distributed.

Min - Minimum Elevation:
L - Lowlands; **?** - Uncertain value; numeric values in meters.

Max - Maximum Elevation:
L - Lowlands; **?** - Uncertain value; **+** - species occurs at least to given elevation but likely occurs higher; numeric values in meters.

Micro - Microhabitats:
A - Army ants; **B** - Bamboo; **T** - Treefalls; **G** - Ground bromeliads; **C** - Rocky outcrops and caves; **S** - Streamside; **V** - Vine tangles; **B/V** -Bamboo/vine tangles.

Habitats:
F1 - Tropical lowland evergreen forest; **F2** - Flooded tropical evergreen forest; **F3** - River-edge forest; **F4** - Montane evergreen forest; **F5** - Elfin forest; **F6** - *Polylepis* woodland; **F7** - Tropical deciduous forest; **F8** - Gallery forest; **F9** - Southern temperate forest; **F10** - Pine forest; **F11** - Pine-oak forest; **F12** - White sand forest; **F13** - Palm forest; **F14** - Mangrove forest; **F15** - Secondary forest; **N1** - Arid lowland scrub; **N2** - Arid montane scrub; **N3** - Semihumid/humid montane scrub; **N4** - Cerrado; **N5** - Campo grasslands; **N6** - Low, seasonally wet grassland; **N7** - Southern temperate grassland; **N8** - Northern temperate grassland; **N9** - Puna grassland; **N10** - Paramo grassland; **N11** - Riparian thickets; **N12** - River island scrub; **N13** - Pastures/agricultural lands; **N14** - Second-growth scrub; **A1** - Freshwater marshes; **A2** - Saltwater/brackish marshes; **A3** - Coastal sand beaches/mudflats; **A4** - Coastal rocky beaches; **A5** - Riverine sand beaches; **A6** - Freshwater lakes and ponds; **A7** - Alkaline lakes; **A8** - Rivers; **A9** - Streams; **A10** - Bogs; **A11** - Coastal waters; **A12** - Pelagic waters.
E - Edge (used as a modifer to particular habitats).

Sub - Subregions:
ARC - Arid Caribbean Coast; **AWA** - Altiplano and Western Andes; **BAH** - Bahamas; **BAJ** - Baja California; **CAA** - Caatinga; **CAH** - Central American Highlands; **CER** - Cerrado; **CHA** - Chaco; **CHG** - Chiapas-Guanacaste; **CHL** - Chilean Desert; **CHR** - Chiriquí; **CIS** - Cocos Island; **CMV** - Cauca-Magdalena Valley; **COC** - Cuzco-Cochabamba; **CUB** - Cuba; **DOM** - Dominica; **EAS** - Eastern Slope Andes; **FDN** - Fernando de Noronha; **GAL** - Galápagos; **GCM** - Gulf Coast-Mexico; **GRE** - Grenada; **GUA** - Guadeloupe; **GUI** - Guianan; **HIS** - Hispaniola; **HPC** - Humid Pacific Coast; **ISA** - Isla Providencia and Isla San Andrés; **JAM** - Jamaica; **JFI** - Juan Fernández Islands; **MAN** - Manabí-Tumbes; **MAR** - Marañón Valley; **MID** - Madeira-Tapajós; **MON** - Montserrat; **MRT** - Martinique; **MTC** - Marañón-Cuzco; **NMM** - Northern Mexican Mountains; **NOR** - Northern Coastal Brazil; **PAR** - Pará; **PER** - Peruvian Desert; **PUE** - Puerto Rico; **RDJ** - Rio de Janeiro-Bahia Lowlands; **RMW** - Rio Madeira West; **RNW** - Rio Negro West; **SCA** - Southern Central America; **SCT** - Santa Cruz-Tucumán; **SIN** - Sinaloa-Oaxaca; **SMH** - Southern Mexican Highlands; **SMT** - Santa Marta; **SOC** - Islas Revillagigedo (Socorro Island group); **SON** - Sonoran Desert; **SOU** - Southern Atlantic Coast; **STL** - St. Lucia; **STV** - St. Vincent; **TAC** - Tacarcuna; **VAN** - Venezuelan Andes; **VNZ** - Venezuelan Coastal Mountains; **WES** - Western Andes; **YUC** - Yucatán Peninsula.
o - Endemic to region, but not restricted to a single subregion.

Zoogeographic Regions:
AMN - Northern Amazonia; **AMS** - Southern Amazonia; **ATL** - Atlantic Forest; **BSR** - Baja-Sonora; **CAN** - Central Andes; **CDH** - Chiriquí-Darién Highlands; **CHO** - Chocó Lowlands; **CSA** - Central South America; **EPC** - Equatorial Pacific Coast; **GAN** - Greater Antilles; **GCS** - Gulf-Caribbean Slope; **LAN** - Lesser Antilles; **MAH** - Madrean Highlands; **MPL** - Mexican Plateau; **NAN** - Northern Andes; **NSA** - Northern South America; **PAM** - Pampas; **PAS** - Pacific Arid Slope; **PAT** - Patagonia; **SAN** - Southern Andes; **STP** - Subtropical Pacific; **TEP** - Tepuis.

CP -Conservation Priority:
1 - Urgent; **2** - High; **3** - Medium; **4** - Low.

RP - Research Priority:
1 - High; **2** - Medium; **3** - Low.

	Snst	Strat	Cntab	Rel	Min	Max	Micro	Habitats	Sub	Zoogeographic Regions
Streptopelia decaocto	L	T/C	LS	C	L	L		N14, F15		GAN
Zenaida asiatica	L	T/M	LT	C	L	2500		F7, F8, N11, N14, N1		GAN, BSR, MPL, PAS, MAH, GCS, EPC, STP
Zenaida auriculata	L	T/M	LT	C	L	3400		N14, N1, N2		LAN, STP, NAN, CAN, SAN, NSA, AMN, AMS, CSA, ATL, PAM, PAT
Zenaida aurita	L	T	LT	F	L	600+		F7, N1, N14		GAN, LAN, GCS
Zenaida galapagoensis	L	T	LT	F	L	L		F7, N1	GAL	EPC
Zenaida graysoni	H	T	LT	R	L	L		N1	SOC	PAS
Zenaida macroura	L	T/M	LS	C	L	3200		N13, N14, F15, F7, N1, N2		GAN, BSR, MPL, PAS, MAH, GCS, CDH
Columbina cruziana	L	T	LT	C	L	2500		N14, N1, N11, N2		EPC, STP, CAN
Columbina cyanopis	H	T?	HT	R	L	800		N5?	CER	CSA
Columbina minuta	L	T	LT	F/P	L	1400		N1, N6, N2, N14, N5		PAS, GCS, STP, NSA, AMN, AMS, CSA
Columbina passerina	L	T	LT	C	L	2300		N1, N2, N14, N13		GAN, LAN, BSR, MPL, PAS, MAH, GCS, NAN, NSA, AMN, AMS, CSA
Columbina picui	L	T	LS	C	L	1250		N14, N11, N1, N2		STP, CAN, CSA, PAM, PAT
Columbina talpacoti										
buckleyi	M	T	LT	F	L	900		F7, N1	MAN	EPC
talpacoti	L	T	LT	C	L	1200		N14, N11, N1, N13		PAS, GCS, CAN, NSA, AMN, AMS, CSA, ATL, PAM
Claravis godefrida	H	T/M	UT	R/P	L	1400+	B	F4, F1	SOU	ATL
Claravis mondetoura	M	T/M	MM	U/P	900	3000	B	F4		MAH, CDH, NAN, CAN
Claravis pretiosa	L	T/M	LT	F	L	1200		F1E, F15, F3, F8		PAS, GCS, CHO, EPC, NSA, AMN, AMS, CSA, ATL
Metriopelia aymara	M	T	UM	F	2800	4700		N9, N2		CAN, SAN
Metriopelia ceciliae	L	T	MM	C	2000	4000		N2	AWA	CAN
Metriopelia melanoptera	M	T	UM	F	2000	4400		N2, F6		NAN, CAN, SAN
Metriopelia morenoi	M	T	MM?	R?	1800	3200+		N2		CAN, SAN
Scardafella inca	L	T	LS	C	L	2400		N14, N11, N1, N2		BSR, MPL, PAS, MAH, GCS
Scardafella squammata	L	T	LT	C	L	1200		N14, N11, N1, N6		NSA, AMN, AMS, CSA, ATL
Uropelia campestris	M	T	LT	U/P	L	1100		N6, N5		AMN, AMS, CSA
Leptotila cassini	M	T	LT	F	L	1400		F1E, F15		GCS, CHO, NSA
Leptotila conoveri	M	T	MM	?	1600	2300		F4E?, F15?	EAS	NAN
Leptotila jamaicensis	M	T	LT	F	L	L?		F7, F1E, F15		GAN, GCS
Leptotila megalura	M	T	MM	U	900	2800		F4	SCT	CAN
Leptotila ochraceiventris	M	T	HT	U	700	1800		F7, F1	MAN	EPC
Leptotila pallida	M	T	HT	C	L	800		F1E, F15	o	CHO
Leptotila rufaxilla										
plumbeiceps	M	T	LT	F	L	1000		F1E, F15		PAS, GCS
rufaxilla	M	T	LT	C	L	1900		F3, F8, F15, F1E		NSA, AMN, AMS, CSA, ATL
wellsi	M	T	LT	R	L	L?		F7	GRE	LAN
Leptotila verreauxi	L	T/U	UT	C	L	2800		F7, F8, F15, F3, F1E		PAS, MAH, GCS, CDH, EPC, NAN, CAN, NSA, AMN, AMS, CSA, ATL, PAM
Geotrygon albifacies	H	T	MM	U	1200	2700		F4	o	MAH
Geotrygon caniceps	M	T	UT?	U	L	1800+		F1, F4	o	GAN
Geotrygon chiriquensis	M	T	MM	U	600	3100		F4	CHR	CDH
Geotrygon chrysia	M	T	LT	F	L	500+		F7	o	GAN
Geotrygon costaricensis	H	T	MM	F	1000	3000		F4	CHR	CDH
Geotrygon frenata	H	T	MM	U	900	3000		F4		NAN, CAN
Geotrygon goldmani	H	T	UT	U	750	1600		F4	TAC	CDH
Geotrygon lawrencii	H	T	HT	U/P	400	1400		F4, F1		MAH, CDH
Geotrygon linearis	H	T	UT	F	L	2500		F4, F1		NAN, NSA
Geotrygon montana	M	T	LT	F	L	1400		F1, F4, F7		GAN, LAN, PAS, MAH, GCS, CDH, CHO, NAN, CAN, NSA, TEP, AMN, AMS, CSA, ATL
Geotrygon mystacea	M	T	LT	U	L	700+		F7, F1		GAN, LAN
Geotrygon saphirina	H	T	HT	U/P	600	1100		F1, F4		CHO, NAN, CAN, AMN, AMS

CP	RP	Notes
4	3	Introduced in Bahamas and spreading.
4	3	Monitor hunting; probably contains two species.
4	3	Locally to 4,000 m+.
4	3	
4	3	
1	1	Extinct in wild.
4	3	
4	3	
2	1	Poorly known; habitat destruction.
4	3	Occasionally to 2,100 m (Peru).
4	3	Locally to 2,900 m (Ecuador).
4	3	Locally to 2,700 m (Bolivia).
4	3	
4	3	Occasionally to 2,600 m.
1	1	Declining; deforestation; movements tied to bamboo seeding; survey.
3	2	Movements poorly known.
4	3	Occasionally to 1,800 m (Colombia).
4	2	Seasonal movements poorly known.
4	3	Locally to 600 m.
4	3	Locally to 1,000 m.
4	3	
4	3	
4	3	
3	2	Poorly known; habitat destruction.
4	3	
2	1	Status uncertain; deforestation.
4	3	
4	2	Poorly known.
2	1	Formerly to sea level; status uncertain; deforestation.
4	2	
4	3	
4	3	Locally to 2,200 m+ (southeastern Brazil).
2	1	Habitat destruction,introduced predators.
4	3	Occasionally to 3,200 m.
3	2	Occasionally to 300 m; probably declining with deforestation.
3	2	Probably declining.
4	3	
4	3	
3	3	Probably declining with deforestation.
4	3	Occasionally to 700 m.
3	3	
3	2	Deforestation.
4	2	Deforestation.
4	3	Occasionally to 2,600 m (Colombia).
3	2	
3	2	Distribution poorly known; local in lowlands.

Abbreviations Used

Snst - Sensitivity:
L - Low; **M** - Medium; **H** - High.

Strat - Foraging Strata:
T - Terrestrial; **U** - Understory; **M** - Midstory; **C** - Canopy; **A** - Aerial; **W** - Water.

Cntab - Center of Abundance:
LT - Lower tropical; **LS** - Lower subtropical; **HT** - Hill tropical; **UT** - Upper tropical; **US** - Upper subtropical; **MM** - Middle montane; **UM** - Upper montane.

Rel - Relative Abundance:
R - Rare; **U** - Uncommon; **F** - Fairly common; **C** - Common; **P** - Patchily distributed.

Min - Minimum Elevation:
L - Lowlands; **?** - Uncertain value; numeric values in meters.

Max - Maximum Elevation:
L - Lowlands; **?** - Uncertain value; **+** - species occurs at least to given elevation but likely occurs higher; numeric values in meters.

Micro - Microhabitats:
A - Army ants; **B** - Bamboo; **T** - Treefalls; **G** - Ground bromeliads; **C** - Rocky outcrops and caves; **S** - Streamside; **V** - Vine tangles; **B/V** -Bamboo/vine tangles.

Habitats:
F1 - Tropical lowland evergreen forest; **F2** - Flooded tropical evergreen forest; **F3** - River-edge forest; **F4** - Montane evergreen forest; **F5** - Elfin forest; **F6** - *Polylepis* woodland; **F7** - Tropical deciduous forest; **F8** - Gallery forest; **F9** - Southern temperate forest; **F10** - Pine forest; **F11** - Pine-oak forest; **F12** - White sand forest; **F13** - Palm forest; **F14** - Mangrove forest; **F15** - Secondary forest; **N1** - Arid lowland scrub; **N2** - Arid montane scrub; **N3** - Semihumid/humid montane scrub; **N4** - Cerrado; **N5** - Campo grasslands; **N6** - Low, seasonally wet grassland; **N7** - Southern temperate grassland; **N8** - Northern temperate grassland; **N9** - Puna grassland; **N10** - Paramo grassland; **N11** - Riparian thickets; **N12** - River island scrub; **N13** - Pastures/agricultural lands; **N14** - Second-growth scrub; **A1** - Freshwater marshes; **A2** - Saltwater/brackish marshes; **A3** - Coastal sand beaches/mudflats; **A4** - Coastal rocky beaches; **A5** - Riverine sand beaches; **A6** - Freshwater lakes and ponds; **A7** - Alkaline lakes; **A8** - Rivers; **A9** - Streams; **A10** - Bogs; **A11** - Coastal waters; **A12** - Pelagic waters.
E - Edge (used as a modifer to particular habitats).

Sub - Subregions:
ARC - Arid Caribbean Coast; **AWA** - Altiplano and Western Andes; **BAH** - Bahamas; **BAJ** - Baja California; **CAA** - Caatinga; **CAH** - Central American Highlands; **CER** - Cerrado; **CHA** - Chaco; **CHG** - Chiapas-Guanacaste; **CHL** - Chilean Desert; **CHR** - Chiriquí; **CIS** - Cocos Island; **CMV** - Cauca-Magdalena Valley; **COC** - Cuzco-Cochabamba; **CUB** - Cuba; **DOM** - Dominica; **EAS** - Eastern Slope Andes; **FDN** - Fernando de Noronha; **GAL** - Galápagos; **GCM** - Gulf Coast-Mexico; **GRE** - Grenada; **GUA** - Guadeloupe; **GUI** - Guianan; **HIS** - Hispaniola; **HPC** - Humid Pacific Coast; **ISA** - Isla Providencia and Isla San Andrés; **JAM** - Jamaica; **JFI** - Juan Fernández Islands; **MAN** - Manabí-Tumbes; **MAR** - Marañón Valley; **MID** - Madeira-Tapajós; **MON** - Montserrat; **MRT** - Martinique; **MTC** - Marañón-Cuzco; **NMM** - Northern Mexican Mountains; **NOR** - Northern Coastal Brazil; **PAR** - Pará; **PER** - Peruvian Desert; **PUE** - Puerto Rico; **RDJ** - Rio de Janeiro-Bahia Lowlands; **RMW** - Rio Madeira West; **RNW** - Rio Negro West; **SCA** - Southern Central America; **SCT** - Santa Cruz-Tucumán; **SIN** - Sinaloa-Oaxaca; **SMH** - Southern Mexican Highlands; **SMT** - Santa Marta; **SOC** - Islas Revillagigedo (Socorro Island group); **SON** - Sonoran Desert; **SOU** - Southern Atlantic Coast; **STL** - St. Lucia; **STV** - St. Vincent; **TAC** - Tacarcuna; **VAN** - Venezuelan Andes; **VNZ** - Venezuelan Coastal Mountains; **WES** - Western Andes; **YUC** - Yucatán Peninsula.
o - Endemic to region, but not restricted to a single subregion.

Zoogeographic Regions:
AMN - Northern Amazonia; **AMS** - Southern Amazonia; **ATL** - Atlantic Forest; **BSR** - Baja-Sonora; **CAN** - Central Andes; **CDH** - Chiriquí-Darién Highlands; **CHO** - Chocó Lowlands; **CSA** - Central South America; **EPC** - Equatorial Pacific Coast; **GAN** - Greater Antilles; **GCS** - Gulf-Caribbean Slope; **LAN** - Lesser Antilles; **MAH** - Madrean Highlands; **MPL** - Mexican Plateau; **NAN** - Northern Andes; **NSA** - Northern South America; **PAM** - Pampas; **PAS** - Pacific Arid Slope; **PAT** - Patagonia; **SAN** - Southern Andes; **STP** - Subtropical Pacific; **TEP** - Tepuis.

CP -Conservation Priority:
1 - Urgent; **2** - High; **3** - Medium; **4** - Low.

RP - Research Priority:
1 - High; **2** - Medium; **3** - Low.

	Snst	Strat	Cntab	Rel	Min	Max	Micro	Habitats	Sub	Zoogeographic Regions
Geotrygon veraguensis	M	T	LT	U	L	900		F1		GCS, CHO
Geotrygon versicolor	H	T	UT	U	100	1800		F4	JAM	GAN
Geotrygon violacea	H	T	HT	U/P	L	1600		F1, F15		PAS, GCS, NAN, NSA, AMS, CSA, ATL
Starnoenas cyanocephala	M	T	LT	U	L	L?		F1, F7?	CUB	GAN
PSITTACIFORMES										
Psittacidae										
Anodorhynchus glaucus	H	C	LT	R	L	L		F8, F1	CHA	CSA
Anodorhynchus hyacinthinus	H	C	LT	R	L	800		F8, F7, F1, F2, F13		AMS, CSA
Anodorhynchus leari	H	C	LT	R	400	800	R	F7, F13	CAA	CSA
Cyanopsitta spixii	H	C	LT	R	L	L		F8, F13	CAA	CSA
Ara ambigua	M	C	LT	R/U	L	700		F1		GCS, CHO
Ara ararauna	M	C	LT	U	L	700		F8, F13, F2, F1		GCS, CHO, NSA, AMN, AMS, CSA
Ara auricollis	M	C	LT	F	L	600		F7, F8	o	CSA
Ara chloroptera	H	C	LT	F	L	1400		F1, F4		GCS, CHO, NSA, TEP, AMN, AMS, CSA, ATL
Ara couloni	M	C	HT	U/P	L	800		F1E	RMW	AMS
Ara glaucogularis	H	C	LT	R	L	L		F8, F13	CHA	CSA
Ara macao	M	C	LT	F	L	900		F1, F7, F8		PAS, GCS, NSA, AMN, AMS
Ara manilata	M	C	LT	F	L	1200		F13, F8		NSA, TEP, AMN, AMS, CSA
Ara maracana	M	C	LT	R	L	1000		F1, F8		CSA, ATL
Ara militaris	M	C	UT	U/P	600	2600+	R	F4, F7, F11, F1		PAS, MAH, GCS, NAN, CAN, NSA
Ara nobilis	M	T/C	LT	F	L	1400		F8, F13		NSA, AMN, AMS, CSA, ATL
Ara rubrogenys	M	C	MM	R	1300	2200		F7	COC	CAN
Ara severa	M	C	LT	F	L	800		F3, F8, F1E, F2		GCS, CHO, NSA, AMN, AMS, ATL
Aratinga acuticaudata	M	C	LT	C	L	1800		F7, F8, F4E		CAN, NSA, CSA, PAM
Aratinga aurea	M	U/C	LT	C	L	1100		N6, N4, F8, F15		AMN, AMS, CSA, ATL
Aratinga auricapilla	M	C	LT	R	L	1400		F1, F7		CSA, ATL
Aratinga cactorum	M	C	LT	F	L	800+		F7		AMS, CSA
Aratinga canicularis	L	C	LT	F	L	1500		F7, F8, F15		PAS, GCS
Aratinga chloroptera	M	C	UT?	U	L	2000+		F4, F1	HIS	GAN
Aratinga erythrogenys	M	C	LT	C	L	800		F7, F8	MAN	EPC
Aratinga euops	M	C	HT	R/U	L	800+		F1, F7	CUB	GAN
Aratinga finschi	M	C	LT	F	L	1600		F1E, F15		GCS, CDH
Aratinga guarouba	H	C	LT	R	L	L		F1	PAR	AMS
Aratinga holochlora										
brevipes	M	C	HT	F	450	1000		F7	SOC	PAS
holochlora	M	C	UT	F	L	2200		F1, F7, F15, F11		MAH, GCS
rubritorquis	M	C	MM	F	800?	2600		F11, F10, F7	CAH	MAH
strenua	M	C	LT	F?	L	1300?		F7, F8, F11, F15	CHG	PAS
Aratinga jandaya	M	C	LT	R	L	1200?		F1, F8, F15?		AMS, CSA, ATL
Aratinga leucophthalmus	L	C	LT	C	L	1000		F3, F8, F1E, F15		NSA, AMN, AMS, CSA, ATL, PAM
Aratinga mitrata	M	C	MM	C/P	1000	3400		F4E, F15, N3		CAN, SAN
Aratinga nana	L	C	LT	F	L	800		F1E, F8, F15		GAN, GCS
Aratinga pertinax	M	C	LT	C	L	1200		F7, F8, F12, F1E		GCS, NSA, AMN, AMS
Aratinga solstitialis	M	C	LT	R	L	1400		F8, F1E		TEP, AMN
Aratinga wagleri	M	C	MM	C	900	2800		F4E, F15, F7, F8, N3		NAN, CAN
Aratinga weddellii	L	C	LT	C	L	750		F3, F1E, F15		AMN, AMS
Nandayus nenday	M	C	LT	F	L	800+		F8, F7	o	CSA
Leptosittaca branickii	H	C	UM	R/P	2500	3350		F4, F5		NAN, CAN
Ognorhynchus icterotis	H	C	UM	R	2000	3400		F4	o	NAN
Rhynchopsitta pachyrhyncha	H	C	UM	R	1500	3400		F10, F11	NMM	MAH
Rhynchopsitta terrisi	H	C	MM	R	2000	3300	R	F10, F11	NMM	MAH
Cyanoliseus patagonus	M	T/C	LS	U/P	L	1800+	R	N1, N2, N13		STP, CSA, PAT

CP	RP	Notes
3	2	Deforestation.
3	2	Survey.
4	2	Distribution and seasonal movements poorly known.
3	2	Deforestation; survey.
1	1	Probably extinct.
1	1	Often associated with palms; declining; survey.
1	1	Survey.
1	1	Nearly extinct; captive breeding needed.
2	1	Occasionally to 1,500 m; declining; survey.
3	2	Declining in many areas; monitor populations.
3	2	Monitor; capture for bird trade.
3	3	Declining outside Amazonia; extinct in eastern Brazil?
4	2	Occasionally to 1,550 m; monitor; may increase with deforestation.
2	1	Poorly known; associated with palms (*Attalea* sp.)? capture for bird trade; survey.
3	2	Declining outside Amazonia; endangered in Middle America.
4	3	Closely associated with *Mauritia* palm swamp.
2	1	Declining; survey.
3	2	Occasionally to lowlands; declining; survey.
4	3	Frequently associated with *Mauritia* palms.
2	1	Survey.
4	3	Occasionally to 1,500 m.
4	3	Regularly to 2,600 m (Bolivia).
4	3	
2	1	Locally 2,200 m; survey; capture for bird trade.
3	2	Monitor.
4	2	
2	1	Survey.
3	2	Monitor; capture for bird trade.
2	1	Probably declining; monitor.
4	2	Apparently increasing; monitor.
2	1	Survey; deforestation and bird trade.
2	2	Formerly to lowlands; habitat destruction.
3	2	Locally to Pacific lowlands in winter; probably declining.
3	2	
4	2	Locally to 2,500 m; monitor.
2	1	Declining; survey.
4	3	Occasionally to 2,500 m.
4	2	May contain two species.
4	2	Taxonomy and status of nominate *nana* (Jamaica) uncertain.
4	3	Locally to 1,600 m (Venezuela).
3	1	Survey.
4	2	Occasionally to lowlands; may contain two species.
4	3	
3	2	Monitor; capture for bird trade.
2	1	Nomadic? study and monitor; associated with *Podocarpus*.
1	1	Occasionally to 1,200 m; associated with *Ceroxylon* palms; survey.
2	1	Nomadic; survey.
2	1	Occasionally to 1,300 and 3,700 m; nomadic; survey.
3	2	Nomadic?; survey.

Abbreviations Used

Snst - Sensitivity:
L - Low; **M** - Medium; **H** - High.

Strat - Foraging Strata:
T - Terrestrial; **U** - Understory; **M** - Midstory; **C** - Canopy; **A** - Aerial; **W** - Water.

Cntab - Center of Abundance:
LT - Lower tropical; **LS** - Lower subtropical; **HT** - Hill tropical; **UT** - Upper tropical; **US** - Upper subtropical; **MM** - Middle montane; **UM** - Upper montane.

Rel - Relative Abundance:
R - Rare; **U** - Uncommon; **F** - Fairly common; **C** - Common; **P** - Patchily distributed.

Min - Minimum Elevation:
L - Lowlands; **?** - Uncertain value; numeric values in meters.

Max - Maximum Elevation:
L - Lowlands; **?** - Uncertain value; **+** - species occurs at least to given elevation but likely occurs higher; numeric values in meters.

Micro - Microhabitats:
A - Army ants; **B** - Bamboo; **T** - Treefalls; **G** - Ground bromeliads; **C** - Rocky outcrops and caves; **S** - Streamside; **V** - Vine tangles; **B/V** -Bamboo/vine tangles.

Habitats:
F1 - Tropical lowland evergreen forest; **F2** - Flooded tropical evergreen forest; **F3** - River-edge forest; **F4** - Montane evergreen forest; **F5** - Elfin forest; **F6** - *Polylepis* woodland; **F7** - Tropical deciduous forest; **F8** - Gallery forest; **F9** - Southern temperate forest; **F10** - Pine forest; **F11** - Pine-oak forest; **F12** - White sand forest; **F13** - Palm forest; **F14** - Mangrove forest; **F15** - Secondary forest; **N1** - Arid lowland scrub; **N2** - Arid montane scrub; **N3** - Semihumid/humid montane scrub; **N4** - Cerrado; **N5** - Campo grasslands; **N6** - Low, seasonally wet grassland; **N7** - Southern temperate grassland; **N8** - Northern temperate grassland; **N9** - Puna grassland; **N10** - Paramo grassland; **N11** - Riparian thickets; **N12** - River island scrub; **N13** - Pastures/agricultural lands; **N14** - Second-growth scrub; **A1** - Freshwater marshes; **A2** - Saltwater/brackish marshes; **A3** - Coastal sand beaches/mudflats; **A4** - Coastal rocky beaches; **A5** - Riverine sand beaches; **A6** - Freshwater lakes and ponds; **A7** - Alkaline lakes; **A8** - Rivers; **A9** - Streams; **A10** - Bogs; **A11** - Coastal waters; **A12** - Pelagic waters.
E - Edge (used as a modifer to particular habitats).

Sub - Subregions:
ARC - Arid Caribbean Coast; **AWA** - Altiplano and Western Andes; **BAH** - Bahamas; **BAJ** - Baja California; **CAA** - Caatinga; **CAH** - Central American Highlands; **CER** - Cerrado; **CHA** - Chaco; **CHG** - Chiapas-Guanacaste; **CHL** - Chilean Desert; **CHR** - Chiriquí; **CIS** - Cocos Island; **CMV** - Cauca-Magdalena Valley; **COC** - Cuzco-Cochabamba; **CUB** - Cuba; **DOM** - Dominica; **EAS** - Eastern Slope Andes; **FDN** - Fernando de Noronha; **GAL** - Galápagos; **GCM** - Gulf Coast-Mexico; **GRE** - Grenada; **GUA** - Guadeloupe; **GUI** - Guianan; **HIS** - Hispaniola; **HPC** - Humid Pacific Coast; **ISA** - Isla Providencia and Isla San Andrés; **JAM** - Jamaica; **JFI** - Juan Fernández Islands; **MAN** - Manabí-Tumbes; **MAR** - Marañón Valley; **MID** - Madeira-Tapajós; **MON** - Montserrat; **MRT** - Martinique; **MTC** - Marañón-Cuzco; **NMM** - Northern Mexican Mountains; **NOR** - Northern Coastal Brazil; **PAR** - Pará; **PER** - Peruvian Desert; **PUE** - Puerto Rico; **RDJ** - Rio de Janeiro-Bahia Lowlands; **RMW** - Rio Madeira West; **RNW** - Rio Negro West; **SCA** - Southern Central America; **SCT** - Santa Cruz-Tucumán; **SIN** - Sinaloa-Oaxaca; **SMH** - Southern Mexican Highlands; **SMT** - Santa Marta; **SOC** - Islas Revillagigedo (Socorro Island group); **SON** - Sonoran Desert; **SOU** - Southern Atlantic Coast; **STL** - St. Lucia; **STV** - St. Vincent; **TAC** - Tacarcuna; **VAN** - Venezuelan Andes; **VNZ** - Venezuelan Coastal Mountains; **WES** - Western Andes; **YUC** - Yucatán Peninsula.
o - Endemic to region, but not restricted to a single subregion.

Zoogeographic Regions:
AMN - Northern Amazonia; **AMS** - Southern Amazonia; **ATL** - Atlantic Forest; **BSR** - Baja-Sonora; **CAN** - Central Andes; **CDH** - Chiriquí-Darién Highlands; **CHO** - Chocó Lowlands; **CSA** - Central South America; **EPC** - Equatorial Pacific Coast; **GAN** - Greater Antilles; **GCS** - Gulf-Caribbean Slope; **LAN** - Lesser Antilles; **MAH** - Madrean Highlands; **MPL** - Mexican Plateau; **NAN** - Northern Andes; **NSA** - Northern South America; **PAM** - Pampas; **PAS** - Pacific Arid Slope; **PAT** - Patagonia; **SAN** - Southern Andes; **STP** - Subtropical Pacific; **TEP** - Tepuis.

CP -Conservation Priority:
1 - Urgent; **2** - High; **3** - Medium; **4** - Low.

RP - Research Priority:
1 - High; **2** - Medium; **3** - Low.

	Snst	Strat	Cntab	Rel	Min	Max	Micro	Habitats	Sub	Zoogeographic Regions
Pyrrhura albipectus	H	C	UT	?	1200	2000		F4	EAS	NAN
Pyrrhura calliptera	M	C	UM	U?	1700	3400		F4, F5	EAS	NAN
Pyrrhura cruentata	M	C	LT	U	L	400		F1, F15?	RDJ	ATL
Pyrrhura devillei	M	C	LT	U	L	L?		F8, F7?	CHA	CSA
Pyrrhura egregia	H	C	UT	F	700	1800		F4	o	TEP
Pyrrhura frontalis	M	C	HT	C	L	1850		F4, F9, F1	o	ATL
Pyrrhura hoematotis	M	C	UT	F	1000	2000+		F4, F15	VNZ	NAN
Pyrrhura hoffmanni	M	C	UT/MM	F	1200	3000		F4, F15	CHR	CDH
Pyrrhura lepida	H	C	LT	F	L	L		F1	PAR	AMS
Pyrrhura leucotis										
emma	H	C	HT?	F	L	1700		F4, F1		NAN, NSA
griseipectus	H	C	HT	F	500	800		F1	NOR	ATL
leucotis	M	C	LT	F	L	L		F1, F15	RDJ	ATL
pfrimeri	H	C	LT	F	L	700		F7	CER	CSA
Pyrrhura melanura										
chapmani	H	C	MM	F?	1600	2800		F4	EAS	NAN
melanura	H	C	LT	F	L	1500		F1, F4		NAN, CAN, AMN, AMS
pacifica	H	C	LT	F	L	300		F1	o	CHO
Pyrrhura molinae	M	C	LT	C	L	2600+		F7, F4, F15?		CAN, CSA
Pyrrhura orcesi	H	C	HT	U	600	1300		F4	WES	NAN
Pyrrhura perlata	H	C	LT	F	L	L		F1	MID	AMS
Pyrrhura picta										
caeruleiceps	H	C	LT	U	L	2000		F1, F4		GCS, NAN, NSA
picta	H	C	LT	F	L	1200		F1, F4		AMN, AMS
Pyrrhura rhodocephala	M	C	UT/MM	?	800	3100		F4, F5, F15	VAN	NAN
Pyrrhura rupicola	H	C	LT	F	L	1100		F1	RMW	AMS
Pyrrhura viridicata	M	C	MM	F	2000	2500		F4	SMT	NAN
Enicognathus ferrugineus	M	C	US?	F	L	2000		F9	o	SAN
Enicognathus leptorhynchus	M	C	LS	?	L	1000		F9		STP, SAN
Myiopsitta monachus	L	C	LS	C	L	1800		F15, F8		CAN, CSA, PAM
Bolborhynchus aurifrons	L	T/C	UM	F	2500	4500		N2, N3		CAN, SAN
Bolborhynchus aymara	L	T/C	UM	F	1800	3400		N2, N3		CAN, SAN
Bolborhynchus ferrugineifrons	M	C	UM	U	3200	4000		N3, F5	EAS	NAN
Bolborhynchus lineola	H	T/C	UM	F/P	800	3300	B	F4		MAH, CDH, NAN, CAN
Bolborhynchus orbygnesius	M	C	UM	F/P	2200	3800		N3, F5, F6	o	CAN
Forpus coelestis	M	C	LT	C	L	1500		F7, F8, F15, N1	MAN	EPC
Forpus conspicillatus	L	C	LT	C	L	1800		F7, F15, F1E		GCS, CHO, NSA
Forpus crassirostris	L	C	LT	C	L	1200		F3, F8, F1E, F15		NSA, AMN, AMS, CSA, ATL
Forpus cyanopygius	L	C	LT	C	L	1300		F7, F15	SIN	PAS
Forpus passerinus	L	C	LT	C	L	900		F7, F8, F1E, F15		GAN, NSA, AMN, AMS
Forpus sclateri	H	C	LT	F	L	800		F2, F1		AMN, AMS
Forpus xanthops	M	C	UT	F	600	1800		F7, F8, N2	MAR	CAN
Brotogeris chrysopterus	M	C	LT	C	L	1200		F1, F15		NSA, AMN, AMS
Brotogeris cyanoptera	M	C	LT	C	L	900		F3, F1, F15		AMN, AMS
Brotogeris jugularis	L?	C	LT	C	L	1200		F7, F1E, F8, F15		PAS, GCS, CHO, NSA
Brotogeris pyrrhopterus	M	C	LT	U?	L	800+		F7, F8, F15?	MAN	EPC
Brotogeris sanctithomae	M	C	LT	C	L	L		F3, F2, F15		AMN, AMS
Brotogeris tirica	L	C	LT	C	L	1300		F1, F4, F15	o	ATL
Brotogeris versicolurus										
chiriri	M	C	HT	F	L	1200		F8, F15	o	CSA
versicolurus	M	C	LT	C	L	1000		F3, F8, F15		AMN, AMS
Nannopsittaca dachilleae	H	C	LT	F	L	L?		F3	RMW	AMS
Nannopsittaca panychlora	H	C	UT	F/P	750	1850		F4, F1		NSA, TEP

CP	RP	Notes
2	1	Deforestation; survey; relationship to *P. melanurus* uncertain.
2	1	Deforestation; survey.
2	1	Locally to 950 m; probably declining; survey.
3	2	Poorly known; survey.
4	3	Range largely inaccessible.
4	3	
3	2	Survey.
4	3	Occasionally to lowlands.
2	1	Declining; deforestation; survey; formerly *P. perlata*(Arndt 1983).
3	2	
2	1	Poorly known; deforestation.
3	2	Deforestation; survey.
3	2	
3	2	Restricted to upper Magdalena valley; deforestation.
3	1	
3	2	Occasionally to 1,400 m.
4	3	
2	1	Deforestation; survey.
3	2	Formerly *P. rhodogaster* (Arndt 1983); deforestation; monitor.
3	2	Poorly known.
4	2	To 2,000 m; possibly contains multiple species.
3	2	Survey.
4	3	Very locally to 2,100 m+.
3	2	Monitor.
4	3	
3	2	Survey.
4	2	Bolivian race *luchsi* poorly known and possibly rare.
4	3	Wanders to coast of Peru.
4	3	
2	1	
3	1	Occasionally to 400 m; movements poorly known, tied to flowering of bamboo.
4	3	Occasionally to 4,200 m.
4	3	
4	3	
4	3	Usually called *F. xanthopterygius* (see Pinto 1978).
4	3	
4	3	Locally to 1,800 m (Venezuela).
4	3	
3	2	Survey.
4	3	
4	3	
4	3	
2	1	Survey; declining; deforestation and bird trade.
4	3	
4	3	
4	2	
4	2	Monitor.
3	2	Recently described (O'Neill, Munn and Franke 1991);
4	3	Apparently nomadic.

Abbreviations Used

Snst - Sensitivity:
L - Low; **M** - Medium; **H** - High.

Strat - Foraging Strata:
T - Terrestrial; **U** - Understory; **M** - Midstory; **C** - Canopy; **A** - Aerial; **W** - Water.

Cntab - Center of Abundance:
LT - Lower tropical; **LS** - Lower subtropical; **HT** - Hill tropical; **UT** - Upper tropical; **US** - Upper subtropical; **MM** - Middle montane; **UM** - Upper montane.

Rel - Relative Abundance:
R - Rare; **U** - Uncommon; **F** - Fairly common; **C** - Common; **P** - Patchily distributed.

Min - Minimum Elevation:
L - Lowlands; **?** - Uncertain value; numeric values in meters.

Max - Maximum Elevation:
L - Lowlands; **?** - Uncertain value; **+** - species occurs at least to given elevation but likely occurs higher; numeric values in meters.

Micro - Microhabitats:
A - Army ants; **B** - Bamboo; **T** - Treefalls; **G** - Ground bromeliads; **C** - Rocky outcrops and caves; **S** - Streamside; **V** - Vine tangles; **B/V** -Bamboo/vine tangles.

Habitats:
F1 - Tropical lowland evergreen forest; **F2** - Flooded tropical evergreen forest; **F3** - River-edge forest; **F4** - Montane evergreen forest; **F5** - Elfin forest; **F6** - *Polylepis* woodland; **F7** - Tropical deciduous forest; **F8** - Gallery forest; **F9** - Southern temperate forest; **F10** - Pine forest; **F11** - Pine-oak forest; **F12** - White sand forest; **F13** - Palm forest; **F14** - Mangrove forest; **F15** - Secondary forest; **N1** - Arid lowland scrub; **N2** - Arid montane scrub; **N3** - Semihumid/humid montane scrub; **N4** - Cerrado; **N5** - Campo grasslands; **N6** - Low, seasonally wet grassland; **N7** - Southern temperate grassland; **N8** - Northern temperate grassland; **N9** - Puna grassland; **N10** - Paramo grassland; **N11** - Riparian thickets; **N12** - River island scrub; **N13** - Pastures/agricultural lands; **N14** - Second-growth scrub; **A1** - Freshwater marshes; **A2** - Saltwater/brackish marshes; **A3** - Coastal sand beaches/mudflats; **A4** - Coastal rocky beaches; **A5** - Riverine sand beaches; **A6** - Freshwater lakes and ponds; **A7** - Alkaline lakes; **A8** - Rivers; **A9** - Streams; **A10** - Bogs; **A11** - Coastal waters; **A12** - Pelagic waters.
E - Edge (used as a modifer to particular habitats).

Sub - Subregions:
ARC - Arid Caribbean Coast; **AWA** - Altiplano and Western Andes; **BAH** - Bahamas; **BAJ** - Baja California; **CAA** - Caatinga; **CAH** - Central American Highlands; **CER** - Cerrado; **CHA** - Chaco; **CHG** - Chiapas-Guanacaste; **CHL** - Chilean Desert; **CHR** - Chiriquí; **CIS** - Cocos Island; **CMV** - Cauca-Magdalena Valley; **COC** - Cuzco-Cochabamba; **CUB** - Cuba; **DOM** - Dominica; **EAS** - Eastern Slope Andes; **FDN** - Fernando de Noronha; **GAL** - Galápagos; **GCM** - Gulf Coast-Mexico; **GRE** - Grenada; **GUA** - Guadeloupe; **GUI** - Guianan; **HIS** - Hispaniola; **HPC** - Humid Pacific Coast; **ISA** - Isla Providencia and Isla San Andrés; **JAM** - Jamaica; **JFI** - Juan Fernández Islands; **MAN** - Manabí-Tumbes; **MAR** - Marañón Valley; **MID** - Madeira-Tapajós; **MON** - Montserrat; **MRT** - Martinique; **MTC** - Marañón-Cuzco; **NMM** - Northern Mexican Mountains; **NOR** - Northern Coastal Brazil; **PAR** - Pará; **PER** - Peruvian Desert; **PUE** - Puerto Rico; **RDJ** - Rio de Janeiro-Bahia Lowlands; **RMW** - Rio Madeira West; **RNW** - Rio Negro West; **SCA** - Southern Central America; **SCT** - Santa Cruz-Tucumán; **SIN** - Sinaloa-Oaxaca; **SMH** - Southern Mexican Highlands; **SMT** - Santa Marta; **SOC** - Islas Revillagigedo (Socorro Island group); **SON** - Sonoran Desert; **SOU** - Southern Atlantic Coast; **STL** - St. Lucia; **STV** - St. Vincent; **TAC** - Tacarcuna; **VAN** - Venezuelan Andes; **VNZ** - Venezuelan Coastal Mountains; **WES** - Western Andes; **YUC** - Yucatán Peninsula.
o - Endemic to region, but not restricted to a single subregion.

Zoogeographic Regions:
AMN - Northern Amazonia; **AMS** - Southern Amazonia; **ATL** - Atlantic Forest; **BSR** - Baja-Sonora; **CAN** - Central Andes; **CDH** - Chiriquí-Darién Highlands; **CHO** - Chocó Lowlands; **CSA** - Central South America; **EPC** - Equatorial Pacific Coast; **GAN** - Greater Antilles; **GCS** - Gulf-Caribbean Slope; **LAN** - Lesser Antilles; **MAH** - Madrean Highlands; **MPL** - Mexican Plateau; **NAN** - Northern Andes; **NSA** - Northern South America; **PAM** - Pampas; **PAS** - Pacific Arid Slope; **PAT** - Patagonia; **SAN** - Southern Andes; **STP** - Subtropical Pacific; **TEP** - Tepuis.

CP -Conservation Priority:
1 - Urgent; **2** - High; **3** - Medium; **4** - Low.

RP - Research Priority:
1 - High; **2** - Medium; **3** - Low.

	Snst	Strat	Cntab	Rel	Min	Max	Micro	Habitats	Sub	Zoogeographic Regions
Touit batavica	M	C	HT	F	L	1700		F4, F1		NSA, AMN
Touit costaricensis	H	C	HT	U	500	1000		F4	CHR	CDH
Touit dilectissima	H	C	UT	U	800	1700		F4, F1		CDH, NAN
Touit huetii	H	C	LT	U/P	L	900		F1		NSA, AMN, AMS
Touit melanonota	H	C	HT	R	500	1700		F1, F4	SOU	ATL
Touit purpurata	H	C	LT	U	L	1400+		F1, F2, F4		AMN, AMS
Touit stictoptera	H	C	UT	U	600	2400		F4		NAN, CAN
Touit surda	H	C	HT	R	L	900		F1	o	ATL
Pionites leucogaster	H	C	LT	F	L	800		F1, F2	o	AMS
Pionites melanocephala	H	C	LT	F	L	800		F1, F2	o	AMN
Pionopsitta barrabandi	H	C	LT	U	L	800		F1		AMN, AMS
Pionopsitta caica	H	C	LT	U	L	1100		F1	GUI	AMN
Pionopsitta haematotis	M	C	LT	F	L	1200		F1, F4		GCS, CHO
Pionopsitta pileata	M	C	HT	U	L	2100		F4, F1	o	ATL
Pionopsitta pulchra	M	C	HT	U/P	L	1200		F1, F4	o	CHO
Pionopsitta pyrilia	M	C	HT	U	L	1000		F1, F4		GCS, CHO, NAN, NSA
Gypopsitta vulturina	H	C	LT	U	L	L		F1, F2?	o	AMS
Hapalopsittaca amazonina										
amazonina	H	C	UM	R/P	2000	3000		F4	EAS	NAN
fuertesi	H	C	UM	R	2900	3800		F4	EAS	NAN
pyrrhops	H	C	UM	R	2500	3500		F4	EAS	NAN
Hapalopsittaca melanotis	H	C	UM	R/P	2000	3400		F4	o	CAN
Graydidascalus brachyurus	M	C	LT	F	L	L		F2, F3		AMN, AMS
Pionus chalcopterus	M	C	UT	U	800	2400		F4, F1	o	NAN
Pionus fuscus	H	C	LT	U	L	1200		F1		AMN, AMS
Pionus maximiliani	M	C	HT	F	L	1300		F1, F7, F8, F4		CSA, ATL
Pionus menstruus	L	C	LT	C	L	1200		F3, F8, F1E, F15		GCS, CHO, NSA, AMN, AMS, ATL
Pionus senilis	M	C	HT	U	L	1600		F4, F1, F15		MAH, GCS, CDH
Pionus sordidus	M	C	UT	F	800	1800		F4, F1, F15?		NAN, CAN, NSA
Pionus tumultuosus										
seniloides	M	C	UM	F/P	1600	3100		F4	o	NAN
tumultuosus	M	C	UM	F/P	2000	3300		F4	o	CAN
Amazona aestiva	M	C	LT	F	L	1600		F8, F7, N4, N6		CSA, ATL
Amazona agilis	M	C	HT/UT	U	500	1600+		F4, F1	JAM	GAN
Amazona albifrons	M	C	LT	F	L	1800		F7, F1, F15		PAS, GCS
Amazona amazonica	M	C	LT	F	L	800		F2, F3, F8, N6, F1		NSA, AMN, AMS, CSA, ATL
Amazona arausiaca	M	C	HT	R	L	1200		F1, F4	DOM	LAN
Amazona autumnalis										
autumnalis	M	C	LT	F	L	1100		F1E, F7, F8, F15		GCS, CHO, NSA
diadema	H	C	LT	F	L	L		F1E	o	AMN
Amazona barbadensis	M	C	LT	R/U	L	L		N1, F7	ARC	NSA
Amazona brasiliensis	H	C	LT	R	L	L		F1, F12	SOU	ATL
Amazona collaria	M	C	HT	F	L	1200		F4, F1	JAM	GAN
Amazona dufresniana	H	C	UT	R/U	700	1700		F4, F1		TEP, AMN
Amazona farinosa	M	C	LT	F	L	1200		F1		GCS, CHO, NSA, AMN, AMS, ATL
Amazona festiva	M	C	LT	U	L	L		F2, F3, F8		NSA, AMN, AMS
Amazona finschi	M	C	UT	U	L	2200		F11, F1, F7		PAS, MAH
Amazona guildingii	M	C	HT	R	L?	1000		F4, F1	STV	LAN
Amazona imperialis	M	C	HT	R	500	1400		F4	DOM	LAN
Amazona kawalli	H	C	LT	R?	L	L		F1?	o	AMS

CP	RP	Notes
4	2	Monitor.
3	2	Survey; seasonal movements to lowlands and 3,000 m.
3	2	Occasionally to lowlands.
4	2	Occasionally to 1,300 m; distribution poorly known; nomadic?
1	1	Locally to lowlands; poorly known; deforestation; survey.
4	3	
3	2	Survey.
2	1	Survey.
4	3	
4	3	Occasionally to 1,100 m.
4	3	
4	3	
4	3	Locally to 1,600 m.
3	2	Probably declining; monitor.
3	2	Locally to 2,100 m (Colombia); deforestation; monitor.
3	2	Occasionally to 1,700 m; deforestation; monitor.
3	2	May be declining locally; monitor.
2	1	Survey; see Graves 1987 for details on species group.
1	1	No recent records; survey.
2	1	Declining; deforestation; survey.
3	2	Survey.
4	3	
3	1	Occasionally to lowlands and 2,800 m; declining; survey; elevational movements.
4	3	Occasionally to 1,800 m (Colombia).
4	3	
4	3	Occasionally to 1,600 m+ (Bolivia); declining in eastern Brazil.
3	2	Probably declining in much of range; monitor.
3	2	Occasionally to 200 and 2,400 m; monitor.
4	3	Probably conspecific with *tumultuosus* (O'Neill and Parker 1977).
4	3	
4	2	Monitor.
2	1	Monitor.
4	3	
4	3	
2	1	Habitat destruction.
3	2	Declining; monitor.
3	2	Seasonal movements poorly known.
3	2	Status uncertain; survey.
1	1	Habitat destruction; capture for bird trade.
2	1	Monitor.
3	2	Monitor; seasonal movements to lowlands?
4	3	Occasionally to 1,600 m+ (Bolivia).
3	3	Common locally only; monitor.
3	2	Survey.
1	1	Habitat destruction, capture for bird trade.
1	1	Occasionally to lowlands; deforestation, hunting.
3	1	May be variant of *A. farinosa*; recently described (Grantsau and Camargo 1989).

Abbreviations Used

Snst - Sensitivity:
L - Low; **M** - Medium; **H** - High.

Strat - Foraging Strata:
T - Terrestrial; **U** - Understory; **M** - Midstory; **C** - Canopy; **A** - Aerial; **W** - Water.

Cntab - Center of Abundance:
LT - Lower tropical; **LS** - Lower subtropical; **HT** - Hill tropical; **UT** - Upper tropical; **US** - Upper subtropical; **MM** - Middle montane; **UM** - Upper montane.

Rel - Relative Abundance:
R - Rare; **U** - Uncommon; **F** - Fairly common; **C** - Common; **P** - Patchily distributed.

Min - Minimum Elevation:
L - Lowlands; **?** - Uncertain value; numeric values in meters.

Max - Maximum Elevation:
L - Lowlands; **?** - Uncertain value; **+** - species occurs at least to given elevation but likely occurs higher; numeric values in meters.

Micro - Microhabitats:
A - Army ants; **B** - Bamboo; **T** - Treefalls; **G** - Ground bromeliads; **C** - Rocky outcrops and caves; **S** - Streamside; **V** - Vine tangles; **B/V** -Bamboo/vine tangles.

Habitats:
F1 - Tropical lowland evergreen forest; **F2** - Flooded tropical evergreen forest; **F3** - River-edge forest; **F4** - Montane evergreen forest; **F5** - Elfin forest; **F6** - *Polylepis* woodland; **F7** - Tropical deciduous forest; **F8** - Gallery forest; **F9** - Southern temperate forest; **F10** - Pine forest; **F11** - Pine-oak forest; **F12** - White sand forest; **F13** - Palm forest; **F14** - Mangrove forest; **F15** - Secondary forest; **N1** - Arid lowland scrub; **N2** - Arid montane scrub; **N3** - Semihumid/humid montane scrub; **N4** - Cerrado; **N5** - Campo grasslands; **N6** - Low, seasonally wet grassland; **N7** - Southern temperate grassland; **N8** - Northern temperate grassland; **N9** - Puna grassland; **N10** - Paramo grassland; **N11** - Riparian thickets; **N12** - River island scrub; **N13** - Pastures/agricultural lands; **N14** - Second-growth scrub; **A1** - Freshwater marshes; **A2** - Saltwater/brackish marshes; **A3** - Coastal sand beaches/mudflats; **A4** - Coastal rocky beaches; **A5** - Riverine sand beaches; **A6** - Freshwater lakes and ponds; **A7** - Alkaline lakes; **A8** - Rivers; **A9** - Streams; **A10** - Bogs; **A11** - Coastal waters; **A12** - Pelagic waters.
E - Edge (used as a modifer to particular habitats).

Sub - Subregions:
ARC - Arid Caribbean Coast; **AWA** - Altiplano and Western Andes; **BAH** - Bahamas; **BAJ** - Baja California; **CAA** - Caatinga; **CAH** - Central American Highlands; **CER** - Cerrado; **CHA** - Chaco; **CHG** - Chiapas-Guanacaste; **CHL** - Chilean Desert; **CHR** - Chiriquí; **CIS** - Cocos Island; **CMV** - Cauca-Magdalena Valley; **COC** - Cuzco-Cochabamba; **CUB** - Cuba; **DOM** - Dominica; **EAS** - Eastern Slope Andes; **FDN** - Fernando de Noronha; **GAL** - Galápagos; **GCM** - Gulf Coast-Mexico; **GRE** - Grenada; **GUA** - Guadeloupe; **GUI** - Guianan; **HIS** - Hispaniola; **HPC** - Humid Pacific Coast; **ISA** - Isla Providencia and Isla San Andrés; **JAM** - Jamaica; **JFI** - Juan Fernández Islands; **MAN** - Manabí-Tumbes; **MAR** - Marañón Valley; **MID** - Madeira-Tapajós; **MON** - Montserrat; **MRT** - Martinique; **MTC** - Marañón-Cuzco; **NMM** - Northern Mexican Mountains; **NOR** - Northern Coastal Brazil; **PAR** - Pará; **PER** - Peruvian Desert; **PUE** - Puerto Rico; **RDJ** - Rio de Janeiro-Bahia Lowlands; **RMW** - Rio Madeira West; **RNW** - Rio Negro West; **SCA** - Southern Central America; **SCT** - Santa Cruz-Tucumán; **SIN** - Sinaloa-Oaxaca; **SMH** - Southern Mexican Highlands; **SMT** - Santa Marta; **SOC** - Islas Revillagigedo (Socorro Island group); **SON** - Sonoran Desert; **SOU** - Southern Atlantic Coast; **STL** - St. Lucia; **STV** - St. Vincent; **TAC** - Tacarcuna; **VAN** - Venezuelan Andes; **VNZ** - Venezuelan Coastal Mountains; **WES** - Western Andes; **YUC** - Yucatán Peninsula.
o - Endemic to region, but not restricted to a single subregion.

Zoogeographic Regions:
AMN - Northern Amazonia; **AMS** - Southern Amazonia; **ATL** - Atlantic Forest; **BSR** - Baja-Sonora; **CAN** - Central Andes; **CDH** - Chiriquí-Darién Highlands; **CHO** - Chocó Lowlands; **CSA** - Central South America; **EPC** - Equatorial Pacific Coast; **GAN** - Greater Antilles; **GCS** - Gulf-Caribbean Slope; **LAN** - Lesser Antilles; **MAH** - Madrean Highlands; **MPL** - Mexican Plateau; **NAN** - Northern Andes; **NSA** - Northern South America; **PAM** - Pampas; **PAS** - Pacific Arid Slope; **PAT** - Patagonia; **SAN** - Southern Andes; **STP** - Subtropical Pacific; **TEP** - Tepuis.

CP -Conservation Priority:
1 - Urgent; **2** - High; **3** - Medium; **4** - Low.

RP - Research Priority:
1 - High; **2** - Medium; **3** - Low.

	Snst	Strat	Cntab	Rel	Min	Max	Micro	Habitats	Sub	Zoogeographic Regions
Amazona leucocephala	M	C	LT	U/F	L	800+		F1, F4, F7	o	GAN
Amazona mercenaria	M	C	MM	F	1100	3300		F4, F1		NAN, CAN
Amazona ochrocephala										
auropalliata	M	C	LT	F	L	600		F7, F8, F15	o	PAS
ochrocephala	M	C	LT	F	L	850		F2, F3, F8, F7		GCS, CHO, NSA, AMN, AMS
oratrix	M	C	LT	R	L	700		F7, F8, F1		PAS, GCS
Amazona pretrei	M	C	UT	R	500	1000		F9	SOU	ATL
Amazona rhodocorytha	M	C	LT	U	L	900		F1	RDJ	ATL
Amazona tucumana	M	C	UT	U?	1000	2200		F4, F1	SCT	CAN
Amazona ventralis	M	C	HT/UT	U	L	1500+		F4, F1	HIS	GAN
Amazona versicolor	M	C	HT	R	L	1000		F1	STL	LAN
Amazona vinacea	M	C	UT	R	500	1700		F9, F1	SOU	ATL
Amazona viridigenalis	M	C	LT	U	L	1200		F8, F7, F11	GCM	GCS
Amazona vittata	H	C	HT	R	200	900		F4	PUE	GAN
Amazona xantholora	M	C	LT	U/F	L	L		F7, F15	YUC	GCS
Amazona xanthops	M	C	HT	U	600	1200		N4, F8	CER	CSA
Deroptyus accipitrinus	H	C	LT	F	L	L		F1, F3		AMN, AMS
Triclaria malachitacea	M	M/C	HT	R	500	1100		F1, F4	SOU	ATL
CUCULIFORMES										
Cuculidae										
Coccyzus americanus	M	M/C	LT	F	L	1500		F8, F7, F15		GAN, LAN, BSR, MPL, PAS, MAH, GCS
Coccyzus cinereus	M	M/C	LT	U	L	900		F7, F8, F3		CSA, PAM
Coccyzus euleri	M	M/C	LT	R	L	900		F1, F8, F15		NSA, AMN, AMS, CSA, ATL
Coccyzus ferrugineus	M	U/M	LT	U	L	L		F1	CIS	PAS
Coccyzus lansbergi	M	M/C	LT	R	L	800		F7, F8		CHO, EPC, NSA
Coccyzus melacoryphus	L	M/C	LT	F	L	1200+		F7, F8, F15, F3, F1		CHO, EPC, AMN, AMS, CSA, ATL, PAM
Coccyzus minor	M	M/C	LT	U/F	L	1250		F7, F8, F14, F15		GAN, LAN, PAS, GCS, NSA
Coccyzus pumilus	M	M/C	LT	F	L	1000		F7, F8, F15	o	NSA
Piaya cayana	L	C	LT	C	L	2500		F1, F7, F15, F8, F2		PAS, MAH, GCS, CDH, CHO, EPC, NAN, CAN, NSA, AMN, AMS, CSA, ATL, PAM
Piaya melanogaster	H	C	LT	U	L	800		F1		AMN, AMS
Piaya minuta	L	U/M	LT	F	L	900+		F1E, F15, F3, N14		GCS, NSA, AMN, AMS
Piaya pluvialis	M	M/C	HT	U	L	1500+		F1, F15	JAM	GAN
Piaya rufigularis	M	M/C	LT	R	L	900+		F7, F1?	HIS	GAN
Saurothera longirostris	M	M/C	LT	F	L	2000+		F7, F1	HIS	GAN
Saurothera merlini	M	M/C	LT	F	L	1200+		F1, F7, F15, F10	o	GAN
Saurothera vetula	M	M/C	LT	U	L	1200+		F1, F7?	JAM	GAN
Saurothera vielloti	M	M/C	LT	R	L	800+		F7, F1	PUE	GAN
Crotophaga ani	L	T/C	LT	C	L	2000		N14, N12		GAN, LAN, GCS, NSA, AMN, AMS, CSA, ATL
Crotophaga major	M	T/C	LT	F	L	800		F2, F3, F8, F14?		GCS, CHO, NSA, AMN, AMS, CSA, ATL, PAM
Crotophaga sulcirostris	L	T/M	LT	C	L	2300		N14, N11		PAS, MAH, GCS, CHO, EPC, STP, NSA, CSA
Guira guira	L	T	LT	C	L	1200+		N14		AMS, CSA, ATL, PAM
Tapera naevia	L	T/U	LT	C	L	1500		N14, N6, N11, N12		PAS, GCS, CHO?, EPC, NSA, AMN, AMS, CSA, ATL
Morococcyx erythropygus	L	T/U	LT	F	L	1500		N1, F7E, N14	o	PAS
Dromococcyx pavoninus	H	T/U	LT	U/P	L	1600	B	F1, F4		NAN, CAN, NSA, AMN, AMS, ATL
Dromococcyx phasianellus	M	T	LT	U	L	1600		F1, F2, F7		PAS, GCS, NSA, AMN, AMS, CSA, ATL
Geococcyx californianus	L	T	LS	F	L	2500		N1, N2		BSR, MPL, MAH, GCS
Geococcyx velox	L	T	LT	F	L	2800		N1, N2		PAS, MAH, GCS
Neomorphus geoffroyi	H	T	LT	R	L	1200		F1		GCS, CHO, AMN, AMS, ATL
Neomorphus pucheranii	H	T	LT	R	L	700		F1		AMN, AMS
Neomorphus radiolosus	H	T	HT	R	500	1200		F1	o	CHO
Neomorphus rufipennis	H	T	LT	R	L	1100?		F1	GUI	AMN

CP	RP	Notes
2	1	Monitor.
4	3	Occasionally to lowlands.
3	2	Declining in most areas; monitor.
4	2	Occasionally to 1,400 m (Peru); monitor.
2	1	Declining; capture for bird trade; status of race *tresmariae* unknown.
1	1	Declining; deforestation; survey.
2	1	Declining; deforestation; survey.
2	1	Occasionally to 300 m; survey; seasonal movements poorly known.
2	1	Monitor.
1	1	Very rare; conservation measures.
2	1	Locally to lowlands; declining; survey.
2	1	Habitat destruction; survey.
1	1	Introduced nest competitors, habitat destruction.
3	2	Monitor.
2	1	Declining with habitat destruction.
4	3	
2	1	Seasonally to lowlands; declining locally; survey.
4	3	
4	3	
4	2	Distribution poorly known.
2	2	Poorly known; monitor.
4	2	Occasionally to 1,400 m (Venezuela); distribution poorly known.
4	3	Occasionally to 2,400 m; rarely to 3,600 m in migration.
4	3	
4	3	Occasionally to 2,600 m (Colombia).
4	3	
4	3	
4	3	Occasionally to 1,600 m (Colombia).
3	2	Survey.
3	2	Survey.
4	3	
4	3	
4	2	
4	3	
4	3	
4	2	Occasionally to 2,600 m (Colombia); movements poorly known.
4	3	
4	3	
4	3	Occasionally to 2,500 m (Venezuela).
4	3	Locally to 1,800 m+ (Guatemala).
4	3	Occasionally to 1,900 m+ (Venezuela).
4	3	
4	3	
4	3	
3	2	Locally to 1,650 m (Bolivia); population in eastern Brazil threatened.
4	3	
2	1	Poorly known; habitat destruction.
4	2	Poorly known.

Abbreviations Used

Snst - Sensitivity:
L - Low; **M** - Medium; **H** - High.

Strat - Foraging Strata:
T - Terrestrial; **U** - Understory; **M** - Midstory; **C** - Canopy; **A** - Aerial; **W** - Water.

Cntab - Center of Abundance:
LT - Lower tropical; **LS** - Lower subtropical; **HT** - Hill tropical; **UT** - Upper tropical; **US** - Upper subtropical; **MM** - Middle montane; **UM** - Upper montane.

Rel - Relative Abundance:
R - Rare; **U** - Uncommon; **F** - Fairly common; **C** - Common; **P** - Patchily distributed.

Min - Minimum Elevation:
L - Lowlands; **?** - Uncertain value; numeric values in meters.

Max - Maximum Elevation:
L - Lowlands; **?** - Uncertain value; **+** - species occurs at least to given elevation but likely occurs higher; numeric values in meters.

Micro - Microhabitats:
A - Army ants; **B** - Bamboo; **T** - Treefalls; **G** - Ground bromeliads; **C** - Rocky outcrops and caves; **S** - Streamside; **V** - Vine tangles; **B/V** -Bamboo/vine tangles.

Habitats:
F1 - Tropical lowland evergreen forest; **F2** - Flooded tropical evergreen forest; **F3** - River-edge forest; **F4** - Montane evergreen forest; **F5** - Elfin forest; **F6** - *Polylepis* woodland; **F7** - Tropical deciduous forest; **F8** - Gallery forest; **F9** - Southern temperate forest; **F10** - Pine forest; **F11** - Pine-oak forest; **F12** - White sand forest; **F13** - Palm forest; **F14** - Mangrove forest; **F15** - Secondary forest; **N1** - Arid lowland scrub; **N2** - Arid montane scrub; **N3** - Semihumid/humid montane scrub; **N4** - Cerrado; **N5** - Campo grasslands; **N6** - Low, seasonally wet grassland; **N7** - Southern temperate grassland; **N8** - Northern temperate grassland; **N9** - Puna grassland; **N10** - Paramo grassland; **N11** - Riparian thickets; **N12** - River island scrub; **N13** - Pastures/agricultural lands; **N14** - Second-growth scrub; **A1** - Freshwater marshes; **A2** - Saltwater/brackish marshes; **A3** - Coastal sand beaches/mudflats; **A4** - Coastal rocky beaches; **A5** - Riverine sand beaches; **A6** - Freshwater lakes and ponds; **A7** - Alkaline lakes; **A8** - Rivers; **A9** - Streams; **A10** - Bogs; **A11** - Coastal waters; **A12** - Pelagic waters.
E - Edge (used as a modifer to particular habitats).

Sub - Subregions:
ARC - Arid Caribbean Coast; **AWA** - Altiplano and Western Andes; **BAH** - Bahamas; **BAJ** - Baja California; **CAA** - Caatinga; **CAH** - Central American Highlands; **CER** - Cerrado; **CHA** - Chaco; **CHG** - Chiapas-Guanacaste; **CHL** - Chilean Desert; **CHR** - Chiriquí; **CIS** - Cocos Island; **CMV** - Cauca-Magdalena Valley; **COC** - Cuzco-Cochabamba; **CUB** - Cuba; **DOM** - Dominica; **EAS** - Eastern Slope Andes; **FDN** - Fernando de Noronha; **GAL** - Galápagos; **GCM** - Gulf Coast-Mexico; **GRE** - Grenada; **GUA** - Guadeloupe; **GUI** - Guianan; **HIS** - Hispaniola; **HPC** - Humid Pacific Coast; **ISA** - Isla Providencia and Isla San Andrés; **JAM** - Jamaica; **JFI** - Juan Fernández Islands; **MAN** - Manabí-Tumbes; **MAR** - Marañón Valley; **MID** - Madeira-Tapajós; **MON** - Montserrat; **MRT** - Martinique; **MTC** - Marañón-Cuzco; **NMM** - Northern Mexican Mountains; **NOR** - Northern Coastal Brazil; **PAR** - Pará; **PER** - Peruvian Desert; **PUE** - Puerto Rico; **RDJ** - Rio de Janeiro-Bahia Lowlands; **RMW** - Rio Madeira West; **RNW** - Rio Negro West; **SCA** - Southern Central America; **SCT** - Santa Cruz-Tucumán; **SIN** - Sinaloa-Oaxaca; **SMH** - Southern Mexican Highlands; **SMT** - Santa Marta; **SOC** - Islas Revillagigedo (Socorro Island group); **SON** - Sonoran Desert; **SOU** - Southern Atlantic Coast; **STL** - St. Lucia; **STV** - St. Vincent; **TAC** - Tacarcuna; **VAN** - Venezuelan Andes; **VNZ** - Venezuelan Coastal Mountains; **WES** - Western Andes; **YUC** - Yucatán Peninsula.
o - Endemic to region, but not restricted to a single subregion.

Zoogeographic Regions:
AMN - Northern Amazonia; **AMS** - Southern Amazonia; **ATL** - Atlantic Forest; **BSR** - Baja-Sonora; **CAN** - Central Andes; **CDH** - Chiriquí-Darién Highlands; **CHO** - Chocó Lowlands; **CSA** - Central South America; **EPC** - Equatorial Pacific Coast; **GAN** - Greater Antilles; **GCS** - Gulf-Caribbean Slope; **LAN** - Lesser Antilles; **MAH** - Madrean Highlands; **MPL** - Mexican Plateau; **NAN** - Northern Andes; **NSA** - Northern South America; **PAM** - Pampas; **PAS** - Pacific Arid Slope; **PAT** - Patagonia; **SAN** - Southern Andes; **STP** - Subtropical Pacific; **TEP** - Tepuis.

CP -Conservation Priority:
1 - Urgent; **2** - High; **3** - Medium; **4** - Low.

RP - Research Priority:
1 - High; **2** - Medium; **3** - Low.

	Snst	Strat	Cntab	Rel	Min	Max	Micro	Habitats	Sub	Zoogeographic Regions
Neomorphus squamiger	H	T	LT	R	L	L		F1	PAR	AMS
Opisthocomidae										
Opisthocomus hoazin	M	U/C	LT	C	L	L		F8E, A1		NSA, AMN, AMS, CSA
STRIGIFORMES										
Tytonidae										
Tyto alba	L	C	LT	F	L	4000		N14, N1, N2		GAN, LAN, BSR, MPL, PAS, MAH, GCS, CDH, CHO, EPC, STP, NAN, CAN, SAN, NSA, TEP, AMN, AMS, CSA, ATL, PAM, PAT
Tyto glaucops	?	C	?	U?	L	2000+		N1, N2, N14	HIS	GAN
Strigidae										
Otus albogularis	H	C	UM	F	2000	3600		F4, F5		NAN, CAN
Otus asio	L	C	LS	F	L	1500+		F7, F8, F15		GCS
Otus atricapillus	L	C	LT	F/P	L	1150		F1, F15, F9	SOU	ATL
Otus barbarus	M	C	MM	?	1400	2500		F10, F4	CAH	MAH
Otus choliba	L	C	LT	C	L	2800		F15, F1E, F3, F8		GCS, NAN, CAN, NSA, TEP, AMN, AMS, CSA, ATL
Otus clarkii	H	C	MM	U	900	3300		F4	o	CDH
Otus colombianus	H	C	UT	U	1250	1600		F4	EAS	NAN
Otus cooperi	M	C	LT	F	L	950		F7, F8, F15, F14, F1E	CHG	PAS
Otus flammeolus	H	C	UM	F	1350	3100		F10, F11		MAH
Otus guatemalae	M	C	UT	F	L	1800		F1, F4, F15, F7, F11?		PAS, MAH, GCS, CHO, NAN, CAN, NSA, TEP, CSA
Otus ingens	H	M/C	UT	F	1000	2200		F4		NAN, CAN
Otus kennicotti	L	C	LS	C	L	2200		F8, F11, F15, F7		BSR, MPL, MAH
Otus koepckeae	M	C	UM	?	1500	3200		F6	AWA	CAN
Otus marshalli	H	C	MM	?	1700	2250		F4	MTC	CAN
Otus nudipes	M	C	HT	C	L	900+		F1, F7	PUE	GAN
Otus petersoni	H	C	MM	U	1900	2200		F4	EAS	NAN
Otus roboratus	M	C	LT	F	L	1800		F7, F8, F15		EPC, CAN
Otus seductus	M	C	LT	U	L	1200+		F7, F15	SIN	PAS
Otus trichopsis	H	C	MM	F	600	2950		F11, F10	o	MAH
Otus watsonii	H	M/C	LT	C	L	800		F1, F2		AMN, AMS
Lophostrix cristata	H	C	LT	U/F	L	1000		F1, F4		GCS, CHO, NSA, AMN, AMS
Bubo virginianus	L	C	LS	F	L	4400		F4, F1, F7, F8, F11, N1, N2		BSR, MPL, PAS, MAH, GCS, CDH, CHO, EPC, STP, NAN, CAN, SAN, NSA, AMN, AMS, CSA, ATL, PAM, PAT
Pulsatrix koeniswaldiana	H	C	HT	U	L	1500		F4, F1	SOU	ATL
Pulsatrix melanota	M	C	HT	F	600	1250		F4, F1, F15		NAN, CAN, AMS
Pulsatrix perspicillata	M	C	LT	F	L	1000		F2, F1, F8, F15		GCS, CHO, NSA, AMN, AMS, CSA, ATL
Glaucidium brasilianum	L	C	LT	C	L	2000		N1, N2, N14, F7, F1E, F15		BSR, PAS, MAH, GCS, SAN, NSA, TEP, AMN, AMS, CSA, ATL, PAM, PAT
Glaucidium gnoma	M	C	UM	U	1200	4000		F11, F10		BSR, MAH
Glaucidium hardyi	H	M/C	LT	U	L	800		F1		AMN, AMS, ATL
Glaucidium jardinii	M	C	UM	F	2000	3400		F4		CDH, NAN, CAN
Glaucidium minutissimum	M	C	LT	U	L	2100		F1, F7, F4, F11		PAS, MAH, GCS, CHO?, AMN, AMS, CSA, ATL
Glaucidium peruanum	M	M/C	MM	C	L	3500		N11, N2, N1, F15		EPC, STP, CAN
Glaucidium siju	M	C	LT	F	L	1500+		F1, F7, F10, F15	CUB	GAN
Xenoglaux loweryi	H	U/M	MM	R	1900	2350		F5	MTC	CAN
Micrathene whitneyi	M	C	US	F	L	2100+		N1, F8, F11		BSR, MPL, MAH, GCS
Gymnoglaux lawrencii	M	C	LT?	F	L	L?		F1, F7, F15?	CUB	GAN
Speotyto cunicularia	M	T	LS	F/P	L	4000		N8, N7, N5, N1, N2		GAN, LAN, BSR, MPL, PAS, MAH, GCS, EPC, STP, CAN, SAN, NSA, AMN, CSA, ATL, PAM, PAT

CP	RP	Notes
3	2	Poorly known; may be conspecific with *N. geoffroyi*.
4	3	
4	3	
3	2	Monitor.
4	3	
4	3	
4	2	Probably contains two species.
3	2	Poorly known.
4	3	
4	3	
3	2	Poorly known.
4	3	
4	3	
4	2	Distribution poorly known.
4	3	
4	3	Includes *O. vinaceus*.
3	2	Poorly known.
3	2	Poorly known.
4	3	
3	2	Poorly known.
4	3	
2	1	Habitat destruction.
4	3	
4	2	Population above 2,000 m (Venezuela) needs study.
4	3	Occasionally to 2,000 m (Honduras).
4	3	
3	2	
3	2	Occasionally to lowlands(?) and 1,650 m (Bolivia); deforestation.
4	3	Occasionally to 1,500 m.
4	3	Mainly below 1,200 m; includes *G. nanum*.
4	3	Occasionally to 400 m; may contain multiple species.
4	3	Recently described (Vielliard 1989).
4	3	Locally to 900 m; may contain two species (König 1991b).
4	2	Below 900 m in South America; may contain multiple species.
4	3	Recently described (König 1991b); may include two species.
4	3	
2	1	Poorly known.
4	2	
3	2	Monitor.
4	3	

Abbreviations Used

Snst - Sensitivity:
L - Low; **M** - Medium; **H** - High.

Strat - Foraging Strata:
T - Terrestrial; **U** - Understory; **M** - Midstory; **C** - Canopy; **A** - Aerial; **W** - Water.

Cntab - Center of Abundance:
LT - Lower tropical; **LS** - Lower subtropical; **HT** - Hill tropical; **UT** - Upper tropical; **US** - Upper subtropical; **MM** - Middle montane; **UM** - Upper montane.

Rel - Relative Abundance:
R - Rare; **U** - Uncommon; **F** - Fairly common; **C** - Common; **P** - Patchily distributed.

Min - Minimum Elevation:
L - Lowlands; **?** - Uncertain value; numeric values in meters.

Max - Maximum Elevation:
L - Lowlands; **?** - Uncertain value; **+** - species occurs at least to given elevation but likely occurs higher; numeric values in meters.

Micro - Microhabitats:
A - Army ants; **B** - Bamboo; **T** - Treefalls; **G** - Ground bromeliads; **C** - Rocky outcrops and caves; **S** - Streamside; **V** - Vine tangles; **B/V** -Bamboo/vine tangles.

Habitats:
F1 - Tropical lowland evergreen forest; **F2** - Flooded tropical evergreen forest; **F3** - River-edge forest; **F4** - Montane evergreen forest; **F5** - Elfin forest; **F6** - *Polylepis* woodland; **F7** - Tropical deciduous forest; **F8** - Gallery forest; **F9** - Southern temperate forest; **F10** - Pine forest; **F11** - Pine-oak forest; **F12** - White sand forest; **F13** - Palm forest; **F14** - Mangrove forest; **F15** - Secondary forest; **N1** - Arid lowland scrub; **N2** - Arid montane scrub; **N3** - Semihumid/humid montane scrub; **N4** - Cerrado; **N5** - Campo grasslands; **N6** - Low, seasonally wet grassland; **N7** - Southern temperate grassland; **N8** - Northern temperate grassland; **N9** - Puna grassland; **N10** - Paramo grassland; **N11** - Riparian thickets; **N12** - River island scrub; **N13** - Pastures/agricultural lands; **N14** - Second-growth scrub; **A1** - Freshwater marshes; **A2** - Saltwater/brackish marshes; **A3** - Coastal sand beaches/mudflats; **A4** - Coastal rocky beaches; **A5** - Riverine sand beaches; **A6** - Freshwater lakes and ponds; **A7** - Alkaline lakes; **A8** - Rivers; **A9** - Streams; **A10** - Bogs; **A11** - Coastal waters; **A12** - Pelagic waters.
E - Edge (used as a modifer to particular habitats).

Sub - Subregions:
ARC - Arid Caribbean Coast; **AWA** - Altiplano and Western Andes; **BAH** - Bahamas; **BAJ** - Baja California; **CAA** - Caatinga; **CAH** - Central American Highlands; **CER** - Cerrado; **CHA** - Chaco; **CHG** - Chiapas-Guanacaste; **CHL** - Chilean Desert; **CHR** - Chiriquí; **CIS** - Cocos Island; **CMV** - Cauca-Magdalena Valley; **COC** - Cuzco-Cochabamba; **CUB** - Cuba; **DOM** - Dominica; **EAS** - Eastern Slope Andes; **FDN** - Fernando de Noronha; **GAL** - Galápagos; **GCM** - Gulf Coast-Mexico; **GRE** - Grenada; **GUA** - Guadeloupe; **GUI** - Guianan; **HIS** - Hispaniola; **HPC** - Humid Pacific Coast; **ISA** - Isla Providencia and Isla San Andrés; **JAM** - Jamaica; **JFI** - Juan Fernández Islands; **MAN** - Manabí-Tumbes; **MAR** - Marañón Valley; **MID** - Madeira-Tapajós; **MON** - Montserrat; **MRT** - Martinique; **MTC** - Marañón-Cuzco; **NMM** - Northern Mexican Mountains; **NOR** - Northern Coastal Brazil; **PAR** - Pará; **PER** - Peruvian Desert; **PUE** - Puerto Rico; **RDJ** - Rio de Janeiro-Bahia Lowlands; **RMW** - Rio Madeira West; **RNW** - Rio Negro West; **SCA** - Southern Central America; **SCT** - Santa Cruz-Tucumán; **SIN** - Sinaloa-Oaxaca; **SMH** - Southern Mexican Highlands; **SMT** - Santa Marta; **SOC** - Islas Revillagigedo (Socorro Island group); **SON** - Sonoran Desert; **SOU** - Southern Atlantic Coast; **STL** - St. Lucia; **STV** - St. Vincent; **TAC** - Tacarcuna; **VAN** - Venezuelan Andes; **VNZ** - Venezuelan Coastal Mountains; **WES** - Western Andes; **YUC** - Yucatán Peninsula.
o - Endemic to region, but not restricted to a single subregion.

Zoogeographic Regions:
AMN - Northern Amazonia; **AMS** - Southern Amazonia; **ATL** - Atlantic Forest; **BSR** - Baja-Sonora; **CAN** - Central Andes; **CDH** - Chiriquí-Darién Highlands; **CHO** - Chocó Lowlands; **CSA** - Central South America; **EPC** - Equatorial Pacific Coast; **GAN** - Greater Antilles; **GCS** - Gulf-Caribbean Slope; **LAN** - Lesser Antilles; **MAH** - Madrean Highlands; **MPL** - Mexican Plateau; **NAN** - Northern Andes; **NSA** - Northern South America; **PAM** - Pampas; **PAS** - Pacific Arid Slope; **PAT** - Patagonia; **SAN** - Southern Andes; **STP** - Subtropical Pacific; **TEP** - Tepuis.

CP -Conservation Priority:
1 - Urgent; **2** - High; **3** - Medium; **4** - Low.

RP - Research Priority:
1 - High; **2** - Medium; **3** - Low.

	Snst	Strat	Cntab	Rel	Min	Max	Micro	Habitats	Sub	Zoogeographic Regions
Ciccaba albitarsus	M	C	UM	F	1500	3000		F4		NAN, CAN
Ciccaba huhula	M	C	LT	F/P	L	900+		F1, F4, F2		AMN, AMS, CSA
Ciccaba nigrolineata	M	C	LT	F	L	1500		F1, F8, F7, F4		PAS, GCS, CHO, EPC, NSA
Ciccaba virgata	M	C	LT	F	L	2200		F1, F4, F7, F8		PAS, MAH, GCS, CDH, CHO, NAN, NSA, AMN, AMS, ATL
Strix fulvescens	H	C	MM	U	1200	3100		F4, F11	CAH	MAH
Strix hylophila	H	C	UT	U	L	2000+		F4, F1, F9	SOU	ATL
Strix occidentalis	M	C	MM	U	1250	2500		F11, F10		BSR, MAH
Strix rufipes	M	C	LS	U/F	L	1000		F7, F9		SAN, CSA
Strix varia	M	C	MM	R	1300	3100		F11, F10		MAH
Rhinoptynx clamator	L	T/U	LT	U/P	L	1400		N6, N14		PAS, GCS, NSA, AMN, AMS, CSA, ATL, PAM
Asio flammeus	L	T	UM	U/P	L	4300		N8, N7, N13, N9		GAN, EPC, NAN, CAN, SAN, NSA, CSA, PAM, PAT
Asio otus	M	C	LS	R	L	1450+		F11, F8		BSR, MAH
Asio stygius	M	C	MM	R/P	L	3100		F4, F11, F10, F1, F7		GAN, MAH, NAN, CAN, NSA, AMN, AMS, CSA
Pseudoscops grammicus	L	C	LT/HT	F	L	600+		F1, F15	JAM	GAN
Aegolius acadicus	M	C	MM	U	1900	3100		F11, F10		MAH
Aegolius harrisii	H	C	UM	U/P	1600	3100		F4, F5, F7		NAN, CAN, TEP, CSA, ATL
Aegolius ridgwayi	M	C	UM	U	1600	3300		F4, F11		MAH, CDH
CAPRIMULGIFORMES										
Steatornithidae										
Steatornis caripensis	M	C/A	HT	U/P	L	2200	R	F1, F4		CHO, NAN, CAN, NSA, TEP, AMN, AMS
Nyctibiidae										
Nyctibius aethereus	H	C	LT	U/P	L	1200		F1		CHO, AMN, AMS, ATL
Nyctibius bracteatus	H	M?	LT	R	L	L		F1		AMN, AMS
Nyctibius grandis	M	C	LT	F	L	L		F1, F8		GCS, CHO?, NSA, AMN, AMS
Nyctibius griseus	L	C	LT	C	L	1800		F1E, F15, F8, F4E, F3		GAN, PAS, GCS, CHO, EPC, NSA, AMN, AMS, CSA, ATL
Nyctibius leucopterus	H	C	LT	R?	L	L		F1		AMN, ATL
Nyctibius maculosus	H	C	MM	U	1800	2800		F4E		NAN, CAN
Caprimulgidae										
Lurocalis semitorquatus										
rufiventris	H	A	MM	U	1600	2800		F4		NAN, CAN
semitorquatus	M	A	LT	F/P	L	1700		F1, F2		PAS, GCS, NSA, AMN, AMS, ATL
Chordeiles acutipennis	L	A	LT	C	L	2500		N1, N2, N6, N14		BSR, MPL, PAS, MAH, GCS, EPC, STP, NSA, AMN, AMS, CSA, ATL
Chordeiles gundlachii	L	A	LT	F	L	600+		N14, N1	o	GAN
Chordeiles minor	L	A	LT	F	L	2500+		N8, F10		MPL, MAH, GCS
Chordeiles pusillus	M	A	LT	F/P	L	900+		N6, N5		NSA, AMN, AMS, CSA, ATL
Chordeiles rupestris	M	A	LT	F	L	700		A8, A5, N12, N14		NSA, AMN, AMS
Nyctiprogne leucopyga	M	A	LT	F/P	L	L		F8E, F3E, A8, A1		NSA, AMN, AMS
Podager nacunda	L	A	LT	F	L	1400		N6, N5, N14		NSA, AMN, AMS, CSA
Nyctidromus albicollis	L	T	LT	C	L	1700		F1E, F15, F8, F7		PAS, GCS, CHO, EPC, NSA, AMN, AMS, CSA, ATL
Phalaenoptilus nuttallii	M	T	LT	F	L	2200		N1, N2		BSR, MPL, MAH
Siphonorhis americanus	H	T?	LT	R	L	L		F7?	JAM	GAN
Siphonorhis brewsteri	M	T	LT?	U?	L	900+		F7	HIS	GAN
Otophanes mcleodii	M	T/U	UT	U	1100	2400		F11, F7	NMM	MAH
Otophanes yucatanicus	M	T?	LT	U?	L	L		F7, N1	YUC	GCS
Nyctiphrynus ocellatus	M	T	LT	F/P	L	1350		F1, F4?		GCS, CHO, NSA, AMN, AMS, CSA, ATL
Nyctiphrynus rosenbergi	H	T	LT	F	L	900		F1	o	CHO
Caprimulgus anthonyi	M	T	LT	U/P	L	800		N1		EPC, CAN
Caprimulgus candicans	H	T	LT	U/P	L	900		N5	CER	CSA

CP	RP	Notes
4	3	
4	3	Occasionally to 1,350 m (Bolivia).
4	3	Occasionally to 2,400 m (Colombia).
4	3	
4	2	Monitor.
3	3	
3	2	Distribution in Mexico poorly known.
4	3	
4	2	Distribution in Mexico poorly known.
4	3	
3	2	Survey resident populations.
4	3	
3	1	Distribution poorly known; some populations vulnerable.
3	2	
4	2	Distribution poorly known.
4	2	Locally to lowlands (southern Brazil); distribution poorly known.
4	2	Occasionally to 1,400 m (Guatemala); distribution poorly known.
4	2	
4	2	Poorly known; Atlantic Forest population threatened.
4	2	Poorly known.
4	3	
4	3	Probably contains two species.
3	1	Poorly known; Atlantic Forest population threatened?.
4	2	Distribution and status poorly known.
4	3	
4	3	Southern populations migratory.
4	3	
4	2	Winter range unknown.
4	2	Extent of breeding range uncertain.
4	3	
4	3	
4	3	
4	3	
4	3	Occasionally to 2,300 m.
4	3	
1	1	Apparently extinct.
2	1	Poorly known.
2	1	Poorly known.
3	2	Poorly known.
4	2	Regularly to 900 m.
3	2	See Robbins & Ridgely (1992) for taxonomic status.
3	2	Habitat poorly known; overgrazing a problem?
2	1	Poorly known, but in threatened habitat (campo grassland).

Abbreviations Used

Snst - Sensitivity:
L - Low; **M** - Medium; **H** - High.

Strat - Foraging Strata:
T - Terrestrial; **U** - Understory; **M** - Midstory; **C** - Canopy; **A** - Aerial; **W** - Water.

Cntab - Center of Abundance:
LT - Lower tropical; **LS** - Lower subtropical; **HT** - Hill tropical; **UT** - Upper tropical; **US** - Upper subtropical; **MM** - Middle montane; **UM** - Upper montane.

Rel - Relative Abundance:
R - Rare; **U** - Uncommon; **F** - Fairly common; **C** - Common; **P** - Patchily distributed.

Min - Minimum Elevation:
L - Lowlands; **?** - Uncertain value; numeric values in meters.

Max - Maximum Elevation:
L - Lowlands; **?** - Uncertain value; **+** - species occurs at least to given elevation but likely occurs higher; numeric values in meters.

Micro - Microhabitats:
A - Army ants; **B** - Bamboo; **T** - Treefalls; **G** - Ground bromeliads; **C** - Rocky outcrops and caves; **S** - Streamside; **V** - Vine tangles; **B/V** -Bamboo/vine tangles.

Habitats:
F1 - Tropical lowland evergreen forest; **F2** - Flooded tropical evergreen forest; **F3** - River-edge forest; **F4** - Montane evergreen forest; **F5** - Elfin forest; **F6** - *Polylepis* woodland; **F7** - Tropical deciduous forest; **F8** - Gallery forest; **F9** - Southern temperate forest; **F10** - Pine forest; **F11** - Pine-oak forest; **F12** - White sand forest; **F13** - Palm forest; **F14** - Mangrove forest; **F15** - Secondary forest; **N1** - Arid lowland scrub; **N2** - Arid montane scrub; **N3** - Semihumid/humid montane scrub; **N4** - Cerrado; **N5** - Campo grasslands; **N6** - Low, seasonally wet grassland; **N7** - Southern temperate grassland; **N8** - Northern temperate grassland; **N9** - Puna grassland; **N10** - Paramo grassland; **N11** - Riparian thickets; **N12** - River island scrub; **N13** - Pastures/agricultural lands; **N14** - Second-growth scrub; **A1** - Freshwater marshes; **A2** - Saltwater/brackish marshes; **A3** - Coastal sand beaches/mudflats; **A4** - Coastal rocky beaches; **A5** - Riverine sand beaches; **A6** - Freshwater lakes and ponds; **A7** - Alkaline lakes; **A8** - Rivers; **A9** - Streams; **A10** - Bogs; **A11** - Coastal waters; **A12** - Pelagic waters.
E - Edge (used as a modifer to particular habitats).

Sub - Subregions:
ARC - Arid Caribbean Coast; **AWA** - Altiplano and Western Andes; **BAH** - Bahamas; **BAJ** - Baja California; **CAA** - Caatinga; **CAH** - Central American Highlands; **CER** - Cerrado; **CHA** - Chaco; **CHG** - Chiapas-Guanacaste; **CHL** - Chilean Desert; **CHR** - Chiriquí; **CIS** - Cocos Island; **CMV** - Cauca-Magdalena Valley; **COC** - Cuzco-Cochabamba; **CUB** - Cuba; **DOM** - Dominica; **EAS** - Eastern Slope Andes; **FDN** - Fernando de Noronha; **GAL** - Galápagos; **GCM** - Gulf Coast-Mexico; **GRE** - Grenada; **GUA** - Guadeloupe; **GUI** - Guianan; **HIS** - Hispaniola; **HPC** - Humid Pacific Coast; **ISA** - Isla Providencia and Isla San Andrés; **JAM** - Jamaica; **JFI** - Juan Fernández Islands; **MAN** - Manabí-Tumbes; **MAR** - Marañón Valley; **MID** - Madeira-Tapajós; **MON** - Montserrat; **MRT** - Martinique; **MTC** - Marañón-Cuzco; **NMM** - Northern Mexican Mountains; **NOR** - Northern Coastal Brazil; **PAR** - Pará; **PER** - Peruvian Desert; **PUE** - Puerto Rico; **RDJ** - Rio de Janeiro-Bahia Lowlands; **RMW** - Rio Madeira West; **RNW** - Rio Negro West; **SCA** - Southern Central America; **SCT** - Santa Cruz-Tucumán; **SIN** - Sinaloa-Oaxaca; **SMH** - Southern Mexican Highlands; **SMT** - Santa Marta; **SOC** - Islas Revillagigedo (Socorro Island group); **SON** - Sonoran Desert; **SOU** - Southern Atlantic Coast; **STL** - St. Lucia; **STV** - St. Vincent; **TAC** - Tacarcuna; **VAN** - Venezuelan Andes; **VNZ** - Venezuelan Coastal Mountains; **WES** - Western Andes; **YUC** - Yucatán Peninsula.
o - Endemic to region, but not restricted to a single subregion.

Zoogeographic Regions:
AMN - Northern Amazonia; **AMS** - Southern Amazonia; **ATL** - Atlantic Forest; **BSR** - Baja-Sonora; **CAN** - Central Andes; **CDH** - Chiriquí-Darién Highlands; **CHO** - Chocó Lowlands; **CSA** - Central South America; **EPC** - Equatorial Pacific Coast; **GAN** - Greater Antilles; **GCS** - Gulf-Caribbean Slope; **LAN** - Lesser Antilles; **MAH** - Madrean Highlands; **MPL** - Mexican Plateau; **NAN** - Northern Andes; **NSA** - Northern South America; **PAM** - Pampas; **PAS** - Pacific Arid Slope; **PAT** - Patagonia; **SAN** - Southern Andes; **STP** - Subtropical Pacific; **TEP** - Tepuis.

CP -Conservation Priority:
1 - Urgent; **2** - High; **3** - Medium; **4** - Low.

RP - Research Priority:
1 - High; **2** - Medium; **3** - Low.

	Snst	Strat	Cntab	Rel	Min	Max	Micro	Habitats	Sub	Zoogeographic Regions
Caprimulgus cayennensis	L	T	LT	F	L	1000		N6, N14		LAN, GCS, NSA, AMN
Caprimulgus cubanensis	M	T?	?	F	L	2000+		F1, F10	o	GAN
Caprimulgus hirundinaceus	M	T?	LT	?	L	L?		F7	CAA	CSA
Caprimulgus longirostris	L	T	UM	F	L	4000		N2, N14, N10, N1		STP, NAN, CAN, SAN, TEP, CSA, ATL, PAT
Caprimulgus maculicaudus	M	T?	LT	F/P	L	1500		N6, N5		GCS, NSA, AMN, AMS, CSA, ATL
Caprimulgus maculosus	?	T?	LT	?	L	L		F1?	GUI	AMN
Caprimulgus nigrescens	M	T	LT	F/P	L	1100	R	F12, F1E, F8E, F3E		TEP, AMN, AMS
Caprimulgus noctitherus	M	T	LT	F	L	L		F7	PUE	GAN
Caprimulgus parvulus	L	T	LT	F	L	1000		F8, F7E, F15E		CHO, NSA, AMN, AMS, CSA, ATL
Caprimulgus ridgwayi	M	T	LT	F	L	2000		F7, N2, N1, F11?		BSR, PAS, MAH
Caprimulgus rufus										
otiosus	L	T	LT	F	L	L		F7		LAN, NSA?
rufus	L	T	LT	F	L	800		F7, F15, F8		PAS, GCS, NSA, AMN, AMS, CSA, ATL
Caprimulgus salvini										
badius	M	T?	LT	U	L	L		F7	YUC	GCS
salvini	M	T	LT	F	L	500?		F7	GCM	GCS
Caprimulgus saturatus	M	T	MM	F	1500	3100		F4, F15E	CHR	CDH
Caprimulgus sericocaudatus	M	T?	LT	R/P	L	600		F1, F8		AMS, CSA
Caprimulgus vociferus	M	T/U	MM	F	1300	3100		F10, F11		BSR, MPL, MAH
Caprimulgus whitelyi	M	T	UT	F	1300	1800		F5E, N3	o	TEP
Hydropsalis brasiliana	L	T	LT	F	L	1100		N14, N5, N6		AMS, CSA, ATL
Hydropsalis climacocerca	M	U	LT	F	L	700		N12, A8, A6		AMN, AMS
Uropsalis segmentata	M	T	UM	U	2250	3500		F5E, F4E, N10		NAN, CAN
Uropsalis lyra	M	T	UT	U	1100	2100		F4E		NAN, CAN
Macropsalis creagra	M	T	UT	U/P	600	2000+		F4E	SOU	ATL
Eleothreptus anomalus	M	T?	HT	R?	L	1100		A1?		CSA, ATL, PAM
APODIFORMES										
Apodidae										
Cypseloides cherriei	M	A	UT	R	1100	2200	R	F4		CDH, NAN
Cypseloides cryptus	M	A	UT?	U/P	L	3000		F4, F1		GCS, CDH, NAN, CAN, TEP
Cypseloides fumigatus										
fumigatus	M	A	UT	F/P	700	2100+	R	F4, F1, F9, N14		CSA, ATL
major	?	A	?	?	500?	2000?	R	F4	o	CAN
Cypseloides lemosi	L	A	UT	R/P	1000	1300	R?	F15, N14	WES	NAN
Cypseloides phelpsi	M	A	UT	F	400	1400	R	F4, F1, N6	o	TEP
Cypseloides rutilus	L	A	UT	C	800	2800	R	F4, F15, N14		MAH, CDH, NAN, CAN
Cypseloides storeri	M	A	MM	R	2500	2500		F4	SMH	MAH
Nephoecetes niger	M	A	MM	U/P	1000	3400	R	F4E, F15		GAN, LAN, MAH, CDH
Aerornis senex	M	A	LT	F/P	L	1000+	R	F1, F9, N14		CSA, ATL
Streptoprocne biscutata	M	A	LT?	F/P	L	2000+	R	F1, F4, F9, N14, F7		CSA, ATL
Streptoprocne semicollaris	L	A	MM	F	800	3000	R	F11, F7, N14	o	MAH
Streptoprocne zonaris	L	A	LT	F	L	3600	R	F4, F1, F15, N14		GAN, PAS, MAH, GCS, CDH, NAN, CAN, SAN, NSA, TEP, AMN, AMS, CSA, ATL
Chaetura andrei	L	A	LT	C	L	1600		F1E, F15, N14		NSA, CSA, ATL
Chaetura brachyura	L	A	LT	C	L	1050		F15, F1E, F7, N14		GCS, CHO, EPC, NSA, AMN, AMS
Chaetura chapmani	M	A	LT	U/P	L	1500		F1, F15, N14		GCS, NSA, AMN, AMS
Chaetura cinereiventris	M	A	UT	F	L	1800	R	F1, F4, F2, F15		LAN, GCS, CHO, EPC, NAN, CAN, NSA, TEP, AMN, AMS, ATL
Chaetura egregia	M	A	LT	F	L	1100		F1	o	AMS
Chaetura martinica	M	A	LT?	F	L	1000+		F1, F15?	o	LAN
Chaetura spinicauda	L	A	LT	C	L	1000		F1E, F15		PAS, GCS, CHO, NSA, AMN, AMS, ATL
Chaetura vauxi	M	A	LT	F	L	2800		F1, F4, F7, F15, N14		PAS, MAH, GCS, CDH, NAN, NSA
Aeronautes andecolus	L	A	UM	F	2000	3900	R	N2, N3		CAN, SAN

CP	RP	Notes
4	3	Locally to 2,100 m.
3	2	Poorly known.
3	2	Poorly known.
4	3	
3	2	Local and disjunct; may be migratory.
3	1	Taxonomy and status uncertain.
4	3	Regularly to 1,350 m?
3	2	Poorly known.
4	3	
4	3	
3	2	Status on mainland uncertain.
4	3	Locally to 1,800 m.
4	2	Poorly known.
4	3	
4	3	
3	2	Range poorly known; habitat requirements unknown.
4	3	
3	2	
4	3	Locally to 1,550 m (Bolivia).
4	3	
4	3	
4	3	Occasionally to 900 and 3,000 m.
3	2	Poorly known.
3	2	Habitat and status uncertain.
2	2	Range and status poorly known.
3	2	Range and status uncertain; breeding range poorly known.
4	2	Nonbreeding range poorly known.
3	2	Poorly known.
2	1	Poorly known.
4	3	
3	2	Occasionally to lowlands and 3,500 m.
3	1	Recently described (Navarro et al. 1992); poorly known.
3	2	Range south of U. S. poorly known.
3	1	Local as breeder; dams may affect breeding populations; migratory?
3	2	Range poorly known; monitor.
4	3	Wanders to coast.
4	3	
4	3	
4	3	
4	2	Range poorly known.
4	3	
4	3	Range poorly known.
4	3	
4	3	Occasionally to 1,500 m.
4	3	
4	3	Occasionally to Pacific coast.

Abbreviations Used

Snst - Sensitivity:
L - Low; **M** - Medium; **H** - High.

Strat - Foraging Strata:
T - Terrestrial; **U** - Understory; **M** - Midstory; **C** - Canopy; **A** - Aerial; **W** - Water.

Cntab - Center of Abundance:
LT - Lower tropical; **LS** - Lower subtropical; **HT** - Hill tropical; **UT** - Upper tropical; **US** - Upper subtropical; **MM** - Middle montane; **UM** - Upper montane.

Rel - Relative Abundance:
R - Rare; **U** - Uncommon; **F** - Fairly common; **C** - Common; **P** - Patchily distributed.

Min - Minimum Elevation:
L - Lowlands; **?** - Uncertain value; numeric values in meters.

Max - Maximum Elevation:
L - Lowlands; **?** - Uncertain value; **+** - species occurs at least to given elevation but likely occurs higher; numeric values in meters.

Micro - Microhabitats:
A - Army ants; **B** - Bamboo; **T** - Treefalls; **G** - Ground bromeliads; **C** - Rocky outcrops and caves; **S** - Streamside; **V** - Vine tangles; **B/V** -Bamboo/vine tangles.

Habitats:
F1 - Tropical lowland evergreen forest; **F2** - Flooded tropical evergreen forest; **F3** - River-edge forest; **F4** - Montane evergreen forest; **F5** - Elfin forest; **F6** - *Polylepis* woodland; **F7** - Tropical deciduous forest; **F8** - Gallery forest; **F9** - Southern temperate forest; **F10** - Pine forest; **F11** - Pine-oak forest; **F12** - White sand forest; **F13** - Palm forest; **F14** - Mangrove forest; **F15** - Secondary forest; **N1** - Arid lowland scrub; **N2** - Arid montane scrub; **N3** - Semihumid/humid montane scrub; **N4** - Cerrado; **N5** - Campo grasslands; **N6** - Low, seasonally wet grassland; **N7** - Southern temperate grassland; **N8** - Northern temperate grassland; **N9** - Puna grassland; **N10** - Paramo grassland; **N11** - Riparian thickets; **N12** - River island scrub; **N13** - Pastures/agricultural lands; **N14** - Second-growth scrub; **A1** - Freshwater marshes; **A2** - Saltwater/brackish marshes; **A3** - Coastal sand beaches/mudflats; **A4** - Coastal rocky beaches; **A5** - Riverine sand beaches; **A6** - Freshwater lakes and ponds; **A7** - Alkaline lakes; **A8** - Rivers; **A9** - Streams; **A10** - Bogs; **A11** - Coastal waters; **A12** - Pelagic waters.
E - Edge (used as a modifer to particular habitats).

Sub - Subregions:
ARC - Arid Caribbean Coast; **AWA** - Altiplano and Western Andes; **BAH** - Bahamas; **BAJ** - Baja California; **CAA** - Caatinga; **CAH** - Central American Highlands; **CER** - Cerrado; **CHA** - Chaco; **CHG** - Chiapas-Guanacaste; **CHL** - Chilean Desert; **CHR** - Chiriquí; **CIS** - Cocos Island; **CMV** - Cauca-Magdalena Valley; **COC** - Cuzco-Cochabamba; **CUB** - Cuba; **DOM** - Dominica; **EAS** - Eastern Slope Andes; **FDN** - Fernando de Noronha; **GAL** - Galápagos; **GCM** - Gulf Coast-Mexico; **GRE** - Grenada; **GUA** - Guadeloupe; **GUI** - Guianan; **HIS** - Hispaniola; **HPC** - Humid Pacific Coast; **ISA** - Isla Providencia and Isla San Andrés; **JAM** - Jamaica; **JFI** - Juan Fernández Islands; **MAN** - Manabí-Tumbes; **MAR** - Marañón Valley; **MID** - Madeira-Tapajós; **MON** - Montserrat; **MRT** - Martinique; **MTC** - Marañón-Cuzco; **NMM** - Northern Mexican Mountains; **NOR** - Northern Coastal Brazil; **PAR** - Pará; **PER** - Peruvian Desert; **PUE** - Puerto Rico; **RDJ** - Rio de Janeiro-Bahia Lowlands; **RMW** - Rio Madeira West; **RNW** - Rio Negro West; **SCA** - Southern Central America; **SCT** - Santa Cruz-Tucumán; **SIN** - Sinaloa-Oaxaca; **SMH** - Southern Mexican Highlands; **SMT** - Santa Marta; **SOC** - Islas Revillagigedo (Socorro Island group); **SON** - Sonoran Desert; **SOU** - Southern Atlantic Coast; **STL** - St. Lucia; **STV** - St. Vincent; **TAC** - Tacarcuna; **VAN** - Venezuelan Andes; **VNZ** - Venezuelan Coastal Mountains; **WES** - Western Andes; **YUC** - Yucatán Peninsula.
o - Endemic to region, but not restricted to a single subregion.

Zoogeographic Regions:
AMN - Northern Amazonia; **AMS** - Southern Amazonia; **ATL** - Atlantic Forest; **BSR** - Baja-Sonora; **CAN** - Central Andes; **CDH** - Chiriquí-Darién Highlands; **CHO** - Chocó Lowlands; **CSA** - Central South America; **EPC** - Equatorial Pacific Coast; **GAN** - Greater Antilles; **GCS** - Gulf-Caribbean Slope; **LAN** - Lesser Antilles; **MAH** - Madrean Highlands; **MPL** - Mexican Plateau; **NAN** - Northern Andes; **NSA** - Northern South America; **PAM** - Pampas; **PAS** - Pacific Arid Slope; **PAT** - Patagonia; **SAN** - Southern Andes; **STP** - Subtropical Pacific; **TEP** - Tepuis.

CP -Conservation Priority:
1 - Urgent; **2** - High; **3** - Medium; **4** - Low.

RP - Research Priority:
1 - High; **2** - Medium; **3** - Low.

	Snst	Strat	Cntab	Rel	Min	Max	Micro	Habitats	Sub	Zoogeographic Regions
Aeronautes montivagus	M	A	MM	F/P	500	2600	R	F4, F15, F1		NAN, CAN, TEP
Aeronautes saxatalis	L	A	MM	C	1200	2800	R	N2, F11, N14		BSR, MPL, MAH
Tachornis furcata	L?	A	LT	?	L	L		F1, F15, N14	ARC	NSA
Tachornis phoenicobia	L	A	LT	F	L	L		N6, N14	o	GAN
Tachornis squamata	L	A	LT	C	L	900		F13, F3, N6, N14		NSA, AMN, AMS, CSA, ATL
Panyptila cayennensis	M	A	LT	U/P	L	1200		F1, F15		PAS, GCS, NSA, AMN, AMS, ATL
Panyptila sanctihieronymi	M	A	UT	U/P	600	1850	R	F4, F10, F15, N2	o	MAH
Trochilidae										
Doryfera johannae	M	U/M	HT	U	400	1600	R	F4, F1		NAN, CAN, TEP
Doryfera ludoviciae	M	U/M	MM	U	1200	2800	R	F4		CDH, NAN, CAN
Androdon aequatorialis	M	U/M	UT	U	750	1550		F4, F1		CDH, CHO, NAN
Ramphodon naevius	M	U	LT	F	L	900		F1, F15	SOU	ATL
Glaucis aenea	H	U	LT	F	L	800		F1, F15		GCS, CHO
Glaucis dohrnii	H	U	LT	R	L	L	S?	F1	RDJ	ATL
Glaucis hirsuta	L	U	LT	F	L	1100		F1, F15, F2		LAN, GCS, CHO, AMN, AMS, ATL
Threnetes leucurus	M	U	LT	U	L	1050		F1, F2, F3		AMN, AMS
Threnetes loehkeni	H	U?	LT	?	L	L		F1	GUI	AMN
Threnetes niger	?	U?	LT	?	L	L		F1?	GUI	AMN
Threnetes ruckeri	H	U	LT	U	L	1050		F1, F15		GCS, CHO, NSA
Phaethornis anthophilus	L	U	LT	F	L	900		F1, F15		GCS, NSA
Phaethornis augusti	M	U	UT	F	L	1600		F4, F1, F7, F15		NAN, NSA, TEP
Phaethornis bourcieri	H	U/M	LT	F	L	1600		F1, F4		TEP, AMN, AMS
Phaethornis eurynome	M	U	HT	F	300	2000		F4, F1	SOU	ATL
Phaethornis gounellei	?	U?	LT	?	L	900+		F7	CAA	CSA
Phaethornis griseogularis										
griseogularis	M	U	UT	F	500	1800		F4, F15		NAN, TEP
porcullae	M	U	UT	U/P	1100?	2100?		F7, F4		NAN, CAN
Phaethornis guy	M	U	UT	F	800	2000		F4		CDH, NAN, CAN
Phaethornis hispidus	M	U	LT	C	L	L		F2, F3, F8		AMN, AMS
Phaethornis idaliae	M	U	LT	F	L	L		F1	RDJ	ATL
Phaethornis koepckeae	H	U	HT	F	500	1300		F1, F4	MTC	CAN
Phaethornis longuemareus	M	U	LT	F	L	1200		F1, F15		PAS, GCS, CHO, NSA, AMN, AMS
Phaethornis malaris	H	U	LT	F	L	500+		F1	GUI	AMN
Phaethornis nattereri	M	U	LT	?	L	1000+		F7	CER	CSA
Phaethornis philippii	H	U	LT	F	L	L		F1	o	AMS
Phaethornis pretrei	L	U	LT	F	L	1900		F7, F1, F15		CAN, CSA, ATL
Phaethornis ruber	M	U	LT	C	L	900+		F1, F2, F15		AMN, AMS, ATL
Phaethornis squalidus	M	U	LT	F	L	1100		F1, F4, F8, F15		NSA, AMN, AMS, ATL
Phaethornis stuarti	H	U	HT	F/P	500	1050	B	F1	o	CAN
Phaethornis subochraceus	M	U	LT	U	L	700		F7	CHA	CSA
Phaethornis superciliosus										
margarettae	H	U	LT	R	L	L		F1	o	ATL
superciliosus	H	U	LT	C	L	1400		F1, F4, F7		PAS, MAH, GCS, CHO, NSA, AMN, AMS
Phaethornis syrmatophorus	M	U	MM	F	1100	2400		F4		NAN, CAN
Phaethornis yaruqui	H	U	LT	C	L	1100		F1, F4	o	CHO
Eutoxeres aquila	M	U	UT	U	L	2100		F4, F1		GCS, CHO, NAN
Eutoxeres condamini	M	U	UT	U	L	2750		F4, F1		NAN, CAN
Phaeochroa cuvierii	L	M/C	LT	C	L	1200		F15, N14, F1E		GCS, NSA
Campylopterus curvipennis										
curvipennis	M	U/M	LT	F	L	1400		F1, F15	o	GCS
excellens	M	U/M	?	F	L?	1050+		F1, F4	GCM	GCS
Campylopterus duidae	L	U/M	MM	C	1200	2400		F4, F5, N3	o	TEP

CP	RP	Notes
4	3	
4	3	Locally to lowlands.
4	2	
4	3	
4	3	
4	3	Occasionally to 1,500 m.
3	2	Occasionally to 500 m; monitor.
4	3	Occasionally to lowlands and 2,000 m.
4	3	Locally to 750 m.
3	2	Locally to lowlands (Pacific Colombia).
3	2	
4	3	
1	1	Deforestation; habitat requirements poorly known; survey.
4	3	
4	3	
3	1	Probably pale morph of *T. niger*.
3	2	Poorly known.
4	3	Wanders to 1,200 m.
4	3	Occasionally to 1,500 m.
4	3	Occasionally to 2,500 m?
4	3	Montane in the Tepuis.
4	3	
3	2	Poorly known.
4	3	
3	2	
4	3	Locally to 500 m, occasionally to 3,000 m.
4	3	Occasionally to 900 m.
3	2	
3	2	Rapid deforestation in its elevational range.
4	3	Locally to 1,500 m.
4	3	
3	2	Poorly known.
4	3	
4	3	Locally to 2,500 m in Bolivia.
4	3	
4	2	Probably contains two species.
3	2	Relationship to *P. ruber*, and of race *longipennis* uncertain.
3	2	Poorly known.
1	1	Deforestation; no viable populations known; survey.
4	3	Locally to 1,900 m; may contains multiple species.
4	3	Occasionally to 800 m.
4	3	Occasionally to 2,500 m.
4	3	Most numerous 900 to 1,400 m in South America, 300 to 1,000 m in Central America.
4	3	Mainly above 700 m.
4	3	
4	3	
2	2	Taxonomic status uncertain; deforestation.
4	3	

Abbreviations Used

Snst - Sensitivity:
L - Low; **M** - Medium; **H** - High.

Strat - Foraging Strata:
T - Terrestrial; **U** - Understory; **M** - Midstory; **C** - Canopy; **A** - Aerial; **W** - Water.

Cntab - Center of Abundance:
LT - Lower tropical; **LS** - Lower subtropical; **HT** - Hill tropical; **UT** - Upper tropical; **US** - Upper subtropical; **MM** - Middle montane; **UM** - Upper montane.

Rel - Relative Abundance:
R - Rare; **U** - Uncommon; **F** - Fairly common; **C** - Common; **P** - Patchily distributed.

Min - Minimum Elevation:
L - Lowlands; **?** - Uncertain value; numeric values in meters.

Max - Maximum Elevation:
L - Lowlands; **?** - Uncertain value; **+** - species occurs at least to given elevation but likely occurs higher; numeric values in meters.

Micro - Microhabitats:
A - Army ants; **B** - Bamboo; **T** - Treefalls; **G** - Ground bromeliads; **C** - Rocky outcrops and caves; **S** - Streamside; **V** - Vine tangles; **B/V** -Bamboo/vine tangles.

Habitats:
F1 - Tropical lowland evergreen forest; **F2** - Flooded tropical evergreen forest; **F3** - River-edge forest; **F4** - Montane evergreen forest; **F5** - Elfin forest; **F6** - *Polylepis* woodland; **F7** - Tropical deciduous forest; **F8** - Gallery forest; **F9** - Southern temperate forest; **F10** - Pine forest; **F11** - Pine-oak forest; **F12** - White sand forest; **F13** - Palm forest; **F14** - Mangrove forest; **F15** - Secondary forest; **N1** - Arid lowland scrub; **N2** - Arid montane scrub; **N3** - Semihumid/humid montane scrub; **N4** - Cerrado; **N5** - Campo grasslands; **N6** - Low, seasonally wet grassland; **N7** - Southern temperate grassland; **N8** - Northern temperate grassland; **N9** - Puna grassland; **N10** - Paramo grassland; **N11** - Riparian thickets; **N12** - River island scrub; **N13** - Pastures/agricultural lands; **N14** - Second-growth scrub; **A1** - Freshwater marshes; **A2** - Saltwater/brackish marshes; **A3** - Coastal sand beaches/mudflats; **A4** - Coastal rocky beaches; **A5** - Riverine sand beaches; **A6** - Freshwater lakes and ponds; **A7** - Alkaline lakes; **A8** - Rivers; **A9** - Streams; **A10** - Bogs; **A11** - Coastal waters; **A12** - Pelagic waters.
E - Edge (used as a modifer to particular habitats).

Sub - Subregions:
ARC - Arid Caribbean Coast; **AWA** - Altiplano and Western Andes; **BAH** - Bahamas; **BAJ** - Baja California; **CAA** - Caatinga; **CAH** - Central American Highlands; **CER** - Cerrado; **CHA** - Chaco; **CHG** - Chiapas-Guanacaste; **CHL** - Chilean Desert; **CHR** - Chiriquí; **CIS** - Cocos Island; **CMV** - Cauca-Magdalena Valley; **COC** - Cuzco-Cochabamba; **CUB** - Cuba; **DOM** - Dominica; **EAS** - Eastern Slope Andes; **FDN** - Fernando de Noronha; **GAL** - Galápagos; **GCM** - Gulf Coast-Mexico; **GRE** - Grenada; **GUA** - Guadeloupe; **GUI** - Guianan; **HIS** - Hispaniola; **HPC** - Humid Pacific Coast; **ISA** - Isla Providencia and Isla San Andrés; **JAM** - Jamaica; **JFI** - Juan Fernández Islands; **MAN** - Manabí-Tumbes; **MAR** - Marañón Valley; **MID** - Madeira-Tapajós; **MON** - Montserrat; **MRT** - Martinique; **MTC** - Marañón-Cuzco; **NMM** - Northern Mexican Mountains; **NOR** - Northern Coastal Brazil; **PAR** - Pará; **PER** - Peruvian Desert; **PUE** - Puerto Rico; **RDJ** - Rio de Janeiro-Bahia Lowlands; **RMW** - Rio Madeira West; **RNW** - Rio Negro West; **SCA** - Southern Central America; **SCT** - Santa Cruz-Tucumán; **SIN** - Sinaloa-Oaxaca; **SMH** - Southern Mexican Highlands; **SMT** - Santa Marta; **SOC** - Islas Revillagigedo (Socorro Island group); **SON** - Sonoran Desert; **SOU** - Southern Atlantic Coast; **STL** - St. Lucia; **STV** - St. Vincent; **TAC** - Tacarcuna; **VAN** - Venezuelan Andes; **VNZ** - Venezuelan Coastal Mountains; **WES** - Western Andes; **YUC** - Yucatán Peninsula.
o - Endemic to region, but not restricted to a single subregion.

Zoogeographic Regions:
AMN - Northern Amazonia; **AMS** - Southern Amazonia; **ATL** - Atlantic Forest; **BSR** - Baja-Sonora; **CAN** - Central Andes; **CDH** - Chiriquí-Darién Highlands; **CHO** - Chocó Lowlands; **CSA** - Central South America; **EPC** - Equatorial Pacific Coast; **GAN** - Greater Antilles; **GCS** - Gulf-Caribbean Slope; **LAN** - Lesser Antilles; **MAH** - Madrean Highlands; **MPL** - Mexican Plateau; **NAN** - Northern Andes; **NSA** - Northern South America; **PAM** - Pampas; **PAS** - Pacific Arid Slope; **PAT** - Patagonia; **SAN** - Southern Andes; **STP** - Subtropical Pacific; **TEP** - Tepuis.

CP -Conservation Priority:
1 - Urgent; **2** - High; **3** - Medium; **4** - Low.

RP - Research Priority:
1 - High; **2** - Medium; **3** - Low.

	Snst	Strat	Cntab	Rel	Min	Max	Micro	Habitats	Sub	Zoogeographic Regions
Campylopterus ensipennis	M	U/M	UT	F	500	1850		F4	VNZ	NAN
Campylopterus falcatus	M	U/M	MM	U/P	900	3000		F4, F15	o	NAN
Campylopterus hemileucurus	M	U/M	UT	F	900	2400		F4		MAH, CDH
Campylopterus hyperythrus	L	U/M	MM	F	1200	2600		F4	o	TEP
Campylopterus largipennis	M	U/M	LT	U	L	900		F3, F1, F15		AMN, AMS, CSA
Campylopterus phainopeplus	?	U/M	UT	F	1200	3500		F4, F15	SMT	NAN
Campylopterus rufus	M	U/M	UT	U	950	2000		F4, F15	CAH	MAH
Campylopterus villaviscensio	M	U/M	UT	F	1050	1500		F4, F5		NAN, CAN
Eupetomena macroura	L	U/C	LT	F	L	1800		N4, N14, F7		AMN, AMS, CSA, ATL
Florisuga mellivora	L	M/C	LT	F	L	900		F1, F15		PAS?, GCS, CHO, AMN, AMS
Melanotrochilus fuscus	M	M/C	HT	F	L	1250		F1, F4, F15	o	ATL
Colibri coruscans	L	U/C	MM	C	1300	3600		F15, N14, N3, F4		NAN, CAN, TEP
Colibri delphinae	M	M/C	UT	U/P	600	2500		F4, F15		MAH, CDH, NAN, CAN, TEP, CSA
Colibri serrirostris	L	U/M	UT	C	L	2100+		N4, F7, N14		CAN, CSA, ATL
Colibri thalassinus	L	M/C	UT	C	1400	3000		F11, F15, N14		MAH, CDH, NAN, CAN
Anthracothorax dominicus	L	M/C	LT	C	L	1500		F1, F7, F15	o	GAN
Anthracothorax mango	L	M/C	LT	F	L	L		F1, F15	JAM	GAN
Anthracothorax nigricollis	L	M/C	LT	F	L	1000		F15, F8, F1E, N14		GCS, NSA, AMN, AMS, CSA, ATL
Anthracothorax prevostii	L	M/C	LT	F	L	1000		F15, F8		PAS, GCS, EPC, NSA
Anthracothorax viridigula	L	M/C	LT	U	L	L		F15, F1E, N14		AMN, AMS
Anthracothorax viridis	L	M/C	HT	U	L	900		F1, F15	PUE	GAN
Avocettula recurvirostris	H	?	LT	R/P	L	L		F1		AMN, AMS
Eulampis jugularis	M	M/C	HT	C	L	1100		F1, F15	o	LAN
Sericotes holosericeus	L	U/C	LT	C	L	900		N14, F15		GAN, LAN
Chrysolampis mosquitus	L	C	LT	U	L	1300		F8, F7, N6		NSA, AMN, CSA
Orthorhyncus cristatus	L	U/C	LT	C	L	1000		N14, F15, F1		GAN, LAN
Klais guimeti	M	U	UT	U/P	300	1400		F4, F1, F15		GCS, CDH, NAN, CAN
Abeillia abeillei	M	U/M	UT	U	1000	1850		F4, F15	CAH	MAH
Stephanoxis lalandi	M	M/C	UT	U	L	2150		N14, F15, F4	SOU	ATL
Lophornis chalybea	L	C	LT	U	L	600		F3, F1E, F15		AMN, AMS, ATL
Lophornis delattrei										
brachylopha	M	C	UT?	R	900	1800		F4	SMH	MAH
delattrei	M	C	UT	R/P	L	2000		F15, F1, F4E		GCS, CDH, NAN, NSA, AMN?, AMS
Lophornis gouldii	L	C	LT	?	L	L		F15, F8		AMS, CSA
Lophornis magnifica	L	C	LT	U	L	1100		F15, F1		CSA, ATL
Lophornis ornata	L	C	LT	U	L	950		F15, F8, F1E		NSA, TEP, AMN
Lophornis pavonina	M	C	UT	U	1100	2000		F15, F4	o	TEP
Lophornis stictolopha	M	C	HT	R/P	500	1300		F15, F1, F7		NSA, AMN
Paphosia adorabilis	L	C	HT	U	300	1200		F1E, F15, N14	CHR	CDH
Paphosia helenae	M	C	UT	U	300	1450		F4, F1, F15		MAH, CDH
Popelairia conversii	M	C	UT	U	700	1400		F4, F1E		GCS, CDH, CHO, NAN
Popelairia langsdorffi	M	C	LT	U	L	800		F1, F15		AMN, AMS, ATL
Popelairia letitiae	?	C?	LT?	R?	L?	L?		F1?	o	?
Popelairia popelairii	M	C	UT	U	500	1200		F4, F1		NAN, CAN, AMN, AMS
Discosura longicauda	M	C	LT	U	L	700		F1, F15		AMN, AMS, ATL
Chlorestes notatus	L	U/C	LT	F	L	1000		F3, F8, F15, F7?		NSA, AMN, AMS, CSA, ATL
Chlorostilbon alice	L	U/C	UT	F	750	1800		F4E, F15, F1	VNZ	NAN
Chlorostilbon assimilis	L	U/C	LT	C	L	800+		F1E, N14, F15	HPC	GCS
Chlorostilbon aureoventris	L	U/C	LT	C	L	2500		N14, F1E, F4E, F15, N11		CSA, ATL, PAM
Chlorostilbon canivetii	L	U/C	LT	C	L	1800		F1E, F8, F7, N14, F15		PAS, MAH, GCS
Chlorostilbon gibsoni	L	U/C	LT	U/P	L	2300		F7, N1, F15		NAN, NSA
Chlorostilbon maugaeus	L	U/C	HT	C	L	1000+		F4, F1, F7, F15, N14	PUE	GAN
Chlorostilbon mellisugus	L	U/M	LT	C	L	2200		F4E, F15, F1E, N14, F8		NAN, NSA, AMN, AMS

CP	RP	Notes
3	2	Monitor.
4	3	
3	3	Occasionally to lowlands; probably declining; monitor.
4	3	
4	3	Occasionally to 1,650 m (Bolivia).
3	2	Occasionally to 4,800 m; elevational movements; breeds at upper elevations?
3	2	Deforestation; monitor.
3	2	Deforestation; survey.
4	3	
4	3	Occasionally to 1,600 m.
4	3	Locally to 1,800 m+; leaves high elevations in winter.
4	3	Occasionally to 600 m.
4	2	Occasionally to lowlands and 3,350 m; movements poorly understood.
4	3	
4	3	Seasonally to 900 m; occasionally to 600 m; may contain two species.
4	3	Occasionally to 2,200 m.
4	3	
4	3	Occasionally to 1,750 m (Colombia).
4	3	
4	3	
4	3	Mainly above 400 m.
4	2	Poorly known.
4	3	Mainly montane.
4	3	
4	3	Occasionally to 1,750 m (Colombia).
4	3	
4	3	Occasionally to lowlands and 1,800 m.
3	3	Deforestation; survey.
4	3	Mainly montane except in Paraná drainage.
4	3	
2	2	Poorly known; deforestation.
3	2	Distribution poorly known.
4	3	
4	3	
4	3	
4	3	Occasionally to 500 m?
4	3	
3	2	Survey.
4	3	Occasionally to lowlands.
4	3	Occasionally to lowlands.
4	3	
3	1	Known from two specimens "from Bolivia."
4	3	
4	3	
4	3	
4	3	
4	3	
4	3	
4	3	May contain multiple species.
4	3	
4	3	
4	3	Locally to 2,700 m.

Abbreviations Used

Snst - Sensitivity:
L - Low; **M** - Medium; **H** - High.

Strat - Foraging Strata:
T - Terrestrial; **U** - Understory; **M** - Midstory; **C** - Canopy; **A** - Aerial; **W** - Water.

Cntab - Center of Abundance:
LT - Lower tropical; **LS** - Lower subtropical; **HT** - Hill tropical; **UT** - Upper tropical; **US** - Upper subtropical; **MM** - Middle montane; **UM** - Upper montane.

Rel - Relative Abundance:
R - Rare; **U** - Uncommon; **F** Fairly common; **C** - Common; **P** - Patchily distributed.

Min - Minimum Elevation:
L - Lowlands; **?** - Uncertain value; numeric values in meters.

Max - Maximum Elevation:
L - Lowlands; **?** - Uncertain value; **+** - species occurs at least to given elevation but likely occurs higher; numeric values in meters.

Micro - Microhabitats:
A - Army ants; **B** - Bamboo; **T** - Treefalls; **G** - Ground bromeliads; **C** - Rocky outcrops and caves; **S** - Streamside; **V** - Vine tangles; **B/V** -Bamboo/vine tangles.

Habitats:
F1 - Tropical lowland evergreen forest; **F2** - Flooded tropical evergreen forest; **F3** - River-edge forest; **F4** - Montane evergreen forest; **F5** - Elfin forest; **F6** - *Polylepis* woodland; **F7** - Tropical deciduous forest; **F8** - Gallery forest; **F9** - Southern temperate forest; **F10** - Pine forest; **F11** - Pine-oak forest; **F12** - White sand forest; **F13** - Palm forest; **F14** - Mangrove forest; **F15** - Secondary forest; **N1** - Arid lowland scrub; **N2** - Arid montane scrub; **N3** - Semihumid/humid montane scrub; **N4** - Cerrado; **N5** - Campo grasslands; **N6** - Low, seasonally wet grassland; **N7** - Southern temperate grassland; **N8** - Northern temperate grassland; **N9** - Puna grassland; **N10** - Paramo grassland; **N11** - Riparian thickets; **N12** - River island scrub; **N13** - Pastures/agricultural lands; **N14** - Second-growth scrub; **A1** - Freshwater marshes; **A2** - Saltwater/brackish marshes; **A3** - Coastal sand beaches/mudflats; **A4** - Coastal rocky beaches; **A5** - Riverine sand beaches; **A6** - Freshwater lakes and ponds; **A7** - Alkaline lakes; **A8** - Rivers; **A9** - Streams; **A10** - Bogs; **A11** - Coastal waters; **A12** - Pelagic waters.
E - Edge (used as a modifer to particular habitats).

Sub - Subregions:
ARC - Arid Caribbean Coast; **AWA** - Altiplano and Western Andes; **BAH** - Bahamas; **BAJ** - Baja California; **CAA** - Caatinga; **CAH** - Central American Highlands; **CER** - Cerrado; **CHA** - Chaco; **CHG** - Chiapas-Guanacaste; **CHL** - Chilean Desert; **CHR** - Chiriquí; **CIS** - Cocos Island; **CMV** - Cauca-Magdalena Valley; **COC** - Cuzco-Cochabamba; **CUB** - Cuba; **DOM** - Dominica; **EAS** - Eastern Slope Andes; **FDN** - Fernando de Noronha; **GAL** - Galápagos; **GCM** - Gulf Coast-Mexico; **GRE** - Grenada; **GUA** - Guadeloupe; **GUI** - Guianan; **HIS** - Hispaniola; **HPC** - Humid Pacific Coast; **ISA** - Isla Providencia and Isla San Andrés; **JAM** - Jamaica; **JFI** - Juan Fernández Islands; **MAN** - Manabí-Tumbes; **MAR** - Marañón Valley; **MID** - Madeira-Tapajós; **MON** - Montserrat; **MRT** - Martinique; **MTC** - Marañón-Cuzco; **NMM** - Northern Mexican Mountains; **NOR** - Northern Coastal Brazil; **PAR** - Pará; **PER** - Peruvian Desert; **PUE** - Puerto Rico; **RDJ** - Rio de Janeiro-Bahia Lowlands; **RMW** - Rio Madeira West; **RNW** - Rio Negro West; **SCA** - Southern Central America; **SCT** - Santa Cruz-Tucumán; **SIN** - Sinaloa-Oaxaca; **SMH** - Southern Mexican Highlands; **SMT** - Santa Marta; **SOC** - Islas Revillagigedo (Socorro Island group); **SON** - Sonoran Desert; **SOU** - Southern Atlantic Coast; **STL** - St. Lucia; **STV** - St. Vincent; **TAC** - Tacarcuna; **VAN** - Venezuelan Andes; **VNZ** - Venezuelan Coastal Mountains; **WES** - Western Andes; **YUC** - Yucatán Peninsula.
o - Endemic to region, but not restricted to a single subregion.

Zoogeographic Regions:
AMN - Northern Amazonia; **AMS** - Southern Amazonia; **ATL** - Atlantic Forest; **BSR** - Baja-Sonora; **CAN** - Central Andes; **CDH** - Chiriquí-Darién Highlands; **CHO** - Chocó Lowlands; **CSA** - Central South America; **EPC** - Equatorial Pacific Coast; **GAN** - Greater Antilles; **GCS** - Gulf-Caribbean Slope; **LAN** - Lesser Antilles; **MAH** - Madrean Highlands; **MPL** - Mexican Plateau; **NAN** - Northern Andes; **NSA** - Northern South America; **PAM** - Pampas; **PAS** - Pacific Arid Slope; **PAT** - Patagonia; **SAN** - Southern Andes; **STP** - Subtropical Pacific; **TEP** - Tepuis.

CP -Conservation Priority:
1 - Urgent; **2** - High; **3** - Medium; **4** - Low.

RP - Research Priority:
1 - High; **2** - Medium; **3** - Low.

	Snst	Strat	Cntab	Rel	Min	Max	Micro	Habitats	Sub	Zoogeographic Regions
Chlorostilbon poortmanni	L	U/C	UT	U	800	2800		F4E, F1E, F15, N14?		NAN, NSA
Chlorostilbon ricordii	L	U/C	LT	C	L	1200+		F1, F15, N10, F10	o	GAN
Chlorostilbon russatus	M	U/C	UT	U/P	600	2600		F4E, N14	o	NAN
Chlorostilbon stenura	L	U/C	UT	F	1000	3000		F4E, F15, N14	o	NAN
Chlorostilbon swainsonii	L	U/C	UT	C	L	2400+		F4, F1, F15, N14	HIS	GAN
Cynanthus latirostris	L	U/M	UT	F	L	2100+		F7, F8		BSR, PAS, MAH, GCS
Cynanthus sordidus	L	U/M	UT	F	900	2250		N2, F8	SMH	MAH
Cyanophaia bicolor	M	U/C	HT	F	L	900+		F1, F15	o	LAN
Thalurania colombica										
colombica	M	U/M	LT	C	L	1900		F1, F15, F4, F7		GCS, CHO, NAN, NSA
hypochlora	M	U/M	LT	C	L	800		F7	MAN	EPC
ridgwayi	M	U/M	MM	F\P	200	2100?		F4, F1, F15	NMM	MAH
Thalurania furcata	M	U/M	LT	C	L	1700		F1, F15, F4		NAN, CAN, NSA, AMN, AMS, CSA
Thalurania glaucopis	M	U/M	LT	C	L	1200		F1, F4, F15	o	ATL
Thalurania watertonii	M	U	LT	?	L	700+		F1, F15?		AMS, ATL
Panterpe insignis	M	U/M	MM	C	1400	3100		F4E, N10, N14	CHR	CDH
Damophila julie	M	U/M	LT	F	L	900		F1E, F15, F7		GCS, CHO, EPC, NSA
Lepidopyga coeruleogularis	L	U	LT	U/P	L	700		F1E, F15E, N14		GCS, NSA
Lepidopyga goudoti	M	U/C	LT	F	L	1600		F7, F15, N1	o	NSA
Lepidopyga lilliae	M?	U/C	LT	R?	L	L		F14	ARC	NSA
Hylocharis chrysura	M	U/M	LT	F	L	1100		F8E, N4		CSA, PAM
Hylocharis cyanus	L	U/C	LT	F	L	1000		F1E, F3, F12, F15, F8		NSA, AMN, AMS, CSA, ATL
Hylocharis eliciae	M	U/C	LT	F	L	1100		F1, F8, F15		PAS, GCS
Hylocharis grayi	M	U/C	LT	U	L	2000		F1E, F15, F14?		CHO, NSA
Hylocharis leucotis	M	U/C	MM	C	900	3100+		F10, F11	o	MAH
Hylocharis sapphirina	M	U/C	LT	F	L	L		F1E, F15		NSA?, AMN, AMS, CSA, ATL
Hylocharis xantusii	M	U/M	LT	F	L	1900		N1, N2	BAJ	BSR
Chrysuronia oenone	L	U/C	LT	U	L	1650		F1E, F4E, F15, F8, F3		NAN, CAN, NSA, AMN, AMS
Goldmania violiceps	H	U	HT	F	600	1000		F1	TAC	CDH
Goethalsia bella	H	U	UT	U	600	1650		F4	TAC	CDH
Trochilus polytmus	L	U/C	UT	C	L	1500		F4, F1, F15	JAM	GAN
Leucochloris albicollis	L	U/C	HT	C	L	2000+		F4E, F1E, F15, F9	SOU	ATL
Polytmus guainumbi	M	U	LT	F	L	600		N6, N5		NSA, AMN, AMS, CSA, ATL
Polytmus milleri	M	U	UT	F	1300	2200		N6?, F4E?	o	TEP
Polytmus theresiae	M	U	LT	U/P	L	L		N6, F8E, N14		NSA, AMN, AMS
Leucippus baeri	M	U/M	LT	F	L	L?		N1, F7	MAN	EPC
Leucippus chlorocercus	M	U/C	LT	F	L	L		N12	RNW	AMN
Leucippus fallax	M	U/C	LT	F	L	800		N1, F7, F14	ARC	NSA
Leucippus taczanowskii	M	U/M	LT	F	L	1500		N1, F7		EPC, CAN
Taphrospilus hypostictus	M	U	HT	U	750	1350		F4, F1		NAN, CAN
Amazilia amabilis	L	U	LT	F	L	L		F1E, F15		GCS, CHO, NSA
Amazilia amazilia	L	U/M	LT	C	L	1200		F7, N1, F15, N14		EPC, STP
Amazilia beryllina	M	M/C	MM	F	600	2200		F11, F10, F7, F15		PAS, MAH
Amazilia boucardi	M	U/C	LT	F	L	L		F14	HPC	GCS
Amazilia candida	M	U/C	LT	C	L	1600		F1, F7		PAS, GCS
Amazilia castaneiventris	?	?	UT	?	850	2050		F1E?	EAS	NAN
Amazilia chionogaster	L	U/C	MM	C	L	2800		N3, F4E, F15, N1		CAN, SAN, CSA
Amazilia chionopectus	M	U/C	LT	F	L	L		F1, F7, F15		NSA, AMN
Amazilia cyanifrons	L	M/C	UT	F	400	2000		F15, F4E?, F1E?		CDH?, NAN, NSA
Amazilia cyanocephala	M	M/C	UT	F	600	1800+		F11, F10, F4		MAH, GCS
Amazilia cyanura	L	M/C	LT	F	L	1500		F15, F7, F1E		PAS, GCS
Amazilia decora	M	U/M	LT	C	L	L		F1E, F15	HPC	GCS
Amazilia distans	?	C?	LT	?	L	800?		F1?	ARC	NSA
Amazilia edward	L	U/C	HT	F	L	1800		F1E, F4E, F15		GCS, CDH

CP	RP	Notes
4	3	Occasionally to 150 m.
4	3	
4	3	
4	3	
4	3	
4	3	
4	2	
4	3	
4	3	
3	2	Habitat destruction.
3	2	Survey.
4	3	
4	3	
3	2	Poorly known.
4	3	Seasonally to 750 m.
4	3	Occasionally to 1,750 m.
4	3	
4	3	
3	2	Poorly known; may be conspecific with *L. coeruleogularis*.
4	3	
4	3	Occasionally to 1,750 m (Venezuela).
4	3	
4	3	Locally to 2,600 m.
4	3	
4	3	Occasionally to 1,850 m (Tepuis).
4	3	
4	3	
3	2	Occasionally to 1,400 m; deforestation.
3	2	
4	3	
4	3	
4	3	Occasionally to 1,500 m (Tepuis).
4	2	Habitat requirements unknown.
4	2	Poorly known; populations widely disjunct.
4	2	Habitat requirements poorly known.
3	2	Poorly known.
4	3	
4	2	Habitat requirements poorly known.
3	2	
4	3	Locally to 1,400 m.
4	3	
4	2	Locally to sea level (seasonally?) and 3,100 m.
3	2	
4	3	
2	1	Poorly known.
4	3	North of Bolivia mainly above 1,100 m.
4	3	
4	3	Occasionally at sea level; Costa Rica population unknown.
3	3	Occasionally to lowlands; deforestation?.
4	2	Range poorly known.
4	3	Locally to 1,200 m.
2	2	Known from one specimen; status uncertain.
4	3	

Abbreviations Used

Snst - Sensitivity:
L - Low; **M** - Medium; **H** - High.

Strat - Foraging Strata:
T - Terrestrial; **U** - Understory; **M** - Midstory; **C** - Canopy; **A** - Aerial; **W** - Water.

Cntab - Center of Abundance:
LT - Lower tropical; **LS** - Lower subtropical; **HT** - Hill tropical; **UT** - Upper tropical; **US** - Upper subtropical; **MM** - Middle montane; **UM** - Upper montane.

Rel - Relative Abundance:
R - Rare; **U** - Uncommon; **F** - Fairly common; **C** - Common; **P** - Patchily distributed.

Min - Minimum Elevation:
L - Lowlands; **?** - Uncertain value; numeric values in meters.

Max - Maximum Elevation:
L - Lowlands; **?** - Uncertain value; **+** - species occurs at least to given elevation but likely occurs higher; numeric values in meters.

Micro - Microhabitats:
A - Army ants; **B** - Bamboo; **T** - Treefalls; **G** - Ground bromeliads; **C** - Rocky outcrops and caves; **S** - Streamside; **V** - Vine tangles; **B/V** -Bamboo/vine tangles.

Habitats:
F1 - Tropical lowland evergreen forest; **F2** - Flooded tropical evergreen forest; **F3** - River-edge forest; **F4** - Montane evergreen forest; **F5** - Elfin forest; **F6** - *Polylepis* woodland; **F7** - Tropical deciduous forest; **F8** - Gallery forest; **F9** - Southern temperate forest; **F10** - Pine forest; **F11** - Pine-oak forest; **F12** - White sand forest; **F13** - Palm forest; **F14** - Mangrove forest; **F15** - Secondary forest; **N1** - Arid lowland scrub; **N2** - Arid montane scrub; **N3** - Semihumid/humid montane scrub; **N4** - Cerrado; **N5** - Campo grasslands; **N6** - Low, seasonally wet grassland; **N7** - Southern temperate grassland; **N8** - Northern temperate grassland; **N9** - Puna grassland; **N10** - Paramo grassland; **N11** - Riparian thickets; **N12** - River island scrub; **N13** - Pastures/agricultural lands; **N14** - Second-growth scrub; **A1** - Freshwater marshes; **A2** - Saltwater/brackish marshes; **A3** - Coastal sand beaches/mudflats; **A4** - Coastal rocky beaches; **A5** - Riverine sand beaches; **A6** - Freshwater lakes and ponds; **A7** - Alkaline lakes; **A8** - Rivers; **A9** - Streams; **A10** - Bogs; **A11** - Coastal waters; **A12** - Pelagic waters.
E - Edge (used as a modifer to particular habitats).

Sub - Subregions:
ARC - Arid Caribbean Coast; **AWA** - Altiplano and Western Andes; **BAH** - Bahamas; **BAJ** - Baja California; **CAA** - Caatinga; **CAH** - Central American Highlands; **CER** - Cerrado; **CHA** - Chaco; **CHG** - Chiapas-Guanacaste; **CHL** - Chilean Desert; **CHR** - Chiriquí; **CIS** - Cocos Island; **CMV** - Cauca-Magdalena Valley; **COC** - Cuzco-Cochabamba; **CUB** - Cuba; **DOM** - Dominica; **EAS** - Eastern Slope Andes; **FDN** - Fernando de Noronha; **GAL** - Galápagos; **GCM** - Gulf Coast-Mexico; **GRE** - Grenada; **GUA** - Guadeloupe; **GUI** - Guianan; **HIS** - Hispaniola; **HPC** - Humid Pacific Coast; **ISA** - Isla Providencia and Isla San Andrés; **JAM** - Jamaica; **JFI** - Juan Fernández Islands; **MAN** - Manabí-Tumbes; **MAR** - Marañón Valley; **MID** - Madeira-Tapajós; **MON** - Montserrat; **MRT** - Martinique; **MTC** - Marañón-Cuzco; **NMM** - Northern Mexican Mountains; **NOR** - Northern Coastal Brazil; **PAR** - Pará; **PER** - Peruvian Desert; **PUE** - Puerto Rico; **RDJ** - Rio de Janeiro-Bahia Lowlands; **RMW** - Rio Madeira West; **RNW** - Rio Negro West; **SCA** - Southern Central America; **SCT** - Santa Cruz-Tucumán; **SIN** - Sinaloa-Oaxaca; **SMH** - Southern Mexican Highlands; **SMT** - Santa Marta; **SOC** - Islas Revillagigedo (Socorro Island group); **SON** - Sonoran Desert; **SOU** - Southern Atlantic Coast; **STL** - St. Lucia; **STV** - St. Vincent; **TAC** - Tacarcuna; **VAN** - Venezuelan Andes; **VNZ** - Venezuelan Coastal Mountains; **WES** - Western Andes; **YUC** - Yucatán Peninsula.
o - Endemic to region, but not restricted to a single subregion.

Zoogeographic Regions:
AMN - Northern Amazonia; **AMS** - Southern Amazonia; **ATL** - Atlantic Forest; **BSR** - Baja-Sonora; **CAN** - Central Andes; **CDH** - Chiriquí-Darién Highlands; **CHO** - Chocó Lowlands; **CSA** - Central South America; **EPC** - Equatorial Pacific Coast; **GAN** - Greater Antilles; **GCS** - Gulf-Caribbean Slope; **LAN** - Lesser Antilles; **MAH** - Madrean Highlands; **MPL** - Mexican Plateau; **NAN** - Northern Andes; **NSA** - Northern South America; **PAM** - Pampas; **PAS** - Pacific Arid Slope; **PAT** - Patagonia; **SAN** - Southern Andes; **STP** - Subtropical Pacific; **TEP** - Tepuis.

CP -Conservation Priority:
1 - Urgent; **2** - High; **3** - Medium; **4** - Low.

RP - Research Priority:
1 - High; **2** - Medium; **3** - Low.

	Snst	Strat	Cntab	Rel	Min	Max	Micro	Habitats	Sub	Zoogeographic Regions
Amazilia fimbriata	L	U/C	LT	C	L	800		F3, F8, F15, F12		NSA, AMN, AMS, CSA, ATL
Amazilia franciae	L	U/C	UT	F	900	2000		F4E, F7, F15		NAN, CAN
Amazilia lactea	L	M/C	LT	F	L	900		F1E, F3, F15		TEP, AMS, ATL
Amazilia leucogaster	L	U/C	LT	?	L	L		F7, F15, F14?		NSA, AMN, AMS, CSA
Amazilia luciae	M	U/C	LT	F/P	L	L		F7	SCA	GCS
Amazilia rosenbergi	L	U	LT	U	L	L		F1E, F15	o	CHO
Amazilia rutila	L	U/C	LT	C	L	1600		F7, F15, F8, N1		PAS, GCS
Amazilia saucerrottei	L	U/C	LT	C	L	2000		F1E, F8E, F15, N14		PAS, NSA
Amazilia tobaci	L	U/C	LT	C	L	1800		F1E, F4?, F7, F15, F8, F14	o	NSA
Amazilia tzacatl	L	U/C	LT	C	L	1800		F1E, F15, F7		GCS, CHO, NAN, NSA
Amazilia versicolor	L	U/C	LT	F	L	900		F1E, F7, F8, F15, F12		NSA, AMN, AMS, CSA, ATL
Amazilia violiceps	M	U/C	UT	F	L	2200		F7, F8, F15		PAS, MAH
Amazilia viridicauda	L	U/C	MM	F	900	2800		F4E, F15	o	CAN
Amazilia viridifrons	M	U/C	LT	F	L	1550		F7, N1, N2, F1E		PAS, MAH
Amazilia viridigaster	L	U/M	HT	F	L	2100		F4E, F1E, F15, F7?		NSA, TEP, AMN
Amazilia yucatanensis	L	U/M	LT	C	L	1250		F7, F8, F15, F1E	o	GCS
Eupherusa cyanophrys	M	U	UT	F	700	2600		F4, F7	SMH	MAH
Eupherusa eximia	M	U	UT	U	800	2000		F1, F15		MAH, CDH
Eupherusa nigriventris	M	U	UT	?	900	2000		F4	CHR	CDH
Eupherusa poliocerca	M	U	UT	U	900	2200		F4, F7	SMH	MAH
Elvira chionura	M	U	UT	F	900	2000		F4	CHR	CDH
Elvira cupreiceps	M	U	UT	F	700	1500		F4	CHR	CDH
Microchera albocoronata	M	U	HT	U	300	1000		F1E, F4E		MAH, CDH
Chalybura buffonii	L	U/M	LT	F	L	900		F1, F7, F15		GCS, CHO, EPC, NSA
Chalybura urochrysia	M	U	LT	U	L	900		F1		GCS, CHO
Aphantochroa cirrhochloris	M	U/M	LT	F	L	700		F15, F1E, N14	o	ATL
Lampornis amethystinus	M	U/M	MM	U	1300	3400		F11, F4	o	MAH
Lampornis castaneoventris										
calolaema	M	U/M	MM	F	800	3200		F4, F15		MAH, CDH
castaneoventris	M	U/M	MM	C	1250	3150		F4, F15	o	CDH
cinereicauda	M	U/M	MM	F	1800	3100		F4, F15	CHR	CDH
Lampornis clemenciae	M	U/M	MM	F	1500	3400		F11, F10, F15?	NMM	MAH
Lampornis hemileucus	M	U/M	UT	F	700	1400		F4	CHR	CDH
Lampornis sybillae	M	U/M	UT	F	1000	2400+		F4, F11?	CAH	MAH
Lampornis viridipallens	M	U/M	MM	F	1000	3100		F4, F11	CAH	MAH
Lamprolaima rhami	M	U/M	MM	U	1100	3100		F4, F11	o	MAH
Adelomyia melanogenys	M	U	MM	F	1100	2300		F4		NAN, CAN, SAN
Anthocephala floriceps	M	U	UT	R	1200	2300		F4, F15?	o	NAN
Urosticte benjamini										
benjamini	M	U	UT	F	900	1500		F4		NAN, CAN
ruficrissa	M	U	MM	U/P	1350	2300		F4	EAS	NAN
Phlogophilus hemileucurus	M	U	UT	U?	800	1500		F4		NAN, CAN
Phlogophilus harterti	M	U	UT	U	750	1200		F4	MTC	CAN
Clytolaema rubricauda	M	U/M	UT	F	750	2000		F4, F15, F1	SOU	ATL
Polyplancta aurescens	M	U/C	LT	U	L	1050		F3, F1, F2		AMN, AMS
Heliodoxa branickii	H	U	HT	F	700	1550		F4, F1	o	CAN
Heliodoxa gularis	H	U	HT	U	900?	1050		F1, F4?	EAS	NAN
Heliodoxa imperatrix	H	U/M	UT	F	900	1800		F4, F1	WES	NAN
Heliodoxa jacula	M	U	UT	F/P	500	2150		F4, F1		CDH, CHO, NAN
Heliodoxa leadbeateri	M	U/M	UT	F	1050	2300		F4		NAN, CAN
Heliodoxa rubinoides	H	U/M	MM	U/P	1700	2650		F4		NAN, CAN
Heliodoxa schreibersii	H	U	HT	U	L	1100		F1, F4		NAN, CAN, AMN
Heliodoxa xanthogonys	H	U/C	UT	F	950	2000+		F4, N3	o	TEP
Eugenes fulgens	M	U/M	MM	F	1300	3300		F11, F10, F4		MAH, CDH

CP	RP	Notes
4	3	
4	3	
4	3	Locally to 1,400 m (Tepuis).
4	3	
2	2	Locally to 1,200 m; poorly known.
4	3	
4	3	Occasionally to 1,700 m in Honduras.
4	3	Occasionally to 3,000 m in Venezuela.
4	3	
4	3	Occasionally to 2,500 m (Andes).
4	3	Occasionally to 1,700 m.
4	3	Mainly above 1,500 m.
4	3	
4	3	
4	3	
4	3	
2	1	Locally to 700 m; deforestation.
4	3	Seasonally to lowlands.
3	2	Seasonally to 600 m; poorly known.
2	1	Deforestation may be problem; poorly known.
4	3	
3	2	Seasonally to 300 m.
3	2	Seasonally to lowlands; poorly known.
4	3	Occasionally to 2,000 m.
3	2	Poorly known.
3	2	
4	3	Locally to 900 m.
4	3	Seasonally to 300 m.
4	2	Relationship to other forms uncertain.
4	3	
4	3	
4	3	
3	2	Poorly known.
4	3	Occasionally to 900 m.
3	2	Deforestation.
4	3	Occasionally to 3,000 m.
3	2	
4	3	Occasionally to 700 m.
3	2	Deforestation.
3	2	Deforestation.
3	2	Deforestation.
4	3	
4	3	Occasionally to 1,300 m (Peru).
3	2	
2	1	Poorly known; deforestation.
4	3	Occasionally to 400 m.
4	3	Seasonally to lowlands.
4	3	Occasionally to 700 m.
4	3	
4	3	Primarily in humid foothills.
4	3	Occasionally to 700 m?
4	3	

Abbreviations Used

Snst - Sensitivity:
L - Low; **M** - Medium; **H** - High.

Strat - Foraging Strata:
T - Terrestrial; **U** - Understory; **M** - Midstory; **C** - Canopy; **A** - Aerial; **W** - Water.

Cntab - Center of Abundance:
LT - Lower tropical; **LS** - Lower subtropical; **HT** - Hill tropical; **UT** - Upper tropical; **US** - Upper subtropical; **MM** - Middle montane; **UM** - Upper montane.

Rel - Relative Abundance:
R - Rare; **U** - Uncommon; **F** - Fairly common; **C** - Common; **P** - Patchily distributed.

Min - Minimum Elevation:
L - Lowlands; **?** - Uncertain value; numeric values in meters.

Max - Maximum Elevation:
L - Lowlands; **?** - Uncertain value; **+** - species occurs at least to given elevation but likely occurs higher; numeric values in meters.

Micro - Microhabitats:
A - Army ants; **B** - Bamboo; **T** - Treefalls; **G** - Ground bromeliads; **C** - Rocky outcrops and caves; **S** - Streamside; **V** - Vine tangles; **B/V** -Bamboo/vine tangles.

Habitats:
F1 - Tropical lowland evergreen forest; **F2** - Flooded tropical evergreen forest; **F3** - River-edge forest; **F4** - Montane evergreen forest; **F5** - Elfin forest; **F6** - *Polylepis* woodland; **F7** - Tropical deciduous forest; **F8** - Gallery forest; **F9** - Southern temperate forest; **F10** - Pine forest; **F11** - Pine-oak forest; **F12** - White sand forest; **F13** - Palm forest; **F14** - Mangrove forest; **F15** - Secondary forest; **N1** - Arid lowland scrub; **N2** - Arid montane scrub; **N3** - Semihumid/humid montane scrub; **N4** - Cerrado; **N5** - Campo grasslands; **N6** - Low, seasonally wet grassland; **N7** - Southern temperate grassland; **N8** - Northern temperate grassland; **N9** - Puna grassland; **N10** - Paramo grassland; **N11** - Riparian thickets; **N12** - River island scrub; **N13** - Pastures/agricultural lands; **N14** - Second-growth scrub; **A1** - Freshwater marshes; **A2** - Saltwater/brackish marshes; **A3** - Coastal sand beaches/mudflats; **A4** - Coastal rocky beaches; **A5** - Riverine sand beaches; **A6** - Freshwater lakes and ponds; **A7** - Alkaline lakes; **A8** - Rivers; **A9** - Streams; **A10** - Bogs; **A11** - Coastal waters; **A12** - Pelagic waters.
E - Edge (used as a modifer to particular habitats).

Sub - Subregions:
ARC - Arid Caribbean Coast; **AWA** - Altiplano and Western Andes; **BAH** - Bahamas; **BAJ** - Baja California; **CAA** - Caatinga; **CAH** - Central American Highlands; **CER** - Cerrado; **CHA** - Chaco; **CHG** - Chiapas-Guanacaste; **CHL** - Chilean Desert; **CHR** - Chiriquí; **CIS** - Cocos Island; **CMV** - Cauca-Magdalena Valley; **COC** - Cuzco-Cochabamba; **CUB** - Cuba; **DOM** - Dominica; **EAS** - Eastern Slope Andes; **FDN** - Fernando de Noronha; **GAL** - Galápagos; **GCM** - Gulf Coast-Mexico; **GRE** - Grenada; **GUA** - Guadeloupe; **GUI** - Guianan; **HIS** - Hispaniola; **HPC** - Humid Pacific Coast; **ISA** - Isla Providencia and Isla San Andrés; **JAM** - Jamaica; **JFI** - Juan Fernández Islands; **MAN** - Manabí-Tumbes; **MAR** - Marañón Valley; **MID** - Madeira-Tapajós; **MON** - Montserrat; **MRT** - Martinique; **MTC** - Marañón-Cuzco; **NMM** - Northern Mexican Mountains; **NOR** - Northern Coastal Brazil; **PAR** - Pará; **PER** - Peruvian Desert; **PUE** - Puerto Rico; **RDJ** - Rio de Janeiro-Bahia Lowlands; **RMW** - Rio Madeira West; **RNW** - Rio Negro West; **SCA** - Southern Central America; **SCT** - Santa Cruz-Tucumán; **SIN** - Sinaloa-Oaxaca; **SMH** - Southern Mexican Highlands; **SMT** - Santa Marta; **SOC** - Islas Revillagigedo (Socorro Island group); **SON** - Sonoran Desert; **SOU** - Southern Atlantic Coast; **STL** - St. Lucia; **STV** - St. Vincent; **TAC** - Tacarcuna; **VAN** - Venezuelan Andes; **VNZ** - Venezuelan Coastal Mountains; **WES** - Western Andes; **YUC** - Yucatán Peninsula.
o - Endemic to region, but not restricted to a single subregion.

Zoogeographic Regions:
AMN - Northern Amazonia; **AMS** - Southern Amazonia; **ATL** - Atlantic Forest; **BSR** - Baja-Sonora; **CAN** - Central Andes; **CDH** - Chiriquí-Darién Highlands; **CHO** - Chocó Lowlands; **CSA** - Central South America; **EPC** - Equatorial Pacific Coast; **GAN** - Greater Antilles; **GCS** - Gulf-Caribbean Slope; **LAN** - Lesser Antilles; **MAH** - Madrean Highlands; **MPL** - Mexican Plateau; **NAN** - Northern Andes; **NSA** - Northern South America; **PAM** - Pampas; **PAS** - Pacific Arid Slope; **PAT** - Patagonia; **SAN** - Southern Andes; **STP** - Subtropical Pacific; **TEP** - Tepuis.

CP -Conservation Priority:
1 - Urgent; **2** - High; **3** - Medium; **4** - Low.

RP - Research Priority:
1 - High; **2** - Medium; **3** - Low.

	Snst	Strat	Cntab	Rel	Min	Max	Micro	Habitats	Sub	Zoogeographic Regions
Hylonympha macrocerca	M	M?	UT	F	550	1200		F4	VNZ	NAN
Sternoclyta cyanopectus	M	?	UT	F	900	1900		F4, F1, F15?	o	NAN
Topaza pella	M	U/M	LT	U	L	600	S	F1, F3		AMN, AMS
Topaza pyra	M	U/M	LT	R	L	L	S	F1	RNW	AMN
Oreotrochilus adela	M	U	UM	?	2550	4000		N2	o	CAN
Oreotrochilus estella										
chimborazo	M	T/U	UM	C/P	3500	5000		N10	EAS	NAN
estella	M	T/U	UM	F	3500	4600		N9, N10		NAN, CAN
Oreotrochilus leucopleurus	M	U	UM	U	1200	4000		N9, N2		CAN, SAN
Oreotrochilus melanogaster	M	T/U	UM	U/P	3700	4800		N9	AWA	CAN
Urochroa bougueri	H	U/M	UT	U	1050	2100		F4		NAN, CAN
Patagona gigas	L	U/C	UM	U	2100	3700		N2		NAN, CAN, SAN
Aglaeactis aliciae	M	U/C	UM	R?	3000	3200		N3	MAR	CAN
Aglaeactis castelnaudii	M	U/C	UM	C/P	3100	4200		N3, F5	MTC	CAN
Aglaeactis cupripennis	M	U/C	UM	C/P	2800	4300		N3, F6, F5		NAN, CAN
Aglaeactis pamela	M	U/C	UM	U/P	3000	3500		N3, F5	COC	CAN
Lafresnaya lafresnayi	M	U	UM	F/P	2300	3350		F4, F15		NAN, CAN
Pterophanes cyanopterus	M	U/M	UM	F	2600	3700		F5, F4E		NAN, CAN
Coeligena bonapartei	M	U/M	MM/UM	U/P	2150	3200		F4, F5	o	NAN
Coeligena coeligena	H	U/M	MM	F	1100	2650		F4		NAN, CAN
Coeligena helianthea	L	U/C	MM	F	1900	3300		F4, F5, N3	o	NAN
Coeligena iris	L	U/M	UM	F	1500	3500		F4, F5, F15, N3		NAN, CAN
Coeligena lutetiae	M	U/M	UM	F	3000	3750		F5, F4	o	NAN
Coeligena phalerata	M	U/C	MM?	F	1400	3400		F4, F5	SMT	NAN
Coeligena prunellei	H	M/C	MM	U	1650	2600		F4	EAS	NAN
Coeligena torquata	M	U/C	MM	F	1700	2800		F4		NAN, CAN
Coeligena violifer	M	U/M	UM	F	2800	3600		F4, F5	o	CAN
Coeligena wilsoni	H	U	UT	C	1000	1500		F4	WES	NAN
Ensifera ensifera	M	U/C	UM	U/P	2200	3600		F4, F5		NAN, CAN
Sephanoides fernandensis	M	U/M	LS	R	L	800+		N3	JFI	STP
Sephanoides sephanoides	L	U/M	LT	F	L	2000+		N14, F9, N3, F15?		STP, PAT
Boissonneaua flavescens	L	M/C	MM	F	1400	2800		F4, F5, F15	o	NAN
Boissonneaua jardini	L?	M	UT	U/P	800	2200		F4, F15	WES	NAN
Boissonneaua matthewsii	L	M/C	MM	F	1550	2700		F4, F15		NAN, CAN
Heliangelus amethysticollis	M	U/M	UM	F	1800	3300		F4, F15		NAN, CAN
Heliangelus exortis										
exortis	M	U/M	UM	C	2300	3400		F4, F15	o	NAN
micrastur	M	U/M	UM	U	2400	2900		F4	EAS	NAN
Heliangelus mavors	M	U/M	UM?	F	2000	3200		F4, F5, F15	o	NAN
Heliangelus regalis	H	U	MM	U	1450	2200		F5		NAN, CAN
Heliangelus spencei	M	U/M	UM	F	2000	3600		F4, F5	VAN	NAN
Heliangelus strophianus	M	U/M	UM	F	1200	2800		F4, F15	WES	NAN
Heliangelus viola	M	U/M	UM	F	2150	3050		F4, F15	WES	NAN
Heliangelus zusii	H?	?	MM?	?	?	?		F4?	EAS	NAN?
Eriocnemis alinae	M	U/M	MM	U	2000	2800		F4, F15		NAN, CAN
Eriocnemis cupreoventris	M?	?	UM	U	2200	3200		F5, F4	o	NAN
Eriocnemis derbyi	M	U/M	UM	U/P	2900	3600		F15	EAS	NAN
Eriocnemis glaucopoides	M	U	MM	U	1900	2900		F15, F4	SCT	CAN
Eriocnemis godini	M	?	MM	R	2100	2300?		F4	WES	NAN
Eriocnemis luciani	M	U/M	UM	F	2600	3750		F4, F5		NAN, CAN
Eriocnemis mirabilis	M	U	MM	R	2200	2450		F4, F15	WES	NAN
Eriocnemis mosquera	M	U	UM	C	2600	3300		F5, F4	o	NAN
Eriocnemis nigrivestis	M	?	UM	R?	2400	3600		F5, F4	o	NAN
Eriocnemis vestitus	M	?	UM	C	2250	3850		F5, F15?	o	NAN

CP	RP	Notes
2	1	Poorly known.
4	3	Occasionally to lowlands.
4	3	
4	3	
4	2	Poorly known.
3	2	
4	3	Occasionally to 2,400 m.
4	3	
4	2	Poorly known.
3	2	Occasionally (seasonally?) to 500 and 2,500 m.
4	3	Occasionally to 1,600 and 4,000 m.
2	1	
3	3	Occasionally to 2,500 m?
4	3	Occasionally to 2,500 m; seasonal movements.
3	3	
4	3	Occasionally to 1,500 and 3,700 m; marked seasonal movements.
4	3	
3	2	Locally to 1,400 m (Venezuela); status poorly known.
4	2	Occasionally to lower elevations; seasonal movements in Columbia.
4	3	Mainly 2,400 to 2,900 m (Colombia).
4	3	
4	3	Occasionally to 2,600 m.
4	2	Monitor.
2	1	
4	3	Occasionally to 1,500 and 3,300 m.
4	3	Mainly above 2,800 m.
3	2	Occasionally to 700 and 1,900 m; monitor.
4	3	Occasionally to 1,700 m.
2	1	Population under 1,000; monitor.
4	3	
4	3	Occasionally to 850 and 3,350 m.
3	2	Occasionally to 300 m.
4	3	
4	3	
4	3	Occasionally to 1,500 m.
4	3	
4	3	
2	2	Poorly known.
4	3	
4	3	
4	3	
1	1	Known from single "Bogota" specimen (Graves 1993).
4	3	
2	2	
3	3	Occasionally to 2,500 m.
4	3	
2	2	Taxonomic and general status uncertain.
4	3	Occasionally to 2,000 and 4,800 m?
2	1	Known from one locality.
4	3	Occasionally to 1,200 and 3,600 m.
2	2	Occasionally or seasonally to 4,500 m.
4	3	

Abbreviations Used

Snst - Sensitivity:
L - Low; **M** - Medium; **H** - High.

Strat - Foraging Strata:
T - Terrestrial; **U** - Understory; **M** - Midstory; **C** - Canopy; **A** - Aerial; **W** - Water.

Cntab - Center of Abundance:
LT - Lower tropical; **LS** - Lower subtropical; **HT** - Hill tropical; **UT** - Upper tropical; **US** - Upper subtropical; **MM** - Middle montane; **UM** - Upper montane.

Rel - Relative Abundance:
R - Rare; **U** - Uncommon; **F** - Fairly common; **C** - Common; **P** - Patchily distributed.

Min - Minimum Elevation:
L - Lowlands; **?** - Uncertain value; numeric values in meters.

Max - Maximum Elevation:
L - Lowlands; **?** - Uncertain value; **+** - species occurs at least to given elevation but likely occurs higher; numeric values in meters.

Micro - Microhabitats:
A - Army ants; **B** - Bamboo; **T** - Treefalls; **G** - Ground bromeliads; **C** - Rocky outcrops and caves; **S** - Streamside; **V** - Vine tangles; **B/V** -Bamboo/vine tangles.

Habitats:
F1 - Tropical lowland evergreen forest; **F2** - Flooded tropical evergreen forest; **F3** - River-edge forest; **F4** - Montane evergreen forest; **F5** - Elfin forest; **F6** - *Polylepis* woodland; **F7** - Tropical deciduous forest; **F8** - Gallery forest; **F9** - Southern temperate forest; **F10** - Pine forest; **F11** - Pine-oak forest; **F12** - White sand forest; **F13** - Palm forest; **F14** - Mangrove forest; **F15** - Secondary forest; **N1** - Arid lowland scrub; **N2** - Arid montane scrub; **N3** - Semihumid/humid montane scrub; **N4** - Cerrado; **N5** - Campo grasslands; **N6** - Low, seasonally wet grassland; **N7** - Southern temperate grassland; **N8** - Northern temperate grassland; **N9** - Puna grassland; **N10** - Paramo grassland; **N11** - Riparian thickets; **N12** - River island scrub; **N13** - Pastures/agricultural lands; **N14** - Second-growth scrub; **A1** - Freshwater marshes; **A2** - Saltwater/brackish marshes; **A3** - Coastal sand beaches/mudflats; **A4** - Coastal rocky beaches; **A5** - Riverine sand beaches; **A6** - Freshwater lakes and ponds; **A7** - Alkaline lakes; **A8** - Rivers; **A9** - Streams; **A10** - Bogs; **A11** - Coastal waters; **A12** - Pelagic waters.
E - Edge (used as a modifer to particular habitats).

Sub - Subregions:
ARC - Arid Caribbean Coast; **AWA** - Altiplano and Western Andes; **BAH** - Bahamas; **BAJ** - Baja California; **CAA** - Caatinga; **CAH** - Central American Highlands; **CER** - Cerrado; **CHA** - Chaco; **CHG** - Chiapas-Guanacaste; **CHL** - Chilean Desert; **CHR** - Chiriquí; **CIS** - Cocos Island; **CMV** - Cauca-Magdalena Valley; **COC** - Cuzco-Cochabamba; **CUB** - Cuba; **DOM** - Dominica; **EAS** - Eastern Slope Andes; **FDN** - Fernando de Noronha; **GAL** - Galápagos; **GCM** - Gulf Coast-Mexico; **GRE** - Grenada; **GUA** - Guadeloupe; **GUI** - Guianan; **HIS** - Hispaniola; **HPC** - Humid Pacific Coast; **ISA** - Isla Providencia and Isla San Andrés; **JAM** - Jamaica; **JFI** - Juan Fernández Islands; **MAN** - Manabí-Tumbes; **MAR** - Marañón Valley; **MID** - Madeira-Tapajós; **MON** - Montserrat; **MRT** - Martinique; **MTC** - Marañón-Cuzco; **NMM** - Northern Mexican Mountains; **NOR** - Northern Coastal Brazil; **PAR** - Pará; **PER** - Peruvian Desert; **PUE** - Puerto Rico; **RDJ** - Rio de Janeiro-Bahia Lowlands; **RMW** - Rio Madeira West; **RNW** - Rio Negro West; **SCA** - Southern Central America; **SCT** - Santa Cruz-Tucumán; **SIN** - Sinaloa-Oaxaca; **SMH** - Southern Mexican Highlands; **SMT** - Santa Marta; **SOC** - Islas Revillagigedo (Socorro Island group); **SON** - Sonoran Desert; **SOU** - Southern Atlantic Coast; **STL** - St. Lucia; **STV** - St. Vincent; **TAC** - Tacarcuna; **VAN** - Venezuelan Andes; **VNZ** - Venezuelan Coastal Mountains; **WES** - Western Andes; **YUC** - Yucatán Peninsula.
o - Endemic to region, but not restricted to a single subregion.

Zoogeographic Regions:
AMN - Northern Amazonia; **AMS** - Southern Amazonia; **ATL** - Atlantic Forest; **BSR** - Baja-Sonora; **CAN** - Central Andes; **CDH** - Chiriquí-Darién Highlands; **CHO** - Chocó Lowlands; **CSA** - Central South America; **EPC** - Equatorial Pacific Coast; **GAN** - Greater Antilles; **GCS** - Gulf-Caribbean Slope; **LAN** - Lesser Antilles; **MAH** - Madrean Highlands; **MPL** - Mexican Plateau; **NAN** - Northern Andes; **NSA** - Northern South America; **PAM** - Pampas; **PAS** - Pacific Arid Slope; **PAT** - Patagonia; **SAN** - Southern Andes; **STP** - Subtropical Pacific; **TEP** - Tepuis.

CP -Conservation Priority:
1 - Urgent; **2** - High; **3** - Medium; **4** - Low.

RP - Research Priority:
1 - High; **2** - Medium; **3** - Low.

	Snst	Strat	Cntab	Rel	Min	Max	Micro	Habitats	Sub	Zoogeographic Regions
Haplophaedia aureliae	M	U	MM	F	1400	2500		F4, F15		CDH, NAN, CAN
Haplophaedia lugens	H	U	UT	F	1100	2500		F4	WES	NAN
Ocreatus underwoodii	L	U	UM	F	1050	2500		F4, F15		NAN, CAN
Lesbia nuna	L	U/C	UM	F	2200	3000		N3, N14, F15		NAN, CAN
Lesbia victoriae	L	U/C	UM	F	2500	4000		N3, N14, F15, F6		NAN, CAN
Sappho sparganura	L	U/C	UM	F	2000?	3600		N2		CAN, SAN
Polyonymus caroli	L	U/C	MM	U	1500	2800		N2	AWA	CAN
Ramphomicron dorsale	M	U/C	UM	U	2000	4500		F4, F5, N10	SMT	NAN
Ramphomicron microrhynchum	M	M/C	UM	U	2500	3750		F4, F5		NAN, CAN
Metallura aeneocauda	M	U/C	UM	F	2800	3600		F5	COC	CAN
Metallura baroni	M	U/C	UM	F	3100	3700		F5, F6, N3	o	NAN
Metallura eupogon	M	U/C	UM	F	3000	3400		F5	MTC	CAN
Metallura iracunda	M	U/C	UM	?	2800	3100		F5	VAN	NAN
Metallura odomae	M	U/C	UM	U/F	2850	3350		F5	EAS	NAN
Metallura phoebe	L	T/U	UM	F	2500	4400		N2, F6	AWA	CAN
Metallura theresiae	M	U/C	UM	F	3100	3550		F5	MTC	CAN
Metallura tyrianthina	L	U/M	UM	C	2400	3500		F5, F4, F15		NAN, CAN
Metallura williami	M	U/C	UM	U	2900	3800		F5, N10	o	NAN
Chalcostigma herrani	M	U/C	UM	U	2700	3400		N10	o	NAN
Chalcostigma heteropogon	M	U/C	UM	U	2900	3500		N10	o	NAN
Chalcostigma olivaceum	L	U/C	UM	U	3150	4500		N9, N10	o	CAN
Chalcostigma ruficeps	L	U/M	UM	U	2250	3300		F4, F15		NAN, CAN
Chalcostigma stanleyi	M	U/C	UM	F/P	3350	4400		N10, F6		NAN, CAN
Oxypogon guerinii	M?	T/U	UM	U	3200	4500		N10	o	NAN
Opisthoprora euryptera	H	U	UM	R/P	2600	3600		F5, F4		NAN, CAN
Taphrolesbia griseiventris	L	U	UM	R	2750	3200		N2	AWA	CAN
Aglaiocercus coelestis	M	M/C	UT	F	900	2100		F4	WES	NAN
Aglaiocercus kingi	M	M/C	MM	F	1300	2600		F4		NAN, CAN
Oreonympha nobilis	L	U/M	UM	U	2500	3700		N2	AWA	CAN
Augastes lumachellus	M	U/M	UT	F?	950	1600		N2	CER	CSA
Augastes scutatus	M	U/C	UT	F	900	2000		N2	CER	CSA
Schistes geoffroyi	M	U	UT	U	1100	2250		F4		NAN, CAN
Heliothryx aurita	M	M/C	LT	U	L	1100		F1		AMN, AMS, ATL
Heliothryx barroti	M	M/C	LT	U	L	1300		F1, F15		GCS, CHO
Heliactin bilophum	M	U/M	LT	U	L	1000		N5, N4		AMN, CSA
Loddigesia mirabilis	M	U	MM	U	2100	2800		N3, F4E	MAR	CAN
Heliomaster constantii	M	C	LT	F	L	1250		F7, F8, N1		BSR, PAS
Heliomaster furcifer	M	C	LT	U	L	1000+		F8, F3, N4, F7	o	CSA
Heliomaster longirostris	M	C	LT	U	L	1500		F1E, F7, F8, F15		PAS, GCS, CHO, EPC, AMN, AMS, CSA
Heliomaster squamosus	M	C	LT	U/P	L	1100		F8, F1E, F15, F7		CSA, ATL
Rhodopis vesper	M	U/C	MM	F	L	3100		N1, N2, N11		STP, CAN
Thaumastura cora	L	U/C	MM	F	L	3000		N1, N2, N11, N14		STP, CAN
Philodice bryantae	M	U/C	UT	U/P	700	1900		F4E, F15, N14	CHR	CDH
Philodice evelynae	L	U/C	LT	F	L	L		F15, N14, F1E, N1	BAH	GAN
Philodice mitchellii	L?	U/C	UT	U/P	1000	1900		F4, N14?	WES	NAN
Doricha eliza	L	U/C	LT	U	L	L		N1	YUC	GCS
Doricha enicura	L	U/C	UT	F/P	1000	2100		F4E, N14	CAH	MAH
Tilmatura dupontii	M	U/C	UM	U	900	2500		F11, F4E, N14	o	MAH
Microstilbon burmeisteri	M	?	?	U	L	2000+		F7, N2		CAN, SAN, CSA
Calothorax lucifer	M	U/C	MM	U	1200	2500		N2, F11?		MPL, MAH
Calothorax pulcher	M	U/C	MM	U	1000	2250		N2	o	MAH
Archilochus alexandri	L	U/C	HT	F	L	1800		F8, N1, N2, N14		BSR, MPL
Calliphlox amethystina	L	U/C	HT	U	L	1050		F1E, F4E		NSA, AMN, AMS, CSA, ATL
Mellisuga minima	L	U/C	LT	C	L	2400+		N14, F1E	o	GAN

CP	RP	Notes
4	3	Occasionally to 700 and 3,100 m.
3	2	Deforestation.
4	3	Occasionally to 850 and 3,100 m.
4	3	Locally to 3,800 m.
4	3	
4	3	
4	3	
4	3	Occasionally to 900 m.
4	3	Occasionally to 1,700 m.
4	3	
3	3	Occasionally to 1,900 m?
4	3	
3	2	Occasionally to 1,850 m (Venezuela)?
3	2	
4	3	
4	3	
4	3	Occasionally to 600 m?
4	3	Occasionally to 2,100 m.
4	3	
4	3	
4	3	
4	3	Occasionally to 3,800 m.
3	2	Destruction of *Polylepis* may threaten locally.
4	3	
3	2	
2	2	Habitat requirements unknown.
4	3	Occasionally to 300 m.
4	3	Occasionally to 900 m and 3,000 m.
4	3	
4	3	In "campo rupestre".
4	2	In "campo rupestre".
4	3	
4	3	
4	3	Occasionally to 2,200 m.
3	2	Usually called *H. cornuta* (see Mees 1985); in "campo sujo."
2	1	Poorly known.
4	3	
4	3	
4	3	Locally to 2,500 m.
4	3	
4	3	
4	3	
4	3	
4	3	
4	3	
3	2	
4	3	
4	3	Occasionally to lowlands.
4	3	
4	3	
4	3	
4	3	
4	3	Occasionally to 1,500 m.
4	3	Mainly below 1,600 m in winter.

Abbreviations Used

Snst - Sensitivity:
L - Low; **M** - Medium; **H** - High.

Strat - Foraging Strata:
T - Terrestrial; **U** - Understory; **M** - Midstory; **C** - Canopy; **A** - Aerial; **W** - Water.

Cntab - Center of Abundance:
LT - Lower tropical; **LS** - Lower subtropical; **HT** - Hill tropical; **UT** - Upper tropical; **US** - Upper subtropical; **MM** - Middle montane; **UM** - Upper montane.

Rel - Relative Abundance:
R - Rare; **U** - Uncommon; **F** - Fairly common; **C** - Common; **P** - Patchily distributed.

Min - Minimum Elevation:
L - Lowlands; **?** - Uncertain value; numeric values in meters.

Max - Maximum Elevation:
L - Lowlands; **?** - Uncertain value; **+** - species occurs at least to given elevation but likely occurs higher; numeric values in meters.

Micro - Microhabitats:
A - Army ants; **B** - Bamboo; **T** - Treefalls; **G** - Ground bromeliads; **C** - Rocky outcrops and caves; **S** - Streamside; **V** - Vine tangles; **B/V** -Bamboo/vine tangles.

Habitats:
F1 - Tropical lowland evergreen forest; **F2** - Flooded tropical evergreen forest; **F3** - River-edge forest; **F4** - Montane evergreen forest; **F5** - Elfin forest; **F6** - *Polylepis* woodland; **F7** - Tropical deciduous forest; **F8** - Gallery forest; **F9** - Southern temperate forest; **F10** - Pine forest; **F11** - Pine-oak forest; **F12** - White sand forest; **F13** - Palm forest; **F14** - Mangrove forest; **F15** - Secondary forest; **N1** - Arid lowland scrub; **N2** - Arid montane scrub; **N3** - Semihumid/humid montane scrub; **N4** - Cerrado; **N5** - Campo grasslands; **N6** - Low, seasonally wet grassland; **N7** - Southern temperate grassland; **N8** - Northern temperate grassland; **N9** - Puna grassland; **N10** - Paramo grassland; **N11** - Riparian thickets; **N12** - River island scrub; **N13** - Pastures/agricultural lands; **N14** - Second-growth scrub; **A1** - Freshwater marshes; **A2** - Saltwater/brackish marshes; **A3** - Coastal sand beaches/mudflats; **A4** - Coastal rocky beaches; **A5** - Riverine sand beaches; **A6** - Freshwater lakes and ponds; **A7** - Alkaline lakes; **A8** - Rivers; **A9** - Streams; **A10** - Bogs; **A11** - Coastal waters; **A12** - Pelagic waters.
E - Edge (used as a modifer to particular habitats).

Sub - Subregions:
ARC - Arid Caribbean Coast; **AWA** - Altiplano and Western Andes; **BAH** - Bahamas; **BAJ** - Baja California; **CAA** - Caatinga; **CAH** - Central American Highlands; **CER** - Cerrado; **CHA** - Chaco; **CHG** - Chiapas-Guanacaste; **CHL** - Chilean Desert; **CHR** - Chiriquí; **CIS** - Cocos Island; **CMV** - Cauca-Magdalena Valley; **COC** - Cuzco-Cochabamba; **CUB** - Cuba; **DOM** - Dominica; **EAS** - Eastern Slope Andes; **FDN** - Fernando de Noronha; **GAL** - Galápagos; **GCM** - Gulf Coast-Mexico; **GRE** - Grenada; **GUA** - Guadeloupe; **GUI** - Guianan; **HIS** - Hispaniola; **HPC** - Humid Pacific Coast; **ISA** - Isla Providencia and Isla San Andrés; **JAM** - Jamaica; **JFI** - Juan Fernández Islands; **MAN** - Manabí-Tumbes; **MAR** - Marañón Valley; **MID** - Madeira-Tapajós; **MON** - Montserrat; **MRT** - Martinique; **MTC** - Marañón-Cuzco; **NMM** - Northern Mexican Mountains; **NOR** - Northern Coastal Brazil; **PAR** - Pará; **PER** - Peruvian Desert; **PUE** - Puerto Rico; **RDJ** - Rio de Janeiro-Bahia Lowlands; **RMW** - Rio Madeira West; **RNW** - Rio Negro West; **SCA** - Southern Central America; **SCT** - Santa Cruz-Tucumán; **SIN** - Sinaloa-Oaxaca; **SMH** - Southern Mexican Highlands; **SMT** - Santa Marta; **SOC** - Islas Revillagigedo (Socorro Island group); **SON** - Sonoran Desert; **SOU** - Southern Atlantic Coast; **STL** - St. Lucia; **STV** - St. Vincent; **TAC** - Tacarcuna; **VAN** - Venezuelan Andes; **VNZ** - Venezuelan Coastal Mountains; **WES** - Western Andes; **YUC** - Yucatán Peninsula.
o - Endemic to region, but not restricted to a single subregion.

Zoogeographic Regions:
AMN - Northern Amazonia; **AMS** - Southern Amazonia; **ATL** - Atlantic Forest; **BSR** - Baja-Sonora; **CAN** - Central Andes; **CDH** - Chiriquí-Darién Highlands; **CHO** - Chocó Lowlands; **CSA** - Central South America; **EPC** - Equatorial Pacific Coast; **GAN** - Greater Antilles; **GCS** - Gulf-Caribbean Slope; **LAN** - Lesser Antilles; **MAH** - Madrean Highlands; **MPL** - Mexican Plateau; **NAN** - Northern Andes; **NSA** - Northern South America; **PAM** - Pampas; **PAS** - Pacific Arid Slope; **PAT** - Patagonia; **SAN** - Southern Andes; **STP** - Subtropical Pacific; **TEP** - Tepuis.

CP -Conservation Priority:
1 - Urgent; **2** - High; **3** - Medium; **4** - Low.

RP - Research Priority:
1 - High; **2** - Medium; **3** - Low.

	Snst	Strat	Cntab	Rel	Min	Max	Micro	Habitats	Sub	Zoogeographic Regions
Calypte anna	L	U/C	US	F	L	1800		F8, N14		BSR
Calypte costae	M	U/C	LT	F	L	800		N1, N2		BSR
Calypte helenae	L	U/C	LT/HT	U	L	1200+		N14, F4E, F10E, F1E, F15	CUB	GAN
Stellula calliope	M	U/C	MM	U	2000	2900		F10, F11		BSR
Atthis ellioti	M	U/C	MM	U	900	3000		F11, F4E, N14	CAH	MAH
Atthis heloisa	M	U/C	MM	U	1200	3100		F11, F4E	o	MAH
Myrtis fanny	M	U/C	MM	F	L	3200		N2, N11, N14		EPC, STP, CAN
Eulidia yarrellii	M	U/C	LT	U	L	800+		N11, N14	CHL	STP
Myrmia micrura	M	U/C	LT	U	L	L		N1	MAN	EPC
Acestrura berlepschi	?	C	LT	?	L	L		F1E?	o	CHO
Acestrura bombus	?	M/C	UT?	U/P	L	2150		F4E, F1E, F7?		EPC, NAN, CAN
Acestrura heliodor	M	U/C	UT	U	1200	3000		F4, F15	o	NAN
Acestrura mulsant	M	U/C	MM	F	900	2800		F4E, F15		NAN, CAN
Chaetocercus jourdanii	M	U/C	MM	U/P	900	1800		F4, F15	o	NAN
Selasphorus ardens	M	U/C	MM	F	750	1800		N14, F4E, F15	CHR	CDH
Selasphorus flammula	L	U/C	UM	C	1850	3400		N10, N14, F4E, F15	CHR	CDH
Selasphorus platycercus	M	U/C	MM	C	1900	3750		F11, F10, N14		MAH
Selasphorus scintilla	M	U/C	MM	C	900	2100		N14, F4E, F15	CHR	CDH
TROGONIFORMES										
Trogonidae										
Pharomachrus antisianus	M	M	UT	U	1050	2800		F4		NAN, CAN
Pharomachrus auriceps	M	M	UT	F	1000	2700		F4, F15		CDH, NAN, CAN
Pharomachrus fulgidus	M	M	UT	U	1500	2500		F4	o	NAN
Pharomachrus mocinno	M	M	MM	U	1300	3000		F4		MAH, CDH
Pharomachrus pavoninus	H	M/C	LT	U/P	L	1200		F1		AMN, AMS
Euptilotis neoxenus	M	M/C	MM	U/P	1900	3100		F10, F11	NMM	MAH
Priotelus temnurus	L	M/C	?	C	L	2000+		F1, F7, F10, F15	CUB	GAN
Temnotrogon roseigaster	M	M/C	MM	F	L	3000		F4, F10, F15?	HIS	GAN
Trogon aurantiiventris	M	M	UT	F	750	2100		F4, F15	o	CDH
Trogon bairdii	M	C	LT	U	L	1250		F1	HPC	GCS
Trogon citreolus	L	M/C	LT	C	L	950+		F7, F8, F15	SIN	PAS
Trogon clathratus	H	C	HT	U	L	1100		F1	SCA	GCS
Trogon collaris	M	M/C	LT	C	L	2500		F1, F4, F2, F7		PAS, MAH, GCS, CDH, CHO, NAN, CAN, NSA, AMN, AMS, ATL
Trogon comptus	M	M/C	HT	U	L	1800		F1, F4		CHO, NSA
Trogon curucui	M	C	LT	F	L	1600		F3, F1, F15		AMN, AMS, CSA, ATL?
Trogon elegans	M	M/C	UT	F	L	2500		F7, F11		PAS, MAH
Trogon massena	M	M/C	LT	F	L	1200		F1, F15		PAS, GCS, CHO
Trogon melanocephalus	L	M/C	LT	C	L	800		F1, F7, F8, F15		PAS, GCS
Trogon melanurus	M	C	LT	C	L	1000		F1, F2, F8		GCS, NSA, AMN, AMS
Trogon mexicanus	M	M/C	MM	C	1200	3100		F11, F10, F4	o	MAH
Trogon personatus	M	M	UT	F	1300	3400		F4, F5?		NAN, CAN, TEP
Trogon rufus	M	U/M	LT	U/P	L	900		F1, F15		GCS, NSA, AMN, AMS, ATL
Trogon surrucura	M	C	HT	C	L	2000+		F1, F4	o	ATL
Trogon violaceus	M	C	LT	F	L	1300		F1, F15		PAS, GCS, CHO, EPC, NSA, AMN, AMS
Trogon viridis	M	C	LT	C	L	1300		F1		GCS, NSA, AMN, AMS, ATL
CORACIIFORMES										
Alcedinidae										
Ceryle torquata	L	U/C	LT	C	L	2000		A8, A6, A11, F14		LAN, PAS, GCS, CHO, EPC, SAN, NSA, AMN, AMS, CSA, ATL, PAM, PAT
Chloroceryle aenea	M	U	LT	F	L	L		A9, A6, F14		PAS, GCS, CHO, NSA, AMN, AMS, ATL
Chloroceryle amazona	L	U/M	LT	C	L	1000		A8, A6, F14		PAS, GCS, CHO, NSA, AMN, AMS, CSA, ATL, PAM

CP	RP	Notes
4	3	
4	3	Locally to 2,200 m.
4	3	
4	3	
4	3	Mainly above 1,500 m.
4	3	
4	3	Occasionally to 4,000 m?
3	1	Monitor.
4	3	
2	1	Poorly known.
3	2	Locally to 3,000 m; poorly known.
4	3	Occasionally to 500 m.
4	3	
4	3	Occasionally to 3,300 m (Venezuela)?
3	2	Occasionally to 2,700 m?
4	3	
4	3	Occasionally to 900 m.
4	3	
3	2	Mainly 1,200 to 2,500 m; declining; deforestation; monitor.
4	3	Occasionally to 3,100 m.
3	2	Locally to 900 m (Venezuela); declining; deforestation; monitor.
3	2	Occasionally to 900 m; declining; deforestation; monitor.
4	3	
3	2	Locally to 1,400 m; deforestation.
4	3	
3	2	Deforestation; monitor.
4	3	
3	2	Declining with deforestation; monitor.
4	3	
4	3	Occasionally to 1,400 m; monitor.
4	3	
3	2	Monitor; deforestation.
4	3	In Amazonia, uses *terra firme* forest only along edge.
4	3	
4	3	
4	3	
4	3	Occasionally to 2,200 m.
4	3	Occasionally to 600 m.
4	3	Locally to 700 m.
4	3	Occasionally to 1,400 m.
4	3	
4	3	Occasionally to 1,850 m.
4	3	
4	3	Occasionally wanders to 2,600 m.
4	3	Mostly forest streams.
4	3	Occasionally to 2,500 m.

Abbreviations Used

Snst - Sensitivity:
L - Low; **M** - Medium; **H** - High.

Strat - Foraging Strata:
T - Terrestrial; **U** - Understory; **M** - Midstory; **C** - Canopy; **A** - Aerial; **W** - Water.

Cntab - Center of Abundance:
LT - Lower tropical; **LS** - Lower subtropical; **HT** - Hill tropical; **UT** - Upper tropical; **US** - Upper subtropical; **MM** - Middle montane; **UM** - Upper montane.

Rel - Relative Abundance:
R - Rare; **U** - Uncommon; **F** - Fairly common; **C** - Common; **P** - Patchily distributed.

Min - Minimum Elevation:
L - Lowlands; **?** - Uncertain value; numeric values in meters.

Max - Maximum Elevation:
L - Lowlands; **?** - Uncertain value; **+** - species occurs at least to given elevation but likely occurs higher; numeric values in meters.

Micro - Microhabitats:
A - Army ants; **B** - Bamboo; **T** - Treefalls; **G** - Ground bromeliads; **C** - Rocky outcrops and caves; **S** - Streamside; **V** - Vine tangles; **B/V** -Bamboo/vine tangles.

Habitats:
F1 - Tropical lowland evergreen forest; **F2** - Flooded tropical evergreen forest; **F3** - River-edge forest; **F4** - Montane evergreen forest; **F5** - Elfin forest; **F6** - *Polylepis* woodland; **F7** - Tropical deciduous forest; **F8** - Gallery forest; **F9** - Southern temperate forest; **F10** - Pine forest; **F11** - Pine-oak forest; **F12** - White sand forest; **F13** - Palm forest; **F14** - Mangrove forest; **F15** - Secondary forest; **N1** - Arid lowland scrub; **N2** - Arid montane scrub; **N3** - Semihumid/humid montane scrub; **N4** - Cerrado; **N5** - Campo grasslands; **N6** - Low, seasonally wet grassland; **N7** - Southern temperate grassland; **N8** - Northern temperate grassland; **N9** - Puna grassland; **N10** - Paramo grassland; **N11** - Riparian thickets; **N12** - River island scrub; **N13** - Pastures/agricultural lands; **N14** - Second-growth scrub; **A1** - Freshwater marshes; **A2** - Saltwater/brackish marshes; **A3** - Coastal sand beaches/mudflats; **A4** - Coastal rocky beaches; **A5** - Riverine sand beaches; **A6** - Freshwater lakes and ponds; **A7** - Alkaline lakes; **A8** - Rivers; **A9** - Streams; **A10** - Bogs; **A11** - Coastal waters; **A12** - Pelagic waters.
E - Edge (used as a modifer to particular habitats).

Sub - Subregions:
ARC - Arid Caribbean Coast; **AWA** - Altiplano and Western Andes; **BAH** - Bahamas; **BAJ** - Baja California; **CAA** - Caatinga; **CAH** - Central American Highlands; **CER** - Cerrado; **CHA** - Chaco; **CHG** - Chiapas-Guanacaste; **CHL** - Chilean Desert; **CHR** - Chiriquí; **CIS** - Cocos Island; **CMV** - Cauca-Magdalena Valley; **COC** - Cuzco-Cochabamba; **CUB** - Cuba; **DOM** - Dominica; **EAS** - Eastern Slope Andes; **FDN** - Fernando de Noronha; **GAL** - Galápagos; **GCM** - Gulf Coast-Mexico; **GRE** - Grenada; **GUA** - Guadeloupe; **GUI** - Guianan; **HIS** - Hispaniola; **HPC** - Humid Pacific Coast; **ISA** - Isla Providencia and Isla San Andrés; **JAM** - Jamaica; **JFI** - Juan Fernández Islands; **MAN** - Manabí-Tumbes; **MAR** - Marañón Valley; **MID** - Madeira-Tapajós; **MON** - Montserrat; **MRT** - Martinique; **MTC** - Marañón-Cuzco; **NMM** - Northern Mexican Mountains; **NOR** - Northern Coastal Brazil; **PAR** - Pará; **PER** - Peruvian Desert; **PUE** - Puerto Rico; **RDJ** - Rio de Janeiro-Bahia Lowlands; **RMW** - Rio Madeira West; **RNW** - Rio Negro West; **SCA** - Southern Central America; **SCT** - Santa Cruz-Tucumán; **SIN** - Sinaloa-Oaxaca; **SMH** - Southern Mexican Highlands; **SMT** - Santa Marta; **SOC** - Islas Revillagigedo (Socorro Island group); **SON** - Sonoran Desert; **SOU** - Southern Atlantic Coast; **STL** - St. Lucia; **STV** - St. Vincent; **TAC** - Tacarcuna; **VAN** - Venezuelan Andes; **VNZ** - Venezuelan Coastal Mountains; **WES** - Western Andes; **YUC** - Yucatán Peninsula.
o - Endemic to region, but not restricted to a single subregion.

Zoogeographic Regions:
AMN - Northern Amazonia; **AMS** - Southern Amazonia; **ATL** - Atlantic Forest; **BSR** - Baja-Sonora; **CAN** - Central Andes; **CDH** - Chiriquí-Darién Highlands; **CHO** - Chocó Lowlands; **CSA** - Central South America; **EPC** - Equatorial Pacific Coast; **GAN** - Greater Antilles; **GCS** - Gulf-Caribbean Slope; **LAN** - Lesser Antilles; **MAH** - Madrean Highlands; **MPL** - Mexican Plateau; **NAN** - Northern Andes; **NSA** - Northern South America; **PAM** - Pampas; **PAS** - Pacific Arid Slope; **PAT** - Patagonia; **SAN** - Southern Andes; **STP** - Subtropical Pacific; **TEP** - Tepuis.

CP -Conservation Priority:
1 - Urgent; **2** - High; **3** - Medium; **4** - Low.

RP - Research Priority:
1 - High; **2** - Medium; **3** - Low.

	Snst	Strat	Cntab	Rel	Min	Max	Micro	Habitats	Sub	Zoogeographic Regions
Chloroceryle americana	L	U	LT	C	L	2000		A9, A6, A8, F14		BSR, PAS, MAH, GCS, CHO, EPC, STP, NSA, AMN, AMS, CSA, ATL, PAM
Chloroceryle inda	M	U	LT	U	L	L		A9, A6, F2		GCS, CHO, NSA, AMN, AMS, CSA, ATL
Todidae										
Todus angustirostris	M	U/M	UT	F	900	2400		F4, F15	HIS	GAN
Todus mexicanus	L	U/M	HT	C	L	1000		F4, F1, F7, F15, N14	PUE	GAN
Todus multicolor	L	U/M	LT	C	L	2400		N1, N2, F7, F1, F4, F10	CUB	GAN
Todus subulatus	L	U/M	LT	C	L	1700		F7, N1, F15, F1E, N14	HIS	GAN
Todus todus	L	U/M	LT	F	L	1800+		F1, F7, F15, F14	JAM	GAN
Momotidae										
Hylomanes momotula	H	U	HT	U	L	1200		F1, F4		PAS, MAH, GCS, CDH, CHO, NAN
Aspatha gularis	H	U	MM	U	1500	3100		F4, F11	CAH	MAH
Electron carinatum	H	M	LT	R	L	900		F1, F4		PAS, MAH, GCS
Electron platyrhynchum	M	M	LT	F/P	L	1100		F1, F15?		GCS, CHO, AMN, AMS
Eumomota superciliosa	L	U/M	LT	C	L	900		F7, F8, F15		PAS, GCS
Baryphthengus martii	M	U/M	LT	F	L	1400		F1		GCS, CHO, AMN, AMS
Baryphthengus ruficapillus	M	U/M	LT	C	L	1250		F1, F4, F15	o	ATL
Momotus mexicanus	M	U/M	LT	C	L	1900		F7, F8, F15	o	PAS
Momotus momota										
aequatorialis	M	U/M	UT	F	1250	2200		F4, F15		NAN, CAN
momota	M	U/M	LT	C	L	1300		F1, F4, F15, F8, F7, F2		GCS, CHO, NSA, AMN, AMS, CSA
PICIFORMES										
Galbulidae										
Galbalcyrhynchus leucotis	M	M/C	LT	C	L	L		F2E, F15	RNW	AMN
Galbalcyrhynchus purusianus	M	M/C	LT	C	L	L		F2E, F15	RMW	AMS
Brachygalba albogularis	M	C	LT	U/P	L	L		F3E	RMW	AMS
Brachygalba goeringi	M	C	LT	U/P	L	L		F8, F7E	ARC	NSA
Brachygalba lugubris	L	C	LT	U/P	L	900		F1E, F8, F3, F15E		AMN, AMS, CSA
Brachygalba salmoni	M	C	LT	U/P	L	600		F1E, F15E		GCS, NSA
Jacamaralcyon tridactyla	M	C?	LT	U/P	L	1000		F1E, F8, F15	o	ATL
Galbula albirostris	H	M	LT	U	L	900	T	F1	o	AMN
Galbula cyanescens	L	M	LT	C	L	1050		F1E	RMW	AMS
Galbula cyanicollis	H	M	LT	U	L	L	T	F1	o	AMS
Galbula dea	M	C	LT	F	L	800		F1, F3		AMN, AMS
Galbula galbula	L	M	LT	F	L	700		F1E, F8, F15		AMN, AMS
Galbula leucogastra										
chalcothorax	H	?	LT	U	L	600		F1		AMN, AMS
leucogastra	H	C	LT	U/P	L	900		F12, F1E		AMN, AMS
Galbula pastazae	H	M?	UT	U	1000	1700		F4	EAS	NAN
Galbula ruficauda	L	M	LT	C	L	900	S	F1E, F8, F7E, F3		PAS, GCS, CHO, NSA, AMN, AMS, CSA, ATL
Galbula tombacea	L	M	LT	F	L	1200		F1E, F2E, F8		AMN, AMS
Jacamerops aurea	H	M/C	LT	U/P	L	1100		F1		GCS, CHO, AMN, AMS
Bucconidae										
Notharchus macrorhynchos	M	C	LT	F	L	900		F1, F15		PAS, GCS, CHO, NSA, AMN, AMS, ATL
Notharchus ordii	H	C	LT	R/P	L	L		F1		AMN, AMS
Notharchus pectoralis	H	C	LT	U	L	1000		F1, F15?		GCS, CHO, NSA
Notharchus tectus	M	C	LT	F/P	L	1000		F1E, F15		GCS, NSA, AMN, AMS
Bucco capensis	H	C	LT	F	L	1100		F1		AMN, AMS
Bucco macrodactylus	M	M	LT	F	L	L		F3, F2E, F8, F1E		AMN, AMS
Bucco noanamae	M	C	LT	R?	L	L		F1, F15?	o	CHO
Bucco tamatia	M	C	LT	F	L	L		F2, F15		AMN, AMS
Nystalus chacuru	M	C	LT	F	L	1400		F7, N4, F8E, F15		AMS, CSA, ATL
Nystalus maculatus	M	C	LT	F	L	1300		F7, N4		AMS, CSA

CP	RP	Notes
4	3	Occasionally to 3,000 m+.
4	3	Mostly forest streams.
4	3	
4	3	
4	3	
4	3	
4	3	
3	2	Occasionally to 1,850 m; declining with deforestation.
3	2	Occasionally to 1,300 m; declining with deforestation.
3	2	Locally to 1,500 m; poorly known.
4	3	
4	3	
4	3	
4	3	
4	3	
4	3	Occasionally to 3,100 m?
4	3	Locally to 2,100 m (Central America).
4	3	
4	3	
4	3	
4	3	Locally to 1,100 m (Venezuela).
4	3	Occasionally to 1,500 m.
4	3	
2	1	Poorly known; habitat destruction.
4	3	Occasionally to 1,300 m.
4	3	
4	3	
4	3	Occasionally to 1,100 m.
4	3	
4	2	Poorly known.
4	3	
2	2	Poorly known; survey.
4	3	Locally to 1,300 m.
4	3	
4	3	
4	3	
3	2	Poorly known.
4	3	
4	3	
4	3	
4	3	
2	1	Poorly known.
4	3	
4	3	
4	3	Locally to 2,500 m (Bolivia).

Abbreviations Used

Snst - Sensitivity:
L - Low; **M** - Medium; **H** - High.

Strat - Foraging Strata:
T - Terrestrial; **U** - Understory; **M** - Midstory; **C** - Canopy; **A** - Aerial; **W** - Water.

Cntab - Center of Abundance:
LT - Lower tropical; **LS** - Lower subtropical; **HT** - Hill tropical; **UT** - Upper tropical; **US** - Upper subtropical; **MM** - Middle montane; **UM** - Upper montane.

Rel - Relative Abundance:
R - Rare; **U** - Uncommon; **F** - Fairly common; **C** - Common; **P** - Patchily distributed.

Min - Minimum Elevation:
L - Lowlands; **?** - Uncertain value; numeric values in meters.

Max - Maximum Elevation:
L - Lowlands; **?** - Uncertain value; **+** - species occurs at least to given elevation but likely occurs higher; numeric values in meters.

Micro - Microhabitats:
A - Army ants; **B** - Bamboo; **T** - Treefalls; **G** - Ground bromeliads; **C** - Rocky outcrops and caves; **S** - Streamside; **V** - Vine tangles; **B/V** -Bamboo/vine tangles.

Habitats:
F1 - Tropical lowland evergreen forest; **F2** - Flooded tropical evergreen forest; **F3** - River-edge forest; **F4** - Montane evergreen forest; **F5** - Elfin forest; **F6** - *Polylepis* woodland; **F7** - Tropical deciduous forest; **F8** - Gallery forest; **F9** - Southern temperate forest; **F10** - Pine forest; **F11** - Pine-oak forest; **F12** - White sand forest; **F13** - Palm forest; **F14** - Mangrove forest; **F15** - Secondary forest; **N1** - Arid lowland scrub; **N2** - Arid montane scrub; **N3** - Semihumid/humid montane scrub; **N4** - Cerrado; **N5** - Campo grasslands; **N6** - Low, seasonally wet grassland; **N7** - Southern temperate grassland; **N8** - Northern temperate grassland; **N9** - Puna grassland; **N10** - Paramo grassland; **N11** - Riparian thickets; **N12** - River island scrub; **N13** - Pastures/agricultural lands; **N14** - Second-growth scrub; **A1** - Freshwater marshes; **A2** - Saltwater/brackish marshes; **A3** - Coastal sand beaches/mudflats; **A4** - Coastal rocky beaches; **A5** - Riverine sand beaches; **A6** - Freshwater lakes and ponds; **A7** - Alkaline lakes; **A8** - Rivers; **A9** - Streams; **A10** - Bogs; **A11** - Coastal waters; **A12** - Pelagic waters.
E - Edge (used as a modifer to particular habitats).

Sub - Subregions:
ARC - Arid Caribbean Coast; **AWA** - Altiplano and Western Andes; **BAH** - Bahamas; **BAJ** - Baja California; **CAA** - Caatinga; **CAH** - Central American Highlands; **CER** - Cerrado; **CHA** - Chaco; **CHG** - Chiapas-Guanacaste; **CHL** - Chilean Desert; **CHR** - Chiriquí; **CIS** - Cocos Island; **CMV** - Cauca-Magdalena Valley; **COC** - Cuzco-Cochabamba; **CUB** - Cuba; **DOM** - Dominica; **EAS** - Eastern Slope Andes; **FDN** - Fernando de Noronha; **GAL** - Galápagos; **GCM** - Gulf Coast-Mexico; **GRE** - Grenada; **GUA** - Guadeloupe; **GUI** - Guianan; **HIS** - Hispaniola; **HPC** - Humid Pacific Coast; **ISA** - Isla Providencia and Isla San Andrés; **JAM** - Jamaica; **JFI** - Juan Fernández Islands; **MAN** - Manabí-Tumbes; **MAR** - Marañón Valley; **MID** - Madeira-Tapajós; **MON** - Montserrat; **MRT** - Martinique; **MTC** - Marañón-Cuzco; **NMM** - Northern Mexican Mountains; **NOR** - Northern Coastal Brazil; **PAR** - Pará; **PER** - Peruvian Desert; **PUE** - Puerto Rico; **RDJ** - Rio de Janeiro-Bahia Lowlands; **RMW** - Rio Madeira West; **RNW** - Rio Negro West; **SCA** - Southern Central America; **SCT** - Santa Cruz-Tucumán; **SIN** - Sinaloa-Oaxaca; **SMH** - Southern Mexican Highlands; **SMT** - Santa Marta; **SOC** - Islas Revillagigedo (Socorro Island group); **SON** - Sonoran Desert; **SOU** - Southern Atlantic Coast; **STL** - St. Lucia; **STV** - St. Vincent; **TAC** - Tacarcuna; **VAN** - Venezuelan Andes; **VNZ** - Venezuelan Coastal Mountains; **WES** - Western Andes; **YUC** - Yucatán Peninsula.
o - Endemic to region, but not restricted to a single subregion.

Zoogeographic Regions:
AMN - Northern Amazonia; **AMS** - Southern Amazonia; **ATL** - Atlantic Forest; **BSR** - Baja-Sonora; **CAN** - Central Andes; **CDH** - Chiriquí-Darién Highlands; **CHO** - Chocó Lowlands; **CSA** - Central South America; **EPC** - Equatorial Pacific Coast; **GAN** - Greater Antilles; **GCS** - Gulf-Caribbean Slope; **LAN** - Lesser Antilles; **MAH** - Madrean Highlands; **MPL** - Mexican Plateau; **NAN** - Northern Andes; **NSA** - Northern South America; **PAM** - Pampas; **PAS** - Pacific Arid Slope; **PAT** - Patagonia; **SAN** - Southern Andes; **STP** - Subtropical Pacific; **TEP** - Tepuis.

CP -Conservation Priority:
1 - Urgent; **2** - High; **3** - Medium; **4** - Low.

RP - Research Priority:
1 - High; **2** - Medium; **3** - Low.

	Snst	Strat	Cntab	Rel	Min	Max	Micro	Habitats	Sub	Zoogeographic Regions
Nystalus radiatus	M	C	LT	U	L	900		F1E, F15		GCS, CHO, NSA
Nystalus striolatus	M	C	LT	F	L	1700		F1, F3		AMN, AMS
Hypnelus ruficollis	L?	M/C	LT	F	L	1200		F7, F8, F15	o	NSA
Malacoptila fulvogularis	H	U	UT	U	1050	2100		F4		NAN, CAN
Malacoptila fusca	H	U	LT	U	L	900		F1		AMN, AMS
Malacoptila mystacalis	M	U	UT	U	700	2100		F4, F1, F7, F15		NAN, NSA
Malacoptila panamensis	M	U	LT	F	L	1250		F1, F15		GCS, CHO, NSA
Malacoptila rufa	H	U	LT	F	L	L		F1	o	AMS
Malacoptila semicincta	H	U	LT	U	L	1050		F1	RMW	AMS
Malacoptila striata	M	U/M	LT	U	L	1000		F1, F4	o	ATL
Micromonacha lanceolata	H	C	UT	R/P	300	2100		F4, F1		GCS, CHO, NAN, CAN
Nonnula amaurocephala	M	U	LT	?	L	L		F2?	RNW	AMN
Nonnula brunnea	H	U	LT	U	L	600		F1	RNW	AMN
Nonnula rubecula	H	U/M	LT	U	L	L		F1, F2		AMN, AMS, CSA, ATL
Nonnula ruficapilla										
frontalis	L	U/M	LT	U	L	1000		F1E, F15		GCS, CHO, NSA
ruficapilla	M	U/M	LT	U/P	L	1650	B	F1		AMN, AMS
Nonnula sclateri	H	U	LT	U	L	L	B	F1	RMW	AMS
Hapaloptila castanea	H	C	MM	R/P	750	2900		F4		NAN, CAN
Monasa atra	M	M/C	LT	F	L	900		F1, F8	o	AMN
Monasa flavirostris	M	M/C	LT	R/P	L	1400	B/V	F1E, F2E, F15		AMN, AMS
Monasa morphoeus	H	M/C	LT	F	L	1100		F1, F4		PAS, GCS, CHO, AMN, AMS, ATL
Monasa nigrifrons	M	M/C	LT	C	L	900		F2, F3, F1E, F15		AMN, AMS, CSA
Chelidoptera tenebrosa	L	C	LT	C	L	1200		F1E, F2E, F3, F8E, F15E		NSA, AMN, AMS, CSA, ATL
Capitonidae										
Capito aurovirens	M	C	LT	C	L	L		F2, F3, F15		AMN, AMS
Capito dayi	H	C	LT	F	L	L		F1	MID	AMS
Capito hypoleucus	?	C	UT	F	800	1500		F1	CMV	NSA
Capito maculicoronatus	M	C	LT	F	L	1000		F1, F15		PAS, GCS, CHO, NSA
Capito niger	M	M/C	LT	C	L	1350		F1, F15, F2		AMN, AMS
Capito quinticolor	M	C	LT	U/P	L	L		F1, F15	o	CHO
Capito squamatus	M	C	LT	?	L	1500		F1, F15?	o	CHO
Eubucco bourcierii	M	C	UT	F	900	2400		F4, F15		CDH, NAN
Eubucco richardsoni	H	C	LT	F	L	900		F1, F2		AMN, AMS
Eubucco tucinkae	M	C	LT	R/P	L	800		F3, F15	RMW	AMS
Eubucco versicolor	M	C	UT	U	850	2500		F4	o	CAN
Semnornis frantzii	M	C	MM	U	1200	2450		F4	CHR	CDH
Semnornis ramphastinus	M	C	UT	U	1000	2400		F4	WES	NAN
Ramphastidae										
Aulacorhynchus calorhynchus	M	C	UT	F	1200	1900		F4, F15	o	NAN
Aulacorhynchus coeruleicinctis	H	C	MM	U	1500	2700		F4	o	CAN
Aulacorhynchus derbianus	H	C	UT	U	800	2400		F4		NAN, CAN, TEP
Aulacorhynchus haematopygus	M	C	UT	F	800	2200		F4, F15	o	NAN
Aulacorhynchus huallagae	H	C	MM	U	2000	2600		F4	MTC	CAN
Aulacorhynchus prasinus	M	C	UT	F	L	3000		F4, F1		MAH, GCS, CDH, NAN, CAN, AMS
Aulacorhynchus sulcatus	M	C	UT	F	600	2000		F4, F15	VNZ	NAN
Pteroglossus aracari	M	C	LT	C	L	600		F1, F15		NSA, AMN, AMS, CSA, ATL
Pteroglossus azara	H	C	LT	F	L	900		F1		AMN, AMS
Pteroglossus beauharnaesii	H	C	LT	U	L	800		F1	o	AMS
Pteroglossus bitorquatus	M	C	LT	F	L	L		F1, F15	o	AMS
Pteroglossus castanotis	H	C	LT	C	L	900		F3, F15, F2, F1		AMN, AMS, CSA
Pteroglossus frantzii	M	C	LT	F	L	1500		F1, F15	HPC	GCS
Pteroglossus inscriptus	M	C	LT	F	L	700		F2, F3, F15		AMN, AMS

CP	RP	Notes
4	3	
4	3	
4	3	
4	3	
4	3	
4	3	Locally to 400 m.
4	3	
4	3	
4	3	
4	3	
4	3	Very local in upper Amazonian basin; poorly known.
3	2	Poorly known.
4	3	
4	3	
4	3	
4	3	
4	3	
3	2	Poorly known.
4	3	
4	2	Poorly known.
4	3	
4	3	
4	3	
4	3	
4	2	
2	1	Poorly known; deforestation.
4	3	
4	3	
3	2	Poorly known; survey.
3	2	Poorly known.
4	3	Locally to 400 m.
4	3	Occasionally to 1,200 m.
4	3	
4	3	Occasionally to 750 m; deforestation; monitor.
4	3	Locally to 750 m; occasionally to 450 m.
4	2	Survey.
4	3	
4	3	
4	3	
4	3	Occasionally to 300 m on Pacific slope.
2	2	Survey.
4	3	Lowland populations uncommon and local.
4	3	
4	3	
4	3	Occasionally to 1,350 m; usually called *P. flavirostris*.
4	3	
4	3	
4	3	Occasionally to 1,300 m (Bolivia).
3	2	Occasionally to 1,900 m; deforestation.
4	3	

Abbreviations Used

Snst - Sensitivity:
L - Low; **M** - Medium; **H** - High.

Strat - Foraging Strata:
T - Terrestrial; **U** - Understory; **M** - Midstory; **C** - Canopy; **A** - Aerial; **W** - Water.

Cntab - Center of Abundance:
LT - Lower tropical; **LS** - Lower subtropical; **HT** - Hill tropical; **UT** - Upper tropical; **US** - Upper subtropical; **MM** - Middle montane; **UM** - Upper montane.

Rel - Relative Abundance:
R - Rare; **U** - Uncommon; **F** - Fairly common; **C** - Common; **P** - Patchily distributed.

Min - Minimum Elevation:
L - Lowlands; **?** - Uncertain value; numeric values in meters.

Max - Maximum Elevation:
L - Lowlands; **?** - Uncertain value; **+** - species occurs at least to given elevation but likely occurs higher; numeric values in meters.

Micro - Microhabitats:
A - Army ants; **B** - Bamboo; **T** - Treefalls; **G** - Ground bromeliads; **C** - Rocky outcrops and caves; **S** - Streamside; **V** - Vine tangles; **B/V** -Bamboo/vine tangles.

Habitats:
F1 - Tropical lowland evergreen forest; **F2** - Flooded tropical evergreen forest; **F3** - River-edge forest; **F4** - Montane evergreen forest; **F5** - Elfin forest; **F6** - *Polylepis* woodland; **F7** - Tropical deciduous forest; **F8** - Gallery forest; **F9** - Southern temperate forest; **F10** - Pine forest; **F11** - Pine-oak forest; **F12** - White sand forest; **F13** - Palm forest; **F14** - Mangrove forest; **F15** - Secondary forest; **N1** - Arid lowland scrub; **N2** - Arid montane scrub; **N3** - Semihumid/humid montane scrub; **N4** - Cerrado; **N5** - Campo grasslands; **N6** - Low, seasonally wet grassland; **N7** - Southern temperate grassland; **N8** - Northern temperate grassland; **N9** - Puna grassland; **N10** - Paramo grassland; **N11** - Riparian thickets; **N12** - River island scrub; **N13** - Pastures/agricultural lands; **N14** - Second-growth scrub; **A1** - Freshwater marshes; **A2** - Saltwater/brackish marshes; **A3** - Coastal sand beaches/mudflats; **A4** - Coastal rocky beaches; **A5** - Riverine sand beaches; **A6** - Freshwater lakes and ponds; **A7** - Alkaline lakes; **A8** - Rivers; **A9** - Streams; **A10** - Bogs; **A11** - Coastal waters; **A12** - Pelagic waters.
E - Edge (used as a modifer to particular habitats).

Sub - Subregions:
ARC - Arid Caribbean Coast; **AWA** - Altiplano and Western Andes; **BAH** - Bahamas; **BAJ** - Baja California; **CAA** - Caatinga; **CAH** - Central American Highlands; **CER** - Cerrado; **CHA** - Chaco; **CHG** - Chiapas-Guanacaste; **CHL** - Chilean Desert; **CHR** - Chiriquí; **CIS** - Cocos Island; **CMV** - Cauca-Magdalena Valley; **COC** - Cuzco-Cochabamba; **CUB** - Cuba; **DOM** - Dominica; **EAS** - Eastern Slope Andes; **FDN** - Fernando de Noronha; **GAL** - Galápagos; **GCM** - Gulf Coast-Mexico; **GRE** - Grenada; **GUA** - Guadeloupe; **GUI** - Guianan; **HIS** - Hispaniola; **HPC** - Humid Pacific Coast; **ISA** - Isla Providencia and Isla San Andrés; **JAM** - Jamaica; **JFI** - Juan Fernández Islands; **MAN** - Manabí-Tumbes; **MAR** - Marañón Valley; **MID** - Madeira-Tapajós; **MON** - Montserrat; **MRT** - Martinique; **MTC** - Marañón-Cuzco; **NMM** - Northern Mexican Mountains; **NOR** - Northern Coastal Brazil; **PAR** - Pará; **PER** - Peruvian Desert; **PUE** - Puerto Rico; **RDJ** - Rio de Janeiro-Bahia Lowlands; **RMW** - Rio Madeira West; **RNW** - Rio Negro West; **SCA** - Southern Central America; **SCT** - Santa Cruz-Tucumán; **SIN** - Sinaloa-Oaxaca; **SMH** - Southern Mexican Highlands; **SMT** - Santa Marta; **SOC** - Islas Revillagigedo (Socorro Island group); **SON** - Sonoran Desert; **SOU** - Southern Atlantic Coast; **STL** - St. Lucia; **STV** - St. Vincent; **TAC** - Tacarcuna; **VAN** - Venezuelan Andes; **VNZ** - Venezuelan Coastal Mountains; **WES** - Western Andes; **YUC** - Yucatán Peninsula.
o - Endemic to region, but not restricted to a single subregion.

Zoogeographic Regions:
AMN - Northern Amazonia; **AMS** - Southern Amazonia; **ATL** - Atlantic Forest; **BSR** - Baja-Sonora; **CAN** - Central Andes; **CDH** - Chiriquí-Darién Highlands; **CHO** - Chocó Lowlands; **CSA** - Central South America; **EPC** - Equatorial Pacific Coast; **GAN** - Greater Antilles; **GCS** - Gulf-Caribbean Slope; **LAN** - Lesser Antilles; **MAH** - Madrean Highlands; **MPL** - Mexican Plateau; **NAN** - Northern Andes; **NSA** - Northern South America; **PAM** - Pampas; **PAS** - Pacific Arid Slope; **PAT** - Patagonia; **SAN** - Southern Andes; **STP** - Subtropical Pacific; **TEP** - Tepuis.

CP -Conservation Priority:
1 - Urgent; **2** - High; **3** - Medium; **4** - Low.

RP - Research Priority:
1 - High; **2** - Medium; **3** - Low.

	Snst	Strat	Cntab	Rel	Min	Max	Micro	Habitats	Sub	Zoogeographic Regions
Pteroglossus pluricinctus	H	C	LT	U	L	900		F1		NSA, AMN
Pteroglossus torquatus	M	C	LT	C	L	1200		F1, F15		PAS, GCS, CHO, NSA
Pteroglossus viridis	H	C	LT	U	L	800		F1	GUI	AMN
Selenidera culik	L	C	LT	U	L	900		F1	GUI	AMN
Selenidera maculirostris										
gouldi	M	C	LT	F	L	L		F1	o	AMS
maculirostris	M	C	LT	U	L	1000		F1, F4	o	ATL
Selenidera nattereri	H	C	LT	U	L	L?		F1	o	AMN
Selenidera reinwardtii	H	C	LT	U	L	1100		F1, F4		AMN, AMS
Selenidera spectabilis	H	C	UT	U	L	1500		F1, F4		PAS, GCS, CHO, NSA
Baillonius bailloni	H	C	HT	F	L	1550		F4, F1	SOU	ATL
Andigena cucullata	H	C	UM	U	2500	3300		F4	COC	CAN
Andigena hypoglauca	H	C	UM	U	2400	3350		F4		NAN, CAN
Andigena laminirostris	H	C	MM	F	1200	3200		F4	WES	NAN
Andigena nigrirostris	H	C	MM	F	1600	3200		F4	o	NAN
Ramphastos ambiguus	H	C	UT	F	500	2400		F4		NAN, CAN
Ramphastos brevis	H	C	LT	?	L	1000		F1	o	CHO
Ramphastos dicolorus	M	C	UT	F	L	1800		F1, F4	SOU	ATL
Ramphastos sulfuratus	M	C	LT	C	L	1600		F1, F15		PAS, GCS, NSA
Ramphastos swainsonii	M	C	LT	F	L	2000		F1, F4		PAS, GCS, CHO, NSA
Ramphastos toco	M	C	LT	F	L	1200		N6, F8, F3		AMN, AMS, CSA, ATL
Ramphastos tucanus	H	C	LT	C	L	1100		F1		NSA, AMN, AMS
Ramphastos vitellinus	H	C	LT	F	L	1250		F1		NSA, AMN, AMS, ATL
Picidae										
Picumnus albosquamatus	L	M/C	LT	F	L	2100		F8, F7, F1E, N4		CAN, CSA
Picumnus aurifrons	M	M/C	LT	F	L	1100		F1, F15	o	AMS
Picumnus castelnau	L	M/C	LT	F	L	950		F3, F15		AMN, AMS
Picumnus cinnamomeus	M	C?	LT	C	L	L		F7, N1, F14	ARC	NSA
Picumnus cirratus										
cirratus	L	M/C	LT	C	L	2200		F1, F15, F8, F7		AMN, AMS, CSA, ATL
dorbygnianus	M	M/C	UT	F	1100	2200		F4, F15	o	CAN
temminckii	M	M/C	LT	F	L	800		F1, F15, F12	SOU	ATL
Picumnus exilis										
exilis	M	M/C	LT	F	L	1900?		F1, F8, F15		AMN, CSA, ATL
salvini	L?	M/C	LT	R?	L	L		F15, F8?	ARC	NSA
Picumnus fulvescens	H	?	LT	?	L	950?		F7?	CAA	CSA
Picumnus fuscus	H	?	LT	?	L	L		F3?, F8?	CER	CSA
Picumnus granadensis	L	M/C	UT	F	800	2200		F1E, F7, F15		NAN, NSA
Picumnus lafresnayi										
lafresnayi	M	M/C	LT	U	L	1400		F1, F3	RNW	AMN
pumilis	M	?	LT	?	L	L		F8?	RNW	AMN
Picumnus limae	M	?	LT	?	L	1000		F7	CAA	CSA
Picumnus minutissimus	L	M/C	LT	F	L	L?		F1E, F8, F15, F14?	GUI	AMN
Picumnus nebulosus	M	U/M	LT	U	L	1100	B?	F9, F1		ATL, PAM
Picumnus olivaceus	L	M/C	LT	F	L	1700		F1E, F15, F7?		PAS, GCS, CHO
Picumnus pygmaeus	M	M/C	LT	?	L	800+		F7	CAA	CSA
Picumnus rufiventris	L	U/M	LT	U/P	L	900		F3, F1E, F15		AMN, AMS
Picumnus sclateri	M	M/C	LT	F	L	1400		F7	MAN	EPC
Picumnus spilogaster	L	M/C	LT	F	L	L		F8, F15, F7		NSA, AMN
Picumnus squamulatus	L	U/C	LT	F	L	1900		F7, F8, F15	o	NSA
Picumnus steindachneri	H	C	UT	U	1100	1900		F4	MTC	CAN
Picumnus subtilis	L	M/C	LT	U	L	1100		F3, F15	RMW	AMS
Picumnus varzeae	M	C	LT	?	L	L		F2, F3, F12?, F15?		AMN, AMS

CP	RP	Notes
4	3	
4	3	
4	3	
4	3	
4	3	
3	2	Declining outside reserves; deforestation.
4	2	Poorly known.
4	3	Occasionally to 1,550 m (Peru).
3	2	Deforestation; monitor.
3	2	Declining outside reserves.
4	3	
4	3	Occasionally to 2,000 m.
3	3	Occasionally to 300 m.
3	2	Locally to 1,200 m; habitat destruction.
3	2	Locally to lowlands; declining locally; deforestation.
3	2	Deforestation.
3	2	Declining outside reserves; monitor; elevational movements.
4	3	
3	2	Declining outside reserves.
4	3	
4	3	Occasionally to 1,350 m.
4	3	Occasionally to 1,650 m.
4	3	Usually below 1,200 m.
4	3	
4	3	
4	3	
4	2	Taxonomic relationships needs study.
4	2	
4	3	
4	3	May contain two species.
3	2	Poorly known; often called *P. nigropunctatus* (see Short 1982).
2	1	Poorly known; habitat destruction.
3	2	Poorly known.
3	3	
4	3	
3	2	Poorly known.
3	2	Poorly known.
4	3	
3	2	
4	3	Occasionally to 2,600 m.
3	2	Poorly known.
4	2	
4	2	Occasionally to 2,100 m; monitor.
4	3	
4	3	
3	2	Poorly known.
4	2	Poorly known; relationship to *P. castelnau* uncertain.
3	2	Poorly known; habitat destruction.

Abbreviations Used

Snst - Sensitivity:
L - Low; **M** - Medium; **H** - High.

Strat - Foraging Strata:
T - Terrestrial; **U** - Understory; **M** - Midstory; **C** - Canopy; **A** - Aerial; **W** - Water.

Cntab - Center of Abundance:
LT - Lower tropical; **LS** - Lower subtropical; **HT** - Hill tropical; **UT** - Upper tropical; **US** - Upper subtropical; **MM** - Middle montane; **UM** - Upper montane.

Rel - Relative Abundance:
R - Rare; **U** - Uncommon; **F** - Fairly common; **C** - Common; **P** - Patchily distributed.

Min - Minimum Elevation:
L - Lowlands; **?** - Uncertain value; numeric values in meters.

Max - Maximum Elevation:
L - Lowlands; **?** - Uncertain value; **+** - species occurs at least to given elevation but likely occurs higher; numeric values in meters.

Micro - Microhabitats:
A - Army ants; **B** - Bamboo; **T** - Treefalls; **G** - Ground bromeliads; **C** - Rocky outcrops and caves; **S** - Streamside; **V** - Vine tangles; **B/V** -Bamboo/vine tangles.

Habitats:
F1 - Tropical lowland evergreen forest; **F2** - Flooded tropical evergreen forest; **F3** - River-edge forest; **F4** - Montane evergreen forest; **F5** - Elfin forest; **F6** - *Polylepis* woodland; **F7** - Tropical deciduous forest; **F8** - Gallery forest; **F9** - Southern temperate forest; **F10** - Pine forest; **F11** - Pine-oak forest; **F12** - White sand forest; **F13** - Palm forest; **F14** - Mangrove forest; **F15** - Secondary forest; **N1** - Arid lowland scrub; **N2** - Arid montane scrub; **N3** - Semihumid/humid montane scrub; **N4** - Cerrado; **N5** - Campo grasslands; **N6** - Low, seasonally wet grassland; **N7** - Southern temperate grassland; **N8** - Northern temperate grassland; **N9** - Puna grassland; **N10** - Paramo grassland; **N11** - Riparian thickets; **N12** - River island scrub; **N13** - Pastures/agricultural lands; **N14** - Second-growth scrub; **A1** - Freshwater marshes; **A2** - Saltwater/brackish marshes; **A3** - Coastal sand beaches/mudflats; **A4** - Coastal rocky beaches; **A5** - Riverine sand beaches; **A6** - Freshwater lakes and ponds; **A7** - Alkaline lakes; **A8** - Rivers; **A9** - Streams; **A10** - Bogs; **A11** - Coastal waters; **A12** - Pelagic waters.
E - Edge (used as a modifer to particular habitats).

Sub - Subregions:
ARC - Arid Caribbean Coast; **AWA** - Altiplano and Western Andes; **BAH** - Bahamas; **BAJ** - Baja California; **CAA** - Caatinga; **CAH** - Central American Highlands; **CER** - Cerrado; **CHA** - Chaco; **CHG** - Chiapas-Guanacaste; **CHL** - Chilean Desert; **CHR** - Chiriquí; **CIS** - Cocos Island; **CMV** - Cauca-Magdalena Valley; **COC** - Cuzco-Cochabamba; **CUB** - Cuba; **DOM** - Dominica; **EAS** - Eastern Slope Andes; **FDN** - Fernando de Noronha; **GAL** - Galápagos; **GCM** - Gulf Coast-Mexico; **GRE** - Grenada; **GUA** - Guadeloupe; **GUI** - Guianan; **HIS** - Hispaniola; **HPC** - Humid Pacific Coast; **ISA** - Isla Providencia and Isla San Andrés; **JAM** - Jamaica; **JFI** - Juan Fernández Islands; **MAN** - Manabí-Tumbes; **MAR** - Marañón Valley; **MID** - Madeira-Tapajós; **MON** - Montserrat; **MRT** - Martinique; **MTC** - Marañón-Cuzco; **NMM** - Northern Mexican Mountains; **NOR** - Northern Coastal Brazil; **PAR** - Pará; **PER** - Peruvian Desert; **PUE** - Puerto Rico; **RDJ** - Rio de Janeiro-Bahia Lowlands; **RMW** - Rio Madeira West; **RNW** - Rio Negro West; **SCA** - Southern Central America; **SCT** - Santa Cruz-Tucumán; **SIN** - Sinaloa-Oaxaca; **SMH** - Southern Mexican Highlands; **SMT** - Santa Marta; **SOC** - Islas Revillagigedo (Socorro Island group); **SON** - Sonoran Desert; **SOU** - Southern Atlantic Coast; **STL** - St. Lucia; **STV** - St. Vincent; **TAC** - Tacarcuna; **VAN** - Venezuelan Andes; **VNZ** - Venezuelan Coastal Mountains; **WES** - Western Andes; **YUC** - Yucatán Peninsula.
o - Endemic to region, but not restricted to a single subregion.

Zoogeographic Regions:
AMN - Northern Amazonia; **AMS** - Southern Amazonia; **ATL** - Atlantic Forest; **BSR** - Baja-Sonora; **CAN** - Central Andes; **CDH** - Chiriquí-Darién Highlands; **CHO** - Chocó Lowlands; **CSA** - Central South America; **EPC** - Equatorial Pacific Coast; **GAN** - Greater Antilles; **GCS** - Gulf-Caribbean Slope; **LAN** - Lesser Antilles; **MAH** - Madrean Highlands; **MPL** - Mexican Plateau; **NAN** - Northern Andes; **NSA** - Northern South America; **PAM** - Pampas; **PAS** - Pacific Arid Slope; **PAT** - Patagonia; **SAN** - Southern Andes; **STP** - Subtropical Pacific; **TEP** - Tepuis.

CP -Conservation Priority:
1 - Urgent; **2** - High; **3** - Medium; **4** - Low.

RP - Research Priority:
1 - High; **2** - Medium; **3** - Low.

	Snst	Strat	Cntab	Rel	Min	Max	Micro	Habitats	Sub	Zoogeographic Regions
Nesoctites micromegas	M	M/C	LT	U	L	1800		F7, F1, N1	HIS	GAN
Melanerpes aurifrons	L	M/C	LT	C	L	2400		N1, N2, F8, F1E, F15, F7		MPL, PAS, MAH, GCS
Melanerpes cactorum	M	M/C	LT	C	L	2500		F7, N2, N1		CAN, CSA
Melanerpes candidus	L	M/C	LT	U/P	L	1200		N6, N5, F7E, F8E, F1E		AMN, AMS, CSA, ATL
Melanerpes chrysauchen	L	C	LT	C	L	1550		F1E, F15		GCS, NSA
Melanerpes chrysogenys	L	C	LT	C	L	1500		F7, F8, F15		PAS, MAH
Melanerpes cruentatus	L	C	LT	C	L	1350		F3, F1E, F15		NSA, AMN, AMS
Melanerpes flavifrons	M	C	LT	F	L	950		F1, F15	o	ATL
Melanerpes formicivorus	L	M/C	MM	C	L	3300		F11, F10, F4E		BSR, MAH, GCS, CDH, NAN
Melanerpes herminieri	L?	?	LT	F	L	700		F1, F15	GUA	LAN
Melanerpes hoffmannii	L	C	LT	C	L	2050		F7, F15, N14		PAS, CDH
Melanerpes hypopolius	L	M/C	UT	F	900	2450		N2, F8	SMH	MAH
Melanerpes portoricensis	L	M/C	LT	F	L	1000		F1, F7, F15	PUE	GAN
Melanerpes pucherani	M	C	LT	C	L	800		F1, F15		PAS, GCS, CHO, NSA
Melanerpes pygmaeus	L	M/C	LT	F	L	L		N1, F7, F15	YUC	GCS
Melanerpes radiolatus	L	C	LT	C	L	1800+		F1, F15	JAM	GAN
Melanerpes rubricapillus	L	C	LT	C	L	1800		F1E, F15, F8, F7, F14		GCS, NSA, AMN
Melanerpes striatus	L	C	LT	C	L	2400+		F1, F15, F7, F14	HIS	GAN
Melanerpes superciliaris	L	C	LT	C	L	2000+		F1E, F7, F15, F14	o	GAN
Melanerpes uropygialis	M	C	LS	C	L	1550		N1, N2, F7, F8, N14, F15		BSR, MPL
Sphyrapicus thyroideus	M	M/C	US	F	1900	2800		F11, F10		BSR
Xiphidiopicus percussus	M	M/C	LT	F	L	2000		F1, F7, F15?	CUB	GAN
Picoides lignarius	M	M/C	MM	U	L	2800		N2, F9E, F15		STP, SAN
Picoides mixtus	M	M/C	LT	U?	L	600+		N4, F7, N11	o	CSA
Picoides nuttallii	M	M/C	LS	U	L	1250		F8, F11		BSR
Picoides scalaris	L	M/C	LS	C	L	2600		N1, N2, F8, F11, F7		BSR, MPL, PAS, MAH, GCS
Picoides stricklandi	H	M/C	MM	F	1250	4200		F11	NMM	MAH
Picoides villosus	M	M/C	UM	F	950	3450		F10, F11, F4		BSR, MAH, CDH
Veniliornis affinis	M	C	LT	F	L	1050		F1, F8		CHO, AMN, AMS, ATL
Veniliornis callonotus	L	M/C	LT	C	L	1200		N1, F7, F8		NAN, EPC
Veniliornis cassini	H	C	LT	C	L	1500		F1	GUI	AMN
Veniliornis dignus	H	C	MM	U	1200	2300		F4		NAN, CAN
Veniliornis frontalis	M	M/C	UT	C	L?	2000		F4, F7	SCT	CAN
Veniliornis fumigatus	L	M/C	UT	C	L	2800		F4, F1, F15, F6		PAS, MAH, GCS, CDH, NAN, CAN
Veniliornis kirkii	M	C	LT	F	L	1900		F1, F7, F4		GCS, CHO, NSA, TEP
Veniliornis maculifrons	M	C	HT	F	L	1300		F1, F15	o	ATL
Veniliornis nigriceps	H	M/C	UM	F	2300	3600		F4, F5		NAN, CAN
Veniliornis passerinus	L	C	LT	C	L	1200+		F3, F15, F8		NSA, AMN, AMS, CSA
Veniliornis sanguineus	M	C	LT	F	L	L		F1, F15, F14	GUI	AMN
Veniliornis spilogaster	M	U/C	HT	C	L	2000+		F4, F1, F15	SOU	ATL
Piculus auricularis	M	C	UT	U	900	2000		F11, F4	NMM	MAH
Piculus aurulentus	M	M/C	UT	U	750	2000		F4, F1, F9	SOU	ATL
Piculus chrysochloros	M	C	LT	U	L	650		F1, F8, F7		AMN, AMS, CSA, ATL
Piculus flavigula	H	C	LT	F	L	700		F1, F2		AMN, AMS, ATL
Piculus leucolaemus										
leucolaemus	H	C	LT	U	L	1400		F1		GCS, CHO, NSA, AMN, AMS
simplex	M	C	LT	U	L	900		F1	o	GCS
Piculus rivolii	M	M/C	MM	U	1800	3300		F4, F5		NAN, CAN
Piculus rubiginosus	L	C	UT	F	L	2200		F4, F1, F7, F15, F11		PAS, MAH, GCS, CDH, CHO, EPC, NAN, CAN, NSA, TEP
Colaptes atricollis	L	M/C	MM	U	900	3400		N2, F8, F15		STP, CAN
Colaptes auratus	L	T/C	MM	F	L	3500		N1, F10, F11, F8		GAN, BSR, MPL, MAH
Colaptes campestris	L	T/C	LT	C	L	2100		N6, N4, N5, N13		AMN, CSA, ATL, PAM
Colaptes fernandinae	M	M/C	LT	R	L	L?		N6, F1E	CUB	GAN

CP	RP	Notes
4	3	Poorly known.
4	3	
4	3	
4	3	Occasionally to 2,350 m.
4	3	
4	3	
4	3	
4	3	Occasionally to 1,800 m (southeastern Brazil)?
4	3	
4	2	Monitor.
4	3	Occasionally to 2,200 m; local on Caribbean slope.
4	3	
4	3	
4	3	Occasionally to 1,250 m.
4	3	
4	3	
4	3	Occasionally to 1,900 m.
4	3	
4	3	
4	3	
4	3	Breeding status uncertain.
4	3	
4	3	Occasionally to 3,800 m?
4	3	
4	3	Occasionally to 2,000 m.
4	3	
4	3	
4	3	
4	3	Occasionally to 1,350 m.
4	3	
4	3	
4	3	Occasionally to 700 and 2,700 m.
4	2	Poorly known.
4	3	Locally to 4,000 m in *Polylepis* (Peru).
4	3	
3	3	
4	3	Mainly above 2,800 m.
4	3	Occasionally to 1,650 m (Bolivia).
4	3	
4	3	
4	3	Occasionally in lowlands.
4	3	
4	3	
4	3	
4	3	Includes *P. callopterus*.
3	2	Poorly known.
4	3	Occasionally to 700 m and 3,700 m.
4	3	Occasionally to 3,100 m (Colombia).
4	2	Rare and local at sea level; survey.
4	2	Probably contains multiple species.
4	3	
2	1	Associated with palms; survey; conservation measures needed.

Abbreviations Used

Snst - Sensitivity:
L - Low; **M** - Medium; **H** - High.

Strat - Foraging Strata:
T - Terrestrial; **U** - Understory; **M** - Midstory; **C** - Canopy; **A** - Aerial; **W** - Water.

Cntab - Center of Abundance:
LT - Lower tropical; **LS** - Lower subtropical; **HT** - Hill tropical; **UT** - Upper tropical; **US** - Upper subtropical; **MM** - Middle montane; **UM** - Upper montane.

Rel - Relative Abundance:
R - Rare; **U** - Uncommon; **F** - Fairly common; **C** - Common; **P** - Patchily distributed.

Min - Minimum Elevation:
L - Lowlands; **?** - Uncertain value; numeric values in meters.

Max - Maximum Elevation:
L - Lowlands; **?** - Uncertain value; **+** - species occurs at least to given elevation but likely occurs higher; numeric values in meters.

Micro - Microhabitats:
A - Army ants; **B** - Bamboo; **T** - Treefalls; **G** - Ground bromeliads; **C** - Rocky outcrops and caves; **S** - Streamside; **V** - Vine tangles; **B/V** -Bamboo/vine tangles.

Habitats:
F1 - Tropical lowland evergreen forest; **F2** - Flooded tropical evergreen forest; **F3** - River-edge forest; **F4** - Montane evergreen forest; **F5** - Elfin forest; **F6** - *Polylepis* woodland; **F7** - Tropical deciduous forest; **F8** - Gallery forest; **F9** - Southern temperate forest; **F10** - Pine forest; **F11** - Pine-oak forest; **F12** - White sand forest; **F13** - Palm forest; **F14** - Mangrove forest; **F15** - Secondary forest; **N1** - Arid lowland scrub; **N2** - Arid montane scrub; **N3** - Semihumid/humid montane scrub; **N4** - Cerrado; **N5** - Campo grasslands; **N6** - Low, seasonally wet grassland; **N7** - Southern temperate grassland; **N8** - Northern temperate grassland; **N9** - Puna grassland; **N10** - Paramo grassland; **N11** - Riparian thickets; **N12** - River island scrub; **N13** - Pastures/agricultural lands; **N14** - Second-growth scrub; **A1** - Freshwater marshes; **A2** - Saltwater/brackish marshes; **A3** - Coastal sand beaches/mudflats; **A4** - Coastal rocky beaches; **A5** - Riverine sand beaches; **A6** - Freshwater lakes and ponds; **A7** - Alkaline lakes; **A8** - Rivers; **A9** - Streams; **A10** - Bogs; **A11** - Coastal waters; **A12** - Pelagic waters.
E - Edge (used as a modifer to particular habitats).

Sub - Subregions:
ARC - Arid Caribbean Coast; **AWA** - Altiplano and Western Andes; **BAH** - Bahamas; **BAJ** - Baja California; **CAA** - Caatinga; **CAH** - Central American Highlands; **CER** - Cerrado; **CHA** - Chaco; **CHG** - Chiapas-Guanacaste; **CHL** - Chilean Desert; **CHR** - Chiriquí; **CIS** - Cocos Island; **CMV** - Cauca-Magdalena Valley; **COC** - Cuzco-Cochabamba; **CUB** - Cuba; **DOM** - Dominica; **EAS** - Eastern Slope Andes; **FDN** - Fernando de Noronha; **GAL** - Galápagos; **GCM** - Gulf Coast-Mexico; **GRE** - Grenada; **GUA** - Guadeloupe; **GUI** - Guianan; **HIS** - Hispaniola; **HPC** - Humid Pacific Coast; **ISA** - Isla Providencia and Isla San Andrés; **JAM** - Jamaica; **JFI** - Juan Fernández Islands; **MAN** - Manabí-Tumbes; **MAR** - Marañón Valley; **MID** - Madeira-Tapajós; **MON** - Montserrat; **MRT** - Martinique; **MTC** - Marañón-Cuzco; **NMM** - Northern Mexican Mountains; **NOR** - Northern Coastal Brazil; **PAR** - Pará; **PER** - Peruvian Desert; **PUE** - Puerto Rico; **RDJ** - Rio de Janeiro-Bahia Lowlands; **RMW** - Rio Madeira West; **RNW** - Rio Negro West; **SCA** - Southern Central America; **SCT** - Santa Cruz-Tucumán; **SIN** - Sinaloa-Oaxaca; **SMH** - Southern Mexican Highlands; **SMT** - Santa Marta; **SOC** - Islas Revillagigedo (Socorro Island group); **SON** - Sonoran Desert; **SOU** - Southern Atlantic Coast; **STL** - St. Lucia; **STV** - St. Vincent; **TAC** - Tacarcuna; **VAN** - Venezuelan Andes; **VNZ** - Venezuelan Coastal Mountains; **WES** - Western Andes; **YUC** - Yucatán Peninsula.
o - Endemic to region, but not restricted to a single subregion.

Zoogeographic Regions:
AMN - Northern Amazonia; **AMS** - Southern Amazonia; **ATL** - Atlantic Forest; **BSR** - Baja-Sonora; **CAN** - Central Andes; **CDH** - Chiriquí-Darién Highlands; **CHO** - Chocó Lowlands; **CSA** - Central South America; **EPC** - Equatorial Pacific Coast; **GAN** - Greater Antilles; **GCS** - Gulf-Caribbean Slope; **LAN** - Lesser Antilles; **MAH** - Madrean Highlands; **MPL** - Mexican Plateau; **NAN** - Northern Andes; **NSA** - Northern South America; **PAM** - Pampas; **PAS** - Pacific Arid Slope; **PAT** - Patagonia; **SAN** - Southern Andes; **STP** - Subtropical Pacific; **TEP** - Tepuis.

CP -Conservation Priority:
1 - Urgent; **2** - High; **3** - Medium; **4** - Low.

RP - Research Priority:
1 - High; **2** - Medium; **3** - Low.

	Snst	Strat	Cntab	Rel	Min	Max	Micro	Habitats	Sub	Zoogeographic Regions
Colaptes melanochloros	L	T/C	LT	F	L	1250		F1E, F8, F7		CAN, AMS, CSA, ATL, PAM
Colaptes pitius	L	T/C	US	F	L	1500		F9E, F15, N2, N14		STP, SAN, PAT
Colaptes punctigula	L	M/C	LT	F	L	800		F3, F15, F14		GCS, CHO, NSA, AMN, AMS
Colaptes rupicola	M	T	UM	F	2900	4600		N9, N10, N13	AWA	CAN
Celeus castaneus	M	M/C	LT	U	L	750		F1	o	GCS
Celeus elegans	M	M/C	LT	U	L	800		F1, F2		NSA, AMN, AMS
Celeus flavescens	M	M/C	LT	F	L	1200		F1, F8, F12, F15		AMN, AMS, CSA, ATL
Celeus flavus	M	C	LT	F	L	700		F2, F3, F8		NSA, AMN, AMS, ATL
Celeus grammicus	H	C	LT	U	L	900		F1		AMN, AMS
Celeus loricatus	H	C	LT	U	L	800		F1		GCS, CHO, NSA
Celeus lugubris	M	M/C	LT	U	L	800+		F7, F8	o	CSA
Celeus spectabilis										
obrieni	H	U/M	LT	R	L	L?		F7?	CAA	CSA
spectabilis	H	U/M	LT	R/P	L	L		F3		AMN, AMS
Celeus torquatus	H	C	LT	R	L	L		F1, F2		AMN, AMS, ATL
Celeus undatus	H	C	LT	U	L	500+		F1		NSA, AMN, AMS
Dryocopus galeatus	H	M/C	LT	R	L	800		F1	SOU	ATL
Dryocopus lineatus	L	C	LT	C	L	1550		F3, F8, F15, F1E, F7, F4E		PAS, GCS, CHO, EPC, NSA, AMN, AMS, CSA, ATL
Dryocopus schulzi	H	C	LT	U	L	L		F7, F15	CHA	CSA
Campephilus gayaquilensis	M	C	LT	F	L	1500+		F7, F1E		CHO, EPC
Campephilus guatemalensis	M	C	LT	F	L	1550		F1E, F8, F15, F7		PAS, GCS
Campephilus haematogaster	H	U/M	UT	U	L	2200		F4, F1		CDH, NAN, CAN
Campephilus imperialis	H	U/C	UM	R	1900	3150		F10	NMM	MAH
Campephilus leucopogon	M	?	LT	U?	L	1750		F7	CHA	CSA
Campephilus magellanicus	H	U/M	LS	U	L	2000+		F9	o	SAN
Campephilus melanoleucos	M	C	LT	F	L	2500		F3, F1E, F8, F15		GCS, CHO, NAN, NSA, AMN, AMS, CSA
Campephilus pollens	H	U/M	MM	U	1500	3350		F4		NAN, CAN
Campephilus principalis	H	U/C	LT	R	L	900+		F10	CUB	GAN
Campephilus robustus	M	M	LT	U	L	1200		F1, F4	o	ATL
Campephilus rubricollis	H	M	LT	F	L	1250		F1, F4		AMN, AMS
Passeriformes										
Dendrocolaptidae										
Dendrocincla anabatina	H	U	LT	U	L	1250	A	F1	o	GCS
Dendrocincla fuliginosa										
fuliginosa	H	U/M	LT	F	L	1200	A	F1		GCS, CHO, NSA, AMN, AMS
turdina	M	U/M	LT	F	L	1250	A	F1, F4	o	ATL
Dendrocincla homochroa	H	U	LT	F	L	1500	A	F1, F4, F7		PAS, MAH, GCS, CDH, CHO, NSA
Dendrocincla merula	H	U	LT	U	L	600	A	F1		AMN, AMS
Dendrocincla tyrannina	H	U/M	MM	U	1300	2500		F4		NAN, CAN
Deconychura longicauda	H	M	LT	U	L	1400		F1		GCS, CDH, NAN, CAN, AMN, AMS
Deconychura stictolaema	H	M	LT	U/P	L	L		F1		AMN, AMS
Sittasomus griseicapillus	M	M	LT	C	L	1550		F1, F2, F4, F15, F7		PAS, MAH, GCS, CDH, CHO, EPC, NAN, CAN, NSA, AMN, AMS, CSA, ATL
Glyphorynchus spirurus	M	U/M	LT	F	L	1250		F1, F4		GCS, CHO, NSA, AMN, AMS, ATL
Drymornis bridgesii	M	T/M	LT	?	L	1000+		F7, N1	CHA	CSA
Nasica longirostris	H	M/C	LT	U/F	L	500		F2, F3		AMN, AMS
Dendrexetastes rufigula	H	M	LT	F	L	950		F1, F2		AMN, AMS
Hylexetastes perrotii	H	U/M	LT	U	L	L		F1		AMN, AMS
Hylexetastes stresemanni	H	U/M	LT	R	L	L		F1		AMN, AMS
Xiphocolaptes albicollis	M	M	HT	U	L	1800+		F1, F4, F8		CSA, ATL

CP	RP	Notes
4	3	Locally to 2,800 m in Andes.
4	3	
4	3	Locally to 1,500 m.
4	3	
4	3	
4	3	Occasionally to 1,100 m (Venezuela); may contain two species.
4	3	
4	2	
4	3	Occasionally to 1,150 m.
4	2	Occasionally to 1,500 m.
4	3	
2	1	Known from one specimen; survey.
3	2	Survey; poorly known.
4	2	Atlantic Forest population threatened.
4	3	
1	1	No viable populations known; several recent records.
4	3	Occasionally to 2,150 m; mainly below 900 m.
3	2	Survey; relationship to *D. lineatus* uncertain.
3	2	Deforestation; monitor.
4	3	Locally to 2,500 m.
4	2	Deforestation; monitor.
1	1	Nearly extinct; habitat destruction.
3	2	Poorly known.
4	3	
4	3	Occasionally to 3,100 m; mainly lowlands.
4	3	Occasionally to 900 and 3,750 m.
1	1	Nearly extinct; habitat destruction.
3	2	Occasionally to 2,250 m; declining outside reserves; survey.
4	3	Occasionally to 1,650 m.
3	3	Occasionally to 1,400 m (Costa Rica); deforestation.
4	3	Occasionally to 1,650 m (Bolivia).
3	3	
4	3	
4	3	
4	3	Occasionally to 3,000 m (Colombia).
4	3	Occasionally to 1,700 m (Ecuador).
4	3	
4	2	Occasionally to 2,300 m; may contain multiple species.
4	3	
4	2	
4	3	
4	3	
4	3	
3	2	Poorly known.
3	3	Declining in many areas outside reserves.

Abbreviations Used

Snst - Sensitivity:
L - Low; **M** - Medium; **H** - High.

Strat - Foraging Strata:
T - Terrestrial; **U** - Understory; **M** - Midstory; **C** - Canopy; **A** - Aerial; **W** - Water.

Cntab - Center of Abundance:
LT - Lower tropical; **LS** - Lower subtropical; **HT** - Hill tropical; **UT** - Upper tropical; **US** - Upper subtropical; **MM** - Middle montane; **UM** - Upper montane.

Rel - Relative Abundance:
R - Rare; **U** - Uncommon; **F** - Fairly common; **C** - Common; **P** - Patchily distributed.

Min - Minimum Elevation:
L - Lowlands; **?** - Uncertain value; numeric values in meters.

Max - Maximum Elevation:
L - Lowlands; **?** - Uncertain value; **+** - species occurs at least to given elevation but likely occurs higher; numeric values in meters.

Micro - Microhabitats:
A - Army ants; **B** - Bamboo; **T** - Treefalls; **G** - Ground bromeliads; **C** - Rocky outcrops and caves; **S** - Streamside; **V** - Vine tangles; **B/V** -Bamboo/vine tangles.

Habitats:
F1 - Tropical lowland evergreen forest; **F2** - Flooded tropical evergreen forest; **F3** - River-edge forest; **F4** - Montane evergreen forest; **F5** - Elfin forest; **F6** - *Polylepis* woodland; **F7** - Tropical deciduous forest; **F8** - Gallery forest; **F9** - Southern temperate forest; **F10** - Pine forest; **F11** - Pine-oak forest; **F12** - White sand forest; **F13** - Palm forest; **F14** - Mangrove forest; **F15** - Secondary forest; **N1** - Arid lowland scrub; **N2** - Arid montane scrub; **N3** - Semihumid/humid montane scrub; **N4** - Cerrado; **N5** - Campo grasslands; **N6** - Low, seasonally wet grassland; **N7** - Southern temperate grassland; **N8** - Northern temperate grassland; **N9** - Puna grassland; **N10** - Paramo grassland; **N11** - Riparian thickets; **N12** - River island scrub; **N13** - Pastures/agricultural lands; **N14** - Second-growth scrub; **A1** - Freshwater marshes; **A2** - Saltwater/brackish marshes; **A3** - Coastal sand beaches/mudflats; **A4** - Coastal rocky beaches; **A5** - Riverine sand beaches; **A6** - Freshwater lakes and ponds; **A7** - Alkaline lakes; **A8** - Rivers; **A9** - Streams; **A10** - Bogs; **A11** - Coastal waters; **A12** - Pelagic waters.
E - Edge (used as a modifer to particular habitats).

Sub - Subregions:
ARC - Arid Caribbean Coast; **AWA** - Altiplano and Western Andes; **BAH** - Bahamas; **BAJ** - Baja California; **CAA** - Caatinga; **CAH** - Central American Highlands; **CER** - Cerrado; **CHA** - Chaco; **CHG** - Chiapas-Guanacaste; **CHL** - Chilean Desert; **CHR** - Chiriquí; **CIS** - Cocos Island; **CMV** - Cauca-Magdalena Valley; **COC** - Cuzco-Cochabamba; **CUB** - Cuba; **DOM** - Dominica; **EAS** - Eastern Slope Andes; **FDN** - Fernando de Noronha; **GAL** - Galápagos; **GCM** - Gulf Coast-Mexico; **GRE** - Grenada; **GUA** - Guadeloupe; **GUI** - Guianan; **HIS** - Hispaniola; **HPC** - Humid Pacific Coast; **ISA** - Isla Providencia and Isla San Andrés; **JAM** - Jamaica; **JFI** - Juan Fernández Islands; **MAN** - Manabí-Tumbes; **MAR** - Marañón Valley; **MID** - Madeira-Tapajós; **MON** - Montserrat; **MRT** - Martinique; **MTC** - Marañón-Cuzco; **NMM** - Northern Mexican Mountains; **NOR** - Northern Coastal Brazil; **PAR** - Pará; **PER** - Peruvian Desert; **PUE** - Puerto Rico; **RDJ** - Rio de Janeiro-Bahia Lowlands; **RMW** - Rio Madeira West; **RNW** - Rio Negro West; **SCA** - Southern Central America; **SCT** - Santa Cruz-Tucumán; **SIN** - Sinaloa-Oaxaca; **SMH** - Southern Mexican Highlands; **SMT** - Santa Marta; **SOC** - Islas Revillagigedo (Socorro Island group); **SON** - Sonoran Desert; **SOU** - Southern Atlantic Coast; **STL** - St. Lucia; **STV** - St. Vincent; **TAC** - Tacarcuna; **VAN** - Venezuelan Andes; **VNZ** - Venezuelan Coastal Mountains; **WES** - Western Andes; **YUC** - Yucatán Peninsula.
o - Endemic to region, but not restricted to a single subregion.

Zoogeographic Regions:
AMN - Northern Amazonia; **AMS** - Southern Amazonia; **ATL** - Atlantic Forest; **BSR** - Baja-Sonora; **CAN** - Central Andes; **CDH** - Chiriquí-Darién Highlands; **CHO** - Chocó Lowlands; **CSA** - Central South America; **EPC** - Equatorial Pacific Coast; **GAN** - Greater Antilles; **GCS** - Gulf-Caribbean Slope; **LAN** - Lesser Antilles; **MAH** - Madrean Highlands; **MPL** - Mexican Plateau; **NAN** - Northern Andes; **NSA** - Northern South America; **PAM** - Pampas; **PAS** - Pacific Arid Slope; **PAT** - Patagonia; **SAN** - Southern Andes; **STP** - Subtropical Pacific; **TEP** - Tepuis.

CP -Conservation Priority:
1 - Urgent; **2** - High; **3** - Medium; **4** - Low.

RP - Research Priority:
1 - High; **2** - Medium; **3** - Low.

	Snst	Strat	Cntab	Rel	Min	Max	Micro	Habitats	Sub	Zoogeographic Regions
Xiphocolaptes falcirostris										
falcirostris	M	M	LT	U?	L	800+		F8, F1	CAA	CSA
franciscanus	H	M	LT	R	400	400		F7	CER	CSA
Xiphocolaptes major	M	U/M	LT	U	L	1800		F7, F8	CHA	CSA
Xiphocolaptes promeropirhynchus										
orenocensis	H	M/C	LT	U/P	L	800		F1		AMN, AMS
promeropirhynchus	H	M	MM	U	700	3100		F4, F11		MAH, CDH, EPC, NAN, CAN, TEP
Dendrocolaptes certhia										
certhia	H	U/M	LT	F	L	1300	A	F1		MAH, GCS, CHO, NSA, AMN, AMS, ATL
concolor	H	U/M	LT	F	L	L	A	F1	o	AMS
Dendrocolaptes hoffmannsi	H	U/M	LT	U	L	L	A	F1	MID	AMS
Dendrocolaptes picumnus	H	M	LT	U	L	2800	A	F1, F4		MAH, CDH, NAN, CAN, AMN, AMS, CSA
Dendrocolaptes platyrostris	M	M	LT	F	L	2100		F1, F4, F8		CSA, ATL
Xiphorhynchus erythropygius	M	M	UT	F	900	2200		F4, F1		MAH, CDH, CHO, NAN
Xiphorhynchus flavigaster	M	U/M	LT	C	L	1500		F1, F4, F7, F15, F11		PAS, MAH, GCS
Xiphorhynchus guttatus										
eytoni	M	U/C	LT	F	L	L		F1		AMN, AMS
guttatus	L	U/C	LT	C	L	1100		F1, F2, F15		GCS, NSA, AMN, AMS, ATL
Xiphorhynchus lachrymosus	M	M	LT	F	L	1200		F1, F14		GCS, CHO, NSA
Xiphorhynchus necopinus	?	?	LT	?	L	L		F2		AMN, AMS
Xiphorhynchus obsoletus	M	U/M	LT	F	L	500		F2, F8, F12		AMN, AMS
Xiphorhynchus ocellatus	H	U/M	UT	F	L	1600		F1, F4		CAN, AMN, AMS
Xiphorhynchus pardalotus	H	U/M	LT	F	L	1800		F1, F4		TEP, AMN, AMS
Xiphorhynchus picus	L	M	LT	C	L	900		F3, F7, F8, F15, F14		GCS, NSA, AMN, AMS
Xiphorhynchus spixii										
elegans	H	U/M	LT	F	L	500		F1		AMN, AMS
spixii	H	U/M	LT	F	L	600		F1		NAN, AMN, AMS
Xiphorhynchus triangularis	H	M	UT	F	1100	2400		F4		NAN, CAN
Lepidocolaptes affinis	M	M	UT/MM	F	1000	3100		F4, F11, F15		MAH, CDH, NAN, CAN
Lepidocolaptes albolineatus	H	C	LT	U	L	1100		F1		AMN, AMS
Lepidocolaptes angustirostris	M	U/M	LT	F	L	1200+		F7, N4		AMS, CSA
Lepidocolaptes fuscus	H	U/M	LT	F	L	1300		F1, F4	o	ATL
Lepidocolaptes leucogaster	M	M/C	MM	F	950	4000		F11, F10, F7?	o	MAH
Lepidocolaptes souleyetii	L	U/M	LT	F	L	1600		F7, F8, F1, F14, F15		PAS, GCS, CHO, EPC, NSA, AMN
Lepidocolaptes squamatus	H	M/C	UT	F	L	2000+		F4, F1	o	ATL
Campylorhamphus falcularius	H	U/M	UT	U	L	1600+	B	F4, F1	SOU	ATL
Campylorhamphus procurvoides	H	U/M	LT	U/P	L	500	B	F1		AMN, AMS
Campylorhamphus pucherani	H	U/M	MM	R/P	2100	2950		F4		NAN, CAN
Campylorhamphus pusillus	H	U/M	UT	U	L	2200		F4, F1		GCS, CDH, NAN, CAN
Campylorhamphus trochilirostris	H	U/M	LT	F/P	L	1200	B	F1, F4, F7		GCS, CHO, EPC, NAN, CAN, NSA, AMN, AMS, CSA
Furnariidae										
Geobates poecilopterus	M	T	UT	U/P	700	1250		N5	CER	CSA
Geositta antarctica	M	T	LS	F	L	L		N7	o	PAT
Geositta crassirostris	M	T	MM	U	600	2500		N2		STP, CAN
Geositta cunicularia	M	T	LS	F	L	4800		N7, N9, N1		STP, CAN, SAN, PAM, PAT
Geositta isabellina	M	T	UM	F	1800	3100		N9	o	SAN
Geositta maritima	L	T	LT	F	L	2300		N1		STP, CAN
Geositta peruviana	L	T	LT	F	L	700		N1		EPC, STP
Geositta punensis	M	T	UM	U	3200	4600		N9	AWA	CAN
Geositta rufipennis	M	T	UM	F	3100	4400		N9, N2		STP, CAN, SAN
Geositta saxicolina	M	T	UM	F	3700	4900		N9	AWA	CAN
Geositta tenuirostris	L	T	UM	F	2500	4600		N9, N13		NAN, CAN

CP	RP	Notes
3	2	Poorly known; taxonomy of group needs study.
1	1	Deforestation; relationship to *X. falcirostris* uncertain.
4	3	
4	3	
4	3	Locally to 3,600 m (Mexico).
4	3	Locally to 1,800 m (Mexico, Honduras).
4	3	
3	3	
4	3	Above 1,000 m west of Andes.
4	3	
4	3	Locally to 200 m; occasionally to 2,400 m.
4	3	Occasionally (regularly?) to 2,500 m.
4	3	
4	3	
4	3	Locally to 1,500 m (Colombia).
4	2	Poorly known; taxonomic status uncertain.
4	3	
4	2	Local in lowlands?
4	3	
4	3	Occasionally to 1,400 m (Venezuela).
		Allocation of some subspecies to *X. elegans* or *X. spixii* uncertain.
4	3	
4	3	Locally to 1,400 m; occasionally to 2,400 m(Colombia).
4	3	Occasionally to 2,700 m (Colombia).
4	3	Occasionally to 550 and 3,600 m (Mexico).
4	3	Occasionally to 2,200 m? may contain two species.
4	3	
4	3	
4	3	Occasionally to 400 m.
4	3	
4	3	
3	2	Deforestation; monitor.
4	3	Distribution poorly known.
4	2	Poorly known; patchily distributed.
4	3	Mainly above 1,250 m in Andes.
4	3	Occasionally to 2,100 m.
2	1	Survey; colonizes recently burned areas.
4	3	
4	3	
4	3	
4	3	
4	3	
4	3	
4	3	Occasionally to 3,050 and 5,000 m.
4	3	
4	3	
4	3	

Abbreviations Used

Snst - Sensitivity:
L - Low; **M** - Medium; **H** - High.

Strat - Foraging Strata:
T - Terrestrial; **U** - Understory; **M** - Midstory; **C** - Canopy; **A** - Aerial; **W** - Water.

Cntab - Center of Abundance:
LT - Lower tropical; **LS** - Lower subtropical; **HT** - Hill tropical; **UT** - Upper tropical; **US** - Upper subtropical; **MM** - Middle montane; **UM** - Upper montane.

Rel - Relative Abundance:
R - Rare; **U** - Uncommon; **F** - Fairly common; **C** - Common; **P** - Patchily distributed.

Min - Minimum Elevation:
L - Lowlands; **?** - Uncertain value; numeric values in meters.

Max - Maximum Elevation:
L - Lowlands; **?** - Uncertain value; **+** - species occurs at least to given elevation but likely occurs higher; numeric values in meters.

Micro - Microhabitats:
A - Army ants; **B** - Bamboo; **T** - Treefalls; **G** - Ground bromeliads; **C** - Rocky outcrops and caves; **S** - Streamside; **V** - Vine tangles; **B/V** -Bamboo/vine tangles.

Habitats:
F1 - Tropical lowland evergreen forest; **F2** - Flooded tropical evergreen forest; **F3** - River-edge forest; **F4** - Montane evergreen forest; **F5** - Elfin forest; **F6** - *Polylepis* woodland; **F7** - Tropical deciduous forest; **F8** - Gallery forest; **F9** - Southern temperate forest; **F10** - Pine forest; **F11** - Pine-oak forest; **F12** - White sand forest; **F13** - Palm forest; **F14** - Mangrove forest; **F15** - Secondary forest; **N1** - Arid lowland scrub; **N2** - Arid montane scrub; **N3** - Semihumid/humid montane scrub; **N4** - Cerrado; **N5** - Campo grasslands; **N6** - Low, seasonally wet grassland; **N7** - Southern temperate grassland; **N8** - Northern temperate grassland; **N9** - Puna grassland; **N10** - Paramo grassland; **N11** - Riparian thickets; **N12** - River island scrub; **N13** - Pastures/agricultural lands; **N14** - Second-growth scrub; **A1** - Freshwater marshes; **A2** - Saltwater/brackish marshes; **A3** - Coastal sand beaches/mudflats; **A4** - Coastal rocky beaches; **A5** - Riverine sand beaches; **A6** - Freshwater lakes and ponds; **A7** - Alkaline lakes; **A8** - Rivers; **A9** - Streams; **A10** - Bogs; **A11** - Coastal waters; **A12** - Pelagic waters.
E - Edge (used as a modifer to particular habitats).

Sub - Subregions:
ARC - Arid Caribbean Coast; **AWA** - Altiplano and Western Andes; **BAH** - Bahamas; **BAJ** - Baja California; **CAA** - Caatinga; **CAH** - Central American Highlands; **CER** - Cerrado; **CHA** - Chaco; **CHG** - Chiapas-Guanacaste; **CHL** - Chilean Desert; **CHR** - Chiriquí; **CIS** - Cocos Island; **CMV** - Cauca-Magdalena Valley; **COC** - Cuzco-Cochabamba; **CUB** - Cuba; **DOM** - Dominica; **EAS** - Eastern Slope Andes; **FDN** - Fernando de Noronha; **GAL** - Galápagos; **GCM** - Gulf Coast-Mexico; **GRE** - Grenada; **GUA** - Guadeloupe; **GUI** - Guianan; **HIS** - Hispaniola; **HPC** - Humid Pacific Coast; **ISA** - Isla Providencia and Isla San Andrés; **JAM** - Jamaica; **JFI** - Juan Fernández Islands; **MAN** - Manabí-Tumbes; **MAR** - Marañón Valley; **MID** - Madeira-Tapajós; **MON** - Montserrat; **MRT** - Martinique; **MTC** - Marañón-Cuzco; **NMM** - Northern Mexican Mountains; **NOR** - Northern Coastal Brazil; **PAR** - Pará; **PER** - Peruvian Desert; **PUE** - Puerto Rico; **RDJ** - Rio de Janeiro-Bahia Lowlands; **RMW** - Rio Madeira West; **RNW** - Rio Negro West; **SCA** - Southern Central America; **SCT** - Santa Cruz-Tucumán; **SIN** - Sinaloa-Oaxaca; **SMH** - Southern Mexican Highlands; **SMT** - Santa Marta; **SOC** - Islas Revillagigedo (Socorro Island group); **SON** - Sonoran Desert; **SOU** - Southern Atlantic Coast; **STL** - St. Lucia; **STV** - St. Vincent; **TAC** - Tacarcuna; **VAN** - Venezuelan Andes; **VNZ** - Venezuelan Coastal Mountains; **WES** - Western Andes; **YUC** - Yucatán Peninsula.
o - Endemic to region, but not restricted to a single subregion.

Zoogeographic Regions:
AMN - Northern Amazonia; **AMS** - Southern Amazonia; **ATL** - Atlantic Forest; **BSR** - Baja-Sonora; **CAN** - Central Andes; **CDH** - Chiriquí-Darién Highlands; **CHO** - Chocó Lowlands; **CSA** - Central South America; **EPC** - Equatorial Pacific Coast; **GAN** - Greater Antilles; **GCS** - Gulf-Caribbean Slope; **LAN** - Lesser Antilles; **MAH** - Madrean Highlands; **MPL** - Mexican Plateau; **NAN** - Northern Andes; **NSA** - Northern South America; **PAM** - Pampas; **PAS** - Pacific Arid Slope; **PAT** - Patagonia; **SAN** - Southern Andes; **STP** - Subtropical Pacific; **TEP** - Tepuis.

CP -Conservation Priority:
1 - Urgent; **2** - High; **3** - Medium; **4** - Low.

RP - Research Priority:
1 - High; **2** - Medium; **3** - Low.

	Snst	Strat	Cntab	Rel	Min	Max	Micro	Habitats	Sub	Zoogeographic Regions
Upucerthia albigula	M	T	UM	U	3050	3700		N2	AWA	CAN
Upucerthia andaecola	M	T	UM	U?	2500	4500		N2, N9	AWA	CAN
Upucerthia dumetaria	M	T	LS	F	L	4000		N2, N1, N9		CAN, SAN, PAT
Upucerthia jelskii	M	T	UM	F	3250	4600		N9, N2	AWA	CAN
Upucerthia serrana	M	T	UM	U	2750	4300		N2, F6	AWA	CAN
Upucerthia validirostris	M	T	UM	F	2700	5000		N9		CAN, SAN
Ochetorhynchus certhioides										
certhioides	M	T	LT	F	L	1300		N1	CHA	CSA
harterti	M	T	MM	U	1400	2900	G	N2	SCT	CAN
Ochetorhynchus ruficauda	M	T	UM	F	1800	4200		N2		CAN, SAN
Eremobius phoenicurus	M	T/U	LS	F/U	L	1200		N1, N7		CSA, PAT
Chilia melanura	M	T	MM	U	L	3000		N2, N1		STP, SAN
Cinclodes antarcticus	H	T	LS	F	L	L		A4	o	PAT
Cinclodes atacamensis	M	T	UM	F	2800	4900		N9, A9		CAN, SAN
Cinclodes comechingonus	M	T	UM	?	1600	2800	S	N2?	o	SAN
Cinclodes excelsior										
aricomae	M	T	UM	R	3500	4600		F6, N3	AWA	CAN
excelsior	M	T	UM	R/U	3200	5200		N10, N3	EAS	NAN
Cinclodes fuscus	M	T	UM	C	L	4900		N10, N9, N7, N2		NAN, CAN, SAN, PAT
Cinclodes nigrofumosus										
nigrofumosus	H	T	LS	F	L	L		A4	CHL	STP
taczanowskii	H	T	LS	F	L	L		A4	PER	STP
Cinclodes olrogi	M	T	UM	C	1600	2800	S	N2	o	SAN
Cinclodes oustaleti	M	T	LS	F	L	3700	S	N2, N1		STP, SAN
Cinclodes pabsti	L	T	UT	U	750	1100	S	N7, N13	SOU	ATL
Cinclodes palliatus	M	T	UM	R/P	4400	5000		A10, N9	AWA	CAN
Cinclodes patagonicus	M	T	LS	F	L	3400		A9, A4		STP, SAN, PAT
Clibanornis dendrocolaptoides	M	T/U	HT	R/U	L	1000+	B	F1	SOU	ATL
Furnarius cristatus	M	T	LT	F	L	1000		N1	CHA	CSA
Furnarius figulus	L	T	LT	F	L	900	S	F3, F15, N14		AMN, AMS, CSA, ATL
Furnarius leucopus										
cinnamomeus	L	T	LT	C	L	2700		F8, F15, N13	MAN	EPC
leucopus	L	T	LT	F	L	800		F2, F3, F8, F15, N14		NSA, AMN, AMS, CSA
Furnarius minor	M	T	LT	F	L	L		N12		AMN, AMS
Furnarius rufus	L	T	LT	C	L	3500		N14, N13		CAN, CSA, ATL, PAM
Furnarius torridus	M	T	LT	F	L	L		F2, F3		AMN, AMS
Limnornis curvirostris	M	U	LS	F	L	L		A1, A3	o	PAM
Sylviorthorhynchus desmursii	M	U	LS	U	L	1000	B	F9, F15	o	SAN
Aphrastura masafuerae	M	M/C	US	F	600	1300		N3	JFI	STP
Aphrastura spinicauda	M	M/C	LS	C	L	1800		F9, N1	o	SAN
Phleocryptes melanops	M	U	LS	F	L	4300+		A1, A1, A1		STP, CAN, SAN, ATL, PAM, PAT
Leptasthenura aegithaloides	M	U/C	LS	C	L	4300+		N1, N2		STP, CAN, SAN, CSA
Leptasthenura andicola	M	U/M	UM	F	3200	4700		N2, N3, N10, F6		NAN, CAN
Leptasthenura fuliginiceps	M	U/C	UM	F	1500	4200		N2, N3, F6		CAN, SAN
Leptasthenura pileata	M	U/C	UM	F	2800	4400		N2, F6	AWA	CAN
Leptasthenura platensis	M	U/C	LS	U	L	800		F8, N11, N1		CSA, PAM, PAT
Leptasthenura setaria	L	C	UT	C	750	1900		F9, F15	SOU	ATL
Leptasthenura striata	M	U/C	MM	C	1550	3800		N2, F6	AWA	CAN
Leptasthenura striolata	L	U/M	UT	F	750	1200+		F9, N11	SOU	ATL
Leptasthenura xenothorax	H	U/C	UM	U	3900	4300		F6	AWA	CAN
Leptasthenura yanacensis	H	U/C	UM	U/P	3700	4500		F6, N3	AWA	CAN
Spartonoica maluroides	M	U	LS	F	L	L		A1, A2, A1	o	PAM
Schizoeaca coryi	H	U	UM	F	2800	4100	B	N10	VAN	NAN

CP	RP	Notes
4	3	
4	3	Occasionally to 2,100 m.
4	3	
4	3	
4	3	
4	3	
4	3	
4	2	Poorly known.
4	3	Occasionally to 1,300 m.
4	3	
4	3	
4	3	
4	3	Locally to 1,600 m (Argentina); to lower elevations in winter.
3	2	Poorly known.
2	1	*Polylepis* destruction; survey.
4	2	Poorly known.
4	3	Above 3,200 m in Andes.
4	3	
4	3	
4	3	Winters to 900 m.
4	3	
3	2	Poorly known; winters to lower elevations.
3	2	Poorly known; habitat appears safe.
4	3	
2	2	Poorly known; habitat destruction; survey.
4	2	
4	3	
4	3	
4	3	Locally to 2,700 m (Bolivia).
4	3	
4	3	
4	3	
4	3	
4	3	
2	1	Population <1,000; humid scrub with tree ferns; effects of livestock?
4	3	
4	3	
4	3	
4	3	Occasionally to 2,600 and 5,200 m.
4	3	Winters to lowlands.
4	3	
4	3	Occasionally to 3,000 m?
3	3	Dependent on *Araucaria* trees.
4	3	Locally to 4,000 m.
4	3	
2	1	Occasionally to 3,600 m.
2	1	Occasionally to 3,200 and 5,200 m.
4	3	
3	2	Occasionally to 2,300 m; burning, overgrazing.

Abbreviations Used

Snst - Sensitivity:
L - Low; **M** - Medium; **H** - High.

Strat - Foraging Strata:
T - Terrestrial; **U** - Understory; **M** - Midstory; **C** - Canopy; **A** - Aerial; **W** - Water.

Cntab - Center of Abundance:
LT - Lower tropical; **LS** - Lower subtropical; **HT** - Hill tropical; **UT** - Upper tropical; **US** - Upper subtropical; **MM** - Middle montane; **UM** - Upper montane.

Rel - Relative Abundance:
R - Rare; **U** - Uncommon; **F** - Fairly common; **C** - Common; **P** - Patchily distributed.

Min - Minimum Elevation:
L - Lowlands; **?** - Uncertain value; numeric values in meters.

Max - Maximum Elevation:
L - Lowlands; **?** - Uncertain value; **+** - species occurs at least to given elevation but likely occurs higher; numeric values in meters.

Micro - Microhabitats:
A - Army ants; **B** - Bamboo; **T** - Treefalls; **G** - Ground bromeliads; **C** - Rocky outcrops and caves; **S** - Streamside; **V** - Vine tangles; **B/V** -Bamboo/vine tangles.

Habitats:
F1 - Tropical lowland evergreen forest; **F2** - Flooded tropical evergreen forest; **F3** - River-edge forest; **F4** - Montane evergreen forest; **F5** - Elfin forest; **F6** - *Polylepis* woodland; **F7** - Tropical deciduous forest; **F8** - Gallery forest; **F9** - Southern temperate forest; **F10** - Pine forest; **F11** - Pine-oak forest; **F12** - White sand forest; **F13** - Palm forest; **F14** - Mangrove forest; **F15** - Secondary forest; **N1** - Arid lowland scrub; **N2** - Arid montane scrub; **N3** - Semihumid/humid montane scrub; **N4** - Cerrado; **N5** - Campo grasslands; **N6** - Low, seasonally wet grassland; **N7** - Southern temperate grassland; **N8** - Northern temperate grassland; **N9** - Puna grassland; **N10** - Paramo grassland; **N11** - Riparian thickets; **N12** - River island scrub; **N13** - Pastures/agricultural lands; **N14** - Second-growth scrub; **A1** - Freshwater marshes; **A2** - Saltwater/brackish marshes; **A3** - Coastal sand beaches/mudflats; **A4** - Coastal rocky beaches; **A5** - Riverine sand beaches; **A6** - Freshwater lakes and ponds; **A7** - Alkaline lakes; **A8** - Rivers; **A9** - Streams; **A10** - Bogs; **A11** - Coastal waters; **A12** - Pelagic waters.
E - Edge (used as a modifer to particular habitats).

Sub - Subregions:
ARC - Arid Caribbean Coast; **AWA** - Altiplano and Western Andes; **BAH** - Bahamas; **BAJ** - Baja California; **CAA** - Caatinga; **CAH** - Central American Highlands; **CER** - Cerrado; **CHA** - Chaco; **CHG** - Chiapas-Guanacaste; **CHL** - Chilean Desert; **CHR** - Chiriquí; **CIS** - Cocos Island; **CMV** - Cauca-Magdalena Valley; **COC** - Cuzco-Cochabamba; **CUB** - Cuba; **DOM** - Dominica; **EAS** - Eastern Slope Andes; **FDN** - Fernando de Noronha; **GAL** - Galápagos; **GCM** - Gulf Coast-Mexico; **GRE** - Grenada; **GUA** - Guadeloupe; **GUI** - Guianan; **HIS** - Hispaniola; **HPC** - Humid Pacific Coast; **ISA** - Isla Providencia and Isla San Andrés; **JAM** - Jamaica; **JFI** - Juan Fernández Islands; **MAN** - Manabí-Tumbes; **MAR** - Marañón Valley; **MID** - Madeira-Tapajós; **MON** - Montserrat; **MRT** - Martinique; **MTC** - Marañón-Cuzco; **NMM** - Northern Mexican Mountains; **NOR** - Northern Coastal Brazil; **PAR** - Pará; **PER** - Peruvian Desert; **PUE** - Puerto Rico; **RDJ** - Rio de Janeiro-Bahia Lowlands; **RMW** - Rio Madeira West; **RNW** - Rio Negro West; **SCA** - Southern Central America; **SCT** - Santa Cruz-Tucumán; **SIN** - Sinaloa-Oaxaca; **SMH** - Southern Mexican Highlands; **SMT** - Santa Marta; **SOC** - Islas Revillagigedo (Socorro Island group); **SON** - Sonoran Desert; **SOU** - Southern Atlantic Coast; **STL** - St. Lucia; **STV** - St. Vincent; **TAC** - Tacarcuna; **VAN** - Venezuelan Andes; **VNZ** - Venezuelan Coastal Mountains; **WES** - Western Andes; **YUC** - Yucatán Peninsula.
o - Endemic to region, but not restricted to a single subregion.

Zoogeographic Regions:
AMN - Northern Amazonia; **AMS** - Southern Amazonia; **ATL** - Atlantic Forest; **BSR** - Baja-Sonora; **CAN** - Central Andes; **CDH** - Chiriquí-Darién Highlands; **CHO** - Chocó Lowlands; **CSA** - Central South America; **EPC** - Equatorial Pacific Coast; **GAN** - Greater Antilles; **GCS** - Gulf-Caribbean Slope; **LAN** - Lesser Antilles; **MAH** - Madrean Highlands; **MPL** - Mexican Plateau; **NAN** - Northern Andes; **NSA** - Northern South America; **PAM** - Pampas; **PAS** - Pacific Arid Slope; **PAT** - Patagonia; **SAN** - Southern Andes; **STP** - Subtropical Pacific; **TEP** - Tepuis.

CP -Conservation Priority:
1 - Urgent; **2** - High; **3** - Medium; **4** - Low.

RP - Research Priority:
1 - High; **2** - Medium; **3** - Low.

	Snst	Strat	Cntab	Rel	Min	Max	Micro	Habitats	Sub	Zoogeographic Regions
Schizoeaca fuliginosa										
fuliginosa	H	U	UM	F	3000	4300	B	N10, F5		NAN, CAN
griseomurina	H	U	UM	F	2750	3200	B	N10	EAS	NAN
harterti	H	U	UM	F	2900	3500	B	N10, F5	COC	CAN
helleri	H	U	UM	F	2800	3750	B	N10, F5	COC	CAN
palpebralis	H	U	UM	?	3000	3500	B	N10	MTC	CAN
perijana	H	U	UM	?	3000	3400	B?	N10	VAN	NAN
vilcabambae	H	U	UM	F?	2800	3400	B	N10, F5	MTC	CAN
Schoeniophylax phryganophila	L	U	LT	F	L	L?		N11, N14		CSA, PAM
Oreophylax moreirae	M	U	MM	F/C	2000	2800	B	N3	SOU	ATL
Synallaxis albescens	L	U	LT	C	L	1500		N4, N5, N13, N14		GCS, NSA, AMN, AMS, CSA
Synallaxis albigularis	L	U	LT	F	L	800		N12, N14		AMN, AMS
Synallaxis azarae										
azarae	L	U	MM	C	1250	3100		F4E, F15	o	CAN
courseni	M	U	MM/UM	F	2700	3500		F4E, F15	MTC	CAN
elegantior	L	U	MM	C	700	3000		F4E, F15	o	NAN
superciliosa	M	U	UT	F	600	2900		F4E, F15, F7	o	CAN
Synallaxis brachyura	L	U	LT	C	L	2000		N14, N11, F4E, F1E		GCS, CHO, EPC, NAN, NSA
Synallaxis cabanisi										
cabanisi	L	U	LT	F	L	1400		F1E, F15, F3E	o	AMS
macconnelli	M	U	UT	F	L	1900		F1E, F4E, F15		TEP, AMN
Synallaxis castanea	M	U	MM	F	1300	2900	B	F4, F15	VNZ	NAN
Synallaxis cherriei	M	U	LT	U/P	L	1050	B	F1, F15?		AMN, AMS
Synallaxis cinerascens	M	U/M	LT	U	L	2000		F1, F4		ATL, PAM
Synallaxis cinnamomea	L	U	UT	F	900	2100		F15, N14, F4, F7, F1		NAN, NSA
Synallaxis erythrothorax	L	T/U	LT	C	L	1000		F15, N14, F1E		PAS, GCS
Synallaxis frontalis	L	U	LT	F	L	2300		F7, F8E, F15		CAN, CSA, PAM
Synallaxis fuscorufa	L	U	MM	C	900	3000		F4E, N14	SMT	NAN
Synallaxis gujanensis										
albilora	L	U	LT	C	L	600		F8, F15	CER	CSA
gujanensis	L	U	LT	C	L	900		F3, F15, F8		AMN, AMS
maranonica	L	U	UT	F	L	1500		F8, F15	MAR	CAN
Synallaxis hypospodia	M	U	LT	U/P	L	700		N6, N14		AMS, CSA
Synallaxis moesta	M	U	LT	F	L	1200		F3E, F1E, F15		AMN, AMS
Synallaxis propinqua	M	U	LT	C/P	L	L		N12		AMN, AMS
Synallaxis ruficapilla										
infuscata	M	U	HT	F	L	800?		F1	NOR	ATL
ruficapilla	M	U	HT	F	L	1400+		F4, F1, F15	SOU	ATL
Synallaxis rutilans	H	U	LT	F	L	900	T	F1		AMN, AMS
Synallaxis spixi	L	U	LT	C	L	2200		N14, N11, N4		ATL, PAM
Synallaxis stictothorax	M	U	LT	C	L	400		N1	MAN	EPC
Synallaxis subpudica	L	U	MM	C	1200	3200		F4E, F15E, N14	EAS	NAN
Synallaxis tithys	M	U	LT	F	L	750		F7	MAN	EPC
Synallaxis unirufa	M	U	UM	F	1700	3300	B	F4, F5		NAN, CAN
Synallaxis zimmeri	M	U	MM	U	1900	3000		N2	AWA	CAN
Hellmayrea gularis	H	U	UM	U	2500	3200	B	F4, F5		NAN, CAN
Gyalophylax hellmayri	M	T	LT	?	L	400	G	F7?	CAA	CSA
Certhiaxis cinnamomea	M	T/U	LT	C	L	1000		A1, F14		NSA, AMN, AMS, CSA, ATL, PAM
Certhiaxis mustelina	M	U	LT	F	L	L		A1, A8		AMN, AMS
Limnoctites rectirostris	M	U	LS	F/P	L	1000		A1		ATL, PAM
Poecilurus candei	M	T/U	LT	F	L	1100		F7, N1	ARC	NSA
Poecilurus kollari	M	U?	LT	R?	L	L		F8?, N1?	GUI	AMN
Poecilurus scutatus	M	T/U	LT	U	L	1500	V	F7, F8	o	CSA
Cranioleuca albicapilla	L	U	UM	F	2400	3600		N3, F6	AWA	CAN

CP	RP	Notes
4	3	Occasionally to 2,300 m; burning, overgrazing.
3	2	Poorly known; burning, overgrazing.
3	2	Occasionally to 2,500 m; burning, overgrazing.
3	2	Burning, overgrazing.
3	2	Burning, overgrazing.
3	2	Poorly known; burning, overgrazing.
3	2	Burning, overgrazing.
4	3	
3	3	
4	3	Occasionally to 2,100 m.
4	3	Locally to 1,200 m.
4	3	
3	2	
4	3	Occasionally to 3,750 m (Colombia).
4	3	
4	3	
4	3	
4	3	
4	3	
3	1	Poorly known; local.
3	2	
4	3	Locally to lowlands (Trinidad).
3	3	
4	3	
4	3	Occasionally to 750 m; mainly above 2,000 m.
4	3	
4	3	Occasionally to 1,200 m.
3	2	Survey.
3	2	Burning, overgrazing; monitor.
4	3	Occasionally to 1,400 m.
4	3	
2	1	Deforestation.
4	3	
4	3	
4	3	
3	3	
4	3	
3	2	Deforestation.
4	3	Occasionally to 1,000 m.
3	2	
4	3	Occasionally to 3,800 m.
3	2	
4	3	
4	3	
3	2	
3	3	
3	2	Poorly known; survey.
3	2	Dry and gallery forest habitat decreasing.
4	3	

Abbreviations Used

Snst - Sensitivity:
L - Low; **M** - Medium; **H** - High.

Strat - Foraging Strata:
T - Terrestrial; **U** - Understory; **M** - Midstory; **C** - Canopy; **A** - Aerial; **W** - Water.

Cntab - Center of Abundance:
LT - Lower tropical; **LS** - Lower subtropical; **HT** - Hill tropical; **UT** - Upper tropical; **US** - Upper subtropical; **MM** - Middle montane; **UM** - Upper montane.

Rel - Relative Abundance:
R - Rare; **U** - Uncommon; **F** - Fairly common; **C** - Common; **P** - Patchily distributed.

Min - Minimum Elevation:
L - Lowlands; **?** - Uncertain value; numeric values in meters.

Max - Maximum Elevation:
L - Lowlands; **?** - Uncertain value; **+** - species occurs at least to given elevation but likely occurs higher; numeric values in meters.

Micro - Microhabitats:
A - Army ants; **B** - Bamboo; **T** - Treefalls; **G** - Ground bromeliads; **C** - Rocky outcrops and caves; **S** - Streamside; **V** - Vine tangles; **B/V** -Bamboo/vine tangles.

Habitats:
F1 - Tropical lowland evergreen forest; **F2** - Flooded tropical evergreen forest; **F3** - River-edge forest; **F4** - Montane evergreen forest; **F5** - Elfin forest; **F6** - *Polylepis* woodland; **F7** - Tropical deciduous forest; **F8** - Gallery forest; **F9** - Southern temperate forest; **F10** - Pine forest; **F11** - Pine-oak forest; **F12** - White sand forest; **F13** - Palm forest; **F14** - Mangrove forest; **F15** - Secondary forest; **N1** - Arid lowland scrub; **N2** - Arid montane scrub; **N3** - Semihumid/humid montane scrub; **N4** - Cerrado; **N5** - Campo grasslands; **N6** - Low, seasonally wet grassland; **N7** - Southern temperate grassland; **N8** - Northern temperate grassland; **N9** - Puna grassland; **N10** - Paramo grassland; **N11** - Riparian thickets; **N12** - River island scrub; **N13** - Pastures/agricultural lands; **N14** - Second-growth scrub; **A1** - Freshwater marshes; **A2** - Saltwater/brackish marshes; **A3** - Coastal sand beaches/mudflats; **A4** - Coastal rocky beaches; **A5** - Riverine sand beaches; **A6** - Freshwater lakes and ponds; **A7** - Alkaline lakes; **A8** - Rivers; **A9** - Streams; **A10** - Bogs; **A11** - Coastal waters; **A12** - Pelagic waters.
E - Edge (used as a modifer to particular habitats).

Sub - Subregions:
ARC - Arid Caribbean Coast; **AWA** - Altiplano and Western Andes; **BAH** - Bahamas; **BAJ** - Baja California; **CAA** - Caatinga; **CAH** - Central American Highlands; **CER** - Cerrado; **CHA** - Chaco; **CHG** - Chiapas-Guanacaste; **CHL** - Chilean Desert; **CHR** - Chiriquí; **CIS** - Cocos Island; **CMV** - Cauca-Magdalena Valley; **COC** - Cuzco-Cochabamba; **CUB** - Cuba; **DOM** - Dominica; **EAS** - Eastern Slope Andes; **FDN** - Fernando de Noronha; **GAL** - Galápagos; **GCM** - Gulf Coast-Mexico; **GRE** - Grenada; **GUA** - Guadeloupe; **GUI** - Guianan; **HIS** - Hispaniola; **HPC** - Humid Pacific Coast; **ISA** - Isla Providencia and Isla San Andrés; **JAM** - Jamaica; **JFI** - Juan Fernández Islands; **MAN** - Manabí-Tumbes; **MAR** - Marañón Valley; **MID** - Madeira-Tapajós; **MON** - Montserrat; **MRT** - Martinique; **MTC** - Marañón-Cuzco; **NMM** - Northern Mexican Mountains; **NOR** - Northern Coastal Brazil; **PAR** - Pará; **PER** - Peruvian Desert; **PUE** - Puerto Rico; **RDJ** - Rio de Janeiro-Bahia Lowlands; **RMW** - Rio Madeira West; **RNW** - Rio Negro West; **SCA** - Southern Central America; **SCT** - Santa Cruz-Tucumán; **SIN** - Sinaloa-Oaxaca; **SMH** - Southern Mexican Highlands; **SMT** - Santa Marta; **SOC** - Islas Revillagigedo (Socorro Island group); **SON** - Sonoran Desert; **SOU** - Southern Atlantic Coast; **STL** - St. Lucia; **STV** - St. Vincent; **TAC** - Tacarcuna; **VAN** - Venezuelan Andes; **VNZ** - Venezuelan Coastal Mountains; **WES** - Western Andes; **YUC** - Yucatán Peninsula.
o - Endemic to region, but not restricted to a single subregion.

Zoogeographic Regions:
AMN - Northern Amazonia; **AMS** - Southern Amazonia; **ATL** - Atlantic Forest; **BSR** - Baja-Sonora; **CAN** - Central Andes; **CDH** - Chiriquí-Darién Highlands; **CHO** - Chocó Lowlands; **CSA** - Central South America; **EPC** - Equatorial Pacific Coast; **GAN** - Greater Antilles; **GCS** - Gulf-Caribbean Slope; **LAN** - Lesser Antilles; **MAH** - Madrean Highlands; **MPL** - Mexican Plateau; **NAN** - Northern Andes; **NSA** - Northern South America; **PAM** - Pampas; **PAS** - Pacific Arid Slope; **PAT** - Patagonia; **SAN** - Southern Andes; **STP** - Subtropical Pacific; **TEP** - Tepuis.

CP -Conservation Priority:
1 - Urgent; **2** - High; **3** - Medium; **4** - Low.

RP - Research Priority:
1 - High; **2** - Medium; **3** - Low.

	Snst	Strat	Cntab	Rel	Min	Max	Micro	Habitats	Sub	Zoogeographic Regions
Cranioleuca albiceps	H	M/C	UM	F	2200	3300	B	F4	COC	CAN
Cranioleuca antisiensis										
antisiensis	H	M/C	UM	F	1200	3100		F4		NAN, CAN
baroni	M	M/C	UM	F/P	2600	4400		F6, F15	MTC	CAN
Cranioleuca curtata	H	C	UT	U	800	2500		F4		NAN, CAN
Cranioleuca demissa	H	M/C	UT	F	1100	2450		F4	o	TEP
Cranioleuca erythrops	M	M/C	UT	F	700	2300		F4		CDH, NAN
Cranioleuca gutturata	H	C	LT	F	L	850		F2, F1		AMN, AMS
Cranioleuca hellmayri	M	M/C	MM	C	1500	3000		F4, F15	SMT	NAN
Cranioleuca marcapatae	H	U	UM	F	2400	3300	B	F4, F5	COC	CAN
Cranioleuca muelleri	M	?	LT	?	L	L		F2?		AMN, AMS
Cranioleuca obsoleta	M	M/C	LT	F	L	1000		F1, F9	SOU	ATL
Cranioleuca pallida	M	M/C	UT	F	800	2200		F4	SOU	ATL
Cranioleuca pyrrhophia	M	M	LT	F	L	2500		F1, F7, F8		CAN, CSA, PAM
Cranioleuca semicinerea	M	M/C	LT	U	L	900		F7	o	CSA
Cranioleuca subcristata	M	M/C	UT	C	300	2300		F4, F1		NAN, NSA
Cranioleuca sulphurifera	H	U	LT	U/P	L	L		A1	o	PAM
Cranioleuca vulpina										
dissita	M	M	LT	F	L	L		F7	HPC	GCS
vulpina	M	M/C	LT	C/P	L	800		F8, N12, N11		NSA, AMN, AMS, CSA
Siptornopsis hypochondriacus	M	T/U	MM	U	2450	2800		N2	MAR	CAN
Asthenes anthoides	M	T	LS	U	L	1500		N7, N1?		SAN, PAT
Asthenes baeri	M	T/U	LS	F	L	L		N1		CSA, PAM
Asthenes berlepschi	?	T/U?	UM	?	2600	3700		N2	AWA	CAN
Asthenes cactorum	M	T/U?	US	U/P	L	2400		N2		STP, CAN
Asthenes dorbignyi	M	T/U	UM	C	1800	4300		N2, F6		CAN, SAN
Asthenes flammulata	M	T/U	UM	F	3300	4500		N10		NAN, CAN
Asthenes heterura	M	T/U	UM	F	3000	4150		N2, F6	AWA	CAN
Asthenes hudsoni	L	T/U	LS	U	L	L		N7		PAM, PAT
Asthenes humicola	M	U	LS/US	F	L	2200		N2, N1		STP, SAN
Asthenes humilis	M	T	UM	F	3500	4800		N9	AWA	CAN
Asthenes luizae	M	U/M	UT	U	900	1500		N2	CER	CSA
Asthenes maculicauda	M	T/U	UM	U	2900	4300		N10	o	CAN
Asthenes modesta	M	T	UM	C	L	4600		N9, N7		CAN, SAN, PAT
Asthenes ottonis	L	T/U	UM	F	2800	3700		N2, N3, F6	AWA	CAN
Asthenes patagonica	M	T	LS	F	L	L		N1	o	PAT
Asthenes pudibunda	M	T/U	UM	F	2500	4000		N2, F6	AWA	CAN
Asthenes punensis	M	T	UM	U	2150	4000		N10, N9		CAN, SAN
Asthenes pyrrholeuca	M	T/U	LS	C	L	3000		N1, N2, N7		STP, SAN, PAT
Asthenes sclateri	M	T	UM	F	2000	2900		N7	o	SAN
Asthenes steinbachi	?	T/U?	MM?	?	800	3000		N2	o	SAN
Asthenes urubambensis	H	U	UM	U	2750	3800		N10, F6	o	CAN
Asthenes virgata	M	T/U	UM	U/P	3300	4300		N10, N9	AWA	CAN
Asthenes wyatti	M	T	UM	F	3000	4300		N10, N9		NAN, CAN
Thripophaga berlepschi	H	U/M	UM	U	3050	3300		F5	MTC	CAN
Thripophaga cherriei	H	M?	LT	?	L	L		F3?	RNW	AMN
Thripophaga fusciceps	H	M	LT	U/P	L	L		F2, F3, F7		AMN, AMS
Thripophaga macroura	M	M/C	LT	U	L	800		F1	RDJ	ATL
Phacellodomus dorsalis	M	T/C	MM	U	2050	2800		N2	MAR	CAN
Phacellodomus erythrophthalmus										
erythrophthalmus	M	U/M	LT	?	L	1250		F4, F1, F15	o	ATL
ferrugineigula	M	U	LT	U	L	900		A1, N11, F8	o	ATL
Phacellodomus ruber	L	T/C	LT	C	L	700+		N11, N14		CSA, PAM

CP	RP	Notes
3	3	
3	2	
3	2	Occasionally to 1,700 m?
3	2	Deforestation.
4	3	
3	2	
4	3	
3	2	
3	3	
3	2	Poorly known.
4	3	
4	3	
4	3	Occasionally to 3,100 m.
3	2	Poorly known.
3	3	
4	3	
3	2	
4	3	
3	2	Survey.
3	2	Overgrazing.
4	3	
3	2	Poorly known.
3	2	Distribution and behavior poorly known.
3	1	Occasionally to 4,600 m; habitat destruction; probably contains multiple species, of which some may be threatened.
4	3	Occasionally to 2,800 m.
4	3	
4	3	
4	3	
4	3	Occasionally to 2,750 m.
2	1	Recently described (Vielliard 1990).
4	3	Occasionally to 2,250 m.
4	3	In Central Andes above 3,200 m.
4	3	
4	3	
4	3	
4	2	
4	3	
3	2	Poorly known.
4	2	Poorly known.
3	2	Ecology poorly known.
4	3	
4	3	Occasionally to 5,500 m.
3	2	Locally to 2,500 m.
3	2	Poorly known.
4	2	Poorly known.
2	2	Poorly known; local; deforestation.
3	1	
2	1	Poorly known.
3	2	
4	3	

Abbreviations Used

Snst - Sensitivity:
L - Low; **M** - Medium; **H** - High.

Strat - Foraging Strata:
T - Terrestrial; **U** - Understory; **M** - Midstory; **C** - Canopy; **A** - Aerial; **W** - Water.

Cntab - Center of Abundance:
LT - Lower tropical; **LS** - Lower subtropical; **HT** - Hill tropical; **UT** - Upper tropical; **US** - Upper subtropical; **MM** - Middle montane; **UM** - Upper montane.

Rel - Relative Abundance:
R - Rare; **U** - Uncommon; **F** - Fairly common; **C** - Common; **P** - Patchily distributed.

Min - Minimum Elevation:
L - Lowlands; **?** - Uncertain value; numeric values in meters.

Max - Maximum Elevation:
L - Lowlands; **?** - Uncertain value; **+** - species occurs at least to given elevation but likely occurs higher; numeric values in meters.

Micro - Microhabitats:
A - Army ants; **B** - Bamboo; **T** - Treefalls; **G** - Ground bromeliads; **C** - Rocky outcrops and caves; **S** - Streamside; **V** - Vine tangles; **B/V** -Bamboo/vine tangles.

Habitats:
F1 - Tropical lowland evergreen forest; **F2** - Flooded tropical evergreen forest; **F3** - River-edge forest; **F4** - Montane evergreen forest; **F5** - Elfin forest; **F6** - *Polylepis* woodland; **F7** - Tropical deciduous forest; **F8** - Gallery forest; **F9** - Southern temperate forest; **F10** - Pine forest; **F11** - Pine-oak forest; **F12** - White sand forest; **F13** - Palm forest; **F14** - Mangrove forest; **F15** - Secondary forest; **N1** - Arid lowland scrub; **N2** - Arid montane scrub; **N3** - Semihumid/humid montane scrub; **N4** - Cerrado; **N5** - Campo grasslands; **N6** - Low, seasonally wet grassland; **N7** - Southern temperate grassland; **N8** - Northern temperate grassland; **N9** - Puna grassland; **N10** - Paramo grassland; **N11** - Riparian thickets; **N12** - River island scrub; **N13** - Pastures/agricultural lands; **N14** - Second-growth scrub; **A1** - Freshwater marshes; **A2** - Saltwater/brackish marshes; **A3** - Coastal sand beaches/mudflats; **A4** - Coastal rocky beaches; **A5** - Riverine sand beaches; **A6** - Freshwater lakes and ponds; **A7** - Alkaline lakes; **A8** - Rivers; **A9** - Streams; **A10** - Bogs; **A11** - Coastal waters; **A12** - Pelagic waters.
E - Edge (used as a modifer to particular habitats).

Sub - Subregions:
ARC - Arid Caribbean Coast; **AWA** - Altiplano and Western Andes; **BAH** - Bahamas; **BAJ** - Baja California; **CAA** - Caatinga; **CAH** - Central American Highlands; **CER** - Cerrado; **CHA** - Chaco; **CHG** - Chiapas-Guanacaste; **CHL** - Chilean Desert; **CHR** - Chiriquí; **CIS** - Cocos Island; **CMV** - Cauca-Magdalena Valley; **COC** - Cuzco-Cochabamba; **CUB** - Cuba; **DOM** - Dominica; **EAS** - Eastern Slope Andes; **FDN** - Fernando de Noronha; **GAL** - Galápagos; **GCM** - Gulf Coast-Mexico; **GRE** - Grenada; **GUA** - Guadeloupe; **GUI** - Guianan; **HIS** - Hispaniola; **HPC** - Humid Pacific Coast; **ISA** - Isla Providencia and Isla San Andrés; **JAM** - Jamaica; **JFI** - Juan Fernández Islands; **MAN** - Manabí-Tumbes; **MAR** - Marañón Valley; **MID** - Madeira-Tapajós; **MON** - Montserrat; **MRT** - Martinique; **MTC** - Marañón-Cuzco; **NMM** - Northern Mexican Mountains; **NOR** - Northern Coastal Brazil; **PAR** - Pará; **PER** - Peruvian Desert; **PUE** - Puerto Rico; **RDJ** - Rio de Janeiro-Bahia Lowlands; **RMW** - Rio Madeira West; **RNW** - Rio Negro West; **SCA** - Southern Central America; **SCT** - Santa Cruz-Tucumán; **SIN** - Sinaloa-Oaxaca; **SMH** - Southern Mexican Highlands; **SMT** - Santa Marta; **SOC** - Islas Revillagigedo (Socorro Island group); **SON** - Sonoran Desert; **SOU** - Southern Atlantic Coast; **STL** - St. Lucia; **STV** - St. Vincent; **TAC** - Tacarcuna; **VAN** - Venezuelan Andes; **VNZ** - Venezuelan Coastal Mountains; **WES** - Western Andes; **YUC** - Yucatán Peninsula.
o - Endemic to region, but not restricted to a single subregion.

Zoogeographic Regions:
AMN - Northern Amazonia; **AMS** - Southern Amazonia; **ATL** - Atlantic Forest; **BSR** - Baja-Sonora; **CAN** - Central Andes; **CDH** - Chiriquí-Darién Highlands; **CHO** - Chocó Lowlands; **CSA** - Central South America; **EPC** - Equatorial Pacific Coast; **GAN** - Greater Antilles; **GCS** - Gulf-Caribbean Slope; **LAN** - Lesser Antilles; **MAH** - Madrean Highlands; **MPL** - Mexican Plateau; **NAN** - Northern Andes; **NSA** - Northern South America; **PAM** - Pampas; **PAS** - Pacific Arid Slope; **PAT** - Patagonia; **SAN** - Southern Andes; **STP** - Subtropical Pacific; **TEP** - Tepuis.

CP -Conservation Priority:
1 - Urgent; **2** - High; **3** - Medium; **4** - Low.

RP - Research Priority:
1 - High; **2** - Medium; **3** - Low.

	Snst	Strat	Cntab	Rel	Min	Max	Micro	Habitats	Sub	Zoogeographic Regions
Phacellodomus rufifrons	M	U/C	LT	C	L	2000		N1, N2, F7, N4, F15		NSA, AMN, AMS, CSA
Phacellodomus sibilatrix	M	T/C	LT	F	L	L		F7, N1		CSA, PAM
Phacellodomus striaticeps	M	T/C	UM	U	2600	4000+		N2, F6	AWA	CAN
Phacellodomus striaticollis										
maculipectus	M	U	MM	U	1000	2500		N2, F7		CAN, SAN
striaticollis	M	U/M	LT	F	L	800		N11, F8, N1		CSA, PAM
Coryphistera alaudina	M	T	LT	F	L	700+		N1		CSA, PAM
Anumbius annumbi	M	T	LT	F	L	1000		N6, N13, N14		CSA, ATL, PAM
Siptornis striaticollis	H	C	UT	U	1300	2400		F4	EAS	NAN
Xenerpestes minlosi	H	C	HT	U	L	1000		F4, F1		GCS, CDH, CHO
Xenerpestes singularis	H	C	UT	U	1050	1700		F4		NAN, CAN
Metopothrix aurantiacus	L	C	LT	U/P	L	1100		F3, F15		AMN, AMS
Roraimia adusta	H	U/M	UT	U	1200	2500		F4, F5	o	TEP
Margarornis bellulus	H	M	UT	U	1350	1600		F4, F5	TAC	CDH
Margarornis rubiginosus	M	M	MM	F	1200	3000		F4	CHR	CDH
Margarornis squamiger	H	M	UM	C	1400	3600		F4, F5		NAN, CAN
Margarornis stellatus	H	M	UT	C	900	2200		F4, F5	WES	NAN
Premnornis guttuligera	H	U/M	MM	U	1300	2500		F4		NAN, CAN
Premnoplex brunnescens	H	U	UT	F	950	2500		F4		CDH, NAN, CAN
Premnoplex tatei	H	U	UT	F	800	2400		F4	VNZ	NAN
Pseudocolaptes boissonneautii	H	M/C	MM	F	1400	3400		F4, F5		NAN, CAN
Pseudocolaptes lawrencii										
johnsoni	H	M/C	UT	U/P	800	2000		F4	WES	NAN
lawrencii	H	M/C	MM	U	1800	3100		F4	CHR	CDH
Berlepschia rikeri	M	C	LT	U/P	L	L		F13		AMN, AMS
Pseudoseisura cristata	M	T/C	LT	F	L	500+		F7, F8E, N14	o	CSA
Pseudoseisura gutturalis	M	T/C	LS	U	L	1000		N1		CSA, PAT
Pseudoseisura lophotes	M	T/C	LT	F	L	800		F7, F8, N14		CSA, PAM
Hyloctistes subulatus	H	M	LT	U	L	1300		F1, F4		GCS, CHO, NAN, NSA, AMN, AMS
Ancistrops strigilatus	H	M/C	LT	F	L	900		F1		AMN, AMS
Anabazenops fuscus	H	M	UT	U/P	350	1250	B	F4	SOU	ATL
Syndactyla guttulata	M	U	UT	C	900	2100		F4, F15	VNZ	NAN
Syndactyla rufosuperciliata	M	U	UT	C	L	2600		F1, F4, F8		NAN, CAN, SAN, CSA, ATL, PAM
Syndactyla subalaris	H	U	UT	F	1000	2300		F4		CDH, NAN, CAN
Simoxenops striatus	H	U	HT	U?	650	800	B/V	F1	COC	CAN
Simoxenops ucayalae	M	U	LT	U	L	1000	B	F1, F3	o	AMS
Anabacerthia amaurotis	H	M	HT	U	600	1500		F4	SOU	ATL
Anabacerthia striaticollis	H	M	UT	F	950	2200		F4		NAN, CAN
Anabacerthia variegaticeps	H	M	UT	F	700	2100		F4, F1		MAH, CDH, NAN
Philydor atricapillus	H	M	LT	F	L	1050		F1	o	ATL
Philydor dimidiatus	H	M	LT	U	L	1200+		F8, F1	CER	CSA
Philydor erythrocercus										
erythrocercus	H	M	LT	F	L	700+		F1, F4		AMN, AMS
ochrogaster	H	M/C	UT	F	750	1650		F4	o	CAN
Philydor erythropterus	H	C	LT	F	L	900		F1		AMN, AMS
Philydor fuscipennis	H	M	HT	F	L	1400		F1, F4		GCS, CDH, CHO, NAN
Philydor lichtensteini	H	M	LT	C	L	950		F1	SOU	ATL
Philydor novaesi	H	M	HT	R	500	700		F1	NOR	ATL
Philydor pyrrhodes	H	M	LT	U	L	750		F1, F2		AMN, AMS
Philydor ruficaudatus	H	M	LT	U/P	L	1050		F1		AMN, AMS
Philydor rufus	M	C	LT	F	L	2200		F4, F1, F3		CDH, NAN, CAN, TEP, AMS, CSA, ATL
Automolus dorsalis	M	U/M	HT	U/P	L	1100	B	F1, F3		AMN, AMS
Automolus infuscatus	H	U	LT	C	L	800		F1		AMN, AMS
Automolus leucophthalmus	M	U	LT	F	L	1000	B	F1	o	ATL

CP	RP	Notes
4	3	
4	3	
4	3	Occasionally to 5,000 m.
4	2	See Nores and Yzurieta (1981) for taxonomy.
4	3	
4	3	
4	3	
3	2	Poorly known; habitat destruction.
3	2	Habitat destruction.
2	1	Habitat destruction.
4	3	Mainly below 600 m; locally in foothill terra firme forest.
4	3	Occasionally to 1,000 m.
3	2	Occasionally to 900 m; poorly known.
4	3	
4	3	Occasionally to 4,100 m.
3	3	Occasionally to 2,500 m.
4	3	Occasionally to 2,750 m?
4	3	Occasionally to 600 and 3,000 m.
2	1	Survey; habitat destruction.
4	3	Occasionally to 4,400 m.
3	2	
4	3	Locally to 1,200 m.
4	2	Poorly known; local.
4	3	
4	3	Locally to 2,400 m.
4	3	
4	2	Occasionally to 1,700 m; may contain two species.
4	3	
4	3	
4	3	
4	3	Occasionally to 3,000 m.
4	3	Occasionally to 600 and 2,800 m.
2	1	Deforestation.
4	2	Distribution in Brazil uncertain.
3	2	
4	3	Occasionally to 2,600 m.
3	2	Occasionally to 2,750 m; deforestation.
4	2	Deforestation.
3	2	Gallery forest destruction in central Brazil.
4	3	
3	2	Deforestation.
4	3	
3	2	Deforestation.
3	2	Deforestation.
1	1	Deforestation immediate threat; survey.
4	3	Usually associated with palms.
4	2	
4	3	Mainly above 900 m in Andes and Central America.
4	2	Occasionally to 2,150 m.
4	3	Occasionally to 1,300 m.
4	2	

Abbreviations Used

Snst - Sensitivity:
L - Low; **M** - Medium; **H** - High.

Strat - Foraging Strata:
T - Terrestrial; **U** - Understory; **M** - Midstory; **C** - Canopy; **A** - Aerial; **W** - Water.

Cntab - Center of Abundance:
LT - Lower tropical; **LS** - Lower subtropical; **HT** - Hill tropical; **UT** - Upper tropical; **US** - Upper subtropical; **MM** - Middle montane; **UM** - Upper montane.

Rel - Relative Abundance:
R - Rare; **U** - Uncommon; **F** - Fairly common; **C** - Common; **P** - Patchily distributed.

Min - Minimum Elevation:
L - Lowlands; **?** - Uncertain value; numeric values in meters.

Max - Maximum Elevation:
L - Lowlands; **?** - Uncertain value; **+** - species occurs at least to given elevation but likely occurs higher; numeric values in meters.

Micro - Microhabitats:
A - Army ants; **B** - Bamboo; **T** - Treefalls; **G** - Ground bromeliads; **C** - Rocky outcrops and caves; **S** - Streamside; **V** - Vine tangles; **B/V** -Bamboo/vine tangles.

Habitats:
F1 - Tropical lowland evergreen forest; **F2** - Flooded tropical evergreen forest; **F3** - River-edge forest; **F4** - Montane evergreen forest; **F5** - Elfin forest; **F6** - *Polylepis* woodland; **F7** - Tropical deciduous forest; **F8** - Gallery forest; **F9** - Southern temperate forest; **F10** - Pine forest; **F11** - Pine-oak forest; **F12** - White sand forest; **F13** - Palm forest; **F14** - Mangrove forest; **F15** - Secondary forest; **N1** - Arid lowland scrub; **N2** - Arid montane scrub; **N3** - Semihumid/humid montane scrub; **N4** - Cerrado; **N5** - Campo grasslands; **N6** - Low, seasonally wet grassland; **N7** - Southern temperate grassland; **N8** - Northern temperate grassland; **N9** - Puna grassland; **N10** - Paramo grassland; **N11** - Riparian thickets; **N12** - River island scrub; **N13** - Pastures/agricultural lands; **N14** - Second-growth scrub; **A1** - Freshwater marshes; **A2** - Saltwater/brackish marshes; **A3** - Coastal sand beaches/mudflats; **A4** - Coastal rocky beaches; **A5** - Riverine sand beaches; **A6** - Freshwater lakes and ponds; **A7** - Alkaline lakes; **A8** - Rivers; **A9** - Streams; **A10** - Bogs; **A11** - Coastal waters; **A12** - Pelagic waters.
E - Edge (used as a modifer to particular habitats).

Sub - Subregions:
ARC - Arid Caribbean Coast; **AWA** - Altiplano and Western Andes; **BAH** - Bahamas; **BAJ** - Baja California; **CAA** - Caatinga; **CAH** - Central American Highlands; **CER** - Cerrado; **CHA** - Chaco; **CHG** - Chiapas-Guanacaste; **CHL** - Chilean Desert; **CHR** - Chiriquí; **CIS** - Cocos Island; **CMV** - Cauca-Magdalena Valley; **COC** - Cuzco-Cochabamba; **CUB** - Cuba; **DOM** - Dominica; **EAS** - Eastern Slope Andes; **FDN** - Fernando de Noronha; **GAL** - Galápagos; **GCM** - Gulf Coast-Mexico; **GRE** - Grenada; **GUA** - Guadeloupe; **GUI** - Guianan; **HIS** - Hispaniola; **HPC** - Humid Pacific Coast; **ISA** - Isla Providencia and Isla San Andrés; **JAM** - Jamaica; **JFI** - Juan Fernández Islands; **MAN** - Manabí-Tumbes; **MAR** - Marañón Valley; **MID** - Madeira-Tapajós; **MON** - Montserrat; **MRT** - Martinique; **MTC** - Marañón-Cuzco; **NMM** - Northern Mexican Mountains; **NOR** - Northern Coastal Brazil; **PAR** - Pará; **PER** - Peruvian Desert; **PUE** - Puerto Rico; **RDJ** - Rio de Janeiro-Bahia Lowlands; **RMW** - Rio Madeira West; **RNW** - Rio Negro West; **SCA** - Southern Central America; **SCT** - Santa Cruz-Tucumán; **SIN** - Sinaloa-Oaxaca; **SMH** - Southern Mexican Highlands; **SMT** - Santa Marta; **SOC** - Islas Revillagigedo (Socorro Island group); **SON** - Sonoran Desert; **SOU** - Southern Atlantic Coast; **STL** - St. Lucia; **STV** - St. Vincent; **TAC** - Tacarcuna; **VAN** - Venezuelan Andes; **VNZ** - Venezuelan Coastal Mountains; **WES** - Western Andes; **YUC** - Yucatán Peninsula.
o - Endemic to region, but not restricted to a single subregion.

Zoogeographic Regions:
AMN - Northern Amazonia; **AMS** - Southern Amazonia; **ATL** - Atlantic Forest; **BSR** - Baja-Sonora; **CAN** - Central Andes; **CDH** - Chiriquí-Darién Highlands; **CHO** - Chocó Lowlands; **CSA** - Central South America; **EPC** - Equatorial Pacific Coast; **GAN** - Greater Antilles; **GCS** - Gulf-Caribbean Slope; **LAN** - Lesser Antilles; **MAH** - Madrean Highlands; **MPL** - Mexican Plateau; **NAN** - Northern Andes; **NSA** - Northern South America; **PAM** - Pampas; **PAS** - Pacific Arid Slope; **PAT** - Patagonia; **SAN** - Southern Andes; **STP** - Subtropical Pacific; **TEP** - Tepuis.

CP -Conservation Priority:
1 - Urgent; **2** - High; **3** - Medium; **4** - Low.

RP - Research Priority:
1 - High; **2** - Medium; **3** - Low.

	Snst	Strat	Cntab	Rel	Min	Max	Micro	Habitats	Sub	Zoogeographic Regions
Automolus melanopezus	H	U	LT	U/P	L	L	B	F2, F1		AMN, AMS
Automolus ochrolaemus	M	U	LT	C	L	1400		F1, F2?		GCS, AMN, AMS
Automolus roraimae	H	U	UT	U	1250	2500		F4	o	TEP
Automolus rubiginosus	M	U	UT	U	L	2400		F4, F1		MAH, CDH, CHO, NAN, CAN, NSA, TEP, AMS
Automolus ruficollis	H	U/M	UT	U	500	2900	B	F4, F7		EPC, NAN
Automolus rufipileatus	M	U	LT	F	L	850		F3, F2		NSA, AMN, AMS
Hylocryptus erythrocephalus	M	T	HT	R	600	1800		F7	MAN	EPC
Hylocryptus rectirostris	H	T	HT	R	600	1200		F8	CER	CSA
Cichlocolaptes leucophrus	H	C	HT	U	L	1450		F1, F4	o	ATL
Heliobletus contaminatus	H	C	UT	F	750	1800		F4, F1	SOU	ATL
Thripadectes flammulatus	H	U	UM	U	1400	3250		F4, F5	o	NAN
Thripadectes holostictus	M	U	MM	F	1600	2700		F4		NAN, CAN
Thripadectes ignobilis	H	U	UT	U?	800	2500		F4, F1	WES	NAN
Thripadectes melanorhynchus	H	U	UT	U	900	1750		F4		NAN, CAN
Thripadectes rufobrunneus	H	U	MM	F	1200	2500		F4	CHR	CDH
Thripadectes scrutator	H	U	UM	U	2100	3500		F4, F5	o	CAN
Thripadectes virgaticeps	H	U	UT	?	1000	2500		F4	o	NAN
Xenops milleri	H	C	LT	U/P	L	L		F1		AMN, AMS
Xenops minutus	M	U/M	LT	F	L	1500		F1, F2		GCS, CDH, CHO, EPC, NSA, AMN, AMS, CSA, ATL
Xenops rutilans	M	C	UT	F	L	2400		F4, F1, F7		CDH, EPC, NAN, CAN, SAN, AMS, CSA, ATL
Xenops tenuirostris	M	C	LT	U	L	L		F3, F2		AMN, AMS
Megaxenops parnaguae	H	M	HT	?	300	800		F7, F8	CAA	CSA
Pygarrhichas albogularis	M	M/C	LS	F	L	2000+		F9	o	SAN
Sclerurus albigularis	H	T	UT	U	700	2100		F4, F1		CDH, NAN, CAN, NSA, AMS
Sclerurus caudacutus	H	T	LT	U/F	L	1100		F1		AMN, AMS, ATL
Sclerurus guatemalensis	H	T	LT	U	L	1250		F1, F4	o	GCS
Sclerurus mexicanus	H	T	LT	U	L	1800		F1, F4		MAH, CDH, CHO, NAN, CAN, NSA, AMN, ATL
Sclerurus rufigularis	H	T	LT	U	L	900		F1		AMN, AMS
Sclerurus scansor	H	T	LT	U	L	1250		F1, F4	o	ATL
Lochmias nematura	M	T	UT	U	L	2450	S	F4, F1, F8		CDH, NAN, CAN, TEP, CSA, ATL, PAM
Formicariidae										
Cymbilaimus lineatus	M	C	LT	F	L	1000	V	F1		GCS, CHO, NSA, AMN, AMS
Cymbilaimus sanctaemariae	M	M/C	LT	F	L	1100	B/V	F3, F1	o	AMS
Hypoedaleus guttatus	H	C	LT	U	L	900+	V	F1	SOU	ATL
Batara cinerea	M	U/M	UT	U	L	2600	B	F4, F1, F15		CAN, SAN, CSA, ATL
Mackenziaena leachii	M	U	UT	U/F	L	2150	B	F4, F1	SOU	ATL
Mackenziaena severa	M	U	UT	U	L	1250	B	F4, F1, F15	SOU	ATL
Frederickena unduligera	H	U	LT	U	L	1050	T	F1		AMN, AMS
Frederickena viridis	H	U	LT	U	L	700	T	F1	GUI	AMN
Taraba major	L	U	LT	C	L	1400		F1E, F15, F8, N11, N14		GCS, CHO, EPC, NSA, TEP, AMN, AMS, CSA, ATL
Sakesphorus bernardi	L	U/C	LT	C	L	900		F7, N1, N11	MAN	EPC
Sakesphorus canadensis	M	U/M	LT	C	L	900		F7, F8		NSA, AMN, AMS?
Sakesphorus cristatus	M	U/M	LT	F	L	800		F7, N1	CAA	CSA
Sakesphorus luctuosus	M	U/M	LT	F	L	L		F3, F2		AMN, AMS
Sakesphorus melanonotus	M?	M	LT	U	L	500		F7	ARC	NSA
Sakesphorus melanothorax	M	U?	LT	?	L	L		F2	GUI	AMN
Biatas nigropectus	M	U/M	HT	R	500	1200	B	F4, F1	SOU	ATL
Thamnophilus aethiops	H	U	LT	U/F	L	950	T	F1		AMN, AMS, ATL
Thamnophilus amazonicus	L	U/M	LT	F	L	L		F1E, F8, F2, F3		AMN, AMS

CP	RP	Notes
4	3	
4	3	Locally to 1,650 m.
4	3	
4	2	Local in lowlands; may contain multiple species.
2	1	Survey; deforestation.
4	3	
2	2	In semideciduous forests; deforestation.
2	2	Habitat destruction.
4	2	
4	2	Mainly montane.
4	3	Occasionally to 800 m.
4	3	Locally to 900 and 3,100 m.
3	2	Occasionally to 200 m; deforestation.
3	2	Occasionally to 750 m; deforestation.
3	2	Occasionally to 750 and 3,000 m; deforestation.
4	3	
3	3	
4	2	Distribution poorly known.
4	3	Locally to 2,200 m (Venezuela).
4	3	Locally common in Amazonian lowlands; occasionally to 2,800 m.
4	2	Distribution poorly known.
2	1	Locally to 1,100 m; poorly known; habitat destruction.
4	3	
4	2	Locally in lowlands.
4	3	
3	3	Deforestation.
4	3	Occasionally to 2,200 m (Honduras).
4	3	Occasionally to 1,800 m.
3	2	Deforestation outside reserves.
4	3	
4	3	Occasionally to 1,300 m (Venezuela).
4	3	Occasionally to 1,300 m.
3	1	Scarce outside reserves.
3	3	
3	2	
3	2	
4	3	
4	3	
4	3	Occasionally to 2,200 m (Venezuela); mostly below 800 m.
4	3	
4	3	
4	3	
4	3	
3	2	Survey.
4	1	Poorly known; record from south of Amazon erroneous.
2	1	Survey.
4	3	Locally to 1,700 m (Ecuador).
4	2	

Abbreviations Used

Snst - Sensitivity:
L - Low; **M** - Medium; **H** - High.

Strat - Foraging Strata:
T - Terrestrial; **U** - Understory; **M** - Midstory; **C** - Canopy; **A** - Aerial; **W** - Water.

Cntab - Center of Abundance:
LT - Lower tropical; **LS** - Lower subtropical; **HT** - Hill tropical; **UT** - Upper tropical; **US** - Upper subtropical; **MM** - Middle montane; **UM** - Upper montane.

Rel - Relative Abundance:
R - Rare; **U** - Uncommon; **F** - Fairly common; **C** - Common; **P** - Patchily distributed.

Min - Minimum Elevation:
L - Lowlands; **?** - Uncertain value; numeric values in meters.

Max - Maximum Elevation:
L - Lowlands; **?** - Uncertain value; **+** - species occurs at least to given elevation but likely occurs higher; numeric values in meters.

Micro - Microhabitats:
A - Army ants; **B** - Bamboo; **T** - Treefalls; **G** - Ground bromeliads; **C** - Rocky outcrops and caves; **S** - Streamside; **V** - Vine tangles; **B/V** -Bamboo/vine tangles.

Habitats:
F1 - Tropical lowland evergreen forest; **F2** - Flooded tropical evergreen forest; **F3** - River-edge forest; **F4** - Montane evergreen forest; **F5** - Elfin forest; **F6** - *Polylepis* woodland; **F7** - Tropical deciduous forest; **F8** - Gallery forest; **F9** - Southern temperate forest; **F10** - Pine forest; **F11** - Pine-oak forest; **F12** - White sand forest; **F13** - Palm forest; **F14** - Mangrove forest; **F15** - Secondary forest; **N1** - Arid lowland scrub; **N2** - Arid montane scrub; **N3** - Semihumid/humid montane scrub; **N4** - Cerrado; **N5** - Campo grasslands; **N6** - Low, seasonally wet grassland; **N7** - Southern temperate grassland; **N8** - Northern temperate grassland; **N9** - Puna grassland; **N10** - Paramo grassland; **N11** - Riparian thickets; **N12** - River island scrub; **N13** - Pastures/agricultural lands; **N14** - Second-growth scrub; **A1** - Freshwater marshes; **A2** - Saltwater/brackish marshes; **A3** - Coastal sand beaches/mudflats; **A4** - Coastal rocky beaches; **A5** - Riverine sand beaches; **A6** - Freshwater lakes and ponds; **A7** - Alkaline lakes; **A8** - Rivers; **A9** - Streams; **A10** - Bogs; **A11** - Coastal waters; **A12** - Pelagic waters.
E - Edge (used as a modifer to particular habitats).

Sub - Subregions:
ARC - Arid Caribbean Coast; **AWA** - Altiplano and Western Andes; **BAH** - Bahamas; **BAJ** - Baja California; **CAA** - Caatinga; **CAH** - Central American Highlands; **CER** - Cerrado; **CHA** - Chaco; **CHG** - Chiapas-Guanacaste; **CHL** - Chilean Desert; **CHR** - Chiriquí; **CIS** - Cocos Island; **CMV** - Cauca-Magdalena Valley; **COC** - Cuzco-Cochabamba; **CUB** - Cuba; **DOM** - Dominica; **EAS** - Eastern Slope Andes; **FDN** - Fernando de Noronha; **GAL** - Galápagos; **GCM** - Gulf Coast-Mexico; **GRE** - Grenada; **GUA** - Guadeloupe; **GUI** - Guianan; **HIS** - Hispaniola; **HPC** - Humid Pacific Coast; **ISA** - Isla Providencia and Isla San Andrés; **JAM** - Jamaica; **JFI** - Juan Fernández Islands; **MAN** - Manabí-Tumbes; **MAR** - Marañón Valley; **MID** - Madeira-Tapajós; **MON** - Montserrat; **MRT** - Martinique; **MTC** - Marañón-Cuzco; **NMM** - Northern Mexican Mountains; **NOR** - Northern Coastal Brazil; **PAR** - Pará; **PER** - Peruvian Desert; **PUE** - Puerto Rico; **RDJ** - Rio de Janeiro-Bahia Lowlands; **RMW** - Rio Madeira West; **RNW** - Rio Negro West; **SCA** - Southern Central America; **SCT** - Santa Cruz-Tucumán; **SIN** - Sinaloa-Oaxaca; **SMH** - Southern Mexican Highlands; **SMT** - Santa Marta; **SOC** - Islas Revillagigedo (Socorro Island group); **SON** - Sonoran Desert; **SOU** - Southern Atlantic Coast; **STL** - St. Lucia; **STV** - St. Vincent; **TAC** - Tacarcuna; **VAN** - Venezuelan Andes; **VNZ** - Venezuelan Coastal Mountains; **WES** - Western Andes; **YUC** - Yucatán Peninsula.
o - Endemic to region, but not restricted to a single subregion.

Zoogeographic Regions:
AMN - Northern Amazonia; **AMS** - Southern Amazonia; **ATL** - Atlantic Forest; **BSR** - Baja-Sonora; **CAN** - Central Andes; **CDH** - Chiriquí-Darién Highlands; **CHO** - Chocó Lowlands; **CSA** - Central South America; **EPC** - Equatorial Pacific Coast; **GAN** - Greater Antilles; **GCS** - Gulf-Caribbean Slope; **LAN** - Lesser Antilles; **MAH** - Madrean Highlands; **MPL** - Mexican Plateau; **NAN** - Northern Andes; **NSA** - Northern South America; **PAM** - Pampas; **PAS** - Pacific Arid Slope; **PAT** - Patagonia; **SAN** - Southern Andes; **STP** - Subtropical Pacific; **TEP** - Tepuis.

CP -Conservation Priority:
1 - Urgent; **2** - High; **3** - Medium; **4** - Low.

RP - Research Priority:
1 - High; **2** - Medium; **3** - Low.

	Snst	Strat	Cntab	Rel	Min	Max	Micro	Habitats	Sub	Zoogeographic Regions
Thamnophilus aroyae	M	U	UT	F	800	1700	B?	F4E, F15	COC	CAN
Thamnophilus bridgesi	M	U/M	LT	F	L	1150		F1E, F8, F15, F14	HPC	GCS
Thamnophilus caerulescens	L	U/M	UT	C	L	2300		F4E, F1E, F8, F7		CAN, CSA, ATL, PAM
Thamnophilus cryptoleucus	L	U/M	LT	F	L	L		F3, F15		AMN, AMS
Thamnophilus doliatus										
doliatus	L	U/M	LT	C	L	2000		N14, N11, N12, F3		PAS, GCS, CHO, NSA, AMN, AMS, CSA
zarumae	M	U/C	HT	U	L	1700		F7	MAN	EPC
Thamnophilus insignis	M	U/M	UT	U	900	2000		F4, F5	o	TEP
Thamnophilus multistriatus	L	U	UT	F	900	2200		N14, F7E, F4E	o	NAN
Thamnophilus murinus	H	M	LT	C	L	1000+		F1		AMN, AMS
Thamnophilus nigriceps	M	U	LT	F	L	600		F1E, F15		GCS, NSA
Thamnophilus nigrocinereus	M	U/M	LT	F	L	L		F3, F2, F8	o	AMN
Thamnophilus palliatus	L	U/M	LT	F	L	1700		N14, F1E, F4E		NAN, CAN, AMN, AMS, ATL
Thamnophilus praecox	?	U	LT	U	L	L		F2	RNW	AMN
Thamnophilus punctatus	L	U/M	LT	C	L	1500		F7, F15, F1E, F12, F8		GCS, CHO, EPC, AMN, AMS, CSA, ATL
Thamnophilus ruficapillus	L	U	UT	F	L	2200		N11, F4E, N3		CAN, CSA, ATL, PAM
Thamnophilus schistaceus	H	M	LT	C	L	1100		F1, F2		AMN, AMS
Thamnophilus torquatus	M	U	LT?	F	L	1200+		N11, F8E, N4	o	CSA
Thamnophilus unicolor	M	U	MM	F	1200	2300		F4		NAN, CAN
Pygiptila stellaris	H	C	LT	C	L	700		F1		AMN, AMS
Megastictus margaritatus	H	U	LT	U/P	L	L		F1		AMN, AMS
Neoctantes niger	H	U	LT	R/P	L	800	T	F1		AMN, AMS
Clytoctantes alixi	H	U	HT	R	L	1000	V	F1		NAN, NSA
Clytoctantes atrogularis	H	U	LT	R	L	L	V	F1	MID	AMS
Xenornis setifrons	H	U	HT	R	L	600+		F1		GCS, CDH, CHO
Thamnistes anabatinus	M	C	UT	U	L	1700		F4, F1		GCS, CDH, CHO, NAN, CAN
Dysithamnus mentalis	M	U/M	UT	C	600	2200		F4, F1		MAH, GCS, CDH, CHO, EPC, NAN, CAN, NSA, CSA, ATL
Dysithamnus puncticeps	H	U/M	LT	U	L	1000		F1		GCS, CHO
Dysithamnus stictothorax	M	M	HT	F	L	1200		F1, F4	SOU	ATL
Dysithamnus striaticeps	M	U/M	HT	U?	L	800		F1	o	GCS
Dysithamnus xanthopterus	M	M/C	UT	U/P	800	1700		F4	SOU	ATL
Thamnomanes ardesiacus	H	U	LT	C	L	900		F1		AMN, AMS
Thamnomanes caesius	H	U/M	LT	C	L	850+		F1		AMN, AMS, ATL
Thamnomanes occidentalis	H	U	UT	U	900	2100	T?	F4, F1	WES	NAN
Thamnomanes plumbeus										
leucostictus	H	U	UT	U	900	1900		F4	o	NAN
plumbeus	H	U	LT	U	L	L		F1	RDJ	ATL
Thamnomanes saturninus	H	U	LT	C	L	L		F1		AMN?, AMS
Thamnomanes schistogynus	H	U/M	LT	C	L	1050		F1, F3	RMW	AMS
Myrmotherula ambigua	H	C	LT	F	L	L		F1	RNW	AMN
Myrmotherula assimilis	M	M	LT	F/P	L	L		F3		AMN, AMS
Myrmotherula axillaris	M	U/M	LT	C	L	1100		F1, F2, F15		GCS, CHO, NSA, AMN, AMS, ATL
Myrmotherula behni	H	U/M	UT	U	900	1800		F4		NAN, TEP
Myrmotherula brachyura										
brachyura	L	C	LT	F	L	1100		F1E, F2, F15		AMN, AMS
ignota	L	C	LT	F	L	900		F1E, F15		GCS, CHO
Myrmotherula cherriei	M	U/M	LT	F	L	550		F12, F8E, F3E		NSA?, AMN
Myrmotherula erythronotos	M	U/M	LT	R	L	L		F15	SOU	ATL
Myrmotherula erythrura	H	U/M	HT	F	L	900		F1		AMN, AMS
Myrmotherula fluminensis	M	?	LT	R	L	L?		F1	RDJ	ATL

CP	RP	Notes
3	3	
3	2	Deforestation.
4	2	May contain multiple species.
4	3	
4	3	Mostly below 1,000 m.
2	1	
4	3	
4	3	Locally to 400 m (Pacific slope Colombia).
4	3	Occasionally to 1,300 m (Venezuela).
4	3	
4	3	
4	2	May contain two species; Andean population mainly in bamboo.
3	1	Poorly known.
4	2	Probably contains two species.
4	2	Mainly above 800 m except in southeastern Brazil; may contain two species.
4	3	
4	2	Behavior and distribution poorly known.
4	3	Occasionally to 900 and 2,700 m (Colombia).
4	3	
4	2	Poorly known; associated with forest on sandy soil?
4	2	Poorly known.
2	1	Poorly known; deforestation.
2	1	Essentially unknown; deforestation.
2	1	Poorly known; deforestation.
4	2	Mainly above 900 m in Andes; may contain two species; deforestation.
4	3	Mainly above 900 m in Andes; locally in lowlands.
3	2	Deforestation.
3	2	Deforestation.
3	2	Deforestation.
3	2	
4	3	Occasionally to 1,100 m (Venezuela).
4	3	
2	1	Poorly known.
3	2	
2	2	Deforestation.
4	3	
4	3	Occasionally to 1,400 m.
3	2	
4	3	
4	3	
4	2	Occasionally to lowlands; poorly known; status of Andean population uncertain.
4	3	Occasionally to 1,300 m?
4	2	
3	2	
1	1	Rediscovered recently (Pacheco 1988); habitat unprotected.
4	3	Local east of Andean foothills.
2	1	Recently described (Gonzaga 1988); status uncertain.

Abbreviations Used

Snst - Sensitivity:
L - Low; **M** - Medium; **H** - High.

Strat - Foraging Strata:
T - Terrestrial; **U** - Understory; **M** - Midstory; **C** - Canopy; **A** - Aerial; **W** - Water.

Cntab - Center of Abundance:
LT - Lower tropical; **LS** - Lower subtropical; **HT** - Hill tropical; **UT** - Upper tropical; **US** - Upper subtropical; **MM** - Middle montane; **UM** - Upper montane.

Rel - Relative Abundance:
R - Rare; **U** - Uncommon; **F** - Fairly common; **C** - Common; **P** - Patchily distributed.

Min - Minimum Elevation:
L - Lowlands; **?** - Uncertain value; numeric values in meters.

Max - Maximum Elevation:
L - Lowlands; **?** - Uncertain value; **+** - species occurs at least to given elevation but likely occurs higher; numeric values in meters.

Micro - Microhabitats:
A - Army ants; **B** - Bamboo; **T** - Treefalls; **G** - Ground bromeliads; **C** - Rocky outcrops and caves; **S** - Streamside; **V** - Vine tangles; **B/V** -Bamboo/vine tangles.

Habitats:
F1 - Tropical lowland evergreen forest; **F2** - Flooded tropical evergreen forest; **F3** - River-edge forest; **F4** - Montane evergreen forest; **F5** - Elfin forest; **F6** - *Polylepis* woodland; **F7** - Tropical deciduous forest; **F8** - Gallery forest; **F9** - Southern temperate forest; **F10** - Pine forest; **F11** - Pine-oak forest; **F12** - White sand forest; **F13** - Palm forest; **F14** - Mangrove forest; **F15** - Secondary forest; **N1** - Arid lowland scrub; **N2** - Arid montane scrub; **N3** - Semihumid/humid montane scrub; **N4** - Cerrado; **N5** - Campo grasslands; **N6** - Low, seasonally wet grassland; **N7** - Southern temperate grassland; **N8** - Northern temperate grassland; **N9** - Puna grassland; **N10** - Paramo grassland; **N11** - Riparian thickets; **N12** - River island scrub; **N13** - Pastures/agricultural lands; **N14** - Second-growth scrub; **A1** - Freshwater marshes; **A2** - Saltwater/brackish marshes; **A3** - Coastal sand beaches/mudflats; **A4** - Coastal rocky beaches; **A5** - Riverine sand beaches; **A6** - Freshwater lakes and ponds; **A7** - Alkaline lakes; **A8** - Rivers; **A9** - Streams; **A10** - Bogs; **A11** - Coastal waters; **A12** - Pelagic waters.
E - Edge (used as a modifer to particular habitats).

Sub - Subregions:
ARC - Arid Caribbean Coast; **AWA** - Altiplano and Western Andes; **BAH** - Bahamas; **BAJ** - Baja California; **CAA** - Caatinga; **CAH** - Central American Highlands; **CER** - Cerrado; **CHA** - Chaco; **CHG** - Chiapas-Guanacaste; **CHL** - Chilean Desert; **CHR** - Chiriquí; **CIS** - Cocos Island; **CMV** - Cauca-Magdalena Valley; **COC** - Cuzco-Cochabamba; **CUB** - Cuba; **DOM** - Dominica; **EAS** - Eastern Slope Andes; **FDN** - Fernando de Noronha; **GAL** - Galápagos; **GCM** - Gulf Coast-Mexico; **GRE** - Grenada; **GUA** - Guadeloupe; **GUI** - Guianan; **HIS** - Hispaniola; **HPC** - Humid Pacific Coast; **ISA** - Isla Providencia and Isla San Andrés; **JAM** - Jamaica; **JFI** - Juan Fernández Islands; **MAN** - Manabí-Tumbes; **MAR** - Marañón Valley; **MID** - Madeira-Tapajós; **MON** - Montserrat; **MRT** - Martinique; **MTC** - Marañón-Cuzco; **NMM** - Northern Mexican Mountains; **NOR** - Northern Coastal Brazil; **PAR** - Pará; **PER** - Peruvian Desert; **PUE** - Puerto Rico; **RDJ** - Rio de Janeiro-Bahia Lowlands; **RMW** - Rio Madeira West; **RNW** - Rio Negro West; **SCA** - Southern Central America; **SCT** - Santa Cruz-Tucumán; **SIN** - Sinaloa-Oaxaca; **SMH** - Southern Mexican Highlands; **SMT** - Santa Marta; **SOC** - Islas Revillagigedo (Socorro Island group); **SON** - Sonoran Desert; **SOU** - Southern Atlantic Coast; **STL** - St. Lucia; **STV** - St. Vincent; **TAC** - Tacarcuna; **VAN** - Venezuelan Andes; **VNZ** - Venezuelan Coastal Mountains; **WES** - Western Andes; **YUC** - Yucatán Peninsula.
o - Endemic to region, but not restricted to a single subregion.

Zoogeographic Regions:
AMN - Northern Amazonia; **AMS** - Southern Amazonia; **ATL** - Atlantic Forest; **BSR** - Baja-Sonora; **CAN** - Central Andes; **CDH** - Chiriquí-Darién Highlands; **CHO** - Chocó Lowlands; **CSA** - Central South America; **EPC** - Equatorial Pacific Coast; **GAN** - Greater Antilles; **GCS** - Gulf-Caribbean Slope; **LAN** - Lesser Antilles; **MAH** - Madrean Highlands; **MPL** - Mexican Plateau; **NAN** - Northern Andes; **NSA** - Northern South America; **PAM** - Pampas; **PAS** - Pacific Arid Slope; **PAT** - Patagonia; **SAN** - Southern Andes; **STP** - Subtropical Pacific; **TEP** - Tepuis.

CP -Conservation Priority:
1 - Urgent; **2** - High; **3** - Medium; **4** - Low.

RP - Research Priority:
1 - High; **2** - Medium; **3** - Low.

	Snst	Strat	Cntab	Rel	Min	Max	Micro	Habitats	Sub	Zoogeographic Regions
Myrmotherula fulviventris	M	U	LT	F	L	1100		F1		GCS, CHO, NSA
Myrmotherula grisea	H	M	HT	U	500	1650		F1, F4	COC	CAN
Myrmotherula gularis	M	U	HT	U	400	1550		F4, F1	SOU	ATL
Myrmotherula guttata	H	U	LT	F	L	700		F1	GUI	AMN
Myrmotherula gutturalis	H	U	LT	F	L	1000		F1	GUI	AMN
Myrmotherula haematonota										
haematonota	H	U	LT	F	L	900		F1		AMN, AMS
spodionota	H	U	HT	F	600	1300		F1, F4		NAN, CAN
Myrmotherula hauxwelli	H	U	LT	F	L	L		F1		AMN, AMS
Myrmotherula iheringi	H	M	LT	U	L	650	B/V	F1	o	AMS
Myrmotherula klagesi	?	?	LT	?	L	L		F3?		AMN, AMS
Myrmotherula leucophthalma	H	U	LT	F	L	800		F1	o	AMS
Myrmotherula longicauda	L	U	HT	F	600	1200		F4E, F1E, N14		NAN, CAN
Myrmotherula longipennis	H	U/M	LT	F	L	700		F1		AMN, AMS
Myrmotherula menetriesii	H	M/C	LT	C	L	900		F1		AMN, AMS
Myrmotherula minor	H	M	HT	U	L	900		F1	SOU	ATL
Myrmotherula obscura	M	C	LT	F	L	L		F1E, F2		AMN, AMS
Myrmotherula ornata	H	U/M	LT	F	L	1200	B/V	F1, F2		AMN, AMS
Myrmotherula schisticolor	M	U	UT	F	900	2200		F4, F1		MAH, GCS, CDH, CHO, NAN, CAN
Myrmotherula sclateri	M	C	LT	F	L	700		F1	o	AMS
Myrmotherula sunensis	H	U/M	HT	U	L	900		F1		AMN, AMS
Myrmotherula surinamensis	L	U/M	LT	F	L	700		F2E, F1E, F15		GCS, CHO, NSA, AMN, AMS
Myrmotherula unicolor	M	M	LT	U	L	350		F1, F12, F15	o	ATL
Myrmotherula urosticta	M	U/M	LT	U	L	L		F1	RDJ	ATL
Dichrozona cincta	H	T	LT	U	L	800		F1		AMN, AMS
Myrmorchilus strigilatus	M	T	LT	F	L	1200+	G	F7	o	CSA
Herpsilochmus atricapillus	M	C	LT	C	L	1200+		F8, F7	o	CSA
Herpsilochmus axillaris	H	C	UT	U	900	1800	V	F4		NAN, CAN
Herpsilochmus dorsimaculatus	H	C	LT	F	L	L		F1	o	AMN
Herpsilochmus longirostris	M	C	HT	F	L	1200		F8	CER	CSA
Herpsilochmus motacilloides	H	C	UT	F/P	900	2050		F4	MTC	CAN
Herpsilochmus parkeri	H	C	UT	F	1350	1350		F4	MTC	CAN
Herpsilochmus pectoralis	M	C	LT	U	L	L?		F7	CAA	CSA
Herpsilochmus pileatus	M	C	LT	U?	L	800		F7	CAA	CSA
Herpsilochmus roraimae	H	C	UT	C	700	2000		F4	o	TEP
Herpsilochmus rufimarginatus	M	C	HT	C	L	1200		F1, F4, F7, F8, F12		GCS, CDH, NAN, CAN, NSA, AMN, AMS, CSA, ATL
Herpsilochmus stictocephalus	H	C	LT	U	L	L		F1	GUI	AMN
Herpsilochmus sticturus										
dugandi	H	C	LT	U	L	L	V	F1	RNW	AMN
sticturus	H	C	LT	U	L	L	V	F1	GUI	AMN
Microrhopias quixensis	M	M	LT	C/P	L	1100	B/V	F1		GCS, CHO, NSA, AMN, AMS
Formicivora grisea	L	U/M	LT	C	L	1500		F7, F15, F8, F12		GCS, NSA, AMN, AMS, CSA, ATL
Formicivora iheringi	H	M	HT	U	600	900	V	F7	CAA	CSA
Formicivora melanogaster	M	U/M	LT	F	L	1000		F7	o	CSA
Formicivora rufa	L	U	LT	F/P	L	1200		N6, N14, F12		AMN, CSA, ATL
Formicivora serrana										
littoralis	M	U/M	LT	F	L	L		F12	RDJ	ATL
serrana	?	U/M	LT	U	L	1100		F1E, N14	o	ATL
Drymophila caudata	M	U	UT	F/P	1200	2500	B	F4, F15		NAN, CAN
Drymophila devillei										
devillei	H	U	LT	F/P	L	1050	B	F1		AMN, AMS
subochracea	H	U	LT	F/P	L	L	B	F1	o	AMS

CP	RP	Notes
4	3	Occasionally to 2,000 m (Colombia).
2	1	Deforestation.
3	2	
4	3	
4	3	
4	2	
3	2	
4	3	
4	3	
4	2	Poorly known.
4	3	
4	3	Locally to lowlands.
4	3	
4	3	Occasionally to 1,000 m (Venezuela).
2	1	Poorly known; deforestation.
4	3	
4	3	
4	3	Locally to lowlands (Middle America).
4	3	
3	2	Poorly known.
4	3	Occasionally to 1,100 m (Colombia); usually at edge of lake or stream.
3	2	
2	1	Poorly known; deforestation.
4	3	
4	3	
4	3	See Davis and O'Neill (1986) for taxonomy
3	2	Occasionally to 700 m.
4	3	
3	2	Habitat destruction.
3	2	Deforestation.
2	1	Recently described (Davis and O'Neill 1986); deforestation.
3	2	Poorly known.
3	1	Poorly known.
4	3	
4	3	
4	3	
4	2	Poorly known.
4	3	
4	2	Occasionally to 1,350 m; may contain multiple species.
4	3	
2	1	Poorly known; deforestation.
4	3	
4	2	
2	2	Recently described (Gonzaga & Pacheco 1990); habitat destruction.
3	2	
4	3	Occasionally to 600 and 2,700 m (Colombia).
4	3	Occasionally to 1,300 m (Peru).
3	2	Poorly known.

Abbreviations Used

Snst - Sensitivity:
L - Low; **M** - Medium; **H** - High.

Strat - Foraging Strata:
T - Terrestrial; **U** - Understory; **M** - Midstory; **C** - Canopy; **A** - Aerial; **W** - Water.

Cntab - Center of Abundance:
LT - Lower tropical; **LS** - Lower subtropical; **HT** - Hill tropical; **UT** - Upper tropical; **US** - Upper subtropical; **MM** - Middle montane; **UM** - Upper montane.

Rel - Relative Abundance:
R - Rare; **U** - Uncommon; **F** - Fairly common; **C** - Common; **P** - Patchily distributed.

Min - Minimum Elevation:
L - Lowlands; **?** - Uncertain value; numeric values in meters.

Max - Maximum Elevation:
L - Lowlands; **?** - Uncertain value; **+** - species occurs at least to given elevation but likely occurs higher; numeric values in meters.

Micro - Microhabitats:
A - Army ants; **B** - Bamboo; **T** - Treefalls; **G** - Ground bromeliads; **C** - Rocky outcrops and caves; **S** - Streamside; **V** - Vine tangles; **B/V** -Bamboo/vine tangles.

Habitats:
F1 - Tropical lowland evergreen forest; **F2** - Flooded tropical evergreen forest; **F3** - River-edge forest; **F4** - Montane evergreen forest; **F5** - Elfin forest; **F6** - *Polylepis* woodland; **F7** - Tropical deciduous forest; **F8** - Gallery forest; **F9** - Southern temperate forest; **F10** - Pine forest; **F11** - Pine-oak forest; **F12** - White sand forest; **F13** - Palm forest; **F14** - Mangrove forest; **F15** - Secondary forest; **N1** - Arid lowland scrub; **N2** - Arid montane scrub; **N3** - Semihumid/humid montane scrub; **N4** - Cerrado; **N5** - Campo grasslands; **N6** - Low, seasonally wet grassland; **N7** - Southern temperate grassland; **N8** - Northern temperate grassland; **N9** - Puna grassland; **N10** - Paramo grassland; **N11** - Riparian thickets; **N12** - River island scrub; **N13** - Pastures/agricultural lands; **N14** - Second-growth scrub; **A1** - Freshwater marshes; **A2** - Saltwater/brackish marshes; **A3** - Coastal sand beaches/mudflats; **A4** - Coastal rocky beaches; **A5** - Riverine sand beaches; **A6** - Freshwater lakes and ponds; **A7** - Alkaline lakes; **A8** - Rivers; **A9** - Streams; **A10** - Bogs; **A11** - Coastal waters; **A12** - Pelagic waters.
E - Edge (used as a modifer to particular habitats).

Sub - Subregions:
ARC - Arid Caribbean Coast; **AWA** - Altiplano and Western Andes; **BAH** - Bahamas; **BAJ** - Baja California; **CAA** - Caatinga; **CAH** - Central American Highlands; **CER** - Cerrado; **CHA** - Chaco; **CHG** - Chiapas-Guanacaste; **CHL** - Chilean Desert; **CHR** - Chiriquí; **CIS** - Cocos Island; **CMV** - Cauca-Magdalena Valley; **COC** - Cuzco-Cochabamba; **CUB** - Cuba; **DOM** - Dominica; **EAS** - Eastern Slope Andes; **FDN** - Fernando de Noronha; **GAL** - Galápagos; **GCM** - Gulf Coast-Mexico; **GRE** - Grenada; **GUA** - Guadeloupe; **GUI** - Guianan; **HIS** - Hispaniola; **HPC** - Humid Pacific Coast; **ISA** - Isla Providencia and Isla San Andrés; **JAM** - Jamaica; **JFI** - Juan Fernández Islands; **MAN** - Manabí-Tumbes; **MAR** - Marañón Valley; **MID** - Madeira-Tapajós; **MON** - Montserrat; **MRT** - Martinique; **MTC** - Marañón-Cuzco; **NMM** - Northern Mexican Mountains; **NOR** - Northern Coastal Brazil; **PAR** - Pará; **PER** - Peruvian Desert; **PUE** - Puerto Rico; **RDJ** - Rio de Janeiro-Bahia Lowlands; **RMW** - Rio Madeira West; **RNW** - Rio Negro West; **SCA** - Southern Central America; **SCT** - Santa Cruz-Tucumán; **SIN** - Sinaloa-Oaxaca; **SMH** - Southern Mexican Highlands; **SMT** - Santa Marta; **SOC** - Islas Revillagigedo (Socorro Island group); **SON** - Sonoran Desert; **SOU** - Southern Atlantic Coast; **STL** - St. Lucia; **STV** - St. Vincent; **TAC** - Tacarcuna; **VAN** - Venezuelan Andes; **VNZ** - Venezuelan Coastal Mountains; **WES** - Western Andes; **YUC** - Yucatán Peninsula.
o - Endemic to region, but not restricted to a single subregion.

Zoogeographic Regions:
AMN - Northern Amazonia; **AMS** - Southern Amazonia; **ATL** - Atlantic Forest; **BSR** - Baja-Sonora; **CAN** - Central Andes; **CDH** - Chiriquí-Darién Highlands; **CHO** - Chocó Lowlands; **CSA** - Central South America; **EPC** - Equatorial Pacific Coast; **GAN** - Greater Antilles; **GCS** - Gulf-Caribbean Slope; **LAN** - Lesser Antilles; **MAH** - Madrean Highlands; **MPL** - Mexican Plateau; **NAN** - Northern Andes; **NSA** - Northern South America; **PAM** - Pampas; **PAS** - Pacific Arid Slope; **PAT** - Patagonia; **SAN** - Southern Andes; **STP** - Subtropical Pacific; **TEP** - Tepuis.

CP -Conservation Priority:
1 - Urgent; **2** - High; **3** - Medium; **4** - Low.

RP - Research Priority:
1 - High; **2** - Medium; **3** - Low.

	Snst	Strat	Cntab	Rel	Min	Max	Micro	Habitats	Sub	Zoogeographic Regions
Drymophila ferruginea	M	U	HT	C	L	1250	B	F1, F4	o	ATL
Drymophila genei	M	U	UT	C	1150	2200	B	F4	SOU	ATL
Drymophila malura	M	U	LT	F/P	L	950	V	F1	SOU	ATL
Drymophila ochropyga	M	U	UT	F	650	1300	B	F1, F4	SOU	ATL
Drymophila rubricollis	M	U	UT	C	L	2000	B	F4, F1	SOU	ATL
Drymophila squamata	M	U	LT	C	L	600		F1, F15	o	ATL
Terenura callinota	H	C	UT	U	750	2000		F4		CDH, NAN, CAN, TEP
Terenura humeralis	H	C	LT	U	L	650		F1		AMN?, AMS
Terenura maculata	M	C	HT	F	L	1200		F1, F4	o	ATL
Terenura sharpei	H	C	UT	U	1100	1650		F4	COC	CAN
Terenura sicki	M	C	HT	U	400	700		F1	NOR	ATL
Terenura spodioptila	H	C	LT	F	L	1100		F1		AMN, AMS
Cercomacra brasiliana	M	?	HT	R	600	1000		F1E	RDJ	ATL
Cercomacra carbonaria	M	U	LT	F	L	L		F8	GUI	AMN
Cercomacra cinerascens	H	C	LT	C	L	1100	V	F1		AMN, AMS
Cercomacra ferdinandi	M	U/M	LT	F	L	L	V	F3	PAR	AMS
Cercomacra laeta	L	U	LT	F	L	900		F1E, F15		AMN, AMS, ATL
Cercomacra manu	M	M	LT	U/P	L	1100	B	F3, F1E	o	AMS
Cercomacra melanaria	M	U	LT	F	L	L		F8, F7E	CHA	CSA
Cercomacra nigrescens	M	U	LT	F/P	L	1800		F3, F4E, F1, F15		NAN, CAN, AMN, AMS
Cercomacra nigricans	M	U/M	LT	F?	L	1500	V	F1E		GCS, CHO, NSA
Cercomacra serva	M	U	LT	U/P	L	1100	T	F1		AMN, AMS
Cercomacra tyrannina	L	U	LT	C	L	1800		F1E, F4E, F15		MAH, GCS, CDH, CHO, NAN, NSA, AMN
Sipia berlepschi	H	U	LT	F/P	L	600		F1	o	CHO
Sipia nigricauda	M	U	HT	U	400	1100		F4, F1	WES	NAN
Pyriglena atra	M	U	LT	R	L	L		F1E	RDJ	ATL
Pyriglena leuconota										
castanoptera	M	U	MM	C	1000	2500		F4E		NAN, CAN
leuconota	M	U	LT	F	L	1650		F1E, F4E, F7		CAN, AMS, ATL
pacifica	M	U	HT	F	L	900		F7, F1E		CHO, EPC
Pyriglena leucoptera	M	U	LT	C	L	1250	B?	F1E, F4E	o	ATL
Rhopornis ardesiaca	H	T/U	HT	U	700	1000	G	F7	CAA	CSA
Myrmoborus leucophrys	M	U	LT	F	L	1400	B	F1, F4, F3		NSA, AMN, AMS
Myrmoborus lugubris	M	U	LT	F	L	L		F3		AMN, AMS
Myrmoborus melanurus	H	U	LT	F	L	L		F2	RMW	AMS
Myrmoborus myotherinus	H	U	LT	C	L	1200		F1		AMN, AMS
Hypocnemis cantator	M	U/M	LT	C	L	1100		F1, F2, F15		AMN, AMS
Hypocnemis hypoxantha	H	U/M	LT	U	L	L	T	F1		AMN, AMS
Hypocnemoides maculicauda	M	U	LT	F	L	L	S	F2	o	AMS
Hypocnemoides melanopogon	M	U	LT	F	L	L	S	F2		AMN, AMS
Myrmochanes hemileucus	M	U	LT	F	L	L		N12, F3		AMN, AMS
Gymnocichla nudiceps	M	U	LT	U	L	L	S?	F1E		GCS, CHO, NSA
Sclateria naevia	M	T	LT	F	L	500	S	F2		NSA, AMN, AMS
Percnostola caurensis	H	U	?	U?	L	1300		F1		TEP, AMN
Percnostola leucostigma	H	T/U	HT	U	L	1100	S	F1, F4		NAN, CAN, TEP, AMN, AMS
Percnostola lophotes	L	T/U	LT	F	L	1050	B	F3, F1E, F15	RMW	AMS
Percnostola rufifrons	H	U	LT	F/P	L	L	T	F1	o	AMN
Percnostola schistacea	H	U	LT	U	L	L		F1		AMN, AMS
Myrmeciza atrothorax	L	U	LT	F	L	600		F1E, F15, F3		AMN, AMS
Myrmeciza disjuncta	H	U	LT	R?	L	L		F1	RNW	AMN
Myrmeciza exsul	M	U	LT	C	L	900		F1		GCS, CHO, NSA
Myrmeciza ferruginea	H	T	LT	F	L	L	T	F1		AMN, AMS

CP	RP	Notes
4	2	
3	2	Monitor.
3	2	Occasionally to 1,700 m.
3	2	Monitor.
3	2	Monitor.
4	2	
3	2	Occasionally to 2,400 m; deforestation.
4	3	
3	3	
2	1	Deforestation.
1	1	Deforestation immediate threat.
4	3	
2	1	Poorly known; deforestation, but apparently tolerates disturbed woodlands.
3	2	Poorly known.
4	3	
3	2	
4	2	
3	2	
4	3	
4	3	Occasionally to 2,100 m (Peru).
4	3	
4	3	
4	3	May contain multiple species.
3	2	Deforestation; survey.
3	2	Occasionally to 200 m; deforestation; usually called *S. rosenbergi* (see Robbins & Ridgely 1991).
1	1	May be conspecific with other *Pyriglena*.
4	3	
4	3	
3	2	Deforestation.
4	3	
1	1	Deforestation, most remaining habitat degraded.
4	3	
4	3	
3	2	Poorly known; habitat destruction?
4	3	Mainly below 800 m.
4	3	Occasionally to 1,400 m (Peru).
4	3	
4	3	
4	3	
4	3	
3	2	Deforestation; probably declining in most of range.
4	3	
3	2	Poorly known.
4	3	
4	3	Occasionally to 1,350 m.
4	3	May contain two species.
4	3	
4	3	Occasionally to 1,600 m (Venezuela).
3	2	Poorly known.
4	3	
4	3	

Abbreviations Used

Snst - Sensitivity:
L - Low; **M** - Medium; **H** - High.

Strat - Foraging Strata:
T - Terrestrial; **U** - Understory; **M** - Midstory; **C** - Canopy; **A** - Aerial; **W** - Water.

Cntab - Center of Abundance:
LT - Lower tropical; **LS** - Lower subtropical; **HT** - Hill tropical; **UT** - Upper tropical; **US** - Upper subtropical; **MM** - Middle montane; **UM** - Upper montane.

Rel - Relative Abundance:
R - Rare; **U** - Uncommon; **F** - Fairly common; **C** - Common; **P** - Patchily distributed.

Min - Minimum Elevation:
L - Lowlands; **?** - Uncertain value; numeric values in meters.

Max - Maximum Elevation:
L - Lowlands; **?** - Uncertain value; **+** - species occurs at least to given elevation but likely occurs higher; numeric values in meters.

Micro - Microhabitats:
A - Army ants; **B** - Bamboo; **T** - Treefalls; **G** - Ground bromeliads; **C** - Rocky outcrops and caves; **S** - Streamside; **V** - Vine tangles; **B/V** -Bamboo/vine tangles.

Habitats:
F1 - Tropical lowland evergreen forest; **F2** - Flooded tropical evergreen forest; **F3** - River-edge forest; **F4** - Montane evergreen forest; **F5** - Elfin forest; **F6** - *Polylepis* woodland; **F7** - Tropical deciduous forest; **F8** - Gallery forest; **F9** - Southern temperate forest; **F10** - Pine forest; **F11** - Pine-oak forest; **F12** - White sand forest; **F13** - Palm forest; **F14** - Mangrove forest; **F15** - Secondary forest; **N1** - Arid lowland scrub; **N2** - Arid montane scrub; **N3** - Semihumid/humid montane scrub; **N4** - Cerrado; **N5** - Campo grasslands; **N6** - Low, seasonally wet grassland; **N7** - Southern temperate grassland; **N8** - Northern temperate grassland; **N9** - Puna grassland; **N10** - Paramo grassland; **N11** - Riparian thickets; **N12** - River island scrub; **N13** - Pastures/agricultural lands; **N14** - Second-growth scrub; **A1** - Freshwater marshes; **A2** - Saltwater/brackish marshes; **A3** - Coastal sand beaches/mudflats; **A4** - Coastal rocky beaches; **A5** - Riverine sand beaches; **A6** - Freshwater lakes and ponds; **A7** - Alkaline lakes; **A8** - Rivers; **A9** - Streams; **A10** - Bogs; **A11** - Coastal waters; **A12** - Pelagic waters.
E - Edge (used as a modifer to particular habitats).

Sub - Subregions:
ARC - Arid Caribbean Coast; **AWA** - Altiplano and Western Andes; **BAH** - Bahamas; **BAJ** - Baja California; **CAA** - Caatinga; **CAH** - Central American Highlands; **CER** - Cerrado; **CHA** - Chaco; **CHG** - Chiapas-Guanacaste; **CHL** - Chilean Desert; **CHR** - Chiriquí; **CIS** - Cocos Island; **CMV** - Cauca-Magdalena Valley; **COC** - Cuzco-Cochabamba; **CUB** - Cuba; **DOM** - Dominica; **EAS** - Eastern Slope Andes; **FDN** - Fernando de Noronha; **GAL** - Galápagos; **GCM** - Gulf Coast-Mexico; **GRE** - Grenada; **GUA** - Guadeloupe; **GUI** - Guianan; **HIS** - Hispaniola; **HPC** - Humid Pacific Coast; **ISA** - Isla Providencia and Isla San Andrés; **JAM** - Jamaica; **JFI** - Juan Fernández Islands; **MAN** - Manabí-Tumbes; **MAR** - Marañón Valley; **MID** - Madeira-Tapajós; **MON** - Montserrat; **MRT** - Martinique; **MTC** - Marañón-Cuzco; **NMM** - Northern Mexican Mountains; **NOR** - Northern Coastal Brazil; **PAR** - Pará; **PER** - Peruvian Desert; **PUE** - Puerto Rico; **RDJ** - Rio de Janeiro-Bahia Lowlands; **RMW** - Rio Madeira West; **RNW** - Rio Negro West; **SCA** - Southern Central America; **SCT** - Santa Cruz-Tucumán; **SIN** - Sinaloa-Oaxaca; **SMH** - Southern Mexican Highlands; **SMT** - Santa Marta; **SOC** - Islas Revillagigedo (Socorro Island group); **SON** - Sonoran Desert; **SOU** - Southern Atlantic Coast; **STL** - St. Lucia; **STV** - St. Vincent; **TAC** - Tacarcuna; **VAN** - Venezuelan Andes; **VNZ** - Venezuelan Coastal Mountains; **WES** - Western Andes; **YUC** - Yucatán Peninsula.
o - Endemic to region, but not restricted to a single subregion.

Zoogeographic Regions:
AMN - Northern Amazonia; **AMS** - Southern Amazonia; **ATL** - Atlantic Forest; **BSR** - Baja-Sonora; **CAN** - Central Andes; **CDH** - Chiriquí-Darién Highlands; **CHO** - Chocó Lowlands; **CSA** - Central South America; **EPC** - Equatorial Pacific Coast; **GAN** - Greater Antilles; **GCS** - Gulf-Caribbean Slope; **LAN** - Lesser Antilles; **MAH** - Madrean Highlands; **MPL** - Mexican Plateau; **NAN** - Northern Andes; **NSA** - Northern South America; **PAM** - Pampas; **PAS** - Pacific Arid Slope; **PAT** - Patagonia; **SAN** - Southern Andes; **STP** - Subtropical Pacific; **TEP** - Tepuis.

CP -Conservation Priority:
1 - Urgent; **2** - High; **3** - Medium; **4** - Low.

RP - Research Priority:
1 - High; **2** - Medium; **3** - Low.

	Snst	Strat	Cntab	Rel	Min	Max	Micro	Habitats	Sub	Zoogeographic Regions
Myrmeciza fortis	H	T/U	LT	U	L	1050	A	F1		AMN, AMS
Myrmeciza goeldii	H	T	LT	F	L	L	B	F3, F1	RMW	AMS
Myrmeciza griseiceps	M	U	UT	U	650	2900	B	F4, F7		EPC, NAN
Myrmeciza hemimelaena	M	T/U	LT	F	L	1350	T	F1, F4		CAN, AMN, AMS
Myrmeciza hyperythra	M	T/U	LT	C	L	L		F2		AMN, AMS
Myrmeciza immaculata	H	U	HT	U	L	2000	A	F1		CDH, CHO, NAN, NSA
Myrmeciza laemosticta	H	T/U	HT	U	L	1100	S	F1		GCS, NSA
Myrmeciza longipes	L	T/U	LT	C	L	1700		F7, F1, F8		GCS, NSA, AMN
Myrmeciza loricata	M	T	HT	U	700	1300		F1, F4	SOU	ATL
Myrmeciza melanoceps	M	T	LT	F	L	L		F2		AMN, AMS
Myrmeciza pelzelni	H	U?	LT	?	L	L		F1	RNW	AMN
Myrmeciza ruficauda	M	T	LT	U/P	L	600		F1	o	ATL
Myrmeciza squamosa	M	T	HT	C	L	1000		F4, F1	SOU	ATL
Pithys albifrons	H	U	LT	F	L	1100	A	F1		AMN, AMS
Pithys castanea	?	U	LT	?	L	L		F1?	RNW	AMN
Gymnopithys leucaspis	M	U	LT	F	L	900	A	F1		GCS, CHO, AMN
Gymnopithys lunulata	H	U	LT	F	L	L	A	F1		AMN, AMS
Gymnopithys rufigula	M	U	LT	F	L	900	A	F1	GUI	AMN
Gymnopithys salvini	H	U	LT	F	L	L	A	F1	RMW	AMS
Rhegmatorhina berlepschi	H	U	LT	U	L	L	A	F1	MID	AMS
Rhegmatorhina cristata	H	U	LT	?	L	L	A	F1	RNW	AMN
Rhegmatorhina gymnops	H	U	LT	?	L	L	A	F1	PAR	AMS
Rhegmatorhina hoffmannsi	H	U	LT	C	L	L	A	F1	MID	AMS
Rhegmatorhina melanosticta	H	U	LT	F/P	L	1050	A	F1		AMN, AMS
Hylophylax naevia	H	U	LT	F	L	1150	T	F1, F2		AMN, AMS
Hylophylax naevioides	M	U	LT	F	L	900	A	F1		GCS, CHO, NSA
Hylophylax poecilinota	M	U	LT	F	L	950		F1		AMN, AMS
Hylophylax punctulata	M	U	LT	U/P	L	L		F2		AMN, AMS
Phlegopsis borbae	H	U	LT	U	L	L	A	F1	MID	AMS
Phlegopsis erythroptera	H	U	LT	R	L	L	A	F1		AMN, AMS
Phlegopsis nigromaculata	M	U	LT	F	L	700	A	F1, F2		AMN, AMS
Phaenostictus mcleannani	H	U	LT	U	L	1200	A	F1		GCS, CHO, NSA
Formicarius analis	M	T	LT	C	L	1400		F1, F2		GCS, CHO, NSA, AMN, AMS
Formicarius colma	H	T	LT	C	L	750		F1		AMN, AMS, ATL
Formicarius nigricapillus	H	T	HT	U	L	1800		F4, F1		GCS, CDH, CHO, NAN
Formicarius rufifrons	M	T	LT	R	L	L		F3	RMW	AMS
Formicarius rufipectus	H	T	UT	U	1100	2200		F4		CDH, NAN, CAN
Chamaeza campanisona	H	T	UT	F	L	1800		F4, F1		NAN, CAN, TEP, ATL
Chamaeza meruloides	M	T	HT	C	500	1900		F4, F1	SOU	ATL
Chamaeza mollissima	H	T	MM	U/P	1850	3100		F4		NAN, CAN
Chamaeza nobilis	H	T	LT	U	L	L		F1		AMN, AMS
Chamaeza ruficauda										
ruficauda	H	T	UT	F	700	2100+		F4	SOU	ATL
turdina	H	T	MM	F	1500	2600		F4	o	NAN
Myrmornis torquata	H	T	LT	U/P	L	1200		F1		GCS, CDH, AMN, AMS
Pittasoma michleri	H	T	HT	U	L	1050	T	F1		GCS, CDH, CHO
Pittasoma rufopileatum	H	T	LT	F	L	1100		F1	o	CHO
Grallaria albigula	M	T	MM	U	1500	3200	B?	F4	o	CAN
Grallaria alleni	H?	T	MM	R?	2100	2100		F4	EAS	NAN
Grallaria andicola	M	T	UM	F	3350	4400		F6, F5	o	CAN
Grallaria bangsi	M	T	MM	C	1600	2400		F4	SMT	NAN
Grallaria blakei	H	T	MM	U	2100	2500		F4	MTC	CAN
Grallaria capitalis	M	T	MM	F	1300	2800		F4E, F15	MTC	CAN

CP	RP	Notes
4	3	Occasionally to 1,200 m.
4	3	
2	1	Deforestation.
4	3	
4	3	
4	3	
3	1	
4	3	
3	2	
4	3	
3	2	Poorly known; associated with sandy soils?
2	1	Deforestation.
4	2	
4	3	Occasionally to 1,350 m.
3	1	Taxonomy uncertain; possibly a hybrid, one specimen known.
4	3	May contain two species.
4	3	Probably occurs into foothills.
4	3	
4	3	
3	2	Poorly known; deforestation.
3	2	Poorly known; deforestation.
3	2	Poorly known; deforestation.
3	2	Deforestation.
4	3	Occasionally to 1,350 m (Peru).
4	3	
4	3	
4	3	Occasionally to 1,350 m (Peru).
4	2	Distribution poorly known.
3	2	Poorly known.
4	3	
4	3	
4	3	
4	3	Locally to 2,050 m (Guatemala).
4	3	Occasionally to 1,100 m (Venezuela).
3	2	Mainly above 500 m; deforestation.
3	2	Poorly known.
4	3	One record for 3,100 m (Colombia).
4	2	Occasionally to 2,200 m; above 1,000 m in Andes, below 1,000 m in eastern Brazil; probably contains multiple species.
4	3	For taxonomy see Willis (1992).
4	2	To 1,400 m (Colombia); distribution poorly known.
4	3	
3	3	To 500 m in Rio Grande do Sul.
3	2	Deforestation?
4	2	Distribution poorly known in South America.
3	2	Deforestation.
3	2	Deforestation.
3	3	
1	1	Essentially unknown; deforestation.
3	3	Polylepis forests declining.
3	3	Occasionally to 1,200 m.
3	2	Poorly known; allocation of some populations uncertain.
3	3	

Abbreviations Used

Snst - Sensitivity:
L - Low; **M** - Medium; **H** - High.

Strat - Foraging Strata:
T - Terrestrial; **U** - Understory; **M** - Midstory; **C** - Canopy; **A** - Aerial; **W** - Water.

Cntab - Center of Abundance:
LT - Lower tropical; **LS** - Lower subtropical; **HT** - Hill tropical; **UT** - Upper tropical; **US** - Upper subtropical; **MM** - Middle montane; **UM** - Upper montane.

Rel - Relative Abundance:
R - Rare; **U** - Uncommon; **F** - Fairly common; **C** - Common; **P** - Patchily distributed.

Min - Minimum Elevation:
L - Lowlands; **?** - Uncertain value; numeric values in meters.

Max - Maximum Elevation:
L - Lowlands; **?** - Uncertain value; **+** - species occurs at least to given elevation but likely occurs higher; numeric values in meters.

Micro - Microhabitats:
A - Army ants; **B** - Bamboo; **T** - Treefalls; **G** - Ground bromeliads; **C** - Rocky outcrops and caves; **S** - Streamside; **V** - Vine tangles; **B/V** -Bamboo/vine tangles.

Habitats:
F1 - Tropical lowland evergreen forest; **F2** - Flooded tropical evergreen forest; **F3** - River-edge forest; **F4** - Montane evergreen forest; **F5** - Elfin forest; **F6** - *Polylepis* woodland; **F7** - Tropical deciduous forest; **F8** - Gallery forest; **F9** - Southern temperate forest; **F10** - Pine forest; **F11** - Pine-oak forest; **F12** - White sand forest; **F13** - Palm forest; **F14** - Mangrove forest; **F15** - Secondary forest; **N1** - Arid lowland scrub; **N2** - Arid montane scrub; **N3** - Semihumid/humid montane scrub; **N4** - Cerrado; **N5** - Campo grasslands; **N6** - Low, seasonally wet grassland; **N7** - Southern temperate grassland; **N8** - Northern temperate grassland; **N9** - Puna grassland; **N10** - Paramo grassland; **N11** - Riparian thickets; **N12** - River island scrub; **N13** - Pastures/agricultural lands; **N14** - Second-growth scrub; **A1** - Freshwater marshes; **A2** - Saltwater/brackish marshes; **A3** - Coastal sand beaches/mudflats; **A4** - Coastal rocky beaches; **A5** - Riverine sand beaches; **A6** - Freshwater lakes and ponds; **A7** - Alkaline lakes; **A8** - Rivers; **A9** - Streams; **A10** - Bogs; **A11** - Coastal waters; **A12** - Pelagic waters.
E - Edge (used as a modifer to particular habitats).

Sub - Subregions:
ARC - Arid Caribbean Coast; **AWA** - Altiplano and Western Andes; **BAH** - Bahamas; **BAJ** - Baja California; **CAA** - Caatinga; **CAH** - Central American Highlands; **CER** - Cerrado; **CHA** - Chaco; **CHG** - Chiapas-Guanacaste; **CHL** - Chilean Desert; **CHR** - Chiriquí; **CIS** - Cocos Island; **CMV** - Cauca-Magdalena Valley; **COC** - Cuzco-Cochabamba; **CUB** - Cuba; **DOM** - Dominica; **EAS** - Eastern Slope Andes; **FDN** - Fernando de Noronha; **GAL** - Galápagos; **GCM** - Gulf Coast-Mexico; **GRE** - Grenada; **GUA** - Guadeloupe; **GUI** - Guianan; **HIS** - Hispaniola; **HPC** - Humid Pacific Coast; **ISA** - Isla Providencia and Isla San Andrés; **JAM** - Jamaica; **JFI** - Juan Fernández Islands; **MAN** - Manabí-Tumbes; **MAR** - Marañón Valley; **MID** - Madeira-Tapajós; **MON** - Montserrat; **MRT** - Martinique; **MTC** - Marañón-Cuzco; **NMM** - Northern Mexican Mountains; **NOR** - Northern Coastal Brazil; **PAR** - Pará; **PER** - Peruvian Desert; **PUE** - Puerto Rico; **RDJ** - Rio de Janeiro-Bahia Lowlands; **RMW** - Rio Madeira West; **RNW** - Rio Negro West; **SCA** - Southern Central America; **SCT** - Santa Cruz-Tucumán; **SIN** - Sinaloa-Oaxaca; **SMH** - Southern Mexican Highlands; **SMT** - Santa Marta; **SOC** - Islas Revillagigedo (Socorro Island group); **SON** - Sonoran Desert; **SOU** - Southern Atlantic Coast; **STL** - St. Lucia; **STV** - St. Vincent; **TAC** - Tacarcuna; **VAN** - Venezuelan Andes; **VNZ** - Venezuelan Coastal Mountains; **WES** - Western Andes; **YUC** - Yucatán Peninsula.
o - Endemic to region, but not restricted to a single subregion.

Zoogeographic Regions:
AMN - Northern Amazonia; **AMS** - Southern Amazonia; **ATL** - Atlantic Forest; **BSR** - Baja-Sonora; **CAN** - Central Andes; **CDH** - Chiriquí-Darién Highlands; **CHO** - Chocó Lowlands; **CSA** - Central South America; **EPC** - Equatorial Pacific Coast; **GAN** - Greater Antilles; **GCS** - Gulf-Caribbean Slope; **LAN** - Lesser Antilles; **MAH** - Madrean Highlands; **MPL** - Mexican Plateau; **NAN** - Northern Andes; **NSA** - Northern South America; **PAM** - Pampas; **PAS** - Pacific Arid Slope; **PAT** - Patagonia; **SAN** - Southern Andes; **STP** - Subtropical Pacific; **TEP** - Tepuis.

CP -Conservation Priority:
1 - Urgent; **2** - High; **3** - Medium; **4** - Low.

RP - Research Priority:
1 - High; **2** - Medium; **3** - Low.

	Snst	Strat	Cntab	Rel	Min	Max	Micro	Habitats	Sub	Zoogeographic Regions
Grallaria carrikeri	H	T	UM	U	2400	2800	B	F4	MTC	CAN
Grallaria chthonia	H	T	MM	?	1800	2100		F4	VAN	NAN
Grallaria dignissima	H	T	LT	R	L	L		F1	RNW	AMN
Grallaria eludens	H	T	LT	R	L	500		F1	RMW	AMS
Grallaria erythroleuca	L	T	UM	U	2500	2950		F4, F15	COC	CAN
Grallaria erythrotis	M	T	UM	F	2000	3000		F4, F15	COC	CAN
Grallaria excelsa	H	T	MM	?	1700	2300		F4	VAN	NAN
Grallaria flavotincta	M	T	UT	F	1300	1800		F4	WES	NAN
Grallaria gigantea	H	T	MM	R?	1400	3000		F4	o	NAN
Grallaria griseonucha	H	T	MM	F	2300	2800		F4	VAN	NAN
Grallaria guatimalensis	H	T	UT	U	600	3000		F4, F1		MAH, GCS, CDH, NAN, CAN, TEP
Grallaria haplonota	M	T	UT	F	900	2000		F4, F15		NAN, CAN
Grallaria hypoleuca	L	T	MM	F	1500	2200	B	F4, F15	EAS	NAN
Grallaria kaestneri	M	T	MM	F	2000	2300		F4, F15	EAS	NAN
Grallaria milleri	H	T	UM	?	2700	3100		F4	EAS	NAN
Grallaria nuchalis	H	T	UM	F	2200	3300	B	F4	o	NAN
Grallaria przewalskii	L	T	MM	F	1900	2800		F4E, F15	MTC	CAN
Grallaria quitensis	M	T	UM	C	2200	3400		F6, F5		NAN, CAN
Grallaria ruficapilla										
ruficapilla	M	T	MM	C	1300	3100		F4E, F15		NAN, CAN
watkinsi	M	T	HT	F	600	1400		F7	MAN	EPC
Grallaria rufocinerea	H	T	MM	U	2400	3100		F4	EAS	NAN
Grallaria rufula	H	T	UM	C	2400	3600		F4, F5		NAN, CAN
Grallaria squamigera	H	T	UM	U	2000	3350		F4, F5		NAN, CAN
Grallaria varia	H	T	LT	U	L	1550		F4, F1		AMN, AMS, ATL
Hylopezus fulviventris										
berlepschi	M	T	LT	U	L	L		F3, F1E, F15	o	AMS
dives	M	T	LT	F	L	900	T	F1E, F15		GCS, CHO, NSA
fulviventris	L	T	LT	U/P	L	800		F1E, F3, F15	RNW	AMN
Hylopezus macularius	M	T	LT	F	L	L		F1		AMN, AMS
Hylopezus ochroleucus										
nattereri	H	T	UT	F	700	1700	B	F4, F1	SOU	ATL
ochroleucus	M	T	HT	R	500	900		F8	CAA	CSA
Hylopezus perspicillatus	H	T	LT	F	L	1250		F1		GCS, CHO, NSA
Myrmothera campanisona	H	T	LT	F	L	850	T	F1		AMN, AMS
Myrmothera simplex	H	T	UT	F	900	2400		F4, F5	o	TEP
Grallaricula cucullata	H	U	MM	F/P	1500	2700		F4	o	NAN
Grallaricula ferrugineipectus	H	U	MM	F	800	3350		F4, F15		NAN, CAN
Grallaricula flavirostris	H	U	UT	F	900	2200		F4		CDH, NAN, CAN
Grallaricula lineifrons	H	U	UM	F/P	3000	3400		F4, F5	EAS	NAN
Grallaricula loricata	H	U	MM	U	1400	2100		F4	VNZ	NAN
Grallaricula nana	H	U	MM	F	1900	2950		F4, F5		NAN, TEP
Grallaricula ochraceifrons	H?	T/U	MM	R	1900	2000		F4		NAN, CAN
Grallaricula peruviana	H	U	MM	R	1700	2100		F4	EAS	NAN
Conopophaga ardesiaca	H	U	UT	F	1000	1650		F4	COC	CAN
Conopophaga aurita	H	U	LT	U	L	L		F1		AMN, AMS
Conopophaga castaneiceps	H	U	UT	F	1100	2100		F4		NAN, CAN
Conopophaga lineata										
cearae	M	U	LT?	?	500	800		F7?	NOR	ATL
lineata	M	U	UT	C	L	2150		F4, F1, F15	SOU	ATL
Conopophaga melanogaster	H	U	LT	U	L	L	T	F1	MID	AMS
Conopophaga melanops	H	U	LT	U	L	800		F1	o	ATL
Conopophaga peruviana	H	U	LT	U	L	850		F1		AMN, AMS
Conopophaga roberti	?	U	LT	R/U	L	L?		F1, F7?		AMS, CSA

CP	RP	Notes
3	2	
2	1	Essentially unknown; deforestation.
4	2	Poorly known.
4	2	Essentially unknown.
3	2	
4	3	
2	2	Poorly known.
3	2	
3	2	Poorly known.
3	2	
3	3	Mainly above 900 m, occasionally to 200 m and 3,600 m.
4	2	Range poorly known.
4	3	
3	2	Recently described (Stiles 1992).
1	1	Range mostly deforested; almost unknown.
4	3	
3	3	
4	3	
4	3	
2	1	Deforestation; mainly in semideciduous forest.
3	2	Poorly known.
4	2	Occasionally to 2,000 m; may contain multiple species.
4	3	Occasionally to 1,850 and 3,800 m.
4	3	
4	3	Probably conspecific with *H. fulviventris*.
4	3	
4	3	
4	3	
3	2	Declining outside reserves.
2	1	Poorly known; deforestation.
4	3	
4	3	
4	3	Locally to 600 m.
3	1	Poorly known.
4	3	Locally to 600 m (Colombia); rarely to 200 m (Venezuela).
4	3	Occasionally to 500 m (Colombia).
3	2	
3	2	
4	3	Locally to 700m (Venezuela).
3	2	
2	1	
3	3	
4	3	
4	3	Occasionally to 500 m.
2	2	Ecology unknown.
4	3	
4	2	
3	2	Most common in lowlands; deforestation.
4	3	
2	2	Deforestation; poorly known.

Abbreviations Used

Snst - Sensitivity:
L - Low; **M** - Medium; **H** - High.

Strat - Foraging Strata:
T - Terrestrial; **U** - Understory; **M** - Midstory; **C** - Canopy; **A** - Aerial; **W** - Water.

Cntab - Center of Abundance:
LT - Lower tropical; **LS** - Lower subtropical; **HT** - Hill tropical; **UT** - Upper tropical; **US** - Upper subtropical; **MM** - Middle montane; **UM** - Upper montane.

Rel - Relative Abundance:
R - Rare; **U** - Uncommon; **F** - Fairly common; **C** - Common; **P** - Patchily distributed.

Min - Minimum Elevation:
L - Lowlands; **?** - Uncertain value; numeric values in meters.

Max - Maximum Elevation:
L - Lowlands; **?** - Uncertain value; **+** - species occurs at least to given elevation but likely occurs higher; numeric values in meters.

Micro - Microhabitats:
A - Army ants; **B** - Bamboo; **T** - Treefalls; **G** - Ground bromeliads; **C** - Rocky outcrops and caves; **S** - Streamside; **V** - Vine tangles; **B/V** -Bamboo/vine tangles.

Habitats:
F1 - Tropical lowland evergreen forest; **F2** - Flooded tropical evergreen forest; **F3** - River-edge forest; **F4** - Montane evergreen forest; **F5** - Elfin forest; **F6** - *Polylepis* woodland; **F7** - Tropical deciduous forest; **F8** - Gallery forest; **F9** - Southern temperate forest; **F10** - Pine forest; **F11** - Pine-oak forest; **F12** - White sand forest; **F13** - Palm forest; **F14** - Mangrove forest; **F15** - Secondary forest; **N1** - Arid lowland scrub; **N2** - Arid montane scrub; **N3** - Semihumid/humid montane scrub; **N4** - Cerrado; **N5** - Campo grasslands; **N6** - Low, seasonally wet grassland; **N7** - Southern temperate grassland; **N8** - Northern temperate grassland; **N9** - Puna grassland; **N10** - Paramo grassland; **N11** - Riparian thickets; **N12** - River island scrub; **N13** - Pastures/agricultural lands; **N14** - Second-growth scrub; **A1** - Freshwater marshes; **A2** - Saltwater/brackish marshes; **A3** - Coastal sand beaches/mudflats; **A4** - Coastal rocky beaches; **A5** - Riverine sand beaches; **A6** - Freshwater lakes and ponds; **A7** - Alkaline lakes; **A8** - Rivers; **A9** - Streams; **A10** - Bogs; **A11** - Coastal waters; **A12** - Pelagic waters.
E - Edge (used as a modifer to particular habitats).

Sub - Subregions:
ARC - Arid Caribbean Coast; **AWA** - Altiplano and Western Andes; **BAH** - Bahamas; **BAJ** - Baja California; **CAA** - Caatinga; **CAH** - Central American Highlands; **CER** - Cerrado; **CHA** - Chaco; **CHG** - Chiapas-Guanacaste; **CHL** - Chilean Desert; **CHR** - Chiriquí; **CIS** - Cocos Island; **CMV** - Cauca-Magdalena Valley; **COC** - Cuzco-Cochabamba; **CUB** - Cuba; **DOM** - Dominica; **EAS** - Eastern Slope Andes; **FDN** - Fernando de Noronha; **GAL** - Galápagos; **GCM** - Gulf Coast-Mexico; **GRE** - Grenada; **GUA** - Guadeloupe; **GUI** - Guianan; **HIS** - Hispaniola; **HPC** - Humid Pacific Coast; **ISA** - Isla Providencia and Isla San Andrés; **JAM** - Jamaica; **JFI** - Juan Fernández Islands; **MAN** - Manabí-Tumbes; **MAR** - Marañón Valley; **MID** - Madeira-Tapajós; **MON** - Montserrat; **MRT** - Martinique; **MTC** - Marañón-Cuzco; **NMM** - Northern Mexican Mountains; **NOR** - Northern Coastal Brazil; **PAR** - Pará; **PER** - Peruvian Desert; **PUE** - Puerto Rico; **RDJ** - Rio de Janeiro-Bahia Lowlands; **RMW** - Rio Madeira West; **RNW** - Rio Negro West; **SCA** - Southern Central America; **SCT** - Santa Cruz-Tucumán; **SIN** - Sinaloa-Oaxaca; **SMH** - Southern Mexican Highlands; **SMT** - Santa Marta; **SOC** - Islas Revillagigedo (Socorro Island group); **SON** - Sonoran Desert; **SOU** - Southern Atlantic Coast; **STL** - St. Lucia; **STV** - St. Vincent; **TAC** - Tacarcuna; **VAN** - Venezuelan Andes; **VNZ** - Venezuelan Coastal Mountains; **WES** - Western Andes; **YUC** - Yucatán Peninsula.
o - Endemic to region, but not restricted to a single subregion.

Zoogeographic Regions:
AMN - Northern Amazonia; **AMS** - Southern Amazonia; **ATL** - Atlantic Forest; **BSR** - Baja-Sonora; **CAN** - Central Andes; **CDH** - Chiriquí-Darién Highlands; **CHO** - Chocó Lowlands; **CSA** - Central South America; **EPC** - Equatorial Pacific Coast; **GAN** - Greater Antilles; **GCS** - Gulf-Caribbean Slope; **LAN** - Lesser Antilles; **MAH** - Madrean Highlands; **MPL** - Mexican Plateau; **NAN** - Northern Andes; **NSA** - Northern South America; **PAM** - Pampas; **PAS** - Pacific Arid Slope; **PAT** - Patagonia; **SAN** - Southern Andes; **STP** - Subtropical Pacific; **TEP** - Tepuis.

CP -Conservation Priority:
1 - Urgent; **2** - High; **3** - Medium; **4** - Low.

RP - Research Priority:
1 - High; **2** - Medium; **3** - Low.

	Snst	Strat	Cntab	Rel	Min	Max	Micro	Habitats	Sub	Zoogeographic Regions
Rhinocryptidae										
Pteroptochos castaneus	M	T	US	U	L	1600		F9, F15		STP, SAN
Pteroptochos megapodius	M	T	US	F	L	3150		N2, N1		STP, SAN
Pteroptochos tarnii	M	T	US	F	L	1500		F9	o	SAN
Scelorchilus albicollis	M	T	LS?	F	L	1600		N1, N2		STP, SAN
Scelorchilus rubecula	M	T	LS	F	L	1500	B	F9		STP, SAN
Rhinocrypta lanceolata	M	T	LT	U	L	1800		N1, F7	CHA	CSA
Teledromas fuscus	M	T	LT	F	L	2500		N1	CHA	CSA
Liosceles thoracicus	H	T	LT	F	L	1050		F1		AMN, AMS
Melanopareia elegans	M	T	LT/HT	F	L	1250		F7	MAN	EPC
Melanopareia maranonica	M	T	LT	?	400	800		F7, N1	MAR	CAN
Melanopareia maximiliani	M	T/U	HT	F	L	2150		F7, N1, N2		CAN, SAN, CSA
Melanopareia torquata	M	T/U	LT	F/P	L	1400		N4, N5	CER	CSA
Psilorhamphus guttatus	M	U	LT	U	L	900	B	F1	SOU	ATL
Merulaxis ater	H	T	UT	U	800	1800		F4	SOU	ATL
Merulaxis stresemanni	H	T	LT	R	L	L		F1	RDJ	ATL
Eugralla paradoxa	M	U	LS	?	L	1000		F9	o	SAN
Myornis senilis	H	U	UM	U	2300	3350	B	F4, F5		NAN, CAN
Scytalopus argentifrons	M	U	UT/MM	F	1000	3100		F4	CHR	CDH
Scytalopus femoralis										
atratus	H	U	UT/MM	F	800	2200		F4		NAN, CAN
bolivianus	H	U	MM	U	1200	2150		F4	COC	CAN
femoralis	H	U	MM	F	850	2500		F4		NAN, CAN
sanctaemariae	H	U	UT	F	1350	1700		F4	SMT	NAN
Scytalopus indigoticus										
indigoticus	M	U	LT	U	L	1000		F1	o	ATL
psychopompas	M	U	LT	?	L	L?		F1	RDJ	ATL
Scytalopus latebricola										
caracae	H	U	MM	F	1600	1900		F4	VNZ	NAN
latebricola	H	U	MM	F	2150	3300		F4	SMT	NAN
meridanus	H	U	MM	F	2000	3700		F4	o	NAN
spillmanni	H	U	MM	F	2200	3200		F4	o	NAN
sp.nov.	H	U	UM	F	2550	3200	B	F4, F5	EAS	NAN
Scytalopus macropus	H	U	UM	U	2400	3300	S	F4	MTC	CAN
Scytalopus magellanicus										
acutirostris	M	U/T	UM	C	2500	3500		F4	MTC	CAN
canus	M	U/T	UM	F	3100	4000		F4	o	NAN
fuscus	H	U/T	?	?	950	4000		F9	o	SAN
griseicollis	M	U/T	UM	?	2500	3650		F4		NAN, CAN
magellanicus	M	U/T	LS	C	L	2000		F9, N3	o	SAN
simonsi	M	U/T	UM	F	2600	4300		F5, F6, N3		NAN, CAN
superciliaris	M	U	MM	?	1500	3350		F4	SCT	CAN
Scytalopus novacapitalis	H	U	UT	R	1000	1200+	S	F8	CER	CSA
Scytalopus panamensis	H	U	UT	F	1050	1500		F4		CDH, NAN
Scytalopus speluncae	M	U	UT	C	750	2500	B	F4, F1	SOU	ATL
Scytalopus unicolor										
latrans	H	U	UM	C	1500	3700		F4		NAN, CAN
parvirostris	H	U	UM	C	1800	3200		F4	o	CAN
unicolor	H	U	UM	?	2000	3150		N3?	AWA	CAN
Scytalopus vicinior	H	U	UT	U	1200	2800		F4	o	CDH
Syctalopus sp. nov.	H	U	UT	U	250	1500		F4, F1		CDH, NAN
Acropternis orthonyx	H	T/U	UM	U/P	2250	3300	B	F4, F5		NAN, CAN

CP	RP	Notes
3	2	
4	3	
4	3	
4	3	
4	3	
4	3	
4	3	
4	3	
4	2	Entire genus needs ecological and taxonomic study.
3	2	
4	2	
3	2	
3	2	Poorly known.
3	2	Locally to lowlands.
1	1	May not be a valid species.
4	2	Poorly known.
4	3	
4	3	
4	2	
4	2	
4	3	Occasionally to 2,950 m.
4	2	
3	1	Deforestation.
2	1	Poorly known; deforestation.
4	3	
4	3	Occasionally to 3,600 m.
4	3	May contain two species.
4	3	
3	2	
4	3	
4	2	Taxonomic relationships and nomenclature uncertain.
4	2	
4	2	Poorly known.
4	2	May contain two species.
4	2	
4	2	Occasionally to 2,450 m.
3	2	Mainly in alder (*Alnus*) forests.
2	1	Poorly known; habitat destruction.
3	2	
4	3	Occasionally to 400 m.
4	2	
4	2	Mainly below 2,500 m.
4	2	Poorly known.
4	2	May contain two species.
4	2	May contain two species.
4	3	

Abbreviations Used

Snst - Sensitivity:
L - Low; **M** - Medium; **H** - High.

Strat - Foraging Strata:
T - Terrestrial; **U** - Understory; **M** - Midstory; **C** - Canopy; **A** - Aerial; **W** - Water.

Cntab - Center of Abundance:
LT - Lower tropical; **LS** - Lower subtropical; **HT** - Hill tropical; **UT** - Upper tropical; **US** - Upper subtropical; **MM** - Middle montane; **UM** - Upper montane.

Rel - Relative Abundance:
R - Rare; **U** - Uncommon; **F** - Fairly common; **C** - Common; **P** - Patchily distributed.

Min - Minimum Elevation:
L - Lowlands; **?** - Uncertain value; numeric values in meters.

Max - Maximum Elevation:
L - Lowlands; **?** - Uncertain value; **+** - species occurs at least to given elevation but likely occurs higher; numeric values in meters.

Micro - Microhabitats:
A - Army ants; **B** - Bamboo; **T** - Treefalls; **G** - Ground bromeliads; **C** - Rocky outcrops and caves; **S** - Streamside; **V** - Vine tangles; **B/V** -Bamboo/vine tangles.

Habitats:
F1 - Tropical lowland evergreen forest; **F2** - Flooded tropical evergreen forest; **F3** - River-edge forest; **F4** - Montane evergreen forest; **F5** - Elfin forest; **F6** - *Polylepis* woodland; **F7** - Tropical deciduous forest; **F8** - Gallery forest; **F9** - Southern temperate forest; **F10** - Pine forest; **F11** - Pine-oak forest; **F12** - White sand forest; **F13** - Palm forest; **F14** - Mangrove forest; **F15** - Secondary forest; **N1** - Arid lowland scrub; **N2** - Arid montane scrub; **N3** - Semihumid/humid montane scrub; **N4** - Cerrado; **N5** - Campo grasslands; **N6** - Low, seasonally wet grassland; **N7** - Southern temperate grassland; **N8** - Northern temperate grassland; **N9** - Puna grassland; **N10** - Paramo grassland; **N11** - Riparian thickets; **N12** - River island scrub; **N13** - Pastures/agricultural lands; **N14** - Second-growth scrub; **A1** - Freshwater marshes; **A2** - Saltwater/brackish marshes; **A3** - Coastal sand beaches/mudflats; **A4** - Coastal rocky beaches; **A5** - Riverine sand beaches; **A6** - Freshwater lakes and ponds; **A7** - Alkaline lakes; **A8** - Rivers; **A9** - Streams; **A10** - Bogs; **A11** - Coastal waters; **A12** - Pelagic waters.
E - Edge (used as a modifer to particular habitats).

Sub - Subregions:
ARC - Arid Caribbean Coast; **AWA** - Altiplano and Western Andes; **BAH** - Bahamas; **BAJ** - Baja California; **CAA** - Caatinga; **CAH** - Central American Highlands; **CER** - Cerrado; **CHA** - Chaco; **CHG** - Chiapas-Guanacaste; **CHL** - Chilean Desert; **CHR** - Chiriquí; **CIS** - Cocos Island; **CMV** - Cauca-Magdalena Valley; **COC** - Cuzco-Cochabamba; **CUB** - Cuba; **DOM** - Dominica; **EAS** - Eastern Slope Andes; **FDN** - Fernando de Noronha; **GAL** - Galápagos; **GCM** - Gulf Coast-Mexico; **GRE** - Grenada; **GUA** - Guadeloupe; **GUI** - Guianan; **HIS** - Hispaniola; **HPC** - Humid Pacific Coast; **ISA** - Isla Providencia and Isla San Andrés; **JAM** - Jamaica; **JFI** - Juan Fernández Islands; **MAN** - Manabí-Tumbes; **MAR** - Marañón Valley; **MID** - Madeira-Tapajós; **MON** - Montserrat; **MRT** - Martinique; **MTC** - Marañón-Cuzco; **NMM** - Northern Mexican Mountains; **NOR** - Northern Coastal Brazil; **PAR** - Pará; **PER** - Peruvian Desert; **PUE** - Puerto Rico; **RDJ** - Rio de Janeiro-Bahia Lowlands; **RMW** - Rio Madeira West; **RNW** - Rio Negro West; **SCA** - Southern Central America; **SCT** - Santa Cruz-Tucumán; **SIN** - Sinaloa-Oaxaca; **SMH** - Southern Mexican Highlands; **SMT** - Santa Marta; **SOC** - Islas Revillagigedo (Socorro Island group); **SON** - Sonoran Desert; **SOU** - Southern Atlantic Coast; **STL** - St. Lucia; **STV** - St. Vincent; **TAC** - Tacarcuna; **VAN** - Venezuelan Andes; **VNZ** - Venezuelan Coastal Mountains; **WES** - Western Andes; **YUC** - Yucatán Peninsula.
o - Endemic to region, but not restricted to a single subregion.

Zoogeographic Regions:
AMN - Northern Amazonia; **AMS** - Southern Amazonia; **ATL** - Atlantic Forest; **BSR** - Baja-Sonora; **CAN** - Central Andes; **CDH** - Chiriquí-Darién Highlands; **CHO** - Chocó Lowlands; **CSA** - Central South America; **EPC** - Equatorial Pacific Coast; **GAN** - Greater Antilles; **GCS** - Gulf-Caribbean Slope; **LAN** - Lesser Antilles; **MAH** - Madrean Highlands; **MPL** - Mexican Plateau; **NAN** - Northern Andes; **NSA** - Northern South America; **PAM** - Pampas; **PAS** - Pacific Arid Slope; **PAT** - Patagonia; **SAN** - Southern Andes; **STP** - Subtropical Pacific; **TEP** - Tepuis.

CP -Conservation Priority:
1 - Urgent; **2** - High; **3** - Medium; **4** - Low.

RP - Research Priority:
1 - High; **2** - Medium; **3** - Low.

	Snst	Strat	Cntab	Rel	Min	Max	Micro	Habitats	Sub	Zoogeographic Regions
Tyrannidae										
Phyllomyias burmeisteri										
burmeisteri	M	C	HT	U	L	1400		F1, F4		CAN, ATL
leucogonys	M	C	UT	U/P	800	1500		F4		NAN, CAN, TEP
zeledoni	H	C	UT	R?	900	1850		F4	CHR	CDH
Phyllomyias cinereiceps	H	C	MM	F	1150	2700		F4		NAN, CAN
Phyllomyias fasciatus	M	C	UT	F	L	1900		F4, F1, F8		CAN, CSA, ATL
Phyllomyias griseiceps	L	C	LT	F/P	L	1300		F1E, F7, F15		GCS, CHO, NAN, NSA, AMN
Phyllomyias griseocapilla	M	C	UT	U/P	750	1850		F4, F1	SOU	ATL
Phyllomyias nigrocapillus	H	C	UM	U	2600	3400		F4, F5		NAN, CAN
Phyllomyias plumbeiceps	H	C	MM	U/P	1300	2200		F4		NAN, CAN
Phyllomyias sclateri	M	C	UT	C	400	2200		F4, F15	o	CAN
Phyllomyias uropygialis	M	C	UM	U/P	1500	3600		F4, F5, F15		NAN, CAN
Phyllomyias virescens										
reiseri	M	C	HT	?	700	1000		F7, F8?	o	CSA
urichi	M	C	HT	?	L?	1100		F1?	VNZ	NAN
virescens	M	C	UT	U/P	L	1800		F1, F4, F9	SOU	ATL
Zimmerius bolivianus	M	C	UT/MM	F/P	1200	2850		F4	COC	CAN
Zimmerius cinereicapillus	M	C	HT	U/P	500	1200		F1, F4		NAN, CAN
Zimmerius gracilipes	M	C	LT	C	L	1300		F1, F2		AMN, AMS, ATL?
Zimmerius vilissimus	M	C	UT?	C	L	3000		F4, F1, F15		MAH, GCS, CDH, CHO, NAN
Zimmerius viridiflavus										
chrysops	M	C	UT	F	700	2400		F4, F15		NAN, CAN
viridiflavus	M	C	MM	F	1250	2700		F4	MTC	CAN
Ornithion brunneicapillum	M	C	LT	U/F	L	900		F1, F15		GCS, CHO, NSA
Ornithion inerme	M	C	LT	F/P	L	950		F1E, F2		AMN, AMS, ATL
Ornithion semiflavum	M	C	LT	F	L	1250		F1E, F15	o	GCS
Camptostoma imberbe	L	C	LT	F	L	2100		F8, F15, N11		PAS, MAH, GCS
Camptostoma obsoletum	L	C	LT	F	L	1500		F15, F8, F3, F12, N14, N11		GCS, EPC, STP, NAN, CAN, NSA, AMN, AMS, CSA, ATL, PAM
Phaeomyias murina	L	C	LT	F/P	L	1750		N1, N4, N14, F7, F8, F3, F14		GCS, EPC, NSA, AMN, AMS, CSA, ATL
Sublegatus modestus										
arenarum	M	C	LT	U	L	L		F7, F8, F14, N1		PAS, GCS, NSA, AMN
modestus	M	C	LT	F	L	800		F7, F8, N1		AMS, CSA
obscurior	M	C	LT	U	L	1050		F3, F1E, F7		NSA, AMN, AMS
Suiriri suiriri	M	C	LT	F	L	1500		N4, F7		CAN, AMN, AMS, CSA
Tyrannulus elatus	L	C	LT	C	L	1000		F3, F2, F1, F15		GCS, CHO, NSA, AMN, AMS
Myiopagis caniceps	M	C	LT	F/P	L	900		F1		GCS, CHO, NSA, AMN, AMS, ATL
Myiopagis cotta	M	C	HT	F	L	1400		F1, F4, F15	JAM	GAN
Myiopagis flavivertex	H	M	LT	U	L	L		F2		AMN, AMS
Myiopagis gaimardii	M	C	LT	C	L	1000		F1, F8, F15		GCS, NSA, AMN, AMS, CSA
Myiopagis leucospodia	M	C	LT	F	L	800		N1, N11	MAN	EPC
Myiopagis subplacens	H	C	HT	F	L	1750		F7, F8	MAN	EPC
Myiopagis viridicata	M	C	LT	F	L	1700		F1, F7, F8, F15		PAS, GCS, EPC, NSA, AMN, AMS, CSA, ATL
Elaenia albiceps	L	C	LS	C	L	3300		F9, F4E, F15, N3		STP, NAN, CAN, SAN, CSA, PAT
Elaenia chiriquensis	L	C	LT	C	L	3000		N4, N6, F12, N14		GCS, CDH, NAN, NSA, AMN, AMS, CSA, ATL
Elaenia cristata	M	C	LT	F	L	1350		N4, N6, F12, N1		NSA, AMN, AMS, CSA
Elaenia dayi	M	C	MM	U/F	1500	2600		F5, N3	o	TEP
Elaenia fallax	M	C	UT	F	500	2000		F4, F1	o	GAN
Elaenia flavogaster	L	C	LT	C	L	1700		N14, N11, F15E, N4		PAS, GCS, CHO, EPC, NSA, AMN, AMS, CSA, ATL
Elaenia frantzii	L	C	MM	C	900	3600		F4, F15		MAH, CDH, NAN
Elaenia gigas	L	C	HT	U/P	L	1200		N11, N14, F15		AMN, AMS

CP	RP	Notes
3	2	Taxonomy of species group poorly understood.
3	2	
3	2	
4	2	Poorly known.
4	2	Distribution poorly known.
4	3	
4	2	Locally to sea level.
4	3	Occasionally to 1,600 m.
4	2	Poorly known.
4	3	
4	3	
2	2	Survey; deforestation.
2	2	Poorly known; deforestation; survey.
3	2	May be declining, more information needed.
4	3	
3	2	Poorly known.
4	3	Occasionally to 2,000 m (Venezuela).
4	3	
4	3	Occasionally to 300 m (Colombia).
3	3	
4	3	Locally to 1,200 m (Venezuela).
4	3	
4	3	
4	3	
4	2	Locally to 2,950 m (Bolivia).
4	3	
4	3	
4	3	
4	2	Taxonomic status uncertain (see Traylor 1982).
4	3	
4	3	Occasionally to 1,200 m.
4	3	
4	3	
4	3	
4	3	
4	3	
3	3	Habitat destruction.
4	3	Locally to 2,200 m (Mexico).
4	3	
4	2	
4	3	
4	3	
3	2	Monitor.
4	3	Occasionally to 2,100 m.
4	2	Seasonal movements poorly known.
4	2	Poorly known.

Abbreviations Used

Snst - Sensitivity:
L - Low; **M** - Medium; **H** - High.

Strat - Foraging Strata:
T - Terrestrial; **U** - Understory; **M** - Midstory; **C** - Canopy; **A** - Aerial; **W** - Water.

Cntab - Center of Abundance:
LT - Lower tropical; **LS** - Lower subtropical; **HT** - Hill tropical; **UT** - Upper tropical; **US** - Upper subtropical; **MM** - Middle montane; **UM** - Upper montane.

Rel - Relative Abundance:
R - Rare; **U** - Uncommon; **F** - Fairly common; **C** - Common; **P** - Patchily distributed.

Min - Minimum Elevation:
L - Lowlands; **?** - Uncertain value; numeric values in meters.

Max - Maximum Elevation:
L - Lowlands; **?** - Uncertain value; **+** - species occurs at least to given elevation but likely occurs higher; numeric values in meters.

Micro - Microhabitats:
A - Army ants; **B** - Bamboo; **T** - Treefalls; **G** - Ground bromeliads; **C** - Rocky outcrops and caves; **S** - Streamside; **V** - Vine tangles; **B/V** -Bamboo/vine tangles.

Habitats:
F1 - Tropical lowland evergreen forest; **F2** - Flooded tropical evergreen forest; **F3** - River-edge forest; **F4** - Montane evergreen forest; **F5** - Elfin forest; **F6** - *Polylepis* woodland; **F7** - Tropical deciduous forest; **F8** - Gallery forest; **F9** - Southern temperate forest; **F10** - Pine forest; **F11** - Pine-oak forest; **F12** - White sand forest; **F13** - Palm forest; **F14** - Mangrove forest; **F15** - Secondary forest; **N1** - Arid lowland scrub; **N2** - Arid montane scrub; **N3** - Semihumid/humid montane scrub; **N4** - Cerrado; **N5** - Campo grasslands; **N6** - Low, seasonally wet grassland; **N7** - Southern temperate grassland; **N8** - Northern temperate grassland; **N9** - Puna grassland; **N10** - Paramo grassland; **N11** - Riparian thickets; **N12** - River island scrub; **N13** - Pastures/agricultural lands; **N14** - Second-growth scrub; **A1** - Freshwater marshes; **A2** - Saltwater/brackish marshes; **A3** - Coastal sand beaches/mudflats; **A4** - Coastal rocky beaches; **A5** - Riverine sand beaches; **A6** - Freshwater lakes and ponds; **A7** - Alkaline lakes; **A8** - Rivers; **A9** - Streams; **A10** - Bogs; **A11** - Coastal waters; **A12** - Pelagic waters.
E - Edge (used as a modifer to particular habitats).

Sub - Subregions:
ARC - Arid Caribbean Coast; **AWA** - Altiplano and Western Andes; **BAH** - Bahamas; **BAJ** - Baja California; **CAA** - Caatinga; **CAH** - Central American Highlands; **CER** - Cerrado; **CHA** - Chaco; **CHG** - Chiapas-Guanacaste; **CHL** - Chilean Desert; **CHR** - Chiriquí; **CIS** - Cocos Island; **CMV** - Cauca-Magdalena Valley; **COC** - Cuzco-Cochabamba; **CUB** - Cuba; **DOM** - Dominica; **EAS** - Eastern Slope Andes; **FDN** - Fernando de Noronha; **GAL** - Galápagos; **GCM** - Gulf Coast-Mexico; **GRE** - Grenada; **GUA** - Guadeloupe; **GUI** - Guianan; **HIS** - Hispaniola; **HPC** - Humid Pacific Coast; **ISA** - Isla Providencia and Isla San Andrés; **JAM** - Jamaica; **JFI** - Juan Fernández Islands; **MAN** - Manabí-Tumbes; **MAR** - Marañón Valley; **MID** - Madeira-Tapajós; **MON** - Montserrat; **MRT** - Martinique; **MTC** - Marañón-Cuzco; **NMM** - Northern Mexican Mountains; **NOR** - Northern Coastal Brazil; **PAR** - Pará; **PER** - Peruvian Desert; **PUE** - Puerto Rico; **RDJ** - Rio de Janeiro-Bahia Lowlands; **RMW** - Rio Madeira West; **RNW** - Rio Negro West; **SCA** - Southern Central America; **SCT** - Santa Cruz-Tucumán; **SIN** - Sinaloa-Oaxaca; **SMH** - Southern Mexican Highlands; **SMT** - Santa Marta; **SOC** - Islas Revillagigedo (Socorro Island group); **SON** - Sonoran Desert; **SOU** - Southern Atlantic Coast; **STL** - St. Lucia; **STV** - St. Vincent; **TAC** - Tacarcuna; **VAN** - Venezuelan Andes; **VNZ** - Venezuelan Coastal Mountains; **WES** - Western Andes; **YUC** - Yucatán Peninsula.
o - Endemic to region, but not restricted to a single subregion.

Zoogeographic Regions:
AMN - Northern Amazonia; **AMS** - Southern Amazonia; **ATL** - Atlantic Forest; **BSR** - Baja-Sonora; **CAN** - Central Andes; **CDH** - Chiriquí-Darién Highlands; **CHO** - Chocó Lowlands; **CSA** - Central South America; **EPC** - Equatorial Pacific Coast; **GAN** - Greater Antilles; **GCS** - Gulf-Caribbean Slope; **LAN** - Lesser Antilles; **MAH** - Madrean Highlands; **MPL** - Mexican Plateau; **NAN** - Northern Andes; **NSA** - Northern South America; **PAM** - Pampas; **PAS** - Pacific Arid Slope; **PAT** - Patagonia; **SAN** - Southern Andes; **STP** - Subtropical Pacific; **TEP** - Tepuis.

CP -Conservation Priority:
1 - Urgent; **2** - High; **3** - Medium; **4** - Low.

RP - Research Priority:
1 - High; **2** - Medium; **3** - Low.

	Snst	Strat	Cntab	Rel	Min	Max	Micro	Habitats	Sub	Zoogeographic Regions
Elaenia martinica	L	C	LT	C	L	700+		F1, F7, F15		GAN, LAN, GCS
Elaenia mesoleuca	L	C	UT	C	L	2100		F4, F1, F15, F9, F8		CSA, ATL
Elaenia obscura	M	M/C	UT	U	750	2800		F4E, F1E, F15, F8, N11		CAN, CSA, ATL
Elaenia pallatangae	L	C	MM	F	2200	3300		F4E, F15		NAN, CAN, TEP
Elaenia parvirostris	L	C	LT	C	L	1000+		F8, F7, F15		CSA, PAM
Elaenia pelzelni	M	C	LT	U/P	L	L		F3		AMN, AMS
Elaenia ridleyana	L	M/C	LT	F	L	L		F7, N14	FDN	ATL
Elaenia ruficeps	M	C	LT	F	L	1400		F12, F8E		AMN, AMS
Elaenia spectabilis	L	C	LT	C	L	1000+		F8, F15		CSA, PAM
Elaenia strepera	M	C	MM	U?	1500	2400		F7		CAN, CSA
Mecocerculus calopterus	M	C	UT	U	800	1950		F4, F7		NAN, CAN
Mecocerculus hellmayri	H	C	UT	F	1300	2400		F4	o	CAN
Mecocerculus leucophrys	M	C	UM	C	1500	4400		F5, F4, F6		NAN, CAN, TEP
Mecocerculus minor	M	C	MM	F	1600	2650		F4, F4E		NAN, CAN
Mecocerculus poecilocercus	H	C	MM	F	1600	2600		F4		NAN, CAN
Mecocerculus stictopterus	H	C	UM	C	2600	3600		F4		NAN, CAN
Serpophaga cinerea	L	T/U	MM	F	1100	3200		A8, A9		CDH, NAN, CAN
Serpophaga hypoleuca	M	U/C	LT	U/P	L	L		N12		AMN, AMS
Serpophaga munda	L	M/C	UT	F	L	2600		F7		CAN, CSA
Serpophaga nigricans	L	T/U	LT	F	L	1000+		N11, A1, A9		CSA, ATL, PAM
Serpophaga subcristata	L	M/C	LT	F	L	1500		F1E, F15, F7		CSA, ATL, PAM
Inezia inornata	L	C	LT	F	L	600		F7, F8	o	CSA
Inezia subflava	M	M/C	LT	F	L	L		F8, F7, F15		NSA, AMN, AMS
Inezia tenuirostris	M	C	LT	F	L	600		F7, N1	ARC	NSA
Stigmatura budytoides	M	U/C	LT	F/C	L	2300		N1, N2, N11	o	CSA
Stigmatura napensis										
bahiae	?	?	LT	?	L	1000		N1	CAA	CSA
napensis	M	C	LT	F	L	L		N12		AMN, AMS
Anairetes agilis	H	U/M	UM	F	2700	3400	B	F5	EAS	NAN
Anairetes agraphia	H	U/M	UM	F	2650	3600	B	F5	MTC	CAN
Anairetes alpinus	H	M/C	UM	R/P	3900	4400		F6	AWA	CAN
Anairetes fernandezianus	?	C	LS	?	L	1000		F4	JFI	STP
Anairetes flavirostris	M	U/C	UM	F	1400	3700		N2, F6		CAN, SAN, PAT
Anairetes parulus	L	U/C	UM	C	L	4000		N3, F15, F5, F9		STP, NAN, CAN, SAN, PAT
Anairetes reguloides										
nigrocristatus	L	U/M	UM	U	2350	4200		N2, F6	AWA	CAN
reguloides	L	U/M	LS	F	L	2900		N11, N2		STP, CAN
Tachuris rubrigastra	M	U	LS	C	L	4200		A1		STP, CAN, SAN, ATL, PAM, PAT
Culicivora caudacuta	M	U	LT	U/P	L	1400		N5, N6	CER	CSA
Polystictus pectoralis	H	U	UT	U/P	L	1300		N5, N6		NAN, NSA, CSA, PAM
Polystictus superciliaris	M	U	UT	U	900	1400		N2	CER	CSA
Pseudocolopteryx acutipennis	M	U	MM	U/P	1500	2600		N11, A1		NAN, CAN
Pseudocolopteryx dinellianus	H	U	LT	?	L	L?		N1	CHA	CSA
Pseudocolopteryx flaviventris	L	U	LT	F	L	L		A1, A1		STP, CSA, PAM, PAT
Pseudocolopteryx sclateri	M	U	LT	F?	L	L		A1		AMN, CSA, ATL, PAM
Euscarthmus meloryphus	L	U	LT	C	L	2100		N1, N2, N4		EPC, NSA, CSA, ATL, PAM
Euscarthmus rufomarginatus	H	U	LT	R/P	L	1000+		N4, N5		AMN, CSA
Mionectes macconnelli	H	U/M	LT	F/P	L	2000		F1, F4		CAN, TEP, AMN, AMS
Mionectes oleagineus	M	U/C	LT	F	L	1200		F1, F2, F15		PAS, GCS, CHO, EPC, NSA, AMN, AMS, ATL
Mionectes olivaceus	M	U/M	HT	F/P	L	1800		F1, F4, F15		CDH, NAN, CAN, AMN, AMS
Mionectes rufiventris	M	U/M	HT	F/P	L	1900		F1, F4	SOU	ATL
Mionectes striaticollis	M	U/M	MM	C	1200	3350		F4, F15		NAN, CAN
Leptopogon amaurocephalus	M	U/M	LT	F	L	1300		F1, F15		GCS, NSA, TEP, AMN, AMS, CSA, ATL
Leptopogon rufipectus	H	U/M	MM	F	1600	2700		F4	o	NAN

CP	RP	Notes
4	3	
4	3	
4	2	Locally to lowlands in southeastern Brazil; distribution poorly known.
4	3	Locally to 900 m.
4	3	
4	2	Distribution and behavior poorly known.
4	2	
4	2	Poorly known.
4	3	
4	2	Distribution poorly known.
3	3	
4	3	
4	3	Mainly above 2,600 m.
4	3	
4	3	Occasionally to 3,100 m.
4	3	Occasionally to 1,800 m.
4	3	Locally to lowlands.
4	3	
4	3	
4	3	
4	3	
4	3	
4	3	
4	3	
4	3	
3	2	Poorly known; survey.
4	3	
4	3	Occasionally to 1,800 m.
4	3	Occasionally to 1,800 m.
2	1	Deforestation; survey.
3	2	Survey.
4	3	Locally to lowlands in the south.
4	3	
3	2	
3	2	
4	3	
2	1	Rapid habitat destruction.
2	1	Locally to 2,700 m (Colombia); survey; grassland destruction.
3	2	Habitat currently not at risk.
4	2	Northern limits of breeding range uncertain.
4	2	Poorly known.
4	3	
4	2	Poorly known.
4	3	
2	1	Habitat destruction.
4	3	
4	3	Locally to 1,800 m (Central America).
4	3	Locally to 3,000 m (Venezuela).
4	3	
4	3	Occasionally to 650 m; elevational movements poorly known.
4	3	Locally to 1,600 m (Venezuela).
4	3	

Abbreviations Used

Snst - Sensitivity:
L - Low; **M** - Medium; **H** - High.

Strat - Foraging Strata:
T - Terrestrial; **U** - Understory; **M** - Midstory; **C** - Canopy; **A** - Aerial; **W** - Water.

Cntab - Center of Abundance:
LT - Lower tropical; **LS** - Lower subtropical; **HT** - Hill tropical; **UT** - Upper tropical; **US** - Upper subtropical; **MM** - Middle montane; **UM** - Upper montane.

Rel - Relative Abundance:
R - Rare; **U** - Uncommon; **F** - Fairly common; **C** - Common; **P** - Patchily distributed.

Min - Minimum Elevation:
L - Lowlands; **?** - Uncertain value; numeric values in meters.

Max - Maximum Elevation:
L - Lowlands; **?** - Uncertain value; **+** - species occurs at least to given elevation but likely occurs higher; numeric values in meters.

Micro - Microhabitats:
A - Army ants; **B** - Bamboo; **T** - Treefalls; **G** - Ground bromeliads; **C** - Rocky outcrops and caves; **S** - Streamside; **V** - Vine tangles; **B/V** -Bamboo/vine tangles.

Habitats:
F1 - Tropical lowland evergreen forest; **F2** - Flooded tropical evergreen forest; **F3** - River-edge forest; **F4** - Montane evergreen forest; **F5** - Elfin forest; **F6** - *Polylepis* woodland; **F7** - Tropical deciduous forest; **F8** - Gallery forest; **F9** - Southern temperate forest; **F10** - Pine forest; **F11** - Pine-oak forest; **F12** - White sand forest; **F13** - Palm forest; **F14** - Mangrove forest; **F15** - Secondary forest; **N1** - Arid lowland scrub; **N2** - Arid montane scrub; **N3** - Semihumid/humid montane scrub; **N4** - Cerrado; **N5** - Campo grasslands; **N6** - Low, seasonally wet grassland; **N7** - Southern temperate grassland; **N8** - Northern temperate grassland; **N9** - Puna grassland; **N10** - Paramo grassland; **N11** - Riparian thickets; **N12** - River island scrub; **N13** - Pastures/agricultural lands; **N14** - Second-growth scrub; **A1** - Freshwater marshes; **A2** - Saltwater/brackish marshes; **A3** - Coastal sand beaches/mudflats; **A4** - Coastal rocky beaches; **A5** - Riverine sand beaches; **A6** - Freshwater lakes and ponds; **A7** - Alkaline lakes; **A8** - Rivers; **A9** - Streams; **A10** - Bogs; **A11** - Coastal waters; **A12** - Pelagic waters.
E - Edge (used as a modifer to particular habitats).

Sub - Subregions:
ARC - Arid Caribbean Coast; **AWA** - Altiplano and Western Andes; **BAH** - Bahamas; **BAJ** - Baja California; **CAA** - Caatinga; **CAH** - Central American Highlands; **CER** - Cerrado; **CHA** - Chaco; **CHG** - Chiapas-Guanacaste; **CHL** - Chilean Desert; **CHR** - Chiriquí; **CIS** - Cocos Island; **CMV** - Cauca-Magdalena Valley; **COC** - Cuzco-Cochabamba; **CUB** - Cuba; **DOM** - Dominica; **EAS** - Eastern Slope Andes; **FDN** - Fernando de Noronha; **GAL** - Galápagos; **GCM** - Gulf Coast-Mexico; **GRE** - Grenada; **GUA** - Guadeloupe; **GUI** - Guianan; **HIS** - Hispaniola; **HPC** - Humid Pacific Coast; **ISA** - Isla Providencia and Isla San Andrés; **JAM** - Jamaica; **JFI** - Juan Fernández Islands; **MAN** - Manabí-Tumbes; **MAR** - Marañón Valley; **MID** - Madeira-Tapajós; **MON** - Montserrat; **MRT** - Martinique; **MTC** - Marañón-Cuzco; **NMM** - Northern Mexican Mountains; **NOR** - Northern Coastal Brazil; **PAR** - Pará; **PER** - Peruvian Desert; **PUE** - Puerto Rico; **RDJ** - Rio de Janeiro-Bahia Lowlands; **RMW** - Rio Madeira West; **RNW** - Rio Negro West; **SCA** - Southern Central America; **SCT** - Santa Cruz-Tucumán; **SIN** - Sinaloa-Oaxaca; **SMH** - Southern Mexican Highlands; **SMT** - Santa Marta; **SOC** - Islas Revillagigedo (Socorro Island group); **SON** - Sonoran Desert; **SOU** - Southern Atlantic Coast; **STL** - St. Lucia; **STV** - St. Vincent; **TAC** - Tacarcuna; **VAN** - Venezuelan Andes; **VNZ** - Venezuelan Coastal Mountains; **WES** - Western Andes; **YUC** - Yucatán Peninsula.
o - Endemic to region, but not restricted to a single subregion.

Zoogeographic Regions:
AMN - Northern Amazonia; **AMS** - Southern Amazonia; **ATL** - Atlantic Forest; **BSR** - Baja-Sonora; **CAN** - Central Andes; **CDH** - Chiriquí-Darién Highlands; **CHO** - Chocó Lowlands; **CSA** - Central South America; **EPC** - Equatorial Pacific Coast; **GAN** - Greater Antilles; **GCS** - Gulf-Caribbean Slope; **LAN** - Lesser Antilles; **MAH** - Madrean Highlands; **MPL** - Mexican Plateau; **NAN** - Northern Andes; **NSA** - Northern South America; **PAM** - Pampas; **PAS** - Pacific Arid Slope; **PAT** - Patagonia; **SAN** - Southern Andes; **STP** - Subtropical Pacific; **TEP** - Tepuis.

CP -Conservation Priority:
1 - Urgent; **2** - High; **3** - Medium; **4** - Low.

RP - Research Priority:
1 - High; **2** - Medium; **3** - Low.

	Snst	Strat	Cntab	Rel	Min	Max	Micro	Habitats	Sub	Zoogeographic Regions
Leptopogon superciliaris	M	U/M	UT	F	600	2100		F4		CDH, NAN, CAN
Leptopogon taczanowskii	H	U/M	MM	F	1700	2650		F4	MTC	CAN
Phylloscartes ceciliae	M	C	HT	U?	500	800		F1	NOR	ATL
Phylloscartes chapmani	H	M	UT	U	1000	2000		F4	o	TEP
Phylloscartes difficilis	M	U/M	MM	U/F	950	2150		F4	SOU	ATL
Phylloscartes eximius	M	M	LT	F	L	1800		F1, F4	SOU	ATL
Phylloscartes flaveolus	L	U/M	LT	F/P	L	1250	B	F1E, F15, F7, F8		GCS, CHO, NSA, AMN, AMS, CSA, ATL
Phylloscartes flaviventris	H	C	UT	U	750	1000		F4	VNZ	NAN
Phylloscartes flavovirens	M	C	LT	U/P	L	500		F1	HPC	GCS
Phylloscartes gualaquizae	H	C	UT	U	1050	2000		F4		NAN, CAN
Phylloscartes kronei	M	U/C	LT	F	L	L		F12, F15	SOU	ATL
Phylloscartes lanyoni	M?	C	HT	U?	450	750		F1?	CMV	NSA
Phylloscartes nigrifrons	H	C	UT	F	900	1800		F4	o	TEP
Phylloscartes ophthalmicus	H	M/C	UT	F	900	1800		F4		NAN, CAN
Phylloscartes orbitalis	H	C	HT	F	600	1150		F1, F4		NAN, CAN
Phylloscartes oustaleti	H	C	HT	F	500	900		F1	SOU	ATL
Phylloscartes paulistus	M	M	LT	U	L	300		F1	SOU	ATL
Phylloscartes poecilotis	H	C	MM	U/F	1500	2400		F4		NAN, CAN
Phylloscartes roquettei	M?	C	HT?	?	400	500?		F7	CER	CSA
Phylloscartes sp. nov.	H	C	UT	U	750	1900		F4	o	CAN
Phylloscartes superciliaris	H	C	UT	U	600	1700		F4		CDH, NAN
Phylloscartes sylviolus	M	C	LT	U/P	L	600		F1	o	ATL
Phylloscartes venezuelanus	H	C	UT	F	1000	1400		F4	VNZ	NAN
Phylloscartes ventralis	M	C	UT	F	1100	2300		F4, F1, F9		CAN, ATL
Phylloscartes virescens	H	C	LT	R/U	L	L		F1	GUI	AMN
Pseudotriccus pelzelni	H	U	UT	F	700	2000		F4		CDH, NAN, CAN
Pseudotriccus ruficeps	H	U	UM	F	1850	3350		F4		NAN, CAN
Pseudotriccus simplex	H	U	UT	U	1300	2100		F4	COC	CAN
Corythopis delalandi	M	T	LT	C	L	1200+		F1, F8		CSA, ATL
Corythopis torquata	H	T	LT	F	L	800		F1		AMN, AMS
Myiornis albiventris	H	C	HT	F/U	600	1200	V	F1	o	CAN
Myiornis atricapillus	M	C	LT	U	L	700		F1		GCS, CHO
Myiornis auricularis	L	M/C	LT	F	L	1250		F1, F15	o	ATL
Myiornis ecaudatus	M	C	LT	F	L	950		F2, F1		NSA, AMN, AMS
Lophotriccus eulophotes	M	U/M	LT	U/P	L	L	B	F1	RMW	AMS
Lophotriccus galeatus	M	M/C	LT	F	L	1100		F15, F1		NSA, AMN, AMS
Lophotriccus pileatus	M	U/M	UT	F	750	2100		F4, F1		CDH, NAN, CAN
Lophotriccus vitiosus	M	U/M	LT	F	L	800		F1, F2		AMN, AMS
Atalotriccus pilaris	L	M/C	LT	F	L	800		F7, F1		GCS, NSA, AMN
Poecilotriccus albifacies	H	M	LT	U/P	L	1050	B	F1	RMW	AMS
Poecilotriccus andrei	H	U	LT	R/P	L	L	B	F1		AMN, AMS
Poecilotriccus capitalis	M	U/C	LT	U	L	1100	B/V	F1, F2		NAN, CAN, AMN, AMS
Poecilotriccus ruficeps	M	U	MM	F/P	1600	2700	B	F4		NAN, CAN
Poecilotriccus sp. nov.	M	U	MM	F	1900	2600	B	F4	MTC	CAN
Oncostoma cinereigulare	L	U/M	LT	F	L	1200		F1E, F7, F15		PAS, GCS
Oncostoma olivaceum	L	U/M	LT	F	L	1000		F1E, F15		GCS, NSA
Hemitriccus cinnamomeipectus	H	U	MM	U	1700	2200		F5, F4		NAN, CAN
Hemitriccus diops	M	U	HT	F/P	L	1300	B	F1, F4	o	ATL
Hemitriccus flammulatus	M	U/M	LT	F/P	L	700	B	F1	o	AMS
Hemitriccus furcatus	M	U/M	HT?	R	L	1200	B	F1	o	ATL
Hemitriccus granadensis	M	U	MM	F/P	2000	3300		F4E		NAN, CAN
Hemitriccus inornatus	H?	U?	LT	?	L	L		F12?	RNW	AMN
Hemitriccus iohannis	M	M	LT	U	L	600	V	F3, F15		AMN, AMS

CP	RP	Notes
4	3	Locally to 100 m (Pacific Colombia).
4	3	
1	1	Deforestation; habitat unprotected.
4	3	
3	3	
2	2	Mainly in Paraná drainage.
4	3	
4	2	Survey.
3	2	Deforestation.
3	2	
2	2	Recently described (Willis 1992); deforestation.
1	1	Recently described (Graves 1988); deforestation; only specimen from secondary forest.
4	3	
4	3	Occasionally to 600 m (Pacific Colombia) and 2,400 m.
3	2	Deforestation.
3	2	Locally to lowlands.
2	2	Occasionally to 750 m; survey; declining outside reserves.
4	3	
1	1	Survey; deforestation; not found recently at type locality.
3	2	Distribution poorly known.
3	2	Distribution poorly known.
3	2	Declining outside reserves; coastal population scarce.
4	2	Survey.
4	3	Regularly in lowlands in southeastern Brazil and Uruguay.
4	2	Poorly known.
4	3	Locally to 2,500 m.
4	3	Occasionally to 400 m.
3	3	
4	3	
4	3	Occasionally to 1,350 m.
3	2	Poorly known.
4	3	
4	3	
4	3	
3	2	Poorly known.
4	3	
4	3	Locally to 300 m and 2,300 m.
4	3	
4	3	Occasionally to 2,000 m.
3	2	Distribution poorly known.
4	2	Distribution poorly known.
3	2	
4	3	Occasionally to 1,000 m (Colombia).
3	2	
4	3	Locally to 1,450 m.
4	3	
2	1	Deforestation.
4	3	
4	3	Occasionally to 1,300 m.
1	1	Survey; few currently occupied sites protected.
4	3	
2	1	
4	3	

Abbreviations Used

Snst - Sensitivity:
L - Low; **M** - Medium; **H** - High.

Strat - Foraging Strata:
T - Terrestrial; **U** - Understory; **M** - Midstory; **C** - Canopy; **A** - Aerial; **W** - Water.

Cntab - Center of Abundance:
LT - Lower tropical; **LS** - Lower subtropical; **HT** - Hill tropical; **UT** - Upper tropical; **US** - Upper subtropical; **MM** - Middle montane; **UM** - Upper montane.

Rel - Relative Abundance:
R - Rare; **U** - Uncommon; **F** - Fairly common; **C** - Common; **P** - Patchily distributed.

Min - Minimum Elevation:
L - Lowlands; **?** - Uncertain value; numeric values in meters.

Max - Maximum Elevation:
L - Lowlands; **?** - Uncertain value; **+** - species occurs at least to given elevation but likely occurs higher; numeric values in meters.

Micro - Microhabitats:
A - Army ants; **B** - Bamboo; **T** - Treefalls; **G** - Ground bromeliads; **C** - Rocky outcrops and caves; **S** - Streamside; **V** - Vine tangles; **B/V** -Bamboo/vine tangles.

Habitats:
F1 - Tropical lowland evergreen forest; **F2** - Flooded tropical evergreen forest; **F3** - River-edge forest; **F4** - Montane evergreen forest; **F5** - Elfin forest; **F6** - *Polylepis* woodland; **F7** - Tropical deciduous forest; **F8** - Gallery forest; **F9** - Southern temperate forest; **F10** - Pine forest; **F11** - Pine-oak forest; **F12** - White sand forest; **F13** - Palm forest; **F14** - Mangrove forest; **F15** - Secondary forest; **N1** - Arid lowland scrub; **N2** - Arid montane scrub; **N3** - Semihumid/humid montane scrub; **N4** - Cerrado; **N5** - Campo grasslands; **N6** - Low, seasonally wet grassland; **N7** - Southern temperate grassland; **N8** - Northern temperate grassland; **N9** - Puna grassland; **N10** - Paramo grassland; **N11** - Riparian thickets; **N12** - River island scrub; **N13** - Pastures/agricultural lands; **N14** - Second-growth scrub; **A1** - Freshwater marshes; **A2** - Saltwater/brackish marshes; **A3** - Coastal sand beaches/mudflats; **A4** - Coastal rocky beaches; **A5** - Riverine sand beaches; **A6** - Freshwater lakes and ponds; **A7** - Alkaline lakes; **A8** - Rivers; **A9** - Streams; **A10** - Bogs; **A11** - Coastal waters; **A12** - Pelagic waters.
E - Edge (used as a modifer to particular habitats).

Sub - Subregions:
ARC - Arid Caribbean Coast; **AWA** - Altiplano and Western Andes; **BAH** - Bahamas; **BAJ** - Baja California; **CAA** - Caatinga; **CAH** - Central American Highlands; **CER** - Cerrado; **CHA** - Chaco; **CHG** - Chiapas-Guanacaste; **CHL** - Chilean Desert; **CHR** - Chiriquí; **CIS** - Cocos Island; **CMV** - Cauca-Magdalena Valley; **COC** - Cuzco-Cochabamba; **CUB** - Cuba; **DOM** - Dominica; **EAS** - Eastern Slope Andes; **FDN** - Fernando de Noronha; **GAL** - Galápagos; **GCM** - Gulf Coast-Mexico; **GRE** - Grenada; **GUA** - Guadeloupe; **GUI** - Guianan; **HIS** - Hispaniola; **HPC** - Humid Pacific Coast; **ISA** - Isla Providencia and Isla San Andrés; **JAM** - Jamaica; **JFI** - Juan Fernández Islands; **MAN** - Manabí-Tumbes; **MAR** - Marañón Valley; **MID** - Madeira-Tapajós; **MON** - Montserrat; **MRT** - Martinique; **MTC** - Marañón-Cuzco; **NMM** - Northern Mexican Mountains; **NOR** - Northern Coastal Brazil; **PAR** - Pará; **PER** - Peruvian Desert; **PUE** - Puerto Rico; **RDJ** - Rio de Janeiro-Bahia Lowlands; **RMW** - Rio Madeira West; **RNW** - Rio Negro West; **SCA** - Southern Central America; **SCT** - Santa Cruz-Tucumán; **SIN** - Sinaloa-Oaxaca; **SMH** - Southern Mexican Highlands; **SMT** - Santa Marta; **SOC** - Islas Revillagigedo (Socorro Island group); **SON** - Sonoran Desert; **SOU** - Southern Atlantic Coast; **STL** - St. Lucia; **STV** - St. Vincent; **TAC** - Tacarcuna; **VAN** - Venezuelan Andes; **VNZ** - Venezuelan Coastal Mountains; **WES** - Western Andes; **YUC** - Yucatán Peninsula.
o - Endemic to region, but not restricted to a single subregion.

Zoogeographic Regions:
AMN - Northern Amazonia; **AMS** - Southern Amazonia; **ATL** - Atlantic Forest; **BSR** - Baja-Sonora; **CAN** - Central Andes; **CDH** - Chiriquí-Darién Highlands; **CHO** - Chocó Lowlands; **CSA** - Central South America; **EPC** - Equatorial Pacific Coast; **GAN** - Greater Antilles; **GCS** - Gulf-Caribbean Slope; **LAN** - Lesser Antilles; **MAH** - Madrean Highlands; **MPL** - Mexican Plateau; **NAN** - Northern Andes; **NSA** - Northern South America; **PAM** - Pampas; **PAS** - Pacific Arid Slope; **PAT** - Patagonia; **SAN** - Southern Andes; **STP** - Subtropical Pacific; **TEP** - Tepuis.

CP -Conservation Priority:
1 - Urgent; **2** - High; **3** - Medium; **4** - Low.

RP - Research Priority:
1 - High; **2** - Medium; **3** - Low.

	Snst	Strat	Cntab	Rel	Min	Max	Micro	Habitats	Sub	Zoogeographic Regions
Hemitriccus josephinae	H	M?	LT	U	L	L		F1	GUI	AMN
Hemitriccus kaempferi	H	M	LT	R	L	L		F1	SOU	ATL
Hemitriccus margaritaceiventer	M	U/M	LT	C	L	1800		F7, F8, N1		NSA, TEP, AMS, CSA
Hemitriccus minimus	H	C	LT	U/P	L	L		F12	o	AMS
Hemitriccus minor	H	M	LT	U	L	700		F1		AMN, AMS
Hemitriccus mirandae	H	M	HT	?	600?	900		F1	NOR	ATL
Hemitriccus nidipendulus	L	U/M	HT	F	L	900		F1E, F15	o	ATL
Hemitriccus obsoletus	M	U	UT	F	900	2100	B	F4	SOU	ATL
Hemitriccus orbitatus	M	M	LT	F	L	600		F1	SOU	ATL
Hemitriccus rufigularis	H	M	UT	U/P	800	1350	V	F4	o	CAN
Hemitriccus spodiops	H	U	UT	U	800	1600	B	F4E	COC	CAN
Hemitriccus striaticollis	M	M	LT	F	L	700		F8, F12		AMN, AMS, CSA
Hemitriccus zosterops	H	M	LT	F/P	L	850		F1, F12		AMN, AMS, ATL
Todirostrum calopterum										
calopterum	M	U	HT	U/P	L	800		F1E		AMN, AMS
pulchellum	M	U	HT	U/P	500	950		F1E	RMW	AMS
Todirostrum chrysocrotaphum	M	C	LT	F	L	900		F1, F2, F15		AMN, AMS
Todirostrum cinereum	L	U/C	LT	C	L	1200		F1E, F15, F8, F4E, F7E		GCS, CHO, EPC, NSA, AMN, AMS, CSA, ATL
Todirostrum fumifrons	L	U	LT	F	L	L		F1E, F7, F8		AMN, AMS, CSA
Todirostrum latirostre	L	U	LT	C	L	900		F3, F15, F8		AMN, AMS, CSA
Todirostrum maculatum	L	C	LT	C	L	L		F3, N12, F15, F14		AMN, AMS
Todirostrum nigriceps	M	C	LT	U/F	L	1100		F1		GCS, CHO, NSA
Todirostrum pictum	M	C	LT	F	L	L		F1, F15	GUI	AMN
Todirostrum plumbeiceps	M	U	UT	F	L	2600		F4E, F1E, F15		CAN, ATL
Todirostrum poliocephalum	L	M/C	HT	U	L	1100		F1E, F15	SOU	ATL
Todirostrum russatum	H	U	MM	F	1300	2500		F4	o	TEP
Todirostrum senex	M	U/M	LT	U	L	L		F2	MID	AMS
Todirostrum sylvia	L	U	LT	F	L	1100		F1E, F7, F8, F15, N14		GCS, CHO, NSA, AMN, AMS, CSA
Todirostrum viridanum	L	M/C	LT	F	L	L		F7, F8, N1?	ARC	NSA
Cnipodectes subbrunneus	H	U	LT	U/P	L	700		F1		GCS, CHO, AMN, AMS
Ramphotrigon fuscicauda	M	M	LT	F	L	900	B	F1		AMN, AMS
Ramphotrigon megacephala	M	M	LT	F/P	L	1200	B	F1, F4		NSA, AMN, AMS, ATL
Ramphotrigon ruficauda	M	M	LT	F	L	600		F1		AMN, AMS
Rhynchocyclus brevirostris										
brevirostris	M	M	LT	U	L	2250		F1, F4		PAS, MAH, GCS, CDH
pacificus	M	M	LT	U	L	1100		F1	o	CHO
Rhynchocyclus fulvipectus	H	M	UT	U	750	2300		F4		NAN, CAN
Rhynchocyclus olivaceus	H	M	LT	U/P	L	950		F1, F2		GCS, NSA, AMN, AMS, ATL
Tolmomyias assimilis										
assimilis	H	C	LT	F	L	950		F1		NSA, AMN, AMS
flavotectus	H	C	LT	F	L	1000		F1		GCS, CHO
Tolmomyias flaviventris										
flaviventris	L	C	LT	C	L	800		F1E, F3, F8, F15, F7		NSA, AMN, AMS, CSA, ATL
viridiceps	L	C	LT	F	L	1100		F3, F1E, F15		AMN, AMS
Tolmomyias poliocephalus	M	C	LT	F	L	800		F2, F3, F1E		AMN, AMS, ATL
Tolmomyias sulphurescens	M	C	LT	F	L	2100		F1, F4, F7, F3, F8, F15		PAS, MAH, GCS, CDH, CHO, EPC, NAN, CAN, NSA, AMN, AMS, CSA, ATL
Tolmomyias sp. nov.	H	C	LT	U	L	L		F2	RNW	AMN
Platyrinchus coronatus	H	U/M	LT	F	L	900		F1		GCS, CHO, AMN, AMS
Platyrinchus flavigularis	H	U	MM	R/U	1250	2300		F4		NAN, CAN
Platyrinchus leucoryphus	H	M	LT	R/P	L	900		F1	SOU	ATL

CP	RP	Notes
3	2	Poorly known.
2	1	Survey.
4	3	
3	2	Usually called *H. aenigma* (see Stotz 1992).
4	3	
2	1	Deforestation; survey.
4	3	
3	3	
3	2	Occasionally to 1,000 m.
3	2	Deforestation.
3	2	
4	3	
4	2	Probably contains two species; status in northeastern Brazil uncertain.
4	3	
3	2	
4	2	Occasionally to 1,150 m.
4	3	Occasionally to 2,300 m.
4	3	
4	3	
4	3	
4	3	Occasionally to 1,500 m (Costa Rica).
4	3	
4	3	
4	3	
4	3	
4	1	Poorly known.
4	3	
4	3	
4	3	Locally to 1,200 m (Pacific Colombia).
4	2	Poorly known.
4	2	Regularly to 1,500 m in southeastern Brazil.
4	3	
4	3	
3	2	
4	3	
4	3	
4	3	
4	3	
4	3	
4	3	
4	3	
4	1	Almost certainly contains multiple species.
3	2	
4	3	Occasionally to 1,200 m (Costa Rica).
4	2	Distribution and behavior poorly known.
2	1	Deforestation; survey.

Abbreviations Used

Snst - Sensitivity:
L - Low; **M** - Medium; **H** - High.

Strat - Foraging Strata:
T - Terrestrial; **U** - Understory; **M** - Midstory; **C** - Canopy; **A** - Aerial; **W** - Water.

Cntab - Center of Abundance:
LT - Lower tropical; **LS** - Lower subtropical; **HT** - Hill tropical; **UT** - Upper tropical; **US** - Upper subtropical; **MM** - Middle montane; **UM** - Upper montane.

Rel - Relative Abundance:
R - Rare; **U** - Uncommon; **F** - Fairly common; **C** - Common; **P** - Patchily distributed.

Min - Minimum Elevation:
L - Lowlands; **?** - Uncertain value; numeric values in meters.

Max - Maximum Elevation:
L - Lowlands; **?** - Uncertain value; **+** - species occurs at least to given elevation but likely occurs higher; numeric values in meters.

Micro - Microhabitats:
A - Army ants; **B** - Bamboo; **T** - Treefalls; **G** - Ground bromeliads; **C** - Rocky outcrops and caves; **S** - Streamside; **V** - Vine tangles; **B/V** -Bamboo/vine tangles.

Habitats:
F1 - Tropical lowland evergreen forest; **F2** - Flooded tropical evergreen forest; **F3** - River-edge forest; **F4** - Montane evergreen forest; **F5** - Elfin forest; **F6** - *Polylepis* woodland; **F7** - Tropical deciduous forest; **F8** - Gallery forest; **F9** - Southern temperate forest; **F10** - Pine forest; **F11** - Pine-oak forest; **F12** - White sand forest; **F13** - Palm forest; **F14** - Mangrove forest; **F15** - Secondary forest; **N1** - Arid lowland scrub; **N2** - Arid montane scrub; **N3** - Semihumid/humid montane scrub; **N4** - Cerrado; **N5** - Campo grasslands; **N6** - Low, seasonally wet grassland; **N7** - Southern temperate grassland; **N8** - Northern temperate grassland; **N9** - Puna grassland; **N10** - Paramo grassland; **N11** - Riparian thickets; **N12** - River island scrub; **N13** - Pastures/agricultural lands; **N14** - Second-growth scrub; **A1** - Freshwater marshes; **A2** - Saltwater/brackish marshes; **A3** - Coastal sand beaches/mudflats; **A4** - Coastal rocky beaches; **A5** - Riverine sand beaches; **A6** - Freshwater lakes and ponds; **A7** - Alkaline lakes; **A8** - Rivers; **A9** - Streams; **A10** - Bogs; **A11** - Coastal waters; **A12** - Pelagic waters.
E - Edge (used as a modifer to particular habitats).

Sub - Subregions:
ARC - Arid Caribbean Coast; **AWA** - Altiplano and Western Andes; **BAH** - Bahamas; **BAJ** - Baja California; **CAA** - Caatinga; **CAH** - Central American Highlands; **CER** - Cerrado; **CHA** - Chaco; **CHG** - Chiapas-Guanacaste; **CHL** - Chilean Desert; **CHR** - Chiriquí; **CIS** - Cocos Island; **CMV** - Cauca-Magdalena Valley; **COC** - Cuzco-Cochabamba; **CUB** - Cuba; **DOM** - Dominica; **EAS** - Eastern Slope Andes; **FDN** - Fernando de Noronha; **GAL** - Galápagos; **GCM** - Gulf Coast-Mexico; **GRE** - Grenada; **GUA** - Guadeloupe; **GUI** - Guianan; **HIS** - Hispaniola; **HPC** - Humid Pacific Coast; **ISA** - Isla Providencia and Isla San Andrés; **JAM** - Jamaica; **JFI** - Juan Fernández Islands; **MAN** - Manabí-Tumbes; **MAR** - Marañón Valley; **MID** - Madeira-Tapajós; **MON** - Montserrat; **MRT** - Martinique; **MTC** - Marañón-Cuzco; **NMM** - Northern Mexican Mountains; **NOR** - Northern Coastal Brazil; **PAR** - Pará; **PER** - Peruvian Desert; **PUE** - Puerto Rico; **RDJ** - Rio de Janeiro-Bahia Lowlands; **RMW** - Rio Madeira West; **RNW** - Rio Negro West; **SCA** - Southern Central America; **SCT** - Santa Cruz-Tucumán; **SIN** - Sinaloa-Oaxaca; **SMH** - Southern Mexican Highlands; **SMT** - Santa Marta; **SOC** - Islas Revillagigedo (Socorro Island group); **SON** - Sonoran Desert; **SOU** - Southern Atlantic Coast; **STL** - St. Lucia; **STV** - St. Vincent; **TAC** - Tacarcuna; **VAN** - Venezuelan Andes; **VNZ** - Venezuelan Coastal Mountains; **WES** - Western Andes; **YUC** - Yucatán Peninsula.
o - Endemic to region, but not restricted to a single subregion.

Zoogeographic Regions:
AMN - Northern Amazonia; **AMS** - Southern Amazonia; **ATL** - Atlantic Forest; **BSR** - Baja-Sonora; **CAN** - Central Andes; **CDH** - Chiriquí-Darién Highlands; **CHO** - Chocó Lowlands; **CSA** - Central South America; **EPC** - Equatorial Pacific Coast; **GAN** - Greater Antilles; **GCS** - Gulf-Caribbean Slope; **LAN** - Lesser Antilles; **MAH** - Madrean Highlands; **MPL** - Mexican Plateau; **NAN** - Northern Andes; **NSA** - Northern South America; **PAM** - Pampas; **PAS** - Pacific Arid Slope; **PAT** - Patagonia; **SAN** - Southern Andes; **STP** - Subtropical Pacific; **TEP** - Tepuis.

CP -Conservation Priority:
1 - Urgent; **2** - High; **3** - Medium; **4** - Low.

RP - Research Priority:
1 - High; **2** - Medium; **3** - Low.

	Snst	Strat	Cntab	Rel	Min	Max	Micro	Habitats	Sub	Zoogeographic Regions
Platyrinchus mystaceus										
cancrominus	M	U	LT	F	L	1400		F1, F7, F8		PAS, GCS
mystaceus	M	U	UT	F	L	2000+		F4, F1		CDH, NAN, CAN, TEP, CSA, ATL
Platyrinchus platyrhynchos	H	M	LT	U/P	L	900		F1		AMN, AMS
Platyrinchus saturatus	H	U	LT	U	L	900		F1		AMN, AMS
Onychorhynchus coronatus										
coronatus	H	M	LT	U	L	1200?	S	F1		AMN, AMS
mexicanus	H	M	LT	U	L	1200	S	F1		GCS, NSA
occidentalis	H	M	HT	U	L	900	S	F7, F1	MAN	EPC
swainsoni	H	M	LT	R	L	800	S?	F1	SOU	ATL
Myiotriccus ornatus	H	U/M	UT	F	750	1800		F4		NAN, CAN
Terenotriccus erythrurus	M	M/C	LT	F	L	1200		F1		GCS, CHO, NSA, AMN, AMS
Myiobius atricaudus	M	U/M	LT	U/P	L	1400		F1, F8, F15		GCS, CHO, EPC, NSA, AMN, AMS, CSA, ATL
Myiobius barbatus	H	U/M	LT	U	L	900		F1		AMN, AMS, ATL
Myiobius sulphureipygius	M	U/M	LT	F	L	1200		F1, F8, F15		GCS, CHO
Myiobius villosus	H	U/M	UT	U	800	2100		F4		CDH, NAN, CAN
Myiophobus cryptoxanthus	M	U	UT	U	900	1100		F4E		NAN, CAN
Myiophobus fasciatus	L	U	LT	F	L	2000		N14, N11, N12		GCS, CHO, EPC, STP, NSA, AMN, AMS, CSA, ATL, PAM
Myiophobus flavicans	M	M	MM	F	1500	2700		F4		NAN, CAN
Myiophobus inornatus	H	U	UT	U	1350	2000		F4	COC	CAN
Myiophobus lintoni	H	M/C	MM	U	2250	2750		F4	EAS	NAN
Myiophobus ochraceiventris	H	M/C	UM	F	2800	3350		F4, F5	o	CAN
Myiophobus phoenicomitra	H	U	UT	U	1100	1400		F4		NAN, CAN
Myiophobus pulcher	H	M/C	MM	F/P	1500	2600		F4		NAN, CAN
Myiophobus roraimae	H	U	UT	F/P	900	1900		F4		NAN, CAN, TEP
Aphanotriccus audax	H	U	HT	U	L	600		F1		GCS, CHO
Aphanotriccus capitalis	M	U/M	LT	U	L	1000		F1, F15	SCA	GCS
Xenotriccus callizonus	M	U/M	MM	U	1200	1850		F7	CAH	MAH
Xenotriccus mexicanus	M	U/M	UT	U	950	1850		N2	SMH	MAH
Pyrrhomyias cinnamomea	M	C	UT/MM	C	1000	3350		F4, F4E		NAN, CAN
Mitrephanes olivaceus	M	U/M	UT	U	1300	2000		F4, F4E	o	CAN
Mitrephanes phaeocercus	M	U/M	UT/MM	U/F	600	3600		F4, F11, F4E		MAH, CDH, NAN
Contopus albogularis	H	C	LT	R/U	L	700		F1	GUI	AMN
Contopus borealis	M	C	US	U	2000	2800		F10		BSR
Contopus caribaeus	L	C	LT	F/C	L	1000+		F1, F10, F7, F15	o	GAN
Contopus cinereus	L	U/C	HT	F/P	L	2200		F1E, F4E, F7, F8, F15		PAS, GCS, CHO, EPC, STP, NAN, CAN, NSA, AMN, AMS, CSA, ATL
Contopus fumigatus	M	C	MM	F	500	2600		F4, F15, F7		NAN, CAN, TEP
Contopus latirostris	L	C	LT	U?	L	900+		F1, F4, F7		GAN, LAN
Contopus lugubris	M	C	MM	F	1200	2700		F4, F4E, F15	CHR	CDH
Contopus nigrescens	H	C	UT	R/P	800	1100		F4, F1		NAN, CAN, TEP, AMS
Contopus ochraceus	H	C	MM	R	2100	3000		F4	CHR	CDH
Contopus pertinax	M	C	MM	F	900	3400		F10, F11, F4	o	MAH
Contopus sordidulus	M	C	MM	F	900	3000		F11, F8		MAH
Empidonax affinis	M	M/C	UM	U/F	1800	4000		F10, F11	NMM	MAH
Empidonax albigularis	L	U/M	UT	U	900	2600		N14, N11		PAS, MAH, GCS, CDH
Empidonax atriceps	M	U/M	UM	F	2100	3300		F4, F15	CHR	CDH
Empidonax difficilis	L	U/M	LS	F	1500	3000		F8		BSR
Empidonax euleri	M	M	LT	F	L	1350		F1, F4, F15		LAN, CAN, NSA, AMN, AMS, CSA, ATL
Empidonax flavescens	L	U/M	UT	F	900	2800		F4, F11		MAH, CDH
Empidonax fulvifrons	M	U/M	MM	U	600	2500		F11, F10, F7, N2	o	MAH
Empidonax griseipectus	M	M	HT	U	L	1700		F7, F1	MAN	EPC

CP	RP	Notes
4	3	
4	3	Mainly above 900 m in Andes.
4	3	
4	2	Distribution poorly known.
4	3	
4	3	Occasionally to 2,000 m.
2	1	In semideciduous forest; deforestation.
2	1	Poorly known; survey.
3	3	Occasionally to 400 m.
4	3	
4	2	Probably contains two species.
4	3	
4	3	
4	3	Occasionally to 600 m.
4	2	Poorly known.
4	3	Locally to 2,600 m.
4	3	Locally to 1,100 m (coastal Venezuela).
4	2	Occasionally to 2,600 m? poorly known.
2	2	
4	3	Occasionally to 2,450 m.
4	3	Lower elevations in Pacific Colombia.
4	2	Occasionally to 800 m (Colombia); poorly known.
3	2	Locally to 250 m.
2	2	Deforestation.
4	3	
2	1	Deforestation; survey.
3	2	Deforestation; survey.
4	3	Locally to 600 m.
4	3	
4	3	Locally to 100 m (Pacific Colombia).
3	1	Poorly known; survey.
4	3	
4	3	
4	2	
4	3	Occasionally to 300 m (Colombia).
4	2	May contain two species.
4	3	
2	1	To 300 m and seasonally to lowlands in eastern Amazonian Brazil; deforestation.
3	2	Poorly known; in humid oak forests?
4	3	
4	2	Nonbreeding distribution poorly known.
4	2	Poorly known.
4	3	
4	3	Occasionally to 1,850 m.
4	3	
4	3	Occasionally to 1,650 m (Bolivia).
4	3	
4	3	
2	2	Deforestation.

Abbreviations Used

Snst - Sensitivity:
L - Low; **M** - Medium; **H** - High.

Strat - Foraging Strata:
T - Terrestrial; **U** - Understory; **M** - Midstory; **C** - Canopy; **A** - Aerial; **W** - Water.

Cntab - Center of Abundance:
LT - Lower tropical; **LS** - Lower subtropical; **HT** - Hill tropical; **UT** - Upper tropical; **US** - Upper subtropical; **MM** - Middle montane; **UM** - Upper montane.

Rel - Relative Abundance:
R - Rare; **U** - Uncommon; **F** - Fairly common; **C** - Common; **P** - Patchily distributed.

Min - Minimum Elevation:
L - Lowlands; **?** - Uncertain value; numeric values in meters.

Max - Maximum Elevation:
L - Lowlands; **?** - Uncertain value; **+** - species occurs at least to given elevation but likely occurs higher; numeric values in meters.

Micro - Microhabitats:
A - Army ants; **B** - Bamboo; **T** - Treefalls; **G** - Ground bromeliads; **C** - Rocky outcrops and caves; **S** - Streamside; **V** - Vine tangles; **B/V** -Bamboo/vine tangles.

Habitats:
F1 - Tropical lowland evergreen forest; **F2** - Flooded tropical evergreen forest; **F3** - River-edge forest; **F4** - Montane evergreen forest; **F5** - Elfin forest; **F6** - *Polylepis* woodland; **F7** - Tropical deciduous forest; **F8** - Gallery forest; **F9** - Southern temperate forest; **F10** - Pine forest; **F11** - Pine-oak forest; **F12** - White sand forest; **F13** - Palm forest; **F14** - Mangrove forest; **F15** - Secondary forest; **N1** - Arid lowland scrub; **N2** - Arid montane scrub; **N3** - Semihumid/humid montane scrub; **N4** - Cerrado; **N5** - Campo grasslands; **N6** - Low, seasonally wet grassland; **N7** - Southern temperate grassland; **N8** - Northern temperate grassland; **N9** - Puna grassland; **N10** - Paramo grassland; **N11** - Riparian thickets; **N12** - River island scrub; **N13** - Pastures/agricultural lands; **N14** - Second-growth scrub; **A1** - Freshwater marshes; **A2** - Saltwater/brackish marshes; **A3** - Coastal sand beaches/mudflats; **A4** - Coastal rocky beaches; **A5** - Riverine sand beaches; **A6** - Freshwater lakes and ponds; **A7** - Alkaline lakes; **A8** - Rivers; **A9** - Streams; **A10** - Bogs; **A11** - Coastal waters; **A12** - Pelagic waters.
E - Edge (used as a modifer to particular habitats).

Sub - Subregions:
ARC - Arid Caribbean Coast; **AWA** - Altiplano and Western Andes; **BAH** - Bahamas; **BAJ** - Baja California; **CAA** - Caatinga; **CAH** - Central American Highlands; **CER** - Cerrado; **CHA** - Chaco; **CHG** - Chiapas-Guanacaste; **CHL** - Chilean Desert; **CHR** - Chiriquí; **CIS** - Cocos Island; **CMV** - Cauca-Magdalena Valley; **COC** - Cuzco-Cochabamba; **CUB** - Cuba; **DOM** - Dominica; **EAS** - Eastern Slope Andes; **FDN** - Fernando de Noronha; **GAL** - Galápagos; **GCM** - Gulf Coast-Mexico; **GRE** - Grenada; **GUA** - Guadeloupe; **GUI** - Guianan; **HIS** - Hispaniola; **HPC** - Humid Pacific Coast; **ISA** - Isla Providencia and Isla San Andrés; **JAM** - Jamaica; **JFI** - Juan Fernández Islands; **MAN** - Manabí-Tumbes; **MAR** - Marañón Valley; **MID** - Madeira-Tapajós; **MON** - Montserrat; **MRT** - Martinique; **MTC** - Marañón-Cuzco; **NMM** - Northern Mexican Mountains; **NOR** - Northern Coastal Brazil; **PAR** - Pará; **PER** - Peruvian Desert; **PUE** - Puerto Rico; **RDJ** - Rio de Janeiro-Bahia Lowlands; **RMW** - Rio Madeira West; **RNW** - Rio Negro West; **SCA** - Southern Central America; **SCT** - Santa Cruz-Tucumán; **SIN** - Sinaloa-Oaxaca; **SMH** - Southern Mexican Highlands; **SMT** - Santa Marta; **SOC** - Islas Revillagigedo (Socorro Island group); **SON** - Sonoran Desert; **SOU** - Southern Atlantic Coast; **STL** - St. Lucia; **STV** - St. Vincent; **TAC** - Tacarcuna; **VAN** - Venezuelan Andes; **VNZ** - Venezuelan Coastal Mountains; **WES** - Western Andes; **YUC** - Yucatán Peninsula.
o - Endemic to region, but not restricted to a single subregion.

Zoogeographic Regions:
AMN - Northern Amazonia; **AMS** - Southern Amazonia; **ATL** - Atlantic Forest; **BSR** - Baja-Sonora; **CAN** - Central Andes; **CDH** - Chiriquí-Darién Highlands; **CHO** - Chocó Lowlands; **CSA** - Central South America; **EPC** - Equatorial Pacific Coast; **GAN** - Greater Antilles; **GCS** - Gulf-Caribbean Slope; **LAN** - Lesser Antilles; **MAH** - Madrean Highlands; **MPL** - Mexican Plateau; **NAN** - Northern Andes; **NSA** - Northern South America; **PAM** - Pampas; **PAS** - Pacific Arid Slope; **PAT** - Patagonia; **SAN** - Southern Andes; **STP** - Subtropical Pacific; **TEP** - Tepuis.

CP -Conservation Priority:
1 - Urgent; **2** - High; **3** - Medium; **4** - Low.

RP - Research Priority:
1 - High; **2** - Medium; **3** - Low.

	Snst	Strat	Cntab	Rel	Min	Max	Micro	Habitats	Sub	Zoogeographic Regions
Empidonax occidentalis	L	U/M	MM	F	1250	3400		F11, F10, F4		MAH
Nesotriccus ridgwayi	M	M/C	LT	C	L	500		F1	CIS	PAS
Cnemotriccus fuscatus	L	U/M	LT	F	L	1100		F3, F1E, F7, F8, F15, F12		NSA, AMN, AMS, CSA, ATL
Sayornis nigricans	L	T/C	UT	F	L	2800+		N11, A9, A8		MAH, CDH, NAN, CAN
Sayornis saya	L	T/C	UT	F	L	2500+		N8, N2, N13, N1		BSR, MPL
Pyrocephalus rubinus	L	T/C	LT	F	L	2600		N13, N11, N14, N12, F7E, F8E		BSR, PAS, MAH, GCS, CHO, EPC, STP, NSA, AMN, CSA, ATL, PAM
Ochthoeca cinnamomeiventris	M	U/M	UM	F	1900	3350	S	F4, F15		NAN, CAN
Ochthoeca diadema	M	U	MM	F	1700	3150		F4, F15	o	NAN
Ochthoeca frontalis	H	U	UM	F	2300	3600		F4, F5		NAN, CAN
Ochthoeca fumicolor	M	T/C	UM	C	2400	4400		N10, N14, F5E, F6		NAN, CAN
Ochthoeca jelskii	M	U	UM	U	1300	3400		F4, F6		NAN, CAN
Ochthoeca leucophrys	L	T/C	MM	C	500	3700+		N2, N3		CAN, SAN
Ochthoeca littoralis	M	T/U	LT	F	L	L		A5		AMN, AMS
Ochthoeca oenanthoides	M	T/C	UM	F	2800	4400		N2, N3, F6	o	CAN
Ochthoeca parvirostris	L	C	US	C	L	2000		F9	o	SAN
Ochthoeca piurae	M	T/C	UT	U	1200	3000		N2, N11	AWA	CAN
Ochthoeca pulchella	M	U	MM	F	1800	2800		F4	o	CAN
Ochthoeca rufipectoralis	L	U/C	UM	C	2600	3600		F5, F4E, F15, F6		NAN, CAN
Myiotheretes erythropygius	M	T/C	UM	U/P	2900	4100		F5, N10, F6		NAN, CAN
Myiotheretes fumigatus	M	C	UM	U	1800	3600		F4		NAN, CAN
Myiotheretes fuscorufus	M	C	UM	U	2200	3500		F4, F15	o	CAN
Myiotheretes pernix	L	C	MM?	U	2100	2900		F4E, N14	SMT	NAN
Myiotheretes rufipennis	M	T/U	UM	U/P	3100	4400		F6, N2	AWA	CAN
Myiotheretes striaticollis	L	C	UM	F	1500	3600		F4E, F15, N3, N14		NAN, CAN
Xolmis cinerea	L	T/U	LT	U/P	L	1200		N6, N5, N13		AMN, AMS, CSA, PAM
Xolmis coronata	M	T/U	LS	F	L	1000		N1	o	PAT
Xolmis dominicana	L	T/U	LT	U/P	L	1100		N7, N13		ATL, PAM
Xolmis irupero	L	T/U	LS	U	L	1200		N14, N1		CSA, PAM
Xolmis pyrope	M	U/C	LS	F	L	1800		F9E	o	SAN
Xolmis velata	M	T/U	LT	F/P	L	1000		N4, N13		AMN?, AMS, CSA
Neoxolmis rubetra	M	T	LS	F	L	L?		N1, N13	o	PAT
Neoxolmis rufiventris	M	T	LS	U/P	L	1200		N7	o	PAT
Agriornis andicola	L	T/U	UM	U	3000	4500		N2, N9		NAN, CAN
Agriornis livida	L	T/U	LS	U	L	1800		N2, N1, N13		STP, SAN, PAT
Agriornis microptera	L	T/U	UM	U	L	4000		N2, N1, N9		CAN, SAN, PAT
Agriornis montana	L	T/U	UM	U	1800	4000+		N2, N9, N13		NAN, CAN, SAN, PAT
Agriornis murina	M	T/U	LS	F	L	2000		N1	o	PAT
Muscisaxicola albifrons	M	T	UM	U	3600	5200		N9, A10	AWA	CAN
Muscisaxicola albilora	M	T	UM	F	1500	2500		N9	o	SAN
Muscisaxicola alpina	M	T	UM	C	3300	4600		N10, N9, N2		NAN, CAN
Muscisaxicola capistrata	M	T	LS	U	L	L		N7	o	PAT
Muscisaxicola cinerea	M	T	UM	F	2700	4300		N9		CAN, SAN
Muscisaxicola flavinucha	M	T	UM	F	1800	4300		N7, N9		SAN, PAT
Muscisaxicola fluviatilis	M	T	LT	U	L	800		A5, N12		AMN, AMS
Muscisaxicola frontalis	M	T	UM	U	2800	4000		N9	o	SAN
Muscisaxicola juninensis	M	T	UM	F	3300	5000		N9, A10	AWA	CAN
Muscisaxicola macloviana	L	T	LS	F	L	1200		N7		SAN, PAT
Muscisaxicola maculirostris	L	T	UM	C	1000	3800		N2, N13		NAN, CAN, SAN
Muscisaxicola rufivertex	M	T	UM	F	600	4500		N9, N2		CAN, SAN
Lessonia oreas	M	T	UM	F	2800	4300		A6, A7	AWA	CAN
Lessonia rufa	L	T	LS	F	L	2000		A6, A7		STP, SAN, PAT

CP	RP	Notes
4	3	
3	3	
4	3	Occasionally to 2,400 m (Bolivia); probably contains two species.
4	3	
4	3	
4	3	
4	3	Occasionally to 900 m?
4	3	
4	3	
4	3	Occasionally to 1,800 m? mainly above 3,050 m.
3	3	See Traylor 1985 for taxonomic status.
4	3	Occasionally to sea level.
4	3	
4	3	Locally to 2,000 m in southern part of range.
4	3	Seasonal movements poorly known.
3	2	Occasionally to lower elevations.
4	3	Occasionally to 3,300 m.
4	3	Locally to 2,000 m.
4	2	Basis for patchy distribution not known.
4	3	
4	3	
4	2	Survey.
3	2	Survey.
4	3	
4	3	
4	3	
3	1	Monitor; declining? survives in degraded grasslands; nests in small marshes.
4	3	
4	3	
4	3	
4	3	
4	2	Monitor.
3	2	
4	3	
4	3	
4	3	Occasionally to lowlands in south.
4	3	
4	3	
4	3	
4	3	Occasionally to 2,400 m.
4	3	
4	3	
4	3	Breeds to lowlands in southern Argentina.
4	3	
4	3	
4	3	
4	3	
4	3	
4	3	
4	3	Occasionally to 1,000 m? along lakeshores.
4	3	Along lakeshores.

Abbreviations Used

Snst - Sensitivity:
L - Low; **M** - Medium; **H** - High.

Strat - Foraging Strata:
T - Terrestrial; **U** - Understory; **M** - Midstory; **C** - Canopy; **A** - Aerial; **W** - Water.

Cntab - Center of Abundance:
LT - Lower tropical; **LS** - Lower subtropical; **HT** - Hill tropical; **UT** - Upper tropical; **US** - Upper subtropical; **MM** - Middle montane; **UM** - Upper montane.

Rel - Relative Abundance:
R - Rare; **U** - Uncommon; **F** - Fairly common; **C** - Common; **P** - Patchily distributed.

Min - Minimum Elevation:
L - Lowlands; **?** - Uncertain value; numeric values in meters.

Max - Maximum Elevation:
L - Lowlands; **?** - Uncertain value; **+** - species occurs at least to given elevation but likely occurs higher; numeric values in meters.

Micro - Microhabitats:
A - Army ants; **B** - Bamboo; **T** - Treefalls; **G** - Ground bromeliads; **C** - Rocky outcrops and caves; **S** - Streamside; **V** - Vine tangles; **B/V** -Bamboo/vine tangles.

Habitats:
F1 - Tropical lowland evergreen forest; **F2** - Flooded tropical evergreen forest; **F3** - River-edge forest; **F4** - Montane evergreen forest; **F5** - Elfin forest; **F6** - *Polylepis* woodland; **F7** - Tropical deciduous forest; **F8** - Gallery forest; **F9** - Southern temperate forest; **F10** - Pine forest; **F11** - Pine-oak forest; **F12** - White sand forest; **F13** - Palm forest; **F14** - Mangrove forest; **F15** - Secondary forest; **N1** - Arid lowland scrub; **N2** - Arid montane scrub; **N3** - Semihumid/humid montane scrub; **N4** - Cerrado; **N5** - Campo grasslands; **N6** - Low, seasonally wet grassland; **N7** - Southern temperate grassland; **N8** - Northern temperate grassland; **N9** - Puna grassland; **N10** - Paramo grassland; **N11** - Riparian thickets; **N12** - River island scrub; **N13** - Pastures/agricultural lands; **N14** - Second-growth scrub; **A1** - Freshwater marshes; **A2** - Saltwater/brackish marshes; **A3** - Coastal sand beaches/mudflats; **A4** - Coastal rocky beaches; **A5** - Riverine sand beaches; **A6** - Freshwater lakes and ponds; **A7** - Alkaline lakes; **A8** - Rivers; **A9** - Streams; **A10** - Bogs; **A11** - Coastal waters; **A12** - Pelagic waters.
E - Edge (used as a modifer to particular habitats).

Sub - Subregions:
ARC - Arid Caribbean Coast; **AWA** - Altiplano and Western Andes; **BAH** - Bahamas; **BAJ** - Baja California; **CAA** - Caatinga; **CAH** - Central American Highlands; **CER** - Cerrado; **CHA** - Chaco; **CHG** - Chiapas-Guanacaste; **CHL** - Chilean Desert; **CHR** - Chiriquí; **CIS** - Cocos Island; **CMV** - Cauca-Magdalena Valley; **COC** - Cuzco-Cochabamba; **CUB** - Cuba; **DOM** - Dominica; **EAS** - Eastern Slope Andes; **FDN** - Fernando de Noronha; **GAL** - Galápagos; **GCM** - Gulf Coast-Mexico; **GRE** - Grenada; **GUA** - Guadeloupe; **GUI** - Guianan; **HIS** - Hispaniola; **HPC** - Humid Pacific Coast; **ISA** - Isla Providencia and Isla San Andrés; **JAM** - Jamaica; **JFI** - Juan Fernández Islands; **MAN** - Manabí-Tumbes; **MAR** - Marañón Valley; **MID** - Madeira-Tapajós; **MON** - Montserrat; **MRT** - Martinique; **MTC** - Marañón-Cuzco; **NMM** - Northern Mexican Mountains; **NOR** - Northern Coastal Brazil; **PAR** - Pará; **PER** - Peruvian Desert; **PUE** - Puerto Rico; **RDJ** - Rio de Janeiro-Bahia Lowlands; **RMW** - Rio Madeira West; **RNW** - Rio Negro West; **SCA** - Southern Central America; **SCT** - Santa Cruz-Tucumán; **SIN** - Sinaloa-Oaxaca; **SMH** - Southern Mexican Highlands; **SMT** - Santa Marta; **SOC** - Islas Revillagigedo (Socorro Island group); **SON** - Sonoran Desert; **SOU** - Southern Atlantic Coast; **STL** - St. Lucia; **STV** - St. Vincent; **TAC** - Tacarcuna; **VAN** - Venezuelan Andes; **VNZ** - Venezuelan Coastal Mountains; **WES** - Western Andes; **YUC** - Yucatán Peninsula.
o - Endemic to region, but not restricted to a single subregion.

Zoogeographic Regions:
AMN - Northern Amazonia; **AMS** - Southern Amazonia; **ATL** - Atlantic Forest; **BSR** - Baja-Sonora; **CAN** - Central Andes; **CDH** - Chiriquí-Darién Highlands; **CHO** - Chocó Lowlands; **CSA** - Central South America; **EPC** - Equatorial Pacific Coast; **GAN** - Greater Antilles; **GCS** - Gulf-Caribbean Slope; **LAN** - Lesser Antilles; **MAH** - Madrean Highlands; **MPL** - Mexican Plateau; **NAN** - Northern Andes; **NSA** - Northern South America; **PAM** - Pampas; **PAS** - Pacific Arid Slope; **PAT** - Patagonia; **SAN** - Southern Andes; **STP** - Subtropical Pacific; **TEP** - Tepuis.

CP -Conservation Priority:
1 - Urgent; **2** - High; **3** - Medium; **4** - Low.

RP - Research Priority:
1 - High; **2** - Medium; **3** - Low.

	Snst	Strat	Cntab	Rel	Min	Max	Micro	Habitats	Sub	Zoogeographic Regions
Knipolegus aterrimus										
aterrimus	L	C	MM	F	L	3200		F4E, N11, F15		CAN, CSA, PAT
franciscanus	M	U/C	LT	U	L	500		F7	CER	CSA
Knipolegus cyanirostris	L	T/C	UT	C	L	2100		F9E, F4E, F15, N3, N14		ATL, PAM
Knipolegus hudsoni	M?	U/C	LS	F	L	800+		N1		PAM, PAT
Knipolegus lophotes	L	T/C	UT	F	L	1250+		N4, N13		CSA, ATL, PAM
Knipolegus nigerrimus	M	T/C	UT	U	900	2200		F4E, F9, N3	SOU	ATL
Knipolegus orenocensis	M	M/C	LT	U/P	L	L		N12		AMN, AMS
Knipolegus poecilocercus	M	U	LT	U/P	L	L		F2		AMN, AMS
Knipolegus poecilurus	L	U/M	UT	U	900	2600		F4E, N14, N3		NAN, CAN, TEP
Knipolegus signatus										
cabanisi	H	U	UT	U	800	2500	B	F4E	o	CAN
signatus	M	U	MM	R	1900	2900	B	F4E	MTC	CAN
Knipolegus striaticeps	M?	M/C	LS	F	L	1900		N1	CHA	CSA
Hymenops perspicillata	M	T/C	LS	F	L	1250		A1, N1		STP, SAN, CSA, PAM, PAT
Fluvicola nengeta										
atripennis	L	T	LT	F	L	L		N11, N14, F14	MAN	EPC
nengeta	L	T	LT	F	L	800		N11, N14		CSA, ATL
Fluvicola leucocephala	M	T/C	LT	F	L	600		A1, N11		NSA, AMN, AMS, CSA, ATL
Fluvicola pica										
albiventer	M	T	LT	F	L	L		A1		AMN, AMS, CSA, ATL
pica	M	T	LT	F	L	1000		A1, N11, F14		GCS, NSA, AMN
Colonia colonus	L	C	UT	F/P	L	1800		F4E, F1E, F15		GCS, CHO, NAN, CAN, AMN, AMS, CSA, ATL
Alectrurus risorus	M	U	LT	U/P	L	1200		N6, N7		CSA, PAM
Alectrurus tricolor	H	U	HT	U/P	L	1200		N5, N6	CER	CSA
Gubernetes yetapa	M	T/C	LT	U/P	L	1200		N6, N5	CER	CSA
Satrapa icterophrys	L	M/C	LT	F	L	2000		N13, N14, F3, F8		CSA, ATL, PAM
Tumbezia salvini	L	M	LT	F	L	900		F8, N1	MAN	EPC
Muscigralla brevicauda	L	T	LT	U	L	1000		N1, N13		EPC, STP
Hirundinea ferruginea										
bellicosa	L	C	LT	U/P	L	2600	R	F1E, F4E, F15, F7		CAN, SAN, CSA, ATL
ferruginea	L	C	HT	F/P	500	1700	R	F1E, F4E, F15E		NAN, CAN, TEP, AMN
Machetornis rixosus	L	T	LT	C	L	1000		N13, N14		NSA, CSA, ATL, PAM
Muscipipra vetula	M	C	UT	U/P	L	1850		F4E, F1E, F15	SOU	ATL
Attila bolivianus	H	M/C	LT	F	L	450		F2		AMN, AMS
Attila cinnamomeus	H	C	LT	F	L	500+		F2		AMN, AMS
Attila citriniventris	H	C	LT	U/P	L	L		F1		AMN, AMS
Attila phoenicurus	H	M/C	HT	U/P	L	1700		F1, F4		AMS, CSA, ATL
Attila rufus	M	M/C	HT	F	L	1400		F1, F4	o	ATL
Attila spadiceus	M	M/C	LT	F	L	1800		F1, F7, F4		PAS, GCS, CDH, CHO, NSA, AMN, AMS, ATL
Attila torridus	M	M/C	HT	U	L	1200		F1		CHO, EPC
Casiornis fusca	M	M/C	LT	?	L	500+		F7		AMS, CSA
Casiornis rufa	M	M/C	LT	F	L	800		F7, F8	o	CSA
Rhytipterna holerythra	M	M/C	LT	F	L	1200		F1, F15		GCS, CHO
Rhytipterna immunda	M	U/C	LT	U/P	L	L?		F12		AMN, AMS
Rhytipterna simplex	H	M/C	LT	F	L	800		F1		AMN, AMS, ATL
Laniocera hypopyrra	H	M/C	LT	U/P	L	850		F1		AMN, AMS, ATL
Laniocera rufescens	M	M	LT	U/P	L	1350		F1		GCS, CHO, NSA
Sirystes sibilator	M	C	LT	F/P	L	1250		F1, F8		GCS, CHO, AMN, AMS, CSA, ATL
Myiarchus antillarum	L	M/C	LT	U?	L	800+		F7, N1, F14, F1	PUE	GAN
Myiarchus apicalis	L	M/C	UT	F	400	2300		F7, F8, F1E, F15		NAN, NSA
Myiarchus barbirostris	L	M/C	HT	F	L	2000		F1, F4, F15	JAM	GAN
Myiarchus cephalotes	L	M/C	MM	U	800	3000		F4E, F15		NAN, CAN
Myiarchus cinerascens	L	U/C	LT	C	L	2200+		N1, N2, F8, F7E		BSR, MPL, PAS, MAH

CP	RP	Notes
4	3	Locally to 3,700 m
3	2	
4	3	
4	2	Nonbreeding range poorly known.
4	3	
4	3	Occasionally to lowlands in winter.
4	3	
4	2	
4	3	
4	3	
3	2	Poorly known.
4	2	Nonbreeding range poorly known.
4	3	Occasionally to 2,800 m (during migration only?).
4	2	
4	2	
4	3	
4	2	Migratory movements poorly understood.
4	2	
4	3	
2	1	Movements poorly understood; habitat destruction.
2	1	Movements poorly understood; habitat destruction.
3	2	Survey.
4	3	
4	3	
4	3	
4	3	Locally to 3,600 m.
4	3	Locally to lowlands and 2,400 m.
4	3	Locally to 1,800 m.
3	2	Poorly known; seasonal movements poorly known.
4	3	
4	3	
4	2	Distribution and behavior poorly known.
3	1	Nonbreeding range poorly known.
3	2	
4	3	Occasionally to 2,500 m.
2	1	Deforestation; declining.
3	2	Distribution and behavior poorly known.
4	3	
4	3	
4	2	Poorly known.
4	3	Locally to 1,400 m.
4	3	
3	2	Deforestation.
4	2	May contain two species.
3	3	Monitor.
4	3	
3	3	
4	3	
4	3	

Abbreviations Used

Snst - Sensitivity:
L - Low; **M** - Medium; **H** - High.

Strat - Foraging Strata:
T - Terrestrial; **U** - Understory; **M** - Midstory; **C** - Canopy; **A** - Aerial; **W** - Water.

Cntab - Center of Abundance:
LT - Lower tropical; **LS** - Lower subtropical; **HT** - Hill tropical; **UT** - Upper tropical; **US** - Upper subtropical; **MM** - Middle montane; **UM** - Upper montane.

Rel - Relative Abundance:
R - Rare; **U** - Uncommon; **F** - Fairly common; **C** - Common; **P** - Patchily distributed.

Min - Minimum Elevation:
L - Lowlands; **?** - Uncertain value; numeric values in meters.

Max - Maximum Elevation:
L - Lowlands; **?** - Uncertain value; **+** - species occurs at least to given elevation but likely occurs higher; numeric values in meters.

Micro - Microhabitats:
A - Army ants; **B** - Bamboo; **T** - Treefalls; **G** - Ground bromeliads; **C** - Rocky outcrops and caves; **S** - Streamside; **V** - Vine tangles; **B/V** -Bamboo/vine tangles.

Habitats:
F1 - Tropical lowland evergreen forest; **F2** - Flooded tropical evergreen forest; **F3** - River-edge forest; **F4** - Montane evergreen forest; **F5** - Elfin forest; **F6** - *Polylepis* woodland; **F7** - Tropical deciduous forest; **F8** - Gallery forest; **F9** - Southern temperate forest; **F10** - Pine forest; **F11** - Pine-oak forest; **F12** - White sand forest; **F13** - Palm forest; **F14** - Mangrove forest; **F15** - Secondary forest; **N1** - Arid lowland scrub; **N2** - Arid montane scrub; **N3** - Semihumid/humid montane scrub; **N4** - Cerrado; **N5** - Campo grasslands; **N6** - Low, seasonally wet grassland; **N7** - Southern temperate grassland; **N8** - Northern temperate grassland; **N9** - Puna grassland; **N10** - Paramo grassland; **N11** - Riparian thickets; **N12** - River island scrub; **N13** - Pastures/agricultural lands; **N14** - Second-growth scrub; **A1** - Freshwater marshes; **A2** - Saltwater/brackish marshes; **A3** - Coastal sand beaches/mudflats; **A4** - Coastal rocky beaches; **A5** - Riverine sand beaches; **A6** - Freshwater lakes and ponds; **A7** - Alkaline lakes; **A8** - Rivers; **A9** - Streams; **A10** - Bogs; **A11** - Coastal waters; **A12** - Pelagic waters.
E - Edge (used as a modifer to particular habitats).

Sub - Subregions:
ARC - Arid Caribbean Coast; **AWA** - Altiplano and Western Andes; **BAH** - Bahamas; **BAJ** - Baja California; **CAA** - Caatinga; **CAH** - Central American Highlands; **CER** - Cerrado; **CHA** - Chaco; **CHG** - Chiapas-Guanacaste; **CHL** - Chilean Desert; **CHR** - Chiriquí; **CIS** - Cocos Island; **CMV** - Cauca-Magdalena Valley; **COC** - Cuzco-Cochabamba; **CUB** - Cuba; **DOM** - Dominica; **EAS** - Eastern Slope Andes; **FDN** - Fernando de Noronha; **GAL** - Galápagos; **GCM** - Gulf Coast-Mexico; **GRE** - Grenada; **GUA** - Guadeloupe; **GUI** - Guianan; **HIS** - Hispaniola; **HPC** - Humid Pacific Coast; **ISA** - Isla Providencia and Isla San Andrés; **JAM** - Jamaica; **JFI** - Juan Fernández Islands; **MAN** - Manabí-Tumbes; **MAR** - Marañón Valley; **MID** - Madeira-Tapajós; **MON** - Montserrat; **MRT** - Martinique; **MTC** - Marañón-Cuzco; **NMM** - Northern Mexican Mountains; **NOR** - Northern Coastal Brazil; **PAR** - Pará; **PER** - Peruvian Desert; **PUE** - Puerto Rico; **RDJ** - Rio de Janeiro-Bahia Lowlands; **RMW** - Rio Madeira West; **RNW** - Rio Negro West; **SCA** - Southern Central America; **SCT** - Santa Cruz-Tucumán; **SIN** - Sinaloa-Oaxaca; **SMH** - Southern Mexican Highlands; **SMT** - Santa Marta; **SOC** - Islas Revillagigedo (Socorro Island group); **SON** - Sonoran Desert; **SOU** - Southern Atlantic Coast; **STL** - St. Lucia; **STV** - St. Vincent; **TAC** - Tacarcuna; **VAN** - Venezuelan Andes; **VNZ** - Venezuelan Coastal Mountains; **WES** - Western Andes; **YUC** - Yucatán Peninsula.
o - Endemic to region, but not restricted to a single subregion.

Zoogeographic Regions:
AMN - Northern Amazonia; **AMS** - Southern Amazonia; **ATL** - Atlantic Forest; **BSR** - Baja-Sonora; **CAN** - Central Andes; **CDH** - Chiriquí-Darién Highlands; **CHO** - Chocó Lowlands; **CSA** - Central South America; **EPC** - Equatorial Pacific Coast; **GAN** - Greater Antilles; **GCS** - Gulf-Caribbean Slope; **LAN** - Lesser Antilles; **MAH** - Madrean Highlands; **MPL** - Mexican Plateau; **NAN** - Northern Andes; **NSA** - Northern South America; **PAM** - Pampas; **PAS** - Pacific Arid Slope; **PAT** - Patagonia; **SAN** - Southern Andes; **STP** - Subtropical Pacific; **TEP** - Tepuis.

CP -Conservation Priority:
1 - Urgent; **2** - High; **3** - Medium; **4** - Low.

RP - Research Priority:
1 - High; **2** - Medium; **3** - Low.

	Snst	Strat	Cntab	Rel	Min	Max	Micro	Habitats	Sub	Zoogeographic Regions
Myiarchus ferox	L	M/C	LT	F	L	950		F3, F8, F1E, F15		NSA, AMN, AMS, CSA, ATL, PAM
Myiarchus magnirostris	M	M/C	LT	F	L	1500		F7, N1	GAL	EPC
Myiarchus nugator	L	M/C	LT	F	L	900?		F1, F15	o	LAN
Myiarchus nuttingi	M	U/M	LT	F	L	1800+		F7, F8, N1, N14		PAS, GCS
Myiarchus oberi	M	M/C	HT?	F/U	L	900+		F1	o	LAN
Myiarchus panamensis	L	M/C	LT	F	L	1400		F7, F8, F15, F14, N1		GCS, NSA
Myiarchus phaeocephalus	L	M/C	HT	F	L	1500		F7, F8	MAN	EPC
Myiarchus sagrae	L	M/C	LT	F	L	1500+		F1, F15, F10, F14	o	GAN
Myiarchus semirufus	M	M/C	LT	U	L	500+		N1, F8	MAN	EPC
Myiarchus stolidus	L	M/C	LT	F	L	1800+		F7, F15, F1E, F14	o	GAN
Myiarchus swainsoni	L	M/C	LT	F	L	1700		F1E, F8, F15, F7		AMN, AMS, CSA, ATL, PAM
Myiarchus tuberculifer	L	M/C	LT	C	L	3400		F4, F1, F7, F11, F15		BSR, PAS, MAH, GCS, CDH, CHO, NAN, CAN, NSA, AMN, AMS, CSA, ATL
Myiarchus tyrannulus	L	M/C	LT	F/C	L	1700+		F7, F8, F15, N1, F14, F12		BSR, PAS, GCS, NSA, AMN, CSA, ATL
Myiarchus validus	L	M/C	HT	U	L	2000		F1, F4, F15	JAM	GAN
Myiarchus venezuelensis	L	M/C	LT	F	L	600		F7, F8, F15, N14	ARC	NSA
Myiarchus yucatanensis	L	M/C	LT	F	L	L		F7, F15	YUC	GCS
Deltarhynchus flammulatus	M	M	LT	U	L	1250		F7	SIN	PAS
Pitangus lictor	L	U	LT	F	L	L		N11, A1		GCS, NSA, AMN, AMS, CSA, ATL
Pitangus sulphuratus	L	T/C	LT	C	L	1600		F15, N11, F8, N14, F14		PAS, GCS, NSA, AMN, AMS, CSA, ATL, PAM PAT
Megarynchus pitangua	L	C	LT	F	L	1850		F1E, F15, F8, F7, F3		PAS, MAH, GCS, CDH, CHO, EPC, NSA, AMN, AMS, CSA, ATL
Myiozetetes cayanensis	L	C	LT	C	L	1500		N14, F1E, F15		GCS, CHO, NSA, AMN, AMS, CSA, ATL
Myiozetetes granadensis	L	C	LT	C	L	1200		F3, F1E, F15		GCS, CHO, AMN, AMS
Myiozetetes luteiventris	M	C	LT	U	L	L	T	F1, F2		AMN, AMS
Myiozetetes similis	L	M/C	LT	C	L	1500		F1E, F7E, F8, F15		PAS, GCS, EPC, NSA, AMN, AMS, CSA, ATL
Conopias albovittata										
albovittata	M	C	LT	F	L	900		F1, F15		GCS, CHO
parva	M	C	LT	F	L	1300		F1	o	AMN
Conopias cinchoneti	M	C	UT	F/P	750	2150		F4		NAN, CAN
Conopias inornatus	L	U/M	LT	U	L	L		F8E, N14	o	NSA
Conopias trivirgata	M	C	LT	U	L	950		F1, F2		AMN, AMS, ATL
Myiodynastes bairdi	L	C	LT	C	L	1200		F7, F8, F15	MAN	EPC
Myiodynastes chrysocephalus	M	M/C	UT	C	800	2400		F4, F15		CDH, NAN, CAN
Myiodynastes hemichrysus	M	M/C	UT	F	700	1850		F4	CHR	CDH
Myiodynastes luteiventris	L	M/C	HT	F	L	1850		F7, F8, F1E		PAS, MAH, GCS, CDH
Myiodynastes maculatus										
maculatus	L	M/C	LT	C	L	1500		F1E, F15, F8, F3		GCS, CHO, NSA, AMN, AMS
solitarius	L	M/C	LT	F	L	1100+		F1E, F7, F8, F15		CAN?, CSA, ATL, PAM
Legatus leucophaius	L	C	LT	F/C	L	1500		F1E, F8, F15, F4E		GCS, CDH, CHO, NSA, AMN, AMS, CSA, ATL
Empidonomus aurantioatrocristatus	L	C	LT	F	L	1800		F7, F8		AMS, CSA, PAM
Empidonomus varius	L	C	LT	F	L	1200+		F7E, F1E, F8, F15		NSA, AMN, AMS, CSA, ATL
Tyrannopsis sulphurea	M	C	LT	U/P	L	700		F13		NSA, AMN, AMS
Tyrannus albogularis	L	C	LT	F/P	L	950		F8, F3, N12		TEP, AMN, AMS, CSA
Tyrannus caudifasciatus	M	M/C	HT	F	L	2000		F1, F10	o	GAN
Tyrannus couchii	L	C	LT	F	L	800		F8, F7, F15, N11	o	GCS
Tyrannus crassirostris	M	C	UT	F	L	1850		F8, F7E		BSR, PAS, MAH
Tyrannus cubensis	M	C	HT	R?	L	1100		F10	CUB	GAN
Tyrannus dominicensis	L	C	LT	C	L	900+		F1E, F15, F14, N14		GAN, LAN, NSA
Tyrannus forficatus	L	C	LT	C	L	1500		N13, N8, N14		MPL, GCS
Tyrannus melancholicus	L	C	LT	C	L	1800		F15, F8, F3, N14, F1E		BSR, PAS, GCS, CHO, EPC, STP, NSA, AMN, AMS, CSA, ATL, PAM
Tyrannus niveigularis	M	C	LT	F	L	1200		F8, N1		CHO, EPC

CP	RP	Notes
4	3	Occasionally to 1,400 m (Peru).
4	3	
4	3	Probably conspecific with *M. tyrannulus*.
4	3	
3	3	
4	3	
4	3	
4	3	
3	2	
4	3	
4	3	
4	3	
4	3	
3	2	Monitor.
4	3	
4	3	
3	2	Poorly known.
4	3	
4	3	Occasionally to 3,300 m.
4	3	Occasionally to 2,000 m.
4	3	
4	3	Occasionally to 1,650 m.
4	3	
4	3	Occasionally to 2,000 m.
4	3	Occasionally to 1,350 m.
4	3	
4	3	Locally to 400 m.
4	3	
4	3	Local in Amazonia.
4	3	
4	3	Occasionally to 400 m.
4	3	Occasionally to 2,300 m.
4	3	
4	2	
4	3	
4	3	Occasionally to 1,850 m.
4	3	
4	3	Nonbreeding range poorly known.
4	3	
4	2	Often with *Mauritia* palms; nonbreeding range poorly known.
4	3	
4	3	
4	3	Occasionally to 2,400 m.
2	1	Survey.
4	3	
4	3	Occasionally to 2,300 m.
4	3	Locally to 2,700 m.
4	3	Mainly below 600 m.

Abbreviations Used

Snst - Sensitivity:
L - Low; **M** - Medium; **H** - High.

Strat - Foraging Strata:
T - Terrestrial; **U** - Understory; **M** - Midstory; **C** - Canopy; **A** - Aerial; **W** - Water.

Cntab - Center of Abundance:
LT - Lower tropical; **LS** - Lower subtropical; **HT** - Hill tropical; **UT** - Upper tropical; **US** - Upper subtropical; **MM** - Middle montane; **UM** - Upper montane.

Rel - Relative Abundance:
R - Rare; **U** - Uncommon; **F** - Fairly common; **C** - Common; **P** - Patchily distributed.

Min - Minimum Elevation:
L - Lowlands; **?** - Uncertain value; numeric values in meters.

Max - Maximum Elevation:
L - Lowlands; **?** - Uncertain value; **+** - species occurs at least to given elevation but likely occurs higher; numeric values in meters.

Micro - Microhabitats:
A - Army ants; **B** - Bamboo; **T** - Treefalls; **G** - Ground bromeliads; **C** - Rocky outcrops and caves; **S** - Streamside; **V** - Vine tangles; **B/V** -Bamboo/vine tangles.

Habitats:
F1 - Tropical lowland evergreen forest; **F2** - Flooded tropical evergreen forest; **F3** - River-edge forest; **F4** - Montane evergreen forest; **F5** - Elfin forest; **F6** - *Polylepis* woodland; **F7** - Tropical deciduous forest; **F8** - Gallery forest; **F9** - Southern temperate forest; **F10** - Pine forest; **F11** - Pine-oak forest; **F12** - White sand forest; **F13** - Palm forest; **F14** - Mangrove forest; **F15** - Secondary forest; **N1** - Arid lowland scrub; **N2** - Arid montane scrub; **N3** - Semihumid/humid montane scrub; **N4** - Cerrado; **N5** - Campo grasslands; **N6** - Low, seasonally wet grassland; **N7** - Southern temperate grassland; **N8** - Northern temperate grassland; **N9** - Puna grassland; **N10** - Paramo grassland; **N11** - Riparian thickets; **N12** - River island scrub; **N13** - Pastures/agricultural lands; **N14** - Second-growth scrub; **A1** - Freshwater marshes; **A2** - Saltwater/brackish marshes; **A3** - Coastal sand beaches/mudflats; **A4** - Coastal rocky beaches; **A5** - Riverine sand beaches; **A6** - Freshwater lakes and ponds; **A7** - Alkaline lakes; **A8** - Rivers; **A9** - Streams; **A10** - Bogs; **A11** - Coastal waters; **A12** - Pelagic waters.
E - Edge (used as a modifer to particular habitats).

Sub - Subregions:
ARC - Arid Caribbean Coast; **AWA** - Altiplano and Western Andes; **BAH** - Bahamas; **BAJ** - Baja California; **CAA** - Caatinga; **CAH** - Central American Highlands; **CER** - Cerrado; **CHA** - Chaco; **CHG** - Chiapas-Guanacaste; **CHL** - Chilean Desert; **CHR** - Chiriquí; **CIS** - Cocos Island; **CMV** - Cauca-Magdalena Valley; **COC** - Cuzco-Cochabamba; **CUB** - Cuba; **DOM** - Dominica; **EAS** - Eastern Slope Andes; **FDN** - Fernando de Noronha; **GAL** - Galápagos; **GCM** - Gulf Coast-Mexico; **GRE** - Grenada; **GUA** - Guadeloupe; **GUI** - Guianan; **HIS** - Hispaniola; **HPC** - Humid Pacific Coast; **ISA** - Isla Providencia and Isla San Andrés; **JAM** - Jamaica; **JFI** - Juan Fernández Islands; **MAN** - Manabí-Tumbes; **MAR** - Marañón Valley; **MID** - Madeira-Tapajós; **MON** - Montserrat; **MRT** - Martinique; **MTC** - Marañón-Cuzco; **NMM** - Northern Mexican Mountains; **NOR** - Northern Coastal Brazil; **PAR** - Pará; **PER** - Peruvian Desert; **PUE** - Puerto Rico; **RDJ** - Rio de Janeiro-Bahia Lowlands; **RMW** - Rio Madeira West; **RNW** - Rio Negro West; **SCA** - Southern Central America; **SCT** - Santa Cruz-Tucumán; **SIN** - Sinaloa-Oaxaca; **SMH** - Southern Mexican Highlands; **SMT** - Santa Marta; **SOC** - Islas Revillagigedo (Socorro Island group); **SON** - Sonoran Desert; **SOU** - Southern Atlantic Coast; **STL** - St. Lucia; **STV** - St. Vincent; **TAC** - Tacarcuna; **VAN** - Venezuelan Andes; **VNZ** - Venezuelan Coastal Mountains; **WES** - Western Andes; **YUC** - Yucatán Peninsula.
o - Endemic to region, but not restricted to a single subregion.

Zoogeographic Regions:
AMN - Northern Amazonia; **AMS** - Southern Amazonia; **ATL** - Atlantic Forest; **BSR** - Baja-Sonora; **CAN** - Central Andes; **CDH** - Chiriquí-Darién Highlands; **CHO** - Chocó Lowlands; **CSA** - Central South America; **EPC** - Equatorial Pacific Coast; **GAN** - Greater Antilles; **GCS** - Gulf-Caribbean Slope; **LAN** - Lesser Antilles; **MAH** - Madrean Highlands; **MPL** - Mexican Plateau; **NAN** - Northern Andes; **NSA** - Northern South America; **PAM** - Pampas; **PAS** - Pacific Arid Slope; **PAT** - Patagonia; **SAN** - Southern Andes; **STP** - Subtropical Pacific; **TEP** - Tepuis.

CP -Conservation Priority:
1 - Urgent; **2** - High; **3** - Medium; **4** - Low.

RP - Research Priority:
1 - High; **2** - Medium; **3** - Low.

	Snst	Strat	Cntab	Rel	Min	Max	Micro	Habitats	Sub	Zoogeographic Regions
Tyrannus savana	L	C	LT	C	L	1600		N6, N7, N13, N14		GCS, NSA, AMN, AMS, CSA, ATL, PAM, PAT
Tyrannus verticalis	L	C	US	C	L	2300		N13, N8, N14		BSR, MPL
Tyrannus vociferans	M	C	US	F	900	2200		F11, F8		BSR, MPL, MAH
Xenopsaris albinucha	M	C	LT	U/P	L	600		F8, F7		NSA, CSA
Pachyramphus aglaiae	M	C	LT	F	L	1250		F8, F7, F1E, F11		BSR, PAS, GCS
Pachyramphus albogriseus	M	C	UT	U	500	3050		F4, F7		CDH, EPC, NAN, CAN
Pachyramphus castaneus	M	C	LT	F	L	1900		F1, F4, F3, F15		NAN, CAN, NSA, TEP, AMN, AMS, CSA, ATL
Pachyramphus cinnamomeus	L	C	LT	F	L	1300		F1E, F15		GCS, CHO, NSA
Pachyramphus homochrous	L	C	LT	F	L	900		F1, F7, F8, F15		GCS, CHO, EPC, NSA
Pachyramphus major	M	C	UT	F	800	2300		F4, F11, F7, F1E		PAS, MAH, GCS
Pachyramphus marginatus	H	C	LT	F	L	1000		F1		AMN, AMS, ATL
Pachyramphus minor	H	C	LT	U	L	1050		F1		AMN, AMS
Pachyramphus niger	M	C	HT?	F	L	1800		F1, F4	JAM	GAN
Pachyramphus polychopterus	L	C	LT	C	L	1800		F1E, F3, F8, F15		GCS, CHO, NSA, AMN, AMS, CSA, ATL
Pachyramphus rufus	L	C	LT	U/P	L	1500		F3, F8, F15, F1E, F12		GCS, NSA, AMN, AMS
Pachyramphus spodiurus	M	C	HT	U	L	900		F7	MAN	EPC
Pachyramphus surinamus	H	C	LT	U/P	L	L		F1	GUI	AMN
Pachyramphus validus	M	C	HT	U	L	2500		F1, F4, F15		CAN, AMS, CSA, ATL
Pachyramphus versicolor	H	C	MM	F	1500	3400		F4, F5		CDH, NAN, CAN
Pachyramphus viridis	M	C	HT	U/P	L	1700		F1, F4		CAN, TEP, AMN, AMS, CSA, ATL
Tityra cayana	M	C	LT	F	L	1100		F2, F1		NSA, AMN, AMS, CSA, ATL
Tityra inquisitor	M	C	LT	F	L	1200		F1, F15		GCS, CHO, NSA, AMN, AMS, ATL
Tityra semifasciata	M	C	LT	C	L	1200		F1, F4, F15		PAS, GCS, CHO, NSA, AMN, AMS
Pipridae										
Schiffornis major	H	U	LT	F	L	L		F2		AMN, AMS
Schiffornis turdinus	H	U	LT	F	L	1500		F1, F4		GCS, CDH, CHO, NSA, AMN, AMS, ATL
Schiffornis virescens	M	U	HT	F	L	1700		F1, F4, F15	SOU	ATL
Sapayoa aenigma	H	M	HT	U	L	1350		F1		GCS, CHO
Piprites chloris	H	C	LT	F	L	1500		F1, F4		NAN, CAN, NSA, AMN, AMS, ATL
Piprites griseiceps	M	C	LT	U	L	800		F1	SCA	GCS
Piprites pileatus	M	C	UT	U	900	1900		F9, F4	SOU	ATL
Neopipo cinnamomea	H	U	LT	R/P	L	700		F1, F12		AMN, AMS
Chloropipo flavicapilla	M	U	UT	U/P	1200	2400		F4, F15	o	NAN
Chloropipo holochlora	H	U	HT	F/P	600	1300		F1		GCS, CHO, NAN, CAN
Chloropipo unicolor	H	U	UT	F/P	950	2500		F4		NAN, CAN
Chloropipo uniformis	H	U/M	UT	F	800	2100		F4	o	TEP
Xenopipo atronitens	M	U	LT	F/P	L	1200		F8, F12		AMN, AMS
Antilophia galeata	M	M/C	LT	F	L	1000		F8	CER	CSA
Tyranneutes stolzmanni	H	M	LT	F	L	800		F1		AMN, AMS
Tyranneutes virescens	H	M	LT	F	L	L		F1	GUI	AMN
Neopelma aurifrons										
aurifrons	?	U	LT	?	L	L?		F1?	RDJ	ATL
chrysolophum	M	U	HT	U/P	750	1500		F4, F1, F15	SOU	ATL
Neopelma chrysocephalum	M	U	LT	F	L	700		F12, F8	o	AMN
Neopelma pallescens	M	U	LT	F/P	L	900		F7, F8, F12		AMN, AMS, CSA
Neopelma sulphureiventer	H	U	LT	U/P	L	900	B	F1	o	AMS
Heterocercus aurantiivertex	H?	U	LT	?	L	L		F2, F12	RNW	AMN
Heterocercus flavivertex	H	U	LT	F/P	L	L		F8, F12	o	AMN
Heterocercus linteatus	M	U/M	LT	U/P	L	L		F2, F3	o	AMS
Machaeropterus deliciosus	M	U/M	UT	U/P	400	1900		F4, F15	WES	NAN
Machaeropterus pyrocephalus	M	U/M	LT	F/P	L	1050	B	F1		AMN, AMS
Machaeropterus regulus	M	U/M	LT	F/P	L	1500		F1, F4		NSA, TEP, AMN, AMS, ATL
Manacus candei	M	U	LT	F	L	950		F1E, F15	o	GCS

CP	RP	Notes
4	3	
4	3	
4	3	Locally to lowlands.
4	2	Poorly known.
4	3	Locally to 2,700 m (southern Mexico).
4	3	Occasionally to 100 and 3,750 m (Peru).
4	3	
4	3	
4	3	
4	3	Locally to lowlands (Yucatán).
4	3	
4	3	
3	2	Monitor.
4	3	
4	2	
3	2	In semideciduous forest; poorly known.
4	2	Poorly known.
4	3	
4	3	Occasionally to 400 m (Colombia).
4	2	Distribution poorly understood.
4	3	
4	3	
4	3	Occasionally to 2,500 m.
4	3	
4	2	Probably contains multiple species.
4	3	
3	2	Poorly known.
4	3	Occasionally to 200 m.
3	2	Occasionally to 1,500 m? deforestation; poorly known.
2	1	Deforestation; poorly known.
4	2	Habitat requirements poorly known.
3	2	
4	3	Locally to lowlands.
3	2	
4	3	
4	3	
4	3	
4	3	
4	3	
2	1	Deforestation; poorly known.
3	2	Deforestation, but tolerates secondary forest.
4	3	
4	3	
4	3	
4	2	Poorly known.
4	2	
4	3	
3	2	
4	3	Occasionally to 1,350 m.
4	3	
3	3	

Abbreviations Used

Snst - Sensitivity:
L - Low; **M** - Medium; **H** - High.

Strat - Foraging Strata:
T - Terrestrial; **U** - Understory; **M** - Midstory; **C** - Canopy; **A** - Aerial; **W** - Water.

Cntab - Center of Abundance:
LT - Lower tropical; **LS** - Lower subtropical; **HT** - Hill tropical; **UT** - Upper tropical; **US** - Upper subtropical; **MM** - Middle montane; **UM** - Upper montane.

Rel - Relative Abundance:
R - Rare; **U** - Uncommon; **F** - Fairly common; **C** - Common; **P** - Patchily distributed.

Min - Minimum Elevation:
L - Lowlands; **?** - Uncertain value; numeric values in meters.

Max - Maximum Elevation:
L - Lowlands; **?** - Uncertain value; **+** - species occurs at least to given elevation but likely occurs higher; numeric values in meters.

Micro - Microhabitats:
A - Army ants; **B** - Bamboo; **T** - Treefalls; **G** - Ground bromeliads; **C** - Rocky outcrops and caves; **S** - Streamside; **V** - Vine tangles; **B/V** -Bamboo/vine tangles.

Habitats:
F1 - Tropical lowland evergreen forest; **F2** - Flooded tropical evergreen forest; **F3** - River-edge forest; **F4** - Montane evergreen forest; **F5** - Elfin forest; **F6** - *Polylepis* woodland; **F7** - Tropical deciduous forest; **F8** - Gallery forest; **F9** - Southern temperate forest; **F10** - Pine forest; **F11** - Pine-oak forest; **F12** - White sand forest; **F13** - Palm forest; **F14** - Mangrove forest; **F15** - Secondary forest; **N1** - Arid lowland scrub; **N2** - Arid montane scrub; **N3** - Semihumid/humid montane scrub; **N4** - Cerrado; **N5** - Campo grasslands; **N6** - Low, seasonally wet grassland; **N7** - Southern temperate grassland; **N8** - Northern temperate grassland; **N9** - Puna grassland; **N10** - Paramo grassland; **N11** - Riparian thickets; **N12** - River island scrub; **N13** - Pastures/agricultural lands; **N14** - Second-growth scrub; **A1** - Freshwater marshes; **A2** - Saltwater/brackish marshes; **A3** - Coastal sand beaches/mudflats; **A4** - Coastal rocky beaches; **A5** - Riverine sand beaches; **A6** - Freshwater lakes and ponds; **A7** - Alkaline lakes; **A8** - Rivers; **A9** - Streams; **A10** - Bogs; **A11** - Coastal waters; **A12** - Pelagic waters.
E - Edge (used as a modifer to particular habitats).

Sub - Subregions:
ARC - Arid Caribbean Coast; **AWA** - Altiplano and Western Andes; **BAH** - Bahamas; **BAJ** - Baja California; **CAA** - Caatinga; **CAH** - Central American Highlands; **CER** - Cerrado; **CHA** - Chaco; **CHG** - Chiapas-Guanacaste; **CHL** - Chilean Desert; **CHR** - Chiriquí; **CIS** - Cocos Island; **CMV** - Cauca-Magdalena Valley; **COC** - Cuzco-Cochabamba; **CUB** - Cuba; **DOM** - Dominica; **EAS** - Eastern Slope Andes; **FDN** - Fernando de Noronha; **GAL** - Galápagos; **GCM** - Gulf Coast-Mexico; **GRE** - Grenada; **GUA** - Guadeloupe; **GUI** - Guianan; **HIS** - Hispaniola; **HPC** - Humid Pacific Coast; **ISA** - Isla Providencia and Isla San Andrés; **JAM** - Jamaica; **JFI** - Juan Fernández Islands; **MAN** - Manabí-Tumbes; **MAR** - Marañón Valley; **MID** - Madeira-Tapajós; **MON** - Montserrat; **MRT** - Martinique; **MTC** - Marañón-Cuzco; **NMM** - Northern Mexican Mountains; **NOR** - Northern Coastal Brazil; **PAR** - Pará; **PER** - Peruvian Desert; **PUE** - Puerto Rico; **RDJ** - Rio de Janeiro-Bahia Lowlands; **RMW** - Rio Madeira West; **RNW** - Rio Negro West; **SCA** - Southern Central America; **SCT** - Santa Cruz-Tucumán; **SIN** - Sinaloa-Oaxaca; **SMH** - Southern Mexican Highlands; **SMT** - Santa Marta; **SOC** - Islas Revillagigedo (Socorro Island group); **SON** - Sonoran Desert; **SOU** - Southern Atlantic Coast; **STL** - St. Lucia; **STV** - St. Vincent; **TAC** - Tacarcuna; **VAN** - Venezuelan Andes; **VNZ** - Venezuelan Coastal Mountains; **WES** - Western Andes; **YUC** - Yucatán Peninsula.
o - Endemic to region, but not restricted to a single subregion.

Zoogeographic Regions:
AMN - Northern Amazonia; **AMS** - Southern Amazonia; **ATL** - Atlantic Forest; **BSR** - Baja-Sonora; **CAN** - Central Andes; **CDH** - Chiriquí-Darién Highlands; **CHO** - Chocó Lowlands; **CSA** - Central South America; **EPC** - Equatorial Pacific Coast; **GAN** - Greater Antilles; **GCS** - Gulf-Caribbean Slope; **LAN** - Lesser Antilles; **MAH** - Madrean Highlands; **MPL** - Mexican Plateau; **NAN** - Northern Andes; **NSA** - Northern South America; **PAM** - Pampas; **PAS** - Pacific Arid Slope; **PAT** - Patagonia; **SAN** - Southern Andes; **STP** - Subtropical Pacific; **TEP** - Tepuis.

CP -Conservation Priority:
1 - Urgent; **2** - High; **3** - Medium; **4** - Low.

RP - Research Priority:
1 - High; **2** - Medium; **3** - Low.

	Snst	Strat	Cntab	Rel	Min	Max	Micro	Habitats	Sub	Zoogeographic Regions
Manacus manacus	L	U	LT	F	L	1000		F1E, F15, F8, F12		CHO, EPC, NSA, AMN, AMS, ATL
Manacus vitellinus	M	U	LT	C	L	1200		F1E, F15		GCS, CHO, NSA
Corapipo gutturalis	H	U/M	HT	F	L	1100		F1	GUI	AMN
Corapipo leucorrhoa	H	U	HT	U	L	1500		F1, F4		GCS, CDH, CHO, NAN, NSA
Ilicura militaris	M	M/C	HT	F	500	1250		F4, F1	SOU	ATL
Masius chrysopterus	M	U	UT	U	1100	2300		F4, F15		NAN, CAN
Chiroxiphia caudata	L	U/M	HT	C	L	1900		F1, F4, F15	SOU	ATL
Chiroxiphia lanceolata	L	U/M	LT	F	L	1400		F7, F8, F1		GCS, NSA
Chiroxiphia linearis	M	U/M	LT	F	L	1500		F7, F8, F15	CHG	PAS
Chiroxiphia pareola										
boliviana	M	U	UT	C	900	1650		F4	COC	CAN
pareola	H	U/M	LT	F	L	750		F1		NSA, AMN, AMS, ATL
Pipra aureola	M	U/M	LT	F	L	800		F2, F15		NSA, AMN, AMS
Pipra chloromeros	H	U/M	HT	F	L	1400		F1, F4		CAN, AMS
Pipra coeruleocapilla	H	U	UT	F	800	1900		F4	o	CAN
Pipra cornuta	H	U/M	UT	F	800	1800		F4	o	TEP
Pipra coronota	M	U/M	LT	C	L	1400		F1, F15		GCS, CDH, CHO, NSA, AMN, AMS
Pipra erythrocephala	H	U/M	LT	F	L	1100		F1		GCS, CHO, NSA, AMN, AMS
Pipra fasciicauda	M	U/M	LT	F	L	800		F2, F15, F8, F3		AMS, CSA
Pipra filicauda	M	U/M	LT	F/P	L	800		F2, F1		NSA, AMN, AMS
Pipra iris	M	U/M	LT	F	L	L		F1	PAR	AMS
Pipra isidorei	H	U	UT	F	700	1700		F4		NAN, CAN
Pipra mentalis	M	U/M	LT	F	L	1050		F1		GCS, CHO
Pipra nattereri	H	U/M	LT	F	L	L		F1	MID	AMS
Pipra pipra	H	U	LT	U/P	L	2150		F1, F4		GCS, CDH, NAN, CAN, NSA, AMN, AMS, ATL
Pipra rubrocapilla	H	U/M	LT	F	L	700		F1		AMS, ATL
Pipra serena										
serena	H	U/M	LT	F	L	L		F1	GUI	AMN
suavissima	H	U/M	UT	F	900	1800		F1, F4	o	TEP
Pipra vilasboasi	H	U	LT	?	L	L		F1	PAR	AMS
Cotingidae										
Phoenicircus carnifex	H	C	LT	U/P	L	700		F1		AMN, AMS
Phoenicircus nigricollis	H	C	LT	U/P	L	L		F1		AMN, AMS
Laniisoma elegans	H	M/C	UT	R	700	1800		F4, F1		NAN, CAN, ATL
Phibalura flavirostris	M	C	UT	U/P	L	2000+		F4, F1		CAN, ATL
Tijuca atra	H	C	MM	U	1100	2100		F4	SOU	ATL
Tijuca condita	H	C	MM	R	1400	2000		F5	SOU	ATL
Carpornis cucullatus	H	M/C	HT	U	400	1600		F4, F1	o	ATL
Carpornis melanocephalus	H	M/C	LT	U	L	700		F1	o	ATL
Ampelion remseni	H	C	UM	U	3100	3650		F5	EAS	NAN
Ampelion rubrocristatus	L	C	UM	C	2800	4050		F5, F4, F15		NAN, CAN
Ampelion rufaxilla	M	C	MM	U/P	2200	2750		F4		NAN, CAN
Ampelion sclateri	H	C	UM	U	2500	3350		F5	MTC	CAN
Ampelion stresemanni	H	C	UM	U	2700	4300		F6	AWA	CAN
Pipreola arcuata	M	M/C	UM	C	1800	3350		F4, F5		NAN, CAN
Pipreola aureopectus	M	C	MM	F	800	2300		F4	o	NAN
Pipreola chlorolepidota	H	C	UT	U/P	800	1700		F4, F1		NAN, CAN
Pipreola formosa	M	C	UT	F	800	2200		F4	VNZ	NAN
Pipreola frontalis	H	C	UT	F	1100	2000		F4		NAN, CAN
Pipreola intermedia	M	C	UM	F	2000	3300		F4	o	CAN
Pipreola jucunda	M	C	UT	F	900	2300		F4	WES	NAN
Pipreola lubomirskii	H	C	MM	U	1600	2300		F4	EAS	NAN
Pipreola pulchra	H	C	MM	F	1500	2250		F4	MTC	CAN

CP	RP	Notes
4	3	Occasionally to 1,900 m.
4	3	
4	3	
4	3	
3	2	Locally to 1,800 m.
4	3	Occasionally to 600 m.
4	3	
4	3	Rarely to 1,650 m.
4	3	
4	3	Occasionally to 600 m.
4	3	
4	3	Rarely to 1,700 m (Venezuela).
4	3	Rarely to 1,650 m (Bolivia).
3	2	Deforestation.
4	3	Occasionally to lowlands?
4	3	Below 900 m in the Andes.
4	3	Occasionally to 2,000 m (Venezuela).
4	3	Occasionally to 950 m (Peru).
4	3	
3	3	Deforestation?.
3	2	Occasionally to 500 m.
4	3	
3	3	
4	2	May contain multiple species.
4	3	
4	3	
4	3	
2	1	Poorly known; not encountered recently.
4	3	
4	3	
2	1	Poorly known; occasionally to lowlands.
2	1	Poorly known; seasonal movements not understood.
2	1	Habitat mostly protected.
2	1	Mainly in protected areas; survey; needs ecological study.
3	1	
2	1	Deforestation.
4	2	Recently described (Robbins et al. 1994).
4	3	Locally to 2,200 m.
4	2	Distribution poorly known; locally to 1,900 m.
4	2	Poorly known.
2	1	Narrow food preferences (see Parker 1981); *Polylepis destruction.*
4	3	Occasionally to 1,200 m? mainly above 2,200 m.
4	3	Occasionally to 300 m.
2	1	Poorly known; occasionally to 200 m?
3	2	
3	2	Occasionally to 650 and 2,300 m.
4	3	Occasionally to 1,100 m.
3	2	
4	2	Poorly known.
3	2	

Abbreviations Used

Snst - Sensitivity:
L - Low; **M** - Medium; **H** - High.

Strat - Foraging Strata:
T - Terrestrial; **U** - Understory; **M** - Midstory; **C** - Canopy; **A** - Aerial; **W** - Water.

Cntab - Center of Abundance:
LT - Lower tropical; **LS** - Lower subtropical; **HT** - Hill tropical; **UT** - Upper tropical; **US** - Upper subtropical; **MM** - Middle montane; **UM** - Upper montane.

Rel - Relative Abundance:
R - Rare; **U** - Uncommon; **F** - Fairly common; **C** - Common; **P** - Patchily distributed.

Min - Minimum Elevation:
L - Lowlands; **?** - Uncertain value; numeric values in meters.

Max - Maximum Elevation:
L - Lowlands; **?** - Uncertain value; **+** - species occurs at least to given elevation but likely occurs higher; numeric values in meters.

Micro - Microhabitats:
A - Army ants; **B** - Bamboo; **T** - Treefalls; **G** - Ground bromeliads; **C** - Rocky outcrops and caves; **S** - Streamside; **V** - Vine tangles; **B/V** -Bamboo/vine tangles.

Habitats:
F1 - Tropical lowland evergreen forest; **F2** - Flooded tropical evergreen forest; **F3** - River-edge forest; **F4** - Montane evergreen forest; **F5** - Elfin forest; **F6** - *Polylepis* woodland; **F7** - Tropical deciduous forest; **F8** - Gallery forest; **F9** - Southern temperate forest; **F10** - Pine forest; **F11** - Pine-oak forest; **F12** - White sand forest; **F13** - Palm forest; **F14** - Mangrove forest; **F15** - Secondary forest; **N1** - Arid lowland scrub; **N2** - Arid montane scrub; **N3** - Semihumid/humid montane scrub; **N4** - Cerrado; **N5** - Campo grasslands; **N6** - Low, seasonally wet grassland; **N7** - Southern temperate grassland; **N8** - Northern temperate grassland; **N9** - Puna grassland; **N10** - Paramo grassland; **N11** - Riparian thickets; **N12** - River island scrub; **N13** - Pastures/agricultural lands; **N14** - Second-growth scrub; **A1** - Freshwater marshes; **A2** - Saltwater/brackish marshes; **A3** - Coastal sand beaches/mudflats; **A4** - Coastal rocky beaches; **A5** - Riverine sand beaches; **A6** - Freshwater lakes and ponds; **A7** - Alkaline lakes; **A8** - Rivers; **A9** - Streams; **A10** - Bogs; **A11** - Coastal waters; **A12** - Pelagic waters.
E - Edge (used as a modifer to particular habitats).

Sub - Subregions:
ARC - Arid Caribbean Coast; **AWA** - Altiplano and Western Andes; **BAH** - Bahamas; **BAJ** - Baja California; **CAA** - Caatinga; **CAH** - Central American Highlands; **CER** - Cerrado; **CHA** - Chaco; **CHG** - Chiapas-Guanacaste; **CHL** - Chilean Desert; **CHR** - Chiriquí; **CIS** - Cocos Island; **CMV** - Cauca-Magdalena Valley; **COC** - Cuzco-Cochabamba; **CUB** - Cuba; **DOM** - Dominica; **EAS** - Eastern Slope Andes; **FDN** - Fernando de Noronha; **GAL** - Galápagos; **GCM** - Gulf Coast-Mexico; **GRE** - Grenada; **GUA** - Guadeloupe; **GUI** - Guianan; **HIS** - Hispaniola; **HPC** - Humid Pacific Coast; **ISA** - Isla Providencia and Isla San Andrés; **JAM** - Jamaica; **JFI** - Juan Fernández Islands; **MAN** - Manabí-Tumbes; **MAR** - Marañón Valley; **MID** - Madeira-Tapajós; **MON** - Montserrat; **MRT** - Martinique; **MTC** - Marañón-Cuzco; **NMM** - Northern Mexican Mountains; **NOR** - Northern Coastal Brazil; **PAR** - Pará; **PER** - Peruvian Desert; **PUE** - Puerto Rico; **RDJ** - Rio de Janeiro-Bahia Lowlands; **RMW** - Rio Madeira West; **RNW** - Rio Negro West; **SCA** - Southern Central America; **SCT** - Santa Cruz-Tucumán; **SIN** - Sinaloa-Oaxaca; **SMH** - Southern Mexican Highlands; **SMT** - Santa Marta; **SOC** - Islas Revillagigedo (Socorro Island group); **SON** - Sonoran Desert; **SOU** - Southern Atlantic Coast; **STL** - St. Lucia; **STV** - St. Vincent; **TAC** - Tacarcuna; **VAN** - Venezuelan Andes; **VNZ** - Venezuelan Coastal Mountains; **WES** - Western Andes; **YUC** - Yucatán Peninsula.
o - Endemic to region, but not restricted to a single subregion.

Zoogeographic Regions:
AMN - Northern Amazonia; **AMS** - Southern Amazonia; **ATL** - Atlantic Forest; **BSR** - Baja-Sonora; **CAN** - Central Andes; **CDH** - Chiriquí-Darién Highlands; **CHO** - Chocó Lowlands; **CSA** - Central South America; **EPC** - Equatorial Pacific Coast; **GAN** - Greater Antilles; **GCS** - Gulf-Caribbean Slope; **LAN** - Lesser Antilles; **MAH** - Madrean Highlands; **MPL** - Mexican Plateau; **NAN** - Northern Andes; **NSA** - Northern South America; **PAM** - Pampas; **PAS** - Pacific Arid Slope; **PAT** - Patagonia; **SAN** - Southern Andes; **STP** - Subtropical Pacific; **TEP** - Tepuis.

CP -Conservation Priority:
1 - Urgent; **2** - High; **3** - Medium; **4** - Low.

RP - Research Priority:
1 - High; **2** - Medium; **3** - Low.

	Snst	Strat	Cntab	Rel	Min	Max	Micro	Habitats	Sub	Zoogeographic Regions
Pipreola riefferii	M	C	MM	F	1200	3050		F4		NAN, CAN
Pipreola whitelyi	H	C	UT	U	1300	2250		F4	o	TEP
Ampelioides tschudii	H	C	UT	U	900	2300		F4		NAN, CAN
Iodopleura fusca	M	C	LT	U/P	L	L		F1	GUI	AMN
Iodopleura isabellae	M	C	LT	U/P	L	900		F1		AMN, AMS
Iodopleura pipra	M	C	LT	R/P	L	900		F1	o	ATL
Calyptura cristata	H	M?	HT?	R	L	900?		F1	RDJ	ATL
Lipaugus cryptolophus	H	M	UT	U	900	2300		F4		NAN, CAN
Lipaugus fuscocinereus	H	C	UM	U	1700	3000		F4	o	NAN
Lipaugus lanioides	H	M/C	HT	U	L	900		F1	SOU	ATL
Lipaugus streptophorus	H	C	UT	F	1000	1800		F4	o	TEP
Lipaugus subalaris	H	M/C	UT	U/P	800	1350		F4		NAN, CAN
Lipaugus unirufus	M	M/C	LT	F	L	1000		F1		GCS, CHO, NSA
Lipaugus vociferans	H	M/C	LT	C	L	800		F1		NSA, AMN, AMS, ATL
Chirocylla uropygialis	H	M/C	MM	U	1800	2600		F4	COC	CAN
Porphyrolaema porphyrolaema	M	C	LT	U/P	L	L		F2, F15		AMN, AMS
Cotinga amabilis	M	C	LT	F	L	1700		F1, F15	o	GCS
Cotinga cayana	H	C	LT	U	L	800		F1		AMN, AMS
Cotinga cotinga	M	C	LT	U	L	600		F1		AMN, AMS
Cotinga maculata	M	C	LT	R	L	L		F1	RDJ	ATL
Cotinga maynana	M	C	LT	F	L	L		F2, F3, F15		AMN, AMS
Cotinga nattererii	M	C	LT	F	L	1250		F1, F15		GCS, CHO, NSA
Cotinga ridgwayi	M	C	LT	F	L	1400		F1, F15	HPC	GCS
Xipholena atropurpurea	M	C	LT	U	L	700		F1	o	ATL
Xipholena lamellipennis	H	C	LT	U	L	L		F1	PAR	AMS
Xipholena punicea	M	C	LT	F/P	L	L		F1		AMN, AMS
Carpodectes antoniae	H	C	LT	U	L	800		F1, F14	HPC	GCS
Carpodectes hopkei	H	C	LT	U	L	900		F1	o	CHO
Carpodectes nitidus	M	C	LT	U	L	750		F1, F15	SCA	GCS
Conioptilon mcilhennyi	H	C	LT	F/P	L	L		F3	RMW	AMS
Gymnoderus foetidus	M	C	LT	F	L	700		F2, F3		AMN, AMS
Haematoderus militaris	H	C	LT	U/P	L	L		F1		AMN, AMS
Querula purpurata	M	C	LT	F	L	1050		F1		GCS, CHO, NSA, AMN, AMS
Pyroderus scutatus										
granadensis	M	M	UT	U/P	700	2700		F4, F1		NAN, CAN, AMN
scutatus	M	M	LT	R/P	L	1100		F1, F4	o	ATL
Cephalopterus glabricollis	H	M/C	UT	R/P	800	2000		F1, F4	CHR	CDH
Cephalopterus ornatus	M	M/C	LT	U/P	L	1300		F3, F4		NAN, CAN, AMN, AMS
Cephalopterus penduliger	M	M/C	UT	R/P	700	1800		F4	WES	NAN
Perissocephalus tricolor	H	C	LT	U	L	1400		F1	o	AMN
Procnias alba	M	C	HT	U	450	1500		F1		NSA, TEP, AMN, AMS
Procnias averano	H	C	HT	U/P	L	1900		F1, F4		NSA, TEP, ATL
Procnias nudicollis	M	C	HT	F	L	1150		F1, F4	o	ATL
Procnias tricarunculata	M	C	UT	U	600	2400		F4, F1		MAH, CDH
Rupicola peruviana	M	U/M	UT	U/P	900	2400	R	F4		NAN, CAN
Rupicola rupicola	H	U/M	HT	U/P	L	1500	R	F1, F4		TEP, AMN
Oxyruncidae										
Oxyruncus cristatus	H	C	UT	U/P	L	1800		F4, F1		CDH, CAN, TEP, AMS, ATL
Phytotomidae										
Phytotoma raimondii	M	C	LT	R/U	L	500		N1	MAN	EPC
Phytotoma rara	M	C	US	U	L	2700		F9, F15		STP, SAN

CP	RP	Notes
4	3	Locally to 900 m (Colombia).
4	3	
3	2	Occasionally to 650 and 2,700 m; deforestation.
4	2	Biology and distribution poorly known.
4	2	
2	1	Poorly known; deforestation; old record from Guyana doubtful.
1	1	May be extinct, no reliable reports this century.
3	2	Locally to 600 m.
4	2	
2	1	Poorly known; deforestation.
4	3	
3	1	Poorly known; deforestation.
4	3	
4	3	Occasionally to 1,400 m (Venezuela).
3	2	Poorly known.
4	2	Occasionally to 900 m; poorly known.
4	3	
4	3	
4	3	
1	1	Deforestation; restricted to a few reserves.
4	3	
3	3	
3	2	Occasionally to 1,850 m; deforestation.
2	1	Deforestation; mainly in a few reserves.
3	2	Deforestation; status uncertain.
4	3	Locally to 1,300 m in Tepuis.
2	2	Deforestation; status uncertain.
3	2	Occasionally to 1,450 m; deforestation; status uncertain.
3	2	Deforestation; seasonal elevational movements.
3	2	Deforestation?
4	3	
3	2	Poorly known.
4	3	
3	2	Local in Guianan lowlands; declining in some areas.
2	2	Occasionally to 2,000 m; declining; deforestation and hunting.
2	1	Seasonally to lowlands; deforestation.
4	2	
2	1	Occasionally to sea level; declining with deforestation.
4	3	
4	3	Occasionally to lowlands; breeds locally in hilly regions of eastern Amazonia.
3	2	
3	1	Movements poorly known; deforestation; survives in small forest patches.
3	2	Seasonally to sea level.
3	2	Deforestation;
4	3	
3	2	Mainly 800 to 1,400 m outside Brazil; deforestation.
2	1	Possibly declining; survey
4	3	

Abbreviations Used

Snst - Sensitivity:
L - Low; **M** - Medium; **H** - High.

Strat - Foraging Strata:
T - Terrestrial; **U** - Understory; **M** - Midstory; **C** - Canopy; **A** - Aerial; **W** - Water.

Cntab - Center of Abundance:
LT - Lower tropical; **LS** - Lower subtropical; **HT** - Hill tropical; **UT** - Upper tropical; **US** - Upper subtropical; **MM** - Middle montane; **UM** - Upper montane.

Rel - Relative Abundance:
R - Rare; **U** - Uncommon; **F** - Fairly common; **C** - Common; **P** - Patchily distributed.

Min - Minimum Elevation:
L - Lowlands; **?** - Uncertain value; numeric values in meters.

Max - Maximum Elevation:
L - Lowlands; **?** - Uncertain value; **+** - species occurs at least to given elevation but likely occurs higher; numeric values in meters.

Micro - Microhabitats:
A - Army ants; **B** - Bamboo; **T** - Treefalls; **G** - Ground bromeliads; **C** - Rocky outcrops and caves; **S** - Streamside; **V** - Vine tangles; **B/V** -Bamboo/vine tangles.

Habitats:
F1 - Tropical lowland evergreen forest; **F2** - Flooded tropical evergreen forest; **F3** - River-edge forest; **F4** - Montane evergreen forest; **F5** - Elfin forest; **F6** - *Polylepis* woodland; **F7** - Tropical deciduous forest; **F8** - Gallery forest; **F9** - Southern temperate forest; **F10** - Pine forest; **F11** - Pine-oak forest; **F12** - White sand forest; **F13** - Palm forest; **F14** - Mangrove forest; **F15** - Secondary forest; **N1** - Arid lowland scrub; **N2** - Arid montane scrub; **N3** - Semihumid/humid montane scrub; **N4** - Cerrado; **N5** - Campo grasslands; **N6** - Low, seasonally wet grassland; **N7** - Southern temperate grassland; **N8** - Northern temperate grassland; **N9** - Puna grassland; **N10** - Paramo grassland; **N11** - Riparian thickets; **N12** - River island scrub; **N13** - Pastures/agricultural lands; **N14** - Second-growth scrub; **A1** - Freshwater marshes; **A2** - Saltwater/brackish marshes; **A3** - Coastal sand beaches/mudflats; **A4** - Coastal rocky beaches; **A5** - Riverine sand beaches; **A6** - Freshwater lakes and ponds; **A7** - Alkaline lakes; **A8** - Rivers; **A9** - Streams; **A10** - Bogs; **A11** - Coastal waters; **A12** - Pelagic waters.
E - Edge (used as a modifer to particular habitats).

Sub - Subregions:
ARC - Arid Caribbean Coast; **AWA** - Altiplano and Western Andes; **BAH** - Bahamas; **BAJ** - Baja California; **CAA** - Caatinga; **CAH** - Central American Highlands; **CER** - Cerrado; **CHA** - Chaco; **CHG** - Chiapas-Guanacaste; **CHL** - Chilean Desert; **CHR** - Chiriquí; **CIS** - Cocos Island; **CMV** - Cauca-Magdalena Valley; **COC** - Cuzco-Cochabamba; **CUB** - Cuba; **DOM** - Dominica; **EAS** - Eastern Slope Andes; **FDN** - Fernando de Noronha; **GAL** - Galápagos; **GCM** - Gulf Coast-Mexico; **GRE** - Grenada; **GUA** - Guadeloupe; **GUI** - Guianan; **HIS** - Hispaniola; **HPC** - Humid Pacific Coast; **ISA** - Isla Providencia and Isla San Andrés; **JAM** - Jamaica; **JFI** - Juan Fernández Islands; **MAN** - Manabí-Tumbes; **MAR** - Marañón Valley; **MID** - Madeira-Tapajós; **MON** - Montserrat; **MRT** - Martinique; **MTC** - Marañón-Cuzco; **NMM** - Northern Mexican Mountains; **NOR** - Northern Coastal Brazil; **PAR** - Pará; **PER** - Peruvian Desert; **PUE** - Puerto Rico; **RDJ** - Rio de Janeiro-Bahia Lowlands; **RMW** - Rio Madeira West; **RNW** - Rio Negro West; **SCA** - Southern Central America; **SCT** - Santa Cruz-Tucumán; **SIN** - Sinaloa-Oaxaca; **SMH** - Southern Mexican Highlands; **SMT** - Santa Marta; **SOC** - Islas Revillagigedo (Socorro Island group); **SON** - Sonoran Desert; **SOU** - Southern Atlantic Coast; **STL** - St. Lucia; **STV** - St. Vincent; **TAC** - Tacarcuna; **VAN** - Venezuelan Andes; **VNZ** - Venezuelan Coastal Mountains; **WES** - Western Andes; **YUC** - Yucatán Peninsula.
o - Endemic to region, but not restricted to a single subregion.

Zoogeographic Regions:
AMN - Northern Amazonia; **AMS** - Southern Amazonia; **ATL** - Atlantic Forest; **BSR** - Baja-Sonora; **CAN** - Central Andes; **CDH** - Chiriquí-Darién Highlands; **CHO** - Chocó Lowlands; **CSA** - Central South America; **EPC** - Equatorial Pacific Coast; **GAN** - Greater Antilles; **GCS** - Gulf-Caribbean Slope; **LAN** - Lesser Antilles; **MAH** - Madrean Highlands; **MPL** - Mexican Plateau; **NAN** - Northern Andes; **NSA** - Northern South America; **PAM** - Pampas; **PAS** - Pacific Arid Slope; **PAT** - Patagonia; **SAN** - Southern Andes; **STP** - Subtropical Pacific; **TEP** - Tepuis.

CP -Conservation Priority:
1 - Urgent; **2** - High; **3** - Medium; **4** - Low.

RP - Research Priority:
1 - High; **2** - Medium; **3** - Low.

	Snst	Strat	Cntab	Rel	Min	Max	Micro	Habitats	Sub	Zoogeographic Regions
Phytotoma rutila	M	C	US	F	L	3100		N2, N1, N11		CAN, SAN, CSA
Alaudidae										
Eremophila alpestris	L	T	US	U/P	L	3750		N8, N13, N1		BSR, GCS, MPL, MAH, NAN
Hirundinidae										
Tachycineta albilinea	L	A	LT	C/P	L	L		F14, A6, A8, N13		BSR, PAS, GCS, EPC
Tachycineta albiventer	L	A	LT	C	L	600		A8, A6, A9		NSA, AMN, AMS, CSA, ATL
Tachycineta leucopyga	L	A	LS	F	L	1500		N7, N13, N14		STP, SAN, PAT
Tachycineta leucorrhoa	L	A	LT	C	L	1100		N6, N5, N13, N14		CSA, ATL, PAM
Tachycineta thalassina	L	A	UM	C	L	3200		F10, F11		BSR, MPL, MAH
Callichelidon cyaneoviridis	L	A	LT	U	L	L		F10	BAH	GAN
Kalochelidon euchrysea	M	A	UT	R/P	L	2000+		F10, F4	o	GAN
Progne chalybea	L	A	LT	C	L	1700		N14, N13		PAS, MAH, GCS, CDH, CHO, EPC, NSA, AMN, AMS, CSA, ATL, PAM
Progne cryptoleuca	L	A	LT	F/P	L	1500+		N1, N13, N14, F10	CUB	GAN
Progne dominicensis	L	A	LT	F/P	L	1500+		N14, N13		GAN, LAN, NSA
Progne modesta										
elegans	L	A	LT	F	L	L		N14, N6		CSA, PAM, PAT
modesta	L	A	LT	F	L	1500		N1	GAL	EPC
murphyi	L	A	LT	U/P	L	L		N14, N13		EPC, STP
Progne sinaloae	M	A	MM	F/P	1100	2800		F11	NMM	MAH
Progne subis	L	A	LT	C	L	3200		F10, N1, N14		BSR, MPL, MAH
Progne tapera	L	A	LT	C	L	1600		N6, N4, N14, A8		EPC, NSA, AMN, AMS, CSA, ATL, PAM
Notiochelidon cyanoleuca	L	A	LS	C	L	3600		N14, N13, N7		CDH, STP, NAN, CAN, SAN, NSA, TEP, CSA, ATL, PAM, PAT
Notiochelidon flavipes	H	A	UM	F/P	2100	3400		F5, F4		NAN, CAN
Notiochelidon murina	L	A	UM	F	2500	4100		N10, N13, N2, N3		NAN, CAN
Notiochelidon pileata	L	A	MM	F	1600	3100		F11, F4, F15	CAH	MAH
Atticora fasciata	M	A	LT	C/P	L	800		A8		AMN, AMS
Atticora melanoleuca	M	A	LT	F/P	L	L	R	A8		AMN, AMS, CSA, ATL
Neochelidon tibialis	M	A	HT	U/P	L	1200		F1E		GCS, CHO, NSA, TEP, AMN, AMS, ATL
Alopochelidon fucata	M	A	LS	U/P	L	1600		N5, N6		NAN, TEP, AMS?, CSA, ATL, PAM
Stelgidopteryx ruficollis	L	A	LT	C	L	2000		N14, N13, A8, A9		GCS, CDH, CHO, EPC, NAN, CAN, NSA, AMN, AMS, CSA, ATL, PAM
Stelgidopteryx serripennis	L	A	LS	F	L	2500		N14, N13, A8, A9		BSR, PAS, MAH, GCS, CDH
Riparia riparia	L	A	LS	U/P	L	L		N14, N13, A8, A9		GCS
Hirundo rustica	L	A	US	C	L	2700		N13, N8, N14		BSR, MPL, MAH
Petrochelidon andecola	M	A	UM	F/P	3300	4400+		N9, N2	AWA	CAN
Petrochelidon fulva										
fulva	L	A	LT	F	L	2100		N8, N13, N14, N1		GAN, MPL, MAH, GCS
ruficollis	L	A	LT	F	L	1500		N13, N14		EPC, STP
Petrochelidon pyrrhonota	L	A	US	C	L	3000		N8, N13		BSR, MPL, MAH
Motacillidae										
Anthus bogotensis	M	T	UM	F	2100	4200		N10, N13, N9		NAN, CAN
Anthus chacoensis	?	T	LT	?	L	L		N7	CHA	CSA
Anthus correndera	L	T	LS	F	L	4400		N9, N7, N13		STP, CAN, SAN, CSA, PAM, PAT
Anthus furcatus	M	T	LS	F	L	4000		N9, N7		CAN, CSA, PAM, PAT
Anthus hellmayri	L	T	LS	F	L	3600		N7, N9, N13		CAN, SAN, ATL, PAM
Anthus lutescens	L	T	LT	F	L	1300		N13, N7, N6		GCS, STP, NSA, AMN, AMS, CSA, ATL, PAM
Anthus nattereri	M	T	LS	R	L	900		N5		ATL, PAM
Laniidae										
Lanius ludovicianus	L	C	LS	F	L	3000		N1, N2, N14, N13, N8		BSR, MPL, PAS, MAH
Bombycillidae										
Ptilogonys caudatus	L	C	MM	C	1800	3000		F4, F15	CHR	CDH

CP	RP	Notes
4	3	
4	2	Monitor Andean population.
4	2	May contain two species.
4	3	
4	2	Limits of winter range unknown.
4	3	
4	3	
2	1	Survey.
3	2	Survey; probably more widespread than suspected.
4	3	
4	2	Winter range unknown.
4	2	Winter range unknown.
4	2	Occasionally to 2,000 m during migration (Bolivia).
4	3	
3	2	Monitor; may be declining.
4	2	Winter range unknown.
4	2	
4	2	Occasionally to 3,000 m during migration.
4	3	
4	2	Range poorly known.
4	3	Locally to 2,100 m.
4	3	Occasionally to 700 m.
4	3	Occasionally to 1,400 m.
4	2	Range outside of Amazonia poorly known.
4	2	Range poorly known.
3	2	Seasonal movements poorly known.
4	3	
4	3	
4	3	
4	3	
4	3	
4	2	Increasing; nonbreeding range of U.S./Mexico population uncertain.
4	3	
4	3	
4	3	
2	1	Poorly known; relationship to *A. lutescens* uncertain.
4	3	
4	3	
4	2	Andean form poorly known; seasonal movements?
4	3	
2	1	Poorly known; overgrazing, conversion to cropland.
4	3	
4	3	Seasonally to 1,200 m.

Abbreviations Used

Snst - Sensitivity:
L - Low; **M** - Medium; **H** - High.

Strat - Foraging Strata:
T - Terrestrial; **U** - Understory; **M** - Midstory; **C** - Canopy; **A** - Aerial; **W** - Water.

Cntab - Center of Abundance:
LT - Lower tropical; **LS** - Lower subtropical; **HT** - Hill tropical; **UT** - Upper tropical; **US** - Upper subtropical; **MM** - Middle montane; **UM** - Upper montane.

Rel - Relative Abundance:
R - Rare; **U** - Uncommon; **F** - Fairly common; **C** - Common; **P** - Patchily distributed.

Min - Minimum Elevation:
L - Lowlands; **?** - Uncertain value; numeric values in meters.

Max - Maximum Elevation:
L - Lowlands; **?** - Uncertain value; **+** - species occurs at least to given elevation but likely occurs higher; numeric values in meters.

Micro - Microhabitats:
A - Army ants; **B** - Bamboo; **T** - Treefalls; **G** - Ground bromeliads; **C** - Rocky outcrops and caves; **S** - Streamside; **V** - Vine tangles; **B/V** -Bamboo/vine tangles.

Habitats:
F1 - Tropical lowland evergreen forest; **F2** - Flooded tropical evergreen forest; **F3** - River-edge forest; **F4** - Montane evergreen forest; **F5** - Elfin forest; **F6** - *Polylepis* woodland; **F7** - Tropical deciduous forest; **F8** - Gallery forest; **F9** - Southern temperate forest; **F10** - Pine forest; **F11** - Pine-oak forest; **F12** - White sand forest; **F13** - Palm forest; **F14** - Mangrove forest; **F15** - Secondary forest; **N1** - Arid lowland scrub; **N2** - Arid montane scrub; **N3** - Semihumid/humid montane scrub; **N4** - Cerrado; **N5** - Campo grasslands; **N6** - Low, seasonally wet grassland; **N7** - Southern temperate grassland; **N8** - Northern temperate grassland; **N9** - Puna grassland; **N10** - Paramo grassland; **N11** - Riparian thickets; **N12** - River island scrub; **N13** - Pastures/agricultural lands; **N14** - Second-growth scrub; **A1** - Freshwater marshes; **A2** - Saltwater/brackish marshes; **A3** - Coastal sand beaches/mudflats; **A4** - Coastal rocky beaches; **A5** - Riverine sand beaches; **A6** - Freshwater lakes and ponds; **A7** - Alkaline lakes; **A8** - Rivers; **A9** - Streams; **A10** - Bogs; **A11** - Coastal waters; **A12** - Pelagic waters.
E - Edge (used as a modifer to particular habitats).

Sub - Subregions:
ARC - Arid Caribbean Coast; **AWA** - Altiplano and Western Andes; **BAH** - Bahamas; **BAJ** - Baja California; **CAA** - Caatinga; **CAH** - Central American Highlands; **CER** - Cerrado; **CHA** - Chaco; **CHG** - Chiapas-Guanacaste; **CHL** - Chilean Desert; **CHR** - Chiriquí; **CIS** - Cocos Island; **CMV** - Cauca-Magdalena Valley; **COC** - Cuzco-Cochabamba; **CUB** - Cuba; **DOM** - Dominica; **EAS** - Eastern Slope Andes; **FDN** - Fernando de Noronha; **GAL** - Galápagos; **GCM** - Gulf Coast-Mexico; **GRE** - Grenada; **GUA** - Guadeloupe; **GUI** - Guianan; **HIS** - Hispaniola; **HPC** - Humid Pacific Coast; **ISA** - Isla Providencia and Isla San Andrés; **JAM** - Jamaica; **JFI** - Juan Fernández Islands; **MAN** - Manabí-Tumbes; **MAR** - Marañón Valley; **MID** - Madeira-Tapajós; **MON** - Montserrat; **MRT** - Martinique; **MTC** - Marañón-Cuzco; **NMM** - Northern Mexican Mountains; **NOR** - Northern Coastal Brazil; **PAR** - Pará; **PER** - Peruvian Desert; **PUE** - Puerto Rico; **RDJ** - Rio de Janeiro-Bahia Lowlands; **RMW** - Rio Madeira West; **RNW** - Rio Negro West; **SCA** - Southern Central America; **SCT** - Santa Cruz-Tucumán; **SIN** - Sinaloa-Oaxaca; **SMH** - Southern Mexican Highlands; **SMT** - Santa Marta; **SOC** - Islas Revillagigedo (Socorro Island group); **SON** - Sonoran Desert; **SOU** - Southern Atlantic Coast; **STL** - St. Lucia; **STV** - St. Vincent; **TAC** - Tacarcuna; **VAN** - Venezuelan Andes; **VNZ** - Venezuelan Coastal Mountains; **WES** - Western Andes; **YUC** - Yucatán Peninsula.
o - Endemic to region, but not restricted to a single subregion.

Zoogeographic Regions:
AMN - Northern Amazonia; **AMS** - Southern Amazonia; **ATL** - Atlantic Forest; **BSR** - Baja-Sonora; **CAN** - Central Andes; **CDH** - Chiriquí-Darién Highlands; **CHO** - Chocó Lowlands; **CSA** - Central South America; **EPC** - Equatorial Pacific Coast; **GAN** - Greater Antilles; **GCS** - Gulf-Caribbean Slope; **LAN** - Lesser Antilles; **MAH** - Madrean Highlands; **MPL** - Mexican Plateau; **NAN** - Northern Andes; **NSA** - Northern South America; **PAM** - Pampas; **PAS** - Pacific Arid Slope; **PAT** - Patagonia; **SAN** - Southern Andes; **STP** - Subtropical Pacific; **TEP** - Tepuis.

CP -Conservation Priority:
1 - Urgent; **2** - High; **3** - Medium; **4** - Low.

RP - Research Priority:
1 - High; **2** - Medium; **3** - Low.

	Snst	Strat	Cntab	Rel	Min	Max	Micro	Habitats	Sub	Zoogeographic Regions
Ptilogonys cinereus	M	C	MM	C/P	1100	3200		F11, F10	o	MAH
Phainopepla nitens	L	C	US	F/P	L	2400		N1, N2, F8		BSR, MPL, MAH
Phainoptila melanoxantha	M	U/M	MM	U	1200	3000		F4	CHR	CDH
Dulidae										
Dulus dominicus	L	C	LT	C	L	1800		F15, F7E, F1E	HIS	GAN
Cinclidae										
Cinclus leucocephalus	M	T	MM	F/P	900	3900	R	A9, A8		NAN, CAN
Cinclus mexicanus	M	T	MM	U/P	700	3100	R	A9, A8		MAH, CDH
Cinclus schulzi	M	T	UT	U	1400	2800	R	A9, A8	SCT	CAN
Troglodytidae										
Donacobius atricapillus	M	U	LT	C	L	800		A1		GCS, NSA, AMN, AMS, CSA, ATL
Campylorhynchus albobrunneus	M	M/C	LT	U/P	L	1500		F1E, F15		GCS, CHO
Campylorhynchus brunneicapillus	L	U/C	LT	C	L	2200		N1, N2		BSR, MPL, PAS
Campylorhynchus chiapensis	L	M/C	LT	U/F	L	500		F1E, N14, F15	CHG	PAS
Campylorhynchus fasciatus	L	M/C	LT	C	L	2600		F7, F8, N1, N2		EPC, CAN
Campylorhynchus griseus	L	U/C	LT	C	L	2100		N1, N2, F7, F8, F1E, F15		NSA, AMN
Campylorhynchus gularis	M	M/C	UT	F	450	2500		F11, F7, N2		PAS, MAH, GCS
Campylorhynchus jocosus	M	M/C	UT	F	1000	2400		F11, N2	SMH	MAH
Campylorhynchus megalopterus	M	M/C	UM	F	2000	3200		F10, F11	o	MAH
Campylorhynchus nuchalis	L	M/C	LT	C	L	800		F7E, F8, F1E, F15, F14	ARC	NSA
Campylorhynchus rufinucha	L	M/C	LT	C	L	1500		F7, F8, F15, N1		PAS, GCS
Campylorhynchus turdinus	L	M/C	LT	C	L	1100		F1E, F15, F7, F2		AMN, AMS, CSA, ATL
Campylorhynchus yucatanicus	M	U/C	LT	F	L	L		N1	YUC	GCS
Campylorhynchus zonatus	L	M/C	UT	C	L	2300		F11, F4E, F1E, N2		PAS, MAH, GCS, CDH, CHO, NSA
Odontorchilus branickii	H	C	UT	U	800	2000		F4		NAN, CAN
Odontorchilus cinereus	H	C	LT	U	L	600		F1	o	AMS
Salpinctes mexicanus	L	T	US	F	L	3600	R	N2, N1		BSR, MPL, MAH
Salpinctes obsoletus	L	T	US	F	L	3100	R	N2, N1		BSR, MPL, MAH, CDH
Hylorchilus sumichrasti	H	T	LT	R	L	950	R	F1		PAS, GCS
Cinnycerthia peruana	H	U	UM	C	1500	3350	B	F4		NAN, CAN
Cinnycerthia unirufa	H	U	UM	F	2200	3400	B	F4, F5	o	NAN
Cistothorus apolinari	M	U	UM	F/P	2000	4000		N10	EAS	NAN
Cistothorus meridae	M	U	UM	F	3000	4100		N10	VAN	NAN
Cistothorus palustris	M	U	US	F	L	2500		A1, A2		BSR, MPL
Cistothorus platensis										
platensis	L	U	UM	F/P	L	4600		N10, N5, N6, A1, N13		NAN, CAN, SAN, NSA, TEP, CSA, PAM, PAT,
stellaris	M	U	MM	U/P	L	2700		N6, A1		MAH, GCS, CDH
Thryomanes bewickii	M	U/M	US	F	L	2900		N1, F11, N2, N11, F8		BSR, MPL, MAH
Thryomanes sissonii	M	U	LT	U	L	1050		F7, N1	SOC	PAS
Ferminia cerverai	H	U	LT	R	L	L		A1	CUB	GAN
Thryothorus atrogularis	L	U	LT	F	L	1100		F1E, F15	SCA	GCS
Thryothorus coraya	L	U	LT	F	L	1400		F1, F2, F15		TEP, AMN, AMS
Thryothorus eisenmanni	L	U	UM	F	1800	3400	B	F4	MTC	CAN
Thryothorus euophrys	L	U	UM	F	1900	3300	B	F4		NAN, CAN
Thryothorus fasciatoventris	M	U	LT	F	L	1000	S	F1E, F15, N14		GCS, CHO, NSA
Thryothorus felix	L	U	LT	F	L	1900		F7, F8, F15, N1?		PAS, MAH
Thryothorus genibarbis										
genibarbis	L	U	LT	F	L	1600		F1E, F4E, F3, F8, F15		CAN, AMS, CSA, ATL
mystacalis	L	U	UT	F	800	2400		F4E, F1E, F8, F15		CHO, EPC, NAN
Thryothorus griseus	L	U/M	LT	F	L	L	V	F2	RMW	AMS
Thryothorus guarayanus	L	U	LT	C	L	600		F1E, F8, F15, F2, F7E	CER	CSA
Thryothorus leucopogon	M	U/M	LT	U	L	900		F1E		GCS, CHO
Thryothorus leucotis	L	U	LT	C	L	600		F1E, F8, F15, F2, F14		NSA, AMN, AMS, CSA

CP	RP	Notes
4	3	
4	3	Mistletoe specialist.
4	3	
4	3	
4	2	Monitor (water pollution).
4	3	Occasionally to 100 m.
3	1	Seasonally to 700 m; water pollution; survey
4	3	Mainly near forest.
4	3	
4	3	
4	3	
4	3	
4	3	
4	3	
4	3	Occasionally to 300 m.
4	3	Occasionally to 1,500 m.
4	3	
4	3	
4	3	
4	3	
4	3	Locally to 3,000 m.
3	2	Occasionally to 2,400 m; deforestation.
3	2	
4	3	Also occurs on tall buildings in Mexican cities.
4	3	
2	1	Deforestation; not known from reserves; survey.
4	3	Occasionally to 900 m.
4	3	Locally to 1,800 m (Venezuela) and 3,800 m (Colombia).
2	2	Survey.
3	2	Monitor.
4	3	
3	2	Habitat destruction.
3	2	Some Middle American populations threatened.
4	3	
2	1	Survey.
1	1	Endemic to Zapata Swamp; habitat destruction; burning.
4	3	
4	3	Locally to 2,400 m.
4	3	
4	2	May contain two species.
4	3	
4	3	
4	3	Occasionally to 2,300 m.
4	2	Locally to lowlands (western Ecuador).
4	2	Poorly known.
4	3	
4	3	
4	3	Occasionally to 950 m.

Abbreviations Used

Snst - Sensitivity:
L - Low; **M** - Medium; **H** - High.

Strat - Foraging Strata:
T - Terrestrial; **U** - Understory; **M** - Midstory; **C** - Canopy; **A** - Aerial; **W** - Water.

Cntab - Center of Abundance:
LT - Lower tropical; **LS** - Lower subtropical; **HT** - Hill tropical; **UT** - Upper tropical; **US** - Upper subtropical; **MM** - Middle montane; **UM** - Upper montane.

Rel - Relative Abundance:
R - Rare; **U** - Uncommon; **F** - Fairly common; **C** - Common; **P** - Patchily distributed.

Min - Minimum Elevation:
L - Lowlands; **?** - Uncertain value; numeric values in meters.

Max - Maximum Elevation:
L - Lowlands; **?** - Uncertain value; **+** - species occurs at least to given elevation but likely occurs higher; numeric values in meters.

Micro - Microhabitats:
A - Army ants; **B** - Bamboo; **T** - Treefalls; **G** - Ground bromeliads; **C** - Rocky outcrops and caves; **S** - Streamside; **V** - Vine tangles; **B/V** -Bamboo/vine tangles.

Habitats:
F1 - Tropical lowland evergreen forest; **F2** - Flooded tropical evergreen forest; **F3** - River-edge forest; **F4** - Montane evergreen forest; **F5** - Elfin forest; **F6** - *Polylepis* woodland; **F7** - Tropical deciduous forest; **F8** - Gallery forest; **F9** - Southern temperate forest; **F10** - Pine forest; **F11** - Pine-oak forest; **F12** - White sand forest; **F13** - Palm forest; **F14** - Mangrove forest; **F15** - Secondary forest; **N1** - Arid lowland scrub; **N2** - Arid montane scrub; **N3** - Semihumid/humid montane scrub; **N4** - Cerrado; **N5** - Campo grasslands; **N6** - Low, seasonally wet grassland; **N7** - Southern temperate grassland; **N8** - Northern temperate grassland; **N9** - Puna grassland; **N10** - Paramo grassland; **N11** - Riparian thickets; **N12** - River island scrub; **N13** - Pastures/agricultural lands; **N14** - Second-growth scrub; **A1** - Freshwater marshes; **A2** - Saltwater/brackish marshes; **A3** - Coastal sand beaches/mudflats; **A4** - Coastal rocky beaches; **A5** - Riverine sand beaches; **A6** - Freshwater lakes and ponds; **A7** - Alkaline lakes; **A8** - Rivers; **A9** - Streams; **A10** - Bogs; **A11** - Coastal waters; **A12** - Pelagic waters.
E - Edge (used as a modifer to particular habitats).

Sub - Subregions:
ARC - Arid Caribbean Coast; **AWA** - Altiplano and Western Andes; **BAH** - Bahamas; **BAJ** - Baja California; **CAA** - Caatinga; **CAH** - Central American Highlands; **CER** - Cerrado; **CHA** - Chaco; **CHG** - Chiapas-Guanacaste; **CHL** - Chilean Desert; **CHR** - Chiriquí; **CIS** - Cocos Island; **CMV** - Cauca-Magdalena Valley; **COC** - Cuzco-Cochabamba; **CUB** - Cuba; **DOM** - Dominica; **EAS** - Eastern Slope Andes; **FDN** - Fernando de Noronha; **GAL** - Galápagos; **GCM** - Gulf Coast-Mexico; **GRE** - Grenada; **GUA** - Guadeloupe; **GUI** - Guianan; **HIS** - Hispaniola; **HPC** - Humid Pacific Coast; **ISA** - Isla Providencia and Isla San Andrés; **JAM** - Jamaica; **JFI** - Juan Fernández Islands; **MAN** - Manabí-Tumbes; **MAR** - Marañón Valley; **MID** - Madeira-Tapajós; **MON** - Montserrat; **MRT** - Martinique; **MTC** - Marañón-Cuzco; **NMM** - Northern Mexican Mountains; **NOR** - Northern Coastal Brazil; **PAR** - Pará; **PER** - Peruvian Desert; **PUE** - Puerto Rico; **RDJ** - Rio de Janeiro-Bahia Lowlands; **RMW** - Rio Madeira West; **RNW** - Rio Negro West; **SCA** - Southern Central America; **SCT** - Santa Cruz-Tucumán; **SIN** - Sinaloa-Oaxaca; **SMH** - Southern Mexican Highlands; **SMT** - Santa Marta; **SOC** - Islas Revillagigedo (Socorro Island group); **SON** - Sonoran Desert; **SOU** - Southern Atlantic Coast; **STL** - St. Lucia; **STV** - St. Vincent; **TAC** - Tacarcuna; **VAN** - Venezuelan Andes; **VNZ** - Venezuelan Coastal Mountains; **WES** - Western Andes; **YUC** - Yucatán Peninsula.
o - Endemic to region, but not restricted to a single subregion.

Zoogeographic Regions:
AMN - Northern Amazonia; **AMS** - Southern Amazonia; **ATL** - Atlantic Forest; **BSR** - Baja-Sonora; **CAN** - Central Andes; **CDH** - Chiriquí-Darién Highlands; **CHO** - Chocó Lowlands; **CSA** - Central South America; **EPC** - Equatorial Pacific Coast; **GAN** - Greater Antilles; **GCS** - Gulf-Caribbean Slope; **LAN** - Lesser Antilles; **MAH** - Madrean Highlands; **MPL** - Mexican Plateau; **NAN** - Northern Andes; **NSA** - Northern South America; **PAM** - Pampas; **PAS** - Pacific Arid Slope; **PAT** - Patagonia; **SAN** - Southern Andes; **STP** - Subtropical Pacific; **TEP** - Tepuis.

CP -Conservation Priority:
1 - Urgent; **2** - High; **3** - Medium; **4** - Low.

RP - Research Priority:
1 - High; **2** - Medium; **3** - Low.

	Snst	Strat	Cntab	Rel	Min	Max	Micro	Habitats	Sub	Zoogeographic Regions
Thryothorus longirostris	L	U	LT	F	L	800		F1E, F15, F7, F12		CSA, ATL
Thryothorus ludovicianus										
albinucha	L	U	LT	F	L	L		F7, F8, F15	o	GCS
ludovicianus	L	U	LT	C	L	2200		F7, F8, F15		MAH, GCS
Thryothorus maculipectus										
colombianus	?	U	UT	?	1300	2000		F4E, F15	EAS	NAN
maculipectus	L	U/M	LT	F	L	1300		F1E, F15, F7		PAS, GCS
paucimaculatus	M	U	LT	C	L	1250		F7, F15	MAN	EPC
sclateri	M	U	UT?	F	L	1700		F7, N11, F4E	MAR	CAN
Thryothorus modestus	L	U	LT	C	L	1900		F7E, F1E, N14		PAS, MAH, GCS, CDH
Thryothorus nicefori	?	U	UT	?	1100	1100		N2?	EAS	NAN
Thryothorus nigricapillus	L	U	LT	C	L	1400		F1E, N14, F15		GCS, CHO
Thryothorus pleurostictus	M	U	LT	C	L	1750		F7, N1		PAS, MAH
Thryothorus rufalbus	M	U	LT	F	L	1600		F1E, F4E, F7, F8, F15		PAS, MAH, GCS, CDH, NSA
Thryothorus rutilus	L	U/M	LT	F	L	1700		F1E, F15		GCS, NSA
Thryothorus semibadius	L	U	LT	U/P	L	1200	S	F1E	HPC	GCS
Thryothorus sinaloa	L	U	LT	C	L	2100		F7, F8, F14?		PAS, MAH
Thryothorus spadix	H	U/M	HT	F	400	1800		F4, F1		GCS, CDH, CHO, NAN
Thryothorus superciliaris	L	U	LT	C	L	1200		F7, F8, N1, F1E, F14	MAN	EPC
Thryothorus thoracicus	M	U/M	LT	U/F	L	1000		F1E, F15	o	GCS
Troglodytes aedon										
aedon	L	T/U	LT	C	L	4600		N14, N1, N2, N3, N4		BSR, MPL, PAS, MAH, GCS, CDH, CHO, EPC, STP, NAN, CAN, SAN, NSA, TEP, AMN, AMS, CSA, ATL, PAM, PAT
beani	L	U	LT	F	L	L		F7, N14, F15	YUC	GCS
martinicensis	L	U	LT	R	L	900		F1, F7, F15, N14	o	LAN
Troglodytes browni	M	U	UM	F	2800	3600	B	F5, F4E	CHR	CDH
Troglodytes ochraceus	M	M	MM	F	900	2500		F4	o	CDH
Troglodytes rufociliatus	M	M	MM	F	1700	3200		F4, F11	CAH	MAH
Troglodytes rufulus	H	U	MM	U/P	1000	2800		F4E, F5	o	TEP
Troglodytes solstitialis										
monticola	?	M	UM	?	3200	4500		F5	SMT	NAN
solstitialis	M	M	MM	F	1100	3600		F4, F5		NAN, CAN
Troglodytes tanneri	L	U	LT	F	L	L		N1	SOC	PAS
Uropsila leucogastra	M	U/M	LT	F	L	L	V	F7, F1, F15		PAS, GCS
Henicorhina leucophrys	M	U	UT	C	900	3000		F4		MAH, CDH, NAN, CAN
Henicorhina leucoptera	H	U	MM	F	1350	2450		F5		NAN, CAN
Henicorhina leucosticta	M	U	HT	F	L	1100		F1, F4		PAS, MAH, GCS, CDH, CHO, NSA, TEP, AMN, AMS
Microcerculus bambla	H	T/U	LT	F/P	L	1100		F1		AMN, AMS
Microcerculus marginatus	H	T/U	LT	F	L	1200		F1		GCS, CHO, NSA, AMN, AMS
Microcerculus philomela	H	T/U	HT	F	L	1400		F1	o	GCS
Microcerculus ustulatus	H	T/U	UT	F	1200	2100		F4	o	TEP
Cyphorhinus aradus	H	T/U	LT	F	L	1100		F1		AMN, AMS
Cyphorhinus phaeocephalus	M	T/U	LT	F	L	1000		F1		GCS, CHO
Cyphorhinus thoracicus	H	T/U	UT	F/P	800	2650		F4		NAN, CAN
Mimidae										
Melanoptila glabrirostris	M	U	LT	F	L	L		F7E, F1E, F15	YUC	GCS
Melanotis caerulescens	M	U	UT/MM	F	L	3200		F4E, F11, F7, F15		PAS, MAH, GCS
Melanotis hypoleucus	M	U	UT/MM	F	900	3000		F4E, F11, F15	CAH	MAH
Mimus dorsalis	M	C	UM	F	2300	3500		N2, N14, N13	AWA	CAN
Mimus gilvus	L	C	LT	C	L	2600		N1, N2, N14, F15, F7E, F1E, F12		PAS, MAH, GCS, NAN, NSA, AMN, AMS, ATL
Mimus gundlachii	L	C	LT	F	L	L		N1, N14, F7E, F1E	o	GAN

CP	RP	Notes
4	3	
3	2	Locally to 1,200 m (Guatemala).
4	3	
3	2	Poorly known.
4	3	
3	2	
3	2	Poorly known.
4	3	
2	1	Poorly known; relationship to *T. rufalbus* needs study.
4	2	Rarely to 1,800 m.
4	3	
4	3	
4	3	Locally to 1,900 m (Colombia).
4	3	
4	3	
4	3	
4	3	
4	3	
4	2	May contain multiple species.
3	2	
2	1	Many races very rare or extinct.
4	3	Occasionally to 2,200 m.
4	3	Locally to 3,000 m.
4	3	
4	2	Poorly known.
3	2	Poorly known.
4	3	Occasionally to 700 m.
2	1	Poorly known; declining? habitat destruction.
4	3	
4	3	Occasionally to 400 m.
2	1	Deforestation.
4	3	Locally to 1,800 m (Middle America and Tepuis).
4	2	Occasionally to 1,500 m.
4	3	Locally to 1,700 m; may contain two species.
3	2	Deforestation; see Stiles (1983b) for taxonomy.
4	3	Occasionally to 850 m.
4	3	
4	3	
4	3	Occasionally to 3,000 m.
4	3	
4	3	Mainly breeds above 700 m.
4	3	Occasionally to 600 m.
4	3	
4	3	
4	3	

Abbreviations Used

Snst - Sensitivity:
L - Low; **M** - Medium; **H** - High.

Strat - Foraging Strata:
T - Terrestrial; **U** - Understory; **M** - Midstory; **C** - Canopy; **A** - Aerial; **W** - Water.

Cntab - Center of Abundance:
LT - Lower tropical; **LS** - Lower subtropical; **HT** - Hill tropical; **UT** - Upper tropical; **US** - Upper subtropical; **MM** - Middle montane; **UM** - Upper montane.

Rel - Relative Abundance:
R - Rare; **U** - Uncommon; **F** - Fairly common; **C** - Common; **P** - Patchily distributed.

Min - Minimum Elevation:
L - Lowlands; **?** - Uncertain value; numeric values in meters.

Max - Maximum Elevation:
L - Lowlands; **?** - Uncertain value; **+** - species occurs at least to given elevation but likely occurs higher; numeric values in meters.

Micro - Microhabitats:
A - Army ants; **B** - Bamboo; **T** - Treefalls; **G** - Ground bromeliads; **C** - Rocky outcrops and caves; **S** - Streamside; **V** - Vine tangles; **B/V** -Bamboo/vine tangles.

Habitats:
F1 - Tropical lowland evergreen forest; **F2** - Flooded tropical evergreen forest; **F3** - River-edge forest; **F4** - Montane evergreen forest; **F5** - Elfin forest; **F6** - *Polylepis* woodland; **F7** - Tropical deciduous forest; **F8** - Gallery forest; **F9** - Southern temperate forest; **F10** - Pine forest; **F11** - Pine-oak forest; **F12** - White sand forest; **F13** - Palm forest; **F14** - Mangrove forest; **F15** - Secondary forest; **N1** - Arid lowland scrub; **N2** - Arid montane scrub; **N3** - Semihumid/humid montane scrub; **N4** - Cerrado; **N5** - Campo grasslands; **N6** - Low, seasonally wet grassland; **N7** - Southern temperate grassland; **N8** - Northern temperate grassland; **N9** - Puna grassland; **N10** - Paramo grassland; **N11** - Riparian thickets; **N12** - River island scrub; **N13** - Pastures/agricultural lands; **N14** - Second-growth scrub; **A1** - Freshwater marshes; **A2** - Saltwater/brackish marshes; **A3** - Coastal sand beaches/mudflats; **A4** - Coastal rocky beaches; **A5** - Riverine sand beaches; **A6** - Freshwater lakes and ponds; **A7** - Alkaline lakes; **A8** - Rivers; **A9** - Streams; **A10** - Bogs; **A11** - Coastal waters; **A12** - Pelagic waters.
E - Edge (used as a modifer to particular habitats).

Sub - Subregions:
ARC - Arid Caribbean Coast; **AWA** - Altiplano and Western Andes; **BAH** - Bahamas; **BAJ** - Baja California; **CAA** - Caatinga; **CAH** - Central American Highlands; **CER** - Cerrado; **CHA** - Chaco; **CHG** - Chiapas-Guanacaste; **CHL** - Chilean Desert; **CHR** - Chiriquí; **CIS** - Cocos Island; **CMV** - Cauca-Magdalena Valley; **COC** - Cuzco-Cochabamba; **CUB** - Cuba; **DOM** - Dominica; **EAS** - Eastern Slope Andes; **FDN** - Fernando de Noronha; **GAL** - Galápagos; **GCM** - Gulf Coast-Mexico; **GRE** - Grenada; **GUA** - Guadeloupe; **GUI** - Guianan; **HIS** - Hispaniola; **HPC** - Humid Pacific Coast; **ISA** - Isla Providencia and Isla San Andrés; **JAM** - Jamaica; **JFI** - Juan Fernández Islands; **MAN** - Manabí-Tumbes; **MAR** - Marañón Valley; **MID** - Madeira-Tapajós; **MON** - Montserrat; **MRT** - Martinique; **MTC** - Marañón-Cuzco; **NMM** - Northern Mexican Mountains; **NOR** - Northern Coastal Brazil; **PAR** - Pará; **PER** - Peruvian Desert; **PUE** - Puerto Rico; **RDJ** - Rio de Janeiro-Bahia Lowlands; **RMW** - Rio Madeira West; **RNW** - Rio Negro West; **SCA** - Southern Central America; **SCT** - Santa Cruz-Tucumán; **SIN** - Sinaloa-Oaxaca; **SMH** - Southern Mexican Highlands; **SMT** - Santa Marta; **SOC** - Islas Revillagigedo (Socorro Island group); **SON** - Sonoran Desert; **SOU** - Southern Atlantic Coast; **STL** - St. Lucia; **STV** - St. Vincent; **TAC** - Tacarcuna; **VAN** - Venezuelan Andes; **VNZ** - Venezuelan Coastal Mountains; **WES** - Western Andes; **YUC** - Yucatán Peninsula.
o - Endemic to region, but not restricted to a single subregion.

Zoogeographic Regions:
AMN - Northern Amazonia; **AMS** - Southern Amazonia; **ATL** - Atlantic Forest; **BSR** - Baja-Sonora; **CAN** - Central Andes; **CDH** - Chiriquí-Darién Highlands; **CHO** - Chocó Lowlands; **CSA** - Central South America; **EPC** - Equatorial Pacific Coast; **GAN** - Greater Antilles; **GCS** - Gulf-Caribbean Slope; **LAN** - Lesser Antilles; **MAH** - Madrean Highlands; **MPL** - Mexican Plateau; **NAN** - Northern Andes; **NSA** - Northern South America; **PAM** - Pampas; **PAS** - Pacific Arid Slope; **PAT** - Patagonia; **SAN** - Southern Andes; **STP** - Subtropical Pacific; **TEP** - Tepuis.

CP -Conservation Priority:
1 - Urgent; **2** - High; **3** - Medium; **4** - Low.

RP - Research Priority:
1 - High; **2** - Medium; **3** - Low.

	Snst	Strat	Cntab	Rel	Min	Max	Micro	Habitats	Sub	Zoogeographic Regions
Mimus longicaudatus	L	C	LT	C	L	2100		N1, N2, F8, F7E		EPC, STP, CAN
Mimus patagonicus	L	C	LS	F	L	1000		N1, N14?		SAN, CSA, PAM, PAT
Mimus polyglottos	L	C	LS	C	L	3100		N1, N2, N14, F15E, F7E		GAN, BSR, MPL, PAS, MAH, GCS
Mimus saturninus	L	C	LT	C	L	1200		N1, N2, N4, N14		CAN, AMN, AMS, CSA, ATL, PAM
Mimus thenca	L	C	LS	F	L	800		N1, N14	CHL	STP
Mimus triurus	L	C	LS	F	L	700		N1, N14, N2		CSA, PAM, PAT
Nesomimus macdonaldi	L	T/U	LT	C	L	L		N1, F7	GAL	EPC
Nesomimus melanotis	L	T/U	LT	C	L	L		N1, F7	GAL	EPC
Nesomimus parvulus	L	T/U	LT	C	L	1500		N1, F7	GAL	EPC
Nesomimus trifasciatus	L	T/U	LT	U	L	L		N1, F7	GAL	EPC
Mimodes graysoni	M	T/C	HT	R	L	900		F7, N1	SOC	PAS
Toxostoma bendirei	M	T/U	LS	F	L	1600		N1		BSR, PAS
Toxostoma cinereum	H	T/U	LS	F	L	1500		N1	BAJ	BSR
Toxostoma crissale	M	T	LS	F	L	2400		N11, N2, N1		BSR, MPL
Toxostoma curvirostre	L	T/U	LS	C	L	3300		N1, N2		BSR, MPL, PAS, MAH, GCS
Toxostoma guttatum	L	T/U	LT	U	L	L		N1, F7E	YUC	GCS
Toxostoma lecontei	M	T	LS	U	L	L		N1		BSR
Toxostoma longirostre	L	T/U	LS	F	L	1550		N11, N1, F7E		MAH, GCS
Toxostoma ocellatum	H	T/U	MM	U	1500	2900		N2, F11	SMH	MAH
Toxostoma redivivum	L	T	LS	C	L	2000		N1, N11		BSR
Cinclocerthia ruficauda	L	U/M	LT	C	L	900+		F1, F7, F15	o	LAN
Ramphocinclus brachyurus	M	T/U	LT	R	L	300		F7	o	LAN
Margarops fuscatus	L	U/C	LT	C	L	900+		N1, F1, F7, F15		GAN, LAN
Allenia fusca	L	U/C	LT	C	L	900+		N1, F1, F7, F15	o	LAN
Muscicapidae										
Turdinae										
Sialia mexicana	L	M/C	MM	F	1200	4000		F10, F11		BSR, MPL, MAH
Sialia sialis	L	M/C	MM	F	700	3000		F11, N2		MPL, MAH, GCS
Myadestes coloratus	M	M/C	UT	F	800	2200		F4	TAC	CDH
Myadestes elisabeth	M	C	UT?	F	L	2000+		F10, F1	CUB	GAN
Myadestes genibarbis	H	C	HT	F	L	1800+		F1, F4		GAN, LAN
Myadestes leucogenys	H	M/C	UT	U/P	550	1400		F1, F4		NAN, CAN, TEP, ATL
Myadestes melanops	M	M/C	MM	C	900	2800		F4	CHR	CDH
Myadestes obscurus	H	M/C	MM	C	900	3050		F11, F4, F1		PAS, MAH
Myadestes ralloides	M	M/C	MM	C	800	2900		F4, F15		NAN, CAN
Myadestes townsendi	M	C	US	F	1600	3100		F10, N2		MPL, MAH
Myadestes unicolor	M	M/C	UT	F	800	2500		F4, F11	o	MAH
Entomodestes coracinus	H	M/C	UT	U/P	400	1900		F4, F1	WES	NAN
Entomodestes leucotis	H	M/C	MM	F	900	2700		F4	o	CAN
Zoothera pinicola	H	T/M	MM	U/P	1850	3100		F11, F10	o	MAH
Cichlherminia lherminieri	M	?	LT	U	L	1000		F1, F15	o	LAN
Catharus aurantiirostris	L	T/U	UT	C	400	2300		F4E, F1E, F15, F11, F7		MAH, CDH, NAN, NSA
Catharus dryas	H	T/U	UT	F	700	2300		F4		MAH, CDH, NAN, CAN
Catharus frantzii	M	T/U	UM	C	1250	3100		F4, F11		MAH, CDH
Catharus fuscater	H	T/U	MM	F	800	3000		F4		CDH, NAN, CAN
Catharus gracilirostris	L	T/U	UM	C	2100	3500		F4, F5, N14	CHR	CDH
Catharus mexicanus	M	T/U	UT	F	600	1800		F4, F1		MAH, GCS, CDH
Catharus occidentalis	M	T/U	UM	F	1500	3700		F11, F4	o	MAH
Platycichla flavipes	M	M/C	UT	C	600	2500		F4, F1, F15		NAN, NSA, TEP, ATL
Platycichla leucops	H	M/C	UT	F/P	900	2100		F4		NAN, CAN, TEP
Turdus albicollis	M	U/M	LT	F	L	1900		F1		NSA, AMN, AMS, ATL
Turdus amaurochalinus	L	T/C	LT	C	L	1250		F1E, F7, F15, F8		CSA, ATL, PAM

CP	RP	Notes
4	3	Occasionally to 2,700 m.
4	3	Locally to 1,800 m.
4	3	
4	3	Locally to 2,500 m (Andes).
4	3	
4	2	Locally to 2,500 m+; breeding range poorly known.
4	3	
4	3	
4	3	
3	2	Small population.
1	1	Occasionally to 950 m; introduced predators, habitat destruction; monitor.
4	3	
4	3	
4	3	
4	3	
3	2	Survey.
4	2	
4	3	
3	2	Poorly known.
4	3	
4	3	
1	1	Habitat destruction.
4	3	
4	3	
4	3	Winters locally in lowlands.
4	3	Locally in lowlands; lower elevations in winter.
3	3	Deforestation.
4	3	
4	2	
3	2	Occasionally to 300 m; deforestation; survey.
4	3	Seasonally to 450 m (Costa Rica).
4	3	Locally to lowlands (Tres Marias Islands).
4	3	Occasionally to 3,300 m.
4	3	Winters irregularly at lower elevations.
3	3	Deforestation.
4	2	Elevational movements?
4	3	Nonbreeders wander to 3,350 m.
4	2	Distribution and behavior poorly known.
2	1	Deforestation; survey.
4	3	Occasionally to 2,900 m; locally to lowlands.
4	3	Occasionally to 3,000 m.
4	3	
4	3	Locally to 600 m.
4	3	Seasonally to 1,500 m.
4	3	Locally to 300 m.
4	3	
4	2	Seasonal movements poorly understood.
4	3	Locally to 3,000 m.
4	2	May include two species.
4	3	Locally to 2,600 m.

Abbreviations Used

Snst - Sensitivity:
L - Low; **M** - Medium; **H** - High.

Strat - Foraging Strata:
T - Terrestrial; **U** - Understory; **M** - Midstory; **C** - Canopy; **A** - Aerial; **W** - Water.

Cntab - Center of Abundance:
LT - Lower tropical; **LS** - Lower subtropical; **HT** - Hill tropical; **UT** - Upper tropical; **US** - Upper subtropical; **MM** - Middle montane; **UM** - Upper montane.

Rel - Relative Abundance:
R - Rare; **U** - Uncommon; **F** - Fairly common; **C** - Common; **P** - Patchily distributed.

Min - Minimum Elevation:
L - Lowlands; **?** - Uncertain value; numeric values in meters.

Max - Maximum Elevation:
L - Lowlands; **?** - Uncertain value; **+** - species occurs at least to given elevation but likely occurs higher; numeric values in meters.

Micro - Microhabitats:
A - Army ants; **B** - Bamboo; **T** - Treefalls; **G** - Ground bromeliads; **C** - Rocky outcrops and caves; **S** - Streamside; **V** - Vine tangles; **B/V** -Bamboo/vine tangles.

Habitats:
F1 - Tropical lowland evergreen forest; **F2** - Flooded tropical evergreen forest; **F3** - River-edge forest; **F4** - Montane evergreen forest; **F5** - Elfin forest; **F6** - *Polylepis* woodland; **F7** - Tropical deciduous forest; **F8** - Gallery forest; **F9** - Southern temperate forest; **F10** - Pine forest; **F11** - Pine-oak forest; **F12** - White sand forest; **F13** - Palm forest; **F14** - Mangrove forest; **F15** - Secondary forest; **N1** - Arid lowland scrub; **N2** - Arid montane scrub; **N3** - Semihumid/humid montane scrub; **N4** - Cerrado; **N5** - Campo grasslands; **N6** - Low, seasonally wet grassland; **N7** - Southern temperate grassland; **N8** - Northern temperate grassland; **N9** - Puna grassland; **N10** - Paramo grassland; **N11** - Riparian thickets; **N12** - River island scrub; **N13** - Pastures/agricultural lands; **N14** - Second-growth scrub; **A1** - Freshwater marshes; **A2** - Saltwater/brackish marshes; **A3** - Coastal sand beaches/mudflats; **A4** - Coastal rocky beaches; **A5** - Riverine sand beaches; **A6** - Freshwater lakes and ponds; **A7** - Alkaline lakes; **A8** - Rivers; **A9** - Streams; **A10** - Bogs; **A11** - Coastal waters; **A12** - Pelagic waters.
E - Edge (used as a modifer to particular habitats).

Sub - Subregions:
ARC - Arid Caribbean Coast; **AWA** - Altiplano and Western Andes; **BAH** - Bahamas; **BAJ** - Baja California; **CAA** - Caatinga; **CAH** - Central American Highlands; **CER** - Cerrado; **CHA** - Chaco; **CHG** - Chiapas-Guanacaste; **CHL** - Chilean Desert; **CHR** - Chiriquí; **CIS** - Cocos Island; **CMV** - Cauca-Magdalena Valley; **COC** - Cuzco-Cochabamba; **CUB** - Cuba; **DOM** - Dominica; **EAS** - Eastern Slope Andes; **FDN** - Fernando de Noronha; **GAL** - Galápagos; **GCM** - Gulf Coast-Mexico; **GRE** - Grenada; **GUA** - Guadeloupe; **GUI** - Guianan; **HIS** - Hispaniola; **HPC** - Humid Pacific Coast; **ISA** - Isla Providencia and Isla San Andrés; **JAM** - Jamaica; **JFI** - Juan Fernández Islands; **MAN** - Manabí-Tumbes; **MAR** - Marañón Valley; **MID** - Madeira-Tapajós; **MON** - Montserrat; **MRT** - Martinique; **MTC** - Marañón-Cuzco; **NMM** - Northern Mexican Mountains; **NOR** - Northern Coastal Brazil; **PAR** - Pará; **PER** - Peruvian Desert; **PUE** - Puerto Rico; **RDJ** - Rio de Janeiro-Bahia Lowlands; **RMW** - Rio Madeira West; **RNW** - Rio Negro West; **SCA** - Southern Central America; **SCT** - Santa Cruz-Tucumán; **SIN** - Sinaloa-Oaxaca; **SMH** - Southern Mexican Highlands; **SMT** - Santa Marta; **SOC** - Islas Revillagigedo (Socorro Island group); **SON** - Sonoran Desert; **SOU** - Southern Atlantic Coast; **STL** - St. Lucia; **STV** - St. Vincent; **TAC** - Tacarcuna; **VAN** - Venezuelan Andes; **VNZ** - Venezuelan Coastal Mountains; **WES** - Western Andes; **YUC** - Yucatán Peninsula.
o - Endemic to region, but not restricted to a single subregion.

Zoogeographic Regions:
AMN - Northern Amazonia; **AMS** - Southern Amazonia; **ATL** - Atlantic Forest; **BSR** - Baja-Sonora; **CAN** - Central Andes; **CDH** - Chiriquí-Darién Highlands; **CHO** - Chocó Lowlands; **CSA** - Central South America; **EPC** - Equatorial Pacific Coast; **GAN** - Greater Antilles; **GCS** - Gulf-Caribbean Slope; **LAN** - Lesser Antilles; **MAH** - Madrean Highlands; **MPL** - Mexican Plateau; **NAN** - Northern Andes; **NSA** - Northern South America; **PAM** - Pampas; **PAS** - Pacific Arid Slope; **PAT** - Patagonia; **SAN** - Southern Andes; **STP** - Subtropical Pacific; **TEP** - Tepuis.

CP -Conservation Priority:
1 - Urgent; **2** - High; **3** - Medium; **4** - Low.

RP - Research Priority:
1 - High; **2** - Medium; **3** - Low.

	Snst	Strat	Cntab	Rel	Min	Max	Micro	Habitats	Sub	Zoogeographic Regions
Turdus assimilis	M	U/M	UT	F	L	3100		F4, F1, F7		PAS, MAH, GCS, CDH, CHO
Turdus aurantius	L	T/M	HT	F	L	1800		F4, F1, F15	JAM	GAN
Turdus chiguanco	L	T/C	UM	C	1200	4300		F15, N3, N2, N14		STP, NAN, CAN, SAN
Turdus falcklandii	L	T/C	LS	C	L	2100		F9, F15, N14		STP, SAN, PAT
Turdus fulviventris	M	T/C	MM	U	1300	2700		F4, F15	o	NAN
Turdus fumigatus	M	T/M	LT	F	L	1400		F2, F8, F1		LAN, NSA, AMN, AMS, ATL
Turdus fuscater	L	T/C	UM	C	1800	4100		F4, F4E, F15, N3, N14		NAN, CAN
Turdus grayi	L	T/M	LT	C	L	2500		F1E, F7, F15		PAS, MAH, GCS, CDH, NSA
Turdus haplochrous	H	U/M	LT	U	L	L		F8	CHA	CSA
Turdus hauxwelli	H	U/M	LT	F	L	800		F2, F3, F1?		AMN, AMS
Turdus ignobilis	L	T/C	LT	C	L	2100		F3, F8, F12, F15, F1E, F4E		NSA, TEP, AMN, AMS
Turdus infuscatus	H	M/C	MM	F	900	3100		F4, F11	o	MAH
Turdus jamaicensis	M	T/C	UT	F	L	1800		F4, F1, F15	JAM	GAN
Turdus lawrencii	H	C	LT	U/P	L	L		F2, F1		AMN, AMS
Turdus leucomelas	L	T/C	LT	C	L	1800		F1E, F7, F8, F15		NSA, AMN, AMS, CSA, ATL
Turdus maranonicus	M	C	UT	F	600	2200		F7, F8	MAR	CAN
Turdus migratorius	L	T/C	MM	C	1200	4000		F11, F10, F15		BSR, MPL, MAH
Turdus nigrescens	L	T/M	UM	F	2200	3500		F4E, N3, N14	CHR	CDH
Turdus nigriceps										
nigriceps	M	C	UT	F	600	2100		F4, F1		NAN, SAN
subalaris	L	C	LT	F	L	1200		F1, F15, F9	SOU	ATL
Turdus nudigenis										
maculirostris	M	T/M	HT	U	L	1600		F7	MAN	EPC
nudigenis	L	T/M	LT	F	L	1600		F7, F8, F15, F1E		LAN, NSA, AMN
Turdus obsoletus	M	U/M	HT	F	500	1900		F4, F1, F15		GCS?, CDH, CHO, NAN
Turdus olivater	L	C	UT	C	800	2600		F4, N3, F15		NAN, TEP
Turdus plebejus	M	T/C	MM	C	1200	3000		F4, F11, F15		MAH, CDH
Turdus plumbeus	L	T/C	LT	C	L	1200+		F7, F1, F4, F15		GAN, LAN
Turdus reevei	M	C	LT	F	L	1500		F7, F8, F4E	MAN	EPC
Turdus rufitorques	M	T/C	UM	F	1500	3300		F10, F11, F15	CAH	MAH
Turdus rufiventris	L	T/C	LT	C	L	2200		F1E, F4E, F15		CSA, ATL, PAM
Turdus rufopalliatus										
graysoni	?	?	LT	?	L	L		F7	SIN	PAS
rufopalliatus	M	T/C	LT	F	L	2500		F7, F8		PAS, MAH
Turdus serranus	M	C	MM	F	900	2800		F4		NAN, CAN
Turdus swalesi	H	U	MM	F	1400	2100		F4	HIS	GAN
Timaliinae										
Chamaea fasciata	M	U	LS	F	L	2600		N1, N2		BSR
Polioptilinae										
Microbates cinereiventris	H	U	HT	F	L	1200		F1		GCS, CHO, AMN, AMS
Microbates collaris	H	U	LT	U	L	900	T	F1	o	AMN
Ramphocaenus melanurus	L	U/M	LT	F/P	L	1500	V	F1E, F15		PAS, GCS, CHO, NSA, AMN, AMS, ATL
Polioptila albiloris	M	M/C	LT	F	L	1900		F7, N1, N2, F8		PAS, MAH, GCS
Polioptila caerulea	L	M/C	US	F	L	2100		F7, F1E, F15, N2		GAN, BSR, MAH, GCS
Polioptila californica	M	U	LS	F	L	700		N1	BAJ	BSR
Polioptila dumicola	M	U/C	LT	F	L	2400		F7, F8, N1, N2		CSA, PAM
Polioptila guianensis	H	C	LT	U	L	L		F1		AMN, AMS
Polioptila lactea	M	C	LT	F	L	L		F1, F15	SOU	ATL
Polioptila lembeyei	M	U	LT	F	L	L?		N1	CUB	GAN
Polioptila melanura	M	U	LS	F	L	2100		N1, N2		BSR, MPL
Polioptila nigriceps	M	U/M	LT	F	L	1200		F8, F7, N1		BSR, PAS

CP	RP	Notes
4	3	Mainly above 700 m in Central America.
4	3	
4	3	To sea level in western Peru and Chile.
4	3	
4	3	
4	3	Occasionally to 1,800 m (Venezuela).
4	3	Occasionally to 1,400 m.
4	3	
3	2	Poorly known.
4	2	Relationship to *T. fumigatus* and *T. obsoletus* needs study.
4	3	Locally to 2,800 m (Tepuis).
4	3	Occasionally to 3,600 m.
4	3	Mainly montane.
4	3	Locally to 1,200 m.
4	3	
3	2	Poorly known; survey.
4	3	
4	3	
4	2	Limits of breeding range uncertain.
4	2	
3	2	In semideciduous forest.
4	3	Occasionally to 1,800 m.
4	3	
4	3	Status of Cauca population unknown.
4	3	Locally to 900 m and 3,500 m.
4	2	May contain multiple species.
4	3	Occasionally to 2,300 m.
4	3	
4	3	Locally to 2,600 m (Bolivia).
2	1	Poorly known; taxonomy and mainland distribution uncertain.
4	3	
4	3	Locally to 3,500 m.
2	1	Deforestation; survey.
4	3	
4	3	
4	3	
4	3	
4	3	
4	3	
4	3	Locally to 2,000 m.
4	3	May contain two species.
4	2	Range poorly known; may contain multiple species.
2	2	Poorly known; deforestation; mainly in Paraná drainage.
3	2	Survey.
4	3	
4	3	

Abbreviations Used

Snst - Sensitivity:
L - Low; **M** - Medium; **H** - High.

Strat - Foraging Strata:
T - Terrestrial; **U** - Understory; **M** - Midstory; **C** - Canopy; **A** - Aerial; **W** - Water.

Cntab - Center of Abundance:
LT - Lower tropical; **LS** - Lower subtropical; **HT** - Hill tropical; **UT** - Upper tropical; **US** - Upper subtropical; **MM** - Middle montane; **UM** - Upper montane.

Rel - Relative Abundance:
R - Rare; **U** - Uncommon; **F** - Fairly common; **C** - Common; **P** - Patchily distributed.

Min - Minimum Elevation:
L - Lowlands; **?** - Uncertain value; numeric values in meters.

Max - Maximum Elevation:
L - Lowlands; **?** - Uncertain value; **+** - species occurs at least to given elevation but likely occurs higher; numeric values in meters.

Micro - Microhabitats:
A - Army ants; **B** - Bamboo; **T** - Treefalls; **G** - Ground bromeliads; **C** - Rocky outcrops and caves; **S** - Streamside; **V** - Vine tangles; **B/V** -Bamboo/vine tangles.

Habitats:
F1 - Tropical lowland evergreen forest; **F2** - Flooded tropical evergreen forest; **F3** - River-edge forest; **F4** - Montane evergreen forest; **F5** - Elfin forest; **F6** - *Polylepis* woodland; **F7** - Tropical deciduous forest; **F8** - Gallery forest; **F9** - Southern temperate forest; **F10** - Pine forest; **F11** - Pine-oak forest; **F12** - White sand forest; **F13** - Palm forest; **F14** - Mangrove forest; **F15** - Secondary forest; **N1** - Arid lowland scrub; **N2** - Arid montane scrub; **N3** - Semihumid/humid montane scrub; **N4** - Cerrado; **N5** - Campo grasslands; **N6** - Low, seasonally wet grassland; **N7** - Southern temperate grassland; **N8** - Northern temperate grassland; **N9** - Puna grassland; **N10** - Paramo grassland; **N11** - Riparian thickets; **N12** - River island scrub; **N13** - Pastures/agricultural lands; **N14** - Second-growth scrub; **A1** - Freshwater marshes; **A2** - Saltwater/brackish marshes; **A3** - Coastal sand beaches/mudflats; **A4** - Coastal rocky beaches; **A5** - Riverine sand beaches; **A6** - Freshwater lakes and ponds; **A7** - Alkaline lakes; **A8** - Rivers; **A9** - Streams; **A10** - Bogs; **A11** - Coastal waters; **A12** - Pelagic waters.
E - Edge (used as a modifer to particular habitats).

Sub - Subregions:
ARC - Arid Caribbean Coast; **AWA** - Altiplano and Western Andes; **BAH** - Bahamas; **BAJ** - Baja California; **CAA** - Caatinga; **CAH** - Central American Highlands; **CER** - Cerrado; **CHA** - Chaco; **CHG** - Chiapas-Guanacaste; **CHL** - Chilean Desert; **CHR** - Chiriquí; **CIS** - Cocos Island; **CMV** - Cauca-Magdalena Valley; **COC** - Cuzco-Cochabamba; **CUB** - Cuba; **DOM** - Dominica; **EAS** - Eastern Slope Andes; **FDN** - Fernando de Noronha; **GAL** - Galápagos; **GCM** - Gulf Coast-Mexico; **GRE** - Grenada; **GUA** - Guadeloupe; **GUI** - Guianan; **HIS** - Hispaniola; **HPC** - Humid Pacific Coast; **ISA** - Isla Providencia and Isla San Andrés; **JAM** - Jamaica; **JFI** - Juan Fernández Islands; **MAN** - Manabí-Tumbes; **MAR** - Marañón Valley; **MID** - Madeira-Tapajós; **MON** - Montserrat; **MRT** - Martinique; **MTC** - Marañón-Cuzco; **NMM** - Northern Mexican Mountains; **NOR** - Northern Coastal Brazil; **PAR** - Pará; **PER** - Peruvian Desert; **PUE** - Puerto Rico; **RDJ** - Rio de Janeiro-Bahia Lowlands; **RMW** - Rio Madeira West; **RNW** - Rio Negro West; **SCA** - Southern Central America; **SCT** - Santa Cruz-Tucumán; **SIN** - Sinaloa-Oaxaca; **SMH** - Southern Mexican Highlands; **SMT** - Santa Marta; **SOC** - Islas Revillagigedo (Socorro Island group); **SON** - Sonoran Desert; **SOU** - Southern Atlantic Coast; **STL** - St. Lucia; **STV** - St. Vincent; **TAC** - Tacarcuna; **VAN** - Venezuelan Andes; **VNZ** - Venezuelan Coastal Mountains; **WES** - Western Andes; **YUC** - Yucatán Peninsula.
o - Endemic to region, but not restricted to a single subregion.

Zoogeographic Regions:
AMN - Northern Amazonia; **AMS** - Southern Amazonia; **ATL** - Atlantic Forest; **BSR** - Baja-Sonora; **CAN** - Central Andes; **CDH** - Chiriquí-Darién Highlands; **CHO** - Chocó Lowlands; **CSA** - Central South America; **EPC** - Equatorial Pacific Coast; **GAN** - Greater Antilles; **GCS** - Gulf-Caribbean Slope; **LAN** - Lesser Antilles; **MAH** - Madrean Highlands; **MPL** - Mexican Plateau; **NAN** - Northern Andes; **NSA** - Northern South America; **PAM** - Pampas; **PAS** - Pacific Arid Slope; **PAT** - Patagonia; **SAN** - Southern Andes; **STP** - Subtropical Pacific; **TEP** - Tepuis.

CP -Conservation Priority:
1 - Urgent; **2** - High; **3** - Medium; **4** - Low.

RP - Research Priority:
1 - High; **2** - Medium; **3** - Low.

	Snst	Strat	Cntab	Rel	Min	Max	Micro	Habitats	Sub	Zoogeographic Regions
Polioptila plumbea										
maior	M	U/C	UT	F	500	2100		N1, N2, F7	MAR	CAN
plumbea	L	U/C	LT	F	L	1500+		F7, F1E, F8, F15, N1, N2		GCS, CDH, CHO, EPC, NSA, AMN, AMS, CSA
Polioptila schistaceigula	M	C	LT	U	L	1000		F1		CDH, CHO
Sylviinae										
Regulus calendula	H	C	US	R	L	1300		F10		BSR
Regulus satrapa	M	M/C	UM	F	2300	3700		F10, F11		MAH
Aegithalidae										
Psaltriparus minimus	L	U/C	MM/UM	C	1200	3600		F11, N2		BSR, MAH
Remizidae										
Auriparus flaviceps	L	U/M	LS	F	L	2100		N1, N2, F8		BSR, MPL
Paridae										
Parus bicolor										
atricristatus	L	C	LS	C	L	2300		F7, F15, F8		MPL, GCS
Parus gambeli	M	C	UM	C	1250	3000		F10, F11		BSR
Parus inornatus	M	C	LS	U	L	2500		N1, N2, F8, F11		BSR
Parus sclateri	M	C	UM	F	1500	3900		F10, F11	o	MAH
Parus wollweberi	M	C	US	F	1200	2700		F11, F8		BSR, MAH
Sittidae										
Sitta canadensis	M	C	LS	U	L	1000		F10		BSR
Sitta carolinensis	M	C	US	F	1250	3600		F10, F11, F8		BSR, MAH
Sitta pusilla	M	M/C	LS	U	L	L		F10		GAN
Sitta pygmaea	M	C	UM	C	1700	3900		F10		BSR, MAH
Certhiidae										
Certhia americana	M	U/C	UM	F	1700	4000		F10, F11		MAH
Emberizidae										
Emberizinae										
Zonotrichia capensis	L	T/U	UM	C	L	4000		N1, N2, N14, F15, N3, N5, N13		GAN, MAH, CDH, STP, NAN, CAN, SAN, TEP, AMN, AMS, CSA, ATL, PAM, PAT
Zonotrichia melodia	L	T/U	LS	C	L	2800		A1, N11		BSR, MPL, MAH
Junco hyemalis										
hyemalis	M	T	MM	F	1800	2800		F10	o	BSR
insularis	M	T	LS	U	L	1300		F10, F11	BAJ	BSR
Junco phaeonotus	M	T	UM	C	1200	4300		F10, F11		BSR, MAH
Junco vulcani	M	T	UM	F	2700	3600		N3, N10	CHR	CDH
Ammodramus aurifrons	L	T	LT	C	L	900		N12, N14, N13		NSA, AMN, AMS
Ammodramus baileyi	M	T	UM	R	2400	3050		F10, N8	NMM	MAH
Ammodramus humeralis	L	T	LT	C	L	1700		N5, N6, N13		NSA, AMN, AMS, CSA, ATL, PAM
Ammodramus sandwichensis										
beldingi	M	T	LS	U	L	L		A2	BAJ	BSR
rostratus	M	T	LS	F	L	L		A2	o	BSR
sandwichensis	M	T	MM	F/P	1500	3300		N8, N13		MPL, MAH
Ammodramus savannarum	M	T/U	MM	U/P	L	2500		N8, N5, N13		GAN, BSR, MPL, PAS, GCS, NAN, NSA
Spizella atrogularis	M	T	US	F/P	1200	2400		N2		BSR, MPL, MAH
Spizella passerina	L	T	MM	C	L	3800		F10, F11		BSR, MAH, GCS
Spizella wortheni	M	T	MM	R	1200	2500		N8	o	MPL
Chondestes grammacus	L	T	US	F	1100	2400		N1, N2, N8, N14		MPL
Amphispiza belli	M	T	LS	F	L	1200		N1, N2		BSR
Amphispiza bilineata	M	T	LS	C	L	2200		N1, N2		BSR, MPL
Aimophila botterii										
botterii	L	T	UT	F/P	L	2400		N8		BSR, MPL, PAS, GCS
petenica	M	T	LT	U	L	1600		N8, F10		MAH, GCS
Aimophila carpalis	M	T	UT	F/P	L	1500		N1		BSR, PAS

CP	RP	Notes
4	2	Poorly known.
4	3	
3	2	Deforestation.
3	2	Status of breeding population on Guadalupe Island unknown.
4	3	
4	3	To sea level in northwestern Baja.
4	3	
4	2	
4	3	
4	3	
4	3	
4	3	
3	2	Resident Guadalupe Island.
4	3	
4	3	
4	3	
4	3	
4	3	Locally to 5,000 m+.
4	3	
4	2	Taxonomy uncertain, breeding forms belong to *J. oreganus* complex.
2	1	Habitat destruction.
4	2	
4	3	Locally to 2,100 m.
4	3	
2	1	Habitat destruction; survey.
4	3	
3	2	Habitat destruction.
4	3	
4	3	
3	2	Monitor resident populations; overgrazing.
4	3	
4	3	
2	1	Survey.
4	3	
4	3	
4	3	
4	2	Monitor; grazing.
4	2	Poorly known; monitor; grazing.
4	2	Monitor.

Abbreviations Used

Snst - Sensitivity:
L - Low; **M** - Medium; **H** - High.

Strat - Foraging Strata:
T - Terrestrial; **U** - Understory; **M** - Midstory; **C** - Canopy; **A** - Aerial; **W** - Water.

Cntab - Center of Abundance:
LT - Lower tropical; **LS** - Lower subtropical; **HT** - Hill tropical; **UT** - Upper tropical; **US** - Upper subtropical; **MM** - Middle montane; **UM** - Upper montane.

Rel - Relative Abundance:
R - Rare; **U** - Uncommon; **F** - Fairly common; **C** - Common; **P** - Patchily distributed.

Min - Minimum Elevation:
L - Lowlands; **?** - Uncertain value; numeric values in meters.

Max - Maximum Elevation:
L - Lowlands; **?** - Uncertain value; **+** - species occurs at least to given elevation but likely occurs higher; numeric values in meters.

Micro - Microhabitats:
A - Army ants; **B** - Bamboo; **T** - Treefalls; **G** - Ground bromeliads; **C** - Rocky outcrops and caves; **S** - Streamside; **V** - Vine tangles; **B/V** -Bamboo/vine tangles.

Habitats:
F1 - Tropical lowland evergreen forest; **F2** - Flooded tropical evergreen forest; **F3** - River-edge forest; **F4** - Montane evergreen forest; **F5** - Elfin forest; **F6** - *Pclylepis* woodland; **F7** - Tropical deciduous forest; **F8** - Gallery forest; **F9** - Southern temperate forest; **F10** - Pine forest; **F11** - Pine-oak forest; **F12** - White sand forest; **F13** - Palm forest; **F14** - Mangrove forest; **F15** - Secondary forest; **N1** - Arid lowland scrub; **N2** - Arid montane scrub; **N3** - Semihumid/humid montane scrub; **N4** - Cerrado; **N5** - Campo grasslands; **N6** - Low, seasonally wet grassland; **N7** - Southern temperate grassland; **N8** - Northern temperate grassland; **N9** - Puna grassland; **N10** - Paramo grassland; **N11** - Riparian thickets; **N12** - River island scrub; **N13** - Pastures/agricultural lands; **N14** - Second-growth scrub; **A1** - Freshwater marshes; **A2** - Saltwater/brackish marshes; **A3** - Coastal sand beaches/mudflats; **A4** - Coastal rocky beaches; **A5** - Riverine sand beaches; **A6** - Freshwater lakes and ponds; **A7** - Alkaline lakes; **A8** - Rivers; **A9** - Streams; **A10** - Bogs; **A11** - Coastal waters; **A12** - Pelagic waters.
E - Edge (used as a modifer to particular habitats).

Sub - Subregions:
ARC - Arid Caribbean Coast; **AWA** - Altiplano and Western Andes; **BAH** - Bahamas; **BAJ** - Baja California; **CAA** - Caatinga; **CAH** - Central American Highlands; **CER** - Cerrado; **CHA** - Chaco; **CHG** - Chiapas-Guanacaste; **CHL** - Chilean Desert; **CHR** - Chiriquí; **CIS** - Cocos Island; **CMV** - Cauca-Magdalena Valley; **COC** - Cuzco-Cochabamba; **CUB** - Cuba; **DOM** - Dominica; **EAS** - Eastern Slope Andes; **FDN** - Fernando de Noronha; **GAL** - Galápagos; **GCM** - Gulf Coast-Mexico; **GRE** - Grenada; **GUA** - Guadeloupe; **GUI** - Guianan; **HIS** - Hispaniola; **HPC** - Humid Pacific Coast; **ISA** - Isla Providencia and Isla San Andrés; **JAM** - Jamaica; **JFI** - Juan Fernández Islands; **MAN** - Manabí-Tumbes; **MAR** - Marañón Valley; **MID** - Madeira-Tapajós; **MON** - Montserrat; **MRT** - Martinique; **MTC** - Marañón-Cuzco; **NMM** - Northern Mexican Mountains; **NOR** - Northern Coastal Brazil; **PAR** - Pará; **PER** - Peruvian Desert; **PUE** - Puerto Rico; **RDJ** - Rio de Janeiro-Bahia Lowlands; **RMW** - Rio Madeira West; **RNW** - Rio Negro West; **SCA** - Southern Central America; **SCT** - Santa Cruz-Tucumán; **SIN** - Sinaloa-Oaxaca; **SMH** - Southern Mexican Highlands; **SMT** - Santa Marta; **SOC** - Islas Revillagigedo (Socorro Island group); **SON** - Sonoran Desert; **SOU** - Southern Atlantic Coast; **STL** - St. Lucia; **STV** - St. Vincent; **TAC** - Tacarcuna; **VAN** - Venezuelan Andes; **VNZ** - Venezuelan Coastal Mountains; **WES** - Western Andes; **YUC** - Yucatán Peninsula.
o - Endemic to region, but not restricted to a single subregion.

Zoogeographic Regions:
AMN - Northern Amazonia; **AMS** - Southern Amazonia; **ATL** - Atlantic Forest; **BSR** - Baja-Sonora; **CAN** - Central Andes; **CDH** - Chiriquí-Darién Highlands; **CHO** - Chocó Lowlands; **CSA** - Central South America; **EPC** - Equatorial Pacific Coast; **GAN** - Greater Antilles; **GCS** - Gulf-Caribbean Slope; **LAN** - Lesser Antilles; **MAH** - Madrean Highlands; **MPL** - Mexican Plateau; **NAN** - Northern Andes; **NSA** - Northern South America; **PAM** - Pampas; **PAS** - Pacific Arid Slope; **PAT** - Patagonia; **SAN** - Southern Andes; **STP** - Subtropical Pacific; **TEP** - Tepuis.

CP -Conservation Priority:
1 - Urgent; **2** - High; **3** - Medium; **4** - Low.

RP - Research Priority:
1 - High; **2** - Medium; **3** - Low.

	Snst	Strat	Cntab	Rel	Min	Max	Micro	Habitats	Sub	Zoogeographic Regions
Aimophila cassinii	L	T	UT	C	L	2200		N8, N1		BSR, MPL, GCS
Aimophila humeralis	M	T	UT	F	L	1500		N1, N2		PAS, MAH
Aimophila mystacalis	M	T	UT	F	900	1900		N2	SMH	MAH
Aimophila notosticta	M	T	MM	R	1500	1900		N2	SMH	MAH
Aimophila quinquestriata	M	T	UT	F/P	500	1850	R	N2		BSR, PAS, MAH
Aimophila rufescens	L	T	UT	F	600	2700		N2, F11, F7		PAS, MAH, GCS
Aimophila ruficauda	L	T	LT	F	L	2000		N1, N2, F7		PAS, MAH
Aimophila ruficeps	M	T	US	C	L	2400	R	N2, N1		BSR, MPL, MAH
Aimophila stolzmanni	M	T	LT	F	L	1200		N1, F7	MAN	EPC
Aimophila strigiceps	M	T	LT	U	L	1000		F7, N1	CHA	CSA
Aimophila sumichrasti	M	T	LT	F	L	950		N1, F7E	SIN	PAS
Torreornis inexpectata	M	T	LT	R	L	L		N1, F7	CUB	GAN
Oriturus superciliosus	M	T	UM	F	2100	3300		N8, F10, F11	o	MAH
Phrygilus alaudinus	L	T	UM	F/P	L	4000		N2, N1		STP, NAN, CAN, SAN
Phrygilus atriceps	M	T/U	UM	F	3000	4200		N2, F6		CAN, SAN
Phrygilus carbonarius	M	T	LS	F	L	700		N7, N1	o	PAT
Phrygilus dorsalis	H	T	UM	U	3700	4500		N9	AWA	CAN
Phrygilus erythronotus	H	T	UM	U	3600	4700		N9	AWA	CAN
Phrygilus fruticeti	M	T/U	UM	C	L	4000		N2, N3, N1		STP, CAN, SAN, PAT
Phrygilus gayi	M	T/U	UM	C	L	3600		N2, N3, N1		STP, SAN, PAT
Phrygilus patagonicus	L	T/U	LS	F	L	1800		F9E, N1, N7		SAN, PAT
Phrygilus plebejus	L	T	UM	C/P	L	4000		N2, N1, N9		EPC, NAN, CAN, SAN
Phrygilus punensis	L	T/U	UM	C	2900	4300		N2, N3	AWA	CAN
Phrygilus unicolor	M	T	UM	F	2700	4500		N10, N9, N13		NAN, CAN, SAN
Melanodera melanodera	L	T	LS	U	L	L?		N7, N13	o	PAT
Melanodera xanthogramma	M	T	UM	U/P	L	3300		N7, N13, N9	o	SAN
Haplospiza rustica	M	U/M	MM	U/P	1500	2500	B	F4E, F15?		MAH, CDH, NAN, CAN, TEP
Haplospiza unicolor	M	M/C	UT	U/P	L	2100	B	F4, F1	SOU	ATL
Acanthidops bairdi	M	T/M	MM	U/P	1500	3000	B	F4E	CHR	CDH
Lophospingus griseocristatus	L	T/U	MM	C	1000	2800		N2, N14	SCT	CAN
Lophospingus pusillus	M	T/U	LT	F	L	900		N1, N2		CAN, CSA
Donacospiza albifrons	L	U	LT	F/P	L	1000		N6, N7, A1		CSA, ATL, PAM
Diuca diuca	L	T	LS	C	L	2000		N1, N2, N14		STP, SAN, CSA, PAT
Diuca speculifera	M	T	UM	F/P	4300	5200		N9	AWA	CAN
Idiopsar brachyurus	M	T	UM	U/P	3300	4500	R	N9	AWA	CAN
Piezorhina cinerea	M	T	LT	C	L	L		N1	MAN	EPC
Xenospingus concolor	M	U/C	LT	U/P	L	800		N1, N11	o	STP
Incaspiza laeta	M	T/U	MM	F	1400	3000		N2, F7	MAR	CAN
Incaspiza ortizi	M	T	MM	U/P	1800	2200		N2	MAR	CAN
Incaspiza personata	M	T	UM	U/P	2200	3400		N2	MAR	CAN
Incaspiza pulchra	M	T	MM	U/P	1000	2500		N2	AWA	CAN
Incaspiza watkinsi	M	T	HT	F	500	900		N1	MAR	CAN
Poospiza alticola	M	U/M	UM	U	3000	4300		F6, N2, N3	AWA	CAN
Poospiza baeri	M	U/M	MM	U	2000	2800		N3, F4E?	o	CAN
Poospiza boliviana	M	U/M	UM	F	1500	3100		N2, N3	SCT	CAN
Poospiza caesar	L	T/U	UM	U	2600	3800		N3, N2	COC	CAN
Poospiza cinerea	H	?	UT	R	600	1200		N5	CER	CSA
Poospiza erythrophrys	M	C	MM?	F	1600	2800		F4E	SCT	CAN
Poospiza garleppi	M	U/M	UM	U	3000	3800		F6, N3	COC	CAN
Poospiza hispaniolensis	L	U	LT	F	L	1500		N1, N2, N11, N14		EPC, STP
Poospiza hypochondria	M	U/M	UM	F	2500	4200		N2, N3		CAN, SAN
Poospiza lateralis	M	M/C	UT	C	L	2100		F4E, F9, N3		ATL, PAM
Poospiza melanoleuca	M	U/M	LS	C	L	1800		N1, F7, N2	CHA	CSA

CP	RP	Notes
4	2	Range south of U. S. poorly known.
4	3	
4	3	
2	1	Habitat disturbance; survey.
4	3	Locally to lowlands.
4	3	Locally to sea level.
4	3	
4	3	
4	3	
4	3	
4	3	
2	1	Habitat poorly known; survey.
4	2	Monitor.
4	3	
4	3	Occasionally to 2,400 m.
4	3	
4	2	Poorly known.
4	2	Distribution and behavior poorly known.
4	3	Mainly above 2,400 m in the Andes.
4	3	
4	3	
4	3	
4	3	
4	3	
2	1	Overgrazing; apparently declining except in Malvinas; survey.
2	1	Overgrazing; monitor.
4	2	Occasionally to 1,000 and 2,800 m; nomadic?
3	2	Movements poorly known, follows bamboo seeding.
3	2	Seasonally to 1,200 m; monitor; movements poorly known.
4	3	
4	3	Occasionally to 2,200 m.
4	3	Locally to 2,200 m.
4	3	
4	3	Occasionally to 4,000 m.
4	2	Poorly known.
4	3	
2	1	Occasionally to 3,500 m? habitat destruction; survey.
4	2	Poorly known.
3	2	Poorly known.
4	2	Occasionally to 4,800 m? poorly known.
4	2	Poorly known.
3	2	Poorly known.
3	2	Poorly known.
3	2	Poorly known.
4	3	Occasionally to 3,800 m.
3	3	
2	1	Apparently declining; habitat degradation.
4	3	Occasionally to 1,200 m.
2	1	Poorly known.
4	3	Occasionally to 2,500 m.
4	3	Occasionally to 1,000 m (Argentina).
4	3	
4	3	

Abbreviations Used

Snst - Sensitivity:
L - Low; **M** - Medium; **H** - High.

Strat - Foraging Strata:
T - Terrestrial; **U** - Understory; **M** - Midstory; **C** - Canopy; **A** - Aerial; **W** - Water.

Cntab - Center of Abundance:
LT - Lower tropical; **LS** - Lower subtropical; **HT** - Hill tropical; **UT** - Upper tropical; **US** - Upper subtropical; **MM** - Middle montane; **UM** - Upper montane.

Rel - Relative Abundance:
R - Rare; **U** - Uncommon; **F** - Fairly common; **C** - Common; **P** - Patchily distributed.

Min - Minimum Elevation:
L - Lowlands; **?** - Uncertain value; numeric values in meters.

Max - Maximum Elevation:
L - Lowlands; **?** - Uncertain value; **+** - species occurs at least to given elevation but likely occurs higher; numeric values in meters.

Micro - Microhabitats:
A - Army ants; **B** - Bamboo; **T** - Treefalls; **G** - Ground bromeliads; **C** - Rocky outcrops and caves; **S** - Streamside; **V** - Vine tangles; **B/V** -Bamboo/vine tangles.

Habitats:
F1 - Tropical lowland evergreen forest; **F2** - Flooded tropical evergreen forest; **F3** - River-edge forest; **F4** - Montane evergreen forest; **F5** - Elfin forest; **F6** - *Polylepis* woodland; **F7** - Tropical deciduous forest; **F8** - Gallery forest; **F9** - Southern temperate forest; **F10** - Pine forest; **F11** - Pine-oak forest; **F12** - White sand forest; **F13** - Palm forest; **F14** - Mangrove forest; **F15** - Secondary forest; **N1** - Arid lowland scrub; **N2** - Arid montane scrub; **N3** - Semihumid/humid montane scrub; **N4** - Cerrado; **N5** - Campo grasslands; **N6** - Low, seasonally wet grassland; **N7** - Southern temperate grassland; **N8** - Northern temperate grassland; **N9** - Puna grassland; **N10** - Paramo grassland; **N11** - Riparian thickets; **N12** - River island scrub; **N13** - Pastures/agricultural lands; **N14** - Second-growth scrub; **A1** - Freshwater marshes; **A2** - Saltwater/brackish marshes; **A3** - Coastal sand beaches/mudflats; **A4** - Coastal rocky beaches; **A5** - Riverine sand beaches; **A6** - Freshwater lakes and ponds; **A7** - Alkaline lakes; **A8** - Rivers; **A9** - Streams; **A10** - Bogs; **A11** - Coastal waters; **A12** - Pelagic waters.
E - Edge (used as a modifer to particular habitats).

Sub - Subregions:
ARC - Arid Caribbean Coast; **AWA** - Altiplano and Western Andes; **BAH** - Bahamas; **BAJ** - Baja California; **CAA** - Caatinga; **CAH** - Central American Highlands; **CER** - Cerrado; **CHA** - Chaco; **CHG** - Chiapas-Guanacaste; **CHL** - Chilean Desert; **CHR** - Chiriquí; **CIS** - Cocos Island; **CMV** - Cauca-Magdalena Valley; **COC** - Cuzco-Cochabamba; **CUB** - Cuba; **DOM** - Dominica; **EAS** - Eastern Slope Andes; **FDN** - Fernando de Noronha; **GAL** - Galápagos; **GCM** - Gulf Coast-Mexico; **GRE** - Grenada; **GUA** - Guadeloupe; **GUI** - Guianan; **HIS** - Hispaniola; **HPC** - Humid Pacific Coast; **ISA** - Isla Providencia and Isla San Andrés; **JAM** - Jamaica; **JFI** - Juan Fernández Islands; **MAN** - Manabí-Tumbes; **MAR** - Marañón Valley; **MID** - Madeira-Tapajós; **MON** - Montserrat; **MRT** - Martinique; **MTC** - Marañón-Cuzco; **NMM** - Northern Mexican Mountains; **NOR** - Northern Coastal Brazil; **PAR** - Pará; **PER** - Peruvian Desert; **PUE** - Puerto Rico; **RDJ** - Rio de Janeiro-Bahia Lowlands; **RMW** - Rio Madeira West; **RNW** - Rio Negro West; **SCA** - Southern Central America; **SCT** - Santa Cruz-Tucumán; **SIN** - Sinaloa-Oaxaca; **SMH** - Southern Mexican Highlands; **SMT** - Santa Marta; **SOC** - Islas Revillagigedo (Socorro Island group); **SON** - Sonoran Desert; **SOU** - Southern Atlantic Coast; **STL** - St. Lucia; **STV** - St. Vincent; **TAC** - Tacarcuna; **VAN** - Venezuelan Andes; **VNZ** - Venezuelan Coastal Mountains; **WES** - Western Andes; **YUC** - Yucatán Peninsula.
o - Endemic to region, but not restricted to a single subregion.

Zoogeographic Regions:
AMN - Northern Amazonia; **AMS** - Southern Amazonia; **ATL** - Atlantic Forest; **BSR** - Baja-Sonora; **CAN** - Central Andes; **CDH** - Chiriquí-Darién Highlands; **CHO** - Chocó Lowlands; **CSA** - Central South America; **EPC** - Equatorial Pacific Coast; **GAN** - Greater Antilles; **GCS** - Gulf-Caribbean Slope; **LAN** - Lesser Antilles; **MAH** - Madrean Highlands; **MPL** - Mexican Plateau; **NAN** - Northern Andes; **NSA** - Northern South America; **PAM** - Pampas; **PAS** - Pacific Arid Slope; **PAT** - Patagonia; **SAN** - Southern Andes; **STP** - Subtropical Pacific; **TEP** - Tepuis.

CP -Conservation Priority:
1 - Urgent; **2** - High; **3** - Medium; **4** - Low.

RP - Research Priority:
1 - High; **2** - Medium; **3** - Low.

	Snst	Strat	Cntab	Rel	Min	Max	Micro	Habitats	Sub	Zoogeographic Regions
Poospiza nigrorufa										
nigrorufa	M	U/M	LS	F	L	900		N11, A1, N14		ATL, PAM
whitii	M	U	US	F	600	2700		N11, N2, N1		CAN, SAN, CSA
Poospiza ornata	M?	?	LS	U/F	L	1000+		N1, N14, F7?	CHA	CSA
Poospiza rubecula	M	U	UM	R	2300	3500		N3, F6?	AWA	CAN
Poospiza thoracica	M	M/C	UT	U	900	2100		F4, F9	SOU	ATL
Poospiza torquata	M	U/M	LS	F	L	2800		N1, F7, N2		CAN, SAN, CSA
Sicalis auriventris	L	T	MM	C	1800	2500		N2, N7?, N14	o	SAN
Sicalis citrina	M	T	UT	F/P	600	2800		N5, N13		NAN, CAN, TEP, AMN, CSA
Sicalis columbiana	L	T	LT	F/P	L	L		N12, N14, N11		NSA, AMN, AMS, CSA
Sicalis flaveola	L	T	LT	C	L	800		N1, N14, N2?		EPC, CAN, NSA, CSA, ATL, PAM
Sicalis lebruni	M	T	LS	U	L	1200		N7, N1	o	PAT
Sicalis lutea	M	T	UM	F/P	3700	4400		N9	AWA	CAN
Sicalis luteocephala	M	T	UM	F	2600	3500		N2	AWA	CAN
Sicalis luteola	L	T	LT	C/P	L	3500		N7, N6, N13, N5		GCS, STP, NAN, CAN, SAN, NSA, AMN, AMS, CSA, PAM, PAT
Sicalis olivascens	L	T	UM	C	2350	3700		N2, N14		CAN, SAN
Sicalis raimondii	M	T	US	C/P	500	2500		N2, N1	AWA	CAN
Sicalis taczanowskii	L	T	LT	C/P	L	L		N1	MAN	EPC
Sicalis uropygialis	M	T	UM	C	3600	4800		N9, N14	AWA	CAN
Emberizoides herbicola										
duidae	H	U	MM	?	1300	2100		N5	o	TEP
herbicola	L	U	LT	C	L	1900		N6, N5, N14		GCS, NSA, AMN, AMS, CSA
Emberizoides ypiranganus	M	U	LT	F	L	1100		A1, N7		ATL, PAM
Embernagra longicauda	M	T/U	UT	U	700	1300		N2	CER	CSA
Embernagra platensis	L	T/U	LS	C	L	1200		N6, N7, N2, A1		CAN, CSA, PAM
Volatinia jacarina	L	T/U	LT	C	L	1100		N14, N6, N5, N1, N13, N4, N11		PAS, GCS, CHO, EPC, STP, NSA, AMN, AMS, CSA, ATL
Sporophila albogularis	M	U	LT	F	L	1200		N1, F7E, N14		CSA, ATL
Sporophila americana										
americana	L	U/M	LT	C	L	800+		N14, N11, N12, F15, F3		NSA, AMN, AMS
aurita	L	U/M	LT	C	L	1500		N14, F1E, F7, F15		GCS, CHO, EPC
Sporophila ardesiaca	M	U	LT	U	L	900		N11, A1, N14	RDJ	ATL
Sporophila bouvreuil	M	U	LT	U/P	L	1100		N5		AMN, AMS, CSA, ATL
Sporophila caerulescens	L	U	LS	C	L	2100		N14, N11, N13		CSA, ATL, PAM
Sporophila castaneiventris	L	U	LT	C	L	950		N14, N11, N12		AMN, AMS
Sporophila cinnamomea	M	U	LT	U	L	L		N6, A1, N5	o	PAM
Sporophila collaris	L	U	LT	F	L	800		N6, A1, N14		CSA, ATL, PAM
Sporophila falcirostris	M	U/M	LT	R/P	L	1200+	B	F1	o	ATL
Sporophila frontalis	M	U	UT	R/P	900	1500	B	F4, F1	SOU	ATL
Sporophila hypochroma	M	U	LT	U/P	L	1100+		N6, N5?	CER	CSA
Sporophila hypoxantha	M	U	LT	C	L	1100+		N6, N5	o	CSA
Sporophila insulata	?	?	LT	?	L	L		N1?	o	CHO
Sporophila intermedia	L	T/U	LT	F	L	1200		N14, N6		CHO, NSA, AMN
Sporophila leucoptera	L	U	LT	U	L	1100		N11, A1, N14		AMN, AMS, CSA, ATL
Sporophila lineola										
bouvronides	L	U	LT	F	L	900		N14, N11		NSA, AMN, AMS
lineola	L	U	LT	C	L	1200		N14, N11, N13	o	CSA
Sporophila luctuosa	L	U	MM	C/P	L	3100		N14, N3, N11		NAN, CAN, AMN?, AMS
Sporophila melanogaster	M	U	HT	U	700	1100		A1, N7	SOU	ATL
Sporophila minuta	L	U	LT	F	L	1100		N6, N5, N14		PAS, GCS, CHO, NSA, AMN, AMS

CP	RP	Notes
4	3	
4	3	
4	3	
2	1	Poorly known.
4	3	
4	3	Locally to 3,200 m.
4	3	
3	2	Locally to 3,700 m; poorly known.
4	2	
4	3	Locally to 3,000 m.
4	3	
4	2	Poorly known.
4	3	
4	2	Mainly above 2,000 m in Andes.
4	3	Occasionally to 1,500 m.
4	3	Occasionally to sea level.
4	2	Nomadic; movements poorly known.
4	3	Locally to 2,500 m (Chile).
3	1	Poorly known.
4	3	Mainly below 1,100 m.
3	2	Habitat destruction.
3	1	Poorly known.
4	3	
4	3	Locally to 2,000 m.
4	3	
4	3	
4	3	
3	1	Bird trapping; possibly hybrid or race of *S. nigricollis*.
3	2	Habitat destruction; distinctive populations near Rio de Janeiro and São Paulo threatened.
4	3	
4	3	
3	2	Survey.
4	3	
2	1	Movements tied to bamboo seeding; deforestation; bird trapping.
2	1	Locally to sea level; movements tied to bamboo seeding.
4	2	Movements and status uncertain; taxonomic relationship to other *Sporophila* uncertain.
4	2	Taxonomic relationship to other *Sporophila* uncertain.
2	1	Poorly known; no recent records; survey.
4	3	Occasionally to 2,300 m.
4	2	May contain two species.
4	2	Amazonian records away from Guianas probably migrants.
4	2	Nonbreeding range poorly known.
4	2	Mainly 1,200 to 2,700 m; possible seasonal movements? nomadic?
3	2	Nonbreeding range poorly known.
4	3	Locally to 2,300 m.

Abbreviations Used

Snst - Sensitivity:
L - Low; **M** - Medium; **H** - High.

Strat - Foraging Strata:
T - Terrestrial; **U** - Understory; **M** - Midstory; **C** - Canopy; **A** - Aerial; **W** - Water.

Cntab - Center of Abundance:
LT - Lower tropical; **LS** - Lower subtropical; **HT** - Hill tropical; **UT** - Upper tropical; **US** - Upper subtropical; **MM** - Middle montane; **UM** - Upper montane.

Rel - Relative Abundance:
R - Rare; **U** - Uncommon; **F** - Fairly common; **C** - Common; **P** - Patchily distributed.

Min - Minimum Elevation:
L - Lowlands; **?** - Uncertain value; numeric values in meters.

Max - Maximum Elevation:
L - Lowlands; **?** - Uncertain value; **+** - species occurs at least to given elevation but likely occurs higher; numeric values in meters.

Micro - Microhabitats:
A - Army ants; **B** - Bamboo; **T** - Treefalls; **G** - Ground bromeliads; **C** - Rocky outcrops and caves; **S** - Streamside; **V** - Vine tangles; **B/V** -Bamboo/vine tangles.

Habitats:
F1 - Tropical lowland evergreen forest; **F2** - Flooded tropical evergreen forest; **F3** - River-edge forest; **F4** - Montane evergreen forest; **F5** - Elfin forest; **F6** - *Polylepis* woodland; **F7** - Tropical deciduous forest; **F8** - Gallery forest; **F9** - Southern temperate forest; **F10** - Pine forest; **F11** - Pine-oak forest; **F12** - White sand forest; **F13** - Palm forest; **F14** - Mangrove forest; **F15** - Secondary forest; **N1** - Arid lowland scrub; **N2** - Arid montane scrub; **N3** - Semihumid/humid montane scrub; **N4** - Cerrado; **N5** - Campo grasslands; **N6** - Low, seasonally wet grassland; **N7** - Southern temperate grassland; **N8** - Northern temperate grassland; **N9** - Puna grassland; **N10** - Paramo grassland; **N11** - Riparian thickets; **N12** - River island scrub; **N13** - Pastures/agricultural lands; **N14** - Second-growth scrub; **A1** - Freshwater marshes; **A2** - Saltwater/brackish marshes; **A3** - Coastal sand beaches/mudflats; **A4** - Coastal rocky beaches; **A5** - Riverine sand beaches; **A6** - Freshwater lakes and ponds; **A7** - Alkaline lakes; **A8** - Rivers; **A9** - Streams; **A10** - Bogs; **A11** - Coastal waters; **A12** - Pelagic waters.
E - Edge (used as a modifer to particular habitats).

Sub - Subregions:
ARC - Arid Caribbean Coast; **AWA** - Altiplano and Western Andes; **BAH** - Bahamas; **BAJ** - Baja California; **CAA** - Caatinga; **CAH** - Central American Highlands; **CER** - Cerrado; **CHA** - Chaco; **CHG** - Chiapas-Guanacaste; **CHL** - Chilean Desert; **CHR** - Chiriquí; **CIS** - Cocos Island; **CMV** - Cauca-Magdalena Valley; **COC** - Cuzco-Cochabamba; **CUB** - Cuba; **DOM** - Dominica; **EAS** - Eastern Slope Andes; **FDN** - Fernando de Noronha; **GAL** - Galápagos; **GCM** - Gulf Coast-Mexico; **GRE** - Grenada; **GUA** - Guadeloupe; **GUI** - Guianan; **HIS** - Hispaniola; **HPC** - Humid Pacific Coast; **ISA** - Isla Providencia and Isla San Andrés; **JAM** - Jamaica; **JFI** - Juan Fernández Islands; **MAN** - Manabí-Tumbes; **MAR** - Marañón Valley; **MID** - Madeira-Tapajós; **MON** - Montserrat; **MRT** - Martinique; **MTC** - Marañón-Cuzco; **NMM** - Northern Mexican Mountains; **NOR** - Northern Coastal Brazil; **PAR** - Pará; **PER** - Peruvian Desert; **PUE** - Puerto Rico; **RDJ** - Rio de Janeiro-Bahia Lowlands; **RMW** - Rio Madeira West; **RNW** - Rio Negro West; **SCA** - Southern Central America; **SCT** - Santa Cruz-Tucumán; **SIN** - Sinaloa-Oaxaca; **SMH** - Southern Mexican Highlands; **SMT** - Santa Marta; **SOC** - Islas Revillagigedo (Socorro Island group); **SON** - Sonoran Desert; **SOU** - Southern Atlantic Coast; **STL** - St. Lucia; **STV** - St. Vincent; **TAC** - Tacarcuna; **VAN** - Venezuelan Andes; **VNZ** - Venezuelan Coastal Mountains; **WES** - Western Andes; **YUC** - Yucatán Peninsula.
o - Endemic to region, but not restricted to a single subregion.

Zoogeographic Regions:
AMN - Northern Amazonia; **AMS** - Southern Amazonia; **ATL** - Atlantic Forest; **BSR** - Baja-Sonora; **CAN** - Central Andes; **CDH** - Chiriquí-Darién Highlands; **CHO** - Chocó Lowlands; **CSA** - Central South America; **EPC** - Equatorial Pacific Coast; **GAN** - Greater Antilles; **GCS** - Gulf-Caribbean Slope; **LAN** - Lesser Antilles; **MAH** - Madrean Highlands; **MPL** - Mexican Plateau; **NAN** - Northern Andes; **NSA** - Northern South America; **PAM** - Pampas; **PAS** - Pacific Arid Slope; **PAT** - Patagonia; **SAN** - Southern Andes; **STP** - Subtropical Pacific; **TEP** - Tepuis.

CP -Conservation Priority:
1 - Urgent; **2** - High; **3** - Medium; **4** - Low.

RP - Research Priority:
1 - High; **2** - Medium; **3** - Low.

	Snst	Strat	Cntab	Rel	Min	Max	Micro	Habitats	Sub	Zoogeographic Regions
Sporophila nigricollis	L	U	UT	F	L	2300		N14, N3, N13		LAN, GCS, CHO, NAN, CAN, AMN, AMS, CSA, ATL
Sporophila nigrorufa	M	U	LT	R?	L	L		N6, N5?	CER	CSA
Sporophila obscura	L	U	UT	U/P	L	2000+		N14, N11, F1E, F4E, N2		STP, NAN, CAN
Sporophila palustris	M	U	LS	F/P	L	L		N6, A1, N11	o	PAM
Sporophila peruviana	L	U	LT	C/P	L	700		N1, N11		EPC, STP
Sporophila plumbea	M	U	LT	U/P	L	1500		N6, N5		NSA, AMN, AMS, CSA, ATL
Sporophila ruficollis	M	U	LT	F/P	L	1100+		N6, N5		CSA, PAM
Sporophila schistacea	M	U/M	LT	U/P	L	1500	B	F1E, N14, F15		GCS, CHO, NSA, AMN, AMS
Sporophila simplex	L	U	LT	U	L	1800		N1, N11, N2		EPC, STP, CAN
Sporophila telasco	L	U	LT	C	L	1200		N1, N11, N14, A1		CHO, EPC, STP
Sporophila torqueola										
morelleti	L	U	LT	C	L	1550+		N14, N1, N11		PAS, GCS
torqueola	L	U	LT	C	L	2000+		N14, N1, N2, N11	SIN	PAS
Sporophila zelichi	M	U	LS	R	L	L?		N11?	o	PAM
Oryzoborus angolensis										
angolensis	L	U/M	LT	C	L	1400		N14, F1E, F15E		NSA, AMN, AMS, CSA, ATL
funereus	L	U/M	LT	F	L	1100		N14, F15E, F1E		GCS, CHO
Oryzoborus crassirostris	M	U	LT	U/P	L	700		N11, A1, N14		NSA, AMN, AMS
Oryzoborus maximiliani										
maximiliani	L	U	LT	U/P	L	1100?		N11, A1, N14		CHO, EPC, AMN, AMS, CSA, ATL
nuttingi	L	U/M	LT	U/P	L	500		N11, A1, N14	SCA	GCS
Amaurospiza concolor	M?	U/M	UT	R/P	1000	2200	B	F4E, F15		MAH, CDH, NAN
Amaurospiza moesta	M	U/M	UT	R/P	L	1600	B	F4, F1	SOU	ATL
Melopyrrha nigra	L	U/M	LT	F	L	900+		F1, F10, F15	CUB	GAN
Dolospingus fringilloides	M	U	LT	U	L	L		F12	RNW	AMN
Catamenia analis	L	T/U	UM	C	1800	3300		N2, N3, N14		NAN, CAN, SAN
Catamenia homochroa	L	T/U	UM	U/P	2500	3600		N3, F5E, F4E, N14		NAN, CAN, TEP
Catamenia inornata	L	T/U	UM	F	2800	4400		N2, N3, F6, N10, N9		NAN, CAN, SAN
Tiaris bicolor	L	T/M	LT	C	L	1300		N1, N14, F7E, F1E		GAN, LAN, NSA
Tiaris canora	L	T/M	LT	U	L	L?		F1E, F15, F10, N1, N14	CUB	GAN
Tiaris fuliginosa	L	U/M	LT	U/P	L	1700		F1E, F4E, F15E, N1, N14		NAN, NSA, CSA, ATL
Tiaris olivacea	L	T/M	LT	C	L	2300		N14, N1		GAN, PAS, GCS, CHO?, NAN
Loxipasser anoxanthus	L	T/M	LT	U	L	1800?		F1E, F15E, F4E	JAM	GAN
Loxigilla noctis	L	M/C	LT	C	L	900+		F1, F15, F7		GAN, LAN
Loxigilla portoricensis	L	M/C	HT	F	L	1000		F4, F1, F7, F15, F14?	PUE	GAN
Loxigilla violacea	L	M/C	LT	F	L	2000+		F1, F4, F7, F15, N1?	o	GAN
Melanospiza richardsoni	M	U/M	HT	U	L	1000		F1E, F7	STL	LAN
Geospiza conirostris	L	U/M	LT	F	L	L		N1, F7	GAL	EPC
Geospiza difficilis	L	T/M	LT	F	L	1000		N1, F7	GAL	EPC
Geospiza fortis	L	T/M	LT	F	L	1000		N1, F7	GAL	EPC
Geospiza fulginosa	L	T/M	LT	C	L	1700		N1, F7	GAL	EPC
Geospiza magnirostris	L	T/M	LT	F	L	L		N1, F7	GAL	EPC
Geospiza scandens	L	U/M	LT	F	L	L		N1, F7	GAL	EPC
Camarhynchus crassirostris	M	U/C	LT	F	L	500		F7, F4	GAL	EPC
Camarhynchus heliobates	H	M/C	LT	R	L	L		F14	GAL	EPC
Camarhynchus pallidus	M	U/C	LT	U	L	500		N1, F7	GAL	EPC
Camarhynchus parvulus	L	U/C	HT	F	L	700		F7, N1	GAL	EPC
Camarhynchus pauper	M	U/C	HT	C	L	600		F4, F7	GAL	EPC
Camarhynchus psittacula	M	U/C	HT	U	300	700		F4, F7	GAL	EPC
Certhidea olivacea	L	U/C	LT	C	L	800?		N1, F7, F4	GAL	EPC
Pinaroloxias inornata	L	U/C	LT	C	L	800		F1	CIS	PAS
Pipilo aberti	L	T	LT	F	L	1250		N11, N1	o	BSR

CP	RP	Notes
4	3	
2	1	Poorly known.
4	3	
3	2	Status uncertain; bird trapping.
4	3	
4	2	Monitor; absent from central Amazonia.
4	2	Movements and status uncertain.
3	1	Mainly below 900 m; movements tied to bamboo seeding.
3	2	Poorly known.
4	3	
4	2	
4	2	
2	1	Taxonomic status uncertain, may be hybrid; bird trapping.
4	2	
4	3	Locally to 1,600 m (Colombia).
3	2	Status and range poorly known.
3	1	May contain two species; bird trapping.
3	2	Occasionally to 900 m.
3	1	Locally to sea level; habitat requirements and movements poorly known.
2	1	Habitat requirements and movements poorly known.
4	3	
4	2	Poorly known.
4	3	To sea level on Pacific slope and locally to 4,600 m.
4	2	Locally to 1,600 m (Venezuela); follows bamboo fruiting?
4	3	Locally to 2,300 m (Colombia).
4	3	Local on mainland.
4	3	
4	3	
4	3	
4	2	
4	2	
4	3	
4	3	
3	2	Monitor.
4	3	
4	3	
4	3	
4	3	
4	3	
4	3	
4	3	
2	1	Habitat patches small and local; survey.
4	3	
4	3	
2	2	Survey.
4	3	
4	3	
4	3	
4	3	

Abbreviations Used

Snst - Sensitivity:
L - Low; **M** - Medium; **H** - High.

Strat - Foraging Strata:
T - Terrestrial; **U** - Understory; **M** - Midstory; **C** - Canopy; **A** - Aerial; **W** - Water.

Cntab - Center of Abundance:
LT - Lower tropical; **LS** - Lower subtropical; **HT** - Hill tropical; **UT** - Upper tropical; **US** - Upper subtropical; **MM** - Middle montane; **UM** - Upper montane.

Rel - Relative Abundance:
R - Rare; **U** - Uncommon; **F** - Fairly common; **C** - Common; **P** - Patchily distributed.

Min - Minimum Elevation:
L - Lowlands; **?** - Uncertain value; numeric values in meters.

Max - Maximum Elevation:
L - Lowlands; **?** - Uncertain value; **+** - species occurs at least to given elevation but likely occurs higher; numeric values in meters.

Micro - Microhabitats:
A - Army ants; **B** - Bamboo; **T** - Treefalls; **G** - Ground bromeliads; **C** - Rocky outcrops and caves; **S** - Streamside; **V** - Vine tangles; **B/V** -Bamboo/vine tangles.

Habitats:
F1 - Tropical lowland evergreen forest; **F2** - Flooded tropical evergreen forest; **F3** - River-edge forest; **F4** - Montane evergreen forest; **F5** - Elfin forest; **F6** - *Polylepis* woodland; **F7** - Tropical deciduous forest; **F8** - Gallery forest; **F9** - Southern temperate forest; **F10** - Pine forest; **F11** - Pine-oak forest; **F12** - White sand forest; **F13** - Palm forest; **F14** - Mangrove forest; **F15** - Secondary forest; **N1** - Arid lowland scrub; **N2** - Arid montane scrub; **N3** - Semihumid/humid montane scrub; **N4** - Cerrado; **N5** - Campo grasslands; **N6** - Low, seasonally wet grassland; **N7** - Southern temperate grassland; **N8** - Northern temperate grassland; **N9** - Puna grassland; **N10** - Paramo grassland; **N11** - Riparian thickets; **N12** - River island scrub; **N13** - Pastures/agricultural lands; **N14** - Second-growth scrub; **A1** - Freshwater marshes; **A2** - Saltwater/brackish marshes; **A3** - Coastal sand beaches/mudflats; **A4** - Coastal rocky beaches; **A5** - Riverine sand beaches; **A6** - Freshwater lakes and ponds; **A7** - Alkaline lakes; **A8** - Rivers; **A9** - Streams; **A10** - Bogs; **A11** - Coastal waters; **A12** - Pelagic waters.
E - Edge (used as a modifer to particular habitats).

Sub - Subregions:
ARC - Arid Caribbean Coast; **AWA** - Altiplano and Western Andes; **BAH** - Bahamas; **BAJ** - Baja California; **CAA** - Caatinga; **CAH** - Central American Highlands; **CER** - Cerrado; **CHA** - Chaco; **CHG** - Chiapas-Guanacaste; **CHL** - Chilean Desert; **CHR** - Chiriquí; **CIS** - Cocos Island; **CMV** - Cauca-Magdalena Valley; **COC** - Cuzco-Cochabamba; **CUB** - Cuba; **DOM** - Dominica; **EAS** - Eastern Slope Andes; **FDN** - Fernando de Noronha; **GAL** - Galápagos; **GCM** - Gulf Coast-Mexico; **GRE** - Grenada; **GUA** - Guadeloupe; **GUI** - Guianan; **HIS** - Hispaniola; **HPC** - Humid Pacific Coast; **ISA** - Isla Providencia and Isla San Andrés; **JAM** - Jamaica; **JFI** - Juan Fernández Islands; **MAN** - Manabí-Tumbes; **MAR** - Marañón Valley; **MID** - Madeira-Tapajós; **MON** - Montserrat; **MRT** - Martinique; **MTC** - Marañón-Cuzco; **NMM** - Northern Mexican Mountains; **NOR** - Northern Coastal Brazil; **PAR** - Pará; **PER** - Peruvian Desert; **PUE** - Puerto Rico; **RDJ** - Rio de Janeiro-Bahia Lowlands; **RMW** - Rio Madeira West; **RNW** - Rio Negro West; **SCA** - Southern Central America; **SCT** - Santa Cruz-Tucumán; **SIN** - Sinaloa-Oaxaca; **SMH** - Southern Mexican Highlands; **SMT** - Santa Marta; **SOC** - Islas Revillagigedo (Socorro Island group); **SON** - Sonoran Desert; **SOU** - Southern Atlantic Coast; **STL** - St. Lucia; **STV** - St. Vincent; **TAC** - Tacarcuna; **VAN** - Venezuelan Andes; **VNZ** - Venezuelan Coastal Mountains; **WES** - Western Andes; **YUC** - Yucatán Peninsula.
o - Endemic to region, but not restricted to a single subregion.

Zoogeographic Regions:
AMN - Northern Amazonia; **AMS** - Southern Amazonia; **ATL** - Atlantic Forest; **BSR** - Baja-Sonora; **CAN** - Central Andes; **CDH** - Chiriquí-Darién Highlands; **CHO** - Chocó Lowlands; **CSA** - Central South America; **EPC** - Equatorial Pacific Coast; **GAN** - Greater Antilles; **GCS** - Gulf-Caribbean Slope; **LAN** - Lesser Antilles; **MAH** - Madrean Highlands; **MPL** - Mexican Plateau; **NAN** - Northern Andes; **NSA** - Northern South America; **PAM** - Pampas; **PAS** - Pacific Arid Slope; **PAT** - Patagonia; **SAN** - Southern Andes; **STP** - Subtropical Pacific; **TEP** - Tepuis.

CP -Conservation Priority:
1 - Urgent; **2** - High; **3** - Medium; **4** - Low.

RP - Research Priority:
1 - High; **2** - Medium; **3** - Low.

	Snst	Strat	Cntab	Rel	Min	Max	Micro	Habitats	Sub	Zoogeographic Regions
Pipilo albicollis	L	T	MM	C	1150	2800		N2, F11	SMH	MAH
Pipilo crissalis	L	T	LS	C	L	2400		N1, N2, N11		BSR
Pipilo erythrophthalmus	L	T	UM	C	L	3500		F11E, N14, N11, N2		BSR, MPL, MAH
Pipilo fuscus	L	T	US	C	L	3100		N1, N2, N11		BSR, MPL, MAH
Pipilo ocai	M	T	US	F	1500	3750		F11E, F4E, N14	o	MAH
Melozone biarcuatum	L	T	UT	F	600	1800		F7, F4E, F15		MAH, CDH
Melozone kieneri	L	T	LT	F	L	1500		F7, F15, N2		PAS, MAH
Melozone leucotis	M	T	UT	F	500	2000		F4E		MAH, CDH
Arremon abeillei	M	T	HT	F	L	800		F7, F8	MAN	EPC
Arremon aurantiirostris	M	T	LT	F	L	1200		F1		GCS, AMN, AMS
Arremon flavirostris	M	T	LT	F	L	1400		F1E, F8, F7		CSA, ATL
Arremon schlegeli	M	T	LT	F	L	1400		F7, N1	ARC	NSA
Arremon taciturnus										
semitorquatus	M	T	HT	?	L	1000		F1, F15?	SOU	ATL
taciturnus	M	T	LT	F	L	1100		F1		NSA, AMN, AMS, ATL
Arremonops chloronotus	L	T/U	LT	C	L	900		F1E, F7E, F15, N14	o	GCS
Arremonops conirostris	L	T/U	LT	C	L	1600		F1E, F7E, F15, N11, N14		GCS, CHO, EPC, NSA, AMN
Arremonops rufivirgatus	M	T	LT	C	L	1550		F7, N1, N11		PAS, GCS
Arremonops tocuyensis	M	T	LT	F	L	1100		F7, N1	ARC	NSA
Atlapetes albiceps	M	T/U	HT	C	L	1200		F7, F8	MAN	EPC
Atlapetes albinucha	M	T/U	UT	F	900	2300		F4E, F11	o	MAH
Atlapetes albofrenatus	L	U	MM	F	1300	2500		F4E, N14	o	NAN
Atlapetes brunneinucha	L	T/U	UT	F	700	3100		F4, F11, F15		MAH, CDH, NAN, CAN
Atlapetes citrinellus	L?	U	UT	F	700	2400+		F4E, N3	SCT	CAN
Atlapetes flaviceps	M	U	MM?	F/P	1300	2200		F4E, N14?	EAS	NAN
Atlapetes fulviceps	L	U	MM	F	1600	3000		F4E, F15	SCT	CAN
Atlapetes fuscoolivaceus	L	U	MM	F	1600	2400		N14, F4E	EAS	NAN
Atlapetes gutturalis	L	T/U	MM	C	900	2500		F4E, F11, F15, N3, N14		MAH, CDH, NAN
Atlapetes leucopis	M	T/U	MM	R	2100	3200		F4, F5, F15, N14	EAS	NAN
Atlapetes leucopterus										
leucopterus	M	T/M	UT	C	700	2900		F4, F7, F8, F15		EPC, NAN, CAN
paynteri	M	U	MM	?	1700	2200		F4E	EAS	NAN
Atlapetes melanocephalus	M	T/U	MM	C	1300	3200		F4E, F15	SMT	NAN
Atlapetes nationi	L	U	UM	F	1800	4000		N2, N3, F6	AWA	CAN
Atlapetes pallidiceps	M	U/M	MM	R	1500	2100		N3	WES	NAN
Atlapetes pallidinucha	M	T/U	UM	F	2000	3600		F5, F4E	o	NAN
Atlapetes personatus	M	U/M	UT	F	1000	2500		F4	o	TEP
Atlapetes pileatus	M	U	MM	C	1300	3400		F11, F4E, N3?	o	MAH
Atlapetes rufigenis	L	U/M	UM	F/P	2600	4000		F6, F4E, N3, N14	AWA	CAN
Atlapetes rufinucha	L	U	MM	C	1100	3800		F4E, F15, N14		NAN, CAN
Atlapetes schistaceus	M	U/M	UM	F	1900	3300		F4E, F5		NAN, CAN
Atlapetes seebohmi	M	T/M	MM	U	800	2500+		F7, F4E		NAN, CAN
Atlapetes semirufus	L	T/M	UM	C	1600	3500		F4E, F15, N14	o	NAN
Atlapetes torquatus										
atricapillus	M	T/U	HT	U	300	1500		F4, F1, F15, F5		CDH, NAN
torquatus	H	T/U	MM	C	1700	3300		F4, F5		NAN, CAN
virenticeps	H	T/U	MM	F	1500	3000+		F4, F11	NMM	MAH
Atlapetes tricolor	L	U	MM	F	800	2200		F4, F15		NAN, CAN
Pezopetes capitalis	M	T/U	MM	F	2150	3350		F4E, N3, N14	CHR	CDH
Oreothraupis arremonops	M	T/U	MM	U/P	1700	2500		F4	WES	NAN
Pselliophorus luteoviridis	M	U/M	UT	?	1200	1800		F4	CHR	CDH
Pselliophorus tibialis	M	T/C	MM	F	1500	3400		F4, F15	CHR	CDH
Lysurus castaneiceps	M	T/U	MM	U/P	700	2200		F4	o	NAN, CAN
Lysurus crassirostris	M	T/U	MM	U	600	2000		F4	o	CDH

CP	RP	Notes
4	3	
4	3	
4	3	
4	3	
4	3	
4	3	Occasionally to 2,900 m.
4	3	
4	3	
4	3	
4	3	
4	3	
4	3	
3	2	Poorly known; deforestation.
4	3	Locally to 1,400 m (Colombia).
4	3	
4	3	
4	3	
4	3	
4	3	
4	3	
4	3	Mainly above 1,600 m.
4	3	Locally to 400 m (Veracruz).
4	3	
2	1	Deforestation; survey.
4	3	Seasonally to 400 m.
4	3	
4	3	
3	2	Poorly known.
4	3	
2	1	Almost unknown.
4	3	Occasionally to 600 m.
4	3	
1	1	Deforestation; nearly extinct? survey.
4	3	
4	3	
4	3	
3	3	
4	3	
4	3	Occasionally to 3,700 m (Colombia).
3	2	May be conspecific with *A. nationi*.
4	3	Locally to 600 m (northern Venezuela).
4	2	Relationship of various forms with *A. torquatus* uncertain.
4	3	Locally to 600 m (Colombia, Venezuela).
4	3	
4	3	Occasionally to 300 m and 3,000 m.
4	3	Locally to 1,500 m.
3	2	Locally to 1,200 m; poorly known.
3	2	Poorly known.
4	3	Seasonally to 1,200 m.
4	2	Poorly known.
4	2	Occasionally to 3,100 m (Panama).

Abbreviations Used

Snst - Sensitivity:
L - Low; **M** - Medium; **H** - High.

Strat - Foraging Strata:
T - Terrestrial; **U** - Understory; **M** - Midstory; **C** - Canopy; **A** - Aerial; **W** - Water.

Cntab - Center of Abundance:
LT - Lower tropical; **LS** - Lower subtropical; **HT** - Hill tropical; **UT** - Upper tropical; **US** - Upper subtropical; **MM** - Middle montane; **UM** - Upper montane.

Rel - Relative Abundance:
R - Rare; **U** - Uncommon; **F** - Fairly common; **C** - Common; **P** - Patchily distributed.

Min - Minimum Elevation:
L - Lowlands; **?** - Uncertain value; numeric values in meters.

Max - Maximum Elevation:
L - Lowlands; **?** - Uncertain value; **+** - species occurs at least to given elevation but likely occurs higher; numeric values in meters.

Micro - Microhabitats:
A - Army ants; **B** - Bamboo; **T** - Treefalls; **G** - Ground bromeliads; **C** - Rocky outcrops and caves; **S** - Streamside; **V** - Vine tangles; **B/V** -Bamboo/vine tangles.

Habitats:
F1 - Tropical lowland evergreen forest; **F2** - Flooded tropical evergreen forest; **F3** - River-edge forest; **F4** - Montane evergreen forest; **F5** - Elfin forest; **F6** - *Polylepis* woodland; **F7** - Tropical deciduous forest; **F8** - Gallery forest; **F9** - Southern temperate forest; **F10** - Pine forest; **F11** - Pine-oak forest; **F12** - White sand forest; **F13** - Palm forest; **F14** - Mangrove forest; **F15** - Secondary forest; **N1** - Arid lowland scrub; **N2** - Arid montane scrub; **N3** - Semihumid/humid montane scrub; **N4** - Cerrado; **N5** - Campo grasslands; **N6** - Low, seasonally wet grassland; **N7** - Southern temperate grassland; **N8** - Northern temperate grassland; **N9** - Puna grassland; **N10** - Paramo grassland; **N11** - Riparian thickets; **N12** - River island scrub; **N13** - Pastures/agricultural lands; **N14** - Second-growth scrub; **A1** - Freshwater marshes; **A2** - Saltwater/brackish marshes; **A3** - Coastal sand beaches/mudflats; **A4** - Coastal rocky beaches; **A5** - Riverine sand beaches; **A6** - Freshwater lakes and ponds; **A7** - Alkaline lakes; **A8** - Rivers; **A9** - Streams; **A10** - Bogs; **A11** - Coastal waters; **A12** - Pelagic waters.
E - Edge (used as a modifer to particular habitats).

Sub - Subregions:
ARC - Arid Caribbean Coast; **AWA** - Altiplano and Western Andes; **BAH** - Bahamas; **BAJ** - Baja California; **CAA** - Caatinga; **CAH** - Central American Highlands; **CER** - Cerrado; **CHA** - Chaco; **CHG** - Chiapas-Guanacaste; **CHL** - Chilean Desert; **CHR** - Chiriquí; **CIS** - Cocos Island; **CMV** - Cauca-Magdalena Valley; **COC** - Cuzco-Cochabamba; **CUB** - Cuba; **DOM** - Dominica; **EAS** - Eastern Slope Andes; **FDN** - Fernando de Noronha; **GAL** - Galápagos; **GCM** - Gulf Coast-Mexico; **GRE** - Grenada; **GUA** - Guadeloupe; **GUI** - Guianan; **HIS** - Hispaniola; **HPC** - Humid Pacific Coast; **ISA** - Isla Providencia and Isla San Andrés; **JAM** - Jamaica; **JFI** - Juan Fernández Islands; **MAN** - Manabí-Tumbes; **MAR** - Marañón Valley; **MID** - Madeira-Tapajós; **MON** - Montserrat; **MRT** - Martinique; **MTC** - Marañón-Cuzco; **NMM** - Northern Mexican Mountains; **NOR** - Northern Coastal Brazil; **PAR** - Pará; **PER** - Peruvian Desert; **PUE** - Puerto Rico; **RDJ** - Rio de Janeiro-Bahia Lowlands; **RMW** - Rio Madeira West; **RNW** - Rio Negro West; **SCA** - Southern Central America; **SCT** - Santa Cruz-Tucumán; **SIN** - Sinaloa-Oaxaca; **SMH** - Southern Mexican Highlands; **SMT** - Santa Marta; **SOC** - Islas Revillagigedo (Socorro Island group); **SON** - Sonoran Desert; **SOU** - Southern Atlantic Coast; **STL** - St. Lucia; **STV** - St. Vincent; **TAC** - Tacarcuna; **VAN** - Venezuelan Andes; **VNZ** - Venezuelan Coastal Mountains; **WES** - Western Andes; **YUC** - Yucatán Peninsula.
o - Endemic to region, but not restricted to a single subregion.

Zoogeographic Regions:
AMN - Northern Amazonia; **AMS** - Southern Amazonia; **ATL** - Atlantic Forest; **BSR** - Baja-Sonora; **CAN** - Central Andes; **CDH** - Chiriquí-Darién Highlands; **CHO** - Chocó Lowlands; **CSA** - Central South America; **EPC** - Equatorial Pacific Coast; **GAN** - Greater Antilles; **GCS** - Gulf-Caribbean Slope; **LAN** - Lesser Antilles; **MAH** - Madrean Highlands; **MPL** - Mexican Plateau; **NAN** - Northern Andes; **NSA** - Northern South America; **PAM** - Pampas; **PAS** - Pacific Arid Slope; **PAT** - Patagonia; **SAN** - Southern Andes; **STP** - Subtropical Pacific; **TEP** - Tepuis.

CP -Conservation Priority:
1 - Urgent; **2** - High; **3** - Medium; **4** - Low.

RP - Research Priority:
1 - High; **2** - Medium; **3** - Low.

	Snst	Strat	Cntab	Rel	Min	Max	Micro	Habitats	Sub	Zoogeographic Regions
Urothraupis stolzmanni	H	U/M	UM	F	3000	3600		F5	EAS	NAN
Charitospiza eucosma	H	T/U	LT	U/P	L	1200		N4	CER	CSA
Coryphaspiza melanotis	H	T/U	LT	U/P	L	1200		N5, N6		AMS, CSA
Saltatricula multicolor	M	T	LS	C	L	600		N1, F7E	CHA	CSA
Gubernatrix cristata	M?	T	LS	U	L	700		N1, N11		CSA, PAM
Coryphospingus cucullatus	L	T/U	LS	C	L	1600		N1, F7E, F1E, F15		CAN, AMS, CSA, ATL, PAM
Coryphospingus pileatus	L	T/U	LT	F	L	1200		N1, F7E, F1E, F15		NSA, CSA, ATL
Rhodospingus cruentus	M	T/M	LT	F	L	800		F7, F1E	MAN	EPC
Paroaria baeri	M	?	LT	F	L	L		N11, F3	PAR	AMS
Paroaria capitata	L	T/M	LT	C	L	L		N11, N14, A1		CSA, PAM
Paroaria coronata	L	T/U	LT	F	L	L		N1, N14		CSA, PAM
Paroaria dominicana	L	T/U	LT	C	L	1200		N1, F7	CAA	CSA
Paroaria gularis	L	T/M	LT	C	L	700		N11, N14, F3, F15		NSA, AMN, AMS
Catamblyrhynchinae										
Catamblyrhynchus diadema	H	U	UM	F	1800	3500	B	F5, F4		NAN, CAN
Cardinalinae										
Pheucticus aureoventris	L	C	MM	C	L	3100		F4E, F15, N3, N2, N1		NAN, CAN, SAN, CSA
Pheucticus chrysogaster	L	C	UT	F	950	2500		F4E, F7, F15, N1		EPC, STP, NAN, CAN
Pheucticus chrysopeplus	M	C	LT	F	L	2800		F4E, F1E, F7, F8		PAS, MAH
Pheucticus melanocephalus	M	C	MM	C	1200	3400		F11, F8		BSR, MPL, MAH
Pheucticus tibialis	M	C	UT	F	1000	2600		F4E	CHR	CDH
Cardinalis cardinalis	L	T/C	LS	C	L	2500		N11, N14, N1, F8, F15		BSR, MPL, PAS, MAH, GCS
Cardinalis phoeniceus	L	T/C	LT	F	L	L		N1	ARC	NSA
Cardinalis sinuatus	L	T/C	US	F	L	2200		N1, N2, N11		BSR, MPL, PAS, GCS
Caryothraustes canadensis	M	C	LT	F/P	L	900		F1, F15?		GCS, AMN, AMS, ATL
Caryothraustes humeralis	H	C	LT	U/P	L	1000		F1		AMN, AMS
Caryothraustes poliogaster	M	M/C	LT	F	L	900		F1, F15?	o	GCS
Rhodothraupis celaeno	L	U/C	LT	F	L	1200		F7, F8, F15	GCM	GCS
Periporphyrus erythromelas	L	U/M	LT	U/P	L	900		F1		AMN, AMS
Pitylus fuliginosus	M	C	HT	U	L	1200+		F1	o	ATL
Pitylus grossus	M	M/C	LT	F/P	L	1200		F1		GCS, CHO, AMN, AMS
Saltator albicollis	L	M/C	LT	C	L	1850		F7, F15		LAN, GCS, EPC, STP, CAN, NSA
Saltator atriceps	M	U/C	LT	F	L	1300		F1E, F15, N14		PAS, GCS
Saltator atricollis	M	U/C	HT	F/P	600	1200		N4, F7	o	CSA
Saltator atripennis	M	C	UT	F	800	2200		F4	o	NAN
Saltator aurantiirostris										
aurantiirostris	L	U/C	LS	C	L	3600		F7, F15, N1, N2, N3		CAN, SAN, CSA, PAM
nigriceps	M	U/C	MM	U	800	2400		F7, F8		EPC, CAN
Saltator cinctus	H	U/C	UM	R/P	1700	3100		F4, F5		NAN, CAN
Saltator coerulescens	L	M/C	LT	C	L	1300		N14, N12, F1E, F7, F8, F15		PAS, GCS, NSA, AMN, AMS, CSA
Saltator maxillosus	M	M/C	UT	F	900	2200		F4E, F1E, F15	SOU	ATL
Saltator maximus	L	M/C	LT	C	L	1500		F1E, F15, F4E		GCS, CHO, EPC, NSA, AMN, AMS, CSA, ATL
Saltator orenocensis	M	U/C	LT	F	L	600		N1, F7, F8	ARC	NSA
Saltator rufiventris	M	U/C	UM	U	2600	4000		F6, N3	SCT	CAN
Saltator similis	L	M/C	LT	C	L	1250		F1E, F15, F8		CSA, ATL
Passerina amoena	L	T/C	LS	F	L	2400		N1, N11		BSR
Passerina brissonii	M	U	LT	F	L	900		F1, F7, N1		NSA, CSA, ATL
Passerina caerulea	L	T/M	US	C	L	2500		F8, N11, N1, F15, N14		GAN, BSR, MPL, PAS, MAH, GCS, CDH
Passerina caerulescens	M	U/C	HT	U/P	600	1100		N5	CER	CSA
Passerina ciris	L	T/M	US	F	L	1700		N11, N2, N14		MPL, GCS
Passerina cyanoides	M	U	LT	F	L	1250		F1, F15		GCS, CHO, EPC, NSA, AMN, AMS
Passerina glaucocaerulea	L	U/M	LT	U	L	1000		F1E, F15, N14, N11		ATL, PAM
Passerina leclancherii	M	T/M	LT	F	L	1200		F7, N1	SIN	PAS

CP	RP	Notes
4	3	
2	1	Monitor; habitat destruction; local movements need study.
2	1	Habitat destruction; survey
4	3	
2	1	Declining; capture for bird trade.
4	3	
4	3	
3	2	Seasonal movements poorly known.
3	2	
4	3	
3	2	Declining in many areas; capture for bird trade.
4	3	
4	3	
4	3	
4	3	
4	3	Locally to lowlands.
4	3	
4	3	Locally to sea level (Baja California).
4	3	
4	3	
4	2	Poorly known.
4	3	
4	3	
4	3	
4	3	
3	2	Deforestation? monitor.
4	3	
4	3	
4	3	
4	3	Occasionally to 2,700 m.
3	2	
3	2	Habitat destruction; monitor.
4	3	Locally to sea level (Pacific slope).
4	3	Mainly above 1,700 m in Andes.
3	2	
3	2	Associated with *Podocarpus*?
4	3	
3	3	Locally to sea level.
4	3	
4	3	
3	2	Some habitat destruction; monitor.
4	3	
4	3	
4	3	Occasionally to 1,600 m (Colombia).
4	3	
2	1	Habitat destruction.
4	3	
4	3	
3	2	Declining? monitor.
3	2	Capture for bird trade.

Abbreviations Used

Snst - Sensitivity:
L - Low; **M** - Medium; **H** - High.

Strat - Foraging Strata:
T - Terrestrial; **U** - Understory; **M** - Midstory; **C** - Canopy; **A** - Aerial; **W** - Water.

Cntab - Center of Abundance:
LT - Lower tropical; **LS** - Lower subtropical; **HT** - Hill tropical; **UT** - Upper tropical; **US** - Upper subtropical; **MM** - Middle montane; **UM** - Upper montane.

Rel - Relative Abundance:
R - Rare; **U** - Uncommon; **F** - Fairly common; **C** - Common; **P** - Patchily distributed.

Min - Minimum Elevation:
L - Lowlands; **?** - Uncertain value; numeric values in meters.

Max - Maximum Elevation:
L - Lowlands; **?** - Uncertain value; **+** - species occurs at least to given elevation but likely occurs higher; numeric values in meters.

Micro - Microhabitats:
A - Army ants; **B** - Bamboo; **T** - Treefalls; **G** - Ground bromeliads; **C** - Rocky outcrops and caves; **S** - Streamside; **V** - Vine tangles; **B/V** -Bamboo/vine tangles.

Habitats:
F1 - Tropical lowland evergreen forest; **F2** - Flooded tropical evergreen forest; **F3** - River-edge forest; **F4** - Montane evergreen forest; **F5** - Elfin forest; **F6** - *Polylepis* woodland; **F7** - Tropical deciduous forest; **F8** - Gallery forest; **F9** - Southern temperate forest; **F10** - Pine forest; **F11** - Pine-oak forest; **F12** - White sand forest; **F13** - Palm forest; **F14** - Mangrove forest; **F15** - Secondary forest; **N1** - Arid lowland scrub; **N2** - Arid montane scrub; **N3** - Semihumid/humid montane scrub; **N4** - Cerrado; **N5** - Campo grasslands; **N6** - Low, seasonally wet grassland; **N7** - Southern temperate grassland; **N8** - Northern temperate grassland; **N9** - Puna grassland; **N10** - Paramo grassland; **N11** - Riparian thickets; **N12** - River island scrub; **N13** - Pastures/agricultural lands; **N14** - Second-growth scrub; **A1** - Freshwater marshes; **A2** - Saltwater/brackish marshes; **A3** - Coastal sand beaches/mudflats; **A4** - Coastal rocky beaches; **A5** - Riverine sand beaches; **A6** - Freshwater lakes and ponds; **A7** - Alkaline lakes; **A8** - Rivers; **A9** - Streams; **A10** - Bogs; **A11** - Coastal waters; **A12** - Pelagic waters.
E - Edge (used as a modifer to particular habitats).

Sub - Subregions:
ARC - Arid Caribbean Coast; **AWA** - Altiplano and Western Andes; **BAH** - Bahamas; **BAJ** - Baja California; **CAA** - Caatinga; **CAH** - Central American Highlands; **CER** - Cerrado; **CHA** - Chaco; **CHG** - Chiapas-Guanacaste; **CHL** - Chilean Desert; **CHR** - Chiriquí; **CIS** - Cocos Island; **CMV** - Cauca-Magdalena Valley; **COC** - Cuzco-Cochabamba; **CUB** - Cuba; **DOM** - Dominica; **EAS** - Eastern Slope Andes; **FDN** - Fernando de Noronha; **GAL** - Galápagos; **GCM** - Gulf Coast-Mexico; **GRE** - Grenada; **GUA** - Guadeloupe; **GUI** - Guianan; **HIS** - Hispaniola; **HPC** - Humid Pacific Coast; **ISA** - Isla Providencia and Isla San Andrés; **JAM** - Jamaica; **JFI** - Juan Fernández Islands; **MAN** - Manabí-Tumbes; **MAR** - Marañón Valley; **MID** - Madeira-Tapajós; **MON** - Montserrat; **MRT** - Martinique; **MTC** - Marañón-Cuzco; **NMM** - Northern Mexican Mountains; **NOR** - Northern Coastal Brazil; **PAR** - Pará; **PER** - Peruvian Desert; **PUE** - Puerto Rico; **RDJ** - Rio de Janeiro-Bahia Lowlands; **RMW** - Rio Madeira West; **RNW** - Rio Negro West; **SCA** - Southern Central America; **SCT** - Santa Cruz-Tucumán; **SIN** - Sinaloa-Oaxaca; **SMH** - Southern Mexican Highlands; **SMT** - Santa Marta; **SOC** - Islas Revillagigedo (Socorro Island group); **SON** - Sonoran Desert; **SOU** - Southern Atlantic Coast; **STL** - St. Lucia; **STV** - St. Vincent; **TAC** - Tacarcuna; **VAN** - Venezuelan Andes; **VNZ** - Venezuelan Coastal Mountains; **WES** - Western Andes; **YUC** - Yucatán Peninsula.
o - Endemic to region, but not restricted to a single subregion.

Zoogeographic Regions:
AMN - Northern Amazonia; **AMS** - Southern Amazonia; **ATL** - Atlantic Forest; **BSR** - Baja-Sonora; **CAN** - Central Andes; **CDH** - Chiriquí-Darién Highlands; **CHO** - Chocó Lowlands; **CSA** - Central South America; **EPC** - Equatorial Pacific Coast; **GAN** - Greater Antilles; **GCS** - Gulf-Caribbean Slope; **LAN** - Lesser Antilles; **MAH** - Madrean Highlands; **MPL** - Mexican Plateau; **NAN** - Northern Andes; **NSA** - Northern South America; **PAM** - Pampas; **PAS** - Pacific Arid Slope; **PAT** - Patagonia; **SAN** - Southern Andes; **STP** - Subtropical Pacific; **TEP** - Tepuis.

CP -Conservation Priority:
1 - Urgent; **2** - High; **3** - Medium; **4** - Low.

RP - Research Priority:
1 - High; **2** - Medium; **3** - Low.

	Snst	Strat	Cntab	Rel	Min	Max	Micro	Habitats	Sub	Zoogeographic Regions
Passerina parellina	M	U/M	LT	F	L	1850		F7, F1E, F11		PAS, GCS
Passerina rositae	M	U/M	LT	U	L	1100		F7	CHG	PAS
Passerina versicolor	L	U/M	US	F	L	1900		N2, N1, N11		BSR, MPL, PAS, MAH, GCS
Thraupinae										
Orchesticus abeillei	M	C	UT	U	750	1500		F4	o	ATL
Schistochlamys melanopis	L	U/C	LT	F	L	1700		F8, N4, N5, F12		NSA, AMN, AMS, CSA, ATL
Schistochlamys ruficapillus	L	U/C	LT	F	L	1100		F7, N4, F12, N14		CSA, ATL
Neothraupis fasciata	M	U/C	LT	F	L	1100		N4	CER	CSA
Cypsnagra hirundinacea	H	T/C	LT	F/P	L	1000		N5, N4	CER	CSA
Conothraupis mesoleuca	M	?	LT	R?	L	L		F7?	CER	CSA
Conothraupis speculigera	M	U/C	UT	U/P	L	1800		F7, F8, N11		EPC, AMS
Lamprospiza melanoleuca	H	C	LT	U/P	L	700		F1		AMN, AMS
Cissopis leveriana	L	U/C	LT	F	L	1200		F15, F3, F1		AMN, AMS, CSA, ATL
Chlorornis riefferii	M	C	MM	F	2300	3350		F4		NAN, CAN
Sericossypha albocristata	H	C	MM	U/P	1600	3200		F4		NAN, CAN
Compsothraupis loricata	H	C	LT	U	L	1000		F8, F7	CER	CSA
Nesospingus speculiferus	L	U/C	HT	F	200	1200		F4, F15	PUE	GAN
Chlorospingus canigularis	M	C	UT	F	300	2600		F4, F1, F7		CDH, NAN, CAN
Chlorospingus flavigularis	M	U/C	UT	F	250	1600		F4, F15		CDH, NAN, CAN
Chlorospingus flavovirens	H	M/C	UT	U/P	950	1050		F4	WES	NAN
Chlorospingus inornatus	H	M/C	UT	C	800	1550		F4, F5	TAC	CDH
Chlorospingus ophthalmicus	M	U/M	UT	C	1000	2500		F4, F15		MAH, CDH, NAN, CAN
Chlorospingus parvirostris	M	U/C	MM	F	1400	2600		F4		NAN, CAN
Chlorospingus pileatus	M	U/C	MM	C	1500	3000		F4, F5, F15	CHR	CDH
Chlorospingus semifuscus	H	U/M	UT	F	900	2500		F4	WES	NAN
Chlorospingus tacarcunae	H	U/M	UT	U	850	1500		F4, F5	TAC	CDH
Cnemoscopus rubrirostris	H	C	MM	F	1900	3350		F4, F5		NAN, CAN
Hemispingus atropileus	H	U/M	UM	F	2300	3350	B	F4, F5		NAN, CAN
Hemispingus calophrys	H	U	UM	F	2300	3350	B	F4, F5	COC	CAN
Hemispingus frontalis	M	U/M	MM	F	1300	2900		F4, F15		NAN, CAN
Hemispingus goeringi	H	U	UM	R	2600	3200		F5	VAN	NAN
Hemispingus melanotis	M	U	MM	F/P	1500	2700	B	F4, F15		NAN, CAN
Hemispingus parodii	H	U	UM	F	2750	3500	B	F5	MTC	CAN
Hemispingus reyi	M	U	UM	F	1900	3200	B	F4, F5	VAN	NAN
Hemispingus rufosuperciliaris	H	U	UM	U	2500	3350	B	F5	MTC	CAN
Hemispingus superciliaris	L	C	UM	F	2100	3350		F4, F15, F6		NAN, CAN
Hemispingus trifasciatus	H	C	UM	F	2800	4250		F5	o	CAN
Hemispingus verticalis	H	C	UM	F	2600	3500		F5, F4	o	NAN
Hemispingus xanthophthalmus	H	C	UM	F	2400	3500		F4, F5	o	CAN
Pyrrhocoma ruficeps	M	U	LT	F/P	L	1500	B	F1, F4, F15	SOU	ATL
Thlypopsis fulviceps	L	U/C	UT	C	750	2000		F15, F4	o	NAN
Thlypopsis inornata	L	U/C	UT	F	450	2000		N3, N2	o	CAN
Thlypopsis ornata	L	U/C	UM	F	2000	3400		F15, F4E, N3		NAN, CAN
Thlypopsis pectoralis	L	U/C	UM	U	2500	3100		F15, N3	AWA	CAN
Thlypopsis ruficeps	L	U/C	UM	F	1300	3600		F15, F4	o	CAN
Thlypopsis sordida	L	U/C	LT	F	L	800		F8, F15, F3, N12		NSA, AMN, AMS, CSA, ATL
Hemithraupis flavicollis	M	C	LT	F	L	1000		F1, F15		NSA, AMN, AMS, ATL
Hemithraupis guira	L	C	LT	C	L	1000		F1, F8, F15		EPC, NSA, AMN, AMS, CSA
Hemithraupis ruficapilla	L	C	HT	C	L	1350		F4, F1, F15	o	ATL
Chrysothlypis chrysomelas	M	C	UT	F	350	1600		F4, F1		GCS, CDH
Chrysothlypis salmoni	L	C	HT	F	L	1100		F15, F1	o	CHO
Nemosia pileata	L	C	LT	F	L	800		F8, F15, F3, F14		NSA, AMN, AMS, CSA, ATL
Nemosia rourei	?	C	LT	R	L	900		F1?	RDJ	ATL

CP	RP	Notes
4	3	
3	2	Survey.
4	3	
3	2	
4	3	Occasionally to 2,400 m; local in Amazonia.
4	3	Occasionally to 1,850 m.
4	2	
3	2	Local in Amazonian savannas; survey.
2	1	Known from one specimen; habitat destruction; survey.
3	1	Nomadic? survey.
4	3	
4	3	Occasionally to 2,000 m.
4	3	Occasionally to 1,500 m.
3	2	
4	3	
4	3	
4	2	
4	3	
2	2	Survey.
3	3	
4	3	Occasionally to 3,500 m; may contain multiple species.
4	3	
4	3	
3	3	
3	2	
4	3	May contain two species.
4	3	
3	3	
4	3	
3	2	Poorly known.
3	2	Locally to 1,200 and 3,050 m; may contain multiple species.
3	3	
3	3	
3	3	Mainly above 2,800 m.
4	3	Occasionally to 1,900 m.
4	3	
4	3	
4	3	
3	2	
4	3	
3	3	
4	3	Occasionally to 1,400 m.
3	3	
4	3	
4	3	Occasionally to 1,300 m.
4	3	
4	3	Occasionally to 2,000 m.
3	3	
3	3	Deforestation.
4	3	
4	3	
1	1	One specimen, one sight record known; possibly extinct.

Abbreviations Used

Snst - Sensitivity:
L - Low; **M** - Medium; **H** - High.

Strat - Foraging Strata:
T - Terrestrial; **U** - Understory; **M** - Midstory; **C** - Canopy; **A** - Aerial; **W** - Water.

Cntab - Center of Abundance:
LT - Lower tropical; **LS** - Lower subtropical; **HT** - Hill tropical; **UT** - Upper tropical; **US** - Upper subtropical; **MM** - Middle montane; **UM** - Upper montane.

Rel - Relative Abundance:
R - Rare; **U** - Uncommon; **F** - Fairly common; **C** - Common; **P** - Patchily distributed.

Min - Minimum Elevation:
L - Lowlands; **?** - Uncertain value; numeric values in meters.

Max - Maximum Elevation:
L - Lowlands; **?** - Uncertain value; **+** - species occurs at least to given elevation but likely occurs higher; numeric values in meters.

Micro - Microhabitats:
A - Army ants; **B** - Bamboo; **T** - Treefalls; **G** - Ground bromeliads; **C** - Rocky outcrops and caves; **S** - Streamside; **V** - Vine tangles; **B/V** -Bamboo/vine tangles.

Habitats:
F1 - Tropical lowland evergreen forest; **F2** - Flooded tropical evergreen forest; **F3** - River-edge forest; **F4** - Montane evergreen forest; **F5** - Elfin forest; **F6** - *Polylepis* woodland; **F7** - Tropical deciduous forest; **F8** - Gallery forest; **F9** - Southern temperate forest; **F10** - Pine forest; **F11** - Pine-oak forest; **F12** - White sand forest; **F13** - Palm forest; **F14** - Mangrove forest; **F15** - Secondary forest; **N1** - Arid lowland scrub; **N2** - Arid montane scrub; **N3** - Semihumid/humid montane scrub; **N4** - Cerrado; **N5** - Campo grasslands; **N6** - Low, seasonally wet grassland; **N7** - Southern temperate grassland; **N8** - Northern temperate grassland; **N9** - Puna grassland; **N10** - Paramo grassland; **N11** - Riparian thickets; **N12** - River island scrub; **N13** - Pastures/agricultural lands; **N14** - Second-growth scrub; **A1** - Freshwater marshes; **A2** - Saltwater/brackish marshes; **A3** - Coastal sand beaches/mudflats; **A4** - Coastal rocky beaches; **A5** - Riverine sand beaches; **A6** - Freshwater lakes and ponds; **A7** - Alkaline lakes; **A8** - Rivers; **A9** - Streams; **A10** - Bogs; **A11** - Coastal waters; **A12** - Pelagic waters.
E - Edge (used as a modifer to particular habitats).

Sub - Subregions:
ARC - Arid Caribbean Coast; **AWA** - Altiplano and Western Andes; **BAH** - Bahamas; **BAJ** - Baja California; **CAA** - Caatinga; **CAH** - Central American Highlands; **CER** - Cerrado; **CHA** - Chaco; **CHG** - Chiapas-Guanacaste; **CHL** - Chilean Desert; **CHR** - Chiriquí; **CIS** - Cocos Island; **CMV** - Cauca-Magdalena Valley; **COC** - Cuzco-Cochabamba; **CUB** - Cuba; **DOM** - Dominica; **EAS** - Eastern Slope Andes; **FDN** - Fernando de Noronha; **GAL** - Galápagos; **GCM** - Gulf Coast-Mexico; **GRE** - Grenada; **GUA** - Guadeloupe; **GUI** - Guianan; **HIS** - Hispaniola; **HPC** - Humid Pacific Coast; **ISA** - Isla Providencia and Isla San Andrés; **JAM** - Jamaica; **JFI** - Juan Fernández Islands; **MAN** - Manabí-Tumbes; **MAR** - Marañón Valley; **MID** - Madeira-Tapajós; **MON** - Montserrat; **MRT** - Martinique; **MTC** - Marañón-Cuzco; **NMM** - Northern Mexican Mountains; **NOR** - Northern Coastal Brazil; **PAR** - Pará; **PER** - Peruvian Desert; **PUE** - Puerto Rico; **RDJ** - Rio de Janeiro-Bahia Lowlands; **RMW** - Rio Madeira West; **RNW** - Rio Negro West; **SCA** - Southern Central America; **SCT** - Santa Cruz-Tucumán; **SIN** - Sinaloa-Oaxaca; **SMH** - Southern Mexican Highlands; **SMT** - Santa Marta; **SOC** - Islas Revillagigedo (Socorro Island group); **SON** - Sonoran Desert; **SOU** - Southern Atlantic Coast; **STL** - St. Lucia; **STV** - St. Vincent; **TAC** - Tacarcuna; **VAN** - Venezuelan Andes; **VNZ** - Venezuelan Coastal Mountains; **WES** - Western Andes; **YUC** - Yucatán Peninsula.
o - Endemic to region, but not restricted to a single subregion.

Zoogeographic Regions:
AMN - Northern Amazonia; **AMS** - Southern Amazonia; **ATL** - Atlantic Forest; **BSR** - Baja-Sonora; **CAN** - Central Andes; **CDH** - Chiriquí-Darién Highlands; **CHO** - Chocó Lowlands; **CSA** - Central South America; **EPC** - Equatorial Pacific Coast; **GAN** - Greater Antilles; **GCS** - Gulf-Caribbean Slope; **LAN** - Lesser Antilles; **MAH** - Madrean Highlands; **MPL** - Mexican Plateau; **NAN** - Northern Andes; **NSA** - Northern South America; **PAM** - Pampas; **PAS** - Pacific Arid Slope; **PAT** - Patagonia; **SAN** - Southern Andes; **STP** - Subtropical Pacific; **TEP** - Tepuis.

CP -Conservation Priority:
1 - Urgent; **2** - High; **3** - Medium; **4** - Low.

RP - Research Priority:
1 - High; **2** - Medium; **3** - Low.

	Snst	Strat	Cntab	Rel	Min	Max	Micro	Habitats	Sub	Zoogeographic Regions
Phaenicophilus palmarum	L	U/C	LT	C	L	2000+		F15, F1, F7, F4, F14	HIS	GAN
Phaenicophilus poliocephalus	L	U/C	LT	C	L	2400		F15, F1, F4, F14	HIS	GAN
Calyptophilus frugivorus	M	T/U	UT	F/P	1000	2200		F4, F7, F10	HIS	GAN
Rhodinocichla rosea	M	T/U	LT	F/P	L	1700		F7, F15, F8		PAS, GCS, NSA
Mitrospingus cassinii	M	U/M	LT	F	L	1200		F1E, F15		GCS, CHO
Mitrospingus oleagineus	H	U/M	UT	F	900	1800		F4	o	TEP
Chlorothraupis carmioli	M	U/M	HT	F/P	L	1200		F1, F15		GCS, CDH, NAN, CAN
Chlorothraupis olivacea	M	U/M	LT	F	L	1500		F1, F4, F15		CDH, CHO, NSA
Chlorothraupis stolzmanni	H	U/M	UT	F	400	2100		F1, F4	WES	NAN
Orthogonys chloricterus	M	C	UT	U/P	700	1800		F4, F15	SOU	ATL
Eucometis penicillata	M	U/M	LT	F/P	L	600	A	F1, F8, F2, F15		PAS, GCS, NSA, AMN, AMS, CSA
Lanio aurantius	H	M/C	LT	F	L	750		F1	o	GCS
Lanio fulvus	H	C	LT	F	L	1300		F1	o	AMN
Lanio leucothorax	H	M/C	LT	F	L	750		F1	o	GCS
Lanio versicolor	H	C	LT	F	L	900		F1	o	AMS
Creurgops dentata	H	C	MM	U	1500	2150		F4	COC	CAN
Creurgops verticalis	H	C	MM	U	1150	2700		F4		NAN, CAN
Heterospingus rubrifrons	H	U/C	HT	U	L	900		F1	o	GCS
Heterospingus xanthopygius	H	M/C	LT	U	L	1100		F1		GCS, CHO, NSA
Tachyphonus coronatus	L	M/C	LT	C	L	1200		F1E, F4E, F15	SOU	ATL
Tachyphonus cristatus	M	C	LT	F	L	1100		F1, F12		AMN, AMS, ATL
Tachyphonus delatrii	M	U/M	LT	C	L	900		F1, F4, F15		GCS, CHO, NSA
Tachyphonus luctuosus	M	M/C	LT	F/P	L	1000		F1, F3, F15		GCS, CHO, NSA, AMN, AMS
Tachyphonus phoenicius	M	U/C	LT	F/P	L	2000		F12, N6		AMN, AMS
Tachyphonus rufiventer	H	C	LT	F	L	1400		F1	RMW	AMS
Tachyphonus rufus	L	U/C	LT	C/P	L	1500		F15, F8, F1, N14		GCS, NSA, AMN, AMS, CSA, PAM
Tachyphonus surinamus	M	U/M	LT	F/P	L	600		F1		AMN, AMS
Trichothraupis melanops	M	U/M	UT	F/P	L	1700		F1, F4, F15		CAN, CSA, ATL
Habia atrimaxillaris	M	U	LT	F	L	L		F1, F15	HPC	GCS
Habia cristata	M	U	UT	U	700	1800		F1, F4	WES	NAN
Habia fuscicauda	M	U	LT	F	L	1200		F1E, F2, F15		PAS, GCS, NSA
Habia gutturalis	L	U	HT	F	100	1000		F15, F1	CMV	NSA
Habia rubica	H	U/M	LT	F	L	1000		F1		PAS, GCS, NSA, AMN, AMS, ATL
Piranga bidentata	M	C	MM	F	800	2800		F4, F11, F15		MAH, CDH
Piranga erythrocephala	M	U/C	MM	F	900	2600		F11, F4	o	MAH
Piranga flava	L	C	UT	F	600	3000		F11, F8, F7, F15, F4E, F1E, N4		MAH, CDH, NAN, CAN, TEP, CSA, ATL
Piranga leucoptera	M	C	UT	F	800	2200		F4, F1, F11		MAH, CDH, NAN, CAN, TEP
Piranga ludoviciana	M	C	MM	?	1600	2500+		F11, F10		BSR
Piranga roseogularis	M	M/C	LT	F	L	L		F7, F15	YUC	GCS
Piranga rubra	L	C	LT	F	L	1800		F8		BSR, MPL
Piranga rubriceps	H	C	MM	U/P	1700	3000		F4		NAN, CAN
Calochaetes coccineus	H	C	UT	U	1100	2400		F4		NAN, CAN
Ramphocelus bresilius	L	U/M	LT	F	L	800		F15, F8, F3, F12	o	ATL
Ramphocelus carbo	L	U/C	LT	C	L	1200		F15, F1E, F8, F3, N14		NSA, AMN, AMS, CSA
Ramphocelus dimidiatus	L	U/M	LT	C	L	1700		F15, F1E		GCS, CHO, NSA
Ramphocelus flammigerus	L	U/C	LT	C	L	800		F1E, F15, N14		GCS, CHO, NSA
Ramphocelus melanogaster	L	U/M	HT	C	600	2100		F15, F1E, F3, N14		CAN, AMS
Ramphocelus nigrogularis	M	U/C	LT	F	L	600		F2, N11		AMN, AMS
Ramphocelus passerinii	L	U/C	LT	C	L	1000		F1E, F15, N14	o	GCS
Ramphocelus sanguinolentus	L	U/M	LT	F	L	1200		F1E, F15	o	GCS
Spindalis zena	L	U/C	LT	C	L	2000		F4, F1, F15, N14	o	GAN
Thraupis abbas	L	C	LT	C	L	1600		F1E, F15, F8		PAS, GCS
Thraupis bonariensis	L	C	LT	C	L	3000		F4E, F15, F7, F8, N3		NAN, CAN, SAN, PAM
Thraupis cyanocephala	M	C	MM	C	1500	3000		F4, F15		NAN, CAN

CP	RP	Notes
4	3	
3	2	
2	2	Locally to lowlands; deforestation.
4	3	
4	3	
4	3	
4	2	Occasionally to 1,450 m (Panama); may contain two species.
3	3	
3	3	
3	2	Locally to sea level; monitor.
4	3	Occasionally to 1,700 m.
3	3	Rarely to 1,200 m.
4	3	
3	2	
4	3	Locally to 1,200 m.
3	3	
4	3	
3	3	
3	3	
4	3	
4	3	
4	3	Locally to 1,500 m (Colombia).
4	3	Occasionally to 2,200 m (Colombia).
4	3	
4	3	Locally to 1,650 m (Bolivia).
4	3	Occasionally to 2,200 m.
4	3	Locally to 1,400 m (Venezuela).
4	3	Mainly above 1,000 m in Andes.
3	3	
3	2	Survey.
4	3	Locally to 1,500 m.
3	3	
4	3	Occasionally to 2,250 m (Panama).
4	3	
4	3	
4	2	Locally to sea level; probably contains multiple species.
4	3	Occasionally to sea level and 2,500 m.
4	2	Status as breeding species in Mexico uncertain.
3	3	
4	3	
4	2	Survey.
3	2	Occasionally to 600 m.
4	2	Declining locally because of trapping for cagebirds.
4	3	Occasionally to 1,900 m.
4	3	
4	3	Occasionally to 2,100 m (Colombia).
4	3	
4	3	
4	3	Occasionally to 1,700 m.
4	3	
4	3	
4	3	
4	3	Occasionally to 3,600 m.
4	3	Occasionally to 3,300 m; locally to 600 m.

Abbreviations Used

Snst - Sensitivity:
L - Low; **M** - Medium; **H** - High.

Strat - Foraging Strata:
T - Terrestrial; **U** - Understory; **M** - Midstory; **C** - Canopy; **A** - Aerial; **W** - Water.

Cntab - Center of Abundance:
LT - Lower tropical; **LS** - Lower subtropical; **HT** - Hill tropical; **UT** - Upper tropical; **US** - Upper subtropical; **MM** - Middle montane; **UM** - Upper montane.

Rel - Relative Abundance:
R - Rare; **U** - Uncommon; **F** - Fairly common; **C** - Common; **P** - Patchily distributed.

Min - Minimum Elevation:
L - Lowlands; **?** - Uncertain value; numeric values in meters.

Max - Maximum Elevation:
L - Lowlands; **?** - Uncertain value; **+** - species occurs at least to given elevation but likely occurs higher; numeric values in meters.

Micro - Microhabitats:
A - Army ants; **B** - Bamboo; **T** - Treefalls; **G** - Ground bromeliads; **C** - Rocky outcrops and caves; **S** - Streamside; **V** - Vine tangles; **B/V** -Bamboo/vine tangles.

Habitats:
F1 - Tropical lowland evergreen forest; **F2** - Flooded tropical evergreen forest; **F3** - River-edge forest; **F4** - Montane evergreen forest; **F5** - Elfin forest; **F6** - *Polylepis* woodland; **F7** - Tropical deciduous forest; **F8** - Gallery forest; **F9** - Southern temperate forest; **F10** - Pine forest; **F11** - Pine-oak forest; **F12** - White sand forest; **F13** - Palm forest; **F14** - Mangrove forest; **F15** - Secondary forest; **N1** - Arid lowland scrub; **N2** - Arid montane scrub; **N3** - Semihumid/humid montane scrub; **N4** - Cerrado; **N5** - Campo grasslands; **N6** - Low, seasonally wet grassland; **N7** - Southern temperate grassland; **N8** - Northern temperate grassland; **N9** - Puna grassland; **N10** - Paramo grassland; **N11** - Riparian thickets; **N12** - River island scrub; **N13** - Pastures/agricultural lands; **N14** - Second-growth scrub; **A1** - Freshwater marshes; **A2** - Saltwater/brackish marshes; **A3** - Coastal sand beaches/mudflats; **A4** - Coastal rocky beaches; **A5** - Riverine sand beaches; **A6** - Freshwater lakes and ponds; **A7** - Alkaline lakes; **A8** - Rivers; **A9** - Streams; **A10** - Bogs; **A11** - Coastal waters; **A12** - Pelagic waters.
E - Edge (used as a modifer to particular habitats).

Sub - Subregions:
ARC - Arid Caribbean Coast; **AWA** - Altiplano and Western Andes; **BAH** - Bahamas; **BAJ** - Baja California; **CAA** - Caatinga; **CAH** - Central American Highlands; **CER** - Cerrado; **CHA** - Chaco; **CHG** - Chiapas-Guanacaste; **CHL** - Chilean Desert; **CHR** - Chiriquí; **CIS** - Cocos Island; **CMV** - Cauca-Magdalena Valley; **COC** - Cuzco-Cochabamba; **CUB** - Cuba; **DOM** - Dominica; **EAS** - Eastern Slope Andes; **FDN** - Fernando de Noronha; **GAL** - Galápagos; **GCM** - Gulf Coast-Mexico; **GRE** - Grenada; **GUA** - Guadeloupe; **GUI** - Guianan; **HIS** - Hispaniola; **HPC** - Humid Pacific Coast; **ISA** - Isla Providencia and Isla San Andrés; **JAM** - Jamaica; **JFI** - Juan Fernández Islands; **MAN** - Manabí-Tumbes; **MAR** - Marañón Valley; **MID** - Madeira-Tapajós; **MON** - Montserrat; **MRT** - Martinique; **MTC** - Marañón-Cuzco; **NMM** - Northern Mexican Mountains; **NOR** - Northern Coastal Brazil; **PAR** - Pará; **PER** - Peruvian Desert; **PUE** - Puerto Rico; **RDJ** - Rio de Janeiro-Bahia Lowlands; **RMW** - Rio Madeira West; **RNW** - Rio Negro West; **SCA** - Southern Central America; **SCT** - Santa Cruz-Tucumán; **SIN** - Sinaloa-Oaxaca; **SMH** - Southern Mexican Highlands; **SMT** - Santa Marta; **SOC** - Islas Revillagigedo (Socorro Island group); **SON** - Sonoran Desert; **SOU** - Southern Atlantic Coast; **STL** - St. Lucia; **STV** - St. Vincent; **TAC** - Tacarcuna; **VAN** - Venezuelan Andes; **VNZ** - Venezuelan Coastal Mountains; **WES** - Western Andes; **YUC** - Yucatán Peninsula.
o - Endemic to region, but not restricted to a single subregion.

Zoogeographic Regions:
AMN - Northern Amazonia; **AMS** - Southern Amazonia; **ATL** - Atlantic Forest; **BSR** - Baja-Sonora; **CAN** - Central Andes; **CDH** - Chiriquí-Darién Highlands; **CHO** - Chocó Lowlands; **CSA** - Central South America; **EPC** - Equatorial Pacific Coast; **GAN** - Greater Antilles; **GCS** - Gulf-Caribbean Slope; **LAN** - Lesser Antilles; **MAH** - Madrean Highlands; **MPL** - Mexican Plateau; **NAN** - Northern Andes; **NSA** - Northern South America; **PAM** - Pampas; **PAS** - Pacific Arid Slope; **PAT** - Patagonia; **SAN** - Southern Andes; **STP** - Subtropical Pacific; **TEP** - Tepuis.

CP -Conservation Priority:
1 - Urgent; **2** - High; **3** - Medium; **4** - Low.

RP - Research Priority:
1 - High; **2** - Medium; **3** - Low.

	Snst	Strat	Cntab	Rel	Min	Max	Micro	Habitats	Sub	Zoogeographic Regions
Thraupis cyanoptera	M	C	HT	U	200	1200		F1, F4, F15?	SOU	ATL
Thraupis episcopus	L	C	LT	C	L	2600		F1E, F15, F3, N14		PAS, GCS, CHO, EPC, NSA, AMN, AMS
Thraupis glaucocolpa	L	C	LT	F	L	800		F1E, F8, F15	ARC	NSA
Thraupis ornata	M	C	LT	C	L	1750		F1E, F4, F15	SOU	ATL
Thraupis palmarum	L	C	LT	C	L	1200		F1E, F15, F8, F4, F2, F12		GCS, CHO, NSA, AMN, AMS, CSA, ATL
Thraupis sayaca	L	C	LT	C	L	2000		F1E, F15, F8, N14		CAN, CSA, ATL, PAM
Cyanicterus cyanicterus	H	C	LT	U	L	600		F1	GUI	AMN
Buthraupis arcaei	M	C	HT	U	300	1200		F1, F4	o	CDH
Buthraupis aureocincta	H	C	MM	?	1600	2200		F4	WES	NAN
Buthraupis aureodorsalis	H	C	UM	U	3150	3500		F5	MTC	CAN
Buthraupis edwardsi	M	C	UT	F	900	2100		F4, F1	WES	NAN
Buthraupis eximia	H	C	UM	U	2700	3400		F5	o	NAN
Buthraupis melanochlamys	H	C	MM	R	1300	2450		F4	o	NAN
Buthraupis montana	M	C	MM	C	2000	3500		F4		NAN, CAN
Buthraupis rothschildi	M	C	LT	F	L	1100		F1, F4	WES	NAN
Buthraupis wetmorei	H	C	UM	R/P	2900	3650		F5	EAS	NAN
Wetmorethraupis sterrhopteron	H	C	HT	U	600	1000		F1	EAS	NAN
Anisognathus flavinucha	M	M/C	MM	C	900	2300		F4		NAN, CAN
Anisognathus igniventris	M	U/C	UM	C	2600	3600		F4, F5, F15		NAN, CAN
Anisognathus lacrymosus	M	M/C	UM	C	2100	3800		F4, F5, F15		NAN, CAN
Anisognathus melanogenys	M	U/C	MM	C	1600	3200		F4, F15	SMT	NAN
Anisognathus notabilis	M	C	UT	F	900	2200		F4	WES	NAN
Stephanophorus diadematus	L	U/C	UT	F	L	2400		F4, F9, F1, N11, F15		ATL, PAM
Iridosornis analis	H	U/M	MM	F	1150	2600		F4		NAN, CAN
Iridosornis jelskii	H	U/C	UM	U/P	3000	3600		F5	o	CAN
Iridosornis porphyrocephala	M	U/M	MM	U	1500	2200		F4, F15?	o	NAN
Iridosornis reinhardti	H	U/M	UM	F	2050	3500		F4, F5	MTC	CAN
Iridosornis rufivertex	H	U/M	UM	F	2600	3800		F5	o	NAN
Dubusia taeniata	H	U/M	UM	U	2000	3600		F5, F4		NAN, CAN
Delothraupis castaneoventris	H	C	UM	U	2200	3500		F5, F4	o	CAN
Pipraeidea melanonota	L	M/C	MM	F	L	2500		F4E, F1E, F15		NAN, CAN, TEP, CSA, ATL, PAM
Euphonia affinis	L	C	LT	F	L	1000		F7, F8, F15, F1E		PAS, GCS
Euphonia anneae	M	U/M	UT	F	600	1500		F1, F4, F15	o	CDH
Euphonia cayennensis	M	C	LT	U	L	1100		F1		AMN, AMS
Euphonia chalybea	M	C	LT	U	L	950		F1	SOU	ATL
Euphonia chlorotica	L	C	LT	C	L	1200		F8, F1E, F3, F15		AMN, AMS, ATL, PAM
Euphonia chrysopasta	M	C	LT	F	L	900		F1, F2, F3		AMN, AMS
Euphonia concinna	L	C	LT	U	L	1000		F7, F15	CMV	NSA
Euphonia finschi	L	C	LT	U	L	1200		F1E, F3, F15	GUI	AMN
Euphonia fulvicrissa	M	C	LT	F	L	1000		F1, F15		GCS, CHO, NSA
Euphonia gouldi	M	C	LT	F	L	900		F1	o	GCS
Euphonia hirundinacea	L	C	LT	C	L	1200		F1E, F8, F15, F7		PAS, GCS
Euphonia imitans	M	C	LT	U	L	1350		F1, F15	HPC	GCS
Euphonia jamaica	L	C	LT	F	L	1000+		F1, F15	JAM	GAN
Euphonia laniirostris	L	C	LT	F	L	1800		F3, F8, F15, F7		GCS, EPC, NSA, AMN, AMS, CSA
Euphonia luteicapilla	L	C	LT	C	L	900		F1E, F7, F15	o	GCS
Euphonia mesochrysa	H	C	UT	U	850	2150		F4		NAN, CAN
Euphonia minuta	M	C	LT	U	L	1000		F1, F3, F15		GCS, CHO, NSA, AMN, AMS
Euphonia musica										
cyanocephala	L	C	UT	F/P	L	2600		F4, F1E, F15		NAN, CAN, NSA, TEP, AMN, CSA, ATL
elegantissima	M	C	UT	F/P	1000	2500		F11, F4, F15		MAH, CDH
musica	L	C	LT	F/P	L	2000		F1, F7, F15		GAN, LAN
Euphonia pectoralis	M	C	LT	C	L	1550		F1, F4	o	ATL
Euphonia plumbea	L	C	LT	U	L	1000		F1E, F15, F8	GUI	AMN

CP	RP	Notes
3	2	Seasonal movements poorly known.
4	3	
4	3	
4	3	
4	3	Occasionally to 2,600 m.
4	3	Locally to 3,600 m (Bolivia).
4	2	Poorly known.
3	2	Deforestation.
1	1	Poorly known; deforestation.
3	3	
3	3	Occasionally to 400 m.
4	2	Locally to 2,000 m; distribution poorly known.
2	1	Locally to 1,000 m; poorly known; deforestation.
4	3	
3	2	
3	1	Poorly known.
3	2	Poorly known.
4	3	
4	3	Occasionally to 2,250 m.
4	3	Locally to 1,800 m.
3	3	
3	3	
4	3	
4	3	
4	3	
4	3	Occasionally to 750 m and 2,600 m.
4	3	
4	3	Occasionally to 2,300 m.
4	3	
4	3	
4	3	Mainly above 900 m in Andes; locally to 3,250 m.
4	3	Occasionally to 2,250 m.
3	2	Occasionally to sea level and 2,100 m; deforestation.
4	3	
3	2	Poorly known; deforestation.
4	3	Occasionally to 2,000 m.
4	3	Occasionally to 1,200 m.
3	2	Occasionally to 1,800 m; poorly known.
4	2	Poorly known.
4	3	
4	3	Occasionally to 1,200 m.
4	3	Occasionally to 2,100 m.
3	2	Poorly known; deforestation.
3	3	
4	3	Occasionally to 2,200 m.
4	3	Occasionally to 1,600 m.
3	3	Occasionally to 150 m? deforestation.
4	2	Occasionally to 1,500 m.
4	3	Mainly above 1,000 m; often called *E. aureata*.
4	3	Occasionally to sea level and 3,050 m.
4	3	
4	3	
4	3	

Abbreviations Used

Snst - Sensitivity:
L - Low; **M** - Medium; **H** - High.

Strat - Foraging Strata:
T - Terrestrial; **U** - Understory; **M** - Midstory; **C** - Canopy; **A** - Aerial; **W** - Water.

Cntab - Center of Abundance:
LT - Lower tropical; **LS** - Lower subtropical; **HT** - Hill tropical; **UT** - Upper tropical; **US** - Upper subtropical; **MM** - Middle montane; **UM** - Upper montane.

Rel - Relative Abundance:
R - Rare; **U** - Uncommon; **F** - Fairly common; **C** - Common; **P** - Patchily distributed.

Min - Minimum Elevation:
L - Lowlands; **?** - Uncertain value; numeric values in meters.

Max - Maximum Elevation:
L - Lowlands; **?** - Uncertain value; **+** - species occurs at least to given elevation but likely occurs higher; numeric values in meters.

Micro - Microhabitats:
A - Army ants; **B** - Bamboo; **T** - Treefalls; **G** - Ground bromeliads; **C** - Rocky outcrops and caves; **S** - Streamside; **V** - Vine tangles; **B/V** -Bamboo/vine tangles.

Habitats:
F1 - Tropical lowland evergreen forest; **F2** - Flooded tropical evergreen forest; **F3** - River-edge forest; **F4** - Montane evergreen forest; **F5** - Elfin forest; **F6** - *Polylepis* woodland; **F7** - Tropical deciduous forest; **F8** - Gallery forest; **F9** - Southern temperate forest; **F10** - Pine forest; **F11** - Pine-oak forest; **F12** - White sand forest; **F13** - Palm forest; **F14** - Mangrove forest; **F15** - Secondary forest; **N1** - Arid lowland scrub; **N2** - Arid montane scrub; **N3** - Semihumid/humid montane scrub; **N4** - Cerrado; **N5** - Campo grasslands; **N6** - Low, seasonally wet grassland; **N7** - Southern temperate grassland; **N8** - Northern temperate grassland; **N9** - Puna grassland; **N10** - Paramo grassland; **N11** - Riparian thickets; **N12** - River island scrub; **N13** - Pastures/agricultural lands; **N14** - Second-growth scrub; **A1** - Freshwater marshes; **A2** - Saltwater/brackish marshes; **A3** - Coastal sand beaches/mudflats; **A4** - Coastal rocky beaches; **A5** - Riverine sand beaches; **A6** - Freshwater lakes and ponds; **A7** - Alkaline lakes; **A8** - Rivers; **A9** - Streams; **A10** - Bogs; **A11** - Coastal waters; **A12** - Pelagic waters.
E - Edge (used as a modifer to particular habitats).

Sub - Subregions:
ARC - Arid Caribbean Coast; **AWA** - Altiplano and Western Andes; **BAH** - Bahamas; **BAJ** - Baja California; **CAA** - Caatinga; **CAH** - Central American Highlands; **CER** - Cerrado; **CHA** - Chaco; **CHG** - Chiapas-Guanacaste; **CHL** - Chilean Desert; **CHR** - Chiriquí; **CIS** - Cocos Island; **CMV** - Cauca-Magdalena Valley; **COC** - Cuzco-Cochabamba; **CUB** - Cuba; **DOM** - Dominica; **EAS** - Eastern Slope Andes; **FDN** - Fernando de Noronha; **GAL** - Galápagos; **GCM** - Gulf Coast-Mexico; **GRE** - Grenada; **GUA** - Guadeloupe; **GUI** - Guianan; **HIS** - Hispaniola; **HPC** - Humid Pacific Coast; **ISA** - Isla Providencia and Isla San Andrés; **JAM** - Jamaica; **JFI** - Juan Fernández Islands; **MAN** - Manabí-Tumbes; **MAR** - Marañón Valley; **MID** - Madeira-Tapajós; **MON** - Montserrat; **MRT** - Martinique; **MTC** - Marañón-Cuzco; **NMM** - Northern Mexican Mountains; **NOR** - Northern Coastal Brazil; **PAR** - Pará; **PER** - Peruvian Desert; **PUE** - Puerto Rico; **RDJ** - Rio de Janeiro-Bahia Lowlands; **RMW** - Rio Madeira West; **RNW** - Rio Negro West; **SCA** - Southern Central America; **SCT** - Santa Cruz-Tucumán; **SIN** - Sinaloa-Oaxaca; **SMH** - Southern Mexican Highlands; **SMT** - Santa Marta; **SOC** - Islas Revillagigedo (Socorro Island group); **SON** - Sonoran Desert; **SOU** - Southern Atlantic Coast; **STL** - St. Lucia; **STV** - St. Vincent; **TAC** - Tacarcuna; **VAN** - Venezuelan Andes; **VNZ** - Venezuelan Coastal Mountains; **WES** - Western Andes; **YUC** - Yucatán Peninsula.
o - Endemic to region, but not restricted to a single subregion.

Zoogeographic Regions:
AMN - Northern Amazonia; **AMS** - Southern Amazonia; **ATL** - Atlantic Forest; **BSR** - Baja-Sonora; **CAN** - Central Andes; **CDH** - Chiriquí-Darién Highlands; **CHO** - Chocó Lowlands; **CSA** - Central South America; **EPC** - Equatorial Pacific Coast; **GAN** - Greater Antilles; **GCS** - Gulf-Caribbean Slope; **LAN** - Lesser Antilles; **MAH** - Madrean Highlands; **MPL** - Mexican Plateau; **NAN** - Northern Andes; **NSA** - Northern South America; **PAM** - Pampas; **PAS** - Pacific Arid Slope; **PAT** - Patagonia; **SAN** - Southern Andes; **STP** - Subtropical Pacific; **TEP** - Tepuis.

CP -Conservation Priority:
1 - Urgent; **2** - High; **3** - Medium; **4** - Low.

RP - Research Priority:
1 - High; **2** - Medium; **3** - Low.

	Snst	Strat	Cntab	Rel	Min	Max	Micro	Habitats	Sub	Zoogeographic Regions
Euphonia rufiventris	M	C	LT	C	L	1100		F1		AMN, AMS
Euphonia saturata	L	C	LT	U/P	L	1300		F1E, F7, F15		CHO, EPC
Euphonia trinitatis	L	C	LT	C	L	1100		F7, F1E, F8, F15		NSA, AMN
Euphonia violacea	L	C	LT	F	L	1100		F1E, F8, F15		NSA, AMN, AMS, CSA, ATL
Euphonia xanthogaster	M	U/C	HT	F	L	2300		F4, F1		GCS, CHO, NAN, CAN, NSA, TEP, AMN, AMS, ATL
Chlorophonia callophrys	M	C	MM	U	750	2500		F4	CHR	CDH
Chlorophonia cyanea	M	C	UT	C	L	2100		F4, F1		NAN, CAN, TEP, ATL
Chlorophonia flavirostris	M	C	UT	U	100	1900		F4, F1	WES	NAN
Chlorophonia occipitalis	M	C	UT	U	1000	2500		F4	o	MAH
Chlorophonia pyrrhophrys	H	C	MM	U	1400	3300		F4		NAN, CAN
Chlorochrysa calliparaea	H	C	UT	U	900	2000		F4		NAN, CAN
Chlorochrysa nitidissima	H	C	UT	U	900	2000		F4	o	NAN
Chlorochrysa phoenicotis	H	C	UT	U	700	2200		F4	WES	NAN
Tangara argyrofenges	M	C	MM	U/P	1200	2700		F4	o	CAN
Tangara arthus	H	C	UT	F	700	2500		F4		NAN, CAN
Tangara cabanisi	M	C	UT	F	1000	1700		F4, F1	CAH	MAH
Tangara callophrys	H	C	LT	U/P	L	1000		F1		AMN, AMS
Tangara cayana	M	U/C	LT	F	L	1800		F8, N4, N6, N5, F12		NSA, TEP, AMN, AMS, CSA
Tangara chilensis	M	C	LT	C	L	1100		F1, F2?, F15		AMN, AMS
Tangara chrysotis	H	C	UT	U	900	1750		F4		NAN, CAN
Tangara cucullata	L	C	HT	F	L	850+		F1, F15	o	LAN
Tangara cyanicollis	L	C	UT	F	L	2400		F4, F1, F15		NAN, CAN, AMS, CSA
Tangara cyanocephala	M	C	LT	C	L	1000		F1, F15	o	ATL
Tangara cyanoptera	L	C	UT	C	600	2000		F4, N3, F15		NAN, TEP
Tangara cyanotis	H	C	UT	U	1250	2200		F4		NAN, CAN
Tangara cyanoventris	M	C	HT	C	L	1200		F1, F4, F15	SOU	ATL
Tangara desmaresti	M	C	UT	C	600	2200		F4	SOU	ATL
Tangara dowii	H	C	UT	U	1300	2700		F4	CHR	CDH
Tangara fastuosa	M	C	LT	R	L	850		F1, F15	NOR	ATL
Tangara florida	M	C	HT	F/P	L	1200		F1, F4		CDH, NAN
Tangara fucosa	H	C	MM	F	1400	2000		F4, F5	TAC	CDH
Tangara guttata	H	C	UT	F	700	2000		F4, F1		GCS, CDH, NAN, NSA, TEP
Tangara gyrola	M	C	HT	F/P	L	1800		F4, F1		CDH, CHO, NAN, CAN, TEP, AMN, AMS
Tangara heinei	L	C	MM	U	1300	2700		F15, F4E	o	NAN
Tangara icterocephala	M	C	UT	C	600	1600		F4, F1, F15		GCS, CDH, CHO, NAN
Tangara inornata	L	C	LT	C	L	1000		F1, F15		GCS, NSA
Tangara johannae	M	C	LT	U	L	700		F1	o	CHO
Tangara labradorides	M	C	MM	F	1300	2750		F4		NAN, CAN
Tangara larvata	L	C	LT	C	L	1200		F1E, F15		GCS, CHO
Tangara lavinia	M	C	HT	F	L	1000		F1, F15		GCS, CHO
Tangara mexicana										
brasiliensis	M	C	LT	F	L	L		F1E, F15	RDJ	ATL
mexicana	M	C	LT	C	L	1000		F2, F3, F15, F8, F1E		AMN, AMS
Tangara meyerdeschauenseei	L	C	MM	?	1800	2200		N3	COC	CAN
Tangara nigrocincta	M	C	LT	U	L	900		F1, F15		AMN, AMS
Tangara nigroviridis	M	C	MM	C	1500	3000		F4, F15		NAN, CAN
Tangara palmeri	M	C	HT	U	L	1100		F1, F4		CDH, CHO, NAN
Tangara parzudakii	H	C	MM	F	1000	2600		F4, F5?		NAN, CAN
Tangara peruviana	M	C	LT	F/P	L	600		F12, F1E, F15	SOU	ATL
Tangara phillipsi	H	C	UT	U?	1300	1600		F4	MTC	CAN
Tangara preciosa	L	C	HT	F	L	1000		F9, F15		ATL, PAM
Tangara pulcherrima	M	C	UT	U/P	1000	2150		F4, F15		NAN, CAN
Tangara punctata	H	C	UT	F	L	1700		F1, F4		NAN, CAN, TEP, AMN

CP	RP	Notes
4	3	
4	3	
4	3	May be conspecific with *E. chlorotica*.
4	3	
4	3	Occasionally to 2,600 m.
4	3	
4	3	
3	2	Movements poorly understood.
4	2	
4	2	
3	2	
3	2	Locally to 2,200 m.
3	2	
3	2	Distribution poorly known; survey.
4	3	
2	1	
4	3	
4	3	Occasionally to 2,500 m; patchy in Amazonia.
4	3	Occasionally to 1,400 m.
3	2	Occasionally to 2,400 m.
3	2	Survey.
4	3	
4	2	Northern population poorly known.
4	3	Occasionally to lowlands.
4	3	Occasionally to 2,600 m.
4	2	Distribution poorly known.
4	3	Seasonal movements poorly known.
4	3	Occasionally to 1,100 m and 3,200 m.
2	1	Survey.
4	3	
3	3	Occasionally to 550 m.
4	3	Locally to 300 m.
4	3	Local in lowlands.
4	3	Occasionally to 700 m
4	3	Occasionally to 2,300 m.
4	3	
3	2	Monitor.
3	3	Occasionally to 900 m.
4	3	Occasionally to 1,800 m.
4	3	
3	2	Survey.
4	3	
2	2	Poorly known.
4	3	Locally to 1,400 m.
4	3	Occasionally to 900 m.
3	2	
4	3	
3	2	Occasionally to 900 m in winter.
3	2	Poorly known; recently described (Graves and Weske 1987).
4	3	
4	2	Distribution poorly known.
4	3	Above 700 m in Andes.

Abbreviations Used

Snst - Sensitivity:
L - Low; **M** - Medium; **H** - High.

Strat - Foraging Strata:
T - Terrestrial; **U** - Understory; **M** - Midstory; **C** - Canopy; **A** - Aerial; **W** - Water.

Cntab - Center of Abundance:
LT - Lower tropical; **LS** - Lower subtropical; **HT** - Hill tropical; **UT** - Upper tropical; **US** - Upper subtropical; **MM** - Middle montane; **UM** - Upper montane.

Rel - Relative Abundance:
R - Rare; **U** - Uncommon; **F** - Fairly common; **C** - Common; **P** - Patchily distributed.

Min - Minimum Elevation:
L - Lowlands; **?** - Uncertain value; numeric values in meters.

Max - Maximum Elevation:
L - Lowlands; **?** - Uncertain value; **+** - species occurs at least to given elevation but likely occurs higher; numeric values in meters.

Micro - Microhabitats:
A - Army ants; **B** - Bamboo; **T** - Treefalls; **G** - Ground bromeliads; **C** - Rocky outcrops and caves; **S** - Streamside; **V** - Vine tangles; **B/V** -Bamboo/vine tangles.

Habitats:
F1 - Tropical lowland evergreen forest; **F2** - Flooded tropical evergreen forest; **F3** - River-edge forest; **F4** - Montane evergreen forest; **F5** - Elfin forest; **F6** - *Polylepis* woodland; **F7** - Tropical deciduous forest; **F8** - Gallery forest; **F9** - Southern temperate forest; **F10** - Pine forest; **F11** - Pine-oak forest; **F12** - White sand forest; **F13** - Palm forest; **F14** - Mangrove forest; **F15** - Secondary forest; **N1** - Arid lowland scrub; **N2** - Arid montane scrub; **N3** - Semihumid/humid montane scrub; **N4** - Cerrado; **N5** - Campo grasslands; **N6** - Low, seasonally wet grassland; **N7** - Southern temperate grassland; **N8** - Northern temperate grassland; **N9** - Puna grassland; **N10** - Paramo grassland; **N11** - Riparian thickets; **N12** - River island scrub; **N13** - Pastures/agricultural lands; **N14** - Second-growth scrub; **A1** - Freshwater marshes; **A2** - Saltwater/brackish marshes; **A3** - Coastal sand beaches/mudflats; **A4** - Coastal rocky beaches; **A5** - Riverine sand beaches; **A6** - Freshwater lakes and ponds; **A7** - Alkaline lakes; **A8** - Rivers; **A9** - Streams; **A10** - Bogs; **A11** - Coastal waters; **A12** - Pelagic waters.
E - Edge (used as a modifer to particular habitats).

Sub - Subregions:
ARC - Arid Caribbean Coast; **AWA** - Altiplano and Western Andes; **BAH** - Bahamas; **BAJ** - Baja California; **CAA** - Caatinga; **CAH** - Central American Highlands; **CER** - Cerrado; **CHA** - Chaco; **CHG** - Chiapas-Guanacaste; **CHL** - Chilean Desert; **CHR** - Chiriquí; **CIS** - Cocos Island; **CMV** - Cauca-Magdalena Valley; **COC** - Cuzco-Cochabamba; **CUB** - Cuba; **DOM** - Dominica; **EAS** - Eastern Slope Andes; **FDN** - Fernando de Noronha; **GAL** - Galápagos; **GCM** - Gulf Coast-Mexico; **GRE** - Grenada; **GUA** - Guadeloupe; **GUI** - Guianan; **HIS** - Hispaniola; **HPC** - Humid Pacific Coast; **ISA** - Isla Providencia and Isla San Andrés; **JAM** - Jamaica; **JFI** - Juan Fernández Islands; **MAN** - Manabí-Tumbes; **MAR** - Marañón Valley; **MID** - Madeira-Tapajós; **MON** - Montserrat; **MRT** - Martinique; **MTC** - Marañón-Cuzco; **NMM** - Northern Mexican Mountains; **NOR** - Northern Coastal Brazil; **PAR** - Pará; **PER** - Peruvian Desert; **PUE** - Puerto Rico; **RDJ** - Rio de Janeiro-Bahia Lowlands; **RMW** - Rio Madeira West; **RNW** - Rio Negro West; **SCA** - Southern Central America; **SCT** - Santa Cruz-Tucumán; **SIN** - Sinaloa-Oaxaca; **SMH** - Southern Mexican Highlands; **SMT** - Santa Marta; **SOC** - Islas Revillagigedo (Socorro Island group); **SON** - Sonoran Desert; **SOU** - Southern Atlantic Coast; **STL** - St. Lucia; **STV** - St. Vincent; **TAC** - Tacarcuna; **VAN** - Venezuelan Andes; **VNZ** - Venezuelan Coastal Mountains; **WES** - Western Andes; **YUC** - Yucatán Peninsula.
o - Endemic to region, but not restricted to a single subregion.

Zoogeographic Regions:
AMN - Northern Amazonia; **AMS** - Southern Amazonia; **ATL** - Atlantic Forest; **BSR** - Baja-Sonora; **CAN** - Central Andes; **CDH** - Chiriquí-Darién Highlands; **CHO** - Chocó Lowlands; **CSA** - Central South America; **EPC** - Equatorial Pacific Coast; **GAN** - Greater Antilles; **GCS** - Gulf-Caribbean Slope; **LAN** - Lesser Antilles; **MAH** - Madrean Highlands; **MPL** - Mexican Plateau; **NAN** - Northern Andes; **NSA** - Northern South America; **PAM** - Pampas; **PAS** - Pacific Arid Slope; **PAT** - Patagonia; **SAN** - Southern Andes; **STP** - Subtropical Pacific; **TEP** - Tepuis.

CP -Conservation Priority:
1 - Urgent; **2** - High; **3** - Medium; **4** - Low.

RP - Research Priority:
1 - High; **2** - Medium; **3** - Low.

	Snst	Strat	Cntab	Rel	Min	Max	Micro	Habitats	Sub	Zoogeographic Regions
Tangara ruficervix	M	C	MM	U	1100	2400		F4, F15		NAN, CAN
Tangara rufigenis	M	C	UT	U?	900	1400		F4	VNZ	NAN
Tangara rufigula	M	C	UT	C	400	2100		F4, F15	WES	NAN
Tangara schrankii	H	M/C	LT	C	L	1200		F1, F2		AMN, AMS
Tangara seledon	M	C	LT	C	L	1100		F1, F4, F15	o	ATL
Tangara varia	M	C	LT	U/P	L	L		F1, F15		AMN, AMS
Tangara vassorii	M	C	UM	F	2400	3500		F4, F5, F15		NAN, CAN
Tangara velia										
cyanomelaena	M	C	LT	U	L	L		F1, F15?	RDJ	ATL
velia	H	C	LT	U/P	L	1000		F1		AMN, AMS
Tangara viridicollis	L	C	MM	F	1500	2500		F4, F7, F15		NAN, CAN
Tangara vitriolina	L	T/C	UT	C	300	2500		F15, N3, F4E	o	NAN
Tangara xanthocephala	M	C	MM	C	1100	2600		F4, F15		NAN, CAN
Tangara xanthogastra	H	C	LT	C/P	L	1350		F1, F4		TEP, AMN, AMS
Dacnis albiventris	H	C	LT	R/P	L	L		F1?		AMN, AMS
Dacnis berlepschi	M	C	LT	U/P	200	1200		F1, F15	o	NAN
Dacnis cayana	L	C	LT	F	L	1200		F1, F2, F12, F15		GCS, CHO, NSA, AMN, AMS, CSA, ATL
Dacnis flaviventer	M	C	LT	U/P	L	700		F2, F1E		AMN, AMS
Dacnis hartlaubi	M	C	MM	R/P	1000	2200		F4E, F15	o	NAN
Dacnis lineata	M	C	LT	F	L	1100		F1, F2, F15		CHO, NSA, AMN, AMS
Dacnis nigripes	M	C	HT	R	L	1000		F1	SOU	ATL
Dacnis venusta	M	C	UT	U	L	1450		F4, F1, F15		GCS, CDH, CHO
Dacnis viguieri	M	C	LT	R	L	600		F1		GCS, CHO
Chlorophanes spiza	M	C	LT	F	L	1600		F1, F2, F8, F15		GCS, CHO, NSA, AMN, AMS, ATL
Cyanerpes caeruleus	M	C	LT	C	L	1100		F1, F2, F15, F4		GCS, CHO, NSA, AMN, AMS
Cyanerpes cyaneus	L	C	LT	C/P	L	1200		F1, F15, F8		GAN, PAS, GCS, CHO, NSA, AMN, AMS, CSA, ATL
Cyanerpes lucidus	M	C	HT	F	L	1200		F1		GCS, CDH
Cyanerpes nitidus	H	C	LT	U/P	L	L		F1		AMN, AMS
Nephelornis oneilli	H	U/M	UM	F/P	3000	3800		F5	MTC	CAN
Xenodacnis parina	H	U/C	UM	F/P	3000	4400		F6		NAN, CAN
Oreomanes fraseri	H	U/C	UM	U/P	3200	4500		F6		NAN, CAN
Diglossa albilatera	L	U/M	MM	C	1600	3300		F4E, F15, N14		NAN, CAN
Diglossa baritula										
baritula	L	U/C	UM	F	1500	3350		F4E, F11E, F15, N14	o	MAH
plumbea	L	C	MM	C	1200	3300		F4E, N3, N14, N10	CHR	CDH
sittoides	L	M/C	MM	F	1800	3200		F4E, N3, F15, N14		NAN, CAN
Diglossa caerulescens	M	C	MM	F/P	1350	3200		F4		NAN, CAN
Diglossa carbonaria										
brunneiventris	L	U/C	UM	C	2000	4200		N3, N2, N14, F5, F4E		NAN, CAN
carbonaria	L	U/C	UM	C	2200	4200		N3, F5, F4E, N14	COC	CAN
gloriosa	L	U/C	UM	U	3000	4150		N3, F5, F4E	VAN	NAN
humeralis	L	U/C	UM	F	2200	4000		N3, N14, F5, F4E	o	NAN
Diglossa cyanea	M	C	UM	C	1800	3600		F4, F5		NAN, CAN
Diglossa duidae	H	?	MM	F	1400	2500		F4, F5, N3	o	TEP
Diglossa glauca	M	C	UT	F	1000	2200		F4		NAN, CAN
Diglossa indigotica	M	C	UT	F	700	2200		F4, F15	WES	NAN
Diglossa lafresnayii										
gloriosissima	L	U/C	UM	?	3000	3750		F5, N3, N10	WES	NAN
lafresnayii	L	U/C	UM	C	2700	3800		F5, F4E, F15, N10	o	NAN
mystacalis	L	U/C	UM	F	2500	3600		F5, F4E, F15, N10	o	CAN
Diglossa major	H	C	MM	F/P	1400	2800		F4, F5, N3	o	TEP
Diglossa venezuelensis	L	U/C	MM	U	1600	2500		F4E, F15, N14	VNZ	NAN
Euneornis campestris	L	M/C	HT	F	L	1500+		F1, F15	JAM	GAN

CP	RP	Notes
4	3	
3	2	Occasionally to 2,050 m; poorly known.
4	3	
4	3	Occasionally to 1,650 m.
4	3	
4	2	Poorly known.
4	3	Occasionally to 1,300 m.
3	2	Survey.
4	3	Occasionally to 1,200 m (Venezuela).
4	3	Occasionally to 800 and 3,050 m.
4	3	
4	3	
4	2	1,000 to 1,800 m in Tepuis.
3	1	Poorly known; survey.
3	2	Poorly known.
4	3	Occasionally to 1,650 m (Bolivia).
4	3	
2	1	Occasionally to 300 m; poorly known; survey.
4	3	Occasionally to 1,350 m.
2	1	Poorly known; survey.
4	3	Occasionally to 1,650 m.
3	1	Poorly known; survey.
4	3	Occasionally to 2,300 m (Colombia).
4	3	Occasionally to 1,950 m.
4	3	
4	2	Occasionally to 1,600 m; distribution poorly known.
4	3	
3	3	
3	2	Survey.
3	2	Locally to 2,700 and 4,850 m; monitor; *Polylepis* destruction.
4	3	Occasionally to 1,300 m.
4	3	
4	3	
4	3	Occasionally to 800 and 4,000 m.
4	3	
4	3	
4	3	
4	3	Occasionally to 2,500 m.
4	3	
4	3	Occasionally to 1,400 m.
4	3	
4	3	
3	2	Mainly 1,000 to 1,400 m.
3	2	Poorly known.
4	3	Occasionally to 2,000 m.
4	3	
4	3	
3	2	Locally to 900 m.
4	3	

Abbreviations Used

Snst - Sensitivity:
L - Low; **M** - Medium; **H** - High.

Strat - Foraging Strata:
T - Terrestrial; **U** - Understory; **M** - Midstory; **C** - Canopy; **A** - Aerial; **W** - Water.

Cntab - Center of Abundance:
LT - Lower tropical; **LS** - Lower subtropical; **HT** - Hill tropical; **UT** - Upper tropical; **US** - Upper subtropical; **MM** - Middle montane; **UM** - Upper montane.

Rel - Relative Abundance:
R - Rare; **U** - Uncommon; **F** - Fairly common; **C** - Common; **P** - Patchily distributed.

Min - Minimum Elevation:
L - Lowlands; **?** - Uncertain value; numeric values in meters.

Max - Maximum Elevation:
L - Lowlands; **?** - Uncertain value; **+** - species occurs at least to given elevation but likely occurs higher; numeric values in meters.

Micro - Microhabitats:
A - Army ants; **B** - Bamboo; **T** - Treefalls; **G** - Ground bromeliads; **C** - Rocky outcrops and caves; **S** - Streamside; **V** - Vine tangles; **B/V** -Bamboo/vine tangles.

Habitats:
F1 - Tropical lowland evergreen forest; **F2** - Flooded tropical evergreen forest; **F3** - River-edge forest; **F4** - Montane evergreen forest; **F5** - Elfin forest; **F6** - *Polylepis* woodland; **F7** - Tropical deciduous forest; **F8** - Gallery forest; **F9** - Southern temperate forest; **F10** - Pine forest; **F11** - Pine-oak forest; **F12** - White sand forest; **F13** - Palm forest; **F14** - Mangrove forest; **F15** - Secondary forest; **N1** - Arid lowland scrub; **N2** - Arid montane scrub; **N3** - Semihumid/humid montane scrub; **N4** - Cerrado; **N5** - Campo grasslands; **N6** - Low, seasonally wet grassland; **N7** - Southern temperate grassland; **N8** - Northern temperate grassland; **N9** - Puna grassland; **N10** - Paramo grassland; **N11** - Riparian thickets; **N12** - River island scrub; **N13** - Pastures/agricultural lands; **N14** - Second-growth scrub; **A1** - Freshwater marshes; **A2** - Saltwater/brackish marshes; **A3** - Coastal sand beaches/mudflats; **A4** - Coastal rocky beaches; **A5** - Riverine sand beaches; **A6** - Freshwater lakes and ponds; **A7** - Alkaline lakes; **A8** - Rivers; **A9** - Streams; **A10** - Bogs; **A11** - Coastal waters; **A12** - Pelagic waters.
E - Edge (used as a modifer to particular habitats).

Sub - Subregions:
ARC - Arid Caribbean Coast; **AWA** - Altiplano and Western Andes; **BAH** - Bahamas; **BAJ** - Baja California; **CAA** - Caatinga; **CAH** - Central American Highlands; **CER** - Cerrado; **CHA** - Chaco; **CHG** - Chiapas-Guanacaste; **CHL** - Chilean Desert; **CHR** - Chiriquí; **CIS** - Cocos Island; **CMV** - Cauca-Magdalena Valley; **COC** - Cuzco-Cochabamba; **CUB** - Cuba; **DOM** - Dominica; **EAS** - Eastern Slope Andes; **FDN** - Fernando de Noronha; **GAL** - Galápagos; **GCM** - Gulf Coast-Mexico; **GRE** - Grenada; **GUA** - Guadeloupe; **GUI** - Guianan; **HIS** - Hispaniola; **HPC** - Humid Pacific Coast; **ISA** - Isla Providencia and Isla San Andrés; **JAM** - Jamaica; **JFI** - Juan Fernández Islands; **MAN** - Manabí-Tumbes; **MAR** - Marañón Valley; **MID** - Madeira-Tapajós; **MON** - Montserrat; **MRT** - Martinique; **MTC** - Marañón-Cuzco; **NMM** - Northern Mexican Mountains; **NOR** - Northern Coastal Brazil; **PAR** - Pará; **PER** - Peruvian Desert; **PUE** - Puerto Rico; **RDJ** - Rio de Janeiro-Bahia Lowlands; **RMW** - Rio Madeira West; **RNW** - Rio Negro West; **SCA** - Southern Central America; **SCT** - Santa Cruz-Tucumán; **SIN** - Sinaloa-Oaxaca; **SMH** - Southern Mexican Highlands; **SMT** - Santa Marta; **SOC** - Islas Revillagigedo (Socorro Island group); **SON** - Sonoran Desert; **SOU** - Southern Atlantic Coast; **STL** - St. Lucia; **STV** - St. Vincent; **TAC** - Tacarcuna; **VAN** - Venezuelan Andes; **VNZ** - Venezuelan Coastal Mountains; **WES** - Western Andes; **YUC** - Yucatán Peninsula.
o - Endemic to region, but not restricted to a single subregion.

Zoogeographic Regions:
AMN - Northern Amazonia; **AMS** - Southern Amazonia; **ATL** - Atlantic Forest; **BSR** - Baja-Sonora; **CAN** - Central Andes; **CDH** - Chiriquí-Darién Highlands; **CHO** - Chocó Lowlands; **CSA** - Central South America; **EPC** - Equatorial Pacific Coast; **GAN** - Greater Antilles; **GCS** - Gulf-Caribbean Slope; **LAN** - Lesser Antilles; **MAH** - Madrean Highlands; **MPL** - Mexican Plateau; **NAN** - Northern Andes; **NSA** - Northern South America; **PAM** - Pampas; **PAS** - Pacific Arid Slope; **PAT** - Patagonia; **SAN** - Southern Andes; **STP** - Subtropical Pacific; **TEP** - Tepuis.

CP -Conservation Priority:
1 - Urgent; **2** - High; **3** - Medium; **4** - Low.

RP - Research Priority:
1 - High; **2** - Medium; **3** - Low.

	Snst	Strat	Cntab	Rel	Min	Max	Micro	Habitats	Sub	Zoogeographic Regions
Tersininae										
Tersina viridis	L	C	LT	F	L	1600		F1E, F15, F3, F8		GCS, CHO, NAN, CAN, NSA, AMN, AMS, ATL
Parulinae										
Vermivora celata	L	U/C	LS	F	L	1500		F7, F15, F11		BSR
Vermivora crissalis	M	U/C	US	F	1600	3000		F11, N2	NMM	MAH
Vermivora gutturalis	M	C	UM	F	1800	3000		F4	CHR	CDH
Vermivora luciae	M	C	LT	F	L	1200		F8, N1		BSR
Vermivora superciliosa	M	C	UM	F	900	3400		F11, F4	o	MAH
Parula pitiayumi	M	C	UT	C	L	2600		F4, F1, F7, F15, F8		BSR, PAS, MAH, GCS, CDH, EPC, NAN, CAN, TEP, CSA, ATL, PAM
Dendroica adelaidae	L	M/C	LT	C	L	700		F1, F7, N1		GAN, LAN
Dendroica angelae	H	M/C	UT	U	650	1050		F5, F4	PUE	GAN
Dendroica coronata	L	U/C	UM	C/P	2300	3500		F10, F11		BSR, MAH
Dendroica dominica	L	C	LT	F	L	L		F10		GAN
Dendroica graciae	M	C	MM	F	600	2800		F10, F11		MAH, GCS
Dendroica nigrescens	L	C	US	F	1200	2500		F11		BSR, MAH
Dendroica petechia										
aestiva	L	C	LT	C	L	2600		F8, F15		BSR, MPL, MAH
erithachorides	L	C	LT	C	L	L		F14, F15, N1		BSR, PAS, GCS, CHO, EPC, NSA, AMN
petechia	L	C	LT	C	L	L		F14, N1, F7, F15		GAN, LAN, NSA
Dendroica pharetra	M	M/C	UT	U	300	1600+		F4	JAM	GAN
Dendroica pinus	M	C	LT	F	L	2100+		F10		GAN
Dendroica pityophila	M	C	LT	F	L	2000?		F10	o	GAN
Dendroica plumbea	M	M/C	HT	F	L	900+		F1, F7	o	LAN
Dendroica vitellina	L	U/C	LT	F	L	L		F7, N1	o	GAN
Catharopeza bishopi	M	U/M	HT	U	300	1000		F1	STV	LAN
Geothlypis aequinoctialis	L	U	LT	C	L	2100		N11, A1, N2, N14		CDH, EPC, STP, NAN, CAN, NSA, AMN, AMS, CSA, ATL, PAM
Geothlypis beldingi	H	U	LT	F	L	L		A1, A2?	BAJ	BSR
Geothlypis flavovelata	H	U	LT	F	L	L		A1	GCM	GCS
Geothlypis nelsoni	M	U	UM	U	2000	3100+		F11E, N2	o	MAH
Geothlypis poliocephala	L	U	LT	F	L	1500		N14, N11		PAS, MAH, GCS, CDH
Geothlypis rostrata	M	U	LT	F/P	L	L		N1	BAH	GAN
Geothlypis semiflava	L	U	LT	C/P	L	1800		N11, N14		GCS, CDH, CHO, NAN
Geothlypis speciosa	M	U	MM	R	1700	2800		A1	NMM	MAH
Geothlypis trichas	L	U	US	C	L	2800		A1, A2		BSR, MPL, PAS, MAH
Microligea palustris	M	U	LT	F	L	2000+		F4, F7, F15	HIS	GAN
Teretistris fernandinae	L	U/M	HT/UT	C	L	500		F1, F7	CUB	GAN
Teretistris fornsi	L	U/M	UT?	C	L	1500+		F7, F1, F10, N1	CUB	GAN
Leucopeza semperi	M	U	HT	R	400?	900		F1	STL	LAN
Cardellina rubrifrons	M	U/C	UM	F	1500	3100+		F10, F11, N11	NMM	MAH
Ergaticus ruber	M	U/M	UM	F	2100	3200		F10, F11	o	MAH
Ergaticus versicolor	M	U/C	UM	U	2100	3000		F11, F4	CAH	MAH
Myioborus albifacies	H	C?	UT	?	900	2250		F4	o	TEP
Myioborus albifrons	H	M/C	UM	F/C	2200	3200		F4, F5	VAN	NAN
Myioborus brunniceps										
brunniceps	M	M/C	UT	F	1400	3000		F4, F7, F15		CAN, SAN
castaneocapillus	H	M/C	UT	F	1200	2200		F4, N3	o	TEP
Myioborus cardonai	H	M/C	UT	?	1200	1600		F4	o	TEP
Myioborus flavivertex	M	M/C	MM	C	1500	3000		F4, F15, F5	SMT	NAN
Myioborus melanocephalus	M	M/C	UM	C	2000	3400		F4, F5		NAN, CAN
Myioborus miniatus	L	M/C	UT	C	600	2500		F4, F15, F11		MAH, CDH, NAN, CAN, TEP
Myioborus ornatus	M	M/C	UM	C	1800	3400		F4, F5	o	NAN

CP	RP	Notes
4	2	Occasionally to 2,100 m; movements poorly known.
4	2	
2	1	Poorly known.
4	3	Seasonally to 1,400 m.
4	3	
4	3	
4	3	
4	2	May contain two species.
2	2	Extent of range and status uncertain; survey.
4	3	
4	3	
4	3	Locally in lowland pine savanna.
4	3	
4	2	
4	2	Taxonomic relationships of some subspecies uncertain.
4	2	
4	2	Occasionally (seasonally?) to lowlands.
4	3	
4	3	
4	3	
3	3	
2	1	Survey.
4	2	May contain multiple species.
3	2	Drainage of marshes.
3	2	Drainage of marshes.
3	2	Occasionally to 1,250 m? poorly known.
4	3	Occasionally to 2,500 m.
4	2	Monitor.
4	3	
2	2	Poorly known; drainage of marshes.
4	3	
4	3	
4	3	
4	3	
1	1	Introduced predators; possibly extinct; survey.
4	3	
4	3	To 1,600 m in winter.
3	2	Survey.
4	2	Poorly known; taxonomic relationship to *M. cardonai* uncertain.
4	3	
4	3	Seasonally to 600 m.
4	3	
4	2	Poorly known.
3	2	
4	3	
4	3	Locally to 3,000 m+.
4	3	Mainly above 2,400 m.

Abbreviations Used

Snst - Sensitivity:
L - Low; **M** - Medium; **H** - High.

Strat - Foraging Strata:
T - Terrestrial; **U** - Understory; **M** - Midstory; **C** - Canopy; **A** - Aerial; **W** - Water.

Cntab - Center of Abundance:
LT - Lower tropical; **LS** - Lower subtropical; **HT** - Hill tropical; **UT** - Upper tropical; **US** - Upper subtropical; **MM** - Middle montane; **UM** - Upper montane.

Rel - Relative Abundance:
R - Rare; **U** - Uncommon; **F** - Fairly common; **C** - Common; **P** - Patchily distributed.

Min - Minimum Elevation:
L - Lowlands; **?** - Uncertain value; numeric values in meters.

Max - Maximum Elevation:
L - Lowlands; **?** - Uncertain value; **+** - species occurs at least to given elevation but likely occurs higher; numeric values in meters.

Micro - Microhabitats:
A - Army ants; **B** - Bamboo; **T** - Treefalls; **G** - Ground bromeliads; **C** - Rocky outcrops and caves; **S** - Streamside; **V** - Vine tangles; **B/V** -Bamboo/vine tangles.

Habitats:
F1 - Tropical lowland evergreen forest; **F2** - Flooded tropical evergreen forest; **F3** - River-edge forest; **F4** - Montane evergreen forest; **F5** - Elfin forest; **F6** - *Polylepis* woodland; **F7** - Tropical deciduous forest; **F8** - Gallery forest; **F9** - Southern temperate forest; **F10** - Pine forest; **F11** - Pine-oak forest; **F12** - White sand forest; **F13** - Palm forest; **F14** - Mangrove forest; **F15** - Secondary forest; **N1** - Arid lowland scrub; **N2** - Arid montane scrub; **N3** - Semihumid/humid montane scrub; **N4** - Cerrado; **N5** - Campo grasslands; **N6** - Low, seasonally wet grassland; **N7** - Southern temperate grassland; **N8** - Northern temperate grassland; **N9** - Puna grassland; **N10** - Paramo grassland; **N11** - Riparian thickets; **N12** - River island scrub; **N13** - Pastures/agricultural lands; **N14** - Second-growth scrub; **A1** - Freshwater marshes; **A2** - Saltwater/brackish marshes; **A3** - Coastal sand beaches/mudflats; **A4** - Coastal rocky beaches; **A5** - Riverine sand beaches; **A6** - Freshwater lakes and ponds; **A7** - Alkaline lakes; **A8** - Rivers; **A9** - Streams; **A10** - Bogs; **A11** - Coastal waters; **A12** - Pelagic waters.
E - Edge (used as a modifer to particular habitats).

Sub - Subregions:
ARC - Arid Caribbean Coast; **AWA** - Altiplano and Western Andes; **BAH** - Bahamas; **BAJ** - Baja California; **CAA** - Caatinga; **CAH** - Central American Highlands; **CER** - Cerrado; **CHA** - Chaco; **CHG** - Chiapas-Guanacaste; **CHL** - Chilean Desert; **CHR** - Chiriquí; **CIS** - Cocos Island; **CMV** - Cauca-Magdalena Valley; **COC** - Cuzco-Cochabamba; **CUB** - Cuba; **DOM** - Dominica; **EAS** - Eastern Slope Andes; **FDN** - Fernando de Noronha; **GAL** - Galápagos; **GCM** - Gulf Coast-Mexico; **GRE** - Grenada; **GUA** - Guadeloupe; **GUI** - Guianan; **HIS** - Hispaniola; **HPC** - Humid Pacific Coast; **ISA** - Isla Providencia and Isla San Andrés; **JAM** - Jamaica; **JFI** - Juan Fernández Islands; **MAN** - Manabí-Tumbes; **MAR** - Marañón Valley; **MID** - Madeira-Tapajós; **MON** - Montserrat; **MRT** - Martinique; **MTC** - Marañón-Cuzco; **NMM** - Northern Mexican Mountains; **NOR** - Northern Coastal Brazil; **PAR** - Pará; **PER** - Peruvian Desert; **PUE** - Puerto Rico; **RDJ** - Rio de Janeiro-Bahia Lowlands; **RMW** - Rio Madeira West; **RNW** - Rio Negro West; **SCA** - Southern Central America; **SCT** - Santa Cruz-Tucumán; **SIN** - Sinaloa-Oaxaca; **SMH** - Southern Mexican Highlands; **SMT** - Santa Marta; **SOC** - Islas Revillagigedo (Socorro Island group); **SON** - Sonoran Desert; **SOU** - Southern Atlantic Coast; **STL** - St. Lucia; **STV** - St. Vincent; **TAC** - Tacarcuna; **VAN** - Venezuelan Andes; **VNZ** - Venezuelan Coastal Mountains; **WES** - Western Andes; **YUC** - Yucatán Peninsula.
o - Endemic to region, but not restricted to a single subregion.

Zoogeographic Regions:
AMN - Northern Amazonia; **AMS** - Southern Amazonia; **ATL** - Atlantic Forest; **BSR** - Baja-Sonora; **CAN** - Central Andes; **CDH** - Chiriquí-Darién Highlands; **CHO** - Chocó Lowlands; **CSA** - Central South America; **EPC** - Equatorial Pacific Coast; **GAN** - Greater Antilles; **GCS** - Gulf-Caribbean Slope; **LAN** - Lesser Antilles; **MAH** - Madrean Highlands; **MPL** - Mexican Plateau; **NAN** - Northern Andes; **NSA** - Northern South America; **PAM** - Pampas; **PAS** - Pacific Arid Slope; **PAT** - Patagonia; **SAN** - Southern Andes; **STP** - Subtropical Pacific; **TEP** - Tepuis.

CP -Conservation Priority:
1 - Urgent; **2** - High; **3** - Medium; **4** - Low.

RP - Research Priority:
1 - High; **2** - Medium; **3** - Low.

	Snst	Strat	Cntab	Rel	Min	Max	Micro	Habitats	Sub	Zoogeographic Regions
Myioborus pariae	M	M/C	UT	U	800	1200		F4	VNZ	NAN
Myioborus pictus	M	U/M	MM	F	1100	3100+		F11, F10	o	MAH
Myioborus torquatus	M	M/C	MM	C	1400	3500		F4, F15, F5	CHR	CDH
Euthlypis lachrymosa	M	U	LT	F	L	1900+		F7, F1, F4, F8		PAS, MAH, GCS
Basileuterus basilicus	L	U	UM	U	2100	3000		F4, F5, F15	SMT	NAN
Basileuterus belli	M	U	UM	F	1300	3100		F4, F11	o	MAH
Basileuterus bivittatus	M	U	UT	F	700	1800		F4, F15		CAN, TEP
Basileuterus chrysogaster	M	U/M	HT	U/P	L	1200		F4, F1E, F15		CHO, NAN, CAN
Basileuterus cinereicollis	M	U	UT?	U	800	2100		F4, F15	o	NAN
Basileuterus conspicillatus	M	U	UT	C	750	2200		F4, F15	SMT	NAN
Basileuterus coronatus	M	U	MM	C	1400	2800		F4, F15		NAN, CAN
Basileuterus culicivorus	M	U/M	HT	C	L	2100		F1, F4, F15		PAS, MAH, GCS, CHO, NSA, TEP, CSA, ATL, PAM
Basileuterus flaveolus	M	T/U	HT	F	L	1200		F7, F8		NSA, CSA
Basileuterus fraseri	M	U	LT	F	L	1200		F7, F1, F8	MAN	EPC
Basileuterus griseiceps	M	U	UT	F	1200	2200		F4, F15?	VNZ	NAN
Basileuterus hypoleucus	L	U/M	HT	F	L	1100		F8, F7	CER	CSA
Basileuterus ignotus	H	U	UT	F	1200	1500+		F4, F5	TAC	CDH
Basileuterus leucoblepharus	M	U	UT	C	L	2000		F4, F1, N11, F15	o	ATL
Basileuterus leucophrys	M	T/U	HT	U	L	1100		F8	CER	CSA
Basileuterus luteoviridis	M	U	UM	C	2400	3400		F4, F5		NAN, CAN
Basileuterus melanogenys	M	U	MM	C	1500	3500		F5, F4, F15	CHR	CDH
Basileuterus nigrocristatus	L	U/M	UM	C	1500	3400		F4E, F15, F5, F6		NAN, CAN
Basileuterus rufifrons	L	U	UT	C	L	2800		F7E, F1E, F15, F11, N2		PAS, MAH, GCS, CDH, NAN, NSA
Basileuterus signatus	L	U	MM	F	1800	2800		F4E, F15		NAN?, CAN
Basileuterus trifasciatus	M	U/M	MM	C	1200	3050		F4, F15		NAN, CAN
Basileuterus tristriatus	M	U	UT	C	800	2500		F4, F15		CDH, NAN, CAN
Phaeothlypis fulvicauda	M	T	LT	F	L	1100	S	F1		GCS, CHO, AMN, AMS
Phaeothlypis rivularis	M	T	LT	F	L	1400	S	F1		AMN, AMS
Zeledonia coronata	M	T/U	UM	F	1500	3300		F4, F5	CHR	CDH
Peucedramus taeniatus	M	M/C	UM	F	1700	3100		F10, F11	o	MAH
Xenoligea montana	M	U/M	UT	U	1200	2000		F4	HIS	GAN
Granatellus pelzelni	M	M/C	LT	U/P	L	850		F1		AMN, AMS
Granatellus sallaei	M	U/M	LT	U	L	L		F7	YUC	GCS
Granatellus venustus	M	U/M	LT	U	L	1200		F7	SIN	PAS
Icteria virens	L	U	LT	U	L	1600		F8, F7, N11		BSR, MPL, PAS, MAH
Conirostrum albifrons	L	C	MM	F	1200	3000		F4, F15		NAN, CAN
Conirostrum bicolor	L	U/C	LT	F	L	L		F14, N12, F3, F15		NSA, AMN, AMS, ATL
Conirostrum cinereum	L	U/C	UM	C	L	4000		N3, N2, N11, N14		EPC, STP, NAN, CAN
Conirostrum ferrugineiventre	H	M/C	UM	F	2800	3900		F5	o	CAN
Conirostrum leucogenys	L	C	LT	F	L	600		F1E, F8, F15		GCS, NSA
Conirostrum margaritae	M	C	LT	U/P	L	L		F3		AMN, AMS
Conirostrum rufum	L	U/C	UM	U	2650	3350		N3, F5	o	NAN
Conirostrum sitticolor	M	C	UM	F	2500	3700		F5, F4		NAN, CAN
Conirostrum speciosum	L	C	LT	C	L	700		F1, F8, F3, F15		AMN, AMS, CSA, ATL
Conirostrum tamarugense	M	U/C	UM	F/P	L	4100		F6, N2	AWA	CAN
Coereba flaveola	L	C	LT	C	L	1500		F1, F15, F7, N1, N14		GAN, LAN, GCS, CHO, EPC, NAN, CAN, NSA, AMN, AMS
Vireonidae										
Cyclarhis gujanensis	L	M/C	LT	C	L	2800		F1E, F8, F15, F4E		PAS, MAH, GCS, CDH, CHO, EPC, NSA, AMN, AMS, CSA, ATL, PAM
Cyclarhis nigrirostris	H	M/C	MM	U/P	1300	2700		F4, F15	o	NAN
Vireolanius eximius	H	C	LT	F	L	1500		F1, F4		GCS, CDH, NSA

CP	RP	Notes
2	1	Deforestation; survey.
4	3	
4	3	Occasionally to 1,100 m.
4	3	
3	2	Survey.
4	3	
4	3	Mainly above 1,200 m.
4	2	Distribution and behavior poorly known.
3	2	Survey.
3	3	
4	3	Occasionally to 3,100 m.
4	2	May contain multiple species.
4	3	
4	3	Occasionally to 3,100 m.
2	1	Locally to 2,400 m; deforestation; survey.
4	2	Taxonomic relationship to *B. culicivorus* uncertain.
3	3	Deforestation; monitor.
4	3	
3	2	Monitor; destruction of gallery forests.
4	3	Occasionally to 1,700 m.
4	3	Locally to 1,200 m (Panama).
4	3	Seasonally to 1,300 and 3,800 m.
4	3	May contain two species.
4	2	Occasionally to 3,400 m; status in Colombia unknown.
4	2	Occasionally to sea level; elevational movements?
4	3	Occasionally to 300 m?
4	3	Occasionally to 1,500 m.
4	3	
4	3	
4	3	To 1,200 m in winter.
3	2	Occasionally to 350 m; deforestation; survey.
4	3	
4	3	
3	3	
4	3	Locally to 2,500 m.
4	3	
4	3	
4	3	
4	3	
4	3	Locally to 1,300 m (Venezuela).
3	2	Survey.
3	3	
4	3	
4	3	
3	2	Breeding areas unknown.
4	3	
4	3	
4	2	Poorly known.
4	3	

Abbreviations Used

Snst - Sensitivity:
L - Low; **M** - Medium; **H** - High.

Strat - Foraging Strata:
T - Terrestrial; **U** - Understory; **M** - Midstory; **C** - Canopy; **A** - Aerial; **W** - Water.

Cntab - Center of Abundance:
LT - Lower tropical; **LS** - Lower subtropical; **HT** - Hill tropical; **UT** - Upper tropical; **US** - Upper subtropical; **MM** - Middle montane; **UM** - Upper montane.

Rel - Relative Abundance:
R - Rare; **U** - Uncommon; **F** - Fairly common; **C** - Common; **P** - Patchily distributed.

Min - Minimum Elevation:
L - Lowlands; **?** - Uncertain value; numeric values in meters.

Max - Maximum Elevation:
L - Lowlands; **?** - Uncertain value; **+** - species occurs at least to given elevation but likely occurs higher; numeric values in meters.

Micro - Microhabitats:
A - Army ants; **B** - Bamboo; **T** - Treefalls; **G** - Ground bromeliads; **C** - Rocky outcrops and caves; **S** - Streamside; **V** - Vine tangles; **B/V** -Bamboo/vine tangles.

Habitats:
F1 - Tropical lowland evergreen forest; **F2** - Flooded tropical evergreen forest; **F3** - River-edge forest; **F4** - Montane evergreen forest; **F5** - Elfin forest; **F6** - *Polylepis* woodland; **F7** - Tropical deciduous forest; **F8** - Gallery forest; **F9** - Southern temperate forest; **F10** - Pine forest; **F11** - Pine-oak forest; **F12** - White sand forest; **F13** - Palm forest; **F14** - Mangrove forest; **F15** - Secondary forest; **N1** - Arid lowland scrub; **N2** - Arid montane scrub; **N3** - Semihumid/humid montane scrub; **N4** - Cerrado; **N5** - Campo grasslands; **N6** - Low, seasonally wet grassland; **N7** - Southern temperate grassland; **N8** - Northern temperate grassland; **N9** - Puna grassland; **N10** - Paramo grassland; **N11** - Riparian thickets; **N12** - River island scrub; **N13** - Pastures/agricultural lands; **N14** - Second-growth scrub; **A1** - Freshwater marshes; **A2** - Saltwater/brackish marshes; **A3** - Coastal sand beaches/mudflats; **A4** - Coastal rocky beaches; **A5** - Riverine sand beaches; **A6** - Freshwater lakes and ponds; **A7** - Alkaline lakes; **A8** - Rivers; **A9** - Streams; **A10** - Bogs; **A11** - Coastal waters; **A12** - Pelagic waters.
E - Edge (used as a modifer to particular habitats).

Sub - Subregions:
ARC - Arid Caribbean Coast; **AWA** - Altiplano and Western Andes; **BAH** - Bahamas; **BAJ** - Baja California; **CAA** - Caatinga; **CAH** - Central American Highlands; **CER** - Cerrado; **CHA** - Chaco; **CHG** - Chiapas-Guanacaste; **CHL** - Chilean Desert; **CHR** - Chiriquí; **CIS** - Cocos Island; **CMV** - Cauca-Magdalena Valley; **COC** - Cuzco-Cochabamba; **CUB** - Cuba; **DOM** - Dominica; **EAS** - Eastern Slope Andes; **FDN** - Fernando de Noronha; **GAL** - Galápagos; **GCM** - Gulf Coast-Mexico; **GRE** - Grenada; **GUA** - Guadeloupe; **GUI** - Guianan; **HIS** - Hispaniola; **HPC** - Humid Pacific Coast; **ISA** - Isla Providencia and Isla San Andrés; **JAM** - Jamaica; **JFI** - Juan Fernández Islands; **MAN** - Manabí-Tumbes; **MAR** - Marañón Valley; **MID** - Madeira-Tapajós; **MON** - Montserrat; **MRT** - Martinique; **MTC** - Marañón-Cuzco; **NMM** - Northern Mexican Mountains; **NOR** - Northern Coastal Brazil; **PAR** - Pará; **PER** - Peruvian Desert; **PUE** - Puerto Rico; **RDJ** - Rio de Janeiro-Bahia Lowlands; **RMW** - Rio Madeira West; **RNW** - Rio Negro West; **SCA** - Southern Central America; **SCT** - Santa Cruz-Tucumán; **SIN** - Sinaloa-Oaxaca; **SMH** - Southern Mexican Highlands; **SMT** - Santa Marta; **SOC** - Islas Revillagigedo (Socorro Island group); **SON** - Sonoran Desert; **SOU** - Southern Atlantic Coast; **STL** - St. Lucia; **STV** - St. Vincent; **TAC** - Tacarcuna; **VAN** - Venezuelan Andes; **VNZ** - Venezuelan Coastal Mountains; **WES** - Western Andes; **YUC** - Yucatán Peninsula.
o - Endemic to region, but not restricted to a single subregion.

Zoogeographic Regions:
AMN - Northern Amazonia; **AMS** - Southern Amazonia; **ATL** - Atlantic Forest; **BSR** - Baja-Sonora; **CAN** - Central Andes; **CDH** - Chiriquí-Darién Highlands; **CHO** - Chocó Lowlands; **CSA** - Central South America; **EPC** - Equatorial Pacific Coast; **GAN** - Greater Antilles; **GCS** - Gulf-Caribbean Slope; **LAN** - Lesser Antilles; **MAH** - Madrean Highlands; **MPL** - Mexican Plateau; **NAN** - Northern Andes; **NSA** - Northern South America; **PAM** - Pampas; **PAS** - Pacific Arid Slope; **PAT** - Patagonia; **SAN** - Southern Andes; **STP** - Subtropical Pacific; **TEP** - Tepuis.

CP -Conservation Priority:
1 - Urgent; **2** - High; **3** - Medium; **4** - Low.

RP - Research Priority:
1 - High; **2** - Medium; **3** - Low.

	Snst	Strat	Cntab	Rel	Min	Max	Micro	Habitats	Sub	Zoogeographic Regions
Vireolanius leucotis	H	C	LT/HT	F/P	L	1700		F1, F4		CHO, NAN, CAN, AMN, AMS
Vireolanius melitophrys	M	C	UM	U	1350	3000		F4, F11	o	MAH
Vireolanius pulchellus	M	C	LT	F/P	L	1800		F1	o	GCS
Vireo altiloquus	L	C	LT	C	L	900		F7, F1, F15, F14		GAN, LAN, NSA
Vireo atricapillus	M	U/M	HT	U	700	1800		N2, N1, F7		MPL, MAH
Vireo bairdi	M	U/M	LT	F	L	L		F7, F15	YUC	GCS
Vireo bellii	M	U	LT	F	L	2000		N11, F8, N1, N2		BSR, MPL, GCS?
Vireo brevipennis	H	U	MM	U/P	1200	2100		N2, F11	o	MAH
Vireo caribaeus	M	U/M	LT	?	L	L		F7, F14, N1	ISA	GAN
Vireo carmioli	M	C	UM	F	2000	3300		F4	CHR	CDH
Vireo crassirostris	M	U/M	LT	C	L	L		F7, N1, F14	o	GAN
Vireo flavoviridis	L	C	LT	F	L	1700		F15, F7, F8, F1E		PAS, GCS
Vireo gilvus	L	M/C	MM	F	1100	2500		F11, F10, F8		BSR, MAH
Vireo gracilirostris	L	T/C	LT	C	L	L		F7, N14, F15	FDN	ATL
Vireo griseus	L	U/M	LT	C	L	1200		N1, F15, F8, F7, N14		GCS
Vireo gundlachii	M	U/M	LT	C	L	700+		F1, F7, N1, F15	CUB	GAN
Vireo huttoni	M	C	MM	F	900	3400		F11, F8		BSR, MAH
Vireo hypochryseus	M	M/C	UT?	F	L	2000		F7, F8		PAS, MAH
Vireo latimeri	M	U/M	LT	F	L	900		F7, F1, F15, N1	PUE	GAN
Vireo leucophrys	M	C	UT	F/C	1200	2600		F4, F15		MAH, CDH, NAN, CAN
Vireo magister	M	C	LT	F	L	L		F7, F15, F14	YUC	GCS
Vireo modestus	L	U/M	LT	F	L	1500+		F7, F1, F15, F4	JAM	GAN
Vireo nanus	M	U	LT	U	L	1200		F7	HIS	GAN
Vireo nelsoni	M	U	MM	U	1500	2400		N2	SMH	MAH
Vireo olivaceus										
chivi	L	C	LT	C	L	1500		F1, F15, F7, F8, F3		CHO, EPC, NSA, AMN, AMS, CSA, ATL, PAM
Vireo osburni	M	C	UT	U	600	2000		F4, F1, F15	JAM	GAN
Vireo pallens	M	U/M	LT	F	L	L		F7, F14, N1		PAS, GCS
Vireo solitarius										
cassinii	M	C	US	F	500	2400		F11		BSR
plumbeus	M	C	MM	F	1000	3100		F11, F10		BSR, MAH
Vireo vicinior	M	U/M	US	U/P	1000	1700		F11, N2		BSR, MAH
Hylophilus aurantiifrons	L	C	LT	F	L	1300		F7, F8, F15, F1E		GCS, NSA
Hylophilus brunneiceps	H	C	LT	F?	L	L		F12	RNW	AMN
Hylophilus decurtatus	M	M/C	LT	C	L	1400+		F1, F7, F8, F15		PAS, GCS, CHO, EPC
Hylophilus flavipes	L	M/C	LT	C	L	1000		F7, F8, F15, F14		GCS, NSA
Hylophilus hypoxanthus	H	C	LT	C	L	900		F1		AMN, AMS
Hylophilus muscicapinus	H	C	LT	C	L	1100		F1		AMN, AMS
Hylophilus ochraceiceps	M	U/M	LT	F	L	1200		F1		GCS, CHO, AMN, AMS
Hylophilus olivaceus	H	M/C	UT	F	600?	1600		F4		NAN, CAN
Hylophilus pectoralis	L	C	LT	C	L	600		F8, F7, F1E, F15, F14		AMN, AMS
Hylophilus poicilotis										
amaurocephalus	M	U/C	LT	C	L	1100+		N1, F8, F7, F15, F1E		CSA, ATL
poicilotis	M	M/C	UT	C	L	1900		F1, F4, F15	SOU	ATL
Hylophilus sclateri	H	C	UT	F	900	2000		F4	o	TEP
Hylophilus semibrunneus	M	M?	UT	U/P	1000	2100		F4E, F15	o	NAN
Hylophilus semicinereus	L	C	LT	C	L	600		F15, F3, F1E		AMN, AMS
Hylophilus thoracicus	H	C	LT	U/P	L	700		F2, F1, F15?		AMN, AMS, ATL
Icteridae										
Icterus auratus	M	C	LT	U	L	L		F7, F15	YUC	GCS
Icterus auricapillus	L	C	LT	F	L	800		F7, F1, F15, F8		GCS, NSA
Icterus bonana	L	C	LT	R	L	700		F7, F1, F14, F15	MRT	LAN

CP	RP	Notes
4	3	Occasionally to 2,100 m.
4	3	
4	3	Occasionally to 1,500 m.
4	2	Locally to 1,700 m.
2	1	Declining; cowbird parasitism; survey Mexican population.
4	2	Monitor.
3	2	Declining in some areas.
3	2	Range and status poorly known; survey
3	2	
4	3	Seasonally to 1,500 m (Costa Rica).
4	3	
4	3	
4	2	
3	2	
4	3	
4	3	
4	3	Locally to sea level.
4	3	
4	3	
4	3	Occasionally to 2,800 m (Colombia).
4	3	
4	3	
4	2	Poorly known.
4	2	Poorly known.
4	2	Taxonomic relationships to nominate *V. olivaceus*, and between migrant and resident forms need study.
4	3	Seasonally to 100 m.
4	3	
4	3	
4	3	
4	3	
4	3	
4	3	
4	2	
4	3	
4	2	Occasionally to 1,200 m; includes *inornatus* as subspecies.
4	3	
4	2	Occasionally to 1,500 m; may contain two species.
4	2	Occasionally to 2,000 m; deforestation.
4	2	Isolated population in northern Peru? See Willis (1991) for taxonomy.
4	3	Status of Bolivian population uncertain.
4	3	
4	3	Occasionally to 600 m.
3	2	Occasionally to 450 m; survey.
4	3	
4	2	Southeastern Brazil population in restinga and secondary forest.
4	3	
4	3	Occasionally to 1,400 m?
2	1	Survey.

Abbreviations Used

Snst - Sensitivity:
L - Low; **M** - Medium; **H** - High.

Strat - Foraging Strata:
T - Terrestrial; **U** - Understory; **M** - Midstory; **C** - Canopy; **A** - Aerial; **W** - Water.

Cntab - Center of Abundance:
LT - Lower tropical; **LS** - Lower subtropical; **HT** - Hill tropical; **UT** - Upper tropical; **US** - Upper subtropical; **MM** - Middle montane; **UM** - Upper montane.

Rel - Relative Abundance:
R - Rare; **U** - Uncommon; **F** - Fairly common; **C** - Common; **P** - Patchily distributed.

Min - Minimum Elevation:
L - Lowlands; **?** - Uncertain value; numeric values in meters.

Max - Maximum Elevation:
L - Lowlands; **?** - Uncertain value; **+** - species occurs at least to given elevation but likely occurs higher; numeric values in meters.

Micro - Microhabitats:
A - Army ants; **B** - Bamboo; **T** - Treefalls; **G** - Ground bromeliads; **C** - Rocky outcrops and caves; **S** - Streamside; **V** - Vine tangles; **B/V** -Bamboo/vine tangles.

Habitats:
F1 - Tropical lowland evergreen forest; **F2** - Flooded tropical evergreen forest; **F3** - River-edge forest; **F4** - Montane evergreen forest; **F5** - Elfin forest; **F6** - *Polylepis* woodland; **F7** - Tropical deciduous forest; **F8** - Gallery forest; **F9** - Southern temperate forest; **F10** - Pine forest; **F11** - Pine-oak forest; **F12** - White sand forest; **F13** - Palm forest; **F14** - Mangrove forest; **F15** - Secondary forest; **N1** - Arid lowland scrub; **N2** - Arid montane scrub; **N3** - Semihumid/humid montane scrub; **N4** - Cerrado; **N5** - Campo grasslands; **N6** - Low, seasonally wet grassland; **N7** - Southern temperate grassland; **N8** - Northern temperate grassland; **N9** - Puna grassland; **N10** - Paramo grassland; **N11** - Riparian thickets; **N12** - River island scrub; **N13** - Pastures/agricultural lands; **N14** - Second-growth scrub; **A1** - Freshwater marshes; **A2** - Saltwater/brackish marshes; **A3** - Coastal sand beaches/mudflats; **A4** - Coastal rocky beaches; **A5** - Riverine sand beaches; **A6** - Freshwater lakes and ponds; **A7** - Alkaline lakes; **A8** - Rivers; **A9** - Streams; **A10** - Bogs; **A11** - Coastal waters; **A12** - Pelagic waters.
E - Edge (used as a modifer to particular habitats).

Sub - Subregions:
ARC - Arid Caribbean Coast; **AWA** - Altiplano and Western Andes; **BAH** - Bahamas; **BAJ** - Baja California; **CAA** - Caatinga; **CAH** - Central American Highlands; **CER** - Cerrado; **CHA** - Chaco; **CHG** - Chiapas-Guanacaste; **CHL** - Chilean Desert; **CHR** - Chiriquí; **CIS** - Cocos Island; **CMV** - Cauca-Magdalena Valley; **COC** - Cuzco-Cochabamba; **CUB** - Cuba; **DOM** - Dominica; **EAS** - Eastern Slope Andes; **FDN** - Fernando de Noronha; **GAL** - Galápagos; **GCM** - Gulf Coast-Mexico; **GRE** - Grenada; **GUA** - Guadeloupe; **GUI** - Guianan; **HIS** - Hispaniola; **HPC** - Humid Pacific Coast; **ISA** - Isla Providencia and Isla San Andrés; **JAM** - Jamaica; **JFI** - Juan Fernández Islands; **MAN** - Manabí-Tumbes; **MAR** - Marañón Valley; **MID** - Madeira-Tapajós; **MON** - Montserrat; **MRT** - Martinique; **MTC** - Marañón-Cuzco; **NMM** - Northern Mexican Mountains; **NOR** - Northern Coastal Brazil; **PAR** - Pará; **PER** - Peruvian Desert; **PUE** - Puerto Rico; **RDJ** - Rio de Janeiro-Bahia Lowlands; **RMW** - Rio Madeira West; **RNW** - Rio Negro West; **SCA** - Southern Central America; **SCT** - Santa Cruz-Tucumán; **SIN** - Sinaloa-Oaxaca; **SMH** - Southern Mexican Highlands; **SMT** - Santa Marta; **SOC** - Islas Revillagigedo (Socorro Island group); **SON** - Sonoran Desert; **SOU** - Southern Atlantic Coast; **STL** - St. Lucia; **STV** - St. Vincent; **TAC** - Tacarcuna; **VAN** - Venezuelan Andes; **VNZ** - Venezuelan Coastal Mountains; **WES** - Western Andes; **YUC** - Yucatán Peninsula.
o - Endemic to region, but not restricted to a single subregion.

Zoogeographic Regions:
AMN - Northern Amazonia; **AMS** - Southern Amazonia; **ATL** - Atlantic Forest; **BSR** - Baja-Sonora; **CAN** - Central Andes; **CDH** - Chiriquí-Darién Highlands; **CHO** - Chocó Lowlands; **CSA** - Central South America; **EPC** - Equatorial Pacific Coast; **GAN** - Greater Antilles; **GCS** - Gulf-Caribbean Slope; **LAN** - Lesser Antilles; **MAH** - Madrean Highlands; **MPL** - Mexican Plateau; **NAN** - Northern Andes; **NSA** - Northern South America; **PAM** - Pampas; **PAS** - Pacific Arid Slope; **PAT** - Patagonia; **SAN** - Southern Andes; **STP** - Subtropical Pacific; **TEP** - Tepuis.

CP -Conservation Priority:
1 - Urgent; **2** - High; **3** - Medium; **4** - Low.

RP - Research Priority:
1 - High; **2** - Medium; **3** - Low.

	Snst	Strat	Cntab	Rel	Min	Max	Micro	Habitats	Sub	Zoogeographic Regions
Icterus cayanensis										
cayanensis	M	C	LT	F	L	1300		F1, F3, F15		AMN, AMS, ATL
chrysocephalus	L	C	LT	U	L	L		F2, F3, F1E, F15		NSA, AMN, AMS
pyrrhopterus	M	C	LT	F	L	1300		F8, F1E, N1		CSA, PAM
Icterus chrysater	L	C	UT	F	L	2500		F7, F11, F1E, F15		MAH, GCS, CHO, NAN, NSA
Icterus cucullatus	L	M/C	LT	C	L	1900		F7, F8, F15, N1, N11		BSR, MPL, PAS, MAH, GCS
Icterus dominicensis										
dominicensis	L	C	HT?	F	L	1000		F1E, F15	o	GAN
prosthemelas	L	C	LT	F	L	1200		F1E, F15	o	GCS
Icterus galbula										
abeillei	M	C	MM	?	1600	2800		F11, F8		MPL, MAH
bullockii	L	C	UT	C	L	1800+		F8, F7, F15		BSR, MPL, MAH
Icterus graceannae	M	C	LT	F	L	800		F7, F8	MAN	EPC
Icterus graduacauda	M	C	UT	F	L	2100		F8, F11, F1, F7		PAS, MAH, GCS
Icterus gularis	M	C	LT	F	L	1000		F7, F8, F15		PAS, GCS
Icterus icterus	L	C	LT	F/P	L	700		F8, F15, F3, F7		GAN, NSA, AMN, AMS, CSA, ATL
Icterus laudabilis	L	C	HT	U	L	900		F1, F7, F15	STL	LAN
Icterus leucopteryx	L	C	HT	F	L	1000+		F15, F1, F4	o	GAN
Icterus maculialatus	M	C	UT	U	700	2100		F11, F15	CAH	MAH
Icterus mesomelas	L	C	LT	F	L	1600		F7, F15, F1E, F8		GCS, CHO, EPC, CAN, NSA
Icterus nigrogularis	L	C	LT	F	L	L		F7, F8, N1, F15, N14		NSA, AMN
Icterus oberi	L	C	HT	R	200	900		F1, F4	MON	LAN
Icterus parisorum	M	M/C	US	F	L	2600		N2, N1, F11		BSR, MPL, MAH
Icterus pectoralis	M	C	LT	F	L	600		F7, F8, F15		PAS, GCS
Icterus pustulatus	L	C	LT	F	L	1900		F7, F8, F15, N1		BSR, PAS
Icterus spurius										
fuertesi	M	C	LT	F	L	L?		F8, F15	GCM	GCS
spurius	L	C	US	C	700	1800+		F15, F8, F7		MPL, MAH
Icterus wagleri	M	C	UT	U	750	2400		F11, F7, F8	o	MAH
Psarocolius angustifrons	L	C	LT	C	L	2400		F3, F2, F4E, F1E, F15		NAN, CAN, AMN, AMS
Psarocolius atrovirens	M	C	UT	C	1400	2400		F4, F15	o	CAN
Psarocolius bifasciatus	M	C	LT	F	L	900		F1, F3?, F15?		AMN, AMS
Psarocolius cassini	M	C	LT	R	L	L		F1	o	CHO
Psarocolius decumanus	M	C	LT	C/P	L	1200		F1, F15, F2		GCS, NSA, AMN, AMS, CSA, ATL
Psarocolius guatimozinus	M	C	LT	F	L	800		F1, F3		GCS, NSA
Psarocolius latirostris	M	C	LT	U/P	L	L		F2, F3		AMN, AMS
Psarocolius montezuma	M	C	LT	C	L	800		F1, F15	o	GCS
Psarocolius oseryi	H	C	LT	U/P	L	800		F1		AMN, AMS
Psarocolius viridis	H	C	LT	C/P	L	1100		F1		AMN, AMS
Psarocolius wagleri	M	C	LT	F	L	1200		F1, F15		GCS, CHO, NSA
Cacicus cela	L	M/C	LT	C	L	1100		F3, F2, F1E, F15		GCS, EPC, NSA, AMN, AMS, CSA, ATL
Cacicus chrysopterus	M	C	HT	F	L	2000		F4, F1		CAN, CSA, ATL, PAM
Cacicus haemorrhous	L	M/C	LT	C/P	L	1200		F1E, F2, F15		AMN, AMS, CSA, ATL
Cacicus holosericeus	L	U	UM	F	L	3300	B	F4, F1, F15		PAS, MAH, GCS, CDH, CHO, EPC, NAN, CAN
Cacicus koepckeae	H	U?	LT	R	L	L		F3	RMW	AMS
Cacicus leucoramphus										
chrysonotus	H	C	UM	U/P	2300	3100		F4	o	CAN
leucoramphus	H	C	UM	U/P	1700	3200		F4		NAN, CAN
Cacicus melanicterus	L	M/C	LT	C	L	950		F7, F15	o	PAS
Cacicus sclateri	H	M	LT	F	L	600		F3		AMN, AMS
Cacicus solitarius	L	U/M	LT	F	L	800		F3, F8, F15, F2E		NSA, AMN, AMS, CSA
Cacicus uropygialis										
microrhynchus	L	C	LT/HT	F	L	1100		F1, F15		GCS, CHO
uropygialis	M	C	UT	C/P	1200	2300		F4, F1, F15		NAN, CAN

CP	RP	Notes
4	3	
4	3	
4	2	Taxonomic relationship to *I. cayanensis* needs study.
4	3	Occasionally to 2,900 m.
4	2	
4	3	
4	2	Taxonomic relationship to *I. dominicensis* needs study.
3	2	Poorly known; survey.
4	2	
4	3	Occasionally to 1,500 m.
4	3	
4	3	
4	3	Introduced to Puerto Rico; may contain multiple species.
2	2	Survey.
4	3	
4	2	Poorly known.
4	3	
4	3	Occasionally to 1,000 m?
2	1	Survey.
4	3	
4	3	
4	3	
3	2	Poorly known; survey.
4	3	
4	3	Occasionally to 3,300 m.
4	3	May contain two species.
4	3	Locally to 800 m.
4	3	
2	1	Deforestation; survey.
4	3	Occasionally to 2,600 m.
3	2	Deforestation; monitor.
4	3	Irregularly in terra firme forest.
4	3	Occasionally to 1,700 m.
4	3	
4	3	
4	3	Locally to 1,700 m.
4	3	
4	3	
4	3	Local in Amazonia where mainly associated with palms.
4	3	On eastern slope of Andes, mainly above 2,000 m.
3	1	Almost unknown.
4	2	Probably conspecific with *C. leucoramphus*.
4	3	Mainly above 2,300 m.
4	3	
4	2	Distribution and behavior poorly known.
4	3	Occasionally to 1,400 m.
4	2	
4	3	

Abbreviations Used

Snst - Sensitivity:
L - Low; **M** - Medium; **H** - High.

Strat - Foraging Strata:
T - Terrestrial; **U** - Understory; **M** - Midstory; **C** - Canopy; **A** - Aerial; **W** - Water.

Cntab - Center of Abundance:
LT - Lower tropical; **LS** - Lower subtropical; **HT** - Hill tropical; **UT** - Upper tropical; **US** - Upper subtropical; **MM** - Middle montane; **UM** - Upper montane.

Rel - Relative Abundance:
R - Rare; **U** - Uncommon; **F** - Fairly common; **C** - Common; **P** - Patchily distributed.

Min - Minimum Elevation:
L - Lowlands; **?** - Uncertain value; numeric values in meters.

Max - Maximum Elevation:
L - Lowlands; **?** - Uncertain value; **+** - species occurs at least to given elevation but likely occurs higher; numeric values in meters.

Micro - Microhabitats:
A - Army ants; **B** - Bamboo; **T** - Treefalls; **G** - Ground bromeliads; **C** - Rocky outcrops and caves; **S** - Streamside; **V** - Vine tangles; **B/V** -Bamboo/vine tangles.

Habitats:
F1 - Tropical lowland evergreen forest; **F2** - Flooded tropical evergreen forest; **F3** - River-edge forest; **F4** - Montane evergreen forest; **F5** - Elfin forest; **F6** - *Polylepis* woodland; **F7** - Tropical deciduous forest; **F8** - Gallery forest; **F9** - Southern temperate forest; **F10** - Pine forest; **F11** - Pine-oak forest; **F12** - White sand forest; **F13** - Palm forest; **F14** - Mangrove forest; **F15** - Secondary forest; **N1** - Arid lowland scrub; **N2** - Arid montane scrub; **N3** - Semihumid/humid montane scrub; **N4** - Cerrado; **N5** - Campo grasslands; **N6** - Low, seasonally wet grassland; **N7** - Southern temperate grassland; **N8** - Northern temperate grassland; **N9** - Puna grassland; **N10** - Paramo grassland; **N11** - Riparian thickets; **N12** - River island scrub; **N13** - Pastures/agricultural lands; **N14** - Second-growth scrub; **A1** - Freshwater marshes; **A2** - Saltwater/brackish marshes; **A3** - Coastal sand beaches/mudflats; **A4** - Coastal rocky beaches; **A5** - Riverine sand beaches; **A6** - Freshwater lakes and ponds; **A7** - Alkaline lakes; **A8** - Rivers; **A9** - Streams; **A10** - Bogs; **A11** - Coastal waters; **A12** - Pelagic waters.
E - Edge (used as a modifer to particular habitats).

Sub - Subregions:
ARC - Arid Caribbean Coast; **AWA** - Altiplano and Western Andes; **BAH** - Bahamas; **BAJ** - Baja California; **CAA** - Caatinga; **CAH** - Central American Highlands; **CER** - Cerrado; **CHA** - Chaco; **CHG** - Chiapas-Guanacaste; **CHL** - Chilean Desert; **CHR** - Chiriquí; **CIS** - Cocos Island; **CMV** - Cauca-Magdalena Valley; **COC** - Cuzco-Cochabamba; **CUB** - Cuba; **DOM** - Dominica; **EAS** - Eastern Slope Andes; **FDN** - Fernando de Noronha; **GAL** - Galápagos; **GCM** - Gulf Coast-Mexico; **GRE** - Grenada; **GUA** - Guadeloupe; **GUI** - Guianan; **HIS** - Hispaniola; **HPC** - Humid Pacific Coast; **ISA** - Isla Providencia and Isla San Andrés; **JAM** - Jamaica; **JFI** - Juan Fernández Islands; **MAN** - Manabí-Tumbes; **MAR** - Marañón Valley; **MID** - Madeira-Tapajós; **MON** - Montserrat; **MRT** - Martinique; **MTC** - Marañón-Cuzco; **NMM** - Northern Mexican Mountains; **NOR** - Northern Coastal Brazil; **PAR** - Pará; **PER** - Peruvian Desert; **PUE** - Puerto Rico; **RDJ** - Rio de Janeiro-Bahia Lowlands; **RMW** - Rio Madeira West; **RNW** - Rio Negro West; **SCA** - Southern Central America; **SCT** - Santa Cruz-Tucumán; **SIN** - Sinaloa-Oaxaca; **SMH** - Southern Mexican Highlands; **SMT** - Santa Marta; **SOC** - Islas Revillagigedo (Socorro Island group); **SON** - Sonoran Desert; **SOU** - Southern Atlantic Coast; **STL** - St. Lucia; **STV** - St. Vincent; **TAC** - Tacarcuna; **VAN** - Venezuelan Andes; **VNZ** - Venezuelan Coastal Mountains; **WES** - Western Andes; **YUC** - Yucatán Peninsula.
o - Endemic to region, but not restricted to a single subregion.

Zoogeographic Regions:
AMN - Northern Amazonia; **AMS** - Southern Amazonia; **ATL** - Atlantic Forest; **BSR** - Baja-Sonora; **CAN** - Central Andes; **CDH** - Chiriquí-Darién Highlands; **CHO** - Chocó Lowlands; **CSA** - Central South America; **EPC** - Equatorial Pacific Coast; **GAN** - Greater Antilles; **GCS** - Gulf-Caribbean Slope; **LAN** - Lesser Antilles; **MAH** - Madrean Highlands; **MPL** - Mexican Plateau; **NAN** - Northern Andes; **NSA** - Northern South America; **PAM** - Pampas; **PAS** - Pacific Arid Slope; **PAT** - Patagonia; **SAN** - Southern Andes; **STP** - Subtropical Pacific; **TEP** - Tepuis.

CP -Conservation Priority:
1 - Urgent; **2** - High; **3** - Medium; **4** - Low.

RP - Research Priority:
1 - High; **2** - Medium; **3** - Low.

	Snst	Strat	Cntab	Rel	Min	Max	Micro	Habitats	Sub	Zoogeographic Regions
Nesopsar nigerrimus	M	C	UT	U	500	1500+		F4	JAM	GAN
Xanthopsar flavus	M	T	LT	U/P	L	1100		N7, N13, A1		ATL, PAM
Gymnomystax mexicanus	L	U/M	LT	F	L	1000		F3, F8, N12, N6, A1		NSA, AMN, AMS
Xanthocephalus xanthocephalus	L	T	LS	F	L	1000		A1		BSR
Agelaius cyanopus	M	T/U	LT	F/P	L	L		A1		AMN, AMS, CSA, ATL
Agelaius humeralis	L	T/M	LT	F	L	900		N1, N13, N14	o	GAN
Agelaius icterocephalus	M	U	LT	C	L	600		A1		NSA, AMN, AMS
Agelaius phoeniceus	L	T/M	MM	C	L	3000+		A1, A2, N11		GAN, BSR, MPL, PAS, MAH, GCS
Agelaius ruficapillus	L	T/U	LT	C	L	850		N13, A1		AMN, AMS, CSA, ATL, PAM
Agelaius thilius	M	T/U	LS	C	L	4300		A1, A2, N13		STP, CAN, SAN, CSA, PAM, PAT
Agelaius tricolor	L	T/M	LS	F	L	L		A1		BSR
Agelaius xanthomus	L	T/M	LT	R	L	L		F14, N1, N13, N11	PUE	GAN
Agelaius xanthophthalmus	H	U	LT	U/P	L	750		A1	o	AMS
Sturnella bellicosa	L	T/U	LT	C	L	2500		N13, N2, N1, A2		EPC, STP
Sturnella defilippi	M	T/U	LT	U/P	L	L		N8, N13	o	PAM
Sturnella loyca	L	T	LS	C	L	2500		N7, N13, N1		STP, SAN, PAM, PAT
Sturnella magna	L	T	US	C	L	3500		N8, N5, N13		BSR, MPL, PAS, MAH, GCS, CDH, NAN, NSA, AMN
Sturnella militaris	L	T/U	LT	C	L	1600		N13, N6, A1		GCS, CHO, NSA, AMN, AMS
Sturnella neglecta	L	T	LS	C	L	2800		N8, N13, N1		BSR, MPL, MAH
Sturnella superciliaris	L	T/U	LT	C	L	2500		N13, N6, N5, A1		CSA, ATL, PAM
Pseudoleistes guirahuro	L	T	LT	F/P	L	1100		N13, N5, A1		CSA, ATL, PAM
Pseudoleistes virescens	M	T	LT	F/P	L	L		N13, A1		CSA, PAM
Amblyramphus holosericeus	M	U	LT	U/P	L	600		A1		CSA, PAM
Hypopyrrhus pyrohypogaster	M	C	UT	R/P	1200	2700		F4	o	NAN
Curaeus curaeus	L	T/C	US?	C	L	1500		F9, N3, N2, N14		STP, SAN, PAT
Curaeus forbesi	H	C	LT	U/P	L	600		F1E, A1	o	ATL
Gnorimopsar chopi	L	T/C	LT	C	L	1000		N6, N5, N13, F15		AMS, CSA, ATL, PAM
Oreopsar bolivianus	M	T/C	MM	U	2100	3200		N2, N13	COC	CAN
Lampropsar tanagrinus	M	C	LT	F	L	L		F2, F15		AMN, AMS
Macroagelaius imthurni	H	C	UT	C	700	2000		F4	o	TEP
Macroagelaius subalaris	M	C	MM?	?	1950	3100		F4	EAS	NAN
Dives atroviolacea	L	T/M	LT	C	L	500+		F1E, F8, F15	CUB	GAN
Dives dives	L	T/M	LT	C	L	1000		F1E, F15, F8		PAS, GCS
Dives warszewiczi	L	T/M	LT	C	L	2500		F8, F15		EPC, STP, CAN
Quiscalus lugubris	L	T/C	LT	C	L	600		N14, N13		LAN, NSA, AMN
Quiscalus mexicanus	L	T/C	LT	C	L	2300		N14, N13, F14, F15		BSR, MPL, PAS, GCS, CHO, EPC, NSA
Quiscalus nicaraguensis	L	T?	LT	?	L	L		A1, N13	CHG	PAS
Quiscalus niger	L	T/C	LT	C	L	1800		N13, N14	o	GAN
Euphagus cyanocephalus	L	T/M	LS	C	L	1300?		N13, N14		BSR
Molothrus aeneus										
aeneus	L	T	LT	C	L	2200		F11, F7, N14, N13		BSR, MPL, PAS, MAH, GCS
armenti	L	T	LT	U	L	L		N1, N13	ARC	NSA
Molothrus ater	L	T	LS	C	L	2000+		F8, N1, N14, N13		BSR, MPL, MAH
Molothrus badius	L	T	LT	C	L	2500		N14, N13, F15		CSA, PAM, PAT
Molothrus bonariensis	L	T	LT	C	L	2000		F7, N11, F1E, N1, N14, N13		GAN, LAN, CHO, EPC, STP, NSA, AMN, AMS, CSA, ATL, PAM, PAT
Molothrus rufoaxillaris	L	T	LT	F	L	1000		N14, N13		CSA, PAM
Scaphidura oryzivora	L	T/C	LT	C	L	2000		F1E, N12, N14		GCS, CHO, EPC, NSA, AMN, AMS, CSA, ATL
Fringillidae										
Carduelis atrata	M	C	UM	F/P	3600	4600		N9, N2		CAN, SAN
Carduelis atriceps	M	C	UM	F	2300	3100		F10E, F11E, N14	CAH	MAH
Carduelis barbata	L	C	LS	C	L	1500		F9, F15, N14		STP, SAN, PAT

CP	RP	Notes
3	2	To lowlands in winter; survey.
2	1	Apparently declining; survey.
4	3	
4	3	
4	3	
4	2	
4	3	Locally to 2,600 m (Colombia).
4	3	
4	3	Mainly forages in rice fields.
4	3	
4	3	
2	1	Cowbird parasitism, habitat disturbance.
4	2	Oxbow lake margins; monitor.
4	3	
3	2	Declining? overgrazing; survey.
4	3	
4	3	
4	3	
4	3	
4	3	
3	2	Possibly declining; monitor.
3	2	Seasonal movements; declining locally?
4	3	
2	1	Deforestation; survey.
4	3	
2	1	Poorly known; survey.
4	3	
4	3	Occasionally to 1,500 m.
4	2	
4	3	
2	1	Deforestation; survey.
4	3	
4	3	
4	3	
4	3	Occasionally to 850 m.
4	3	Expanding range.
3	2	Survey.
4	3	
4	3	
4	3	Expanding range.
3	2	Habitat degradation.
4	3	
4	3	
4	2	Expanding range; monitor effect on other species.
4	3	
4	3	Occasionally to 2,200 m.
4	3	
4	3	
4	3	

Abbreviations Used

Snst - Sensitivity:
L - Low; **M** - Medium; **H** - High.

Strat - Foraging Strata:
T - Terrestrial; **U** - Understory; **M** - Midstory; **C** - Canopy; **A** - Aerial; **W** - Water.

Cntab - Center of Abundance:
LT - Lower tropical; **LS** - Lower subtropical; **HT** - Hill tropical; **UT** - Upper tropical; **US** - Upper subtropical; **MM** - Middle montane; **UM** - Upper montane.

Rel - Relative Abundance:
R - Rare; **U** - Uncommon; **F** - Fairly common; **C** - Common; **P** - Patchily distributed.

Min - Minimum Elevation:
L - Lowlands; **?** - Uncertain value; numeric values in meters.

Max - Maximum Elevation:
L - Lowlands; **?** - Uncertain value; **+** - species occurs at least to given elevation but likely occurs higher; numeric values in meters.

Micro - Microhabitats:
A - Army ants; **B** - Bamboo; **T** - Treefalls; **G** - Ground bromeliads; **C** - Rocky outcrops and caves; **S** - Streamside; **V** - Vine tangles; **B/V** -Bamboo/vine tangles.

Habitats:
F1 - Tropical lowland evergreen forest; **F2** - Flooded tropical evergreen forest; **F3** - River-edge forest; **F4** - Montane evergreen forest; **F5** - Elfin forest; **F6** - *Polylepis* woodland; **F7** - Tropical deciduous forest; **F8** - Gallery forest; **F9** - Southern temperate forest; **F10** - Pine forest; **F11** - Pine-oak forest; **F12** - White sand forest; **F13** - Palm forest; **F14** - Mangrove forest; **F15** - Secondary forest; **N1** - Arid lowland scrub; **N2** - Arid montane scrub; **N3** - Semihumid/humid montane scrub; **N4** - Cerrado; **N5** - Campo grasslands; **N6** - Low, seasonally wet grassland; **N7** - Southern temperate grassland; **N8** - Northern temperate grassland; **N9** - Puna grassland; **N10** - Paramo grassland; **N11** - Riparian thickets; **N12** - River island scrub; **N13** - Pastures/agricultural lands; **N14** - Second-growth scrub; **A1** - Freshwater marshes; **A2** - Saltwater/brackish marshes; **A3** - Coastal sand beaches/mudflats; **A4** - Coastal rocky beaches; **A5** - Riverine sand beaches; **A6** - Freshwater lakes and ponds; **A7** - Alkaline lakes; **A8** - Rivers; **A9** - Streams; **A10** - Bogs; **A11** - Coastal waters; **A12** - Pelagic waters.
E - Edge (used as a modifer to particular habitats).

Sub - Subregions:
ARC - Arid Caribbean Coast; **AWA** - Altiplano and Western Andes; **BAH** - Bahamas; **BAJ** - Baja California; **CAA** - Caatinga; **CAH** - Central American Highlands; **CER** - Cerrado; **CHA** - Chaco; **CHG** - Chiapas-Guanacaste; **CHL** - Chilean Desert; **CHR** - Chiriquí; **CIS** - Cocos Island; **CMV** - Cauca-Magdalena Valley; **COC** - Cuzco-Cochabamba; **CUB** - Cuba; **DOM** - Dominica; **EAS** - Eastern Slope Andes; **FDN** - Fernando de Noronha; **GAL** - Galápagos; **GCM** - Gulf Coast-Mexico; **GRE** - Grenada; **GUA** - Guadeloupe; **GUI** - Guianan; **HIS** - Hispaniola; **HPC** - Humid Pacific Coast; **ISA** - Isla Providencia and Isla San Andrés; **JAM** - Jamaica; **JFI** - Juan Fernández Islands; **MAN** - Manabí-Tumbes; **MAR** - Marañón Valley; **MID** - Madeira-Tapajós; **MON** - Montserrat; **MRT** - Martinique; **MTC** - Marañón-Cuzco; **NMM** - Northern Mexican Mountains; **NOR** - Northern Coastal Brazil; **PAR** - Pará; **PER** - Peruvian Desert; **PUE** - Puerto Rico; **RDJ** - Rio de Janeiro-Bahia Lowlands; **RMW** - Rio Madeira West; **RNW** - Rio Negro West; **SCA** - Southern Central America; **SCT** - Santa Cruz-Tucumán; **SIN** - Sinaloa-Oaxaca; **SMH** - Southern Mexican Highlands; **SMT** - Santa Marta; **SOC** - Islas Revillagigedo (Socorro Island group); **SON** - Sonoran Desert; **SOU** - Southern Atlantic Coast; **STL** - St. Lucia; **STV** - St. Vincent; **TAC** - Tacarcuna; **VAN** - Venezuelan Andes; **VNZ** - Venezuelan Coastal Mountains; **WES** - Western Andes; **YUC** - Yucatán Peninsula.
o - Endemic to region, but not restricted to a single subregion.

Zoogeographic Regions:
AMN - Northern Amazonia; **AMS** - Southern Amazonia; **ATL** - Atlantic Forest; **BSR** - Baja-Sonora; **CAN** - Central Andes; **CDH** - Chiriquí-Darién Highlands; **CHO** - Chocó Lowlands; **CSA** - Central South America; **EPC** - Equatorial Pacific Coast; **GAN** - Greater Antilles; **GCS** - Gulf-Caribbean Slope; **LAN** - Lesser Antilles; **MAH** - Madrean Highlands; **MPL** - Mexican Plateau; **NAN** - Northern Andes; **NSA** - Northern South America; **PAM** - Pampas; **PAS** - Pacific Arid Slope; **PAT** - Patagonia; **SAN** - Southern Andes; **STP** - Subtropical Pacific; **TEP** - Tepuis.

CP -Conservation Priority:
1 - Urgent; **2** - High; **3** - Medium; **4** - Low.

RP - Research Priority:
1 - High; **2** - Medium; **3** - Low.

	Snst	Strat	Cntab	Rel	Min	Max	Micro	Habitats	Sub	Zoogeographic Regions
Carduelis crassirostris	M	C	UM	U/P	3000	4400		F6, N2		CAN, SAN
Carduelis cucullata	L	C	UT	R	L	1700		N1, N3, F7		NAN, NSA
Carduelis dominicensis	L	C	MM	U	700	3000		F10, F15, N14	HIS	GAN
Carduelis lawrencei	M	C	LS	F/P	L	2500		F8, F7		BSR
Carduelis magellanica	L	C	LS	C	L	3400		N3, N2, N14, F15, N1		EPC, STP, NAN, CAN, NSA, TEP, AMN?, AMS, CSA, ATL, PAM
Carduelis notata	M	C	MM	F	900	3100		F11, F4, F10, F15		MAH, GCS
Carduelis olivacea	M	C	UT	F	900	2500		F4, F15		NAN, CAN
Carduelis pinus	M	C	UM	F/P	1800	4000		F10, F11		BSR, MAH
Carduelis psaltria	L	C	LS	C	L	3100		N1, N2, N3, N14		BSR, MPL, PAS, MAH, GCS, CDH, CHO, EPC, NAN, CAN, NSA
Carduelis siemiradzkii	M	C	LT	U	L	700		F7, F15, N14	MAN	EPC
Carduelis spinescens	L	C	UM	F/P	1800	4000		N10, N14, N3, F5	o	NAN
Carduelis uropygialis	M	C	UM	F/P	1800	4100		N2, F6		CAN, SAN
Carduelis xanthogastra	L	C	MM	F/P	1400	3000		F4, F15, N14		CDH, NAN, CAN
Carduelis yarrellii	?	C	LT	R	L	900+		F7?		NSA?, ATL
Carpodacus cassinii	M	C	UM	F	2200	2900		F10		BSR
Carpodacus mexicanus	L	C	LS	C	L	3000		N1, N2, N14		BSR, MPL, PAS, MAH
Loxia curvirostra	M	C	UM	F/P	800	4100		F10, F11		BSR, MAH, GCS
Loxia leucoptera										
megaplaga	M	C	MM	U/P	1250	2500+		F10	HIS	GAN
Coccothraustes abeillei	M	C	MM	U/P	900	3200		F4, F11, F10	o	MAH
Coccothraustes vespertinus	M	C	UM	R/P	1500	3500		F10		MAH
Passeridae										
Passer domesticus	L	T/C	LS	C	L	3000		N14, N13, F15		GAN, BSR, MPL, PAS, MAH, GCS, EPC, STP, AMS, CSA, ATL, PAM, PAT
Sturnidae										
Sturnus vulgaris	L	T/C	LS	C	L	2000		F15, N14, N13, F8		BSR, MPL
Corvidae										
Gymnorhinus cyanocephalus	M	C	MM	F	1600	2900		F10		BSR
Cyanocitta stelleri	M	C	UM	C	900	3600		F10, F11		MAH
Aphelocoma coerulescens	L	C	US	C	L	3300		N2, N1, F11		BSR, MPL, MAH
Aphelocoma ultramarina	M	C	MM	F	1200	3400		F11, F8, F10	NMM	MAH
Aphelocoma unicolor	M	C	MM	F	1300	3300		F11, F4, F10	o	MAH
Cyanolyca argentigula	M	C	UM	U	2000	3200		F4	CHR	CDH
Cyanolyca cucullata	M	U/M	UT	U	800	2100		F4		MAH, CDH
Cyanolyca mirabilis	H	C	UM	R	1800	3500		F11, F4	SMH	MAH
Cyanolyca nana	M	C	UM	U	1850	3200		F11, F10	SMH	MAH
Cyanolyca pulchra	H	U/M	UT	R/P	900	2300		F4	WES	NAN
Cyanolyca pumilo	H	C	UM	U	1600	3000		F4, F11	CAH	MAH
Cyanolyca turcosa	M	C	UM	C	2500	3100		F4, F5	o	NAN
Cyanolyca viridicyana										
armillata	H	M/C	MM	U	1600	3100		F4	o	NAN
viridicyana	M	M/C	UM	F	2200	3300		F4, F15	o	CAN
Cyanocorax affinis	L	M/C	LT	C	L	1500		F1E, F15, F7, F8		CHO, NSA
Cyanocorax caeruleus	M	C	HT	U	L	1000		F1, F9, F12, F15	SOU	ATL
Cyanocorax cayanus	L	C	LT	F	L	1100		F12, F1E, F15	GUI	AMN
Cyanocorax chrysops	L	C	LT	F	L	1500		F1, F7, F15, F8		AMS, CSA, ATL
Cyanocorax cristatellus	M	M/C	HT	F	600	1100		N4	CER	CSA
Cyanocorax cyanomelas	L	C	LT	C	L	2000		F7, F8, F15, F3		AMS, CSA
Cyanocorax cyanopogon	M	C	LT	F	L	1300		F7, F8	o	CSA
Cyanocorax dickeyi	M	C	MM	U	1500	2200		F4, F11	NMM	MAH
Cyanocorax heilprini	H	C	LT	F	L	L		F1E, F12, F3?	RNW	AMN

CP	RP	Notes
4	3	
1	1	Capture for bird trade; introduced in Puerto Rico.
3	2	Occasionally to lowlands; survey.
4	3	
4	3	
4	3	Locally to lowlands.
4	3	Occasionally to 3,000 m.
4	3	
4	3	
2	1	Taxonomic relationship to *C. magellanicus* uncertain.
4	3	Occasionally to 1,500 m.
4	2	Seasonal movements poorly known.
4	3	Locally to 3,700 m (Bolivia); occasionally to 800 m.
2	1	Survey.
4	3	
4	3	
4	3	Locally to sea level in winter.
2	2	Survey Hispaniola population.
3	2	
4	3	
4	2	Expanding range; monitor effect on other species.
4	2	Expanding range; monitor effect on other species.
4	3	
4	3	
4	3	
4	3	
4	2	Locally to 3,500 m; monitor; habitat degradation.
4	3	Occasionally to 1,300 m.
4	3	Occasionally to 300 m.
2	1	Deforestation; survey.
2	2	Declining; deforestation; monitor.
3	2	Survey.
3	2	Deforestation; monitor.
4	3	Occasionally to 1,500 m?
4	3	
4	3	Locally to 1,600 m.
4	3	Occasionally to 2,200 m (Colombia).
3	2	Monitor, may be declining.
4	3	
4	3	Occasionally to 2,800 m.
3	2	Monitor; habitat destruction.
4	3	
3	2	Declining in parts of its range? survey.
2	1	Occasionally to 1,200 m; deforestation; survey.
4	2	Poorly known.

Abbreviations Used

Snst - Sensitivity:
L - Low; **M** - Medium; **H** - High.

Strat - Foraging Strata:
T - Terrestrial; **U** - Understory; **M** - Midstory; **C** - Canopy; **A** - Aerial; **W** - Water.

Cntab - Center of Abundance:
LT - Lower tropical; **LS** - Lower subtropical; **HT** - Hill tropical; **UT** - Upper tropical; **US** - Upper subtropical; **MM** - Middle montane; **UM** - Upper montane.

Rel - Relative Abundance:
R - Rare; **U** - Uncommon; **F** - Fairly common; **C** - Common; **P** - Patchily distributed.

Min - Minimum Elevation:
L - Lowlands; **?** - Uncertain value; numeric values in meters.

Max - Maximum Elevation:
L - Lowlands; **?** - Uncertain value; **+** - species occurs at least to given elevation but likely occurs higher; numeric values in meters.

Micro - Microhabitats:
A - Army ants; **B** - Bamboo; **T** - Treefalls; **G** - Ground bromeliads; **C** - Rocky outcrops and caves; **S** - Streamside; **V** - Vine tangles; **B/V** -Bamboo/vine tangles.

Habitats:
F1 - Tropical lowland evergreen forest; **F2** - Flooded tropical evergreen forest; **F3** - River-edge forest; **F4** - Montane evergreen forest; **F5** - Elfin forest; **F6** - *Polylepis* woodland; **F7** - Tropical deciduous forest; **F8** - Gallery forest; **F9** - Southern temperate forest; **F10** - Pine forest; **F11** - Pine-oak forest; **F12** - White sand forest; **F13** - Palm forest; **F14** - Mangrove forest; **F15** - Secondary forest; **N1** - Arid lowland scrub; **N2** - Arid montane scrub; **N3** - Semihumid/humid montane scrub; **N4** - Cerrado; **N5** - Campo grasslands; **N6** - Low, seasonally wet grassland; **N7** - Southern temperate grassland; **N8** - Northern temperate grassland; **N9** - Puna grassland; **N10** - Paramo grassland; **N11** - Riparian thickets; **N12** - River island scrub; **N13** - Pastures/agricultural lands; **N14** - Second-growth scrub; **A1** - Freshwater marshes; **A2** - Saltwater/brackish marshes; **A3** - Coastal sand beaches/mudflats; **A4** - Coastal rocky beaches; **A5** - Riverine sand beaches; **A6** - Freshwater lakes and ponds; **A7** - Alkaline lakes; **A8** - Rivers; **A9** - Streams; **A10** - Bogs; **A11** - Coastal waters; **A12** - Pelagic waters.
E - Edge (used as a modifer to particular habitats).

Sub - Subregions:
ARC - Arid Caribbean Coast; **AWA** - Altiplano and Western Andes; **BAH** - Bahamas; **BAJ** - Baja California; **CAA** - Caatinga; **CAH** - Central American Highlands; **CER** - Cerrado; **CHA** - Chaco; **CHG** - Chiapas-Guanacaste; **CHL** - Chilean Desert; **CHR** - Chiriquí; **CIS** - Cocos Island; **CMV** - Cauca-Magdalena Valley; **COC** - Cuzco-Cochabamba; **CUB** - Cuba; **DOM** - Dominica; **EAS** - Eastern Slope Andes; **FDN** - Fernando de Noronha; **GAL** - Galápagos; **GCM** - Gulf Coast-Mexico; **GRE** - Grenada; **GUA** - Guadeloupe; **GUI** - Guianan; **HIS** - Hispaniola; **HPC** - Humid Pacific Coast; **ISA** - Isla Providencia and Isla San Andrés; **JAM** - Jamaica; **JFI** - Juan Fernández Islands; **MAN** - Manabí-Tumbes; **MAR** - Marañón Valley; **MID** - Madeira-Tapajós; **MON** - Montserrat; **MRT** - Martinique; **MTC** - Marañón-Cuzco; **NMM** - Northern Mexican Mountains; **NOR** - Northern Coastal Brazil; **PAR** - Pará; **PER** - Peruvian Desert; **PUE** - Puerto Rico; **RDJ** - Rio de Janeiro-Bahia Lowlands; **RMW** - Rio Madeira West; **RNW** - Rio Negro West; **SCA** - Southern Central America; **SCT** - Santa Cruz-Tucumán; **SIN** - Sinaloa-Oaxaca; **SMH** - Southern Mexican Highlands; **SMT** - Santa Marta; **SOC** - Islas Revillagigedo (Socorro Island group); **SON** - Sonoran Desert; **SOU** - Southern Atlantic Coast; **STL** - St. Lucia; **STV** - St. Vincent; **TAC** - Tacarcuna; **VAN** - Venezuelan Andes; **VNZ** - Venezuelan Coastal Mountains; **WES** - Western Andes; **YUC** - Yucatán Peninsula.
o - Endemic to region, but not restricted to a single subregion.

Zoogeographic Regions:
AMN - Northern Amazonia; **AMS** - Southern Amazonia; **ATL** - Atlantic Forest; **BSR** - Baja-Sonora; **CAN** - Central Andes; **CDH** - Chiriquí-Darién Highlands; **CHO** - Chocó Lowlands; **CSA** - Central South America; **EPC** - Equatorial Pacific Coast; **GAN** - Greater Antilles; **GCS** - Gulf-Caribbean Slope; **LAN** - Lesser Antilles; **MAH** - Madrean Highlands; **MPL** - Mexican Plateau; **NAN** - Northern Andes; **NSA** - Northern South America; **PAM** - Pampas; **PAS** - Pacific Arid Slope; **PAT** - Patagonia; **SAN** - Southern Andes; **STP** - Subtropical Pacific; **TEP** - Tepuis.

CP -Conservation Priority:
1 - Urgent; **2** - High; **3** - Medium; **4** - Low.

RP - Research Priority:
1 - High; **2** - Medium; **3** - Low.

	Snst	Strat	Cntab	Rel	Min	Max	Micro	Habitats	Sub	Zoogeographic Regions
Cyanocorax mystacalis	L	C	LT	F	L	1200		F7, F8	MAN	EPC
Cyanocorax violaceus	L	C	LT	F	L	1100		F8, F1E, F15, F3		AMN, AMS
Cyanocorax yncas	L	C	UT	F/P	L	2800		F4, F7, F15		PAS, GCS, NAN, CAN
Cissilopha beecheii	M	C	LT	F	L	700		F7	SIN	PAS
Cissilopha melanocyaneus	M	C	UT	F	600	2400		F4, F11, F15	CAH	MAH
Cissilopha sanblasianus	M	C	LT	F	L	1200		F7	SIN	PAS
Cissilopha yucatanicus	M	C	LT	F	L	L		F7, F15	YUC	GCS
Psilorhinus morio	L	C	LT	F	L	1500		F8, F15, F7, F1E		PAS, GCS
Calocitta colliei	M	C	LT	F	L	1700		F7, F8, F15	SIN	PAS
Calocitta formosa	M	C	LT	F	L	1500		F7, F8, F15	o	PAS
Nucifraga columbiana	M	C	UM	R	2000	3100		F10		BSR, MAH?
Corvus brachyrhynchos	L	T/C	LS	F	L	L		N13, F8, F15		BSR
Corvus corax	M	T/C	US	F	L	4200		F10, F7, F15, N8, N2, N1		BSR, MPL, PAS, MAH
Corvus cryptoleucus	M	T/C	US	F	L	2400		N8, N1, N2		BSR, MPL, GCS
Corvus imparatus										
imparatus	L	T/C	LT	F	L	900		F8, F7, F15, N13	GCM	GCS
sinaloae	L	T/C	LT	C	L	1000		F8, F7, F15, N13	SIN	PAS
Corvus jamaicensis	L?	C	HT	F	L	1200+		F1, F15, F4	JAM	GAN
Corvus leucognaphalus	M	C	?	R	L	1500		F10, F15, F14	HIS	GAN
Corvus nasicus	L	C	LT	F	L	1500		F1, F15, F10	o	GAN
Corvus palmarum	M	C	MM	U	L	2000		F10, F1	o	GAN

CP	RP	Notes
4	3	
4	3	Occasionally to 1,350 m.
4	3	Above 1,200 m in Andes.
4	3	
4	3	Occasionally to lowlands.
4	3	
4	3	
4	3	
4	3	Occasionally to 1,700 m.
4	3	
4	3	
4	3	Mexican status uncertain.
4	3	Locally to 5,500 m.
4	3	
4	3	
4	3	
4	3	
1	1	Declining rapidly; survey.
3	2	Monitor.
2	1	Declining throughout its range? survey.

Abbreviations Used

Snst - Sensitivity:
L - Low; **M** - Medium; **H** - High.

Strat - Foraging Strata:
T - Terrestrial; **U** - Understory; **M** - Midstory; **C** - Canopy; **A** - Aerial; **W** - Water.

Cntab - Center of Abundance:
LT - Lower tropical; **LS** - Lower subtropical; **HT** - Hill tropical; **UT** - Upper tropical; **US** - Upper subtropical; **MM** - Middle montane; **UM** - Upper montane.

Rel - Relative Abundance:
R - Rare; **U** - Uncommon; **F** - Fairly common; **C** - Common; **P** - Patchily distributed.

Min - Minimum Elevation:
L - Lowlands; **?** - Uncertain value; numeric values in meters.

Max - Maximum Elevation:
L - Lowlands; **?** - Uncertain value; **+** - species occurs at least to given elevation but likely occurs higher; numeric values in meters.

Micro - Microhabitats:
A - Army ants; **B** - Bamboo; **T** - Treefalls; **G** - Ground bromeliads; **C** - Rocky outcrops and caves; **S** - Streamside; **V** - Vine tangles; **B/V** -Bamboo/vine tangles.

Habitats:
F1 - Tropical lowland evergreen forest; **F2** - Flooded tropical evergreen forest; **F3** - River-edge forest; **F4** - Montane evergreen forest; **F5** - Elfin forest; **F6** - *Polylepis* woodland; **F7** - Tropical deciduous forest; **F8** - Gallery forest; **F9** - Southern temperate forest; **F10** - Pine forest; **F11** - Pine-oak forest; **F12** - White sand forest; **F13** - Palm forest; **F14** - Mangrove forest; **F15** - Secondary forest; **N1** - Arid lowland scrub; **N2** - Arid montane scrub; **N3** - Semihumid/humid montane scrub; **N4** - Cerrado; **N5** - Campo grasslands; **N6** - Low, seasonally wet grassland; **N7** - Southern temperate grassland; **N8** - Northern temperate grassland; **N9** - Puna grassland; **N10** - Paramo grassland; **N11** - Riparian thickets; **N12** - River island scrub; **N13** - Pastures/agricultural lands; **N14** - Second-growth scrub; **A1** - Freshwater marshes; **A2** - Saltwater/brackish marshes; **A3** - Coastal sand beaches/mudflats; **A4** - Coastal rocky beaches; **A5** - Riverine sand beaches; **A6** - Freshwater lakes and ponds; **A7** - Alkaline lakes; **A8** - Rivers; **A9** - Streams; **A10** - Bogs; **A11** - Coastal waters; **A12** - Pelagic waters.
E - Edge (used as a modifer to particular habitats).

Sub - Subregions:
ARC - Arid Caribbean Coast; **AWA** - Altiplano and Western Andes; **BAH** - Bahamas; **BAJ** - Baja California; **CAA** - Caatinga; **CAH** - Central American Highlands; **CER** - Cerrado; **CHA** - Chaco; **CHG** - Chiapas-Guanacaste; **CHL** - Chilean Desert; **CHR** - Chiriquí; **CIS** - Cocos Island; **CMV** - Cauca-Magdalena Valley; **COC** - Cuzco-Cochabamba; **CUB** - Cuba; **DOM** - Dominica; **EAS** - Eastern Slope Andes; **FDN** - Fernando de Noronha; **GAL** - Galápagos; **GCM** - Gulf Coast-Mexico; **GRE** - Grenada; **GUA** - Guadeloupe; **GUI** - Guianan; **HIS** - Hispaniola; **HPC** - Humid Pacific Coast; **ISA** - Isla Providencia and Isla San Andrés; **JAM** - Jamaica; **JFI** - Juan Fernández Islands; **MAN** - Manabí-Tumbes; **MAR** - Marañón Valley; **MID** - Madeira-Tapajós; **MON** - Montserrat; **MRT** - Martinique; **MTC** - Marañón-Cuzco; **NMM** - Northern Mexican Mountains; **NOR** - Northern Coastal Brazil; **PAR** - Pará; **PER** - Peruvian Desert; **PUE** - Puerto Rico; **RDJ** - Rio de Janeiro-Bahia Lowlands; **RMW** - Rio Madeira West; **RNW** - Rio Negro West; **SCA** - Southern Central America; **SCT** - Santa Cruz-Tucumán; **SIN** - Sinaloa-Oaxaca; **SMH** - Southern Mexican Highlands; **SMT** - Santa Marta; **SOC** - Islas Revillagigedo (Socorro Island group); **SON** - Sonoran Desert; **SOU** - Southern Atlantic Coast; **STL** - St. Lucia; **STV** - St. Vincent; **TAC** - Tacarcuna; **VAN** - Venezuelan Andes; **VNZ** - Venezuelan Coastal Mountains; **WES** - Western Andes; **YUC** - Yucatán Peninsula.
o - Endemic to region, but not restricted to a single subregion.

Zoogeographic Regions:
AMN - Northern Amazonia; **AMS** - Southern Amazonia; **ATL** - Atlantic Forest; **BSR** - Baja-Sonora; **CAN** - Central Andes; **CDH** - Chiriquí-Darién Higlands; **CHO** - Chocó Lowlands; **CSA** - Central South America; **EPC** - Equatorial Pacific Coast; **GAN** - Greater Antilles; **GCS** - Gulf-Caribbean Slope; **LAN** - Lesser Antilles; **MAH** - Madrean Highlands; **MPL** - Mexican Plateau; **NAN** - Northern Andes; **NSA** - Northern South America; **PAM** - Pampas; **PAS** - Pacific Arid Slope; **PAT** - Patagonia; **SAN** - Southern Andes; **STP** - Subtropical Pacific; **TEP** - Tepuis.

CP -Conservation Priority:
1 - Urgent; **2** - High; **3** - Medium; **4** - Low.

RP - Research Priority:
1 - High; **2** - Medium; **3** - Low.

Database B

Distribution of Neotropical Bird Species by Country

	Baha	Cuba	Hisp	Jama	Puer	Lant	Nant	Mexi	Guat	Beli	Elsa	Hond	Nica	Cost	Pana	Colo	Vene	Trin	Guya	Suri	Fren	Ecua	Peru	Boli	Braz	Parg	Urug	Argn	Chil
RHEIFORMES																													
Rheidae																													
Rhea americana																								X	X	X	X	X	
Pterocnemia pennata																													
pennata																												X	X
tarapacensis																							X	X				X	X
TINAMIFORMES																													
Tinamidae																													
Tinamus guttatus																X	X					X	X	X	X				
Tinamus major								X	X	X		X	X	X	X	X	X		X	X	X	X	X	X	X				
Tinamus osgoodi																X							X						
Tinamus solitarius																									X	X		X	
Tinamus tao																X	X		X			X	X	X	X				
Nothocercus bonapartei														X	X	X	X					X	X						
Nothocercus julius																X	X					X	X						
Nothocercus nigrocapillus																							X	X					
Crypturellus atrocapillus																							X	X					
Crypturellus bartletti																							X	X	X				
Crypturellus berlepschi																X						X							
Crypturellus boucardi								X	X	X		X	X	X		X													
Crypturellus brevirostris																X					X		X		X				
Crypturellus casiquiare																X	X								X				
Crypturellus cinereus																X	X		X	X	X	X	X	X	X				
Crypturellus cinnamomeus								X	X	X	X	X	X	X															
Crypturellus duidae																X	X								X				
Crypturellus erythropus																													
columbianus																XR													
erythropus																X	X		X	X	X				X				
idoneus																X	X												
saltuarius																XR													
Crypturellus kerriae															X	X													
Crypturellus noctivagus																									XR				
Crypturellus obsoletus																X	X					X	X	X	X	X		X	
Crypturellus parvirostris																							X	X	X	X		X	
Crypturellus ptaritepui																	XR												
Crypturellus soui								X	X	X		X	X	X	X	X	X	X	X	X	X	X	X	X	X				
Crypturellus strigulosus																							X	X	X				
Crypturellus tataupa																							X	X	X	X		X	
Crypturellus transfasciatus																						X	X						
Crypturellus undulatus																X	X		X		SX	X	X	X	X	X		X	
Crypturellus variegatus																X	X		X	X	X	X	X	X	X				
Rhynchotus rufescens																							X	X	X	X	X	X	
Nothoprocta cinerascens																								X		X		X	
Nothoprocta curvirostris																						X	X						
Nothoprocta kalinowskii																							XR						
Nothoprocta ornata																							X	X				X	X
Nothoprocta pentlandii																						X	X	X				X	X
Nothoprocta perdicaria																													XR
Nothoprocta taczanowskii																							XR						
Nothura boraquira																								X	X	X			
Nothura chacoensis																										X		X	
Nothura darwinii																							X	X				X	

Countries: Argn - Argentina; **Baha** - Bahamas; **Beli** - Belize; **Boli** - Bolivia; **Braz** - Brazil; **Chil** - Chile; **Colo** - Colombia; **Cost** - Costa Rica; **Cuba** - Cuba; **Ecua** - Ecuador; **Elsa** - El Salvador; **Fren** - French Guiana; **Guat** - Guatemala; **Guya** - Guyana; **Hisp** - Hispaniola; **Hond** - Honduras; **Jama** - Jamaica; **Lant** - Lesser Antilles; **Mexi** - Mexico; **Nant** - Netherland Antilles; **Nica** - Nicaragua; **Pana** - Panama; **Parg** - Paraguay; **Peru** - Peru; **Puer** - Puerto Rico; **Suri** - Suriname; **Trin** - Trinidad; **Urug** - Uruguay; **Vene** - Venezuela.

	Baha	Cuba	Hisp	Jama	Puer	Lant	Nant	Mexi	Guat	Beli	Elsa	Hond	Nica	Cost	Pana	Colo	Vene	Trin	Guya	Suri	Fren	Ecua	Peru	Boli	Braz	Parg	Urug	Argn	Chil
Nothura maculosa																									X	X	X	X	
Nothura minor																									X			X	
Taoniscus nanus																									XR				
Eudromia elegans																								?				X	X
Eudromia formosa																										X		X	
Tinamotis ingoufi																												X	X
Tinamotis pentlandii																							X	X				X	X
SPHENISCIFORMES																													
Spheniscidae																													
Aptenodytes forsteri																												XN	XN
Aptenodytes patagonicus																												X	X
Pygoscelis adeliae																												V	
Pygoscelis antarcticus																													X?
Pygoscelis papua																												X	X?
Eudyptes chrysocome																									V		XN	X	X
Eudyptes chrysolophus																									XN			X	X
Eudyptes robustus																												V	
Eudyptes sclateri																												V	
Spheniscus humboldti																						XN	X						X
Spheniscus magellanicus																									XN		XN	X	X
Spheniscus mendiculus																						XR							
GAVIIFORMES																													
Gaviidae																													
Gavia adamsii								V																					
Gavia immer		V						XN																					
Gavia pacifica								XN																					
Gavia stellata								XN																					
PODICIPEDIFORMES																													
Podicipedidae																													
Tachybaptus dominicus	X	X	X	X	X		X	X	X	X	X	X	X	X	X	X	X	X	X	X	X	X	X	X	X	X		X	
Podilymbus gigas									+																				
Podilymbus podiceps	X	X	X	X	X	X	X	X	X	X	X	X	X	X	X	X	X	X	X	X	S?	X	X	X	X	X	X	X	X
Rollandia micropterum																							X	X					
Rollandia rolland																							X	X	X	X	X	X	X
Podiceps auritus								XN																					
Podiceps gallardoi																												XR	
Podiceps major																							X		X	X	X	X	X
Podiceps nigricollis																													
andinus																XR													
nigricollis								X	XN		XN			V															
Podiceps occipitalis																X						X	X	X				X	X
Podiceps taczanowskii																							XR						
Aechmophorus clarkii								X																					
Aechmophorus occidentalis								X																					
PROCELLARIIFORMES																													
Diomedeidae																													
Diomedea albatrus								V																					
Diomedea bulleri																							XN						XN
Diomedea cauta																							XN					XN	XN
Diomedea chlororhynchos																									XN		XN	XN	
Diomedea chrysostoma																							XN		V			XN	X
Diomedea epomophora																							SV		V		XN	XN	XN

Status: **X** - Breeding species; **XN** - Regular non-breeding species; **XR** - Endemic breeding species; **X?** - Regular species, breeding status uncertain; **XI** - Introduced species; **XD** - Dubious species; **XF** - Formerly bred; **V** - Vagrants; **SX** - Breeding species, sight records only; **SN** - Regular non-breeding species, sight records only; **S?** - Uncertain breeding status; sight records only; **SI** -Introduced; sight records only; **SV** - Vagrant; sight records only. **?** - Occurrence uncertain; **+** - Extinct.

	Baha	Cuba	Hisp	Jama	Puer	Lant	Nant	Mexi	Guat	Beli	Elsa	Hond	Nica	Cost	Pana	Colo	Vene	Trin	Guya	Suri	Fren	Ecua	Peru	Boli	Braz	Parg	Urug	Argn	Chil
Diomedea exulans																									V		XN	XN	XN
Diomedea immutabilis								X																					
Diomedea irrorata															SV	XN						X	XN						
Diomedea melanophris						V																XN	XN		XN		XN	X	X
Diomedea nigripes								XN														SV							
Phoebetria fusca																									V			V	V
Phoebetria palpebrata																									XN			XN	XN
Procellariidae																													
Macronectes giganteus																						SV	XN		XN		XN	XN	X
Macronectes halli																													V
Fulmarus glacialis					SV			XN																					
Fulmarus glacialoides																						V	XN		XN		XN	XN	XN
Thalassoica antarctica																									XN			XN	XN
Daption capense																V						XN	XN		XN		XN	XN	XN
Pterodroma arminjoniana					V																				X				
Pterodroma cooki																													
cooki								XN															XN						XN
defilippiana																													XR
Pterodroma externa								SN																				XN	XR
Pterodroma hasitata	XN	X?	X	XF	XN	X	SN							SV		XN									V				
Pterodroma incerta																									V			XN	
Pterodroma inexpectata																						V							
Pterodroma lessoni																									V			XN	XN
Pterodroma longirostris																													
longirostris																													XR
Pterodroma macroptera																									V			XN	
Pterodroma mollis																									SV			XN	
Pterodroma neglecta								XN																					X
Pterodroma phaeopygia								SN						XN	SV	XN						X	XN						
Pterodroma rostrata								SN																					
Halobaena caerulea																									V		XN	XN	X
Pachyptila belcheri																							XN		XN		XN	X	XN
Pachyptila desolata																						V	XN		XN		XN	XN	XN
Pachyptila salvini																							XN						
Pachyptila turtur																												X	XN
Pachyptila vittata																							XN		V				
Bulweria bulwerii							SV											V			SV								
Procellaria aequinoctialis																							XN		XN		XN	XN	XN
Procellaria cinerea																							XN		V		XN	V	XN
Procellaria parkinsoni								XN	XN			?	?	XN	SN							XN	XN						
Procellaria westlandica																												V	XN
Calonectris diomedea	XN	V				XN		SV										XN	XN		SN				XN		XN		
Puffinus assimilis				XN	V																SV		SV		V		XN	XN	X?
Puffinus auricularis								XR							SV														
Puffinus bulleri								SN														?	XN						XN
Puffinus carneipes								SN																					XN
Puffinus creatopus								XN						SN		SV						XN	XN						X
Puffinus gravis	XN				V	XN	V	V									XN	XN	XN	XN	XN				XN		XN	X	XN
Puffinus griseus	XN	XN			V	V		XN	XN	XN			XN	XN	XN	XN						XN	XN		XN		XN	X	X
Puffinus lherminieri	X	XN	SN	?	X	X	X?	XN	XN			?	XN	XN	XN	X	X	X	?			X							
Puffinus nativitatis								XN																					XN
Puffinus opisthomelas								XR																					
Puffinus pacificus								X	XN			?	XN	XN	XN	XN						XN							

Countries: Argn - Argentina; **Baha** - Bahamas; **Beli** - Belize; **Boli** - Bolivia; **Braz** - Brazil; **Chil** - Chile; **Colo** - Colombia; **Cost** - Costa Rica; **Cuba** - Cuba; **Ecua** - Ecuador; **Elsa** - El Salvador; **Fren** - French Guiana; **Guat** - Guatemala; **Guya** - Guyana; **Hisp** - Hispaniola; **Hond** - Honduras; **Jama** - Jamaica; **Lant** - Lesser Antilles; **Mexi** - Mexico; **Nant** - Netherland Antilles; **Nica** - Nicaragua; **Pana** - Panama; **Parg** - Paraguay; **Peru** - Peru; **Puer** - Puerto Rico; **Suri** - Suriname; **Trin** - Trinidad; **Urug** - Uruguay; **Vene** - Venezuela.

	Baha	Cuba	Hisp	Jama	Puer	Lant	Nant	Mexi	Guat	Beli	Elsa	Hond	Nica	Cost	Pana	Colo	Vene	Trin	Guya	Suri	Fren	Ecua	Peru	Boli	Braz	Parg	Urug	Argn	Chil
Puffinus puffinus					V												?	XN			XN				XN		XN	XN	XN
Puffinus tenuirostris								XN						SV															
Hydrobatidae																													
Oceanites gracilis																XN						XN	X						X
Oceanites oceanicus		XN		?	XN		XN	SN	XN					XN	XN		XN	SV	XN	XN	XN	XN	XN		XN		XN	X	X
Garrodia nereis																												X	XN
Pelagodroma marina														V								XN	XN				XN	XN	
Fregetta grallaria																						XN			SN			XN	X
Fregetta tropica																							XN		SV		XN	XN	XN
Halocyptena microsoma								X						XN	XN	XN						XN	XN						
Oceanodroma castro		V						V						XN		SV						X							
Oceanodroma homochroa								X																					
Oceanodroma hornbyi																XN						XN	X						X
Oceanodroma leucorhoa	XN	XN	V		XN	SV	V	X	XN					XN			XN	XN	XN	XN	XN	XN			XN				
Oceanodroma macrodactyla								+																					
Oceanodroma markhami														V		SV						XN	X						XN
Oceanodroma melania								X	SN				XN	XN	XN	XN						XN	XN						
Oceanodroma tethys								XN	XN					XN	XN	XN						X	X						XN
Pelecanoididae																													
Pelecanoides garnotii																							X						X
Pelecanoides georgicus																												V	
Pelecanoides magellani																									V			X	X
Pelecanoides urinatrix																											V	X	X
PELECANIFORMES																													
Phaethontidae																													
Phaethon aethereus	?	V	?	?	X	X	XN	X			V			X	X	X	X	X			XN	X	SV		X				XN
Phaethon lepturus	X	X	X	X	X	X	SV	V	SV	V					V	V		SV							X				V
Phaethon rubricauda								X?																					V
Pelecanidae																													
Pelecanus erythrorhynchos	V	V	SV	V	V			X	XN		XN		XN	XN															
Pelecanus occidentalis	X	X	X	X	X	X	X	X	X	X	XN	X	XN	X	X	X	X	X	X	X	X	X	X		XN				
Pelecanus thagus																							X						X
Sulidae																													
Morus bassanus	V							XN																					
Morus capensis																									?				
Morus serrator																									V				
Sula dactylatra	X	XN	XN	XN	X	X	XN	X	SN	V			XN	X	XN	XN	X	V				X	XN		X				X
Sula leucogaster	X	X	X	X	X	X	XN	X	X	X	X	X	X	X	X	X	X	X	X	X	XN	X			X		X	X	V
Sula nebouxii								X			X	XN	XN	XN	X	X						X	X						V
Sula sula	X	XN	XN	?	X	X	XN	X	SN	X		X		X	XN	XN	X	X			SN	X			X				
Sula variegata															XN	XN						XN	X						X
Phalacrocoracidae																													
Phalacrocorax albiventer																											XN	X	X
Phalacrocorax atriceps																											XN	X	X
Phalacrocorax auritus	X	X	XN	X?	XN	V	V	X		X																			
Phalacrocorax bougainvillii															SV	XN						XN	X					X	X
Phalacrocorax brasilianus	X	X		V	XN	V	XN	X	X	X	X	X	X	X	X	X	X	XN	X	X	X	X	X	X	X	X	X	X	X
Phalacrocorax gaimardi																							X					X	X
Phalacrocorax magellanicus																											XN	X	X
Phalacrocorax pelagicus								X																					
Phalacrocorax penicillatus								X																					
Nannopterum harrisi																						XR							

Status: **X** - Breeding species; **XN** - Regular non-breeding species; **XR** - Endemic breeding species; **X?** - Regular species, breeding status uncertain; **XI** - Introduced species; **XD** - Dubious species; **XF** - Formerly bred; **V** - Vagrants; **SX** - Breeding species, sight records only; **SN** - Regular non-breeding species, sight records only; **S?** - Uncertain breeding status; sight records only; **SI** -Introduced; sight records only; **SV** - Vagrant; sight records only. **?** - Occurrence uncertain; **+** - Extinct.

	Baha	Cuba	Hisp	Jama	Puer	Lant	Nant	Mexi	Guat	Beli	Elsa	Hond	Nica	Cost	Pana	Colo	Vene	Trin	Guya	Suri	Fren	Ecua	Peru	Boli	Braz	Parg	Urug	Argn	Chil
Anhingidae																													
Anhinga anhinga	V	X	V			X?		X	X	X	X	X	X	X	X	X	X	X	X	X	X	X	X	X	X	X	X	X	
Fregatidae																													
Fregata ariel																									X				
Fregata magnificens	X	X	X	X	X	X	XN	X	XN	X	XN	X	XN	X	X	X	X	X	X	X	X	X	XN		X		XN	XN	XN
Fregata minor								X						X								X			X				XN
CICONIIFORMES																													
Ardeidae																													
Botaurus lentiginosus	XN	XN	XN	XN	XN	XN		X	XN	XN	XN	XN	XN	XN	V														
Botaurus pinnatus							V	X		X	X?			X		X	X	X	X	X	X	X	SV		X	X	X	X	
Ixobrychus exilis	XN	X	XN	XN	X	XN		X	X	XN	+	X	X	X	X	X	X	X	X	X	X	X	X	X	X	X		X	
Ixobrychus involucris																X	X	X	X	X	X		V	X	X	X	X	X	X
Tigrisoma fasciatum														X	X	X	X					X	X	X	X			X	
Tigrisoma lineatum												V	X	X	X	X	X	X	X	X	X	X	X	X	X	X	X	X	
Tigrisoma mexicanum								X	X	X	X	X	X	X	X	X													
Zebrilus undulatus																X	X		X	X	X	X	X	X	X				
Nycticorax nycticorax	X	X	X	X	X	XN	X	X	X	X	X	X	X	X	X	X	X	X	X	X	X	X	X	X	X	X	X	X	X
Nycticorax pileatus															X	X	X		X	X	X	X	X	X	X	X			
Nycticorax violaceus	X	X	X	X	X	X	X	X	X	X	X	X	X	X	X	X	X	X	X	X	X	X	X		X				
Cochlearius cochlearius							V	X	X	X	X	X	X	X	X	X	X	X	X	X	X	X	X	X	X	X		X	
Ardeola ibis	X	X	X	X	X	X	X	X	X	X	X	X	X	X	X	X	X	X	X	X	X	X	X	X	X	X	X	X	X
Ardeola ralloides																									SV				
Syrigma sibilatrix																X	X							X	X	X	X	X	
Butorides striatus																													
striatus						V								V	X	X	X	X	X	X	X	X	X	X	X	X	X	X	X
sundevalli																						XR							
virescens	X	X	X	X	X	X	X	X	X	X	X	X	X	X	X	XN	XN	X	SV	V		V							
Hydranassa caerulea	X	X	X	X	X	X	XN	X	X	X	X	X	X	X	X	X	X	X	X	X	X	X	X	X	X	XN	X		XN
Hydranassa rufescens	X	X	X	XN	XN	XN	X	X	XN	XN	XN	XN	XN	XN	SV	X	XN	SV											
Hydranassa tricolor	X	X	X	X	X	XN	X	X	X	X	X	X	X	X	X	X	X	X	X	X	X	X	XN		X				
Egretta alba	X	X	X	X	X	X	X	X	X	X	X	X	X	X	X	X	X	X	X	X	X	X	X	X	X	X	X	X	X
Egretta garzetta						V												V		V									
Egretta gularis						V												V											
Egretta thula	X	X	X	X	X	X	X	X	X	X	X	X	X	X	X	X	X	X	X	X	X	X	X	X	X	X	X	X	X
Ardea cinerea						V												V							V				
Ardea cocoi															X	X	X	XN	X	X	X	X	X	X	X	X	X	X	X
Ardea herodias	XN	X	X	X	X	XN	XN	X	XN	XN	XN	XN	XN	XN	XN	XN	X	XN				X							
Ardea purpurea																									SV				
Agamia agami								X	X	X		X		X	X	X	X	XN	X	X	X	X	X	X	X				
Ciconiidae																													
Mycteria americana	V	X	X	V			V	X	X	X	X	X	X	X	X	X	X	XN	X	X	X	X	X	X	X	X	X	X	V
Ciconia maguari																X	X		X	X	XN			X	X	X	X	X	X
Jabiru mycteria								X	X?	X	SV	X	X	X	V	X	X	SV	X	X	X	X	X	X	X	X	X	X	
Threskiornithidae																													
Harpiprion caerulescens																								X	X	X	X	X	
Theristicus caudatus																													
branickii																						X	X	X				X	X
caudatus															V	X	X		X	X	X				X	X	X	X	
melanopis																							X	X				X	X
Cercibis oxycerca																X	X		X						X				
Mesembrinibis cayennensis												X		X	X	X	X		X	X	X	X	X	X	X	X		X	
Phimosus infuscatus																X	X		X			X		X	X	X	X	X	

Countries: Argn - Argentina; **Baha** - Bahamas; **Beli** - Belize; **Boli** - Bolivia; **Braz** - Brazil; **Chil** - Chile; **Colo** - Colombia; **Cost** - Costa Rica; **Cuba** - Cuba; **Ecua** - Ecuador; **Elsa** - El Salvador; **Fren** - French Guiana; **Guat** - Guatemala; **Guya** - Guyana; **Hisp** - Hispaniola; **Hond** - Honduras; **Jama** - Jamaica; **Lant** - Lesser Antilles; **Mexi** - Mexico; **Nant** - Netherland Antilles; **Nica** - Nicaragua; **Pana** - Panama; **Parg** - Paraguay; **Peru** - Peru; **Puer** - Puerto Rico; **Suri** - Suriname; **Trin** - Trinidad; **Urug** - Uruguay; **Vene** - Venezuela.

	Baha	Cuba	Hisp	Jama	Puer	Lant	Nant	Mexi	Guat	Beli	Elsa	Hond	Nica	Cost	Pana	Colo	Vene	Trin	Guya	Suri	Fren	Ecua	Peru	Boli	Braz	Parg	Urug	Argn	Chil
Eudocimus albus	XN	X	X	X	XN		X?	X	X?	X	X	X	X	X	X	X	X	SV			S?	X	XN						
Eudocimus ruber		?					V									X	X	X	X?	X	?	X			X				
Plegadis chihi							?	X	XN		V			V									XV	X	X	X	X	X	X
Plegadis falcinellus	X?	X	X	X	X?	XN	XN	X		XN				X	XN	XN	X	SN				SV							
Plegadis ridgwayi																							X	X				X	X
Ajaia ajaja	X	X	X	XN	XN	XN	X	X	X	X	X	X	X	X	X	X	X	XN	X	X	X	X	X	X	X	X	X	X	X
PHOENICOPTERIFORMES																													
Phoenicopteridae																													
Phoenicopterus chilensis																						XN	X	X	XN	XN	XN	X	X
Phoenicopterus ruber	X	X	X		XN		X	X		XN		?				XN	XN	SV	XN	XN	SN	X			X				
Phoenicoparrus andinus																							XN	X	V			X	X
Phoenicoparrus jamesi																							XN	X				X	X
ANSERIFORMES																													
Anhimidae																													
Anhima cornuta																X	X	XF	X?	X	X	X	X	X	X			X	
Chauna chavaria																X	X												
Chauna torquata																							SV	X	X	X	X	X	
Anatidae																													
Dendrocygna arborea	X	X	X	X	X	X																							
Dendrocygna autumnalis		?			XN	V	V	X	X	X	X	X	X	X	X	X	X	X	X	X	X	X	XN	XN	X	X		X	
Dendrocygna bicolor	XN	X	X		X	V	V	X	SV	SV	X	X		X	X	X	X	X	X	X	X?	X	XN	XN	X	X	X	X	XN
Dendrocygna viduata		V	V			V	V						X	X	X	X	X	X	X	X	SV		XN	XN	X	X	X	X	V
Cygnus buccinator								V																					
Cygnus columbianus		V			V			XN																					
Cygnus melanocoryphus																									X		X	X	X
Coscoroba coscoroba																									X	X	X	X	X
Anser albifrons		XN					V	XN		V																			
Anser caerulescens	XN	XN			V			XN		XN		V						SV											
Anser rossi								V																					
Branta bernicla								XN																					
Branta canadensis	V	V		?				XN																					
Chloephaga hybrida																												X	X
Chloephaga melanoptera																							X	X				X	X
Chloephaga picta																											V	X	X
Chloephaga poliocephala																												X	X
Chloephaga rubidiceps																												X	X
Neochen jubata																X	X		X		X	?	X	X	X	X?		X	
Tachyeres brachypterus																												XR	
Tachyeres leucocephala																												XR	
Tachyeres patachonicus																												X	X
Tachyeres pteneres																												X	X
Cairina moschata								X	X	X	X	X	X	X	X	X	X	X	X	X	X	X	X	X	X	X	X	X	V
Sarkidiornis melanotos							V								X	X	X	SV	X			X	X	X	X	X	X	X	
Callonetta leucophrys																								X	X	X	X	X	
Aix sponsa	XN	X		V	V	V		XN																					
Amazonetta brasiliensis																X	X		X					X	X	X	X	X	
Merganetta armata																X	X					X	X	X				X	X
Anas acuta	XN	XN	XN	XN	XN	XN	SV	XN	XN	XN	XN	XN	XN	XN	XN	XN	V		V	V					SV				
Anas americana	XN	XN	XN	XN	XN	XN	XN	XN	XN	XN	XN	XN	XN	XN	XN	XN	XN	XN											
Anas bahamensis	X	X	X	X	X	X	X									X	X	X	X	X	X	X	X	X	X	X	X	X	X
Anas clypeata	XN	XN	XN	XN	XN	XN	V	XN	XN	XN	XN	XN	XN	XN	XN	XN		XN											
Anas crecca		XN	V		XN	V		XN	XN	XN	SN	XN		V		V		V											

Status: **X** - Breeding species; **XN** - Regular non-breeding species; **XR** - Endemic breeding species; **X?** - Regular species, breeding status uncertain; **XI** - Introduced species; **XD** - Dubious species; **XF** - Formerly bred; **V** - Vagrants; **SX** - Breeding species, sight records only; **SN** - Regular non-breeding species, sight records only; **S?** - Uncertain breeding status; sight records only; **SI** -Introduced; sight records only; **SV** - Vagrant; sight records only. **?** - Occurrence uncertain; **+** - Extinct.

	Baha	Cuba	Hisp	Jama	Puer	Lant	Nant	Mexi	Guat	Beli	Elsa	Hond	Nica	Cost	Pana	Colo	Vene	Trin	Guya	Suri	Fren	Ecua	Peru	Boli	Braz	Parg	Urug	Argn	Chil
Anas cyanoptera	V	XN		V				X	XN	XN		XN	XN	SN	XN	X	V					XN	X	X	XN	X	X	X	X
Anas discors	XN	XN	XN	XN	XN	XN	XN	XN	XN	XN	XN	XN	XN	XN	XN	XN	XN	XN	XN	XN	XN	XN	XN		XN		XN	XN	V
Anas flavirostris																X	X					X	X	X	X	SN	X	X	X
Anas fulvigula								X																					
Anas georgica																X						X	X	X	X	?	X	X	X
Anas penelope			V		V	V		XN																					
Anas platalea																							X	X	X	X	X	X	X
Anas platyrhynchos																													
diazi								X																					
platyrhynchos	XN	XN			XN		SV	X	XN	V		V	V	V	SV														
Anas puna																							X	X				X	X
Anas rubripes					XN																								
Anas sibilatrix																									XN	XN	X	X	X
Anas specularioides																							X	X				X	X
Anas specularis																												X	X
Anas strepera	XN	XN		XN	XN			XN																					
Anas versicolor																								X	X	X	X	X	X
Netta erythrophthalma																X	X	V				X	X	?	X			X	X?
Netta peposaca																									X	X	X	X	X
Aythya affinis	XN	XN	XN	XN	XN	XN	XN	XN	XN	XN	XN	XN	XN	XN	XN	XN	XN	XN		SV		X							
Aythya americana	XN	XN		XN				X	XN																				
Aythya collaris	XN	XN	XN	XN	XN	XN	SV	XN	XN	XN		XN	XN	XN	XN	SN	V	V											
Aythya marila	?	SV						XN						V															
Aythya valisineria		XN			SN			XN	V			V																	
Histrionicus histrionicus								V																					
Clangula hyemalis								V																					
Melanitta fusca								XN																					
Melanitta nigra								XN																					
Melanitta perspicillata								XN																					
Bucephala albeola		V		XN	V			XN																					
Bucephala clangula								XN																					
Mergus cucullatus	SN	XN			V	V		XN																					
Mergus merganser								X																					
Mergus octosetaceus																									X	XF		X	
Mergus serrator	XN	XN			V			XN																					
Heteronetta atricapilla																								X	X	X	X	X	X
Oxyura dominica	V	X	X	X	X	X	SV	X	X	X	X	X		X	X	X	X	X	X	X	X	X	X	X	X	X	X	X	
Oxyura jamaicensis																													
ferruginea																X						X	X	X				X	X
jamaicensis	X	X	X	X	X	X		X	X		XN	XN	SV			X													
Oxyura vittata																									X	XN	X	X	X
FALCONIFORMES																													
Cathartidae																													
Cathartes aura	X	X	XN	X	XI			X	X	X	X	X	X	X	X	X	X	SX	X	X	X	X	X	X	X	X	X	X	X
Cathartes burrovianus								X	X	X	?	X	X	X	X	X	X		X	X	X	?	X	X	X	X	X	X	
Cathartes melambrotus																X	X		X	X	X	X	X	X	X				
Coragyps atratus		SV		SV		SV		X	X	X	X	X	X	X	X	X	X	X	X	X	X	X	X	X	X	X	X	X	X
Sarcoramphus papa								X	X	X	X	X	X	X	X	X	X	XN	X	X	X	X	X	X	X	X		X	
Vultur gryphus																X	X					X	X	X	V			X	X
Accipitridae																													
Pandion haliaetus	X	X	XN	XN	X?	XN	XN	X	XN	X	XN	XN	XN	XN	XN	XN	XN	XN	XN	XN	XN	XN	XN	XN	XN	XN	XN	XN	XN
Leptodon cayanensis								X	X	X	X	X	X	X	X	X	X	X	X	X	X	X	X	X	X	X		X	

Countries: Argn - Argentina; **Baha** - Bahamas; **Beli** - Belize; **Boli** - Bolivia; **Braz** - Brazil; **Chil** - Chile; **Colo** - Colombia; **Cost** - Costa Rica; **Cuba** - Cuba; **Ecua** - Ecuador; **Elsa** - El Salvador; **Fren** - French Guiana; **Guat** - Guatemala; **Guya** - Guyana; **Hisp** - Hispaniola; **Hond** - Honduras; **Jama** - Jamaica; **Lant** - Lesser Antilles; **Mexi** - Mexico; **Nant** - Netherland Antilles; **Nica** - Nicaragua; **Pana** - Panama; **Parg** - Paraguay; **Peru** - Peru; **Puer** - Puerto Rico; **Suri** - Suriname; **Trin** - Trinidad; **Urug** - Uruguay; **Vene** - Venezuela.

	Baha	Cuba	Hisp	Jama	Puer	Lant	Nant	Mexi	Guat	Beli	Elsa	Hond	Nica	Cost	Pana	Colo	Vene	Trin	Guya	Suri	Fren	Ecua	Peru	Boli	Braz	Parg	Urug	Argn	Chil
Leptodon forbesi																									XR				
Chondrohierax uncinatus																													
uncinatus						X		X	X	X	X	X	X	X	X	X	X	X	X	X	X	X	X	X	X	X		X	
wilsonii		XR																											
Elanoides forficatus	SV	XN		XN				X	X	X	SN	X	X	X	X	X	X	X	X	X	X	X	X	X	X	X	V	X	
Gampsonyx swainsonii													X		X	X	X	X	X	X	?	X	X	X	X	X		X	
Elanus leucurus							V	X	X	X	X	X	X	X	X	X	X	X	X	X		XN		SX	X	X	X	X	X
Rostrhamus hamatus															X	X	X			X	X	X	X	X	X				
Rostrhamus sociabilis		X						X	X	X		X	X	X	X	X	X	XN	X	X	X	X	X	X	X	X	X	X	
Harpagus bidentatus								X	X	X	X	X	X	X	X	X	X	X	X	X	X	X	X	X	X				
Harpagus diodon																			XN	XN	XN	XN		X	X	X		X	
Ictinia mississippiensis								XN	XN	XN	SV	XN	XN	XN	SN	XN							SV	XN	SN	XN		XN	
Ictinia plumbea								X	X	X	X	X	X	X	X	X	X	X	X	X	X	X	X	X	X	X		X	
Haliaeetus leucocephalus					SV			X																					
Geranospiza caerulescens								X	X	X	X	X	X	X	X	X	X		X	X	X	X	X	X	X	X	X	X	
Circus buffoni																X	X	X	X	X	X			X	X	X	X	X	X
Circus cinereus																X						X	X	X	XN	X	X	X	X
Circus cyaneus	V	XN	XN	SN	XN	V		X	XN	XN	XN	XN	XN	XN	XN	XN	V												
Accipiter bicolor								X	X	X		X	X	X	X	X	X		X	X	X	X	X	X	X	X	X	X	X
Accipiter collaris																X	X					X	X						
Accipiter cooperii								X	XN	XN		XN		V		V													
Accipiter gentilis								X																					
Accipiter gundlachi		XR																											
Accipiter poliogaster																X?	X?		X?			X?	X?	X	X	X		X	
Accipiter superciliosus													X	X	X	X	X		X	X	X	X	X	X	X	X		X	
Accipiter striatus																													
chionogaster								X	X		X	X	X																
erythronemius																X	X					X	X	X	X	X	X	X	
striatus	XN	X	X	XN	X			X	XN	XN	XN	XN	XN	XN	XN														
Leucopternis albicollis								X	X	X	X	X	X	X	X	X	X	X	X	X	X	X	X	X	X				
Leucopternis kuhli																							X	SX	X				
Leucopternis lacernulata																									XR				
Leucopternis melanops																X	X		X	X	X	X	X		X				
Leucopternis occidentalis																						X	X						
Leucopternis plumbea															X	X						X	X						
Leucopternis polionota																									X	X		X	
Leucopternis princeps														X	X	X						X	X						
Leucopternis schistacea																X	X				X	X	X	X	X				
Leucopternis semiplumbea												X		X	X	X						X							
Buteogallus aequinoctialis																	X	SX	X	X	X				X				
Buteogallus anthracinus		X			V?	X		X	X	X	X	X	X	X	X	X	X	X	X		S?								
Buteogallus subtilis								X	X		X	X		X	X	X						X	X						
Buteogallus urubitinga								X	X	X	X	X	X	X	X	X	X	X	X	X	X	X	X	X	X	X	X	X	
Harpyhaliaetus coronatus																								X	X	X	X	X	
Harpyhaliaetus solitarius								X	X	X		X		X	X	X	X					X	X	X				X	
Heterospizias meridionalis														X	X	X	X	X	X	X	X	X	X	X	X	X	X	X	
Busarellus nigricollis								X	X	X	X	X	X	X	X	X	X	SX	X	X	X	X	X	X	X	X	X	X	
Geranoaetus melanoleucus																X	X					X	X	X	X	X	X	X	X
Parabuteo unicinctus								X	X		X		X	X	X	X	X					X	X	X	X	X	X	X	X
Buteo albicaudatus						SV	X	X	X	X	X	X	X	X	X	X	X	X	X	X	X		SX	X	X	X	X	X	
Buteo albigula																X	X					X	X	SX					X
Buteo albonotatus								X	X	SN	SX	X	X	X	X	X	X	X	X	X	X	X	X	X	X	X			

Status: **X** - Breeding species; **XN** - Regular non-breeding species; **XR** - Endemic breeding species; **X?** - Regular species, breeding status uncertain; **XI** - Introduced species; **XD** - Dubious species; **XF** - Formerly bred; **V** - Vagrants; **SX** - Breeding species, sight records only; **SN** - Regular non-breeding species, sight records only; **S?** - Uncertain breeding status; sight records only; **SI** -Introduced; sight records only; **SV** - Vagrant; sight records only. **?** - Occurrence uncertain; **+** - Extinct.

	Baha	Cuba	Hisp	Jama	Puer	Lant	Nant	Mexi	Guat	Beli	Elsa	Hond	Nica	Cost	Pana	Colo	Vene	Trin	Guya	Suri	Fren	Ecua	Peru	Boli	Braz	Parg	Urug	Argn	Chil
Buteo brachyurus								X	X	X	X	X	X	X	X	X	X	SX	X	X	X	X	X	X	X	X		X	
Buteo galapagoensis																						XR							
Buteo jamaicensis	X	X	X	X	X	X		X	X	X	X	X	X	X	X														
Buteo lagopus								XN																					
Buteo leucorrhous																X	X					X	X	X	X	X		X	
Buteo lineatus								X																					
Buteo magnirostris								X	X	X	X	X	X	X	X	X	X		X	X	X	X	X	X	X	X	X	X	
Buteo nitidus								X	X	X	X	X	X	X	X	X	X	X	X	X	X	X	X	X	X	X		X	
Buteo platypterus		X	V		X	X		XN	XN	XN	XN	XN	XN	XN	XN	XN	XN	X	XN	SV	V	XN	XN	XN	XN				
Buteo poecilochrous																X						X	X	X				X	X
Buteo polyosoma																X						X	X	X			X	X	X
Buteo regalis								XN																					
Buteo ridgwayi			XR																										
Buteo swainsoni								X	XN	XN	XN	XN	XN	XN	XN	XN	XN	SV				XN	XN	XN	XN	XN	XN	XN	
Buteo ventralis																												X	X
Morphnus guianensis									X			X		X	X	X	X		X	X	X	X	X	X	X	X		X	
Harpia harpyja								X	X	X		X	X	X	X	X	X		X	X	X	X	X	X	X	X		X	
Aquila chrysaetos								X																					
Spizastur melanoleucus								X	X	X		X	X	X	X	X	X		X	X	X	X	X	X	X	X		X	
Spizaetus ornatus								X	X	X	X	X	X	X	X	X	X	X	X	X	X	X	X	X	X	X		X	
Spizaetus tyrannus								X	X	X	X	X	X	X	X	X	X	X?	X	X	X	X	X	X	X	X		X	
Oroaetus isidori																X	X					X	X	X				X	
Falconidae																													
Daptrius americanus								XF	X			X	X	X	X	X	X		X	X	X	X	X	X	X				
Daptrius ater																X	X		X	X	X	X	X	X	X				
Phalcoboenus albogularis																												X	X
Phalcoboenus australis																												X	X
Phalcoboenus carunculatus																X						X							
Phalcoboenus megalopterus																							X	X				X	X
Polyborus plancus		X		V			X	X	X		X	X	X	X	X	X	X	SN	X	X	X	X	X	X	X	X	X	X	X
Milvago chimachima							SV							X	X	X	X	SX	X	X	X	X	X	X	X	X	X	X	
Milvago chimango																									X	X	X	X	X
Herpetotheres cachinnans								X	X	X	X	X	X	X	X	X	X		X	X	X	X	X	X	X	X		X	X
Micrastur buckleyi																						X	X						
Micrastur gilvicollis																X	X		X	X	X	X	X	X	X				
Micrastur mirandollei														X	X	X	X		X	X	X	X	X	X	X				
Micrastur plumbeus																X						X							
Micrastur ruficollis								X	X	X	X	X	X	X	X	X	X		X	X	X	X	X	X	X	X		X	
Micrastur semitorquatus								X	X	X	X	X	X	X	X	X	X		X	X	X	X	X	X	X	X		X	
Spiziapteryx circumcinctus																								X		X		X	
Falco columbarius	XN	XN	XN	XN	XN	XN	XN	XN	XN	XN	XN	XN	XN	XN	XN	XN	XN	XN	SV		SV	XN	XN		XN				
Falco deiroleucus								X	X	X		X	X	X	X	X	X	X	X	X	X	X	X	X	X	X		X	
Falco femoralis								X	X?	X		X	X	V	X	X	X	X	X	X		X	X	X	X	X	X	X	X
Falco mexicanus								X																					
Falco peregrinus	XN	XN	XN	XN	XN	XN	XN	X	XN	XN	SN	XN	XN	XN	XN	XN	XN	XN	XN	XN	XN	X	XN	XN	XN	XN	XN	X	X
Falco rufigularis								X	X	X	X	X	X	X	X	X	X	X	X	X	X	X	X	X	X	X		X	
Falco sparverius	X	X	X	X	X	X	X	X	X	X	X	X	X	XN	XN	X	X	SX	X		X	X	X	X	X	X	X	X	X
Falco tinnunculus						V															SV								
GALLIFORMES																													
Cracidae																													
Ortalis canicollis																								X	X	X		X	
Ortalis cinereiceps												X	X	X	X	X													

Countries: Argn - Argentina; **Baha** - Bahamas; **Beli** - Belize; **Boli** - Bolivia; **Braz** - Brazil; **Chil** - Chile; **Colo** - Colombia; **Cost** - Costa Rica; **Cuba** - Cuba; **Ecua** - Ecuador; **Elsa** - El Salvador; **Fren** - French Guiana; **Guat** - Guatemala; **Guya** - Guyana; **Hisp** - Hispaniola; **Hond** - Honduras; **Jama** - Jamaica; **Lant** - Lesser Antilles; **Mexi** - Mexico; **Nant** - Netherland Antilles; **Nica** - Nicaragua; **Pana** - Panama; **Parg** - Paraguay; **Peru** - Peru; **Puer** - Puerto Rico; **Suri** - Suriname; **Trin** - Trinidad; **Urug** - Uruguay; **Vene** - Venezuela.

	Baha	Cuba	Hisp	Jama	Puer	Lant	Nant	Mexi	Guat	Beli	Elsa	Hond	Nica	Cost	Pana	Colo	Vene	Trin	Guya	Suri	Fren	Ecua	Peru	Boli	Braz	Parg	Urug	Argn	Chil
Ortalis erythroptera																						X	X						
Ortalis garrula																XR													
Ortalis leucogastra								X	X		X	X	X	X															
Ortalis motmot																													
araucuan																									XR				
colombiana																XR													
guttata																X						X	X	X	X				
motmot																	X		X	X	X				X				
superciliaris																									XR				
Ortalis poliocephala																													
poliocephala								XR																					
wagleri								XR																					
Ortalis ruficauda																X	X	X											
Ortalis vetula								X	X	X		X	X	X															
Penelope albipennis																							XR						
Penelope argyrotis																X	X					X							
Penelope barbata																						X	X						
Penelope dabbenei																								X				X	
Penelope jacquacu																X	X		X			X	X	X	X				
Penelope jacucaca																									XR				
Penelope marail																	X		X	X	X				X				
Penelope montagnii																X	X					X	X	X				X	
Penelope obscura																								X	X	X	X	X	
Penelope ochrogaster																									XR				
Penelope ortoni																X						X							
Penelope perspicax																XR													
Penelope pileata																									XR				
Penelope purpurascens								X	X	X	X	X	X	X	X	X	X					X							
Penelope superciliaris																								X	X	X		X	
Aburria aburri																X	X					X	X						
Aburria cujubi																								X	X				
Aburria jacutinga																									X	X		X	
Aburria pipile																X	X	X	X	X	X	X	X	X	X	X			
Chamaepetes goudotii																X						X	X	X					
Chamaepetes unicolor														X	X														
Penelopina nigra								X	X		X	X	X																
Oreophasis derbianus								X	X																				
Nothocrax urumutum																X	X					X	X		X				
Crax alberti																XR													
Crax alector																X	X		X	X	X				X				
Crax blumenbachii																									XR				
Crax daubentoni																X	X												
Crax fasciolata																								X	X	X		X	
Crax globulosa																X						X	X	X	X				
Crax mitu																													
mitu																									XR				
tuberosa																X							X	X	X				
Crax pauxi																X	X												
Crax rubra								X	X	X	X	X	X	X	X	X						X							
Crax salvini																X						X	X						
Crax tomentosa																X	X		X						X				
Crax unicornis																							X	X					

Status: X - Breeding species; **XN** - Regular non-breeding species; **XR** - Endemic breeding species; **X?** - Regular species, breeding status uncertain; **XI** - Introduced species; **XD** - Dubious species; **XF** - Formerly bred; **V** - Vagrants; **SX** - Breeding species, sight records only; **SN** - Regular non-breeding species, sight records only; **S?** - Uncertain breeding status; sight records only; **SI** -Introduced; sight records only; **SV** - Vagrant; sight records only. **?** - Occurrence uncertain; **+** - Extinct.

	Baha	Cuba	Hisp	Jama	Puer	Lant	Nant	Mexi	Guat	Beli	Elsa	Hond	Nica	Cost	Pana	Colo	Vene	Trin	Guya	Suri	Fren	Ecua	Peru	Boli	Braz	Parg	Urug	Argn	Chil
Phasianidae																													
Meleagris gallopavo								X																					
Agriocharis ocellata								X	X	X																			
Dendrortyx barbatus								XR																					
Dendrortyx leucophrys								X	X		X	X	X	X															
Dendrortyx macroura								XR																					
Oreortyx pictus								X																					
Callipepla squamata								X																					
Lophortyx californica								X																					XI
Lophortyx douglasii								XR																					
Lophortyx gambelii								X																					
Philortyx fasciatus								XR																					
Colinus cristatus							X		X		X	X	X	X	X	X	X		X	X	X				X				
Colinus nigrogularis								X	X	X		X	X																
Colinus virginianus																													
ridgwayi								XR																					
virginianus	XI	X	XI		XI			X	X																				
Odontophorus atrifrons																X	X												
Odontophorus balliviani																							X	X					
Odontophorus capueira																									X	X		X	
Odontophorus columbianus																	XR												
Odontophorus dialeucos															X	X													
Odontophorus erythrops												X	X	X	X	X						X							
Odontophorus gujanensis														X	X	X	X		X	X	X	X	X	X	X				
Odontophorus guttatus								X	X	X		X	X	X	X														
Odontophorus hyperthyrus																XR													
Odontophorus leucolaemus														X	X														
Odontophorus melanonotus																X						X							
Odontophorus speciosus																						X	X	X					
Odontophorus stellatus																						X	X	X	X				
Odontophorus strophium																XR													
Dactylortyx thoracicus								X	X	X	X	X																	
Cyrtonyx montezumae								X																					
Cyrtonyx ocellatus								X	X		X	X	X																
Rhynchortyx cinctus												X	X	X	X	X						X							
GRUIFORMES																													
Gruidae																													
Grus americana								+																					
Grus canadensis		X						XN																					
Aramidae																													
Aramus guarauna	XN	X	X	X	X		V	X	X	X	X	X	X	X	X	X	X	X	X	X	X	X	X	X	X	X	X	X	
Psophidae																													
Psophia crepitans																X	X		X	X	X	X	X		X				
Psophia leucoptera																							X	X	X				
Psophia viridis																									XR				
Rallidae																													
Rallus antarcticus																												X	X
Rallus elegans																													
elegans		X						X																					
tenuirostris								XR																					
Rallus limicola		V			SV			X	XN							X						X	X						

Countries: **Argn** - Argentina; **Baha** - Bahamas; **Beli** - Belize; **Boli** - Bolivia; **Braz** - Brazil; **Chil** - Chile; **Colo** - Colombia; **Cost** - Costa Rica; **Cuba** - Cuba; **Ecua** - Ecuador; **Elsa** - El Salvador; **Fren** - French Guiana; **Guat** - Guatemala; **Guya** - Guyana; **Hisp** - Hispaniola; **Hond** - Honduras; **Jama** - Jamaica; **Lant** - Lesser Antilles; **Mexi** - Mexico; **Nant** - Netherland Antilles; **Nica** - Nicaragua; **Pana** - Panama; **Parg** - Paraguay; **Peru** - Peru; **Puer** - Puerto Rico; **Suri** - Suriname; **Trin** - Trinidad; **Urug** - Uruguay; **Vene** - Venezuela.

	Baha	Cuba	Hisp	Jama	Puer	Lant	Nant	Mexi	Guat	Beli	Elsa	Hond	Nica	Cost	Pana	Colo	Vene	Trin	Guya	Suri	Fren	Ecua	Peru	Boli	Braz	Parg	Urug	Argn	Chil
Rallus longirostris																													
longirostris	X	X	X	X	X	X		X		X						X	X	X	X	X	X	X	X		X				
obsoletus								X																					
Rallus semiplumbeus																XR													
Rallus wetmorei																	XR												
Ortygonax nigricans																X	X					X	X	SX	X	X		X	
Ortygonax sanguinolentus																							X	X	X	X	X	X	X
Pardirallus maculatus		X	X	X				X		X	X?			X	X	X	X	X		X	X?	X?	X	X	X	X	X	X	V
Amaurolimnas concolor				+	XI			X	X	X		X	X	X	X	X	X		X		?	X	X	X	X				
Cyanolimnas cerverai		XR																											
Aramides axillaris								X		X	X	X	X	X	X	X	X	X	X	X	SX	X	X						
Aramides cajanea								X	X	X	X	X	X	X	X	X	X	X	X	X	X	X	X	X	X	X	X	X	
Aramides calopterus																						X	X		X				
Aramides mangle																									XR				
Aramides saracura																									X	X		X	
Aramides wolfi																X						X							
Aramides ypecaha																									X	X	X	X	
Anurolimnas castaneiceps																X						X	X	X					
Porzana albicollis																X	X	X	X	X	X		X	X	X	X		X	
Porzana carolina	XN	XN	XN	XN	XN	XN	XN	X	XN	XN	XN	XN	XN	XN	XN	XN	XN	XN	XN			XN	XN						
Porzana flaviventer		X	X	X	X			X	X	X	X		X	X	X	X	X	X	X	X	X			SX	X	X	V	X	
Porzana spiloptera																											X	X	
Laterallus albigularis												X	X	X	X	X						X							
Laterallus exilis									X	X		X	X	SX	X	X	X	X	X	X	X	X	X	X	X	X			
Laterallus fasciatus																X						X	X		X				
Laterallus jamaicensis		X	V	X?	XN			X	XN	X				SX		?							X					X	X
Laterallus leucopyrrhus																									X	X	X	X	
Laterallus levraudi																	XR												
Laterallus melanophaius																X	X		X	X		X	X	X	X	X	X	X	
Laterallus ruber								X	X	X	X	X	X	SX															
Laterallus spilonotus																						XR							
Laterallus viridis																X	X		X	X	X	X	X	X	X				
Laterallus xenopterus																									X	X			
Micropygia schomburgkii														X?		X	X		X		X		X	X	X				
Coturnicops notatus																X	X		X						X	X	X	X	
Coturnicops noveboracensis	V							X																					
Neocrex columbianus															X	X						X							
Neocrex erythrops															V	X	X	X?	X	X	SX	X	X	X	X	X		X	
Porphyriops melanops																X							?	X	X	X	X	X	X
Gallinula chloropus	X	X	X	X	X	X	X	X	X	X	X	X	X	X	X	X	X	X	X	X	X	X	X	X	X	X	X	X	X
Porphyrula flavirostris																X	X	SN	X	X	X	X	X	X	X	X		X	
Porphyrula martinica	XN	X	X	X	X	X	X	X	X	X	X	X	X	X	X	X	X	X	X	X	X	X	X	X	X	X	X	X	V
Fulica americana	X	X	X	X	X	XN		X	X	X	X	X	X	X	XN	X	SV												
Fulica ardesiaca																X						X	X	X				X	X
Fulica armillata																									X	X	X	X	X
Fulica caribaea	X	X	X	X	X	X	X									X	X	X?											
Fulica cornuta																								X				X	X
Fulica gigantea																							X	X				?	X
Fulica leucoptera																								X	X	X	X	X	X
Fulica rufifrons																							X		X	X?	X	X	X
Heliornithidae																													
Heliornis fulica								X	X	X		X	X	X	X	X	X	V	X	X	X	X	X	X	X	X		X	

Status: **X** - Breeding species; **XN** - Regular non-breeding species; **XR** - Endemic breeding species; **X?** - Regular species, breeding status uncertain; **XI** - Introduced species; **XD** - Dubious species; **XF** - Formerly bred; **V** - Vagrants; **SX** - Breeding species, sight records only; **SN** - Regular non-breeding species, sight records only; **S?** - Uncertain breeding status; sight records only; **SI** -Introduced; sight records only; **SV** - Vagrant; sight records only. **?** - Occurrence uncertain; **+** - Extinct.

	Baha	Cuba	Hisp	Jama	Puer	Lant	Nant	Mexi	Guat	Beli	Elsa	Hond	Nica	Cost	Pana	Colo	Vene	Trin	Guya	Suri	Fren	Ecua	Peru	Boli	Braz	Parg	Urug	Argn	Chil
Eurypygidae																													
Eurypyga helias								?	X			X	X	X	X	X	X		X	X	X	X	X	X	X				
Cariamidae																													
Cariama cristata																								X	X	X	X	X	
Chunga burmeisteri																								X		X		X	
CHARADRIIFORMES																													
Jacanidae																													
Jacana jacana							V								X	X	X	X	X	X	X	X	X	X	X	X	X	X	V
Jacana spinosa		X	X	X	V			X	X	X	X	X	X	V	X														
Rostratulidae																													
Nycticryphes semicollaris																									X	X	X	X	X
Haematopodidae																													
Haematopus ater																							X				V	X	X
Haematopus bachmani								X																					
Haematopus leucopodus																												X	X
Haematopus palliatus	X	X?	X	X	X	X	X	X	X?	XN	S?	XN		X	X	X	X	V			SV	X	X		X		X	X	X
Recurvirostridae																													
Himantopus mexicanus	X	X	X	X	X	X	X	X	X	XN	X	XN	X	X	X	X	X	SN	X	X	X	XN	XN	X	X	X	X	X	X
Recurvirostra americana	V	V		SV	V	V	SV	X	XN	XN		V		V	V			V				V							
Recurvirostra andina																							X	X				X	X
Burhinidae																													
Burhinus bistriatus			X				V	X	X		X	X	X	X		X	X	SV	X						X				
Burhinus superciliaris																						X	X						X
Charadriidae																													
Vanellus cayanus																X	X		X	X	X?	V	X	X	X	X		V	
Vanellus chilensis							V								X	X	X	X	X	X	X	X	SV	X	X	X	X	X	X
Vanellus resplendens																X						X	X	X				X	X
Vanellus vanellus	V				V	V																							
Pluvialis dominicus																													
dominicus	XN	XN	XN		XN		XN	XN	XN	XN				XN	XN	XN	XN	XN	XN	XN	XN	XN	XN	XN	XN	XN	XN	XN	XN
fulva								XN																					
Pluvialis squatarola	XN	XN	XN	XN	XN	XN	XN	XN	XN	XN	XN	XN	XN	XN	XN	XN	XN	XN	XN	XN	XN	XN	XN	SV	XN	V	XN	XN	XN
Charadrius alexandrinus	X	X	X	X	X	X	X	X	V			V		V	XN	XN	X	SV				X	X						X
Charadrius alticola																							X	X				X	X
Charadrius collaris						X	X	X	X	?	SV	X	X	X	X	X	X	X	X	X	X	X	X	X	X	?	X	X	X
Charadrius falklandicus																									XN		XN	X	X
Charadrius hiaticula						V												V										V	
Charadrius melodus	XN	XN	XN	XN	XN	V		XN														V							
Charadrius modestus																							V		XN		XN	X	X
Charadrius montanus								XN		?																			
Charadrius semipalmatus	XN	XN	XN	XN	XN	XN	XN	XN	XN	XN	XN	XN	XN	XN	XN	XN	XN	XN	XN	XN	XN	XN	XN	XN	XN		XN	XN	XN
Charadrius vociferus	X	X	X	X	X		X	X	XN	XN	XN	XN	XN	X	XN	XN	XN	SN			SV	XN	X						X?
Charadrius wilsonia	X	X	X	X	X	X	X	X	X	X	X	X		X	X	X?	X	X	X	X	SX	X	X		XN				
Phegornis mitchellii																							X	X				X	X
Eudromias ruficollis																						X?	X	X	XN		XN	X	X
Pluvianellus socialis																												X	X
Scolopacidae																													
Limosa fedoa	XN	XN	XN	XN	XN	XN		XN	XN	XN	SV	XN	XN	XN	XN	SV	XN	XN				XN	XN						V
Limosa haemastica	V	XN	XN		XN	XN	V	XN	XN	XN				X	V	SV	XN	XN		SV	SN	XN	XN	V	XN	XN	XN	XN	XN
Limosa lapponica					V			V									V								SV				
Limosa limosa					SV																								

Countries: **Argn** - Argentina; **Baha** - Bahamas; **Beli** - Belize; **Boli** - Bolivia; **Braz** - Brazil; **Chil** - Chile; **Colo** - Colombia; **Cost** - Costa Rica; **Cuba** - Cuba; **Ecua** - Ecuador; **Elsa** - El Salvador; **Fren** - French Guiana; **Guat** - Guatemala; **Guya** - Guyana; **Hisp** - Hispaniola; **Hond** - Honduras; **Jama** - Jamaica; **Lant** - Lesser Antilles; **Mexi** - Mexico; **Nant** - Netherland Antilles; **Nica** - Nicaragua; **Pana** - Panama; **Parg** - Paraguay; **Peru** - Peru; **Puer** - Puerto Rico; **Suri** - Suriname; **Trin** - Trinidad; **Urug** - Uruguay; **Vene** - Venezuela.

	Baha	Cuba	Hisp	Jama	Puer	Lant	Nant	Mexi	Guat	Beli	Elsa	Hond	Nica	Cost	Pana	Colo	Vene	Trin	Guya	Suri	Fren	Ecua	Peru	Boli	Braz	Parg	Urug	Argn	Chil
Numenius americanus		V		V				XN	XN	XN	SV	XN		XN	V		XN				SV								
Numenius borealis					V	V		V	V									V							V	V	V	V	V
Numenius phaeopus	XN	XN	SN	XN	XN	XN	XN	XN	XN	XN	XN	XN	XN	XN	XN	XN	XN	XN	XN	XN	XN	XN	XN	SV	XN			XN	XN
Bartramia longicauda	XN	XN	XN	XN	XN	XN	V	XN	XN	XN		XN	XN	XN	XN	XN	XN	XN	XN	XN	XN	XN	XN	XN	XN	XN	XN	XN	V
Tringa erythropus						V												SV											
Tringa flavipes	XN	XN	XN	XN	XN	XN	XN	XN	XN	XN	XN	XN	XN	XN	XN	XN	XN	XN	XN	XN	XN	XN	XN	XN	XN	XN	XN	XN	XN
Tringa glareola						V																							
Tringa melanoleuca	XN	XN	XN	XN	XN	XN	XN	XN	XN	XN	XN	XN	XN	XN	XN	XN	XN	XN	XN	XN	XN	XN	XN	XN	XN	XN	XN	XN	XN
Tringa nebularia																		SV											
Tringa solitaria	XN	XN	XN	XN	XN	XN	XN	XN	XN	XN	XN	XN	XN	XN	XN	XN	XN	XN	XN	XN	XN	XN	XN	XN	XN	XN	XN	XN	V
Catoptrophorus semipalmatus	X	X	X?	XN	X	X	XN	X	XN	XN	XN	XN	XN	XN	XN	XN	X	XN	XN	XN	XN	XN	XN		XN				XN
Actitis macularia	XN	XN	XN	XN	XN	XN	XN	XN	XN	XN	XN	XN	XN	XN	XN	XN	XN	XN	XN	XN	XN	XN	XN	XN	XN	XN	XN	XN	XN
Heteroscelus incanus								XN			XN	XN		XN	XN	V						XN	XN						V
Arenaria interpres	XN	XN	XN	XN	XN	XN	XN	XN	XN	XN	XN	XN	XN	XN	XN	XN	XN	XN	XN	XN	XN	XN	XN		XN		XN	XN	XN
Arenaria melanocephala								XN														V							
Phalaropus fulicaria		V						XN	SN					SN		XN						XN	XN		V	V		V	XN
Phalaropus lobatus	V	V		V	V		V	XN	V		?	XN		XN	XN	XN						XN	XN					V	XN
Phalaropus tricolor	V			SV	XN	V	XN	XN	XN	?	XN	XN	XN	XN	XN	XN	V			SV		XN	XN	XN	XN	XN	XN	XN	XN
Scolopax minor								SV																					
Gallinago andina																							X	X				X	X
Gallinago gallinago	XN	XN	XN	XN	XN	XN	XN	X?	XN	X	XN	X	XN	XN	XN	XN	XN	XN	XN	V									
Gallinago imperialis																X						X	X						
Gallinago nobilis																X	X					X	SX						
Gallinago paraguaiae																X	X	X	X	X	X	X	X	X	X	X		X	X
Gallinago stricklandii																X	X					X	X	X				?	X
Gallinago undulata																X	X		X	X	X				X	X		V	
Lymnocryptes minimus						V																							
Limnodromus griseus	XN	XN	XN	XN	XN	XN	XN	XN	XN	XN	XN	XN	XN	XN	XN	XN	XN	XN	XN	XN	XN	XN	XN		XN			SV	
Limnodromus scolopaceus		XN		XN	?		XN	XN	XN	XN	?	XN	XN	XN	XN	?												V	
Aphriza virgata								XN	SN		V			XN	XN							XN	XN						XN
Calidris alba	XN	XN	XN	XN	XN	XN	XN	XN	XN	XN	XN	XN	XN	XN	XN	XN	XN	XN	XN	XN	XN	XN	XN		XN	V	XN	XN	XN
Calidris alpina	XN			SV	SV	XN		XN	V	SV				XN	V						V		SV						
Calidris bairdii					SN	V	SV	XN	V	XN	V	SV		XN	XN	XN	XN	SV		SN	SV	XN	XN	XN	XN		XN	XN	XN
Calidris canutus	XN	XN	XN	XN	XN	XN	XN	XN	SN	XN	SN	XN		XN	XN	SN	XN	XN	XN	XN	SN	XN	XN	SV	XN	V	XN	XN	XN
Calidris ferruginea						XN																	V					V	
Calidris fuscicollis	XN	XN	XN	XN	XN	XN	XN	XN	XN	XN		XN	XN	XN	XN	XN	XN	XN	XN	XN	XN	XN	XN	XN	XN	XN	XN	XN	XN
Calidris mauri	XN	XN	XN	XN	XN	XN	XN	XN	XN	XN	XN	XN	XN	XN	XN	XN	XN	XN	XN	XN	XN	XN	XN						V
Calidris melanotos	XN	XN	XN	XN	XN	XN	XN	XN	XN	XN	XN	XN	XN	XN	XN	XN	XN	XN	XN	XN	SN	XN	XN	XN	XN	XN	XN	XN	XN
Calidris minutilla	XN	XN	XN	XN	XN	XN	XN	XN	XN	XN	XN	XN	XN	XN	XN	XN	XN	XN	XN	XN	XN	XN	XN	XN	XN	V			XN
Calidris pusilla	XN	XN	XN	XN	XN	XN	XN	XN	XN	XN	XN	XN	XN	XN	XN	XN	XN	XN	XN	XN	XN	XN	XN		XN		XN	XN	XN
Calidris ruficollis																							V						
Micropalama himantopus	XN	XN	?	XN	XN	XN	XN	XN	XN		SV	XN	XN	XN	XN	XN	XN	XN	SN	XN	SN	XN	XN	XN	XN	XN	XN	XN	XN
Tryngites subruficollis	XN	XN	V	XN	V	XN	V	XN	?	XN	V	XN	XN	XN	XN	XN	XN	XN	SN	XN	?	XN	XN	XN	XN	XN	XN	XN	XN
Philomachus pugnax				V	XN	XN			V					SV	V	V	SV	V					SV		SV				
Thinocoridae																													
Attagis gayi																						X	X	X				X	X
Attagis malouinus																												X	X
Thinocorus orbignyianus																							X	X				X	X
Thinocorus rumicivorus																						X	X	X			X	X	X
Chionididae																													
Chionis alba																									V		XN	X?	X?

Status: X - Breeding species; **XN** - Regular non-breeding species; **XR** - Endemic breeding species; **X?** - Regular species, breeding status uncertain; **XI** - Introduced species; **XD** - Dubious species; **XF** - Formerly bred; **V** - Vagrants; **SX** - Breeding species, sight records only; **SN** - Regular non-breeding species, sight records only; **S?** - Uncertain breeding status; sight records only; **SI** -Introduced; sight records only; **SV** - Vagrant; sight records only. **?** - Occurrence uncertain; **+** - Extinct.

	Baha	Cuba	Hisp	Jama	Puer	Lant	Nant	Mexi	Guat	Beli	Elsa	Hond	Nica	Cost	Pana	Colo	Vene	Trin	Guya	Suri	Fren	Ecua	Peru	Boli	Braz	Parg	Urug	Argn	Chil
Laridae																													
Catharacta chilensis																							XN		XN			X	X
Catharacta maccormicki						V		SN						SN	SN			SV		?	SV		XN		XN		XN	XN	?
Catharacta skua																													
antarctica																									XN		XN	X	
skua					?	?	SV			V						?			V		SV				V				
Stercorarius longicaudus		V				V		XN	SV					V								XN	XN		SV			XN	XN
Stercorarius parasiticus	XN	XN		XN		XN	XN	XN	?	V		XN	XN	XN	XN	SN	V	SN	XN		SN	XN	XN		XN		XN	XN	XN
Stercorarius pomarinus	XN	XN			XN	XN	XN	XN	XN	V			XN	XN	SN	SN	XN	SN	XN	SV	SN	XN	XN		XN		XN		XN
Gabianus scoresbii																												X	X
Larus argentatus	XN	XN	XN	XN	XN	XN	XN	XN	XN	XN	XN	XN	XN	XN	XN	SN	XN	V											
Larus atricilla	X	X	X	X	X	X	X	X	X	X	SN	X	XN	X	XN	XN	X	X	XN	X	X	X	XN		XN				
Larus belcheri																													
atlanticus																									SV		X	X	
belcheri															V								X						X
Larus californicus								XN																					
Larus canus								XN																					
Larus cirrocephalus															SV							X	X		X	X?	X	X	
Larus delawarensis	XN	XN	XN	XN	XN	V	V	XN	SN	XN	XN	XN		XN	XN	SV		SN				SV			V				
Larus dominicanus								V														X	X		X		X	X	X
Larus fuliginosus																						XR							
Larus fuscus					V	V	XN	V							V		SV				SV								
Larus glaucescens								XN																					
Larus heermanni								X	XN																				
Larus hyperboreus								XN																					
Larus livens								XR																					
Larus maculipennis																									X	X?	X	X	X
Larus marinus		V	V		V	V	V			V																			
Larus minutus								SV								V													
Larus modestus														V	SV	V						XN	XN						X
Larus occidentalis								X																					
Larus philadelphia	V	XN	XN		V	V	SV	XN		V				SV	V														
Larus pipixcan					V		SV	XN	XN	V	XN	XN	XN	XN	XN	XN					SV	XN	XN	SN	SV				XN
Larus ridibundus					XN	XN	V	V										XN		SV	SN								
Larus serranus																						X	X	X				X	X
Larus thayeri								XN																					
Rissa tridactyla	V	V		V		V		XN															V						
Creagrus furcatus															V	X						X	XN						XN
Xema sabini		V						XN	SN		XN			XN	XN	XN		V				XN	XN						XN
Chlidonias leucopterus	V				V	V																							
Chlidonias niger	XN	XN	?	XN	XN	XN	SN	XN	XN	XN	XN	XN	XN	XN	XN	XN	XN	XN	XN	XN	SN	XN	XN		V			V	V
Phaetusa simplex		V					V								XN	X	X	X	X	X	X	X	X	X	X	X	X	X	
Gelochelidon nilotica	X	SV	XN	XN	X	XN	XN	X	XN	XN	XN	XN	XN	XN	XN	XN	XN	XN	XN	XN	SN	X	XN		X		X	X	
Hydroprogne caspia	XN	XN	XN	XN	XN		XN	X	XN			XN	XN	XN	XN	XN	XN	V			SV								
Sterna anaethetus	X	X	X	X	X	X	X	X		X	XN			X	X?	X?	X	X	XN										V
Sterna antillarum	X	X	X	X	X	X	X	X	XN	X	SN	X		XN	XN	XN	X	XN	XN	XN	XN		V		XN			XN	
Sterna dougallii	X	X	X	X	X	X	X	SN		X	V	X				XN	X	XN	XN	XN	V				XN				
Sterna forsteri	XN	XN	XN	XN	XN			X	XN	XN	V	V		XN											V				
Sterna fuscata	X	X	X	X	X	X	X	X	?	X	V	X	XN	XN	X	XN	X	X	XN	XN	X	X	SN		X				XN
Sterna hirundinacea																							X		X		X	X	X
Sterna hirundo	XN	XN	X	XN	X	XN	X	XN	XN	XN	SN	XN	XN	XN	XN	XN	X	XN	XN	XN	XN	XN	XN	XN	XN		V	XN	
Sterna lorata																						X	X						X

Countries: Argn - Argentina; **Baha** - Bahamas; **Beli** - Belize; **Boli** - Bolivia; **Braz** - Brazil; **Chil** - Chile; **Colo** - Colombia; **Cost** - Costa Rica; **Cuba** - Cuba; **Ecua** - Ecuador; **Elsa** - El Salvador; **Fren** - French Guiana; **Guat** - Guatemala; **Guya** - Guyana; **Hisp** - Hispaniola; **Hond** - Honduras; **Jama** - Jamaica; **Lant** - Lesser Antilles; **Mexi** - Mexico; **Nant** - Netherland Antilles; **Nica** - Nicaragua; **Pana** - Panama; **Parg** - Paraguay; **Peru** - Peru; **Puer** - Puerto Rico; **Suri** - Suriname; **Trin** - Trinidad; **Urug** - Uruguay; **Vene** - Venezuela.

	Baha	Cuba	Hisp	Jama	Puer	Lant	Nant	Mexi	Guat	Beli	Elsa	Hond	Nica	Cost	Pana	Colo	Vene	Trin	Guya	Suri	Fren	Ecua	Peru	Boli	Braz	Parg	Urug	Argn	Chil
Sterna paradisaea		V			SV			XN								V						XN	XN	V	XN	V		XN	XN
Sterna superciliaris															V	X	X	XN	X	X	X	X	X	X	X	X	X	X	
Sterna trudeaui																							V		X		X	X	X
Sterna vittata																									XN		X	X	XN
Thalasseus elegans								X	XN		V		XN	XN	SN	SV					SV	XN	XN						XN
Thalasseus maximus	X	X	X	X	X	X	X	X	XN	XN	XN	XN	XN	XN	XN	XN	X	X	SN	XN	X	XN	XN		X		X	XN	
Thalasseus sandvicensis	X	X	X?	XN	X	XN	X	X	XN	X	SV		XN	XN	XN	XN	X	X	XN	X	X	XN	XN		X		XN	X	V
Procelsterna cerulea																													X
Larosterna inca															XN	SV						XN	X						X
Anous minutus						SV	V			X				X											X				
Anous stolidus	X	X	X	X	X	X	XN	X	XN	X	SV	XN	XN	X	X?	X	X	X	XN	XN	X	X			X				X
Gygis alba								V						X		SV		V				V			X				
Rhynchopidae																													
Rhynchops niger	XN	XN	XN	XN	XN	V	XN	X	X	X	XN	X	XN	X	X	X	X	X	X	X	X	X	X	X	X	X	X	X	X
Alcidae																													
Alle alle	V	V																											
Uria aalge								XN																					
Cepphus columba								V																					
Brachyramphus craveri								XR	SV																				
Brachyramphus hypoleucus								X																					
Synthliboramphus antiquus								V																					
Ptychoramphus aleuticus								X																					
Aethia cristatella								SV																					
Cerorhinca monocerata								XN																					
COLUMBIFORMES																													
Columbidae																													
Columba araucana																												X	X
Columba caribaea				XR																									
Columba cayennensis								X	X	X		X	X	X	X	X	X	X	X	X	X	X	X	X	X	X	X	X	
Columba corensis							X									X	X												
Columba fasciata								X	X		X	X	X	X	X	X	X	X				X	X	X	X			X	
Columba flavirostris								X	X	X	X	X	X	X															
Columba goodsoni															S?	X						X							
Columba inornata		X	X	X	X																								
Columba leucocephala	X	X	X	X	X	X		X		X		X		SV	X	X													
Columba livia	XI	XI	XI	XI	XI	XI	XI	XI	XI	XI	XI	XI	XI	XI	XI	XI	XI	XI	XI	XI	XI	XI	XI	XI	XI	XI	XI	XI	XI
Columba maculosa																							X	X	X	X	X	X	
Columba nigrirostris								X	X	X		X	X	X	X	X													
Columba oenops																							XR						
Columba picazuro																								X	X	X	X	X	
Columba plumbea																X	X		X	X	X	X	X	X	X	X			
Columba speciosa								X	X	X		X	X	X	X	X	X	X	X	X	X	X	X	X	X	X		X	
Columba squamosa		X	X	X	X	X	X										X												
Columba subvinacea														X	X	X	X		X	X	X	X	X	X	X				
Streptopelia decaocto	XI																												
Zenaida asiatica	XN	X	X	X	X		V?	X	X	X	X	X	X	X	X	X?						X	X						X
Zenaida auriculata						X	X									X	X	X	X	X	SN	X	X	X	X	X	X	X	X
Zenaida aurita	X	X	X	X	X	X		X																					
Zenaida galapagoensis																						XR							
Zenaida graysoni								XR																					
Zenaida macroura	X	X	X	X	X			X	X	X	X	X	X?	X	X	V													
Columbina cruziana																						X	X						X

Status: **X** - Breeding species; **XN** - Regular non-breeding species; **XR** - Endemic breeding species; **X?** - Regular species, breeding status uncertain; **XI** - Introduced species; **XD** - Dubious species; **XF** - Formerly bred; **V** - Vagrants; **SX** - Breeding species, sight records only; **SN** - Regular non-breeding species, sight records only; **S?** - Uncertain breeding status; sight records only; **SI** -Introduced; sight records only; **SV** - Vagrant; sight records only. **?** - Occurrence uncertain; **+** - Extinct.

	Baha	Cuba	Hisp	Jama	Puer	Lant	Nant	Mexi	Guat	Beli	Elsa	Hond	Nica	Cost	Pana	Colo	Vene	Trin	Guya	Suri	Fren	Ecua	Peru	Boli	Braz	Parg	Urug	Argn	Chil
Columbina cyanopis																									XR				
Columbina minuta								X	X	X	X	?	X	X	X	X	X	X	X	X	X	X	X	X	X	X		V	
Columbina passerina	X	X	X	X	X	X	X	X	X	X	X	X	X	X	X	X	X	X	X	X	X	X			X				
Columbina picui																V							XN	X	X	X	X	X	X
Columbina talpacoti																													
buckleyi																						X	X						
talpacoti							V	X	X	X	X	X	X	X	X	X	X	X	X	X	X	X	X	X	X	X	V	X	XN
Claravis godefrida																									X	X			
Claravis mondetoura								X	X		X	X		X	X	X	X					X	X	X					
Claravis pretiosa								X	X	X	X	X	X	X	X	X	X	X	X	X	X	X	X	X	X	X		X	
Metriopelia aymara																							X?	X				X	X
Metriopelia ceciliae																							X	X				X	X
Metriopelia melanoptera																X						X	X	X				X	X
Metriopelia morenoi																												XR	
Scardafella inca								X	X		X	X	X	X															
Scardafella squammata																X	X	V			X			X?	X	X		X	
Uropelia campestris																								X	X				
Leptotila cassini								X	X	X		X	X	X	X	X													
Leptotila conoveri																XR													
Leptotila jamaicensis	X			X				X				X				X													
Leptotila megalura																								X				X	
Leptotila ochraceiventris																						X	X						
Leptotila pallida																X						X							
Leptotila rufaxilla																													
plumbeiceps								X	X	X		X	X	X	X	X													
rufaxilla																X	X	X	X	X	X	X	X	X	X	X	X	X	
wellsi						XR																							
Leptotila verreauxi							X	X	X	X	X	X	X	X	X	X	X	X	X	X	X	X	X	X	X	X	X	X	
Geotrygon albifacies								X	X		X	X	X																
Geotrygon caniceps		X	X																										
Geotrygon chiriquensis														X	X														
Geotrygon chrysia	X	X	X		X																								
Geotrygon costaricensis														X	X														
Geotrygon frenata																X						X	X	X				X	
Geotrygon goldmani															X	X													
Geotrygon lawrencii								X						X	X														
Geotrygon linearis																X	X	X											
Geotrygon montana		X	X	X	X	X		X	X	X	X	X	X	X	X	X	X	X	X	X	X	X	X	X	X	X		X	
Geotrygon mystacea					X	X																							
Geotrygon saphirina																X						X	X		SX				
Geotrygon veraguensis														X	X	X						X							
Geotrygon versicolor				XR																									
Geotrygon violacea													X	X	X	X	X			X			X	X	X	X		X	
Starnoenas cyanocephala		XR																											
PSITTACIFORMES																													
Psittacidae																													
Anodorhynchus glaucus																									?	X	X	X?	
Anodorhynchus hyacinthinus																								X	X	SX			
Anodorhynchus leari																									XR				
Cyanopsitta spixii																									XR				
Ara ambigua												X	X	X	X	X						X							
Ara ararauna															X	X	X	XF	X	X	X	X	X	X	X	XF			

Countries: Argn - Argentina; **Baha** - Bahamas; **Beli** - Belize; **Boli** - Bolivia; **Braz** - Brazil; **Chil** - Chile; **Colo** - Colombia; **Cost** - Costa Rica; **Cuba** - Cuba; **Ecua** - Ecuador; **Elsa** - El Salvador; **Fren** - French Guiana; **Guat** - Guatemala; **Guya** - Guyana; **Hisp** - Hispaniola; **Hond** - Honduras; **Jama** - Jamaica; **Lant** - Lesser Antilles; **Mexi** - Mexico; **Nant** - Netherland Antilles; **Nica** - Nicaragua; **Pana** - Panama; **Parg** - Paraguay; **Peru** - Peru; **Puer** - Puerto Rico; **Suri** - Suriname; **Trin** - Trinidad; **Urug** - Uruguay; **Vene** - Venezuela.

	Baha	Cuba	Hisp	Jama	Puer	Lant	Nant	Mexi	Guat	Beli	Elsa	Hond	Nica	Cost	Pana	Colo	Vene	Trin	Guya	Suri	Fren	Ecua	Peru	Boli	Braz	Parg	Urug	Argn	Chil
Ara auricollis																								X	X	X		X	
Ara chloroptera															X	X	X		X	X	X	X	X	X	X	X		X	
Ara couloni																							X	X	SX				
Ara glaucogularis																								XR		?		?	
Ara macao								X	X	X	+	X	X	X	X	X	X	SV	X	X	X	X	X	X	X				
Ara manilata																X	X	X	X	X	X	X	X	X	X				
Ara maracana																									X	X		X	
Ara militaris								X								X	X					X	X	X				X	
Ara nobilis																	X		X	X	X		X	X	X				
Ara rubrogenys																								XR					
Ara severa															X	X	X		X	X	X	X	X	X	X				
Aratinga acuticaudata																X	X							X	X	X	X	X	
Aratinga aurea																				X?			X	X	X	X		X	
Aratinga auricapilla																									XR				
Aratinga cactorum																									XR				
Aratinga canicularis					XI			X	X		X	X	X	X															
Aratinga chloroptera			XR		XI																								
Aratinga erythrogenys																						X	X						
Aratinga euops		XR																											
Aratinga finschi													X	X	X														
Aratinga guarouba																									XR				
Aratinga holochlora																													
brevipes								XR																					
holochlora								XR																					
rubritorquis									X		X	X	X																
strenua								X	X		X	X	X																
Aratinga jandaya																									XR				
Aratinga leucophthalmus																X	X		X	X	X	X	X	X	X	X	X	X	
Aratinga mitrata																							X	X				X	
Aratinga nana				X				X	X	X		X	X	X	X														
Aratinga pertinax					XI		X								X	X	X		X	X	X				X				
Aratinga solstitialis																	X		X	X	X				X				
Aratinga wagleri																X	X					X	X						
Aratinga weddellii																X						X	X	X	X				
Nandayus nenday																								X	X	X		X	
Leptosittaca branickii																X						X	X						
Ognorhynchus icterotis																X						X							
Rhynchopsitta pachyrhyncha								XR																					
Rhynchopsitta terrisi								XR																					
Cyanoliseus patagonus																											XN	X	X
Pyrrhura albipectus																						XR							
Pyrrhura calliptera																XR													
Pyrrhura cruentata																									XR				
Pyrrhura devillei																									X	X			
Pyrrhura egregia																	X		X						X				
Pyrrhura frontalis																									X	X	X	X	
Pyrrhura hoematotis																	XR												
Pyrrhura hoffmanni														X	X														
Pyrrhura lepida																									XR				
Pyrrhura leucotis																													
emma																	XR												
griseipectus																									XR				

Status: **X** - Breeding species; **XN** - Regular non-breeding species; **XR** - Endemic breeding species; **X?** - Regular species, breeding status uncertain; **XI** - Introduced species; **XD** - Dubious species; **XF** - Formerly bred; **V** - Vagrants; **SX** - Breeding species, sight records only; **SN** - Regular non-breeding species, sight records only; **S?** - Uncertain breeding status; sight records only; **SI** -Introduced; sight records only; **SV** - Vagrant; sight records only. **?** - Occurrence uncertain; **+** - Extinct.

	Baha	Cuba	Hisp	Jama	Puer	Lant	Nant	Mexi	Guat	Beli	Elsa	Hond	Nica	Cost	Pana	Colo	Vene	Trin	Guya	Suri	Fren	Ecua	Peru	Boli	Braz	Parg	Urug	Argn	Chil
Pyrrhura leucotis (cont.)																													
leucotis																									XR				
pfrimeri																									XR				
Pyrrhura melanura																													
chapmani																XR													
melanura																X	X					X	X		X				
pacifica																X						X							
Pyrrhura molinae																								X	X			X	
Pyrrhura orcesi																						XR							
Pyrrhura perlata																								X	X				
Pyrrhura picta																													
caeruleiceps																X	X												
picta															X		X		X	X	X	SX	X	X	X				
Pyrrhura rhodocephala																	XR												
Pyrrhura rupicola																							X	X	X				
Pyrrhura viridicata																XR													
Enicognathus ferrugineus																												X	X
Enicognathus leptorhynchus																													XR
Myiopsitta monachus					XN																			X	X	X	X	X	
Bolborhynchus aurifrons																							X	X				X	X
Bolborhynchus aymara																								X				X	
Bolborhynchus ferrugineifrons																XR													
Bolborhynchus lineola								X	X			X		X	X	X	X					SX	X						
Bolborhynchus orbygnesius																							X	X					
Forpus coelestis																						X	X						
Forpus conspicillatus															X	X	X												
Forpus crassirostris																X						X	X	X	X	X		X	
Forpus cyanopygius								XR																					
Forpus passerinus				XI			XI									X	X	X	X	X	X				X				
Forpus sclateri																X	X		X		SX	X	X	X	X				
Forpus xanthops																							XR						
Brotogeris chrysopterus																	X		X	X	X				X				
Brotogeris cyanoptera																X	X					X	X	X	X				
Brotogeris jugularis								X	X		X	X	X	X	X	X	X												
Brotogeris pyrrhopterus																						X	X						
Brotogeris sanctithomae																X							X	X	X				
Brotogeris tirica																									XR				
Brotogeris versicolurus																													
chiriri																								X	X	X		X	
versicolurus					XI											X					X	X	X	X	X				
Nannopsittaca dachilleae																							X	X					
Nannopsittaca panychlora																	X		X						SX				
Touit batavica																	X	X	X	X	SX								
Touit costaricensis														X	X														
Touit dilectissima															X	X	X					X							
Touit huetii																X	X	X	X			X	X	X	X				
Touit melanonota																									XR				
Touit purpurata																X	X		X	X	X	X	X		X				
Touit stictoptera																X						X	X						
Touit surda																									XR				
Pionites leucogaster																							X	X	X				
Pionites melanocephala																X	X		X	X	X	X	X		X				

Countries: Argn - Argentina; **Baha** - Bahamas; **Beli** - Belize; **Boli** - Bolivia; **Braz** - Brazil; **Chil** - Chile; **Colo** - Colombia; **Cost** - Costa Rica; **Cuba** - Cuba; **Ecua** - Ecuador; **Elsa** - El Salvador; **Fren** - French Guiana; **Guat** - Guatemala; **Guya** - Guyana; **Hisp** - Hispaniola; **Hond** - Honduras; **Jama** - Jamaica; **Lant** - Lesser Antilles; **Mexi** - Mexico; **Nant** - Netherland Antilles; **Nica** - Nicaragua; **Pana** - Panama; **Parg** - Paraguay; **Peru** - Peru; **Puer** - Puerto Rico; **Suri** - Suriname; **Trin** - Trinidad; **Urug** - Uruguay; **Vene** - Venezuela.

	Baha	Cuba	Hisp	Jama	Puer	Lant	Nant	Mexi	Guat	Beli	Elsa	Hond	Nica	Cost	Pana	Colo	Vene	Trin	Guya	Suri	Fren	Ecua	Peru	Boli	Braz	Parg	Urug	Argn	Chil
Pionopsitta barrabandi																X	X					X	X	X	X				
Pionopsitta caica																	X		X	X	X				X				
Pionopsitta haematotis								X	X	X		X	X	X	X	X						X							
Pionopsitta pileata																									X	X		X	
Pionopsitta pulchra																X						X							
Pionopsitta pyrilia															X	X	X												
Gypopsitta vulturina																									XR				
Hapalopsittaca amazonina																													
amazonina																X	X												
fuertesi																XR													
pyrrhops																						X	X						
Hapalopsittaca melanotis																							X	X					
Graydidascalus brachyurus																X					X	X	X		X				
Pionus chalcopterus																X	X					X	X						
Pionus fuscus																X	X		X	X	X				X				
Pionus maximiliani																								X	X	X		X	
Pionus menstruus														X	X	X	X	X	X	X	X	X	X	X	X				
Pionus senilis								X	X	X		X	X	X	X														
Pionus sordidus																X	X					X	X	X					
Pionus tumultuosus																													
seniloides																	X					X	X						
tumultuosus																X							X	X					
Amazona aestiva																								X	X	X		X	
Amazona agilis				XR																									
Amazona albifrons								X	X	X	X	X	X	X															
Amazona amazonica																X	X	X	X	X	X	X	X	X	X				
Amazona arausiaca						XR																							
Amazona autumnalis																													
autumnalis								X	X	X		X	X	X	X	X	X					X							
diadema																									XR				
Amazona barbadensis							X										X												
Amazona brasiliensis																									XR				
Amazona collaria				XR																									
Amazona dufresniana																	X		X	X	X								
Amazona farinosa								X	X	X		X	X	X	X	X	X		X	X	X	X	X	X	X				
Amazona festiva																X	X		X?			X	X		X				
Amazona finschi								XR																					
Amazona guildingii						XR																							
Amazona imperialis						XR																							
Amazona kawalli																									XR				
Amazona leucocephala	X	X																											
Amazona mercenaria																X	X					X	X	X					
Amazona ochrocephala																													
auropalliata								X	X		X	X	X	X															
ochrocephala												X			X	X	X		X	X	X	X	X	X	X				
oratrix								X		X																			
Amazona pretrei																									X	SV		X	
Amazona rhodocorytha																									XR				
Amazona tucumana																								X				X	
Amazona ventralis			XR		XI																								
Amazona versicolor						XR																							
Amazona vinacea																									X	X		X	

Status: **X** - Breeding species; **XN** - Regular non-breeding species; **XR** - Endemic breeding species; **X?** - Regular species, breeding status uncertain; **XI** - Introduced species; **XD** - Dubious species; **XF** - Formerly bred; **V** - Vagrants; **SX** - Breeding species, sight records only; **SN** - Regular non-breeding species, sight records only; **S?** - Uncertain breeding status; sight records only; **SI** -Introduced; sight records only; **SV** - Vagrant; sight records only. **?** - Occurrence uncertain; **+** - Extinct.

	Baha	Cuba	Hisp	Jama	Puer	Lant	Nant	Mexi	Guat	Beli	Elsa	Hond	Nica	Cost	Pana	Colo	Vene	Trin	Guya	Suri	Fren	Ecua	Peru	Boli	Braz	Parg	Urug	Argn	Chil
Amazona viridigenalis								XR																					
Amazona vittata					XR																								
Amazona xantholora								X		X		X?																	
Amazona xanthops																								X	X				
Deroptyus accipitrinus																X	X		X	X	X	X	X		X				
Triclaria malachitacea																									XR				
CUCULIFORMES																													
Cuculidae																													
Cuculus canorus						V																							
Coccyzus americanus	X	X	X	X	X	X	XN	X	XN	XN	XN	XN	XN	XN	XN	XN	XN	XN	XN	XN	XN	XN	XN	XN	XN	XN	V	XN	
Coccyzus cinereus																SV							SN	XN	X	X	X	X	
Coccyzus erythropthalmus	XN	XN		XN	V	V		XN	XN	XN		XN	XN	XN	XN	XN	XN	V				XN	XN	XN	SV	XN		XN	
Coccyzus euleri																X	X		X	X	SV				X			X	
Coccyzus ferrugineus														XR															
Coccyzus lansbergi							V								SV	X	X					X	XN						
Coccyzus melacoryphus						V										X	X	X	X?	XN	XN	X	X	X	X	X	X	X	V
Coccyzus minor	X	X	X	X	X	X	XN	X	X	X	X	X	X	XN	XN	X	X	X	X	X	X				X				
Coccyzus pumilus															SV	X	X												
Piaya cayana								X	X	X	X	X	X	X	X	X	X	X	X	X	X	X	X	X	X	X	X	X	
Piaya melanogaster																X	X		X	X	X	X	X	X	X				
Piaya minuta															X	X	X	X	X	X	X	X	X	X	X				
Piaya pluvialis				XR																									
Piaya rufigularis			XR																										
Saurothera longirostris			XR																										
Saurothera merlini	X	X																											
Saurothera vetula				XR																									
Saurothera vielloti					XR																								
Crotophaga ani	X	X	X	X	X	X		X		X		X	X	X	X	X	X	X	X	X	X	X	X	X	X	X	X	X	
Crotophaga major															X	X	X	X	X	X	X	X	X	X	X	X	X	X	
Crotophaga sulcirostris							X	X	X	X	X	X	X	X	X	X	X					X	X					X	X
Guira guira							V																	X	X	X	X	X	
Tapera naevia								X	X	X	X	X	X	X	X	X	X	X	X	X	X	X	X	X	X	X	X	X	
Morococcyx erythropygus								X	X		X	X	X	X															
Dromococcyx pavoninus																	X		X			X	X	X	X	X		X	
Dromococcyx phasianellus								X	X	X	X	X	X	X	X	X	X					X	X	X	X	X		X	
Geococcyx californianus								X																					
Geococcyx velox								X	X		X	X	X																
Neomorphus geoffroyi													X	X	X	X						X	X	X	X				
Neomorphus pucheranii																SX							X		X				
Neomorphus radiolosus																X						X							
Neomorphus rufipennis																	X		X						X				
Neomorphus squamiger																									XR				
Opisthocomidae																													
Opisthocomus hoazin																X	X		X	X	X	X	X	X	X				
STRIGIFORMES																													
Tytonidae																													
Tyto alba	X	X	X	X	V	X	X	X	X	X	X	X	X	X	X	X	X	X	X	X	X	X	X	X	X	X	X	X	X
Tyto glaucops			XR																										
Strigidae																													
Otus albogularis																X	X					X	X	X					
Otus asio								X																					
Otus atricapillus																									X	X	X	X	

Countries: Argn - Argentina; **Baha** - Bahamas; **Beli** - Belize; **Boli** - Bolivia; **Braz** - Brazil; **Chil** - Chile; **Colo** - Colombia; **Cost** - Costa Rica; **Cuba** - Cuba; **Ecua** - Ecuador; **Elsa** - El Salvador; **Fren** - French Guiana; **Guat** - Guatemala; **Guya** - Guyana; **Hisp** - Hispaniola; **Hond** - Honduras; **Jama** - Jamaica; **Lant** - Lesser Antilles; **Mexi** - Mexico; **Nant** - Netherland Antilles; **Nica** - Nicaragua; **Pana** - Panama; **Parg** - Paraguay; **Peru** - Peru; **Puer** - Puerto Rico; **Suri** - Suriname; **Trin** - Trinidad; **Urug** - Uruguay; **Vene** - Venezuela.

	Baha	Cuba	Hisp	Jama	Puer	Lant	Nant	Mexi	Guat	Beli	Elsa	Hond	Nica	Cost	Pana	Colo	Vene	Trin	Guya	Suri	Fren	Ecua	Peru	Boli	Braz	Parg	Urug	Argn	Chil
Otus barbarus								X	X																				
Otus choliba														X	X	X	X	X	X	X	X	X	X	X	X	X	X	X	
Otus clarkii														X	X	X													
Otus colombianus																X						X							
Otus cooperi								X	X		X	X	X	X															
Otus flammeolus								X	X		XN																		
Otus guatemalae								X	X	X		X	X	X	X	X	X		?			X	X	X	X				
Otus ingens																X	X					X	X	X					
Otus kennicotti								X																					
Otus koepckeae																							XR						
Otus marshalli																							XR						
Otus nudipes					XR																								
Otus petersoni																						X	X						
Otus roboratus																						X	X						
Otus seductus								XR																					
Otus trichopsis								X	X		X	X	X																
Otus watsonii																X	X		X	X	X	X	X	X	X				
Lophostrix cristata								X	X	X	X	X	X	X	X	X	X		X	X	SX	X	X	X	X				
Bubo virginianus								X	X	X	X	X	X	X	X	X	X		X	X	SX	X	X	X	X	X	X	X	X
Pulsatrix koeniswaldiana																									X	X		X	
Pulsatrix melanota																X						X	X	X					
Pulsatrix perspicillata								X	X	X	X	X	X	X	X	X	X	X	X	X	X	X	X	X	X	X		X	
Glaucidium brasilianum								X	X	X	X	X	X	X	X	X	X	X	X	X	?	X	X	X	X	X	X	X	X
Glaucidium gnoma								X	X	SX		X																	
Glaucidium hardyi																	X		X		X		X	X	X				
Glaucidium jardinii														X	X	X	X					X	X	X					
Glaucidium minutissimum								X	X	X		X		X	X	X						X	X		X	X		X	
Glaucidium peruanum																						X	X						
Glaucidium siju		XR																											
Xenoglaux loweryi																							XR						
Micrathene whitneyi								X																					
Gymnoglaux lawrencii		XR																											
Speotyto cunicularia	X	X	X			X	X	X	XN	XN	XN	V		V	V	X	X		X			X	X	X	X	X	X	X	X
Ciccaba albitarsus																X	X					X	X	X					
Ciccaba huhula																X	X		X	X	X	X	X	X	X	X		X	
Ciccaba nigrolineata								X	X	X	X	X	X	X	X	X	X					X	X						
Ciccaba virgata								X	X	X	X	X	X	X	X	X	X	X	X	X	X	X	X	X	X	X		X	
Strix fulvescens								X	X		X	X																	
Strix hylophila																									X	X		X	
Strix occidentalis								X																					
Strix rufipes																								X		X		X	X
Strix varia								X																					
Rhinoptynx clamator								X	X	SX	X	X	X	X	X	X	X	X	X	X	X	X	X	X	X	X	X	X	
Asio flammeus	V	X	X		X	V		XN	V					V		X	X		X		S?	X	X	X	X	X	X	X	X
Asio otus		V						X																					
Asio stygius		X	X					X	X	X			X			X	X					X		X	X	X		X	
Pseudoscops grammicus				XR																									
Aegolius acadicus								X																					
Aegolius harrisii																X	X					X	X	X	X	X	X	X	
Aegolius ridgwayi								X	X		X			X	X?														

Status: X - Breeding species; **XN** - Regular non-breeding species; **XR** - Endemic breeding species; **X?** - Regular species, breeding status uncertain; **XI** - Introduced species; **XD** - Dubious species; **XF** - Formerly bred; **V** - Vagrants; **SX** - Breeding species, sight records only; **SN** - Regular non-breeding species, sight records only; **S?** - Uncertain breeding status; sight records only; **SI** -Introduced; sight records only; **SV** - Vagrant; sight records only. **?** - Occurrence uncertain; **+** - Extinct.

	Baha	Cuba	Hisp	Jama	Puer	Lant	Nant	Mexi	Guat	Beli	Elsa	Hond	Nica	Cost	Pana	Colo	Vene	Trin	Guya	Suri	Fren	Ecua	Peru	Boli	Braz	Parg	Urug	Argn	Chil
CAPRIMULGIFORMES																													
Steatornithidae																													
Steatornis caripensis							V							V	V	X	X	X	X			X	X	X					
Nyctibiidae																													
Nyctibius aethereus																X	X		X			X	X	X	X	X		X	
Nyctibius bracteatus																?			X			X	X		X				
Nyctibius grandis								X	X	X		X	X	X	X	X	X		X	X	X	X	X	X	X				
Nyctibius griseus			X	X	V			X	X	X	X	X	X	X	X	X	X	X	X	X	X	X	X	X	X	X	X	X	
Nyctibius leucopterus																			X						X				
Nyctibius maculosus																X	X					X	X	X					
Caprimulgidae																													
Lurocalis semitorquatus																													
rufiventris																X	X					X	X	X					
semitorquatus								S?	S?			S?	X	X	X	X	X	X	X	X	X	X	X	X	X	X		X	
Chordeiles acutipennis							SV	X	X	X	X	X	X	X	X	X	X	X	X	X	X	X	X	X	X	X			V
Chordeiles gundlachii	X	X	X	X	X		V					V																	
Chordeiles minor	XN	XN	XN	XN	XN	XN	XN	X	XN	X		X	X	X	X	XN	XN	?				XN	XN		XN	XN	XN	XN	
Chordeiles pusillus																X	X		X					X	X				
Chordeiles rupestris																X	X					X	X	X	X				
Nyctiprogne leucopyga																X	X		X		X		S?	X	X	X			
Podager nacunda																X	X	X	X	X	X	X	X	X	X	X	X	X	
Nyctidromus albicollis								X	X	X	X	X	X	X	X	X	X	X	X	X	X	X	X	X	X	X		X	
Phalaenoptilus nuttallii								X																					
Siphonorhis americanus				+																									
Siphonorhis brewsteri			XR																										
Otophanes mcleodii								XR																					
Otophanes yucatanicus								X	X	X																			
Nyctiphrynus ocellatus													X?	X		X						X	X	X	X	X		X	
Nyctiphrynus rosenbergi																X						X							
Caprimulgus anthonyi																						X	X						
Caprimulgus candicans																								X	X	X			
Caprimulgus carolinensis	X?	XN	XN	XN	XN	V	XN	XN	XN	V	XN	XN	XN	XN	XN	XN	V												
Caprimulgus cayennensis					V	X	X							X	X	X	X	X	X	X	X	X			X				
Caprimulgus cubanensis		X	X																										
Caprimulgus hirundinaceus																									XR				
Caprimulgus longirostris																X	X					X	X	X	X	X	X	X	X
Caprimulgus maculicaudus								X				V	X			X	X		X	X	X		X	X	X				
Caprimulgus maculosus																					XR								
Caprimulgus nigrescens																X	X		X	X	X	X	X	X	X				
Caprimulgus noctitherus					XR																								
Caprimulgus parvulus																X	X						X	X	X	X	X	X	
Caprimulgus ridgwayi								X	X			X	X																
Caprimulgus rufus																													
otiosus						X											X												
rufus														X	X	X	X	X	?	X	X		SX	X	X	X		X	
Caprimulgus salvini																													
badius								X	X	X																			
salvini								X					V																
Caprimulgus saturatus														X	X														
Caprimulgus sericocaudatus																							X	X	X	X		X	
Caprimulgus vociferus		V						X	X	X	X	X		XN	XN														
Caprimulgus whitelyi																	XR												

Countries: Argn - Argentina; **Baha** - Bahamas; **Beli** - Belize; **Boli** - Bolivia; **Braz** - Brazil; **Chil** - Chile; **Colo** - Colombia; **Cost** - Costa Rica; **Cuba** - Cuba; **Ecua** - Ecuador; **Elsa** - El Salvador; **Fren** - French Guiana; **Guat** - Guatemala; **Guya** - Guyana; **Hisp** - Hispaniola; **Hond** - Honduras; **Jama** - Jamaica; **Lant** - Lesser Antilles; **Mexi** - Mexico; **Nant** - Netherland Antilles; **Nica** - Nicaragua; **Pana** - Panama; **Parg** - Paraguay; **Peru** - Peru; **Puer** - Puerto Rico; **Suri** - Suriname; **Trin** - Trinidad; **Urug** - Uruguay; **Vene** - Venezuela.

	Baha	Cuba	Hisp	Jama	Puer	Lant	Nant	Mexi	Guat	Beli	Elsa	Hond	Nica	Cost	Pana	Colo	Vene	Trin	Guya	Suri	Fren	Ecua	Peru	Boli	Braz	Parg	Urug	Argn	Chil
Hydropsalis brasiliana																				X?			XN	X	X	X	X	X	
Hydropsalis climacocerca																X	X		X	X	X	X	X	X	X				
Uropsalis segmentata																X						X	X	X					
Uropsalis lyra																X	X					X	X	X				X	
Macropsalis creagra																									X			X	
Eleothreptus anomalus																									X	X		X	
APODIFORMES																													
Apodidae																													
Cypseloides cherriei														X		X	X					X							
Cypseloides cryptus										X		X	X?	X	X?	X	X		X			X	X						
Cypseloides fumigatus																													
fumigatus																									X	SX		X	
major																								X				X	
Cypseloides lemosi																XR													
Cypseloides phelpsi																	X		X						SX				
Cypseloides rutilus								X	X	?	?	X		X	X	X	X	X				X	X	X					
Cypseloides storeri								XR																					
Nephoecetes niger		X	X	X	X	X		X	X?			X	X	X				S?	V										
Aerornis senex																									X	X		X	
Streptoprocne biscutata																									X			X	
Streptoprocne semicollaris								XR																					
Streptoprocne zonaris		X	X	X	V	X		X	X	X	X	X	X	X	X	X	X	XN	X	X	S?	X	X	X	X		V	X	
Chaetura andrei															V	XN	X			X	SN			X	X	X		X	
Chaetura brachyura					V	X									X	X	X	X	X	X	X	X	X	X	X				
Chaetura chapmani															X?	X	X	X	X	X	X		X	SX	X				
Chaetura cinereiventris						X							X	X	X	X	X	X	X			X	X	X	X	X		X	
Chaetura egregia																						X	X	X	X				
Chaetura martinica						XR																							
Chaetura pelagica	XN	SN	XN	XN	SN		SV	XN	?	XN		XN	XN	XN	XN	XN	XN					XN	XN						XN
Chaetura spinicauda														X	X	X	X	X	X	X	X	X			X				
Chaetura vauxi								X	X	X	X	X	X	X	X		X												
Aeronautes andecolus																							X	X				X	X
Aeronautes montivagus																X	X		SX			X	X	X	X			X	
Aeronautes saxatalis								X	X	X?	X	X																	
Tachornis furcata																X	X												
Tachornis phoenicobia		X	X	X	V																								
Tachornis squamata																X	X	X	X	X	X	X	X	X	X				
Panyptila cayennensis								X	X	X		X	X	X	X	X	X	X	X	X	X	X	X	X	X				
Panyptila sanctihieronymi								X	X			X	V	V															
Trochilidae																													
Doryfera johannae																X	X		X			X	X		X				
Doryfera ludoviciae														X	X	X	X					X	X	X					
Androdon aequatorialis															X	X						X							
Ramphodon naevius																									XR				
Glaucis aenea													X	X	X	X						X							
Glaucis dohrnii																									XR				
Glaucis hirsuta						X	V								X	X	X	X	X	X	X	X	X	X	X				
Threnetes leucurus																X	X		X	X	X	X	X	X	X				
Threnetes loehkeni																									XR				
Threnetes niger																					X				X				
Threnetes ruckeri									X	X		X	X	X	X	X	X					X							
Phaethornis anthophilus															X	X	X												

Status: **X** - Breeding species; **XN** - Regular non-breeding species; **XR** - Endemic breeding species; **X?** - Regular species, breeding status uncertain; **XI** - Introduced species; **XD** - Dubious species; **XF** - Formerly bred; **V** - Vagrants; **SX** - Breeding species, sight records only; **SN** - Regular non-breeding species, sight records only; **S?** - Uncertain breeding status; sight records only; **SI** -Introduced; sight records only; **SV** - Vagrant; sight records only. **?** - Occurrence uncertain; + - Extinct.

	Baha	Cuba	Hisp	Jama	Puer	Lant	Nant	Mexi	Guat	Beli	Elsa	Hond	Nica	Cost	Pana	Colo	Vene	Trin	Guya	Suri	Fren	Ecua	Peru	Boli	Braz	Parg	Urug	Argn	Chil
Phaethornis augusti																X	X		X										
Phaethornis bourcieri																X	X		X	X	X	X	X		X				
Phaethornis eurynome																									X	X		X	
Phaethornis gounellei																									XR				
Phaethornis griseogularis																													
griseogularis																X	X					X	X		X				
porcullae																							XR						
Phaethornis guy														X	X	X	X	X				X	X						
Phaethornis hispidus																X	X					X	X	X	X				
Phaethornis idaliae																									XR				
Phaethornis koepckeae																							XR						
Phaethornis longuemareus								X	X	X		X	X	X	X	X	X	X	X	X	X	X	X		X				
Phaethornis malaris																				X	X				X				
Phaethornis nattereri																								X	X				
Phaethornis philippii																							X	X	X				
Phaethornis pretrei																								X	X	X		X	
Phaethornis ruber																X	X		X	X	X	X	X	X	X				
Phaethornis squalidus																X	X		X						X				
Phaethornis stuarti																							X	X					
Phaethornis subochraceus																								X	X				
Phaethornis superciliosus																													
margarettae																									XR				
superciliosus								X	X	X		X	X	X	X	X	X		X	X	X	X	X	X	X				
Phaethornis syrmatophorus																X						X	X						
Phaethornis yaruqui																X						X							
Eutoxeres aquila														X	X	X						X	X						
Eutoxeres condamini																X						X	X	X					
Phaeochroa cuvierii								X	X	X		X	X	X	X	X													
Campylopterus curvipennis																													
curvipennis								X	X	X		X																	
excellens								XR																					
Campylopterus duidae																	X								X				
Campylopterus ensipennis																	X	X											
Campylopterus falcatus																X	X					X							
Campylopterus hemileucurus								X	X	X	X	X	X	X	X														
Campylopterus hyperythrus																	X								X				
Campylopterus largipennis																X	X		X	X	X	X	X	X	X				
Campylopterus phainopeplus																XR													
Campylopterus rufus								X	X		X																		
Campylopterus villaviscensio																						X	X						
Eupetomena macroura																				X	X		X	X	X	X			
Florisuga mellivora						V	V	X	X	X		X	X	X	X	X	X	X	X	X	X	X	X	X	X				
Melanotrochilus fuscus																									X		X		
Colibri coruscans																X	X					X	X	X	X			X	X
Colibri delphinae									X	X		X	X	X	X	X	X	X	X	SX		X	X	X	X				
Colibri serrirostris																								X	X	X		X	
Colibri thalassinus								X	X		X	X		X	X	X	X					X	X	X					
Anthracothorax dominicus			X		X																								
Anthracothorax mango				XR																									
Anthracothorax nigricollis															X	X	X	X	X	X	X	X	X	X	X	X		X	
Anthracothorax prevostii								X	X	X	X	X	X	X	X	X	X					X	X						
Anthracothorax viridigula						SV											X	X	X	X	X				X				

Countries: Argn - Argentina; **Baha** - Bahamas; **Beli** - Belize; **Boli** - Bolivia; **Braz** - Brazil; **Chil** - Chile; **Colo** - Colombia; **Cost** - Costa Rica; **Cuba** - Cuba; **Ecua** - Ecuador; **Elsa** - El Salvador; **Fren** - French Guiana; **Guat** - Guatemala; **Guya** - Guyana; **Hisp** - Hispaniola; **Hond** - Honduras; **Jama** - Jamaica; **Lant** - Lesser Antilles; **Mexi** - Mexico; **Nant** - Netherland Antilles; **Nica** - Nicaragua; **Pana** - Panama; **Parg** - Paraguay; **Peru** - Peru; **Puer** - Puerto Rico; **Suri** - Suriname; **Trin** - Trinidad; **Urug** - Uruguay; **Vene** - Venezuela.

	Baha	Cuba	Hisp	Jama	Puer	Lant	Nant	Mexi	Guat	Beli	Elsa	Hond	Nica	Cost	Pana	Colo	Vene	Trin	Guya	Suri	Fren	Ecua	Peru	Boli	Braz	Parg	Urug	Argn	Chil
Anthracothorax viridis					XR																								
Avocettula recurvirostris																	X		X	SX	X	X			X				
Eulampis jugularis					V	XR																							
Sericotes holosericeus					X	X																							
Chrysolampis mosquitus						SV	X								V	X	X	X	X	X	X			X	X				
Orthorhyncus cristatus					X	X																							
Klais guimeti												X	X	X	X	X	X					X	X	X					
Abeillia abeillei								X	X	X	X	X	X																
Stephanoxis lalandi																									X	X		X	
Lophornis chalybea																X	X					X	X	X	X				
Lophornis delattrei																													
brachylopha								XR																					
delattrei														X	X	X							X	X					
Lophornis gouldii																								X	X				
Lophornis magnifica																									XR				
Lophornis ornata																	X	X	X	X	X				X				
Lophornis pavonina																	X		X						X				
Lophornis stictolopha																X	X					X	X						
Paphosia adorabilis														X	X														
Paphosia helenae								X	X	X		X	X	X															
Popelairia conversii														X	X	X						X							
Popelairia langsdorffi																X	X					X	X	X	X				
Popelairia letitiae																								XR					
Popelairia popelairii																X						X	X						
Discosura longicauda																	X		X	X	X				X				
Chlorestes notatus																X	X	X	X	X	X	X	X		X				
Chlorostilbon alice																	XR												
Chlorostilbon assimilis														X	X														
Chlorostilbon aureoventris																								X	X	X	X	X	
Chlorostilbon canivetii								X	X	X	X	X	X	X															
Chlorostilbon gibsoni																X	X												
Chlorostilbon maugaeus					XR																								
Chlorostilbon mellisugus							X									X	X	X	X	X	X	X	X	X	X				
Chlorostilbon poortmanni																X	X												
Chlorostilbon ricordii	X	X																											
Chlorostilbon russatus																X	X												
Chlorostilbon stenura																X	X												
Chlorostilbon swainsonii			XR																										
Cynanthus latirostris								X																					
Cynanthus sordidus								XR																					
Cyanophaia bicolor						XR																							
Thalurania colombica																													
colombica									X	X		X	X	X	X	X	X					X							
hypochlora																						X	SX						
ridgwayi								XR																					
Thalurania furcata																X	X		X	X	X	X	X	X	X	X		X	
Thalurania glaucopis																									X	X	X	X	
Thalurania watertonii																									XR				
Panterpe insignis														X	X														
Damophila julie															X	X						X	X						
Lepidopyga coeruleogularis														?	X	X													
Lepidopyga goudoti																X	X												

Status: **X** - Breeding species; **XN** - Regular non-breeding species; **XR** - Endemic breeding species; **X?** - Regular species, breeding status uncertain; **XI** - Introduced species; **XD** - Dubious species; **XF** - Formerly bred; **V** - Vagrants; **SX** - Breeding species, sight records only; **SN** - Regular non-breeding species, sight records only; **S?** - Uncertain breeding status; sight records only; **SI** -Introduced; sight records only; **SV** - Vagrant; sight records only. **?** - Occurrence uncertain; **+** - Extinct.

	Baha	Cuba	Hisp	Jama	Puer	Lant	Nant	Mexi	Guat	Beli	Elsa	Hond	Nica	Cost	Pana	Colo	Vene	Trin	Guya	Suri	Fren	Ecua	Peru	Boli	Braz	Parg	Urug	Argn	Chil
Lepidopyga lilliae																XR													
Hylocharis chrysura																								X	X	X	X	X	
Hylocharis cyanus																X	X		X	X	X	X	X	X	X			V	
Hylocharis eliciae								X	X		X	X	X	X	X	X													
Hylocharis grayi															X	X						X							
Hylocharis leucotis								X	X		X	X	X																
Hylocharis sapphirina																X	X		X	X	X	X	X	X	X	X		X	
Hylocharis xantusii								XR																					
Chrysuronia oenone																X	X					X	X	X	X				
Goldmania violiceps															X	X													
Goethalsia bella															X	X													
Trochilus polytmus				XR																									
Leucochloris albicollis																									X	X	X	X	
Polytmus guainumbi																X	X	X	X	X	X		X	X	X	X		X	
Polytmus milleri																	XR												
Polytmus theresiae																X	X		X	X	X	X	X		X				
Leucippus baeri																							XR						
Leucippus chlorocercus																X						X	X		X				
Leucippus fallax																X	X												
Leucippus taczanowskii																							XR						
Taphrospilus hypostictus																						X	X	X	X			X	
Amazilia amabilis													X	X	X	X						X							
Amazilia amazilia																						X	X						
Amazilia beryllina								X	X		X	X																	
Amazilia boucardi														XR															
Amazilia candida								X	X	X		X	X	X?															
Amazilia castaneiventris																XR													
Amazilia chionogaster																							X	X	X			X	
Amazilia chionopectus																	X	X	X	X	X				X				
Amazilia cyanifrons														X?		XR													
Amazilia cyanocephala								X	X	X	X	X	X																
Amazilia cyanura								X	X		X	X	X	X?															
Amazilia decora														X	X														
Amazilia distans																	XR												
Amazilia edward														X	X														
Amazilia fimbriata																X	X		X	X	X	X	X	X	X	X			
Amazilia franciae																X						X	X						
Amazilia lactea																	X						X	X	X				
Amazilia leucogaster																	X		X	X	X				X				
Amazilia luciae												XR																	
Amazilia rosenbergi																X						X							
Amazilia rutila								X	X	X	X	X	X	X															
Amazilia saucerrottei													X	X		X	X												
Amazilia tobaci																	X	X											
Amazilia tzacatl								X	X	X		X	X	X	X	X	X		SX			X							
Amazilia versicolor																X	X							X	X	X		X	
Amazilia violiceps								X	SV																				
Amazilia viridicauda																							XR						
Amazilia viridifrons								XR																					
Amazilia viridigaster																X	X		X						X				
Amazilia yucatanensis								X	X	X		X																	
Eupherusa cyanophrys								XR																					

Countries: Argn - Argentina; **Baha** - Bahamas; **Beli** - Belize; **Boli** - Bolivia; **Braz** - Brazil; **Chil** - Chile; **Colo** - Colombia; **Cost** - Costa Rica; **Cuba** - Cuba; **Ecua** - Ecuador; **Elsa** - El Salvador; **Fren** - French Guiana; **Guat** - Guatemala; **Guya** - Guyana; **Hisp** - Hispaniola; **Hond** - Honduras; **Jama** - Jamaica; **Lant** - Lesser Antilles; **Mexi** - Mexico; **Nant** - Netherland Antilles; **Nica** - Nicaragua; **Pana** - Panama; **Parg** - Paraguay; **Peru** - Peru; **Puer** - Puerto Rico; **Suri** - Suriname; **Trin** - Trinidad; **Urug** - Uruguay; **Vene** - Venezuela.

	Baha	Cuba	Hisp	Jama	Puer	Lant	Nant	Mexi	Guat	Beli	Elsa	Hond	Nica	Cost	Pana	Colo	Vene	Trin	Guya	Suri	Fren	Ecua	Peru	Boli	Braz	Parg	Urug	Argn	Chil
Eupherusa eximia								X	X	X		X	X	X	X														
Eupherusa nigriventris														X	X														
Eupherusa poliocerca								XR																					
Elvira chionura														X	X														
Elvira cupreiceps														XR															
Microchera albocoronata												X	X	X	X														
Chalybura buffonii															X	X	X					X	X						
Chalybura urochrysia												X	X	X	X	X						X							
Aphantochroa cirrhochloris																									XR				
Lampornis amethystinus								X	X		X	X																	
Lampornis castaneoventris																													
calolaema													X	X	X														
castaneoventris															XR														
cinereicauda														XR															
Lampornis clemenciae								X																					
Lampornis hemileucus														X	X														
Lampornis sybillae												X	X																
Lampornis viridipallens								X	X		X	X																	
Lamprolaima rhami								X	X		X	X																	
Adelomyia melanogenys																X	X					X	X	X				X	
Anthocephala floriceps																XR													
Urosticte benjamini																													
benjamini																X						X	X						
ruficrissa																X						X							
Phlogophilus hemileucurus																X						X	X						
Phlogophilus harterti																							XR						
Clytolaema rubricauda																									XR				
Polyplancta aurescens																X	X					X	X	X	X				
Heliodoxa branickii																							XR	?					
Heliodoxa gularis																X						X	X						
Heliodoxa imperatrix																X						X							
Heliodoxa jacula														X	X	X						X							
Heliodoxa leadbeateri																X	X					X	X	X					
Heliodoxa rubinoides																X						X	X						
Heliodoxa schreibersii																X						X	X		X				
Heliodoxa xanthogonys																	X		X						X				
Eugenes fulgens								X	X		X	X	X	X	X														
Hylonympha macrocerca																	XR												
Sternoclyta cyanopectus																	XR												
Topaza pella																	X		X	X	X	X			X				
Topaza pyra																X	X					X	X		X				
Oreotrochilus adela																								XR					
Oreotrochilus estella																													
chimborazo																X						X							
estella																							X	X				X	X
Oreotrochilus leucopleurus																								X				X	X
Oreotrochilus melanogaster																							XR						
Urochroa bougueri																X						X	X						
Patagona gigas																S?						X	X	X				X	X
Aglaeactis aliciae																							XR						
Aglaeactis castelnaudii																							XR						
Aglaeactis cupripennis																X						X	X						

Status: X - Breeding species; **XN** - Regular non-breeding species; **XR** - Endemic breeding species; **X?** - Regular species, breeding status uncertain; **XI** - Introduced species; **XD** - Dubious species; **XF** - Formerly bred; **V** - Vagrants; **SX** - Breeding species, sight records only; **SN** - Regular non-breeding species, sight records only; **S?** - Uncertain breeding status; sight records only; **SI** -Introduced; sight records only; **SV** - Vagrant; sight records only. **?** - Occurrence uncertain; **+** - Extinct.

	Baha	Cuba	Hisp	Jama	Puer	Lant	Nant	Mexi	Guat	Beli	Elsa	Hond	Nica	Cost	Pana	Colo	Vene	Trin	Guya	Suri	Fren	Ecua	Peru	Boli	Braz	Parg	Urug	Argn	Chil
Aglaeactis pamela																								XR					
Lafresnaya lafresnayi																X	X					X	X						
Pterophanes cyanopterus																X						X	X	X					
Coeligena bonapartei																X	X												
Coeligena coeligena																X	X					X	X	X					
Coeligena helianthea																X	X												
Coeligena iris																						X	X						
Coeligena lutetiae																X						X	X						
Coeligena phalerata																XR													
Coeligena prunellei																XR													
Coeligena torquata																X	X					X	X	X					
Coeligena violifer																							X	X					
Coeligena wilsoni																X						X							
Ensifera ensifera																X	X					X	X	X					
Sephanoides fernandensis																													XR
Sephanoides sephanoides																												X	X
Boissonneaua flavescens																X	X					X							
Boissonneaua jardini																X						X							
Boissonneaua matthewsii																X						X	X						
Heliangelus amethysticollis																X	X					X	X	X					
Heliangelus exortis																													
exortis																X						X							
micrastur																						X	X						
Heliangelus mavors																X	X												
Heliangelus regalis																							XR						
Heliangelus spencei																	XR												
Heliangelus strophianus																?						X							
Heliangelus viola																						X	X						
Heliangelus zusii																XR													
Eriocnemis alinae																X						X	X						
Eriocnemis cupreoventris																X	X												
Eriocnemis derbyi																X						X							
Eriocnemis glaucopoides																								X				X	
Eriocnemis godini																?						X							
Eriocnemis luciani																X						X	X						
Eriocnemis mirabilis																XR													
Eriocnemis mosquera																X						X							
Eriocnemis nigrivestis																						XR							
Eriocnemis vestitus																X	X					X	X						
Haplophaedia aureliae															X	X						X	X	X					
Haplophaedia lugens																X						X							
Ocreatus underwoodii																X	X					X	X	X					
Lesbia nuna																X	X?					X	X	X					
Lesbia victoriae																X						X	X						
Sappho sparganura																							?	X				X	
Polyonymus caroli																							XR						
Ramphomicron dorsale																XR													
Ramphomicron microrhynchum																X	X					X	X	X					
Metallura aeneocauda																							X	X					
Metallura baroni																						XR							
Metallura eupogon																							XR						
Metallura iracunda																X	X												

Countries: Argn - Argentina; **Baha** - Bahamas; **Beli** - Belize; **Boli** - Bolivia; **Braz** - Brazil; **Chil** - Chile; **Colo** - Colombia; **Cost** - Costa Rica; **Cuba** - Cuba; **Ecua** - Ecuador; **Elsa** - El Salvador; **Fren** - French Guiana; **Guat** - Guatemala; **Guya** - Guyana; **Hisp** - Hispaniola; **Hond** - Honduras; **Jama** - Jamaica; **Lant** - Lesser Antilles; **Mexi** - Mexico; **Nant** - Netherland Antilles; **Nica** - Nicaragua; **Pana** - Panama; **Parg** - Paraguay; **Peru** - Peru; **Puer** - Puerto Rico; **Suri** - Suriname; **Trin** - Trinidad; **Urug** - Uruguay; **Vene** - Venezuela.

	Baha	Cuba	Hisp	Jama	Puer	Lant	Nant	Mexi	Guat	Beli	Elsa	Hond	Nica	Cost	Pana	Colo	Vene	Trin	Guya	Suri	Fren	Ecua	Peru	Boli	Braz	Parg	Urug	Argn	Chil
Metallura odomae																							XR						
Metallura phoebe																							XR	?					
Metallura theresiae																							XR						
Metallura tyrianthina																X	X					X	X	X					
Metallura williami																X						X							
Chalcostigma herrani																X						X	X						
Chalcostigma heteropogon																X	X												
Chalcostigma olivaceum																							X	X					
Chalcostigma ruficeps																						X	X	X					
Chalcostigma stanleyi																						X	X	X					
Oxypogon guerinii																X	X												
Opisthoprora euryptera																X						X	X						
Taphrolesbia griseiventris																							XR						
Aglaiocercus coelestis																X						X							
Aglaiocercus kingi																X	X					X	X	X					
Oreonympha nobilis																							XR						
Augastes lumachellus																									XR				
Augastes scutatus																									XR				
Schistes geoffroyi																X	X					X	X	X					
Heliothryx aurita																X	X		X	X	X	X	X	X	X				
Heliothryx barroti								X	X	X		X	X	X	X	X						X							
Heliactin bilophum																				X				X	X				
Loddigesia mirabilis																							XR						
Heliomaster constantii								X	X		X	X	X	X															
Heliomaster furcifer																X?								X	X	X	X	X	
Heliomaster longirostris								X	X		X	X	X	X	X	X	X	X	X	X	X	X	X	X	X				
Heliomaster squamosus																									XR				
Rhodopis vesper																							X						X
Thaumastura cora																							X						SX
Philodice bryantae														X	X														
Philodice evelynae	XR																												
Philodice mitchellii															V	X						X							
Doricha eliza								XR																					
Doricha enicura								X	X		X	X																	
Tilmatura dupontii								X	X		X	X	X																
Microstilbon burmeisteri																								X				X	
Calothorax lucifer								X																					
Calothorax pulcher								XR																					
Archilochus alexandri								X																					
Archilochus colubris	XN	XN	SV	V	V			XN	XN	XN	XN	XN	XN	XN	XN														
Calliphlox amethystina																X	X		X	X	X	X	X	X	X	X		X	
Mellisuga minima			X	X	V																								
Calypte anna								X																					
Calypte costae								X																					
Calypte helenae		XR																											
Stellula calliope								X																					
Atthis ellioti								X	X		X	X																	
Atthis heloisa								XR																					
Myrtis fanny																						X	X						
Eulidia yarrellii																							SX						X
Myrmia micrura																						X	X						
Acestrura berlepschi																						XR							

Status: X - Breeding species; **XN** - Regular non-breeding species; **XR** - Endemic breeding species; **X?** - Regular species, breeding status uncertain; **XI** - Introduced species; **XD** - Dubious species; **XF** - Formerly bred; **V** - Vagrants; **SX** - Breeding species, sight records only; **SN** - Regular non-breeding species, sight records only; **S?** - Uncertain breeding status; sight records only; **SI** -Introduced; sight records only; **SV** - Vagrant; sight records only. **?** - Occurrence uncertain; **+** - Extinct.

	Baha	Cuba	Hisp	Jama	Puer	Lant	Nant	Mexi	Guat	Beli	Elsa	Hond	Nica	Cost	Pana	Colo	Vene	Trin	Guya	Suri	Fren	Ecua	Peru	Boli	Braz	Parg	Urug	Argn	Chil
Acestrura bombus																						X	X						
Acestrura heliodor																X	X					X							
Acestrura mulsant																X						X	X	X					
Chaetocercus jourdanii																X	X	X											
Selasphorus ardens															XR														
Selasphorus flammula														X	X														
Selasphorus platycercus								X	X																				
Selasphorus rufus	V							XN																					
Selasphorus sasin								XN																					
Selasphorus scintilla														X	X														
TROGONIFORMES																													
Trogonidae																													
Pharomachrus antisianus																X	X					X	X	X					
Pharomachrus auriceps															X	X	X					X	X	X					
Pharomachrus fulgidus																X	X		?										
Pharomachrus mocinno								X	X		X	X	X	X	X														
Pharomachrus pavoninus																X	X					X	X	X	X				
Euptilotis neoxenus								XR																					
Priotelus temnurus		XR																											
Temnotrogon roseigaster			XR																										
Trogon aurantiiventris														X	X														
Trogon bairdii														X	X														
Trogon citreolus								XR																					
Trogon clathratus														X	X														
Trogon collaris								X	X	X	X	X	X	X	X	X	X	X	X	X	X	X	X	X	X				
Trogon comptus																X						X							
Trogon curucui																X						X	X	X	X	X		X	
Trogon elegans								X	X		X	X	X	X															
Trogon massena								X	X	X		X	X	X	X	X						X							
Trogon melanocephalus								X	X	X	X	X	X	X															
Trogon melanurus															X	X	X		X	X	X	X	X	X	X				
Trogon mexicanus								X	X		X	X																	
Trogon personatus																X	X		X			X	X	X	X				
Trogon rufus												X	X	X	X	X	X		X	X	X	X	X		X	X		X	
Trogon surrucura																									X	X		X	
Trogon violaceus								X	X	X	X	X	X	X	X	X	X	X	X	X	X	X	X	X	X				
Trogon viridis															X	X	X	X	X	X	X	X	X	X	X				
CORACIIFORMES																													
Alcedinidae																													
Ceryle alcyon	XN	XN	XN	XN	XN	XN	XN	XN	XN	XN	XN	XN	XN	XN	XN	XN	XN	XN	SV			XN							
Ceryle torquata					V	X		X	X	X	X	X	X	X	X	X	X	X	X	X	X	X	X	X	X	X	X	X	X
Chloroceryle aenea								X	X	X	X	X	X	X	X	X	X	X	X	X	X	X	X	X	X	X		SX	
Chloroceryle amazona							SV	X	X	X	X	X	X	X	X	X	X	X	X	X	X	X	X	X	X	X	X	X	
Chloroceryle americana								X	X	X	X	X	X	X	X	X	X	X	X	X	X	X	X	X	X	X	X	X	X
Chloroceryle inda													X	X	X	X	X		X	X	X	X	X	X	X	X			
Todidae																													
Todus angustirostris			XR																										
Todus mexicanus					XR																								
Todus multicolor		XR																											
Todus subulatus			XR																										
Todus todus				XR																									

Countries: Argn - Argentina; **Baha** - Bahamas; **Beli** - Belize; **Boli** - Bolivia; **Braz** - Brazil; **Chil** - Chile; **Colo** - Colombia; **Cost** - Costa Rica; **Cuba** - Cuba; **Ecua** - Ecuador; **Elsa** - El Salvador; **Fren** - French Guiana; **Guat** - Guatemala; **Guya** - Guyana; **Hisp** - Hispaniola; **Hond** - Honduras; **Jama** - Jamaica; **Lant** - Lesser Antilles; **Mexi** - Mexico; **Nant** - Netherland Antilles; **Nica** - Nicaragua; **Pana** - Panama; **Parg** - Paraguay; **Peru** - Peru; **Puer** - Puerto Rico; **Suri** - Suriname; **Trin** - Trinidad; **Urug** - Uruguay; **Vene** - Venezuela.

	Baha	Cuba	Hisp	Jama	Puer	Lant	Nant	Mexi	Guat	Beli	Elsa	Hond	Nica	Cost	Pana	Colo	Vene	Trin	Guya	Suri	Fren	Ecua	Peru	Boli	Braz	Parg	Urug	Argn	Chil
Momotidae																													
Hylomanes momotula								X	X	X	X	X	X	X	X	X													
Aspatha gularis								X	X		X	X																	
Electron carinatum								X	X	X		X	X	X															
Electron platyrhynchum												X	X	X	X	X						X	X	X	X				
Eumomota superciliosa								X	X		X	X	X	X															
Baryphthengus martii												X	X	X	X	X						X	X	X	X				
Baryphthengus ruficapillus																									X	X		X	
Momotus mexicanus								X	X																				
Momotus momota																													
aequatorialis																X						X	X	X					
momota								X	X	X	X	X	X	X	X	X	X	X	X	X	X	X	X	X	X	X		X	
PICIFORMES																													
Galbulidae																													
Galbalcyrhynchus leucotis																X						X	X		X				
Galbalcyrhynchus purusianus																							X	X	X				
Brachygalba albogularis																							X	SX	X				
Brachygalba goeringi																X	X												
Brachygalba lugubris																X	X		X	X	X	X	X	X	X				
Brachygalba salmoni															X	X													
Jacamaralcyon tridactyla																									XR				
Galbula albirostris																X	X		X	X	X	X	X		X				
Galbula cyanescens																							X	X	X				
Galbula cyanicollis																							X		X				
Galbula dea																X	X		X	X	X	X	X	X	X				
Galbula galbula																X	X		X	X	X				X				
Galbula leucogastra																													
chalcothorax																						X	X		X				
leucogastra																SX	X		X	X	X			X	X				
Galbula pastazae																X						X	X						
Galbula ruficauda								X	X	X		X	X	X	X	X	X	X	X		X	X		X	X	X		X	
Galbula tombacea																X						X	X		X				
Jacamerops aurea														X	X	X	X		X	X	X	X	X	X	X				
Bucconidae																													
Notharchus macrorhynchos								X	X	X	X	X	X	X	X	X	X		X	X	X	X	X	X	X	X		X	
Notharchus ordii																	X						X	X	X				
Notharchus pectoralis															X	X						X							
Notharchus tectus														X	X	X	X		X	X	X	X	X	X	X				
Bucco capensis																X	X		X	X	X	X	X		X				
Bucco macrodactylus																X	X					X	X	X	X				
Bucco noanamae																XR													
Bucco tamatia																X	X		X	X	X	X	X	X	X				
Nystalus chacuru																							X	X	X	X		X	
Nystalus maculatus																								X	X	X		X	
Nystalus radiatus															X	X						X							
Nystalus striolatus																						X	X	X	X				
Hypnelus ruficollis																X	X												
Malacoptila fulvogularis																X						X	X	X					
Malacoptila fusca																X	X		X	X	X	X	X		X				
Malacoptila mystacalis																X	X												
Malacoptila panamensis								X	X	X		X	X	X	X	X						X							
Malacoptila rufa																							X	X	X				

Status: **X** - Breeding species; **XN** - Regular non-breeding species; **XR** - Endemic breeding species; **X?** - Regular species, breeding status uncertain; **XI** - Introduced species; **XD** - Dubious species; **XF** - Formerly bred; **V** - Vagrants; **SX** - Breeding species, sight records only; **SN** - Regular non-breeding species, sight records only; **S?** - Uncertain breeding status; sight records only; **SI** -Introduced; sight records only; **SV** - Vagrant; sight records only. **?** - Occurrence uncertain; **+** - Extinct.

	Baha	Cuba	Hisp	Jama	Puer	Lant	Nant	Mexi	Guat	Beli	Elsa	Hond	Nica	Cost	Pana	Colo	Vene	Trin	Guya	Suri	Fren	Ecua	Peru	Boli	Braz	Parg	Urug	Argn	Chil
Malacoptila semicincta																							X	X	X				
Malacoptila striata																									XR				
Micromonacha lanceolata														X	X	X						X	X		X				
Nonnula amaurocephala																									XR				
Nonnula brunnea																X						X	X						
Nonnula rubecula																X	X			X	SX		X		X	X		X	
Nonnula ruficapilla																													
frontalis															X	X													
ruficapilla																							X	X	X				
Nonnula sclateri																							X	X	X				
Hapaloptila castanea																X						X	X						
Monasa atra																	X		X	X	X				X				
Monasa flavirostris																X						X	X		X				
Monasa morphoeus												X	X	X	X	X	X					X	X	X	X				
Monasa nigrifrons																X						X	X	X	X				
Chelidoptera tenebrosa																X	X		X	X	X	X	X	X	X				
Capitonidae																													
Capito aurovirens																X						X	X		X				
Capito dayi																								X	X				
Capito hypoleucus																XR													
Capito maculicoronatus															X	X													
Capito niger																X	X		X	X	X	X	X	X	X				
Capito quinticolor																XR													
Capito squamatus																X						X							
Eubucco bourcierii														X	X	X	X					X	X						
Eubucco richardsoni																X						X	X	X	X				
Eubucco tucinkae																							X	X					
Eubucco versicolor																							X	X					
Semnornis frantzii														X	X														
Semnornis ramphastinus																X						X							
Ramphastidae																													
Aulacorhynchus calorhynchus																X	X												
Aulacorhynchus coeruleicinctis																							X	X					
Aulacorhynchus derbianus																X	X		X	SX		X	X	X	X				
Aulacorhynchus haematopygus																X	X					X							
Aulacorhynchus huallagae																							XR						
Aulacorhynchus prasinus								X	X	X	X	X	X	X	X	X	X					X	X	X	S?				
Aulacorhynchus sulcatus																	XR												
Pteroglossus aracari																	X		X	X	X				X				
Pteroglossus azara																X	X					X	X	X	X				
Pteroglossus beauharnaesii																							X	X	X				
Pteroglossus bitorquatus																								X	X				
Pteroglossus castanotis																X						X	X	X	X	X		X	
Pteroglossus frantzii														X	X														
Pteroglossus inscriptus																X						X	X	X	X				
Pteroglossus pluricinctus																X	X					X	X		X				
Pteroglossus torquatus								X	X	X	X	X	X	X	X	X	X					X							
Pteroglossus viridis																	X		X	X	X				X				
Selenidera culik																	X		X	X	X				X				
Selenidera maculirostris																													
gouldi																								X	X				
maculirostris																									X			X	

Countries: Argn - Argentina; **Baha** - Bahamas; **Beli** - Belize; **Boli** - Bolivia; **Braz** - Brazil; **Chil** - Chile; **Colo** - Colombia; **Cost** - Costa Rica; **Cuba** - Cuba; **Ecua** - Ecuador; **Elsa** - El Salvador; **Fren** - French Guiana; **Guat** - Guatemala; **Guya** - Guyana; **Hisp** - Hispaniola; **Hond** - Honduras; **Jama** - Jamaica; **Lant** - Lesser Antilles; **Mexi** - Mexico; **Nant** - Netherland Antilles; **Nica** - Nicaragua; **Pana** - Panama; **Parg** - Paraguay; **Peru** - Peru; **Puer** - Puerto Rico; **Suri** - Suriname; **Trin** - Trinidad; **Urug** - Uruguay; **Vene** - Venezuela.

	Baha	Cuba	Hisp	Jama	Puer	Lant	Nant	Mexi	Guat	Beli	Elsa	Hond	Nica	Cost	Pana	Colo	Vene	Trin	Guya	Suri	Fren	Ecua	Peru	Boli	Braz	Parg	Urug	Argn	Chil
Selenidera nattereri																X	X		X		SX				X				
Selenidera reinwardtii																X						X	X	X	X				
Selenidera spectabilis												X	X	X	X	X						X							
Baillonius bailloni																									X	X		X	
Andigena cucullata																							X	X					
Andigena hypoglauca																X						X	X						
Andigena laminirostris																X						X							
Andigena nigrirostris																X	X					X							
Ramphastos ambiguus																X	X						X						
Ramphastos brevis															?	X						X							
Ramphastos dicolorus																									X	X		X	
Ramphastos sulfuratus								X	X	X		X	X	X	X	X	X												
Ramphastos swainsonii												X	X	X	X	X						X							
Ramphastos toco																			X	X	X		X	X	X	X		X	
Ramphastos tucanus																X	X		X	X	X	X	X	X	X				
Ramphastos vitellinus																X	X	X	X	X	X	X	X	X	X				
Picidae																													
Picumnus albosquamatus																								X	X				
Picumnus aurifrons																							X	X	X				
Picumnus castelnau																X						X	X						
Picumnus cinnamomeus																X	X												
Picumnus cirratus																													
cirratus																			X		X			X	X	X		X	
dorbygnianus																							XD	X					
temminckii																									X	X		X	
Picumnus exilis																													
exilis																SX	X		X	X	X				X				
salvini																	XR												
Picumnus fulvescens																									XR				
Picumnus fuscus																								X	X				
Picumnus granadensis																XR													
Picumnus lafresnayi																													
lafresnayi																X						X	X		X				
pumilis																X									X				
Picumnus limae																									XR				
Picumnus minutissimus																			X	X	X								
Picumnus nebulosus																									X	?	X	X	
Picumnus olivaceus									X			X	X	X	X	X	X					X	SX						
Picumnus pygmaeus																									XR				
Picumnus rufiventris																X						X	X	X	X				
Picumnus sclateri																						X	X						
Picumnus spilogaster																	X		X	X	X				X				
Picumnus squamulatus																X	X												
Picumnus steindachneri																							XR						
Picumnus subtilis																							XR						
Picumnus varzeae																									XR				
Nesoctites micromegas			XR																										
Melanerpes aurifrons								X	X	X	X	X	X																
Melanerpes cactorum																							?	X	X	X		X	
Melanerpes candidus																				X	S?		SX	X	X	X	X	X	
Melanerpes chrysauchen														X	X	X													
Melanerpes chrysogenys								XR																					

Status: X - Breeding species; **XN** - Regular non-breeding species; **XR** - Endemic breeding species; **X?** - Regular species, breeding status uncertain; **XI** - Introduced species; **XD** - Dubious species; **XF** - Formerly bred; **V** - Vagrants; **SX** - Breeding species, sight records only; **SN** - Regular non-breeding species, sight records only; **S?** - Uncertain breeding status; sight records only; **SI** -Introduced; sight records only; **SV** - Vagrant; sight records only. **?** - Occurrence uncertain; **+** - Extinct.

	Baha	Cuba	Hisp	Jama	Puer	Lant	Nant	Mexi	Guat	Beli	Elsa	Hond	Nica	Cost	Pana	Colo	Vene	Trin	Guya	Suri	Fren	Ecua	Peru	Boli	Braz	Parg	Urug	Argn	Chil
Melanerpes cruentatus																X	X		X	X	X	X	X	X	X				
Melanerpes flavifrons																									X	X		X	
Melanerpes formicivorus								X	X	X	X	X	X	X	X	X													
Melanerpes herminieri						XR																							
Melanerpes hoffmannii												X	X	X															
Melanerpes hypopolius								XR																					
Melanerpes lewis								XN																					
Melanerpes portoricensis					XR																								
Melanerpes pucherani								X	X	X		X	X	X	X	X						X							
Melanerpes pygmaeus								X		X		X																	
Melanerpes radiolatus				XR																									
Melanerpes rubricapillus														X	X	X	X	X	X	X									
Melanerpes striatus			XR																										
Melanerpes superciliaris	X	X																											
Melanerpes uropygialis								X																					
Sphyrapicus nuchalis								XN	XN																				
Sphyrapicus ruber								XN																					
Sphyrapicus thyroideus								X																					
Sphyrapicus varius	XN	XN	XN	XN	XN	XN	XN	XN	XN	XN	XN	XN	XN	XN	XN	XN													
Xiphidiopicus percussus		XR																											
Picoides lignarius																								X				X	X
Picoides mixtus																								X	X	X	X	X	
Picoides nuttallii								X																					
Picoides scalaris								X	SX	X		X	X																
Picoides stricklandi								X																					
Picoides villosus	X				SV			X	X		X	X	X	X	X														
Veniliornis affinis																X	X					X	X	X	X				
Veniliornis callonotus																X						X	X						
Veniliornis cassini																	X		X	X	X				X				
Veniliornis dignus																X	X					X	X						
Veniliornis frontalis																								X				X	
Veniliornis fumigatus								X	X	X	X	X	X	X	X	X	X					X	X	X				X	
Veniliornis kirkii														X	X	X	X	X				X	X		X				
Veniliornis maculifrons																									XR				
Veniliornis nigriceps																X						X	X	X					
Veniliornis passerinus																X	X		X		X	X	X	X	X	X		X	
Veniliornis sanguineus																			X	X	X								
Veniliornis spilogaster																									X	X	X	X	
Piculus auricularis								XR																					
Piculus aurulentus																									X	X		X	
Piculus chrysochloros															X	X	X		X	X	X	X	X	X	X	X		X	
Piculus flavigula																X	X		X	X	X	X	X	X	X				
Piculus leucolaemus																													
leucolaemus															X	X						X	X	X	X				
simplex												X	X	X	X														
Piculus rivolii																X	X					X	X	X					
Piculus rubiginosus								X	X	X	X	X	X	X	X	X	X	X	X	X	X	X	X	X	X			X	
Colaptes atricollis																							XR						
Colaptes auratus		X						X	X		X	X	X																
Colaptes campestris																				X				X	X	X	X	X	
Colaptes fernandinae		XR																											
Colaptes melanochloros																								X	X	X	X	X	

Countries: **Argn** - Argentina; **Baha** - Bahamas; **Beli** - Belize; **Boli** - Bolivia; **Braz** - Brazil; **Chil** - Chile; **Colo** - Colombia; **Cost** - Costa Rica; **Cuba** - Cuba; **Ecua** - Ecuador; **Elsa** - El Salvador; **Fren** - French Guiana; **Guat** - Guatemala; **Guya** - Guyana; **Hisp** - Hispaniola; **Hond** - Honduras; **Jama** - Jamaica; **Lant** - Lesser Antilles; **Mexi** - Mexico; **Nant** - Netherland Antilles; **Nica** - Nicaragua; **Pana** - Panama; **Parg** - Paraguay; **Peru** - Peru; **Puer** - Puerto Rico; **Suri** - Suriname; **Trin** - Trinidad; **Urug** - Uruguay; **Vene** - Venezuela.

	Baha	Cuba	Hisp	Jama	Puer	Lant	Nant	Mexi	Guat	Beli	Elsa	Hond	Nica	Cost	Pana	Colo	Vene	Trin	Guya	Suri	Fren	Ecua	Peru	Boli	Braz	Parg	Urug	Argn	Chil
Colaptes pitius																												X	X
Colaptes punctigula															X	X	X		X	X	X	X	X	X	X				
Colaptes rupicola																							X	X				X	X
Celeus castaneus								X	X	X		X	X	X	X														
Celeus elegans																X	X	X	X	X	X	X	X	X	X				
Celeus flavescens																									X	X		X	
Celeus flavus																X	X		X	X	X	X	X	X	X				
Celeus grammicus																X	X				?	X	X	X	X				
Celeus loricatus													X	X	X	X						X							
Celeus lugubris																								X	X	X		X	
Celeus spectabilis																													
obrieni																									XR				
spectabilis																						X	X	X					
Celeus torquatus																X	X		X	X	X	X	X	X	X				
Celeus undatus																	X		X	X	X				X				
Dryocopus galeatus																									X	X		X	
Dryocopus lineatus								X	X	X	X	X	X	X	X	X	X	X	X	X	X	X	X	X	X	X		X	
Dryocopus schulzi																								X		X		X	
Campephilus gayaquilensis																X						X	X						
Campephilus guatemalensis								X	X	X	X	X	X	X	X														
Campephilus haematogaster															X	X						X	X						
Campephilus imperialis								XR																					
Campephilus leucopogon																								X	X	X	X	X	
Campephilus magellanicus																												X	X
Campephilus melanoleucos															X	X	X	X	X	X	X	X	X	X	X	X		X	
Campephilus pollens																X	X					X	X						
Campephilus principalis		X																											
Campephilus robustus																									X	X		X	
Campephilus rubricollis																X	X		X	X	X	X	X	X	X				
PASSERIFORMES																													
Dendrocolaptidae																													
Dendrocincla anabatina								X	X	X		X	X	X	X														
Dendrocincla fuliginosa																													
fuliginosa												X	X	X	X	X	X	X	X	X	X	X	X	X	X				
turdina																									X	X		X	
Dendrocincla homochroa								X	X	X	X	X	X	X	X	X	X												
Dendrocincla merula																X	X		X	X	X	X	X	X	X				
Dendrocincla tyrannina																X	X					X	X						
Deconychura longicauda												X		X	X	X	X		X	X	X	X	X	X	X				
Deconychura stictolaema																X	X				X	X	X		X				
Sittasomus griseicapillus								X	X	X	X	X	X	X	X	X	X	X	X	?	X	X	X	X	X	X		X	
Glyphorynchus spirurus								X	X	X		X	X	X	X	X	X		X	X	X	X	X	X	X				
Drymornis bridgesii																								X	X	X	X	X	
Nasica longirostris																X	X				X	X	X	X	X				
Dendrexetastes rufigula																X	X		X	X	X	X	X	X	X				
Hylexetastes perrotii																	X		X	X	X			X	X				
Hylexetastes stresemanni																							X	X	X				
Xiphocolaptes albicollis																									X	X		X	
Xiphocolaptes falcirostris																													
falcirostris																									XR				
franciscanus																									XR				
Xiphocolaptes major																								X	X	X		X	

Status: X - Breeding species; **XN** - Regular non-breeding species; **XR** - Endemic breeding species; **X?** - Regular species, breeding status uncertain; **XI** - Introduced species; **XD** - Dubious species; **XF** - Formerly bred; **V** - Vagrants; **SX** - Breeding species, sight records only; **SN** - Regular non-breeding species, sight records only; **S?** - Uncertain breeding status; sight records only; **SI** -Introduced; sight records only; **SV** - Vagrant; sight records only. **?** - Occurrence uncertain; **+** - Extinct.

	Baha	Cuba	Hisp	Jama	Puer	Lant	Nant	Mexi	Guat	Beli	Elsa	Hond	Nica	Cost	Pana	Colo	Vene	Trin	Guya	Suri	Fren	Ecua	Peru	Boli	Braz	Parg	Urug	Argn	Chil
Xiphocolaptes promeropirhynchus																													
orenocensis																X	X				X	X	X	X	X				
promeropirhynchus								X	X	X	X	X	X	X	X	X	X		X			X	X	X					
Dendrocolaptes certhia																													
certhia								X	X	X	X	X	X	X	X	X	X		X	X	X	X	X	X	X				
concolor																								X	X				
Dendrocolaptes hoffmannsi																									XR				
Dendrocolaptes picumnus								X	X			X		X	X	X	X		X	X	X	X	X	X	X	X		X	
Dendrocolaptes platyrostris																									X	X		X	
Xiphorhynchus erythropygius								X	X	X		X	X	X	X	X						X							
Xiphorhynchus flavigaster								X	X	X	X	X	X	X															
Xiphorhynchus guttatus																													
eytoni																									XR				
guttatus									X			X	X	X	X	X	X	X	X	X	X	X	X	X	X				
Xiphorhynchus lachrymosus													X	X	X	X						X							
Xiphorhynchus necopinus																									XR				
Xiphorhynchus obsoletus																X	X		X	X	X	X	X	X	X				
Xiphorhynchus ocellatus																X	X					X	X	X	X				
Xiphorhynchus pardalotus																	X		X	X	X				X				
Xiphorhynchus picus															X	X	X	X	X	X	X	X	X	X	X				
Xiphorhynchus spixii																													
elegans																X						X	X	X	X				
spixii																									XR				
Xiphorhynchus triangularis																X	X					X	X	X					
Lepidocolaptes affinis								X	X		X	X	X	X	X	X	X					X	X	X					
Lepidocolaptes albolineatus																SX	X		X	X	X	X	X	X	X				
Lepidocolaptes angustirostris																				X				X	X	X	X	X	
Lepidocolaptes fuscus																									X	X		X	
Lepidocolaptes leucogaster								XR																					
Lepidocolaptes souleyetii								X	X	X	X	X	X	X	X	X	X	X	X			X	X		X				
Lepidocolaptes squamatus																									X	X		X	
Campylorhamphus falcularius																									X	X		X	
Campylorhamphus procurvoides																X	X		X	X	X	X	X		X				
Campylorhamphus pucherani																X						X	X						
Campylorhamphus pusillus														X	X	X	X					X	X						
Campylorhamphus trochilirostris															X	X	X					X	X	X	X	X		X	
Furnariidae																													
Geobates poecilopterus																								X	X				
Geositta antarctica																												X	X
Geositta crassirostris																							XR						
Geositta cunicularia																							X	X	X	X?	X	X	X
Geositta isabellina																												X	X
Geositta maritima																							X						X
Geositta peruviana																							XR						
Geositta punensis																							X	X				X	X
Geositta rufipennis																								X				X	X
Geositta saxicolina																							XR						
Geositta tenuirostris																						X	X	X				X	SX
Upucerthia albigula																							X						X
Upucerthia andaecola																								X				X	X
Upucerthia dumetaria																							X	X			XN	X	X
Upucerthia jelskii																							X	X				X	X

Countries: Argn - Argentina; **Baha** - Bahamas; **Beli** - Belize; **Boli** - Bolivia; **Braz** - Brazil; **Chil** - Chile; **Colo** - Colombia; **Cost** - Costa Rica; **Cuba** - Cuba; **Ecua** - Ecuador; **Elsa** - El Salvador; **Fren** - French Guiana; **Guat** - Guatemala; **Guya** - Guyana; **Hisp** - Hispaniola; **Hond** - Honduras; **Jama** - Jamaica; **Lant** - Lesser Antilles; **Mexi** - Mexico; **Nant** - Netherland Antilles; **Nica** - Nicaragua; **Pana** - Panama; **Parg** - Paraguay; **Peru** - Peru; **Puer** - Puerto Rico; **Suri** - Suriname; **Trin** - Trinidad; **Urug** - Uruguay; **Vene** - Venezuela.

	Baha	Cuba	Hisp	Jama	Puer	Lant	Nant	Mexi	Guat	Beli	Elsa	Hond	Nica	Cost	Pana	Colo	Vene	Trin	Guya	Suri	Fren	Ecua	Peru	Boli	Braz	Parg	Urug	Argn	Chil
Upucerthia serrana																							XR						
Upucerthia validirostris																								X				X	
Ochetorhynchus certhioides																													
certhioides																								X		X		X	
harterti																								XR					
Ochetorhynchus ruficauda																							X	X				X	X
Eremobius phoenicurus																												X	X
Chilia melanura																													XR
Cinclodes antarcticus																												X	X
Cinclodes atacamensis																							X	X				X	X
Cinclodes comechingonus																												XR	
Cinclodes excelsior																													
aricomae																							X	X					
excelsior																X						X							
Cinclodes fuscus																X	X					X	X	X	XN	XN	XN	X	X
Cinclodes nigrofumosus																													
nigrofumosus																													XR
taczanowskii																							XR						
Cinclodes olrogi																												XR	
Cinclodes oustaleti																												X	X
Cinclodes pabsti																									XR				
Cinclodes palliatus																							XR						
Cinclodes patagonicus																												X	X
Clibanornis dendrocolaptoides																									X	X		X	
Furnarius cristatus																								X		X		X	
Furnarius figulus																									XR				
Furnarius leucopus																													
cinnamomeus																						X	X						
leucopus																X	X		X				X	X	X				
Furnarius minor																X						X	X		X				
Furnarius rufus																								X	X	X	X	X	
Furnarius torridus																						SX	X		X				
Limnornis curvirostris																									X		X	X	
Sylviorthorhynchus desmursii																												X	X
Aphrastura masafuerae																													XR
Aphrastura spinicauda																												X	X
Phleocryptes melanops																							X	X	X	X?	X	X	X
Leptasthenura aegithaloides																							X	X				X	X
Leptasthenura andicola																X	X					X	X	X					
Leptasthenura fuliginiceps																								X				X	
Leptasthenura pileata																							XR						
Leptasthenura platensis																									X	X	X	X	
Leptasthenura setaria																									X			X	
Leptasthenura striata																							X						X
Leptasthenura striolata																									XR				
Leptasthenura xenothorax																							XR						
Leptasthenura yanacensis																							X	X					
Spartonoica maluroides																									X		X	X	
Schizoeaca coryi																	XR												
Schizoeaca fuliginosa																													
fuliginosa																X	X					X	X						
griseomurina																						X	X						

Status: X - Breeding species; **XN** - Regular non-breeding species; **XR** - Endemic breeding species; **X?** - Regular species, breeding status uncertain; **XI** - Introduced species; **XD** - Dubious species; **XF** - Formerly bred; **V** - Vagrants; **SX** - Breeding species, sight records only; **SN** - Regular non-breeding species, sight records only; **S?** - Uncertain breeding status; sight records only; **SI** -Introduced; sight records only; **SV** - Vagrant; sight records only. **?** - Occurrence uncertain; **+** - Extinct.

	Baha	Cuba	Hisp	Jama	Puer	Lant	Nant	Mexi	Guat	Beli	Elsa	Hond	Nica	Cost	Pana	Colo	Vene	Trin	Guya	Suri	Fren	Ecua	Peru	Boli	Braz	Parg	Urug	Argn	Chil
Schizoeaca fuliginosa (cont.)																													
harterti																								XR					
helleri																							XR						
palpebralis																							XR						
perijana																X	X												
vilcabambae																							XR						
Schoeniophylax phryganophila																								X	X	X	X	X	
Oreophylax moreirae																									XR				
Synallaxis albescens														X	X	X	X	X	X	X	X		X	X	X	X		X	
Synallaxis albigularis																X						X	X		X				
Synallaxis azarae																													
azarae																							X	X					
courseni																							XR						
elegantior																X	X					X	X						
superciliosa																								X				X	
Synallaxis brachyura												X	X	X	X	X						X	X						
Synallaxis cabanisi																													
cabanisi																							X	X	X				
macconnelli																	X			X	X				X				
Synallaxis castanea																	XR												
Synallaxis cherriei																X						X	X		X				
Synallaxis cinerascens																									X	X	X	X	
Synallaxis cinnamomea																X	X	X											
Synallaxis erythrothorax								X	X	X	X	X																	
Synallaxis frontalis																								X	X	X	X	X	
Synallaxis fuscorufa																XR													
Synallaxis gujanensis																													
albilora																								X	X	X			
gujanensis																X	X		X	X	X	X	X	X	X				
maranonica																						X	X						
Synallaxis hypospodia																							X	X	X				
Synallaxis moesta																X						X	X						
Synallaxis propinqua																SX					X	X	X	X	X				
Synallaxis ruficapilla																													
infuscata																									XR				
ruficapilla																									X	X		X	
Synallaxis rutilans																X	X		X	X	X	X	X	X	X				
Synallaxis spixi																									X	X	X	X	
Synallaxis stictothorax																						X	X						
Synallaxis subpudica																XR													
Synallaxis tithys																						X	X						
Synallaxis unirufa																X	X					X	X						
Synallaxis zimmeri																							XR						
Hellmayrea gularis																X	X					X	X						
Gyalophylax hellmayri																									XR				
Certhiaxis cinnamomea																X	X	X	X	X	X		X	X	X	X	X	X	
Certhiaxis mustelina																X							X		X				
Limnoctites rectirostris																									X		X	X	
Poecilurus candei																X	X												
Poecilurus kollari																			SX						X				
Poecilurus scutatus																								X	X			X	
Cranioleuca albicapilla																							XR						

Countries: Argn - Argentina; **Baha** - Bahamas; **Beli** - Belize; **Boli** - Bolivia; **Braz** - Brazil; **Chil** - Chile; **Colo** - Colombia; **Cost** - Costa Rica; **Cuba** - Cuba; **Ecua** - Ecuador; **Elsa** - El Salvador; **Fren** - French Guiana; **Guat** - Guatemala; **Guya** - Guyana; **Hisp** - Hispaniola; **Hond** - Honduras; **Jama** - Jamaica; **Lant** - Lesser Antilles; **Mexi** - Mexico; **Nant** - Netherland Antilles; **Nica** - Nicaragua; **Pana** - Panama; **Parg** - Paraguay; **Peru** - Peru; **Puer** - Puerto Rico; **Suri** - Suriname; **Trin** - Trinidad; **Urug** - Uruguay; **Vene** - Venezuela.

	Baha	Cuba	Hisp	Jama	Puer	Lant	Nant	Mexi	Guat	Beli	Elsa	Hond	Nica	Cost	Pana	Colo	Vene	Trin	Guya	Suri	Fren	Ecua	Peru	Boli	Braz	Parg	Urug	Argn	Chil
Cranioleuca albiceps																							X	X					
Cranioleuca antisiensis																													
antisiensis																						X	X						
baroni																							XR						
Cranioleuca curtata																X						X	X	X					
Cranioleuca demissa																	X		X						X				
Cranioleuca erythrops														X	X	X						X							
Cranioleuca gutturata																X	X			X	X	X	X	X	X				
Cranioleuca hellmayri																XR													
Cranioleuca marcapatae																							XR						
Cranioleuca muelleri																									XR				
Cranioleuca obsoleta																									X	X		X	
Cranioleuca pallida																									XR				
Cranioleuca pyrrhophia																								X	X	X	X	X	
Cranioleuca semicinerea																									XR				
Cranioleuca subcristata																X	X												
Cranioleuca sulphurifera																									X		X	X	
Cranioleuca vulpina																													
dissita															XR														
vulpina																X	X					X	X	X	X				
Siptornopsis hypochondriacus																							XR						
Asthenes anthoides																												X	X
Asthenes baeri																								X	X	X	X	X	
Asthenes berlepschi																								XR					
Asthenes cactorum																							XR						
Asthenes dorbignyi																							X	X				X	X
Asthenes flammulata																X						X	X						
Asthenes heterura																								XR					
Asthenes hudsoni																									X		X	X	
Asthenes humicola																												?	XR
Asthenes humilis																							X	X					
Asthenes luizae																									XR				
Asthenes maculicauda																							X	X				X	
Asthenes modesta																							X	X				X	X
Asthenes ottonis																							XR						
Asthenes patagonica																												XR	
Asthenes pudibunda																							XR						
Asthenes punensis																							X	X				X	
Asthenes pyrrholeuca																								XN		XN	XN	X	X
Asthenes sclateri																												XR	
Asthenes steinbachi																												XR	
Asthenes urubambensis																							X	X					
Asthenes virgata																							XR						
Asthenes wyatti																X	X					X	X						
Thripophaga berlepschi																							XR						
Thripophaga cherriei																	XR												
Thripophaga fusciceps																						X	X	X	X				
Thripophaga macroura																									XR				
Phacellodomus dorsalis																							XR						
Phacellodomus erythrophthalmus																													
erythrophthalmus																									XR				
ferrugineigula																									XR				

Status: **X** - Breeding species; **XN** - Regular non-breeding species; **XR** - Endemic breeding species; **X?** - Regular species, breeding status uncertain; **XI** - Introduced species; **XD** - Dubious species; **XF** - Formerly bred; **V** - Vagrants; **SX** - Breeding species, sight records only; **SN** - Regular non-breeding species, sight records only; **S?** - Uncertain breeding status; sight records only; **SI** -Introduced; sight records only; **SV** - Vagrant; sight records only. **?** - Occurrence uncertain; **+** - Extinct.

	Baha	Cuba	Hisp	Jama	Puer	Lant	Nant	Mexi	Guat	Beli	Elsa	Hond	Nica	Cost	Pana	Colo	Vene	Trin	Guya	Suri	Fren	Ecua	Peru	Boli	Braz	Parg	Urug	Argn	Chil
Phacellodomus ruber																								X	X	X		X	
Phacellodomus rufifrons																X	X					X	X	X	X	X		X	
Phacellodomus sibilatrix																								X		X	X	X	
Phacellodomus striaticeps																							X	X				X	
Phacellodomus striaticollis																													
maculipectus																								X				X	
striaticollis																									X		X	X	
Coryphistera alaudina																								X	X	X	X	X	
Anumbius annumbi																									X	X	X	X	
Siptornis striaticollis																X						X	X						
Xenerpestes minlosi															X	X													
Xenerpestes singularis																						X	X						
Metopothrix aurantiacus																X						X	X	X	X				
Roraimia adusta																	X		X						X				
Margarornis bellulus															XR														
Margarornis rubiginosus														X	X														
Margarornis squamiger																X	X					X	X	X				SX	
Margarornis stellatus																X						X							
Premnornis guttuligera																X	X					X	X	SX					
Premnoplex brunnescens														X	X	X	X					X	X	X					
Premnoplex tatei																	XR												
Pseudocolaptes boissonneautii																X	X					X	X	X					
Pseudocolaptes lawrencii																													
johnsoni																X						X							
lawrencii														X	X														
Berlepschia rikeri																SX	X		X	X	SX	X	X	X	X				
Pseudoseisura cristata																								X	X	X			
Pseudoseisura gutturalis																												XR	
Pseudoseisura lophotes																								X	X	X	X	X	
Hyloctistes subulatus													X	X	X	X	X					X	X	X	X				
Ancistrops strigilatus																X						X	X	X	X				
Anabazenops fuscus																									XR				
Syndactyla guttulata																	XR												
Syndactyla rufosuperciliata																						X	X	X	X	X	X	X	
Syndactyla subalaris														X	X	X	X					X	X						
Simoxenops striatus																								XR					
Simoxenops ucayalae																							X	X	X				
Anabacerthia amaurotis																									X	SX		X	
Anabacerthia striaticollis																X	X					X	X	X					
Anabacerthia variegaticeps								X	X	SX	X	X		X	X	X						X							
Philydor atricapillus																									X	X		X	
Philydor dimidiatus																									X	X			
Philydor erythrocercus																													
erythrocercus																X			X	X	X	X	X	X	X				
ochrogaster																							X	X					
Philydor erythropterus																X	X					X	X	X	X				
Philydor fuscipennis															X	X						X							
Philydor lichtensteini																									X	X		X	
Philydor novaesi																									XR				
Philydor pyrrhodes																X	X		X	X	X	X	X	X	X				
Philydor ruficaudatus																X	X		X	X	X	X	X	X	X				
Philydor rufus														X	X	X	X					X	X	X	X	X		X	

Countries: Argn - Argentina; **Baha** - Bahamas; **Beli** - Belize; **Boli** - Bolivia; **Braz** - Brazil; **Chil** - Chile; **Colo** - Colombia; **Cost** - Costa Rica; **Cuba** - Cuba; **Ecua** - Ecuador; **Elsa** - El Salvador; **Fren** - French Guiana; **Guat** - Guatemala; **Guya** - Guyana; **Hisp** - Hispaniola; **Hond** - Honduras; **Jama** - Jamaica; **Lant** - Lesser Antilles; **Mexi** - Mexico; **Nant** - Netherland Antilles; **Nica** - Nicaragua; **Pana** - Panama; **Parg** - Paraguay; **Peru** - Peru; **Puer** - Puerto Rico; **Suri** - Suriname; **Trin** - Trinidad; **Urug** - Uruguay; **Vene** - Venezuela.

	Baha	Cuba	Hisp	Jama	Puer	Lant	Nant	Mexi	Guat	Beli	Elsa	Hond	Nica	Cost	Pana	Colo	Vene	Trin	Guya	Suri	Fren	Ecua	Peru	Boli	Braz	Parg	Urug	Argn	Chil
Automolus dorsalis																X						X	X	X	X				
Automolus infuscatus																X	X		X	X	X	X	X	X	X				
Automolus leucophthalmus																									X	X		X	
Automolus melanopezus																X						X	X	X	X				
Automolus ochrolaemus								X	X	X		X	X	X	X	X	X		X	X	X	X	X	X	X				
Automolus roraimae																	X								X				
Automolus rubiginosus								X	X		X	X	X	X	X	X	X		X	X	X	X	X	X	X				
Automolus ruficollis																						X	X						
Automolus rufipileatus																X	X		X	X	X	X	X	X	X				
Hylocryptus erythrocephalus																						X	X						
Hylocryptus rectirostris																									X	X			
Cichlocolaptes leucophrus																									XR				
Heliobletus contaminatus																									X	X		X	
Thripadectes flammulatus																X	X					X	X						
Thripadectes holostictus																X	X					X	X	X					
Thripadectes ignobilis																X						X							
Thripadectes melanorhynchus																X						X	X						
Thripadectes rufobrunneus														X	X														
Thripadectes scrutator																							X	X					
Thripadectes virgaticeps																X	X					X							
Xenops milleri																X	X			X	X	X	X	SX	X				
Xenops minutus								X	X	X		X	X	X	X	X	X		X	X	X	X	X	X	X	X		X	
Xenops rutilans														X	X	X	X	X				X	X	X	X	X		X	
Xenops tenuirostris																X	X			X	X	X	X	X	X				
Megaxenops parnaguae																									XR				
Pygarrhichas albogularis																												X	X
Sclerurus albigularis														X	X	X	X	X				X	X	X	X?				
Sclerurus caudacutus																X	X		X	X	X	X	X	X	X				
Sclerurus guatemalensis								X	X	X		X	X	X	X	X						X							
Sclerurus mexicanus								X	X			X		X	X	X	X		X	X	X	X	X	X	X				
Sclerurus rufigularis																X	X		X	X	X	X	X	X	X				
Sclerurus scansor																									X	X		X	
Lochmias nematura															X	X	X					X	X	X	X	X	X	X	
Formicariidae																													
Cymbilaimus lineatus												X	X	X	X	X	X		X	X	X	X	X	X	X				
Cymbilaimus sanctaemariae																							X	X	X				
Hypoedaleus guttatus																									X	X		X	
Batara cinerea																								X	X	X		X	
Mackenziaena leachii																									X	X		X	
Mackenziaena severa																									X	X		X	
Frederickena unduligera																X						X	X	X	X				
Frederickena viridis																	X		X	X	X				X				
Taraba major								X	X	X		X	X	X	X	X	X	X	X	X	X	X	X	X	X	X	?	X	
Sakesphorus bernardi																						X	X						
Sakesphorus canadensis																X	X	X	X	X	X		X		X				
Sakesphorus cristatus																									XR				
Sakesphorus luctuosus																									XR				
Sakesphorus melanonotus																X	X												
Sakesphorus melanothorax																				X	X				X				
Biatas nigropectus																									X			X	
Thamnophilus aethiops																X	X					X	X	X	X				
Thamnophilus amazonicus																X	X		X	X	X	X	X	X	X				

Status: **X** - Breeding species; **XN** - Regular non-breeding species; **XR** - Endemic breeding species; **X?** - Regular species, breeding status uncertain; **XI** - Introduced species; **XD** - Dubious species; **XF** - Formerly bred; **V** - Vagrants; **SX** - Breeding species, sight records only; **SN** - Regular non-breeding species, sight records only; **S?** - Uncertain breeding status; sight records only; **SI** -Introduced; sight records only; **SV** - Vagrant; sight records only. **?** - Occurrence uncertain; **+** - Extinct.

	Baha	Cuba	Hisp	Jama	Puer	Lant	Nant	Mexi	Guat	Beli	Elsa	Hond	Nica	Cost	Pana	Colo	Vene	Trin	Guya	Suri	Fren	Ecua	Peru	Boli	Braz	Parg	Urug	Argn	Chil
Thamnophilus aroyae																							X	X					
Thamnophilus bridgesi														X	X														
Thamnophilus caerulescens																							X	X	X	X	X	X	
Thamnophilus cryptoleucus																X						X	X		X				
Thamnophilus doliatus																													
doliatus								X	X	X	X	X	X	X	X	X	X	X	X	X	X	SX	X	X	X	X		X	
zarumae																						X	X						
Thamnophilus insignis																	X								X				
Thamnophilus multistriatus																X	X												
Thamnophilus murinus																X	X		X	X	X	X	X		X				
Thamnophilus nigriceps															X	X													
Thamnophilus nigrocinereus																X	X				X				X				
Thamnophilus palliatus																X						X	X	X	X				
Thamnophilus praecox																						XR							
Thamnophilus punctatus									X	X		X	X	X	X	X	X		X	X	X	X	X	X	X				
Thamnophilus ruficapillus																							X	X	X	X	X	X	
Thamnophilus schistaceus																X						X	X	X	X				
Thamnophilus torquatus																								X	X				
Thamnophilus unicolor																X						X	X						
Pygiptila stellaris																X	X			X	X	X	X	X	X				
Megastictus margaritatus																X	X					X	X		X				
Neoctantes niger																X						X	X		X				
Clytoctantes alixi																X	X												
Clytoctantes atrogularis																									XR				
Xenornis setifrons															X	X													
Thamnistes anabatinus								X	X	X		X	X	X	X	X	X					X	X	X					
Dysithamnus mentalis								X	X	X		X		X	X	X	X	X				X	X	X	X	X		X	
Dysithamnus puncticeps														X	X	X						X							
Dysithamnus stictothorax																									X			X	
Dysithamnus striaticeps												X	X	X															
Dysithamnus xanthopterus																									XR				
Thamnomanes ardesiacus																X	X		X	X	X	X	X	X	X				
Thamnomanes caesius																X	X		X	X	X	X	X	X	X				
Thamnomanes occidentalis																X						X							
Thamnomanes plumbeus																													
leucostictus																X	X					X	X						
plumbeus																									XR				
Thamnomanes saturninus																							X	X	X				
Thamnomanes schistogynus																							X	X	X				
Myrmotherula ambigua																X	X								X				
Myrmotherula assimilis																SX							X	X	X				
Myrmotherula axillaris								X				X	X	X	X	X	X	X	X	X	X	X	X	X	X				
Myrmotherula behni																X	X		X		SX				X				
Myrmotherula brachyura																													
brachyura																X	X		X	X	X	X	X	X	X				
ignota															X	X													
Myrmotherula cherriei																X	X								X				
Myrmotherula erythronotos																									XR				
Myrmotherula erythrura																X						X	X		X				
Myrmotherula fluminensis																									XR				
Myrmotherula fulviventris												X	X	X	X	X						X							
Myrmotherula grisea																								XR					

Countries: Argn - Argentina; **Baha** - Bahamas; **Beli** - Belize; **Boli** - Bolivia; **Braz** - Brazil; **Chil** - Chile; **Colo** - Colombia; **Cost** - Costa Rica; **Cuba** - Cuba; **Ecua** - Ecuador; **Elsa** - El Salvador; **Fren** - French Guiana; **Guat** - Guatemala; **Guya** - Guyana; **Hisp** - Hispaniola; **Hond** - Honduras; **Jama** - Jamaica; **Lant** - Lesser Antilles; **Mexi** - Mexico; **Nant** - Netherland Antilles; **Nica** - Nicaragua; **Pana** - Panama; **Parg** - Paraguay; **Peru** - Peru; **Puer** - Puerto Rico; **Suri** - Suriname; **Trin** - Trinidad; **Urug** - Uruguay; **Vene** - Venezuela.

	Baha	Cuba	Hisp	Jama	Puer	Lant	Nant	Mexi	Guat	Beli	Elsa	Hond	Nica	Cost	Pana	Colo	Vene	Trin	Guya	Suri	Fren	Ecua	Peru	Boli	Braz	Parg	Urug	Argn	Chil
Myrmotherula gularis																									XR				
Myrmotherula guttata																	X		X	X	X				X				
Myrmotherula gutturalis																	X		X	X	X				X				
Myrmotherula haematonota																													
haematonota																X	X					X	X	X	X				
spodionota																X						X	X						
Myrmotherula hauxwelli																X						X	X	X	X				
Myrmotherula iheringi																							X		X				
Myrmotherula klagesi																									XR				
Myrmotherula leucophthalma																							X	X	X				
Myrmotherula longicauda																X						X	X	X					
Myrmotherula longipennis																X	X		X	X	X	X	X	X	X				
Myrmotherula menetriesii																X	X		X	X	X	X	X	X	X				
Myrmotherula minor																									XR				
Myrmotherula obscura																X						X	X		X				
Myrmotherula ornata																X						X	X	X	X				
Myrmotherula schisticolor								X	X	X		X	X	X	X	X	X					X	X						
Myrmotherula sclateri																							X	X	X				
Myrmotherula sunensis																X						X	X		X				
Myrmotherula surinamensis															X	X	X		X	X	X	X	X	X	X				
Myrmotherula unicolor																									XR				
Myrmotherula urosticta																									XR				
Dichrozona cincta																X	X					X	X	X	X				
Myrmorchilus strigilatus																								X	X	X		X	
Herpsilochmus atricapillus																								X	X	X		X	
Herpsilochmus axillaris																X						X	X						
Herpsilochmus dorsimaculatus																X	X								X				
Herpsilochmus longirostris																								X	X				
Herpsilochmus motacilloides																							XR						
Herpsilochmus parkeri																							XR						
Herpsilochmus pectoralis																									XR				
Herpsilochmus pileatus																									XR				
Herpsilochmus roraimae																	X		X						X				
Herpsilochmus rufimarginatus															X	X	X			SX		X	X	X	X	X		X	
Herpsilochmus stictocephalus																	X		X	X	X				X				
Herpsilochmus sticturus																													
dugandi																X						X	X						
sticturus																	X		X	X	X				X				
Microrhopias quixensis								X	X	X		X	X	X	X	X			X	X	X	X	X	X	X				
Formicivora grisea															X	X	X	X	X	X	X			X	X				
Formicivora iheringi																									XR				
Formicivora melanogaster																								X	X	X			
Formicivora rufa																				X			X	X	X	X			
Formicivora serrana																													
littoralis																									XR				
serrana																									XR				
Drymophila caudata																X	X					X	X	X					
Drymophila devillei																													
devillei																X						X	X	X	X				
subochracea																								X	X				
Drymophila ferruginea																									XR				
Drymophila genei																									XR				

Status: X - Breeding species; **XN** - Regular non-breeding species; **XR** - Endemic breeding species; **X?** - Regular species, breeding status uncertain; **XI** - Introduced species; **XD** - Dubious species; **XF** - Formerly bred; **V** - Vagrants; **SX** - Breeding species, sight records only; **SN** - Regular non-breeding species, sight records only; **S?** - Uncertain breeding status; sight records only; **SI** -Introduced; sight records only; **SV** - Vagrant; sight records only. **?** - Occurrence uncertain; **+** - Extinct.

	Baha	Cuba	Hisp	Jama	Puer	Lant	Nant	Mexi	Guat	Beli	Elsa	Hond	Nica	Cost	Pana	Colo	Vene	Trin	Guya	Suri	Fren	Ecua	Peru	Boli	Braz	Parg	Urug	Argn	Chil
Drymophila malura																									X	X		X	
Drymophila ochropyga																									XR				
Drymophila rubricollis																									X	X		X	
Drymophila squamata																									XR				
Terenura callinota														X	X	X	X		X	X		X	X						
Terenura humeralis																						X	X	X	X				
Terenura maculata																									X	X		X	
Terenura sharpei																							X	X					
Terenura sicki																									XR				
Terenura spodioptila																X	X		X	X	X	SX	X		X				
Cercomacra brasiliana																									XR				
Cercomacra carbonaria																			SX						X				
Cercomacra cinerascens																X	X		X	X	X	X	X	X	X				
Cercomacra ferdinandi																									XR				
Cercomacra laeta																									XR				
Cercomacra manu																							X	X	X				
Cercomacra melanaria																								X	X	X			
Cercomacra nigrescens																X				X	X	X	X	X	X				
Cercomacra nigricans															X	X	X					X							
Cercomacra serva																X						X	X	X	X				
Cercomacra tyrannina								X	X	X		X	X	X	X	X	X		X	X	X	X			X				
Sipia berlepschi																X						X							
Sipia nigricauda																X						X							
Pyriglena atra																									XR				
Pyriglena leuconota																													
castanoptera																X						X	X						
leuconota																							X	X	X	X			
pacifica																						X	X						
Pyriglena leucoptera																									X	X		X	
Rhopornis ardesiaca																									XR				
Myrmoborus leucophrys																X	X		X	X	X	X	X	X	X				
Myrmoborus lugubris																X						X	X		X				
Myrmoborus melanurus																							XR						
Myrmoborus myotherinus																X	X					X	X	X	X				
Hypocnemis cantator																X	X		X	X	X	X	X	X	X				
Hypocnemis hypoxantha																X						X	X		X				
Hypocnemoides maculicauda																							X	X	X				
Hypocnemoides melanopogon																X	X		X	X	X	X	X		X				
Myrmochanes hemileucus																X						X	X	X	X				
Gymnocichla nudiceps									X	X		X	X	X	X	X													
Sclateria naevia																X	X	X	X	X	X	X	X	X	X				
Percnostola caurensis																	X								X				
Percnostola leucostigma																X	X		X	X	X	X	X	X	X				
Percnostola lophotes																							X	X					
Percnostola rufifrons																X	X		X	X	X		X		X				
Percnostola schistacea																X						X	X		X				
Myrmeciza atrothorax																X	X		X	X	X	X	X	X	X				
Myrmeciza disjuncta																X	X												
Myrmeciza exsul													X	X	X	X						X							
Myrmeciza ferruginea																	X		X	X	X				X				
Myrmeciza fortis																X						X	X	X	X				
Myrmeciza goeldii																							X	X	X				

Countries: Argn - Argentina; **Baha** - Bahamas; **Beli** - Belize; **Boli** - Bolivia; **Braz** - Brazil; **Chil** - Chile; **Colo** - Colombia; **Cost** - Costa Rica; **Cuba** - Cuba; **Ecua** - Ecuador; **Elsa** - El Salvador; **Fren** - French Guiana; **Guat** - Guatemala; **Guya** - Guyana; **Hisp** - Hispaniola; **Hond** - Honduras; **Jama** - Jamaica; **Lant** - Lesser Antilles; **Mexi** - Mexico; **Nant** - Netherland Antilles; **Nica** - Nicaragua; **Pana** - Panama; **Parg** - Paraguay; **Peru** - Peru; **Puer** - Puerto Rico; **Suri** - Suriname; **Trin** - Trinidad; **Urug** - Uruguay; **Vene** - Venezuela.

	Baha	Cuba	Hisp	Jama	Puer	Lant	Nant	Mexi	Guat	Beli	Elsa	Hond	Nica	Cost	Pana	Colo	Vene	Trin	Guya	Suri	Fren	Ecua	Peru	Boli	Braz	Parg	Urug	Argn	Chil
Myrmeciza griseiceps																						X	X						
Myrmeciza hemimelaena																X						X	X	X	X				
Myrmeciza hyperythra																X						X	X	X	X				
Myrmeciza immaculata														X	X	X	X					X							
Myrmeciza laemosticta														X	X	X	X												
Myrmeciza longipes															X	X	X	X	X		SX				X				
Myrmeciza loricata																									XR				
Myrmeciza melanoceps																X						X	X		X				
Myrmeciza pelzelni																X	X								X				
Myrmeciza ruficauda																									XR				
Myrmeciza squamosa																									XR				
Pithys albifrons																X	X		X	X	X	X	X		X				
Pithys castanea																							XR						
Gymnopithys leucaspis												X	X	X	X	X						X	X		X				
Gymnopithys lunulata																						X	X						
Gymnopithys rufigula																	X		X	X	X				X				
Gymnopithys salvini																							X	X	X				
Rhegmatorhina berlepschi																									XR				
Rhegmatorhina cristata																X									X				
Rhegmatorhina gymnops																									XR				
Rhegmatorhina hoffmannsi																									XR				
Rhegmatorhina melanosticta																X						X	X	X	X				
Hylophylax naevia																X	X		X	X	X	X	X	X	X				
Hylophylax naevioides												X	X	X	X	X						X							
Hylophylax poecilinota																X	X		X	X	X	X	X	X	X				
Hylophylax punctulata																X	X				SX	X?	X	X	X				
Phlegopsis borbae																									XR				
Phlegopsis erythroptera																X	X					X	X	X	X				
Phlegopsis nigromaculata																X						X	X	X	X				
Phaenostictus mcleannani												X	X	X	X	X						X							
Formicarius analis								X	X	X		X	X	X	X	X	X	X	X	X	X	X	X	X	X				
Formicarius colma																X	X		X	X	X	X	X	X	X				
Formicarius nigricapillus														X	X	X						X							
Formicarius rufifrons																							XR						
Formicarius rufipectus														X	X	X	X					X	X						
Chamaeza campanisona																X	X		X			X	X	X	X	X		X	
Chamaeza meruloides																									XR				
Chamaeza mollissima																X						X	X	X					
Chamaeza nobilis																X						X	X	X	X				
Chamaeza ruficauda																													
ruficauda																									XR				
turdina																X	X												
Myrmornis torquata													X		X	X	X		X	X	X	X	X		X				
Pittasoma michleri														X	X	X													
Pittasoma rufopileatum																X						X							
Grallaria albigula																							X	X				X	
Grallaria alleni																XR													
Grallaria andicola																							X	X					
Grallaria bangsi																XR													
Grallaria blakei																							XR						
Grallaria capitalis																							XR						
Grallaria carrikeri																							XR						

Status: **X** - Breeding species; **XN** - Regular non-breeding species; **XR** - Endemic breeding species; **X?** - Regular species, breeding status uncertain; **XI** - Introduced species; **XD** - Dubious species; **XF** - Formerly bred; **V** - Vagrants; **SX** - Breeding species, sight records only; **SN** - Regular non-breeding species, sight records only; **S?** - Uncertain breeding status; sight records only; **SI** -Introduced; sight records only; **SV** - Vagrant; sight records only. **?** - Occurrence uncertain; **+** - Extinct.

	Baha	Cuba	Hisp	Jama	Puer	Lant	Nant	Mexi	Guat	Beli	Elsa	Hond	Nica	Cost	Pana	Colo	Vene	Trin	Guya	Suri	Fren	Ecua	Peru	Boli	Braz	Parg	Urug	Argn	Chil
Grallaria chthonia																	XR												
Grallaria dignissima																X						X	X						
Grallaria eludens																							X		SX				
Grallaria erythroleuca																							XR						
Grallaria erythrotis																								XR					
Grallaria excelsa																	XR												
Grallaria flavotincta																X						X							
Grallaria gigantea																X						X							
Grallaria griseonucha																	XR												
Grallaria guatimalensis								X	X		X	X	X	X	X	X	X	X				X	X	X	X				
Grallaria haplonota																	X					X	X						
Grallaria hypoleuca																X						X	X						
Grallaria kaestneri																XR													
Grallaria milleri																XR													
Grallaria nuchalis																X						X	X						
Grallaria przewalskii																							XR						
Grallaria quitensis																X						X	X						
Grallaria ruficapilla																													
ruficapilla																X	X					X	X						
watkinsi																						X	X						
Grallaria rufocinerea																XR													
Grallaria rufula																X	X					X	X	X					
Grallaria squamigera																X	X					X	X	X					
Grallaria varia																	X		X	X	X		X		X	X		X	
Hylopezus fulviventris																													
berlepschi																							X	X	X				
dives												X	X	X	X	X													
fulviventris																X						X	X						
Hylopezus macularius																X	X		X	X	X	X	X	X	X				
Hylopezus ochroleucus																													
nattereri																									X	X		X	
ochroleucus																									XR				
Hylopezus perspicillatus												X	X	X	X	X						X							
Myrmothera campanisona																X	X		X	X	X	X	X	X	X				
Myrmothera simplex																	X								X				
Grallaricula cucullata																X	X												
Grallaricula ferrugineipectus																X	X						X	X					
Grallaricula flavirostris														X	X	X						X	X	X					
Grallaricula lineifrons																X						X							
Grallaricula loricata																	XR												
Grallaricula nana																X	X					X	X						
Grallaricula ochraceifrons																							XR						
Grallaricula peruviana																						X	X						
Conopophaga ardesiaca																							X	X					
Conopophaga aurita																X			X	X	X	X	X		X				
Conopophaga castaneiceps																X						X	X						
Conopophaga lineata																													
cearae																									XR				
lineata																									X	X		X	
Conopophaga melanogaster																								X	X				
Conopophaga melanops																									XR				
Conopophaga peruviana																						X	X	X	X				

Countries: Argn - Argentina; **Baha** - Bahamas; **Beli** - Belize; **Boli** - Bolivia; **Braz** - Brazil; **Chil** - Chile; **Colo** - Colombia; **Cost** - Costa Rica; **Cuba** - Cuba; **Ecua** - Ecuador; **Elsa** - El Salvador; **Fren** - French Guiana; **Guat** - Guatemala; **Guya** - Guyana; **Hisp** - Hispaniola; **Hond** - Honduras; **Jama** - Jamaica; **Lant** - Lesser Antilles; **Mexi** - Mexico; **Nant** - Netherland Antilles; **Nica** - Nicaragua; **Pana** - Panama; **Parg** - Paraguay; **Peru** - Peru; **Puer** - Puerto Rico; **Suri** - Suriname; **Trin** - Trinidad; **Urug** - Uruguay; **Vene** - Venezuela.

	Baha	Cuba	Hisp	Jama	Puer	Lant	Nant	Mexi	Guat	Beli	Elsa	Hond	Nica	Cost	Pana	Colo	Vene	Trin	Guya	Suri	Fren	Ecua	Peru	Boli	Braz	Parg	Urug	Argn	Chil
Conopophaga roberti																									XR				
Rhinocryptidae																													
Pteroptochos castaneus																													XR
Pteroptochos megapodius																													XR
Pteroptochos tarnii																												X	X
Scelorchilus albicollis																													XR
Scelorchilus rubecula																												X	X
Rhinocrypta lanceolata																								X		X		X	
Teledromas fuscus																												XR	
Liosceles thoracicus																X						X	X		X				
Melanopareia elegans																						X	X						
Melanopareia maranonica																						X	X						
Melanopareia maximiliani																								X		X		X	
Melanopareia torquata																								X	X	X			
Psilorhamphus guttatus																									X			X	
Merulaxis ater																									XR				
Merulaxis stresemanni																									XR				
Eugralla paradoxa																												X	X
Myornis senilis																X						X	X						
Scytalopus argentifrons														X	X														
Scytalopus femoralis																													
atratus																X	X					X	X	X					
bolivianus																							X	X					
femoralis																X						X	X						
sanctaemariae																XR													
Scytalopus indigoticus																													
indigoticus																									XR				
psychopompas																									XR				
Scytalopus latebricola																													
caracae																	XR												
latebricola																XR													
meridanus																X	X												
spillmanni																						X	X						
sp.nov.																						X	X						
Scytalopus macropus																							XR						
Scytalopus magellanicus																													
acutirostris																							XR						
canus																X						X							
fuscus																												X	X
griseicollis																X	X												
magellanicus																												X	X
simonsi																							X	X					
superciliaris																								X				X	
Scytalopus novacapitalis																									XR				
Scytalopus panamensis															X	X													
Scytalopus speluncae																									XR				
Scytalopus unicolor																													
latrans																X	X					X	X						
parvirostris																							X	X					
unicolor																							XR						
Scytalopus vicinior																X						X							
Scytalopus sp.nov.															X	X						X							

Status: **X** - Breeding species; **XN** - Regular non-breeding species; **XR** - Endemic breeding species; **X?** - Regular species, breeding status uncertain; **XI** - Introduced species; **XD** - Dubious species; **XF** - Formerly bred; **V** - Vagrants; **SX** - Breeding species, sight records only; **SN** - Regular non-breeding species, sight records only; **S?** - Uncertain breeding status; sight records only; **SI** -Introduced; sight records only; **SV** - Vagrant; sight records only. **?** - Occurrence uncertain; **+** - Extinct.

	Baha	Cuba	Hisp	Jama	Puer	Lant	Nant	Mexi	Guat	Beli	Elsa	Hond	Nica	Cost	Pana	Colo	Vene	Trin	Guya	Suri	Fren	Ecua	Peru	Boli	Braz	Parg	Urug	Argn	Chil
Acropternis orthonyx																X	X					X	X						
Tyrannidae																													
Phyllomyias burmeisteri																													
burmeisteri																								X	X	X		X	
leucogonys																X	X		X			X	X						
zeledoni														X	X														
Phyllomyias cinereiceps																X						X	X						
Phyllomyias fasciatus																								X	X	X		X	
Phyllomyias griseiceps															X	X	X		X			X	X		X				
Phyllomyias griseocapilla																									XR				
Phyllomyias nigrocapillus																X	X					X	X						
Phyllomyias plumbeiceps																X						X	X						
Phyllomyias sclateri																							X	X				X	
Phyllomyias uropygialis																X	X					X	X	X					
Phyllomyias virescens																													
reiseri																									X	X			
urichi																	XR												
virescens																									X	X		X	
Zimmerius bolivianus																							X	X					
Zimmerius cinereicapillus																						X	X						
Zimmerius gracilipes																X	X		X	X	X	X	X	X	X				
Zimmerius vilissimus								X	X	X	X	X	X	X	X	X	X												
Zimmerius viridiflavus																													
chrysops																X	X					X	X						
viridiflavus																							XR						
Ornithion brunneicapillum														X	X	X	X					X							
Ornithion inerme																X	X		X	X	X	X	X	X	X				
Ornithion semiflavum								X	X	X		X	X	X															
Camptostoma imberbe								X	X	X	X	X	X	X															
Camptostoma obsoletum														X	X	X	X	X	X	X	X	X	X	X	X	X	X	X	
Phaeomyias murina															X	X	X	X	X	X	X	X	X	X	X	X		X	
Sublegatus modestus																													
arenarum							X							X	X	X	X	X	X	X	X								
modestus																							X	X	X	X	X	X	
obscurior																X	X		X	X	X	X	X	X	X				
Suiriri suiriri																				X				X	X	X	X	X	
Tyrannulus elatus														X	X	X	X		X	X	X	X	X	X	X				
Myiopagis caniceps															X	X	X		X		X	X	X	X	X	X		X	
Myiopagis cotta				XR																									
Myiopagis flavivertex																	X		X	X	X	X	X		X				
Myiopagis gaimardii															X	X	X	X	X	X	X	X	X	X	X				
Myiopagis leucospodia																						X	X						
Myiopagis subplacens																						X	X						
Myiopagis viridicata								X	X	X	X	X	X	X	X	X	X		X			X	X	X	X	X		X	
Elaenia albiceps																X						X	X	X	XN	XN	XN	X	X
Elaenia chiriquensis							X?							X	X	X	X	X	X	X	X	X	X	X	X	X		X	
Elaenia cristata																	X		X	X	X		X	X?	X				
Elaenia dayi																	XR												
Elaenia fallax			X	X																									
Elaenia flavogaster						X		X	X	X	X	X	X	X	X	X	X	X	X	X	X	X	X	X	X	X		X	
Elaenia frantzii									X		X	X	X	X	X	X	X												
Elaenia gigas																X						X	X	X					

Countries: Argn - Argentina; **Baha** - Bahamas; **Beli** - Belize; **Boli** - Bolivia; **Braz** - Brazil; **Chil** - Chile; **Colo** - Colombia; **Cost** - Costa Rica; **Cuba** - Cuba; **Ecua** - Ecuador; **Elsa** - El Salvador; **Fren** - French Guiana; **Guat** - Guatemala; **Guya** - Guyana; **Hisp** - Hispaniola; **Hond** - Honduras; **Jama** - Jamaica; **Lant** - Lesser Antilles; **Mexi** - Mexico; **Nant** - Netherland Antilles; **Nica** - Nicaragua; **Pana** - Panama; **Parg** - Paraguay; **Peru** - Peru; **Puer** - Puerto Rico; **Suri** - Suriname; **Trin** - Trinidad; **Urug** - Uruguay; **Vene** - Venezuela.

	Baha	Cuba	Hisp	Jama	Puer	Lant	Nant	Mexi	Guat	Beli	Elsa	Hond	Nica	Cost	Pana	Colo	Vene	Trin	Guya	Suri	Fren	Ecua	Peru	Boli	Braz	Parg	Urug	Argn	Chil
Elaenia martinica					X	X	X	X		X						X													
Elaenia mesoleuca																									X	X	?	X	
Elaenia obscura																							X	X	X	X		X	
Elaenia pallatangae																X	X		X			X	X	X	X				
Elaenia parvirostris							V									XN	XN	V	XN	XN	XN	XN	XN	X	X	X	X	X	
Elaenia pelzelni																SX							XN	X	X				
Elaenia ridleyana																									XR				
Elaenia ruficeps																X	X		X	X	X				X				
Elaenia spectabilis																XN						XN	XN	X	X	X		X	
Elaenia strepera																XN	XN						XN	X				X	
Mecocerculus calopterus																						X	X						
Mecocerculus hellmayri																							X	X				X	
Mecocerculus leucophrys																X	X					X	X	X	X			X	
Mecocerculus minor																X	X					X	X						
Mecocerculus poecilocercus																X						X	X						
Mecocerculus stictopterus																X	X					X	X	X					
Serpophaga cinerea														X	X	X	X					X	X	X					
Serpophaga hypoleuca																SX	X					X	X	X	X				
Serpophaga munda																								X	X?	X?	X?	X	
Serpophaga nigricans																								X	X	X	X	X	
Serpophaga subcristata																								X	X	X	X	X	
Inezia inornata																							XN	X	X	X		X	
Inezia subflava																X	X		X	X	X			X	X				
Inezia tenuirostris																X	X												
Stigmatura budytoides																								X	X	X		X	
Stigmatura napensis																													
bahiae																									XR				
napensis																SX						X	X		X				
Anairetes agilis																X	X					X							
Anairetes agraphia																							XR						
Anairetes alpinus																							X	X					
Anairetes fernandezianus																													XR
Anairetes flavirostris																							X	X				X	X
Anairetes parulus																X						X	X	X				X	X
Anairetes reguloides																													
nigrocristatus																						SX	X						
reguloides																							X						X
Tachuris rubrigastra																							X	X	X	X	X	X	X
Culicivora caudacuta																								X	X	X		X	
Polystictus pectoralis																X	X		X	X	SX			X	X	X	X	X	
Polystictus superciliaris																									XR				
Pseudocolopteryx acutipennis																X?						X	X?	X		X?		X	
Pseudocolopteryx dinellianus																								XN		XN		XR	
Pseudocolopteryx flaviventris																								X	X	XN	X	X	X
Pseudocolopteryx sclateri																	X	X	X?					X	X	X	?	X	
Euscarthmus meloryphus																X	X					X	X	X	X	X	X	X	
Euscarthmus rufomarginatus																				X				X	X	X			
Mionectes macconnelli																	X		X	X	X		X	X	X				
Mionectes oleagineus								X	X	X	X	X	X	X	X	X	X	X	X	X	X	X	X	X	X				
Mionectes olivaceus														X	X	X	X	X				X	X	X					
Mionectes rufiventris																									X	X		X	
Mionectes striaticollis																X						X	X	X					

Status: **X** - Breeding species; **XN** - Regular non-breeding species; **XR** - Endemic breeding species; **X?** - Regular species, breeding status uncertain; **XI** - Introduced species; **XD** - Dubious species; **XF** - Formerly bred; **V** - Vagrants; **SX** - Breeding species, sight records only; **SN** - Regular non-breeding species, sight records only; **S?** - Uncertain breeding status; sight records only; **SI** -Introduced; sight records only; **SV** - Vagrant; sight records only. **?** - Occurrence uncertain; **+** - Extinct.

	Baha	Cuba	Hisp	Jama	Puer	Lant	Nant	Mexi	Guat	Beli	Elsa	Hond	Nica	Cost	Pana	Colo	Vene	Trin	Guya	Suri	Fren	Ecua	Peru	Boli	Braz	Parg	Urug	Argn	Chil
Leptopogon amaurocephalus								X	X	X		X	X	X	X	X	X		X	X	X	X	X	X	X	X		X	
Leptopogon rufipectus																X	X					X	X						
Leptopogon superciliaris														X	X	X	X	X				X	X	X					
Leptopogon taczanowskii																							XR						
Phylloscartes ceciliae																									XR				
Phylloscartes chapmani																	X								X				
Phylloscartes difficilis																									XR				
Phylloscartes eximius																									X	X		X	
Phylloscartes flaveolus													X	X	X	X	X		X	X	X	X	X	X	X	X		X	
Phylloscartes flaviventris																	XR												
Phylloscartes flavovirens															XR														
Phylloscartes gualaquizae																						X	X						
Phylloscartes kronei																									XR				
Phylloscartes lanyoni																XR													
Phylloscartes nigrifrons																	XR												
Phylloscartes ophthalmicus																X	X					X	X	X					
Phylloscartes orbitalis																X						X	X	X					
Phylloscartes oustaleti																									XR				
Phylloscartes paulistus																									X	X		X	
Phylloscartes poecilotis																X	X					X	X						
Phylloscartes roquettei																									XR				
Phylloscartes superciliaris														X	X	X	X					X	SX						
Phylloscartes sylviolus																									X	X		X	
Phylloscartes venezuelanus																	XR												
Phylloscartes ventralis																							X	X	X	X	X	X	
Phylloscartes virescens																			X	X	X				X				
Phylloscartes sp.nov.																							X	X					
Pseudotriccus pelzelni															X	X						X	X						
Pseudotriccus ruficeps																X						X	X	X					
Pseudotriccus simplex																							X	X					
Corythopis delalandi																								X	X	X		X	
Corythopis torquata																X	X		X	X	X	X	X	X	X				
Myiornis albiventris																							X	X					
Myiornis atricapillus														X	X	X						X							
Myiornis auricularis																									X	X		X	
Myiornis ecaudatus																X	X	X	X	X	SX	X	X	X	X				
Lophotriccus eulophotes																							X	X	X				
Lophotriccus galeatus																X	X		X	X	X				X				
Lophotriccus pileatus														X	X	X	X					X	X						
Lophotriccus vitiosus																X			X	X	X	X	X		X				
Atalotriccus pilaris															X	X	X		X						SX				
Poecilotriccus albifacies																							XR						
Poecilotriccus andrei																	X			X					X				
Poecilotriccus capitalis																X						X	X		X				
Poecilotriccus ruficeps																X	X					X	X						
Poecilotriccus sp.nov.																													
Oncostoma cinereigulare								X	X	X	X	X	X	X	X	?													
Oncostoma olivaceum															X	X													
Hemitriccus cinnamomeipectus																						X	X						
Hemitriccus diops																									X	X		X	
Hemitriccus flammulatus																							X	X	X				
Hemitriccus furcatus																									XR				

Countries: Argn - Argentina; **Baha** - Bahamas; **Beli** - Belize; **Boli** - Bolivia; **Braz** - Brazil; **Chil** - Chile; **Colo** - Colombia; **Cost** - Costa Rica; **Cuba** - Cuba; **Ecua** - Ecuador; **Elsa** - El Salvador; **Fren** - French Guiana; **Guat** - Guatemala; **Guya** - Guyana; **Hisp** - Hispaniola; **Hond** - Honduras; **Jama** - Jamaica; **Lant** - Lesser Antilles; **Mexi** - Mexico; **Nant** - Netherland Antilles; **Nica** - Nicaragua; **Pana** - Panama; **Parg** - Paraguay; **Peru** - Peru; **Puer** - Puerto Rico; **Suri** - Suriname; **Trin** - Trinidad; **Urug** - Uruguay; **Vene** - Venezuela.

	Baha	Cuba	Hisp	Jama	Puer	Lant	Nant	Mexi	Guat	Beli	Elsa	Hond	Nica	Cost	Pana	Colo	Vene	Trin	Guya	Suri	Fren	Ecua	Peru	Boli	Braz	Parg	Urug	Argn	Chil
Hemitriccus granadensis																X	X					X	X	X					
Hemitriccus inornatus																									XR				
Hemitriccus iohannis																X							X	X	X				
Hemitriccus josephinae																			X	X	SX				X				
Hemitriccus kaempferi																									XR				
Hemitriccus margaritaceiventer																X	X						X	X	X	X		X	
Hemitriccus minimus																								X	X				
Hemitriccus minor																	X							X	X				
Hemitriccus mirandae																									XR				
Hemitriccus nidipendulus																									XR				
Hemitriccus obsoletus																									XR				
Hemitriccus orbitatus																									XR				
Hemitriccus rufigularis																						X	X	X					
Hemitriccus spodiops																								XR					
Hemitriccus striaticollis																X							X	X	X				
Hemitriccus zosterops																X	X			X	X	X	X	X	X				
Todirostrum calopterum																													
calopterum																X						X	X						
pulchellum																							XR						
Todirostrum chrysocrotaphum																X	X					X	X	X	X				
Todirostrum cinereum								X	X	X	X	X	X	X	X	X	X		X	X	X	X	X	X	X	X			
Todirostrum fumifrons																				X	X				X				
Todirostrum latirostre																X						X	X	X	X				
Todirostrum maculatum																X	X	X?	X	X	X	X	X	X	X				
Todirostrum nigriceps														X	X	X	X					X							
Todirostrum pictum																	X		X	X	X				X				
Todirostrum plumbeiceps																							X	X	X	X		X	
Todirostrum poliocephalum																									XR				
Todirostrum russatum																	X								X				
Todirostrum senex																									XR				
Todirostrum sylvia								X	X	X		X	X	X	X	X	X		X		X				X				
Todirostrum viridanum																	XR												
Cnipodectes subbrunneus															X	X						X	X	X	X				
Ramphotrigon fuscicauda																X						X	X	X	X				
Ramphotrigon megacephala																X	X					X	X	X	X	X		X	
Ramphotrigon ruficauda																X	X		X	X	X	X	X	X	X				
Rhynchocyclus brevirostris																													
brevirostris								X	X	X	X	X	X	X	X	X													
pacificus																X						X							
Rhynchocyclus fulvipectus																X	X					X	X	X					
Rhynchocyclus olivaceus															X	X	X		X	X	X	X	X	X	X				
Tolmomyias assimilis																													
assimilis																X	X		X	X	X	X	X	X	X				
flavotectus														X	X	X						X							
Tolmomyias flaviventris																													
flaviventris																X	X	X	X	X	X		X	X	X				
viridiceps																X						X	X	X	X				
Tolmomyias poliocephalus																X	X		X	X	X	X	X	X	X				
Tolmomyias sulphurescens								X	X	X	X	X	X	X	X	X	X	X	X	X	X	X	X	X	X	X		X	
Tolmomyias sp.nov.																													
Platyrinchus coronatus												X	X	X	X	X	X		X	X	X	X	X	X	X				
Platyrinchus flavigularis																X	X					X	X						

Status: **X** - Breeding species; **XN** - Regular non-breeding species; **XR** - Endemic breeding species; **X?** - Regular species, breeding status uncertain; **XI** - Introduced species; **XD** - Dubious species; **XF** - Formerly bred; **V** - Vagrants; **SX** - Breeding species, sight records only; **SN** - Regular non-breeding species, sight records only; **S?** - Uncertain breeding status; sight records only; **SI** -Introduced; sight records only; **SV** - Vagrant; sight records only. **?** - Occurrence uncertain; **+** - Extinct.

	Baha	Cuba	Hisp	Jama	Puer	Lant	Nant	Mexi	Guat	Beli	Elsa	Hond	Nica	Cost	Pana	Colo	Vene	Trin	Guya	Suri	Fren	Ecua	Peru	Boli	Braz	Parg	Urug	Argn	Chil
Platyrinchus leucoryphus																									X	X		X	
Platyrinchus mystaceus																													
cancrominus								X	X	X	X	X	X	X	X														
mystaceus														X	X	X	X	X	X		X	X	X	X	X	X		X	
Platyrinchus platyrhynchos																X	X		X	X	X	X	X	X	X				
Platyrinchus saturatus																X	X		X	X	X		X		X				
Onychorhynchus coronatus																													
coronatus																X	X		X	X	X	X	X	X	X				
mexicanus								X	X	X	X	X	X	X	X	X	X												
occidentalis																						X	X						
swainsoni																									XR				
Myiotriccus ornatus																X						X	X						
Terenotriccus erythrurus								X	X	X		X	X	X	X	X	X		X	X	X	X	X	X	X				
Myiobius atricaudus														X	X	X	X					X	X		X				
Myiobius barbatus																X	X		X	X	X	X	X		X				
Myiobius sulphureipygius								X	X	X		X	X	X	X	X						X							
Myiobius villosus															X	X	X					X	X	X					
Myiophobus cryptoxanthus																						X	X						
Myiophobus fasciatus														X	X	X	X	X	X	X	X	X	X	X	X	X	X	X	X
Myiophobus flavicans																X	X					X	X						
Myiophobus inornatus																							X	X					
Myiophobus lintoni																						X	X						
Myiophobus ochraceiventris																							X	X					
Myiophobus phoenicomitra																X						X	X						
Myiophobus pulcher																X						X	X						
Myiophobus roraimae																X	X		X			X	X		X				
Aphanotriccus audax															X	X													
Aphanotriccus capitalis													X	X															
Xenotriccus callizonus								X	X		X																		
Xenotriccus mexicanus								XR																					
Pyrrhomyias cinnamomea																X	X					X	X	X				X	
Mitrephanes olivaceus																							X	X					
Mitrephanes phaeocercus								X	X		X	X	X	X	X	X						X							
Contopus albogularis																				X	X				X				
Contopus borealis							V	X	XN	XN	XN	XN	XN	XN	XN	XN	XN	XN	SV	V	XN	XN	XN	XN	XN				
Contopus caribaeus	X	X	X	X	V																								
Contopus cinereus								X	X	X	X	X	X	X	X	X	X	X	X	X	X	X	X	X	X	X		X	
Contopus fumigatus																X	X		X			X	X	X				X	
Contopus latirostris					X	X																							
Contopus lugubris														X	X														
Contopus nigrescens																			X			X	X		X				
Contopus ochraceus														X	X														
Contopus pertinax								X	X	X	X	X	X																
Contopus sordidulus		V		V				X	X	V	XN	XN	X?	XN	XN	XN	XN					XN	XN	XN					
Contopus virens	XN	XN		XN			SV	XN	XN	XN	XN	XN	XN	XN	XN	XN	XN				SV	XN	XN	XN	XN			XN	
Empidonax affinis								X	XN																				
Empidonax albigularis								X	X	X	X	X	X	X	X														
Empidonax alnorum		V						XN	XN	XN	?	SN	?	XN	XN	XN	XN					XN	XN	XN	XN			XN	
Empidonax atriceps														X	X														
Empidonax difficilis								X																					
Empidonax euleri						X										X	X	X		X	X	X	X	X	X	X	X	X	
Empidonax flavescens								X	X		X	X	X	X	X														

Countries: Argn - Argentina; **Baha** - Bahamas; **Beli** - Belize; **Boli** - Bolivia; **Braz** - Brazil; **Chil** - Chile; **Colo** - Colombia; **Cost** - Costa Rica; **Cuba** - Cuba; **Ecua** - Ecuador; **Elsa** - El Salvador; **Fren** - French Guiana; **Guat** - Guatemala; **Guya** - Guyana; **Hisp** - Hispaniola; **Hond** - Honduras; **Jama** - Jamaica; **Lant** - Lesser Antilles; **Mexi** - Mexico; **Nant** - Netherland Antilles; **Nica** - Nicaragua; **Pana** - Panama; **Parg** - Paraguay; **Peru** - Peru; **Puer** - Puerto Rico; **Suri** - Suriname; **Trin** - Trinidad; **Urug** - Uruguay; **Vene** - Venezuela.

	Baha	Cuba	Hisp	Jama	Puer	Lant	Nant	Mexi	Guat	Beli	Elsa	Hond	Nica	Cost	Pana	Colo	Vene	Trin	Guya	Suri	Fren	Ecua	Peru	Boli	Braz	Parg	Urug	Argn	Chil
Empidonax flaviventris		V						XN	XN	XN	XN	XN	XN	XN	XN														
Empidonax fulvifrons								X	X		X	X																	
Empidonax griseipectus																						X	X						
Empidonax hammondii								XN	XN		XN	XN	XN																
Empidonax minimus	V			V				XN	XN	XN	XN	XN	XN	XN	XN														
Empidonax oberholseri								X?	V																				
Empidonax occidentalis								X																					
Empidonax traillii		?		?				XF	XN	XN	XN	XN	XN	XN	XN	XN						?							
Empidonax virescens	XN	V						XN	XN	XN		XN	XN	XN	XN	XN	XN					XN							
Empidonax wrightii								XN																					
Nesotriccus ridgwayi														XR															
Cnemotriccus fuscatus																X	X	X	X	X	X	X	X	X	X	X		X	
Sayornis nigricans								X	X	X	X	X	X	X	X	X	X					X	X	X				X	
Sayornis phoebe	XN	V						XN		V?																			
Sayornis saya								X																					
Pyrocephalus rubinus							V	X	X	X		X	X		V	X	X		X			X	X	X	X	X	X	X	X
Ochthoeca cinnamomeiventris																X	X					X	X	X					
Ochthoeca diadema																X	X					X	X						
Ochthoeca frontalis																X						X	X	X					
Ochthoeca fumicolor																X	X					X	X	X					
Ochthoeca jelskii																						X	X						
Ochthoeca leucophrys																							X	X				X	X
Ochthoeca littoralis																X	X		X		X	X	X	X	X				
Ochthoeca oenanthoides																							X	X				X	X
Ochthoeca parvirostris																												X	X
Ochthoeca piurae																							XR						
Ochthoeca pulchella																							X	X					
Ochthoeca rufipectoralis																X	X					X	X	X					
Myiotheretes erythropygius																X						X	X	X					
Myiotheretes fumigatus																X	X					X	X						
Myiotheretes fuscorufus																							X	X					
Myiotheretes pernix																XR													
Myiotheretes rufipennis																							X	X				SX	
Myiotheretes striaticollis																X	X					X	X	X				X	
Xolmis cinerea																				X			X	X	X	X	X	X	
Xolmis coronata																								XN	XN	XN	XN	XR	
Xolmis dominicana																									X	X	X	X	
Xolmis irupero																								X	X	X	X	X	
Xolmis pyrope																												X	X
Xolmis velata																								X	X	X			
Neoxolmis rubetra																											V	XR	
Neoxolmis rufiventris																									XN		XN	X	X
Agriornis andicola																						X	X	X				X	X
Agriornis livida																												X	X
Agriornis microptera																							X	X		X		X	X
Agriornis montana																X						X	X	X				X	X
Agriornis murina																								XN		XN		X	
Muscisaxicola albifrons																							X	X					X
Muscisaxicola albilora																V						XN	XN	XN				X	X
Muscisaxicola alpina																X						X	X	X					
Muscisaxicola capistrata																							XN	XN				X	X
Muscisaxicola cinerea																							X?	X				X	X

Status: **X** - Breeding species; **XN** - Regular non-breeding species; **XR** - Endemic breeding species; **X?** - Regular species, breeding status uncertain; **XI** - Introduced species; **XD** - Dubious species; **XF** - Formerly bred; **V** - Vagrants; **SX** - Breeding species, sight records only; **SN** - Regular non-breeding species, sight records only; **S?** - Uncertain breeding status; sight records only; **SI** -Introduced; sight records only; **SV** - Vagrant; sight records only. ? - Occurrence uncertain; + -- - Extinct.

	Baha	Cuba	Hisp	Jama	Puer	Lant	Nant	Mexi	Guat	Beli	Elsa	Hond	Nica	Cost	Pana	Colo	Vene	Trin	Guya	Suri	Fren	Ecua	Peru	Boli	Braz	Parg	Urug	Argn	Chil
Muscisaxicola flavinucha																							XN	XN				X	X
Muscisaxicola fluviatilis																X?						X?	X	X	X			?	
Muscisaxicola frontalis																							XN	XN				X	X
Muscisaxicola juninensis																							X	X				X	X
Muscisaxicola macloviana																						SV	XN				XN	X	X
Muscisaxicola maculirostris																X						X	X	X				X	X
Muscisaxicola rufivertex																							X	X				X	X
Lessonia oreas																							X	X				X	X
Lessonia rufa																								XN	XN	XN	XN	X	X
Knipolegus aterrimus																													
aterrimus																							X	X		XN		X	
franciscanus																									XR				
Knipolegus cyanirostris																									X	X	X	X	
Knipolegus hudsoni																								XN	XN	XN		XR	
Knipolegus lophotes																									X		X		
Knipolegus nigerrimus																									XR				
Knipolegus orenocensis																X	X					X	X		X				
Knipolegus poecilocercus																X	X		X			X	X		X				
Knipolegus poecilurus																X	X					X	X	X	X				
Knipolegus signatus																													
cabanisi																							X	X				X	
signatus																							XR						
Knipolegus striaticeps																								XN	XN	X		X	
Hymenops perspicillata																							V	XN	X	X?	X	X	X
Fluvicola nengeta																													
atripennis																						X	X						
nengeta																									XR				
Fluvicola leucocephala																X	X	X	X	X	X	SX	X	X	X	X		X	
Fluvicola pica																													
albiventer																							XN	X	X	X	X	X	
pica															X	X	X	X	X	X	X	S?			X				
Colonia colonus												X	X	X	X	X	X		X	X	X	X	X	X	X	X		X	
Alectrurus risorus																									X	X	X	X	
Alectrurus tricolor																								X	X	X		X	
Gubernetes yetapa																								X	X	X		X	
Satrapa icterophrys																	X						XN	X	X	X	X	X	
Tumbezia salvini																							XR						
Muscigralla brevicauda																						X	X						SX
Hirundinea ferruginea																													
bellicosa																								X	X	X	X	X	SV
ferruginea																X	X		X	X	X	X	X						
Machetornis rixosus															SV	X	X							X	X	X	X	X	
Muscipipra vetula																									X	X		X	
Attila bolivianus																X							X	X	X				
Attila cinnamomeus																X	X		X	X	X	X	X	X	X				
Attila citriniventris																X	X					X	X		X				
Attila phoenicurus																	XN							X?	X	X?		X	
Attila rufus																									XR				
Attila spadiceus								X	X	X	X	X	X	X	X	X	X	X	X	X	X	X	X	X	X				
Attila torridus																X						X	SX						
Casiornis fusca																									XR				
Casiornis rufa																							XN	X	X	X		X	

Countries: Argn - Argentina; **Baha** - Bahamas; **Beli** - Belize; **Boli** - Bolivia; **Braz** - Brazil; **Chil** - Chile; **Colo** - Colombia; **Cost** - Costa Rica; **Cuba** - Cuba; **Ecua** - Ecuador; **Elsa** - El Salvador; **Fren** - French Guiana; **Guat** - Guatemala; **Guya** - Guyana; **Hisp** - Hispaniola; **Hond** - Honduras; **Jama** - Jamaica; **Lant** - Lesser Antilles; **Mexi** - Mexico; **Nant** - Netherland Antilles; **Nica** - Nicaragua; **Pana** - Panama; **Parg** - Paraguay; **Peru** - Peru; **Puer** - Puerto Rico; **Suri** - Suriname; **Trin** - Trinidad; **Urug** - Uruguay; **Vene** - Venezuela.

	Baha	Cuba	Hisp	Jama	Puer	Lant	Nant	Mexi	Guat	Beli	Elsa	Hond	Nica	Cost	Pana	Colo	Vene	Trin	Guya	Suri	Fren	Ecua	Peru	Boli	Braz	Parg	Urug	Argn	Chil
Rhytipterna holerythra								X	X	X		X	X	X	X	X						X							
Rhytipterna immunda																X	X			X	X				X				
Rhytipterna simplex																X	X		X	X	X	X	X	X	X				
Laniocera hypopyrra																X	X		X	X	X	X	X	X	X				
Laniocera rufescens								X	X	X		X	X	X	X	X						X							
Sirystes sibilator															X	X	X		X	X	X	X	X	X	X	X		X	
Myiarchus antillarum					XR																								
Myiarchus apicalis																XR													
Myiarchus barbirostris				XR																									
Myiarchus cephalotes																X	X					X	X	X					
Myiarchus cinerascens								X	XN		XN	XN	XN																
Myiarchus crinitus	XN	XN	SV		V			XN	XN	XN	XN	XN	XN	XN	XN	XN	XN					SN	SV						
Myiarchus ferox																X	X		X	X	X	X	X	X	X	X		X	
Myiarchus magnirostris																						XR							
Myiarchus nugator						XR																							
Myiarchus nuttingi								X	X		X	X	X	X															
Myiarchus oberi						XR																							
Myiarchus panamensis														X	X	X	X												
Myiarchus phaeocephalus																						X	X						
Myiarchus sagrae	X	X																											
Myiarchus semirufus																							XR						
Myiarchus stolidus			X	X																									
Myiarchus swainsoni																XN	X	XN	X	X	X	XN	X	X	X	X	X	X	
Myiarchus tuberculifer								X	X	X	X	X	X	X	X	X	X	X	X	X	X	X	X	X	X			X	
Myiarchus tyrannulus						X	X	X	X	X	X	X	X	X		X	X	X	X	X	X		X	X	X	X		X	
Myiarchus validus				XR																									
Myiarchus venezuelensis																X	X	X											
Myiarchus yucatanensis								X	X	X																			
Deltarhynchus flammulatus								XR																					
Pitangus lictor															X	X	X		X	X	X	X	X	X	X				
Pitangus sulphuratus								X	X	X	X	X	X	X	X	X	X	X	X	X	X	X	X	X	X	X	X	X	XN
Megarynchus pitangua								X	X	X	X	X	X	X	X	X	X	X	X	X	X	X	X	X	X	X		X	
Myiozetetes cayanensis															X	X	X		X	X	X	X	X	X	X				
Myiozetetes granadensis												X	X	X	X	X	X					X	X	X	X				
Myiozetetes luteiventris																X	X			X	X	X	X	X	X				
Myiozetetes similis								X	X	X	X	X	X	X	X	X	X				X	X	X	X	X	X		X	
Conopias albovittata																													
albovittata												X		X	X	X						X							
parva																X	X		X	X	X	X	X		X				
Conopias cinchoneti																X	X					X	X						
Conopias inornatus																	XR												
Conopias trivirgata																	X					X	X	X	X	X		X	
Myiodynastes bairdi																						X	X						
Myiodynastes chrysocephalus															X	X	X					X	X	X				SX	
Myiodynastes hemichrysus														X	X														
Myiodynastes luteiventris								X	X	X	X	X	X	X	XN	XN						XN	XN	XN	SN				
Myiodynastes maculatus																													
maculatus								X	X	X		X	X?	X	X	X	X	X	X	X	X	X	X		X				
solitarius																XN	XN		XN	XN	XN	XN	X	X	X	X	X	X	V
Legatus leucophaius								X	X	X		X	X	X	X	X	X	X	X	X	X	X	X	X	X	X	?	X	
Empidonomus aurantioatrocristatus																XN	XN					XN	XN	XN	X	X	X	X	
Empidonomus varius																XN	X	XN	X	X	X	XN	XN	X	X	X		X	

Status: **X** - Breeding species; **XN** - Regular non-breeding species; **XR** - Endemic breeding species; **X?** - Regular species, breeding status uncertain; **XI** - Introduced species; **XD** - Dubious species; **XF** - Formerly bred; **V** - Vagrants; **SX** - Breeding species, sight records only; **SN** - Regular non-breeding species, sight records only; **S?** - Uncertain breeding status; sight records only; **SI** -Introduced; sight records only; **SV** - Vagrant; sight records only. **?** - Occurrence uncertain; **+** -- - Extinct.

	Baha	Cuba	Hisp	Jama	Puer	Lant	Nant	Mexi	Guat	Beli	Elsa	Hond	Nica	Cost	Pana	Colo	Vene	Trin	Guya	Suri	Fren	Ecua	Peru	Boli	Braz	Parg	Urug	Argn	Chil
Tyrannopsis sulphurea																X	X	X	X	X	X	X	X	X	X				
Tyrannus albogularis																SN	X		X	X	X	XN	XN	X	X				
Tyrannus caudifasciatus	X	X	X	X	X																								
Tyrannus couchii								X	X	X																			
Tyrannus crassirostris								X	V																				
Tyrannus cubensis	XN	XR																											
Tyrannus dominicensis	X	X	X	X	X	X	X	XN		X?		V	V	XN	XN	X?	X	X	XN	XN	XN				SV				
Tyrannus forficatus	V	V			V			X	XN	XN	XN	XN	XN	XN	XN														
Tyrannus melancholicus		V				X	X	X	X	X	X	X	X	X	X	X	X	X	X	X	X	X	X	X	X	X	X	X	SV
Tyrannus niveigularis																X						X	X						
Tyrannus savana		XN				V	XN	X	X	X		X	X	X	X	X	X	XN	X?	XN	XN	XN	XN	X	X	X	X	X	V
Tyrannus tyrannus	XN	XN		XN	V		V	XN	XN	XN	SN	XN	XN	XN	XN	XN	XN		XN	XN		XN	XN	XN	XN	XN		XN	XN
Tyrannus verticalis	XN							X	XN	SN	XN	XN	XN	XN															
Tyrannus vociferans								X	XN	SV		V																	
Xenopsaris albinucha																	X							X	X	X		X	
Pachyramphus aglaiae								X	X	X	X	X	X	X	SV														
Pachyramphus albogriseus														X	X	X	X					X	X						
Pachyramphus castaneus																X	X					X	X	X	X	X		X	
Pachyramphus cinnamomeus								X	X	X		X	X	X	X	X	X					X							
Pachyramphus homochrous															X	X	X					X	X						
Pachyramphus major								X	X	X	X	X	X																
Pachyramphus marginatus																X	X		X	X	X	X	X	X	X				
Pachyramphus minor																X	X		X	X	X	X	X	X	X				
Pachyramphus niger				XR																									
Pachyramphus polychopterus									X	X		X	X	X	X	X	X	X	X	X	X	X	X	X	X	X	X	X	
Pachyramphus rufus															X	X	X		X	X	X	X	X		X				
Pachyramphus spodiurus																						X	X						
Pachyramphus surinamus																				X	X				X				
Pachyramphus validus																							X	X	X	X		X	
Pachyramphus versicolor														X	X	X	X					X	X	X					
Pachyramphus viridis																	X		X			X	X	X	X	X	X	X	
Tityra cayana																X	X	X	X	X	X	X	X	X	X	X		X	
Tityra inquisitor								X	X	X		X	X	X	X	X	X		X	X	X	X	X	X	X	X		X	
Tityra semifasciata								X	X	X	X	X	X	X	X	X	X				X	X	X	X	X				
Pipridae																													
Schiffornis major																X	X					X	X	X	X				
Schiffornis turdinus								X	X	X		X	X	X	X	X	X		X	X	X	X	X	X	X				
Schiffornis virescens																									X	X		X	
Sapayoa aenigma															X	X						X							
Piprites chloris																X	X		X	X	X	X	X	X	X	X		X	
Piprites griseiceps									X			X	X	X															
Piprites pileatus																									X			X	
Neopipo cinnamomea																X	X		X	X	X	X	X		X				
Chloropipo flavicapilla																X						X							
Chloropipo holochlora															X	X						X	X						
Chloropipo unicolor																						X	X						
Chloropipo uniformis																	X		X						X				
Xenopipo atronitens																X	X		X	X	X		X	X	X				
Antilophia galeata																								X	X	X			
Tyranneutes stolzmanni																X	X					X	X	X	X				
Tyranneutes virescens																	X		X	X	X				X				

Countries: Argn - Argentina; **Baha** - Bahamas; **Beli** - Belize; **Boli** - Bolivia; **Braz** - Brazil; **Chil** - Chile; **Colo** - Colombia; **Cost** - Costa Rica; **Cuba** - Cuba; **Ecua** - Ecuador; **Elsa** - El Salvador; **Fren** - French Guiana; **Guat** - Guatemala; **Guya** - Guyana; **Hisp** - Hispaniola; **Hond** - Honduras; **Jama** - Jamaica; **Lant** - Lesser Antilles; **Mexi** - Mexico; **Nant** - Netherland Antilles; **Nica** - Nicaragua; **Pana** - Panama; **Parg** - Paraguay; **Peru** - Peru; **Puer** - Puerto Rico; **Suri** - Suriname; **Trin** - Trinidad; **Urug** - Uruguay; **Vene** - Venezuela.

	Baha	Cuba	Hisp	Jama	Puer	Lant	Nant	Mexi	Guat	Beli	Elsa	Hond	Nica	Cost	Pana	Colo	Vene	Trin	Guya	Suri	Fren	Ecua	Peru	Boli	Braz	Parg	Urug	Argn	Chil
Neopelma aurifrons																													
aurifrons																									XR				
chrysolophum																									XR				
Neopelma chrysocephalum																X	X		X	X	X				X				
Neopelma pallescens																								X	X				
Neopelma sulphureiventer																							X	X	X				
Heterocercus aurantiivertex																						X	X						
Heterocercus flavivertex																X	X								X				
Heterocercus linteatus																							X	X	X				
Machaeropterus deliciosus																X						X							
Machaeropterus pyrocephalus																	X						X	X	X				
Machaeropterus regulus																X	X					X	X		X				
Manacus candei								X	X	X		X	X	X	X														
Manacus manacus																X	X	X	X	X	X	X	X	X	X	X		X	
Manacus vitellinus														X	X	X													
Corapipo gutturalis																	X		X	X	X				X				
Corapipo leucorrhoa												X	X	X	X	X	X												
Ilicura militaris																									XR				
Masius chrysopterus																X	X					X	X						
Chiroxiphia caudata																									X	X		X	
Chiroxiphia lanceolata														X	X	X	X												
Chiroxiphia linearis								X	X		X	X	X	X															
Chiroxiphia pareola																													
boliviana																							X	X					
pareola																X	X	X	X	X	X	X	X	X	X				
Pipra aureola																	X		X	X	X				X				
Pipra chloromeros																							X	X					
Pipra coeruleocapilla																							XR						
Pipra cornuta																	X		X						X				
Pipra coronota														X	X	X	X					X	X	X	X				
Pipra erythrocephala															X	X	X	X	X	X	X	X	X		X				
Pipra fasciicauda																							X	X	X	X		X	
Pipra filicauda																X	X					X	X		X				
Pipra iris																									XR				
Pipra isidorei																X						X	X						
Pipra mentalis								X	X	X		X	X	X	X	X						X							
Pipra nattereri																								X	X				
Pipra pipra														X	X	X	X		X	X	X	X	X		X				
Pipra rubrocapilla																							X	X	X				
Pipra serena																													
serena																			X	X	X				X				
suavissima																	X		X						X				
Pipra vilasboasi																									XR				
Cotingidae																													
Phoenicircus carnifex																	X		X	X	X				X				
Phoenicircus nigricollis																X	X					X	X		X				
Laniisoma elegans																X	X					X	X	X	X				
Phibalura flavirostris																								X	X	X		X	
Tijuca atra																									XR				
Tijuca condita																									XR				
Carpornis cucullatus																									XR				
Carpornis melanocephalus																									XR				

Status: X - Breeding species; **XN** - Regular non-breeding species; **XR** - Endemic breeding species; **X?** - Regular species, breeding status uncertain; **XI** - Introduced species; **XD** - Dubious species; **XF** - Formerly bred; **V** - Vagrants; **SX** - Breeding species, sight records only; **SN** - Regular non-breeding species, sight records only; **S?** - Uncertain breeding status; sight records only; **SI** -Introduced; sight records only; **SV** - Vagrant; sight records only. **?** - Occurrence uncertain; + -- - Extinct.

	Baha	Cuba	Hisp	Jama	Puer	Lant	Nant	Mexi	Guat	Beli	Elsa	Hond	Nica	Cost	Pana	Colo	Vene	Trin	Guya	Suri	Fren	Ecua	Peru	Boli	Braz	Parg	Urug	Argn	Chil
Ampelion remseni																SX						X	X						
Ampelion rubrocristatus																X	X					X	X	X					
Ampelion rufaxilla																X						X	X	X					
Ampelion sclateri																							XR						
Ampelion stresemanni																							XR						
Pipreola arcuata																X	X					X	X	X					
Pipreola aureopectus																X	X												
Pipreola chlorolepidota																X						X	X						
Pipreola formosa																	XR												
Pipreola frontalis																						X	X	X					
Pipreola intermedia																							X	X					
Pipreola jucunda																X						X							
Pipreola lubomirskii																X						X	X						
Pipreola pulchra																							XR						
Pipreola riefferii																X	X					X	X						
Pipreola whitelyi																	X		X										
Ampelioides tschudii																X	X					X	X	X					
Iodopleura fusca																	X		X	X	X				SX				
Iodopleura isabellae																X	X					X	X	X	X				
Iodopleura pipra																			?						X				
Calyptura cristata																									XR				
Lipaugus cryptolophus																X						X	X						
Lipaugus fuscocinereus																X						X	X						
Lipaugus lanioides																									XR				
Lipaugus streptophorus																	X		X						X				
Lipaugus subalaris																X						X	X						
Lipaugus unirufus								X	X	X		X	X	X	X	X						X							
Lipaugus vociferans																X	X		X	X	X	X	X	X	X				
Chirocylla uropygialis																							X	X					
Porphyrolaema porphyrolaema																X						X	X		X				
Cotinga amabilis								X	X	X		X	X	X															
Cotinga cayana																X	X		X	X	X	X	X	X	X				
Cotinga cotinga																X	X		X	X	X		S?		X				
Cotinga maculata																									XR				
Cotinga maynana																X						X	X	X	X				
Cotinga nattererii															X	X	X					X							
Cotinga ridgwayi														X	X														
Xipholena atropurpurea																									XR				
Xipholena lamellipennis																									XR				
Xipholena punicea																X	X		X	X	X	X		X	X				
Carpodectes antoniae														X	X														
Carpodectes hopkei															X	X						X							
Carpodectes nitidus												X	X	X	X														
Conioptilon mcilhennyi																							XR						
Gymnoderus foetidus																X	X		X	X	X	X	X	X	X				
Haematoderus militaris																			X	X	X				X				
Querula purpurata														X	X	X	X		X	X	X	X	X	X	X				
Pyroderus scutatus																													
granadensis																X	X		X			X	X						
scutatus																									X	X		X	
Cephalopterus glabricollis														X	X														
Cephalopterus ornatus																X	X		X			X	X	X	X				

Countries: Argn - Argentina; **Baha** - Bahamas; **Beli** - Belize; **Boli** - Bolivia; **Braz** - Brazil; **Chil** - Chile; **Colo** - Colombia; **Cost** - Costa Rica; **Cuba** - Cuba; **Ecua** - Ecuador; **Elsa** - El Salvador; **Fren** - French Guiana; **Guat** - Guatemala; **Guya** - Guyana; **Hisp** - Hispaniola; **Hond** - Honduras; **Jama** - Jamaica; **Lant** - Lesser Antilles; **Mexi** - Mexico; **Nant** - Netherland Antilles; **Nica** - Nicaragua; **Pana** - Panama; **Parg** - Paraguay; **Peru** - Peru; **Puer** - Puerto Rico; **Suri** - Suriname; **Trin** - Trinidad; **Urug** - Uruguay; **Vene** - Venezuela.

	Baha	Cuba	Hisp	Jama	Puer	Lant	Nant	Mexi	Guat	Beli	Elsa	Hond	Nica	Cost	Pana	Colo	Vene	Trin	Guya	Suri	Fren	Ecua	Peru	Boli	Braz	Parg	Urug	Argn	Chil
Cephalopterus penduliger																X						X							
Perissocephalus tricolor																SX	X		X	X	X				X				
Procnias alba																	X	X	X	X	X				X				
Procnias averano																X	X	X	X						X				
Procnias nudicollis																									X	X		X	
Procnias tricarunculata												X	X	X	X														
Rupicola peruviana																X	X					X	X	X					
Rupicola rupicola																X	X		X	X	X				X				
Oxyruncidae																													
Oxyruncus cristatus														X	X		X		X	X	X		X	SX	X	X		SX	
Phytotomidae																													
Phytotoma raimondii																							XR						
Phytotoma rara																												X	X
Phytotoma rutila																								X	V	X	X	X	
Alaudidae																													
Eremophila alpestris								X								X													
Hirundinidae																													
Tachycineta albilinea								X	X	X	X	X		X	X								X						
Tachycineta albiventer							SV									X	X	X	X	X	X	X	X	X	X	X		X	
Tachycineta bicolor	XN	XN	XN	XN	XN			XN	XN	XN		XN	XN	XN	XN	XN	V		SV		SV								
Tachycineta leucopyga																							SN	V	XN	XN	XN	X	X
Tachycineta leucorrhoa																							XN	X	X	X	X	X	
Tachycineta thalassina								X	XN		XN	XN		XN	XN	SV													
Callichelidon cyaneoviridis	X	XN																											
Kalochelidon euchrysea			X	X																									
Progne chalybea								X	X	X	X	X	X	X	X	X	X	X	X	X	X	X	X	X	X	X	X	X	
Progne cryptoleuca		XR					V																						
Progne dominicensis	V		X	X	X	X	XN											X	SV										
Progne modesta																													
elegans															V	SN				XN			XN	X	XN		X	X	V
modesta																						XR							
murphyi																							XR						V
Progne sinaloae								X	V																				
Progne subis	XN	XN	V		SV		XN	X	XN	XN		XN	XN	XN	XN	XN	XN		XN	XN		XN	XN	XN	XN	XN		XN	
Progne tapera					V									SN	XN	X	X		X	X	X	X	X	X	X	X	X	X	
Notiochelidon cyanoleuca								V					V	X	X	X	X	X	X	X	X?	X	X	X	X	X	X	X	X
Notiochelidon flavipes																X	X					SX	X	X					
Notiochelidon murina																X	X					X	X	X					
Notiochelidon pileata								X	X		X	XN																	
Atticora fasciata																X	X		X	X	X	X	X	X	X				
Atticora melanoleuca																X	X		X	X	X				X			X	
Neochelidon tibialis															X	X	X			X	X	X	X	X	X				
Alopochelidon fucata																XN	X						XN	X	X	X	X	X	
Stelgidopteryx ruficollis												X	X	X	X	X	X	X	X	X	X	X	X	X	X	X	X	X	
Stelgidopteryx serripennis	XN	XN		XN	XN		SV	X	X	X	X	X	X	X	XN														
Riparia riparia	XN	XN	XN	XN	XN	XN	XN	X	XN	XN	XN	XN	XN	XN	XN	XN	XN	XN	XN	XN	XN	XN	XN	XN	XN	XN	XN	XN	XN
Hirundo rustica	XN	XN	XN	XN	XN	XN	XN	X	XN	XN	XN	XN	XN	XN	XN	XN	XN	XN	XN	XN	XN	XN	XN	XN	XN	XN	XN	XN	XN
Petrochelidon andecola																							X	X					X
Petrochelidon fulva																													
fulva		X	X	X	X		V	X		X					SV														
ruficollis																						X	X						
Petrochelidon pyrrhonota	XN	XN	V		XN	XN	XN	X	XN	XN	XN	XN	XN	XN	XN	XN	XN	SV				XN	XN	XN	XN	XN	XN	XN	XN

Status: **X** - Breeding species; **XN** - Regular non-breeding species; **XR** - Endemic breeding species; **X?** - Regular species, breeding status uncertain; **XI** - Introduced species; **XD** - Dubious species; **XF** - Formerly bred; **V** - Vagrants; **SX** - Breeding species, sight records only; **SN** - Regular non-breeding species, sight records only; **S?** - Uncertain breeding status; sight records only; **SI** -Introduced; sight records only; **SV** - Vagrant; sight records only. **?** - Occurrence uncertain; **+** --- Extinct.

	Baha	Cuba	Hisp	Jama	Puer	Lant	Nant	Mexi	Guat	Beli	Elsa	Hond	Nica	Cost	Pana	Colo	Vene	Trin	Guya	Suri	Fren	Ecua	Peru	Boli	Braz	Parg	Urug	Argn	Chil
Motacillidae																													
Motacilla alba						SV		V										V											
Anthus bogotensis																X	X					X	X	X				X	
Anthus cervinus								V																					
Anthus chacoensis																										X?		X	
Anthus correndera																							X	X	X	X	X	X	X
Anthus furcatus																							X	X	X	XN	X	X	
Anthus hellmayri																							X	X	X		X	X	X
Anthus lutescens															X	X	X		X	X	X		X	X	X	X	X	X	X
Anthus nattereri																									X	X		X	
Anthus rubescens	XN			SV				XN	XN		V	V																	
Anthus spragueii								XN																					
Laniidae																													
Lanius ludovicianus	XN							X																					
Bombycillidae																													
Ptilogonys caudatus														X	X														
Ptilogonys cinereus								X	X																				
Phainopepla nitens								X																					
Phainoptila melanoxantha														X	X														
Bombycilla cedrorum	XN	XN	XN	XN	V	V	V	XN	XN	XN	XN	XN	XN	XN	XN	V	V												
Dulidae																													
Dulus dominicus			XR																										
Cinclidae																													
Cinclus leucocephalus																X	X					X	X	X					
Cinclus mexicanus								X	X			X	X	X	X														
Cinclus schulzi																								X				X	
Troglodytidae																													
Donacobius atricapillus															X	X	X		X	X	X	X	X	X	X	X		X	
Campylorhynchus albobrunneus															X	X													
Campylorhynchus brunneicapillus								X																					
Campylorhynchus chiapensis								XR																					
Campylorhynchus fasciatus																						X	X						
Campylorhynchus griseus																X	X		X						X				
Campylorhynchus gularis								XR																					
Campylorhynchus jocosus								XR																					
Campylorhynchus megalopterus								XR																					
Campylorhynchus nuchalis																X	X												
Campylorhynchus rufinucha								X	X		X	X	X	X															
Campylorhynchus turdinus																X						X	X	X	X	X		X	
Campylorhynchus yucatanicus								XR																					
Campylorhynchus zonatus								X	X	X	X	X	X	X	X	X						X							
Odontorchilus branickii																X						X	X	SX					
Odontorchilus cinereus																								X	X				
Salpinctes mexicanus								X																					
Salpinctes obsoletus								X	X		X	X	X	X															
Hylorchilus sumichrasti								XR																					
Cinnycerthia peruana																X						X	X	X					
Cinnycerthia unirufa																X	X					X	X						
Cistothorus apolinari																XR													
Cistothorus meridae																	XR												
Cistothorus palustris								X																					

Countries: Argn - Argentina; **Baha** - Bahamas; **Beli** - Belize; **Boli** - Bolivia; **Braz** - Brazil; **Chil** - Chile; **Colo** - Colombia; **Cost** - Costa Rica; **Cuba** - Cuba; **Ecua** - Ecuador; **Elsa** - El Salvador; **Fren** - French Guiana; **Guat** - Guatemala; **Guya** - Guyana; **Hisp** - Hispaniola; **Hond** - Honduras; **Jama** - Jamaica; **Lant** - Lesser Antilles; **Mexi** - Mexico; **Nant** - Netherland Antilles; **Nica** - Nicaragua; **Pana** - Panama; **Parg** - Paraguay; **Peru** - Peru; **Puer** - Puerto Rico; **Suri** - Suriname; **Trin** - Trinidad; **Urug** - Uruguay; **Vene** - Venezuela.

	Baha	Cuba	Hisp	Jama	Puer	Lant	Nant	Mexi	Guat	Beli	Elsa	Hond	Nica	Cost	Pana	Colo	Vene	Trin	Guya	Suri	Fren	Ecua	Peru	Boli	Braz	Parg	Urug	Argn	Chil
Cistothorus platensis																													
platensis																X	X		X			X	X	X	X			X	X
stellaris								X	X		X	X	X	X	X														
Thryomanes bewickii								X																					
Thryomanes sissonii								XR																					
Ferminia cerverai		XR																											
Thryothorus atrogularis													X	X	X														
Thryothorus coraya																X	X		X	X	X	X	X		X				
Thryothorus eisenmanni																							XR						
Thryothorus euophrys																X						X	X						
Thryothorus fasciatoventris														X	X	X													
Thryothorus felix								XR																					
Thryothorus genibarbis																													
genibarbis																							X	X	X				
mystacalis																X	X					X							
Thryothorus griseus																									XR				
Thryothorus guarayanus																								X	X	X			
Thryothorus leucopogon															X	X						X							
Thryothorus leucotis															X	X	X		X	X	X	X	X	X	X				
Thryothorus longirostris																									XR				
Thryothorus ludovicianus																													
albinucha								X	X	SX			X																
ludovicianus								X																					
Thryothorus maculipectus																													
colombianus																XR													
maculipectus								X	X	X	X	X	X	X															
paucimaculatus																						X	X						
sclateri																							XR						
Thryothorus modestus								X	X	X	X	X	X	X	X														
Thryothorus nicefori																XR													
Thryothorus nigricapillus													X	X	X	X						X							
Thryothorus pleurostictus								X	X		X	X	X	X															
Thryothorus rufalbus								X	X		X	X		X	X	X	X												
Thryothorus rutilus														X	X	X	X	X											
Thryothorus semibadius														X	X														
Thryothorus sinaloa								XR																					
Thryothorus spadix															X	X													
Thryothorus superciliaris																						X	X						
Thryothorus thoracicus													X	X	X														
Troglodytes aedon																													
aedon	V	V				X		X	X	X	X	X	X	X	X	X	X	X	X	X	X	X	X	X	X	X	X	X	X
beani								XR																					
martinicensis						XR																							
Troglodytes browni														X	X														
Troglodytes ochraceus														X	X														
Troglodytes rufociliatus								X	X		X	X																	
Troglodytes rufulus																	X								X				
Troglodytes solstitialis																													
monticola																XR													
solstitialis																X	X					X	X	X				X	
Troglodytes tanneri								XR																					
Troglodytes troglodytes								XN																					

Status: X - Breeding species; **XN** - Regular non-breeding species; **XR** - Endemic breeding species; **X?** - Regular species, breeding status uncertain; **XI** - Introduced species; **XD** - Dubious species; **XF** - Formerly bred; **V** - Vagrants; **SX** - Breeding species, sight records only; **SN** - Regular non-breeding species, sight records only; **S?** - Uncertain breeding status; sight records only; **SI** -Introduced; sight records only; **SV** - Vagrant; sight records only. **?** - Occurrence uncertain; **+** -- - Extinct.

	Baha	Cuba	Hisp	Jama	Puer	Lant	Nant	Mexi	Guat	Beli	Elsa	Hond	Nica	Cost	Pana	Colo	Vene	Trin	Guya	Suri	Fren	Ecua	Peru	Boli	Braz	Parg	Urug	Argn	Chil
Uropsila leucogastra								X	X	X		X																	
Henicorhina leucophrys								X	X		X	X		X	X	X	X					X	X	X					
Henicorhina leucoptera																						X	X						
Henicorhina leucosticta								X	X	X		X	X	X	X	X	X		X	X	X	X	X		X				
Microcerculus bambla																	X		X	X	X	X	X		X				
Microcerculus marginatus														X	X	X	X					X	X	X	X				
Microcerculus philomela								X	X	X		X	X	X															
Microcerculus ustulatus																	X		X						X				
Cyphorhinus aradus																X	X		X	X	X	X	X	X	X				
Cyphorhinus phaeocephalus												X	X	X	X	X						X							
Cyphorhinus thoracicus																X						X	X	SX					
Mimidae																													
Dumetella carolinensis	XN	XN	XN	XN	XN	V		XN	XN	XN		XN	XN	XN	XN	XN													
Melanoptila glabrirostris								X	X	X		X																	
Melanotis caerulescens								XR																					
Melanotis hypoleucus								X	X		X	X																	
Mimus dorsalis																								X				X	
Mimus gilvus						X	X	X	X	X		X			XI	X	X	X	X	X	X				X				
Mimus gundlachii	X	X		X																									
Mimus longicaudatus																						X	X						
Mimus patagonicus																												X	X
Mimus polyglottos	X	X	X	X	X			X																					
Mimus saturninus																				X				X	X	X	X	X	
Mimus thenca																													XR
Mimus triurus																								X	XN	X	X?	X	XN
Nesomimus macdonaldi																						XR							
Nesomimus melanotis																						XR							
Nesomimus parvulus																						XR							
Nesomimus trifasciatus																						XR							
Mimodes graysoni								XR																					
Oreoscoptes montanus								XN																					
Toxostoma bendirei								X																					
Toxostoma cinereum								XR																					
Toxostoma crissale								X																					
Toxostoma curvirostre								X																					
Toxostoma guttatum								XR																					
Toxostoma lecontei								X																					
Toxostoma longirostre								X																					
Toxostoma ocellatum								XR																					
Toxostoma redivivum								X																					
Toxostoma rufum	XN	V					V	V																					
Cinclocerthia ruficauda					V	X																							
Ramphocinclus brachyurus						XR																							
Margarops fuscatus	X				X	X	X										XF												
Allenia fusca						XR																							
Musicapidae																													
Turdinae																													
Sialia currucoides								XN																					
Sialia mexicana								X																					
Sialia sialis		XN						X	X	X	X	X	X																
Myadestes coloratus															X	X													
Myadestes elisabeth		XR																											

Countries: Argn - Argentina; **Baha** - Bahamas; **Beli** - Belize; **Boli** - Bolivia; **Braz** - Brazil; **Chil** - Chile; **Colo** - Colombia; **Cost** - Costa Rica; **Cuba** - Cuba; **Ecua** - Ecuador; **Elsa** - El Salvador; **Fren** - French Guiana; **Guat** - Guatemala; **Guya** - Guyana; **Hisp** - Hispaniola; **Hond** - Honduras; **Jama** - Jamaica; **Lant** - Lesser Antilles; **Mexi** - Mexico; **Nant** - Netherland Antilles; **Nica** - Nicaragua; **Pana** - Panama; **Parg** - Paraguay; **Peru** - Peru; **Puer** - Puerto Rico; **Suri** - Suriname; **Trin** - Trinidad; **Urug** - Uruguay; **Vene** - Venezuela.

	Baha	Cuba	Hisp	Jama	Puer	Lant	Nant	Mexi	Guat	Beli	Elsa	Hond	Nica	Cost	Pana	Colo	Vene	Trin	Guya	Suri	Fren	Ecua	Peru	Boli	Braz	Parg	Urug	Argn	Chil
Myadestes genibarbis			X	X		X																							
Myadestes leucogenys																X	X		X	SX		X	X		X				
Myadestes melanops														X	X														
Myadestes obscurus								X	X	X	X	X																	
Myadestes ralloides																X	X					X	X	X					
Myadestes townsendi								X																					
Myadestes unicolor								X	X	X	X	X	X																
Entomodestes coracinus																X						X							
Entomodestes leucotis																							X	X					
Oenanthe oenanthe		V			SV	V	V	V																					
Zoothera naevia								XN																					
Zoothera pinicola								XR																					
Cichlherminia lherminieri						XR																							
Catharus aurantiirostris								X	X		X	X	X	X	X	X	X	X											
Catharus bicknelli	XN	XN	XN	XN	V																								
Catharus dryas								X	X		X	X				X	X					X	X	X				X	
Catharus frantzii								X	X		X	X	X	X	X														
Catharus fuscater														X	X	X	X					X	X	X					
Catharus fuscescens	XN	XN		XN	V		XN	XN	XN	XN		XN		XN	XN	XN	XN	V	XN		SV		V	V	XN				V
Catharus gracilirostris														X	X														
Catharus guttatus	XN							X?	XN		XN																		
Catharus mexicanus								X	X			X	X	X	X														
Catharus minimus						V	XN	XN	XN	XN		XN		XN	XN	XN	XN	V	XN	SV		XN	XN		XN				
Catharus occidentalis								XR																					
Catharus ustulatus	XN	XN	XN	XN			XN	XN	XN	XN	XN	XN	XN	XN	XN	XN	XN					XN	XN	XN	XN	?		XN	
Hylocichla mustelina	XN	XN			V		V	XN	XN	XN	XN	XN	XN	XN	XN	V													
Platycichla flavipes																X	X	X	X						X	X		X	
Platycichla leucops																X	X		X			X	X	X	X				
Turdus albicollis																X	X	X	X	X	X	X	X	X	X	X	X	X	
Turdus amaurochalinus																							XN	X	X	X	X	X	V
Turdus assimilis								X	X	X	X	X	X	X	X	X						X							
Turdus aurantius				XR																									
Turdus chiguanco																						X	X	X				X	X
Turdus falcklandii																												X	X
Turdus fulviventris																X	X					X	X						
Turdus fumigatus						X										X	X	X	X	X	X				X				
Turdus fuscater																X	X					X	X	X					
Turdus grayi								X	X	X	X	X	X	X	X	X													
Turdus haplochrous																								XR					
Turdus hauxwelli																X						X	X	X	X				
Turdus ignobilis																X	X		X	X		X	X	X	X				
Turdus infuscatus								X	X		X	X																	
Turdus jamaicensis				XR																									
Turdus lawrencii																X	X					X	X	X	X				
Turdus leucomelas																X	X		X	X	X		X	X	X	X		X	
Turdus maranonicus																							XR						
Turdus migratorius	XN	XN		SV	SV			X	XN																				
Turdus nigrescens														X	X														
Turdus nigriceps																													
nigriceps																						X?	X	X				X	
subalaris																									X	X		X	

Status: X - Breeding species; **XN** - Regular non-breeding species; **XR** - Endemic breeding species; **X?** - Regular species, breeding status uncertain; **XI** - Introduced species; **XD** - Dubious species; **XF** - Formerly bred; **V** - Vagrants; **SX** - Breeding species, sight records only; **SN** - Regular non-breeding species, sight records only; **S?** - Uncertain breeding status; sight records only; **SI** -Introduced; sight records only; **SV** - Vagrant; sight records only. **?** - Occurrence uncertain; **+** -- - Extinct.

	Baha	Cuba	Hisp	Jama	Puer	Lant	Nant	Mexi	Guat	Beli	Elsa	Hond	Nica	Cost	Pana	Colo	Vene	Trin	Guya	Suri	Fren	Ecua	Peru	Boli	Braz	Parg	Urug	Argn	Chil
Turdus nudigenis																													
maculirostris																						X	X						
nudigenis						X										X	X	X	X	X	X				X				
Turdus obsoletus														X	X	X						X							
Turdus olivater																X	X		X	SX					X				
Turdus plebejus								X	X		X	X	X	X	X														
Turdus plumbeus	X	X	X		X	X																							
Turdus reevei																						X	X						
Turdus rufitorques								X	X		X	X																	
Turdus rufiventris																								X	X	X	X	X	
Turdus rufopalliatus																													
graysoni								XR																					
rufopalliatus								XR																					
Turdus serranus																X	X					X	X	X				X	
Turdus swalesi			XR																										
Timaliinae																													
Chamaea fasciata								X																					
Polioptilinae																													
Microbates cinereiventris													X	X	X	X						X	X						
Microbates collaris																X	X		X	X	X		X		X				
Ramphocaenus melanurus								X	X	X	X	X	X	X	X	X	X	X	X	X	X	X	X	X	X				
Polioptila albiloris								X	X		X	X	X	X															
Polioptila caerulea	X	XN						X	X?	XN		XN																	
Polioptila californica								X																					
Polioptila dumicola																								X	X	X	X	X	
Polioptila guianensis																SX	X		X	X	X				X				
Polioptila lactea																									X	X		X	
Polioptila lembeyei		XR																											
Polioptila melanura								X																					
Polioptila nigriceps								X																					
Polioptila plumbea																													
maior																							XR						
plumbea								X	X	X		X	X	X	X	X	X		X	X	X	X	X		X				
Polioptila schistaceigula															X	X						X							
Sylviinae																													
Phylloscopus borealis								SV																					
Phylloscopus fuscatus								SV																					
Regulus calendula	XN	V		V				X	XN																				
Regulus satrapa								X	X																				
Aegithalidae																													
Psaltriparus minimus								X	X																				
Remizidae																													
Auriparus flaviceps								X																					
Paridae																													
Parus bicolor																													
atricristatus								X																					
Parus gambeli								X																					
Parus inornatus								X																					
Parus sclateri								X																					
Parus wollweberi								X																					
Sittidae																													
Sitta canadensis								X																					

Countries: Argn - Argentina; **Baha** - Bahamas; **Beli** - Belize; **Boli** - Bolivia; **Braz** - Brazil; **Chil** - Chile; **Colo** - Colombia; **Cost** - Costa Rica; **Cuba** - Cuba; **Ecua** - Ecuador; **Elsa** - El Salvador; **Fren** - French Guiana; **Guat** - Guatemala; **Guya** - Guyana; **Hisp** - Hispaniola; **Hond** - Honduras; **Jama** - Jamaica; **Lant** - Lesser Antilles; **Mexi** - Mexico; **Nant** - Netherland Antilles; **Nica** - Nicaragua; **Pana** - Panama; **Parg** - Paraguay; **Peru** - Peru; **Puer** - Puerto Rico; **Suri** - Suriname; **Trin** - Trinidad; **Urug** - Uruguay; **Vene** - Venezuela.

	Baha	Cuba	Hisp	Jama	Puer	Lant	Nant	Mexi	Guat	Beli	Elsa	Hond	Nica	Cost	Pana	Colo	Vene	Trin	Guya	Suri	Fren	Ecua	Peru	Boli	Braz	Parg	Urug	Argn	Chil
Sitta carolinensis								X																					
Sitta pusilla	X																												
Sitta pygmaea								X																					
Certhiidae																													
Certhia americana								X	X		X?	X	X																
Emberizidae																													
Emberizinae																													
Calcarius lapponicus								V																					
Calcarius mccownii								XN																					
Calcarius ornatus								XN																					
Plectrophenax nivalis	V																												
Calamospiza melanocorys								XN		V																			
Zonotrichia albicollis					SV		?	XN																					
Zonotrichia atricapilla								XN																					
Zonotrichia capensis			X				X	X	X		X	X		X	X	X	X		X	X	X	X	X	X	X	X	X	X	X
Zonotrichia georgiana	V							XN																					
Zonotrichia iliaca								XN																					
Zonotrichia leucophrys	XN	XN		XN				XN		SV																			
Zonotrichia lincolnii	XN	XN	V	XN	V			XN	XN	XN	XN	XN		XN	XN														
Zonotrichia melodia	V							X																					
Junco hyemalis																													
hyemalis	V			V	V			X																					
insularis								XR																					
Junco phaeonotus								X	X																				
Junco vulcani														X	X														
Ammodramus aurifrons																X	X					X	X	X	X				
Ammodramus baileyi								XR																					
Ammodramus bairdii								XN																					
Ammodramus caudacutus								XN																					
Ammodramus humeralis																X	X		X	X	X		X	X	X	X	X	X	
Ammodramus leconteii								V																					
Ammodramus maritima								SV																					
Ammodramus sandwichensis																													
beldingi								X																					
rostratus								XR																					
sandwichensis	XN	XN						X	X	XN	XN	XN		SV															
Ammodramus savannarum	XN	XN	X	X	X		X	X	X	X	X	X	X	X	X	X						X							
Spizella atrogularis								X																					
Spizella breweri								XN																					
Spizella pallida	V	V						XN	V																				
Spizella passerina	XN	V						X	X	X	X	X	X	SV															
Spizella pusilla								XN																					
Spizella wortheni								XR																					
Pooecetes gramineus	V							XN	XN																				
Chondestes grammacus	XN	XN						X	XN	V	V	V																	
Amphispiza belli								X																					
Amphispiza bilineata								X																					
Aimophila botterii																													
botterii								X																					
petenica								X	X	X		X	X	X															
Aimophila carpalis								X																					
Aimophila cassinii								X																					

Status: X - Breeding species; **XN** - Regular non-breeding species; **XR** - Endemic breeding species; **X?** - Regular species, breeding status uncertain; **XI** - Introduced species; **XD** - Dubious species; **XF** - Formerly bred; **V** - Vagrants; **SX** - Breeding species, sight records only; **SN** - Regular non-breeding species, sight records only; **S?** - Uncertain breeding status; sight records only; **SI** -Introduced; sight records only; **SV** - Vagrant; sight records only. **?** - Occurrence uncertain; **+** -- - Extinct.

	Baha	Cuba	Hisp	Jama	Puer	Lant	Nant	Mexi	Guat	Beli	Elsa	Hond	Nica	Cost	Pana	Colo	Vene	Trin	Guya	Suri	Fren	Ecua	Peru	Boli	Braz	Parg	Urug	Argn	Chil
Aimophila humeralis								XR																					
Aimophila mystacalis								XR																					
Aimophila notosticta								XR																					
Aimophila quinquestriata								X																					
Aimophila rufescens								X	X		X	X	X	X															
Aimophila ruficauda								X	X		X	X	X	X															
Aimophila ruficeps								X																					
Aimophila stolzmanni																						X	X						
Aimophila strigiceps																								X		X		X	
Aimophila sumichrasti								XR																					
Torreornis inexpectata		XR																											
Oriturus superciliosus								XR																					
Phrygilus alaudinus																						X	X	X				X	X
Phrygilus atriceps																							X	X				X	X
Phrygilus carbonarius																												XR	
Phrygilus dorsalis																								X				X	X
Phrygilus erythronotus																							X	X					X
Phrygilus fruticeti																							X	X				X	X
Phrygilus gayi																												X	X
Phrygilus patagonicus																												X	X
Phrygilus plebejus																						X	X	X				X	X
Phrygilus punensis																							X	X					
Phrygilus unicolor																X	X					X	X	X				X	X
Melanodera melanodera																												X	X
Melanodera xanthogramma																												X	X
Haplospiza rustica								X			X	X		X	X	X	X					X	X	X					
Haplospiza unicolor																									X	X		X	
Acanthidops bairdi														X	X														
Lophospingus griseocristatus																								X				X	
Lophospingus pusillus																								X		X		X	
Donacospiza albifrons																								X	X	X	X	X	
Diuca diuca																								X	XN		XN	X	X
Diuca speculifera																							X	X				X	X
Idiopsar brachyurus																							X	X				X	
Piezorhina cinerea																							XR						
Xenospingus concolor																							X						X
Incaspiza laeta																							XR						
Incaspiza ortizi																							XR						
Incaspiza personata																							XR						
Incaspiza pulchra																							XR						
Incaspiza watkinsi																							XR						
Poospiza alticola																							XR						
Poospiza baeri																												XR	
Poospiza boliviana																								XR					
Poospiza caesar																							XR						
Poospiza cinerea																								X	X				
Poospiza erythrophrys																								X				X	
Poospiza garleppi																								XR					
Poospiza hispaniolensis																						X	X						
Poospiza hypochondriaca																								X				X	
Poospiza lateralis																									X	X	X	X	
Poospiza melanoleuca																								X	X	X	X	X	

Countries: Argn - Argentina; **Baha** - Bahamas; **Beli** - Belize; **Boli** - Bolivia; **Braz** - Brazil; **Chil** - Chile; **Colo** - Colombia; **Cost** - Costa Rica; **Cuba** - Cuba; **Ecua** - Ecuador; **Elsa** - El Salvador; **Fren** - French Guiana; **Guat** - Guatemala; **Guya** - Guyana; **Hisp** - Hispaniola; **Hond** - Honduras; **Jama** - Jamaica; **Lant** - Lesser Antilles; **Mexi** - Mexico; **Nant** - Netherland Antilles; **Nica** - Nicaragua; **Pana** - Panama; **Parg** - Paraguay; **Peru** - Peru; **Puer** - Puerto Rico; **Suri** - Suriname; **Trin** - Trinidad; **Urug** - Uruguay; **Vene** - Venezuela.

	Baha	Cuba	Hisp	Jama	Puer	Lant	Nant	Mexi	Guat	Beli	Elsa	Hond	Nica	Cost	Pana	Colo	Vene	Trin	Guya	Suri	Fren	Ecua	Peru	Boli	Braz	Parg	Urug	Argn	Chil
Poospiza nigrorufa																													
nigrorufa																									X	X	X	X	
whitii																								X				X	
Poospiza ornata																												XR	
Poospiza rubecula																							XR						
Poospiza thoracica																									XR				
Poospiza torquata																								X		X?		X	
Sicalis auriventris																												X	X
Sicalis citrina																X	X		X	X			X	X	X			X	
Sicalis columbiana																X	X	X?					X		X				
Sicalis flaveola				XI	XI		XI								XI	X	X	X	X	X	X	X	X	X	X	X	X	X	
Sicalis lebruni																												X	X
Sicalis lutea																							X	X				X	
Sicalis luteocephala																								X				SX	
Sicalis luteola						XI		X	X	X		X	X	V	X	X	X		X		X	X	X	X	X	X	X	X	X
Sicalis olivascens																							X	X				X	X
Sicalis raimondii																							XR						
Sicalis taczanowskii																						X	X						
Sicalis uropygialis																							X	X				X	X
Emberizoides herbicola																													
duidae																	XR												
herbicola														X	X	X	X		X	X	X		X	X	X	X		X	
Emberizoides ypiranganus																									X	X		X	
Embernagra longicauda																									XR				
Embernagra platensis																								X	X	X	X	X	
Volatinia jacarina						X	V	X	X	X	X	X	X	X	X	X	X	X	X	X	X	X	X	X	X	X	X	X	X
Sporophila albogularis																									XR				
Sporophila americana																													
americana																X	X	X	X	X	X	X	X		X				
aurita								X	X	X		X	X	X	X	X						X	X						
Sporophila ardesiaca																									XR				
Sporophila bouvreuil																				X					X	X		X	
Sporophila caerulescens																XN							XN	X	X	X	X	X	
Sporophila castaneiventris																X	X		X	X	X	X	X	X	X				
Sporophila cinnamomea																									X	X?		X	
Sporophila collaris																								X	X	X	X	X	
Sporophila falcirostris																									X			X?	
Sporophila frontalis																									X	X		X	
Sporophila hypochroma																			?					X	X			X	
Sporophila hypoxantha																								X	X	X		X	
Sporophila insulata																XR													
Sporophila intermedia																X	X	X	X						X				
Sporophila leucoptera																				X			SV	X	X	X		X	
Sporophila lineola																													
bouvronides															SV	X	X.	X	X	X	X	X?	X?		X?				
lineola																XN	XN		XN	XN	XN	XN	XN	X	X	X		X	
Sporophila luctuosa																X	X					X	X	X	S?				
Sporophila melanogaster																									XR				
Sporophila minuta								X	X		X	X	X	X	X	X	X	X	X	X	X	X			X				
Sporophila nigricollis						X								X	X	X	X	X	X	X		X	X	X	X				
Sporophila nigrorufa																								X	X				
Sporophila obscura																X	X					X	X	X		X		X	

Status: **X** - Breeding species; **XN** - Regular non-breeding species; **XR** - Endemic breeding species; **X?** - Regular species, breeding status uncertain; **XI** - Introduced species; **XD** - Dubious species; **XF** - Formerly bred; **V** - Vagrants; **SX** - Breeding species, sight records only; **SN** - Regular non-breeding species, sight records only; **S?** - Uncertain breeding status; sight records only; **SI** -Introduced; sight records only; **SV** - Vagrant; sight records only. **?** - Occurrence uncertain; **+** -- - Extinct.

	Baha	Cuba	Hisp	Jama	Puer	Lant	Nant	Mexi	Guat	Beli	Elsa	Hond	Nica	Cost	Pana	Colo	Vene	Trin	Guya	Suri	Fren	Ecua	Peru	Boli	Braz	Parg	Urug	Argn	Chil
Sporophila palustris																									X	X	X	X	
Sporophila peruviana																						X	X						
Sporophila plumbea																X	X		X	X	X		X	X	X	X		X	
Sporophila ruficollis																								X	X	X	X	X	
Sporophila schistacea								?		X		X		X	X	X	X	X	X	X		X	X	X	X				
Sporophila simplex																						X	X						
Sporophila telasco																X						X	X						X
Sporophila torqueola																													
morelleti								X	X	X	X	X	X	X	X														
torqueola								XR																					
Sporophila zelichi																												XR	
Oryzoborus angolensis																													
angolensis																X	X	X	X	X	X	X	X	X	X	X		X	
funereus								X	X	X		X	X	X	X	X						X							
Oryzoborus crassirostris																X	X	X	X	X	X		X		X				
Oryzoborus maximiliani																													
maximiliani																X	X		X?		X	X	X	X	X				
nuttingi													X	X	X														
Amaurospiza concolor								X		X?	V	X	X	X	X	X						X							
Amaurospiza moesta																									X	X		X	
Melopyrrha nigra		X																											
Dolospingus fringilloides																X	X								X				
Catamenia analis																X						X	X	X				X	X
Catamenia homochroa																X	X					X	X	X	X				
Catamenia inornata																X	X					X	X	X				X	SX
Tiaris bicolor	X	X	X	X	X	X	X									X	X	X											
Tiaris canora	XI	XR																											
Tiaris fuliginosa																X	X	X	X					X	X	S?			
Tiaris olivacea	XI	X	X	X	X			X	X	SX	X	X	X	X	X	X	X					X							
Loxipasser anoxanthus				XR																									
Loxigilla noctis					XI	XR																							
Loxigilla portoricensis					XR																								
Loxigilla violacea	X		X	X																									
Melanospiza richardsoni						XR																							
Geospiza conirostris																						XR							
Geospiza difficilis																						XR							
Geospiza fortis																						XR							
Geospiza fulginosa																						XR							
Geospiza magnirostris																						XR							
Geospiza scandens																						XR							
Camarhynchus crassirostris																						XR							
Camarhynchus heliobates																						XR							
Camarhynchus pallidus																						XR							
Camarhynchus parvulus																						XR							
Camarhynchus pauper																						XR							
Camarhynchus psittacula																						XR							
Certhidea olivacea																						XR							
Pinaroloxias inornata														XR															
Pipilo aberti								X																					
Pipilo albicollis								XR																					
Pipilo chlorurus		V						X?																					
Pipilo crissalis								X																					

Countries: Argn - Argentina; **Baha** - Bahamas; **Beli** - Belize; **Boli** - Bolivia; **Braz** - Brazil; **Chil** - Chile; **Colo** - Colombia; **Cost** - Costa Rica; **Cuba** - Cuba; **Ecua** - Ecuador; **Elsa** - El Salvador; **Fren** - French Guiana; **Guat** - Guatemala; **Guya** - Guyana; **Hisp** - Hispaniola; **Hond** - Honduras; **Jama** - Jamaica; **Lant** - Lesser Antilles; **Mexi** - Mexico; **Nant** - Netherland Antilles; **Nica** - Nicaragua; **Pana** - Panama; **Parg** - Paraguay; **Peru** - Peru; **Puer** - Puerto Rico; **Suri** - Suriname; **Trin** - Trinidad; **Urug** - Uruguay; **Vene** - Venezuela.

	Baha	Cuba	Hisp	Jama	Puer	Lant	Nant	Mexi	Guat	Beli	Elsa	Hond	Nica	Cost	Pana	Colo	Vene	Trin	Guya	Suri	Fren	Ecua	Peru	Boli	Braz	Parg	Urug	Argn	Chil
Pipilo erythrophthalmus								X	X																				
Pipilo fuscus								X																					
Pipilo ocai								XR																					
Melozone biarcuatum								X	X		X	X		X															
Melozone kieneri								XR																					
Melozone leucotis								X	X		X		X	X															
Arremon abeillei																						X	X						
Arremon aurantiirostris								X	X	X		X	X	X	X	X						X	X						
Arremon flavirostris																								X	X	X		X	
Arremon schlegeli																X	X												
Arremon taciturnus																													
semitorquatus																									XR				
taciturnus																X	X		X	X	X		X	X	X				
Arremonops chloronotus								X	X	X		X																	
Arremonops conirostris												X	X	X	X	X	X					X	SX		X				
Arremonops rufivirgatus								X	X	X		X	X	X															
Arremonops tocuyensis																X	X												
Atlapetes albiceps																						X	X						
Atlapetes albinucha								XR																					
Atlapetes albofrenatus																X	X												
Atlapetes brunneinucha								X	X		X	X	X	X	X	X	X					X	X						
Atlapetes citrinellus																										?		XR	
Atlapetes flaviceps																XR													
Atlapetes fulviceps																								X				X	
Atlapetes fuscoolivaceus																XR													
Atlapetes gutturalis								X	X		X	X	X	X	X	X													
Atlapetes leucopis																X						X							
Atlapetes leucopterus																													
leucopterus																						X	X						
paynteri																							XR						
Atlapetes melanocephalus																XR													
Atlapetes nationi																							XR						
Atlapetes pallidiceps																						XR							
Atlapetes pallidinucha																X	X					X	X						
Atlapetes personatus																	X								X				
Atlapetes pileatus								XR																					
Atlapetes rufigenis																							XR						
Atlapetes rufinucha																X	X					X	X	X					
Atlapetes schistaceus																X	X					X	X						
Atlapetes seebohmi																						X	X						
Atlapetes semirufus																X	X												
Atlapetes torquatus																													
atricapillus														X	X	X													
torquatus																X	X					X	X	X				X	
virenticeps								XR																					
Atlapetes tricolor																X						X	X						
Pezopetes capitalis														X	X														
Oreothraupis arremonops																X						X							
Pselliophorus luteoviridis															XR														
Pselliophorus tibialis														X	X														
Lysurus castaneiceps																X						X	X						
Lysurus crassirostris														X	X	X													

Status: **X** - Breeding species; **XN** - Regular non-breeding species; **XR** - Endemic breeding species; **X?** - Regular species, breeding status uncertain; **XI** - Introduced species; **XD** - Dubious species; **XF** - Formerly bred; **V** - Vagrants; **SX** - Breeding species, sight records only; **SN** - Regular non-breeding species, sight records only; **S?** - Uncertain breeding status; sight records only; **SI** -Introduced; sight records only; **SV** - Vagrant; sight records only. **?** - Occurrence uncertain; **+** -- - Extinct.

	Baha	Cuba	Hisp	Jama	Puer	Lant	Nant	Mexi	Guat	Beli	Elsa	Hond	Nica	Cost	Pana	Colo	Vene	Trin	Guya	Suri	Fren	Ecua	Peru	Boli	Braz	Parg	Urug	Argn	Chil
Urothraupis stolzmanni																X						X							
Charitospiza eucosma																								X	X			X	
Coryphaspiza melanotis																							X	X	X	X		X	
Saltatricula multicolor																								X		X	X	X	
Gubernatrix cristata																									X		X	X	
Coryphospingus cucullatus																			X	X			X	X	X	X	X	X	
Coryphospingus pileatus																X	X				SX				X				
Rhodospingus cruentus																						X	X						
Paroaria baeri																									XR				
Paroaria capitata																								X	X	X	X	X	
Paroaria coronata																								X	X	X	X	X	
Paroaria dominicana																									XR				
Paroaria gularis																X	X	X	X	X		X	X	X	X				
Catamblyrhynchinae																													
Catamblyrhynchus diadema																X	X					X	X	X				X	
Cardinalinae																													
Spiza americana	XN	XN		XN	V		XN	XN	XN	XN	XN	XN	XN	XN	XN	XN	XN	XN	XN	XN					V				
Pheucticus aureoventris																X	X					X	X	X	X	X		X	
Pheucticus chrysogaster																X	X					X	X						
Pheucticus chrysopeplus								X	X																				
Pheucticus ludovicianus	XN	XN	XN	XN	XN	XN	XN	XN	XN	XN	XN	XN	XN	XN	XN	XN	XN	SV	V		V	XN	XN						
Pheucticus melanocephalus							SV	X						SV															
Pheucticus tibialis														X	X														
Cardinalis cardinalis								X	X	X																			
Cardinalis phoeniceus																X	X												
Cardinalis sinuatus								X																					
Caryothraustes canadensis															X	X	X		X	X	X				X				
Caryothraustes humeralis																?						X	X	X	X				
Caryothraustes poliogaster								X	X	X		X	X	X	X														
Rhodothraupis celaeno								XR																					
Periporphyrus erythromelas																	X		X	X	X				X				
Pitylus fuliginosus																									X	X		X	
Pitylus grossus												X	X	X	X	X	X		X	X	X	X	X	X	X				
Saltator albicollis						X								X	X	X	X	X				X	X						
Saltator atriceps								X	X	X	X	X	X	X	X														
Saltator atricollis																								X	X	X			
Saltator atripennis																X						X							
Saltator aurantiirostris																													
aurantiirostris																							X	X	X	X	X	X	X
nigriceps																						X	X						
Saltator cinctus																X						X	X						
Saltator coerulescens								X	X	X	X	X	X	X		X	X	X	X	X	X	X	X	X	X	X	X	X	
Saltator maxillosus																									X	X		X	
Saltator maximus								X	X	X	V	X	X	X	X	X	X		X	X	X	X	X	X	X	X			
Saltator orenocensis																X	X												
Saltator rufiventris																								X				X	
Saltator similis																								X	X	X	X	X	
Passerina amoena								X																					
Passerina brissonii																X	X							X	X	X	X	X	
Passerina caerulea	XN	XN	XN	XN	XN			X	X	X	X	X	X	X	XN	V						V							
Passerina caerulescens																								X	X				
Passerina ciris	XN	XN		XN				X	XN	XN	XN	XN	XN	XN	XN														

Countries: Argn - Argentina; **Baha** - Bahamas; **Beli** - Belize; **Boli** - Bolivia; **Braz** - Brazil; **Chil** - Chile; **Colo** - Colombia; **Cost** - Costa Rica; **Cuba** - Cuba; **Ecua** - Ecuador; **Elsa** - El Salvador; **Fren** - French Guiana; **Guat** - Guatemala; **Guya** - Guyana; **Hisp** - Hispaniola; **Hond** - Honduras; **Jama** - Jamaica; **Lant** - Lesser Antilles; **Mexi** - Mexico; **Nant** - Netherland Antilles; **Nica** - Nicaragua; **Pana** - Panama; **Parg** - Paraguay; **Peru** - Peru; **Puer** - Puerto Rico; **Suri** - Suriname; **Trin** - Trinidad; **Urug** - Uruguay; **Vene** - Venezuela.

	Baha	Cuba	Hisp	Jama	Puer	Lant	Nant	Mexi	Guat	Beli	Elsa	Hond	Nica	Cost	Pana	Colo	Vene	Trin	Guya	Suri	Fren	Ecua	Peru	Boli	Braz	Parg	Urug	Argn	Chil
Passerina cyanea	XN	XN	XN	XN	XN	V	XN	XN	XN	XN	XN	XN	XN	XN	XN	XN	V	SV											
Passerina cyanoides								X	X	X		X	X	X	X	X	X		X	X	X	X	X	X	X				
Passerina glaucocaerulea																									X	X?	X	X	
Passerina leclancherii								XR																					
Passerina parellina								X	X	X	X	X	X																
Passerina rositae								XR																					
Passerina versicolor								X	X																				
Thraupinae																													
Orchesticus abeillei																									XR				
Schistochlamys melanopis																X	X		X	X	X	S?	X	X	X				
Schistochlamys ruficapillus																									XR				
Neothraupis fasciata																								X	X	X			
Cypsnagra hirundinacea																				X	S?			X	X	X			
Conothraupis mesoleuca																									XR				
Conothraupis speculigera																						X	X	SX	X				
Lamprospiza melanoleuca																			X	X	X		X	X	X				
Cissopis leveriana																X	X		X	X	?	X	X	X	X	X		X	
Chlorornis riefferii																X						X	X	X					
Sericossypha albocristata																X	X					X	X						
Compsothraupis loricata																									XR				
Nesospingus speculiferus					XR																								
Chlorospingus canigularis														X	X	X	X					X	X						
Chlorospingus flavigularis															X	X						X	X						
Chlorospingus flavovirens																X						X							
Chlorospingus inornatus															X														
Chlorospingus ophthalmicus								X	X	X	X	X	X	X	X	X	X					X	X	X				X	
Chlorospingus parvirostris																X						X	X	X					
Chlorospingus pileatus														X	X														
Chlorospingus semifuscus																X						X							
Chlorospingus tacarcunae															X	X													
Cnemoscopus rubrirostris																X	X					X	X						
Hemispingus atropileus																X	X					X	X						
Hemispingus calophrys																							X	X					
Hemispingus frontalis																X	X					X	X						
Hemispingus goeringi																	XR												
Hemispingus melanotis																X	X					X	X	X					
Hemispingus parodii																							XR						
Hemispingus reyi																	XR												
Hemispingus rufosuperciliaris																							XR						
Hemispingus superciliaris																X	X					X	X	X					
Hemispingus trifasciatus																							X	X					
Hemispingus verticalis																X	X					X	X						
Hemispingus xanthophthalmus																							X	X					
Pyrrhocoma ruficeps																									X	X		X	
Thlypopsis fulviceps																X	X												
Thlypopsis inornata																							XR						
Thlypopsis ornata																X						X	X						
Thlypopsis pectoralis																							XR						
Thlypopsis ruficeps																							X	X				X	
Thlypopsis sordida																X	X					X	X	X	X	X		X	
Hemithraupis flavicollis															X	X	X		X	X	X	X	X	X	X				
Hemithraupis guira																X	X		X	X	X	X	X	X	X	X		X	

Status: **X** - Breeding species; **XN** - Regular non-breeding species; **XR** - Endemic breeding species; **X?** - Regular species, breeding status uncertain; **XI** - Introduced species; **XD** - Dubious species; **XF** - Formerly bred; **V** - Vagrants; **SX** - Breeding species, sight records only; **SN** - Regular non-breeding species, sight records only; **S?** - Uncertain breeding status; sight records only; **SI** -Introduced; sight records only; **SV** - Vagrant; sight records only. **?** - Occurrence uncertain; **+** -- - Extinct.

	Baha	Cuba	Hisp	Jama	Puer	Lant	Nant	Mexi	Guat	Beli	Elsa	Hond	Nica	Cost	Pana	Colo	Vene	Trin	Guya	Suri	Fren	Ecua	Peru	Boli	Braz	Parg	Urug	Argn	Chil
Hemithraupis ruficapilla																									XR				
Chrysothlypis chrysomelas														X	X														
Chrysothlypis salmoni																X						X							
Nemosia pileata																X	X		X	X	X		X	X	X	X		X	
Nemosia rourei																									XR				
Phaenicophilus palmarum			XR																										
Phaenicophilus poliocephalus			XR																										
Calyptophilus frugivorus			XR																										
Rhodinocichla rosea								X						X	X	X	X												
Mitrospingus cassinii														X	X	X						X							
Mitrospingus oleagineus																	X		X						X				
Chlorothraupis carmioli													X	X	X	X							X	X					
Chlorothraupis olivacea															X	X						X							
Chlorothraupis stolzmanni																X						X							
Orthogonys chloricterus																									XR				
Eucometis penicillata								X	X	X		X	X	X	X	X	X		X	X	X	X	X	X	X	X			
Lanio aurantius								X	X	X		X																	
Lanio fulvus																X	X		X	X	X	X	X		X				
Lanio leucothorax												X	X	X	X														
Lanio versicolor																							X	X	X				
Creurgops dentata																							X	X					
Creurgops verticalis																X	X					X	X						
Heterospingus rubrifrons														X	X														
Heterospingus xanthopygius															X	X						X							
Tachyphonus coronatus																									X	X		X	
Tachyphonus cristatus																X	X		X	X	X	X	X	X	X				
Tachyphonus delatrii												X	X	X	X	X						X							
Tachyphonus luctuosus												X	X	X	X	X	X	X	X	X	X	X	X	X	X				
Tachyphonus phoenicius																X	X		X	X	X		X	X	X				
Tachyphonus rufiventer																							X	X	X				
Tachyphonus rufus														X	X	X	X	X	X	X	X	X	X	X	X	X		X	
Tachyphonus surinamus																X	X		X	X	X	X	X		X				
Trichothraupis melanops																							X	X	X	X		X	
Habia atrimaxillaris														XR															
Habia cristata																XR													
Habia fuscicauda								X	X	X	X	X	X	X	X	X													
Habia gutturalis																XR													
Habia rubica								X	X	X	X	X	X	X	X	X	X	X				X	X	X	X	X		X	
Piranga bidentata								X	X		X	X	X	X	X														
Piranga erythrocephala								XR																					
Piranga flava						V		X	X	X	X	X	X	X	X	X	X	X	X	X	X	X	X	X	X	X	X	X	
Piranga leucoptera								X	X	X	X	X	X	X	X	X	X					X	X	X	X				
Piranga ludoviciana	V	V						X	XN	XN	XN	XN	XN	XN	V														
Piranga olivacea	XN	XN	XN	XN	XN	XN	XN	XN	XN	XN		XN	XN	XN	XN	XN	XN	SV				XN	XN	XN	SV				
Piranga roseogularis								X	X	X																			
Piranga rubra	XN	XN	XN	XN		XN	V	X	XN	XN	XN	XN	XN	XN	XN	XN	XN	XN	XN	XN	SN	XN	XN	XN	XN				V
Piranga rubriceps																X						X	X						
Calochaetes coccineus																X						X	X						
Ramphocelus bresilius																									XR			X?	
Ramphocelus carbo																X	X	X	X	X	X	X	X	X	X	X			
Ramphocelus dimidiatus															X	X	X												
Ramphocelus flammigerus															X	X						X							

Countries: Argn - Argentina; **Baha** - Bahamas; **Beli** - Belize; **Boli** - Bolivia; **Braz** - Brazil; **Chil** - Chile; **Colo** - Colombia; **Cost** - Costa Rica; **Cuba** - Cuba; **Ecua** - Ecuador; **Elsa** - El Salvador; **Fren** - French Guiana; **Guat** - Guatemala; **Guya** - Guyana; **Hisp** - Hispaniola; **Hond** - Honduras; **Jama** - Jamaica; **Lant** - Lesser Antilles; **Mexi** - Mexico; **Nant** - Netherland Antilles; **Nica** - Nicaragua; **Pana** - Panama; **Parg** - Paraguay; **Peru** - Peru; **Puer** - Puerto Rico; **Suri** - Suriname; **Trin** - Trinidad; **Urug** - Uruguay; **Vene** - Venezuela.

	Baha	Cuba	Hisp	Jama	Puer	Lant	Nant	Mexi	Guat	Beli	Elsa	Hond	Nica	Cost	Pana	Colo	Vene	Trin	Guya	Suri	Fren	Ecua	Peru	Boli	Braz	Parg	Urug	Argn	Chil
Ramphocelus melanogaster																							XR						
Ramphocelus nigrogularis																X						X	X	X	X				
Ramphocelus passerinii								X	X	X		X	X	X	X														
Ramphocelus sanguinolentus								X	X	X		X	X	X	X														
Spindalis zena	X	X	X	X	X			X																					
Thraupis abbas								X	X	X	X	X	X																
Thraupis bonariensis																						X	X	X	X	X	X	X	X
Thraupis cyanocephala																X	X	X				X	X	X					
Thraupis cyanoptera																									XR	?			
Thraupis episcopus								X	X	X	X	X	X	X	X	X	X	X	X	X	X	X	X	X	X				
Thraupis glaucocolpa																X	X												
Thraupis ornata																									XR				
Thraupis palmarum												X	X	X	X	X	X	X	X	X	X	X	X	X	X	X		SX	
Thraupis sayaca																							S?	X	X	X	X	X	
Cyanicterus cyanicterus																	X		X	X	X				X				
Buthraupis arcaei														X	X														
Buthraupis aureocincta																XR													
Buthraupis aureodorsalis																							XR						
Buthraupis edwardsi																X						X							
Buthraupis eximia																X	X					X	X						
Buthraupis melanochlamys																XR													
Buthraupis montana																X	X					X	X	X					
Buthraupis rothschildi																X						X							
Buthraupis wetmorei																X						X	X						
Wetmorethraupis sterrhopteron																						X	X						
Anisognathus flavinucha																X	X					X	X	X					
Anisognathus igniventris																X	X					X	X	X					
Anisognathus lacrymosus																X	X					X	X						
Anisognathus melanogenys																XR													
Anisognathus notabilis																X						X							
Stephanophorus diadematus																									X	X	X	X	
Iridosornis analis																?						X	X						
Iridosornis jelskii																							X	X					
Iridosornis porphyrocephala																X						X							
Iridosornis reinhardti																							XR						
Iridosornis rufivertex																X	X					X	X						
Dubusia taeniata																X	X					X	X						
Delothraupis castaneoventris																							X	X					
Pipraeidea melanonota																X	X					X	X	X	X	X	X	X	
Euphonia affinis								X	X	X	X	X	X	X															
Euphonia anneae														X	X	X													
Euphonia cayennensis																	X		X	X	X				X				
Euphonia chalybea																									X	X		X	
Euphonia chlorotica																X	X		X	X	X		X	X	X	X		X	
Euphonia chrysopasta																X	X		X	X	X	X	X	X	X				
Euphonia concinna																XR													
Euphonia finschi																	X		X	X	X				X				
Euphonia fulvicrissa															X	X						X							
Euphonia gouldi								X	X	X		X	X	X	X														
Euphonia hirundinacea								X	X	X	X	X	X	X	X														
Euphonia imitans														X	X														
Euphonia jamaica				XR																									

Status: **X** - Breeding species; **XN** - Regular non-breeding species; **XR** - Endemic breeding species; **X?** - Regular species, breeding status uncertain; **XI** - Introduced species; **XD** - Dubious species; **XF** - Formerly bred; **V** - Vagrants; **SX** - Breeding species, sight records only; **SN** - Regular non-breeding species, sight records only; **S?** - Uncertain breeding status; sight records only; **SI** -Introduced; sight records only; **SV** - Vagrant; sight records only. ? - Occurrence uncertain; + -- - Extinct.

	Baha	Cuba	Hisp	Jama	Puer	Lant	Nant	Mexi	Guat	Beli	Elsa	Hond	Nica	Cost	Pana	Colo	Vene	Trin	Guya	Suri	Fren	Ecua	Peru	Boli	Braz	Parg	Urug	Argn	Chil
Euphonia laniirostris														X	X	X	X					X	X	X	X				
Euphonia luteicapilla													X	X	X														
Euphonia mesochrysa																X						X	X	X					
Euphonia minuta								?	X	X		X	X	X	X	X	X		X	X	X	X	X	X	X				
Euphonia musica																													
cyanocephala																X	X	X	X	X	SX	X	X	X	X	X		X	
elegantissima								X	X	X	X	X	X	X	X														
musica			X		X	X																							
Euphonia pectoralis																									X	X		X	
Euphonia plumbea																SX	X		X	X	SX				X				
Euphonia rufiventris																X	X					X	X	X	X				
Euphonia saturata																X						X	X						
Euphonia trinitatis																X	X	X											
Euphonia violacea																	X	X	X	X	X				X	X		X	
Euphonia xanthogaster															X	X	X		X			X	X	X	X				
Chlorophonia callophrys														X	X														
Chlorophonia cyanea																X	X		X			X	X	X	X	X		X	
Chlorophonia flavirostris															X?	X						X							
Chlorophonia occipitalis								X	X		X	X	X																
Chlorophonia pyrrhophrys																X	X					X	X						
Chlorochrysa calliparaea																X						X	X	X					
Chlorochrysa nitidissima																XR													
Chlorochrysa phoenicotis																X						X							
Tangara argyrofenges																							X	X					
Tangara arthus																X	X					X	X	X					
Tangara cabanisi								X	X																				
Tangara callophrys																X						X	X	X	X				
Tangara cayana																X	X		X	X	X		X	X	X	X		X	
Tangara chilensis																X	X		X	X	X	X	X	X	X				
Tangara chrysotis																X						X	X	X					
Tangara cucullata						XR																							
Tangara cyanicollis																X	X					X	X	X	X				
Tangara cyanocephala																									X	X		X	
Tangara cyanoptera																X	X		X						X				
Tangara cyanotis																X						X	X	X					
Tangara cyanoventris																									XR				
Tangara desmaresti																									XR				
Tangara dowii														X	X														
Tangara fastuosa																									XR				
Tangara florida														X	X	X						X							
Tangara fucosa															X	SX													
Tangara guttata														X	X	X	X	X		SX					X				
Tangara gyrola														X	X	X	X	X	X	X	X	X	X	X	X				
Tangara heinei																X	X					X							
Tangara icterocephala														X	X	X						X							
Tangara inornata														X	X	X													
Tangara johannae																X						X							
Tangara labradorides																X						X	X						
Tangara larvata								X	X	X		X	X	X	X	X						X							
Tangara lavinia									X	X		X	X	X	X	X						X							

Countries: Argn - Argentina; **Baha** - Bahamas; **Beli** - Belize; **Boli** - Bolivia; **Braz** - Brazil; **Chil** - Chile; **Colo** - Colombia; **Cost** - Costa Rica; **Cuba** - Cuba; **Ecua** - Ecuador; **Elsa** - El Salvador; **Fren** - French Guiana; **Guat** - Guatemala; **Guya** - Guyana; **Hisp** - Hispaniola; **Hond** - Honduras; **Jama** - Jamaica; **Lant** - Lesser Antilles; **Mexi** - Mexico; **Nant** - Netherland Antilles; **Nica** - Nicaragua; **Pana** - Panama; **Parg** - Paraguay; **Peru** - Peru; **Puer** - Puerto Rico; **Suri** - Suriname; **Trin** - Trinidad; **Urug** - Uruguay; **Vene** - Venezuela.

	Baha	Cuba	Hisp	Jama	Puer	Lant	Nant	Mexi	Guat	Beli	Elsa	Hond	Nica	Cost	Pana	Colo	Vene	Trin	Guya	Suri	Fren	Ecua	Peru	Boli	Braz	Parg	Urug	Argn	Chil
Tangara mexicana																													
brasiliensis																									XR				
mexicana																X	X	X	X	X	X	X	X	X	X				
Tangara meyerdeschauenseei																							XR						
Tangara nigrocincta																X	X		X			X	X	X	X				
Tangara nigroviridis																X	X					X	X	X					
Tangara palmeri															X	X						X							
Tangara parzudakii																X	X					X	X						
Tangara peruviana																									XR				
Tangara phillipsi																							XR						
Tangara preciosa																									X	X	X	X	
Tangara pulcherrima																X						X	X						
Tangara punctata																	X		X	X	X	X	X	X	X				
Tangara ruficervix																X						X	X	X					
Tangara rufigenis																	XR												
Tangara rufigula																X						X							
Tangara schrankii																X	X					X	X	X	X				
Tangara seledon																									X	X		X	
Tangara varia																	X			X	X				X				
Tangara vassorii																X	X					X	X	X					
Tangara velia																													
cyanomelaena																									XR				
velia																X	X		X	X	X	X	X	X	X				
Tangara viridicollis																						X	X						
Tangara vitriolina																X						X							
Tangara xanthocephala																X	X					X	X	X					
Tangara xanthogastra																X	X					X	X	X	X				
Dacnis albiventris																X	X					X	X		X				
Dacnis berlepschi																X						X							
Dacnis cayana												X	X	X	X	X	X	X	X	X	X	X	X	X	X	X		X	
Dacnis flaviventer																X	X					X	X	X	X				
Dacnis hartlaubi																XR													
Dacnis lineata																X	X		X	X	X	X	X	X	X				
Dacnis nigripes																									XR				
Dacnis venusta														X	X	X						X							
Dacnis viguieri															X	X													
Chlorophanes spiza								X	X	X		X	X	X	X	X	X	X	X	X	X	X	X	X	X				
Cyanerpes caeruleus															X	X	X	X	X	X	X	X	X	X	X				
Cyanerpes cyaneus		X					V	X	X	X	X	X	X	X	X	X	X	X	X	X	X	X	X	X	X				
Cyanerpes lucidus								X	X	X		X	X	X	X	X													
Cyanerpes nitidus																X	X					X	X		X				
Nephelornis oneilli																							XR						
Xenodacnis parina																						SX	X						
Oreomanes fraseri																X						X	X	X					SX
Diglossa albilatera																X	X					X	X						
Diglossa baritula																													
baritula								X	X		X	X																	
plumbea														X	X														
sittoides																X	X					X	X	X				X	
Diglossa caerulescens																X	X					X	X	X					

Status: X - Breeding species; **XN** - Regular non-breeding species; **XR** - Endemic breeding species; **X?** - Regular species, breeding status uncertain; **XI** - Introduced species; **XD** - Dubious species; **XF** - Formerly bred; **V** - Vagrants; **SX** - Breeding species, sight records only; **SN** - Regular non-breeding species, sight records only; **S?** - Uncertain breeding status; sight records only; **SI** -Introduced; sight records only; **SV** - Vagrant; sight records only. **?** - Occurrence uncertain; + -- - Extinct.

	Baha	Cuba	Hisp	Jama	Puer	Lant	Nant	Mexi	Guat	Beli	Elsa	Hond	Nica	Cost	Pana	Colo	Vene	Trin	Guya	Suri	Fren	Ecua	Peru	Boli	Braz	Parg	Urug	Argn	Chil
Diglossa carbonaria																													
brunneiventris																X							X	X					X?
carbonaria																								X				SX	
gloriosa																	XR												
humeralis																X	X					X	X						
Diglossa cyanea																X	X					X	X	X					
Diglossa duidae																	X								X				
Diglossa glauca																X						X	X	X					
Diglossa indigotica																X						X							
Diglossa lafresnayii																													
gloriosissima																XR													
lafresnayii																X	X					X	X						
mystacalis																							X	X					
Diglossa major																	X								X				
Diglossa venezuelensis																	XR												
Euneornis campestris				XR																									
Tersininae																													
Tersina viridis															X	X	X	X	X	X	X	X	X	X	X	X		X	
Parulinae																													
Mniotilta varia	XN	XN	XN	XN	XN	XN	XN	XN	XN	XN	XN	XN	XN	XN	XN	XN	XN	SN				XN	XN		SV				
Vermivora bachmanii	V	XN																											
Vermivora celata	XN							X	XN	XN	SV			V															
Vermivora chrysoptera	XN	XN	XN	XN	XN		SV	XN	XN	XN	XN	XN	XN	XN	XN	XN	XN	SV				SV							
Vermivora crissalis								X																					
Vermivora gutturalis														X	X														
Vermivora luciae								X																					
Vermivora peregrina	XN	XN	XN	V			XN	XN	XN	XN	XN	XN	XN	XN	XN	XN	XN				SV	SN							
Vermivora pinus	XN	XN	XN	XN	V			XN	XN	XN	SV	XN	XN	XN	XN	V													
Vermivora ruficapilla	XN	V		V				XN	XN	XN	XN	XN		V	SV														
Vermivora superciliosa								X	X		X	X	X																
Vermivora virginiae	SV							XN	SV	SV																			
Parula americana	XN	XN	XN	XN	XN	XN	XN	XN	XN	XN	V	XN	XN	XN	SV	SN	V	V											
Parula pitiayumi								X	X	X		X	X	X	X	X	X	X	X	X	X	X	X	X	X	X	X	X	
Dendroica adelaidae					X	X																							
Dendroica angelae					XR																								
Dendroica caerulescens	XN	XN	XN	XN	XN	V	XN	XN	XN	XN		XN		SN	SV	XN	V	SV											
Dendroica castanea	XN	XN	XN	XN	XN	XN	XN	XN	XN	XN		XN	XN	XN	XN	XN	XN	V				SV							
Dendroica cerulea	XN	XN		XN			V	XN	XN	XN		XN		XN	XN	XN	XN					XN	XN	XN	SV				
Dendroica chrysoparia								XN	XN			XN	XN																
Dendroica coronata	XN	XN	XN	XN	XN	XN	XN	X	X	XN	XN	XN	XN	XN	XN	XN	V	SV											
Dendroica discolor	XN	XN	XN	XN	XN	XN	SN	XN	V	XN	V	XN	V	XN	SV	V		SV											
Dendroica dominica	XN	XN	XN	XN	XN	V		XN	XN	XN	V	XN	XN	XN	V	SV		X											
Dendroica fusca	XN	XN	XN		V	XN	XN	XN	XN	XN	XN	XN	XN	XN	XN	XN	XN	SV	SN	SV	SV	XN	XN	SN	XN				
Dendroica graciae								X	X	X	X	X	X																
Dendroica kirtlandii	XN							SV																					
Dendroica magnolia	XN	XN	XN	XN	XN	V		XN	XN	XN	XN	XN	XN	XN	XN	XN	SV	SV											
Dendroica nigrescens								X	SV																				
Dendroica occidentalis								XN	XN		XN	XN	XN	XN	V														
Dendroica palmarum	XN	XN	XN	XN	XN		V	XN	?	XN		XN	XN	XN	V	XN													
Dendroica pensylvanica	XN	XN	XN	XN	XN	V	SV	XN	XN	XN	V	XN	XN	XN	XN	XN	XN	SV				SV							

Countries: Argn - Argentina; **Baha** - Bahamas; **Beli** - Belize; **Boli** - Bolivia; **Braz** - Brazil; **Chil** - Chile; **Colo** - Colombia; **Cost** - Costa Rica; **Cuba** - Cuba; **Ecua** - Ecuador; **Elsa** - El Salvador; **Fren** - French Guiana; **Guat** - Guatemala; **Guya** - Guyana; **Hisp** - Hispaniola; **Hond** - Honduras; **Jama** - Jamaica; **Lant** - Lesser Antilles; **Mexi** - Mexico; **Nant** - Netherland Antilles; **Nica** - Nicaragua; **Pana** - Panama; **Parg** - Paraguay; **Peru** - Peru; **Puer** - Puerto Rico; **Suri** - Suriname; **Trin** - Trinidad; **Urug** - Uruguay; **Vene** - Venezuela.

	Baha	Cuba	Hisp	Jama	Puer	Lant	Nant	Mexi	Guat	Beli	Elsa	Hond	Nica	Cost	Pana	Colo	Vene	Trin	Guya	Suri	Fren	Ecua	Peru	Boli	Braz	Parg	Urug	Argn	Chil
Dendroica petechia																													
aestiva	XN	XN	XN	XN	XN	XN	XN	X	XN	XN	XN	XN	X	XN	XN	XN	XN	XN	XN	XN	XN	XN	XN	SV	XN				
erithachorides								X	X	X	X	X	X	X	X	X	X					X	X						
petechia	X	X	X	X	X	X	X	X								X	X												
Dendroica pharetra				XR																									
Dendroica pinus	X	XN	X					XN		V		XN		SV															
Dendroica pityophila	X	X																											
Dendroica plumbea						XR																							
Dendroica striata	XN	XN	XN	XN	XN	XN	XN	XN						XN	V	XN	XN	XN	XN	XN	XN	XN	XN		XN		V	V	V
Dendroica tigrina	XN	XN	XN	XN	XN	XN	SN	XN	XN	V	V	XN	XN	XN	XN	XN	XN	XN											
Dendroica townsendi								XN	XN		XN	XN	XN	XN	V	V													
Dendroica virens	XN	XN	XN	XN	XN	V	XN	XN	XN	XN	XN	XN	XN	XN	XN	XN	XN	SV											
Dendroica vitellina												X																	
Catharopeza bishopi						XR																							
Setophaga ruticilla	XN	XN	XN	XN	XN	XN	XN	XN	XN	XN	XN	XN	XN	XN	XN	XN	XN	XN	XN	XN	XN	XN	XN		XN				SV
Seiurus aurocapillus	XN	XN	XN	XN	XN	XN	XN	XN	XN	XN	XN	XN	XN	XN	XN	XN	XN	V											
Seiurus motacilla	XN	XN	XN	XN	XN	XN	XN	XN	XN	XN	V	XN	XN	XN	XN	XN	XN												
Seiurus noveboracensis	XN	XN	XN	XN	XN	XN	XN	XN	XN	XN	XN	XN	XN	XN	XN	XN	XN	XN	XN	XN	XN	XN	XN		XN				
Limnothlypis swainsonii	XN	XN		XN	V			XN	SN	XN		XN																	
Helmitheros vermivorus	XN	XN	XN	XN	XN			XN	XN	XN	XN	XN	XN	XN	XN	SV	V												
Protonotaria citrea	XN	XN	XN	XN	XN	XN	XN	XN	XN	XN		XN	XN	XN	XN	XN	XN	XN	XN	V		V							
Geothlypis aequinoctialis														X	X	X	X	X	X	X	X	X	X	X	X	X	X	X	
Geothlypis agilis	XN		V		XN	V	XN			V		V		SV	XN	XN	XN				SV		XN		XN				
Geothlypis beldingi								XR																					
Geothlypis flavovelata								XR																					
Geothlypis formosus	XN	XN	XN	XN	XN	V	XN	XN	XN	XN	XN	XN	XN	XN	XN	XN	XN												
Geothlypis nelsoni								XR																					
Geothlypis philadelphia	V		XN		V		SV	XN	XN	XN	XN	XN	XN	XN	XN	XN	XN					XN							
Geothlypis poliocephala								X	X	X	X	X	X	X	X														
Geothlypis rostrata	XR																												
Geothlypis semiflava												X	X	X	X	X						X							
Geothlypis speciosa								XR																					
Geothlypis tolmiei								XN	XN		XN	XN	XN	XN	XN														
Geothlypis trichas	XN	XN	XN	XN	XN	V	SV	X	XN	XN	XN	XN	XN	XN	XN	XN	V	SV											
Microligea palustris			XR																										
Teretistris fernandinae		XR																											
Teretistris fornsi		XR																											
Leucopeza semperi						XR																							
Wilsonia canadensis	XN	V		XN	XN	V		XN	XN	XN	XN	XN	XN	XN	XN	XN	XN					XN	XN						
Wilsonia citrina	XN	XN	XN	XN	XN		XN	XN	XN	XN	XN	XN	XN	XN	XN	SN	XN	SV											
Wilsonia pusilla	V	V		V	V			XN	XN	XN	XN	XN	XN	XN	XN	SV													
Cardellina rubrifrons								X	XN		XN	XN																	
Ergaticus ruber								XR																					
Ergaticus versicolor								X	X																				
Myioborus albifacies																	XR												
Myioborus albifrons																	XR												
Myioborus brunniceps																													
brunniceps																								X				X	
castaneocapillus																	X		X						X				
Myioborus cardonai																	XR												
Myioborus flavivertex																XR													
Myioborus melanocephalus																X						X	X	X					

Status: X - Breeding species; **XN** - Regular non-breeding species; **XR** - Endemic breeding species; **X?** - Regular species, breeding status uncertain; **XI** - Introduced species; **XD** - Dubious species; **XF** - Formerly bred; **V** - Vagrants; **SX** - Breeding species, sight records only; **SN** - Regular non-breeding species, sight records only; **S?** - Uncertain breeding status; sight records only; **SI** -Introduced; sight records only; **SV** - Vagrant; sight records only. **?** - Occurrence uncertain; **+** -- - Extinct.

	Baha	Cuba	Hisp	Jama	Puer	Lant	Nant	Mexi	Guat	Beli	Elsa	Hond	Nica	Cost	Pana	Colo	Vene	Trin	Guya	Suri	Fren	Ecua	Peru	Boli	Braz	Parg	Urug	Argn	Chil
Myioborus miniatus								X	X		X	X		X	X	X	X		X			X	X	X	X				
Myioborus ornatus																X	X												
Myioborus pariae																	XR												
Myioborus pictus								X	X		X	X	X																
Myioborus torquatus														X	X														
Euthlypis lachrymosa								X	X		X	X	X																
Basileuterus basilicus																XR													
Basileuterus belli								X	X		X	X																	
Basileuterus bivittatus																	X		X				X	X	X			X	
Basileuterus chrysogaster																X						X	X						
Basileuterus cinereicollis																X	X												
Basileuterus conspicillatus																XR													
Basileuterus coronatus																X	X					X	X	X					
Basileuterus culicivorus								X	X	X	X	X	X	X	X	X	X	X	X					X	X	X	X	X	
Basileuterus flaveolus																X	X		X					X	X	X			
Basileuterus fraseri																						X	X						
Basileuterus griseiceps																	XR												
Basileuterus hypoleucus																								X	X	X			
Basileuterus ignotus															X	X													
Basileuterus leucoblepharus																									X	X	X	X	
Basileuterus leucophrys																									XR				
Basileuterus luteoviridis																X	X					X	X	X					
Basileuterus melanogenys														X	X														
Basileuterus nigrocristatus																X	X					X	X						
Basileuterus rufifrons								X	X	X	X	X	X	X	X	X	X												
Basileuterus signatus																X							X	X				X	
Basileuterus trifasciatus																						X	X						
Basileuterus tristriatus														X	X	X	X					X	X	X					
Phaeothlypis fulvicauda												X	X	X	X	X						X	X	X	X				
Phaeothlypis rivularis																	X		X	X	X			X	X	X		X	
Zeledonia coronata														X	X														
Peucedramus taeniatus								X	X		X	X	X																
Xenoligea montana			XR																										
Granatellus pelzelni																	X		X	X	X			X	X				
Granatellus sallaei								X	X	X																			
Granatellus venustus								XR																					
Icteria virens	V	V				V		X	XN	XN	XN	XN	XN	XN	XN														
Conirostrum albifrons																X	X					X	X	X					
Conirostrum bicolor																X	X	X	X	X	X	SX	X		X				
Conirostrum cinereum																X						X	X	X					X
Conirostrum ferrugineiventre																							X	X					
Conirostrum leucogenys															X	X	X												
Conirostrum margaritae																							X		X				
Conirostrum rufum																XR													
Conirostrum sitticolor																X	X					X	X	X					
Conirostrum speciosum																X	X		X	X	X	X	X	X	X	X		X	
Conirostrum tamarugense																							X						X
Coereba flaveola	X	XN	X	X	X	X	X	X	X	X		X	X	X	X	X	X	X	X	X	X	X	X	X	X	X		X	
Vireonidae																													
Cyclarhis gujanensis								X	X	X	X	X	X	X	X	X	X	X	X	X	X	X	X	X	X	X	X	X	
Cyclarhis nigrirostris																X						X							
Vireolanius eximius															X	X	X												

Countries: Argn - Argentina; **Baha** - Bahamas; **Beli** - Belize; **Boli** - Bolivia; **Braz** - Brazil; **Chil** - Chile; **Colo** - Colombia; **Cost** - Costa Rica; **Cuba** - Cuba; **Ecua** - Ecuador; **Elsa** - El Salvador; **Fren** - French Guiana; **Guat** - Guatemala; **Guya** - Guyana; **Hisp** - Hispaniola; **Hond** - Honduras; **Jama** - Jamaica; **Lant** - Lesser Antilles; **Mexi** - Mexico; **Nant** - Netherland Antilles; **Nica** - Nicaragua; **Pana** - Panama; **Parg** - Paraguay; **Peru** - Peru; **Puer** - Puerto Rico; **Suri** - Suriname; **Trin** - Trinidad; **Urug** - Uruguay; **Vene** - Venezuela.

	Baha	Cuba	Hisp	Jama	Puer	Lant	Nant	Mexi	Guat	Beli	Elsa	Hond	Nica	Cost	Pana	Colo	Vene	Trin	Guya	Suri	Fren	Ecua	Peru	Boli	Braz	Parg	Urug	Argn	Chil
Vireolanius leucotis																X	X		X	X	X	X	X	X	X				
Vireolanius melitophrys								X	X																				
Vireolanius pulchellus								X	X	X	X	X	X	X	X														
Vireo altiloquus	X	X	X	X	X	X	X	V		XN				V	XN	X	X	XN	XN	V	XN		XN		XN				
Vireo atricapillus								X																					
Vireo bairdi								XR																					
Vireo bellii								X	XN		XN	XN	XN																
Vireo brevipennis								XR																					
Vireo caribaeus																XR													
Vireo carmioli														X	X														
Vireo crassirostris	X		X													X													
Vireo flavifrons	XN	XN		XN	XN	V	V	XN	XN	XN	XN	XN	XN	XN	XN	XN	XN	V											
Vireo flavoviridis								X	X		X		X	X	X	XN	V					XN	XN	XN	V				
Vireo gilvus		V		V				X	XN	XN	XN	XN	XN	SN															
Vireo gracilirostris																									XR				
Vireo griseus	XN	XN			XN			X	XN	XN		XN	XN	V	V														
Vireo gundlachii		XR																											
Vireo huttoni								X	X																				
Vireo hypochryseus								XR																					
Vireo latimeri					XR																								
Vireo leucophrys								X	X		SX	X		X	X	X	X					X	X	X					
Vireo magister								X		X		X																	
Vireo modestus				XR																									
Vireo nanus			XR																										
Vireo nelsoni								XR																					
Vireo olivaceus																													
chivi																X	X	X	X	X	X	X	X	X	X	X	X	X	
olivaceus	XN	XN		XN	XN	V	XN	XN	XN	XN	XN	XN	XN	XN	XN	XN	XN		XN	XN	XN	XN	XN	XN	XN				V
Vireo osburni				XR																									
Vireo pallens								X	X	X	X	X	X	X															
Vireo philadelphicus	XN	XN		V				XN	XN	XN	XN	XN	XN	XN	XN	XN													
Vireo solitarius																													
cassinii								X	XN																				
plumbeus								X	X	X	X	X																	
solitarius	XN	XN		SV				XN	XN	XN	XN	XN		XN	V														
Vireo vicinior								X																					
Hylophilus aurantiifrons															X	X	X	X											
Hylophilus brunneiceps																X	X								X				
Hylophilus decurtatus								X	X	X	X	X	X	X	X	X						X	X						
Hylophilus flavipes														X	X	X	X	X											
Hylophilus hypoxanthus																X	X					X	X	X	X				
Hylophilus muscicapinus																	X		X	X	X			X	X				
Hylophilus ochraceiceps								X	X	X		X	X	X	X	X	X		X	X	X	X	X	X	X				
Hylophilus olivaceus																						X	X						
Hylophilus pectoralis																	X		X	X	X		X?	X	X				
Hylophilus poicilotis																													
amaurocephalus																								X	X				
poicilotis																									X	X		X	
Hylophilus sclateri																	X		X						X				
Hylophilus semibrunneus																X	X					X							
Hylophilus semicinereus																	X				X			X	X				
Hylophilus thoracicus																?	X		X	X	X		X	X	X				

Status: X - Breeding species; **XN** - Regular non-breeding species; **XR** - Endemic breeding species; **X?** - Regular species, breeding status uncertain; **XI** - Introduced species; **XD** - Dubious species; **XF** - Formerly bred; **V** - Vagrants; **SX** - Breeding species, sight records only; **SN** - Regular non-breeding species, sight records only; **S?** - Uncertain breeding status; sight records only; **SI** -Introduced; sight records only; **SV** - Vagrant; sight records only. **?** - Occurrence uncertain; + --- - Extinct.

	Baha	Cuba	Hisp	Jama	Puer	Lant	Nant	Mexi	Guat	Beli	Elsa	Hond	Nica	Cost	Pana	Colo	Vene	Trin	Guya	Suri	Fren	Ecua	Peru	Boli	Braz	Parg	Urug	Argn	Chil
Icteridae																													
Icterus auratus								XR		X?																			
Icterus auricapillus															X	X	X												
Icterus bonana						XR																							
Icterus cayanensis																													
cayanensis																X?				X	X		X	X	X				
chrysocephalus																X	X	X	X	X	X	X	X		X				
pyrrhopterus																								X	X	X	X	X	
Icterus chrysater								X	X	X	X	X	X		X	X	X												
Icterus cucullatus								X																					
Icterus dominicensis																													
dominicensis	X	X	X		X																								
prosthemelas								X	X	X		X	X	X	X														
Icterus galbula																													
abeillei								XR																					
bullockii								X	XN			SV		XN															
galbula	XN	XN	XN	XN	XN	XN	XN	XN	XN	XN	XN	XN	XN	XN	XN	XN	XN	SV				SV							
Icterus graceannae																						X	X						
Icterus graduacauda								X																					
Icterus gularis								X	X	X	X	X	X																
Icterus icterus					XI		X									X	X		X			X	X	X	X	X		X	
Icterus laudabilis						XR																							
Icterus leucopteryx				X												X													
Icterus maculialatus								X	X		X	X																	
Icterus mesomelas								X	X	X		X	X	X	X	X	X					X	X						
Icterus nigrogularis							X									X	X	X	X	X	X				X				
Icterus oberi						XR																							
Icterus parisorum								X																					
Icterus pectoralis								X	X		X	X	X	X															
Icterus pustulatus								X	X		X	X	X	X															
Icterus spurius																													
fuertesi								XR																					
spurius	XN	XN		XN				X	XN	XN	XN	XN	XN	XN	XN	XN	XN												
Icterus wagleri								X	X		X	X	X																
Psarocolius angustifrons																X	X					X	X	X	X				
Psarocolius atrovirens																							X	X					
Psarocolius bifasciatus																X	X					X	X	X	X				
Psarocolius cassini																XR													
Psarocolius decumanus															X	X	X	X	X	X	X	X	X	X	X	X		X	
Psarocolius guatimozinus															X	X													
Psarocolius latirostris																X						X	X		X				
Psarocolius montezuma								X	X	X		X	X	X	X														
Psarocolius oseryi																						X	X	X	SX				
Psarocolius viridis																X	X		X	X	X	X	X		X				
Psarocolius wagleri								X	X	X		X	X	X	X	X						X							
Cacicus cela															X	X	X	X	X	X	X	X	X	X	X				
Cacicus chrysopterus																								X	X	X	X	X	
Cacicus haemorrhous																X	X		X	X	X	X	X	X	X	X		X	
Cacicus holosericeus								X	X	X	X	X	X	X	X	X	X					X	X	X					
Cacicus koepckeae																							XR						

Countries: **Argn** - Argentina; **Baha** - Bahamas; **Beli** - Belize; **Boli** - Bolivia; **Braz** - Brazil; **Chil** - Chile; **Colo** - Colombia; **Cost** - Costa Rica; **Cuba** - Cuba; **Ecua** - Ecuador; **Elsa** - El Salvador; **Fren** - French Guiana; **Guat** - Guatemala; **Guya** - Guyana; **Hisp** - Hispaniola; **Hond** - Honduras; **Jama** - Jamaica; **Lant** - Lesser Antilles; **Mexi** - Mexico; **Nant** - Netherland Antilles; **Nica** - Nicaragua; **Pana** - Panama; **Parg** - Paraguay; **Peru** - Peru; **Puer** - Puerto Rico; **Suri** - Suriname; **Trin** - Trinidad; **Urug** - Uruguay; **Vene** - Venezuela.

	Baha	Cuba	Hisp	Jama	Puer	Lant	Nant	Mexi	Guat	Beli	Elsa	Hond	Nica	Cost	Pana	Colo	Vene	Trin	Guya	Suri	Fren	Ecua	Peru	Boli	Braz	Parg	Urug	Argn	Chil
Cacicus leucoramphus																													
chrysonotus																							X	X					
leucoramphus																X	X					X	X						
Cacicus melanicterus								X	X																				
Cacicus sclateri																						X	X						
Cacicus solitarius																X	X					X	X	X	X	X	X	X	
Cacicus uropygialis																													
microrhynchus												X	X	X	X	X						X							
uropygialis																X	X					X	X						
Nesopsar nigerrimus				XR																									
Xanthopsar flavus																									X	X	X	X	
Gymnomystax mexicanus																X	X		X		X	X	X		X				
Xanthocephalus xanthocephalus	V	V				V		X						V	V														
Agelaius cyanopus																								X	X	X		X	
Agelaius humeralis		X	X																										
Agelaius icterocephalus							SV									X	X	X	X	X	X		X		X	?			
Agelaius phoeniceus	X	X						X	X	X	X	X	X	X				SV											
Agelaius ruficapillus																					X			X	X	X	X	X	
Agelaius thilius																							X	X	X	X	X	X	X
Agelaius tricolor								X																					
Agelaius xanthomus					XR																								
Agelaius xanthophthalmus																						X	X						
Sturnella bellicosa																						X	X						X
Sturnella defilippi																									X		X	X	
Sturnella loyca																												X	X
Sturnella magna		X					SV	X	X	X		X	X	X	X	X	X		X	X	X				X				
Sturnella militaris														X	X	X	X	X	X	X	X	X	X	X	X				
Sturnella neglecta								X																					
Sturnella superciliaris																							XN	X	X	X	X	X	V
Pseudoleistes guirahuro																									X	X	X	X	
Pseudoleistes virescens																									X	X	X	X	
Amblyramphus holosericeus																								X	X	X	X	X	
Hypopyrrhus pyrohypogaster																XR													
Curaeus curaeus																												X	X
Curaeus forbesi																									XR				
Gnorimopsar chopi																							X	X	X	X	X	X	
Oreopsar bolivianus																								XR					
Lampropsar tanagrinus																X	X		X			X	X	X	X				
Macroagelaius imthurni																	X		X						X				
Macroagelaius subalaris																XR													
Dives atroviolacea		XR																											
Dives dives								X	X	X	X	X	X	V															
Dives warszewiczi																						X	X						
Quiscalus lugubris						X	V									X	X	X	X	X	X				X				
Quiscalus mexicanus								X	X	X	X	X	X	X	X	X	X					X	X						
Quiscalus nicaraguensis													X	X															
Quiscalus niger		X	X	X	X																								
Euphagus carolinus	V	V						V																					
Euphagus cyanocephalus	V							X	V																				
Molothrus aeneus																													
aeneus								X	X	X	X	X	X	X	X														
armenti																XR													

Status: X - Breeding species; **XN** - Regular non-breeding species; **XR** - Endemic breeding species; **X?** - Regular species, breeding status uncertain; **XI** - Introduced species; **XD** - Dubious species; **XF** - Formerly bred; **V** - Vagrants; **SX** - Breeding species, sight records only; **SN** - Regular non-breeding species, sight records only; **S?** - Uncertain breeding status; sight records only; **SI** -Introduced; sight records only; **SV** - Vagrant; sight records only. **?** - Occurrence uncertain; **+** --- - Extinct.

	Baha	Cuba	Hisp	Jama	Puer	Lant	Nant	Mexi	Guat	Beli	Elsa	Hond	Nica	Cost	Pana	Colo	Vene	Trin	Guya	Suri	Fren	Ecua	Peru	Boli	Braz	Parg	Urug	Argn	Chil
Molothrus ater	V	V						X																					
Molothrus badius																								X	X	X	X	X	X?
Molothrus bonariensis		X	X		X	X									X	X	X	X	X	X	X	X	X	X	X	X	X	X	X
Molothrus rufoaxillaris																								X	X	X	X	X	
Scaphidura oryzivora								X	X	X		X	X	X	X	X	X	X	X	X	X	X	X	X	X	X		X	
Dolichonyx oryzivorus	XN	XN	XN	XN	XN	V	XN	XN	V	V		V	V	V	XN	XN	XN	SV	XN	XN	XN	XN	XN	XN	XN	XN		XN	V
Fringillidae																													
Carduelis atrata																							X	X				X	X
Carduelis atriceps								X	X																				
Carduelis barbata																												X	X
Carduelis crassirostris																							X	X				X	X
Carduelis cucullata		XI			XI											X	X	XF											
Carduelis dominicensis			XR																										
Carduelis lawrencei								X																					
Carduelis magellanica																X	X		X			X	X	X	X	X	X	X	X
Carduelis notata								X	X	X	X	X	X																
Carduelis olivacea																						X	X	X					
Carduelis pinus								X																					
Carduelis psaltria			V					X	X	?	X	X	X	X	X	X	X					X	X						
Carduelis siemiradzkii																						X	X						
Carduelis spinescens																X	X					X							
Carduelis tristis	XN							XN																					
Carduelis uropygialis																							X?	X?				X	X
Carduelis xanthogastra														X	X	X	X					X	X	X					
Carduelis yarrellii																	X?								XR				
Carpodacus cassinii								X																					
Carpodacus mexicanus								X																					
Carpodacus purpureus								XN																					
Loxia curvirostra								X	X	X	X	X	X																
Loxia leucoptera megaplaga			XR	SV																									
Coccothraustes abeillei								X	X		X																		
Coccothraustes vespertinus								X																					
Estrildidae																													
Estrilda astrild																									XI				
Passeridae																													
Passer domesticus	XI	XI	XI	XI	XI		XI	X	XI	XI	XI	?	XI	XI	XI	XI						XI	XI	XI	XI	XI	XI	XI	XI
Sturnidae																													
Sturnus vulgaris	XI	XI	?	XI	XI		VI	XI							SI														
Corvidae																													
Gymnorhinus cyanocephalus								X																					
Cyanocitta stelleri								X	X		X	X	X																
Aphelocoma coerulescens								X																					
Aphelocoma ultramarina								X																					
Aphelocoma unicolor								X	X		X	X																	
Cyanolyca argentigula														X	X														
Cyanolyca cucullata								X	X			X		X	X														
Cyanolyca mirabilis								XR																					
Cyanolyca nana								XR																					
Cyanolyca pulchra																X						X							
Cyanolyca pumilo								X	X		X	X																	
Cyanolyca turcosa																X						X	X						

Countries: **Argn** - Argentina; **Baha** - Bahamas; **Beli** - Belize; **Boli** - Bolivia; **Braz** - Brazil; **Chil** - Chile; **Colo** - Colombia; **Cost** - Costa Rica; **Cuba** - Cuba; **Ecua** - Ecuador; **Elsa** - El Salvador; **Fren** - French Guiana; **Guat** - Guatemala; **Guya** - Guyana; **Hisp** - Hispaniola; **Hond** - Honduras; **Jama** - Jamaica; **Lant** - Lesser Antilles; **Mexi** - Mexico; **Nant** - Netherland Antilles; **Nica** - Nicaragua; **Pana** - Panama; **Parg** - Paraguay; **Peru** - Peru; **Puer** - Puerto Rico; **Suri** - Suriname; **Trin** - Trinidad; **Urug** - Uruguay; **Vene** - Venezuela.

	Baha	Cuba	Hisp	Jama	Puer	Lant	Nant	Mexi	Guat	Beli	Elsa	Hond	Nica	Cost	Pana	Colo	Vene	Trin	Guya	Suri	Fren	Ecua	Peru	Boli	Braz	Parg	Urug	Argn	Chil
Cyanolyca viridicyana																													
armillata																X	X					X							
viridicyana																							X	X					
Cyanocorax affinis														X	X	X	X												
Cyanocorax caeruleus																									X	X		X	
Cyanocorax cayanus																	X		X	X	X				X				
Cyanocorax chrysops																								X	X	X	X	X	
Cyanocorax cristatellus																								X	X	X			
Cyanocorax cyanomelas																							X	X	X	X		X	
Cyanocorax cyanopogon																									XR				
Cyanocorax dickeyi								XR																					
Cyanocorax heilprini																X	X								X				
Cyanocorax mystacalis																						X	X						
Cyanocorax violaceus																X	X		X			X	X	X	X				
Cyanocorax yncas								X	X	X		X				X	X					X	X	X					
Cissilopha beecheii								XR																					
Cissilopha melanocyaneus									X		X	X	X																
Cissilopha sanblasianus								XR																					
Cissilopha yucatanicus								X	X	X																			
Psilorhinus morio								X	X	X		X	X	X	X														
Calocitta colliei								XR																					
Calocitta formosa								X	X		X	X	X	X															
Nucifraga columbiana								X																					
Corvus brachyrhynchos								X																					
Corvus corax								X	X		X	X	X																
Corvus cryptoleucus								X																					
Corvus imparatus																													
imparatus								XR																					
sinaloae								XR																					
Corvus jamaicensis				XR																									
Corvus leucognaphalus			X		XF																								
Corvus nasicus	X	X																											
Corvus palmarum		X	X																										

Status: **X** - Breeding species; **XN** - Regular non-breeding species; **XR** - Endemic breeding species; **X?** - Regular species, breeding status uncertain; **XI** - Introduced species; **XD** - Dubious species; **XF** - Formerly bred; **V** - Vagrants; **SX** - Breeding species, sight records only; **SN** - Regular non-breeding species, sight records only; **S?** - Uncertain breeding status; sight records only; **SI** -Introduced; sight records only; **SV** - Vagrant; sight records only. **?** - Occurrence uncertain; **+** -- - Extinct.

Database C

Nearctic Migrants 1: Species Not Breeding in the Neotropics

	Snst	Stat	CP	RP	Min	Max	Habitats	Zoogeographic Regions
GAVIIFORMES								
Gaviidae								
Gavia immer	M	F	4	3	L	L	A11	BSR, PAS, GCS
Gavia pacifica	H	F	4	3	L	L	A11	BSR
Gavia stellata	H	F	4	3	L	L	A11	BSR
PODICIPEDIFORMES								
Podicipedidae								
Podiceps auritus	M	F	4	3	L	L	A11	BSR
ANSERIFORMES								
Anatidae								
Cygnus columbianus	L	F	4	3	L	2000	A6	BSR, MPL
Anser albifrons	L	F	4	2	L	2500	A6, N13, A1	BSR, MPL, PAS, GCS
Anser caerulescens	L	F	4	3	L	2500	N13, A6, A1	BSR, MPL, MAH, GCS
Anser rossii	L	F	4	3	1200	2500	N13, A6, A1	MPL
Branta bernicla	M	F	4	3	L	L	A11, A2	BSR
Branta canadensis	L	F	4	2	L	1800	A6, N13, A1	BSR, MPL, GCS
Anas acuta	L	S	4	3	L	2000	A1, A6	GAN, LAN, BSR, MPL, PAS, MAH, GCS, NSA
Anas americana	L	S	4	2	L	2300	A6, A1	GAN, LAN, BSR, MPL, PAS, MAH, GCS, NSA
Anas clypeata	L	S	4	3	L	2100	A1, A6	GAN, LAN, BSR, MPL, PAS, MAH, GCS, NSA
Anas crecca	L	S	4	3	L	2100	A1, A6	GAN, LAN, BSR, MPL, PAS, MAH, GCS, NSA?
Anas discors	L	S	4	3	L	2600	A1, A6	GAN, LAN, BSR, MPL, PAS, MAH, GCS, CHO, EPC, STP, NAN, NSA, AMN, AMS, CSA, ATL?, PAM
Anas penelope	L	F	4	3	L	L	A6	GAN, LAN, BSR
Anas strepera	L	S	3	2	L	1800	A1, A2, A6	GAN, BSR, MPL, PAS, MAH, GCS
Aythya affinis	M	S	4	2	L	2500	A6, A11	GAN, LAN, BSR, MPL, PAS, MAH, GCS, NSA
Aythya collaris	M	S	4	3	L	2000	A6	GAN, LAN, BSR, MPL, PAS, MAH, GCS
Aythya marila	H	F	4	3	L	L	A11	BSR
Aythya valisineria	M	S	3	2	L	2500	A6, A11	BSR, MPL, PAS, MAH, GCS
Melanitta fusca	H	F	4	3	L	L	A11	BSR
Melanitta nigra	H	F	4	3	L	L	A11	BSR
Melanitta perspicillata	H	F	4	3	L	L	A11	BSR
Bucephala albeola	M	F	4	3	L	2500	A6, A11	BSR, MPL, GCS
Bucephala clangula	M	F	4	3	L	2000	A6, A11	BSR, MPL, GCS
Mergus cucullatus	M	F	4	3	L	2000	A6	GAN, BSR, MPL, GCS
Mergus serrator	M	F	4	3	L	1500	A11, A6	BSR, GCS
FALCONIFORMES								
Accipitridae								
Ictinia mississippiensis	L	A	4	1	L	L?	F7	CSA
Buteo lagopus	L	F	4	3	L	1600	N8	MPL
Buteo regalis	M	S	4	2	L	1900	N8, N2	BSR, MPL
Falconidae								
Falco columbarius	L	S	4	2	L	3400	N13, F8	GAN, BSR, MPL, PAS, MAH, GCS, CDH, CHO, EPC, NAN, NSA
GRUIFORMES								
Gruidae								
Grus americana	M	F	1	1	L	L	A2	GCS
CHARADRIIFORMES								
Charadriidae								
Pluvialis dominicus								
dominicus	L	A	4	3	L	800	N7, N13	AMN, AMS, CSA, PAM, PAT
fulva	L	F	4	3	L	L	A3, N13, N8	BSR, PAS

Notes
Occasionally on large inland lakes.
Winters mainly north of Mexico.
Winters mainly north of Mexico.
Status in Neotropics poorly known.
Local south of U.S..
Monitor.
Monitor.
Monitor.
Rare in Baja California, casual elsewhere.
Monitor; probably declining.
Monitor.
Winters mainly north of Neotropics.
Monitor; apparently declining.
Winters mainly north of Neotropics.
Winters mainly north of Neotropics.
Winters mainly north of Neotropics.
Winters mainly north of Neotropics.
Winters mainly north of Neotropics.
Winters mainly north of Neotropics.
Winters mainly north of Neotropics.
Winter range and habitats poorly known.
Very rare in Mexico.
Monitor.
Winter distribution and habitats poorly known.
Few recent records south of Texas.
Mainly winters on Pacific islands.

Abbreviations Used

Snst - Sensitivity:
L - Low; **M** - Medium; **H** - High.

Stat - Status:
A - All; **F** - Fraction; **S** - Some; **T** - Total;

CP -Conservation Priority:
1 - Urgent; **2** - High; **3** - Medium; **4** - Low.

RP - Research Priority:
1 - High; **2** - Medium; **3** - Low.

Min - Minimum Elevation:
L - Lowlands; **?** - Uncertain value; numeric values in meters.

Max - Maximum Elevation:
L - Lowlands; **?** - Uncertain value; **+** - species occurs at least to given elevation but likely occurs higher; numeric values in meters.

Habitats:
F1 - Tropical lowland evergreen forest; **F2** - Flooded tropical evergreen forest; **F3** - River-edge forest; **F4** - Montane evergreen forest; **F5** - Elfin forest; **F6** - *Polylepis* woodland; **F7** - Tropical deciduous forest; **F8** - Gallery forest; **F9** - Southern temperate forest; **F10** - Pine forest; **F11** - Pine-oak forest; **F12** - White sand forest; **F13** - Palm forest; **F14** - Mangrove forest; **F15** - Secondary forest; **N1** - Arid lowland scrub; **N2** - Arid montane scrub; **N3** - Semihumid/humid montane scrub; **N4** - Cerrado; **N5** - Campo grasslands; **N6** - Low, seasonally wet grassland; **N7** - Southern temperate grassland; **N8** - Northern temperate grassland; **N9** - Puna grassland; **N10** - Paramo grassland; **N11** - Riparian thickets; **N12** - River island scrub; **N13** - Pastures/agricultural lands; **N14** - Second-growth scrub; **A1** - Freshwater marshes; **A2** - Saltwater/brackish marshes; **A3** - Coastal sand beaches/mudflats; **A4** - Coastal rocky beaches; **A5** - Riverine sand beaches; **A6** - Freshwater lakes and ponds; **A7** - Alkaline lakes; **A8** - Rivers; **A9** - Streams; **A10** - Bogs; **A11** - Coastal waters; **A12** - Pelagic waters.
E - Edge (used as a modifer to particular habitats).

Zoogeographic Regions:
AMN - Northern Amazonia; **AMS** - Southern Amazonia; **ATL** - Atlantic Forest; **BSR** - Baja-Sonora; **CAN** - Central Andes; **CDH** - Chiriquí-Darién Highlands; **CHO** - Chocó Lowlands; **CSA** - Central South America; **EPC** - Equatorial Pacific Coast; **GAN** - Greater Antilles; **GCS** - Gulf-Caribbean Slope; **LAN** - Lesser Antilles; **MAH** - Madrean Highlands; **MPL** - Mexican Plateau; **NAN** - Northern Andes; **NSA** - Northern South America; **PAM** - Pampas; **PAS** - Pacific Arid Slope; **PAT** - Patagonia; **SAN** - Southern Andes; **STP** - Subtropical Pacific; **TEP** - Tepuis.

	Snst	Stat	CP	RP	Min	Max	Habitats	Zoogeographic Regions
Pluvialis squatarola	L	S	4	3	L	L	A3, A4	GAN, LAN, BSR, PAS, GCS, CHO, EPC, STP, NSA, AMN, AMS, ATL, PAM, PAT
Charadrius melodus	M	F	2	1	L	L	A3	GAN, GCS
Charadrius montanus	M	S	3	2	L	1800	N8, N13	BSR, MPL, GCS
Charadrius semipalmatus	M	S	4	3	L	L	A3, A1	GAN, LAN, BSR, PAS, GCS, CHO, EPC, STP, NSA, AMN, AMS, ATL, PAM, PAT
Scolopacidae								
Limosa fedoa	M	S	3	2	L	L	A2, A1, A3	BSR, PAS, GCS, CHO, EPC, STP, NSA
Limosa haemastica	M	A	3	2	L	1000	A1, A2, A3	STP, CSA, PAM, PAT
Numenius americanus	M	S	3	2	L	2200+	A3, A1, A2, N13, N8	BSR, MPL, PAS, GCS
Numenius borealis	M	A	1	1	L	L	N7	CSA, PAM, PAT?
Numenius phaeopus	M	S	4	3	L	L	A3, N13	GAN, LAN, BSR, PAS, GCS, CHO, EPC, STP, NSA, AMN, AMS, ATL, PAM, PAT
Bartramia longicauda	M	A	3	2	L	1100	N7, N6, N13	AMN?, AMS, CSA, PAM, PAT
Tringa flavipes	L	S	4	3	L	4000	A1, A2, A3	GAN, LAN, BSR, MPL, PAS, MAH, GCS, CDH, CHO, EPC, STP, NAN, CAN, SAN, NSA, AMN, AMS, CSA, ATL, PAM, PAT
Tringa melanoleuca	L	S	4	3	L	4300	A1, A2, A3, A5	GAN, LAN, BSR, MPL, PAS, MAH, GCS, CDH, CHO, EPC, STP, NAN, CAN, SAN, NSA, AMN, AMS, CSA, ATL, PAM, PAT
Tringa solitaria	L	A	4	3	L	1500	A6, A5	GAN, LAN, BSR, PAS, GCS, CDH, CHO, EPC, STP, NSA, AMN, AMS, CSA, ATL, PAM
Actitis macularia	L	S	4	3	L	2200	A5, A6, A3	GAN, LAN, BSR, MPL, PAS, MAH, GCS, CDH, CHO, EPC, STP, NAN, CAN, NSA, TEP AMN, AMS, CSA, ATL, PAM
Heteroscelus incanus	L	S	4	3	L	900	A4	BSR, PAS, CHO, EPC, STP
Arenaria interpres	H	S	4	3	L	L	A3, A4, A2	GAN, LAN, BSR, PAS, GCS, CHO, EPC, STP, NSA, AMN, AMS, ATL, PAM, PAT
Arenaria melanocephala	M	S	4	3	L	L	A4	BSR
Phalaropus tricolor	M	A	4	3	L	4100	A6, A7, A1, A2	STP, CAN, SAN, AMS?, CSA, PAM, PAT
Gallinago gallinago	L	S	4	3	L	3900	A1, N13	GAN, LAN, BSR, MPL, PAS, MAH, GCS, CDH, CHO, NSA, AMN
Limnodromus griseus	H	S	4	3	L	L	A2, A3, A1	GAN, LAN, BSR, PAS, GCS, CHO, EPC, STP, NSA, AMN, AMS, ATL
Limnodromus scolopaceus	M	S	4	3	L	1600	A1, A2, A3, A6	BSR, MPL, PAS, MAH, GCS
Aphriza virgata	H	S	4	3	L	L	A4	BSR, PAS, CHO, EPC, STP, PAT
Calidris alba	M	S	4	2	L	L	A3	GAN, LAN, BSR, PAS, GCS, CHO, EPC, STP, NSA, AMN, AMS, ATL, PAM, PAT
Calidris alpina	M	S	4	3	L	L	A2, A3	BSR, PAS, GCS
Calidris bairdii	H	A	4	2	L	4600	A6, A7, A3, A1	STP, NAN, CAN, SAN, CSA, PAM, PAT
Calidris canutus	M	A	4	2	L	L	A3	GAN, LAN, BSR, PAS, GCS, CHO, EPC, STP, NSA, AMN, AMS, ATL, PAM, PAT
Calidris ferruginea	M	F	4	3	L	L	A2, A3	LAN
Calidris fuscicollis	M	A	4	3	L	1200	A3, A2, A1	SAN, CSA, PAM, PAT
Calidris mauri	M	S	4	3	L	2000	A3, A2	GAN, LAN, BSR, MPL, PAS, MAH, GCS, CHO, EPC, STP, NSA, AMN
Calidris melanotos	M	A	4	3	L	4000	A1, A2, N13	STP, CAN, SAN, CSA, ATL, PAM, PAT
Calidris minutilla	M	S	4	3	L	2200	A1, A2, A6	GAN, LAN, BSR, MPL, PAS, MAH, GCS, CHO, EPC, STP, NSA, AMN, AMS, CSA, ATL
Calidris pusilla	M	A	4	3	L	L	A3, A2, A1	GAN, LAN, PAS, GCS, CHO, EPC, STP, NSA, AMN, AMS, CSA?, ATL, PAM
Micropalama himantopus	M	A	4	3	L	900	A1, A2	PAS, MAH, GCS, STP?, AMS, CSA, ATL, PAM
Tryngites subruficollis	L	A	3	2	L	L	N7, N13, A1	CSA, PAM

Notes
Casual on mainland coast; monitor; declining.
Monitor.
Monitor; mainly coastal.
Monitor.
Monitor; apparently declining.
Probably extinct.
To 3000m+ in migration; monitor.
Occasionally to 4000m.
To 3400m in migration.
Rarely above 900m.
Mainly winters north of Mexico.
Occasionally to 1600m.
Winters mainly at sea-level.
Monitor.
Accidental in South America.
Winters mainly in high Andean lakes?
Monitor.
Very rare in Neotropics.
Monitor.

Abbreviations Used

Snst - Sensitivity:
L - Low; **M** - Medium; **H** - High.

Stat - Status:
A - All; **F** - Fraction; **S** - Some; **T** - Total;

CP -Conservation Priority:
1 - Urgent; **2** - High; **3** - Medium; **4** - Low.

RP - Research Priority:
1 - High; **2** - Medium; **3** - Low.

Min - Minimum Elevation:
L - Lowlands; **?** - Uncertain value; numeric values in meters.

Max - Maximum Elevation:
L - Lowlands; **?** - Uncertain value; **+** - species occurs at least to given elevation but likely occurs higher; numeric values in meters.

Habitats:
F1 - Tropical lowland evergreen forest; **F2** - Flooded tropical evergreen forest; **F3** - River-edge forest; **F4** - Montane evergreen forest; **F5** - Elfin forest; **F6** - *Polylepis* woodland; **F7** - Tropical deciduous forest; **F8** - Gallery forest; **F9** - Southern temperate forest; **F10** - Pine forest; **F11** - Pine-oak forest; **F12** - White sand forest; **F13** - Palm forest; **F14** - Mangrove forest; **F15** - Secondary forest; **N1** - Arid lowland scrub; **N2** - Arid montane scrub; **N3** - Semihumid/humid montane scrub; **N4** - Cerrado; **N5** - Campo grasslands; **N6** - Low, seasonally wet grassland; **N7** - Southern temperate grassland; **N8** - Northern temperate grassland; **N9** - Puna grassland; **N10** - Páramo grassland; **N11** - Riparian thickets; **N12** - River island scrub; **N13** - Pastures/agricultural lands; **N14** - Second-growth scrub; **A1** - Freshwater marshes; **A2** - Saltwater/brackish marshes; **A3** - Coastal sand beaches/mudflats; **A4** - Coastal rocky beaches; **A5** - Riverine sand beaches; **A6** - Freshwater lakes and ponds; **A7** - Alkaline lakes; **A8** - Rivers; **A9** - Streams; **A10** - Bogs; **A11** - Coastal waters; **A12** - Pelagic waters.
E - Edge (used as a modifer to particular habitats).

Zoogeographic Regions:
AMN - Northern Amazonia; **AMS** - Southern Amazonia; **ATL** - Atlantic Forest; **BSR** - Baja-Sonora; **CAN** - Central Andes; **CDH** - Chiriquí-Darién Highlands; **CHO** - Chocó Lowlands; **CSA** - Central South America; **EPC** - Equatorial Pacific Coast; **GAN** - Greater Antilles; **GCS** - Gulf-Caribbean Slope; **LAN** - Lesser Antilles; **MAH** - Madrean Highlands; **MPL** - Mexican Plateau; **NAN** - Northern Andes; **NSA** - Northern South America; **PAM** - Pampas; **PAS** - Pacific Arid Slope; **PAT** - Patagonia; **SAN** - Southern Andes; **STP** - Subtropical Pacific; **TEP** - Tepuis.

	Snst	Stat	CP	RP	Min	Max	Habitats	Zoogeographic Regions
Philomachus pugnax	L	F	4	3	L	L	A1, A2, N13	LAN
Laridae								
Larus argentatus	L	F	4	3	L	L	A11, A3, A4, A6	GAN, LAN, BSR, MPL, PAS, GCS
Larus californicus	L	S	4	3	L	1600	A11, A3, N13, A6	BSR, MPL?, PAS
Larus canus	M	F	4	3	L	L	A11, A3	BSR
Larus delawarensis	L	F	4	3	L	2600	A11, A3, N13, A6	GAN, BSR, MPL, PAS, MAH, GCS
Larus fuscus	L	F	4	3	L	L	A11, A3	GAN
Larus glaucescens	M	F	4	3	L	L	A11, A3, A4	BSR
Larus philadelphia	M	F	4	3	L	L	A11, A6	GAN, BSR, MPL, PAS, GCS
Larus pipixcan	L	A	4	3	L	L	A3, A11, N13	PAS, CHO, EPC, STP, PAT
Larus ridibundus	L	F	4	3	L	L	A11	GAN, LAN
Larus thayeri	M	F	4	3	L	L	A11, A3	BSR
Rissa tridactyla	H	F	4	3	L	L	A12, A11	BSR
Chlidonias niger	M	A	4	2	L	L	A1, A2, A6, A11	PAS, GCS, CHO, EPC, STP, NSA, AMN
Cuculiformes								
Cuculidae								
Coccyzus erythropthalmus	M	A	4	2	L	900	F1, F15	NSA, AMN, AMS, CSA?
Caprimulgiformes								
Caprimulgidae								
Caprimulgus carolinensis	M	A	4	2	L	2600	F1, F7, F15, F11?	GAN, PAS, GCS, CDH, NAN, NSA
Apodiformes								
Apodidae								
Chaetura pelagica	L	A	4	2	L	L	F3E, F1E, N14	STP, AMN, AMS
Trochilidae								
Archilochus colubris	L	A	4	3	L	1250	F7, F11, F15, N14	PAS, MAH, GCS
Selasphorus rufus	M	A	4	3	400	2700	F10, F11, N14?	PAS, MAH
Selasphorus sasin	?	A	4	2	800	2400	N14, F10?	MAH
Coraciiformes								
Alcedinidae								
Ceryle alcyon	L	S	4	3	L	2500	A9, A8, A6	BSR, MPL, PAS, MAH, GCS, CDH, EPC, NSA
Piciformes								
Picidae								
Melanerpes lewis	M	F	4	3	L	1700	F11, F15	BSR
Sphyrapicus nuchalis	L	S	4	3	L	3300	F10, F11, F8	BSR, MPL, PAS, MAH
Sphyrapicus ruber	M	F	4	2	L	2700	F11, F8	BSR
Sphyrapicus varius	L	S	4	3	L	3350+	F8, F11, F15, F1	GAN, LAN, MPL, PAS, MAH, GCS, CDH
Passeriformes								
Tyrannidae								
Contopus virens	M	A	4	3	L	1200	F1E, F15	GCS?, NSA, AMN, AMS
Empidonax alnorum	L	A	4	2	L	1000	N11, N14, F15	NSA, AMN, AMS, CSA
Empidonax flaviventris	L	A	4	3	L	1200	F1, F15, F7	PAS, GCS
Empidonax hammondii	M	A	4	3	900	2900	F11, N2	MAH
Empidonax minimus	L	A	4	3	L	1200	F1, F7, F15, F4, N1, N2	PAS, GCS
Empidonax oberholseri	L	A	4	3	L	2800+	F11, N11, F8, N2	BSR, MPL, PAS, MAH
Empidonax traillii	L	A	4	2	L	1000	F1E, F15, N14	PAS, GCS, CHO, NSA?
Empidonax virescens	L	A	4	2	L	2700	F1E, F15, F7	GCS, CHO, NSA
Empidonax wrightii	L	S	4	3	L	2100	N1, N2, N11	BSR, MPL, PAS, MAH
Sayornis phoebe	L	S	4	3	L	1500	N11, N13, N14	MPL, GCS
Myiarchus crinitus	L	A	4	3	L	1200	F1, F8, F15	GCS, PAS, CHO, NSA
Tyrannus tyrannus	L	A	4	3	L	800	N14, N13, F1E	NSA, AMN, AMS, CSA

Notes
Very rare in Neotropics.
Rare and local inland.
Winters mainly north of Mexico.
Irregular in Caribbean, accidental elsewhere.
Locally to 2000m in interior.
Occasionally to 4000m.
Very rare in Neotropics.
Winter range poorly known.
To 2900m in migration; winter range poorly known.
Usually below 1500m; winter range not well-known.
Winter range and habitat preference poorly known.
Locally to 2800m.
Winter range and habitats poorly known.
Rare south of US.
Poorly known south of the U.S..
To 2700m in migration.
To 2600+m in migration; winter range poorly known.
To 2900m in migration.
To lowlands, especially in migration.
Occasionally to 2500m.
Mainly above 900m?
To 1500+m in migration; winter range poorly known; may breed NW Mexico.
Winter range poorly known.
Locally to 2500m.
To 1850m in migration.
To 2600m in migration.

Abbreviations Used

Snst - Sensitivity:
L - Low; **M** - Medium; **H** - High.

Stat - Status:
A - All; **F** - Fraction; **S** - Some; **T** - Total;

CP -Conservation Priority:
1 - Urgent; **2** - High; **3** - Medium; **4** - Low.

RP - Research Priority:
1 - High; **2** - Medium; **3** - Low.

Min - Minimum Elevation:
L - Lowlands; **?** - Uncertain value; numeric values in meters.

Max - Maximum Elevation:
L - Lowlands; **?** - Uncertain value; **+** - species occurs at least to given elevation but likely occurs higher; numeric values in meters.

Habitats:
F1 - Tropical lowland evergreen forest; **F2** - Flooded tropical evergreen forest; **F3** - River-edge forest; **F4** - Montane evergreen forest; **F5** - Elfin forest; **F6** - *Polylepis* woodland; **F7** - Tropical deciduous forest; **F8** - Gallery forest; **F9** - Southern temperate forest; **F10** - Pine forest; **F11** - Pine-oak forest; **F12** - White sand forest; **F13** - Palm forest; **F14** - Mangrove forest; **F15** - Secondary forest; **N1** - Arid lowland scrub; **N2** - Arid montane scrub; **N3** - Semihumid/humid montane scrub; **N4** - Cerrado; **N5** - Campo grasslands; **N6** - Low, seasonally wet grassland; **N7** - Southern temperate grassland; **N8** - Northern temperate grassland; **N9** - Puna grassland; **N10** - Paramo grassland; **N11** - Riparian thickets; **N12** - River island scrub; **N13** - Pastures/agricultural lands; **N14** - Second-growth scrub; **A1** - Freshwater marshes; **A2** - Saltwater/brackish marshes; **A3** - Coastal sand beaches/mudflats; **A4** - Coastal rocky beaches; **A5** - Riverine sand beaches; **A6** - Freshwater lakes and ponds; **A7** - Alkaline lakes; **A8** - Rivers; **A9** - Streams; **A10** - Bogs; **A11** - Coastal waters; **A12** - Pelagic waters.
E - Edge (used as a modifer to particular habitats).

Zoogeographic Regions:
AMN - Northern Amazonia; **AMS** - Southern Amazonia; **ATL** - Atlantic Forest; **BSR** - Baja-Sonora; **CAN** - Central Andes; **CDH** - Chiriquí-Darién Highlands; **CHO** - Chocó Lowlands; **CSA** - Central South America; **EPC** - Equatorial Pacific Coast; **GAN** - Greater Antilles; **GCS** - Gulf-Caribbean Slope; **LAN** - Lesser Antilles; **MAH** - Madrean Highlands; **MPL** - Mexican Plateau; **NAN** - Northern Andes; **NSA** - Northern South America; **PAM** - Pampas; **PAS** - Pacific Arid Slope; **PAT** - Patagonia; **SAN** - Southern Andes; **STP** - Subtropical Pacific; **TEP** - Tepuis.

	Snst	Stat	CP	RP	Min	Max	Habitats	Zoogeographic Regions
Hirundinidae								
Tachycineta bicolor	L	S	4	3	L	3100	A6, A9, A1, A2	GAN, BSR, MPL, PAS, MAH, GCS
Motacillidae								
Anthus rubescens	M	S	4	3	L	2700	N13, N8	BSR, MPL, PAS, MAH, GCS
Anthus spragueii	M	S	3	2	L	2500	N8	MPL, GCS
Bombycillidae								
Bombycilla cedrorum	L	S	4	3	L	3000	F11, F8, F15, F1, F4	GAN, BSR, MPL, PAS, MAH, GCS, CDH
Troglodytidae								
Troglodytes troglodytes	M	F	4	3	L	2000	N11, F7	GCS
Mimidae								
Dumetella carolinensis	L	S	4	3	L	1800	F1E, F15, N14	GAN, PAS, GCS
Oreoscoptes montanus	M	S	4	3	L	3000+	N2, N1	BSR, MPL
Toxostoma rufum	L	F	4	3	L	1000	N11, N1	GAN, BSR?, GCS
Muscicapidae								
Turdinae								
Sialia currucoides	L	F	4	3	L	2300	N2, N8, N13, F11	BSR, MPL, MAH
Zoothera naevia	M	F	4	2	L	2500	F10	BSR
Catharus bicknelli	H	A	3	1	L	1800+	F1, F4	GAN
Catharus fuscescens	M	A	4	2	L	L	F1	NSA, AMN, AMS, CSA
Catharus guttatus	L	S	4	3	1000	3600	F10, F11, F8, F15	GAN, BSR, MPL, PAS, MAH, GCS
Catharus minimus	M	A	4	2	L	900	F1	GCS, NSA, AMN, AMS
Catharus ustulatus	M	A	4	3	L	2900	F4, F1, F15, F7	PAS, MAH, CDH, NAN, CAN, NSA, TEP
Hylocichla mustelina	M	A	3	3	L	900	F1, F15	PAS, GCS
Emberizidae								
Emberizinae								
Calcarius lapponicus	L	F	4	3	L	L	N8, N13	BSR
Calcarius mccownii	M	S	3	2	800	2100	N8, N13	MPL
Calcarius ornatus	M	S	4	2	L	2100	N8	BSR, MPL
Calamospiza melanocorys	L	A	4	3	L	2200	N8, N13, N14	BSR, MPL, PAS, GCS
Zonotrichia albicollis	L	F	4	3	L	1200	N11, N14	BSR, MPL, GCS
Zonotrichia atricapilla	L	F	4	3	L	2500	N11, N14	BSR
Zonotrichia georgiana	L	F	4	3	L	2100	N14, A1	BSR, MPL, MAH, GCS
Zonotrichia iliaca	L	F	4	3	L	2700	N11, N2, N14	BSR
Zonotrichia leucophrys	L	S	4	3	L	2600	N11, N14, N13	GAN?, BSR, MPL, MAH, GCS
Zonotrichia lincolnii	L	S	4	3	L	2600	N11, N14, N13	GAN?, BSR, MPL, PAS, MAH, GCS
Ammodramus bairdii	M	S	3	2	1300	2100	N8	MPL
Ammodramus caudacutus	M	F	4	3	L	L	A1, A2	BSR?, GCS
Spizella breweri	M	S	4	3	L	2400	N1, N2, N13	BSR, MPL
Spizella pallida	L	A	4	3	L	2000	N1, N14, N13	BSR, MPL, PAS, MAH, GCS
Spizella pusilla	L	F	4	3	L	1000	N14, N1	MPL, GCS
Pooecetes gramineus	L	S	4	3	L	2400	N8, N13, N2	BSR, MPL, PAS, MAH, GCS
Pipilo chlorurus	M	A	4	3	L	2500	N11	BSR, MPL, PAS, MAH
Cardinalinae								
Spiza americana	L	A	3	2	L	L	N6, N13, N1	PAS, GCS, NSA, AMN
Pheucticus ludovicianus	L	A	4	2	L	2300	F4E, F15, F1E, F7, F8	PAS, MAH, GCS, CDH, CHO, NAN, CAN, NSA, AMN, AMS
Passerina cyanea	L	A	4	3	L	2000	N14, N11, F15	GAN, PAS, MAH, GCS, CDH, NSA
Thraupinae								
Piranga olivacea	M	A	4	2	L	1300	F1, F15	GCS?, AMN, AMS
Parulinae								
Mniotilta varia	L	A	4	3	L	2000	F1, F4, F15, F7	GAN, BSR, MPL, PAS, MAH, GCS, CHO, NAN, CAN, NSA

Notes
Survey Mexican habitat; monitor.
Rare in Mexico.
Very rare in Mexico and Greater Antilles.
Poorly known south of U.S..
Winter range poorly known.
Winter range poorly known.
To lowlands in north and occasionally in south.
To 2600+m in migration; winter range poorly known.
Mainly winters above 900m.
To 2600m in migration.
Very rare in Mexico.
Monitor; overgrazing.
Status south of U.S. poorly known.
To 3000+m in migration.
Survey population; habitat degradation; study winter habitat.
Very rare in Mexico.
Monitor and study; declining?
Occasionally to 3800m; winter distribution poorly known.
Winter distribution poorly known.
To 3000m in migration.

Abbreviations Used

Snst - Sensitivity:
L - Low; **M** - Medium; **H** - High.

Stat - Status:
A - All; **F** - Fraction; **S** - Some; **T** - Total;

CP -Conservation Priority:
1 - Urgent; **2** - High; **3** - Medium; **4** - Low.

RP - Research Priority:
1 - High; **2** - Medium; **3** - Low.

Min - Minimum Elevation:
L - Lowlands; **?** - Uncertain value; numeric values in meters.

Max - Maximum Elevation:
L - Lowlands; **?** - Uncertain value; **+** - species occurs at least to given elevation but likely occurs higher; numeric values in meters.

Habitats:
F1 - Tropical lowland evergreen forest; **F2** - Flooded tropical evergreen forest; **F3** - River-edge forest; **F4** - Montane evergreen forest; **F5** - Elfin forest; **F6** - *Polylepis* woodland; **F7** - Tropical deciduous forest; **F8** - Gallery forest; **F9** - Southern temperate forest; **F10** - Pine forest; **F11** - Pine-oak forest; **F12** - White sand forest; **F13** - Palm forest; **F14** - Mangrove forest; **F15** - Secondary forest; **N1** - Arid lowland scrub; **N2** - Arid montane scrub; **N3** - Semihumid/humid montane scrub; **N4** - Cerrado; **N5** - Campo grasslands; **N6** - Low, seasonally wet grassland; **N7** - Southern temperate grassland; **N8** - Northern temperate grassland; **N9** - Puna grassland; **N10** - Paramo grassland; **N11** - Riparian thickets; **N12** - River island scrub; **N13** - Pastures/agricultural lands; **N14** - Second-growth scrub; **A1** - Freshwater marshes; **A2** - Saltwater/brackish marshes; **A3** - Coastal sand beaches/mudflats; **A4** - Coastal rocky beaches; **A5** - Riverine sand beaches; **A6** - Freshwater lakes and ponds; **A7** - Alkaline lakes; **A8** - Rivers; **A9** - Streams; **A10** - Bogs; **A11** - Coastal waters; **A12** - Pelagic waters.
E - Edge (used as a modifer to particular habitats).

Zoogeographic Regions:
AMN - Northern Amazonia; **AMS** - Southern Amazonia; **ATL** - Atlantic Forest; **BSR** - Baja-Sonora; **CAN** - Central Andes; **CDH** - Chiriquí-Darién Highlands; **CHO** - Chocó Lowlands; **CSA** - Central South America; **EPC** - Equatorial Pacific Coast; **GAN** - Greater Antilles; **GCS** - Gulf-Caribbean Slope; **LAN** - Lesser Antilles; **MAH** - Madrean Highlands; **MPL** - Mexican Plateau; **NAN** - Northern Andes; **NSA** - Northern South America; **PAM** - Pampas; **PAS** - Pacific Arid Slope; **PAT** - Patagonia; **SAN** - Southern Andes; **STP** - Subtropical Pacific; **TEP** - Tepuis.

	Snst	Stat	CP	RP	Min	Max	Habitats	Zoogeographic Regions
Vermivora bachmanii	?	A	1	1	L	L?	F1	GAN
Vermivora chrysoptera	L	A	3	2	L	3000	F15, F4, F1	GAN, GCS, NAN, NSA
Vermivora peregrina	L	A	4	3	L	2600	F15, F1, F4	PAS, GCS, CDH, CHO, NAN, NSA
Vermivora pinus	L	A	4	2	L	2000	F15, F1	PAS, GCS
Vermivora ruficapilla	L	A	4	3	L	2900	F11, F1E, F4, F10, F8, F7, F15	GAN, BSR, PAS, GCS, MAH
Vermivora virginiae	L	A	4	2	800	2000	N2, F7, F11	MAH
Parula americana	L	S	4	3	L	1500	F1, F15, F11, F8	GAN, LAN, PAS, GCS
Dendroica caerulescens	M	A	4	2	L	2000+	F4, F1, F15	GAN
Dendroica castanea	L	A	4	3	L	1200	F1, F15	GCS, CHO, NSA
Dendroica cerulea	M	A	3	2	800	2200	F4, F1	NAN, CAN
Dendroica chrysoparia	M	A	2	1	1500	2600	F11	MAH
Dendroica discolor	L	S	4	3	L	1500+	N1, N14, F7, F1E	GAN, GCS
Dendroica fusca	M	A	4	3	900	3100	F4, F15	CDH, NAN, CAN, NSA, TEP
Dendroica kirtlandii	M	A	1	1	L	L	N1	GAN
Dendroica magnolia	L	A	4	3	L	1500	F1, F15, F8	GAN, PAS, GCS
Dendroica occidentalis	M	A	4	2	1300	3100+	F10, F11	MAH
Dendroica palmarum	L	S	4	3	L	1500	N1, N14, N11	GAN, GCS
Dendroica pensylvanica	L	A	4	2	L	2000	F1, F15	PAS, GCS, CDH, NSA?
Dendroica striata	L	A	4	2	L	800	F3, F15, F1E	NSA, AMN, AMS, ATL
Dendroica tigrina	L	A	4	3	L	1500	F1, F7, F15, F10, N1, N14	GAN, LAN, GCS, NSA
Dendroica townsendi	M	A	4	2	500	3200	F10, F11	BSR, MAH, CDH
Dendroica virens	M	A	4	3	L	3000	F4, F15, F1	GAN, PAS, MAH, GCS, CDH, NAN
Setophaga ruticilla	L	A	4	3	L	1500	F1, F4, F15	GAN, LAN, BSR, PAS, GCS, CHO, NAN, NSA, TEP, AMN
Seiurus aurocapillus	M	A	4	3	L	2000	F1, F15	GAN, LAN, PAS, MAH, GCS, NSA
Seiurus motacilla	M	A	4	3	L	2300	F1, F4, A9	GAN, LAN, BSR, PAS, MAH, GCS, CDH, NAN, NSA
Seiurus noveboracensis	M	A	4	3	L	2000	F1, F15, F14, A9, A8	GAN, LAN, BSR, PAS, MAH, GCS, CDH, CHO, NAN, NSA, AMN
Limnothlypis swainsonii	M	A	3	2	L	L?	F1	GAN, GCS
Helmitheros vermivorus	M	A	3	2	L	1500	F1, F15	GAN, GCS
Protonotaria citrea	M	A	4	3	L	L	F1, F14, F7, N11	GAN, LAN, GCS, NSA
Geothlypis agilis	H	A	4	1	L	L?	F3?, F15?	NSA?, AMN?, AMS?
Geothlypis formosus	M	A	4	3	L	1200	F1, F15	GAN?, GCS, PAS, NSA
Geothlypis philadelphia	L	A	4	2	L	1500	F1, F15, F4	GCS, CDH, CHO, NAN, NSA
Geothlypis tolmiei	L	A	4	3	L	2000+	F4E, N14, N11, F1E, F15	BSR, PAS, MAH, GCS, CDH
Wilsonia canadensis	M	A	4	3	L	2600	F4, F15, F1	GCS?, NAN, CAN, NSA, TEP
Wilsonia citrina	M	A	4	3	L	1200+	F1, F15, F7	PAS, GCS
Wilsonia pusilla	L	A	4	3	L	3500	F4E, F15, F1E, N11, N1	BSR, PAS, MAH, GCS
Vireonidae								
Vireo flavifrons	L	A	4	3	L	1700	F1E, F15, F4, F8	PAS, MAH, GCS, CDH, CHO, NAN, NSA
Vireo olivaceus olivaceus	L	A	4	2	L	1500	F1, F15	CHO, NSA, AMN, AMS
Vireo philadelphicus	L	A	4	2	L	1650	F1E, F7, F15, N1, N14	PAS, MAH, GCS, CDH
Vireo solitarius solitarius	L	S	4	3	L	1400	F1E, F15, F10, F8	GAN, MPL, MAH, GCS
Icteridae								
Icterus galbula galbula	L	A	4	3	L	2000	F15, F8, F7	GAN, PAS, MAH, GCS, CDH, NSA
Dolichonyx oryzivorus	L	A	4	2	L	800	N11, N13, N14, A1	STP?, CSA, PAM
Fringillidae								
Carduelis tristis	L	F	4	3	L	1800	N14, F15, F8	BSR, MPL, GCS
Carpodacus purpureus	L	F	4	3	L	2500	F8, F7, F10	BSR

Notes	Abbreviations Used
May be extinct.	
Winter habitat should be studied.	
Winter habitat needs study.	
Winter habitat poorly known.	
Has bred in NW Mexico.	
Scattered records on mainland during winter; monitor.	
To 2000m in migration; occasionally to 3100m.	
Lowlands in migration; vulnerable to deforestation.	
Survey and monitor; winter range poorly known.	
Occurs in small numbers on Gulf coast in winter.	
To lower and higher elevations in migration.	
To higher elevations in migration.	
Winters mainly above 1500m; survey winter habitats.	
Local in lowlands on Pacific coast (Mexico).	
Occasionally to 1850m; monitor.	
To 3000m in migration; winter range poorly known.	
Local on mainland.	
Occasionally to sea level.	
Mainly above 900m.	
Occasionally to 2500m, especially in migration.	
Occasionally to 2600m in winter; higher in migration?	
Mainly below 1500m.	
Winter range, habitat and behavior poorly known.	
Monitor; habitat destruction.	
Occasionally to 3000+m on migration.	
Winter range and habitats unknown.	
Mainly 1000 - 2000m in winter; may breed in N Mexico.	
Winters mainly from 1200-2100m; irregular in winter in Central America.	
Higher elevation in migration.	
Mainly above 2500m.	
Extent of winter range uncertain, but mainly Amazonia.	
To 2100m during migration.	
Limits of winter range poorly defined.	

Snst - Sensitivity:
L - Low; **M** - Medium; **H** - High.

Stat - Status:
A - All; **F** - Fraction; **S** - Some; **T** - Total;

CP -Conservation Priority:
1 - Urgent; **2** - High; **3** - Medium; **4** - Low.

RP - Research Priority:
1 - High; **2** - Medium; **3** - Low.

Min - Minimum Elevation:
L - Lowlands; **?** - Uncertain value; numeric values in meters.

Max - Maximum Elevation:
L - Lowlands; **?** - Uncertain value; **+** - species occurs at least to given elevation but likely occurs higher; numeric values in meters.

Habitats:
F1 - Tropical lowland evergreen forest; **F2** - Flooded tropical evergreen forest; **F3** - River-edge forest; **F4** - Montane evergreen forest; **F5** - Elfin forest; **F6** - *Polylepis* woodland; **F7** - Tropical deciduous forest; **F8** - Gallery forest; **F9** - Southern temperate forest; **F10** - Pine forest; **F11** - Pine-oak forest; **F12** - White sand forest; **F13** - Palm forest; **F14** - Mangrove forest; **F15** - Secondary forest; **N1** - Arid lowland scrub; **N2** - Arid montane scrub; **N3** - Semihumid/humid montane scrub; **N4** - Cerrado; **N5** - Campo grasslands; **N6** - Low, seasonally wet grassland; **N7** - Southern temperate grassland; **N8** - Northern temperate grassland; **N9** - Puna grassland; **N10** - Paramo grassland; **N11** - Riparian thickets; **N12** - River island scrub; **N13** - Pastures/agricultural lands; **N14** - Second-growth scrub; **A1** - Freshwater marshes; **A2** - Saltwater/brackish marshes; **A3** - Coastal sand beaches/mudflats; **A4** - Coastal rocky beaches; **A5** - Riverine sand beaches; **A6** - Freshwater lakes and ponds; **A7** - Alkaline lakes; **A8** - Rivers; **A9** - Streams; **A10** - Bogs; **A11** - Coastal waters; **A12** - Pelagic waters.
E - Edge (used as a modifer to particular habitats).

Zoogeographic Regions:
AMN - Northern Amazonia; **AMS** - Southern Amazonia; **ATL** - Atlantic Forest; **BSR** - Baja-Sonora; **CAN** - Central Andes; **CDH** - Chiriquí-Darién Highlands; **CHO** - Chocó Lowlands; **CSA** - Central South America; **EPC** - Equatorial Pacific Coast; **GAN** - Greater Antilles; **GCS** - Gulf-Caribbean Slope; **LAN** - Lesser Antilles; **MAH** - Madrean Highlands; **MPL** - Mexican Plateau; **NAN** - Northern Andes; **NSA** - Northern South America; **PAM** - Pampas; **PAS** - Pacific Arid Slope; **PAT** - Patagonia; **SAN** - Southern Andes; **STP** - Subtropical Pacific; **TEP** - Tepuis.

Database D

Nearctic Migrants 2: Species Breeding in the Neotropics

	Snst	Stat	Min	Max	Habitats	Zoogeographic Regions
PODICIPEDIFORMES						
Podicipedidae						
Podiceps nigricollis nigricollis	M	S	L	2500+	A6, A11	BSR, MPL, PAS, MAH, GCS
Aechmophorus clarkii	M	S	L	2200	A6, A11	BSR, MPL, MAH
Aechmophorus occidentalis	M	S	L	2200	A11, A6	BSR, MPL, PAS, MAH
PELECANIFORMES						
Pelecanidae						
Pelecanus erythrorhynchus	M	S	L	L	A11, A1, A6	BSR, MPL, PAS, GCS
Pelecanus occidentalis	L	F	L	L	A11, A12	GAN, LAN, BSR, PAS, GCS, CHO, EPC, NSA, AMN
Phalacrocoracidae						
Phalacrocorax auritus	M	F	L	2200	A11, A6	GAN, BSR, MPL, PAS, GCS
CICONIIFORMES						
Ardeidae						
Botaurus lentiginosus	M	S	L	2800	A1, A2	GAN, BSR, MPL, PAS, MAH, GCS
Nycticorax nycticorax	L	F	L	4400	A1, A6, A8, A9	GAN, LAN, BSR, MPL, PAS, MAH, GCS, CDH, CHO, EPC, STP, NAN, CAN, SAN, NSA, TEP, AMN, AMS, CSA, ATL, PAM, PAT
Nycticorax violaceus	M	S	L	2000	F14, A2, A1, A6	GAN, LAN, BSR, PAS, MAH, GCS, CHO, EPC, NSA, AMN, AMS, ATL
Hydranassa caerulea	M	F	L	2000	A1, A2, F14, A3	GAN, LAN, BSR, PAS, MAH, GCS, CHO, EPC, STP, NSA, AMN, AMS, CSA, ATL
Hydranassa rufescens	H	F	L	L	A3, F14	GAN, BSR, PAS, GCS, NSA
Hydranassa tricolor	M	F	L	1800	A2, A1, A3, F14	GAN, LAN, BSR, PAS, MAH, GCS, CHO, EPC, STP, NSA, AMN, AMS
Egretta alba	L	F	L	2500	A1, A2, A3, A4, A6	GAN, BSR, MPL, PAS, MAH, GCS, CHO, EPC, STP, CAN, SAN, NSA, AMN, AMS, CSA, ATL, PAM, PAT
Egretta thula	L	F	L	2500	A1, A2, A3, A4, A6	GAN, LAN, BSR, MPL, PAS, MAH, GCS, CHO, EPC, STP, NSA, AMN, AMS, CSA, ATL, PAM
Ardea herodias	L	S	L	2500	A1, A2, A3, A6, A8, F14	GAN, LAN, BSR, MPL, PAS, MAH, GCS, EPC, NSA
Threskiornithidae						
Plegadis chihi	L	S	L	2500?	A1, A6	BSR, MPL, PAS, MAH, GCS, STP, NSA, CSA, ATL, PAM, PAT
ANSERIFORMES						
Anatidae						
Aix sponsa	M	F	L	1700	A6, A9	GAN, BSR, MPL, GCS
Anas cyanoptera	L	A	L	4300	A1, A6	BSR, MPL, PAS, MAH, GCS, STP, NAN, CAN, SAN, NSA, CSA, PAM, PAT
Anas platyrhynchos platyrhynchos	L	S	L	2500	A6, A1	GAN, BSR, MPL, PAS, GCS
Aythya americana	M	S	L	2300	A6, A11	GAN, BSR, MPL, PAS, GCS
Mergus merganser	M	F	L	2100	A6, A8	BSR, MPL, GCS
Oxyura jamaicensis jamaicensis	L	S	L	2300	A6, A11	GAN, LAN, BSR, MPL, PAS, MAH, GCS

Notes	Abbreviations Used
Winter distribution, especially coastally, uncertain.	
Irregular in interior of Mexico.	
Mainly coastal, local in interior to 2000m.	
Occasionally to 2200m; increasing in Mexico in winter.	
Monitor migrants from North American.	
Winters mainly north of Neotropics.	

Snst - Sensitivity:
L - Low; **M** - Medium; **H** - High.

Stat - Status:
A - All; **F** - Fraction; **S** - Some; **T** - Total;

Min - Minimum Elevation:
L - Lowlands; **?** - Uncertain value; numeric values in meters.

Max - Maximum Elevation:
L - Lowlands; **?** - Uncertain value; **+** - species occurs at least to given elevation but likely occurs higher; numeric values in meters.

Habitats:
F1 - Tropical lowland evergreen forest; **F2** - Flooded tropical evergreen forest; **F3** - River-edge forest; **F4** - Montane evergreen forest; **F5** - Elfin forest; **F6** - *Polylepis* woodland; **F7** - Tropical deciduous forest; **F8** - Gallery forest; **F9** - Southern temperate forest; **F10** - Pine forest; **F11** - Pine-oak forest; **F12** - White sand forest; **F13** - Palm forest; **F14** - Mangrove forest; **F15** - Secondary forest; **N1** - Arid lowland scrub; **N2** - Arid montane scrub; **N3** - Semihumid/humid montane scrub; **N4** - Cerrado; **N5** - Campo grasslands; **N6** - Low, seasonally wet grassland; **N7** - Southern temperate grassland; **N8** - Northern temperate grassland; **N9** - Puna grassland; **N10** - Paramo grassland; **N11** - Riparian thickets; **N12** - River island scrub; **N13** - Pastures/agricultural lands; **N14** - Second-growth scrub; **A1** - Freshwater marshes; **A2** - Saltwater/brackish marshes; **A3** - Coastal sand beaches/mudflats; **A4** - Coastal rocky beaches; **A5** - Riverine sand beaches; **A6** - Freshwater lakes and ponds; **A7** - Alkaline lakes; **A8** - Rivers; **A9** - Streams; **A10** - Bogs; **A11** - Coastal waters; **A12** - Pelagic waters.
E - Edge (used as a modifer to particular habitats).

Zoogeographic Regions:
AMN - Northern Amazonia; **AMS** - Southern Amazonia; **ATL** - Atlantic Forest; **BSR** - Baja-Sonora; **CAN** - Central Andes; **CDH** - Chiriquí-Darién Highlands; **CHO** - Chocó Lowlands; **CSA** - Central South America; **EPC** - Equatorial Pacific Coast; **GAN** - Greater Antilles; **GCS** - Gulf-Caribbean Slope; **LAN** - Lesser Antilles; **MAH** - Madrean Highlands; **MPL** - Mexican Plateau; **NAN** - Northern Andes; **NSA** - Northern South America; **PAM** - Pampas; **PAS** - Pacific Arid Slope; **PAT** - Patagonia; **SAN** - Southern Andes; **STP** - Subtropical Pacific; **TEP** - Tepuis.

	Snst	Stat	Min	Max	Habitats	Zoogeographic Regions
FALCONIFORMES						
Accipitridae						
Pandion haliaetus	M	S	L	1500	A11, A8, A6	GAN, BSR, PAS, GCS, CHO, EPC, STP, NSA, AMN, AMS, CSA, ATL, PAM
Haliaeetus leucocephalus	M	F	L	2000	A11, A8, A6, A1	BSR, MPL, MAH
Circus cyaneus	L	S	L	2500	N8, N13, N1, A1	GAN, LAN, BSR, MPL, PAS, MAH, GCS, NSA
Accipiter cooperii	M	F	L	3000+	F7, F8, F11, F15	BSR, MPL, PAS, MAH, GCS, CDH
Accipiter striatus striatus	L	F	L	3100	F11, F7, F8, F15	GAN, BSR, MPL, PAS, MAH, GCS, CDH
Buteo jamaicensis	L	S	L	4000	F7E, F10, F11, F4E, N1, N2, F15	GAN, LAN, BSR, MPL, PAS, MAH, GCS, CDH
Buteo lineatus	L	F	L	2200	F8, F15, F11	BSR, MPL, GCS
Buteo platypterus	M	A	L	3000	F1, F4, F7?	GAN, LAN, PAS, MAH, GCS, CDH, NAN, CAN, NSA, AMN, AMS
Buteo swainsoni	L	A	L	600	N1, N6, N7	CSA, PAM
Falconidae						
Falco mexicanus	M	S	L	2300	N8, N2	BSR, MPL, MAH, GCS
Falco peregrinus	L	S	L	4000	A2, A4, A1, A8, N7, N8, A6	GAN, LAN, BSR, MPL, PAS, MAH, GCS, CDH, CHO, EPC, STP, NAN, CAN, SAN, NSA TEP, AMN, AMS, CSA, ATL, PAM, PAT
Falco sparverius	L	S	L	4400	N13, N8, N5, N6, N1, N2, F8	GAN, LAN, BSR, MPL, PAS, MAH, GCS, CDH, CHO, EPC, STP, NAN, CAN, SAN, NSA TEP, AMN, AMS, CSA, ATL, PAM, PAT
GRUIFORMES						
Gruidae						
Grus canadensis	L	S	L	2100	N13, N8	GAN, BSR, MPL, PAS, MAH, GCS
Rallidae						
Rallus limicola	M	S	L	2600	A1	BSR, MPL, PAS, MAH, GCS, EPC, STP, NAN
Porzana carolina	L	S	L	2600	A1	GAN, LAN?, BSR, MPL, PAS, MAH, GCS, CDH, CHO, EPC, STP?, NAN, NSA, AMN
Fulica americana	L	S	L	3400	A1, A2, A6	GAN, LAN, BSR, MPL, PAS, MAH, GCS, NSA?
CHARADRIIFORMES						
Recurvirostridae						
Recurvirostra americana	M	S	L	2500	A1, A2, A3, A6	GAN?, BSR, MPL, PAS, GCS
Charadriidae						
Charadrius vociferus	L	S	L	2600	A1, N13	GAN, LAN, BSR, MPL, PAS, MAH, GCS, CDH, CHO, EPC, STP, NSA
Scolopacidae						
Catoptrophorus semipalmatus	M	S	L	L	A3, A4, A2	GAN, LAN, BSR, PAS, GCS, CHO, EPC, STP, NSA, AMN, AMS
Laridae						
Larus atricilla	M	S	L	L	A11, A3, A4	GAN, LAN, BSR, MPL, PAS, MAH, GCS, CHO, EPC, NSA, AMN, AMS
Gelochelidon nilotica	H	A	L	L	A2, A11	GAN, LAN, BSR, PAS, GCS, CHO, EPC, NSA, AMN, AMS, ATL, PAM
Hydroprogne caspia	H	S	L	L	A1, A2, A11	GAN, BSR, PAS, MAH, GCS, NSA
Sterna antillarum	M	A	L	L	A11, A2	PAS, NSA, AMN, AMS
Sterna dougallii	H	A	L	L	A11, A12	GAN, LAN, NSA, AMN, AMS, ATL
Sterna forsteri	M	S	L	2200	A11, A6, A8, A1, A2	GAN, BSR, MPL, PAS, MAH, GCS
Sterna hirundo	M	A	L	L	A11	GAN, LAN, BSR, PAS, GCS, CHO, EPC, STP, NSA, AMN, AMS, ATL, PAM, PAT
Thalasseus elegans	H	A	L	L	A11	PAS, CHO, EPC, STP

Notes	Abbreviations Used
Higher elevations on migration and occasionally in winter; some summer south of breeding range.	
Monitor.	**Snst - Sensitivity:** L - Low; **M** - Medium; **H** - High.
	Stat - Status: **A** - All; **F** - Fraction; **S** - Some; **T** - Total;
	Min - Minimum Elevation: L - Lowlands; **?** - Uncertain value; numeric values in meters.
To 2600m (Colombia) in migration; winter range poorly known.	**Max - Maximum Elevation:** L - Lowlands; **?** - Uncertain value; **+** - species occurs at least to given elevation but likely occurs higher; numeric values in meters.
Status in Neotropics poorly known.	
Distribution and seasonal status poorly known.	**Habitats:** **F1** - Tropical lowland evergreen forest; **F2** - Flooded tropical evergreen forest; **F3** - River-edge forest; **F4** - Montane evergreen forest; **F5** - Elfin forest; **F6** - *Polylepis* woodland; **F7** - Tropical deciduous forest; **F8** - Gallery forest; **F9** - Southern temperate forest; **F10** - Pine forest; **F11** - Pine-oak forest; **F12** - White sand forest; **F13** - Palm forest; **F14** - Mangrove forest; **F15** - Secondary forest; **N1** - Arid lowland scrub; **N2** - Arid montane scrub; **N3** - Semihumid/humid montane scrub; **N4** - Cerrado; **N5** - Campo grasslands; **N6** - Low, seasonally wet grassland; **N7** - Southern temperate grassland; **N8** - Northern temperate grassland; **N9** - Puna grassland; **N10** - Paramo grassland; **N11** - Riparian thickets; **N12** - River island scrub; **N13** - Pastures/agricultural lands; **N14** - Second-growth scrub; **A1** - Freshwater marshes; **A2** - Saltwater/brackish marshes; **A3** - Coastal sand beaches/mudflats; **A4** - Coastal rocky beaches; **A5** - Riverine sand beaches; **A6** - Freshwater lakes and ponds; **A7** - Alkaline lakes; **A8** - Rivers; **A9** - Streams; **A10** - Bogs; **A11** - Coastal waters; **A12** - Pelagic waters. **E** - Edge (used as a modifer to particular habitats).
	Zoogeographic Regions: **AMN** - Northern Amazonia; **AMS** - Southern Amazonia; **ATL** - Atlantic Forest; **BSR** - Baja-Sonora; **CAN** - Central Andes; **CDH** - Chiriquí-Darién Highlands; **CHO** - Chocó Lowlands; **CSA** - Central South America; **EPC** - Equatorial Pacific Coast; **GAN** - Greater Antilles; **GCS** - Gulf-Caribbean Slope; **LAN** - Lesser Antilles; **MAH** - Madrean Highlands; **MPL** - Mexican Plateau; **NAN** - Northern Andes; **NSA** - Northern South America; **PAM** - Pampas; **PAS** - Pacific Arid Slope; **PAT** - Patagonia; **SAN** - Southern Andes; **STP** - Subtropical Pacific; **TEP** - Tepuis.
Possibly declining; monitor.	
Locally to 2500m.	
Status on Pacific coast of South America unclear.	
Winter distribution poorly known;locally inland during migration.	

	Snst	Stat	Min	Max	Habitats	Zoogeographic Regions
Thalasseus maximus	H	S	L	L	A11	GAN, LAN, BSR, PAS, GCS, CHO, EPC, STP, NSA, AMN, AMS, ATL
Thalasseus sandvicensis	H	A	L	L	A11	GAN, LAN, PAS, GCS, CHO, EPC, STP, NSA, AMN, AMS, ATL, PAM
Rhynchopidae						
Rhynchops niger	H	F	L	600	A8, A11	BSR, PAS, GCS, CHO, EPC, STP, NSA, AMN, AMS, ATL, PAM
CUCULIFORMES						
Cuculidae						
Coccyzus americanus	M	A	L	1200	F8, F7, F1E, F15	CHO, NSA, AMN, AMS, CSA, ATL
STRIGIFORMES						
Strigidae						
Asio flammeus	L	F	L	4300	N7, N8, N13, N9, A1	GAN, BSR, MPL, MAH, GCS, EPC, NAN, CAN, NSA, CSA, PAM, PAT
Asio otus	M	F	L	2200	F11, F8, F7	BSR, MPL, MAH
CAPRIMULGIFORMES						
Caprimulgidae						
Chordeiles gundlachii	?	A	L?	L?	?	?
Chordeiles minor	L	A	L	1200	F1E, N1, N6, N14, N13	AMN, AMS, CSA, ATL, PAM
Caprimulgus vociferus	M	S	L	3100	F11, F4E, F1E, F7	MPL, PAS, MAH, GCS
APODIFORMES						
Trochilidae						
Archilochus alexandri	L	A	L	1250	F8, N1, N2, N14	PAS, MAH
Calypte anna	L	S	L	2200	F8, F15, N14	BSR, MPL, MAH
Calypte costae	M	A	L	1250	N1, N14	BSR, PAS
Stellula calliope	M	A	1250	2800	F10, F11	BSR, MAH
PICIFORMES						
Picidae						
Sphyrapicus thyroideus	M	S	1200	2800	F11, F10	BSR, MAH
PASSERIFORMES						
Tyrannidae						
Contopus borealis	M	A	700	3400	F4E	MAH, CDH, NAN, CAN, NSA
Contopus sordidulus	M	A	500	1600	F4E, F1E	CDH, NAN, CAN
Empidonax albigularis	L	N	L	1800	N14, N11, N1	PAS, MAH, GCS, CDH
Empidonax difficilis	L	A	L	2000	F8, F7, F1, F15	BSR, PAS
Empidonax occidentalis	L	A	L	3400	F11, F4, F8, F7, F15	BSR, PAS, MAH
Sayornis saya	L	S	L	2500	N8, N2, N13, N1	BSR, MPL, MAH, GCS
Myiarchus cinerascens	L	A	L	1800+	N1, N2, F8, F7E	BSR, PAS, MAH, GCS
Myiodynastes luteiventris	L	A	L	1200	F3, F1, F15	AMN, AMS
Tyrannus dominicensis	L	A	L	L	N14, F1E, F15, F14	LAN, NSA, AMN
Tyrannus forficatus	L	A	L	800	F7E, N13, N14	PAS, GCS
Tyrannus verticalis	L	A	L	1500	N13, N8, N14	PAS, GCS
Tyrannus vociferans	M	A	L	2200	F11, F8, N2	BSR, PAS, MAH
Hirundinidae						
Tachycineta thalassina	L	A	L	3100	F10, F11, N8, N1	BSR, MPL, MAH, CDH
Progne cryptoleuca	?	N	L?	L?	?	?
Progne dominicensis	?	N	L?	L?	?	?
Progne sinaloae	?	N	L?	L?	?	?
Progne subis	L	A	L	1200	N6, N14, N13, F1E, N1, N4, A8	NSA, AMN, AMS, CSA, ATL
Stelgidopteryx serripennis	L	A	L	2500	N14, N13	BSR, PAS, MAH, GCS, CDH

Notes
Monitor breeding colonies.
To 2600m+ in migration.
Completely unknown in winter.
To 3000+m in migration; wintering areas not well known.
Occasionally to lowlands in migration.
Occasionally to lowlands; poorly known in winter.
Irregularly winters throughout at edges of evergreen forests.
Nonbreeding distribution poorly known; in lowlands during migration.
To 2600m in migration.
Locally to 2300m.
To 3000+ in migration.
Unknown in winter.
Unknown in winter.
Unknown in winter.
To 3500m in migration; winter range poorly known.

Abbreviations Used

Snst - Sensitivity:
L - Low; **M** - Medium; **H** - High.

Stat - Status:
A - All; **F** - Fraction; **S** - Some; **T** - Total;

Min - Minimum Elevation:
L - Lowlands; **?** - Uncertain value; numeric values in meters.

Max - Maximum Elevation:
L - Lowlands; **?** - Uncertain value; **+** - species occurs at least to given elevation but likely occurs higher; numeric values in meters.

Habitats:
F1 - Tropical lowland evergreen forest; **F2** - Flooded tropical evergreen forest; **F3** - River-edge forest; **F4** - Montane evergreen forest; **F5** - Elfin forest; **F6** - *Polylepis* woodland; **F7** - Tropical deciduous forest; **F8** - Gallery forest; **F9** - Southern temperate forest; **F10** - Pine forest; **F11** - Pine-oak forest; **F12** - White sand forest; **F13** - Palm forest; **F14** - Mangrove forest; **F15** - Secondary forest; **N1** - Arid lowland scrub; **N2** - Arid montane scrub; **N3** - Semihumid/humid montane scrub; **N4** - Cerrado; **N5** - Campo grasslands; **N6** - Low, seasonally wet grassland; **N7** - Southern temperate grassland; **N8** - Northern temperate grassland; **N9** - Puna grassland; **N10** - Paramo grassland; **N11** - Riparian thickets; **N12** - River island scrub; **N13** - Pastures/agricultural lands; **N14** - Second-growth scrub; **A1** - Freshwater marshes; **A2** - Saltwater/brackish marshes; **A3** - Coastal sand beaches/mudflats; **A4** - Coastal rocky beaches; **A5** - Riverine sand beaches; **A6** - Freshwater lakes and ponds; **A7** - Alkaline lakes; **A8** - Rivers; **A9** - Streams; **A10** - Bogs; **A11** - Coastal waters; **A12** - Pelagic waters.
E - Edge (used as a modifer to particular habitats).

Zoogeographic Regions:
AMN - Northern Amazonia; **AMS** - Southern Amazonia; **ATL** - Atlantic Forest; **BSR** - Baja-Sonora; **CAN** - Central Andes; **CDH** - Chiriquí-Darién Highlands; **CHO** - Chocó Lowlands; **CSA** - Central South America; **EPC** - Equatorial Pacific Coast; **GAN** - Greater Antilles; **GCS** - Gulf-Caribbean Slope; **LAN** - Lesser Antilles; **MAH** - Madrean Highlands; **MPL** - Mexican Plateau; **NAN** - Northern Andes; **NSA** - Northern South America; **PAM** - Pampas; **PAS** - Pacific Arid Slope; **PAT** - Patagonia; **SAN** - Southern Andes; **STP** - Subtropical Pacific; **TEP** - Tepuis.

	Snst	Stat	Min	Max	Habitats	Zoogeographic Regions
Riparia riparia	L	A	L	1200	N13, A8, A1	PAS, GCS, NSA, AMN, AMS, CSA, ATL, PAM
Hirundo rustica	L	A	L	3300	N13, N8, N14, A8, N5	GAN, LAN, PAS, MAH, GCS, CDH, CHO, EPC, STP, NAN, CAN, SAN, NSA, TEP, AMN AMS, CSA, ATL, PAM, PAT
Petrochelidon fulva fulva	L	A	L	1500	N8, N13, N14, N1	GAN, MPL, PAS, GCS
Petrochelidon pyrrhonota	L	A	L	1200	N5, N13	CSA, ATL, PAM
Laniidae						
Lanius ludovicianus	L	S	L	3000	N1, N2, N14, N13, N8	BSR, MPL, PAS, MAH, GCS
Troglodytidae						
Cistothorus palustris	L	S	L	2500	A1, A2	BSR, MPL, PAS, MAH, GCS
Cistothorus platensis stellaris	L	F	L	2700	N6, A1, N8	MPL, MAH, GCS, CDH
Mimidae						
Toxostoma bendirei	M	A	L	1600	N1, N13	BSR, PAS
Muscicapidae						
Turdinae						
Myadestes townsendi	M	F	1500	3000+	F10, N2	BSR, MPL, MAH
Turdus migratorius	L	S	L	4000	F15, N14, F11, F10, F7, F8	GAN, BSR, MPL, MAH, GCS
Polioptilinae						
Polioptila caerulea	L	S	L	2500	F7, F1E, F15, N2, F8	BSR, MPL, PAS, MAH, GCS
Regulus calendula	L	S	L	3600	F15, N14, N11, F11, F7	BSR, MPL, PAS, MAH, GCS
Regulus satrapa	M	F	L	3700	F10, F11, F8	BSR, MAH, GCS
Certhiidae						
Certhia americana	M	F	L	4000	F10, F11, F8	BSR, MPL, MAH, GCS
Emberizidae						
Emberizinae						
Junco hyemalis hyemalis	M	F	L	2800	F11, N11, F8, N1, N2, N8	BSR, MPL, MAH, GCS
Ammodramus sandwichensis sandwichensis	L	S	L	3300	N8, N13	GAN, BSR, MPL, PAS, MAH, GCS
Ammodramus savannarum	M	S	L	2500	N8, N5, N13	GAN, BSR, MPL, PAS, MAH, GCS, CDH, NAN, NSA
Spizella passerina	L	S	L	3500	F10, F11, F8, N14, F15	BSR, MPL, PAS, MAH, GCS
Chondestes grammacus	L	S	L	2400	N1, N2, N14	BSR, MPL, PAS, GCS
Amphispiza belli	M	S	L	1800	N1, N2	BSR, MPL
Aimophila cassinii	L	S	L	2200	N8, N1	BSR, MPL, PAS, GCS
Cardinalinae						
Pheucticus melanocephalus	M	A	L	3400	F11, F8	BSR, PAS, MAH
Passerina amoena	L	A	L	2200	N14, N1, N11	BSR, MPL, PAS, MAH
Passerina caerulea	L	A	L	2500	F8, F15, N11, N14	GAN, BSR, MPL, PAS, MAH, GCS, CDH
Passerina ciris	L	A	L	1500	N14, N11	GAN, PAS, MAH, GCS
Thraupinae						
Piranga ludoviciana	M	A	L	2100	F11, F15	BSR, PAS, MAH, GCS, CDH
Piranga rubra	L	A	L	1200	F1E, F15, F3, F8	BSR, PAS, GCS, CHO, NSA, AMN, AMS
Parulinae						
Vermivora celata	L	S	L	2600	N11, F10, F15, N14	BSR, MPL, PAS, MAH, GCS
Vermivora luciae	M	A	L	1800	F8, F7	PAS
Dendroica coronata	L	S	L	4000	F11, F10, F1E, F15, F8, N11	GAN, LAN, BSR, MPL, PAS, MAH, GCS, CDH
Dendroica dominica	L	S	L	1800	F10, F15, F1E	GAN, MAH, GCS
Dendroica nigrescens	L	A	L	2500	F11, F15, F7, N2	BSR, MPL, PAS, MAH

Notes
Mainly below 800m except in migration.
Winter range of northern migrants poorly known.   To 3700m in migration; poorly known in winter.
Winters irregularly at lower elevations.
Monitor? Overgrazing.
Monitor?
Occasionally to 3050m; continue survey on winter range   Occasionally to 3100m.
Poorly known in winter.
To 1800+ in migration.   Winters mainly above 1250m.

Abbreviations Used

Snst - Sensitivity:
L - Low; **M** - Medium; **H** - High.

Stat - Status:
A - All; **F** - Fraction; **S** - Some; **T** - Total;

Min - Minimum Elevation:
L - Lowlands; **?** - Uncertain value; numeric values in meters.

Max - Maximum Elevation:
L - Lowlands; **?** - Uncertain value; **+** - species occurs at least to given elevation but likely occurs higher; numeric values in meters.

Habitats:
F1 - Tropical lowland evergreen forest; **F2** - Flooded tropical evergreen forest; **F3** - River-edge forest; **F4** - Montane evergreen forest; **F5** - Elfin forest; **F6** - *Polylepis* woodland; **F7** - Tropical deciduous forest; **F8** - Gallery forest; **F9** - Southern temperate forest; **F10** - Pine forest; **F11** - Pine-oak forest; **F12** - White sand forest; **F13** - Palm forest; **F14** - Mangrove forest; **F15** - Secondary forest; **N1** - Arid lowland scrub; **N2** - Arid montane scrub; **N3** - Semihumid/humid montane scrub; **N4** - Cerrado; **N5** - Campo grasslands; **N6** - Low, seasonally wet grassland; **N7** - Southern temperate grassland; **N8** - Northern temperate grassland; **N9** - Puna grassland; **N10** - Paramo grassland; **N11** - Riparian thickets; **N12** - River island scrub; **N13** - Pastures/agricultural lands; **N14** - Second-growth scrub; **A1** - Freshwater marshes; **A2** - Saltwater/brackish marshes; **A3** - Coastal sand beaches/mudflats; **A4** - Coastal rocky beaches; **A5** - Riverine sand beaches; **A6** - Freshwater lakes and ponds; **A7** - Alkaline lakes; **A8** - Rivers; **A9** - Streams; **A10** - Bogs; **A11** - Coastal waters; **A12** - Pelagic waters.
E - Edge (used as a modifer to particular habitats).

Zoogeographic Regions:
AMN - Northern Amazonia; **AMS** - Southern Amazonia; **ATL** - Atlantic Forest; **BSR** - Baja-Sonora; **CAN** - Central Andes; **CDH** - Chiriquí-Darién Highlands; **CHO** - Chocó Lowlands; **CSA** - Central South America; **EPC** - Equatorial Pacific Coast; **GAN** - Greater Antilles; **GCS** - Gulf-Caribbean Slope; **LAN** - Lesser Antilles; **MAH** - Madrean Highlands; **MPL** - Mexican Plateau; **NAN** - Northern Andes; **NSA** - Northern South America; **PAM** - Pampas; **PAS** - Pacific Arid Slope; **PAT** - Patagonia; **SAN** - Southern Andes; **STP** - Subtropical Pacific; **TEP** - Tepuis.

	Snst	Stat	Min	Max	Habitats	Zoogeographic Regions
Dendroica petechia						
aestiva	L	A	L	2500+	F8, F3, F15, F1E, F7	GAN, BSR, PAS, MAH, GCS, CDH, NSA, AMN, AMS?
Dendroica pinus	M	F	L	2100+	F10	GAN, GCS
Geothlypis trichas	L	S	L	3100	N11, N14, A1, A2	GAN, BSR, MPL, PAS, MAH, GCS, NSA
Cardellina rubrifrons	M	A	1300	3100	F10, F11, F4, N11	MAH
Icteria virens	L	A	L	1700	F15, F7, N14, N11	PAS, GCS
Vireonidae						
Vireo altiloquus	L	A	L	1200	F7, F1, F15, F14	GAN, LAN, NSA, AMN, AMS
Vireo atricapillus	M	A	L	1600	N2, N1, F7	PAS, MAH
Vireo bellii	M	A	L	2000	N1, F7, N2, N11, N13	BSR, PAS, GCS?
Vireo flavoviridis	L	A	L	1100	F1E, F15	AMN, AMS
Vireo gilvus	L	A	L	2100	F7, F1, F15, F11	BSR, PAS, MAH, GCS
Vireo griseus	L	S	L	1800	F1E, F15, F8, F7, N14	GAN, PAS, GCS
Vireo solitarius						
cassinii	M	A	L	2800	F11, F8, F15, F7	BSR, MPL, PAS, MAH
plumbeus	M	A	L	3100	F11, F10, F8, F15, F4, F7	BSR, MPL, PAS, MAH, GCS, CDH
Vireo vicinior	M	A	L	800	N1	BSR
Icteridae						
Icterus galbula						
bullockii	L	A	L	2800	F11, F7, F4E, F15	PAS, MAH, GCS
Icterus spurius						
fuertesi	M	N	L	1500?	F8, F7, F15	PAS, MAH
spurius	L	A	L	2000	F15, F8, F7	PAS, MAH, GCS, NSA
Xanthocephalus xanthocephalus	L	S	L	2600	N13	BSR, MPL, PAS, MAH, GCS
Sturnella neglecta	L	F	L	2800	N8, N13, N1	BSR, MPL, PAS, MAH, GCS
Euphagus cyanocephalus	L	S	L	2700	N13, N14	BSR, MPL, PAS, MAH, GCS
Molothrus ater	L	S	L	2500	N13, N14, N1	BSR, MPL, PAS, MAH, GCS
Fringillidae						
Carduelis pinus	L	F	L	4000	F10, F11, F8, F15	BSR, MPL, MAH
Carpodacus cassinii	M	F	1500	2900	F10, F11	BSR, MAH
Sturnidae						
Sturnus vulgaris	L	F	L	2200	F15, N14, N13, F8	GAN, BSR, MPL, PAS, GCS
Corvidae						
Gymnorhinus cyanocephalus	M	F	1600	2900	F10, F11	BSR, MAH

Notes
Rare outside breeding range in Neotropics.
Occasionally to lowlands.
Limits of wintering range unknown. Monitor -- declining; survey winter habitat.
Winter range poorly known.
Winter range and habitats poorly known.
Occasionally to lowlands.
Monitor spreading and effect on other species.
Irregular outside breeding range.

Abbreviations Used

Snst - Sensitivity:
L - Low; **M** - Medium; **H** - High.

Stat - Status:
A - All; **F** - Fraction; **S** - Some; **T** - Total;

Min - Minimum Elevation:
L - Lowlands; **?** - Uncertain value; numeric values in meters.

Max - Maximum Elevation:
L - Lowlands; **?** - Uncertain value; **+** - species occurs at least to given elevation but likely occurs higher; numeric values in meters.

Habitats:
F1 - Tropical lowland evergreen forest; **F2** - Flooded tropical evergreen forest; **F3** - River-edge forest; **F4** - Montane evergreen forest; **F5** - Elfin forest; **F6** - *Polylepis* woodland; **F7** - Tropical deciduous forest; **F8** - Gallery forest; **F9** - Southern temperate forest; **F10** - Pine forest; **F11** - Pine-oak forest; **F12** - White sand forest; **F13** - Palm forest; **F14** - Mangrove forest; **F15** - Secondary forest; **N1** - Arid lowland scrub; **N2** - Arid montane scrub; **N3** - Semihumid/humid montane scrub; **N4** - Cerrado; **N5** - Campo grasslands; **N6** - Low, seasonally wet grassland; **N7** - Southern temperate grassland; **N8** - Northern temperate grassland; **N9** - Puna grassland; **N10** - Paramo grassland; **N11** - Riparian thickets; **N12** - River island scrub; **N13** - Pastures/agricultural lands; **N14** - Second-growth scrub; **A1** - Freshwater marshes; **A2** - Saltwater/brackish marshes; **A3** - Coastal sand beaches/mudflats; **A4** - Coastal rocky beaches; **A5** - Riverine sand beaches; **A6** - Freshwater lakes and ponds; **A7** - Alkaline lakes; **A8** - Rivers; **A9** - Streams; **A10** - Bogs; **A11** - Coastal waters; **A12** - Pelagic waters.
E - Edge (used as a modifer to particular habitats).

Zoogeographic Regions:
AMN - Northern Amazonia; **AMS** - Southern Amazonia; **ATL** - Atlantic Forest; **BSR** - Baja-Sonora; **CAN** - Central Andes; **CDH** - Chiriquí-Darién Highlands; **CHO** - Chocó Lowlands; **CSA** - Central South America; **EPC** - Equatorial Pacific Coast; **GAN** - Greater Antilles; **GCS** - Gulf-Caribbean Slope; **LAN** - Lesser Antilles; **MAH** - Madrean Highlands; **MPL** - Mexican Plateau; **NAN** - Northern Andes; **NSA** - Northern South America; **PAM** - Pampas; **PAS** - Pacific Arid Slope; **PAT** - Patagonia; **SAN** - Southern Andes; **STP** - Subtropical Pacific; **TEP** - Tepuis.

Database E

Austral Migrants

	Snst	Rel	CP	RP	Min	Max	Habitats	Zoogeographic Regions
PODICEDIFORMES								
Podicipedidae								
Podiceps occipitalis	M	C	4	3	L	5000	A6	NAN, CAN, SAN, CSA, PAT
PELECANIFORMES								
Phalacrocoracidae								
Phalacrocorax albiventer	H	F	4	2	L	L	A11	PAM, PAT
Phalacrocorax atriceps	H	F	4	2	L	L	A11	PAM, PAT
CICONIIFORMES								
Threskiornithidae								
Theristicus caudatus melanopis	L	U/P	3	2	L	3000	N13, N7	STP, SAN, PAT
ANSERIFORMES								
Anatidae								
Chloephaga picta	L	F	4	3	L	1500	N7, N13	SAN, PAM, PAT
Chloephaga poliocephala	L	F	4	3	L	1500?	N7, N13	SAN, PAM, PAT
Chloephaga rubidiceps	L	R	2	1	L	L	N7, N13	PAM, PAT
Anas platalea	M	F	4	3	L	3500	A1, A6	STP, CAN, SAN, CSA, PAM, PAT
Anas sibilatrix	M	F	3	2	L	1200	A6, A8	STP, CSA, PAM, PAT
Anas specularis	M	U	2	1	L	1800	A8, A6	SAN
Oxyura vittata	M	F	4	3	L	800	A6	STP, CSA, PAM, PAT
FALCONIFORMES								
Accipitridae								
Harpagus diodon	M	F	4	2	L	L	F1	AMN, AMS, CSA, ATL
Falconidae								
Falco peregrinus	M	R	3	2	L	2600	A11, N2, F7E	BSR, MAH, EPC, STP, NAN, CAN, SAN, CSA, PAT
GRUIFORMES								
Rallidae								
Fulica armillata	M	C	4	3	L	1000	A1, A6	STP, SAN, CSA, ATL, PAM, PAT
Fulica rufifrons	M	U	4	3	L	L	A1	STP, CSA, ATL, PAM
CHARADRIIFORMES								
Haematopodidae								
Haematopus leucopodus	L	C	4	3	L	1000	A3, A6	STP, PAM, PAT
Charadriidae								
Charadrius falklandicus	M	F	4	3	L	1200	A3, A4, A6, A7	STP, PAM, PAT
Charadrius modestus	M	F	4	3	L	1000	N7, A3	STP, PAM, PAT
Eudromias ruficollis	L	F	3	2	L	4500	N7, N1, N9, N13	EPC, STP, CAN, SAN, CSA, PAM, PAT

Snst - Sensitivity: **L** - Low; **M** - Medium; **H** - High. **Rel - Relative Abundance:** **R** - Rare; **U** - Uncommon; **F** - Fairly Common; **C** - Common; **P** - Patchily distributed. **CP - Conservation Priority:** **1** - Urgent; **2** - High; **3** - Medium; **4** - Low. **RP - Research Priority:** **1** - High; **2** - Medium; **3** - Low. **Min - Minimum Elevation:** **L** - Lowlands; **?** - Uncertain value; numeric values in meters. **Max - Maximum Elevation:** **L** - Lowlands; **?** - Uncertain value; **+** - species occurs at least to given elevation but likely occurs higher; numeric values in meters.

Zoogeographic Regions: **AMN** - Northern Amazonia; **AMS** - Southern Amazonia; **ATL** - Atlantic Forest; **BSR** - Baja-Sonora; **CAN** - Central Andes; **CDH** - Chiriquí-Darién Highlands; **CHO** - Chocó Lowlands; **CSA** - Central South America; **EPC** - Equatorial Pacific Coast; **GAN** - Greater Antilles; **GCS** - Gulf-Caribbean Slope; **LAN** - Lesser Antilles; **MAH** - Madrean Highlands; **MPL** - Mexican Plateau; **NAN** - Northern Andes; **NSA** - Northern South America; **PAM** - Pampas; **PAS** - Pacific Arid Slope; **PAT** - Patagonia; **SAN** - Southern Andes; **STP** - Subtropical Pacific; **TEP** - Tepuis.

	Snst	Rel	CP	RP	Min	Max	Habitats	Zoogeographic Regions
Chionididae								
Chionis alba	H	F	4	3	L	L	A4, A3	PAM, PAT
Laridae								
Larus modestus	H	C	4	2	L	L	A11, A3	EPC, STP
Sterna hirundinacea	H	F	4	2	L	L	A11	STP, ATL, PAM, PAT
Thalasseus maximus	H	C	4	2	L	L	A11	GAN, LAN, BSR, PAS, GCS, NSA, ATL, PAM
COLUMBIFORMES								
Columbidae								
Columbina picui	L	C	4	3	L	1250	N14, N11, N1	STP, CAN, AMS, CSA, PAM, PAT
PSITTACIFORMES								
Psittacidae								
Cyanoliseus patagonus	M	U/P	3	2	L	1800+	N1, N2, N13	STP, CSA, PAT
CUCULIFORMES								
Cuculidae								
Coccyzus cinereus	M	U	4	3	L	1200	F7, F8, F3	AMS, CSA, ATL, PAM
APODIFORMES								
Apodidae								
Chaetura andrei	L	C	4	3	L	900	F1E, F15, N14	NSA, AMN, AMS?, CSA
PASSERIFORMES								
Furnariidae								
Geositta cunicularia	M	F	4	3	L	4800	N7, N9, N1, N13	STP, CAN, SAN, CSA, PAM, PAT
Upucerthia dumetaria	M	F	4	3	L	4000	N2, N1, N9	CAN, SAN, CSA, PAM, PAT
Cinclodes fuscus	M	C	4	3	L	4900	N10, N9, N7, N2	NAN, CAN, SAN, CSA, PAM, PAT
Asthenes pyrrholeuca	M	C	4	3	L	3000	N1, N2, N7	STP, SAN, CSA, PAM, PAT
Tyrannidae								
Elaenia albiceps	L	C	4	3	L	3300	F4E, F1E, F15, N3	NAN, CAN, AMN, AMS, CSA, ATL
Elaenia parvirostris	L	C	4	3	L	750+	F8, F1E, F15	NSA, AMN, AMS, CSA
Elaenia spectabilis	L	C	4	3	L	800+	F3, F8, F15	AMS, CSA
Elaenia strepera	M	U?	4	2	L	1000?	F7, F1?	NSA, AMN, AMS
Inezia inornata	L	F	4	3	L	600	F7, F3, F8	AMS, CSA
Pseudocolopteryx acutipennis	M	U/P	4	2	L	2600	N11, A1	NAN, CAN, CSA
Pyrocephalus rubinus	L	F	4	3	L	2600	N13, N11, N14, N12, F7E, F8E	BSR, PAS, MAH, GCS, CHO, EPC, STP, NSA, AMN, AMS, CSA, ATL, PAM
Ochthoeca parvirostris	L	C	4	3	L	1200?	F9, F15, F7	STP, SAN
Xolmis coronata	M	F	4	3	L	1000	N1	CSA, PAM, PAT
Neoxolmis rubetra	M	F	4	3	L	L?	N1, N13	CSA, PAT
Neoxolmis rufiventris	M	U/P	4	2	L	L	N7, N1	CSA, PAM, PAT
Agriornis microptera	L	U	4	3	L	4000	N2, N1, N9	CAN, CSA, PAM

Habitats: **F1** - Tropical lowland evergreen forest; **F2** - Flooded tropical evergreen forest; **F3** - River-edge forest; **F4** - Montane evergreen forest; **F5** - Elfin forest; **F6** - *Polylepis* woodland; **F7** - Tropical deciduous forest; **F8** - Gallery forest; **F9** - Southern temperate forest; **F10** - Pine forest; **F11** - Pine- oak forest; **F12** - White sand forest; **F13** - Palm forest; **F14** - Mangrove forest; **F15** - Secondary forest; **N1** - Arid lowland scrub; **N2** - Arid montane scrub; **N3** - Semihumid/humid montane scrub; **N4** - Cerrado; **N5** - Campo grasslands; **N6** - Low, seasonally wet grassland; **N7** - Southern temperate grassland; **N8** - Northern temperate grassland; **N9** - Puna grassland; **N10** - Paramo grassland; **N11** - Riparian thickets; **N12** - River island scrub; **N13** - Pastures/agricultural lands; **N14** - Second-growth scrub; **A1** - Freshwater marshes; **A2** - Saltwater/brackish marshes; **A3** - Coastal sand beaches/mudflats; **A4** - Coastal rocky beaches; **A5** - Riverine sand beaches; **A6** - Freshwater lakes and ponds; **A7** - Alkaline lakes; **A8** - Rivers; **A9** - Streams; **A10** - Bogs; **A11** - Coastal waters; **A12** - Pelagic waters.
E - Edge (used as a modifer to particular habitats).

	Snst	Rel	CP	RP	Min	Max	Habitats	Zoogeographic Regions
Agriornis murina	M	F	4	3	L	800?	N1	CSA, PAT
Muscisaxicola albilora	M	F	4	3	3000	4000	N9	NAN, CAN
Muscisaxicola capistrata	M	U	4	3	1000?	4000	N9, A10, N13	CAN, SAN
Muscisaxicola flavinucha	M	F	4	3	3200	4500	N9, A10	CAN
Muscisaxicola frontalis	M	U	4	3	3600	4000	N9	CAN
Muscisaxicola macloviana	L	F	4	3	L	1200	N13, N1	STP, SAN, CSA, PAM, PAT
Knipolegus hudsoni	M?	F	4	2	L	800+	N1	CSA
Satrapa icterophrys	L	F	4	3	L	2000	N13, N14, F3, F8	NSA, AMN, AMS, CSA, ATL, PAM
Attila phoenicurus	H	U/P	3	1	L	800	F1, F4	AMN?, AMS, CSA, ATL
Casiornis rufa	M	F	4	3	L	800	F7, F8	AMN, AMS, CSA
Myiarchus swainsoni	L	F	4	3	L	1000	F1E, F8, F15, F7	NSA, AMN, AMS, CSA
Myiodynastes maculatus								
solitarius	L	F	4	3	L	1200	F1E, F7, F15	CAN, AMN, AMS, CSA
Empidonomus aurantioatrocristatus	L	F	4	3	L	800	F1E, F7, F8, F15	AMN, AMS, CSA
Tyrannus savana	L	C	4	3	L	1600	N14, N6, N13, N5, F15	LAN, GCS, NSA, AMN, AMS, CSA, ATL?
Hirundinidae								
Tachycineta leucopyga	L	F	4	2	L	1500	N7, N13, N14	STP, SAN, PAM, PAT
Tachycineta leucorrhoa	L	C	4	3	L	1100	N6, N5, N13, N14	AMS, CSA, ATL, PAM
Progne modesta								
elegans	L	F	4	2	L	L	N14, A8	AMN, AMS
Notiochelidon cyanoleuca	L	C	4	3	L	3600	N14, N13, N7	GCS, CDH, STP, NAN, CAN, SAN, NSA, TEP, AMN, AMS, CSA, ATL, PAM
Motacillidae								
Anthus hellmayri	L	F	4	2	L	3600	N7, N9, N13	CAN, SAN, CSA, PAM, PAT
Mimidae								
Mimus patagonicus	L	F	4	3	L	1000	N1, N14?	STP, CSA, PAM, PAT
Mimus triurus	L	F	4	2	L	700	N1, N14, N2	STP, CSA, ATL?, PAM, PAT
Muscicapidae								
Turdinae								
Platycichla flavipes	M	C	4	3	L	800	F1, F4, F12, F15	NSA, TEP, ATL
Turdus amaurochalinus	L	C	4	3	L	1000	F1E, F7, F15, F8, F3	AMS, CSA, ATL
Turdus nigriceps								
nigriceps	M	F	4	2	500	1800	F1, F4	NAN, CAN
subalaris	L	F	4	2	L	1000	F8, F1, F15	CSA, ATL
Emberizidae								
Emberizinae								
Diuca diuca	L	C	4	3	L	2000	N1, N2, N14	STP, SAN, CSA, PAM, PAT
Sporophila caerulescens	L	C	4	3	L	1200	N14, N11, N13	AMN, AMS, CSA, ATL, PAM
Sporophila cinnamomea	M	U	3	2	L	800	N6, N5?	CSA

Snst - Sensitivity: L - Low; **M** - Medium; **H** - High. **Rel - Relative Abundance:** **R** - Rare; **U** - Uncommon; **F** - Fairly Common; **C** - Common; **P** - Patchily distributed. **CP - Conservation Priority:** **1** - Urgent; **2** - High; **3** - Medium; **4** - Low. **RP - Research Priority:** **1** - High; **2** - Medium; **3** - Low. **Min - Minimum Elevation:** **L** - Lowlands; **?** - Uncertain value; numeric values in meters. **Max - Maximum Elevation:** **L** - Lowlands; **?** - Uncertain value; **+** - species occurs at least to given elevation but likely occurs higher; numeric values in meters.

Zoogeographic Regions: **AMN** - Northern Amazonia; **AMS** - Southern Amazonia; **ATL** - Atlantic Forest; **BSR** - Baja-Sonora; **CAN** - Central Andes; **CDH** - Chiriquí-Darién Highlands; **CHO** - Chocó Lowlands; **CSA** - Central South America; **EPC** - Equatorial Pacific Coast; **GAN** - Greater Antilles; **GCS** - Gulf-Caribbean Slope; **LAN** - Lesser Antilles; **MAH** - Madrean Highlands; **MPL** - Mexican Plateau; **NAN** - Northern Andes; **NSA** - Northern South America; **PAM** - Pampas; **PAS** - Pacific Arid Slope; **PAT** - Patagonia; **SAN** - Southern Andes; **STP** - Subtropical Pacific; **TEP** - Tepuis.

	Snst	Rel	CP	RP	Min	Max	Habitats	Zoogeographic Regions
Sporophila lineola lineola	L	C	4	2	L	1200	N14, N11, N13	NSA, AMN, AMS, CSA
Sporophila melanogaster	M	U	3	2	500?	900	N5, N6	CSA
Sporophila palustris	M	F/P	3	2	L	1100	N6, N5	CSA
Sporophila zelichi	M	R	2	1	1000?	1000?	N6?	CSA?
Catamenia analis	L	C	4	3	1800	3300	N2, N3, N14	NAN, CAN, SAN
Thraupinae								
Tangara preciosa	L	F	4	3	L	1000	F9, F15, F12	ATL, PAM
Icteridae								
Sturnella superciliaris	L	C	4	3	L	2600	N13, N6, N5, A1	AMS, CSA, ATL, PAM

Habitats: F1 - Tropical lowland evergreen forest; **F2** - Flooded tropical evergreen forest; **F3** - River-edge forest; **F4** - Montane evergreen forest; **F5** - Elfin forest; **F6** - *Polylepis* woodland; **F7** - Tropical deciduous forest; **F8** - Gallery forest; **F9** - Southern temperate forest; **F10** - Pine forest; **F11** - Pine- oak forest; **F12** - White sand forest; **F13** - Palm forest; **F14** - Mangrove forest; **F15** - Secondary forest; **N1** - Arid lowland scrub; **N2** - Arid montane scrub; **N3** - Semihumid/humid montane scrub; **N4** - Cerrado; **N5** - Campo grasslands; **N6** - Low, seasonally wet grassland; **N7** - Southern temperate grassland; **N8** - Northern temperate grassland; **N9** - Puna grassland; **N10** - Paramo grassland; **N11** - Riparian thickets; **N12** - River island scrub; **N13** - Pastures/agricultural lands; **N14** - Second-growth scrub; **A1** - Freshwater marshes; **A2** - Saltwater/brackish marshes; **A3** - Coastal sand beaches/mudflats; **A4** - Coastal rocky beaches; **A5** - Riverine sand beaches; **A6** - Freshwater lakes and ponds; **A7** - Alkaline lakes; **A8** - Rivers; **A9** - Streams; **A10** - Bogs; **A11** - Coastal waters; **A12** - Pelagic waters.

E - Edge (used as a modifer to particular habitats).

Database F

Seabirds Not Breeding in the Neotropics

Aptenodytes forsteri
Pygoscelis antarcticus
Diomedea albatrus
Diomedea bulleri
Diomedea cauta
Diomedea chlororhynchos
Diomedea epomophora
Diomedea exulans
Diomedea nigripes
Phoebetria palpebrata
Fulmarus glacialis
Fulmarus glacialoides
Thalassoica antarctica
Daption capense
Pterodroma (cooki) cooki
Pterodroma incerta
Pterodroma lessoni
Pterodroma macroptera
Pterodroma mollis
Pterodroma rostrata
Pachyptila desolata
Pachyptila salvini
Pachyptila vittata
Procellaria aequinoctialis
Procellaria cinerea
Procellaria parkinsoni
Procellaria westlandica
Calonectris diomedea
Puffinus assimilis
Puffinus bulleri
Puffinus carneipes
Puffinus nativitatis
Puffinus puffinus
Puffinus tenuirostris
Pelagodroma marina
Fregetta tropica
Phaethon rubricauda
Morus bassanus
Phalaropus fulicaria
Phalaropus lobatus
Catharacta maccormicki
Catharacta (skua) skua
Stercorarius longicauda
Stercorarius parasiticus
Stercorarius pomarinus
Xema sabini
Sterna paradisaea
Uria aalge
Cerorhinca monocerata

Database G

Nearctic Partial Migrants

Species	Status
Podilymbus podiceps	F
Phalacrocorax pelagicus	F
Phalacrocorax penicillatus	F
Anhinga anhinga	S
Ixobrychus exilis	S
Ardeola ibis	F
Butorides (striatus) virescens	S
Eudocimus albus	F
Plegadis falcinellus	F
Dendrocygna autumnalis	S
Dendrocygna bicolor	S
Anas fulvigula	F
Cathartes aura	S
Elanoides forficatus	A
Ictinia plumbea	T
Buteogallus anthracinus	A
Buteo albonotatus	A
Buteo nitidus	A
Aquila chrysaetos	F
Laterallus jamaicensis	S
Gallinula chloropus	S
Porphyrula martinica	S
Haematopus palliatus	F
Himantopus mexicanus	S
Charadrius alexandrinus	S
Charadrius wilsonia	S
Larus heermanni	A
Larus occidentalis	F
Columba fasciata	S
Columba leucocephala	S
Zenaida asiatica	S
Zenaida macroura	S
Columbina passerina	S
Otus flammeolus	A
Micrathene whitneyi	A
Speotyto cunicularia	S
Chordeiles acutipennis	A
Phalaenoptilus nuttallii	A
Caprimulgus ridgwayi	A
Nephoecetes niger	A
Chaetura vauxi	A
Aeronautes saxatalis	S
Anthracothorax prevostii	T
Cynanthus latirostris	A
Hylocharis leucotis	A
Amazilia violiceps	A
Lampornis clemenciae	A
Eugenes fulgens	A
Calothorax lucifer	A
Selasphorus platycercus	A
Trogon elegans	A
Colaptes auratus	S
Camptostoma imberbe	A
Contopus pertinax	A
Empidonax affinis	T
Empidonax fulvifrons	A
Sayornis nigricans	F
Pyrocephalus rubinus	S
Myiarchus tuberculifer	A

Species	Status
Myiarchus tyrannulus	A
Myiodynastes (maculatus) maculatus	T
Legatus leucophaius	T
Tyrannus crassirostris	A
Tyrannus melancholicus	A
Pachyramphus aglaiae	A
Eremophila alpestris	F
Progne chalybea	T
Phainopepla nitens	F
Salpinctes obsoletus	S
Troglodytes (aedon) aedon	S
Sialia mexicana	S
Sialia sialis	F
Sitta canadensis	F
Zonotrichia melodia	S
Spizella atrogularis	S
Amphispiza bilineata	F
Aimophila (botterii) botterii	A
Aimophila quinquestriata	A
Pipilo erythrophthalmus	S
Pheucticus chrysopeplus	T
Passerina versicolor	A
Piranga flava	A
Vermivora crissalis	A
Dendroica graciae	A
Myioborus pictus	A
Euthlypis lachrymosa	T
Basileuterus rufifrons	T
Peucedramus taeniatus	S
Icterus cucullatus	A
Icterus (galbula) abeillei	T
Icterus parisorum	A
Agelaius phoeniceus	F
Sturnella magna	F
Molothrus (aeneus) aeneus	S
Carduelis lawrencei	S
Carduelis pstaltria	F
Loxia curvirostra	F

Status: A - All; **F** - Fraction; **S** - Some; **T** - Total

Database H

Austral Partial Migrants

Rollandia rolland
Phalacrocorax brasilianus
Botaurus pinnatus
Nycticorax nycticorax
Butorides (striatus) striatus
Mycteria americana
Phoenicopterus chilensis
Dendrocygna bicolor
Dendrocygna viduata
Cygnus melanocoryphus
Coscoroba coscoroba
Callonetta leucophrys
Anas cyanoptera
Anas flavirostris
Anas georgica
Anas specularioides
Anas versicolor
Netta peposaca
Heteronetta atricapilla
Cathartes aura
Elanoides forficatus
Rostrhamus sociabilis
Ictinia plumbea
Circus cinereus
Accipiter bicolor
Accipiter poliogaster
Accipiter (striatus) erythronemius
Buteo albigula
Buteo polyosoma
Milvago chimango
Falco femoralis
Ortygonax sanguinolentus
Pardirallus maculatus
Porphyriops melanops
Gallinula chloropus
Porphyrula martinica
Fulica leucoptera
Nycticryphes semicollaris
Vanellus chilensis
Pluvianellus socialis
Gallinago paraguaiae
Thinocorus orbignyianus
Thinocorus rumicivorus
Gabianus scoresbii
Larus (belcheri) atlanticus
Larus maculipennis
Gelochelidon nilotica
Sterna trudeaui
Thalasseus sandvicensis
Rhynchops niger
Columba cayennensis
Coccyzus euleri
Coccyzus melacoryphus
Crotophaga major
Glaucidium brasilianum
Nyctibius griseus
Lurocalis (semitorquatus) semitorquatus
Podager nacunda
Caprimulgus longirostris
Caprimulgus parvulus
Caprimulgus (rufus) rufus
Cypseloides (fumigatus) fumigatus
Melanotrochilus fuscus
Anthracothorax nigricollis
Chlorostilbon aureoventris
Leucochloris albicollis
Sephanoides sephanoides
Calliphlox amethystina
Ceryle torquata
Picoides lignarius
Geositta antarctica
Cinclodes comechingonus
Cinclodes oustaleti
Sylviorthorhynchus desmursii
Synallaxis frontalis
Asthenes anthoides
Phyllomyias (burmeisteri) burmeisteri
Phyllomyias fasciatus
Camptostoma obsoletum
Phaeomyias murina
Sublegatus (modestus) modestus
Myiopagis caniceps
Myiopagis viridicata
Elaenia chiriquensis
Elaenia flavogaster
Elaenia mesoleuca
Serpophaga munda
Serpophaga subcristata
Stigmatura budytoides
Anairetes flavirostris
Anairetes parulus
Tachuris rubrigastra
Pseudocolopteryx dinellianus
Pseudocolopteryx flaviventris
Pseudocolopteryx sclateri
Euscarthmus meloryphus
Myiophobus fasciatus
Contopus cinereus
Empidonax euleri
Xolmis pyrope
Muscisaxicola cinerea
Lessonia rufa
Knipolegus (aterrimus) aterrimus
Knipolegus cyanirostris
Knipolegus striaticeps
Hymenops perspicillata
Fluvicola (pica) albiventer
Hirundinea (ferruginea) bellicosa
Machetornis rixosus
Muscipipra vetula
Sirystes sibilator
Myiarchus tuberculifer
Pitangus sulphuratus
Megarynchus pitangua
Legatus leucophaius
Empidonomus varius

Tyrannus albogularis
Tyrannus melancholicus
Pachyramphus polychopterus
Pachyramphus validus
Tityra cayana
Phibalura flavirostris
Procnias nudicollis
Phytotoma rutila
Tachycineta albiventer
Progne chalybea
Progne tapera
Alopochelidon fucata
Stelgidopteryx ruficollis
Anthus correndera
Troglodytes (aedon) aedon
Zonotrichia capensis
Phrygilus carbonarius
Phrygilus gayi
Phrygilus patagonicus
Melanodera xanthogramma
Poospiza ornata
Poospiza thoracica
Poospiza torquata
Sicalis auriventris
Sicalis luteola
Sicalis olivascens
Volatinia jacarina
Sporophila bouvreuil
Sporophila hypochroma
Sporophila hypoxantha
Sporophila ruficollis
Passerina glaucocaerulea
Hemithraupis guira
Piranga flava
Thraupis bonariensis
Thraupis sayaca
Tangara peruviana
Tersina viridis
Vireo (olivaceus) chivi
Agelaius thilius
Sturnella loyca
Carduelis uropygialis

Database I

Indicator Species

NORTHERN AMAZONIA (AMN)

Bamboo

Dromococcyx pavoninus
Campylorhamphus procurvoides
Campylorhamphus trochilirostris
Synallaxis cherriei
Automolus dorsalis
Automolus melanopezus
Myrmotherula ornata
Microrhopias quixensis
Drymophila devillei
Myrmoborus leucophrys
Phylloscartes flaveolus
Poecilotriccus andrei
Poecilotriccus capitalis
Ramphotrigon fuscicauda
Ramphotrigon megacephala
Machaeropterus pyrocephalus
Sporophila schistacea

Tropical Lowland Evergreen Forest (F1)

Crypturellus variegatus
Micrastur gilvicollis
Crax tuberosa
Crax salvini
Odontophorus gujanensis
Odontophorus stellatus
Psophia crepitans
Phaethornis malaris
Malacoptila fusca
Dendrocincla fuliginosa
Dendrocincla merula
Hylexetastes perrotii
Dendrocolaptes certhia
Xiphorhynchus pardalotus
Campylorhamphus procurvoides
Synallaxis rutilans
Automolus infuscatus
Sclerurus caudacutus
Sclerurus rufigularis
Frederickena viridis
Thamnophilus aethiops
Megastictus margaritatus
Thamnomanes ardesiacus
Thamnomanes caesius
Myrmotherula erythrura
Myrmotherula guttata
Myrmotherula gutturalis
Myrmotherula haematonota
Myrmotherula longipennis
Myrmoborus myotherinus
Percnostola rufifrons
Percnostola schistacea
Myrmeciza ferruginea
Pithys albifrons
Formicarius colma
Chamaeza nobilis
Myrmornis torquata
Myrmothera campanisona
Conopophaga aurita
Conopophaga peruviana
Cnipodectes subbrunneus
Corythopis torquata
Platyrinchus coronatus
Platyrinchus saturatus
Myiobius barbatus
Corapipo gutturalis
Chiroxiphia pareola
Pipra erythrocephala
Pipra serena
Microbates collaris
Lanio fulvus
Hylophilus ochraceiceps

Flooded Tropical Evergreen Forest (F2)

Crypturellus brevirostris
Crypturellus cinereus
Zebrilus undulatus
Agamia agami
Mesembrinibis cayennensis
Leucopternis schistacea
Aramides cajanea
Eurypyga helias
Phaethornis hispidus
Xiphorhynchus obsoletus
Hypocnemoides melanopogon
Sclateria naevia
Myrmeciza melanoceps
Hylophylax punctulata
Knipolegus poecilocercus
Schiffornis major
Heterocercus aurantiivertex
Pipra aureola
Pipra filicauda
Turdus hauxwelli
Lanio versicolor
Hylophilus ochraceiceps

River-Edge/River Island Forest (F3)

Rostrhamus hamatus
Aburria pipile
Laterallus fasciatus
Ara severa
Polyplancta aurescens
Bucco macrodactylus
Celeus spectabilis
Automolus rufipileatus
Xenops tenuirostris
Sakesphorus luctuosus
Thamnophilus nigrocinereus
Myrmotherula assimilis
Myrmoborus lugubris
Sublegatus obscurior
Elaenia pelzelni
Cephalopterus ornatus
Conirostrum margaritae
Cacicus sclateri

NORTHERN AMAZONIA (AMN) (cont.)

White Sand Forest (F12)

Crypturellus erythropus
Aratinga pertinax
Hylocharis cyanus
Galbula leucogastra
Thamnophilus punctatus
Formicivora grisea
Elaenia cristata
Elaenia ruficeps
Rhytipterna immunda
Xenopipo atronitens
Neopelma chrysocephalum
Heterocercus aurantiivertex
Heterocercus flavivertex
Hmitriccus inornatus
Dolospingus fringilloides
Schistochlamys melanopis
Tachyphonus phoenicius
Hylophilus brunneiceps
Cyanocorax cayanus
Cyanocorax heilprini

Campo Grasslands (N5)

Buteo albicaudatus
Falco femoralis
Burhinus bistriatus
Columbina minuta
Uropelia campestris
Speotyto cunicularia
Podager nacunda
Polytmus guainumbi
Melanerpes candidus
Synallaxis albescens
Polystictus pectoralis
Euscarthmus rufomarginatus
Ammodramus humeralis
Sicalis citrina
Sicalis luteola
Emberizoides herbicola
Sporophila minuta
Sporophila plumbea
Schistochlamys melanopis
Tangara cayana

Low, Seasonally Wet Grasslands (N6)

Jabiru mycteria
Theristicus caudatus
Cercibis oxycerca
Cathartes burrovianus
Buteo albicaudatus
Porzana albicollis
Laterallus viridis
Neocrex erythrops
Vanellus chilensis
Gallinago undulata
Aratinga aurea
Rhinoptynx clamator
Podager nacunda
Caprimulgus cayennensis
Polytmus guainumbi
Ramphastos toco
Colaptes campestris
Polystictus pectoralis
Emberizoides herbicola
Sporophila minuta
Sporophila plumbea

SOUTHERN AMAZONIA (AMS)

Bamboo

Dromococcyx pavoninus
Nonnula ruficapilla
Nonnula sclateri
Monasa flavirostris
Campylorhamphus procurvoides
Campylorhamphus trochilirostris
Synallaxis cherriei
Simoxenops ucayalae
Automolus dorsalis
Automolus melanopezus
Cymbilaimus sanctaemariae
Myrmotherula iheringi
Myrmotherula ornata
Microrhopias quixensis
Drymophila devillei
Drymophila subochracea
Cercomacra manu
Percnostola lophotes
Myrmeciza goeldii
Phylloscartes flaveolus
Lophotriccus eulophotes
Poecilotriccus albifacies
Poecilotriccus capitalis
Hemitriccus flammulatus
Ramphotrigon fuscicauda
Ramphotrigon megacephala
Neopelma sulphureiventer
Machaeropterus pyrocephalus
Sporophila schistacea

SOUTHERN AMAZONIA (AMS) (cont.)

Tropical Lowland Evergreen Forest (F1)

Tinamus guttatus
Crypturellus strigulosus
Crypturellus variegatus
Micrastur gilvicollis
Crax tuberosa
Odontophorus stellatus
Psophia leucoptera
Psophia viridis
Phaethornis philippii
Phaethornis stuarti
Malacoptila rufa
Malacoptila semicincta
Dendrocincla fuliginosa
Dendrocincla merula
Hylexetastes perrotii
Dendrocolaptes certhia
Dendrocolaptes concolor
Dendrocolaptes hoffmannsi
Xiphorhynchus elegans
Xiphorhynchus spixii
Synallaxis rutilans
Automolus infuscatus
Sclerurus caudacutus
Sclerurus rufigularis
Thamnophilus aethiops
Megastictus margaritatus
Thamnomanes ardesiacus
Thamnomanes caesius
Thamnomanes saturninus
Myrmotherula haematonota
Myrmotherula hauxwelli
Myrmotherula leucophthalma
Myrmotherula longipennis
Myrmotherula menetriesii
Dichrozona cincta
Myrmoborus myotherinus
Myrmeciza ferruginea
Pithys albifrons
Gymnopithys salvini
Rhegmatorhina berlepschi
Rhegmatorhina gymnops
Rhegmatorhina hoffmannsi
Rhegmatorhina melanosticta
Phlegopsis borbae
Formicarius colma
Chamaeza nobilis
Myrmornis torquata
Myrmothera campanisona
Conopophaga aurita
Conopophaga melanogaster
Conopophaga peruviana
Corythopis torquata
Liosceles thoracicus
Platyrinchus coronatus
Platyrinchus saturatus
Myiobius barbatus
Chiroxiphia pareola
Pipra nattereri
Pipra rubrocapilla
Microcerculus marginatus
Habia rubica

Flooded Tropical Evergreen Forest (F2)

Crypturellus bartletti
Crypturellus cinereus
Zebrilus undulatus
Agamia agami
Mesembrinibis cayennensis
Leucopternis schistacea
Aramides cajanea
Eurypyga helias
Phaethornis hispidus
Xiphorhynchus obsoletus
Furnarius torridus
Myrmoborus melanurus
Hypocnemoides maculicauda
Hypocnemoides melanopogon
Sclateria naevia
Myrmeciza melanoceps
Hylophylax punctulata
Knipolegus poecilocercus
Schiffornis major
Heterocercus linteatus
Pipra aureola
Pipra fasciicauda
Pipra filicauda
Thryothorus griseus
Turdus hauxwelli

River-Edge/River Island Forest (F3)

Rostrhamus hamatus
Aburria cujubi
Aburria pipile
Laterallus fasciatus
Ara severa
Nannopsittaca dachillae
Polyplancta aurescens
Bucco macrodactylus
Celeus spectabilis
Automolus rufipileatus
Xenops tenuirostris
Cymbilaimus sanctaemariae
Sakesphorus luctuosus
Myrmotherula assimilis
Cercomacra ferdinandi
Myrmoborus lugubris
Myrmeciza goeldii
Sublegatus obscurior
Elaenia pelzelni
Conioptilon mcilhennyi
Cephalopterus ornatus
Conirostrum margaritae

White Sand Forest (F12)

Galbula leucogastra
Thamnophilus punctatus
Formicivora grisea
Formicivora rufa
Elaenia cristata
Elaenia ruficeps
Hemitriccus minimus
Rhytipterna immunda
Neopelma pallescens
Xenopipo atronitens
Tachyphonus phoenicius

Atlantic Forest (ATL)

Lowland Bamboo

Claravis godefrida
Campylorhamphus falcularius
Clibanornis dendrocolaptoides
Automolus leucophthalmus
Batara cinerea
Mackenziaena leachii
Mackenziaena severa
Biatas nigropectus
Drymophila ferruginea
Drymophila rubricollis
Psilorhamphus guttatus
Phylloscartes flaveolus
Hemitriccus diops
Ramphotrigon megacephala
Haplospiza unicolor
Sporophila falcirostris
Sporophila frontalis
Amaurospiza moesta
Pyrrhocoma ruficeps

Montane Bamboo

Claravis godefrida
Campylorhamphus falcularius
Clibanornis dendrocolaptoides
Oreophylax moreirae
Anabazenops fuscus
Batara cinerea
Mackenziaena leachii
Mackenziaena severa
Biatas nigropectus
Drymophila ferruginea
Drymophila genei
Drymophila ochropyga
Drymophila rubricollis
Hylopezus ochroleucus
Scytalopus speluncae
Phylloscartes flaveolus
Hemitriccus diops
Hemitriccus obsoletus
Ramphotrigon megacephala
Haplospiza unicolor
Sporophila falcirostris
Sporophila frontalis
Amaurospiza moesta
Pyrrhocoma ruficeps

Tropical Lowland Evergreen Forest (F1)

Tinamus solitarius
Crypturellus variegatus
Leucopternis lacernulata
Crax blumenbachii
Touit surda
Amazona farinosa
Amazona rhodocorytha
Glaucidium minutissimum
Nyctibius aethereus
Phaethornis idaliae
Heliothryx aurita
Trogon viridis
Ramphastos vitellinus
Dryocopus galeatus
Dendrocolaptes certhia
Thripophaga macroura
Philydor atricapillus
Philydor lichtensteini
Automolus leucophthalmus
Sclerurus caudacutus
Hypoedaleus guttatus
Thamnomanes caesius
Thamnomanes plumbeus
Myrmotherula minor
Myrmotherula urosticta
Myrmeciza ruficauda
Formicarius colma
Conopophaga melanops
Scytalopus indigoticus
Myiopagis caniceps
Phylloscartes paulistus
Phylloscartes sylviolus
Hemitriccus orbitatus
Myiobius barbatus
Rhytipterna simplex
Laniocera hypopyrra
Pachyramphus marginatus
Pipra rubrocapilla
Carpornis melanocephalus
Iodopleura pipra
Tangara cyanomelaena
Habia rubica

Humid Broadleaf Forest (F1 or F4), Lower Montane, below 1,000 m

Leucopternis polionota
Odontophorus capueira
Pionopsitta pileata
Pionus maximiliani
Triclaria malachitacea
Pulsatrix koeniswaldiana
Phaethornis eurynome
Trogon surrucura
Baillonius bailloni
Veniliornis maculifrons
Xiphocolaptes albicollis
Anabacerthia amaurotis
Cichlocolaptes leucophrys
Philydor rufus
Dysithamnus stictothorax
Myrmotherula gularis
Myrmotherula minor
Drymophila ferruginea
Terenura maculata
Terenura sicki
Myrmeciza loricata
Myrmeciza squamosa
Chamaeza campanisona
Chamaeza meruloides
Phyllomyias burmeisteri
Mionectes rufiventris
Phylloscartes ceciliae
Phylloscartes oustaleti
Hemitriccus diops
Attila phoenicurus
Pachyramphus viridis
Ilicura militaris
Carpornis cucullatus
Lipaugus lanioides
Procnias averano
Procnias nudicollis
Oxyruncus cristatus
Arremon semitorquatus
Pitylus fuliginosus
Thraupis cyanoptera

Atlantic Forest (ATL) (cont.)

Montane Evergreen Forest (F4), Upper Montane, above 1,000 m

Accipiter erythronemius
Buteo leucorrhous
Penelope obscura
Strix hylophila
Cypseloides fumigatus
Clytolaema rubricauda
Piculus aurulentus
Lepidocolaptes squamatus
Campylorhamphus falcularius
Cranioleuca pallida
Anabazenops fuscus
Heliobletus contaminatus
Xenops rutilans
Lochmias nematura
Mackenziaena leachii
Dysithamnus xanthopterus
Drymophila genei
Drymophila rubricollis
Chamaeza meruloides
Chamaeza ruficauda
Grallaria varia
Hylopezus nattereri
Merulaxis ater
Scytalopus speluncae
Phyllomyias griseocapillus
Phylloscartes difficilis
Phylloscartes ventralis
Hemitriccus obsoletus
Platyrinchus mystaceus
Phibalura flavirostris
Tijuca atra
Oxyruncus cristatus
Platycichla flavipes
Poospiza thoracica
Orchesticus abeillei
Orthogonys chloricterus
Tangara desmaresti
Cacicus chrysopterus

Southern Temperate Forest (F9)

Amazona pretrei
Amazona vinacea
Strix hylophila
Cypseloides fumigatus
Aerornis senex
Streptoprocne biscutata
Picumnus nebulosus
Leptasthenura striolata
Cranioleuca obsoleta
Phyllomyias virescens
Phylloscartes ventralis
Knipolegus nigerrimus
Piprites pileatus
Poospiza lateralis
Poospiza thoracica
Cyanocorax caeruleus

White Sand Forest (F12)

Penelope superciliaris
Columba cayennensis
Amazona brasiliensis
Hylocharis cyanus
Amazilia fimbriata
Amazilia versicolor
Picumnus temminckii
Celeus flavescens
Thamnophilus punctatus
Herpsilochmus rufimarginatus
Formicivora grisea
Formicivora littoralis
Camptostoma obsoletum
Elaenia chiriquensis
Phylloscartes kronei
Cnemotriccus fuscatus
Manacus manacus
Thryothorus longirostris
Mimus gilvus
Tachyphonus cristatus
Ramphocelus bresilius
Tangara peruviana
Cyanocorax caeruleus

Baja- Sonora (BSR)

Pine Forest (F10)

Stellula calliope
Picoides villosus
Parus gambeli
Sitta pygmaea
Turdus migratorius
Junco hyemalis
Spizella passerina
Vermivora celata
Dendroica coronata
Vireo cassini
Carduelis pinus
Carpodacus cassinii
Loxia curvirostra
Gymnorhinus cyanocephalus
Nucifraga columbiana

Baja-Sonora (BSR) (cont.)

Arid Lowland Scrub (N1)

Parabuteo unicinctus
Polyborus plancus
Lophortyx californica
Lophortyx douglasii
Lophortyx gambelii
Geococcyx californianus
Micrathene whitneyi
Chordeiles acutipennis
Phalaenoptilus nuttallii
Hylocharis xantusii
Calypte costae
Melanerpes uropygialis
Picoides scalaris
Colaptes auratus
Myiarchus cinerascens
Phainopepla nitens
Campylorhynchus brunneicapillus
Thryomanes bewickii
Toxostoma bendirei
Toxostoma cinereum
Toxostoma curvirostre
Toxostoma lecontei
Toxostoma redivivum
Chamaea fasciata
Polioptila californica
Polioptila melanura
Parus inornatus
Amphispiza belli
Amphispiza bilineata
Aimophila carpalis

Central Andes (CAN)

Bamboo

Claravis mondetoura
Bolborhynchus lineola
Synallaxis unirufa
Hellmayrea gularis
Cranioleuca albiceps
Cranioleuca marcapatae
Drymophila caudata
Grallaria carrikeri
Anairetes agraphia
Poecilotriccus ruficeps
Poecilotriccus sp.nv.
Hemitriccus spodiops
Knipolegus cabanisi
Knipolegus signatus
Cinnycerthia peruana
Thryothorus eisenmanni
Thryothorus euophrys
Haplospiza rustica
Catamblyrhynchus diadema
Hemispingus atropileus
Hemispingus calophrys
Hemispingus melanotis
Hemispingus parodii
Hemispingus rufosuperciliaris
Cacicus holosericeus

Humid Broadleaf Forest (F1 or F4), Hill Tropical, 500-900 m

Geotrygon saphirina
Pulsatrix melanota
Doryfera johannae
Phaethornis koepckeae
Taphrospilus hypostictus
Heliodoxa branickii
Simoxenops striatus
Myrmotherula grisea
Myrmotherula spodionota
Herpsilochmus rufimarginatus
Percnostola leucostigma
Phyllomyias burmeisteri
Zimmerius cinereicapillus
Phylloscartes orbitalis
Pachyramphus viridis
Chloropipo holochlora
Chlorothraupis carmioli
Euphonia xanthogaster
Tangara gyrola
Basileuterus chrysogaster

CENTRAL ANDES (CAN) (cont.)

Montane Evergreen Forest (F4), Upper Tropical, 900-1,600 m

Phaethornis guy
Eutoxeres condamini
Klais guimeti
Urosticte benjamini
Phlogophilus harterti
Heliodoxa leadbeateri
Urochroa bougueri
Schistes geoffroyi
Pharomachrus antisianus
Pharomachrus auriceps
Trogon personatus
Momotus aequatorialis
Malacoptila fulvogularis
Campephilus haematogaster
Xiphorhynchus ocellatus
Xiphorhynchus triangularis
Premnoplex brunnescens
Syndactyla rufosuperciliatus
Syndactyla subalaris
Anabacerthia striaticollis
Thripadectes melanorhynchus
Sclerurus albigularis
Dysithamnus mentalis
Myrmotherula schisticolor
Formicarius rufipectus
Chamaeza campanisona
Grallaria guatimalensis
Grallaricula flavirostris
Conopophaga ardesiaca
Conopophaga castaneiceps
Leptopogon superciliaris
Pseudotriccus pelzelni
Pseudotriccus simplex
Hemitriccus rufigularis
Rhynchocyclus fulvipectus
Platyrinchus mystaceus
Myiotriccus ornatus
Myiobius villosus
Myiophobus inornatus
Myiophobus roraimae
Mitrephanes olivaceus
Chloropipo unicolor
Masius chrysopterus
Chiroxiphia boliviana
Pipra coeruleocapilla
Pipra isidorei
Lipaugus cryptolophus
Pyroderus granadensis
Rupicola peruviana
Henicorhina leucophrys
Cyphorhinus thoracicus
Catharus dryas
Chlorospingus flavigularis
Chlorospingus ophthalmicus
Trichothraupis melanops
Basileuterus tristriatus

Montane Evergreen Forest (F4), Midmontane, 1,600-2,600 m

Nothocercus nigrocapillus
Odontophorus balliviani
Odontophorus speciosus
Leptotila megalura
Geotrygon frenata
Nyctibius maculosus
Lurocalis rufiventris
Phaethornis syrmatophorus
Adelomyia melanogenys
Coeligena coeligena
Eriocnemis alinae
Eriocnemis glaucopoides
Haplophaedia aureliae
Aulacorhynchus coeruleicinctus
Aulacorhynchus huallagae
Campephilus pollens
Dendrocincla tyrannina
Xiphocolaptes promeropirhynchus
Premnornis guttuligera
Thripadectes holostictus
Thamnophilus unicolor
Chamaeza mollissima
Grallaria albigula
Grallaria blakei
Grallaria capitalis
Grallaricula ferrugineipectus
Phyllomyias cinereiceps
Phyllomyias plumbeiceps
Zimmerius bolivianus
Zimmerius viridiflavus
Mecocerculus poecilocercus
Leptopogon taczanowskii
Phylloscartes poecilotis
Poecilotriccus ruficeps
Platyrinchus flavigularis
Myiophobus flavicans
Ochthoeca pulchella
Ampelion rufaxilla
Pipreola pulchra
Catharus fuscater
Atlapetes torquatus
Chlorospingus parvirostris
Hemispingus frontalis
Hemispingus melanotis
Creurgops dentata
Creurgops verticalis
Piranga rubriceps
Anisognathus flavinucha
Iridosornis analis
Basileuterus coronatus

Montane Evergreen Forest (F4), Upper Montane, 2,600 m to Treeline

Nothocercus julius
Hapalopsittaca melanotis
Lafresnaya lafresnayi
Coeligena violifer
Ensifera ensifera
Heliangelus amethysticollis
Eriocnemis luciani
Opisthoprora euryptera
Andigena cucullata
Andigena hypoglauca
Synallaxis unirufa
Hellmayrea gularis
Cranioleuca marcapatae
Margarornis squamiger
Thripadectes scrutator
Grallaria carrikeri
Grallaria erythrotis
Grallaria rufula
Grallaria squamigera
Scytalopus macropus
Mecoserculus stictopterus
Pseudotriccus ruficeps
Ochthoeca cinnamomeiventris
Ochthoeca frontalis
Ochthoeca jelskii
Myiotheretes fumigatus
Cinnycerthia peruana
Saltator cinctus
Hemispingus atropileus
Hemispingus calophrys
Anisognathus igniventris
Anisognathus lacrymosus
Iridosornis reinhardti
Dubusia taeniata
Basileuterus luteoviridis

Central Andes (CAN) (cont.)

Elfin Forest (F5)

Nothocercus julius
Pterophanes cyanopterus
Metallura aeneocauda
Metallura eupogon
Metallura theresiae
Opisthoprora euryptera
Thripophaga berlepschi
Anairetes agraphia
Myiotheretes erythropygius
Ampelion sclateri
Catamblyrhynchus diadema
Hemispingus parodii
Hemispingus rufosuperciliaris
Hemispingus trifasciatus
Buthraupis aureodorsalis
Iridosornis jelskii
Dubusia taeniata
Delothraupis castaneoventris
Nephelornis oneilli
Conirostrum ferrugineiventre
Conirostrum sitticolor

Polylepis Woodlands (F6)

Otus koepckeae
Veniliornis fumigatus
Cinclodes aricomae
Leptasthenura xenothorax
Leptasthenura yanacensis
Cranioleuca albicapilla
Cranioleuca baroni
Asthenes urubambensis
Grallaria andicola
Grallaria quitensis
Anairetes alpinus
Ochthoeca fumicolor
Ochthoeca oenanthoides
Myiotheretes rufipennis
Ampelion stresemanni
Poospiza alticola
Poospiza garleppi
Atlapetes nationi
Atlapetes rufigenis
Saltator rufiventris
Xenodacnis parina
Oreomanes fraseri
Conirostrum tamarugense
Carduelis crassirostris

Arid Montane Scrub (N2)

Nothoprocta taczanowskii
Metriopelia morenoi
Oreotrochilus adela
Geositta crassirostris
Upucerthia albigula
Upucerthia andaecola
Upucerthia dumetaria
Upucerthia serrana
Ochetorhynchus harterti
Ochetorhynchus ruficauda
Leptasthenura pileata
Leptasthenura striata
Synallaxis zimmeri
Asthenes cactorum
Asthenes dorbignyi
Asthenes heterura
Asthenes pudibunda
Phacellodomus striaticeps
Anairetes flavirostris
Ochthoeca oenanthoides
Ochthoeca piurae
Phytotoma rutila
Mimus dorsalis
Phrygilus atriceps
Phrygilus fruticeti
Incaspiza pulchra
Poospiza boliviana
Poospiza hypochondriaca
Sicalis luteocephala
Sicalis raimondii

Semihumid/Humid Montane Scrub (N3)

Bolborhynchus aurifrons
Aglaeactis aliciae
Aglaeactis castelnaudii
Aglaeactis cupripennis
Aglaeactis pamela
Lesbia nuna
Lesbia victoriae
Loddigesia mirabilis
Leptasthenura andicola
Cranioleuca albicapilla
Asthenes ottonis
Anairetes parulus
Ochthoeca oenanthoides
Poospiza baeri
Poospiza caesar
Poospiza rubecula
Catamenia homochroa
Catamenia inornata
Atlapetes citrinellus
Atlapetes nationi
Thlypopsis inornata
Thlypopsis pectoralis
Diglossa sittoides
Diglossa brunneiventris
Diglossa carbonaria

CENTRAL ANDES (CAN) (cont.)

Puna (N9)

Nothoprocta ornata
Nothura darwinii
Tinamotis pentlandii
Phalcoboenus megalopterus
Attagis gayi
Thinocorus orbignyianus
Metriopelia aymara
Oreotrochilus estella
Oreotrochilus melanogaster
Colaptes rupicola
Geositta punensis
Geositta rufipennis
Geositta saxicolina
Upucerthia jelskii
Cinclodes atacamensis
Cinclodes palliatus
Asthenes humilis
Asthenes modesta
Muscisaxicola albifrons
Muscisaxicola alpina
Muscisaxicola cinerea
Muscisaxicola juninensis
Anthus bogotensis
Anthus furcatus
Phrygilus dorsalis
Phrygilus erythronotus
Phrygilus unicolor
Diuca speculifera
Idiopsar brachyurus
Sicalis lutea
Sicalis uropygialis

CHIRIQUÍ-DARIÉN HIGHLANDS (CDH)
Humid Broadleaf Forest (F1 or F4), Hill Tropical, 500-900 m

Rhynchortyx cinctus
Geotrygon lawrencii
Pionus senilis
Touit costaricensis
Goldmania violiceps
Microchera albocoronata
Hylomanes momotula
Xenerpestes minlosi
Philydor fuscipennis
Xenornis setifrons
Myrmeciza immaculata
Formicarius nigricapillus
Pittasoma michleri
Schiffornis turdinus
Corapipo leucorrhoa
Pipra pipra
Thryothorus spadix
Henicorhina leucosticta
Atlapetes atricapillus
Chlorothraupis carmioli
Chlorothraupis olivacea
Tangara florida
Tangara gyrola
Tangara palmeri

Montane Evergreen Forest (F4), Upper Tropical, 900-1,600 m

Odontophorus dialeucos
Odontophorus guttatus
Odontophorus leucolaemus
Geotrygon goldmani
Androdon aequatorialis
Phaethornis guy
Campylopterus hemileucurus
Goethalsia bella
Elvira chionura
Elvira cupreiceps
Lampornis hemileucus
Heliodoxa jacula
Pharomachrus auriceps
Xiphorhynchus erythropygius
Campylorhamphus pusillus
Premnoplex brunnescens
Syndactyla subalaris
Anabacerthia variegaticeps
Sclerurus albigularis
Myrmotherula schisticolor
Formicarius rufipectus
Grallaricula flavirostris
Leptopogon superciliaris
Myiobius villosus
Henicorhina leucophrys
Catharus dryas
Turdus assimilis
Chlorospingus tacarcunae
Basileuterus tristriatus
Cyanolyca cucullata

Montane Evergreen Forest (F4), Mid- and Upper Montane, 1,600 m to Treeline

Geotrygon chiriquensis
Caprimulgus saturatus
Doryfera ludoviciae
Lampornis calolaema
Lampornis castaneoventris
Lampornis cinereicauda
Pharomachrus mocinno
Margarornis rubiginosus
Thripadectes rufobrunneus
Empidonax atriceps
Phainoptila melanoxantha
Troglodytes ochraceus
Catharus frantzii
Catharus fuscater
Turdus plebejus
Pselliophorus tibialis
Lysurus crassirostris
Chlorospingus pileatus
Zeledonia coronata

Chocó Lowlands (CHO)

Tropical Lowland Humid Forest (F1)

Leucopternis plumbea
Leucopternis semiplumbea
Daptrius americanus
Odontophorus erythrops
Rhynchortyx cinctus
Columba goodsoni
Glaucis aenea
Phaethornis superciliosus
Phaethornis yaruqui
Notharchus pectoralis
Piculus leucolaemus
Celeus loricatus
Dendrocincla fuliginosa
Dendrocolaptes certhia
Campylorhamphus trochilirostris
Hyloctistes subulatus
Philydor fuscipennis
Sclerurus mexicanus
Dysithamnus puncticeps
Sipia berlepschi
Myrmeciza immaculata
Phaenostictus mcleannani
Pittasoma rufopileatum
Hylopezus perspicillatus
Cnipodectes subbrunneus
Tolmomyias flavotectus
Platyrinchus coronatus
Aphanotriccus audax
Schiffornis turdinus
Chloropipo holochlora
Microcerculus marginatus
Microbates cinereiventris
Heterospingus xanthopygius
Vireolanius leucotis

Central South America (CSA)

Gallery Forest (F8)

Penelope ochrogaster
Crax fasciolata
Aramides ypecaha
Leptotila rufaxilla
Ara nobilis
Aratinga aurea
Nandayus nenday
Columba cayennensis
Momotus momota
Xiphocolaptes falcirostris
Xiphocolaptes major
Dendrocolaptes platyrostris
Leptasthenura platensis
Poecilurus scutatus
Philydor dimidiatus
Herpsilochmus atricapillus
Herpsilochmus longirostris
Cercomacra melanaria
Corythopis delalandi
Hemitriccus margaritaceiventer
Xenopsaris albinucha
Neopelma pallescens
Antilophia galeata
Pipra fasciicauda
Arremon flavirostris
Compsothraupis loricata
Eucometis penicillata
Basileuterus flaveolus
Basileuterus hypoleuca
Basileuterus leucophrys

Arid Lowland Scrub (N1)

Nothura boraquira
Geranoaetus melanoleucus
Spiziapteryx circumcinctus
Ochetorhynchus certhioides
Furnarius cristatus
Leptasthenura aegithaloides
Asthenes baeri
Coryphistera alaudina
Myrmorchilus strigilatus
Rhinocrypta lanceolata
Teledromas fuscus
Stigmatura budytoides
Stigmatura bahiae
Knipolegus striaticeps
Lophospingus pusillus
Poospiza melanoleuca
Poospiza ornata
Poospiza torquata
Sporophila albogularis
Saltatricula multicolor
Gubernatrix cristata
Hylophilus amaurocephalus

Arid Montane Scrub (N2)

Geranoaetus melanoleucus
Caprimulgus longirostris
Augastes lumachellus
Augastes scutatus
Asthenes luizae
Polystictus superciliaris
Embernagra longicauda

Campo Grasslands (N5)

Rhea americana
Nothura maculosa
Nothura minor
Falco femoralis
Micropygia schomburgkii
Uropelia campestris
Polytmus guainumbi
Heliactin bilophum
Geobates poecilopterus
Melanopareia torquata
Culicivora caudacuta
Polystictus pectoralis
Euscarthmus rufomarginatus
Alectrurus tricolor
Alopochelidon fucata
Poospiza cinerea
Sicalis citrina
Emberizoides herbicola
Sporophila bouvreuil
Sporophila hypoxantha
Sporophila ruficollis
Coryphaspiza melanotis
Passerina caerulescens
Cypsnagra hirundinacea

Central South America (CSA) (cont.)

Low, Seasonally Wet Grasslands (N6)

Syrigma sibilatrix
Harpiprion caerulescens
Circus buffoni
Porzana albicollis
Gallinago undulata
Uropelia campestris
Aratinga aurea
Chordeiles pusillus
Caprimulgus maculicaudus
Polytmus guainumbi
Ramphastos toco
Synallaxis hypospodia
Anumbius annumbi
Polystictus pectoralis
Gubernetes yetapa
Alopochelidon fucata
Sporophila hypoxantha
Sporophila plumbea
Sporophila ruficollis

Equatorial Pacific Coast (EPC)

Arid Lowland Scrub (N1)

Parabuteo unicinctus
Caprimulgus anthonyi
Leucippus baeri
Leucippus taczanowskii
Myrmia micrura
Veniliornis callonotus
Geositta peruviana
Synallaxis stictothorax
Phaeomyias murina
Myiopagis leucospodia
Euscarthmus meloryphus
Myiarchus semirufus
Muscigralla brevicauda
Phytotoma raimondii
Aimophila stolzmanni
Piezorhina cinerea
Sicalis taczanowskii
Sporophila peruviana
Sporophila simplex

Gulf-Caribbean Slope (GCS)

Tropical Lowland Evergreen Forest (F1)

Odontophorus gujanensis
Geotrygon veraguensis
Ara ambigua
Amazona farinosa
Trogon bairdii
Trogon clathratus
Trogon viridis
Baryphthengus martii
Jacamerops aurea
Piculus leucolaemus
Piculus simplex
Celeus castaneus
Celeus loricatus
Dendrocincla anabatina
Dendrocincla fuliginosa
Deconychura longicauda
Dendrocolaptes certhia
Cymbilaimus lineatus
Dysithamnus puncticeps
Dysithamnus striaticeps
Myrmotherula fulviventris
Myrmeciza exsul
Myrmeciza laemosticta
Gymnopithys leucaspis
Hylophylax naevioides
Phaenostictus mcleannani
Myrmornis torquata
Pittasoma michleri
Hylopezus perspicillatus
Phylloscartes flavovirens
Myiornis atricapillus
Tolmomyias flavotectus
Platyrinchus coronatus
Onychorhynchus mexicanus
Laniocera rufescens
Piprites griseiceps
Pipra mentalis
Lipaugus unirufus
Querula purpurata
Microcerculus marginatus
Microcerculus philomela
Cyphorhinus phaeocephalus
Microbates cinereiventris
Arremon aurantiirostris
Pitylus grossus
Lanio aurantius
Lanio leucothorax
Heterospingus rubrifrons
Habia rubica
Cyanerpes lucidus
Vireolanius pulchellus
Hylophilus ochraceiceps

Madrean Highlands (MAH)

Montane Evergreen Forest (F4), Upper Tropical, 900-1,600 m

Penelopina nigra
Dendrortyx barbatus
Odontophorus guttatus
Dactylortyx thoracicus
Geotrygon lawrencii
Campylopterus hemileucurus
Campylopterus rufus
Colibri delphinae
Abeillia abeillei
Paphosia helenae
Eupherusa cyanophrys
Eupherusa copiocerca
Lampornis sybillae
Xiphorhynchus erythropygius
Anabacerthia variegaticeps
Automolus rubiginosus
Dysithamnus mentalis
Thamnistes anabatinus
Myrmotherula schisticolor
Pachyramphus major
Henicorhina leucophrys
Myadestes unicolor
Catharus dryas
Catharus mexicanus
Turdus assimilis
Atlapetes albinucha
Piranga leucoptera
Cyanolyca cucullata

Madrean Highlands (MAH) (cont.)

Humid Montane Forest (F4), Midmontane, 1,600-2,600 m

Dendrortyx leucophrys
Geotrygon albifacies
Strix fulvescens
Thalurania ridgwayi
Lampornis viridipallens
Lamprolaima rhami
Pharomachrus mocinno
Aspatha gularis
Xiphocolaptes promeropirhynchus
Troglodytes rufociliatus
Catharus frantzii
Turdus infuscatus
Turdus plebejus
Atlapetes virenticeps
Basileuterus belli
Vireolanius melitophrys
Coccothraustes abeillei
Cyanocorax dickeyi

Pine Forest (F10)

Accipiter chionogaster
Rhynchopsitta pachyrhyncha
Rhynchopsitta terrisi
Otus flammeolus
Caprimulgus vociferus
Hylocharis leucotis
Euptilotis neoxenus
Picoides villosus
Contopus pertinax
Empidonax affinis
Progne subis
Campylorhynchus megalopterus
Myadestes townsendi
Parus sclateri
Sitta pygmaea
Junco phaeonotus
Ammodramus baileyi
Dendroica graciae
Cardellina rubrifrons
Ergaticus ruber
Peucedramus taeniatus
Carduelis atriceps
Loxia curvirostra
Coccothraustes vespertinus
Cyanocitta stelleri

Pine-Oak Forest (F11)

Cyrtonyx montezumae
Cyrtonyx ocellatus
Amazilia beryllina
Amazilia cyanocephala
Lampornis amethystinus
Lampornis clemenciae
Eugenes fulgens
Tilmatura dupontii
Atthis ellioti
Atthis heloisa
Trogon mexicanus
Picoides stricklandi
Lepidocolaptes leucogaster
Empidonax fulvifrons
Empidonax occidentalis
Campylorhynchus gularis
Campylorhynchus jocosus
Sialia sialis
Myadestes obscurus
Zoothera pinicola
Catharus occidentalis
Psaltriparus minimus
Atlapetes pileatus
Piranga erythrocephala
Vermivora crissalis
Myioborus pictus
Vireo vicinior

Arid Montane Scrub (N2)

Falco mexicanus
Caprimulgus ridgwayi
Phalaenoptilus nuttallii
Calothorax lucifer
Calothorax pulcher
Xenotriccus mexicanus
Thryomanes bewickii
Toxostoma ocellatum
Spizella atrogularis
Aimophila humeralis
Aimophila mystacalis
Aimophila notosticta
Aimophila quinquestriata
Aimophila ruficeps
Icterus parisorum
Vireo atricapillus
Vireo brevipennis
Vireo nelsoni
Vireo vicinior

Mexican Plateau (MPL)

Montane Arid Scrub (N2)

Falco mexicanus
Speotyto cunicularia
Phalaenoptilus nuttallii
Calothorax lucifer
Thryomanes bewickii
Toxostoma crissale
Polioptila melanura
Spizella atrogularis
Amphispiza bilineata
Aimophila ruficeps
Icterus parisorum

MEXICAN PLATEAU (MPL) (cont.)

Northern Temperate Grasslands (N8)

Buteo swainsoni
Falco femoralis
Falco mexicanus
Falco sparverius
Callipepla squamata
Cyrtonyx montezumae
Speotyto cunicularia
Chordeiles minor
Sayornis saya
Eremophila alpestris
Lanius ludovicianus
Ammodramus sandwichensis
Spizella wortheni
Aimophila botterii
Aimophila cassinii
Sturnella magna

NORTHERN ANDES (NAN)

Bamboo

Claravis mondetoura
Bolborhynchus lineola
Synallaxis castanea
Synallaxis unirufa
Hellmayrea gularis
Drymophila caudata
Myrmeciza griseiceps
Grallaria hypoleuca
Grallaria nuchalis
Myornis senilis
Acropternis orthonyx
Anairetes agilis
Poecilotriccus ruficeps
Cinnycerthia peruana
Cinnycerthia unirufa
Thryothorus euophrys
Haplospiza rustica
Catamblyrhynchus diadema
Hemispingus atropileus
Hemispingus melanotis
Hemispingus reyi
Cacicus holosericeus

Humid Broadleaf Forest (F1 or F4), Hill Tropical, 500-900 m

Geotrygon saphirina
Pyrrhura orcesi
Doryfera johannae
Heliodoxa gularis
Hylomanes momotula
Philydor fuscipennis
Thamnomanes occidentalis
Myrmotherula spodionota
Sipia nigricauda
Percnostola leucostigma
Myrmeciza immaculata
Formicarius nigricapillus
Phylloscartes orbitalis
Chloropipo holochlora
Corapipo leucorrhoa
Thryothorus spadix
Atlapetes atricapillus
Chlorothraupis carmioli
Tangara gyrola
Tangara palmeri

Montane Evergreen Forest (F4), Upper Tropical, 900-1,600 m

Odontophorus melanonotus
Geotrygon linearis
Chaetura cinereiventris
Androdon aequatorialis
Phaethornis augusti
Phaethornis guy
Eutoxeres aquila
Eutoxeres condamini
Campylopterus ensipennis
Klais guimeti
Urosticte benjamini
Phlogophilus hemileucurus
Heliodoxa imperatrix
Heliodoxa jacula
Sternoclyta cyanopectus
Coeligena wilsoni
Haplophaedia lugens
Schistes geoffroyi
Pharomachrus antisianus
Pharomachrus auriceps
Pharomachrus fulgidus
Trogon personatus
Momotus aequatorialis
Galbula pastazae
Malacoptila fulvogularis
Malacoptila mystacalis
Campephilus haematogaster
Xiphorhynchus erythropygius
Campylorhamphus pusillus
Premnoplex brunnescens
Premnoplex tatei
Syndactyla guttulata
Anabacerthia striaticollis
Anabacerthia variegaticeps
Thripadectes ignobilis
Thripadectes virgaticeps
Dysithamnus mentalis
Thamnomanes leucostictus
Thamnomanes occidentalis
Myrmotherula schisticolor
Formicarius rufipectus
Chamaeza campanisona
Grallaria flavotincta
Grallaria haplonota
Grallaricula flavirostris
Conopophaga castaneiceps
Leptopogon superciliaris
Pseudotriccus pelzelni
Rhynchocyclus fulvipectus
Myiotriccus ornatus
Myiobius villosus
Myiophobus phoenicomitra
Myiophobus roraimae
Chloropipo flavicapilla
Machaeropterus deliciosus
Masius chrysopterus
Pipra isidorei
Lipaugus cryptolophus
Pyroderus granadensis
Cyphorhinus thoracicus
Catharus dryas
Chlorospingus flavigularis
Chlorospingus semifuscus
Chlorothraupis stolzmanni
Habia cristata
Basileuterus conspicillatus
Basileuterus griseiceps
Basileuterus tristriatus

NORTHERN ANDES (NAN) (cont.)

Montane Evergreen Forest (F4), Midmontane, 1,600-2,600 m

Nothocercus bonapartei
Odontophorus atrifrons
Odontophorus columbianus
Odontophorus hyperthyrus
Odontophorus speciosus
Geotrygon frenata
Pyrrhura chapmani
Pyrrhura viridcata
Doryfera ludoviciae
Phaethornis syrmatophorus
Campylopterus falcatus
Adelomyia melanogenys
Heliodoxa rubinoides
Coeligena coeligena
Eriocnemis alinae
Haplophaedia aureliae
Andigena laminirostris
Andigena nigrirostris
Campephilus pollens
Dendrocincla tyrannina
Xiphocolaptes promeropirhynchus
Synallaxis castanea
Premnornis guttuligera
Thripadectes holostictus
Thamnophilus unicolor
Chamaeza turdina
Grallaria bangsi
Grallaricula cucullata
Grallaricula ferrugineipectus
Grallaricula loricata
Grallaricula nana
Phyllomyias cinereiceps
Phyllomyias plumbeiceps
Mecocerculus poecilocercus
Leptopogon rufipectus
Phylloscartes poecilotis
Platyrinchus flavigularis
Myiophobus flavicans
Ochthoeca diadema
Ampelion rufaxilla
Catharus fuscater
Atlapetes torquatus
Oreothraupis arremonops
Lysurus castaneiceps
Chlorospingus parvirostris
Hemispingus frontalis
Hemispingus melanotis
Creurgops verticalis
Anisognathus flavinucha
Anisognathus melanogenys
Iridosornis analis
Iridosornis porphyrocephala
Basileuterus coronatus

Montane Evergreen Forest (F4), Upper Montane, 2600m to Treeline

Nothocercus julius
Hapalopsittaca amazonina
Hapalopsittaca pyrrhops
Lafresnaya lafresnayi
Ensifera ensifera
Heliangelus amethysticollis
Heliangelus exortis
Heliangelus micrastur
Heliangelus spencei
Heliangelus viola
Ramphomicron dorsale
Andigena hypoglauca
Synallaxis unirufa
Margarornis squamiger
Thripadectes flammulatus
Grallaria nuchalis
Grallaria rufula
Grallaria squamigera
Mecocerculus stictopterus
Pseudotriccus ruficeps
Ochthoeca cinnamomeiventris
Ochthoeca frontalis
Ochthoeca jelskii
Myiotheretes fumigatus
Cinnycerthia unirufa
Hemispingus atropileus
Hemispingus reyi
Anisognathus lacrymosus
Dubusia taeniata
Basileuterus luteoviridis

Elfin Forest (F5)

Pterophanes cyanopterus
Coeligena lutetiae
Eriocnemis cupreoventris
Eriocnemis mosquera
Eriocnemis vestitus
Metallura iracunda
Metallura odomae
Metallura williami
Anairetes agilis
Myiotheretes erythropygius
Notiochelidon flavipes
Atlapetes pallidinucha
Urothraupis stolzmanni
Catamblyrhynchus diadema
Hemispingus verticalis
Buthraupis eximia
Buthraupis wetmorei
Iridosornis rufivertex
Dubusia taeniata
Conirostrum sitticolor

Semi-Humid/Humid Montane Scrub (N3)

Bolborhynchus ferrugineifrons
Aglaeactis cupripennis
Coeligena iris
Lesbia nuna
Lesbia victoriae
Cinclodes excelsior
Leptasthenura andicola
Notiochelidon murina
Turdus olivator
Catamenia homochroa
Catamenia inornata
Thlypopsis ornata
Tangara vitriolina
Diglossa brunneiventris
Diglossa gloriosa
Diglossa gloriosissima
Diglossa humeralis
Diglossa sittoides
Conirostrum rufum
Carduelis spinescens

NORTHERN ANDES (NAN) (cont.)

Paramo (N10)

Phalcoboenus carunculatus
Gallinago nobilis
Gallinago stricklandii
Oreotrochilus chimbarozo
Chalcostigma herrani
Chalcostigma heteropogon
Chalcostigma stanleyi
Oxypogon guerinii
Cinclodes excelsior
Asthenes flammulata
Asthenes wyatti
Ochthoeca fumicolor
Muscisaxicola alpina
Cistothorus apolinari
Cistothorus meridae
Phrygilus unicolor

NORTHERN SOUTH AMERICA (NSA)

Tropical Lowland Evergreen Forest (F1)

Tinamus tao
Penelope purpurascens
Odontophorus gujanensis
Rhynchortyx cinctus
Psophia crepitans
Geotrygon linearis
Geotryon montana
Geotrygon violacea
Phaethornis superciliosus
Dendrocincla fuliginosa
Dendrocincla homochroa
Dendrocolaptes certhia
Hyloctistes subulatus
Sclerurus albigularis
Sclerurus mexicanus
Myrmeciza immaculata
Myrmeciza laemosticta
Phaenostictus mcleannani
Hylopezus perspicillatus
Rhynchocyclus olivaceus
Onychorhynchus mexicanus
Schiffornis turdinus
Corapipo leucorrhoa
Chiroxiphia pareola
Pipra pipra
Microcerculus marginatus
Habia rubica

Arid Lowland Scrub (N1)

Burhinus bistriatus
Zenaida auriculata
Speotyto cunicularia
Chlorostilbon gibsoni
Lepidopyga goudoti
Leucippus fallax
Picumnus cinnamomeus
Poecilurus candei
Hemitriccus margaritaceiventer
Campylorhynchus griseus
Tiaris bicolor
Arremon schlegeli
Arremonops tocuyensis
Cardinalis phoeniceus
Saltator orenocensis
Molothrus armenti

Low, Seasonally Wet Grasslands (N6)

Syrigma sibilatrix
Theristicus caudatus
Cercibis oxycerca
Circus buffoni
Heterospizias meridionalis
Falco femoralis
Porzana albicollis
Neocrex columbianus
Neocrex erythrops
Burhinus bistriatus
Gallinago undulata
Rhinoptynx clamator
Caprimulgus cayennensis
Caprimulgus maculicaudus
Polytmus guainumbi
Polytmus theresiae
Emberizoides herbicola
Sporophila minuta
Sporophila plumbea

PAMPAS (PAM)

Grasslands (N6, N7)

Falco femoralis
Syrigma sibilatrix
Harpiprion caerulescens
Speotyto cunicularia
Polystictus pectoralis
Alectrurus risorus
Alopochelidon fucata
Anthus furcatus
Emberizoides ypiranganus
Embernagra platensis
Sporophila cinnamomea
Sporophila palustris
Sporophila ruficollis
Xanthopsar flavus

PATAGONIA (PAT)

Arid Lowland Scrub (N1)

Pterocnemia pennata
Eudromia elegans
Geranoaetus melanoleucus
Cyanoliseus patagonus
Geositta cunicularia
Upucerthia dumetaria
Eremobius phoenicurus
Leptasthenura platensis
Asthenes patagonica
Asthenes pyrrholeuca
Pseudoseisura gutturalis
Xolmis coronata
Neoxolmis rubetra
Agriornis murina
Knipolegus hudsoni
Phrygilus carbonarius
Phrygilus fruticeti
Phrygilus gayi
Sicalis lebruni

Southern Temperate Grasslands (N7)

Pterocnemia pennata
Nothura darwinii
Tinamotis ingoufi
Chloephaga picta
Chloephaga poliocephala
Chloephaga rubidiceps
Circus cinereus
Phalcoboenus albogularis
Charadrius modestus
Attagis malouinus
Thinocorus rumicivorus
Geositta antarctica
Geositta cunicularia
Asthenes anthoides
Neoxolmis rufiventris
Muscisaxicola capistrata
Muscisaxicola flavinucha
Muscisaxicola macloviana
Phrygilus carbonarius
Sicalis lebruni
Sicalis luteola

SOUTHERN ANDES (SAN)

Southern Temperate Forests (F9)

Columba araucana
Enicognathus ferrugineus
Enicognathus leptorhynchus
Campephilus magellanicus
Sylviothorhynchus desmursii
Aphrastura spinicauda
Pygarrhichas albogularis
Pteroptochos castaneus
Pteroptochos tarnii
Scytalopus fuscus
Scytalopus magellanicus
Scelorchilus rubecula
Elaenia albiceps
Ochthoeca parvirostris
Phytotoma rara

Arid Montane Scrub (N2)

Nothoprocta perdicaria
Metriopelia melanoptera
Metriopelia morenoi
Picoides lignarius
Upucerthia dumetaria
Ochetorhynchus ruficauda
Chilia melanura
Cinclodes olrogi
Cinclodes oustaleti
Leptasthenura fuliginiceps
Asthenes dorbignyi
Anairetes flavirostris
Phytotoma rutila
Phrygilus atriceps
Phrygilus fruticeti
Phrygilus gayi
Poospiza hypochondriaca
Carduelis uropygialis

Southern Temperate Grasslands (N7)

Pterocnemia pennata
Nothura darwinii
Charadrius modestus
Attagis malouinus
Thinocorus rumicivorus
Geositta cunicularia
Asthenes anthoides
Asthenes sclateri
Muscisaxicola flavinucha
Anthus hellmayri
Melanodera xanthogramma

Puna (N9)

Nothoprocta ornata
Vultur gryphus
Phalcoboenus megalopterus
Attagis gayi
Thinocorus orbignyianus
Metriopelia aymara
Oreotrochilus leucopleurus
Geositta isabellina
Geositta rufipennis
Upucerthia validirostris
Cinclodes atacamensis
Cinclodes fuscus
Asthenes modesta
Asthenes punensis
Muscisaxicola albilora
Muscisaxicola cinerea
Muscisaxicola frontalis
Muscisaxicola rufivertex
Phrygilus unicolor
Carduelis atrata

SUBTROPICAL PACIFIC (STP)

Arid Lowland Scrub (N1)

Geranoaetus melanoleucus
Burhinus superciliaris
Eudromias ruficollis
Cyanoliseeus patagonus
Speotyto cunicularia
Rhodopis vesper
Geositta maritima
Geositta peruviana
Leptasthenura aegithaloides
Asthenes pyrrholeuca
Pteroptochos megapodius
Scelorchilus albicollis
Muscigralla brevicauda
Sporophila peruviana
Sporophila simplex
Thaumastura cora
Xenospingus concolor

Riparian Thickets (N11)

Glaucidium peruanum
Rhodopis vesper
Myrtis fanny
Eulidia yarrellii
Myiophobus fasciatus
Anairetes reguloides
Sporophila peruviana
Sporophila simplex
Xenospingus concolor

TEPUIS (TEP)

Humid Broadleaf Forest (F1 or F4)

Doryfera johannae
Phaethornis augusti
Phaethornis griseogularis
Colibri delphinae
Heliodoxa xanthogonys
Trogon personatus
Cranioleuca demissa
Roraimia adusta
Automolus roraimae
Automolus rubiginosus
Thamnophilus insignis
Myrmotherula behni
Percnostola caurensis
Chamaeza campanisona
Grallaria guatimalensis
Myrmothera simplex
Grallaricula nana
Mionectes macconnelli
Leptopogon superciliaris
Phylloscartes chapmani
Todirostrum russatum
Platyrinchus mystaceus
Myiophobus roraimae
Chloropipo uniformis
Machaeropterus regulus
Pipra cornuta
Pipra suavissima
Procnias alba
Procnias averano
Henicorhina leucosticta
Microcerculus ustulatus
Platycichla flavipes
Platycichla leucops
Atlapetes personatus
Mitrospingus oleagineus
Diglossa duidae
Myioborus albifacies
Myioborus castaneocapillus
Myioborus cardonai
Basileuterus bivittatus
Basileuterus culicivorus

MANGROVE FOREST (F14) (all coastal regions)

Ixobrychus exilis
Nycticorax violaceus
Cochlearius cochlearius
Hydranassa caerulea
Hydranassa rufescens
Eudocimus albus
Eudocimus ruber
Buteogallus aequinoctialis
Buteogallus subtilis
Rallus longirostris
Rallus obsoletus
Rallus wetmorei
Aramides axillaris
Aramides mangle
Aramides wolfi
Columba leucocephala
Coccyzus minor
Otus cooperi
Lepidopyga lilliae
Leucippus fallax
Amazilia boucardi
Veniliornis sanguineus
Xiphorhynchus picus
Thamnophilus bridgesi
Sublegatus arenarum
Todirostrum maculatum
Fluvicola atripennis
Tyrannus dominicensis
Carpodectes antoniae
Tachycineta albilinea
Camarhynchus heliobates
Dendroica erithachorides
Dendroica petechia
Conirostrum bicolor
Vireo altiloquus
Vireo magister
Vireo pallens
Quiscalus mexicanus

TROPICAL DECIDUOUS FORESTS (F7)

Habitat Specialists (with subregion and region for endemics)

Crypturellus idoneus	ARC	NSA
Crypturellus saltuarius	CMV	NSA
Crypturellus transfasciatus	MAN	EPC
Eudromia formosa	CHA	CSA
Penelope albipennis	MAN	EPC
Leptotila wellsi	GRE	LAN
Geotrygon chrysia	o	GAN
Ara rubrogenys	COC	CAN
Aratinga cactorum	Not endemic	
Aratinga brevipes	SOC	PAS
Pyrrhura pfrimeri	CER	CSA
Siphonorhis americanus	JAM	GAN
Siphonorhis brewsteri	HIS	GAN
Caprimulgus hirundinaceus	CAA	CSA
Caprimulgus noctitherus	PUE	GAN
Caprimulgus otiosus	Not endemic	
Caprimulgus badius	YUC	GCS
Caprimulgus salvini	GCM	GCS
Phaethornis gounellei	CAA	CSA
Phaethornis nattereri	CER	CSA
Phaethornis subochraceus	CHA	CSA
Thalurania hypochlorus	MAN	EPC
Amazilia luciae	SCA	GCS
Picumnus fulvescens	CAA	CSA
Picumnus limae	CAA	CSA
Picumnus pygmaeus	CAA	CSA
Picumnus sclateri	MAN	EPC
Celeus obrieni	CAA	CSA
Campephilus leucopogon	CHA	CSA
Xiphocolaptes franciscanus	CER	CSA
Synallaxis tithys	MAN	EPC
Gyalophylax hellmayri	CAA	CSA
Cranioleuca semicinerea	o	CSA
Cranioleuca dissita	HPC	GCS
Hylocryptus erythrocephalus	MAN	EPC
Sakesphorus melanonotus	ARC	NSA
Thamnophilus zarumae	MAN	EPC
Myrmorchilus strigilatus	o	CSA
Herpsilochmus pectoralis	CAA	CSA
Herpsilochmus pileatus	CAA	CSA
Formicivora iheringi	CAA	CSA
Formicivora melanogaster	CSA	
Rhopornis ardesiaca	CAA	CSA
Grallaria watkinsi	MAN	EPC
Melanopareia elegans	MAN	EPC
Elaenia strepera	Not endemic	
Serpophaga munda	Not endemic	
Phylloscartes roquettei	CER	CSA
Xenotriccus callizonus	CAH	MAH
Knipolegus franciscanus	CER	CSA
Casiornis fuscus	Not endemic	
Deltarhynchus flammulatus	SIN	PAS
Pachyramphus spodiurus	MAN	EPC
Ramphocinclus brachyurus	o	LAN
Turdus maculirostris	MAN	EPC
Turdus graysoni	SIN	PAS
Passerina rositae	CHG	PAS
Conothraupis mesoleuca	CER	CSA
Granatellus sallaei	YUC	GCS
Granatellus venustus	SIN	PAS
Vireo nanus	HIS	GAN
Carduelis yarrellii	Not endemic	
Cissilopha beecheii	SIN	PAS
Cissilopha sanblasianus	SIN	PAS

Widespread non-specialists

Crypturellus tataupa
Columba flavirostris
Columba maculosa
Zenaida asiatica
Aratinga acuticaudata
Brotogeris jugularis
Coccyzus melacoryphus
Coccyzus minor
Caprimulgus ridgwayi
Caprimulgus rufus
Lepidocolaptes angustirostris
Lepidocolaptes souleyetii
Synallaxis frontalis
Thamnophilus punctatus
Hemitriccus margaritaceiventer
Myiarchus tyrannulus
Empidonomus aurantioatrocristatus
Polioptila albiloris

Disturbed Habitats (F15, N13, N14)

Crypturellus parvirostris
Cathartes aura
Coragyps atratus
Elanus leucurus
Buteo magnirostris
Milvago chimango
Vanellus chilensis
Zenaida auriculata
Columbina cruziana
Columbina passerina
Columbina picui
Columbina talpacoti
Scardafella inca
Scardafella squammata
Myiopsittaca monachus
Forpus cyanopygius
Brotogeris tirica
Piaya cayana
Crotophaga ani
Crotophaga sulcirostris
Guira guira
Tapera naevia
Tyto alba
Glaucidium brasilianum
Chordeiles acutipennis
Podager nacunda
Nyctidromus albicollis
Chaetura brachyura
Eupetomena macroura
Colibri coruscans
Anthracothorax nigricollis
Anthracothorax prevostii
Amazilia amazilia
Amazilia cyanifrons
Amazilia cyanura
Amazilia fimbriata
Amazilia lactea
Amazilia rutila
Amazilia tzacatl
Lesbia nuna
Lesbia victoriae
Picumnus cirratus
Picumnus rufiventris
Picumnus temminckii
Colaptes auratus
Colaptes campestris
Dryocopus lineatus
Furnarius rufus
Synallaxis albescens
Synallaxis gujanensis
Synallaxis spixi
Taraba major
Thamnophilus doliatus
Thamnophilus multistriatus
Thamnophilus palliatus
Formicivora rufa
Camptostoma imberbe
Camptostoma obsoletum
Phaeomyias murina
Elaenia flavogaster
Serpophaga subcristata
Anairetes parulus
Todirostrum cinereum
Todirostrum maculatum
Myiophobus fasciatus
Xolmis irupero
Knipolegus lophotes
Fluvicola atripennis
Fluvicola nengeta
Satrapa icterophrys
Machetornis rixosus
Myiarchus ferox
Pitangus sulphuratus
Megarynchus pitangua
Myiozetetes cayanensis
Myiozetetes similis
Tyrannus melancholicus
Manacus manacus
Eremophila alpestris
Progne chalybea
Progne cryptoleuca
Progne dominicensis
Progne elegans
Progne tapera
Notiochelidon cyanoleuca
Stelgidopteryx ruficollis
Stelgidopteryx serripennis
Anthus lutescens
Dulus dominicus
Campylorhynchus turdinus
Troglodytes aedon
Mimus gundlachii
Mimus gilvus
Mimus polyglottus
Mimus saturninus
Mimus triurus
Turdus amaurochalinus
Turdus chiguanco
Turdus falcklandii
Turdus leucomelas
Turdus rufiventris
Ammodramus aurifrons
Ammodramus humeralis
Sicalis flaveola
Sicalis olivascens
Volatinia jacarina
Sporophila caerulescens
Sporophila castaneiventris
Sporophila lineola
Sporophila luctuosa
Sporophila morelleti
Sporophila nigricollis
Sporophila telasco
Sporophila torqueola
Oryzoborus funereus
Tiaris olivacea
Paroaria capitata
Paroaria coronata
Paroaria gularis
Cardinalis cardinalis
Saltator coerulescens
Saltator maximus
Saltator similis
Cissopis leveriana
Thlypopsis fulviceps
Thlypopsis sordida
Chrysothlypis salmoni
Ramphocelus bresilius
Ramphocelus carbo
Ramphocelus dimidiatus
Ramphocelus melanogaster
Ramphocelus sanguinolentus
Thraupis abbas
Thraupis bonariensis
Thraupis episcopus
Thraupis palmarum
Thraupis sayaca
Euphonia chlorotica
Tangara mexicana
Dacnis cayana
Cyanerpes cyaneus
Euneornis campestris
Dendroica aestiva
Geothlypis poliocephala
Geothlypis trichas
Conirostrum cinereum
Coereba flaveola
Vireo chivi
Hylophilus semicinereus
Agelaius ruficapillus
Sturnella bellicosa
Sturnella loyca
Sturnella militaris
Sturnella superciliaris
Pseudoleistes guirahuro
Dives warszewiczi
Quiscalus lugubris
Quiscalus mexicanus
Quiscalus niger
Euphagus cyanocephalus
Molothrus badius
Molothrus bonariensis
Molothrus rufoaxillaris
Carduelis magellanicus
Corvus imparatus
Corvus sinaloae

Literature Cited

Ab'Saber, A. N. 1967. Domínios morfo-climáticos e províncias fitogeográficas do Brasil. *Orientação* 3:45–48.

Adis, J. 1981. Comparative ecological studies of the terrestrial arthropod fauna in central Amazonian inundation forest. *Amazoniana* 8:87–173.

———. 1984. Seasonal igapó-forest of central Amazonian blackwater rivers and their terrestrial arthropod fauna. In *The Amazon: Limnology and landscape ecology of a mighty tropical river and its basin,* ed. H. Sioli, 246–68. The Hague: Junk.

Aldrich, J. W., and C. S. Robbins. 1970. Changing abundance of migratory birds in North America. *Smithson. Contrib. Zool.* 26: 17–26.

Alfonso, M. T. A. 1977. Vegetação. In *Geographia do Brasil, Grande Região Sul*, ed. Instituto Brasileiro de Geografia e Estatistica, 81–109. Rio de Janeiro: IBGE.

Ambuel, B., and S. A. Temple. 1982. Songbird populations in southern Wisconsin forests: 1954 and 1979. *J. Field Ornithol.* 53: 149–58.

American Ornithologists' Union (AOU). 1983. *The check-list of North American birds.* 6th ed. Washington, D.C.: American Ornithologists' Union.

———. 1985. Thirty-fifth supplement to the American Ornithologists' Union *Check-list of North American birds. Auk* 102: 680–86.

———. 1987. Thirty-sixth supplement to the American Ornithologists' Union *Check-list of North American birds. Auk* 104: 591–96.

———. 1989. Thirty-seventh supplement to the American Ornithologists' Union *Check-list of North American birds. Auk* 106: 532–38.

———. 1991. Thirty-eighth supplement to the American Ornithologists' Union *Check-list of North American birds. Auk* 108: 750–54.

———. 1993. Thirty-ninth supplement to the American Ornithologists' Union *Check-list of North American birds. Auk* 110: 675–82.

Ames, P. L., M. A. Heimerdinger, and S. L. Warter. 1968. The anatomy and systematic position of the Antpipits *Conopophaga* and *Corythopis. Postilla*, no. 114.

Anderson, A. B. 1981. White-sand vegetation of Brazilian Amazonia. *Biotropica* 13:199–210.

Andrade-Lima, D. 1957. *Estudos fitogeográficos de Pernambuco.* Publ., n.s., no. 2. Recife: Instituto de Pesquisas Agronômicas de Pernambuco.

———. 1960. Estudos fitogeograficos de Pernambuco. *Arquivos do Instituto de Pesquisas Agronômicas* 5:305–41.

———. 1964. Esboços fitoecológicos de alguns "brejos" de Pernambuco. *Instituto de Pesquisas Agronômicas, Public. Bol. Tech.*, n.s., no. 8.

———. 1981. The caatingas dominium. *Revista Brasileira de Botânica* 4:149–53.

Andrén, H., P. Angelstam, E. Lindström, and P. Widén. 1985. Differences in predation pressure in relation to habitat fragmentation: An experiment. *Oikos* 45:273–77.

Askins, R. A., J. F. Lynch, and R. Greenberg. 1990. Population declines in migratory birds in eastern North America. *Current Ornith.* 7:1–57.

Askins, R. A., M. J. Philbrick, and D. S. Sugeno. 1987. Relationship between the regional abundance of forest and the composition of forest bird communities. *Biol. Conserv.* 39:129–52.

Beard, J. S. 1953. The savanna vegetation of northern tropical America. *Ecol. Monogr.* 23:149–215.

———. 1955. The classification of tropical American vegetation-types. *Ecology* 36:89–100.

Beck, S. G. 1984. Comunidades vegetales de las sabanas inundadas del NE de Bolivia. *Phytocoenología* 12:321–50.

Bellrose, F. C. 1976. *Ducks, geese, and swans of North America.* 2d ed. Harrisburg, Pa.: Stackpole.

Belton, W. 1984. Birds of Rio Grande do Sul, Brazil. Part 1, Rheidae through Furnariidae. *Bull. Am. Mus. Nat. Hist.* 178:369–636.

Bibby, C. J., N. J. Collar, M. J. Crosby, M. F. Heath, C. Imboden, T. H. Johnson, A. J. Long, A. J. Stattersfield, and S. J. Thirgood. 1992. *Putting biodiversity on the map: Priority areas for global conservation.* Cambridge: International Council for Bird Preservation.

Bierregaard, R. O., Jr., and T. E. Lovejoy. 1989. Effects of forest fragmentation on Amazonian understory bird communities. *Acta Amazonica* 19:215–41.

Binford, L. C. 1989. *A distributional survey of the birds of the Mexican state of Oaxaca.* Ornithol. Monogr. no. 43. Washington, D.C.: American Ornithologists' Union.

Blake, E. R. 1953. *Birds of Mexico.* Chicago: University of Chicago Press.

Bleiweiss, R. 1988 Plumage ontogeny and taxonomic status of the Dusky Starfrontlet *Coeligena orina* Wetmore. *Bull. Brit. Ornithol. Club* 108:127–31.

Böhning-Gaese, K., M. L. Taper, and J. H. Brown. 1993. Are declines in North American insectivorous songbirds due to causes on the breeding range? *Conserv. Biol.* 7:76–86.

Borland International. 1992a. Paradox version 4.0. Scott's Valley, Calif.: Borland International.

———. 1992b. Paradox for Windows. Scott's Valley, Calif.: Borland International.

———. 1992c. Quattro Pro Version 4.0. Scott's Valley, Calif.: Borland International.

Bosa, M. A. 1993. Conservation in action: Past, present and future of the National Park system in Costa Rica. *Conserv. Biol.* 7:239–47.

Breedlove, D. E. 1973. The phytogeography and vegetation of Chiapas (Mexico). In *Vegetation and vegetational history of northern Latin America,* ed. A. Graham, 149–65. Amsterdam: Elsevier.

Brittingham, M. C., and S. A. Temple. 1983. Have cowbirds caused forest songbirds to decline? *BioScience* 33:31–35.

Brown, D. E. 1982a. Chihuahuan desertscrub. In Biotic communities of the American Southwest—United States and Mexico, ed. D. Brown. *Desert Plants* 4:169–75.

———. 1982b. Grasslands. In Biotic communities of the American Southwest—United States and Mexico, ed. D. Brown. *Desert Plants* 4:107–41.

Bucher, E. H., and M. Nores. 1988. Present status of birds in steppes and savannas of northern and central Argentina. In *Ecology and conservation of grassland birds,* ed. P. D. Goriup, 71–79. ICBP Tech. Pub. no. 7. Cambridge: International Council for Bird Preservation.

Buckley, P. A., M. S. Foster, E. S. Morton, R. S. Ridgely, and F. G. Buckley, eds. 1985. *Neotropical ornithology.* Ornithol. Monogr. 36. Washington, D.C.: American Ornithologists' Union,

Cabrera, A. 1971. Fitogeografia de la Republica Argentina. *Bol. Soc. Arg. Bot.* 14:1–42.

———. 1976. *Regiones fitogeograficas Argentinas.* Enc. Argentina de Agricultura y Ganaderia. Fasc. 1. Buenos Aires: Ed. Acme.

Capparella, A. P. 1988. Genetic variation in Neotropical birds: Implications for the speciation process. In *Acta XIX Congressus Internationalis Ornithologici,* ed. H. Ouellet, 1658–64. Ottawa: University of Ottawa Press.

Cavalcanti, R. B. 1988. Conservation of birds in the *cerrado* of central Brazil. In *Ecology and conservation of grassland birds,* ed. P. D. Goriup, 59–66. ICBP Tech. Pub. no. 7. Cambridge: International Council for Bird Preservation.

Cerrate, E. 1979. *Vegetación del Valle de Chiquián.* Lima: Universidad Nacional Mayor de San Marcos.

Chapman, F. M. 1917. The distribution of bird life in Colombia. *Bull. Am. Mus. Nat. Hist.* 36:1–169.

———. 1929. *My tropical air castle.* New York: Appleton.

———. 1939. The riddle of *Oxyruncus. Am. Mus. Nov.,* no. 1047.

Chesser, R. T. 1994. Migration in South America: An overview of the austral system. *Bird Conserv. Internat.* 4:163–79.

Collar, N. J., and P. Andrew. 1988. *Birds to watch: The ICBP world checklist of threatened birds.* ICBP Tech. Pub. no. 8. Cambridge: International Council for Bird Preservation.

Collar, N. J., L. P. Gonzaga, N. Krabbe, A. Madroño Nieto, L. G. Naranjo, T. A. Parker III, and D. C. Wege. 1992. *Threatened birds of the Americas: The ICBP/IUCN red data book.* Part 2. Cambridge: International Council for Bird Preservation and International Union for Conservation of Nature and Natural Resources.

Connor, E. F. 1988. Digital representation in the analysis of biogeographic data. In *Acta XIX Congressus Internationalis Ornithologici.* ed. H. Ouellet, 1020–29. Ottawa: University of Ottawa Press.

Coupland, R. T. 1992. Overview of South American grasslands. In *Ecosystems of the world 8A: Natural grasslands,* ed. R. T. Coupland, 363–67. Amsterdam: Elsevier.

Cracraft, J. 1983. Species concepts and speciation analysis. *Current Ornithol.* 1:159–87.

———. 1985. Historical biogeography and patterns of differentiation within the South American avifauna: Areas of endemism. In *Neotropical ornithology,* ed. P. A. Buckley, M. S. Foster, E. S. Morton, R. S. Ridgely, and F. G. Buckley, 49–84. Ornithol. Monogr. 36. Washington, D.C.: American Ornithologists' Union.

Croxall, J. P., P. G. H. Evans, and R. W. Schreiber, eds. 1984. *Status and conservation of the world's seabirds.* ICBP Tech. Pub. no. 2. Cambridge: International Council for Bird Preservation.

Cuatracasas, J. 1957. Esquema sumariado de la vegetación de la "Provincia Norteandina." *Suelos Ecuat.* 1:13–30.

———. 1958. Aspectos de la vegetación natural en Colombia. *Rev. Acad. Colomb. Cienc. Exactas Fis. Nat.* 10, no. 40.

Davis, S. E. 1993. Seasonal status, relative abundance, and behavior of the birds of Concepción, Departamento Santa Cruz, Bolivia. *Fieldiana Zool.,* n.s., no. 71.

Delgado B., F. S. 1985. Present situation of the forest birds of Panama. In *Conservation of tropical forest birds,* ed. A. W. Diamond and T. E. Lovejoy, 77–93. ICBP Tech. Pub. no. 4. Cambridge: International Council for Bird Preservation.

Diamond, A. W. 1985. The selection of critical areas and current conservation efforts in tropical forest birds. In *Conservation of tropical forest birds,* ed. A. W. Diamond and T. E. Lovejoy, 33–48. ICBP Tech. Pub. no. 4. Cambridge: International Council for Bird Preservation.

Diamond, A. W., and T. E. Lovejoy, eds. 1985. *Conservation of tropical forest birds.* ICBP Tech. Pub. no. 4. Cambridge: International Council for Bird Preservation.

Diamond, J. M. 1985a. The design of a nature reserve system for Indonesian New Guinea. In *Conservation biology: The science of scarcity and diversity,* ed. M. E. Soulé, 485–503. Sunderland, Mass.: Sinauer.

———. 1985b. New distributional records and taxa from the outlying mountain ranges of New Guinea. *Emu* 85:65–91.

Dickerman, R. W., G. F. Barrowclough, P. F. Cannell, W. H. Phelps Jr., and D. E. Willard. 1986. *Philydor hylobius* Wetmore and Phelps is a synonym of *Automolus roraimae* Hellmayr. *Auk* 103:431–32.

Diels, L. 1937. Beiträge zur Kenntnis der Vegetation und Flora von Ecuador. *Bibliotheca Bot.* 116.

Dixon, J. 1979. Origin and distribution of reptiles in lowland tropical rainforests of South America. *Mus. Nat. Hist., Univ. Kansas, Monogr.* 7:217–40.

Donoghue, M. J. 1985. A critique of the biological species concept and recommendations for a phylogenetic alternative. *Bryologist* 88:172–81.

Duellman, W. E. 1988. Patterns of species diversity in anuran amphibians in the American tropics. *Ann. Missouri Bot. Gard.* 75:79–104.

Duffy, D. C., C. Hays, and M. A. Plenge. 1984. The conservation status of Peruvian seabirds. In *Status and conservation of the world's seabirds,* ed. J. P. Croxall, P. G. H. Evans, and R. W. Schreiber, 245–59. ICBP Tech. Pub. no. 2. Cambridge: International Council for Bird Preservation.

Egler, W. A. 1951. Contribuição ao estudo da caatinga pernambucana. *Rev. Bras. Geogr.* 13:577–90.

Eisenberg, J. F. 1980. The density and biomass of tropical mammals. In *Conservation biology: An evolutionary-ecological perspective,* ed. M. E. Soulé and B. A. Wilcox, 35–55. Sunderland, Mass.: Sinauer.

Eiten, G. 1972. The cerrado vegetation of Brazil. *Bot. Rev.* 38:201–341.

———. 1975. The vegetation of the Serra do Roncador. *Biotropica* 7:112–35.

———. 1978. Delimitation of the cerrado concept. *Vegetatio* 36:169–78.

———. 1984. Vegetation of Brasília. *Phytocoenología* 12:271–92.

Ellis, D. H., and C. P. Garat. 1983. The Pallid Falcon *Falco kreyenborgi* is a color phase of the austral Peregrine Falcon (*Falco peregrinus cassini*). *Auk* 100:269–71.

Emmons, L. H. 1984. Geographic variation in densities and diversities of non-flying mammals in Amazonia. *Biotropica* 16:210–22.

———. 1990. *Neotropical rainforest mammals: A field guide.* Chicago: University of Chicago Press

Emmons, A. H., and A. H. Gentry. 1983. Tropical forest structure and the distribution of gliding and prehensile-tailed vertebrates. *Am. Nat.* 125:513–24.

Endler, J. A. 1982. Pleistocene forest refuges: Fact or fancy? In *Bio-*

logical diversification in the tropics, ed. G. T. Prance, 641–57. New York: Columbia University Press.

Ferreyra, R. 1977. Endangered species and plant communities in Andean and coastal Peru. In *Extinction is forever,* ed. G. Prance and T. Elias, 150–57. New York: New York Botanic Garden.

Ferri, M. G. 1971. *III Simpósio sôbre o cerrado.* São Paulo: S. Editora Universidade de São Paulo.

Fitzpatrick, J. W. 1980. Wintering of North American tyrant flycatchers in the Neotropics. In *Migrant birds in the Neotropics: Ecology, behavior, distribution and conservation,* ed. A. Keast and E. S. Morton, 67–78. Washington, D.C.: Smithsonian Institution Press.

———. 1982. Review of C. Vaurie, *Taxonomy and geographical distribution of the Furnariidae (Aves, Passeriformes). Auk* 9: 810–13.

———. 1985. Form, foraging behavior and adaptive radiation in the Tyrannidae. In *Neotropical ornithology,* ed. P. A. Buckley, M. S. Foster, E. S. Morton, R. S. Ridgely, and F. G. Buckley, 447–70. Ornithol. Monogr. 36. Washington, D.C.: American Ornithologists' Union.

Fjeldså, J. 1987. *Birds of relict forests in the high Andes of Peru and Bolivia.* Copenhagen: Zoological Museum, University of Copenhagen.

———. 1988. Status of birds of steppe habitats of the Andean zone and Patagonia. In *Ecology and conservation of grassland birds,* ed. P. D. Goriup, 81–95. ICBP Tech. Pub. no. 7. Cambridge: International Council for Bird Preservation.

———. 1991. The conservation of biological diversity: Using birds to set priorities. In *Environmental concerns: An interdisciplinary exercise,* ed. J. A. Hansen, 157–75. London: Elsevier.

Fjeldså, J., and N. Krabbe. 1990. *Birds of the high Andes.* Copenhagen: Zoological Museum, University of Copenhagen; Svenborg: Apollo Books.

Flores Mata, G., J. Jiminez Lopez, X. Madrigal Sanchez, F. Moncayo Ruiz, and F. Takaki. 1971. *Tipos de vegetación de la Republica Mexicana.* Mexico City: Subsec. Planeación Dirección General de Estudios, Dirreción de Agrologia, SRH.

Forshaw, J. M. 1973. *Parrots of the world.* Melbourne: Lansdowne Press.

Foster, R. B. 1990. The floristic composition of the Rio Manu floodplain forest. In *Four Neotropical rainforests,* ed. A. H. Gentry, 99–111. New Haven: Yale University Press.

Foster, R. B., J. Arce B., and T. S. Wachter. 1986. Dispersal and the sequential plant communities in Amazonian Peru floodplain. In *Frugivores and seed dispersal,* ed. A. Estrada and T. H. Fleming, 356–70. Dordrecht: Junk.

Garrido, O. H. 1992. Natural and man-induced evolutionary shifts in the birds of some Cuban cays. *Bird Conserv. Internat.* 2:1–6.

Gentry, A. H. 1978. Floristic knowledge and needs in Pacific tropical America. *Brittonia* 30:134–53.

———. 1982a. Neotropical floristic diversity: Phytogeographical connections between Central and South America, Pleistocene climatic fluctuations, or an accident of Andean orogeny. *Ann. Missouri Bot. Gard.* 60:557–93.

———. 1982b. Patterns of Neotropical plant species diversity. *Evol. Biol.* 15:1–84.

———. 1986a. Endemism in tropical versus temperate plant communities. In *Conservation biology: The science of scarcity and diversity,* ed. M. E. Soulé, 153–81. Sunderland, Mass.: Sinauer.

———. 1986b. Species richness and floristic composition of Choco region plant communities. *Caldasia* 15:71–91.

———. 1988a. Changes in plant community diversity and floristic composition on environmental and geographical gradients. *Ann. Missouri Bot. Gard.* 75:1–34.

———. 1988b. Tree species richness of upper Amazonian forests. *Proc. Nat. Acad. Sci. USA* 85:156–59.

———. 1990a. Tropical forests. In *Biogeography and ecology of forest bird communities,* ed. A. Keast, 35–43. The Hague: SPB Academic Publications.

———. 1990b. Floristic similarities and differences between southern Central America and upper and central Amazonia. In *Four Neotropical rainforests,* ed. A. H. Gentry, 141–57. New Haven: Yale University Press.

———. 1993a. *A field guide to the families and genera of woody plants of northwest South America.* Washington, D.C.: Conservation International.

———. 1993b. Diversity and floristic composition of Neotropical dry forests. In *Tropical deciduous forest ecosystems,* ed. H. Mooney, S. Bullock, and E. Medina. Cambridge: Cambridge University Press.

Gentry, A. H., and C. H. Dodson. 1987. Diversity and biogeography of Neotropical vascular epiphytes. *Ann. Missouri Bot. Gard.* 74: 205–33.

Gilbert, L. E. 1980. Food web organization and conservation of Neotropical diversity. In *Conservation biology: An evolutionary-ecological perspective,* ed. M. E. Soulé and B. A. Wilcox, 11–33. Sunderland, Mass.: Sinauer.

Giulietti, A. M., and J. R. Pirani. 1988. Patterns of geographic distribution of some plant species from the Espinhaço Range, Minas Gerais and Bahia, Brazil. In *Proceedings of a workshop on Neotropical distribution patterns,* ed. P. E. Vanzolini and W. R. Heyer. Rio de Janeiro: Academia Brasileira de Ciências.

Goldsmith, F. B. 1974. Multivariate analyses of tropical grassland communities in Mato Grosso, Brazil. *J. Biogeogr.* 1:111–22.

Gradwohl, J., and R. Greenberg. 1982. The effect of a single species of avian predator on the arthropods of aerial leaf litter. *Ecology* 63:581–83.

———. 1984. The search behavior of the Checker-throated Antwren in aerial leaf litter. *Behav. Ecol. Sociobiol.* 15:281–85.

Graves, G. R. 1985. Elevational correlates of speciation and intraspecific geographical variation in plumage in Andean forest birds. *Auk* 105:556–79.

———. 1988. Linearity of geographical ranges and its possible effect on the population structure of Andean birds. *Auk* 105:47–52.

———. 1992. Diagnosis of a hybrid Antbird (*Phlegopsis nigromaculata* × *Phlegopsis erythroptera*) and the rarity of hybridization among suboscines. *Proc. Soc. Biol. Wash.* 105:834–40.

Graves, G. R., and J. S. Weske. 1987. *Tangara phillipsi,* a new species of tanager from the Cerros del Sira, eastern Peru. *Wilson Bull.* 99:1–6.

Greenberg, R., and J. Gradwohl. 1985. A comparative study of the social organization of Antwrens on Barro Colorado Island, Panama. In *Neotropical ornithology,* ed. P. A. Buckley, M. S. Foster, E. S. Morton, R. S. Ridgely, and F. G. Buckley, 845–55. Ornithol. Monogr. 36. Washington, D.C.: American Ornithologists' Union.

Grubb, P. J. 1974. Factors controlling the distribution of forest types on tropical mountains: New facts and a new perspective. In *Altitudinal zonation in Malesia,* ed. J. R. Flenley, 1–25. Geogr. Dept. Misc. Ser. 16. Hull: University of Hull.

———. 1977. Control of forest growth and distribution on wet tropical mountains: With special reference to mineral nutrition. *Ann. Rev. Ecol. Syst.* 8:83–107.

Haase, R., and S. Beck. 1989. Structure and composition of savanna vegetation in northern Bolivia: A preliminary report. *Brittonia* 41:80–100.

Haffer, J. 1974. *Avian speciation in tropical South America.* Publ. Nuttall Ornithol. Club, no. 14. Cambridge, Mass.: Nuttall Ornithological Club.

———. 1985. Avian zoogeography of the Neotropical lowlands. In *Neotropical ornithology,* ed. P. A. Buckley, M. S. Foster, E. S. Morton, R. S. Ridgely, and F. G. Buckley, 113–46. Ornithol. Monogr., no. 36. Washington, D.C.: American Ornithologists' Union.

———. 1990. Avian species richness in tropical South America. *Stud. Neotrop. Fauna Environ.* 25:157–83.

Haffer, J., and J. W. Fitzpatrick. 1985. Geographic variation in some Amazonian forest birds. In *Neotropical ornithology,* ed. P. A. Buckley, M. S. Foster, E. S. Morton, R. S. Ridgely, and F. G. Buckley, 147–68. Ornithol. Monogr., no. 36. Washington, D.C.: American Ornithologists' Union.

Hagan, J. M., III, and D. W. Johnston, eds. 1992. *Ecology and conservation of Neotropical migrant landbirds.* Washington, D.C.: Smithsonian Institution Press.

Hagan, J. M., III, T. L. Lloyd-Evans, J. L. Atwood, and D. S. Wood. 1992. Long-term changes in migratory landbirds in the northeastern United States: Evidence from migration capture data. In *Ecology and conservation of Neotropical migrant landbirds,* ed. J. M. Hagan III and D. W. Johnston, 115–30. Washington, D.C.: Smithsonian Institution Press.

Hall, G. A. 1984. Population decline of Neotropical migrants in an Appalachian forest. *Am. Birds* 38:14–18.

Harper, L. H. 1988. The persistence of ant-following birds in small Amazonian forest fragments. *Acta Amazonica* 118.

Hartman, F. A. 1961. Locomotor mechanisms of birds. *Smithson. Misc. Collect.* 143:1–91

Hartshorn, G. 1980. Neotropical forest dynamics. *Biotropica* 12 (suppl.): 23–30.

———. 1983. Plants: Introduction. In *Costa Rican natural history,* ed. D. H. Janzen, 118–83. Chicago: University of Chicago Press.

———. 1988. Tropical and subtropical vegetation of Meso-America. In *North American terrestrial vegetation,* ed. M. G. Barbour and W. D. Billings, 365–90. Cambridge: Cambridge University Press.

———. 1992. Forest loss and future options in Central America. In *Ecology and conservation of Neotropical migrant landbirds,* ed. J. M. Hagan III and D. W. Johnston, 13–19. Washington, D.C.: Smithsonian Institution Press.

Hayes, F. E., S. M. Goodman, J. A. Fox, T. Granizo Tamayo, and N. E. López. 1990. North American bird migrants in Paraguay. *Condor* 92:947–60.

Hayes, F. E., P. A. Scharf, and R. S. Ridgely. 1994. Austral bird migrants in Paraguay. *Condor* 96:83–97.

Hays, C. 1987. Effects of the 1982–1983 El Niño on Humboldt Penguin colonies. *Biol. Conserv.* 36:169–80.

Heringer, E. P. 1971. Propagação e sucessão de espécies arbóreas do cerrado em função do fogo, do capim, da capina e do aldrin. In *III Simpósio sôbre o Cerrado,* ed. M. G. Ferri, 167–79. São Paulo: S. Editora Universidade de São Paulo.

Hilty, S. L. 1985. Distributional changes in the Colombian avifauna: A preliminary blue list. In *Neotropical ornithology,* ed. P. A. Buckley, M. S. Foster, E. S. Morton, R. S. Ridgely, and F. G. Buckley, 683–712. Ornithol. Monogr. 36. Washington, D.C.: American Ornithologists' Union.

Hilty, S. L., and W. L. Brown. 1986. *A guide to the birds of Colombia.* Princeton: Princeton University Press.

Hinkelmann, C. 1988. On the identity of *Phaethornis maranhaoensis* Grantsau, 1968 (Trochilidae). *Bull. Brit. Ornithol. Club* 108: 14–18.

Holmes, R. T., and T. W. Sherry. 1992. Site fidelity of migratory warblers in temperate breeding annd Neotropical wintering areas: Implications for population dynamics, habitat selection, and conservation. In *Ecology and conservation of Neotropical migrant landbirds,* ed. J. M. Hagan III and D. W. Johnston, 563–75. Washington, D.C.: Smithsonian Institution Press.

Howell, S. N. G., and S. Webb. 1995. *A guide to the birds of Mexico and northern Central America.* Oxford: Oxford University Press.

Howell, T. R., R. A. Paynter Jr., and A. L. Rand. 1968. Subfamily Carduelinae. In *Check-list of birds of the world,* ed. R. A. Paynter Jr., 14:207–306. Cambridge, Mass.: Museum of Comparative Zoology.

Hubbell, S. P. and R. B. Foster. 1985. Biology, chance, and history, and the structure of tropical rain forest communities. In *Community ecology,* ed. T. J. Case and J. Diamond, 314–29. New York: Harper and Row.

———. 1986. Commonness and rarity in a Neotropical forest: Implications for tropical tree conservation. In *Conservation biology: The science of scarcity and diversity,* ed. M. E. Soulé, 205–31. Sunderland, Mass.: Sinauer.

Hughes, R. A. 1985. Notes on the effect of El Niño on the seabirds of the Mollendo district, southwest Peru, in 1983. *Ibis* 127:385–88.

Humphrey, P. S., D. Bridge, P. W. Reynolds, and R. T. Peterson. 1970. *Birds of Isla Grande (Tierra del Fuego).* Lawrence: University of Kansas Museum of Natural History.

Hunter, M. L., Jr., and P. Yonzon. 1993. Altitudinal distributions of birds, mammals, people, forests and parks in Nepal. *Conserv. Biol.* 7:420–23.

Hussell, D. J. T., M. H. Mather, and P. H. Sinclair. 1992. Trends in numbers of tropical- and temperate-wintering migrant landbirds in migration at Long Point, Ontario, 1961–1988. In *Ecology and conservation of Neotropical migrant landbirds,* ed. J. M. Hagan III and D. W. Johnston, 101–14. Washington, D.C.: Smithsonian Institution Press.

Hutto, R. L. 1988. Is tropical deforestation responsible for the reported declines in Neotropical migrant populations? *Am. Birds* 42:375–79.

———. 1989. The effect of habitat alteration on migratory land birds in a west Mexican tropical deciduous forest: A conservation perspective. *Conserv. Biol.* 3:138–48.

———. 1992. Habitat distributions of migratory landbird species in western Mexico. In *Ecology and conservation of Neotropical migrant landbirds,* ed. J. M. Hagan III and D. W. Johnston, 211–39. Washington, D.C.: Smithsonian Institution Press.

Isler, M. L., and P. R. Isler. 1987. *The tanagers: Natural history, distribution, and identification.* Washington, D.C.: Smithsonian Institution Press.

James, F. C. 1991. Signs of trouble in the largest remaining population of Red-cockaded Woodpeckers. *Auk* 108:419–23.

James, H. L., and S. L. Olson. 1991. *Description of thirty-two new species of birds from the Hawaiian Islands.* Part 2, *Passeriformes.* Ornithol. Monogr. 46. Washington, D.C.: American Ornithologists' Union.

Janzen, D. H. 1973a. Sweep samples of tropical foliage insects: Description of study sites, with data on species abundances and size distributions. *Ecology* 54:659–86.

———. 1973b. Sweep samples of tropical foliage insects: Effects of seasons, vegetation types, elevation, time of day, and insularity. *Ecology* 54:687–708.

———. 1976. Why bamboos wait so long to flower. *Ann. Rev. Ecol. Syst.* 7:347–91.

———. 1988. Tropical dry forests: The most endangered major tropical ecosystem. In *Biodiversity,* ed. E. O. Wilson, 130–37. Washington, D.C.: National Academy Press.

Junk, W. J. 1970. Investigations on the ecology and production-biology of the "floating meadows" (Paspalo-Echinochloetum) on the middle Amazon. Part 1, The floating vegetation and its ecology. *Amazoniana* 2:449-95.

Junk, W. J., and Howard-William, C. 1984. Ecology of aquatic macrophytes in Amazonia. In *The Amazon: Limnology and landscape ecology of a mighty tropical river and its basin,* ed. H. Sioli, 269–93. The Hague: Junk.

Karr, J. R. 1976. Seasonality, resource availability, and community diversity in tropical habitats. *Am. Nat.* 110:973–94.

———. 1979. On the use of mist nets in the study of bird communities. *Inland Bird Banding* 51:1–10.

Kaufmann, K. 1990. The changing seasons: Spring 1990. *Am. Birds* 44:384–87.

Keast, A. 1980. Spatial relationships between migratory parulid warblers and their ecological counterparts in the Neotropics. In

Migrant birds in the Neotropics: Ecology, behavior, distribution and conservation, ed. A. Keast and E. S. Morton, 109–30. Washington, D.C.: Smithsonian Institution Press

Keast, A., and E. S. Morton, eds. 1980. *Migrant birds in the Neotropics: Ecology, behavior, distribution and conservation.* Washington, D.C.: Smithsonian Institution Press.

Keeley, J. E., and S. C. Keeley. 1988. Chaparral. In *North American terrestrial vegetation,* ed. M. G. Barbour and W. D. Billings, 165–207. Cambridge: Cambridge University Press.

Killeen, T. J., B. T. Louman, and T. Grimwood. 1990. La ecologia paisajística de la region de Concepción y Lomerío, Santa Cruz, Bolivia. *Ecol. Bolivia* 16:1–45.

King, W. B. 1981. *Endangered birds of the world: The ICBP bird red data book.* Washington, D.C.: Smithsonian Institution Press and the International Council for Bird Preservation.

Koopman, K. F. 1981. The distributional patterns of New World nectar-feeding bats. *Ann. Missouri Bot. Gard.* 68:352–69.

———. 1982. Biogeography of the bats of South America. Special Publs. Ser. *Pymatuning Lab. Ecol.* 6:273–302.

Kruckeberg, A. R., and D. Rabinowitz. 1985. Biological aspects of endemism in higher plants. *Ann. Rev. Ecol. Syst.* 16:447–79.

Lacerda, L. D. de, D. S. D. de Araújo, and N. C. Maciel. 1993. Dry coastal ecosystems of the tropical Brazilian coast. In *Ecosystems of the world 2B: Dry coastal ecosystems—Africa, America, Asia, and Oceania,* ed. E. van der Maarel, 477–93. Amsterdam: Elsevier.

Lamas, G. 1985. Los Papilionoidea (Lepidoptera) de la Zona Reservada de Tambopata, Madre de Dios, Peru. 1. Papilionidae, Pieridae y Nymphalidae (en parte). *Rev. Peru. Entomol.* 27:59–73.

Lewis, W. H. 1971. High floristic endemism in the low cloud forests of Panama. *Biotropica* 3:78–80.

Lovejoy, T. 1983. Tropical deforestation and North American migrant birds. *Bird Conserv.* 1:126–28.

Lovejoy, T. E., R. O. Bierregaard Jr., A. B. Rylands, J. R. Malcolm, C. E. Quintela, L. H. Harper, K. S. Brown Jr., A. H. Powell, G. V. N. Powell, H. O. R. Schubart, and M. B. Hays. 1986. Edge and other effects of isolation on Amazon forest fragments. In *Conservation biology: The science of scarcity and diversity,* ed. M. E. Soulé, 257–85. Sunderland, Mass.: Sinauer.

Lynch, J. F., and D. F. Whigham. 1984. Effects of forest fragmentation on breeding bird communities in Maryland, USA. *Biol. Conserv.* 28:287–324.

MacArthur, R. H. 1972. *Geographical ecology.* Princeton: Princeton University Press.

MacMahon, J. A., and F. H. Wagner. 1985. The Mojave, Sonoran and Chihuahuan Deserts of North America. In *Ecosystems of the world 12A: Hot deserts and arid shrublands, A,* ed. M. Evenari, I. Noy-Meir, and D. W. Goodall, 105–202. Amsterdam: Elsevier.

Mares, M. A. 1992. Neotropical mammals and the myth of Amazonian biodiversity. *Science* 255:976–79.

Mares, M. A., J. Morello, and G. Goldstein. 1985. The Monte desert and other subtropical semi-arid biomes of Argentina. In *Ecosystems of the world 12A: Hot deserts and arid scrublands,* ed. M. Evenari et al., 203–37. Amsterdam: Elsevier.

Marín A., M., L. F. Kiff, and L. Peña G. 1989. Notes on Chilean birds, with descriptions of two new subspecies. *Bull. Brit. Ornithol. Club* 109:66–82.

Marshall, J. T., Jr. 1957. *Birds of pine-oak woodland in southern Arizona and adjacent Mexico.* Pacific Coast Avifauna, no. 32. Columbus, Ohio: Cooper Ornithological Society.

Maurer, B. A., and S. G. Heywood. 1993. Geographic range fragmentation and abundance in Neotropical migratory birds. *Conserv. Biol.* 7:501–9.

Mayr, E. 1963. *Animal species and evolution.* Cambridge: Harvard University Press.

Mayr, E., and W. H. Phelps Jr. 1967. The origin of the bird fauna of the south Venezuelan highlands. *Bull. Am. Mus. Nat. Hist.* 136: 273–327.

McKitrick, M. C., and R. A. Zink. 1988. Species concepts in ornithology. *Condor* 90:1–14.

Meyer de Schauensee, R. 1966. *The species of birds of South America.* Narberth, Pa.: Livingston.

———. 1970. *A guide to the birds of South America.* Wynnewood, Pa.: Livingston.

Minckley, W. L., and D. E. Brown. 1982. Wetlands. In Biotic communities of the American Southwest—United States and Mexico, ed. D. E. Brown, *Desert Plants* 4:223–87.

Mori, S. A., B. M. Boom, A. M. de Carvalino, and T. S. dos Santos. 1983. Ecological importance of Myrtaceae in an eastern Brazilian wet forest. *Biotropica* 15:68–70.

Mori, S. A., B. M. Boom, and G. T. Prance. 1981. Distribution patterns and conservation of eastern Brazilian coastal forest tree species. *Brittonia* 33:233–45.

Morony, J. J., W. J. Bock, and J. Farrand. 1975. *Reference list of birds of the world.* New York: American Museum of Natural History, Department of Ornithology.

Morton, E. S. 1992. What do we know about the future of migrant landbirds? In *Ecology and conservation of Neotropical migrant landbirds,* ed. J. M. Hagan III and D. W. Johnston, 579–89. Washington, D.C.: Smithsonian Institution Press.

Morton, E. S., and R. Greenberg. 1989. The outlook for migratory songbirds: "Future shock" for birders. *Am. Birds* 43:178–83.

Moskovits, D. K., J. W. Fitzpatrick, and D. E. Willard. 1985. Lista preliminar das aves da Estação Ecológica de Maracá, Território de Roraima, Brasil, e áreas adjacentes. *Pap. Avul. Zool.* (São Paulo) 36:51–68.

Munn, C. A. 1985. Permanent canopy and understory flocks in Amazonia: Species composition and population density. In *Neotropical ornithology,* ed. P. A. Buckley, M. S. Foster, E. S. Morton, R. S. Ridgely, and F. G. Buckley, 683–712. Ornithol. Monogr. 36. Washington, D.C.: American Ornithologists' Union.

Munn, C. A., and J. W. Terborgh. 1979. Multi-species flocks territoriality in Neotropical foraging flocks. *Condor* 81:338–47.

Myers, J. P. 1980. The pampas shorebird community: Interactions between breeding and non-breeding members. In *Migrant birds in the Neotropics: Ecology, behavior, distribution and conservation,* ed. A. Keast and E. S. Morton, 37-49. Washington, D.C.: Smithsonian Institution Press.

———. 1983. Conservation of migrating shorebirds: Staging areas, geographic bottlenecks, and regional movements. *Am. Birds* 37: 23–25.

Myers, J. P., R. I. G. Morrison, P. Z. Antas, B. A. Harrington, T. E. Lovejoy, M. Sallaberry, S. E. Senner, and A. Tarak. 1987. Conservation strategy for migratory species. *Am. Scientist* 75:19–26.

Myers, N. 1980. *Conversion of tropical moist forests.* Washington, D.C.: National Research Council.

———. 1986. Tropical deforestation and a mega-extinction spasm. In *Conservation biology: The science of scarcity and diversity,* ed. M. E. Soulé, 394–409. Sunderland, Mass.: Sinauer.

Myers, R. L. 1990. Palm swamps. In *Ecosystems of the world 15: Forested wetlands,* ed. A. E. Lugo, M. Brinson, and S. Brown, 267–86. Amsterdam: Elsevier.

Oliver, I., and A. J. Beattie. 1993. A possible method for the rapid assessment of biodiversity. *Conserv. Biol.* 7:562–68.

Olson, S. L., and H. F. James. 1982. Fossil birds of the Hawaiian Islands: Evidence for wholesale extinction by man before Western contact. *Science* 217:633–35.

———. 1991. *Description of thirty-two new species of birds from the Hawaiian Islands.* Part 1, *Non-Passeriformes.* Ornithol. Monogr. 45. Washington, D.C.: American Ornithologists' Union.

Orejuela, J. E. 1985. Tropical forest birds of Colombia: A survey of problems and a plan for their conservation. In *Conservation of tropical forest birds,* ed. A. W. Diamond and T. E. Lovejoy, 95–114. ICBP Tech. Pub. no. 4. Cambridge: International Council for Bird Preservation.

Oren, D. 1981. *Zoogeographic analysis of the white sand campina avifauna of Amazonia.* Ph.D. diss., Harvard University, Cambridge, Massachusetts.

Ouellet, H., ed. 1988. *Acta XIX Congressus Internationalis Ornithologici.* Ottawa: University of Ottawa Press.

———. 1993. Bicknell's Thrush: Taxonomic status and distribution. *Wilson Bull.* 105:545–72.

Parker, T. A., III. 1982. Observations of some unusual rainforest and marsh birds in southeastern Peru. *Wilson Bull.* 94:477–93.

———. 1991. On the use of tape recorders in avifaunal surveys. *Auk* 108:443–44.

Parker, T. A., P. K. Donahue, and T. S. Schulenberg. 1994. Birds of the Tambopata Reserve (Explorer's Inn Reserve). In *The Tambopata Reserved Zone of southeastern Peru: A biological assessment,* ed. R. B. Foster, T. A. Parker III, A. H. Gentry, L. H. Emmons, A. Chicchón, T. Schulenberg, L. Rodríguez, G. Lamas, H. Ortega, J. Icochea, W. Wust, M. Romo, J. A. Castillo, O. Phillips, C. Reynal, A. Kratter, P. K. Donahue, and L. J. Barkley, 106–24. RAP Working Papers, no. 6. Washington, D.C.: Conservation International.

Pase, C. P., and D. E. Brown. 1982a. Interior chapparal. In Biotic communities of the American Southwest—United States and Mexico, ed. D. E. Brown. *Desert Plants* 4:95–99.

———. 1982b. Rocky Mountain (Petran) and Madrean montane conifer forests. In Biotic communities of the American Southwest—United States and Mexico, ed. D. E. Brown. *Desert Plants* 4:43–48.

Pearson, O. P. 1951. Mammals in the highlands of southern Peru. *Bull. Mus. Comp. Zool.* 106:117–74.

Pearson, O. P., and C. P. Ralph. 1978. The diversity and abundance of vertebrates along an altitudinal gradient in Peru. *Mem. Mus. Hist. Nat. Javier Prado,* no. 18.

Peters, J. L. 1951. *Check-list of birds of the world.* Vol. 7. Cambridge, Mass.: Museum of Comparative Zoology.

Phillips, A. R. 1975. Why neglect the difficult. *Western Birds* 6:69–86.

Pierpont, N., and J. W. Fitzpatrick. 1983. Specific status and behavior of *Cymbilaimus sanctaemariae,* the Bamboo Antshrike, from southwestern Amazonia. *Auk* 100:645–52.

Pimm, S. L. 1986. Community stability and structure. In *Conservation biology: The science of scarcity and diversity,* ed. M. E. Soulé, 309–29. Sunderland, Mass.: Sinauer.

Pires, J. M. 1974. Tipos de vegetação da Amazônia. *Publ. Avuls. Mus. Par. Emilio Goeldi* 20:179–202.

Pires, J. M., and G. T. Prance. 1985. The vegetation types of the Brazilian Amazon. In *Amazonia,* ed. G. T. Prance and T. E. Lovejoy, 109–45. Oxford: Pergamon.

Porneluzi, P., J. C. Bednarz, L. J. Goodrich, N. Zawada, and J. Hoover. 1993. Reproductive performance of territorial ovenbirds occupying forest fragments and a contiguous forest in Pennsylvania. *Conserv. Biol.* 7:618–22.

Powell, G. V. N. 1979. Structure and dynamics of interspecific flocks in a mid-elevation Neotropical forest. *Auk* 96:375–90.

———. 1985. Sociobiology and adaptive significance of interspecific foraging flocks in the Neotropics. In *Neotropical ornithology,* ed. P. A. Buckley, M. S. Foster, E. S. Morton, R. S. Ridgely, and F. G. Buckley, 713–32. Ornithol. Monogr. 36. Washington, D.C.: American Ornithologists' Union.

Powell, G. V. N., and J. H. Rappole. 1986. The Hooded Warbler. In *Audubon Wildlife Report 1986,* ed. R. DiSilvestro, 827–54. New York: National Audubon Society.

Prance, G. T. 1979. Notes on the vegetation of Amazonia III. The terminologoy of Amazonian forest types subject to inundation. *Brittonia* 31:26–38.

———. 1982. Forest refuges: Evidence from woody angiosperms. In *Biological diversification in the tropics,* ed. G. T. Prance, 137–58. New York: Columbia University

———. 1989. American tropical forests. In *Ecosystems of the world 14B: Tropical rain forest ecosystems,* ed. H. Lieth and M. J. A. Werger, 99–132. Amsterdam: Elsevier.

———. 1990. The floristic composition of the forests of central Amazonian Brazil. In *Four Neotropical rainforests,* ed. A. H. Gentry, 112–40. New Haven: Yale University Press.

Pregill, G. K., and S. L. Olson. 1981. Zoogeography of West Indian vertebrates in relation to Pleistocene climatic cycles. *Ann. Rev. Syst. Ecol.* 12:75–98.

Rabinowitz, D. 1981. Seven forms of rarity. In *The biological aspects of rare plant conservation,* ed. H. Synge, 205–17. New York: Wiley.

Rabinowitz, D., S. Cairns, and T. Dillon. 1986. Seven forms of rarity and their frequency in the flora of the British Isles. In *Conservation biology: The science of scarcity and diversity,* ed. M. E. Soulé, 182–204. Sunderland, Mass.: Sinauer.

Ralph, C. J., and C. van Riper III. 1985. Historical and current factors affecting Hawaiian native birds. *Bird Conserv.* 2:7–42.

Rappole, J. H., E. S. Morton, T. E. Lovejoy III, and J. L. Ruos. 1983. *Nearctic avian migrants in the Neotropics.* Washington, D.C.: U.S. Fish and Wildlife Service.

Rauh, W. 1985. The Peruvian-Chilean deserts. In *Ecosystems of the world 12A: Hot deserts and arid shrublands,* ed. M. Evenari, I. Noy-Meir, and D. W. Goodall, 239–67. Amsterdam: Elsevier.

Reed, J. M. 1992. A system for ranking conservation priorities for Neotropical migrant birds based on relative susceptibility to extinction. In *Ecology and conservation of Neotropical migrant landbirds,* ed. J. M. Hagan III and D. W. Johnston, 524–36. Washington, D.C.: Smithsonian Institution Press.

Remsen, J. V., Jr. 1986. Was Bachman's Warbler a bamboo specialist? *Auk* 103:216–19.

Remsen, J. V., and T. A. Parker III. 1983. Contribution of river-created habitats to bird species richness in Amazonia. *Biotropica* 15:223–31.

———. 1984. Arboreal dead-leaf-searching birds of the Neotropics. *Condor* 86:36–41.

———. 1990. Seasonal distribution of the Azure Gallinule (*Porphyrula flavirostris*) with comments on vagrancy in rails and gallinules. *Wilson Bull.* 102:380–99.

Richards, P. W. 1952. *The tropical rain forest.* Cambridge: Cambridge University Press.

Ridgely, R. S., and J. A. Gwynne Jr. 1989. *A guide to the birds of Panama, with Costa Rica, Nicaragua and Honduras.* 2d ed. Princeton: Princeton University Press.

Ridgely, R. S., and M. B. Robbins. 1988. *Pyrrhura orcesi,* a new parakeet from southwestern Ecuador, with systematic notes on the *P. melanura* complex. *Wilson Bull.* 100:173–82.

Ridgely, R. S., and G. Tudor. 1989. *The birds of South America.* Vol. 1, *The oscine passerines.* Austin: University of Texas Press.

Robbins, C. S. 1979. Effect of forest fragmentation on bird populations. In *Workshop proceedings: Management of north central and northeastern forests for nongame birds,* ed. R. M. DeGraaf and K. E. Evans, 198–212. Gen. Tech. Rep. NC-51. Washington, D.C.: U.S. Forest Service.

Robbins, C. S., J. W. Fitzpatrick, and P. B. Hamel. 1992. A warbler in trouble: *Dendroica cerulea.* In *Ecology and conservation of Neotropical migrant landbirds,* ed. J. M. Hagan III and D. W. Johnston, 549–62. Washington, D.C.: Smithsonian Institution Press.

Robbins, C. S., J. R. Sauer, R. S. Greenberg, and S. Droege. 1989. Population declines in North American birds that migrate to the Neotropics. *Proc. Nat. Acad. Sci.* 86:7658–62.

Robbins, C. S., J. R. Sauer, and B. G. Peterjohn. 1993. Population trends and management opportunities for Neotropical migrants.

In *Status and management of Neotropical migratory birds,* ed. D. M. Finch and P. W. Stangel, 17–23. Gen. Tech. Rep. RM-229. Fort Collins, Colo: U.S. Dept. of Agriculture, Rocky Mountain Forest and Range Experimental Station.

Robinson, S. K. 1992. Population dynamics of breeding Neotropical migrants in a fragmented Illinois landscape. In *Ecology and conservation of Neotropical migrant landbirds,* ed. J. M. Hagan III and D. W. Johnston, 408–18. Washington, D.C.: Smithsonian Institution Press.

Robinson, S. K., J. W. Fitzpatrick, and J. Terborgh. 1995. Distribution and abundance of Neotropical migrant land birds in the Amazon basin and Andes. *Bird Conserv. Internat.* 5:305–23.

Robinson, S. K., J. A. Grzybowski, S. I. Rothstein, M. C. Brittingham, L. J. Petit, and F. R. Thompson. 1993. Management implications of cowbird parasitism on Neotropical migrant songbirds. In *Status and management of Neotropical migratory birds,* ed. D. M. Finch and P. W. Stangel, 93–102. Gen. Tech. Rep. RM-229. Fort Collins, Colo.: U.S. Dept. of Agriculture, Rocky Mountain Forest and Range Experimental Station.

Rosenzweig, M. L. 1992. Species diversity gradients: We know more and less than we thought. *J. Mammal.* 73:715–30.

Rzedowski, J. 1978. *Vegetación de México.* Mexico City: Editorial Limusa.

Sader, S. A., and A. T. Joyce. 1988. Deforestation rates and trends in Costa Rica, 1940–1983. *Biotropica* 20:11–19.

Sarmiento, G. 1983. The savannas of tropical America. In *Ecosystems of the world 13: Tropical savannas,* ed. F. Bourlière, 245–88. Amsterdam: Elsevier.

SAS. 1985a. *SAS/STAT guide for personal computers version 6.* Cary, N.C.: SAS Institute.

———. 1985b. *SAS language guide for personal computers version 6.* Cary, N.C.: SAS Institute.

———. 1985c. *SAS procedures guide for personal computers version 6.* Cary, N.C.: SAS Institute

Schmaltz, J. 1991. Deciduous forests in southern South America. In *Ecosystems of the world 7: Temperate deciduous forests,* ed. E. Röhrig and B. Ulrich, 557–78. Amsterdam: Elsevier.

Saville, D. B. O. 1957. Adaptive evolution in the avian wing. *Evolution* 11:212–24.

Schemske, D. W., and N. Brokaw. 1981. Treefalls and the distribution of understory birds in a tropical forest. *Ecology* 62:938–45.

Schimper, A. R. W. 1903. *Plant geography upon a physiological basis.* Oxford: Clarendon Press.

Schulenberg, T. S., and D. F. Stotz. 1990. The taxonomic status of *Myrmeciza stictothorax* (Todd). *Auk* 108:731–33.

Scott, D. A., and M. de L. Brooke. 1985. The endangered avifauna of southeastern Brazil: A report on the BOU/WWF expeditions of 1980/81 and 1981/82. In *Conservation of tropical forest birds,* ed. A. W. Diamond and T. E. Lovejoy, 115–39. ICBP Tech. Pub. no. 4. Cambridge: International Council for Bird Preservation.

Scott, J. M., S. Mountainspring, F. L. Ramsey, and C. B. Kepler. 1986. *Forest bird communities of the Hawaiian Islands: Their dynamics, ecology and conservation.* Studies in Avian Biology no. 9. Lawrence, Kans.: Allen Press.

Segadas-Viana, F. 1968. Ecology of the Itatiaia range, southeastern Brazil—altitudinal zonation of the vegetation. *Arquivos do Museu Nacional, Rio de Janeiro* 53:7–30.

Shelford, V. E. 1963. *The ecology of North America.* Urbana: University of Illinois Press.

Sherry, T. W., and R. T. Holmes 1993. Are populations of Neotropical migrant birds limited in summer or winter? Implications for management. In *Status and management of Neotropical migratory birds,* ed. D. M. Finch and P. W. Stangel, 47–57. Gen. Tech. Rep. RM-229. Fort Collins, Colo.: U.S. Dept. of Argriculture, Rocky Mountain Forest and Range Experimental Station.

Short, L. L. 1975. A zoogeographic analysis of the South American chaco avifauna. *Bull. Am. Mus. Nat. Hist.* 154:165–352.

———. 1982. *Woodpeckers of the world.* Greenville: Delaware Museum of Natural History,

Sibley, C. G., and J. E. Ahlquist. 1990. *Phylogeny and classification of birds: A study in molecular evolution.* New Haven: Yale University Press.

Sick, H. 1985. *Ornitologia brasileira, uma introdução.* Brasília: Editora Universidade de Brasília.

Silberbauer-Gottsberger, I., and G. Gottsberger. 1984. Cerrado-cerradão: A comparison with respect to number of species and growth form. *Phytocoenologia* 12:293–303.

Silva, J. M. C. da. 1989. A reavaluation [*sic*] of *Serpophaga araguayae* Snethlage, 1928 (Aves: Tyrannidae). *Goeldiana Zool.,* no. 1.

Simpson, B. B. 1979. A revision of the genus *Polylepis* (Rosaceae: Sanguisorbeae). *Smithson. Contrib. Bot.* 43:1–59.

Skagen, S. K., and F. L. Knopf. 1993. Toward conservation of mid-continental shorebird migrations. *Conserv. Biol.* 7:533–41.

Slud, P. 1976. Geographic and climatic relationships of avifaunas with special reference to comparative distribution in the Neotropics. *Smithson. Contrib. Zool.* 212.

Smith, W. J., and F. Vuilleumier. 1971. Evolutionary relationships in some South American ground tyrants. *Bull. Mus. Comp. Zool.* 141:181–232.

Snow, D. W. 1979. Family Pipridae. In *Check-list of birds of the world,* ed. M. A. Traylor Jr., 8:245–80. Cambridge, Mass.: Museum of Comparative Zoology.

Soriano, A. 1983. Deserts and semi-deserts of Patagonia. In *Ecosystems of the world 5: Temperate deserts and semi-deserts,* ed. N. E. West, 423–60. Amsterdam: Elsevier.

Soriano, A., R. J. C. León, O. E. Sala, R. S. Lavado, V. A. Deregibus, M. A. Canhépé, O. A. Scaglia, C. A. Velázques, and J. H. Lemcoff. 1992. Río de la Plata grasslands. In *Ecosystems of the world 8A: Natural grasslands,* ed. R. T. Coupland, 367–407. Amsterdam: Elsevier.

Soulé, M. E., and K. A. Kohm, eds. 1989. *Research priorities for conservation biology.* Washington, D.C.: Island Press.

Steadman, D. W., G. K. Pregill, and S. L. Olson. 1984. Fossil vertebrates from Antigua, Lesser Antilles: Evidence for late Holocene human-caused extinctions in the West Indies. *Proc. Natl. Acad. Sci.* 81:4448–51.

Stiles, F. G. 1985a. Conservation of forest birds in Costa Rica: Problems and perspectives. In *Conservation of tropical forest birds,* ed. A. W. Diamond and T. E. Lovejoy, 141–68. ICBP Tech. Pub. no. 4. Cambridge: International Council for Bird Preservation.

———. 1985b. Seasonal patterns and coevolution in the hummingbird-flower community of a Costa Rican subtropical forest. In *Neotropical ornithology,* ed. P. A. Buckley, M. S. Foster, E. S. Morton, R. S. Ridgely, and F. G. Buckley, 757–87. Ornithol. Monogr. 36. Washington, D.C.: American Ornithologists' Union.

———. 1988. Altitudinal movements of birds on the Caribbean slope of Costa Rica: Implications for conservation. *Mem. Calif. Acad. Sci.,* no. 12:243–58.

Stiles, F. G., and A. F. Skutch. 1989. *A guide to the birds of Costa Rica.* Ithaca: Cornell University Press.

Stotz, D. F., and R. O. Bierregaard Jr. 1989. The birds of Fazendas Porto Alegre, Esteio and Dimona, north of Manaus, Amazonas, Brasil. *Rev. Brasil. Biol.* 49:861–72.

Stotz, D. F., R. O. Bierregaard, M. Cohn-Haft, P. Petermann, J. Smith, A. Whittaker, and S. V. Wilson. 1992. The status of North American migrants in central Amazonian Brazil. *Condor* 94:608–21.

Stotz, D. F., S. M. Lanyon, T. S. Schulenberg, D. E. Willard, J. W. Fitzpatrick, and A. T. Peterson. n.d. Results of an avifaunal survey of the middle Rio Jiparanâ, Rondônia, Brazil. *Pap. Avul. Zool.* (São Paulo). In press.

Sturm, H., and O. Rangel Ch. 1985. *Ecologia de los Paramos Andinos: Una visión preliminar integrada.* Bogotá: Universidad Nacional de Colombia.

Terborgh, J. W. 1971. Distribution on environmental gradients: Theory and a preliminary interpretation of distributional patterns in the avifauna of Cordilleira Vilcabamba, Peru. *Ecology* 52: 23–40.

———. 1977. Bird species diversity on an Andean elevation gradient. *Ecology* 58:1007–19.

———. 1980. The conservation status of Neotropical migrants. In *Migrant birds in the Neotropics: Ecology, behavior, distribution and conservation,* ed. A. Keast and E. S. Morton, 21–30. Washington, D.C.: Smithsonian Institution Press.

———. 1983. *Five New World primates: A study in comparative ecology.* Princeton: Princeton University Press.

———. 1989. *Where have all the birds gone?* Princeton: Princeton University Press.

Terborgh, J. W., J. W. Fitzpatrick, and L. Emmons. 1984. Annotated checklist of bird and mammal species of Cocha Cashu Biological Station, Manu National Park, Peru. *Fieldiana Zool.,* n.s., no. 21.

Terborgh, J. W., S. K. Robinson, T. A. Parker III, C. A. Munn, and N. Pierpont. 1990. Structure and organization of an Amazonian forest bird community. *Ecol. Monogr.* 60:213–38.

Terborgh, J. W., and J. S. Weske. 1975. The role of competition in the distribution of Andean birds. *Ecology* 56:562–76.

Terborgh, J. W., and B. Winter. 1980. Some causes of extinction. In *Conservation biology: An evolutionary-ecological perspective,* ed. M. E. Soulé and B. A. Wilcox, 95–117. Sunderland, Mass.: Sinauer.

———. 1982. Evolutionary circumstances of species with small ranges. In *Biological diversification in the tropics,* ed. G. T. Prance, 587–600. New York: Columbia University Press.

———. 1983. A method for siting parks and reserves with special reference to Colombia and Ecuador. *Biol. Conserv.* 27:45–58.

Tomlinson, R. E. 1972. *Review of literature on the endangered Masked Bobwhite.* Res. Publ. 108. Washington, D.C.: Bureau of Sport Fisheries and Wildlife.

Tosi, J. A., Jr. 1960. *Zonas de vida natural en el Peru: Memoria explicativa sobre el mapa ecológico del Perú.* Zona Andina Bol. Tech. no. 5. Turrialba, Costa Rica: Instituto Interamericano de Ciencias y Agricolas, OEA.

Tovar S., H. 1983. Fluctuaciones de poblaciones de aves guaneras en el litoral peruano, 1960–1981. *FAO Fish. Rep.,* no. 291:957–76.

———. 1985. Población de aves guaneras en el litoral peruano, 1960–1981. In *Primer Symposio de Ornitoligia Neotropical* (14–15 October 1983, Arequipa, Peru), ed. F. G. Stiles and P. G. Aguilar F., 119. Lima: Asociación para Conservación de la Naturaleza.

Tramer, F. J. 1974. On latitudinal gradients in avian diversity. *Condor* 76:123–30.

Traylor, M. A., Jr. 1979. Subfamily Elaeninae. In *Check-list of birds of the world,* ed. M. A. Traylor Jr., 8:3–112. Cambridge, Mass.: Museum of Comparative Zoology,

———. 1982. Notes on Tyrant Flycatchers (Aves: Tyrannidae). *Fieldiana Zool.,* n.s., no. 13.

Troll, C. 1959. Die tropischen Gebirge: Ihre dreidimensionale klimatische und pflanzengeographische Zonierung. *Bonn. Geogr. Abh.* 25.

Turner, R. M., and D. E. Brown. 1982. Sonoran desertscrub. In Biotic communities of the American Southwest—United States and Mexico, ed. D. E. Brown. *Desert Plants* 4:181–221.

Vanzolini, P. E. 1972. Miscellaneous notes on the ecology of some Brasilian lizards (Sauria). *Pap. Avul. Zool.* (São Paulo) 26:83–115.

———. 1974. Ecological and geographical distribution of lizards in Pernambuco, northeastern Brasil (Sauria). *Pap. Avul. Zool.* (São Paulo) 28:61–90.

Vari, R. P. 1988. The Curimatidae, a lowland Neotropical fish family (Pisces, Characiformes): Distribution, endemism and phylogenetic biogeography. In *Proceedings of a workshop on Neotropical distribution patterns* (12-16 January 1987), ed. P. E. Vanzolini and W. R. Heyer, 343–77. Rio de Janeiro: Academia Brasileira de Ciências.

Vaurie, C. 1971a. *Classification of the ovenbirds (Furnariidae).* London: H. F. and G. Witherby.

———. 1971b. Systematic status of *Synallaxis demissa* and *Synallaxis poliophrys. Ibis* 113:520–21.

———. 1980. Taxonomy and geographical distribution of the Furnariidae (Aves, Passeriformes). *Bull. Am. Mus. Nat. Hist.* 166: 1–357.

Vincent, J. 1966–71. *Red data book.* Vol. 2, *Aves.* Morges: International Union for the Conservation of Nature.

Vuilleumier, F. 1969. Pleistocene speciation in birds living in the high Andes. *Nature* 223:1179–80.

———. 1985. Forest birds of Patagonia: Ecological geography, speciation, endemism, and faunal history. In *Neotropical ornithology,* ed. P. A. Buckley, M. S. Foster, E. S. Morton, R. S. Ridgely, and F. G. Buckley, 255–304. Ornithol. Monogr. 36. Washington, D.C.: American Ornithologists' Union.

Vuilleumier, F., and D. Ewert. 1978. The distribution of birds in Venezuelan páramos. *Bull. Am. Mus. Nat. Hist.* 162:47–90.

Vuilleumier, F., M. LeCroy, and E. Mayr. 1992. New species of birds described from 1981 to 1990. *Bull. Brit. Ornithol. Club* 112A (suppl.): 267–309.

Vuilleumier, F., and E. Mayr. 1987. New species of birds described from 1976 to 1980. *J. Ornithol.* 128:137–50.

Waechter, J. L., L. A. Cestaro, and S. T. S. Miotto. 1984. Vegetation types in the ecological station of Aracuri, Esmeralda, Rio Grande do Sul, Brazil. *Phytocoenologia* 12:261–69.

Walter, H. 1971. *Ecology of tropical and subtropical vegetation.* New York: Van Nostrand Reinhold.

Weberbauer, A. 1911. *Die Vegetation der Erde XII: Die Pflanzenwelt der peruanischen Anden.* Leipzig: Engelmann.

———. 1936. Phytogeography of the Peruvian Andes. 13–81. In Flora of Peru, part 1, ed. J. F. MacBride. *Fieldiana Bot.,* no. 13 (1).

———. 1945. *El mundo vegetal de los Andes Peruanos.* Lima: Ministerio de Agricultura.

Weitzman, S. H., and M. Weitzman. 1982. Biogeography and evolutionary diversification in Neotropical freshwater fishes, with comments on refuge theory. In *Biological diversification in the tropics,* ed. G. T. Prance, 403–22. New York: Columbia University Press.

Weske, J. S., and J. W. Terborgh. 1971. A new subspecies of curassow of the genus *Pauxi* from Peru. *Auk* 88:233–38.

West, R. C. 1977. Tidal salt-marsh and mangal formations of Middle and South America. In *Ecosystems of the world 1: Wet coastal ecosystems,* ed. V. J. Chapman, 193–213. Amsterdam: Elsevier.

Wetmore, A. 1926. Observations on the birds of Argentina, Paraguay, Uruguay, and Chile. *Bull. U.S. Nat. Mus.* 133.

———. 1972. *Birds of the Republic of Panamá.* Part 3. Washington, D.C.: Smithsonian Institution Press.

Whitcomb, B. L., R. F. Whitcomb, and D. Bystrak. 1977. Island biogeography and "habitat islands" of eastern forest. III. Long-term turnover and effects of selective logging on the avifauna of forest fragments. *Am. Birds* 31:17–23.

Whitcomb, R. F. 1977. Island biogeography and "habitat islands" of eastern forest. *Am. Birds* 31:3–5.

Wilcove, D. S. 1985. Nest predation and the decline of migratory songbirds. *Ecology* 66:1211–14.

Willard, D. E., M. S. Foster, G. F. Barrowclough, R. W. Dickerman, P. F. Cannell, S. L. Coats, J. L. Cracraft, and J. P. O'Neill. 1991. The birds of Cerro de la Neblina, Territorio Federal Amazonas, Venezuela. *Fieldiana Zool.,* n.s., no. 65.

Willis, E. O. 1967. The behavior of Bicolored Antbirds. *Univ. Calif. Publ. Zool.* 79:1–127.

———. 1969. On the behavior of five species of *Rhegmatorhina,* ant-following Antbirds of the Amazon basin. *Wilson Bull.* 81: 363–95.

———. 1973. The behavior of Ocellated Antbirds. *Smithsonian Contrib. Zool.* 144:1–57.

———. 1979a. Comportamento e ecologia da Mãe-de-Taoca, *Phlegopsis nigromaculata* (D'orbigny and Lafresnaye) (Aves, Formicariidae). *Rev. Brasil. Biol.* 37:117–59.

———. 1979b. The composition of avian communities in remanescent woodlots in southern Brazil. *Pap. Avul. Zool.* (São Paulo) 33: 1–25.

———. 1988. Land-bird migration in São Paulo, southeastern Brazil. 754–64. In *Acta XIX Congressus Internationalis Ornithologici,* ed. H. Ouellet, 754–64. Ottawa: University of Ottawa Press.

Willis, E. O., and Y. Oniki. 1978. Birds and army ants. *Ann. Rev. Ecol. Syst.* 9:243–63.

———. 1992. A new *Phylloscartes* (Tyrannidae) from southeastern Brazil. *Bull. Brit. Ornithol. Club* 112:158–65.

Wright, S. 1943. Isolation by distance. *Genetics* 28:114–38.

———. 1978. *Evolution and the genetics of populations.* Vol. 4. *Variability among and within natural populations.* Chicago: University of Chicago Press.

Wright, S. J., and S. P. Hubbell. 1983. Stochastic extinction and reserve size: A focal species approach. *Oikos* 41:466–76.

Zimmer, J. T. 1945. Studies of Peruvian birds. No. 50, The genera *Ramphocelus, Piranga, Habia, Lanio,* and *Tachyphonus. Am. Mus. Novit.,* no. 1304.

Database Sources

Abramson, I. J. 1977. Photographic confirmation of Giant Snipe in Argentina. *Auk* 94:357.

Aguirre, A. C. 1984. Esclarecimento sôbre o pica-pau *Trichopicus cactorum*. *Bol. Inf. Fund. Bras. Conserv. Nat.* 19:155–56.

Albuquerque, J. B. L. 1978. Contribuição ao conhecimento de *Falco peregrinus* Tunstall 1771 na América do Sul (Falconidae, Aves). *Rev. Bras. Biol.* 38 (3): 727–37.

———. 1985. Notes on the distribution of some Brazilian raptors. *Bull. Brit. Ornithol. Club* 105:82-84.

Alexander, W. B. 1963. *Birds of the ocean*. New York: Putnam's.

Altman, A., and C. Parrish. 1978. Sight records of Wilson's Phalarope, Ruff and other shorebirds from Venezuela. *Am. Birds* 32: 309–10.

Alvarez, H. 1975. The social system of the Green Jay in Colombia. *Living Bird* 14:5-43.

American Ornithologists' Union (AOU). 1983. *The checklist of North American birds*. 6th ed. Washington, D.C.: American Ornithologists' Union.

———. 1985. Thirty-fifth supplement to the American Ornithologists' Union *Check-list of North American birds*. *Auk* 102: 680–86.

———. 1987. Thirty-sixth supplement to the American Ornithologists' Union *Check-list of North American birds*. *Auk* 104: 591–96.

———. 1989. Thirty-seventh supplement to the American Ornithologists' Union *Check-list of North American birds*. *Auk* 106: 532–38.

———. 1991. Thirty-eighth supplement to the American Ornithologists' Union *Check-list of North American birds*. *Auk* 108: 750–54.

———. 1993. Thirty-ninth supplement to the American Ornithologists' Union *Check-list of North American birds*. *Auk* 110: 675–82.

Andrade, M. A. de, M. V. de Freitas, and G. T. de Mattos. 1986. A redescoberta de "*Xiphocolaptes franciscanus*" Snethlage 1927 no estado de Minas Gerais, *Brasil. An. Soc. Sul-Riogr. Ornithol.* 7: 18–20.

Andrle, R. F. 1967. The Horned Guan in Mexico and Guatemala. *Condor* 69:93–109.

Ansingh, F. H., H. J. Koelers, P. A. Van der Weft, and K. H. Voous. 1960. The breeding of the Cayenne or Yellow-billed Tern in Curaçao in 1958. *Ardea* 48:51–65.

Araya, B. 1982. *Lista patron de las aves chilenas*. Pubicaciones Ocasionales, Instituto de Oceanologia, no. 1. Valparaiso: Universidad de Valparaiso.

———. 1985. *Lista patron de las aves chilenas*. 2d ed. Pubicaciones Ocasionales, Instituto de Oceanologia, no. 3. Valparaiso: Universidad de Valparaiso.

Arballo, E. 1990. Nuevos registros para avifauna uruguaya. *Hornero* 13:179–87.

Arndt, T. 1983. Neue Erkenntnisse uber den Artstatus des Blausteifssittich *Pyrrhura perlata perlata* Spix 1824. *Spixiana*, suppl. no. 9: 425–28.

Ash, J. S., and G. E. Watson. 1980. Great Shearwater *Puffinus gravis* new to Mexico. *Bull. Brit. Ornithol. Club* 100:194–95.

Atwood, J. L. 1988. *Speciation and geographic variation in Black-tailed Gnatcatchers*. Ornithol. Monogr., no. 42. Washington, D.C.: American Ornithologists' Union.

———. 1992. Elevational distribution of California Gnatcatchers in the United States. *J. Field Ornithol.* 63:159–68.

Avedillo, M. 1977. Communicación: *Passer domesticas* (Gorrión común) en Honduras. *Ceiba* 21:57–62.

Bangs, O., and T. E. Penard. 1918. Notes on a collection of Surinam birds. *Bull. Mus. Comp. Zool.* 62:25–93.

Banks, R. C. 1988a. An old record of the Pearly-breasted Cuckoo in North America and a nomenclatural critique. *Bull. Brit. Ornithol. Club* 108:87–91.

———. 1988b. Supposed northern records of the Southern Fulmar. *Western Birds* 19:121–24.

———. 1990. Taxonomic status of the coquette hummingbird of Guerrero, Mexico. *Auk* 107:191–92.

Baptista, L. F., W. I. Boardman, and P. Kandianidis. 1983. Behavior and taxonomic status of Grayson's Dove. *Auk* 100:907–19.

Barbour, T. 1923. *The birds of Cuba*. Mem. Nuttall Ornithol. Club, no. 6. Cambridge, Mass.: Nuttall Ornithological Club.

Barlow, J. C., J. A. Dick, D. H. Baldwin, and R. A. Davis. 1969. New records of birds from British Honduras. *Ibis* 111:399–402.

Barlow, J. C., J. A. Dick, and E. Pendergast. 1970. Additional records of birds from British Honduras (Belize). *Condor* 72:371–72.

Barlow, J. C., J. A. Dick, D. Weyer, and W. F. Young. 1972. New records of birds from British Honduras (Belize), including a skua. *Condor* 74:486–87.

Barlow, J. C., and R. D. James. 1975. Aspects of the biology of the Chestnut-sided Shrike-Vireo. *Wilson Bull.* 87:320–34.

Barlow, J. C., and S. V. Nash. 1985. Behavior and nesting biology of the St. Andrew Vireo. *Wilson Bull.* 97:265–72.

Bates, J. M. 1993. Winter territorial behavior of Gray Vireos. *Wilson Bull.* 104:425–33.

Bates, J. M., M. C. Garvin, D. C. Schmitt, and C. G. Schmitt. 1989. Notes on bird distribution in northeastern Dpto. Santa Cruz, Bolivia, with 15 species new to Bolivia. *Bull. Brit. Ornithol. Club* 109:236–44.

Bates, J. M., T. A. Parker III, A. P. Capparella, and T. J. Davis. 1992. Observations on the *campo, cerrado* and forest avifaunas of eastern Dpto. Santa Cruz, Bolivia, including 21 species new to the country. *Bull. Brit. Ornithol. Club* 112:86–98.

Beebe, W. 1909. Birds of northeastern Venezuela. *Zoologica* 1: 67–114.

———. 1925. Life history of Variegated Tinamou *C. variegatus*. *Zoologica* 6:195–227.

———. 1947. Avian migration at Rancho Grande in north central Venezuela. *Zoologica* 32:153–68.

———. 1950. Home life of the Bat Falcon, *Falco albigularis albigularis* Daudin. *Zoologica* 35:69–86.

Bege, L. A., and B. T. Pauli. 1990. Two birds new to the Brazilian avifauna. *Bull. Brit. Ornithol. Club* 100:93–94.

Belton, W. 1984. Birds of Rio Grande do Sul, Brazil. Part 1, Rheidae through Furnariidae. *Bull. Am. Mus. Nat. Hist.* 178 (4): 369–631.

———. 1985. Birds of Rio Grande do Sul, Brazil. Part 2, Formicariidae through Corvidae. *Bull. Am. Mus. Nat. Hist.* 180 (1): 1–241.

Benson, R. H., and K. L. P. Benson. 1990. Estimated size of Black-capped Vireo population in northern Coahuila, Mexico. *Condor* 92:777–79.

Berlepsch, H. G. von. 1908. On the birds of Cayenne. *Novit. Zool.* 15:103–64, 261–324.

Berlioz, M.J. 1962. Etude d'une collection d'oiseaux de Guyane française. *Bull. Mus. Nat. Hist. Nat.*, ser. 2, 34:131–43.

Best, B. J., C. T. Clarke, M. Checker, A. L. Bloom, R. M. Thewlis, W. Duckworth, and A. McNab. 1993. Distributional records, natural history notes, and conservation of some poorly known birds from southwestern Ecuador and northwestern Peru. *Bull. Brit. Ornithol. Club* 113:108–19, 234–55.

Binford, L. C. 1989. *A distributional survey of the birds of the Mexican state of Oaxaca*. Ornithol. Monogr., no. 43. Washington, D.C.: American Ornithologists' Union.

Birkenholz, D. E., and D. E. Jenni. 1964. Observations on the Spotted Rail and Pinnated Bittern in Costa Rica. *Auk* 81:558–59.

Blake, E. R. 1950. Birds of the Acary Mts. of southern British Guiana. *Fieldiana Zool.* 32:419–74.

———. 1953. *Birds of Mexico*. Chicago: University of Chicago Press.

———. 1958. Birds of Volcán de Chiriquí, Panama. *Fieldiana Zool.* 36:499–577.

———. 1959. New and rare Colombian birds. *Lozania (Acta Zool. Colomb.)* 11:1–10.

———. 1961. Notes on a collection of birds from northeastern Colombia. *Fieldiana Zool.* 44:25–44.

———. 1962. Birds of the Sierra Macarena, eastern Colombia. *Fieldiana Zool.* 44:69–112.

———. 1968. Family Icteridae. In *Check-list of birds of the world*, ed. R. A. Paynter Jr., 14:138–202. Cambridge, Mass.: Museum of Comparative Zoology.

———. 1971. A new species of spinetail (Synallaxis) from Peru. *Auk* 88:179.

———. 1977. *Manual of Neotropical birds*. Vol. 1. Chicago: University of Chicago Press.

Bleiweiss, R. 1988. Plumage ontogeny and taxonomic status of the Dusky Starfrontlet *Coeligena orina* Wetmore. *Bull. Brit. Ornithol. Club* 108:127–31.

Bleiweiss, R., and M. Ollala P. 1983. Notes on the ecology of the Black-breasted Puffleg on Volcán Pichincha, Ecuador. *Wilson Bull.* 95:656–61.

Blockstein, D. E. 1988. Two endangered birds of Grenada, West Indies: Grenada Dove and Grenada Hook-billed Kite. *Caribbean J. Sci.* 24:127–36.

———. 1991. Population declines of the endangered endemic birds on Grenada, West Indies. *Bird. Conserv. Internat.* 1:83–91.

Blockstein, D. E., and J. W. Hardy. 1989. The Grenada Dove (*Leptotila wellsi*) is a distinct species. *Auk* 106:334–40.

Blokpoel, H., L.-G. Naranjo, and G. D. Tessier. 1984. Immature Little Gull in South America. *Am. Birds* 38:372–73.

Bolster, D. C., and S. K. Robinson. 1990. Habitat use and relative abundance of migrant shorebirds in a western Amazonian site. *Condor* 92:239–42.

Bond, J. 1950. Results of the Cat Lerwood–Chaplin West Indian Expedition, 1948. Part 2, Birds of the Cayo Largo (Cuba), San Andrés and Providencia. *Proc. Acad. Nat. Sci.* 102:43-68.

———. 1965. *Tenth supplement to the check-list of birds of the West Indies*. Philadelphia: Academy of Natural Sciences.

———. 1985. *Birds of the West Indies*. 5th ed. Boston: Houghton Mifflin.

Bond, J., and R. Meyer de Schauensee. 1938. Ecological results of the George Vanderbilt South Pacific Expedition of 1937. Part 2, The birds of Malpelo Island, Colombia. *Proc. Acad. Nat. Sci.* 90: 155–57.

Borrero, J. I. 1947. Aves occasionales en la Sabana de Bogotá y las lagunas de Fúquene y Tota. *Caldasia* 4:495–98.

———. 1952. Algunas aves raras en la Sabana de Bogotá. *Lozania (Acta Zool. Colomb.)* 1:7–12.

———. 1953. Status actual de *Zenaida auriculata* y *Leptotila plumbeiceps* en el Dept. de Caldas y *Cistothorus apolinari* en la región de Bogotá. *Lozania (Acta Zool. Colomb.)* 6:1–6.

———. 1960a. Notas sobre aves de la Amazonia y Ornioquia Colombianas. *Caldasia* 8:485–514.

———. 1960b. Notas sobre *Schizoeaca fuliginosa* y descripción de una nueva subespecie. *Noved. Colomb.* 1:238–42.

———. 1961. Notas sobre aves Colombianas. *Noved. Colomb.* 1: 427–29.

———. 1962. Notas varias sobre *Asio flammeus bogotensis*. *Rev. Biol. Trop.* 10:45–59.

———. 1974. Notes on the structure of the upper eyelid of Potoos (*Nyctibius*). *Condor* 76:210–11.

———. 1975. Notas sobre el comportamiento reproductivo del Colibri *Amazilia tzacatl*. *Ardeola* 21:933–43.

———. 1981. Una nueva ave marina para Colombia: El Petrel del Cabo (*Daption capense*). *Rupicola* 1 (5): 4.

Borrero, J. I., and J. Hernández C. 1958. Apuntas sobre aves Colombianas. *Caldasia* 8:252–94.

———. 1961. Notas sobre aves de Colombia y descripción de una nueva subespecie de *Forpus conspicillatus*. *Noved. Colomb.* 1: 430–45.

Borrero, J. I., A. Olivares, and J. Hernández C. 1962. Notas sobre aves de Colombia. *Caldasia* 8:585–601.

Bourne, G. R. 1974. The Red-billed Toucan in Guyana. *Living Bird* 12:99–126.

Braun, M. J., and D. E. Wolf. 1987. Recent records of vagrant South American land birds in Panama. *Bull. Brit. Ornithol. Club* 107: 115–17.

Brodkorb, P. 1938. Further additions to the avifauna of Paraguay. *Occas. Pap. Mus. Zool. Univ. Mich.* 394:1–5.

Brooke, M. de L. 1988. Distribution and numbers of the Masafuera Rayadito *Aphrastura masafuerae* on Isla Alejandro Selkirk, Juan Fernandez archipelago, Chile. *Bull. Brit. Ornithol. Club* 108: 4–9.

Brown, H. C., and B. L. Monroe Jr. 1974. Bird records from Honduras. *Condor* 76:348–49.

Brown, L., and D. Amadon. 1968. *Eagles, hawks, and falcons of the world*. Vols. 1 and 2. New York: McGraw-Hill.

Brown, R. G., and D. Engleman. 1986. First record of Hudsonian Godwit in Panama. *Am. Birds* 40:429.

——— 1988. First record of American Avocet from the Republic of Panama. *Am. Birds* 42:28.

Browning, M. R. 1989a. The correct citation and spelling of *Ptiliogonys* and type locality of *Ptiliogonys cinereus*. *Auk* 106:743–46.

———. 1989b. The correct name for the Olivaceous Cormorant, "Maigue" of Piso (1658). *Wilson Bull.* 101:101–6.

Buchanan, M. 1971. *Ciccaba virgata* in Trinidad. *Ibis* 113:105–6.

Buden, D. W. 1987. *The birds of the southern Bahamas*. London: British Ornithologists' Union.

Burton, J.A. 1973. *Owls of the world.* New York: E. P. Dutton.

Butler, T. Y. 1979. *The birds of Ecuador and the Galápagos archipelago.* Portsmouth, N.H.: Ramphastos Agency.

Caballero M., L. A., A. Wilinski, and A. E. Seijas. 1984. Una nueva especie de *Rallus* (Gruiformes: Rallidae) para Venezuela. *Boll. Soc. Venez. Cienc. Nat.* 39 (142): 107–10.

Cabot, J. 1990. First record of *Upucerthia validirostris* from Bolivia and new Bolivian distributional data. *Bull. Brit. Ornithol. Club* 110:103–7.

Cabot, J., J. Castroviejo, and V. Urios. 1988. Cuatro nuevas especies de aves para Bolivia. *Donaña Acta Vert.* 15:235–38.

Cabot, J., and P. Serrano. 1988. Distributional data on some non-passerine species in Bolivia. *Bull. Brit. Ornithol. Club* 108: 187–93.

Camargo, H. F. de A., and E. A. Camargo. 1964. Ocorrência de *Iopopleura p. pipra* no estado de São Paulo, Brasil, e algumas notas sôbre *Iodopleura isabellae* (Aves, Cotingidae). *Pap. Avul. Zool.* (São Paulo) 16:45–55.

Capparella, A. P. 1986. First record of Yellow-collared Chlorophonia for Middle America. *Am. Birds* 40:194–95.

Cardiff, S. W. 1983. Three new bird species for Peru, with other distributional records from northern Departamento de Loreto. *Gerfaut* 73: 185–92.

Carriker, M. A., Jr. 1910. An annotated list of the birds of Costa Rica, including Cocos Island. *Ann. Carnegie Mus.* 6:314–915.

———. 1954. Additions to the avifauna of Colombia. *Noved. Colomb.* 1:14–19.

———. 1955. Notes on the occurrence and distribution of certain species of Colombian birds. *Noved. Colomb.* 2:48–64.

———. 1959. New records of rare birds from Nariño and Cauca and notes on others. *Noved. Colomb.* 1:196–99.

Castellanos, A., and R. Rodriguez-Estrella. 1993. Current status of the Socorro Mockingbird. *Wilson Bull.* 105:167–71.

Castro, G., and J. P. Myers. 1988. Snowy Plover (*Charadrius alexandrinus*) records from Panama. *Am. Birds* 42:374.

Chapman, F. M. 1917. The distribution of bird life in Colombia. *Bull. Am. Mus. Nat. Hist.* 36:1–169.

———. 1923. The distribution of the motmots of the genus *Momotus. Bull. Am. Mus. Nat. Hist.* 48:26–59.

———. 1925. Remarks on the life zones of northeastern Venezuela with descriptions of new species of birds. *Am. Mus. Novit.,* no. 191.

———. 1926. The distribution of birdlife in Ecuador. *Bull. Am. Mus. Nat. Hist.* 55.

———. 1927. Description of new birds from northwestern Peru and western Colombia. *Am. Mus. Novit.,* no. 250.

———. 1928. The nesting habits of Wagler's Oropendola (*Zarhynchus wagleri*) on Barro Colorado Island, Canal Zone. *Bull. Am. Mus. Nat. Hist.* 58:123–66.

———. 1939. The riddle of *Oxyruncus. Am. Mus. Nov.,* no. 1047.

Chebez, J. C. 1991. Nuevas registros de aguilas crestadas en el noroeste argentino. *Nuestras Aves,* no. 20:6–7.

Chebez, J. C., H. Casanas, and S. Chichizola. 1984. Nueva cita de *Ramphocelus bresilius* (Linné) (Thraupidae) para la Argentina. *Hornero* 12:221–22.

Chebez, J. C., S. Heinonen, and A. Bosso. 1988. Nidificación del atajacaminos oscuro (*Caprimulgus seicocausatus*) en Misiones, Argentina. *Hornero* 13:90–91.

Cherrie, G. K. 1916. A contribution to the ornithology of the Orinoco region. *Brooklyn Inst. Arts and Sci. Mus. Bull.* 2:133–374.

Chipley, R. M. 1976. The impact of migrant warblers on resident passerines in a subtropical Colombian woodland. *Living Bird* 15: 119–41.

Chubb, C. 1910. On the birds of Paraguay. *Ibis,* ser. 9, 4:53–78, 263–85, 517–34, 571–647.

Clark, G. S., A. J. Goodwin, and A. P. von Meyer. 1984. Extension of the known range of some seabirds on the coast of southern Chile. *Notornis* 31:320–24.

Clark, W. S. and R. C. Banks. 1992. The taxonomic status of the White-tailed Kite. *Wilson Bull.* 104:571–79.

Coats, S., and W. H. Phelps. 1985. The Venezuelan Red Siskin: Case history of an endangered species. In *Neotropical ornithology,* ed. P. A. Buckley, M. S. Foster, E. S. Morton, R. S. Ridgely, and F. G. Buckley, 977–85. Ornithol. Monogr., no. 36. Washington, D.C.: American Ornithologists' Union.

Cohn-Haft, M. 1993. Rediscovery of the White-winged Potoo (*Nyctibius leucopterus*). *Auk* 110:391–94.

Collar, N. J., and P. Andrew. 1988. *Birds to watch: The ICBP world checklist of threatened birds.* ICBP Tech. Pub. no. 8. Cambridge: International Council for Bird Preservation.

Collar, N. J., L. P. Gonzaga, N. Krabbe, A. Madroño Nieto, L. G. Naranjo, T. A. Parker III, and D. C. Wege. 1992. *Threatened birds of the Americas: The ICBP/IUCN red data book.* Part 2. Cambridge: International Council for Bird Preservation and International Union for Conservation of Nature and Natural Resources.

Collins, C. T. 1968. Notes on the biology of Chapman's Swift *Chaetura chapmani. Am. Mus. Novit.,* no. 2320.

Colon, H. E. 1982. A record of the Black Duck—*Anas rubripes* in Puerto Rico. *Caribbean J. Sci.* 17:5–6.

Conover, H. B. 1934. A new species of rail from Paraguay. *Auk* 51: 365–66.

Cottrell, G. W. 1968. The genera of puffbirds (*Bucconidae*). *Breviora* 285:1–5.

Coulter, M. C. 1984. Seabird conservation in the Galápagos Islands, Ecuador. In *Status and conservation of the world's seabirds,* ed. J. P. Croxall, P. G. H. Evans, and R. W. Schreiber, 237–44. ICBP Tech. Pub. no. 2. Cambridge: International Council for Bird Preservation.

Coulter, M. C., F. Cruz, and T. Cruz. 1985. A programme to save the Dark-rumped Petrel, *Pterodroma phaeopygia,* on Floreana Island, Galápagos, Ecuador. In *Conservation of island birds: Case studies for the management of threatened species,* ed. P. J. Moors, 177–80. ICBP Tech. Pub. no. 3. Cambridge: International Council for Bird Preservation.

Cracraft, J. 1985. Historical biogeography and patterns of differentiation within the South American avifauna: Areas of endemism. In *Neotropical ornithology,* ed. P. A. Buckley, M. S. Foster, E. S. Morton, R. S. Ridgely, and F. G. Buckley, 49–84. Ornithol. Monogr., no. 36. Washington, D.C.: American Ornithologists' Union.

Crossin, R. S. 1967. The breeding biology of the Tufted Jay. *Proc. West. Found. Vert. Zool.* 1:265–300.

Croxall, J. P., S. MacInnes, and P. A. Prince. 1984. The status and conservation of seabirds at the Falkland Islands. In *Status and conservation of the world's seabirds,* ed. J. P. Croxall, P. G. H. Evans, and R. W. Schreiber, 271–91. ICBP Tech. Pub. no. 2. Cambridge: International Council for Bird Preservation.

Cruz, A., and C. A. Delannoy. 1984a. Ecology of the Elfin Woods Warbler (*Dendroica angelae*). 1. Distribution, habitat, and population densities. *Caribbean J. Sci.* 20:89–96.

———. 1984b. Ecology of the Elfin Woods Warbler (*Dendroica angelae*). 2. Feeding ecology of the Elfin Woods Warbler and associated insectivorous birds in Puerto Rico. *Caribbean J. Sci.* 20: 153–62.

Cruz, A., T. Manolis, and J. W. Wiley. 1985. The Shiny Cowbird: A brood parasite expanding its range in the Caribbean region. In *Neotropical ornithology,* ed. P. A. Buckley, M. S. Foster, E. S. Morton, R. S. Ridgely, and F. G. Buckley, 607–20. Ornithol. Monogr., no. 36. Washington, D.C.: American Ornithologists' Union.

Cuello, J. P. 1985. Lista de referencia y bibliografía de las aves uruguayas. *Museo Damaso Antorico Larrañaga, Serie de Divulgación,* no. 1.

Cuello, J. P., and E. Gerzenstein. 1962. Las aves del Uruguay: Lista sistemática, distribución y notas. *Com. Zool. Mus. Nat. Hist. Montevideo* 6, no. 93.

Darlington, P. J., Jr. 1931. Notes on the birds of the Río Frío (near Santa Marta), Magdalena, Colombia. *Bull. Mus. Comp. Zool.* 71: 349–421.

Davis, S. E. 1989. Migration of the Mississippi Kite *Ictinia mississippiensis* in Bolivia, with comments on *I. plumbea. Bull. Brit. Ornithol. Club* 109:149–52.

———. 1993. Seasonal status, relative abundance, and behavior of the birds of Concepción, Departamento Santa Cruz, Bolivia. *Fieldiana Zool.*, n.s., no. 71.

Davis, S. E., and E. Flores. 1994. First record of White-winged Nightjar *Caprimulgus candicans* for Bolivia. *Bull. Brit. Ornithol. Club* 114:127–28.

Davis, S. E., O. Rocha O., J. Sarmiento, and W. Hanagarth. 1994. New departmental records and notes for some Bolivian birds. *Bull. Brit. Ornithol. Club* 114:73–85.

Davis, T. A. W. 1935. Some nesting notes from the savannas of the Rupununi district, British Guiana. *Ibis,* ser. 13, 5:530–37.

———. 1949a. Field notes on the Orange-crested Manakin *Neopelma chrysocephalum. Ibis* 91:349–50.

———. 1949b. Display of the White-throated Manakin *Corapipo gutturalis. Ibis* 91:146–47.

Davis, T. H. 1979. Additions to *The birds of Surinam. Continental Birdlife* 1:136–46.

Davis, T. J. 1986. Distribution and natural history of some birds from the Departments of San Martín and Amazonas, northern Peru. *Condor* 88:50–56.

Davis, T. J., and J. P. O'Neill. 1986. A new species of antwren (Formicariidae: *Herpsilochmus*) from Peru, with comments on the systematics of other members of the genus. *Wilson Bull.* 98: 337–52.

Delacour, J., and D. Amadon. 1973. *Curassows and related birds.* New York: American Museum of Natural History.

Devillers, P. 1979. Un goéland brun (*Larus fuscus*) en Guyane française. *Gerfaut* 69:79–80.

Devillers, P., and J. A. Terschuren. 1978a. Midsummer seabird distribution in the Chilean fjords. *Gerfaut* 68:577–88.

———. 1978b. Relationships between the blue-eyed shags of South America. *Gerfaut* 68:53–86.

Dick, J. A. 1991. Grey-tailed Piha in Colombia. *Bull. Brit. Ornithol. Club* 111:172–73.

Dick, J. A., and J. C. Barlow. 1972. The Bran-colored Flycatcher in Guyana. *Condor* 74:101.

———. 1977. L'hirondelle à cuisse blanche en Guyane française. *Oiseau* 47:303.

Dick, J. A., W. B. McGilliuray, and D. J. Brooks. 1984. A list of birds and their weights from Saul, French Guiana. *Wilson Bull.* 96: 347–65.

Dickerman, R. W. 1971. Notes on various rails in Mexico. *Wilson Bull.* 83:49–56.

———. 1975. Nine new specimen records for Guatemala. *Wilson Bull.* 87:412–13.

———. 1977. Three more specimen records for Guatemala. *Wilson Bull.* 89:612–13.

Dickerman, R. W., G. F. Barrowclough, P. F. Cannell, W. H. Phelps Jr., and D. E. Willard. 1986. *Philydor hylobius* Wetmore and Phelps is a synonym of *Automolus roraimae* Hellmayr. *Auk* 103: 431–32.

Dickerman, R. W., A. R. Phillips, and D. W. Warner. 1967. On the Sierra Madre Sparrow, *Xenospiza baileyi,* of Mexico. *Auk* 84: 49–60.

Dickey, D. R., and A. J. van Rossem. 1938. The birds of El Salvador. *Fieldiana Zool.* 23:1–609.

Dod, A. S. 1980. First records of the Spotted Rail (*Pardirallus maculatus*) on the Island of Hispaniola. *Auk* 97:407.

———. 1986. Hispaniola's first Black Rail (*Laterallus jamaicensis*). *Am. Birds* 40:196.

Donahue, P. K. 1985. Notes on some little known or previously unrecorded birds of Surinam. *Am. Birds* 39:229–30.

Dott, H. E. M. 1985. North American migrants in Bolivia. *Condor* 87:343–45.

Duffy, D.C., C. Hays, and M. A. Plenge. 1984. The conservation status of Peruvian seabirds. In *Status and conservation of the world's seabirds,* ed. J. P. Croxall, P. G. H. Evans, and R. W. Schreiber, 245–59. ICBP Tech. Pub. no. 2. Cambridge: International Council for Bird Preservation.

Dujardin, J.-L., and O. Tostain. 1985. Distribution et effectifs d'oiseaux d'eau sur le littoral guyanais. *Alauda* 53:287–94.

———. 1986. Trois Procellaris formes nouveaux en Guyane. *Oiseau* 55:253–54.

Dunlap, E. 1988. Laysan Albatross nesting on Guadalupe Island, Mexico. *Am. Birds* 42:180–81.

Edwards, E. P. 1959. Nesting of the Lesser Swallow-tailed Swift, *Panyptila cayennensis,* in Guatemala. *Auk* 76:358–59.

———. 1989. *A field guide to the birds of Mexico.* 2d ed. Sweet Briar, Va.: E. P. Edwards.

Eisenmann, E. 1955. The species of birds of Middle America. *Trans. Linn. Soc. N.Y.* 7:1–128.

———. 1971. Range expansion and population increase in North and Middle America of the White-tailed Kite (*Elanus leucurus*). *Am. Birds* 25:529–36.

Eisenmann, E., and F. Haverschmidt. 1970. Northward migration to Surinam of South American martins (*Progne*). *Condor* 72: 368–69.

Eisenmann, E., and L. L. Short. 1982. Systematics of the avian genus *Emberizoides* (Emberizidae). *Am. Mus. Novit.,* no. 2740.

Eley, J. W. 1982. Systematic relationships and zoogeography of the White-winged Guan (*Penelope albipennis*) and related forms. *Wilson Bull.* 94:241–59.

Eley, J. W., G. R. Graves, T. A. Parker III, and D. Hunter. 1979. Notes on *Siptornis striaticollis* (Furnariidae) in Peru. *Condor* 81:319.

Ellis, D. H., and C. P. Garat. 1983. The Pallid Falcon *Falco kreyenborgi* is a color phase of the austral Peregrine Falcon (*Falco peregrinus cassini*). *Auk* 100:26–71.

Ellis, D. H., and W. H. Whaley. 1981. Three Crested Eagle records for Guatemala. *Wilson Bull.* 93:284–85.

Erickson, R. 1977. First record of the Knot *Calidris canutus,* and other records, from Belize (British Honduras). *Bull. Brit. Ornithol. Club* 97:78–81.

Escalante, R. 1980. Primera denuncia de un petrel de Kerguelen colectado sobre la Costa Atlantica de Sudamerica. *Hornero* 12: 41–44.

Escalante-Pliego, P., and A. T. Peterson. 1992. Geographic variation and species limits in Middle American woodnymphs (*Thalurania*). *Wilson Bull.* 104:205–19.

Everett, W. T., and D. W. Anderson. 1991. Status and conservation of the breeding seabirds on offshore Pacific islands of Baja California and the Gulf of California. In *Seabird status and conservation: A supplement,* ed. J. P. Croxall, 115–39. ICBP Tech. Pub. no. 11. Cambridge: International Council for Bird Preservation.

Faanes, C. A., and J. C. Haney. 1989. First record of Kirtland's Warbler from the Dominican Republic, and additional bird observations. *Caribbean J. Sci.* 25:30–35.

Faanes, C. A., and S. E. Senner. 1991. Status and conservation of the Eskimo Curlew. *Am. Birds* 45:237–39.

ffrench, R. 1980. *A guide to the birds of Trinidad and Tobago.* Newtown Square, Pa.: Harrowwood Books.

———. 1985. Changes in the avifauna of Trinidad. In *Neotropical ornithology,* ed. P. A. Buckley, M. S. Foster, E. S. Morton, R. S. Ridgely, and F. G. Buckley, 986–91. Ornithol. Monogr., no. 36. Washington, D.C.: American Ornithologists' Union.

———. 1991. *A guide to the birds of Trinidad and Tobago.* 2d ed. Ithaca: Cornell University Press.

Finch, D. W. 1991. Novedades ornitologicas argentinas. *Nuestras Aves,* no. 24:24–25.

Fisher, D. J. 1978. First record of Black-headed Gull *Larus ridibundus* and third record of Herring Gull *Larus argentatus* for South America. *Bull. Brit. Ornithol. Club* 98:113.

Fitzpatrick, J. W. 1976. Systematics and biogeography of the tyrannid genus *Todirostrum* and related genera (Aves). *Bull. Mus. Comp. Zool.* 147:435–63.

———. 1980a. A new race of *Atlapetes leucopterus,* with comments on widespread albinism in *A. l. dresseri* (Taczanowski). *Auk* 97: 883–87.

———. 1980b. Wintering of North American tyrant flycatchers in the Neotropics. In *Migrant birds of the Neotropics: Ecology, behavior, distribution and conservation,* ed. A. Keast and E. S. Morton, 67–78. Washington, D.C.: Smithsonian Institution Press.

Fitzpatrick, J. W., and J. P. O'Neill. 1979. A new tody-tyrant from northern Peru. *Auk* 96:443–47.

———. 1986. *Otus petersoni,* a new screech-owl from the eastern Andes, with systematic notes on *O. colombianus* and *O. ingens. Wilson Bull.* 98:1–14.

Fitzpatrick, J. W., and D. E. Willard. 1982. Twenty-one bird species new or little-known from the Republic of Colombia. *Bull. Brit. Ornithol. Club* 102:153–58.

———. 1990. *Cercomacra manu,* a new species of antbird from southwestern Amazonia. *Auk* 107:239–45.

Fjeldså, J. 1981a. Biological notes on the Giant Coot (*Fulica gigantea*). *Ibis* 123:423–37.

———. 1981b. *Podiceps taczanowskii* (Aves, Podicipedidae), theendemic grebe of Lake Junín, Peru: A review. *Steenstrupia* 7:237–59.

———. 1982. Biology and systematic relations of the Andean Coot "*Fulica americana ardesiaca*" (Aves, Rallidae). *Steenstrupia* 8: 1–21.

———. 1983a. A Black Rail from Junin, central Peru: *Laterallus jamaicensis tuerosi* ssp. n. (Aves, Rallidae). *Steenstrupia* 8:277–82.

———. 1983b. Geographic variation in the Andean Coot, *Fulica ardesiaca. Bull. Brit. Ornithol. Club* 103:18–22.

———. 1985. Origin, evolution, and status of the avifauna of Andean wetlands. In *Neotropical ornithology,* ed. P. A. Buckley, M. S. Foster, E. S. Morton, R. S. Ridgely, and F. G. Buckley, 85–112. Ornithol. Monogr., no. 36. Washington, D.C.: American Ornithologists' Union.

———. 1987. *Birds of relict forests in the high Andes of Peru and Bolivia.* Copenhagen: Zoological Museum, University of Copenhagen.

Fjeldså, J., and N. Krabbe. 1986. Some range extensions and other unusual records of Andean birds. *Bull. Brit. Ornithol. Club* 106: 115–24.

———. 1990. *Birds of the high Andes.* Copenhagen: Zoological Museum, University of Copenhagen; Svenborg: Apollo Books.

Fjeldså, J., N. Krabbe, and T. A. Parker. 1987. Rediscovery of *Cinclodes excelsior aricomae* and notes on the nominate race. *Bull. Brit. Ornithol. Club* 107:112–14.

Forrester, B. C. 1993. *Birding Brazil: A check-list and site guide.* Rankinston, Ayrshire: B. C. Forrester.

Forshaw, J. M. 1973. *Parrots of the world.* Melbourne: Lansdowne Press.

Friedmann, H., L. Griscom, and R. T. Moore. 1950. *Distributional checklist of the birds of Mexico.* Part 1. Pacific Coast Avifauna, no. 29. Columbus, Ohio: Cooper Ornithological Society.

Garrido, O. H. 1984. *Molothrus bonariensis* (Aves: Icteridae), nuevo record para Cuba. *Misc. Zool. Habana,* no. 19:2–3.

———. 1985. Cuban endangered birds. In *Neotropical ornithology,* ed. P. A. Buckley, M. S. Foster, E. S. Morton, R. S. Ridgely, and F. G. Buckley, 992–99. Ornithol. Monogr., no. 36. Washington, D.C.: American Ornithologists' Union.

Garrido, O. H., and F. García-Montaña. 1975. *Catálogo de las aves de Cuba.* Havana: Academia de Ciencias de Cuba.

Gochfeld, M., J. Burger, J. Saliva, and D. Gochfeld. 1988. Herald Petrel new to the West Indies. *Am. Birds* 42:1254–58.

Gonzaga, L. P. 1983. Notas sôbre *Dacnis nigripes* Pelzeln, 1856 (Aves, Coerebidae). *Iheringia (Zool.)* 63:45–58.

———. 1988. A new antwren (*Myrmotherula*) from southeastern Brazil. *Bull. Brit. Ornithol. Club* 108:132–35.

Gonzaga, L. P., and J. F. Pacheco. 1990. Two new subspecies of *Formicivora serrana* (Hellmayr) from southeastern Brazil, and notes on the type locality of *Formicivora deluzae* Ménétriès. *Bull. Brit. Ornithol. Club* 110:187–93.

Goodall, J. D., A. W. Johnson, and R. A. Philippi. 1951. *Las aves de Chile, su conocimiento y sus costumbres,* 2. Buenos Aires: Platt Establecimientos Gráficos.

Goodwin, D. 1976. *Crows of the world.* London: British Museum.

———. 1983. *Pigeons and doves of the world.* 3d ed. Ithaca: Cornell University Press.

Gore, M. E. J., and A. R. M. Gepp. 1978. *Las aves del Uruguay.* Montevideo: Mosca Hermanos,

Graham, D. J. 1984. A sighting of a Black-legged Kittiwake in Saint Lucia. *Am. Birds* 38:256.

Graham, G. L., G. R. Graves, T. S. Schulenberg, and J. P. O'Neill. 1980. Seventeen bird species new to Peru from the Pampas de Heath. *Auk* 97:366–70.

Grantsau, R. 1989. *Os Beija-flores do Brasil.* Rio de Janeiro: Expressão e Cultura.

Grantsau, R., and H. F. de A. Camargo. 1989. Nova espécie brasileira de *Amazona* (Aves, Psittacidae). *Rev. Bras. Biol.* 49: 1017–20.

Graves, G. R. 1980. A new species of metaltail hummingbird from northern Peru. *Wilson Bull.* 92:1–7.

———. 1982. Speciation in the Carbonated Flower-piercer (*Diglossa carbonaria*) complex of the Andes. *Condor* 84:1–14.

———. 1985. Elevational correlates of speciation and intraspecific geographical variation in plumage in Andean forest birds. *Auk* 102:556–79.

———. 1986. The systematic status of *Cranioleuca furcata* Taczanowski (Furnariidae). *Condor* 88:120–22.

———. 1987. A cryptic new species of Antipitta (Formicariidae: *Grallaria*) from the Peruvian Andes. *Wilson Bull.* 99:313–21.

———. 1988. *Phylloscartes lanyoni,* a new species of bristle-tyrant (Tyrannidae) from the lower Cauca Valley of Colombia. *Wilson Bull.* 100:529–34.

———. 1993. Relic of a lost world: A new species of sunangel (Trochilidae: *Heliangelus*) from "Bogotá." *Auk* 110:1–8.

Graves, G. R., and J. A. Giraldo O. 1987. Population status of the Rufous-fronted Parakeet (*Bolborhynchus ferrugineifrons*), a Colombian endemic. *Gerfaut* 77:89–92.

Graves, G. R., J. P. O'Neill, and T. A. Parker III. 1983. *Grallaricula ochraceifrons,* a new species of antpitta from northern Peru. *Wilson Bull.* 95:1–6.

Graves, G. R., and M. A. Plenge. 1978. First record of Curlew Sandpiper in Peru. *Condor* 80:455.

Graves, G. R., and D. Uribe Restrepo. 1989. A new allopatric taxon in the *Hapalopsittaca amazonica* (Psittacidae) superspecies from Colombia. *Wilson Bull.* 101:369–76.

Graves, G. R., and J. S. Weske. 1987. *Tangara phillipsi,* a new species of tanager from the Cerros del Sira, eastern Peru. *Wilson Bull.* 99: 1–6.

Greenwood, J. G. 1983. Dunlin *Calidris alpina* in South America. *Bull. Brit. Ornithol. Club* 103:110–11.

Gregory, P. Notes on new and scarce birds in the Falkland Islands, 1988–1990. *Bull. Brit. Ornithol. Club* 114:12–20.

Greissl, R. 1974. *Burhinus* eu Arica. *Idesia* 3:215–16.

Griscom, L., and J. C. Greenway Jr. 1941. Birds of lower Amazonia. *Bull. Mus. Comp. Zool.* 88:85–334.

Grzybowski, J. A., R. B. Clapp, and J. T. Marshall. 1986. History and current population status of the Black-capped Vireo in Oklahoma. *Am. Birds* 40:1151–61.

Gyldenstolpe, N. 1945a. The bird fauna of Rio Juruá in western Brazil. *Kungl. Sven. Vet. Apsak. Handl.*, ser. 3, 22 (3): 1–338.

———. 1945b. A contribution to the ornithology of northern Bolivia. *Kungl. Sven. Vet. Akad. Handl.*, ser. 3, 23 (1): 1–300.

———. 1951. The ornithology of the Rio Purus region in western Brazil. *Ark. Zool.* 2 (2): 1–320.

Haffer, J. 1967a. Speciation in Colombian forest birds west of the Andes. *Am. Mus. Novit.*, no. 2294.

———. 1967b. Some allopatric species pairs of birds in northwestern Colombia. *Auk* 84:343–65.

———. 1974. *Avian speciation in tropical South America.* Publ. Nuttall Ornithol. Club, no. 14, Cambridge, Mass.: Nuttall Ornithological Club.

———. 1985. Avian zoogeography of the Neotropical lowlands. In *Neotropical ornithology,* ed. P. A. Buckley, M. S. Foster, E. S. Morton, R. S. Ridgely, and F. G. Buckley, 113–46. Ornithol. Monogr., no. 36. Washington, D.C.: American Ornithologists' Union.

Hanagarth, W., and J. Sarmiento. 1988. *Egretta caerulea* Linnaeus 1758 (Ardeidae), una nueva especie para Bolivia. *Ecol. Bolivia* 12: 9–12.

Haney, C. 1983. First sight record of Orange-breasted Falcon for Belize. *Wilson Bull.* 95:314–15.

Harris, M. P. 1974. A complete census of the Flightless Cormorant (*Nannopterum harrisi*) *Biol. Conserv.* 6:188–91.

———. 1982. *A field guide to the birds of Galápagos.* London: Collins.

Harrison, P. 1983. *Seabirds: An identification guide.* Beckenham, Kent: Croom Helm.

Haverschmidt, F. 1968. *Birds of Surinam.* Edinburgh: Oliver and Boyd.

———. 1972. Bird records from Surinam. *Bull. Brit. Ornithol. Club* 92:49–53.

———. 1974. The occurrence of the Giant Snipe *Gallinago undulatus* in Surinam. *Bull. Brit. Ornithol. Club* 92:49–53.

———. 1975. More bird records from Surinam. *Bull. Brit. Ornithol. Club* 95:74–77.

———. 1983. First record of the Little Egret (*Egretta garzetta*) in Suriname. *Wilson Bull.* 95:315.

Hayes, F. E., S. M. Goodman, J. A. Fox, T. Granizo Tamayo, and N. E. López. 1990. North American bird migrants in Paraguay. *Condor* 92:947–60.

Hayes, F. E., S. M. Goodman, and N. E. López. 1990. New or noteworthy bird records from the Matogrosense region of Paraguay. *Bull. Brit. Ornithol. Club* 110:94–103.

Hays, C. 1984. The Humboldt Penguin in Peru. *Oryx* 18:92–95.

Heath, M., and A. Long. 1991. Habitat, distribution and status of the Azure-rumped Tanager *Tangara cabanisi* in Mexico. *Bird Conserv. Internat.* 1:223–54.

Heinonen, S., and J. C. Chebez. 1988. Registro ocular del playerito menor (*Calidris minutilla* Charadriiformes, Scolopacidae) en Uruguay. *Hornero* 13:83–84.

Hellmayr, C. E. 1906. Revision der Spix'schen Typen brasilianischer Vögel. *Abhandl. Königl. Bayer. Akad. Wissensch.* 22 (3): 561–726.

———. 1910. The birds of the Rio Madeira. *Novit. Zool.* 17: 257–428.

———. 1925. Catalogue of the birds of the Americas. Part 4. *Field Mus. Nat. Hist., Zool. Ser.,* vol. 13.

———. 1927. Catalogue of the birds of the Americas. Part 5. *Field Mus. Nat. Hist., Zool. Ser.,* vol. 13.

———. 1929a. A contribution to the ornithology of north-eastern Brazil. *Field Mus. Nat. Hist., Zool. Ser.* 12:235–501.

———. 1929b. Catalogue of the birds of the Americas. Part 7. *Field Mus. Nat. Hist., Zool. Ser.,* vol. 13.

Hellmayr, C. E., and B. Conover 1942. Catalogue of the birds of the Americas. Part 1, no. 1. *Field Mus. Nat. Hist., Zool. Ser.,* vol. 13.

Hilty, S. L. 1974. Notes on birds at swarms of army ants in the highlands of Colombia. *Wilson Bull.* 86:479–81.

———. 1977. *Chlorospingus flavovirens* rediscovered, with notes on other Pacific Colombian and Cauca Valley birds. *Auk* 94: 44–49.

———. 1985. Distributional changes in the Colombian avifauna: A preliminary blue list. In *Neotropical ornithology,* ed. P. A. Buckley, M. S. Foster, E. S. Morton, R. S. Ridgely, and F. G. Buckley, 1000–1012. Ornithol. Monogr., no. 36. Washington, D.C.: American Ornithologists' Union.

Hilty, S. L., and W. L. Brown. 1986. *A guide to the birds of Colombia.* Princeton: Princeton University Press.

Hilty, S. L., and D. Simon. 1977. The Azure-rumped Tanager in Mexico with comparative remarks on the Gray-and-gold Tanager. *Auk* 94:605–6.

Hinkelmann, C. 1988a. On the identity of *Phaethornis maranhaoensis* Grantsau, 1968 (Trochilidae). *Bull. Brit. Ornithol. Club* 108: 14–18.

———. 1988b. Comments on recently described new species of hermit hummingbirds. *Bull. Brit. Ornithol. Club* 108:159–69.

Howell, S. N. G., and B. M. de Montes. 1989. Status of the Glossy Ibis in Mexico. *Am. Birds* 43:43–45.

Howell, S. N. G., B. A. Dowell, D. A. James, R. A. Behrstock, and C. S. Robbins. 1992. New and noteworthy bird records from Belize. *Bull. Brit. Ornithol. Club* 112:235–44.

Howell, S. N. G., and S. J. Engel. 1993. Seabird observations off western Mexico. *Western Birds* 24:167–81.

Howell, S. N. G., and S. Webb. 1989a. Notes on the Honduran Emerald. *Wilson Bull.* 101:642–43.

———. 1989b. Additional notes from Isla Clarión, Mexico. *Condor* 91:1001–8.

———. 1990. The seabirds of Las Islas Revillagigego, Mexico. *Wilson Bull.* 102:140–46.

———. 1992a. New and noteworthy bird records from Guatemala and Honduras. *Bull. Brit. Ornithol. Club* 112:42–49.

———. 1992b. Noteworthy bird observations from Baja California, Mexico. *Western Birds* 23:153–63.

———. 1995. *A guide to the birds of Mexico and northern Central America.* Oxford: Oxford University Press.

Howell, T. R., R. A. Paynter Jr., and A. L. Rand. 1968. Subfamily Carduelinae. In *Check-list of birds of the world,* ed. R. A. Paynter Jr., 14:207–306. Cambridge, Mass.: Museum of Comparative Zoology.

Hughes, R. A. 1980. Additional puna zone bird species on the coast of Peru. *Condor* 82:475.

———. 1982. Broad-billed Prion at Mollendo, Peru: First record for the Pacific Coast of South America. *Condor* 84:130.

———. 1984. Further notes on puna bird species on the coast of Peru. *Condor* 86:93.

———. 1988. Nearctic migrants in southwest Peru. *Bull. Brit. Ornithol. Club* 108:29–43.

Humphrey, P. S., D. Bridge, P. W. Reynolds, and R. T. Peterson. 1970. *Birds of Isla Grande (Tierra del Fuego).* Lawrence: University of Kansas Museum of Natural History.

Humphrey, P. S., and M. C. Thompson. 1981. A new species of steamer-duck (*Tachyeres*) from Argentina. *Occ. Paper Mus. Nat. Hist. Univ. Kans.,* no. 95.

Hunter, L. A. 1988. Status of the endemic Atitlán Grebe of Guatemala: Is it extinct? *Condor* 90:906–12.

Imber, M. J. 1985. Origins, phylogeny and taxonomy of the gadfly-petrels *Pterodroma* spp. *Ibis* 127:197–229.

Ingels, J., K. C. Parkes, and J. Farrand Jr. 1981. The status of the macaw generally but incorrectly called *Ara caninde* (Wagler). *Gerfaut* 71:283–94.

Isler, M. L., and P. R. Isler. 1987. *The tanagers: Natural history, dis-*

tribution, and identification. Washington, D.C:. Smithsonian Institution Press.

Jehl, J. R., Jr. 1973. The distribution of marine birds in Chilean waters in winter. *Auk* 90:114–35.

———. 1974. The near-shore avifauna of the Middle American west coast. *Auk* 91:681–99.

———. 1975. *Pluvianellus socialis*: Biology, ecology and relationships of an enigmatic Patagonian shorebird. *Trans. San Diego Soc. Nat. Hist.* 18:25–74.

———. 1982. The biology and taxonomy of Townsend's Shearwater. *Gerfaut* 72:121–35.

Jehl, J. R., Jr., and W. T. Everett. 1985. History and status of the avifauna of Isla Guadalupe, Mexico. *Trans. San Diego Soc. Nat. Hist.* 20:313–36.

Jehl, J. R., Jr., and K. C. Parkes. 1982. The status of the avifauna of the Revillagigedo Islands, Mexico. *Wilson Bull.* 94:1–19.

Jenny, J. P., F. Ortiz, and M. D. Arnold. 1981. First nesting record of the Peregrine Falcon in Ecuador. *Condor* 83:387.

Johnson, A. W. 1965. *The birds of Chile and adjacent regions of Argentina, Bolivia and Peru.* Vol. 1. Buenos Aires: Platt Establecimientos Gráficos.

———. 1967. *The birds of Chile and adjacent regions of Argentina, Bolivia and Peru.* Vol. 2. Buenos Aires: Platt Establecimientos Gráficos.

———. 1972. *Supplement to "The birds of Chile and adjacent regions of Argentina, Bolivia and Peru," vol. 2.* Buenos Aires: Platt Establecimientos Gráficos.

Johnson, N. K. 1980. Character variation and evolution of sibling species in the *Empidonax difficilis–flavescens* complex (Aves: Tyrannidae). *Univ. Calif. Publs. Zool.* 112:1–151.

Johnson, N. K., and C. B. Johnson. 1985. Speciation in sapsuckers (*Sphyrapicus*): II. Sympatry, hybridization, and mate preference in *S. ruber dagetti* and *S. nuchalis. Auk* 102:1–15.

Johnson, N. K., and J. A. Marten. 1988. Evolutionary genetics of flycatchers: II. Differentiation in the *Empidonax difficilis* group. *Auk* 105:177–91.

Johnson, N. K., and R. M. Zink. 1985. Genetic evidence for relationships among the Red-eyed, Yellow-green, and Chivi Vireos. *Wilson Bull.* 97:421–35.

Jordan, O. C., and C. A. Munn. 1993. First observations of the Blue-throated Macaw in Bolivia. *Wilson Bull.* 105:694–95.

Kepler, C. B., and A. K. Kepler. 1973. The distribution and ecology of the Puerto Rican Whip-poor-will, an endangered species. *Living Bird* 11:207–39.

Kepler, C. B., and K. C. Parkes. 1972. A new species of warbler (Parulidae) from Puerto Rico. *Auk* 89:1–18.

King, J. R. 1989. Notes on the birds of the Rio Mazan Valley, Azuay Province, Ecuador, with special reference to *Leptopsittaca branickii, Hapalopsittaca amazonica pyrrhops,* and *Metallura baroni. Bull. Brit. Ornithol. Club* 109:140–47.

Koepcke, M. 1964. *The birds of the Department of Lima, Peru.* Wynnewood, Pa.: Livingston.

König, C. 1991a. Taxonomische und ökologische Untersuchungen an Kreischeulen (*Otus* sp.) des südlichen Südamerika. *J. Ornithol.* 132:209–14.

———. 1991b. Zur Taxonomie und Ökologie der Sperlingskauze (*Glaucidium* spp.) des Andes raumes. *Oekol. Voegel* 13:15–75.

König, C., and R. Straneck. 1989. Eine neue Eule (Aves: Strigidae) aus Nordargentinien. *Stuttg. Beitr. Naturk.*, ser. A (Biol.), no. 428:1–20.

Krabbe, N. 1992a. Notes on distribution and natural history of some poorly known Ecuadorian birds. *Bull. Brit. Ornithol. Club* 112: 169–74.

———. 1992b. Avifaunistic results of a subtropical camp in the Cordillera del Condor, southeastern Ecuador. *Bull. Brit. Ornithol. Club* 114:55–61.

Kratter, A. W., M. D. Carreño, R. T. Chesser, J. P. O'Neill, and T. S. Sillett. 1992. Further notes on bird distribution in northeastern Dpto. Santa Cruz, Bolivia, with two species new to Bolivia. *Bull. Brit. Ornithol. Club* 112:143–50.

Kratter, A. W., T. S. Sillett, R. T. Chesser, J. P. O'Neill, T. A. Parker, III, and A. Castillo. 1993. Avifauna of a chaco locality in Bolivia. *Wilson Bull.* 105:114–41.

Lack, D. 1976. *Island biology.* Oxford: Blackwell.

Land, H. C. 1970. *Birds of Guatemala.* Wynnewood, Pa.: Livingston.

Lanning, D. V. 1991. Distribution and breeding biology of the Red-fronted Macaw. *Wilson Bull.* 103:357–65.

Lanyon, S. M., D. F. Stotz, and D. E. Willard. 1990. *Clytoctantes atrogularis,* a new species of antbird from western Brasil. *Wilson Bull.* 102:571–80.

Lanyon, W. E. 1967. Revision and probable evolution of the *Myiarchus* flycatchers of the West Indies. *Bull. Am. Mus. Nat. Hist.* 136: 329–70.

———. 1978. Revision of the *Myiarchus* flycatchers of South America. *Bull. Am. Mus. Nat. Hist.* 161:429–627.

Laubmann, A. 1939. *Die Vögel von Paraguay, I.* Stuttgart: Strecker und Schroder.

———. 1940. *Die Vögel von Paraguay, II.* Stuttgart: Strecker und Schroder.

Leck, C. F. 1980. Distributional notes on Ecuadorian birds. *Am. Birds* 34:312–13.

Lee, D. S., and N. Vina. 1993. A re-evaluation of the status of the endangered Black-capped Petrel, *Pterodroma hasitata,* in Cuba. *Ornithol. Neotrop.* 4:99–101.

Lefebvre, G. B. Poulin, and R. McNeil. 1992. Abundance, feeding behavior, and body condition of Nearctic warblers wintering in Venezuelan mangroves. *Wilson Bull.* 104:400–412.

———. 1994. Temporal dynamics of mangrove bird communities in Venezuela with special reference to migrant warblers. *Auk* 111: 405–16.

Lentino R., M. 1988. *Notiochelidon flavipes:* A swallow new to Venezuela. *Bull. Brit. Ornithol. Club* 108:70–71.

Lentino R., M., F. J. Bisbal E., A. A. Ospino B., and R. A. Rivero. 1984. Nuevos registros y extensiones de distribución para especies de aves en Venezuela. *Bol. Soc. Venez. Cienc. Nat.* 39 (142):111–19.

Lizevy, B. C., P. S. Humphrey, and M. C. Thompson. 1985. Notes on coastal birds of Puerto Melo, Chubut, Argentina. *Bull. Brit. Ornithol. Club* 105:17–21.

Lowery, G. H,. and W. W. Dahlquist. 1951. Birds of the state of Veracruz, Mexico. *Univ. Kans. Publ. Mus. Nat. Hist.* 3:531–649.

Mack, A. L., and C. D. Fisher. 1988. Notes on birds from the llanos of Meta, Colombia. *Gerfaut* 78:397–408.

Madroño Nieto, A., and M. Pearman. 1992. Distribution, status and taxonomy of the near-threatened Black-bodied Woodpecker *Dryocopus schulzi. Bird Conserv. Internat.* 2:253–71.

Marcus, M. J. 1983. Additions to the avifauna of Honduras. *Auk* 100:621–29.

Marín A., M. 1993. First record of the White-flanked Antwren (*Myrmotherula axillaris*) in Mexico. *Ornithol. Neotrop.* 4:97–98.

Marín A., M., L. F. Kiff, and L. Peña G. 1989. Notes on Chilean birds, with descriptions of two new subspecies. *Bull. Brit. Ornithol. Club* 109:66–82.

Marín A., M., and F. G. Stiles. 1993. Notes on the biology of the Spot-fronted Swift. *Condor* 95:479–83.

Marshall, J. T., Jr. 1957. *Birds of pine-oak woodland in southern Arizona and adjacent Mexico.* Pacific Coast Avifauna, no. 32. Columbus, Ohio: Cooper Ornithological Society.

Mattos, G. T., and H. Sick. 1985. Sôbre a distribuição e a ecologia de duas espécies crípticas: *Embernagra longicauda* Strickland 1944, e *Embernagra platensis* (Gmelin 1789) (Emberizidae, Aves). *Rev. Bras. Biol.* 45:201–6.

Mayr, E., and G. W. Cottrall, eds. 1979. *Check-list of birds of the world.* Vol. 1. 2d ed. Cambridge, Mass.: Museum of Comparative Zoology.

Mayr, E., and L. L. Short. 1970. *Species taxa of North American birds.* Publ. Nuttall Ornithol. Club, no. 9. Cambridge, Mass.: Nuttall Ornithological Club.

McFarlane, R. W. 1974. Unusual avian migrants in Tarapacá. *Idesia* 3:181–84.

McKenzie, P. M., and R. E. Noble. 1989. Sight records for Connecticut Warbler (*Oporornis agilis*) and Yellow-throated Vireo (*Vireo flavifrons*) in Puerto Rico. *Fla. Field Nat.* 17:60–72.

McKitrick, M. C., and R. A. Zink. 1988. Species concepts in ornithology. *Condor* 90:1–14.

McNeil, R., B. Limoges, F. Mercier, and J. R. Rodríguez S. 1987. Wilson's Phalarope in South America. *Am. Birds* 41:391.

McNeil, R., J. R. Rodriguez S., and F. Mercier. 1985a. Winter range expansion of the Long-billed Curlew (*Numenius americanus*) to South America. *Auk* 102:174–75.

———. 1985b. Eastward range expansion of the Marbled Godwit in South America. *Wilson Bull.* 97:243–44.

Mees, G. F. 1974. Additions to the avifauna of Suriname. *Zool. Meded.* 48:55–67.

———. 1985. Nomenclature and systematics of birds from Suriname. *Proc. K. Ned. Acad. Wet.*, ser. C (Biol. Med. Sci.), 88: 75–91.

———. 1987. The juvenile plumage, systematic position, and range of *Synallaxis macconnelli* Chubb (Aves, Furnariidae). *Proc. K. Ned. Acad. Wet.*, ser. C. (Biol. Med. Sci.), 90:303–9.

Mees, G. F., and Mees-Balchin, V. J. 1990. *Basileuterus flaveolus* (Baird) in Guyana. *Bull. Brit. Ornithol. Club* 110:179–81.

Mercier, F., R. McNeil, and J. R. Rodriguez S. 1987. First occurrence of Bar-tailed Godwit in South America and status of the Marbled Godwit in northeastern Venezuela. *J. Field Ornithol.* 58:78–80.

Meyer de Schauensee, R. 1966. *The species of birds of South America.* Narberth, Pa.: Livingston.

———. 1970. *A guide to the birds of South America.* Wynnewood, Pa.: Livingston.

Meyer de Schauensee, R., and A. L. Mack. 1982. Addenda to *A guide to the birds of South America.* In *A guide to the birds of South America,* by R. Meyer de Schauensee, 429–63. Philadelphia: Academy of Natural Sciences.

Meyer de Schauensee, R., and W. H. Phelps Jr. 1978. *A guide to the birds of Venezuela.* Princeton: Princeton University Press.

Miller, A. H., H. Friedmann, L. Griscom, and R. T. Moore. 1957. *Distributional checklist of the birds of Mexico.* Part 2. Pacific Coast Avifauna, no. 33. Columbus, Ohio: Cooper Ornithological Society.

Miller, B. M., and C. M. Miller. 1992. Distributional notes and new species records for birds in Belize. *Occas. Pap. Belize Nat. Hist. Soc.* 1:6–25.

Mills, E. D., and D. T. Rogers Jr. 1988. First record of the Blue-throated Goldentail (*Hylocharis eliciae*) in Belize. *Wilson Bull.* 100:510.

Mirsky, E. N. 1976. Song divergence in hummingbird and junco populations on Guadalupe Island. *Condor* 78:230–35.

Mitchell, M. H. 1957. *Observations on birds of southeastern Brazil.* Toronto: University of Toronto Press.

Molez, J. F., F. X. Pajot, and G. Chatenay. 1977. Un oiseau nouveau por la Guyane française: Le gros-bec à poitrine rose *Pheucticus ludovicianus* (Linné). *Oiseau* 47:207–10.

Monroe, B. L., Jr. 1963. A revision of the *Lampornis viridipallens* complex (Aves: Trochilidae). *Occas. Pap. Mus. Zool. LA State Univ.*, no. 27.

———. 1968. *A distributional survey of the birds of Honduras.* Ornithol. Monogr., no. 7. Washington, D.C.: American Ornithologists' Union.

———. 1970. Effects of habitat changes on population levels of the avifauna in Honduras. In The avifauna of northern Latin America, ed. H. K. Buechner and J. H. Buechner. *Smithson. Contrib. Zool.* 26:58–61.

Morony, J. J., W. J. Bock, and J. Farrand. 1975. *Reference list of birds of the world.* New York: American Museum of Natural History, Department of Ornithology.

Morton, E. S., and H. T. Gonzáles Alonso. 1982. The biology of *Torreornis inexpectata:* 1, A comparison of vocalizations in *T. i. inexpectata* and *T. i. sigmani. Wilson Bull.* 94:433–46.

Moskovits, D. K., J. W. Fitzpatrick, and D. E. Willard. 1985. Lista preliminar das aves da Estação Ecológica de Maracá, Território de Roraima, Brasil, e áreas adjacentes. *Pap. Avul. Zool.* (São Paulo) 36:51–68.

Murphy, W. L., and W. Nanan. 1987. First confirmed record of Western Reef-Heron (*Egretta gularis*) for South America. *Am. Birds* 41:392–94.

Narosky, S. 1979. Un nuevo picaflor para la Argentina. *Hornero* 12:53.

Narosky, T., and D. Yzurieta. 1987. *Guía para la identificación de las aves de Argentina y Uruguay.* Buenos Aires: Asociación Ornitológica del Plata.

Naumberg, E. M. B. 1930. The birds of Matto Grosso, Brazil: A report on the birds secured by the Roosevelt-Rondon expedition. *Bull. Am. Mus. Nat. Hist.* 60:1–432.

———. 1939. Studies of birds from eastern Brazil and Paraguay, based on a collection made by Emil Kaempfer. *Bull. Am. Mus. Nat. Hist.* 76:231–76.

Navarro S., A. G. 1992. Altitudinal distribution of birds in the Sierra Madre del Sur, Guerrero, Mexico. *Condor* 94:29–39.

Navarro S., A. G., A. T. Peterson, B. P. Escalante P., and H. Benítez D. 1992. *Cypseloides storeri,* a new species of swift from Mexico. *Wilson Bull.* 104:55–64.

Navas, J. R., and N. A. Bó. 1987. *Sporophila falcirostris* (Temminck, 1820), nueva especie para la Argentina (Aves, Emberizinae). *Neotrópica* (La Plata) 33 (90): 96.

Negret, A., and D. M. Teixeira. 1984. The Ocellated Crake (*Micropygia schomburgkii*) of central Brazil. *Condor* 86:220.

Noble, R. E., F. J. Vilella, and P. J. Zwank. 1986. Status of the endangered Puero Rican Nightjar in 1985. *Caribbean J. Sci.* 22: 137–43.

Nores, M. 1986. Nuevos registros para aves de Argentina. *Hornero* 12:304–7.

Nores, M., and D. Yzurieta. 1979. Una nueva especie y dos nuevas subespecies de aves (Passeriformes). *Misc. Acad. Nac. Cienc. Córdoba* 61:4–8.

———. 1984. Registro de aves en el sur de Bolivia. *Donaña Acta. Vert.* 11:329–37.

Norton, D. W., G. Orcés V., and E. Sutter. 1972. Notes on rare and previously unreported birds from Ecuador. *Auk* 89:889–94.

Norton, R. L., and A. Hobbs. 1987. First record of Purple-throated Carib for the Greater Antilles and notes on vagrants in the Virgin Islands. *Caribbean J. Sci.* 23:462–63.

Novaes, F. C. 1957. Contribuição à ornitologia do noroeste do Acre. *Bull. Mus. Para. Emilio Goeldi,* no. 9.

———. 1965. Notas sôbre algumas aves da Serra Parima, Território de Roraima. *Bol. Mus. Para. Emilio Goeldi,* no. 54.

———. 1974. Ornitologia do território do Amapá. Part 1. *Publ. Avul. Mus. Para. Emilio Goeldi,* no. 25.

———. 1978. Ornitologia do território do Amapá. Part 2. *Publ. Avul. Mus. Para. Emilio Goeldi,* no. 29.

———. 1980. Observações sôbre a avifauna do alto curso do Rio Paru de Leste, Estado do Pará. *Bol. Mus. Para. Emilio Goeldi (Zool.),* no. 100.

Olrog, C. C. 1978. Nueva lista de la avifauna Argentina. *Opera Lilloana,* no. 27.

Olson, S. L. 1994. The endemic vireo of Fernando de Noronha (*Vireo gracilirostris*). *Wilson Bull.* 106:1–17.

O'Neill, J. P., C. A. Munn, and I. Franke J. 1991. *Nannopsittaca dachilleae,* a new species of parrotlet from eastern Peru. *Auk* 108: 225–29.

O'Neill, J. P., and T. A. Parker III. 1977. Taxonomy and range of *Pionus "seniloides"* in Peru. *Condor* 79:274.

O'Neill, J. P., and T. S. Schulenberg. 1979. Notes on the Masked Saltator, *Saltator cinctus,* in Peru. *Auk* 96:610–13.

Oren, D. C. 1980. Enormous concentration of martins (*Progne* spp.) in Iquitos, Peru. *Condor* 82:344–45.

———. 1984. Resultados de uma nova expedição a Fernando de Noronha. *Bol. Mus. Para. Emilio Goeldi (Zool.),* n.s., 1:19–44.

Oren, D. C., and F. C. Novaes. 1985. A new subspecies of White Bellbird *Procnias alba* (Hermann). *Bull. Brit. Ornithol. Club* 105: 23–25.

Oren, D. C., and J. M. C. da Silva. 1987. Cherrie's Spinetail (*Synallaxis cherriei* Gyldenstolpe) (Aves: Furnariidae) in Carajas and Gorotire, Pará, Brazil. *Bol. Mus. Para. Emilio Goeldi (Zool.),* n.s., 3:1–9.

Ornelas, J. F. 1987. Rediscovery of the Rufous-crested Coquette (*Lophornis delattrei brachylopha*) in Guerrero, Mexico. *Wilson Bull.* 99:719–21.

Ortíz-Crespo, F., and S. Valarezo-Delgado. 1975. Lista de aves del Ecuador. *Soc. Ecua. Francisco Campos de Amigos Naturaleza, Publ.,* no. 2.

Ortíz-von Halle, B. 1990. Adiciones a la avifauna de Colombia de especies arribadas a la Isla Gorgona. *Caldasia* 16:209–14.

Osbourne, D. R., and S. R. Beissinger. 1979. The Paint-billed Crake in Guyana. *Auk* 96:425.

Ouellet, H. 1993. Bicknell's Thrush: Taxonomic status and distribution. *Wilson Bull.* 105:545–72.

Pacheco, J. F. 1988. Black-hooded Antwren *Formicivora (Myrmotherula) erythronotos* re-discovered in Brazil. *Bull. Brit. Ornithol. Club* 108:179–82.

Parera, A. F. 1990. Zorzolito migrador (*Catharus ustulatus*) en Entre Ríos. *Nuestras Aves,* no. 22:31.

Parker, T. A., III. 1981. Distribution and biology of the White-cheeked Cotinga *Zaratornis stresemanni,* a high Andean frugivore. *Bull. Brit. Ornithol. Club* 101:256–65.

———. 1982a. Observations of some unusual rainforest and marsh birds in southeastern Peru. *Wilson Bull.* 94:477–93.

———. 1982b. First record of the Chilean Woodstar *Eulidia yarellii* in Peru. *Bull. Brit. Ornithol. Club* 102:86.

———. 1983. A record of the Blackburnian Warbler (*Dendroica fusca*) for southeastern Brazil. *Am. Birds* 37:274.

———. 1984a. Notes on the behavior of *Ramphotrigon* flycatchers. *Auk* 101:186–88.

———. 1984b. Rediscovery of the Rufous-fronted Antthrush (*Formicarius rufifrons*) in southeastern Peru. *Gerfaut* 73:287–89.

Parker, T. A., III, and B. Bailey. 1991. *A rapid biological assessment of the Alto Madidi region, and adjacent areas in northern La Paz, Bolivia.* RAP Working Papers, no. 1. Washington, D.C.: Conservation International.

Parker, T. A., III, J. Bates, and G. Cox. 1992. Rediscovery of the Bolivian Recurvebill with notes on other little-known species of the Bolivian Andes. *Wilson Bull.* 104:173–77.

Parker, T. A., III, and J. L. Carr. 1992. *Status of forest remnants in the Cordillera de al Costa and adjacent areas of southwestern Ecuador.* RAP Working Papers, no. 2. Washington, D.C.: Conservation International.

Parker, T. A., III, A. Castillo U., M. Gell-Mann, and O. Rocha O. 1991. Records of new and unusual birds from northern Bolivia. *Bull. Brit. Ornithol. Club* 111:120–38.

Parker, T. A., P. K. Donahue, and T. S. Schulenberg. 1994. Birds of the Tambopata Reserve (Explorer's Inn Reserve). In *The Tambopata Reserved Zone of southeastern Peru: A biological assessment,* ed. R. B. Foster, T. A. Parker III, A. H. Gentry, L. H. Emmons, A. Chicchón, T. Schulenberg, L. Rodríguez, G. Lamas, H. Ortega, J. Icochea, W. Wust, M. Romo, J. A Castillo, O. Phillips, C. Reynal, A. Kratter, P. K. Donahue, and L. J. Barkley, 1062-24. RAP Working Papers, no. 6. Washington, D.C.: Conservation International.

Parker, T. A., III, R. B. Foster, L. H. Emmons, P. Freed, A. B. Forsythe, B. Hoffman, and B. D. Gill. 1993. *A biological assessment of the Kanuku Mountain Region of southwestern Guyana.* RAP Working Papers, no. 5. Washington, D.C.: Conservation International.

Parker, T. A., III, A. H. Gentry, R. B. Foster, L. H. Emmons, and J. V. Remsen. 1993. *The lowland dry forests of Santa Cruz, Bolivia: A global conservation priority.* RAP Working Papers, no. 4. Washington, D.C.: Conservation International.

Parker, T. A., III, B. K. Holst, L. H. Emmons, and J. R. Myers. 1993. *A biological assessment of the Columbia River Forest Reserve, Toledo District, Belize.* RAP Working Papers, no. 3. Washington, D.C.: Conservation International.

Parker, T. A., III, and J. P. O'Neill. 1980. Notes on little known birds of the upper Urubamba Valley, southern Peru. *Auk* 97:167–76.

———. 1985. A new species and a new subspecies of *Thryothorus* wren from Peru. In *Neotropical ornithology,* ed. P. A. Buckley, M. S. Foster, E. S. Morton, R. S. Ridgely, and F. G. Buckley, 9–15. Ornithol. Monogr., no. 36. Washington, D.C.: American Ornithologists' Union.

Parker, T. A., III, and S. A. Parker. 1982. Behavioural and distribution notes on some unusual birds of a lower montane cloud forest in Peru. *Bull. Brit. Ornithol. Club* 102:63–70.

Parker, T. A., III, S. A. Parker, and M. A. Plenge. 1982. *An annotated checklist of Peruvian birds.* Vermilion, S.D: Buteo Books.

Parker, T. A., III, and J. V. Remsen Jr. 1987. Fifty-two Amazonian bird species new to Bolivia. *Bull. Brit. Ornithol. Club* 107: 94–107.

Parker, T. A., III, and O. Rocha O. 1991. Notes on the status and behavior of the Rusty-necked Piculet *Picumnus fuscus. Bull. Brit. Ornithol. Club* 111:91–92.

Parker, T. A., III, T. S. Schulenberg, G. R. Graves, and M. J. Braun. 1985. The avifauna of the Huancabamba region, northern Peru. In *Neotropical Ornithology,* ed. P. A. Buckley, M. S. Foster, E. S. Morton, R. S. Ridgely, and F. G. Buckley, 169–97. Ornithol. Monogr., no. 36. Washington, D.C.: American Ornithologists' Union.

Parkes, K. C. 1982. Nomenclatural notes on the phalaropes. *Bull. Brit. Ornithol. Club* 102:84–85.

Parkes, K. C., D. P. Kibbe, and E. L. Roth. 1978. First records of the Spotted Rail (*Pardirallus maculatus*) for the United States, Chile, Bolivia and western Mexico. *Am. Birds* 32:295–99.

Paulson, D. R., G. H. Orians, and C. F. Leck. 1969. Notes on birds of Isla San Andrés. *Auk* 86:755–58.

Paynter, R. A., Jr. 1977. Biology and evolution of the avian genus *Atlapetes* (Emberizinae). *Bull. Mus. Comp. Zool.* 148:323–69.

———. 1985. *Ornithological gazetteer of Argentina.* Cambridge, Mass.: Museum of Comparative Zoology.

Paynter, R. A., Jr., and M. A. Traylor Jr. 1991. *Ornithological gazetteer of Brazil.* Cambridge, Mass.: Museum of Comparative Zoology.

Pearman, M. 1990. Behaviour and vocalizations of an undescribed canastero *Asthenes* sp. from Brazil. *Bull. Brit. Ornithol. Club* 110:145–53.

———. 1993. Some range extensions and five species new to Colombia, with notes on some scarece or little-known species. *Bull. Brit. Ornithol. Club* 113:66–75.

Pearson, D. L. 1975. Range extensions and new records for bird species in Ecuador, Peru and Bolivia. *Condor* 77:96–99.

———. 1980. Bird migration in Amazonian Ecuador, Peru, and Bolivia. In *Migrant birds of the Neotropics: Ecology, behavior, distribution and conservation,* ed. A. Keast and E. S. Morton, 273–83. Washington, D.C.: Smithsonian Institution Press.

Pearson, D. L., and M. A. Plenge. 1974. Puna bird species on the coast of Peru. *Auk* 91:626–31.

Peters, J. L. 1951. *Check-list of birds of the world.* Vol. 7. Cambridge, Mass.: Museum of Comparative Zoology.

Peterson, R. T., and E. L. Chalif. 1973. *A field guide to Mexican birds.* Boston: Houghton Mifflin.

Peterson, R. T., and G. E. Watson. 1971. Franklin's Gull and Bridled Tern in southern Chile. *Auk* 88:670–71.

Phelps, W. H., and W. H. Phelps Jr. 1948. Descripción de seis aves nuevas de Venezuela y notas sobre veinticuatro adiciones a la avifauna del Brasil. *Bol. Soc. Venez. Cienc. Nat.* 11 (71): 53–74.

———. 1958. Lista de las aves de Venezuela con su distribución: No Passeriformes. *Bol. Soc. Venez. Cienc. Nat.* 19:1–317.

———. 1963. Lista de las aves de Venezuela con su distribución: Passeriformes. *Bol. Soc. Venez. Cienc. Nat.* 24:1–479.

Phelps, W. H., Jr. 1972. Adiciones a las listas de aves de Sur America, Brasil, y Venezuela y notas sobre aves venezolanas. *Bol. Soc. Venez. Cienc. Nat.* 30 (124–25): 23–40.

Philippi, R. A. 1967. Tres especies de aves capturadas por primera vez en Chile. *Bol. Mus. Nac. Hist. Nat. (Chile)* 29 (7): 121–24.

———. 1975. Semipalmated Sandpiper: Identification, migrations, summer and winter ranges. *Am. Birds* 29:799–806.

———. 1981. Subspecies vs. forgotten species: The case of Grayson's Robin (*Turdus graysoni*). *Wilson Bull.* 93:301–9.

———. 1986. *The known birds of North and Middle America.* Part 1. Denver: Allan R. Phillips.

Phillips, A. R., J. Marshall, and G. Monson. 1964. *The birds of Arizona.* Tucson: University of Arizona Press.

Pierpont, N., and J. W. Fitzpatrick. 1983. Specific status and behavior of *Cymbilaimus sanctaemariae,* the Bamboo Antshrike, from southwestern Amazonia. *Auk* 100:645–52.

Pinto, O. M. de O. 1938. Catálogo das aves do Brasil. Part 1a. *Rev. Mus. Paulista* 23:1–566.

———. 1944. *Catálogo das aves do Brasil.* Part 2a. São Paulo: Secretária da Agricultura, Indústria, e Comércio.

———. 1978. *Novo catálogo das aves do Brasil.* Part 1. São Paulo: Empresa Gráfica da Revista dos Tribunais.

Pitman, R. L., M. Newcomer, J. Butler, J. Cotton, and G. Friedrichsen. 1983. A Crested Auklet from Baja California. *Western Birds* 14:47–48.

Post, W. 1981. Biology of the Yellow-shouldered Blackbird—*Agelaius* on a tropical island. *Bull. Fla. State Mus., Biol. Sci.* 26: 125–202.

Pyle, P., and S. N. G. Howell. 1993. An Arctic Warbler in Baja California. *Western Birds* 24:53–56.

Radamaker, K. A., and C. Ludden. 1993. A record of Bar-tailed Godwit for Mexico. *Euphonia* 2:58–65.

Raffaele, H. A. 1989. *A guide to the birds of Puerto Rico and the Virgin Islands.* Rev. ed. San Juan: Fondo Educativo Interamericano.

———. 1993. The raising of a ghost—*Spinus cucullatus* in Puerto Rico. *Auk* 100:737–39.

Rangel-Salazar, J. L., R. Tercero, and P. L. Enriquez. 1991. The Great Potoo as a probable resident in southern Mexico. *Ornitología Neotropical* 2:38–39.

Rappole, J. H., E. S. Morton, T. E. Lovejoy III, and J. L. Ruos. 1983. *Nearctic avian migrants in the Neotropics.* Washington, D.C: U.S. Fish and Wildlife Service.

Rasmussen, P. C. 1991. Relationships between coastal South American King and Blue-eyed Shags. *Condor* 93:825–39.

Ratti, J. T. 1979. Reproductive separation and isolating mechanisms between sympatric dark- and light-phase Western Grebes. *Auk* 96:573–86.

Reed, J. R. 1988. Inca Terns in the Bay of Panama during the 1982–1983 El Niño event. *Am. Birds* 42:172–73.

Remsen, J. V., Jr. 1981. A new subspecies of *Schizoeaca harterti* with notes on taxonomy and natural history of *Schizoeaca* (Aves: Furnariidae) *Proc. Biol. Soc. Wash.* 94:1068–75.

———. 1984a. Geographic variation, zoogeography and possible rapid evolution in some *Cranioleuca* spinetails (Furnariidae) of the Andes. *Wilson Bull.* 96:515–23.

———. 1984b. Natural history notes on some poorly known Bolivian birds. Part 2. *Gerfaut* 74:163–79.

———. 1986. Was Bachman's Warbler a bamboo specialist? *Auk* 103:216–19.

Remsen, J. V., Jr., and T. A. Parker III. 1983. Contribution of river-created habitats to bird species richness in Amazonia. *Biotropica* 15:223–31.

———. 1984. Arboreal dead-leaf-searching birds of the Neotropics. *Condor* 86:36–41.

———. 1990. Seasonal distribution of the Azure Gallinule (*Porphyrula flavirostris*) with comments on vagrancy in rails and gallinules. *Wilson Bull.* 102:380–99.

Remsen, J. V., Jr., T. A. Parker III, and R. S. Ridgely. 1982. Natural history notes on some poorly known Bolivian birds. *Gerfaut* 72: 77–87.

Remsen, J. V., Jr., C. G. Schmitt, and D. C. Schmitt. 1988. Natural history notes on some poorly known Bolivian birds. Part 3. *Gerfaut* 78:363–81.

Remsen, J. V., Jr., and M. A. Traylor Jr. 1989. *An annotated list of the birds of Bolivia.* Vermillion, S.D.: Buteo Books.

Renssen, T. A. 1974. Twelve bird species new for Surinam. *Ardea* 62: 118–29.

Reynard, G. B., O. H. Garrido, and R. L. Sutton. 1993. Taxonomic revision of the Greater Antillean Pewee. *Wilson Bull.* 105: 217–27.

Reynard, G. B., L. L. Short, O. H. Garrido, and G. Alayón García. 1987. Nesting, voice, status, and relationships of the endemic Cuban Gundlach's Hawk (*Accipiter gundlachi*). *Wilson Bull.* 99: 73–77.

Ridgely, R. S. 1980. Notes on some rare or previously unrecorded birds in Ecuador. *Am. Birds* 34:242–48.

Ridgely, R. S., and J. A. Gwynne Jr. 1989. *A guide to the birds of Panama, with Costa Rica, Nicaragua and Honduras.* 2d ed. Princeton: Princeton University Press.

Ridgely, R. S., and M. B. Robbins. 1988. *Pyrrhura orcesi,* a new parakeet from southwestern Ecuador, with systematic notes on the *P. melanura* complex. *Wilson Bull.* 100:173–82.

Ridgely, R. S., and G. Tudor. 1989. *The birds of South America.* Vol. 1, *The oscine passerines.* Austin: University of Texas Press.

———. 1994. *The birds of South America.* Vol. 2, *The suboscine passerines.* Austin: University of Texas Press.

Ridgely, R. S., and D. S. Wilcove. 1979. First nesting record of Gray-hooded Gull from Ecuador. *Condor* 81:438–39.

Ripley, S. D. 1977. *Rails of the world.* Toronto: M. F. Feheley.

Ripley, S. D., and B. M. Beehler. 1985. Rails of the world, a compilation of new information, 1975–1983 (Aves: Rallidae). *Smithson. Contrib. Zool.* 417.

Risebrough, R. W., A. M. Springer, S. A. Temple, C. M. White, J. L. B. Albuquerque, P. H. Bloom, R. W. Fyfe, M. N. Kirven, B. A. Luscombe, D. G. Roseneau, M. Sander, N. J. Schmitt, C. G. Thelander, W. Guillermo Vasina, and W. Walker III. 1990. Observaciones del Halcon Peregrino, *Falco peregrinus* subspp., en America del Sur. *Rev. Bras. Biol.* 50:563–74.

Robbins, C. S., J. W. Fitzpatrick, and P. B. Hamel. 1992. A warbler in trouble: *Dendroica cerulea.* In *Ecology and conservation of Neotropical migrant landbirds,* ed. J. M. Hagen III and D. W. Johnston, 549–62. Washington, D.C.: Smithsonian Institution Press.

Robbins, M. B., N. Krabbe, G. H. Rosenberg, R. S. Ridgely, and F. Sornoza Molina. 1994. Notes on the natural history of Crescent-faced Antpitta. *Wilson Bull.* 106:169–73.

Robbins, M. B., T. A. Parker III., and S. E. Allen. 1985. The avifauna of Cerro Pirre, Darién, Eastern Panama. In *Neotropical ornithology,* ed. P. A. Buckley, M. S. Foster, E. S. Morton, R. S. Ridgely, and F. G. Buckley, 198–232. Ornithol. Monogr., no. 36. Washington, D.C.: American Ornithologists' Union.

Robbins, M. B., and R. S. Ridgely. 1990. The avifauna of an upper

tropical cloud forest in southwestern Ecuador. *Proc. Acad. Nat. Sci.* 142:59–71.
———. 1991. *Sipia rosenbergi* (Formicariidae) is a synonym of *Myrmeciza (laemosticta) nigricauda,* with comments on the validity of the genus *Sipia. Bull. Brit. Ornithol. Club* 111:11–18.
———. 1992. Taxonomy and natural history of *Nyctiphrynus rosenbergi* (Caprimulgidae). *Condor* 94:984–87.
Robbins, M. B., R. S. Ridgely, and S. W. Cardiff. 1994. Voice, plumage and natural history of Anthony's Nightjar (*Caprimulgus anthonyi*). *Condor* 96:224–28.
Robbins, M. B., R. S. Ridgely, T. S. Schulenberg, and F. B. Gill. 1987. The avifauna of the Cordillera de Cutucú, Ecuador, with comparisons to other Andean localities. *Proc. Acad. Nat. Sci.* 139:243–59.
Robbins, M. B., G. H. Rosenberg, and F. Sornoza Molina. 1994. A new species of cotinga (Cotingidae: *Doliornis*) from the Ecuadorian Andes, with comments on plumage sequence in *Doliornis* and *Ampelion. Auk* 111:1–7.
Roberson, D., and L. F. Baptista. 1988. White-shielded coots in North America: A critical evaluation. *Am. Birds* 42:1241–46.
Rodríguez-Estrella, R., E. Mata, and L. Rivera. 1992. Ecological notes on the Green Parakeet of Isla Socorro, Mexico. *Condor* 94: 523–25.
Rosenberg, D. K., C. A. Valle, M. C. Coulter, and S. A. Harcourt. 1990. Monitoring Galápagos Penguins and Flightless Cormorants in the Galápagos Islands. *Wilson Bull.* 102:525–32.
Rosenberg, G. H. 1990. Habitat specialization and foraging behavior by birds of Amazonian river islands in northeastern Peru. *Condor* 92:427–43.
Rumboll, M. A. E. 1990. Tres aves nuevas para la Argentina. *Nuestras Aves,* no. 22:28.
Russell, S. M. 1964. *A distributional study of the birds of British Honduras.* Ornithol. Monogr., no. 1. Washington, D.C.: American Ornithologists' Union.
Russell, S. M., J. C. Barlow, and D. W. Lamm. 1978. Status of some birds on Isla San Andrés and Isla Providencia, Colombia. *Condor* 81:98–100.
Saibene, C. 1985. Registros nuevos para el Chaco. *Nuestras Aves* 3 (7): 6.
Salvador, S., S. Narosky, and R. Fraga. 1986. First description of the nest and eggs of the Rufous-throated Dipper (*Cinclus schulzi*) in northwestern Argentina. Gerfaut 76:63-66.
Salvador, S. A., and L. A. Salvador. 1990. Nuevos hallazgos en Argentina de *Anas discors, Lophornis chalybea,* y *Tyrannus tyrannus. Hornero* 13:178–79.
Santaella, L., and A. M. Sada. 1992. A Cory's Shearwater off Cozumel. *Euphonia* 1:17–18.
Schade F., and R. M. Pallares. 1971. Las aves del Paraguay y un índice. *Rev. Parag. Microbiol.* 6:103–22.
Schlatter, R. P. 1984. Status and conservation of seabirds in Chile. In *Status and conservation of the world's seabirds,* ed. J. P. Croxall, P. G. H. Evans, and R. W. Schreiber, 261–69. ICBP Tech. Pub. no. 2. Cambridge: International Council for Bird Preservation.
Schlatter, R. P., and M. Marin. 1983. Breeding of Elliot's Storm Petrel *Oceanites gracilis* in Chile. *Gerfaut* 73:197–99.
Schmitt, C. G., and D. C. Cole. 1981. First records of Black-legged Seriema (*Chunga burmeisteri*) in Bolivia. *Condor* 83:182–83.
Schmitt, C. G., and J. P. Hubbard. 1974. Eastern Kingbird in Paraguay. *Wilson Bull.* 86:466.
Schmitt, C. G., and D. C. Schmitt. 1990. First record of the White-tailed Nightjar *Caprimulgus cayennensis* in Ecuador. *Bull. Brit. Ornithol. Club* 110:139–40.
Schulenberg, T. S. 1987. Observations on two rare birds, *Upucerthia albigula* and *Conirostrum tamarugense,* from the Andes of southwestern Peru. *Condor* 89:654–58.
Schulenberg, T. S., S. E. Allen, D. F. Stotz, and D. A. Wiedenfeld. 1984. Distributional records from the Cordilleira Yanachaga, central Peru. *Gerfaut* 74:57–70.
Schulenberg, T. S., and L. C. Binford. 1985. A new species of tanager (Emberizidae: Thraupinae, *Tangara*) from southern Peru. *Wilson Bull.* 97:413–20.
Schulenberg, T. S., and T. A. Parker III. 1981. Status and distribution of some northwest Peruvian birds. *Condor* 83:209–16.
Schulenberg, T. S., T. A. Parker III, and R. A. Hughes. 1987. First records of Least Tern, *Sterna antillarum,* for Peru. *Gerfaut* 77: 271–73.
Schulenberg, T. S., and D. F. Stotz. 1990. The taxonomic status of *Myrmeciza stictothorax* (Todd). *Auk* 108:731–33.
Schulenberg, T. S., and M. D. Williams. 1982. A new species of antpitta (*Grallaria*) from northern Peru. *Wilson Bull.* 94:105–13.
Schwartz, P. 1968. Notes on two Neotropical nightjars, *Caprimulgus anthonyi* and *C. parvulus. Condor* 70:223–27.
———. 1972. *Micrastur gilvicollis,* a valid species sympatric with *M. ruficollis* in Amazonia. *Condor* 74:399–415.
———. 1975. Solved and unsolved problems in the *Sporophila lineola/bouvronides* complex (Aves: Emberizidae). *Ann. Carnegie Mus.* 45:277–85.
Scott, D. A., and M. de L. Brooke. 1985. The endangered avifauna of southeastern Brazil: A report on the BOU/WWF expeditions of 1980/81 and 1981/82. In *Conservation of tropical forest birds,* ed. A. W. Diamond and T. E. Lovejoy, 115–39. ICBP Tech. Pub. no. 4. Cambridge: International Council for Bird Preservation.
———. 1993. Rediscovery of the Grey-winged Cotinga *Tijuca condita* in south-eatern Brazil. *Bird Conserv. Internat.* 3:1–12.
Servat, G. P. 1993. First records of the Yellow Tyrannulet (*Capsiempis flaveola*) in Peru. *Wilson Bull.* 105:534.
Shaw, D., and T. C. Maxwell. 1988. First record of the Mississippi Kite for Bolivia. J. Raptor Res. 22:90.
Short, L. L. 1969. Relationships among some South American seedeaters (*Sporophila*), with a record of *S. hypochroma* for Argentina. *Wilson Bull.* 81:216–19.
———. 1972. Two avian species new to Paraguay. *Auk* 89:895.
———. 1975. A zoogeographic analysis of the South American chaco avifauna. *Bull. Am. Mus. Nat. Hist.* 154:163–352.
———. 1976. Notes on a collection of birds from the Paraguayan chaco. *Am. Mus. Novit.,* no. 2597.
———. 1982. *Woodpeckers of the world.* Greenville: Delaware Museum of Natural History,
Short, L. L., and K. C. Parkes. 1975. The status of *Agelaius forbesi* Sclater. *Auk* 96:179–13.
Sibley, C. G. 1954. Hybridization in the red-eyed towhees of Mexico. *Evolution* 8:252–90.
———. 1958. Hybridization in some Colombian tanagers, avian genus *Ramphocelus. Proc. Am. Phil. Soc.* 102:448–53.
Sibley, C. G., and J. E. Ahlquist. 1973. The relationships of the Hoatzin (*Opisthocomus*). *Auk* 90:1–13.
Sibley, C. G., and B. L. Monroe Jr. 1990. *Distribution and taxonomy of birds of the world.* New Haven: Yale University Press.
Sibley, F. C., G. F. Barrowclough, and C. G. Sibley. 1980. Notes on the birds of Honduras. *Wilson Bull.* 92:125–26.
Sick, H. 1965. A fauna do cerrado. *Arq. Zool. São Paulo* 12:71–93.
———. 1979. Notes on some Brazilian birds. *Bull. Brit. Ornithol. Club* 99:115–20.
———. 1985. *Ornitologia brasileira, uma introdução.* Brasília: Editora Universidade de Brasília.
Sick, H., L. P. Gonzaga, and D. M. Teixeira. 1987. A Arara-Azul-de-Lear, *Anodorhynchus leari* Bonaparte, 1856. *Rev. Bras. Zool.* 3:441–63.
Siegel-Causey, D. 1986. The courtship behavior and mixed-species pairing of King and Imperial Blue-eyed Shags (*Phalacrocorax albiventer* and *P. atriceps*). *Wilson Bull.* 98:571–80.
Silva, J. M. C. da. 1989. A reavaluation [*sic*] of *Serpophaga araguayae* Snethlage, 1928 (Aves: Tyrannidae). *Goeldiana Zool.,* no. 1.
———. 1993. The Sharpbill in the Serra dos Carajás, Pará, Brazil,

with comments on altitudinal migration in the Amazon region. *J. Field Ornithol.* 64:310–15.

Slud, P. 1964. The birds of Costa Rica: Distribution and ecology. *Bull. Am. Mus. Nat. Hist.* 128.

Small, A. 1987. Ring-billed Gull: First for Ecuador and the Galapagos. *Am. Birds* 41:390.

Smith, P. W. 1987. The Eurasian Collared-Dove arrives in the Americas. *Am. Birds* 41:1371–79.

Smith, P. W., and M. B. Hutt. 1984. First sight record of Western Reef Heron for Barbados. *Am. Birds* 38:254–55.

Smith, P. W., W. B. Robertson Jr., and H. M. Stevenson. West Indian Cave Swallows nesting in Florida, with comments on the taxonomy of *Hirundo fulva*. *Fla. Field. Nat.* 16:86–90.

Smith, P. W., and S. A. Smith. 1989. The Bahama Swallow *Tachycineta cyaneoviridis*; A summary. *Bull. Brit. Ornithol. Club* 109: 170–80.

Smithe, F. B. 1966. *The birds of Tikal.* New York: Natural History Press.

Snow, D. W. 1979. Family Pipridae. In *Check-list of birds of the world,* ed. M. A. Traylor Jr., 8:245–80. Cambridge, Mass.: Museum of Comparative Zoology.

———. 1980. A new species of cotinga from southeastern Brazil. *Bull. Brit. Ornithol. Club* 100:213–15.

———. 1982. *The cotingas: Bellbirds, umbrellabirds and other species,* London: British Museum; Ithaca: Cornell University Press.

———. 1985. Systematics of the *Turdus fumigatus/hauxwelli* group of thrushes. *Bull. Brit. Ornithol. Club* 105:30–37.

Snyder, D. E. 1966. *The birds of Guyana.* Salem, Mass.: Peabody Museum.

Spaans, A. L., and L. Autar. 1982. First record of Wilson's Phalarope *Phalaropus tricolor* from Surinam. *Bull. Brit. Ornithol. Club* 102: 114–15.

Steinbacher, J. 1962. Beiträge zur Kenntnis der Vögel von Paraguay. *Abhandl. Senckenbergischen Naturf. Gesell.*, no. 502:1–106.

———. 1968. Weitere Beiträge über Vögel von Paragauy. *Senckenbergia Biol.* 49:317–65.

Stiles, F. G. 1981. The taxonomy of Rough-winged Swallows (*Stelgidopteryx*; Hirundinidae) in southern Central America. *Auk* 98: 282–93.

———. 1983a. Systematics of the southern forms of *Selasphorus* (Trochilidae). *Auk* 100:311–25.

———. 1983b. The taxonomy of *Microcerculus* wrens (Troglodytidae) in Central America. *Wilson Bull.* 95:169–83.

———. 1984. The Nicaraguan Seed-Finch (*Oryzoborus nuttingi*) in Costa Rica. *Condor* 86:118–22.

———. 1985. Conservation of forest birds in Costa Rica: Problems and perspectives. In *Conservation of tropical forest birds,* ed. A. W. Diamond and T. E. Lovejoy, 141–68. ICBP Tech. Pub. no. 4. Cambridge: International Council for Bird Preservation.

———. 1992. A new species of antpitta (Formicariidae: *Grallaria*) from the eastern Andes of Colombia. *Wilson Bull.* 104:389–99.

Stiles, F. G., and R. G. Campos. 1983. Identification and occurrence of Blackpoll Warblers in southern Middle America. *Condor* 85: 254–55.

Stiles, F. G., and A. F. Skutch. 1989. *A guide to the birds of Costa Rica.* Ithaca: Cornell University Press.

Storer, R. W. 1981. The Rufous-faced Crake (*Laterallus xenopterus*) and its Paraguayan congeners. *Wilson Bull.* 93:137–44.

———. 1989. Notes on Paraguayan birds. *Occas. Pap. Mus. Zool. Univ. Mich.*, no. 719.

Stotz, D. F. 1990a. First specimens of *Drymophila devillei* from Colombia. *Bull. Brit. Ornithol. Club* 110:37–38.

———. 1990b. The taxonomic status of *Phyllomyias reiseri. Bull. Brit. Ornithol. Club* 110:184–187.

———. 1990c. Additions and corrections to the Brazilian avifauna. *Condor* 92: 1078–79.

———. 1992. Specific status and nomenclature of *Hemitriccus minimus* and *Hemitriccus aenigma. Auk* 109:916–17.

Stotz, D. F., and R. O. Bierregaard Jr. 1989. The birds of Fazendas Porto Alegre, Esteio and Dimona, north of Manaus, Amazonas, Brasil. *Rev. Brasil. Biol.* 49:861–72.

Stotz, D. F., R. O. Bierregaard, M. Cohn-Haft, P. Petermann, J. Smith, A. Whittaker, and S. Wilson. 1992. The status of North American migrants in central Amazonian Brazil. *Condor* 94: 608–21.

Strahl, S. D., P. A. Desenne, T. L. Jimenez, and I. R. Goldstein. Behavior and biology of the Hawk-headed Parrot, *Deroptyus accipitrinus,* in southern Venezuela. *Condor* 93:177–80.

Straneck, R. J. 1987. Aportes sobre el comportamiento y distribución de la cachirla amarillenta, *Anthus lutescens* Pucheran y la cachirla chaqueña, *Anthus chacoensis* Zimmer (Aves, Motacillidae). *Rev. Mus. Argent. Cienc. Nat. "Bernardino Rivadavia" Inst. Nac. Invest. Cienc. Nat. Zool.* 14:95–102.

Studer, A., and J. Vielliard. 1988. Premières données étho-écologiques sur l'Ictéridé brésilien *Curaeus forbesi* (Sclater, 1886) (Aves, Passeriformes). *Rev. Suisse Zool.* 95:1063–77.

Teixeira, D. M. 1986. The avifauna of the northeastern Brazilian Atlantic forests: A case of mass extinctions? *Ibis* 128:167–68.

———. 1987a. A new tyrannulet (*Phylloscartes*) from northeastern Brazil. *Bull. Brit. Ornithol. Club* 107:37–41.

———. 1987b. Notas sôbre *Terenura sicki* Teixeira and Gonzaga, 1983 (Aves, Formicariidae). *Bol. Mus. Para. Emílio Goeldi (Zool.),* n.s., 3:241–51.

Teixeira, D. M., and R. C. Best. 1981. Adendes à ornitologia do território federal do Amapá. *Bol. Mus. Para. Emílio Goeldi (Zool.)* 104:1–25.

Teixeira, D. M., and N. Carnevalli. 1989. Nova espécie de *Scytalopus* Gould 1837, do nordeste do Brasil (Passeriformes, Rhinocryptidae). *Bol. Mus. Nac. Rio de Janeiro (Zool.),* n.s., no. 331.

Teixeira, D. M., and L. P. Gonzaga. 1983a. A new antwren from northeastern Brazil. *Bull. Brit. Ornithol. Club* 103:133–35.

———. 1983b. Um nova Furnariidae do nordeste do Brasil: *Philydor novaesi* sp. nov. (Aves, Passeriformes). *Bol. Mus. Para. Emílio Goeldi (Zool.),* no. 124.

Teixeira, D. M., J. B. Nacinovic, and G. Luigi. 1988. Notes on some birds of northeastern Brazil (3). *Bull. Brit. Ornithol. Club* 108: 75–79.

———. 1989. Notes on some birds of northeastern Brazil (4). *Bull. Brit. Ornithol. Club* 109:152–57.

Teixeira, D. M., J. B. Nacinovic, and R. Novelli. 1985. Notes on some Brazilian seabirds. *Bull. Brit. Ornithol. Club* 105:49–51.

Teixeira, D. M., J. B. Nacinovic, and F. B. Pontual. 1987. Notes on some birds of northeastern Brazil (2). *Bull. Brit. Ornithol. Club* 107:151–57.

Teixeira, D. M., J. B. Nacinovic, I. M. Schloemp, and E. E. Kischlot. 1988. Notes on some Brazilian seabirds (3). *Bull. Brit. Ornithol. Club* 108:136–39.

Teixeira, D. M., J. B. Nacinovic, and M. S. Tavares. 1986. Notes on some birds of northeastern Brazil. *Bull. Brit. Ornithol. Club* 106: 70–74

Teixeira, D. M., and A. Negret. 1984. The Dwarf Tinamou (*Taoniscus nanus*) of central Brazil. *Auk* 101:188–89.

Teixeira, D.M., D. Oren, and R. C. Best. 1986. Notes on Brazilian seabirds, 2. *Bull. Brit. Ornithol. Club* 106:74–77.

Teixeira, D. M., R. Otoch, G Luigi, M. A. Raposa, and A. C. C. de Almeida. 1993. Notes on some birds of northeastern Brazil (5). *Bull. Brit. Ornithol. Club* 113:48–52.

Teixeira, D. M., and M. E. M. Puga. 1984. Notes on the Speckled Crake (*Coturnicops notata*) in Brazil. *Condor* 86:342–43.

Terborgh, J. W., J. W. Fitzpatrick, and L. Emmons. 1984. Annotated checklist of bird and mamal species of Cocha Cashu Biological Station, Manu National Park, Peru. *Fieldiana Zool.*, n.s., no. 21.

Terborgh, J. W., S. K. Robinson, T. A. Parker III, C. A. Munn, and N. Pierpont. 1990. Structure and organization of an Amazonian forest bird community. *Ecol. Monogr.* 60:213–38.

Tershy, B. R., E. Van Gelder, and D. Breese. 1993. Relative abundance and seasonal distribution of seabirds in the Canal de Ballenas, Gulf of California. *Condor* 95:458–64.

Thurber, W. A. 1986. Range expansion of the House Sparrow through Guatemala and El Salvador. *Am. Birds* 40:341.

Thurber, W. A., J. F. Serrano, A. Sermeño, and M. Benitez. 1987. Status of uncommon and previously unreported birds of El Salvador. *Proc. West. Found. Vert. Zool.* 3:109–293.

Tomkins, R. J. 1985. Breeding success and mortality of Dark-rumped Petrels in the Galápagos and control of their predators. In *Conservation of island birds: Case studies for the management of threatened species,* ed. P. J. Moors, 159–76. ICBP Tech. Pub. no. 3. Cambridge: International Council for Bird Preservation.

Tostain, O. 1980. Observations sur quelques dendrocolaptides, furnariides et formicariides de Guyane française. *Gerfaut* 70: 261–71.

———. 1980. Contribution á l'ornithologie de la Guyane française. *Oiseau* 50:47–62.

———. 1987. Deux tyrannidés forestiers nouveaux pour la Guyane: *Empidonax euleri* et *Leptopogon amaurocephalus. Alauda* 55: 150–51.

———. 1987. Le petrel de Bulwer (*Bulweria bulweri*) dans les eaux guyanaises. *Oiseau* 57:45–46.

———. 1988. Découverte du nid de l'Elaéne tête-de-feu *Elaenia ruficeps,* Tyrannidae, en Guyane française. *Alauda* 56:174–75.

Tostain, O., and J.-L. Dujardin. 1985. Le Faucon péterin *Falco peregrinus tundrias* en Guyane française. *Oiseau* 55:251–52.

———. 1988. Nouveaux oiseaux de mer en Guyane française. *Alauda* 56:67–68.

Tostain, O., J.-L. Dujardin, C. Erard, and J.-M. Thiollay. 1992. *Oiseaux de Guyane.* Brunoy, France: Société d'Etudes Ornithologiques.

Toyne, E. P., M. T. Jeffcote, and J. N. Flanagan. 1992. Status, distribution and ecology of the White-breasted Parakeet *Pyrrhura albipectus* in Podocarpus National Park, southern Ecuador. *Bird Conserv. Internat.* 2:237–339.

Trail, P. W. 1978. Sight records of two species new for Surinam. *Ardea* 66:184–85.

Tramer, E. J. 1979. First sight record of Lincoln's Sparrow for Costa Rica. *Wilson Bull.* 91:469–70.

Traylor, M. A., Jr. 1979a. Subfamily Elaeninae. In *Check-list of birds of the world,* ed. M. A. Traylor Jr., 8:3–112. Cambridge, Mass.: Museum of Comparative Zoology.

———. 1979b. Two sibling species of *Tyrannus* (Tyrannidae). *Auk* 96:221–33.

———. 1982. Notes on tyrant flycatchers (Aves: Tyrannidae). *Fieldiana Zool.,* n.s., no. 13.

———. 1985. Species limits in the *Ochtoeca diadema* species-group (Tyrannidae). In *Neotropical ornithology,* ed. P. A. Buckley, M. S. Foster, E. S. Morton, R. S. Ridgely, and F. G. Buckley, 430–42. Ornithol. Monogr., no. 36. Washington, D.C.: American Ornithologists' Union.

———, ed. 1979. *Check-list of birds of the world.* Vol. 8. Cambridge, Mass.: Museum of Comparative Zoology.

Traylor, M. A., Jr., and J. W. Fitzpatrick. 1982. A survey of the tyrant-flycatchers. *Living Bird* 19:7–50.

Tye, A., and H. Tye. 1991. Bird species on St. Andrew and Old Providence Islands, west Caribbean. *Wilson Bull.* 103:493–97.

Udvardy, M. D. F., C. S. de Beausset, and M. Ruby. 1973. New tern records from Caribbean Honduras. *Auk* 90:440–42.

Urban, E. K. 1959. Birds from Coahuila, Mexico. *Univ. Kans. Publ. Mus. Nat. Hist.* 11:443–516.

Valle, C. A., and M. C. Coulter. 1987. Present status of the Flightless Cormorant, Galápagos Penguin and Greater Flamingo populations in the Galápagos Islands, Ecuador, after the 1982–1983 El Niño. *Condor* 89:276–81.

van den Berg, A. B., and C. A. W. Bosman. 1984. Range extensions and rare records of birds in Ecuador. *Bull. Brit. Ornithol. Club* 104:152–54.

van Rossem, A. J. 1929. Nesting of the American Merganser in Chihuahua. *Auk* 46:380.

———. 1945. A distributional survey of the birds of Sonora, Mexico. *Occas. Pap. Mus. Zool. LA State Univ.,* no. 21.

Vanzolini, P. E. 1992. *A supplement to "The Ornithological gazetteer of Brazil."* São Paulo: Museu de Zoologia.

Varty, N. 1991. The status and conservation of Jamaica's threatened and endemic forest avifauna and their habitats following Hurricane Gilbert. *Bird Conserv. Internat.* 1:135–51.

Vaurie, C. 1971. Classification of the ovenbirds (Furnariidae). London: H. F. and G. Witherby.

———. 1980. Taxonomy and geographical distribution of the Furnariidae (Aves, Passeriformes). *Bull. Am. Mus. Nat. Hist.* 166:1–357.

Venegas C., C., and J. Jory H. 1979. Guia de Campo para las Aves de Magallanes. *Publ. Inst. Patagonia,* ser. monog., no. 11.

Vielliard, J. 1989. Uma nova espécie de *Glaucidium* (Aves, Strigidae) da Amazonia. *Rev. Bras. Zool.* 6:685–93.

———. 1990. Uma nova espécie de *Asthenes* da Serra do Cipó, Minas Gerais, Brasil. *Ararajuba* 1:121–22.

Vilella, F. J., and P. J. Zwank. 1993. Geographic distribution and abundance of the Puerto Rican Nightjar. *J. Field Ornithol.* 64: 223–38.

Villaseñor, J. F. 1993. First documented records of the Arctic Tern on the Pacific coast of Mexico. *Wilson Bull.* 105:364–65.

Vooren, C. M., and A. Chiaradia. 1990. Seasonal abundance and behaviour of coastal birds on Cassino Beach, Brazil. *Ornitol. Neotrop.* 1:9–24.

Vooren, C. M., and A. C. Fernandes. 1989. *Guia de albatrozes e petréis do sul de Brasil.* Porto Alegre: Sagra.

Voous, K. H. 1983. *Birds of the Netherlands Antilles.* Zutphen, Netherlands: Walburg.

———. 1985. Additions to the avifauna of Aruba, Curaçao, and Bonaire, South Caribbean. In *Neotropical Ornithology,* ed. P. A. Buckley, M. S. Foster, E. S. Morton, R. S. Ridgely, and F. G. Buckley, 247–54. Ornithol. Monogr., no. 36. Washington, D.C.: American Ornithologists' Union.

Vuilleumier, F., A. P. Capparella, and I. Lazo. 1993. Two notable bird records from Chilean Patagonia. *Bull. Brit. Ornithol. Club* 113: 85–87.

Vuilleumier, F., and E. Mayr. 1987. New species of birds described from 1976 to 1980. *J. Ornithol.* 128:137–50.

Walters, R. 1993. Some records of birds from Belize, Central America, including three first records. *Bull. Brit. Ornithol. Club* 113:145–47.

Wendelken, P. W., and R. F. Martin. 1986. Recent data on the distribution of birds in Guatemala. *Bull. Brit. Ornithol. Club* 106: 16–21.

———. 1989. Recent data on the distribution of birds in Guatemala, 2. *Bull. Brit. Ornithol. Club* 109:31–36.

Weske, J. S. 1972. The distribution of the avifauna in the Apurimac Valley of Peru with respect to environmental gradients, habitats and related species. Ph.D. diss., University of Oklahoma, Norman.

Weske, J. S., and J. W. Terborgh. 1977. *Phaethornis koepckeae,* a new species of hummingbird from Peru *Condor* 79:143–47.

———. 1981. *Otus marshalli,* a new species of screech-owl from Peru. *Auk* 98:1–7.

Wetmore, A. 1926. Observations on the birds of Argentina, Paraguay, Uruguay, and Chile. *Bull. U.S. Nat. Mus.* 133.

———. 1965. *Birds of the Republic of Panamá.* Part 1. Washington, D.C.: Smithsonian Institution Press.

———. 1968. *Birds of the Republic of Panamá.* Part 2. Washington, D.C.: Smithsonian Institution Press.

———. 1972. *Birds of the Republic of Panamá.* Part 3. Washington, D.C.: Smithsonian Institution Press.

Wetmore, A., R. F. Pasquier, and S. L. Olson. 1984. *Birds of the Republic of Panamá.* Part 4. Washington, D.C.: Smithsonian Institution Press.

Wetmore, A., and B. H. Swales. 1931. The birds of Haiti and the Dominican Republic. *Bull. U.S. Nat. Mus.* 155.

White, R. P. 1988. Wintering grounds and migration patterns of the upland sandpiper. *Am. Birds* 42:1247–53.

Whitney, B. M. 1992. Observations on the systematics, behavior and vocalizations of "*Thamnomanes*" *occidentalis* (Formicariidae). *Auk* 109:302–8.

———. 1994. Behavior, vocalizations, and possible relationships of four *Myrmotherula* antwrens (Formicariidae) from eastern Ecuador. *Auk* 111:469–75.

Whitney, B. M., and J. F. Pacheco. 1994. Behavior and vocalizations of *Gyalophylax* and *Megaxenops,* two little-known genera endemic to northeastern Brazil. *Condor* 96:559–65.

Whitney, B. M., and G. H. Rosenberg. 1993. Behavior, vocalizations and possible relationships of *Xenornis setifrons* (Formicariidae), a little-known Chocó endemic. *Condor* 95:227–31.

Wiedenfeld, D. A., T. S. Schulenberg, and M. B. Robbins. 1985. Birds of a tropical deciduous forest in extreme northwestern Peru. In *Neotropical ornithology,* ed. P. A. Buckley, M. S. Foster, E. S. Morton, R. S. Ridgely, and F. G. Buckley, 305–15. Ornithol. Monogr., no. 36. Washington, D.C.: American Ornithologists' Union.

Wiley, J. W. 1991. The status and conservation of parrots and parakeets in the Greater Antilles, Bahama Islands, and Cayman Islands. *Bird Conserv. Internat.* 1:187–214.

Wiley, J. W., W. Post, and A. Cruz. 1991. Conservation of the Yellow-shouldered Blackbird *Agelaius xanthomus,* an endangered West Indian species. *Biol. Conserv.* 55:119–38.

Willard, D. E., M. S. Foster, G. F. Barrowclough, R. W. Dickerman, P. F. Cannell, S. L. Coats, J. L. Cracraft, and J. P. O'Neill. 1991. The birds of Cerro de la Neblina, Territorio Federal Amazonas, Venezuela. *Fieldiana Zool.,* n.s., no. 65.

Williams, E. H., Jr., and L. B. Williams. 1985. A new bird record for Puerto Rico: The Yellow-throated Vireo. *Caribbean J. Sci.* 21:187.

Williams, S. O., III. 1975. Redhead breeding in the state of Jalisco, Mexico. *Auk* 92:152–53.

Willis, E. O. 1972. Taxonomy, ecology and behavior of the Sooty Ant-Tanager (*Habia gutturalis*) and other ant tanagers. *Am. Mus. Novit.,* no. 2480.

———. 1979. The composition of avian communities in remanescent woodlots in southern Brazil. *Pap. Avul. Zool.* (São Paulo) 33: 1–25.

———. 1988a. Behavioral notes, breeding records, and range extensions for Colombian birds. *Rev. Acad. Colomb. Cienc. Exact. Fís. Nat.* 16:137–50.

———. 1988b. *Drymophila rubricollis* (Bertoni, 1901) is a valid species (Aves, Formicariidae). *Rev. Bras. Biol.* 48:431–38.

———. 1988c. Land-bird migration in São Paulo, southeastern Brazil. In *Acta XIX Congressus Internationalis Ornithologici,* ed. H. Ouellet, 754–64. Ottawa: University of Ottawa Press.

———. 1991. Sibling species of greenlets (Vireonidae) in southern Brazil. *Wilson Bull.* 103:559–67.

———. 1992. Three *Chamaeza* antthrushes in eastern Brazil (Formicariidae). *Condor* 94:110–16.

Willis, E. O., and E. Eisenmann. 1979. A revised list of the birds of Barro Colorado Island, Panama. *Smithson. Contrib. Zool.* 291: 1–31.

Willis, E. O., and Y. Oniki. 1981a. Levantamento preliminar de aves em treze áreas do estado de São Paulo. *Rev. Bras. Biol.* 41: 121–35.

———. 1981b. Notes on the Slender Antbird. *Wilson Bull.* 93: 103–7.

———. 1982. Behavior of Fringe-backed Fire-eyes (*Pyriglena atra,* Formicariidae): A test case for taxonomy versus conservation. *Rev. Bras. Biol.* 42:213–23.

———. 1985. Bird specimens new for the state of São Paulo, Brazil. *Rev. Bras. Biol.* 45:105–8.

———. 1991. *Nomes Gerais para as aves Brasileiras.* São Paulo: Sadia.

———. 1992. On a *Phoebetria* specimen from southern Brazil. *Bull. Brit. Ornithol. Club* 113:60–61.

Willis, E. O., D. Snow, D. F. Stotz, and T. A. Parker III. 1993. Olive-sided Flycatchers in southeastern Brazil. *Wilson Bull.* 105: 193–94.

Winker, K., M. A. Ramos, J. H. Rappole, and D. W. Warner. 1992. A note on *Campylopterus excellens* in southern Veracruz, with a guide to sexing captured individuals. *J. Field Ornithol.* 63: 339–44.

Winker, K., J. H. Rappole, and M. A. Ramos. 1990. Population dynamics of the Wood Thrush in southern Veracruz, Mexico. *Condor* 92:444–60.

Wood, D. S., and R. C. Leberman. 1987. Results of the Carnegie Museum of Natural History expeditions to Belize. III. Distributional notes on the birds of Belize. *Ann. Carnegie Mus.* 56:137–60.

Wood, D. S., R. C. Leberman, and D. Weyer. 1986. Checklist of the birds of Belize. *Carnegie Mus. Nat. Hist. Spec. Publ.,* no. 12: 1–24.

Woods, C. A., and J. A. Ottenwalder. 1986. *The birds of Parc National La Visite and Parc National Macaya, Haiti.* Port-au-Prince: USAID/Haiti.

———. 1992. *The natural history of southern Haiti.* Gainesville: Florida Museum of Natural History.

Yamashita, C. 1987. Field observations and comments on the Lear's Macaw (*Anodorhynchus leari*), a highly endangered species from northeastern Brazil. *Wilson Bull.* 99:280–82.

Zimmer, J. T. 1945. Studies of Peruvian birds. No. 50, The genera *Ramphocelus, Piranga, Habia, Lanio,* and *Tachyphonus. Am. Mus. Novit.,* no. 1304.

———. 1955. Further notes on tyrant flycatchers (Tyrannidae). *Am. Mus. Novit.,* no. 1749.

Zink, R. M. 1988. Evolution of Brown Towhees: Allozymes, morphometrics and species limits. *Condor* 90:72–82.

General Index

Index of Scientific Names

Map 1 Neotropical zoogeographic regions

Map 2 Neotropical zoogeographic subregions of Central America

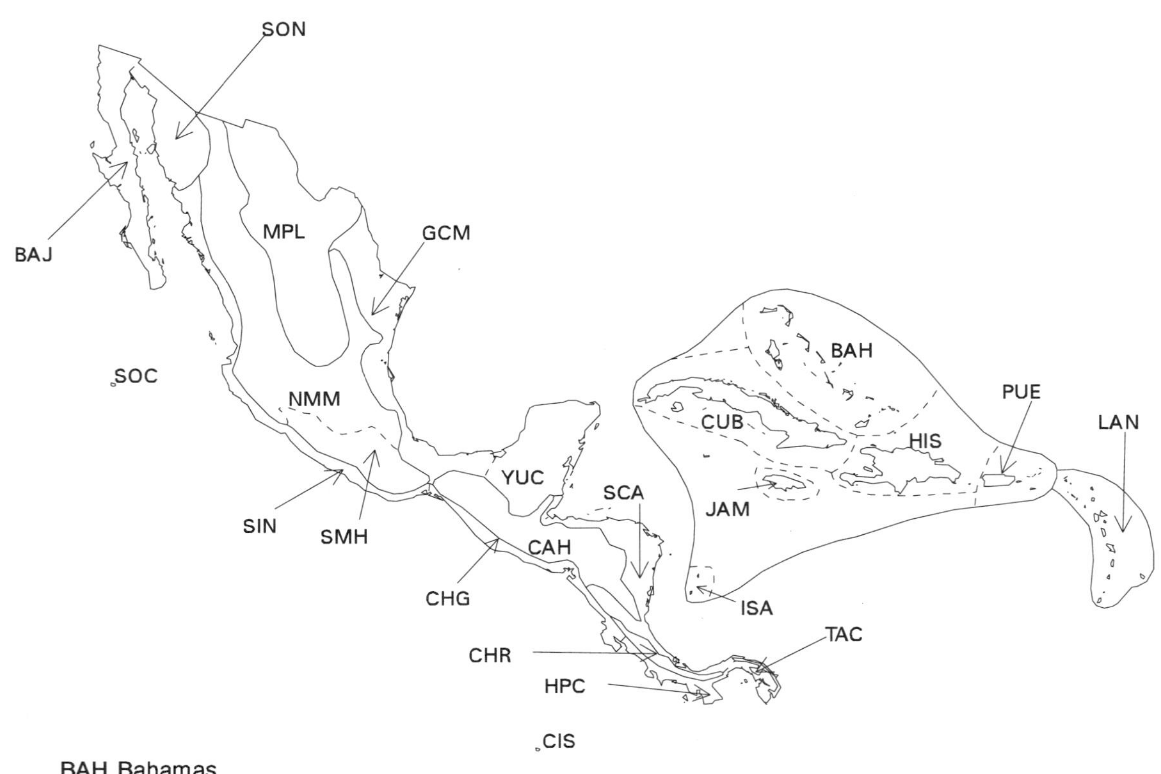

BAH Bahamas
BAJ Baja California
CAH Central American Highlands
CHG Chiapas-Guanacaste
CHR Chiriquí
CIS Cocos Island
CUB Cuba
GCM Gulf Coast-Mexico
HIS Hispaniola
HPC Humid Pacific Coast
ISA Isla Providencia
JAM Jamaica
LAN Lesser Antilles
MPL Mexican Plateau
NMM Northern Mexican Mountains
PUE Puerto Rico
SIN Sinaloa-Oaxaca
SOC Isla Revillagigedo
SON Sonoran Desert
SCA Southern Central America
SMH Southern Mexican Highlands
TAC Tacarcuna
YUC Yucatán

Map 3 Neotropical zoogeographic subregions of South America

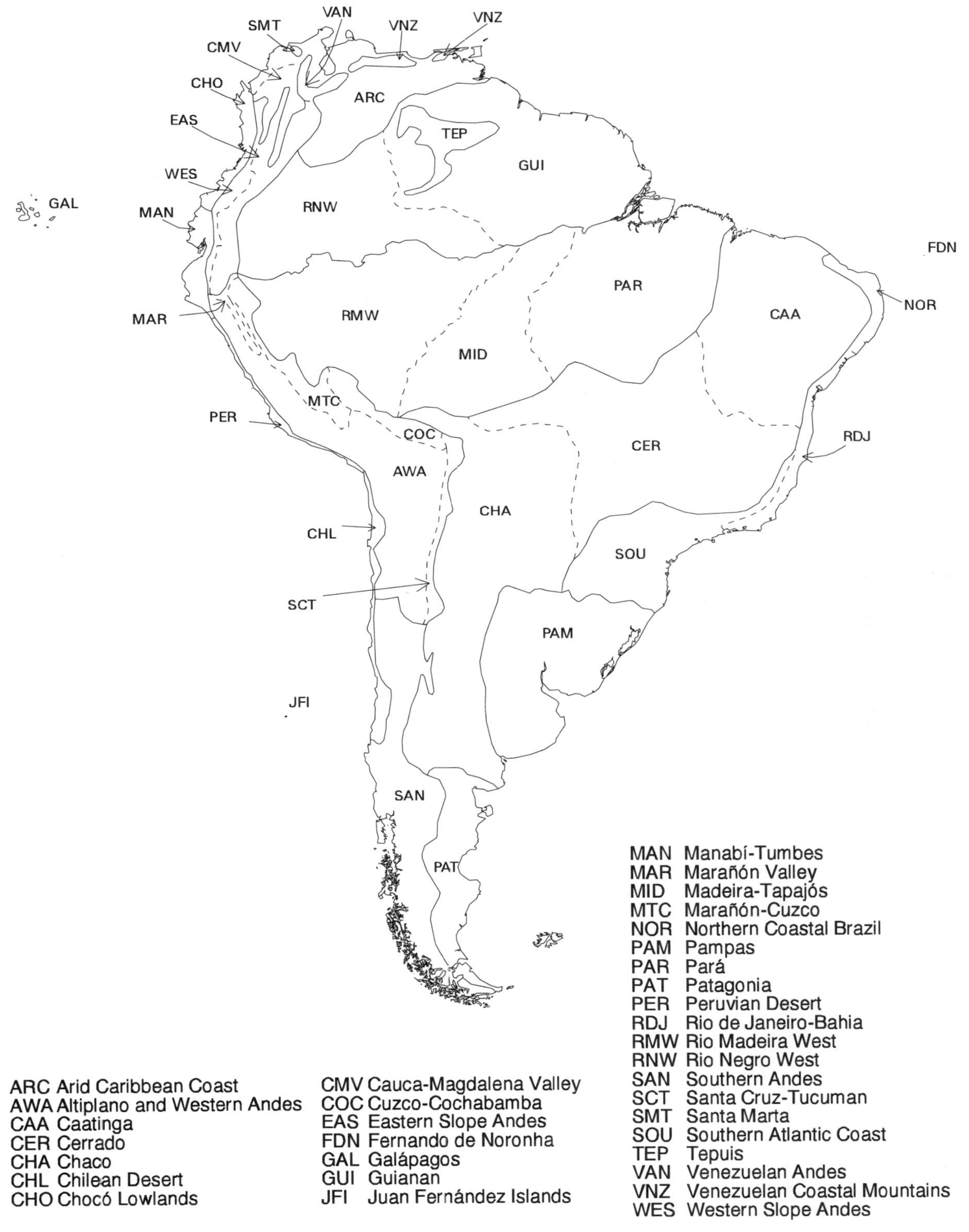